The Gender of Racial Politics and Violence in America

Studies in the Postmodern Theory of Education

Joe L. Kincheloe and Shirley R. Steinberg
General Editors

Vol. 163

PETER LANG
New York • Washington, D.C./Baltimore • Bern
Frankfurt am Main • Berlin • Brussels • Vienna • Oxford

William F. Pinar

The Gender of Racial Politics and Violence in America

Lynching, Prison Rape, & the Crisis of Masculinity

PETER LANG
New York • Washington, D.C./Baltimore • Bern
Frankfurt am Main • Berlin • Brussels • Vienna • Oxford

Library of Congress Cataloging-in-Publication Data

Pinar, William.
The gender of racial politics and violence in America:
lynching, prison rape, and the crisis of masculinity / William F. Pinar.
p. cm. — (Counterpoints; vol. 163)
Includes bibliographical references.
1. United States—Race relations. 2. Racism—United States—History. 3. Sex role—United States—History. 4. Masculinity—United States—History. 5. Homophobia—United States—History. 6. Lynching—United States—Psychological aspects. 7. Prison violence—United States—History. 8. Afro-Americans—Civil rights—History. 9. White men—United States—Psychology. 10. Afro-American men—Psychology. I. Title. II. Counterpoints (New York, N.Y.); vol. 163.
E185.61 .P594 305.8'00973—dc21 00-030643
ISBN 0-8204-5132-0
ISSN 1058-1634

Die Deutsche Bibliothek-CIP-Einheitsaufnahme

Pinar, William F.:
The gender of racial politics and violence in America:
lynching, prison rape, and the crisis of masculinity / William F. Pinar.
–New York; Washington, D.C./Baltimore; Bern;
Frankfurt am Main; Berlin; Brussels; Vienna; Oxford: Lang.
(Counterpoints; Vol. 163)
ISBN 0-8204-5132-0

Cover design by Lisa Dillon

The paper in this book meets the guidelines for permanence and durability
of the Committee on Production Guidelines for Book Longevity
of the Council of Library Resources.

Printed in the United States of America

for JEFF

ACKNOWLEDGMENTS

Grateful acknowledgment is made to the following for permission to reprint from previously published material:

Copyright © 1993. From *Bodies That Matter* by Judith Butler. Reproduced with permission of Taylor and Francis, Inc./Routledge, Inc., http://www.routledge-ny.com

Copyright © 1994. From *Male Impersonators* by Mark Simpson. Reproduced by permission of Taylor and Francis, Inc./Routledge, Inc., http://www.routledge-ny.com

Copyright © 1995 by Bedford/St. Martin's Press, Inc. From: *Adventures of Huckleberry Finn* edited by: Graff/Phelan. Reprinted with permission of Bedford/St. Martin's Press, Inc.

Copyright © 1996. From *Mixed Blessings* edited by Judy Brink and Joan Mencher. Reproduced with permission of Taylor and Francis, Inc./Routledge, Inc., http://www.routledge-ny.com

Excerpts from *Along This Way,* copyright © 1933 by James Weldon Johnson, renewed in 1961 by Grace Nail Johnson. Used by permission of Viking Penguin, a division of Penguin Putnam Inc.

Excerpts from *Brother to Brother* reprinted by permission of Dorothy Beam.

Excerpts from Carolyn A. Haynes' *Divine Destiny: Gender and Race in Nineteenth-Century Protestantism* (1998) reprinted with permission of the University Press of Mississippi.

Excerpts from "Come Back to the Raft Ag'in, Huck Honey!" reprinted with permission of Leslie Fiedler.

Excerpts from Edward L. Ayers' *Vengeance and Justice* reprinted by permission of Oxford University Press.

Excerpts from Harry Brod's "Pornography and the alienation of male sexuality." Reprinted with permission of *Social Theory and Practice,* Department of Philosophy, Florida State University.

Excerpts from Gary Lemons' (1998) "To Be Black, Male, Feminist," reprinted with permission of New York University Press.

Excerpts from Hortense Spillers' "Mama's Baby, Papa's Maybe: An American Grammar Book" reprinted with permission of the Johns Hopkins University Press.

Excerpts from Ida B. Wells' *Crusade for Justice,* reprinted with permission of the University of Chicago Press.

Excerpts from Joel Williamson's (1984) *The Crucible of Race* reprinted with permission of Oxford University Press.

Excerpts from Katherine M. Blee's *Women of the Klan,* reprinted with permission of the Regents of the University of California and the University of California Press.

Excerpts from Larry May and Robert Strikwerda (1996) reprinted with permission of Rowman and Littlefield.

Excerpts from Laurence Goldstein's *The Male Body,* reprinted with permission of the University of Michigan Press.

Excerpts from Leslie Fiedler's *Love and Death in the American Novel* reprinted with permission of Dalkey Archive Press.

Excerpts from Lillian Smith's *Strange Fruit,* reprinted with permission of Harcourt, Inc.

Excerpts from *Lynching and Rape: An Exchange of Views* edited Bettina Aptheker, reprinted with permission from Bettina Aptheker.

Excerpts from *Men Behind Bars: Sexual Exploitation in Prison* by Wayne S. Wooden and Jay Parker. Copyright © 1982 by Wayne S. Wooden and Jay Parker. Reprinted with permission of Perseus Books Publishers, a member of Perseus Books, L.L.C.

Excerpts from *Mothers of Invention* by Drew Gilpin Faust. Copyright © by the University of North Carolina Press. Used by permission of the publisher.

Excerpts from Peter G. Filene's *Him/Her/Self: Gender Identities in Modern America,* copyright © 1999, reprinted with permission of the Johns Hopkins University Press.

Excerpts from Ralph Ginzburg's *100 Years of Lynching* reprinted with permission of Black Classic Press.

Excerpts from *The Black Male in America* reprinted with permission of Burnham, Inc., Publishers.

Excerpts from *The Joint: Language and Culture in a Maximum Security Prison* by Inez Cardozo-Freeman reprinted with permission of Inez Cardozo-Freeman.

Excerpts from *The Memphis Diary of Ida B. Wells* by Miriam Decosta-Willis. Copyright © 1995 by Miriam Decosta-Willis, Reprinted by permission of Beacon Press, Boston.

Excerpts from the *Reveille* reprinted with permission of the L.S.U. Press.

Excerpts from the work of Anthony M. Scacco, Jr., reprinted with permission of Thomas J. Scacco.

Excerpts from the work of Donald Yacovone (1990) reprinted with permission from the University of Chicago Press and Donald Yacovone.

Excerpts from the work of E. Anthony Rotundo (1990) reprinted with permission from the University of Chicago Press and E. Anthony Rotundo.

Excerpts from the work of Ida B. Wells-Barnett reprinted with permission of Ayer Co.

Excerpts from the work of James Baldwin, reprinted with permission of the James Baldwin Estate.

Excerpts from the work of Ron Simmons, reprinted with permission of Ron Simmons.

Excerpts from *Under Sentence of Death: Lynching in the South,* edited by W. Fitzhugh Brundage. Copyright © by the University of North Carolina Press. Used by permission of the publisher.

Excerpts from William Oliver's *The Violent Social World of Black Men,* copyrighted © 1994, by permission by Jossey-Bass, Inc., a subsidiary of John Wiley and Sons, Inc.

Paul Laurence Dunbar's (1920) poem "We Wear the Mask.," excerpted from *The College Poetry of Paul Lawrence,* edited by Joanne Braxton (1993). Reprinted with permission of the University Press of Virginia.

Reprinted by permission of the publisher excerpts from *Homos* by Leo Bersani, Cambridge, Mass: Harvard University Press. Copyright © 1995 by Leo Bersani.

Reprinted by permission of the publisher excerpts from *The Anatomy of Prejudices* by Elizabeth Young-Bruehl, Cambridge, Mass.: Harvard University Press, Copyright © 1996 by Elizabeth Young-Bruehl.

Reprinted with the permission of Scribner, a Division of Simon and Schuster, excerpts from *Terror in Prisons* by Carl Weiss and David James Friar.

Reprinted with the permission of Simon and Schuster excerpts from *Against Our Will,* by Susan Brownmiller. Copyright © 1975 by Susan Brownmiller.

W. E. Du Bois' poem (May, 1919), reprinted with permission of the Crisis Publishing Co.

CONTENTS

INTRODUCTION

I. The Queer Character of Racial Politics and Violence

Perhaps nothing about the history of mob violence is more surprising than how quickly an understanding of the full horror of lynchings has receded from the nation's collective memory.

—W. Fitzhugh Brundage, *Lynching in the New South: Georgia and Virginia, 1880–1930* (1993)

We speak for the strange fruit hung from trees.

—Joseph Beam, ed. *In the Life: A Black Gay Anthology* (1986)

Lynching is not simple murder.

—James Weldon Johnson, "The Practice of Lynching: A Picture, the Problem and What Shall Be Done About It" (1927)

[T]hree hundred years shouted back at him.

—Lillian Smith, *Strange Fruit* (1944/1972)

As a feminist man it is clear to me I must confront my own manhood, understood of course not essentialistically, but historically, socially, racially, in terms of class and culture. The main issue of the twentieth century may have been the color line, but this line did not stay within itself, by itself, dividing what would otherwise be a monolith: humanity. The color line traverses other planes, inhabits other problems, especially educational ones. "Gender and race conflate in a crisis," Henry Louis Gates, Jr. (1996, 84) observed. Mark Ledbetter (1996) employs an even more dramatic image: "Gender and race are the apocalypse" (38), recalling James Baldwin's (1963/1985) famous warning of the "fire next time."

The racial crisis is gendered, and, in the United States at least, the crisis of gender is racialized. Within these intersections of race and gender I want to work autobiographically (however indirectly) to perceive the lives of four men and the historical moments they inhabited. In particular, I want to outline the shadows they cast over me, over "us," European-American men. In so doing, I "sleep" with "bodies of knowledge" which might help reconfigure the lived practices of male self-constitution, and in so doing reformulate self and other: an autobiographics of alterity. Curriculum understood as *currere* is a form of social psychoanalysis, a complicated conversation with myself and others, the point of which is movement: autobiographic, political, cultural. I employ the method of *currere* in search for a passage out of the impasse at this turn-of-the-century America, in this individual life which shares with others the dilemma of being an American, an American man, a white man, in my case, an American white man who is queer.

It is clear that autobiography is not just about oneself but also about the other. It is, in Leigh Gilmore's (1994) phrase, a technology of self-production. It is, as well, a technology of the production of others. How can we understand this production of the "self" as gendered and racialized? How might the European-American male begin to grasp how his masculinity is racialized, and how his "race" is gendered? To answer these questions I have undertaken a study of four men—Robert Musil, Frantz Fanon, Pier Paolo Pasolini, and Eldridge Cleaver—whose lives and times span the twentieth century and traverse the Western world. How might such work enable one to re-experience the gendered and racialized present in America? How might an indirect autobiography, or to borrow from Gilmore (1994), an autobiographics of alterity—one that understands that the "self" comes to form "in the shadow of the other" (Benjamin, 1998)—help us to move through racial and gender sediments which contribute to the stasis that is the present moment? To begin we must return to a time past, still silently in the present.

My argument will be straightforward if queer: racism is in some sense an "affair" between men. Of course, racism is not only an affair between men. Women have been very much victims: white men's assaults on black women from slavery to the present are, for instance, well known. Nor I am suggesting that "race" can be reduced to gender; it cannot. But it does have to do with sex and desire, as Calvin C. Hernton (1965/1988), for one, appreciated.

> The sexualization of racism in the United States is a unique phenomenon in the history of mankind; it is an anomaly of the first order. In fact, there is a sexual involvement, at once real and vicarious, connecting white and black people in America that spans the history of this country from the era of slavery to the present, an involvement so immaculate and yet so perverse, so ethereal and yet so concrete, that all race relations tend to be, however, subtle, sex relations. (6)

Submerged in a heterosexist regime of reason (Leitch 1992), Hernton de-emphasizes the homoerotic content of this "sexualization," although he was, I think, not blind to it. "The central concept and the universal metaphor around which all aspects of the racial situation revolve," Hernton (1987, 38) wrote, "is 'Manhood'." I will focus upon—"blow-up" in a photographic sense—the homoerotic and indeed homosexual elements of racism. In so doing, what becomes visible is a mangled and repressed homoeroticism lacing white men's hatred of black. Repressed does not mean gone, of course, only out of view. As we know, the repressed returns, not always announcing itself (at least in self-evident terms), but recognizable enough, especially for those who have "queered the gaze" (Doll 1998). To make things "perfectly queer" (Doty 1993), I have chosen lynching and prison rape to make explicit the homoeroticism which laces "race relations" and structures, to a remarkable extent, the gender of racial politics and violence in this country. Despite the radical discontinuities between the various historical periods—from the antebellum and post-Reconstruction South to post-1960s prisons—there are certain nightmarish continuities, historical throughlines if you will, in American racial politics and violence.

Predictably, there will be those who protest that I am only "projecting" my own homosexuality onto others, that I am merely repeating the sad faggot fantasy that all men are gay. It is not "sad" and, as it turns out, it is no fantasy; as we will see, the homoerotic is embedded in the self-formation of all subjectivities, and not just in the West (Gilmore 1990). What enables one to "see" this fact is not frustration at being a member of a sexual minority (although that is real enough), but the fact that what is "queer" has sufficiently surfaced in society that it is now no longer invisible. As Roland Barthes (1988) once observed, "History is ... not so much *the real as the intelligible* (1988, 140; Barthes's emphasis). Now that "homosexuality" is on the social surface, we can perceive those heretofore invisible queer elements of "race," and the queer character of American racial politics and violence becomes intelligible.

The Historical Emergence of "Homosexuality"

My use of "homoerotic" and "homosexual" (or the broader and more aggressive term "queer" [see Jagose 1996]) is meant to suggest the ambiguity and complexity of desire circulating among nineteenth-century American men. Particularly in the years before "homosexuality" appeared as a self-conscious discursive practice and sexual identity, fully articulated homosexual narratives (as we might understand that phrase today) were rare, especially given the cultural complexity of erotic desire between men, disavowed as "bestiality" and "sodomy," yet performed variously, including physically, socially, politically, and racially, as we will see in chapter 6. The "prehistory" of homosexual desire in the nineteenth century consists of often buried, sometimes semi-emergent forms of psychosocial and sexual affiliation, at certain moments and in certain classes expressed as "romantic friendship," in others as rituals of fraternal organizations, and, in general, sublimated as "homosociality" in the "separate spheres" ideology of gender. Given that more fully developed ideas of homosexuality do not appear until century's end, homoerotic desire was very much inflected by the nineteenth century's dominant discourses of gender (Derrick 1997). It was inflected as well by "race."

Gender is, of course, a historical, ideological process (Bederman 1995a). So is "race." In the United States, gender and race have merged, conflated in Gates's language, despite the efforts, especially of European Americans, to keep them segregated. Through a complex often convoluted process of gendered racialization and racialized gendering, Americans have positioned and position themselves still as "men" or as "women," as "black" and as "white." Neither set reflects an intrinsic essence or unchanging genetic collection of traits, attributes, racial features, or sex roles. Rather, individuals and groups position themselves by adopting and disclaiming racialized and gendered elements, making racial politics gendered and gender politics racialized. In particular, I will explore how manhood (or "masculinity," as it is more commonly termed today) seemed to be continually (if variably and dynamically) at issue in American racial politics and violence. This, I believe, was no simple reflection of a broadly institutionalized patriarchy, although it was that too. For many European American men, "race" was experienced in a gendered, often explicitly sexualized fashion; gender and sex were often experienced racially.

Broadly speaking, the nineteenth century was characterized by ongoing efforts to "essentialize" and divide men and women on the basis of gender, which had the consequence of producing extremely powerful bonds between members of the same sex, on occasion across "race." This point was dramatically made half a century ago by Leslie Fielder (1948 [1995]; 1966) in his panoramic and perceptive analysis of the American cultural imagination (specifically the male imagination), scholarship I will review in chapter 18. The gender ideology of "separate spheres" created an artificial and exaggerated division between men and women and underlined the role of gender in many aspects of public and private life. As Scott Derrick (1997) comments: "If, for men, aspiration commonly involved identification with a real or imagined figure of the same gender, such identification itself could easily cross into erotic desire" (28). Indeed, Freud (1923; 1977, vol. 11) would suggest that identification represents a sublimation of desire. Derrick recalls Jonathan Dollimore's (1991) observation (while writing about a different historical moment) that an order of homoeroticism inevitably inhabits "the necessary identifications of male bonding." Psychosocial processes of identifications "produce an intensity of admiration some of which just cannot help but transform into deviant desire for, rather than just honorable imitation of, man's most significant other (i.e., man). And it occurs so easily—almost passively—requiring little more than a relinquishing of the effort of emulation, the erasure of 'to be like' and the surrender to what remains: 'I desire … you'" (305).

For the literary texts Derrick (1997) discusses (among them *The Scarlet Letter, The Ambassadors, The Great Gatsby*), "the (inevitable) reality of gender indeterminacy and authority-denying chaos of U.S. culture gives birth to emulative desires of transcendent intensity. … Each text contains an aching desire to achieve a position of acceptable manhood, a desire both blocked and, as a consequence, rendered sublime" (28). Or, in the case of "race relations," a desire rendered violent. While "homosexuality" as a discursive formation and self-conscious social practice and identity option may not have appeared before the twentieth century began, Derrick's (1997) point stands. Namely, the intense and powerful processes of masculine-identity formation, what he terms that "powerful desire for the stuff of masculinity, then, may often create homoerotic desire for the body of the other man as its inevitable by-product" (28). In America, that desire seems to have been expressed racially, as we will see, in two "imprinting" forms of racial politics and violence, nineteenth-century lynching and twentieth-century prison rape.

Witness and Testimony

In one sense, this book is a project of "historical witness," a project that intersects with a more general preoccupation in the West with the remembrance of traumatic historical events. This has become so pervasive that it is now, Claudia Eppert (1999) asserts, "almost cliché to stress memory as a cultural obsession for Western societies" (6). Why is there such a preoccupation now? To answer, Eppert quotes Pierre Nora (1989), who worried that "we speak so much of memory because there is so little of it left" (7). So understood, the obsession with memory appears "melancholic"—a lament not for the past per se as much as a longing for "the traditions of remembrance, in which the past was held in continuity with the present" (Eppert 1999, 7). But it is not only melancholic, Eppert suggests, for "the return to memory concurrently testifies to its struggle to come out from beneath the service and shadows of history to act against the grain of an objectifying and oppressive historical grammar" (7).

What is melancholic for me—or should I say what leaves me in mourning (Eppert 2000)—is to live among and teach white people who remember nothing, who perceive "racism" as merely attitudinal, and as common among black folks as among white, and, most suprisingly, having nothing to do with them. In such a setting, to remember lynching and the struggle against it is perhaps what Eppert (1999) terms a "revisionary task" (7), for it involves, as Eppert suggests, an order of "bearing witness" that requires not merely the evidentiary recounting of historical events but a more active accounting of and for them. "Recounting" denotes a narration of detail. In contrast, accounting is more than description and recall; it demands "a reckoning and reclamation" (Eppert 1999, 8). To pursue this project Eppert examines with subtlety and sensitivity the work of Shosana Felman (1982) and especially Emmanuel Levinas (1966, 1969, 1991, 1994). That larger project I recommend to the reader. For us, suffice to note here her reference to Deborah Britzman's (1998a) observation that education—understood as *Bildung*—involves the risk of the opening of oneself to anxious knowledge, knowledge so awful that one might become inconsolable. For the white male reader, the knowledge of lynching might qualify as such anxious knowledge.

Such knowledge—a curriculum of social psychoanalysis—may be traumatizing, threatening to "shatter the narcissistic unity of the subject," decentering and displacing it "as ego" (Handelman 1991, 221; Eppert 2000). Such "unheard-of" (Levinas 1991, 148) knowledge can have an important effect. By shattering of the narcissistic unity of the (male) subject, subjective space is made for the Other (Handelman 1991). "*Bildung*," Eppert (1999) writes, "is always oriented toward the other; issuing from [what Levinas terms as] a traumatism of astonishment" (133). The education to which this textbook might be said to contribute, then, is "education—*Bildung*—which does not separate learning from its application to oneself ... but encourages a person's development through knowledge, learning as a form of self-encounter and encounter with what is other and different" (Misgeld and Nicholson 1992, xi; also quoted in Eppert 1999, 19). This is curriculum as *currere*, an excavation of the lived—including historical—relations among self, society, and subject matter.

This labor of excavation is made more difficult by the various defenses in place against it. In her study of the Holocaust, Marla Morris (1999) points out that memories of traumatic events are censored, producing what Freud termed "screen memories." These are, Freud (1899/1989) suggested, a form of "recollection ... whose value lies in the fact that it represents in the memory impressions and thoughts of a later date whose content is connected with its own by symbolic or similar links" (126). Screen memories function to "screen" difficult memories by substituting other memories; these are closely connected to the "forgotten" event, but they are not accurate.

Until unconscious memories are made conscious, "acting out" (Freud 1911–1913, 150) typifies the behavior of the repressed. A defense mechanism that allows us not to remember, "acting out" must be repeated, lest the forbidden material surface. Freud terms this defense "repetition compulsion." In repetition compulsion, "the patient does not remember anything of what he has forgotten and repressed, but acts it out. He reproduces it not as a memory but as action; he repeats it, without of course knowing that he is repeating it" (Freud 1911–1913, 150). In the nineteenth century, white men "forgot" their desire for black men by "remembering" black men wanted to rape white women. Lynching was in this sense a kind of repetition compulsion, a defense mechanism in the service of the repression of homosexual desire, the reproduction of misogyny, and the sexual as well as civic subjugation of African Americans.

Scenes of Subjugation and Desire

For many, psychoanalysis is nothing more than hocus-pocus, a fraud perpetrated on humankind (see, for instance, Webster 1995). Even for those more sympathetic, there remain difficulties. Elizabeth Grosz (1995) has observed that "the relationship between psychoanalysis and feminism has always been fraught with complications, qualification, hesitancies" (276). Acknowledging this history, I choose to employ elements of psychoanalytic theory selectively, avoiding, I hope, any wholesale adoption of a particular psychoanalytic scheme. And I do so somewhat promiscuously, something of object relations theory here, a hint of Lacan there, not, as Elizabeth Weed (1994) notes,

> because it is right—the theory that wants to be fully adequate to its object can only speak its nostalgia for metaphysics—but because it works. That is, it [psychoanalysis] yields readings about signification and gaps in signification; about desire, repetition, and interpellation, and about the

> insistent cultural reproduction of fetishistic structures—all of which help us to understand the power and violence of the culture, and all of which are produced by reading something *other* than the already known, the already legible. (267–268)

However bumbling my use of it proves to be, I am, I confess, no virgin. I slept with psychoanalysis during my initial portraits of *currere* in the early 1970s. In the early 1980s, object relations theory helped me to conceive of queer theory in education (1983/1994). In my field—education, specifically curriculum theory—there is a tradition of interest in psychoanalysis. During the Progressive Era there were efforts to theorize a psychoanalysis of education (see, for instance, Cremin 1961, 209ff.), but those efforts disappeared as business thinking and the "national interest" dominated school curriculum (see Pinar et al. 1995, chapter 3). In recent years there has been a renaissance of interest in psychoanalysis among scholars of education, led by Deborah Britzman (1998a), Stephen Appel (1999), Wendy Atwell-Vasey (1998a, 1998b), and Madeleine Grumet (1988).

Psychoanalytic theory might help us understand, however incipiently, the gender of racial politics and violence and, more specifically, the "queer" dimensions of racial subjugation. I focus on the white man, no monolithic category to be sure, but a related series of historically situated, classed, and gendered "subject positions" from which unspeakable acts of violence were—are still—performed. Who is "the white man"? Psychoanalytically considered, what the white male subject takes himself to be as his "self" is other and fictive, deriving from unconscious, historical, and social sources. The concept of the "fantasmatic" is helpful here, a notion that has been theorized by Laplanche and Pontalis (1973), who define it as the unconscious source of dreams and fantasies, the structuring scenario behind social action, especially overdetermined actions structured by transferences and other forms of repetitive behavior. For Laplanche and Pontalis (1973), the fantasmatic "shape[s] and order[s]" the subject life "as a whole" (317). In so doing it becomes "public," as Trevor Hope (1994b) points out: "[f]antasy is necessarily public, and the public, therefore, has a fantasmatic dimension" (215). In American racial politics particularly, the public sphere seems a dreamscape of fantasy, desire, and violence.

Much has been written about the complex relations between fantasy and the ego; suffice to say here that I am focusing on the bodily images through which the white male subject represented himself within the public fantasmatic, as well as on their symbolic placement there. In the nineteenth-century South, for the white male subject, the structuring social fantasmatic was the rape scenario. The fantasy of black male bodies violently penetrating white female bodies in his imagination enabled the white male ego to place himself, identify himself, with white supremacy and political dominance while enjoying, albeit via disavowal, a masochistic, self-shattering sexual ecstasy of being penetrated by a powerful (evil and black) man, in oedipal terms, an absent, loathed longed-for father. To understand the gender of racial politics and violence in America, then, one must move underneath the convoluted social surface to discern "*where* the ego of the subject is" (Lacan, quoted in Silverman 1992, 5). The white male subject is, in this scenario, the vulnerable white girl being raped by the muscular black stud. One hundred years later, the scenario is no longer only in his head. Literally, white men are being raped, by black men, in prison.

There is debate and controversy within psychoanalysis between feminists inspired by Lacan and those working from object relations theory. Despite the current appeal of Lacanian concepts among many in psychoanalysis and in education, I still find utility in object relations theory's positing of an ego in preoedipal and symbiotic identification with the mother, for men a repudiated identification which surfaces in racial and other debates (especially over masculinity) as "matrifocality." This is not the occasion to explicate the complexity of the tensions between object relations theory and Lacanian theory (see, for instance, Benjamin 1998; Chodorow 1996). I shall make a simple and selective use of both.

In employing the trope of the female (i.e., mother's) presence in a man's body, implicit in the matrifocality thesis, I am not essentializing "inversion" as the founding tale of male homosexuality. Nor do I wish to essentialize the notion of "mother" as an object choice; I do not, for instance, assume she is "heterosexual." After Silverman (1992), I am working with a notion—inversion—probably as ancient as the hierarchical binarizing of "man" and "woman." Across time and culture (Gilmore 1990), human creatures have been remarkably resistant to conceptualizing sexual positionality—including, in psychoanalytic theory, object-choice—in terms other than the binary logic of gender. Because the category of masculinity tends to be defined in terms of what it is not, those found guilty of gender "treason" often find themselves banished to the more expansive if devalued category of femininity (Silverman 1992).

We will have to work a while before we return to "mother." First, let us focus on the patriarchal "evidence," those imprinting "scenes of desire" in which racial politics and violence are nightmarishly recorded. Silverman (1992) quotes Laplanche and Pontalis to emphasize not only the specularity of those scenes within which desire is staged—in the present case I am referring to lynching in the nineteenth century and prison rape in the twentieth—but the *placement* of the white male subject within those scenes of desire. Laplanche and Pontalis (1973) suggest that fantasy is less about the visualization and imaginary appropriation of the other—although it is certainly about that—than it is about the expression of a subjective sequence: "not an *object* that the subject imagines and aims at ... but rather a *sequence* in which the subject has his own part to play" (318; quoted in Silverman 1992, 6). In both imprinting episodes of racial politics and violence in America, the black man's phallus is the object around which the sequence of desiring events is structured.

Reminiscent of Freud's notion of infantile polymorphous perversity, Silverman (1992) suggests that at the deepest recesses of its psyche the subject has neither identity nor nameable desire. But toward the psychic surface the fantasmatic and the *moi* (or ego) merge in a mythic and determining version of each. Kim Michasiw (1994) criticizes Silverman for retaining the term desire, "a sign of her enmeshment in the very process she describes, as desire is that organization of the drive allowing it to function in the symbolic order" (158). Michasiw prefers Slavoj Zizek's (1989) characterization of desire as a structuring in fantasy of that self-shattering ecstasy (to borrow Bersani's phrase) which desire presumably facilitates but in fact complicates. Somewhere in the desired object may inhere traces of that against which both the subject and the subject's desire have been structured, sometimes triggering, in the case of lynching, extreme violence in service of repression, psychic in terms of the white man, political in terms of the black, repression of the white man's recognition of his desire inscribed on the black male body.

Silverman too quotes Zizek (1989) to suggest that fantasy not only "provides the co-ordinates of our desire," but "constructs the frame enabling us to desire something." Through fantasy, then *"we learn 'how to desire'"* (118; quoted in Silverman 1992, 6). In the case of nineteenth-century southern white men, one learned how *not* to desire while still fixed in a position of desire. Such are the pleasures of disavowal. Not unlike the homophobe in this respect, the lyncher was fixated on that which he insisted he loathed, a tactic of disavowal which allowed him to visualize the scene in which his desire was embedded while denying his eroticized and desiring position there. Silverman notes that a key element of learning how to desire is the assumption of a desiring position, which nineteenth-century southern white men did by transgendering themselves (in their imaginations) into white women who were then "violated" by muscular young black men.

That enduring fantasy—the nineteenth-century interracial rape scenario—allowed the white male subject to insert himself into a particular desiring syntax or tableau without actually acknowledging himself there and thereby committing himself to the assertion of a sexual identity. In other words, by sexually mutilating black men whom he imagined had raped virginal young white women, the white man experienced "sex" with black men while framing the event heterosexually through self-dissociation and disavowal. That framing meant that black men were sometimes castrated, but no matter, the white man was getting what he wanted while pretending to protect his (imaginary) lady. He remained a "man" (not a sodomite, or, by the early twentieth century, an "invert" or homosexual) while demonstrating "chivalry" and "honor," all in the service of white supremacy, itself both a continuation of the antebellum social order but as well a vicious repudiation of the postwar, Yankee-inseminated "New South."

White men's desire could not, of course, be expressed explicitly or directly, given the racialized regime of "compulsory" heterosexuality (Rich 1980, 637). (Even if the term did not yet exist in nineteenth-century America, sex was nonetheless politicized.) To have sex while disavowing it, white men imaginatively "relocated" that desire onto (imaginary) white women's bodies, bodies with whom they were already unconsciously identified (Chodorow 1978). After inhabiting the bodies of their imaginary white ladies, they then positioned them in the originary fantasy—the interracial rape scenario—enabling them to get laid without anyone being the wiser. While Silverman (1992) is surely right when she asserts that "identity and desire are so completely imbricated that neither can be explained without recourse to the other" (6), in American racial politics, even when its "queer" character gets expressed explicitly in prison, the emphasis in that sentence must be on "imbricated." Desire was not expressed in straightforwardly, easily decodable fashion, in no small measure due to the repression of same-sex desire, especially interracial same-sex desire. (Racial antagonism has never stopped white men from seeking sex with black women.) But the desire of white men was also embedded in political, regional, cultural, economic, and gendered events that masked its nature. And, of course, the heterosexism of scholars of lynching has hardly helped in unraveling the mystery.

What Silverman's appropriation of Lacan and Zizek enables us to understand is that white men's "crises" during the last decade of the nineteenth century—a profoundly gendered event—weakened the seams of imbricated repression, allowing desire to reach the social surface, if in convoluted, violent, ritualistic ways. As Silverman (1992) observes, the "constitutive features of subjectivity are never entirely 'fixed,' neither are they in a state of absolute flux or 'free-play'; on the contrary, they are synonymous with the compulsion to repeat certain images and positionalities, which are relinquished only with difficulty" (6). As we will see in the fight for antilynching legislation in Congress (chapters 10 and 11), white men were utterly compelled to repeat "certain images and positionalities." They were determined never to relinquish them, and indeed antilynching legislation was never enacted, thanks to the compulsions of southern white men (and their complicit white male northern colleagues).

Silverman (1992) argues that the fantasmatic helps form the images within which the *moi* is able to "recognize" itself "by eroticizing those which are commensurate with its representational imperatives" (7). To illustrate, thinking of Rainer Werner Fassbinder's cinema perhaps, she notes that "an external representation might, for instance, pass muster at the level of the fantasmatic through its masochistic connotations, but at the same time involve an identification with a masculine corporeal image" (7–8). Or, Silverman notes that "a subject's structural identification with voyeurism might be ideologically reconfigured through a simultaneous imaginary identification with blackness or femininity" (8). Silverman is suggesting here that it not only makes a political difference where the subject "stands" within the mise-en-scène of its desire. It also makes a political difference what identity it there assumes or—in the case of lynching—by what identity it disavows, transgenders, and relocates in the social fantasmatic. In these simultaneously social and self-structuring moves, sexual, racial and class elements all come into play in key ways, ways will be visible, I trust, in the chapters that follow.

In *The Interpretation of Dreams,* Freud (1900; 1966) suggested that the actual center of subjectivity is the unconscious; he demoted consciousness to a kind of receiving mechanism for stimuli which originate elsewhere. It is, therefore, not within the domain of consciousness where reality is constructed, but rather within another scene, closed off from it by repression: that of the unconscious (Silverman 1992). And for straight white men in America, an identity (or series of identities) constructed in terms of gendered and racial binarisms, that unconscious is necessarily homosexual and black and female, although not necessarily in synchronous relation or sequence. From Freud too we understand that heterosexuality is, in part, repressed homosexuality. From deconstruction we know that binaries are inextricably bound to each other, that "white" exists only in relation to "black," "gay" to "straight." And from object relations theory we know that all men are in a sense women, having become "men" through an arduous, often violent process of oedipal structuration in which preoedipal identification with their mothers is repressed in favor of imaginary identifications with relatively absent, sometimes hostile fathers.

Hegemonic masculinity—typified as it is by a denial of its "lack," as well as "specularity and alterity" (Silverman 1992, 51)—is an inherently unstable concoction vulnerable to destabilization, even breakdown, necessarily and always in "crisis," and very much capable of violence. But to historically surpass its various manifestations requires, as Silverman (1992) suggests, "dismantling the images and undoing the projections and disavowals through which phallic identification is enabled" (50). This is one of the aims to which this project (as is Silverman's *Male Subjectivity at the Margins* upon which I draw here) is dedicated.

We will see how nineteenth-century hegemonic masculinity became destabilized as a result of a series of dramatic historical developments. In the South, as we will see in chapter 4, the Civil War forced women to abandon their fixed, if imaginary, subject positions as "ladies" to do much of the supervisory and managerial labor that absent husbands, fathers, and sons could not perform while off fighting the Yankees. This shift in southern white women's subject positions coupled with the crushingly complete military defeat of southern white men, a profoundly gendered as well as political and military event, set the stage for a beleaguered, regressed, frighteningly de-stabilized series of white male subject positions in the South. Add to that more "gender trouble"—feminism in its various forms and settings, if muted and racialized in the South; shifts in the economy (industrialization swallows artisanal capitalism); in politics (in the 1890s populism threatens what for many southern whites was a political miscegenation), in religion (even conservative Christian women made feminist gains; see chapter 5); in the law (as women gained elementary rights of divorce and property); and in the forms of homosociality (male-male "romantic" friendship ends as homoeroticism surfaces socially and is named and tabooed), and what a number of historians (not without controversy) have termed a general "crisis" of white masculinity in the 1890s—and we have the decade during which lynching was at its zenith.

In contrast to those historians and sociologists who insist that it is finally an economic phenomenon, correlated with cotton price fluctuation, I argue that lynching is also, probably primarily, a gendered form of racial politics and violence in which white men regressed to their "negative" oedipal complex, wherein their repressed, racialized homosexual desire expressed itself in the mutilation and sexual torture of thousands of young black men. I do not doubt that lynching has its economic elements, but I insist it cannot be reduced to them. Lynching was in no small measure a mangled form of queer sex, a fact inaccessible, one supposes, to those white men who participated in the practice, as well as a fact lost on the many white men who later studied the practice (see chapter 3). Black men, however, were not so unconscious; in prison they would perform precisely, if in inverted positions, the gender of racial violence their grandfathers had experienced decades before. As we will see in chapter 18, it would take a literary critic, not a social scientist, to understand that laced throughout racial animosity is stitched the desire, indeed the love, of the white man for the black. As the first judge in the Scottsboro case would exclaim: "My God ... is this whole thing a horrible mistake?" (quoted in Carter 1969/1979, 215; see chapter 12). Obviously the notion of "mistake" does not adequately summarize centuries of white sadism and black subjugation, but it does point to the ego's ability to learn. In that fragile fact resides our hope.

Men, white men particularly, are notorious complainers, as we will be reminded in the final chapter, whining over being forced to pay child support, whining over gay men and women in the military, whining over lost "masculinity" (see chapter 19, section III). I expect those who read this work will complain as well, complain at being forced to read of the legacy and present dangers that accompany the, yes, admittedly variable and complex positionality known as "white straight guys" or, more aptly sequenced for many, "straight white guys." It is essential for my fellow "men" to experience this discomfort, not (just) to cultivate a masochistic pleasure in suffering, but to begin the arduous and probably painful working through (as in dissolving) the reproduced structures of (especially white) "manhood" in America. While such working through requires breaking up the racialized and gendered identification with the "father," it also means re-experiencing that preoedipal relation with the "mother."

I position Ida B. Wells (1862–1931) as the exemplary figure in the tale I tell, not to idealize or sentimentalize her, as many nineteenth-century white men did their unwanted wives, and not only because she merits that pivotal position, but in part to engender racial politics, to position racial politics in the feminine. For heteronormative men, this means confronting one's own castrated status, that is, one's repudiated identification with the mother, one's fabricated masculinity. Perversely as it will seem to some, I consciously valorize the suffering these discursive moves may engender, as I am convinced that only through a kind of educational regression—oddly evocative of that racial regression nineteenth-century white men imagined blacks to be undergoing after Emancipation—which might dissolve identification into its prior state, desire. That is not as improbable as it may seem; as Kaja Silverman (1992) points out, "desire cannot be scrupulously differentiated from identification" (317).

Lynching Today

Lynching reverberates throughout American culture today, faintly but unmistakably. In January 2000, over 60 photographs of lynchings as well as antilynching pamphlets and newspaper reports went on display at the Roth Horowitz gallery on the Upper East Side of Manhattan, and later at the New York Historical Society. Part of the permanent Allen-Littlefield collection at Emory University in Atlanta, these photographs depict charred corpses which were mailed in the thousands as mementos and sometimes as warnings. Not until 1908 did the postmaster general of the United States forbid the mailing of such material.

The American public was reminded of lynching some ten years ago during the confirmation hearings of Clarence Thomas. That drama was reported live over network television, cable, and radio between October 11 and October 13,

1991, reaching an estimated 27 million homes, or 80 percent of the television viewing audience. The hearings and their aftermath were widely debated in the popular and academic press (Bystrom 1996; Roper, Chanslor, and Bystrom 1996; see Ragan, Bystrom, Kaid, and Beck 1996). The testimony of Anita Hill challenged Thomas's claim to be qualified to serve as Supreme Court Justice. Many agreed that the turning point in the proceedings occurred when Thomas likened the hearings to a "high-tech lynching." More than any other statement, that image was pivotal in reversing perceptions of who was on trial and what the trial/hearings themselves were about (Wood 1996).

In March 1996, a black rapper known as Wise Intelligent produced a CD entitled "Killin' U for Fun." On the back cover was a photograph of a charred body, collapsed over a mound of coals, with a group of white men and boys in the background, some of them smiling and laughing. The image was so haunting and horrible that the *Washington Post* printed it, along with a short description of the lynching, which occurred in Coatesville, Pennsylvania, in 1911, near the Worth Brothers Steel Company. "It's a black man being burned on the stake, crucified," Wise Intelligent told the *Post*. "And there's the Establishment looking on, loving the destruction of the black man in this picture" (quoted in Worth 1998, 65).

To Robert Worth (1998) this was no faint historical echo: "I read those words with a jolt of recognition because my great-grandfather owned and ran the steel mills that employed the victim and many of the men who burned him to death. The extended Worth family still lives indirectly on the profits from those mills, but few of us knew anything about the lynching" (65). Thirty or forty years ago, Worth reflects, there might have been some public political point in acknowledging that the Coatesville lynching was an act of barbarism. "By the time I came of age in the 1980s," he continues, "that rhetoric had begun to sound forced. After reading through the grand-jury documents and the old newspaper coverage of the lynching, I couldn't avoid the feeling that an apology ... no matter how eloquent, would no longer mean much" (Worth 1998, 76).

Perhaps not. But by remembering (we will review the Coatesville lynching among others in chapter 1) we can see through layers of scar tissue that deform not just the skin but the entire body of the American nation. Especially during this time of millennial optimism regarding technology and the internet coupled with "end-time" prophecies of TV preachers, perhaps this is exactly the time to remember who we are by reading about who we have been. Why recall such *unpleasant* material? The answer, of course, has to do with memory. Those of us committed to antiracist education accept Jane Flax's (1987) affirmation that "'new' memory" is "a powerful impulse toward political action" (106), including action toward the dissolution of hegemonic masculinity.

Still a fundamental "American dilemma" today, racism requires political and pedagogical action. "The reason we remember the past at all," Maxine Hong Kingston pointed out in an interview, "is that our present-day life is still a working-out of a similar situation"; to "understand the past changes the present. And the ever-evolving present changes the significance of the past" (quoted in Rabinowitz 1987, 179). Toni Morrison too has spoken of the "ways in which the past influences today and tomorrow" (quoted in the *Los Angeles Times,*

October 14, 1987); she has referred to her writing in general as a way of "sorting out the past," of identifying "those things in the past that are useful and those things that are not" (Le Clair 1981, 75–76).

Nor are these recent sentiments only. In 1921 the Austrian novelist and essayist Robert Musil (1990) observed: "Progress itself is not something that unfolds in a single line. Along with the natural weakening an idea suffers as it becomes diffuse, there is also the crisscrossing of influences from new sources of ideas. The innermost core of the life of every age, an inchoate, swelling mass, is poured into molds forged by much earlier times. Every present period is simultaneously now and yet millennia old" (146–147). To recall what I ask us to remember here represents another moment in a curriculum of social psychoanalysis (Pinar, 1991).

"Memory," Marla Morris (1999) reminds, "haunts and hovers like ghosts. Distance in time from these memories does not bring psychological distance for many. In fact, the reverse may be true" (213). Morris is discussing the plight of Holocaust survivors. She quotes Aaron Hass (1996): "As most [survivors] enter old age, a phase characterized by reintegration, reinterpretation, and reminiscence, trauma that had been successful buried may come to life" (23). Freud, Morris reminds, called this failed repression: "Repression has failed because memories which have been buried now push through to consciousness. But the memories that surface do not mirror the original memories; they take on their own shapings and coursings" (Doll, in press; Morris 1999, 213).

To understand white racism today I think we must deliberately work to remember precisely that which we feel compelled to forget, to force our repression to fail, to engender regression. We must return to lynching, that "peculiar" form of vigilante law, social control, and gendered violence that reached its zenith during the last decade of the nineteenth century, a decade of gendered, political, and economic crisis. Often sexualized violence, lynching was a mangled form of interracial homosexual rape, rationalized by a white male fantasy of interracial heterosexual rape. In this sense lynching was parallel to white men's rape of black women.

Always, it seemed, southern white man's "mise-en-scène of desire" (Silverman 1992, 337) featured muscular young black men penetrating fragile young white women, against their will. The southern "lady" was, in this fantasmatic scene, a key site of identification for southern white men, a site of relocated and disavowed desire. As such, it was a site always in peril and in desperate need of protection, drawn taut between fantasized poles of sexual passivity and sublimated agency. For many, perhaps most, southern white men the "lady" was not real, but a pedestalized figment of his imagination, kept safe from concrete reality by the ideology of separate spheres (see chapters 5 and 6). Fictively positioned, southern white women—"ladies"—engendered hysterical loyalty by "honorable" white men. In *The Mind of the South,* W. J. Cash (1960) observed:

> The upshot ... was downright gyneolatry. She was the South's Palladium, the southern woman—shield-bearing Athena gleaming whitely in the clouds, the standard for its rallying, the mystic symbol of its nationality in face of the foe. She was the lily-pure maid of Astolat and the hunting

> goddess of the Boethian hill. And—she was the pitiful Mother of God. Merely to mention her was to send strong men into tears—or shouts. There was hardly a sermon that did not begin and end with tributes in her honor, hardly a brave speech that did not open and close with clashing of shields and flourishing of swords for her glory. (89)

In other words, white women functioned in the nineteenth-century South as symbolic currency in a homosocial economy (Sedgwick 1985; Rubin 1975; Irigaray 1985). In the practice of lynching, they served as justifications for white men's sexual mutilation of black men. White men would have denied that lynching was sexual mutilation, of course. Nor were all victims of lynching black and male; black women and children (and a few whites) were also lynched. However, most victims were young black men. Not all black men who were lynched were also castrated, but many were. What did white men think as they assembled into mobs, tracked their prey, captured then tortured the young black man, now naked before them? White men insisted they were protecting their women, that they were doing nothing less than serving "popular justice," saving "civilization." In such a convoluted state of desire denied, relocated, then performed, how to intervene? Who could possibly break the spell? Not knowing who they were, refusing to see what they were doing, white men would not. Black men were terrorized and politically powerless, although they would survive and they would remember. "I AM A MAN" would become the twentieth-century expression of black men's demand for justice, a succinct conflation of the civic and the gendered.

Why did lynching reach its zenith in the last decade of the nineteenth century? As noted, historians and sociologists point to a combination of economic and political factors. There is little doubt that lynching was a political and economic phenomenon, but I will argue that it was as well, and perhaps most profoundly, a gendered, indeed "queer," phenomenon. In that final decade of the nineteenth century there was, in addition to economic and political turmoil, a certain "crisis" in white masculinity, admittedly a problematic characterization given the wide and variable range of responses white men made to an imperiled sense of manhood. For example, some historians argue that nineteenth-century middle-class manhood was most characterized by a "chest-thumping virility, vigorous outdoor athleticism, and fears of feminization" (Bederman 1995a, 7). Others disagree and stress white middle-class men's growing interest in hitherto strictly "feminine" occupations like parenthood and domesticity. White manhood was—is—no monolith; to appreciate the "polymorphous plurality of [this] subject position" (Zizek 1996, 15) enables us to understand these coextensive and apparently contradictory performances of late nineteenth-century manhood as multiple white sides of one racialized coin.

Black women had no political power in the Jim Crow South, but that fact did not mean defeat or submission. A black woman who had been born a slave would make the first memorable intervention in this white-male compulsion to mutilate the black male body. That black woman was Ida B. Wells, a Memphis schoolteacher and journalist. Her moral courage, pedagogical brilliance, and political acumen mark her as one of the greatest Americans to have ever lived.

She would be joined (be it thirty years later) by a white woman, a woman who sensed that lynching—presumably a practice conducted for white women's sake—had nothing to do with them. This white woman was Jesse Daniel Ames, a Texas suffragist who founded the Association of Southern Women for the Prevention of Lynching. It takes no mystic to divine that it would be men, specifically white men, who would resist these women's efforts—and the efforts of black men, most notably, Walter White and James Weldon Johnson of the N.A.A.C.P.—to end the nightmare that was lynching. A mutilated repressed dynamic is not easily exorcised, especially when it appears masked as "constitutionality" and "states' rights," as we will see in chapters 10 and 11.

A majority of Americans say today they no longer believe in white supremacy, but racial violence continues, albeit less explicitly sexualized. There was the Jasper, Texas, "execution" of James Byrd Jr. Byrd, 49, who was chained at the ankles to a pickup truck and dragged to pieces in the East Texas town of Jasper in 1998 by three white men: John William King, 24, Lawrence Russell Brewer, 32, and Shawn Allen Berry, 24. There is evidence that Brewer and King were organizing a white supremacist organization and wanted to do something to publicize the group. Brewer bragged about the crime in letters written from prison, boasting about "rolling a tire," white slang for assaulting an African American. "Well, I did it," Brewer wrote. "And no longer am I a virgin. It was a rush and I'm still licking my lips for more" (quoted in Graczyk 1999, 16).

Recall too the fate of Michael James and Jackie Burden. On December 8, 1995, they were murdered by two white soldiers in Fayetteville, North Carolina. Like the Jasper, Texas, victim, these two young African Americans were not, as TV news-watching white readers might be quick to assume, gang-bangers, dope dealers, drive-by shooters, or carjackers. These were "regular folks" who were walking along a public street, minding their own business, when they were gunned down. Officials found Klan, Nazi, and right-wing militia literature and paraphernalia in the white soldiers' rooms, yet army spokespersons as well as local police claimed that the murders were not racially motivated (Hutchinson 1997).

These are sensational but not isolated events. The F.B.I. reports approximately 9,000 hate crimes are committed each year. A large number of hate crimes are never reported. In 1999 there were approximately 550 hate groups and 250 web sites devoted to hate (Marshall 1999). Just a decade ago, a poll of 1,500 Americans found that 66 percent of whites still opposed a close relative marrying a black man; in 1993 the Anti-Defamation League found that 31 percent of young whites between eighteen and thirty years old thought blacks were lazy and violence-prone (Hutchinson, 1997). Just over a decade ago ex-Klansman David Duke won 60 percent and 55 percent of the white vote in the 1988 and 1990 Louisiana races for the U.S. Senate and governorship, respectively.

Middle-class African Americans do not escape the material and psychological consequences of continuing white racism. Consider the following incident, reported on the television news program "20/20" in 1998. A middle-class black man shops for clothes with his six-year-old son at a local department store. Suddenly they are surrounded by four security men who announce they have been watching them. They are suspected of shoplifting. Examining their packages, the security men find nothing. Frustrated, they demand that both the father and son "pull their pants down." After seeing what they apparently wanted to see, the two black males are permitted to leave (20/20, 1998).

Between the "races," stereotyping and suspicion remain widespread. A survey commissioned by the National Conference of Christians and Jews in 1994 found that 33 percent of Latinos, 22 percent of Asians, and 12 percent of whites believed that "even if given a chance, African Americans aren't capable of getting ahead" (quoted in Johnson and McCluskey 1997, xv). Another recent survey reported that 35 percent of African Americans believe that AIDS was probably the invention of white scientists plotting to annihilate black people (Johnson and McCluskey 1997).

Such statistics disguise the gender of racial politics. Let us look to the discourses on "men" and the "culture of masculinity" to underline the notion of gender in the preceding sentence. The literature on "men" is too extensive to review in detail, but I present an impressionistic sketch in chapters 13–15. There I examine three discourses: one on white (although not self-consciously), one on black, one on "men" in general. Do we find, for instance, persisting questions concerning the stability of masculinity and "manhood"? Do we find a certain displacement of women, both in the emotional lives of men and in men's conceptions of "race"? Are white men "men"? Are they "white"? What about the so-called "compulsive masculinity" of many lower-class black men? And what can the pervasive homophobia across class and race tell us about the gendered nature of hate, distrust, and prejudice?

If white racism is both expressed and experienced as sexualized, as an assault on "manhood," would we not predict that if there were an opportunity for political revenge, some black men might choose sex as the medium? In American prisons we find exactly that. My reasoning did not proceed as neatly as those sentences imply. I came to the prison rape literature on a whim. If nineteenth-century white men could be so mistaken about their rationale for lynching, namely that black men were raping white women (which was rarely the case), then perhaps (I reasoned) the white-male fantasy about interracial prison rape might be just that, another fiction. To my astonishment I discovered white boys were not making this one up. Even in white majority prisons, heterosexually identified black men bypass willing and available homosexuals (both black and white) to rape and "turn out" young, white, heterosexual men. Rope and faggot—to borrow the title of Walter White's (1929) study of lynching—still describe relations between white and black men, if racially reversed and punned.

Were women only units of exchange in a male-male drama? In one sense yes, as the "southern lady" was used as an excuse by white men to mutilate black men. In another sense no, as white men continued to sexually assault black women and to imprison white women in the domestic sphere as wife and mother. White women were often present at lynchings, and on many occasions apparently encouraged their men. But on no occasion (that I found) did a woman participate in the torture and sexual mutilation of black men. That "job" white men reserved for themselves. Even when white women joined the second Klan (chapter 9), there is only fragmentary evidence of women's violence and no evidence of direct participation in lynching. By the time of the second Klan's demise, white women in the South were calling white men on their bluff, declining their "chivalrous" protection and demanding an end to the white-male assault on black men. White women, however, still circulate in the white male/black male economy, as evident in the controversy surrounding Lisa Olson, the (white female) sports reporter for the *Boston Herald* who was sexually harassed by black athletes in the locker room of the New England Patriots football team in 1990. What peculiar gendered reversals and racial re-enactments were at play when, a century after lynching had peaked, black men cried foul, alleging that a white woman had looked at their naked bodies, and white men rallied to the black men's cause? (see Disch and Kane 1996).

I conclude with an effort to situate these "imprinting" moments—lynching and prison rape—in the American literary imagination. Leslie Fielder (1966) permits me to do that, as he shows (eloquently) how the buried and mangled homoerotic circulating in white racism is not restricted to lynching or prison rape, but is in fact central to American civilization, at least as white men have imagined it. Fielder focuses on *Huckleberry Finn* which, he makes clear, represents a primary and founding national fantasy, at least for the white man. Black-male readers especially may be surprised to learn that behind white male racial hatred is longing. "My God ... is this whole thing a horrible mistake?" (quoted in Carter 1969/1979, 215)

I hope this book will be of interest to you working in African American studies, where complex and changing relationships between gender and race continue to be explored. As bell hooks (1994) has observed: "Feminist and/or queer theory established a broader context for discussions of black body politics" (128). I hope the work will be of some use to those in feminist theory, if only as another disruption of heteronormative masculinity. I take to heart Kaja Silverman's (1992) observation that "masculinity impinges with such force upon femininity [that] to effect a large-scale reconfiguration of male identification and desire would, at the very least, permit female subjectivity to be lived differently than it is at present" (2–3).

At the same time I also take to heart Leo Bersani's (1995) warning: "Male feminism ... risks remaining an affair (yet another one) strictly between men, attesting once more to the extraordinary difficulty men have—not in speaking *for* women or *through* women to each other, but in *addressing* women" (70). Given the largely fictional status of women in many men's minds, some "reproduction" of the culture of masculinity even in "feminist men" seems likely. Relatedly, Steven Schacht and Doris Ewing (1998) have observed: "The problem with the present men's studies emphasis, thinly veiled in feminist theory, is that the focus is almost exclusively on men and their problems, and women are marginalized and ignored, as they are in larger patriarchal realities. At best, most of the research undertaken by those in men's studies treats images of femininity as secondary variables" (128). Late in the game I switched my focus from the "racial politics of masculinity" to the "gender of racial politics," allowing me to attend more fully to women's variegated involvement in struggles against racial violence in the United States. Readers will have to judge whether this more expansive focus has functioned to render women's participation in racial politics more than "secondary variables."

I write as well for those working in queer theory—an important influence to which I hope this volume represents a contribution—as well as for those working in cultural studies generally. Finally, but foremost, I write for colleagues in and students of education, especially for students of multiculturalism and of curriculum theory, especially teachers, practicing and prospective. The literature on multiculturalism has been, it seems to me, too focused on platitudes, on technique (if we just teach or organize subject matter this way, we can teach "tolerance"), and, in "radical" circles, too focused on what sometimes seems to be indignation and self-righteousness posing as political and intellectual activism. How can we dedicate ourselves to "educating citizens in a multicultural society" (Banks 1997) when the very category of the civic is saturated with the sexual in this racist nation?

More recently, the concept of "whiteness," formulated by historians and others (see Roediger 1991/1994; Frankenberg 1993, 1997a, b; Kincheloe, Steinberg, Rodriguez, and Chennault 1998) has structured the multiculturalism debate. For instance, Joe Kincheloe and Shirley Steinberg (1998) suggest: "Indeed, critical multiculturalists understand that questions of whiteness permeate almost every major issue facing Westerners at the end of the twentieth century, from affirmative action and intelligence testing to the deterioration of public space. In this context the study of whiteness becomes a central feature of any critical or multicultural education for the twenty-first century" (4). I agree. But once we settle on the term, the questions begin: What is the psychosexual structure and historical character of "whiteness" that renders it so aggressive, so tortured, so interested in subjugation? Clearly something complex and elusive is at work in the phenomenon beyond "prejudice" (Allport 1958), no matter how sophisticated our typology of that complex phenomenon becomes (see Young-Bruehl 1996).

In *The Long Dream* Richard Wright (1958) has two black characters say: "Now, Tyree, I'm going to say something that'll make you think I'm balmy. Those *whites* suffered more than this boy [a lynching victim]. Only folks who *suffer* can kill like this. … 'But what they suffering *from,* Doc?' Tyree asked. 'I don't know,' the doctor confessed. 'I'm not white. If I were, I'd devote my life to finding out why my kind kills like this" (Wright 1958, 77). Let us, in fact, do that.

II. A Queer Progressive Dream

We have been so ridden with tests and measurements, so leashed and spurred for percentages and retardations that the machinery has run away with the mass production and quite a way back bumped off the driver. I wonder that a robot has not been invented to make the assignments, give the objective tests, mark the scores and—chloroform all teachers who dared bring original thought to the specific problems and needs of their pupils.

—Anna Julia Cooper, in Charles Lemert and Esmé Bhan, *The Voice of Anna Julia Cooper* (1998)

We must employ whichever hybrid combination of interpretative technologies we can access or create that will help us to illuminate precisely the many ways in which difference continues to matter at the end of the twentieth century.
—Michael Awkward, *Negotiating Difference* (1995)

So where is the passion that was once invested in the Left?
—Kobena Mercer, *Welcome to the Jungle: New Positions in Black Cultural Studies* (1994)

In colleges of education—departments of curriculum and instruction specifically—most research is focused on teaching or, as many prefer, "instruction." We are interested in learning how to teach more effectively, so that students can learn more quickly, as measured on standardized examinations, neverendingly prominent in public debates over elementary and secondary school education. In this volume I am suggesting a return to curriculum, but hardly in any traditional sense in which we have studied (bureaucratic) procedures and rationales for "curriculum development." The official or institutional curriculum (especially the secondary school curriculum) was settled, more or less, during the 1960s; it would be directed toward and articulated with postsecondary destinations, primary among them the university and the workplace. What remained of the progressive dream—education for democratization which meant schooling for self-realization—was, as William Pilder noted in 1973, past (in Pinar et al. 1995, 222–223).

We whose interest is the educational significance of the curriculum (i.e., the meaning of the school subjects for self and society) awoke in the aftermath of the 1960s national curriculum reform movement to find that we were "invited" to be, in a word, "facilitators," more bluntly and to the point: bureaucrats. Our job was no longer to think through the complex relations among schooling, society, and self, but rather to accept the conflations of school curriculum with the academic disciplines and the marketplace to ensure that students "learn" what others—politicians, policymakers, university faculty in natural sciences, social sciences, and humanities—declared to be worth learning. Vocationalism, academic and the literal kind, ruled—rule—the day.

What became clear was that our task as curriculum specialists was to assist curriculum to be the means to those ends specified by politicians and corporatists and our well-meaning, if narrowly and academically vocationally focused, arts and sciences colleagues in the university. We were to help teachers forget their historical (if never realized) calling to practice academic freedom, to be authentic individuals not automata. We were to help them become skillful implementers of others' objectives, something like an academic version of the postal service, delivering other people's mail. We were not to participate in what we delivered to the children (except for the sake of its more efficient transmission); our job was to see that the mail—the curriculum—was delivered, opened, read, then learned. "Accountability" was—remains—the chant of the day.

Many of us rejected that occupational description and sought from the outset to understand, not just implement then evaluate, the curriculum. The project of understanding was never a retreat from the everyday world of "practice" into some ivory-tower panopticon. On the contrary, we always took understanding to be a form of praxis. So conceived, such theory and practice involved history, politics, race, gender, phenomenology, postmodernism, autobiography, aesthetics, theology, the institution of schooling, the "global village." These are chapter headings of *Understanding Curriculum* (Pinar et al. 1995), and, with the notable exception of the explosive growth of cultural studies since the early 1990s (which has in effect replaced the effort to understanding curriculum as political text), they remain today the major domains of scholarship in the field.

In other words, we traded the safety of bureaucracy for the excitement of intellectual exploration, hoping all along that we could influence our colleagues and friends in the schools to do the same. Although conditions in the schools have only, in general, deteriorated, we remain determined. Traditionally when curriculum had been conceived as a conversation, the concept connoted "conversing" with those great, usually white-male, minds of Western civilization whose ideas presumably transcended the temporal and cultural locales of their origin. That patriarchal and Eurocentric concept is no longer in fashion, for good reason. European high culture is no longer the center of American civilization—was it ever?—especially as it is codified and theorized in academic scholarship and inquiry. But the political decentering of European knowledges and knowing hardly means that curriculum is no longer students' and teachers' conversation with ideas, including European ones, as these are recorded in primary source material, textbooks, and other curricular artifacts and technologies.

Curriculum remains preeminently that conversation, but it is also a conversation among the participants, one which supports and explores the possibilities of unpredicted and novel events, unplanned destinations, which incorporates life history and politics and popular culture as well as official, institutional, bureaucratized knowledge. The concept of curriculum as "complicated conversation" is a concept I have tried to perform pedagogically in this book: one reads lynching headlines, visits prison cells, listens as Ida B. Wells teaches America (while in Britain) to rethink racial violence. One observes the desire of white men for black, as Leslie Fiedler's breathtaking analysis requires us to do. In so doing I am asking readers to discern how the past inhabits the present.

At the same time I am making curriculum for teachers—prospective and practicing—who study in colleges of education. We education professors may be, in effect, shut out of the school curriculum, but, for now, we are still in charge of ours. Let us teach what we think, in our intellectual and professional judgment, that prospective and practicing teachers ought to know as they try to make sense out of the educational project, a project riddled by the competing, often contradictory claims of parents, politicians, and business leaders. Let our students carry into school classrooms what is missing in their district-mandated textbooks and, as circumstances allow and their professional judgment suggests, complicate the conversations there. Employing research completed in other disciplines as well as our own, let us construct textbooks—like this one, perhaps—which enable public school teachers to reoccupy a vacated "public" domain, not simply as "consumers" of knowledge, but as active participants in conversations they themselves will lead. In drawing—promiscuously but critically—from various academic disciplines and popular culture, I work to create a conceptual montage for the teacher who understands that positionality as aspiring to create a "public" space. By so working, we curriculum theorists are working to resuscitate the progressive project.

While hardly turning away from the problems of the everyday classroom and the practical pedagogue, to understand curriculum as the formation of a new public sphere requires us to acknowledge the limits of teaching technique and bureaucratic procedure. Curriculum conceived as a "complicated conversation" cannot be framed as another conceptual product which will somehow fine-tune the American educational engine, to somehow get it humming smoothly "again." (It never hummed, of course.) Education is—will we ever learn?—no mechanical affair, and yet, astonishingly, much of the field and the public still seems to proceed upon the assumption that if we only make the appropriate adjustments—in the curriculum, teaching, learning, administration, counseling, oh yes, the establishment of "standards"—then those test scores will soar. It is a mad, mostly male fantasy.

The truth is that much of our obsession with technique and procedure in the academic field of education is a doomed effort to make an impossible situation possible. That impossible situation is the official or institutional curriculum. The truth is (surely everyone knows this even if they feign ignorance when they speak publicly of the curriculum) that everyone will not (despite teaching technique, parental involvement, or curriculum reform) and (dare one say it?) need not become terribly interested or even "literate" in everything. That all students must take all the major academic disciplines beyond, say, a middle-school level of acquaintance, is not educationally sensible. The secondary school curriculum as we know it is a somewhat arbitrary political settlement of what Herbert Kliebard (1986) has characterized as the struggle for the American curriculum. We educators lost that struggle; businessmen, in cahoots with our university colleagues in the natural sciences, social sciences, and humanities, won. The children lost.

What we have today—still, unbelievably—is nineteenth-century faculty psychology, contemporary versions of that presumably long-ago discredited idea that the mind is a muscle which must be exercised by all the basic weights (academic disciplines) if it is to bulge. Once bulging, clearly visible by high test scores, America will be rich, powerful, ready for the new millennium. Poverty and crime will disappear and the G.N.P. will seek the sky. In addition to this masculinized fantasy which conflates "mind" with "muscles" and test scores with national supremacy and economic productivity, present-day general curriculum requirements also represent a negotiated settlement among competing constituencies, most powerful of which are the sciences and mathematics. With extensive secondary school curricular prerequisites for college admission closely linked with two years of "general education" at the university level, each of the politically powerful academic disciplines gets a piece of the student enrollment (i.e., budget) pie. While this analysis is too simple, it is sound.

While many are sincere in believing that "general education" makes for "well-rounded" individuals, our colleagues in the politically powerful disciplines are hardly unaware that forcing students to study their fields—academic politics disguised as "general education"—also props up enrollment and employment in those fields. The curricular arrangement that stabilized after Sputnik is not, as we educators know (and despite the pious rhetoric), only about the education of students or the preparation of citizens and workers. At the heart of the present vocationalism—academic and otherwise—is the masculinist, militaristic and economic fantasy that academic achievement (as measured by standardized tests; "excellence" in mathematics and science is especially crucial) creates the conditions for national supremacy, understood today primarily as economic prosperity, but also as world cultural hegemony and continued military dominance.

Serious students of curriculum theory know this sad story already. The progressive dream (Pilder 1974) may have been over long ago, but then it always was a dream, wasn't it? Dewey (1916) must have known his was a losing gamble, even if it was a gamble he was compelled to wage, for his own as well as for the nation's sake. And even while the public sphere in America has almost always been dominated to varying degrees by conservative, sometimes reactionary, political and economic interests, individual teachers have continued—partly due to the influence of much maligned education professors—to try to live out that progressive dream of democratization and self-realization. Individual teachers have always helped to keep hope alive, our faith—"our" denoting those of us in the academic field of education, in teacher preparation, and curriculum studies specifically—that individual educators can somehow find ways to work with children outside official directives and bureaucratic inertia, outside that patriarchal public sphere dominated by right-wing politics and capitalistic economics. We can hear that fundamentally humanitarian hope—and the frustration of it—in the struggles of those who fought lynching; surely our situation is no worse than theirs. Despite the stacked deck, the overwhelming odds, the gamble—the progressive dream of democratization and self-realization, inextricably intertwined as each depends upon the other—must again be waged by those of us committed to the project of public education broadly conceived.

It is, from a pedagogical point of view, inspiring and instructive to read about Ida B. Wells, even if we don't have to go to Britain to gain a hearing. (Actually, we wouldn't get one there either, would we?) Despite our political isolation, how out of tune we are with the business-minded present, we theorists are, thank god, a long way from the dire situation in which Wells found herself. We seem a long way from barricades in the street, although I suppose such chaos is always only an economic crash or racial outrage or unjust war away. Our battles, our efforts toward democratization and self-realization, must take more subtle forms these days. That is why questions of "style" are so very important during times like these, when there are no opportunities for more dramatic protest, more serious insurrection. We might consider "miming" and the "roar of silence," but certainly it is the "micropolitics" of everyday life (see chapter 7 for an explication of these concepts), in these institutions where we live with our own and other people's children, that is the sphere of our possible interventions. It is the sphere of cultural and intellectual politics.

The brilliant postwar Italian filmmaker, poet, novelist, and essayist Pier Paolo Pasolini understood this historical situation exactly. Because we live in a period in which consumer capitalism has triumphed, as Pasolini keenly appreciated, knowledge can be "consumed" like any other "product." Certainly schools and universities become increasingly commercialized, knowledge commodified, teaching more like entertainment. Like Ida B. Wells's, Pasolini's "classroom" was huge; his "students" were the citizens of Italy (as Wells's were European Americans), and his teaching occurred through his art, especially his films, but through his poetry and novels as well. A former schoolteacher like Wells, Pasolini was very clear that simple didacticism—straightforward instruction—was finished, a nineteenth-century fantasy of authority and submission. The twentieth-century triumph of consumption meant that anything that could be easily incorporated into existing structures of self and society would in fact be consumed, could make no political difference, teach no moral lessons, make no social difference. What was required, Pasolini argued, were complex, inassimilable stylistic innovations—forms of "indirect discourse," for instance—which would unsettle one's students, quietly institute a revolution in the self, and thereby unsettle extant social relations. The story of Pasolini's pedagogical efforts in film is extraordinary (Greene 1990). Like Wells's accomplishment, it deserves to be known by many, especially by educators, but that is labor for another day.

What follows is a textbook, albeit a somewhat "unconsumable" one. In part it is the length—not primarily a matter of what, in another context, John Willinsky (1998) terms "the encyclopedic urge" (72)—and in part it is the repetition of violence. Of course it is too long; there is much more than one wants to know. That is, in part, my point. The experience of moving through lynching after lynching after lynching, confounded effort after effort to understand it, prison rape after rape, the myriad of ways men "shatter" then pull themselves together to carry on the racialized patriarchy: this arduous experience of reading violence may begin to unsettle the structures of self created by consumer capitalism, structures which allow the consumption of knowledge as simply "more information," another channel on an apparently infinite range of consumable options.

More than half the chapters are summaries of books, especially, for instance, chapters 4, 5, 9, 12, 19, and, in the case of chapters 6 and 8, summaries of essays. I have paraphrased these works faithfully, I believe, but I urge those readers intrigued by what is reported here, and not only in those chapters, to return to the original works. What I have produced here is finally only a residue and remaking of the original; its value here, I trust, is in the composite picture that the juxtaposition of these summaries and paraphrasings creates. The mosaic that appears in their juxtaposition—the gendered Civil War next to Christian feminism and their relation to the so-called crisis of white masculinity which occurred, not incidentally, during the zenith of lynching—allows us to see patterns of association and meaning not easily evident in the original work read by itself.

To create a textbook that is not easily assimilated and "consumed," therefore, I have emphasized, to the point of sensationalism (I worry) and fatigue (I am sure), the horror that was lynching and the nightmare that is prison rape. In addition to "witnessing" for the dead and the subjugated, one hopes to shock not easily shocked readers into rethinking commonsensical conceptions of racism as only "prejudice," simple "intolerance," and, most importantly perhaps, as in the "past." Racism takes historically and culturally specific forms, yet something "essential" remains, at least in the West, among the American inheritors of Judaic-Christian civilization. That "something," I suggest, is a suppressed erotic, a racialized homoerotic. That fact, I trust, will not be easily consumed, as the images of rape and mutilation are "already immanent in words, in the fabric of description" (Mitchell 1994, 99).

In this regard, drawing upon Marla Morris's (1999) discussion of Mitchell's "picture theory," images and words can be thought of as "image-texts" (Mitchell 1994, 91). Image-texts, Mitchell suggests, are "a site of conflict, a nexus where political, institutional, and social antagonisms play themselves out" (91). Representations of lynching, prison rape and the gender of racial politics, then, are "not a homogeneous field or grid of relationship governed by a single perspective" (57), in the present instance a "queer" perspective, but express multiple if interrelated points of view, concretized and singularized, I hope, in the frequent use of others' work, others' voices.

This move does not insure me, of course, against the tendencies toward positions of imagined omniscience so characteristic of white men. Margaret Whitford's (1991) criticism of Derrida is worth considering here. Whitford accused Derrida of failing to speak "in his own voice," of hiding his voice behind a thick screen of quotations and readings of others texts. Is that what I'm doing here? Whitford described Derrida's position as "elusive," "feminine," difficult to locate, for he slides away from any definite position: "Discourse is citation; meaning is ultimately elusive (feminine)." Where is Derrida's place of enunciation, his positionality, if he is forever quoting someone else? In a masculinist way, it is as if he wants to make his position impregnable, ultimately undecidable. In this sense deconstruction enables him to speak elusively and indefinitely, to hold the floor forevermore. "[H]e 'masters' feminist discourse by speaking about it" (Whitford 1991, 130; quoted in Grosz 1995, 66).

These concerns demand consideration, especially from one who, as a theorist and practitioner of autobiography in education, has written about his self-formation in explicit ways for thirty years (see, for instance, Pinar 1994). For me, at this time of my life, at this historical moment, this explicit self-reflexivity has become implicit, as I search for myself in the "shadow of the other" (Benjamin 1998). The citational structure of *The Gender of Racial Politics and Violence in America* does not, I hope, amount to a masculinist hiding in authorial "drag," as Whitford suggests of Derrida. Rather, I trust it points instead to an interior citationality, a map of how one comes to form in the shadows, the cacophony, of countless others, dead but not gone, spirits all around us still. In a phrase, I want to hint at how (this) one comes to self-formation, and specifically intellectual self-formation, in the history of gendered, racialized violence in America.

How this is specifically about me will have wait for another volume; here I want to raise the dead, and introduce them, and others still living, to our students who say they want to be teachers, to our students who are teachers. In this regard I join my colleague Petra Munro and her co-authors Margaret Crocco Smith and Kathleen Weiler (1999) in broadening the scope of curriculum history, what counts as the "canon" of curriculum knowledge. In particular, I join Munro in asking that concept of educational activism be expanded to include the work of Ida B. Wells and Jane Addams, both great social progressives and, in Wells's case, brilliant antilynching pedagogue. While Addams is incidental to the tale I tell, Wells is joined by other great educator-activists who have not before generally been included in the study of curriculum, among them W. E. B. Du Bois, James Weldon Johnson, Jr., Walter White, and Jesse Daniel Ames.

The field of curriculum studies has been dominated by white men who have, in general, overlooked the importance of black and white women as well as black men. This problem has been exacerbated by the tendency to limit our focus to the school. While it has been frequently observed that we work in a field called "education" not "schooling," that we are professors of "education" not "schooling," the truth is that the two have often been—and remain—conflated. To address "practice" has meant to address issues associated with "the school," and, even more narrowly, the public school. This has meant that we have been pressured to participate in what Herbert Kliebard termed the "ameliorative orientation," trying to improve upon an institution which by its bureaucratic structure may make education more difficult rather than more likely. Certainly this tendency to reduce the discipline of education to schooling has often meant the exclusion of educational phenomena that occur outside the school, such as those pedagogical elements of political and social movements (such as the antilynching campaign), and individuals (such as Ida B. Wells) whose political or racial or feminist labor was in a profound sense performed as pedagogical. In this regard I hope the present volume supports the efforts of scholars like Munro (1998, 1999b, and in press) to "engender" and racialize curriculum history, to expand the canon of what counts as curriculum knowledge, and help us focus on education broadly conceived.

You might join us in this scholarly and pedagogical work. We education professors may have very little jurisdiction over the school curriculum, but we do still enjoy some control over the curriculum—the education major—we teach at colleges and universities, at least in terms of the books we ask students to read, the discussions we lead, the questions on which we examine these prospective and practicing teachers. In these classes, undergraduate and graduate, we can work to demonstrate what it means to teach not as technicians but as progressive intellectuals committed to democratization and self-realization, to the creation of a new public sphere, a sphere that depends very much on them and the children they teach. Drawing upon research in various disciplines in the humanities and social sciences, we can make curricular decisions concerning those configurations of knowledge, interdisciplinary in scope, hybrid in nature, that prospective teachers might study in order to understand the nature of the public project to which they claim allegiance: education.

One version of this is what I have attempted here. In this work I have drawn upon several disciplines to portray the problem of "race"—and by implication its attendant problems of antiracist education—as gendered, as, I argue, "queer." (I borrow from Ida B. Wells the practice of using quotation marks around apparently self-evident terms in order to problematize them.) To make the case, I have paraphrased extant research in history, criminology, feminist and queer theory, as well as literary criticism. In the juxtaposition of these paraphrased portraits of the antilynching campaign, for instance, or the conflation of manliness and civilization in the 1893 Chicago World's Fair, is the possibility of saying something "new," something that is more than the sum of its parts, an effort to persuade those who will teach America's children to teach beyond their contractual obligations, toward self-realization and democratization, the realization of a progressive dream visible now only in the intellectual museums of our minds.

This is, in part, what I meant when I called for an autonomous discipline of curriculum theory (Pinar et al. 1995, 853), a call Dwayne Huebner (1999) misunderstood as "hubris" (see 339–440). Disciplinary "autonomy" is not disciplinary arrogance or self-congratulation; it is a call for greater freedom of inquiry and a renewed commitment to the progressive project. Too many scholarly papers in the field simply summarize others' research not in order to create a conceptual montage that becomes a unique and "autonomous" curricular statement to those struggling to create a public domain, but to squeeze out of it so-called implications for curriculum, implications which tend to leave the curriculum as theorized and as taught undisturbed. To become "autonomous" means to freely select from extant research in the academic disciplines to create interdisciplinary statements that belong to no one discipline and which speak to the historical moment and its intersection with life history (Erikson 1975), that is, to the progressive project Dewey elaborated in his own terms for his own time. The labor of curriculum is not the "facilitation" or "implementation" of others' curriculum content, but the creation of ours, however blocked that creation may be from official endorsement in the schools.

Since the leadership of school curriculum development was assumed in the 1960s by university colleagues in the politically powerful academic disciplines, many curriculum specialists have been left with the bureaucratic labor of implementing others' materials and content. In the postreconceptualization period (see chapters 4–15, Pinar et al. 1995), many of us have been working to understand how the curriculum functions, politically, racially, in terms of gender, self, in a postmodern era. We have focused on how ideas generated in other fields or discourses—such as phenomenology or postmodernism or aesthetics—might help us understand the curriculum as a multifaceted process, involving not only official policy, prescribed textbooks, standardized examinations, but as the "complicated conversation" of the participants. We have reconceived the curriculum; no longer is it only a noun. It is as well a verb: *currere*.

Disciplinary Autonomy

The sharp shift to cultural studies during the 1990s has, perhaps, been too abrupt for a field that, just twenty years earlier, was fundamentally reconceptualized. The disciplinary throughline from, say, the (1950) Tyler Rationale (which established the basic scheme by which curriculum was reduced to objectives measured by standardized examinations) through Madeleine R. Grumet's stunning theoretical synthesis in *Bitter Milk* (1988) to contemporary work in cultural studies in education—on subjects as varied as Disney, Barbie, and Macdonalds restaurants—needs to be articulated. That is not my work here. Much of cultural studies represents a postpolitical scholarship (see chapter 5, Pinar et al. 1995). After the crisis and demise of the twenty-year effort to understand curriculum as political text, the major players in that discursive formation moved to cultural studies, among them Apple (1996), McLaren (1997), Wexler (1996), and most prominently, Giroux (1999). Bowers, the fifth major political theorist whose work was key to understanding curriculum as political text, moved to ecological studies. But cultural studies are not just something for frustrated political theorists to do, although it does represent a continuation of their political interest, with Marx now very much muted. Now political analysis (a hybrid, post-Marxist politics) is applied to subjects outside the school but of obvious relevance to it, such as "youth" in Giroux's case. Does the shift to cultural studies amount to a continued dependency upon more prestigious disciplines or areas of study, or is that interdisciplinary movement itself truly hybrid and internally de-centered?

The question is important in part because the field of education broadly, and curriculum studies more specifically, has suffered—and suffers still—from a colonized relation to the other academic disciplines. We have been occupied by "first-world" (in an academic sense) "foreign powers," such as in the case of educational psychology, whose allegiance clearly is to the parent discipline. While we hardly suffer in any way analogous to colonized peoples worldwide, we do behave, however relatively mild our suffering is, as a subjugated people. We tend to take for granted that what is produced in the colonizer "nations" or disciplines is superior to what we produce, and it often is. When many of us imagine ourselves as "sophisticated" and "independent" we imagine ourselves like scholars in the disciplines who occupy us: computer science or sociology or English. What would it mean to achieve independence on our own terms, for our purposes, to become uniquely ourselves, not fuzzy copies of others? These are questions embedded in my call for disciplinary autonomy; they are hardly prompted by hubris but by an acute awareness that the field of education, in order to mature, must work through its colonization by the occupying fields. We must find our own way, loyal to our own history and constituency, to a world we can only now imagine. But imagine it we must, however foggy the future.

In moving to cultural studies we curriculum specialists are asking, as we once did, what knowledge is of most worth. We take from extant academic knowledge—in the present volume from history, criminology, feminist and queer theory—to devise a mosaic that points to the educational significance of that knowledge for the individual, especially (but hardly only) the individual as a gendered, racialized, male, and tragically human creature. I have juxtaposed the research of historians, feminist and gender theorists, prison researchers, and literary critics to point to a reconceptualization of our understanding of what antiracist education might involve, what "teaching for tolerance" must entail, what the very construct of "multiculturalism" must acknowledge: namely that the pandemic homoeroticism present across among the human species cannot forever be driven underground, quarantined in a segregated and marginalized population known as "homosexuals," without the "return of the repressed" in horrible, violent ways. The history of racial violence in the United States makes such a conclusion inescapable.

Understanding the homoerotic which circulates in "race" does not necessarily dissolve either; even gay white men continue to focus primarily upon the bodies of black men, if often valorizing them positively. There is a historical throughline from the auction blocks to basketball courts, from slave to professional athlete. There is an inextricability of the image of the black rapist/superstud rapper in the white male mind. If these throughlines could be self-reflexively grasped within hegemonic white male subjectivity, perhaps we could begin a complicated, long-term process of dereifying our fictions, appreciating the concrete, independent, and subjective realities of those "others" who are not merely figments of our imagination, constructs of displaced and denied desires, but brothers and sisters, a socially horizontal and not necessarily heterosexualized political metaphor.

As a curriculum theorist, and more broadly as an educator, I am asking that we no longer see our professional obligation as simply devising efficient means to deliver knowledge that others—with their own agendas (business productivity, academic vocationalism)—have directed us to deliver. Of course, we must continue to teach the school subjects, the academic disciplines: those are our passions, not to mention contractual obligations. But the point of such pedagogical labor cannot only be improved test scores on standardized examinations (to establish bragging rights for politicians), or only to prepare students for success in college classrooms, although no educator can be opposed to either.

Our task as the new century begins is nothing less than the intellectual formation of a public sphere in education, a resuscitation of the progressive project in gendered and racialized terms, in which we understand that self-realization and democratization are inevitably intertwined. That is, in addition to providing competent individuals for the workplace and for higher education, we must renew our commitment to the democratization of American society, a sociopolitical and economic process that requires the psychosocial and intellectual development of the self-reflexive individual. Such a pedagogical aspiration is inherently gendered, and for me, focused for the moment upon the construction of "white men," countless millions of whom have mistaken their denied and mangled (homo)sexuality for social reality and in the process undermined both democratization and individualization.

Here the progressive dream of a century ago gets queered. We cannot democratize society or self in America without a radical restructuring of the hegemonic white male self. Full of themselves, too many white men remain impervious to the realities of others, realities of poverty, racism, misogyny, homophobia, and that pervasive commodification of subjectivity consumer capitalism compels. Lost in his own fantasies, he is clueless about the dreams of others. Hegemonic male subjectivity must be brought to ruin, shattered in Leo Bersani's (1995) sense, its narcissistic unity dissolved, its repressed feminine composition reclaimed, homosexual desire (now sublimated into identification with the oedipal "father" and a fascistic fraternalism) re-experienced. A restructured male subjectivity would know that we are "always a priori subjected and indebted to the infinite alterity of the other," that "our ability to think or respond in concrete contexts presupposes a necessary subjection before the infinite alterity of the other" (Nealon 1997, 136; quoted in Eppert 1999, 137). A playful, respectful subjection, perhaps; the Levinasian view seems, finally, too bifurcating, too "absolute" (Grosz 1995, 73), too "straight."

"The straight mind valorizes difference," Bersani (1995, 39) asserts. He is not conflating sexual preference with cognitive practice, as he adds you "[o]bviously don't have to be straight to think straight." The association of compulsory heterosexuality with a hierarchical view of difference—an association elaborated earlier by Monique Wittig (1992)—can be understood psychoanalytically. Bersani (1995) reminds us that Kenneth Lewes (1988) theorized male heterosexual desire as the complicated consequence of flight to the father following a horrified retreat from the mother. So conceptualized, male heterosexuality is constructed upon and actively requires a traumatic privileging of difference. "The cultural consolidation of heterosexuality," Bersani (1995) writes, "is grounded in its more fundamental, nonreflective construction as the compulsive repetition of a traumatic response to difference" (40). In this regard, "the straight mind might be thought of as a sublimation of this privileging of difference" (Bersani 1995, 40).

In addition to psychoanalytically inspired studies, cross-cultural anthropological research (see Gilmore 1990) also underlines the defensive and traumatic character of much male heterosexual desire. The compulsory production of an exclusively heterosexual orientation in men appears to depend upon a misogynous identification with (and suppression of desire for) the father as well as a permanent and ongoing disavowal of femininity, associating it with castration, lack, and loss. In the United States (as well as in other former slave states and colonial powers, although each differently), this gendered formation is racialized, and "race" is gendered. In the social production of hegemonic (white) masculinity, the fabrication of masculine identification requires the relocation of repudiated desire onto others who are already fictionalized (constructed as, for instance, stereotypes)—that is, whose civic existence corresponds to their imagined and often sexualized existence in the white male mind. The genesis of this situation is a civilizational story, but that I reserve for the next project.

For now, suffice to say that the progressive dream might require queering in order to be resuscitated: education for the democratization of society probably requires the democratization of the self, in particular, of the hegemonic white male subject. The political pedagogical project of curriculum today involves the ruination of hegemonic white male subjectivity (which is curiously disembodied and de-subjectified, as we will see in chapter 15), its "regression" to positionalities and subjectivities closer to sites of maternal identification. What we need today, I will argue, is a nation of mama's boys, men who have declined to repudiate their maternal identification, men who preserve within themselves their sense of difference, differentiation, relationality.

Perhaps it is only through a conscious embrace of a rejected maternal identification and the re-experience of homoerotic desire, a position of sexualized tension with (not sublimated resistance to) the father, that the son can eschew the lure of Anglo-American patriarchy, of homosociality, of misogyny and racism, of "power." An uncritical, untheorized homosexual positionality is insufficient here. What is necessary are men who understand and claim their fundamental allegiance and loyalty to women, a male positionality that probably requires a sexualized privileging of anatomical sameness to avoid the idealization/subjugation of women, who, especially for many straight men, have become abstract, "objects," not subjectivities in extricable relation to their own. Bersani (1995) suggests as much when he asserts that the "privileging of sameness has, as its condition of possibility, an indeterminate identity. Homosexual desire is desire for the same from the perspective of a self already identified as different from itself" (59).

Here, then, is a structure of (white, male) self that supports difference within itself, not difference denied, repudiated, relocated, projected onto those who then become "others." Difference does not disappear, of course. But the "difference" that remains is not a projected, imagined difference (women as inferior, black men as rapists or, even, as "absolute alterity" in Levinas' [1969] formulation). The difference that remains is a concrete, volunteered not assumed, not imagined, difference which can be expressed and perceived and appreciated by self-differentiated selves (or, in Bersani's phrase, "indeterminate identities"), negotiating, through dialogical encounters, modalities of horizontal relation to each other across democratized terrains of race, class, gender, and time.

The argument here, as Bersani understands, is not that homosexuals are "better" than heterosexuals. Rather, it is, in Bersani's (1995) words, "to suggest that same-sex desire, while it excludes the other sex as its object, presupposes a desiring subject for whom the antagonism between the different and the same no longer exists" (59–60). Such desire, when educated, should significantly decrease the tendency toward self-division and the multiplication of "others." Men's desire for men does not constitute some "third sex," a genetically based version of left-handedness, as some contemporary scientists fantasize. Nor does it have to do with the existence, as nineteenth-century scientists were so sure, of a woman's soul inside a man's body. But "within what might be called the available social field of desiring subjects, the incorporation of woman's otherness may be a major source of desiring material for male homosexuals" (Bersani 1995, 60). After Kaja Silverman (1992), Bersani is suggesting here that men's conscious embrace of the feminine may prove useful in reconfiguring hegemonic male sexuality, reconfiguring a defensive, compensatory, racialized masculinity into ... well, on this point Silverman and Bersani are less explicit. Certainly the intent of reconceptualizing men's sexuality is to theorize forms of masculine desire that do not eroticize displaced elements of oneself, which then one demands "others" to perform, in various positionalities of subjugation, political versions of S&M.

My queer progressive dream narrates a reconfiguration of men's sexual practices, men's psychic structures, and men's relations to women, children, and to the "othered" men. Bersani (1995) writes, "If queerness means more than simply taking sexuality into account in our political analyses, if it means that modalities of desire are not only effects of social operations but are at the core of our very imagination of the social and the political, then something has to be said about how erotic desire for the same might revolutionize our understanding of how the human subject is, or might be, socially implicated" (73). What that revolution might be, what forms it might take, what its significance might be for contemporary political and economic structures—from "democracy" to "capitalism"—is labor for another day. In this work I focus on the ruination of hegemonic white male positionalities through laboring to understand how they come to form "in the shadow of the other." With Bersani, I realize "there is a more radical possibility: *homo-ness itself necessitates a massive redefining of relationality*. More fundamental than a resistance to normalizing methodologies is a potentially revolutionary inaptitude—perhaps inherent in gay desire—for sociality as it is known" (Bersani 1995, 76). Is he thinking of fluid, ever-changing, always voluntary couplings which, even when anonymous, are devoted to discovering and giving pleasure? As Fassbinder knew, the utter ruination of masculinity can produce a pleasure bordering on ecstasy (Silverman 1992).

One task of the curriculum theorist today, then, is to think beyond the contemporary discourses (see Pinar et al. 1995; Pinar 1999)—while hardly forgetting or de-legitimating them—to extant disciplinary research and popular culture to theorize self-conscious, self-chosen forms of desire and sociality that democratize ourselves and our world. In so doing, we explicate the educational significance of disciplinary research and popular culture for what used to be called (in a thematization of the historical moment) the issues of the day. Despite the nation's distraction by its apparent political and economic and cultural triumph worldwide, by the stock market and technology, we are a nation very much lodged in the shadow of the other, not only the concrete others among us but the ghosts of citizens past and citizens removed from us, imprisoned in the present. In this queer's progressive dream, we the living speak to and honor the dead, work to avenge their murders, remember their dreams, and testify to the lived realities of this gendered and racialized prison-house that is our prosperous pagan America. No one may listen, but the dead among us demand no less.

If we who work in this field of curriculum studies endeavor to understand the educational significance (i.e., its meaning for self and society) of the curriculum across the academic disciplines, we must exhibit in our research an interdisciplinary range and interest. In contrast to subject matter specializations which now dominate departments of curriculum and instruction, specializations which focus, for instance, upon the more effective teaching of English or science or mathematics, curriculum theory aspires to understand the overall educational significance not only of the school curriculum but "curriculum" writ large, including popular culture, historical moment, life history, all intersecting and embodied in (but not restricted to) the students sitting in our classrooms. To focus upon the educational significance of schooling and trends in the culture at large means returning systematized knowledge to the individual him- or herself, teaching not only what is, for instance, historical knowledge, but also suggesting its possible consequences for the individual's self-formation and the gendered remaking of the nation. It means assuming the position of the "public intellectual," especially now that this tradition is so attenuated (Jacoby 1987), and to suggest the significance of academic knowledge for the society at large. We might aspire to become, in Edward Said's (1996) phrase, intellectuals as "amateurs" (82). Teachers, perhaps. With "passionate minds." Like Maxine Greene (see Pinar 1998b, 1998c).

To explicate the relations among curriculum, culture, the individual, and society is to breathe life into a progressive commitment that is currently only a memory. It is to reformulate the Deweyan commitment to democracy and education in light of our situation, our time, our lives, and the lives of children. That, at its most simple and basic, is the historical throughline between the field of education one hundred years ago and the contemporary field, specifically curriculum theory. Such a complex—some would say "chaotic" (Doll, 1993)—view of knowledge is quite congruent with the understanding of curriculum as a "complicated conversation" (Pinar et al. 1995, 848), disclosing as it does the relational character of ideas, in relation not only one to the other, but pointing as well to their embodiment and personification in individual lives, their origin and expression in social movements and trends, their rootedness in the historical past, their foreshadowing of our individual and national futures.

What the present study suggests is that white racism is, in an important sense, queer. White racism, in part, is a mangled but very much still circulating homoerotic desire, a "return of the repressed." When we appreciate that, our understandings of both "race" and "gender" become more complicated and interwoven, our sense of "racial politics" gendered, our sense of gender racialized. The future of the nation depends, I think, upon unraveling these conflated currents and thematics and taking pedagogical action to dissolve them. None of this will be simple or straightforward, of course. It won't be straight at all.

A Cacophony of Voices

As in *Understanding Curriculum,* I wanted to honor the multiplicity of voices that participate in the scholarly conversations regarding these subjects. And so I quote frequently. In so doing I work to "problematize the standard masculinist ways in which the author occupies the position of enunciation" and thereby create, at least by Elizabeth Grosz's (1995) definition, "a feminist text" (23). Sometimes I experience this construction of writing as a parallel to filmmaking, editing bits of film—conversation, interior monologue, visual images—to create a conceptual collage. Such a performance of scholarship might disrupt the patriarchal sense of a single totalizing author; it affirms the "death" of the author as self-made or omniscient. There can be no smooth linear progression of incrementally sequenced thoughts, like steps on a path to a destination I alone have in mind. Instead, I hope there is something of the cacophonous sound of a Charles Ives symphony. One hears a cacophony of voices, the sound and sight of which refer you, the reader, to yourself and your situation, while reminding you of others. After all, one educational point of this study is to prod you to reconsider what you have taken for granted about the gender of racial politics and violence.

This ambition to portray a cacophony of voices comprising that "complicated conversation" that is a field of study suggests another, more troubling, issue concerning style or methodology which has no obvious solution, at least to me. This has to do with the problem of being a white man writing about black men and women, black and white. It has to do with reporting "scenes of subjection," to borrow the title of Saidiya V. Hartman's (1997) extraordinarily thoughtful study of "terror, slavery, and self-making in nineteenth century America." What concerned her and what concerns me is the specular nature of black (and in the case of prison rape, white) suffering, how others' suffering can blur then disappear when it rests in the gaze of the observer. The problem can be understood, in part, as one of empathy—what we might term the queer politics of empathy. It is true that I hope students will be provoked to greater zeal in fighting racism and misogyny, zeal informed by a more complex and perhaps individuated understanding of both. But, as Hartman shows in her consideration of this issue in regard to slavery, this is no easy or self-evident matter. To help us think through the dangers of teaching about lynching, prison rape, and the gender of racial politics and violence, I want to focus, in this final section of the introduction, on Hartman's discussion of these issues in reference to slavery.

III. The Queer Politics of Empathy

While some feminists have begun to take on questions of race and racism, white gay men retain a deafening silence on race.

—Issac Julien and Kobena Mercer, "True Confessions: A Discourse on Images of Black Male Sexuality" (1991)

This obsession of dependency is what makes white Americans, in general, the sickest and certainly the most dangerous people, of any color, to be found in the world today.

—James Baldwin, *The Price of the Ticket* (1985)

I argue that "identification" ... is inimical to a responsive/responsible "learning from."

—Claudia Eppert, "Learning Responsivity/Responsibility" (1999)

Identity is the negative of our desiring fantasies.

—Leo Bersani, *Homos* (1995)

Flesh is only the thermometer of a becoming.

Gilles Deleuze and Félix Guattari, *What Is Philosophy?* (1994)

Abolitionist John Rankin wrote to his brother about the "very dangerous evil" of slavery. What provoked Rankin on this occasion was the witnessing of a coffle ("a train of slaves or animals chained together"). This sight made vivid for him the obscene theatricality of the slave trade. He wrote: "Unfeeling wretches purchased a considerable drove of slaves—how many of them were separated from husbands and wives, I will not pretend to say—and having chained a number of them together, hoisted over the flag of American liberty, and with the music of two violins marched the woe-worn, heart-broken, and sobbing creatures through the town." The spectacle was almost more than he could bear; he was especially shocked by "seeing the most oppressive sorrows of suffering innocence mocked with all the lightness of sportive music." Rankin exclaimed: "My soul abhors the crime." The destruction of domesticity, the parody of liberty, and the callous ignoring of profound suffering characterized the scene in which crime became a theatrical spectacle (Hartman 1997). The "very dangerous evil" of slavery and the "agonizing groans of suffering humanity" were transposed into music (quoted in Hartman 1997, 17).

The sheer cruelty of slavery, Rankin continued, "far exceed[ed] the power of description." Perhaps, but he did not put his pen down. In attempting to describe the horrors of slavery, and this is a point crucial to Hartman's project, Rankin makes clear that the crimes of slavery were not only experienced by the enslaved, not only witnessed by onlookers, but in fact deliberately staged. He makes this explicit by using terms like "stage," "spectacle," and "scene" to convey what he saw. Further, the "abominations of slavery" were disclosed through the reiteration of secondhand accounts, stories from "unquestionable authorities" which positioned Rankin as a surrogate witness to the enslavement of Africans. In the effort to "bring slavery close," these secondhand reports and stories were "performed" in Rankin's letters (Hartman 1997).

Rankin's intention is mine as well: to shock the reader by reducing the comfortable distance of the spectator. How? By providing details, grisly and horrible, Rankin (and I) hope to persuade those indifferent to slavery (racism and the gender of racial politics and violence, in my case) by exhibiting the suffering of the enslaved (the lynched and the raped, in my case). In so doing, Rankin reasoned, perhaps an identification between those free and those enslaved might be built:

> We are naturally too callous to the sufferings of others, and consequently prone to look upon them with cold indifference, until, in imagination we identify ourselves with the sufferers, and make their sufferings our own. ... When I bring it near, inspect it closely, and find that it is inflicted on men and women, who possess the same nature and feelings with myself, my sensibility is aroused. (quoted in Hartman 1997, 18)

In other words, as Hartman poetically puts it: "By bringing suffering near, the ties of sentiment are forged" (18). Then the white man is "aroused"? To bring suffering even nearer to his readers, to suggest to these readers that slaves possess the same nature and feelings as do they—thereby establishing the common humanity of all—Rankin proceeds to imagine that he, his wife and children are enslaved. By becoming the enslaved, he creates a scenario for shared feelings:

> My flight of imagination added much to the tumult of passion by persuading me, for the moment, that I myself was a slave, and with my wife and children placed under the reign of terror. I began in reality to feel for myself, my wife, and my children—the thoughts of being whipped at the pleasure of a morose and capricious master, aroused the strongest feelings of resentment; but when I fancied the cruel lash was approaching my wife and children, and my imagination depicted in lovely colors, their tears, their shrieks, and bloody stripes, every indignant principle of my bloody nature was excited to the highest degree. (Hartman 1997, 18)

Here Rankin and I part company. It seems Rankin's intent has become convoluted; how I hope mine will not. While his fantasy affords him a vicarious firsthand experience of the lash and provokes his indignation and resentment, the fantasy does not seem "clean," not free of his own (submerged) libidinal investment. Of course, no one is free of libidinal investment (certainly I would not claim to be), but it seems here that righteous indignation makes more likely its disguise and distortion. True, Rankin's fantasized scenario results in a renewed protest against the institution of slavery. True too, the point of his identification with himself-as-slave is to make vivid, even intimate, the crime of slavery, but his flight of imagination, his slipping into the male slave's body carries additional baggage, baggage which suggests, in Hartman's phrase, "the difficulty and slipperiness of empathy" (18).

Empathy—Hartman consults Webster's and Peter A. Angeles' (1981) *Dictionary of Philosophy*—is a projection of oneself into another in order to better understand the other or "the projection of one's own personality into an object, with the attribution to the object of one's own emotions" (Angeles 1981; Webster's 1976). This seems straightforward enough, but, Hartman points out, Rankin's practice of empathy confounds his interest in identifying with the enslaved. In making the slave's suffering his own, Rankin's identificatory experience shifts: now he begins to feel for himself rather than for those whom his exercise in imagination presumably represents. Moreover, as Hartman explains, by using the vulnerability of the male slave body as a vessel for his own purposes, his own thoughts and feelings, the humanity he is narratively attempting to extend to the slave inadvertently evaporates in his imagination. With the best of intentions but undermined by the undertow of his own libidinal cathexis, Rankin performs those same expectations and desires which structured chattel slavery. In fact, the ease of Rankin's empathic identification follows not so much upon his good intentions and heartfelt opposition to slavery as to "the fungibility of the captive body" (Hartman 1997, 19). Are white readers—am I—in Rankin's company? By focusing on lynching and prison rape are we, too, reiterating the voyeuristic violence of the white eye? Is somewhere in the hidden labyrinth of the contemporary white unconscious—including my unconscious—an excitation at the sexualized suffering of others, including black others?

The problem is, and here I remain indebted to the perceptive analysis of Saidiya V. Hartman, that Rankin becomes a proxy. The pain of the "other" is acknowledged to the extent that it can be imagined, yet by virtue of the substitution Rankin's object of identification disappears. To convince the white reader that slavery is indeed horrible, Rankin volunteers himself and his family for punishment. Because the black body was perceived not as continuous with the white body but in fact alien to it, Rankin positioned the white body in the place of the black body in hope that then black suffering would be visible and audible to his white audience. "Yet," Hartman (1997) points out, "if this violence can become palpable and indignation can be fully aroused only through the masochistic fantasy, then it becomes clear that empathy is double-edged, for in making the other's suffering one's own, this suffering is occluded by the other's obliteration" (19).

Such are the politics of empathy, or more precisely, the repressive effects of empathy. Hartman quotes Jonathan Boyarin (1994), who suggests that the empathetic "obliteration of otherness" follows from a facile intimacy—an identification—with the "other" dependent on our ability to imagine them to be us. Put simply, "empathy fails to expand the space of the other but merely places the self in its stead" (quoted phrases in Hartman 1997, 20). Gayatri Spivak (1993) too has worried that the ethical position requires imagining the position of the other, with the effect of the self appearing where the "other" had been. Spivak suggests an erotics of surrender, conscious of the impossibility of translation. Hartman is not, however, suggesting that empathy be discarded as an ethical tactic. Nor does she want to dismiss as narcissism Rankin's desire to exist in the place of the other. Rather, Hartman wants to underline the dangers of a facile intimacy which substitutes the self for the other, performing in the imagination what one wants to condemn "out there." Perhaps there is, regardless of one's intentions, a certain "violence of identification" (Hartman 1997, 19; Morrison 1988).

Acknowledgment does not an exorcism make. Does black suffering in particular make a claim on—an appeal to—the white (male) eye? Why would whipping and pain occur to Rankin as the moment of identification? Such a question may seem obvious given the violence, the sadism, of slavery. Abolitionists and other white sympathizers thought so: *Uncle Tom's Cabin* sold well. The slave narrative also contributed to the sense that the feelings and consciousness of the enslaved were most available to whites at the site of suffering. Hartman worries that if the scene of beating is what so readily lends itself to white identification with the black enslaved, does it risk the naturalization of a "pained embodiment?" And if so, contrary to Rankin's good intentions, then does this white identification with black suffering increase the difficulty of empathy by reproducing the spectral position of the white eye, the same position the sadist slaveholder occupied? Hartman (1997) puts the problem this way: "If, on the one hand, pain extends humanity to the dispossessed and the ability to sustain suffering leads to transcendence, on the other, the spectral and spectacular character of this suffering, or, in other words, the shocking and ghostly presence of pain, effaces and restricts black sentience" (20). The living person who is enslaved becomes an "other"—an abstraction which then disappears in the white mind. But then the "living person"—for

Europeans most fundamentally a spirit, a soul—could not be black, for as Isaac Julien and Kobena Mercer (1991) have observed: "Racism defined African peoples as having only bodies" (170).

As Rankin himself said, in order for black suffering to stimulate a reaction among whites, it must be brought close to whites. Yet if empathy is "inextricably tied to human proximity," to quote Zygmunt Bauman, the problem becomes that in the very movement of bringing it near and inspecting it closely, empathy—its moral potential—disappears. Bauman (1991) writes: "Morality conform[s] to the law of optical perspective. It looms large and thick close to the eye" (192). If so, then, how does suffering disappear in the very movement of bringing it near? It disappears, Hartman (1997) explains, precisely because it can only be brought near by way of a proxy, embedded in Rankin's own indignation, in his imagination:

> If the black body is the vehicle of the other's power, pleasure, and profit, then it is no less true that it is the white or near-white body that makes the captive's suffering visible and discernible. Indeed, the elusiveness of black suffering can be attributed to a racist optics in which black flesh is itself identified as the source of opacity, the denial of black humanity, and the effacement of sentience integral to the wanton use of the captive body. (20)

This racist opacity is further complicated, Hartman adds, by the repression of the specular, that is the dynamic by means of which the other functions as a mirror of the self, so that to recognize suffering one must substitute the self for the other.

Rankin's attempts to stimulate white feeling and engender white empathy before the spectacle of black suffering are then erased rather than created by his intervention. Rankin's effort to stimulate empathy, it turns out, increases the distance between white readers and black slaves by literally displacing the slave as his/her pain is brought near. Any white identification made at the site of suffering, Hartman worries, functions to undermine whites' direct experience of black humanity as it reproduces racist assumptions of a limited black sentience, as it reaffirms that the humanity of the enslaved and the violence of the institution of slavery can only be brought into white view by scenes of sadism and dismemberment, and by placing white bodies at (imaginary) risk. "What does it mean," Hartman (1997) asks, "that the violence of slavery or the pained existence of the enslaved, if discernible, is only so in the most heinous and grotesque examples and not in the quotidian routines of slavery? [I]s it not the difficulty of empathy related to both the devaluation and the valuation of black life?" (21). No doubt. But does not the obsession with black suffering, even in service of morality and empathy, suggest another hidden dynamic at work? Does not the apparent opacity of the black man's skin point to an unacknowledged queer grain in the white male eye?

There is a problem with Rankin's empathic identification with the black male slave that is specific to the economy of chattel slavery. While such identification, made possible by the white projection of white feeling upon or into the black object, that is, enfleshed property, and a concomitant fantasized slippage into captivity, while different from those pleasures of white self-inflation which accrued from the ownership of black bodies and all the expectations (including sexual expectations) associated with ownership, is nonetheless entangled in the slave economy. Albeit in an imaginary register, white empathetic identification with the black other amounts to another form of possession or occupation of the enslaved black body. This relation between white pleasure and white possession of black property, in both figurative and literal senses, has to do with what Hartman terms "the fungibility of the slave." That is to say, white pleasure follows in part from the replaceability and interchangeability specific to the commodity, and to "the augmentation of the master subject through his embodiment in external objects and persons." Hartman (1997) explains:

> [T]he fungibility of the commodity makes the captive body an abstract and empty vessel vulnerable to the projection of others' feelings, ideas, desires, and values; and, as property, the dispossessed body of the enslaved is the surrogate for the master's body since it guarantees his disembodied universality and acts as the sign of his power and dominion. Thus, while the beaten and mutilated body presumably establishes the brute materiality of existence, the materiality of suffering regularly eludes (re)cognition by virtue of the body's being replaced by other signs of value, as well as other bodies. (21)

Does Rankin's desire "to don, occupy, or possess blackness or the black body" now appear as straightforward good will and generosity? Is the site of his identification both structured and enabled by the material relations of chattel slavery? Does it not now appear that embedded in Rankin's indignation, outrage, and simulated suffering there is as well some measure of unacknowledged pleasure? While his willingness to abase himself by positioning himself as the beaten does establish a certain moral authority, is there not a hidden and denied masochistic pleasure suggested by this painless embrace of pain? Why does Rankin choose to become the stripped, sweating, muscular black male body in order to testify to the horrors of slavery? What inner and denied passions of his own does this fantasy of being beaten serve? Hartman (1997) suggests that Rankin's fantasy of being beaten "is immune neither to the pleasures to be derived from the masochistic fantasy nor to the sadistic pleasure to be derived from the spectacle of sufferance" (21). While serving the cause of human freedom by performing his moral righteousness, Rankin is getting off.

Like Hartman, I worry that depictions of lynching and prison rape will not just shock but also exploit the perverse. That leaves intact the white male subject and the psychosexual structure of "whiteness" and "masculinity." Yes, I want to teach prospective and practicing teachers, as well as interested others, the gender of racial politics and violence. Students must know what happened, how history is not past but present. But perhaps, in this area, any white and male pedagogical intention cannot be made "clean," free of libidinal investment.

After carefully considering "the complicated nexus of terror and enjoyment" (Hartman 1997, 21) that is Rankin's fantasy of being a black male body in pain, the complicated and queer politics of empathy are clearer but no more resolved. By reminding us how the sadistic sexualized excitations of the white male master are reenacted in Rankin's righteous indignation at the spectacle of black suffering, Hartman (1997) underlines the instability of the scene of suffering and points to our complicity with it even when we testify against it.

By slipping into the black male body and figuratively occupying the position of the enslaved, Rankin plays both captive and attester. In his "occupation" of the black male body Rankin performs what Hartman terms "the crisis of witnessing," a crisis provoked in this instance by the legal incapacity of slaves or even freed blacks to act as witnesses against whites. Since black testimony could not exist, the crimes of slavery had to be witnessed by white observers. But that was not enough, given that whites disagreed over the nature of subjugation. The crimes of slavery had to be made visible to the white eye, perhaps by stripping off his or her shirt and revealing the naked scarred back, by making, in Hartman's phrase, "the body speak." Or the crimes must be made unmistakable by enabling the reader and audience member to experience vicariously the "tragical scenes of cruelty," as Rankin tried to do (Hartman 1997, 22). The "crisis" was doubled in that what the white man's witnessing was sometimes less the black man's suffering and more his own denied desire.

If as a consequence of his abolitionist sentiments Rankin was willing to occupy the enslaved position, it was this white sentimentalism that informed his identification with the enslaved, his risk-free but titillating identification with black male suffering. Rankin refused to accept at face value the pageantry of the coffle, including how slave traders forced slaves to sing in an effort to disguise "the sorrows of suffering innocence" (as Rankin termed their condition). The risk, as Hartman has made plain, is that in the attempt to understand the inner feelings of the enslaved, whites like Rankin managed to efface the horrors of slavery by substituting their own imaginary spectacle for the material suffering of the enslaved. Further, the structure of his fantasy reproduced the specular structure of slavery itself, whereby slaves were extensions of masters' fantasies of themselves, which, among other things, required them to believe in the slaves' presumably unlimited capacity for suffering. Despite these seemingly overwhelming problems, the effort had to be made, for many eyewitnesses of the coffle believed what they saw; for these naïve observers the terrors of slavery were disguised by song, and the violence was exciting, even titillating (Hartman 1997).

What Hartman has pointed to in her perceptive discussion of Rankin, I face in the reporting of lynching and prison rape. What Hartman has underlined so carefully is "the spectacular nature of black suffering and, conversely, the dissimulation of suffering through spectacle." In one sense, these imagined scenes of cruelty made vivid the suffering of the enslaved. In another sense, it was the specular character of slavery itself that produced this crisis of witnessing as much as did the repression of black testimony, given that the body who spoke was forced to speak the master's truth, to provide him with an amplified sense of his own power and manhood by the imposition and intensification of pain. The problem of testimony was further complicated by the "half-articulate" and "incoherent song" that confounds what Hartman nicely terms "the transparency of testimony" and in so doing complicates any portrait of slavery. In light of these concerns, Hartman (1997) poses the following questions:

> Does the extension of humanity to the enslaved ironically reinscribe their subjugated status? Do the figurative capacities of blackness enable white flights of fantasy while increasing the likelihood of the captive's disappearance? Can the moral embrace of pain extricate itself from pleasures borne by subjection? In other words, does the scene of the tyrannized slave at the bloodstained gate delight the loathsome master and provide wholesome pleasures to the upright and the virtuous? Is the act of "witnessing" a kind of looking no less entangled with the wielding of power and the extraction of enjoyment? Does the captive's dance allay grief or articulate the fraught, compromised, and impossible character of agency? Or does it exemplify the use of the body as an instrument against the self? (22)

The scenes of subjugation considered here—the public spectacles of lynching in which the black (usually male) body was sometimes stripped, tortured, mutilated, dismembered and the less public but still horrible spectacles of prison rape in which often young white male bodies are stripped and assaulted—raise these same questions. While I decline to transpose my self into the bodies of the suffering—whether this be the black man being lynched or the white man being raped—I necessarily position myself as spectator, even while in the service of teaching prospective teachers the queer character of white racism and the gendered nature of racial politics. But to document those claims I must report in some detail descriptions and testimonies and analyses which make them credible. Even in the reporting of the struggle against lynching, led by Ida B. Wells, Jesse Daniel Ames, Walter White, James Weldon Johnson, and other leaders of the N.A.A.C.P., I do not escape these questions concerning my positionality. Does my admiration for these activists, for instance, substitute for participation? While teachers need to situate historically and understand in gendered terms the problems of race in schooling and of multiculturalism in the curriculum, have I not unintentionally positioned them—many of whom are middle-class white females—in the bodies of those white wives, daughters and relatives who watched from the edge of the crowd as their "men" savaged—"raped"—black men?

The problem has to do, *au fond,* with the fact that "the constitution of blackness as an abject and degraded condition and the fascination with the other's enjoyment went hand in hand" (Hartman 1997, 22). From the beginning of the slave trade, blacks were seen not as separate individuals but fundamentally as vehicles for white enjoyment, in all of its nightmarishly variegated and often specifically sexual expression. This imaginary subject position of the enslaved African legally encoded the chattel status of the captive and was supported by whites' insistence that the enslaved "act" as if they were free. Whites forced blacks to dance on the decks of slave ships crossing the Middle Passage, step it up lively on the auction block, amuse the master and his friends with good humor while they felt his muscles, fondled his genitals to check for "breeding potential."

Hartman points to the popularity of the "darkies" on the minstrel stage who also have to be understood in these terms, as enabling the white predator to mistake his own motives, to fictionalize the raw reality of southern "society." The subjective and individuated reality of African persons was thereby erased, granting nearly free reign to the white imagination. The nineteenth-century white male imagination was remarkably uniform, unified and congealed by the core fantasy of the black "other." From the proslavery plantation pastoralism to the romantic racialism of abolitionists, all "saw" the African as "childish, primitive, contented, and endowed with great mimetic capacities" (Hartman 1997, 23), features which gathered together in the character of the infamous Sambo. As Hartman understands, these dynamics of the white imagination are key to any evaluation of the politics of pleasure, the uses of slave property, the constitution of the white and black male subject, and the tactics of black dissent. In America, terror and enjoyment converged on the site of the black body (Hartman 1997).

Perhaps the conflation of terror and enjoyment, morality and perversity, can be mitigated by the copious use of the first-person singular. Not "I"—that might support the imaginary inflation of the white male self slipping into the black male other—but the voices of others might help us (the reader, the student) hear the reality of the other, might interrupt our gaze, break the trance that is "whiteness" and "masculinity." By reducing slaves to their bodies—that was their economic as well as sexual value—whites blurred the boundaries between themselves and those they exploited. By forcing slaves to act "happy" and by pretending that slaves were part of the family, by taking the fondled and raped black body as property to be used at will, whites erased black suffering as they inflated white pleasure. In doing, the "whiteness" became invisible (it was "reality") and the white male body disappeared into imagined black ones. Part of the task of antiracist antisexist education is to return white men to themselves so that they might in fact "hear" when the subaltern speaks. By quoting copiously the individual voices of others, I hope to support this project of phenomenological grounding, autobiographical referentiality, and intersubjective sensitivity and relationality, a project which disentangles "identification" and rediscovers "desire."

What I am after is suggested by Kaja Silverman (1992) in the introduction to her study of "male subjectivity at the margins." In this book she examines the work of German filmmaker Rainer Werner Fassbinder. Employing psychoanalytic language, Silverman argues that Fassbinder portrayed masochistic "ecstasy" as an occasion for the "ruination" of masculinity. His cinema was about, Silverman (1992) suggests, "returning to the male body all of the violence which it has historically directed elsewhere, strategies ranging from literal castration and dismembering to homosexual sadomasochism" (9). She further argues there are "moments within that cinema in which the male psyche is in effect 'lifted out' of the male body, and made to feel the pain of other bodies—moments at which identification works according to the logic of 'excorporation' rather than the logic of incorporation" (Silverman 1992, 10). Perhaps another way to understand the problem of empathy is "identification" in its incorporative sense, a sense in which the body of the "other" disappears in the mind of the observer. Perhaps what is required, then, is a "ruination" of the hegemonic male subject so that he may be able to at least glimpse the "otherness" of the "other" while loving, desiring, succoring him. What follows is a textbook that wants to help with the work of just such a perversion, a contribution to the intensification of the continuing "crisis" of white hegemonic masculinity.

IV. Acknowledgments

There are many to thank: Peter Taubman for introducing me to Robert Musil and Pier Paolo Pasolini, initiating the larger project of which this is volume one; Petra Munro for the Bederman essay and the reprint of the Jane Addams/Ida B. Wells-Barnett 1901 exchange in *The Independent* as well as her suggestions regarding chapters 6 and 8; to Claudia Eppert for critiquing chapters 1–4 and for introducing me, through her dissertation, to Levinas and the literature of historical trauma, and to Steve Triche for bringing Adam Fairclough's work to my attention. Thanks as well to John Broughton at Teachers College who encouraged me to pursue my hunch, first articulated in my 1991 essay on education in the South, that the white male fear of black rape was in part a relocated and denied homosexual desire; thanks also to LSU English professors Richard Moreland (for suggesting Christopher Looby) and Elsie Michie (for recommending Kaja Silverman).

I am appreciative of my colleague Ron Good's skepticism regarding psychoanalysis and notions of sexuality that are historical and social rather than genetic, a skepticism that forced me to remain reflective about my most basic assumptions. Thanks to Hongyu Wang and very especially to Seung-bin Roh for help with the references and permissions. Seung-bin not only helped with references, but sent out permissions, hunted down missing page references, and performed a multitude of important if tedious tasks. I'm not sure how I would have done without you, Seung-bin. I am grateful as well to Pam Autrey, Brian Casemore (who also helped with permissions), Nicole Guillory (who also kindly brought Horace Mann and Julia Bond's *Star Creek Papers* to my attention), Denise Taliaferro, and Candace Yang for reading and critiquing the entire manuscript late in the fall term 1999.

I thank the University of Virginia for a mostly free fall term 1995, the time when I first delved into lynching, and Louisiana State University for a sabbatical leave spring term 1998, during which time much was accomplished. Thanks too to Bill Doll and Donna Trueit, who took over, without my asking and much to my relief, the planning of the 2000 LSU Conference on the Internationalization of Curriculum Studies, allowing me to concentrate on finishing this project. I want to express special thanks to Joe Kincheloe and Shirley Steinberg, whose enthusiastic and continuing support of my work has been very important to me. Thanks too to Chris Myers of Peter Lang for his courage in taking on a project of this size, for his willingness to discuss with me matters of production.

I wish to acknowledge my intellectual mentors from my student days at Ohio State. Over thirty years ago Paul Klohr taught me that a serious curriculum scholar pursues developments in disciplines outside the field of education. Retired since 1980, Paul still reads widely, and generously provided material from the *Times Literary Supplement,* the *New York Review of Books,* and from other periodicals I had no time to read. Also thirty years ago Don Bateman introduced me to the work of Paulo Freire and taught me the primacy of the "political" in understanding curriculum. Like Paul, Don remains an inspiration to me today, as he continues to be intellectually and politically engaged, now in the ongoing ecological crisis.

Finally and passionately, I wish to acknowledge Jeffrey Duram Turner, whose love sustains my work and my life. While hardly free of the racial politics described in this volume, our relationship has not succumbed to them.

To you, Jeff, I dedicate this.

William F. Pinar
March, 2000

ONE

Lynching

1 ❖ STRANGE FRUIT

I. The Lynching of Claude Neal

[T]hose strange fruit that Southern trees bore, about which the great Billie Holiday poignantly sang.

—Cornel West, *Race Matters* (1993)

In patriarchy, men (not women) "castrate" each other.

—Calvin C. Hernton, *The Sexual Mountain and Black Women Writers* (1987)

[T]he unconscious itself [is] fundamentally a crowd.

—Gilles Deleuze and Félix Guattari, *A Thousand Plateaus: Capitalism and Schizophrenia* (1987)

[T]he loveliest lynchee was our Lord.

—Gwendolyn Brooks, "The *Chicago Defender* Sends a Man to Little Rock," from *Selected Poems* (1963)

In the early hours of October 27, 1934, in the deep woods of northwest Florida, near Marianna, white men lynched a black laborer named Claude Neal. He had been accused of raping and murdering a young white woman, the daughter of one of his employers, nine days earlier. The murder of Neal, which the N.A.A.C.P.'s Walter White condemned as "one of the most bestial crimes ever committed by a mob" (quoted in McGovern 1982, ix), was overshadowed by the Scottsboro episode, which remains uppermost in the memory of most scholars as the main event in 1930s racial politics. Jean-Paul Sartre wrote a play based on the Scottsboro Nine entitled *The Respectful Prostitute.* I will devote an entire chapter—chapter 12—to the trials of the Scottsboro Nine.

Despite the outrageousness and visibility of the Scottsboro situation, the Neal incident prompted one of America's foremost psychoanalysts, A. A. Brill, to write, "De Sade in all his glory could not have invented a more diabolical situation" (quoted in McGovern 1982, ix). The lynching resulted in national news stories on the victim, produced an outcry from liberal groups, and drew criticisms from several close to President Franklin D. Roosevelt. Both Neal and the Scottsboro Nine were accused of violating the South's most sacred taboo: sex between a black man and a white woman (McGovern 1982). In the American South, such an accusation amounted to a death sentence.

The lynchers of Claude Neal were not poor, as lynchers were often assumed to be (Raper 1933/1969). They and other members of the mob were lower-middle and middle class. During the Great Depression they had remained solvent. They had enough money, cars, and time off from their jobs to support the two-day effort to lynch Neal. Like all lynching mobs, this one felt self-righteous, a seemingly ubiquitous feature of southern religious experience. Certain members made their feelings known through the public media. The Friday afternoon edition of the nearby *Dothan* (Alabama) *Eagle* carried the headline, "Florida to Burn Negro at Stake: Sex Criminal Seized from Brewton Jail, Will be Mutilated, Set Afire in Extralegal Vengeance for Deed" (quoted in McGovern 1982, xxx). The Dothan radio station announced the impending event several times. Someone even notified the sheriff of adjacent Washington County (Florida) of the scheduled time. Word spread that the place would be the Cannidy property, where Neal's alleged victim had lived (McGovern 1982).

Despite the thoroughly public nature of these facts, no police appeared on the Cannidy property. Several hundred cars did park in the vicinity of the Cannidy home on the night of the lynching, but not a one belonged to those public servants dedicated to the preservation of law and order. While the mob waited for darkness, Neal was asked whether he wished to repent. He declined to do so and, by all accounts, maintained an outward calm until the end. He continued to use those deferential formalities of address, which during this era many southern blacks employed in conversations with whites, including "sir" and "kind gentlemen" (quoted in McGovern 1982, 76).

The torture began at 10 P.M. and lasted two hours, producing enough horrors to disturb a number of the lynchers themselves. A few were very disturbed; one man vomited. But the majority evidently enjoyed the event. One man who "accompanied the mob" (they wanted to use his 1930 Ford) explained, "A lot of the boys wanted to get their hands on him so bad they could hardly stand it" (quoted in McGovern 1982, 80). The N.A.A.C.P. investigator, a white North Carolinian named Howard Kester, learned the horrible details ten days after it occurred. For one hour and forty minutes he interviewed a member of the mob. Confessing that he was "quite nauseated by the things which apparently gave this man the greatest delight to relate," Kester reported the man's story, "corroborated by others."

> "After taking the nigger to the woods about four miles from Greenwood, they cut off his penis. He was made to eat it. Then they cut off his testicles and made him eat them and say he liked it." (I gathered that this barbarous act consumed considerable time and that other means of torture were used from time to time on Neal.) "Then they sliced his sides and stomach with knives and every now and then somebody would cut off a finger or toe. Red hot irons were used on the nigger to burn him from top to bottom." From time to time during the torture a rope would be tied around Neal's neck and he was pulled up over a limb and held there until he almost choked to death when he would be let down and the torture began all over again. (quoted in McGovern 1982, 80)

Neal confounded the group by maintaining his composure during the torture. After suffering through a cutting, he asked them, "Kind sirs, do one of you have a cigarette?" (quoted in McGovern 1982, 81). He died calmly, with dignity (McGovern 1982).

Some took pleasure, others solace, when several in the crowd showed fingers and toes from Neal's body in the days and weeks following the lynching. To possess a body part conferred status. One store owner recalled a man entering his store the morning after and announcing with pride, "See what I have here" (quoted in McGovern 1982, 85). What he had was one of Neal's fingers. But not just the lucky few with souvenirs wanted a piece of Neal.

Numbering in the thousands, the crowd wanted to be in on the act too. Howard Kester's informants told him that many people seemed obsessed with the corpse. Several kicked it and others drove cars over it. Children watched and participated: "It is reported from reliable sources that the little children, some of them mere tots, who lived in the Greenwood neighborhood, waited with sharpened sticks for the return of Neal's body and that when it rolled in the dust on the road that awful night these little children drove their weapons deep into the flesh of the dead man" (quoted in McGovern 1982, 82). As a final retribution for the crime allegedly committed by Neal, the crowd then rushed to the slope and burned every shack in the area owned by blacks (McGovern 1982).

The violence in Marianna continued through the next day. Local officials would blame "outsiders." White hatred for blacks became so intense that when a white man accused a black man named Bud Gammons of starting a fight, a riot ensued. Stores were emptied of blacks; streets were cleared. Then the mob moved to rich residential areas where blacks worked as maids. Approximately two hundred black people suffered some form of physical injury during the day-long white riot. The police were conspicuously absent. During the day there were a few individual whites who protected blacks, on occasion, apparently, at risk to themselves. Those black people who were walking toward Marianna recall whites who cautioned them that this was not the day to go to the county seat; they would be safer if they remained at home. Not only humanitarianism was at work here; economic self-interest also prompted the advice (McGovern 1982).

In her 1942 monograph on the changing character of lynching, Jessie Daniel Ames, founder of the Association of Southern Women for the Prevention of Lynching, condemned the lynching at Marianna as one of the worst occasions of white self-delusion and hypocrisy:

> Cannibalism of mobs, revolting souvenir collections carried by lynchers, sadistic acts inspired by diseased and poisoned minds—these facts are played down if they are mentioned at all, while justification is given for any extreme measure of cruelty which a maddened mob may devise. "It was terrible," one white woman remarked about the mob at Marianna, Florida, "but nothing which could have been done to the Negro would have been too much." (Ames 1942, 58)

Such sadism, in the name of moral righteousness and social justice, betrays an undertow of desire, as Hartman's perceptive analysis of John Rankin suggests. Kaja Silverman (1992) has observed, "the inflicting of pain ... turns upon an externalizing identification with the masochist. ... [I]ts goal is the sadist's self-engrossing repudiation of otherness" (266). But it is a racialized and gendered "otherness" to which the sadist is ineluctably drawn.

II. The Rape of the Black Man

The black phallus, of course, was the focus indeed, very often, the site of much of lynching's ritualistic concern and energy.

—Michael Awkward, *Negotiating Difference* (1995)

Temptation and menace twisted together as they see-sawed in the white man's mind.

—Lillian Smith, *Killers of the Dream* (1963)

[T]he question must be asked, what the white man means when he charges the black man with rape.

—Ida B. Wells, *A Red Record* (1892/1969)

Desire plays a central role in what objects mean.

—Lewis R. Gordon, *Bad Faith and Antiblack Racism* (1995)

Neal was hardly the first black man to be lynched in the United States. Nor would he be the last. Between 1882 and 1927, an estimated 4,900 persons were lynched in the United States, although other estimates—including the Tuskegee Institute archival records—place the number slightly lower (R. Brown 1975; Harris 1984; Hall 1979, 141; Zangrando 1980, 4). James Elbert Cutler (1905) estimated that 3,837 human beings were lynched between 1882 and 1903. Contemporary sociologists Stewart Tolnay and E. M. Beck (1995) limit their estimates to the "lynching era," encompassing the five decades between the end of Reconstruction and the beginning of the Great

Depression, 1882 through 1930. During these years they estimate that there were 2,108 separate incidents of lynching in which at least 2,462 African-American men, women, and children met their deaths at the hands of white men. Approximately 14 percent of the 2,018 black lynching incidents involved more than one victim.

Of the 2,462 black victims Tolnay and Beck count, 3 percent (74) were female. (In *A Detailed List of Known Lynchings of Women in the United States: 1889–1922,* Mary Talbert, organizer and national director of the Antilynching Crusade, estimated that during that period 83 women were lynched, several of whom were white [Perkins 1998, 16].) Tolnay and Beck assert that there are no "hard data" for the five-year period between 1877 and 1881, or for the Reconstruction period from 1865 to 1877, even though there were certainly black lynchings before 1882, especially during the early period of Reconstruction (Tolnay and Beck 1995). George C. Wright (1990) agrees; he argues that more lynchings occurred in the fifteen-year period from 1865 to 1880 than during any other fifteen-year period, even the years from 1885 to 1900, which most scholars and contemporary observers characterize as the heyday of lynching. Perhaps it is this knowledge upon which former slave Ida B. Wells relies when she estimates over 10,000 black lives were lost to "rope and faggot."

Lynching statistics are not comprehensive, of course, as they report only recorded lynchings. In an early study of the practice (first published in 1933), appendix B is entitled "Threatened Lynchings Prevented" (Raper 1969, 473). Estimates of the number of prevented lynchings range from 648 during the years 1915–32 (Raper's estimate) to 762 for the 1915–42 period (Jessie Daniel Ames's). While the exact number is not known, these figures suggest that between one-half and two-thirds of threatened lynchings failed, usually due to the active intervention of the authorities (Griffin, Clark, and Sandberg 1997).

Tolnay and Beck (1995) question the accuracy of the data available on prevented lynchings; it can only be considered suggestive of general patterns and trends. Statistics compiled by the Commission on Interracial Cooperation (C.I.C.) suggest that 39 percent of attempted lynchings were prevented between 1916 and 1920. But that percentage rose to 77 percent during the next decade and to 84 percent during the 1930s. The following story printed in Knoxville *East Tennessee News* on December 2, 1920, illustrates what was evidently a common occurrence:

> SHE DENIES RAPIST WAS BLACK. Moultrie, Ga., Nov. 30—Miss Bessie Revere, daughter of one of the most prominent women at Quitman, Ga., gained consciousness just in time to prevent departure of a search party that had been formed to scour the country for "the big, black brute" who had been described in the press as her rapist. Miss Revere said the man who assaulted her was James Harvey, a prominent white man. (quoted in Ginzburg 1962/1988, 143)

When one takes into account how many lynchings were prevented, one can only guess how widespread the practice of lynching actually was (Zangrando 1980).

The victims of lynching mobs were, to repeat, overwhelmingly male. Many were "young black men who may have shown insufficient caution in avoiding situations that older blacks might have perceived as dangerous" (Brundage 1993, 81). Then again, given "ageism," white male mobs may not have felt quite the same frenzy stripping, sexually torturing, and mutilating older black men. How does one avoid hypothesizing a sexual motive in choosing muscular young black men to castrate? Brundage (1993) estimates that approximately one in five mob victims in Georgia and one in three in Virginia were migrant laborers, or "floaters." The demand for unskilled migrant laborers undermined legislative efforts to criminalize vagrancy; the demands of the market ensured that transient black workers, often young, would provide plenty of fantasy material for whites until at least the 1930s. The editors of the *Savannah Morning News* expressed how whites imagined "floaters" when they wrote: "They are worthless vagabonds who wander from place to place, and who do not hesitate to commit the most terrible crimes. They are the ones who commit murder and rape and they are the ones who are lynched. ... These worthless black vagabonds haven't a single redeeming virtue. They are cruel and cowardly" (quoted in Brundage 1993, 81–82).

On rare occasion, lynch mobs were interracial, although whites remained in the majority. After years of living with the unpredictable violence and extreme cruelty of a white farmer named Abe Redmond, in Charlotte County, Virginia, a small number of blacks joined their white neighbors in 1893 and lynched him. On March 24, 1900, in one very unusual instance in Virginia, blacks participated in a huge mob of whites that lynched Walter Cotton, a black "desperado," and Brandt O'Grady, a white transient suspected of being Cotton's accomplice (Brundage 1993).

Significantly, lynch mobs seldom tortured or mutilated their white victims; these sexualized acts, performed as public spectacles of mockery, humiliation, and frenzy, were saved for young black men. The sexual "purity" of a white woman who allegedly had been raped was never questioned, but the arrest of a white man for rape could raise serious questions regarding the virtue of the very woman the lynching was presumed to protect. Therefore, while white women could cry rape with relative ease, certainly without provocation, when frightened by a black man and even for no reason at all, white women were quite reluctant to cry rape when attacked by white men. If they did, they suffered not only the shame of public exposure, but "conventional wisdom," not to mention the double standard, functioned to render women responsible for any sexual aggression committed against them. Put simply, white men never doubted cries of rape when linked to a black man, and rarely believed them when directed toward whites (Brundage 1993).

Walter White notes that the rape myth apparently did not exist before 1830. Given that the first slaves were brought to North America in 1619, that means that for more than two centuries charges of rape against African Americans were virtually unknown. White (1929) emphasizes economic motives, commenting: "Such accusations [of rape] were made only after a defective economic system had been upturned and made enormously profitable through inventions and in doing so had caused slave-labor to become enormously more valuable" (88–89). Some forty years earlier, after three black businessmen had been lynched, Ida B. Wells had perceived that economic motives were at work: "[t]hey [the three lynched men] had committed no crime against white women. This is what opened my eyes to what lynching really was: An excuse to get rid of Negroes who were acquiring wealth and property and thus keep the race terrorized and 'keep the nigger down'" (Wells 1970, 64). No doubt economic motives were at work, but there were others at work as well.

On occasion black men did assault white women, but, as Robert Zangrando (1980) points out, "neither that nor the greater frequency of rape and sexual harassment inflicted on black women by white and black men accounted for mob violence" (4). Although they constituted a minority of all lynchings, some victims were lynched for even the most trivial "violations," including breaches of conduct such as "insulting a white woman," "grave robbing," or "running a bordello" (Tolnay and Beck 1995, 103). Black men were lynched for any reason at all—for instance, "for just acting troublesome" (Zangrando 1980, 4). The fact that most victims were tortured "suggests the presence of sadistic tendencies among the lynchers" (Raper 1969, 1). Indeed, over the history of the phenomenon, "lynching ... seems to have become increasingly sadistic: emasculation, torture, and burning alive replaced the hangman's noose" (Hall 1979, 133). As the nationwide campaign to end the practice intensified, lynchings were slowly replaced by "legal lynchings," a phrase used to describe the mockery of the American judicial system that enabled whites to murder blacks "legally." Nearly all scholars acknowledge that only rarely—if indeed ever—did African Americans receive fair trials in the South.

What was a "typical" lynching like? As Fitzhugh Brundage (1993) points out, there was in fact no "typical" lynching. Sociologists Tolnay and Beck (1995) report: "Although most lynchings were straightforward, albeit illegal, executions with little ceremony or celebration, many went far beyond a mere taking of a human life. At times lynchings acquired a macabre, carnival-like aspect, with the victim being tortured and mutilated for the amusement of onlookers" (23). While not in fact, there was a "typical" lynching in fiction, in the white male imagination, and not infrequently, this fiction became fact.

After a precipitating event occurred (murder was the most common, but anything could be a pretext for violence, including nothing at all), white men assembled, determined to take revenge. Whether the "event" was imaginary or real did not matter; a "guilty party"—usually a young black man—was "identified," and the "manhunt" was on. Once captured, public notices were circulated usually a day or two in advance of the lynching event itself. Sometimes the notices were distributed to distant communities. Sometimes trains made special trips, adding extra cars to meet the demands of crowds wishing to travel in order to watch the spectacle (Harris 1984). (Anna Julia Cooper recalls: "Excursion trains with banners flying were run into place and eager children were heard to exclaim: 'We have seen a hanging, we are now going to see a burning!'" [quoted in Lemert and Bhan 1998, 210].)

The number of spectators on one occasion reached 15,000. The lynching itself was sometimes preceded by hours of torture and mutilation, often climaxed by what whites euphemistically called "surgery below the belt." Those parts of the victim's body that had been dismembered were sometimes photographed for picture postcards, later to be sold as souvenirs. The remains were usually burned. The leaders of lynchings were often well known and seen by thousands. But nearly everyone, including law enforcement officers, participated in a conspiracy of silence; invariably the coroner would declare that the lynching was committed by unknown persons (Brown 1975; Bulhan 1985).

Some of the Allegations Offered by Mobs for Lynching

Acting suspiciously
Adultery
Aiding murderer
Arguing with white man
Arson
Assassination
Attempted murder
Banditry
Being disreputable
Being obnoxious
Boasting about riot
Burglary
Child abuse
Conjuring
Courting white woman
Criminal assault
Cutting levee
Defending rapist
Demanding respect
Disorderly conduct
Eloping with white woman
Entered white woman's room
Enticement
Extortion
Fraud
Frightening white woman
Gambling
Grave robbing
Improper conduct with white woman
Incest
Inciting to riot
Inciting trouble
Indolence
Inflammatory language
Informing
Injuring livestock
Insulting white woman
Insurrection
Kidnapping
Killing livestock
Living with white woman
Looting
Making threats
Miscegenation
Mistaken identity
Molestation
Murder
Nonsexual assault
Peeping Tom
Pillage
Plotting to kill
Poisoning well
Quarreling
Race hatred
Race trouble
Rape
Rape-murders
Resisting mob
Revenge
Robbery
Running a bordello
Sedition
Slander
Spreading disease
Stealing
Suing white man
Swindling
Terrorism
Testifying against white man
Throwing stones
Train wrecking
Trying to colonize blacks
Trying to vote
Unpopularity
Unruly remarks
Using obscene language
Vagrancy
Violated quarantine
Voodooism
Voting for wrong party

(Tolnay and Beck 1995, 47)

Contrary to the popular opinion of the time, then, over the entire forty-nine-year lynching era, murder—not rape—was the most common pretext for lynching African Americans, accounting for 34.3 percent of the total (Tolnay and Beck 1995). In fact, "white womanhood was little more than a thin smoke screen to justify violence toward the African-American community" (Tolnay and Beck 1995, 50). And it was a peculiar, indeed "queer" violence one must say. "Why the rope and faggot rather than the courtroom?" Tolnay and Beck (1995, 113) ask. Why indeed? Lynchings were not substitutions for institutionalized justice. Fully 97.5 percent of the victims of all 1,977 legal executions had been convicted of murder or rape; black men were lynched for nearly any reason white men could imagine. Statistically, Tolnay and Beck (1995) observed virtually no effect of the number of executions in one year on the frequency of lynchings during the next year. Indeed, "the intensity of lynching bore little systematic relationship to the legitimate activities of the formal justice system. ... Lynch mobs appear to have been impressively insensitive to the vigor with which the state imposed the death penalty on blacks" (Tolnay and Beck 1995, 112).

White mobs knew that they had alternatives to lynching, that officials of the institutional justice system would have been eager "to satisfy their appetites" for murder (Tolnay and Beck 1995, 112). Instead, white men, at increasing risk to themselves during the twentieth century, preferred to bypass the formal institutional mechanisms for punishment in order to lynch black men. Tolnay and Beck seem to think whites were employing instrumental reasoning by lynching, which, they write, accomplished several useful purposes. Whites could terrorize blacks under the pretext of popular justice when, as they well knew, there was often insufficient proof to prosecute. But lynching, they argue, functioned to provoke generalized terror in the African-American community: "By conducting the lynching in a circus-like atmosphere, by subjecting the victim to torture and mutilation, and by prominently displaying the corpse, preferably near the black community, they could convey a clear message to the general black population. That message was not necessarily restricted to a simple admonition to obey the law. Rather, it was capable of achieving far broader objectives" (Tolnay and Beck 1995, 113). This is, I submit, far too rational a model of white men's behavior. After all, even in "black belt" counties where African Americans constituted a numerical majority, whites controlled political, economic, and social life. What conceivable purpose could further terrorization serve? No, there was something else at work in the bizarre ritual of lynching.

Whatever the alleged crime, the punishment often exhibited a sexual aspect. In many lynchings white men castrated black men. These castrations were, some have argued, efforts to eliminate the threat of black-male rape of white women. As many have observed, this threat was nearly completely imaginary. To the white man, rape came to mean nearly any intimate or assumed intimate association, however momentary or superficial or invited, between a black man and a white woman. "Invited" was of course not possible in the mind of the white man; in every instance of interracial encounter the white woman had to have been "forced." Especially no southern white man could possibly conceive of any southern white woman voluntarily pursuing or accepting a black man, at least no white women of the planter class (Hodes 1993).

While the rape fantasy may be post–Civil War, white men's obsession with black male sexuality was apparent at slavery's inception in the "new world." From the earliest days, castration was used as a punishment in the colonies, and not simply as one of the many sadistic cruelties which were coded in colonial law. Castration was almost exclusively reserved for black male slaves. In some colonies, laws authorizing castration were worded so that they applied to all black men, whether free or slave, suggesting the white male obsession with the black male phallus overrode any issue of slavery. As a legal punishment castration was a peculiarly American phenomenon; there is no basis of it in English law. In fact, officials in England were shocked and outraged when they learned of the practice, condemning castration as "inhumane and contrary to all Christian laws," "a punishment never inflicted by any Law [in any of] H. M. Dominions" (quoted in Jordan 1974, 81). Many colonists thought the practice necessary to punish and thereby constrain a lecherous, primitive, and barbarous people; many in England appreciated that the barbarity at issue was the colonists' (Jordan 1974).

In attempting to think about the meaning of castration in lynching events, even "empirical" researchers such as sociologists Stewart E. Tolnay and E. M. Beck and historian W. Fitzhugh Brundage resort to "theory," that is, abstractions which purport to explain phenomena they in fact only acknowledge. Tolnay and Beck (1995), who (as we will see later) are convinced that cotton prices played the key role in the lynching phenomenon, discuss a "reinforcement model of social control" that accounts, presumably, for the sexual mutilation of young black men. The two sociologists do allow, however, that the practice was more "expressive" than mere "popular justice" or simple "social control." Determined not to see its explicit sexual elements, they write:

> The number of incidents in which victims were severely tortured and mutilated, or in which the corpses of victims were displayed prominently in the African-American community, illustrate that lynchings had the potential to be considerably more "expressive" than executions. Even if the formal justice system could have executed every black person who committed a capital offense (thereby achieving 100 percent effective specific deterrence), it would have done so in a comparatively facile and unexpressive manner. A residual need may have existed for the white community to continue lynching in order to teach the black community a lesson. ... The reinforcement model of social control depicts lynchings and executions as complementary methods of punishment rather than as alternatives. (Tolnay and Beck 1995, 99–100)

"Residual need," indeed. But this "need" was only ostensibly a matter of social control; was it as well a "need" for sexual control?

Brundage (1993) comes a little closer, writing that "the rituals of mutilation including both the castration of the lynching victim and the collection of gruesome souvenirs, sprang from deeper urges. ... By mutilating the lynching victim, the mob simultaneously stripped his humanity and, not infrequently, his sexuality. Undoubtedly, the bloodthirsty fury of some mob members expressed subconscious envy and *sexual frustration*" (65, emphasis added). Since we are discussing here an event in which men strip other men naked and at some point fondle then mutilate and remove other men's genitalia, are we not, "empirically" and behaviorally speaking, discussing "homosexual" frustration? Is not "subconscious envy" an odd explanatory concept for the scholar who discounts "psychohistorical" explanations (see Brundage 1993, 12)?

Like every other student of lynching who cannot bear to see its queer character, Brundage heterosexualizes the event and dismisses castration as "subconscious envy." No doubt some white men did experience "envy" when they looked at the naked muscular body of the young black man they had hunted and captured. How nice it would be—could white men have thought?—if I were the one stripped naked before this crowd of crazy white men eager to dismember me. Of course, what white scholars like Brundage and black analysts such as Hernton mean, I think, is that heterosexual white men envy the black man's genitals, envy his presumed sexual superiority, a white male fantasy ... unless. Could there have been "empirical trials" that have escaped documentation that established the black man's sexual superiority? Since white women were off limits, were black women the only objects of desire? And from whose point of view was "sexual superiority" established? What seems clear is that "envy" does not adequately account for this gendered insanity; "envy" is a cover for something else. Now what could that "something else" be?

Heterosexist theorists don't want to go there. Instead, let us "hang" with "sexual envy" and "frustration" and start counting. Comparing rates of lynching in Virginia and Georgia, Brundage (1993) found that mass mobs (one of four different types of lynching groups he identifies) mutilated one in three black victims lynched for alleged sexual offenses in Georgia and one in ten blacks lynched in Virginia, although he admits that the extant evidence is open to question. "Almost certainly," Brundage (1993) acknowledges, "we will never know how commonplace the practice was and therefore should be cautious in assuming that the ritual [of castration] was a central, even defining, element of lynchings for rape. Even so, the most relevant measure of the importance of mutilation during lynchings for sexual crimes was never the percentage of black victims who were mutilated, but rather the lasting impression that each incident left upon observers" (66). While he is not clear why we should be cautious—to avoid sensationalizing? to reduce white culpability?—he is clear that the white male mutilation of young black men reverberated in significance far beyond its actual incidence. Calvin Hernton, James Baldwin, Richard Wright, and many others testify to that fact. Parenthetically, Brundage (1993) points out that a very small number of lynchings of blacks for sexual offenses was carried out by black men. In these cases, significantly, murder was punishment enough. Black men did not seem very interested in sexually mutilating other black men.

Winthrop Jordan understood that there has been a gendered dimension to "race relations" in America, dating from the colonial era. "Since the English and colonial American cultures were dominated by males," Jordan (1974) noted, "sexually oriented beliefs about the Negro in America derived principally from the psychological needs of men and were to a considerable extent shaped by specifically masculine modes of thought and behavior" (78–79). But this point seems to startle him, and in the next sentence he backs off: "This is not to say the American attitudes toward the Negro were *male* attitudes but merely that when one talks about *American* attitudes toward anything (the frontier, the city, money, freedom, the Negro) one is using shorthand for attitudes common to both sexes but predominantly male in genesis and tone" (78). Rather than back off, let us dwell on that fact.

Despite the fact that the precipitating events occurred mostly, often only, in the minds of white men, is it not odd that gender has been so undervalued in historical and sociological research on lynching? Only in literary research does the gendered dimension receive serious theorization. In chapter 3 I will review in some detail the most prominent scholarly efforts to understand lynching. For me, the crucial question remains: is it not very curious ("peculiar"?) that lynchings sometimes involved the dismemberment (including castration) of the black man's body and the ritualized distribution of its parts to other white men as mementos? Does this question not require us to focus on the gendered relations between white and black men?

Many lynchings were precipitated only because black men had not been sufficiently deferential to white men, or because they had (allegedly) touched or "whistled" (Sewell 1995; Nordan 1993) or even merely looked at a white woman (Feagin and Hernan 1995). No matter what "happened," sex seemed always involved, if not in fact then in the minds of white men. Some have suggested that the castrations represented an attempt to transfer some of black man's virility to white men (Harris 1984). Even nonsexualized definitions of lynchings employed sexualized terms: "A lynching, the quintessence of passion. ... It is composed of a crowd gathering in the dark, high emotion mixed with hard liquor, and a frightening lust for blood vengeance" (Phillips 1987, 362). Blood vengeance? Yes, but, as Frantz Fanon (1967) asked: "Is not the lynching of the Negro a sexual revenge?" "We know," the French-trained black psychiatrist reminded, "how much of sexuality there is in all cruelties, tortures, beatings" (159). And given that that sexuality is between men and that the act was forced, can we avoid acknowledging it as a kind of mangled homosexual rape?

For Trudier Harris (1984)—whose work I examine in some detail in chapter 3—lynchings represented the final stage of an emasculation process that white men conducted every day by word and deed, a culmination of a psychosexual war on black men. Black men were not allowed to forget that they were commodities, bodies not citizens, objects not men. The military version of the Civil War may have been lost, but the peace would not be, white southern men resolved. If black men dared to claim any privileges of (white) manhood, whether sexual, economic, or political, they risked lynching (Harris 1984). Lynching was then, primarily, an "affair" between men. Is racism itself, in some fundamental sense, a male matter, a systematized and violent white-male sexualized obsession with black men?

The imagery of lynching—in literature, poetry, music, in the minds of men—was inescapably erotic. The character Joe Christmas in Faulkner's *Light in August*, the child of an interracial love affair, was himself doomed to castration and death by lynching. As we will see in a moment, the white lyncher in James Baldwin's "Going to Meet the Man" tosses on his bed in sexual frustration as he remembers a boyhood lynching. Lynching is the culmination of an interracial love affair in Jean Toomer's "Blood-Burning Moon." Billie Holiday, the great jazz singer, made famous the image of the "strange fruit" of race and sex in America:

> Southern trees bear a strange fruit ...
> Black body swinging in the southern breeze,
> Strange fruit hanging from the poplar trees.
>
> Pastoral scene of the gallant South,
> The bulging eyes and the twisted mouth ...
> (Hille 1948, 124–125; quoted in Hall 1979, 150)

Holiday often performed the song at the Café Society, New York City's first interracial club. So controversial was the song that Holiday's label, Columbia Records, refused to record it. Instead, it was recorded by Holiday on Commodore Records in 1939; it made her famous. Written by the white poet Lewis Allan, the song held special and intense meaning for Holiday. She associated it with the death of her father, Clarence Holiday, in 1937 in Dallas, Texas, where he was refused medical treatment by white hospitals. When Holiday performed the song, she felt she was "flailing that audience," but afterward she often suffered severe depression. Despite its content, "Strange Fruit" became one of her most popular recordings. An incident in a Los Angeles nightclub provides a glimpse into the psychosexual dynamics of her white audience: "Billie," requested a patron, "why don't you sing that sexy song you're so famous for? You know, the one about the naked bodies swinging in the trees." "Needless to say," Holiday tells us, "I didn't" (Holiday 1973, 70–71; 86–88; quoted in Hall 1979, 306, n. 57; Perkins 1998).

Going to the Meet the Man

Sexy song? Why would anyone find "sexy" the image of a naked black man hanging from a tree, dead? James Baldwin understood. In his *Going to Meet the Man,* Baldwin (1965/1998) portrays precisely the convoluted homoerotic character of lynching. The story begins with a description of (white, male) Jesse who lies awake one night, frustrated because he finds he is unable to make love to his wife, Grace. Why, he wonders? Baldwin takes us inside the white man's mind:

> And he wasn't old enough to have any trouble getting it up—he was only forty-two. And he was a good man, a God-fearing man, he had tried to do his duty all his life, and he had been a deputy sheriff for several years. ... The niggers. What had the good Lord Almighty had in mind when he made the niggers? Well. They were pretty good at that, all right. Damn. Damn. Goddamn. (Baldwin 1998, 256)

He recalls earlier in the day, in the jail where a young black man was being held for helping black citizens to register to vote. It is the 1960s, and southern white resistance to voter registration drives and to the civil rights movement generally is widespread and savage. Still in bed, he recalls being back in the cell earlier that day, remembering how "he kept prodding the young boy, sweat pouring from beneath the helmet he had not yet taken off. The boy rolled around in his own dirt and water and blood and tried to scream again as the prod hit his testicles, but the scream did not come out, only a kind of rattle and a moan" (Baldwin 1998, 258–259).

From the memory of the young prisoner's testicles he returns to his own childhood when he had a black friend named Otis. Otis was his age, eight, and lived nearby. "They wrestled together in the dirt" (Baldwin 1998, 264). The thought of Otis's body intertwined with his brings to mind the lynching he had observed as an eight-year-old. The black man being lynched, he recalls sitting astride his father's shoulders, "was a big man, a bigger man than his father, and black as an African jungle Cat, and naked. Jesse pulled upward; his father's hands held him firmly by the ankles" (Baldwin 1998, 270). As the lynchers set the pyre on fire, forty-two-year-old Sheriff Jesse recalls being the eight-year-old Jesse. Was he watching the flames? No, his eyes were fixed on the black man's genitals: "There was no hair left on the nigger's privates, and the eyes, now, were wide open, as white as the eyes of a clown or a doll. The smoke now carried a terrible odor across the clearing, the odor of something burning which was both sweet and rotten" (271).

From the dying man's genitals he turned his head to see "the field of faces. He watched his mother's face. Her eyes were very bright, her mouth was open: she was more beautiful than he had ever seen her, and more strange. He began to feel a joy he had never felt before. He watched the hanging, gleaming body, the most beautiful and terrible object he had ever seen till then." Then:

> One of his father's friends reached up and in his hands he held a knife: and Jesse wished that he had been that man. It was a long, bright knife and the sun seemed to catch it, to play with it, to caress it—it was brighter than the fire. And a wave of laughter swept the crowd. Jesse felt his father's hands on his ankles slip and tighten. The man with the knife walked toward the crowd, smiling slightly; as though this were a signal, silence fell; he heard his mother cough. Then the man with the knife walked up to the hanging body. He turned and smiled again. Now there was a silence all over the field. The hanging head looked up. It seemed fully conscious now, as though the fire had burned out terror and pain. The man with the knife took the nigger's privates in his hand, one hand, still smiling, as though he were weighing them. In the cradle of one white hand, the nigger's privates seemed as remote as meat being weighed in the scales; but seemed heavier, too, much heavier, and Jesse felt his scrotum tighten; and huge, huge, much bigger than his father's, flaccid, hairless, the largest thing he had ever seen till then, and the blackest. The white hand stretched them, cradled them, caressed them. Then the dying man's eyes looked straight into Jesse's eyes—it could not have been as long as a second, but it seemed longer than a year. Then Jesse screamed, and the crowd screamed as the knife flashed, first up, then down, cutting the dreadful thing away, and the blood came roaring down. Then the crowd rushed forward, tearing at the body with their hands, with knives, with rocks, with stones, howling and cursing. Jesse's head, of its own weight,

> fell downward toward his father's head. Someone stepped forward and reached the body with kerosene. Where the man had been, a great sheet of flame appeared. Jesse's father lowered him to the ground. (271–272)

The rape and crucifixion of the black man was a very special and profound experience that the young white boy had shared with his father:

> "Well, I told you," said his father, "you wasn't never going to forget this picnic." His father's face was full of sweat, his eyes were very peaceful. At that moment Jesse loved his father more than he had ever loved him. He felt that his father had carried him through a mighty test, had revealed to him a great secret which would be the key to his life forever. (272)

That "great secret" which would be the "key" to his life had to do with the black male body and white men's access to it, a body now burned beyond recognition:

> The black body was on the ground, the chain which had held it was being rolled up by one of his father's friends. Whatever the fire had left undone, the hands and the knives and the stones of the people accomplished. The head was caved in, one eye was torn out, one ear was hanging. But one had to look carefully to realize this, for it was, now, merely a black charred object on the black, charred ground. He lay spread-eagled with what had been a wound between what had been his legs. (272)

Now Baldwin returns us to the present, to the middle-aged sheriff lying in bed with his wife, unable to make love. Having remembered the lynching, now he feels alive. His wife, whose name and depiction convey the white man's idealization of white womanhood, stirs:

> Grace stirred and touched him on the thigh; the moonlight covered her like glory. Something bubbled up in him, his nature again returned to him. He thought of the boy in the cell; he thought of the man in the fire; he thought of the knife and grabbed himself and stroked himself and a terrible sound, something between a high laugh and a howl, came out of him and dragged his sleeping wife up on one elbow. She stared at him in a moonlight which had now grown cold as ice. He thought of the morning and grabbed her, laughing and crying, crying and laughing, and he whispered, as he stroked her, as he took her, "Come on, sugar, I'm going to do you like a nigger, just like a nigger, come on, sugar, and love me just like you'd love a nigger." (272–273)

Jesse's reference to sleeping with his wife "like a nigger" points, Trudier Harris (1984) suggests, to the mix of subservience, sadism, and sexual abandon to which he has consigned all blacks. In identifying with the black man, is he only experiencing a heterosexual event as he imagines the black man? Through his identification with him he enters the body of the black man (Hartman 1997). He must imaginatively enter her body as well, in order to fantasize how she will enjoy the event as if he were a black man fucking her. That is the last line of the passage: "love me just like you'd love a nigger." To imagine that he must imagine himself in her position, too. That is the excitement of fucking her "like a nigger": his sensory experience is not heightened only as a man, but as well like a woman, as a woman he imagines himself to be vis-à-vis the naked, mutilated black man.

Jacquelyn Dowd Hall (1979) understood, if in general terms: "the ritual of lynching, then, served as a dramatization of hierarchical power relationships based both on gender and on race" (156). Based on gender and race, what kind of hierarchical power relationships are we talking about? S&M? Certainly no black victim was a willing masochistic partner in the sadistic sexualized snuff film that was lynching, but the white man: what a work is he! Who can doubt his sadism as he stripped the young black man naked, tortured him slowly, gleamed as he watched his soul depart and the black body was castrated, mutilated, then burned?

III. The Rape Myth

[T]he southern rape complex is central to the history of lynching.

—W. Fitzhugh Brundage, *Lynching in the New South: Georgia and Virginia, 1880–1930* (1993)

[T]he [white] woman is "lynch-bait."

—Trudier Harris, *Exorcising Blackness: Historical and Literary Lynching and Burning Rituals* (1984)

Men and women alike see in outraged womanhood their own mothers or wives or sisters, and they are moved by an invincible force to mete out punishment to the vandals. Something of Arthurian chivalry stirs men's minds; they wear the colors of their own womanhood into a battle for womanhood.

—Jessie Daniel Ames, *The Changing Character of Lynching* (1942)

Sexuality is as much motivated by the fantasy of retrieving prohibited objects as by the desire to remain protected from the threat of punishment such as a retrieval might bring on.

—Judith Butler, *Bodies That Matter: On the Discursive Limits of "Sex"* (1993)

Did those white men who lynched black men have a clue what they were doing? They thought they knew. Presumably it was about (heterosexual, interracial) rape, or so they imagined. Rape and rumors of rape became "a kind of acceptable folk pornography in the Bible Belt." As rumors spread, the attacker became not just a black man but "a ravenous brute, the victim a beautiful, frail, young virgin." She could not possibly be put on the witness stand to suffer the "glare and stare of public curiosity" (and make the truth known, i.e., that there had been no rape). The sexual experience and postrape condition of these imaginary women were sometimes described by their white male "benefactors" in minute and embellished detail. This public performance implies "a kind of group participation in the rape of the woman almost as cathartic as the subsequent lynching of the alleged attacker" (Hall 1979, 150). Perhaps, but because these were tales told by white men, because the victims themselves did not exist but were fragments in the white male imagination, these good old boys were identifying with her not him. *They* were the rape victims. And as we know, fear can be inverted desire. As Freud emphasized in his analysis of the Schreber memoirs, paranoid delusions are often informed by repressed homosexual desire. The nineteenth-century rape fantasy was just that: a collective paranoid delusion.

The percentage of lynchings that was associated with actual (documented) charges of rape (an exact figure is evidently unavailable, but it is clearly much smaller than the 29.2% of lynchings in which sexual assault was employed as a justification by mobs; see Tolnay and Beck 1995, 48) gripped the southern male imagination far out of proportion to statistical reality. A southerner often lucid about the South, Wilbur J. Cash observed that "[t]he actual danger of the southern woman being violated by the Negro has always been comparatively small ... much less, for instance, than the chance that she would be struck by lightning" (1960, 117). Rape was a white-male fantasy, not a black-male reality. In these imaginary rape scenes, often described in the popular press, "the themes of masculinity, rage, and sexual envy were woven into a ritual of death and desire." Unaware of their own sexual motives, participants presumably saw in "lynch law" their ideal selves. Instead of seeing themselves as the aggressors in what we must now think of as nineteenth-century versions of snuff films, these white men fantasized themselves as the "protectors of women, dispensers of justice, and guardians of communal values. But they must also have seen themselves in the victims of their acts." In these vicious sexual murders were caught up "man and beast, good and evil, ego and id, the creative power of an *aroused* masculinity and the destructive power of a loosened animality" (Hall 1979, 151, emphasis added).

The "unspeakable crime" (related to the "love that dare not speak its name"?) gripped the imagination of whites far more than any other. Statistically, as Fitzhugh Brundage (1993) has shown, allegations of murder, not rape, provoked most lynchings. No matter, white southerners still insisted that rape was the key to lynching. Of course, it was, if in a different way than they imagined. Despite the homosocial character of the rape myth, southerners such as Thomas Nelson Page insisted that lynchings represented "the determination [of whites] to put an end to the ravishing of their women by an inferior race." When it was pointed out, as it often was, that rape was not the cause of most lynchings, southerners would not budge, transfixed by their imaginary visions of big black bucks on top of fair blond maidens. A North Carolina farm journal editor, Clarence H. Poe, expressed the convoluted logic of southern white men when he insisted that "to say that men are lynched for other crimes than that against white women, and that therefore lynching cannot be attributed to it, is to be more plausible than accurate." The crime of lynching, he continued, starts as a righteous vengeance for sexual assaults: "here and only there could the furious mob spirit break through the resisting wall of law and order" (quoted in Brundage 1993, 58).

This fantasy of black men's aggressive sexuality was clearly related to white men's obsession with what many thought was an anatomical peculiarity of the black male. That "peculiarity" was an especially large penis. This notion, Winthrop Jordan (1974) tells us, is an ancient one, perhaps older even than exegeses of Ham's offense against his father in Genesis 9:24. Without question, the idea predated the European settlement of America and possibly even the Portuguese explorations of the West African coast. Jordan reports that several fifteenth-century map-makers decorated parts of Africa with naked men, figures which gave the idea graphic expression. In the seventeenth century, English accounts of West Africa carefully described the "extraordinary greatness" of the black men's "members" (quoted in Jordan 1974, 82).

By the close of the eighteenth century the idea that the black man's penis was larger than the white man's had become common knowledge among European scientists. Whether it was common knowledge among the English colonists is more difficult to know, Jordan (1974) tells us, given that such "knowledge" was not likely to find its way into print even if a great many people discussed it. Obviously, however, the fantasy was not unheard of, for an officer in the First Pennsylvania regiment recorded in his journal his thoughts about the black boys waiting on Virginia dinner tables: "I am surpized this does not hurt the feelings of this fair Sex to see these young boys of about Fourteen and Fifteen years Olds to Attend them. These [sic] whole nakedness Expos'd and I can Assure you It would Surprize a person to see these d—d black boys how well they are hung" (quoted in Jordan 1974, 83).

In a letter protesting a specific lynching, Booker T. Washington pointed out that rape or even the suspicion of rape was not at issue in most lynchings. The *New York Tribune* reported in its February 29, 1904, edition sections of the letter. His emphasis upon economic productivity (with an attendant emphasis upon vocationalism in the education of African Americans which earned him the label of "accommodationist") is evident here, as well as his identification with Christianity, and his appreciation that lynching deforms those who tolerate it. Also evident are his pain and outrage:

> Within the last fortnight three members of my race have been burned at the stake. ... Not one of the three was charged with any crime even remotely connected with the abuse of a white woman. ... All of these ... took place in broad daylight, and two of them occurred on Sunday afternoon, in sight of a Christian church. In the midst of the nation's busy and prosperous life, few, I fear, take time to consider whither these brutal and inhuman practices are leading. ... I have always been among those who condemn in the strongest terms crimes of whatsoever character committed by members of my race, and I condemn them now with equal severity, but I maintain that the only protection of our civilization is a fair and calm trial of all people charged with crime and in their legal punishment, if proved guilty. ... These burnings without trial are in the deepest sense unjust to my race. But it is not this injustice alone which stirs my heart. These barbarous scenes are more disgraceful and degrading

> to the people who inflict the punishment than to those who receive it. ... Is it not possible ... to cease bringing shame and ridicule upon our Christian civilization? (quoted in Ginzburg 1962/1988, 64–65)

Lynchings can be linked with poverty and the business cycle, specifically the fluctuating price of commodities such as cotton. But economic factors hardly exclude sexual ones. Hard times may make sublimation more difficult. Vengeance can be lustful. One form that sublimation assumed was a conflation of "sex" and "race." Race is of course a socially constructed, not biological or genetic reality, but for those uneducated southerners who believed otherwise, miscegenation equaled racial impurity. Rape could result in pregnancy, which could result in a mulatto child. Moreover, as a construct in the white man's mind, "race" stood for culture as well as biology, his culture, his biology. When "race" was threatened, it meant he—as a man, a white man—felt threatened. We can begin to decode the complicated conflation of race and sex in the practice of lynching. When the white man cried out that the white race was imperiled, the "threat" to the "white race" was a sublimated recoding of his own personal sense of being sexually aroused and threatened. In this way we can understand the white man, a participant in the Montgomery race conference of 1900, who declared that "the rape of white women by Negroes [can]not [be understood] as ordinary criminality, [but as] an attack on the integrity of the race" (quoted in Hall 1979, 145). "Integrity of the race" equaled "virginity of white man." Somehow the black man would understand this equation. Some sixty years later, in prisons, he would have the opportunity to act it out, as we will see in chapters 16 and 17.

This conflation of sex and race—a "deeply felt taboo"—was the "main rationalization for lynching." Only the threat of immediate and terrible punishment—lynching—stood between the fragile white women (as the white man imagined her) living upon "lonely, isolated farmsteads of the South" and the "overpowering desire of black men." Rape of a white woman was "the most terrible crime on the face of the earth" for which legal punishment was both too uncertain and too lenient (quoted in Hall 1979, 145–146). Does the "lady" protest too much?

One does not doubt the horror of rape, but is it not odd that white men would declare it to be the "most terrible crime on earth" when they did and do continue to practice it, on white women, black women, and gay men (as we will see in chapter 13). Was this "fear" of rape a residue of slavery days? In 1861 there were 12 million whites in the Confederacy and 4 million slaves. During that four-year period nearly every able-bodied white male from 15 to 55 was fighting to preserve the southern way of life. With their men away, were those white women left alone on southern plantations raped by the black men who remained at home? Astonishingly, there are very few documented cases of sexual assaults during that period. Were the losers of southern cause still "men" after this decisive defeat? Yankees didn't think so: when President Jefferson Davis wore a cloak to escape at the War's end, the northern press alleged he wore a dress. He was maligned, one historian explains, because southern white men had asserted they were such "men" that, despite the odds against them, they would defeat northerners in just a few weeks (Faust 1996). The consequent destabilization of gender in the South will be described in chapter 4.

So the fear of rape was nearly completely imaginary. The odds of a white woman being raped by a black man, Cash estimated, were less than being struck dead by lightning. If rape did not occur, why did white men imagine it? Some insist the fabrication was merely cynical: a pretext to act out racial hatred, a "tradition" in the American South, like the Confederate flag, the "stars and bars." It was a tradition all right. But why make this a tradition? Why were white men compelled to enact that fantasy? Why not others? Why would white men obsess over what they imagined as black male desire? Some scholars—among them Winthrop Jordan, Joel Richardson, and Cornel West—have suggested that it is white sexual fears of black men that account for this extreme and savage ritual of racial hatred. But why would white men fear the desire of black men? When it is without basis in reality, fear is inverted desire. Could lynching be a deformed, deflected, displaced expression of desire? Could it have been the mangled, repressed desire of "heterosexual" (the term wasn't invented until the end of the nineteenth century) white men for black men whom they imagined as studs, stallions, bucks? Nearly half a century later, Frantz Fanon (1967) would note: "I have always been struck by the speed with which 'handsome young Negro' turns into 'young colt' or 'stallion'" (167).

Black women were and are also victimized by white fantasies, often expressed as negative sexual stereotypes. Patricia Collins (1991) insists that the image of the sexually aggressive "Jezebel lie[s] at the heart of black women's oppression" by the dominant culture (77). Supplementing the image of the Jezebel is the black matriarch, symbol of the "bad black mother" who emasculates black men because she will not permit them to assume roles as black patriarchs (Collins 1991, 72, 78). Black matriarchs have been held responsible for black men's low educational achievements, inability to earn a living for their families, personality disorders, and delinquency (King 1973; Moynihan 1965). (We will examine that dynamic in chapter 14.) More recently, fantasies of the domineering black matriarch have been expressed as stereotypes of aggressive, career-minded black women. These women are maligned as "egotistical career climbers, better paid, better educated and more socially mobile than [their] male counterparts" (Ransby 1992, 169–170). In her Congressional testimony during the Clarence Thomas confirmation hearings in 1991, Anita Hill was subject to these same vicious stereotypes (Roper, Chanslor, and Bystrom 1996).

Nearly every student of the phenomenon acknowledges that lynching had multiple causes, among them provincialism, poverty, caste solidarity, role preservation, and lack of education (McGovern 1982). It is true, scholars acknowledge, that lynchings reveal something morbid about the personalities and preoccupations of the lynchers. The noted social critic H. L. Mencken hypothesized that the circus-like atmosphere of many lynchings were pathological substitutes for more ordinary community activities (Howard 1995). McGovern (1982) believed that lynchings provided a lurid sensationalism which sustained, for these rural southern white men, the illusion of being alive. Were lynchers "dead men walking," performing their own cultural and spiritual deaths, like sex abusers repeating their own victimization as children? In this view, lynchers were zombies (McGovern 1982). In this regard Richard Dyer (1988) suggested: "If blacks have more 'life' than whites, then it must follow that whites have more 'death' than blacks. ... Living and dead whites are indistinguishable" (59; quoted in Young 1996, 100). While this is highly suggestive, the metaphor of "zombie" seems insufficient. Recall that all but a relatively few lynchings were of black men. At least one black woman—Mary Turner—who was lynched was pregnant, her fetus ripped from her womb as she lay dying. Obviously, such an act was an unimaginably vicious attack on the mother-to-be and her precious child-to-be. But was this not also a maniacal effort to get at the black male seed inside?

White women did not figure prominently in most lynchings. On one occasion a southern (white) "lady" discovered that the local "gentlemen" were reluctant to enter the courtroom, interrupt the trial of an accused black man and "do their duty." She cajoled a group of adolescent boys into ripping down an American flag from the wall of the courthouse corridor, then parade throughout the courthouse and its grounds with stars and stripes overhead, demanding "justice." Using the boys to embarrass the older men, this woman did succeed in shaming them into a performance of their "manly duty" (Raper 1933/1969, 12). On many other occasions white women were present, but it was almost always white men who took it upon themselves to torture, dismember, and burn their black male victims.

Under such (homo)sexually predatory circumstances, what was coming of age like for young black men in the South? "It is doubtful," James McGovern (1982) tells us, "if any black male growing up in the rural South in the period 1909 to 1940 was not traumatized by a fear of being lynched" (6). Somewhere, sometime, like puberty, came another fact of life to the young black man living in the American South: he might be accused of raping a white woman. Without provocation or warning, he might find himself at the center of a circle of savage white men intent on stripping him, torturing, then killing him. A circle of white men who wanted his body, not to love but to cut, mutilate, and burn. Most specifically these white men wanted his penis. They would cut it off, sometimes make the still-alive black man fellate it, then keep it for themselves, a "souvenir" they said. Like war, lynching would seem to be a man's game, in this case, a white man's game. What does that tell us about white men? African American poet, playwright, and novelist Amiri Baraka (1965/1966) had an answer to that question: "Most American white men are ... fags" (216). Now, why would any black man think that?

Beginning her well-known book on rape (to which we return in the final section of chapter 12), Susan Brownmiller (1975/1993) visited the Schomburg Center for Research on Black Culture on 135th Street in Harlem. Brownmiller knew she wanted to have a chapter on rape in slavery; she had gone to the Schomburg to see what documentation was available. Her experience there points to the sexual character of lynching, at least in the mind of one black male librarian:

> "I'm writing a book on rape," I told a librarian. "You wouldn't by any chance have any special files."

> He looked acutely unhappy. I was soon to learn that no library in the world has efficiently catalogued rape material, but that wasn't the cause of this librarian's discomfort. "Why did you come here?" he asked with caution.
>
> "Because I thought this would be the best place to find historical stuff on the rape of black women. I'm writing a serious book."
>
> "Then you mean the lynching of black men. ... To black people, rape has meant the lynching of the black man," he said with his voice rising. (Brownmiller, 1975/1993, 212)

Lynching reached its zenith during the last decade of the nineteenth century. To explain this fact, many students of lynching point to both racial and political considerations. Brundage (1993) argues: "The heightened fears of sexual assaults in the late nineteenth century bespoke profound and growing uneasiness among whites about the proper place for blacks in southern society and the apparent weakening of traditional methods for the social control of blacks" (58–59). A nineteenth-century historian from Virginia, Philip Alexander Bruce (1889) suggested that blacks committed rapes to indicate their disrespect for whites. "Whites" includes, of course, white men. Recall that during slavery black sexual assaults on white women had been virtually unknown (Faust 1996). Did that mean that black men had respected whites until Reconstruction?

But "disrespect" was not, could not be, about "race" or "power" only; it was also about gender, as many scholars pointed out, among them Gail Bederman (1995a, 1995b). Bederman has made clear how white male perceptions of endangered white manhood during the close of the nineteenth century played out in conflations of race, gender, and civilization. Brundage (1993), too, acknowledges that fact: "The preoccupation with sexual attacks also was an expression of concern about the apparent weakening of conventional standards of sexual behavior and traditional gender roles. ... [P]olemics about the threat of sexual assault exposed the desperate efforts of white men to reaffirm their dedication to the idealization of male chivalry and shore up the traditional dependence of white women" (59). Because the sex and gender system, not to mention black sexual attacks on white women (however imaginary), are not separable from popular attitudes regarding power, society, and nationhood, violations of the race/sex barrier were experienced by many whites, many white men, as blows against the very foundations of society. Not only white women were at stake, "civilization" was at stake (Brundage 1993; Bederman 1995a, b). While whites worried, naked black men burned at the stake.

Of course, all this was not exactly obvious to southern (and to most northern) whites at the time. They believed what they imagined, not what they saw. Therefore, white ladies were under constant watch, lest a black "beast" unleash himself upon her, something only a white man might prevent. One is reminded of the famous trial of Lytton Strachey, the well-known and respected author of *Queen Victoria and Eminent Victorians* (despite being a "notorious homosexual"), a member of the "Bloomsbury Group" (which included Virginia and Leonard Woolf, John Maynard Keynes, and other intellectual and artistic luminaries of early twentieth-century Britain), for refusing to fight in World War

I. Frustrated by Strachey's deft verbal maneuvers, the prosecution, in the final days of the trial, grew more and more aggressive. Finally, at wit's end, the prosecutor thundered at Strachey: "Let me put it to you this way, Mr. Strachey. Imagine, if you will, your beautiful, frail young sister lying on the ground, and toward her moves a muscular, virile young German soldier. What would you do then, Mr. Strachey ... would you then fight? What would you do?" After only a brief hesitation, Strachey is said to have flung his scarf around his neck, and in his feminine shrill voice exclaimed: "I would bravely interpose my body between the two!" Case closed (see, for instance, Brownmiller 1975/1993, 263).

Not twenty-five years earlier, European Americans were plagued by fantasies of muscular, virile young black men approaching their frail white sisters and mothers and wives; only their "manly" interposition could protect them. Sexual attacks could occur at any time or any place, even in a taxi, as a late nineteenth-century letter writer to the *Atlanta News* warned. To be driven by a black driver, he advised, was "a thousand times more dangerous than a rattlesnake" to white women because "personal contact often fires the hearts of these drivers with the lusts of hell" (quoted in Brundage 1993, 60). Case closed.

In "an atmosphere saturated with racial and sexual fears," Brundage (1993) writes, "it was tragically predictable that white men interpreted even trifling offenses by black men against white women as ample grounds for summary punishment." In the everyday language usage of white southerners, rape (which applied to white women only) was "an elastic concept" that was by no means restricted to the contemporary legal definition of the crime. As far as southern white men were concerned, "rape" meant attempted rape, aggravated assault, and even acts as apparently innocent and subtle as a nudge. In March 1917, Linton Clinton inadvertently frightened a little white girl when he asked her to read a letter to him. His "attempted outrage" provoked a mob of white men to lynch him (quoted passages Brundage 1993, 61). It seemed that any excuse would do; white men were—are?—just plain obsessed with black men.

Even during the colonial period many white men were decidedly curious about the presumed sexual ardor of black men (Jordan 1968). Despite this "curiosity" and surveillance, antebellum documents reveal that there were, on occasion, liaisons between white women and enslaved black men. There is even evidence to suggest that, on occasion, black men were actually acquitted or pardoned on charges of raping white women; white husbands were, on occasion, denied divorces even when their wives had committed adultery with black men; and there were instances of black men in such adultery cases who suffered no retribution (Hodes 1993).

Such occasions were rare and class-linked. Certainly no white women in the planter class were imagined as desiring black men. But white men did imagine that lower-class white women tended toward a certain sexual depravity, quite capable of illicit liaisons, including unthinkable (for "respectable" white southerners) liaisons with black men. Indeed, white male fantasies regarding lower-class female sexuality were at least as strong as their obsession over black male sexuality (Hodes 1993). For those northern men defending the Scottsboro Nine (see chapter 12), this was probably the case, as Susan Brownmiller (1975/1993) argues.

It was during Reconstruction that black male sexuality first became a major theme in white southern politics, marking a long period of racialized sexual terrorism and lynching. "As part of the same process," Martha Hodes (1993) writes, "white ideology about white female sexuality changed as well, though not as rapidly and never as completely" (403). As we will observe in those southerners who prosecuted the Scottsboro Nine, women who might be regarded by white men as "tramps" were, vis-à-vis black men, flowers of pure southern womanhood. The conditions that made possible the Scottsboro scandal were, while centuries in the making, crystallized after the South's defeat in the Civil War. From that point on, Hodes (1993) argues, "politics and sexuality were inextricably entwined ... in the history of the American South" (404). And not only in the minds of whites. A black Republican representative from Alabama, James Rapier, also expressed the conflation, equating manhood with the right to vote and declaring that "nothing short of a complete acknowledgment of my manhood will satisfy me" (quoted in Hodes 1993, 404).

It was precisely this conflation of political rights and black manhood that surfaced as central during and after the Reconstruction South: "The idea of manhood, which had long implied the rights and responsibilities of citizenship in American political thought, now took on connotations, in white minds, of black male sexual agency, and specifically of sexual transgression with white women" (Hodes 1993, 404). Beginning in the Reconstruction era, black political participation and black male sexuality, were in the minds of southerners, especially southern white men, difficult to disentangle. Although black women and whites who supported the rights of the freedpeople were also victims of white terror during Reconstruction, the most vicious violence would be directed at black men (Hodes 1993).

Most whites found it beyond belief that any sane white woman would voluntarily become sexually involved with a black man, a fact antilynching crusader Ida B. Wells understood well. As Wells suspected and was able to confirm, white women did on occasion choose to become involved with black men. But when white men found out, the liaison was always converted to a case of "rape." A failure to punish such unthinkable behavior meant certain censure not only for her but for her male relatives as well; after all, in a social sense it was not she the black man was entering. "She" was a figment of the white male imagination, a symbolic currency in a homosocial economy (Sedgwick 1985).

So was "he." Both white women and black men (and women) floated within a white male imaginary they mistook for "reality." Even "progressive" white men were liable to such conflations, as a line from a well-known speech made in 1863 before the American Antislavery Convention indicates. There white abolitionist Theodore Tilton (1863) urged "manly" white men to let go of their fear of black men: "In all those intellectual activities which take a strange quickening from the moral faculties—processes which we call instincts, or intuitions—the negro is superior to the white man—equal to the white woman. The negro race is the feminine race of the world" (12; quoted in hooks 1994, 131). This white male fantasy would be repeated by University of

Chicago sociologist Robert Park (1950), who in fact asserted: "The Negro is the lady of the races" (280).

When a black man had sex with a white woman, it was the white man who felt him inside. Nathan Corder, a white farmer in Fauquier County, Virginia, felt it. Surely his daughter, in her right mind, would not have chosen to run off with and marry Arthur Jordan, one of his black farmhands, in 1880. Corder had Jordan arrested in Washington, D.C., where the couple had been married; once back in Fauquier County, his son-in-law stood trial on the charge of bigamy, as Jordan was allegedly already married to a black woman. Four days after Jordan was held in the county jail in Warrenton, a small group of masked men overpowered the jail guards, dragged him from his cell, and lynched him (Brundage 1993). Ida B. Wells (1970) reports a similar case, this one in Mississippi:

> Many cases were like that of the lynching which happened in Tunica County, Mississippi. The Associated Press reporter said, "The big burly brute was lynched because he had raped the seven-year-old daughter of the sheriff." I visited the place afterward and saw the girl, who was a grown woman more than seventeen years old. She had been found in the lynched Negro's cabin by her father, who had led the mob against him in order to save his daughter's reputation. The Negro was a helper on the farm. (65)

The number of lynchings slowly decreased during the opening decades of the twentieth century. Between 50 and 161 lynchings of black men and women were recorded each year from 1889 to 1916. The number dropped to 10–24 a year in the 1930s and 1–6 a year from 1938 to the 1950s, and occasional lynchings occurred during the 1950s, most spectacularly that of Emmett Till. The United States recorded its first lynch-free year in 1950 (Newton and Newton 1991, xiii). The last recorded lynching was Mack Charles Parker in 1959. Yet these figures understate the prevalence of the phenomenon; some believe that the majority of all lynchings were never recorded during the lynching era. Recall that Ida B. Wells estimated that over 10,000 died at white men's hands. Most were carried out with the participation of police authorities, who then erased the event from public record (Feagin and Hernan 1995).

Between 1900 and 1930 it is estimated that only 0.8 percent of lynchings in the United States were followed by criminal conviction of the lyncher (Chadbourn 1933; R. W. Brown 1965). In Florida, where the largest number of blacks were lynched relative to the size of its black population of any state in the country, there was not one conviction for lynchings between 1900 and 1934, the year Claude Neal was executed. Indeed, Florida's fundamentalist governor, Sidney J. Catts (1916–1920), declared that he would himself resort to vigilante "justice." When a N.A.A.C.P. official—John Shillady—criticized the number of unpunished lynchings in Florida, Governor Catts replied, "If any man, white or black, should dishonor one of my family he would meet my pistol square from the shoulder and every white man in the South, who is a red-blooded American, feels the same as I do" (quoted in McGovern 1982, 12; in N.A.A.C.P. 1919, 18). Even as late as the 1930s, only six states had disciplinary statutes prohibiting lynchings (McGovern 1982). Several decades later, Foucault (1988) would link the legal and the sexual in a way that helps make intelligible the good governor's sentiments:

> A last set of dreams in conformity with the law relates to masturbation. These dreams are very closely associated with the theme of slavery, because what is involved is a service that one renders oneself (hands are like servants who do the bidding of their master, the penis) and because the word means "to bind to a post," used in connection with the whipping of slaves, also means "to have an erection." (20)

If sadistic position of the white male torturer got him hard, how did he ignore his crime after he came? Did he not see, the morning after, the pain and suffering he created? White southerners buried whatever guilt they might have felt by invoking biblical rationales for slavery, by feeling the righteousness of their "cause," by, as Lewis Simpson (1983) knew, "forgetting" what happened, simply by not seeing the evidence of their aggression. Of course, in reality the marks left by the whip remained for the life of those beaten, but as Hortense Spillers suggests, whites avoided seeing these indelible signs of their sadism. They perceived only skin color. Spillers wonders about the indelibility of these marks, these scars both literal and metaphoric, as they fester across the generations of subjugated African Americans. She writes: "These indecipherable markings on the captive body render a kind of hieroglyphics of the flesh whose severe disjunctures come to be hidden to the cultural seeing by skin color. We might well ask if this phenomenon of marking and branding actually 'transfers' from one generation to another, finding its various symbolic substitutions in an efficacy of meanings that repeat the initiating moments" (Spillers 1987, 67).

For black men surely these scars are visible as the contemporary "crisis" of black masculinity (see chapter 14); for white men the originary position of the torturer surfaces in his obsession with rape, and later with the positionings of specularity, that is, always watching black men's bodies, sweating, performing, on music stages, basketball courts, and football fields, always caught in the white man's gaze, performing for his pleasure. In the late nineteenth century this originary position of torturer was encoded in white men's absolute obsession with rape. Not his rape of black women, of course, but, in his denial and relocation of desire, his obsessional fantasy of black men lusting after white women.

The rape myth permeated American society; even a (sometimes) progressive reformer like President Theodore Roosevelt pandered to it even while denouncing mob action. Antilynching campaigners committed enormous amounts of time and energy disproving rape as the cause of lynching. Certainly this was true for teacher and journalist Ida B. Wells during the last two decades of the nineteenth century, for former suffragist Jessie Daniel Ames of the Association of Southern Women for the Prevention of Lynching during the 1930s, and Walter White during his long career from 1918 to 1955 with the National Association for the Advancement of Colored People (N.A.A.C.P.). Theirs, however, was an arduous and ultimately failed effort, as we shall see in chapters 10 and 11.

In 1926, Warren A. Candler, senior bishop of the Southern Methodist Church and brother of Coca-Cola founder Asa Candler, expressed the conflation of gender and race made possible by the imaginary status of white women when he warned that a "possible danger to women is inherent in every offense against the white man." Nine years later, he continued to insist that lynching was not caused by "base passion" but righteous indignation over "the most repulsive forms of crime" (quoted in Hall 1979, 147). "Repulsive" as well as "base passion" are words often hurled at homosexuals. Rarely are such terms reserved for heterosexual events. Was that the subtext of these remarks?

In a 1939 survey conducted by Hortense Powdermaker (whose ethnographic research we revisit in chapter 14), 65 percent of her white respondents said that lynching was justified in cases of sexual assault. Politicians knew how their (white) constituents felt. On November 11, 1911, Governor Cole L. Blease told an audience of one thousand assembled in Anderson, South Carolina, that he approved of lynching. He devoted considerable time to the recent lynching of a black man—Willis Jackson—at Honea Path. In that lynching event, the mob had been led by State Representative Joshua W. Ashley and Victor B. Cheshire, editor of a local newspaper, the *Intelligencer;* the governor told his constituents that rather than use the power of his office to deter white men from "punishing that nigger brute" he would have "resigned the office and come to Honea Path and led the mob myself" (quoted in Ginzburg 1962/1988, 74–75).

When Ben Tillman had first been elected governor of South Carolina in 1890, he had in his inaugural address called lynching "a blot on our civilization" and noted that since whites controlled every aspect of the criminal justice system it was "simply infamous that resort should be had to lynch law." After his first term, Tillman's views changed. Realizing that antiblack rhetoric paid handsome political dividends, Tillman came out in favor of lynching during the 1892 election campaign, declaring, "Governor as I am, I'd lead a mob to lynch a man who had ravished a white woman. ... I justify lynching for rape, and, before Almighty God, I'm not ashamed of it" (quoted in Finnegan 1997, 199).

The strategy seems to have paid off. After serving as governor, Tillman was elected to the U.S. Senate, where, in a 1907 speech before Congress, he argued for the abandonment of due process for those black men accused of sex crimes against white women:

> The white women of the South are in a state of siege. ... Some lurking demon who has watched for the opportunity seizes her; she is choked or beaten into insensibility and ravished, her body prostituted, her purity destroyed, her chastity taken from her. ... Shall men ... demand for [the demon] the right to have a fair trial and be punished in the regular course of justice? So far as I am concerned he has put himself outside the pale of the law, human and divine. ... Civilization peels off us ... and we revert to the ... impulses ... to kill! kill! kill! (quoted in Wiegman 1993, 459–460)

While enslaved, Tillman continued, black men had had minds like "those of children." Then they had posed no sexual threat, evidenced by the fact that during the Civil War, with white men away fighting, Tillman thundered: "there is not of record a solitary instance of one white women having been wronged" by the nearly 800,000 black men left on plantations with white women. Only after Emancipation is there "return to barbarism" and rape follows; "the negro becomes a fiend in human form" (quoted in Wiegman 1993, 460).

African Americans didn't take this nonsense lying down. After a lynching in which Tillman communicated to local officials his approval, African Americans mobilized and protested. On April 26, 1893, five hundred black residents traveled to the Columbia courthouse to denounce Governor Tillman for his complicity in the lynching and to exhort their fellow African Americans to join them in protest. Resolutions passed at the meeting which denounced Tillman's actions as "unwarranted, unprecedented, and inhuman" and charged that the lynching proved that the state of South Carolina was unable to protect African Americans, whether guilty or innocent. The time for speaking was over, angry protestors exclaimed; African Americans could no longer wait for a "higher court" to intervene on their behalf. The last speaker was a black mail agent named Shelton; he told his black listeners that they were "too submissive" and were too dependent on whites for protection. With the blood of the lynched man, John Peterson, dripping "from the fingers of the Governor," Shelton pleaded with those gathered to "rise up and defend ourselves against mob law and lynchers." Some black South Carolinians did respond with political action, if on a different occasion. After a black man named Jefferson Crawford was lynched in York County in June 1894, for instance, African Americans registered to vote in the "greatest numbers of the past ten years" (quoted in Finnegan 1997, 200).

Blease's view on lynching hardly hurt him among (white) South Carolina voters. In his campaign for re-election to the Senate in the summer of 1930, Senator Blease toured the state. In Union County, two weeks after a lynching, he spoke once again on the subject. He declared:

> Whenever the Constitution comes between me and the virtue of the white women of South Carolina, I say to hell with the Constitution! Whenever the negro press and associations are to tell me how I am to vote, I ask my God to deprive me of the right to vote. White supremacy and the protection of the virtue of the white women of the South come first with me. When I was governor of South Carolina you did not hear of me calling out the militia to protect negro assaulters. In my South Carolina campaigns you heard me say, "When you catch the brute that assaults a white woman, wait until the next morning to notify me." (quoted in Raper 1933/1969, 293)

The southern obsession with rape reverberated throughout the nation at large. It echoed one of the deepest of American preoccupations: the conflict between "civilization" and "savagery," historically acted out in the genocide of the Indians, the destruction of the forest, the enslavement of Africans, themes to which I return, with Gail Bederman (1995a, 1995b) in chapters 6 and 8, and with Leslie Fielder (1966) in chapter 18. In a Protestant culture predicated upon work, repression, and acquisitiveness, "men struggled to separate themselves from nature," what James Madison had named as "the black race within our bosom [and] the red on our borders" (quoted in Hall 1979, 147–148). The link between Protestantism and white supremacy was, for Walter White, explicit; he termed the Ku Klux Klan an "extreme form of Protestant nationalism" (White 1929, 119).

Native Americans and African Americans did not, perhaps could not, exist outside the Anglo-American imagination and consequently "became the repositories for those parts of the self which, in the process, had to be conquered and repressed" (Hall 1979, 148). This self-division and fragmentation, projected onto the world, meant that white women too were rarely "real." They became "ladies," set apart as "asexual guardians of morality." In the comfort of their affections, men could pursue destruction, acquisition, and expansion, secure in the knowledge that they were not abandoning the values of "civilization." By projecting onto blacks, especially black men, the "animal within," the buried parts of themselves could be objectified, controlled, relocated, re-experienced sexually through fantasies of interracial rape, torture, and other forms of violent, nonreciprocal intimacy.

> But this separation from spontaneous emotional life and heterosexual love generated longings, fantasies, and fears that could never be kept altogether at bay. The result was a society prey to "visions of violent, immoral possession." The image of black over white, of a world turned upside down, symbolized the everpresent danger of the return of the repressed, of a regression to a primitive natural world of sexuality and violence. (Hall 1979, 148)

The myth—the white male fantasy shared by more than a few white women—of muscular, rapacious black rapists reached "pathological proportions at the turn of the century." Some have suggested it was related as well as to sexual tensions associated with a repressive Victorianism that was then waning. The turn to sex was evident in scientific study, associated, for instance, with the work of Freud and Havelock Ellis. It was aggravated by the appearance of the "new woman"—working, independent, demanding her civil rights, including the right to vote. All this, as we will see in chapter 6, intensified a certain "crisis" of white masculinity also associated with shifts in the structure of the economy: "Sexual stirrings—rejected, feared, and projected onto others—beat like a 'distracting savage drum' beneath the genteel discourse of the white middle class. ... No image so dramatically symbolized the most lurid of Victorian fantasies and fears as that of violent sexual congress between a black man and a white woman" (Hall 1979, 148).

In 1915 D. W. Griffith, the son of a Confederate cavalry officer, expressed the white male obsession with the black man in his film version of Thomas R. Dixon's *The Clansman*. Also relying on sections of President Woodrow Wilson's *A History of the American People,* and with the latest in technical innovations, Griffith produced a remarkable film. (Wilson viewed the film appreciatively in the White House.) Set in the Reconstruction South, white Congressional Radicals, attempting to create a biracial, politically just postbellum South, were portrayed as scheming and unprincipled. Their black allies, freed black slaves, were characterized far more harshly. Once a contented labor force under the "peculiar institution," with freedom blacks became vicious, wild, and sexually rapacious. Freedmen in the film were portrayed as coarse, dirty, and ill-behaved, always threatening the welfare of a victimized white society. In sharp contrast, white southerners appeared as cultivated, heroic, well mannered—the epitome of civilization. The attempted rape of the virginal "little Flora" and the lynching of her monstrous attacker was an imprinting moment in the cultural representation and sedimentation of white male fantasy. Heroically, white southern men fought the black "brutes" and overthrew "Negro rule." In the end, their leader proclaimed that "civilization has been saved, and the South redeemed from shame" (quoted in Friedman 1970, 169). *The Birth of a Nation* demonstrated the enormous myth-making potential of the modern movie, especially when it played upon racist stereotypes and sexual obsessions, themselves intertwined (Hall 1979; Friedman 1970).

The "southern rape complex" was never grounded in objective reality. As noted, relatively few of known victims of lynch mobs were even accused of rape or of attempted rape, and these were almost never documented (Guzman 1952; R. W. Brown 1965). Every study of rape has underlined the fact that despite the persistent white fantasies of black male attacks on white women, rape in America has always been an overwhelmingly intraracial event, with the conspicuous exception of white slave owners' repeated rapes of black slave women, and, in all likelihood, of men (Looby 1995; Marsden 1991).

The theory of "projection" has been a prominent interpretation of racism, especially since the 1920s. Several scholars (Resnikoff 1933; Jordan 1968, 1974; Harris 1984; Williamson 1984) have worked to explain lynching by underscoring the intersections among race, gender, and sexuality. In particular, whites have been said to "project" forbidden fantasies onto blacks and then destroyed their projection by murdering the creature of their own creation, the black rapist. Winthrop Jordan (1974) articulated this idea succinctly when he wrote: "For it is apparent that white men projected their own desires onto Negroes. ... It is not we who lust, but they" (80). James Comer (well-known in education circles for his work with black children) said much the same: "The conduct of the whites who participated in murdering and lynching blacks suggests that those grisly events served as a catharsis by purging the evil the whites feared in themselves and 'projected' onto the blacks" (quoted in Harris 1984, 17).

Projection theory begins in the fact that there was no basis in reality for white-male fears of black men. As noted earlier: "No one stopped to consider that, during the years of the Civil War, when white men left their wives, daughters, and homes in the hands of black men, not a single instance of rape was reported. The issue, then, really boils down to one between white men and black men and the mythic conception the former have of the latter" (Harris 1984, 20; see Faust 1996, 59–65). That is not precisely true; as we will see in chapter 4, there were acts of violence, including sexual violence, committed by black male slaves during the Civil War, but they were infrequent. André Green (1986) asserts that "projection is linked to a primary defense mechanism fundamentally defined by the action of expelling; of casting out (to project—

spit, to vomit) something within which is unpleasant" (85). Now what could that "something" "unpleasant" be? Perhaps the clue is Green's observation that projection is "closely linked to paranoia" (85). In the classical psychoanalytical formulation, paranoia in men can follow from the repression of homosexual desire (Freud 1911/1963).

While discussing fascism and anti-Semitism, Max Horkheimer and Theodor Adorno (1944/1972) discuss projection in terms that seem to speak specifically to the nineteenth-century South:

> The psychoanalytical theory of morbid projection views it as consisting of the transference of socially taboo impulses from subject to the object. Under the pressure of the super-ego, the ego projects the aggressive wishes which originate from the id (and are so intense as to be dangerous even to the id), as evil intentions onto the outside world; either in fantasy by identification with the supposed evil, or in reality by supposed self-defense. The forbidden action which is converted into aggression is generally homosexual in nature. Through fear of castration, obedience to the father is taken to the extreme in an anticipation of castration in conscious emotional approximation to the nature of a small girl and actual hatred of the father is suppressed. In paranoia, this hatred leads to a castration wish as a generalized urge to destruction. (192)

The identification with "a small girl" occurred, for most nineteenth-century southern white men, at the site of "vulnerable and virginal southern ladies." The "forbidden action"—recoded heterosexually as the rape scenario—was, as Adorno and Horkheimer note, "generally homosexual in nature."

How did these dynamics of projection and paranoia work in southern white men during the last third of the nineteenth century? Through projection, Freud (1915) wrote in "The Unconscious," "the ego behaves as if the danger of a development of anxiety threatened it not from the direction of an instinctual impulse but from the direction of a perception, and it is thus enabled to react against this external danger with the attempts at flight represented by phobic avoidances" (184). Segregation qualifies—does it not?—as a "phobic avoidance." But key to understanding lynching is that the site of danger was not, as heterosexist critics tend to assume, the body of the white woman. White men were not projecting their own intolerable heterosexual desire for white women onto black men. If that had been the case, the "external danger" (in Freud's words) would have been the white woman herself. There is of course a long history of misogyny associated with such a projection, that is, the woman as whore, seductress, a medusa who emasculates men by her (but in fact his) desire. The "danger" in the late nineteenth-century South was not lascivious white women. They were in general imaginary, safely positioned on pedestals in white men's minds. In the nineteenth century the "danger" was the black man, whom southern white men positioned as a sexualized and racialized "other" vis-à-vis their own identification with "the lady," whom they were then compelled to "defend." Because their own "instinctual" sexual desire for the men they had once subjugated as slaves was now experienced as an intolerable "danger" to an already beleaguered and regressing postbellum white male ego, they projected that homosexual desire onto the black men, in "drag" as it were, as black man's heterosexual desire for the white lady.

A myth is many things, but one thing that it is is a narrative symbolization of desire. Once created, a myth has a life of its own. Once white men had concocted this fantasy of black men as studs, bucks, and stallions, they found themselves imprisoned by it. When they tried to destroy the "myth" of black-male hypersexuality—by destroying black men—they intensified it. During their torture routines, as Trudier Harris (1984) suggests, white men sometimes spent considerable time examining the genitals of the black men whom they were about to murder. Before the final stage of examination—castration—there was fondling, even caressing, of black men's bodies, including their penises. The multiple and apparently unconscious emotions which were surfacing at these moments drove white men to slash even more violently at what was not theirs, but which, with unmistakable intensity, they very much wanted (Harris 1984).

More than one student of lynching would observe, as did Daryl Dance (1978): "[T]he sexual mutilation of the victim—suggests the white man's efforts to wrest from the black man that symbol of manhood (that testament of superiority) which he so fears" (104; quoted in Harris 1984, 22). Fear (without foundation) equals desire (inverted). Several commentators have understood exactly: "the lynched black man becomes a source of sexual pleasure to those who kill him" (Harris 1984, 23). Author of a once-banned and best-selling novel about an illicit interracial love affair in 1920s Georgia entitled *Strange Fruit*, Lillian Smith (1949/1963) observed: "the lynched Negro becomes not an object that must die but a receptacle for every man's damned-up hate, and *a receptacle for every man's forbidden sex feelings*" (158–159; quoted in Harris 1984, 23; second emphasis added). A receptacle? Forbidden? A love that dare not speak its name?

In a lynching the black man was often stripped, sometimes of his penis, and in this act of stripping did the white man imagine the black man's sexual power was transferred to him? Why was the white man compelled to destroy what he wanted? Why would lynchers divide pieces of the black man's body among themselves? (Harris 1984). Such murder is not only racial mutilation; it is not only the "retrieval" of qualities projected onto the "other." It must be regarded also as an explicit sexual act, however deformed. Was lynching precisely that which white men imagined they were punishing: a rape, a (disguised, deformed, denied) homosexual rape? When power relations become reversed—in twentieth-century American prisons—black men acted as if it were so. What constitutes political "revenge" in American prisons? Rape.

Trudier Harris (1984) tells us that the height of sexual tension was reached when the rope was actually around the offender's neck, and the fire had been started. The climactic release began with the crackling of the flames against black flesh. It reached fever pitch with the cries of the black man screaming in unendurable pain. And the climax came in the screams of the white men when they knew the naked, mutilated, burned black man was finally dead. Now, Harris observes, the white men's screams gave way to the silence of satisfaction, a release from tension. The gathering of souvenirs, that is, body parts, begins. The *Chicago Record* for February 27, 1901, records such a scene:

> HOOSIERS HANG NEGRO KILLER. Terre Haute, Ind., Feb. 26. George Ward, the negro who murdered Miss Ida Finkelstein, the school teacher, last evening, was placed in jail at 11 o'clock this morning, and shortly before 1 o'clock was taken out by a mob, dragged face downward to the banks of the Wabash. ... When the crowd near the fire tired of renewing it after two hours, it was seen that the victim's feet were not burned. Someone called an offer of a dollar for one of the toes, and a boy quickly took out his knife and cut off a toe. The offer was followed by others, and the horrible traffic was continued, youths holding up toes and asking for bids. (quoted in Ginzburg 1962/1988, 37)

Something of the white fascination with the now inanimate black male body is captured in the following newspaper account. Note not only what is described but the tone of the description. The reporter appears to share the affect of the onlookers. It is 1930, the day after a lynching, and the *Raleigh News and Observer* published a photograph of the black male body with these comments:

> It was quite the thing to look at the bloody, dead nigger hanging from the limb of a tree near the Edgecombe-Wilson County line this morning. ... Families came together, mothers and fathers, bringing even their youngest children. It was the show of the countryside—a very popular show. Men joked loudly at the sight of the bleeding body ... girls giggled as the flies fed on the blood that dripped from the Negro's nose. (Raper 1933/1969, 114)

There were southern reporters who did not share lynchers' enthusiasm for torture and mutilation, and pretended to a "professional" neutrality on the matter. The September 5, 1899, edition of the *Bangor* (Maine) *Commercial* featured the following story. Notice the "professional distance" the reporter alleges to maintain. At the time he may have been judged a traitor to his southern constituents, but to us now, his neutral tone seems to be one of complicity:

> VISITING SOUTHERN REPORTER DESCRIBES LYNCHINGS SEEN. A veteran reporter on one of the southern newspapers, who is now visiting this city, gives an interesting account of his experiences in "covering" lynching parties. "The news that there is to be a lynching," he begins, "spreads very rapidly in the South, especially in the small cities and towns. To the reporter it is a very disagreeable business to attend these lynchings, for he is usually not overcome by frenzy like the mob made up from the immediate neighborhood, and so cannot sympathize with its method of procedure." (quoted in Ginzburg 1962/1988, 21)

"Frenzy" is a word often associated with sexual excitation. Lynching simultaneously displayed and disguised the white man's sexual obsession with the black man's body. Calling him a "boy," for instance, suggests the strange (pedophiliac?) lens through which the white man saw, then expressed, his mangled desire. In part an effort to control language and thereby control the reality language presumably describes, "boy" both hides and reveals the sexual desirability of the black man to the white man. Castration in this context is hardly a technical, medical procedure:

> The white man—the southerner—secretly worships and fears the sex image he has created in the Negro; therefore, he must destroy that image. Castration represents not only the destruction of that mythical monster, but also the partaking of that monster. It is a disguised form of worship, a primitive pornographic divination rite—and a kind of homosexualism in reverse. (Hernton 1965/1988, 117)

What's "reverse" about it? Perverse, perhaps, but reverse? Does he mean the black guy should be the "top" and the white guy the "bottom," as sex is structured in much interracial prison rape? The homoerotic dimension of lynching is explicit in Hernton's statement, but obscured in those heterosexist interpretations which assert the white man wants to transfer the sexual potency of the black man to himself. When a heterosexual man wants a heterosexual woman, is it to transfer her sexuality to him? Of course there are those Jungian interpretations which imply that the (heterosexual) male wishes to complete himself by "possessing" what he has repressed in himself, that is, the woman or "anima." But phenomenologically, does not heterosexual desire express his literal (as well, perhaps, symbolic) desire for her, to be inside her? Likewise, homoerotic desire cannot be reduced to an attempt to "transfer" sexuality; it *is* sexual desire.

William Faulkner foreshadowed much of what would later be written about white southerners' twin obsessions with race and sex. In *Light in August* (mentioned earlier), Joanna Burden, who is white, is killed by Joe Christmas, a disturbed man of mixed racial ancestry, and the local community responds with a "lust for vengeance." The whites who gathered after the news of the murder of Joanna Burden, "believed it aloud that it was an anonymous negro crime committed not by a negro but by Negro ... and hoped [!] that she had been ravished, too: at least once before her throat was cut and at least once afterward" (Faulkner 1987, 322). At the climax of the novel, Joe Christmas becomes the scapegoat for the repressed sexual longings of Percy Grimm, the leader of the mob that murders and mutilates him. Perhaps with Grimm's twisted psyche in mind, historian Joel Williamson (1984) has suggested that "black men were lynched for having achieved, seemingly, a sexual liberation that white men wanted but could not achieve without great feelings of guilt," an idea we will revisit in the second section of chapter 19. Tortured by their frustration, white men projected their thoughts upon black men "and symbolically killed those thoughts by lynching a hapless black man. ... In effect, the black man lynched was the worst part of themselves" (308).

To suppress the black man, Trudier Harris (1984) asserts, is to position him as "woman." In this position his manhood is stripped from him; he is "castrated." To regain his manhood he must assert it, he must rape. Not just literally, and not just women. Trudier Harris (1984) recalls Richard Wright's (1966/1940) description of Bigger: "But rape was not what one did to women. ... He committed rape every time he looked into a white face" (213–214;

quoted in Harris 1984, 115). As Eldridge Cleaver (1968) made explicit, interracial heterosexual rape is an act of revenge toward the white man. The "traffic" is in women (Rubin 1975), the victimized bodies are female, but the eyes locked together in the sex act are men's, black and white. Slavoj Zizek (1995) tells a story of the 1990s war in the former Yugoslavia; soldiers forced fathers to watch as they gang raped their daughters. Zizek reports that as the soldiers entered the young girls' bodies, their eyes were locked into the eyes of the fathers. This is heterosexual rape? Women's bodies were assaulted ... in the service of a (denied and relocated) homosexual assault.

Calvin Hernton tells the story (he says "there are countless others like it") in which a young black man in Tennessee was picked up by the police while playing in a park. He was arrested, he was told, for breaking into a hair salon. The proprietor, a white woman, lived behind the salon. Once at police headquarters, several officers drilled him to get a "confession." When the boy refused to confess, they approached the white woman. The young man told the following:

> [I] could hear them outside of the room where they kept me, trying to get the woman to cooperate with them. But she was not sure, and she would not say I was the one. They then suggested that maybe I had tried to rape her. She wouldn't go along with that either. She got mad, I think, and left the police station. Later on the cops let me go free, but before they did, they made me take off my clothes, and I had to show them my sex. One of them spilled coffee on me. He pretended it was an accident, but I don't believe him. They said if they ever caught me messing around with one of their women they would fix me for life. (quoted in Hernton 1965/1988, 118–119)

Lynching, and white racism generally, are not, of course, only suppressed, or what Hernton terms "reversed," homosexual desire. Lynching and racism are of course more complex and variegated, and the forms they took differed according to locale and historical period (see Young-Bruehl 1996). They have multiple "causes." Education (or lack of it) would seem to be a variable. "Our real hope of improvement," James Weldon Johnson wrote in 1927, "lies in the slow process of education in public sentiment now going on in the South. ... Educational advance is necessarily slow and must be assisted by every possible outside pressure" (65; quoted in Chadbourn 1933, 17).

Walter Howard (1995) suggests that some lynchings were "diversionary" in nature, noting that many occurred during slack periods of farm work (139). Without question economic issues—specifically the price of cotton (as we will see in chapter 3)—were related. More general links between cycles of economic prosperity and deprivation among rural southern whites and the numbers of lynching victims have been demonstrated statistically. Economic considerations could not have seemed obvious to black observers (of whom there have been few) as they watched the nightmare of mutilation, torture, and murder.

Perhaps in the fetish, the repetition, can be found the truth of lynching. The fetish reveals as it conceals the repressed functioning of the principal structure of a social formation, even of a society (Lemelle 1995). Lynching—

and the black phallus on which the practice was focused—qualifies, I submit, as a key cultural fetish in late nineteenth- and early twentieth-century America. Frederick Douglass put the matter poetically. In what he entitled "What Am I to You" he acknowledged:

> For heart of man though mainly right
> Hides many things from mortal sight
> Which seldom ever come to light
> except upon compulsion.
> (quoted in McDowell 1993, 48)

As Freud (1911/1963) knew, fetishism relies on the psychical defense mechanism of disavowal; he calls it "[a] token of triumph over the threat of castration and a safeguard against it" (116). I say white men destroyed the desire they feared by dismembering the object of their fantasy.

A group's historical memory, Anthony J. Lemelle, Jr. (1995) argues, is communicated both consciously and unconsciously, passed from one generation to the next. But it is exactly this psychohistorical memory that the bourgeoisie requires to be forgotten. Using standard Marxist terms, Lemelle notes that the ideological task of the bourgeoisie requires the revision of history in order to justify their status. I would add that consumer capitalism itself commodifies temporality, leaving the bourgeoisie presentistic, one might even say aphasic. Lemelle points to white ideological fantasies, such as white supremacy, which function to suppress the guilt over and memory of white savagery, white desire. He quotes Frantz Fanon:

> We understand now why the black man cannot take pleasure in his insularity. For him there is only one way out, and it leads into the white world. Whence his constant preoccupation with attracting the attention of the white man, his concern with being powerful like the white man, his determined effort to acquire protective qualities—that is, the proportion of being or having what enters into the composition of an ego. (quoted in Lemelle 1995, 131)

The white man is also preoccupied, is he not? He wants—demands—the attention of the black man; he needs for the black man to remember him, to remember his "place" in their relationship. This is a place in the white man's imagination. It is a sexualized place.

Frances Cress Welsing thinks she knows why the white man is so intrigued with the black male body. In her *Cress Theory of Color Confrontation and Racism (White Supremacy),* Welsing (1991) explains white racism as a function of whites' "inability to produce melanin skin pigment in the skin melanocyte" (232). "All behavioral patterns in the global white collective," she declares, "begin and end with the conscious and/or unconscious consideration of white genetic survival and the corollary consideration of the global threat of white genetic annihilation by the non-white majority" (Welsing 1991, 222). So that's why we're white, why we're so vulnerable to black men. "They" can erase "us" through miscegenation. Her theory, she asserts, "also explains why black males' testicles were the body parts that white males attacked in most lynchings: the testicles store powerful color-producing genetic material." Most accounts focus upon the black male penis, but that would seem, she suggests, to be a displacement of attention from the true object of interest, the testicles:

> Likewise, the repeated and consistent focus on the size of black males' penises by both white males and females is viewed by this theory as a displacement of the fundamental concern with the genetic color-producing capacity residing in the testicles. Since the fact of color-envy must remain repressed, color-desire can never be mentioned or the entire white psychological structure collapses. Therefore, attention is displaced to a less threatening object or symbol—the penis. (Welsing 1991, 7)

The fetish substitutes for the event it represents, shielding the original desire from consciousness and memory. In Marxist terms, for instance, the bourgeoisie fetishize consciousness via commodification, and in their immersion in consumption, have forgotten history, including the sexualized brutality of white political oppression. Black people are everywhere in America but white people do not see them (Ellison 1952). In the rap star, in the basketball celebrity, in the criminal the white man sees the auction block, the shadow of the sweating shining slave, the muscular black male body there to serve him. On the basketball court, in music videos, on the auction block: the white man is always staring at the black man's body. The past remains present.

Not only is a break with the past unlikely, the more revolutionary the movement the more powerful the reactionary undertow, as we have seen these past thirty years in the United States. That is not to say that political movement, a.k.a. "progress," is not possible. It is to say that political gains do not come like economic gains, the apparent reward for hard work not to mention good fortune. The past will not be so easily passed by as was the Dow at 10,000. Because each of us has embedded within us what Jung imagined as the collective unconscious, we as individuals must work through the collective as well as singular past. An individual neurotic may first become aware of his symptoms' history, by dissolving, usually very slowly and free associatively, the various blocks that have been erected to suppress his/her knowledge of the past. Once aware, one can re-experience what was so traumatic once, and release into the present the repressed pain, resentment, and rage. In his *Economic and Philosophical Manuscripts of 1844*, Marx put the matter less psychoanalytically:

> Man, much as he may therefore be a particular individual (and it is precisely his particularity which makes him an individual, and a real individual social being), is just as much the totality—the ideal totality—the subjective existence of thought and experienced society present for itself; just as he exists also in the real world as the awareness and the real enjoyment of social existence, and as a totality of human life-activity. (quoted in Lemelle 1995, 132)

Sartre (1981) conceived of the individual as a "universal singular" in which the social totality is embodied in one's concrete particularity, in a unique, individual way. A generation later, Gilles Deleuze (1993) would put the matter this way: "The world is an infinite series of curvatures or inflections, and the entire world is enclosed in the soul from one point of view" (24).

While in the "raindrop is the ocean," unless the individual has worked through the blocks to his species as well as individual past, he cannot be an individual: "[w]hoever cannot tell himself the truth about his past is trapped in it, is immobilized in the prison of his undiscovered self. Whoever cannot face the truth cannot love" (Baldwin 1985, 24). To be a heterosexual white man—"the man"—is to be an individual variation of a social and gender category, but it is not to be an authentic individual. In fact, the straight white man is not himself; that which he is he is not. He is the desubjectified objectified other that he demands others to be. Baldwin (1985) writes: "The object of one's hatred is never, alas, conveniently outside but is seated in one's lap, stirring in one's bowels and dictating the beat of one's heart. And if one does not know this, one risks becoming an imitation—and, therefore, a continuation—of principles one imagines oneself to despise" (87).

Lynching was rape, if thinly disguised: a snuff film without the celluloid. The victim's fingers, toes, the penis were sometimes severed and saved as souvenirs. Even the corpse was mutilated. Raping a dead person is "necrophilia" ... philia is love. Desire and hate are intertwined; they are not, of course, sharply separable modes of relation. Heterosexual white men want and need women while they simultaneously hate them, as indicated in the crime statistics we review in chapter 13. The "other" is one side of an unstable binary; the relation between the two easily slips from love to hate. Wanting the black male body sexually is not unrelated to hating it, as black gay men testify (see chapter 14, section VIII).

Lynching occurred in public but it was also intrapsychic; what the white man underwent internally he reenacted on the black man. "[It is as if] black male sexuality must be destroyed," Harris (1984, 11) comments, but it was his own sexuality—his own homosexuality—he aimed to kill. In intrapsychic terms, lynching was the white man's public and racialized reenactment of his own self-mutilation. While lynching symbolized a self-self relation, it had a civilizational legacy as well: "It goes without saying that a profound hatred of African people (as seen in slavery, lynching, segregation, and second-class citizenship) sits at the center of American civilization" (West 1993, 73). In the groin, it would seem.

Is "projection" a key that unlocks the structure of the European-American (male) self? "[I]f the white man can attribute his own basest sexual desires to the black man ... then he can remain clean, pure, and morally superior in the eyes of his society," Harris (1984, 91–92) speculates. Is that how compulsory Christianity works, forcing believers, for the sake of moral purity, to deny, then to split off and attach to "others" qualities Christianity—as a repressive political and cultural force, not as an existential self-salvational relationship to one's God—would not allow the faithful to accept in themselves? James Baldwin writes:

> have endured your fire
> and your whip,
> your rope,

and the panic from your hip,
in many ways, false lover,
yet, my love:
You do not know
how desperately I hoped
that you would grow
not so much to love me
as to know
that what you do to me
you do to you.
(Baldwin 1990, 65)

Baldwin, who grew up in New York and lived much of his adult life in France, had never been to the land of lynching, had never been to the African South. He describes his first visit:

> In the fall of last year, my plane hovered over the rust-red earth of Georgia. I was past thirty, and I had never seen this land before. I pressed my face against the window, watching the earth come closer; soon we were just above the tops of trees. I could not suppress the thought that this earth had acquired its color from the blood that had dripped down from these trees. My mind was filled with the image of a black man, younger than I, perhaps, or my own age, hanging from a tree, while white men watched him and cut his sex from him with a knife. (Baldwin 1985, 184)

Strange fruit hanging from southern magnolia trees. But black men are not the only "fruit" circulating in this homosocial racial economy, an economy in which white men felt compelled to kill those whom they desired. Lacan once observed that "[t]he body in pieces [*le corps morcelé*] finds its unity in the image of the Other" (quoted in Butler 1993, 75). Does the repressive monolith that was the nineteenth-century white male self disperse into pieces when the dead black body was carved up into pieces, or did the sight of the muscled black body impart cohesion to a fragmented southern white male self, a self in pieces after the debacle of the Civil War?

IV. Christianity and Lynching

If Christianity is such an effective religion, then why hasn't it helped white people become more humane?

—Nathan McCall, "Makes Me Wanna Holler" (1995/1996)

Accustomed we are to the indifference and apathy of Christian people.

—Ida B. Wells, *Southern Horrors: Lynch Law in All Its Phases* (1892b/1969)

And little lads, lynchers that were to be, Danced round the dreadful thing in fiendish glee.

—Claude McKay, *Selected Poems of Claude McKay* (1953)

Walter White (1929) argued that lynching was interwoven with American, and specifically southern, Protestantism. In fact, he declared, it is "doubtful if lynching could possibly exist under any other religion than Christianity" (40). He pointed out that the Church gave its tacit approval to the concept of Lynch Law and has participated in other less dramatic forms of racial prejudice. But it has been, he knew, those evangelical Christian denominations who must bear primary responsibility for creating that "particular fanaticism which finds an outlet in lynching" (40). "No person," White observed, "who is familiar with the Bible-beating, acrobatic, fanatical preachers of hell-fire in the South, and who has seen the orgies of emotion created by them, can doubt for a moment that dangerous passions are released which contribute to emotional instability and play a part in lynching" (43).

The Christian Church, White argued, must be held responsible not only for lynching but for slavery as well, "for of all the great religions of mankind Christianity is the only one to draw the color line and thus set up an elaborate array of invidious distinctions which assure the white Christian of his immense superiority" (quoted in White 1929, 40). He targeted specifically a Protestantism which, in the United States, "has swung far away from the teachings of tolerance and human brotherhood preached by Jesus" and has become, as André Siegfried pointed out, "the religion of the Anglo-Saxon or 'superior' race," in spite of "sincere protestations to the contrary" (quoted in White 1929, 44).

Sometimes the Church, by "adroit sophistry" as White (1929, 44) put it, dodges the issue of human bondage, but on other occasions, especially in the South, theologians actually quoted scripture to defend the system. Today still we find fanatics and fascists disguised as Christians quoting scripture to justify prejudice, bigotry, and hatred. Even the Puritans, White reminds, managed to salve their conscience over their profits from the slave trade by insisting that their primary motive in bringing Africans to the new world was to confer upon them the blessings of European civilization, specifically Christianity. He quotes Hurd's (1858–1862) *The Law of Freedom and Bondage* which tells us that:

> Opposition to slavery was ... largely stilled when it was stated that this was a method of converting the heathen to Christianity. The corollary was that when a slave was converted he became free. Up to 1660 it seemed accepted ... that baptism into a Christian church would free a Negro slave. Masters, therefore ... were reluctant to have their slaves receive Christian instruction. ... Virginia finally plucked up the courage (in 1667) to attack the issue squarely and declared by law: "Baptism doth not alter the condition of the person as to his bondage or freedom, in order that diverse masters freed from this doubt may more carefully endeavor the propagation of Christianity." (quoted in White 1929, 45)

It was the state of Virginia which provided a spokesman in the U.S. House of Representatives for a theological defense of slavery. A Virginia Congressman reassured his colleagues that the enslavement of Africans was in fact a holy act:

> I believe that the institution of slavery is a noble one; that it is necessary for the good, the well-being of the Negro race. Looking into history, I go further and say, in the presence of this assembly and under all the imposing circumstances surrounding me that I believe it is God's institution. Yes, sir, if there is anything in the action of the greatest Author of us all; if there is anything in the conduct of His chosen people; if there is anything in the conduct of Christ Himself who came upon this earth and yielded His Life as a sacrifice that all through His death might live; if there is anything in the conduct of His apostles who inculcated obedience on the part of slaves towards their masters as a Christian duty then we must believe that the institution is from God. (quoted in White 1929, 45–46)

Is it any accident, White asks, that a Methodist lay preacher named William Joseph Simmons would be the one to resurrect the infamous Ku Klux Klan in the autumn of 1915? No genius was required for Simmons to realize that Baptist and Methodist preachers would prove useful in the reorganization of the Klan. White quotes William J. Robertson (1927), himself a southerner, who in *The Changing South* concluded that the post-World-War Klan "was the direct result of the extra-Christian campaigning of the so-called Christian brethren in the Methodist and Baptist ranks." He also quotes André Siegfried (1927), who, in his *America Comes of Age* reports that the Klan thrived in communities "run by a narrow-minded middle class and inspired by Protestant clergy. ... The Baptist minister is usually in sympathy with the Klan and is often appointed Kleagle or local publicity agent. When a hooded band marches mysteriously out to offer a well-filled purse to some worthy preacher, the choice ... falls ... always on a Baptist or a Methodist" (quoted in White 1929, 46–47).

If it is true that there is a general relationship between racism and evangelical Protestantism, would we not find in those states with the highest number of lynchings that the great majority of the church members are in fact evangelical Protestants? Using the 1920 census figures, Walter White sought an answer to that question. At first, it appeared that Louisiana and Texas, both with a lower percentage of Methodists and Baptists than other southern states yet showing a high number of persons lynched, would answer the question negatively. More careful scrutiny revealed an answer consistent with his hypothesis.

According to the 1920 census, Texas had 402,874 Roman Catholics. In 1920, however, of the 249,652 Mexicans—it is not clear if White means Mexican nationals, Latinos/as or Chicano/as—White assumes that most are probably Catholics. Taking these into consideration, White discovered that Methodists and Baptists numbered 69.3 percent of Texas church membership. The case in Louisiana was even more striking. Louisiana would seem to have the lowest percentage of Methodists and Baptists in relation to total church membership of any of the states with a high number of lynching events.

Quoting figures from the Official Catholic Directory for 1926, the World Almanac for 1927 reported that there were 331,921 Catholics in the diocese of New Orleans alone. White subtracted this number from the total number of Catholics in all of Louisiana, 509, 901, finding that outside of New Orleans, Louisiana was 55.4 percent Methodist or Baptist. His scrutiny of the lynching statistics disclosed that of 168 lynchings in Louisiana since 1900 only one had taken place in New Orleans. "Other factors of necessity enter into the equation," White (1929) concluded, "but it cannot be questioned that an illiterate ministry working with the tools of a primitive, emotional religion does play a not inconsiderable part in the problem of the continued reign of Judge Lynch" (247). Put propositionally, White's conclusion read:

> Lynchings generally are numerous or few in proportion to the percentage of Methodists and Baptists in the total church membership of the various states; less exactly there appears a relationship between the percentage of church members in the total population and that of lynchings. Lynchings appear to decrease in somewhat inverse proportion to the number of communicants of the less emotional and primitive denominations. (White 1929, 268)

Could it be that the extent to which white homoerotic attraction to black men is suppressed—in this case by fanatical Protestantism—is the extent to which violent racism occurs?

In his detailed study of *Race and Democracy: The Civil Rights Struggle in Louisiana, 1915–1972,* contemporary historian Adam Fairclough (1995/1999) confirms White's conclusions. He found that between 1889 and 1922, the peak years of lynching, the north Louisiana parishes of Caddo, Ouachita, and Morehouse, all overwhelmingly Protestant, were home to more lynchings than any other counties in the nation. Over half the lynchings that occurred in Louisiana between 1900 and 1931 took place in seven parishes, all of them primarily Protestant, and all but one in the northern part of the state. The significance of religion was also evident in the bitter opposition of Louisiana Catholics to the second Ku Klux Klan, which began organizing in Louisiana in 1920. Due to the Catholics' opposition—they themselves were the object of Klan propaganda—the Klan never managed to achieve the degree of political influence in Louisiana that it gained in other states, such as Indiana (Fairclough 1999).

On at least one occasion a Protestant preacher was himself responsible for a lynching. In June 1903, in Wilmington, Delaware, "a fiery sermon by a pastor was blamed" for the lynching of George White, "negro, accused ravisher and murderer of Miss Helen S. Bishop." The pastor was the Rev. Robert A. Elwood, pastor of the Olivet Presbyterian Church, who "preached a sensational sermon" on the legitimacy of lynching White. It was widely distributed and is credited with exerting "much influence" in the lynching of White which followed. Elwood took for the text of his sermon Corinthians I, chapter 5, verse 13: "Therefore put away from among ourselves that wicked person." In referring to the urgency for a speedy trial for the accused, evidently the Bible was insufficient justification. Rev. Elwood also cited the U.S. Constitution: "I call special attention to that part of the text found in the constitution which says: 'In all criminal prosecutions the accused shall enjoy the right to a speedy and public trial.'" He thundered to his congregation:

> On the day of this terrible crime the officials arrested a man supposed to be guilty. He was taken before a magistrate and held without bail. Tonight he is in jail, with armed guards parading about for his protection, waiting until the middle of September. Is that speedy? Is that even constitutional? If the judges insist that the trial of the murderer of Miss Bishop be delayed until September, then should he be lynched? I say Yes. (quoted in Ginzburg 1962/1988, 53–54)

The guilt of the accused was, however, uncertain, as the Rev. C. H. Thomas of Belleville, Illinois, later pointed out. "The only evidence against White," he observed, "was the testimony of a woman that a knife found near the spot where the crime was committed had belonged to him. That is no evidence." In the first African Methodist Episcopal Church back in Wilmington the Reverend Mr. Montrose W. Thornton expressed more than doubt regarding the guilt of the victim; he pointed to the guilt of those who committed and those who tolerated the crime of lynching:

> The white man, in face of his boasted civilization, stands before my eyes tonight the demon of the world's races, a monster incarnate, and in so far as the negro race is concerned seems to give no quarter. The white is a heathen, a fiend, a monstrosity before God, and is equal to any act in the calendar of crime. I would sooner trust myself in a den of hyenas as in his arms. (quoted in Ginzburg 1962/1988, 57)

Thornton's and others' criticisms specifically of Elwood, the Presbyterian minister whose sermon provoked the lynching, were rejected by his congregation. Resolutions were read during Sunday services expressing church members' strong faith in the pastor's "honesty, integrity, and Christian character." Meanwhile, the lynching attracted the attention of many whites. Newspaper reports tells us:

> Thousands of persons visited today the scene where White was burned. They came from all the small towns in this vicinity, and hundreds journeyed from Chester, Pa., and Philadelphia. The burning took place in a freshly plowed field, about fifty feet from the roadway, which was hidden by high bushes. The field has been tramped almost as smooth and hard as asphalt by the thousands of person that have visited the farm. The only evidence that remains of the work of the mob are three cobblestones, on one of which this inscription has been placed in indelible ink: "Here is all that remains of White." The bushes behind which the murder was committed have been cut down for a distance of several yards and carried away by relic hunters. Many of those who visited the scene today, among them a large number of young men, carried away a sprig or a branch of the bushes. (quoted in Ginzburg 1962/1988, 58)

Were they in the form of crosses?

On at least one occasion Anna Julia Cooper commented on the hypocrisy of Christian fundamentalists over the lynching issues. Approached by Prohibition enthusiasts to join in opposing the Democratic candidate for president in 1928, Cooper wrote the following:

> A. G. Comings, Treasurer
> Authorized Oberlin Committee
> Campaign Fund of 1928 of the
> Anti-Saloon League of America.
>
> Dear Mr. Comings:
>
> I am sorry I cannot enter wholeheartedly into the Campaign for downing Governor Alfred E. Smith. ... I am unable to warm enthusiastically with religious fervor for Bible "fundamentalists" who have nothing to say about lynching Negroes or reducing whole sections of them to a state of peonage worse than slavery. ...
>
> Very sincerely yours,
> Anna J. Cooper
>
> (quoted in Lemert and Bhan 1998, 336)

Lynching and Christianity, specifically (white) Protestantism, were clearly interrelated. Is there a civilizational legacy of religious fanaticism conflated with white supremacy, misogyny, and homosexual repression? I hope to explore that possibility in volume II. For now, lynching's links to Christianity must remain a mystery. "Mysterious" turns out to be an apt descriptor for lynching generally if its queer aspect is overlooked or denied, as we see in the next chapter. Before we turn to scholarly efforts to explain the practice, let us suspend the abstract and return to the concrete. Space forbids reviewing all cases of mob violence, but, at the risk of sensationalism, let us remember now several of these nightmarish deaths of African Americans, mostly men, at the hands of white men. Because they are nightmarish, because they seem so distant from our everyday reality (they are less distant than we whites think), I want to ground them, as much as one can, in the public world; to help do that I will quote extensively from newspapers. Still, the unreality of the white mind is unnerving. Consider the strange case of "southern chivalry," for example.

Southern Chivalry

While the overwhelming majority of victims was men, women too were lynched. From 1891 to 1921 the South, Hernton reports, lynched forty-five African American women, several of whom were only fourteen to sixteen years old. Walter White (1929) reports that between 1882 and 1927 ninety-two victims were women. He gives us the numbers by state:

> [M]ississippi leads in this exhibition of masculine chivalry, with sixteen women victims; Texas is second with twelve; Alabama and Arkansas are

> tied for third place with nine each; Georgia follows with eight; Tennessee and South Carolina mobs have bravely murdered seven women each; Kentucky and Louisiana five each, Florida and Oklahoma three each; Missouri and North Carolina two each; and Nebraska, Virginia, and Wyoming one each. Three of the twelve Texas victims were a mother and her two young daughters killed by a mob, in 1918, when they "threatened a white man." Thus was white civilization maintained! (227)

"'Southern chivalry' draws no line of sex," White (1929) declared, his bitterness barely contained. The reader appreciates his struggle when we read the following: a white farmer in south Georgia refused to pay his black employee the wages due to him. A few days later the unscrupulous farmer was found shot to death. Unable to find the man who had motive for the murder, mobs began to kill every African American who had even the remotest connection with the victim and the alleged slayer. One of those murdered by a white mob was a black man named Hayes Turner, whose crime was that he knew the accused; both men had worked for the dead farmer. Turner's wife, Mary, was grief-stricken; she cried out in sorrow, cursing those who had left her a widow and her unborn child fatherless. She threatened to swear out warrants to bring her husband's murderers to justice (White 1929).

Her husband's murderers learned of her threat. "We'll teach the damn nigger wench some sense," they responded, and began to search for her. Understanding her peril, her friends hid the grieving woman on a obscure farm, miles away. It was on a Sunday morning, "with a hot May sun beating down," White (1929) reports, when they found her. White, who went to investigate the crime, tells the story:

> Securely they bound her ankles together and, by them, hanged her to a tree. Gasoline and motor oil were thrown upon her dangling clothes; a match wrapped her in sudden flames. Mocking, ribald laughter from her tormentors answered the helpless women's screams of pain and terror.
>
> "Mister, you ought to've heard the nigger wench howl!" a member of the mob boasted to me a few days later as we stood at the place of Mary Turner's death. (quoted in White 1929, 28)

How could White tolerate listening to his informant? How could he contain his horror, his rage, his profound sorrow? Somehow he does, and finishes describing the death of Mary Turner and her child:

> The clothes burned from her crisply toasted body, in which, unfortunately, life still lingered. A man stepped towards the woman and, with his knife, ripped open the abdomen in a crude Cesarean operation. Out tumbled the prematurely born child. Two feeble cries it gave—and received for answer the heel of a stalwart man, as life was ground out of the tiny form. Under the tree of death was scooped a shallow hole. The rope about Mary Turner's charred ankles was cut, and swiftly her body tumbled into its grave. Not without a sense of humor or of appropriateness was some member of the mob, as an empty whisky-bottle, quart size, was given for headstone. Into its neck was stuck a half-smoked cigar—which had saved

> the delicate nostrils of one member of the mob from the stench of burning human flesh. (White 1929, 28–29; see also Hernton 1965/1988, 129)

There are, unfortunately, other instances of "southern chivalry," cases in which the completely vulnerable were singled out for lynching. In September 1925, a mob of white men in Georgia, "not content with murdering sane Negroes" as White (1929) put it, broke into the state insane asylum at Milledgeville and lynched a violently psychotic patient named Dixon who, in one of his periodic violent seizures, had killed one of the white nurses. The "courageous" (as White applauds him) editor of the Columbus, Georgia, *Enquirer-Sun* commented editorially: "We first explain to the world that the Negro is a child, and then, when he commits a heinous crime, we lynch him as if he were a Harvard professor" (quoted in White 1929, 33). The comparison is noteworthy, as Harvard's image was, among many white Protestants in the South, as a predominately Jewish university. In Georgia in 1915, a Jewish businessman named Leo Frank was lynched (Dinnerstein 1968).

Southerners did not tolerate a diversity of point of view on lynching. Nor had southerners tolerated freedom of speech regarding slavery. Nor would they accept criticism of segregation later, even from one of their own. George Washington Cable, the New Orleans novelist, historian, and essayist, questioned southern assumptions regarding race, and worried especially about the effect of racism upon the South. For his trouble he was vilified so intensely that he had decided to move his family to Northampton, Massachusetts, "a school town and college town. There is an atmosphere of intellectual ambition in it such as one is glad to bring his children into." Two years later, he told his wife that "henceforth, more than ever before, my home is in New England. This South may be a free country one of these days; it is not so now" (quoted in Friedman 1970, 116).

Cable—whom Anna Julia Cooper (1892/1998) judged a "brave and just" man (141)—was hardly the only critic of southern life to be vilified for his or her views. In perhaps the most notorious late-nineteenth-century assault on the free discussion of race relations, Andrew Sledd, a young professor at Emory University, was subjected to an unendurable onslaught of public scorn for writing an article in the *Atlantic Monthly* in 1902 that called for an end to lynching and a calm, reasoned discussion of race relations. Enraged by Sledd's willingness to criticize the South in a northern journal, Rebecca Latimer Felton led the campaign that finally forced him to resign his position and move north (Brundage 1993; Williamson 1984; see chapter 7, section V).

In 1898, when Dr. J. B. Hawthorne, a prominent Methodist minister in Nashville, dared suggest that the views of Rebecca Latimer Felton and others were unrepresentative of southern opinion, Mrs. Felton replied by designating him a "slickhaired, slick-tongued Pecksniffian blatherskite" (quoted in Brundage 1993, 199). And that was hardly the end of it, as she carried on a protracted feud with Hawthorne, never missed an opportunity to malign him in her weekly newspaper column (Brundage 1993). As Wilbur J. Cash observed, during the late nineteenth century the South embraced a "savage ideal" of racial orthodoxy, "whereunder dissent and variety are completely suppressed and men become, in all their attitudes, professions, and actions, virtual replicas of one another" (quoted in Brundage 1993, 198–199). In twentieth-century terms, it was a fascist state.

If southerners had little compunction about running one of their own out of town (and out of the region), it takes little imagination to predict their response to "Yankees," even in the twentieth century. The well-known black newspaper *Chicago Defender* carried this story in its March 17, 1927, edition.

> DARROW FORCED TO FLEE AFTER ANTI-LYNCH SPEECH. Mobile, Ala., Mar. 11—Clarence Darrow, internationally known criminal lawyer of Chicago, champion of oppressed people, and advocate of free speech in America, was given an example of southern chivalry early this week when he was forced to leave a hall where he had spoken here, under protection of a squad of riflemen and special police. He was menaced by a mob and although ill and in Alabama for his health, was compelled to leave hastily for Chattanooga, Tenn. where he will rest a few days before returning home to Chicago. Mr. Darrow's only crime was condemning lynchings and other inhuman practices for which Alabama is notorious.
>
> He spoke to two audiences—one composed of white people at the Lyric theater and one to members of our Race at a school. In both speeches he stressed the importance of mutual respect and co-operation, through tolerance, and less mob activity on the part of whites, and independence and backbone on the part of our people.
>
> Immediately following the address to whites he was rushed from the theater back to the home of his host at Fairhope [known to students of education as the site of Marietta Johnson's famous progressive school], where he has been recuperating from a severe illness for several months, and was prevailed upon to board a train at noon Tuesday for the North. He was informed that if he remained in the state even the militia would be unable to make his stay safe. He was denounced from pulpit and by the press and described as a meddling trouble maker from Illinois.
>
> It was during his Lyric theater speech that the first intimation of the temper of an Alabama mob expressed itself. Speaking to what he believed was an audience of the "best people of the South," he had just declared that lynchings are "a disgrace not only to the South but to the North and the entire United States." Suddenly there was a cry, "Lynch him!" But he continued his talk, ignoring the interruption, until it became impossible for him to continue. Then, as he started from the theater, the mob spirit became apparent. Women, children, and others recognized in Mobile's business, professional and social world were conspicuous in the mob that followed him through the street to his car. Police with drawn weapons surrounded him and Mrs. Darrow, holding the mob at bay. As they passed through the crowd handbills signed by the Ku Klux Klan and denouncing him as an advocate of "social equality" were showered upon them. ... Darrow, who is about 65 years old, has long been known as a friend of our people. He takes the position that the white people of America are injured by the lynchings, peonage and segregation in the South as are the people discriminated against. He first aroused the enmity of the South in 1925, when he went to Dayton, Tenn., to defend John T. Scopes, a young schoolteacher, who was being tried for violating the Tennessee law against

> the teaching of evolution. In this case he opposed the late William Jennings Bryan, the idol of the South, who fought valiantly against evolution, but was never known to raise his voice against lynchings. (quoted in Ginzburg 1962/1988, 178–180)

Alabama was, of course, not alone in upholding the "dignity" of the South and the chastity of its "pure ladyhood."

That "purity" must be defended from even the slightest provocation. Insulting a white woman was no slight provocation, as this headline indicates. The *New York World* in its February 18, 1915, edition reported:

> ANOTHER FLORIDA LYNCHING. Tampa, Fla., Feb. 17—John Richards, a negro, was lynched by a mob near Sparr, Fla., last night. He is said to have insulted a white woman. (quoted in Ginzburg 1962/1988, 94)

Sometimes black men lost their lives due to remarks misinterpreted as "insulting," perhaps intentionally misunderstood. On January 2, 1916, in Anderson County, South Carolina, two black men were lynched and one black woman was badly beaten as a result of a remark made to a white girl. According to the newspaper report:

> The three negroes were riding in a buggy when they passed the girl. One of the men made a remark to the white girl, at which she took offense. She reported the encounter to a group of white men who quickly caught up with the blacks, lynched the men, beat the woman and ordered her out of the state. Reports concerning the nature of the allegedly insulting remark are conflicting. Officials of Georgia County say that one of the negro men yelled out, "Hello, Sweetheart." The negro woman asserts that all they said was "Hello." (quoted in Ginzburg 1962/1988, 98)

On at least one occasion the miscommunication was written. The *Knoxville East Tennessee News* for May 1, 1919, carried this story:

> ILLITERATE NEGRO LYNCHED FOR WRITING IMPROPER NOTE. Shreveport, La., Apr. 29—A Vicksburg, Shreveport and Pacific train was held up by an armed mob about five miles from Monroe, La., today, and George Holden, negro, accused of writing an insulting note to a white women named Onlie Elliot, was taken from the train and shot to death. ... The note sent to Mrs. Elliot was written in plain handwriting. Acquaintances of the Negro state that he had no education and could hardly write his name. (quoted in Ginzburg 1962/1988, 118)

Certainly there was risk if a (white) child misunderstood a communication (from a black man). The *St. Louis Argus* for June 8, 1926, carried a story in this category:

> NEGRO LYNCHED FOR "ATTACKING" CHILD HE ONLY STARTLED. Osceola, Ark., June 2—Albert Blades, 22, a negro visiting

> from St. Louis, was hanged and his body was burned Wednesday morning for an alleged attack on a small white girl. Following the lynching, doctors who examined the child said that she had not been attacked. There appears to be some question of whether the child wasn't merely frightened by the unexpected appearance of Blades in a picnic ground where she and her classmates were playing. Blades pleaded his innocence to the last. (quoted in Ginzburg 1962/1988, 174)

Of course, black men were, by definition, not innocent, not even in Pennsylvania.

V. The Lynching of Zachariah Walker

> *[T]he lust for vengeance played a prominent role in lynching.*
>
> —W. Fitzhugh Brundage, *Lynching in the New South: Georgia and Virginia, 1880–1930* (1993)

> *Paradoxically, the death drive and libido do not cancel out but reinforce each other.*
>
> —Elizabeth Grosz, *Space, Time, and Perversion* (1995)

Yes, there were lynchings in the North. In Belleville, Illinois, in June, 1903, for instance, a young black schoolteacher named David Wyatt was dragged from his cell and tortured to death. For undisclosed reasons, Wyatt had been fired by Charles Hertel, County Superintendent. Wyatt went to Hertel's office to request reinstatement. Their discussion escalated into an argument and Wyatt is alleged to have fired one shot at the superintendent while he was sitting at his desk. Not long after Wyatt's arrest, the *New York Herald* reports that a mob dragged him from a supposedly impregnable jail. Wyatt struggled; he was six feet three inches tall and "of powerful build. He tried to defend himself but he was doomed" (quoted in Ginzburg 1962/1988, 49). He was kicked in the face, then stabbed. "Mutilations followed" (52). His body was hung from a telegraph pole in the center of the public square, then burned. The *Herald* also reported that "although the men who lynched David S. Wyatt worked without masks for six hours, in view of hundreds, including all the city and county officials, and although the few men who did the actual killing are known to scores [of residents], it is unlikely their prosecution will follow" (50). Indeed, State Attorney Farmer acknowledged that he had not been able to find anyone who was able to identify any of the lynchers. The report concludes with attention to the wounded superintendent: "Mr. Hertel's condition is improving. His recovery is expected. He greatly regrets the lynching" (52).

In Marion, Indiana, on the night of August 7, 1930, Tom Shipp and Abe Smith, two nineteen-year-old black men, were taken from the Grant County jail. The two men had been accused of murdering a young white man, then raping his female companion, although the evidence was inconclusive. Many in Marion doubted they were guilty. But these "fine points of the law" did not deter "patriotic, law-abiding" citizens hell-bent on "justice." Smith was taken from the jail to the courthouse square where his clothes were torn off. After staring at his naked body, white men covered him in a large cloth. Then a rope was tied around his neck, he was pulled up into a tree, his head facing a second floor window which opened into the courtroom. A few minutes later, Shipp—who had been shot—was also brought to the courthouse square where he was hanged next to Smith (Raper 1933/1969).

But the most famous lynching case in the North occurred forty miles west of Philadelphia, in Coatesville, Pennsylvania, on the evening of August 13, 1911. The lynching of Zachariah Walker, mentioned in the introduction, was the eighth and final lynching to be recorded in Pennsylvania. Walker had moved from his home in rural Virginia to Coatesville because of an abundance of jobs for unskilled workers. Numerous labor agents actively recruited southern blacks for northern steel mills, portraying cities such as Coatesville as idyllic, heaven on earth. No doubt another draw was the absence of Jim Crow segregation laws, a fact that led Walker, and many other African Americans, to assume that there was a greater degree of racial justice in the North. In 1911, Walker was working as a laborer, an obscure lever-puller, in the Worth Brothers Steel Company in Coatesville. Soon he learned that Pennsylvania was not exactly the promised land (Downey and Hyser 1991).

Coatesville rests along the west branch of the Brandywine Creek in Chester County, approximately forty miles west of Philadelphia and twenty miles north of the Maryland border. Surrounded by fertile farmland, the city itself was not exactly an idyllic setting. Two sprawling steel mills dominated the local economy and society in 1911. The Worth Brothers Steel Company was the larger, employing nearly 1,500 workers; the Lukens Steel and Iron Company, although much smaller, was the second leading employer in the borough. Although a Yankee town, "like many other steel towns, Coatesville was permeated by a culture of violence, a central feature of which was a code of honor and an understanding of manhood that fostered a peculiar notion of chivalry in matters of racial etiquette" (Downey and Hyser 1991, 8).

Zachariah Walker worked in Coatesville but he did not live there. Along with European immigrants and fellow African Americans from the South, Walker spent his nonworking hours in The Spruces, a collection of shacks that passed as homes on a bluff overlooking the sprawling steel mills. Located just beyond Brandywine Creek nearly one mile from downtown Coatesville, residents had to travel some distance not only to work, but also to shop for food and supplies, which were sold in Bernardtown, a cluster of small stories at the foot of the hill. On Saturdays, the immigrant workers—European and African American—flocked to the taverns and stores in Coatesville (Downey and Hyser 1991).

August 12, 1911, was the final day of the Harvest Home Festival. Walker and his friend Oscar Starkey spent the day in Coatesville, walking around Main Street near the Smith Hotel, drinking gin. This was a common leisure practice among the workers, especially after the "ghost walked" (Downey and Hyser 1991, 15), as the steelworkers' called payday. As evening came, an intoxicated

Zachariah Walker parted company with Oscar Starkey. He stopped by the Smith Hotel for more liquor, then walked down First Avenue toward his shack in The Spruces. After crossing the covered bridge that spanned Brandywine Creek beyond the Worth Brothers mill, he encountered two Polish workers. By his own admission, Walker was "feeling pretty good" (15–16). He decided to have some fun with the foreigners, and so he took out a revolver that he had tucked into his pants and fired several shots in their general direction. Although Walker was only fooling around and the bullets traveled nowhere near them, the two were understandably terrified and fled, screaming. Walker found their panic amusing; returning the pistol to his pants, he laughed and talked loudly to himself as he staggered toward home (Downey and Hyser 1991).

The commotion had attracted the attention of Edgar Rice, a commissioned coal and iron policeman of the Worth Brothers Steel Company. Rice was on duty at the company substation by which Walker had walked only a few minutes earlier. Intent on investigating the screams, Rice left his post at about 9:00 P.M., crossed the covered bridge, and walked along Youngsburg Road. There he encountered Walker, who, staggering, was making slow progress in the darkness. After asking him a few questions Rice accused him of firing the shots, but Walker vehemently denied that he was the guilty one. Drunkenly he pleaded his case, but Rice would have none of it. Although he could see nothing, Rice decided to place Walker under arrest "for carrying concealed weapons." When Rice insisted on searching for the pistol, Walker resisted. "I protested knowing that I had a gun and was afraid of the penalty," he would say later. Rice was determined, and began to take the drunken man back to the company guardhouse. By his own admission, Walker "got a little sassy with him" (quoted in Downey and Hyser 1991, 16). He leaned into him as Rice tried to gain control of his prisoner (Downey and Hyser 1991).

Well-known about Coatesville for his gentle and patient demeanor, especially with drunks, Rice became uncharacteristically enraged, shouting at the man pressed against him: "Quit leaning against me. If you don't come with me, I will hit you over the head with this club." To show Walker he meant business, Rice drew his nightstick and proceeded to strike him. Having momentarily lost his balance, Walker fell, yelling, "Hit me and I will kill you!" The two started to struggle; Walker threw several wild punches. Rice clubbed him several times with his nightstick before Walker, in his own words, "tore it out of his hand" (quoted in Downey and Hyser 1991, 16). Reaching for his revolver, Rice lunged toward Walker. But Walker beat him to the draw, firing a shot at Rice that sent him rolling down the hill. Walker fired two more shots, both of which hit their target. Critically wounded, Rice struggled to the bottom of the hill where he collapsed on the porch of Sayleon Miclebreck's small store. In moments Edgar Rice, one of the most popular men in Coatesville, was dead (Downey and Hyser 1991).

No one actually witnessed the incident, but moments after the shooting, a small group of immigrants who had been nearby now gathered near the road. They watched Walker search frantically for his hat, which he had lost during the fight. Acting at first as if nothing unusual had happened, Walker asked one of them for a match so he could look for his hat, but he found Rice's police revolver instead. That he tucked into his pants, then grabbed a bystander's hat and ran. He stopped by his shanty, then proceeded to the crest of the bluff overlooking the Brandywine Creek where he sat down and resumed drinking gin (Downey and Hyser 1991).

The first to arrive at Miclebreck's store was William Whitesides, a member of the Worth Brothers police force and Rice's brother-in-law. "My God, it's Edgar," Whitesides exclaimed when he saw the body lying motionless in a pool of blood. He telephoned the police department, the Brandywine Fire Company, and the Rice family. Despite the late hour—it was almost 10:00 P.M.—news traveled fast. Soon, Coatesville residents were pouring into the streets to discuss the shooting and to await further news. Several blocks were crowded with excited people, many in grief over the death of the popular policeman. All available automobiles, including the "big touring car" of William and Sharpless Worth, owners of the steel mill, joined in the search for Rice's assailant. Less than one hour after Rice's murder was communicated by word of mouth, much of Coatesville was choked with vehicles, curious townsfolk, and members of various search parties (Downey and Hyser 1991).

The first search for clues at the murder site produced Walker's hat. Those immigrants who had seen Walker volunteered that they had not witnessed the murder, but they provided a sketchy description of Walker and the general location of his shack. Not long afterward, Oscar Starkey, the two Polish men who had been shot at by Walker, and a few others had been taken to the Coatesville jail, where they were held as witnesses. Then the police found Walker's shack; it was empty. From where he sat on the bluff, Walker watched the frenzy of activity: the Worth brothers' automobile, the police search parties, the crowds. About 1:00 A.M., Walker would say later, "it became quieter" and he went back to his shanty before heading for the countryside south of town. "Being very sleepy and intoxicated," he rested in the haymow of Norm Entrekin's barn, where he slept for the remainder of the night (quoted in Downey and Hyser 1991, 18). Early the next—Sunday—morning, a boy named Louis Townsend discovered Walker while collecting eggs. Walker fled (Downey and Hyser 1991).

Later that afternoon Walker was discovered in a tree by one of the search parties. As men surrounded the tree, "I knew it was all up with me," Walker later explained. "I thought I would end it all and send a bullet in the back of my head." He pointed the pistol at his temple and fired, losing his balance and falling from the tree. One of the men—Al Berry—ran to Walker's side and rolled him over; a large bullet wound from behind the ear to the mouth was visible. His jawbone shattered, Walker was still alive but unconscious and bleeding profusely. The Pennsylvania State Police report mentioned the suicide attempt but also recorded that one witness alleged that a member of the search party had "shot Walker with a rifle, causing him to fall from the tree" (quoted in Downey and Hyser 1991, 19).

Al Berry ordered his search party to take Walker to the patrol wagon and turn him over to police. As they grabbed Walker's feet and began dragging him along the ground unconscious and bleeding, Berry screamed, "Pick him up as you ought to; remember the man is human." As they picked him up, one muttered, "Let us lynch the son of a bitch while we have him here" (quoted in

Downey and Hyser 1991, 19). Berry was not amused, and pointed his shotgun at the men, declaring that there would be no lynching as long as he was in charge. The men muttered as they carried Walker to the road (Downey and Hyser 1991).

The news that Walker had been captured spread quickly. A large crowd had gathered at the Brandywine Fire Company, anxiously awaiting information regarding the search. At about 3:00 P.M. they learned that indeed Walker had been apprehended; they began to celebrate. Cheering wildly as the automobile with Walker stretched across the back seat passed the fire station, several hundred of them ran behind the car as it continued toward the jail. Word spread fast that Rice's murderer had been captured and by the time the car reached the jail, perhaps as many as two thousand people had gathered. Strangely, the police station was locked and everyone waited for several minutes until Chief of Police Umsted arrived. Evidently most thought Walker dead, but when, pressing close to the car observers realized that Walker was only unconscious, not dead, somebody shouted out, "That man ought to be lynched," and another (white) man said, "That damned nigger ought to be lynched" (quoted in Downey and Hyser 1991, 20).

Walker regained consciousness just about the time the police arrived and, according to a witness, "made motions for the officers to kill him" (quoted in Downey and Hyser 1991, 20). As this account passed through the crowd several people shouted that the police should grant his wish. Instead, Walker was taken to lockup and dumped on the floor of a cell. Before entering the station, Chief Umsted told the crowd that the prisoner was dead, but few believed him, certain he was lying to get them to disperse. The crowd did not disperse, but in fact grew in size as word of Walker's capture spread (Downey and Hyser 1991).

A physician, Dr. Artinis Carmichael, examined Walker's head wound and judged it not life-threatening. Still, he told the law enforcement officers, the prisoner had to be taken to the hospital in order to remove the bullet still lodged in his jaw. It was about four o'clock that afternoon when Walker came out of surgery; heavily sedated, he was placed in a private room. Given that he was a prisoner and had attempted suicide, precautionary measures were taken to avoid any escape or suicide attempt. Not only was his right ankle shackled to the post of the iron hospital bed with a pair of police handcuffs, but Walker was also secured in a canvas straitjacket, which was buckled to the four corners of the bed, "to keep him from getting his hands up to his head and tear[ing] the bandage off" or attempting suicide again (quoted in Downey and Hyser 1991, 21). A police officer, Stanley Howe, was stationed outside the room, but neither Chief Charles Umsted, nor anyone else on the Coatesville police force for that matter, seemed concerned that any harm might come to Edgar Rice's killer (Downey and Hyser 1991).

One witness recalled that the small hospital porch was at this time filled with "quite a few people" (approximately two dozen men and boys), but more than two thousand onlookers milled about the hospital grounds and still more were visible on Strode Avenue. Calm was hardly the order of the day, neither inside nor outside the hospital. Someone yelled out, "Don't let a nigger down a white man" (quoted in Downey and Hyser 1991, 31), prompting similar yells from others prowling about the grounds. Several people rang the hospital's entrance bell and even pounded on the glass doors; others even tried to open the front doors, then moved about the building searching for different ways to enter. But, for the moment, the hospital was secure; obscenities and threats were hurled at anyone spotted in a window (Downey and Hyser 1991).

It was not long before those men on the porch began to exchange chants with the larger crowd. "We want more men," someone shouted, and in response more men climbed onto the already crowded porch. The policeman on duty, Stanley Howe, heard a familiar voice demand, "You might as well open the door, the mob is going to get him anyway" (quoted in Downey and Hyser 1991, 31). Then several men began to chant in unison, "The negro or Howe!" and Howe stepped back, allowing the front doors to swing open. An unidentified man was the first to step inside; when no one else on the porch followed him, he turned to them, demanding, "Come on fellows, he is in here in a room by himself." Immediately, twelve to fifteen men stormed into the hospital "yelling like fiends" (quoted in Downey and Hyser 1991, 32).

The mob stormed into Walker's room, "descend[ing] on the hapless black man like vultures." They tried to pull him from the bed, quickly discovering that he was straightjacketed to the bed and that his leg was shackled to the bedpost. Several men ripped the straightjacket away while others looked frantically about the room for keys to unlock the handcuffs. Officer Howe was brusquely pulled into the room and "someone demanded the key." Only Chief Umsted had the keys, he replied; the men became enraged. They tried to break the shackle but only managed to tighten it around Walker's ankle, producing loud moans from the barely conscious man. Someone shouted, "To Hell with the God-damn keys, we will tear the footboard off the bed"—which they promptly did. Walker fell to the floor and squirmed in pain as blood soiled his bandages and flowed from his mouth. A man later identified as Tucker placed his hands on Howe's shoulders advising him "to offer no resistance." (Howe offered none and quickly removed himself through the doorway of an adjacent room.) Then several men grabbed the footboard of the bed and dragged the barely-conscious Walker down the main hospital corridor toward the front porch. Walker twisted and reeled in agony, prompting someone in the building to squeal, "Watch the son of bitch rolling now." Walker "left a trail of blood which flowed from [his] head wound" (quoted in Downey and Hyser 1991, 32–33).

The appearance of the black man on the hospital porch brought a loud roar of approval from the mob of white men. His captors stopped to acknowledge the cheers then dragged him down the twenty-four porch steps. Amid jeers of "Shoot him," "Burn him," "Hang him," Zachariah Walker was dragged behind the footboard to the gate at the base of the knoll. Many men chanted in unison, "Burn him, burn him!" while others took turns kicking and grabbing him or beating him with stones and sticks. Walker's head, particularly his jaw, was a favorite target, as blows to his head produced more blood and excruciating screeches. Walker tried to protect himself, but the blows were too numerous and too widely dispersed over his body for him to deflect. Like other leaders of other white mobs in possession of a black man, the white men who led were careful to ensure that their prey was not rendered unconscious and therefore immune to further suffering. One unidentified man shouted, "Take him up the road! Take him to the woods," and the mob obeyed (quoted in Downey and Hyser 1991, 33).

As the mob dragged Walker into the countryside beyond Coatesville, Police Chief Umsted, Officer Allison, and Dr. Carmichael arrived at the hospital entrance. They were told, "You are too late. They have taken him over the hill," but this information was ignored (quoted in Downey and Hyser 1991, 33). Instead, Umsted chose not to pursue the mob but undertook instead a painstakingly detailed inspection of the hospital. Afterward, despite the fact that Walker's piercing screams and the noise of the mob could be heard on the hospital lawn, Umsted and Carmichael rejoined Allison and the three men returned to Coatesville. "Although informed by different persons that the mob had taken the prisoner up the hill," an official inquiry would later report, "Umsted started in the opposite direction and made absolutely no effort to ascertain the fate of the negro or the identity of the persons who were murdering him" (quoted in Downey and Hyser 1991, 34).

Having dragged Walker for nearly a half mile, the men who were in charge stopped the precession near Sarah J. Newlin's farm. By now the mob approached four thousand people, many of whom were screaming for the black man to die a slow and painful death. Servants of the people, the leaders now dragged Walker about twenty feet off the public road, down a farm lane lined on both sides by a split-rail fence. After a brief exchange, the mob leaders decided, "with an almost inconceivably fiendish brutality," that Zachariah Walker should be burned alive (quoted in Downey and Hyser 1991, 34).

Quickly fuel was gathered and lighted; as the fire grew, the men prepared to throw Walker on the pyre. Barely conscious, Walker begged: "For God's sake, give a man a chance!" For a moment the white men hesitated. Walker continued: "I killed Rice in self-defense. Don't give me no crooked death because I'm not white!" But the black man's pleas fell upon deaf ears as the crowd responded with jeers, hoots, and more demands of "Burn him, burn him." Once again, the leaders did the mob's bidding, and Walker was abruptly thrown into the fire. In a minute the acrid smell of burnt hair and singed skin filled the night air. As Walker was enveloped in flames, a loud roar of approval went up from the crowd. One witness recalled that the "tongues of flame curled over the surface" of his body and "licked" at his skin, as Walker shrieked. (It was learned later that Walker's screams were heard nearly a mile away.) Those close to the fire pressed forward, "eagerly watching the look of mingled horror and terror that distorted his blood-besmeared faced." One teenage boy who was well positioned remembered that "one side of him [was] pretty well burned and the skin was kind of hanging loose" (quoted in Downey and Hyser 1991, 35).

No doubt the mob was shocked when the burned and wounded Walker somehow mustered the strength to emerge from the fire and clung to the split-rail fence, his head touching the ground and his right foot still shacked to the footboard. In a moment their shock passed and several men rushed forward to return the struggling black man to the flames. The teenage boy recalled that "somebody on the other side of the lane beat him over the head with a rail" (quoted in Downey and Hyser 1991, 35). Walker was either pushed with fence rails or was picked up and thrown back into the fire (no one could later recall exactly how it happened) and his screams of pain and terror were once again met with the roar of the white men watching. Several fence rails were removed to prevent Walker from escaping again, but were quickly consumed by the blazing fire. Other rails were used as clubs to beat him over the head while the flames continued to consume the body of the black man (Downey and Hyser 1991).

Unbelievably, Walker somehow managed to crawl once more out of the burning pyre. The mob cheered, immediately appreciating that Walker's desperate act would prolong their viewing pleasure, and the black man's suffering. Once again Walker was clubbed over the head with fence rails and pushed back into the flames, strips of flesh hanging "from his already charred and blistered body." Almost supernaturally it seemed, Walker emerged from the fire a final time. Those nearest the flames allowed him to crawl almost to their feet, mesmerized by the "revolting spectacle his maimed and half-burned body presented to them." But in a moment several men tied a rope around his neck and, holding onto both ends so that he could not escape, pulled him back slowly into the fire. Walker shrieked one time more, then fell back, "while the flames shot higher and higher." In the words of one observer, his pyre was now "an indistinguishable sheet of fire." At about 9:30 P.M., little more than half an hour since he had been dragged from his hospital bed, death freed Zachariah Walker from the white male mob and the unimaginable pain he was forced to endure. Thousands of eyes watched the fire, and as "men and boys danced and capered in the moonlight," the leaders of the mob disappeared into the black of the night (quoted in Downey and Hyser 1991, 35–36). Within an hour, the mob had dissolved; only the burning coals remained (Downey and Hyser 1991).

One newspaper reported that "five thousand watched the proceedings as though it were a ball game or another variety of outdoor sport" (quoted in Downey and Hyser 1991, 38). The *Coatesville Record* emphasized the politeness of the crowd, with men chivalrously stepping aside to allow those women and children who were present a more direct view of the burning. Approximately 150 individuals maintained an all-night vigil, waiting to collect souvenirs after the fire had cooled. Some couldn't wait; they used fence railings to separate Walker's bones from the glowing embers. The manacles and footboard were also retrieved, cooled with water, then broken up as souvenirs. Within hours several enterprising young white men were selling Walker's remains to eager customers in Coatesville streets. A reporter who visited the lynching site several months later found that souvenir-hunters had worn away all the grass near where the burning took place and had taken much of split-rail fence. "Visitors have carried away anything that looked like a souvenir," he reported (quoted in Downey and Hyser 1991, 39).

On Monday morning, Mrs. Annie Rice, widow of the dead policeman, expressed her approval of the lynching. She told reporters that she had "begged" to accompany the mob but that several men had insisted that she remain at home. "I would have done anything to have got near him, but they would not let me, " she complained. "I wanted to apply the match. I wanted to see him burn. He got," Mrs. Rice declared, "just what he deserved" (quoted in Downey and Hyser 1991, 39).

The editor of the Coatesville newspaper, the *Record,* was William Long. Like most Coatesville residents, Long was extremely sensitive to any criticism of the lynching. As Dennis B. Downy and Raymond M. Hyser (1991) suggest, evidently Long saw himself as the chief defender of the community's honor. From the start he and his paper argued for a sympathetic interpretation of events even as many outside Coatesville regarded the incident harshly. On Monday, August 14, the *Record* reported that the "most awful crime in the history of Coatesville" was the murder of Edgar Rice, not the lynching of Zachariah Walker. The newspaper informed its readers that Walker had murdered Rice "in cold blood." The popular Worth Brothers police officer was only performing his duty, it continued. Readers were reminded that Rice had, until a year ago, been a loyal and respected member of the Coatesville police force and had nearly been elected chief of police. Walker was, the paper said, "a floating negro" who had come to Coatesville in recent months to work in the mills (quoted in Downey and Hyser 1991, 44). Not only was he was an outsider, Walker was a drunk, as evidenced by his inebriated state at the time of the altercation. In contrast, Rice was the quintessential insider, raised on a nearby farm. For years he had been a respected member of the community. The paper failed to disclose Walker's insistence that he had killed Rice in self-defense (Downey and Hyser 1991).

Curiously, even in the *Record*'s first account of the crime was the conclusion that those who participated in the lynching, including the leaders of the mob, were unknown. Furthermore, the paper continued, the identities of the participants would probably never be known. Despite detailed coverage of the lynching itself, the *Record* was "unable" to learn the name of a single eyewitness, either at the hospital or at the site of the lynching. Indeed, contrary to fact, the paper claimed that the mob leaders all wore masks. Then, in an apparent contradiction, the *Record* reported: "It has been said on the streets that there were several southern people, strangers in town last night, and there were strange faces in front of the mob who dragged the negro from the hospital." The implication was clear: outsiders—southerners, no doubt—having learned of Rice's murder, traveled to Coatesville on Sunday to look for the Negro murderer, and they were the ones who lynched Walker. As soon as they had appeared they were gone, disappearing into the blackness of night, never to be seen again. On the next day, the *Record* went on to say that the lynching had not even taken place within Coatesville and therefore the city or its residents could not be held responsible "for what was done outside her borders in the heat of inhuman frenzy." The nature of the event itself proved Coatesville residents had not been involved, for "the general temper of the people of Coatesville is peace-loving and law-abiding" (quoted in Downey and Hyser 1991, 45).

The *Record* would maintain this interpretation of events, including its insistence that the facts of the case absolved the town and its residents of any wrongdoing, even as the word spread that the district attorney had the names of persons involved in Walker's murder. Most readers of the newspaper believed what they read, but almost immediately this version of what had occurred would be contested. The editorials of major metropolitan newspapers and periodicals around the state and across the nation treated the event harshly, even though on occasion they reported only rumor and conjecture. In nearby Philadelphia, the *Inquirer* and the *Bulletin* issued scathing indictments. In New York, the *Times* said simply that "nowhere in the United States was a man ever lynched with less excuse or with an equal heaping up of horror on horror." These condemnations of the lynching were repeated in the *World,* the *Herald,* and the *Evening Post.* In Chicago, both the *Tribune* and the *Daily News* took the same line. Indeed, everywhere in the North it seemed, newspaper editors agreed with *The Outlook*'s headline that Coatesville was "A BLOT ON CIVILIZATION" (quoted in Downey and Hyser 1991, 45).

In time, however, these newspapers would stop reporting news concerning the case. African-American newspapers and journals (which, Ida B. Wells [1892a/1969] once declared, "are the only ones which will print the truth" [23]) did not. Developments in the case would continue to be reported in the *Chicago Defender,* the *Washington Bee,* the *Indianapolis Freeman,* and the *Pittsburgh Courier.* In the *Boston Guardian,* Monroe Trotter argued that what happened in Pennsylvania was not unique to one community or state, but rather was symptomatic of the American nation as a whole. Writing in the *New York Age,* T. Thomas Fortune shared Trotter's outrage: "Nothing in Central Africa could have equaled it. Nothing that has occurred in Haiti in its darkest days will compare with this atrocious and barbaric display" (quoted in Downey and Hyser 1991, 47).

For the recently established National Association for the Advancement of Colored People (N.A.A.C.P.), the Coatesville lynching loomed large. The N.A.A.C.P. responded quickly, sending telegraphs to Governor John K. Tener, to State Police Superintendent John Groome, and to Coatesville's chief executive, Burgess Jesse Shallcross, demanding the immediate arrest and prosecution of all those involved in the lynching of Zachariah Walker. For the next nine months, the organization's monthly magazine, *The Crisis,* reported the situation in Coatesville, updating its African-American and white readership. The September 1911 edition, for instance, summarized negative editorial comments from a half-dozen prominent newspapers. Included too was the response from Coatesville's mayor to the telegram he had received: "[w]e are certainly using every effort to bring the perpetrators of the outrageous act of burning a human being while still alive. ... Notwithstanding what may be said by those outside it will develop that the guilty ones will be found and punished to the full extent of the law. ... We are striving to redeem ourselves, which the future will prove" (quoted in Downey and Hyser 1991, 47).

"Let the eagle scream!" W. E. B. Du Bois demanded in an editorial entitled "Triumph" in that same issue. "Again," he wrote with bitterness, "the burden of upholding the best traditions of Anglo-Saxon civilization has fallen on the sturdy shoulders of the American republic." It did not escape him that Walker was lynched on a Sunday evening and that, according to newspaper reports, the evening church services had ended abruptly as word spread that the black man was on his way to meet his maker. "Ah, the splendor of that Sunday night dance. ... Let the eagle scream!/Civilization is again safe." He knew the drill: "Some foolish people talk of punishing the heroic mob, and the Governor of Pennsylvania seems to be real provoked. There may be a few arrests, but the men will be promptly released by the mob sitting as jury—perhaps even as judge. America knows her true heroes. Again, let the eagle scream!" (quoted in Downey and Hyser 1991, 47).

Although the African-American press condemned Coatesville, the local black community remained restrained. There were even newspaper reports that an unidentified black citizen had expressed his horror at Rice's murder by joining the lynch mob, allegedly demanding, "Let me at him! I'll cut his damned heart out" (quoted in Downey and Hyser 1991, 48). Indeed, native black residents of Coatesville evidently felt little kinship with Walker. Five days after the lynching, a group of ten prominent citizens did sign a memorial protesting his death, but the statement was careful to condemn both murders. They condemned the practice of lynching but were cautious in calling for the prosecution of these lynchers. No one in Coatesville, not even this group of respected black ministers, businessmen, and professionals, was prepared to come to Walker's defense. But that, as Downey and Hyser (1991) point out, was not surprising, given Coatesville's—and America's—reactionary racial politics..

The borough council joined the *Record* in an effort to deflect blame from Coatesville; many residents expressed the hope that the controversy would not last long. County and state officials were determined that it would. Like most states, Pennsylvania had no antilynching law in 1911, but murder—even that of a black man who had confessed to killing a white man—was still a capital offense. Within twenty-four hours of Walker's death, District Attorney Robert Gawthrop announced that there would be a full investigation into the lynching and that those proven responsible would be prosecuted. "We will clear this thing up if it takes ten years to do it," he told the *Coatesville Record* (quoted in Downey and Hyser 1991, 49–50).

Pennsylvania Governor John K. Tener issued a statement that the Commonwealth would spare no expense to bring the leaders of the lynching mob to justice. A native of Ireland, Tener had first become famous as a professional baseball player. He was evidently sincere when he said that the Coatesville lynching was nothing less than a challenge to decency and democracy in Pennsylvania, although Downey and Hyser (1991) report that at least one resident of the town recalled that certain civic leaders shared W. E. B. Du Bois's skepticism regarding the governor's resolve. More than a few Coatesville residents apparently considered his statements to be nothing more than public posturing for political gain (Downey and Hyser 1991).

Not everyone was bluffing; the combined efforts of county and state officials led to the most expensive criminal investigation in the history of the Commonwealth of Pennsylvania to that date. For fifteen days the state police patrolled Coatesville's streets, assisting in the investigation and maintaining public order. This in itself infuriated many residents: the proud city of Coatesville needed no patrolling as if it were an enemy city! At District Attorney Gawthrop's request, Coatesville saloons restricted their hours for several weeks as a disciplinary measure; tavern owners complained that the decreased public consumption of liquor and beer was hurting business. The truth of the matter, Downey and Hyser observe, was that residents were staying away from the bars less due to the curfew and more because many feared that if certain individuals drank too much, they might start talking about what they had seen on the evening of August 13. It was widely rumored (but it was no rumor) that undercover agents were in town, drinking in the saloons in an effort to obtain information. These agents were not the Pinkerton detectives who had initially been hired to work with the state police, but four patrolmen from Troop C who had been instructed to remain after the others had departed, their true identities concealed. These plainclothes officers were, it turned out, successful in obtaining leads that led to the arrest of seven men (Downey and Hyser 1991).

The fantasy, carefully constructed by the *Record* and others, that residents of Coatesville played no part in the events of August 13, 1911, was punctured at 10:50 A.M. on September 20, when the grand jury issued a final report. Based on information contained in the report, Richard Tucker and Walter Markward were charged with murder. The more sensational warrants, however, were directed at Charles E. Umsted, who had been chief of police for longer than most people could remember, and Officer Stanley Howe, who, like Umsted, was a longtime and respected citizen of Coatesville. Both men were charged with involuntary manslaughter for their (in)actions on August 13. While not prosecuted, Jesse Shallcross was censured for his failure to act when presented with unmistakable evidence of what was underway at the hospital. As chief executive of the borough, the jurors concluded, Shallcross should have intervened in the clearly deteriorating situation that Sunday evening (Downey and Hyser 1991).

The grand jury report, Downey and Hyser (1991) tell us, was remarkable for its bluntness and detail, and for its blanket indictment of the citizens of Coatesville. In addition to criticizing residents for their "remarkable lack of frankness" during testimony, the jurors noted: "Throughout the whole course of our inquiry, we have been hampered and obstructed by the attitude of the citizens of Coatesville and vicinity, having knowledge of the commissioner of the crime and the identity of the criminals." The jury also charged that, after the crime, "a conspiracy of silence was formed among the citizens of Coatesville"—a cover-up involving in effect the entire community. In their 1912 final report on the incident, the state police underscored this point regarding Coatesville's conspiracy of silence. To illustrate, they pointed to the fact that an unnamed officer of the borough police force had intimidated local black residents into not speaking with detectives for the state police (Downey and Hyser 1991).

The grand jury not only identified those alleged to have participated in the lynching but provided a rather different, more complex, account of the events of August 12–13, 1911. The report raised serious questions regarding the authority of Edgar Rice, employed only as a special policeman for the Worth Brothers, to arrest Zachariah Walker on a public road for carrying a "concealed weapon." Rice was not on company property at the time nor had he seen Walker commit a crime. Moreover, he did not have a warrant for Walker's arrest. In short, Rice acted without authority. This conclusion indirectly corroborated Walker's claim that he shot Rice in self-defense. Regarding the matter of Walker's abduction and lynching—claimed to be spontaneous actions by unidentified outsiders—the report pointed out that for at least two hours before the event rumors had spread throughout the West End that unnamed parties were going to lynch Walker. Even as he was being removed from the police station, white men standing nearby were muttering audibly that they were going to lynch him. By seven o'clock, when a crowd estimated at between 50 and 100 (and later 500) had gathered in front of the Brandywine Fire Station on Main Street, it was clear that more than a few had already decided to lynch the black man (Downey and Hyser 1991).

The evidence against Richard Tucker and Walter Markward seemed conclusive. Tucker declared he was innocent, but Howe insisted that Tucker had convinced him to step aside, and his testimony was corroborated by a witness. Chief Umsted was guilty of failing to pursue the lynchers; nor did he go to the scene of the crime to investigate. Reaction to the grand jury report was immediate and hostile. Once again, the *Record* took the lead in defending the town. Still, as the trials proceeded through the fall and winter, evidence against a few of the ringleaders began to accumulate. Evidence notwithstanding, the juries acquitted every suspect, often after deliberating for only a few minutes. An effort to move the trials to another county failed. In May, prosecutors finally put together what looked like an airtight case. A man named Lewis Denithorne had signed a written confession, admitting to having taken part in almost every phase of the lynching. He was charged with second-degree murder; prosecutors hoped that by not asking for the death penalty they had increased the chances of conviction. The jury took less than half an hour to reach its verdict: not guilty (Worth 1998).

In November, the N.A.A.C.P. held a highly publicized antilynching meeting at the Ethical Culture Hall in New York City. Earlier, in September and October, *The Crisis* had published detailed reports on the Coatesville trials, and W. E. B. Du Bois's editorial had been blistering. In October, the board of directors of the N.A.A.C.P. had discussed at length the Coatesville lynching; a national rally would protest not only Walker's death but all lynchings in the United States. On November 15, 1911, Oswald Garrison Villard, chairman of the board of the N.A.A.C.P., presided over the evening rally attended by some 400, "more than half of them colored," reported the *New York Times* (quoted in Downey and Hyser 1991, 100). This unprecedented event, the N.A.A.C.P. hoped, would heighten public awareness of lynching and raise money for the N.A.A.C.P.'s legal redress fund. In a story buried inside, the *Times* observed that most whites in the audience agreed that lynching must be criminalized, but few of them seemed willing to contribute money to the Association's fund. Despite Dr. John Elliott's appeal for $1,000 in donations, the rally raised a only $260. Undeterred, the N.A.A.C.P. continued to monitor events in Coatesville, determined to bring Walker's lynchers to justice (Downey and Hyser 1991).

The N.A.A.C.P.'s observer during the October trials, William Sinclair, reported to the executive committee that he was satisfied that "the prosecuting attorney had done his job" (quoted in Downey and Hyser 1991, 100). N.A.A.C.P. officials were not convinced, however, and began their own inquiry. This was a brave move for the fledgling civil rights organization, and it indicated the association's willingness to intervene in a sensitive local matter. The managing editor of *The Crisis,* Mary Dunlop Maclean, went to Coatesville in November and conducted a series of interviews; on at least one occasion, Oswald Garrison Villard also visited Coatesville to meet with sympathetic townspeople. In December, following Maclean's and Villard's reports to the board of directors, the N.A.A.C.P. voted to use all the funds raised at that Ethical Culture Hall meeting, as well as resources from its legal redress fund, "to an investigation of the Coatesville lynching with a view of obtaining information which would induce the authorities to continue the work of prosecuting those guilty of this inexcusable and inhuman crime" (quoted in Downey and Hyser 1991, 101). A special Coatesville Committee was to coordinate the N.A.A.C.P.'s investigation (Downey and Hyser 1991).

On Maclean's recommendation, the William Burns Detective Agency was hired. During the winter of 1911–1912, two undercover Burns agents (District Attorney Gawthrop and Deputy Attorney General Cunningham were informed) operated a restaurant in Coatesville as a front to gather information. Over a period of two months they succeeded in befriending a number of local citizens who might have some knowledge of the Walker lynching; then, as the spring court term approached, they abruptly sold the place and disappeared. For its work, the Burns Agency was paid nearly $2,400, a substantial sum for the financially strapped N.A.A.C.P. The detectives' report would prove to be helpful, however, in the Association's efforts to sustain a prosecution that appeared ready to give up. The October trials had failed to produce guilty pleas, but in the winter of 1912 the Commonwealth had not yet given up hope, and its own investigation continued (Downey and Hyser 1991).

With the lynching trials a month away, Coatesville focused on the Republican Party's 1912 presidential primary. In early April it was announced that Theodore Roosevelt, campaigning for the nomination against President William Howard Taft, would visit Coatesville just a few days before the April 14 primary election. The announcement that the former president would give a brief campaign speech in predominantly Republican Coatesville was greeted with enthusiasm. On Wednesday, April 10, thousands of people, many of whom the *Record* said "only come to town once in a while," flocked to see "the man," crowding streets, stores, hotels, and the train station (quoted in Downey and Hyser 1991, 107). It was the largest gathering of people in the history of Coatesville. It was larger, in fact, than the lynching mob and larger than the assemblage for Edgar Rice's funeral: over 6,000 people jammed into a relatively small area. The six-man police force and the entire borough council appeared with Roosevelt on the reviewing stand. Charles Umsted and Stanley Howe, both indicted for involuntary manslaughter in the lynching, stood on either side of the former president during his speech, which lasted only six minutes. Roosevelt was given a "great reception," and the roar of applause and cheers lasted for several minutes (Downey and Hyser 1991, 107). The symbolism of the scene was unmistakable: in the lynching of Zachariah Walker, Coatesville was defiant, Roosevelt complicit.

Four days later, Roosevelt carried Coatesville and the surrounding townships of the county and captured a local delegate's vote in the upcoming Republican party convention. Curiously, just five months earlier, as the first lynching trials began, Theodore Roosevelt had lambasted Coatesville and its leaders for the lynching and the community's defiance. Roosevelt was a contributing editor to the highly respected national magazine *The Outlook* in which he had published an article entitled "Lynching and the Miscarriage of

Justice." In it he declared that Coatesville residents had "not the slightest excuse for ... condoning the actions of the mob." Given that no one tried to stop the lynching or came forward to testify against the mob leaders, all observers were placed "on a level of criminality with their victim" (quoted in Downey and Hyser 1991, 108). Despite the strong condemnation, Roosevelt came to Coatesville and Coastesville residents voted overwhelmingly for Roosevelt in the primary. Curious too that Umsted and Howe proudly stood beside the former president who had so thoroughly condemned them and other Coatesville residents. Perhaps no one in Coatesville had bothered to read *The Outlook,* for the county newspapers (not even the *Record,* which supported Taft) made no mention of Roosevelt's earlier denunciation of the town (Downey and Hyser 1991).

Indeed, public memory of the lynching seemed short. The approaching spring trials rekindled public interest in the lynching, but for most the event had faded. Stories on the disastrous sinking of the *Titanic* shared headlines with the trial preparations, and both the *Record* and the *Daily Local News* reported in some detail the activities of the state police detectives. When the anniversary of the lynching came, only a single sentence, buried on the last page of the *Record,* acknowledged the event: "Just one year tonight from the date of the most deplorable incident in Coatesville's history, but in spite of all her traducers, the town is bigger and better than ever." The *Daily Local News* published only two sentences on the incident and they were buried deep inside the paper, without benefit of a headline. "Fresh in the minds of some," the paper allowed, "most people, however, have forgotten the terrible crime" (quoted in Downey and Hyser 1991, 118).

One individual could not bear for the lynching to be forgotten. John Jay Chapman was a New York essayist and "crusader" who had followed the entire affair with intense interest. In August 1913 he traveled to Coatesville to commemorate the first anniversary of the lynching. He advertised a community prayer meeting, expecting a sizable crowd would attend and join him in asking for forgiveness for the "dreadful crime." Despite all indications that, as the *Daily Local News* had noted, most people were "weary of the lynching case," Chapman came to Coatesville anyway. He scheduled the prayer meeting for Sunday, August 18, in a rented storeroom (the Nagle Building) in downtown Coatesville. No crowd of mourners materialized. Indeed, only two people (one a visitor to Coatesville and the other a black woman from nearby Hayti whom Chapman believed "was a spy sent to see what was going on") showed up. With Chapman and his wife, the total was four. Despite the small audience, Chapman gave a formal speech—Hyser and Downey characterize it as "powerful and persuasive"—in which he blamed the Coatesville lynching on slavery (quoted in Downey and Hyser 1991, 118). He characterized the event as an American tragedy, symptomatic of the corruption and evil inherent in the American character. Indeed, he continued, all Americans were responsible for Zachariah Walker's death. The only hope for the country was to atone for the national sin. Afterward, Chapman delivered a copy of his speech to the *Record* office; William Long published it in its entirety on the front page of the paper without editorial comment, other than to comment that it had been well prepared and contained "no objectionable features" (quoted in Downey and Hyser 1991, 119).

Chapman's "Coatesville Address" was reprinted in several periodicals and newspapers, including *Harper's Weekly*. It also appeared later in pamphlet form and again in a collection of his writings. Coatesville residents may have managed to forget the lynching, but the world would not. As Chapman had declared, the lynching was a national tragedy (Downey and Hyser 1991).

Why was Zachariah Walker lynched? Downey and Hyser point to a confluence of factors. There was, they say first, "something of a siege mentality" throughout Coatesville at the time. The influx of southern blacks and European immigrants left the native white population feeling besieged. Downey and Hyser suggest: "It was as if psychology (individual and collective) were waiting for circumstance, and that occasion came when a recently arrived southern black killed a popular white policeman in what may have been an act of self-defense." They point out that Rice represented institutional authority, "a representative of the established civil and corporate order," and given this symbolism townspeople experienced the murder as an attack on themselves and their community. Downey and Hyser also suggest it was not inconsequential that Rice was killed on a Saturday evening and that Walker was likely drunk at the time and carrying a concealed weapon. It was hardly the first encounter between the police and the residents of Rock Run, Bernardtown, and The Spruces. For many longtime residents the Walker-Rice confrontation was yet another moment in what Kai Erikson (1966) termed the "ongoing social process" (quoted in Downey and Hyser 1991, 140).

For most townspeople, Hyser and Downey note, Walker was the quintessential outsider, a "deviant." (They point out that one Pennsylvania newspaper characterized him as a "negro desperado," even while it acknowledged that little was actually known about him.) Certainly Walker had broken the law in killing Rice, but he had also violated the norm of acceptable conduct for blacks in Coatesville. Downey and Hyser (1991) comment: "Walker had stepped out of his 'place' in this society; his was an offense against the public order. The slaying of Edgar Rice signaled that a new boundary in the web of community relations had been crossed, and the townspeople were determined to do something about it" (quoted on 140). If we gender this comment, we recognize that the "place" Walker left was his place in white male imagination. After all, by and large the "public order" in pre-woman's suffrage Pennsylvania was a male order. The "boundary" the black man had transgressed was the ego boundary of white men.

The gender of white racism in Coatesville was masculine. But the lynching of Zachariah Walker was not only a gendered event. It was also, perhaps primarily, a racial event, and as well a class event. Curiously, Downey and Hyser (1991) reject out of hand any class analysis: "It makes no sense, however, to interpret Walker's death from a class perspective" (140). But in explanation they point only to the absence of class solidarity: "If anything, the lynching transcended class lines. ... No one came to Walker's defense, either during or after his ordeal" (Downey and Hyser 1991, 140–141). I would suggest that the fact that no one came to Walker's defense suggests that race overwhelmed class, although part of what made him expendable was that he was a lower-class worker living in substandard housing, in a tenement-like community.

The absence of (local) racial solidarity had to do with Walker's outsider status, Downey and Hyser suggest. (I would add that class considerations were at work as well, as his job and housing left him estranged from Coatesville's black middle class.) Walker had recently arrived from rural Virginia. By the summer of 1911, the influx of new workers had had the effect of sharpening a division within the African-American community in Coatesville, a division based upon how long individuals and their families had lived there. The lynching had galvanized solidarity based on race and gender within the white (especially male) population; it had the opposite effect for blacks, exposing this division among African Americans, in part due to the effects of the outsider/insider distinction. According to a popular expression of the day, Downey and Hyser (1991) tell us, "Walker may have been skinfolk, but he was not kinfolk" (142).

Downey and Hyser do hint at the gender of racial violence in their analysis of the Walker lynching. They point out that the average steel town in the early 1900s was clearly a "man's place" (144). That is to say, to be a "man" required demonstrations of physical prowess, even violent behavior. Such were the demonstrations, the proof, of a young man's coming of age, becoming a "man." Downey and Hyser point out that nearly half of the defendants in the lynching trials were under the age of twenty-one, and that numerous observers had reported that the teenage boys at the front of the mob were the most agitated; in fact they had to be restrained by older men. [Not incidentally, teenage white boys are most prone to antigay violence; see chapter 13.] Downey and Hyser (1991) comment:

> Manhood could not be assumed; it had to be demonstrated, to be earned and defended when challenged. A man's status in society was confirmed in the company of other men, and the reputation for toughness and a willingness to stand up to a challenge were prized attributes. No man wanted to be branded a coward, perhaps the worst insult he could suffer at the hands of other men. ... For the young men who participated in the burning of Zachariah Walker and then bragged openly for their accomplishment, the events of August 13 served as a rite of passage, a ritual in which they asserted their manhood by the public display of vengeful force. (Downey and Hyser 1991, 144–145)

Later we will read about a more contemporary assertion of "manhood" known as "beaching," when a number of young men, sometimes fraternity brothers, sometimes athletes, serially rape an unconscious or barely conscious young woman. While the lynching of Zachariah Walker involved no genital mutilation, it was, given how it functioned in the coming of age of young white men in Coatesville, a symbolic homosexual rape or "beaching."

After making that revealing statement on manhood, Downey and Hyser retreat to more commonsensical explanations. They suggest that the lynching had to do with Coatesville residents' sense that their way of life was threatened by immigration, industrialization, not to mention racial and gender progress. Those who participated imagined they were acting on a higher purpose, one that the community at large would sanction. On that point they were right. From their perspective, their conduct was not immoral or irrational; rather, it seemed to them to be both reasonable and justified. The "logic" of vigilantism (the more extreme the threat to society, the more severe must be the response by those who claim to be acting for the public good) was very much at work that night in Coatesville. So, too, Downey and Hyser argue, was the idea of honor. That concept will function prominently in traditional interpretations of lynching, and so let us spend a moment on Downey and Hyser's commentary on this aspect.

Downey and Hyser note that much has been made of honor as a dominant cultural trait in the American South. Honor is presumably key to explaining the evolution of a distinctive southern society in the years preceding the Civil War. They quote Elliott Gorn's (1985) definition: "Honor is an intensely social concept, resting on reputation, community standing, and the esteem of kin and compatriots. To possess honor requires acknowledgment from others; it cannot exist in solitary conscience. ... Naked and alone man has dignity; extolled by peers and covered with ribbons, he has honor" (39). They also quote Julian Pitt-Rivers (1968), who argued that honor is a masculine trait that framed public relationships and social etiquette "where the law [is] either not competent or not welcome" (505; both passages quoted in Downey and Hyser 1991, 145). "Honor" privileges the individual's reputation in the eyes of other men; to have one's character impugned in public is an occasion of shame which demands a response. In fact, he who has suffered the affront has the right to demand satisfaction. A homosocial phenomenon, honor requires absolute loyalty to family and kin. A "willingness to stand up to opposition is essential to the acquisition, as to the defense, of honor," Pitt-Rivers (1968) observed, "regardless of the mode of action that is adopted" (505).

Without disputing the argument for the significance of honor in the nineteenth-century American South, Downey and Hyser suggest that the concept has a broader significance. Much of what has been written about the social function of honor, they suggest, is not peculiar to the South; similar dynamics are at work in any society where social relationships are conducted on a familiar, personal level. Despite its accelerated economic and population growth in the early 1900s, Coatesville remained in many respects a small town, a "family place" that lacked the anonymity of larger, more cosmopolitan cities. This relative intimacy among long-term residents provided a certain social cohesion during the decade of rapid growth that preceded the lynching, despite persisting class and status differences. Consequently, they write, "honor, and its connection to masculinity and cowardice, [was] a potent force in male social relationships—so much so, in fact, that in certain situations an affront to one man could be judged an affront to all" (Downey and Hyser 1991, 146). Once again, it appears that the gender of racial violence is masculine. But too, Downey and Hyser add, more mundane human failings were at work: "Clearly, the human capacity for self-deception, the ability to see things as other than they are, was a potent force in rationalizing the lynching" (147).

Eight months after the case was closed, Governor John K. Tener presented his annual address to the Pennsylvania General Assembly in Harrisburg, some sixty-five miles northwest of Coatesville. Tener's initial comments on the lynching, what some local residents termed his "interference," were bitterly resented, and what he told the legislators in January 1913 intensified the feelings of many (white) Coatesville residents. Tener had been governor for not quite a year when the lynching had occurred; he was genuinely embarrassed by it and by Coatesville's defiance. In his annual address to the Pennsylvania legislature, he reminded lawmakers of what had happened. Then, citing a relatively obscure 1901 Commonwealth supreme court decision as precedent, he called on the legislature to revoke the municipal charter of the Borough of Coatesville. "Governmental functions were given her as an arm of the State," Tener declared, "but she has betrayed the trust reposed in her." "People of this Borough," the governor continued, "by fomenting murder and consorting with murderers have not only violated the laws and obstructed the administration of justice, but in my judgment have forfeited the high privilege of further acting as a governmental agency of the State." By their actions, he continued, the inhabitants of Coatesville—officials and citizens—had guaranteed that the Commonwealth of Pennsylvania would be "disgraced and her fair name dishonored." By revoking the privilege of self-government for the borough that "outraged the peace and dignity of the Commonwealth" the legislators could demonstrate to the world their opposition to lynching (quoted in Downey and Hyser 1991, 152–153). To the incredulous ears of a still-defiant Coatesville, the governor was asking that the city be removed from the map as punishment for the lynching of Zachariah Walker. While a few uninformed citizens mistook the governor's speech for reality—that is, that Coatesville had been "wiped off the map"—in reality the corporate charter of the borough was never in jeopardy. The Pennsylvania General Assembly had approved legislation that allowed for the dissolution of municipal charters, but only on the initiative and with the consent of local voters (Downey and Hyser 1991).

More than any other civil rights organization, the N.A.A.C.P. had followed events in the Coatesville lynching and kept its growing membership informed of all developments, including the outrageous outcome of the trials. In June 1912, *The Crisis* printed an editorial entitled "Triumph" in which W. E. B. Du Bois reminded readers that the previous September he had predicted justice would not be served in Pennsylvania. Now, with even more bitterness Du Bois wrote: "The last lyncher is acquitted and the best traditions of Anglo-Saxon civilization are safe. ... Let the eagle scream!" (quoted in Downey and Hyser 1991, 154). Du Bois was not alone in his frustration and bitterness, but the N.A.A.C.P. remained calmly committed to bringing the lynchers to justice (Downey and Hyser 1991).

In a series of meetings between September 1912 and February 1913, N.A.A.C.P. representatives met with Governor Tener and Deputy Attorney General Jesse Cunningham in an effort to persuade them to reopen the cases. Oswald Garrison Villard, legal counsel William Wherry, and several other N.A.A.C.P. officials, presented Pennsylvania officials with new evidence, including the names of unindicted participants, which their investigators had learned. In late January Attorney General John Bell was invited to New York to discuss the case with the N.A.A.C.P.'s board of directors, but he declined. While apparently receptive to the N.A.A.C.P.'s arguments, Governor Tener chose not to renew the prosecutions (Downey and Hyser 1991).

Accepting defeat but undeterred, the N.A.A.C.P. shifted its strategy and became the chief advocate for an antilynching law in Pennsylvania. In a foreshadowing of the resistance that federal antilynching legislation would encounter later (see chapters 10 and 11), the Pennsylvania bill took ten years to clear both legislative houses. Governor Gifford Pinchot signed into law a version of the original legislation on May 19, 1923, but by that time many Pennsylvanians had no memory of the lynching of Zachariah Walker. An incidental consequence of the Association's involvement in the case was the opening of N.A.A.C.P. branch offices in Philadelphia and Harrisburg. In time an office even opened in Coatesville (Downey and Hyser 1991).

The lynching of Zachariah Walker was one of the first cases in which the newly established N.A.A.C.P. became directly involved as part of its campaign to stop lynching in the United States. While the first major *institutional* effort to end lynching, it was, as we will see, by no means the first. The fact that Walker's murder occurred in the North made the case especially important to the Association, for in focusing upon Walker's fate in Coatesville the civil rights organization was emphasizing the national character of the "race question" without appearing to be narrowly antisouthern. The N.A.A.C.P.'s failure to win mass support in the North for its antilynching campaign, and the repeated failure of the U.S. Congress to pass antilynching legislation, were serious defeats for the organization and for the cause of civil rights in America (Downey and Hyser 1991).

Twenty-seven years after the lynching of Zachariah Walker, a second lynching in Coatesville was stopped, thanks to a courageous police chief. In June 1938, a young white woman, a Coatesville teenager, was attacked on South Hill. Word quickly spread that her assailant was black, and a mob quickly formed to search the surrounding countryside. Within hours a young black man was apprehended and brought to the city jail. A crowd had formed by the entrance to the police station, and as the mob arrived, words an older generation of residents had once heard were shouted. Several young men called for the accused to be lynched, but on this occasion the chief of police demonstrated the courage and commitment to duty that Chief Umsted had lacked. Ralph Williams stood up to the crowd on the lawn, telling them that justice required that they disperse, that Coatesville did not need a repetition of August 1911. Upon hearing the reference to the lynching of Walker, the crowd fell silent and its members dispersed without protest. When it was safe to do so, Williams and his deputies transported the accused to a nearby city for his safety. Not a week later, Coatesville police arrested a white man who confessed to the crime (Downey and Hyser 1991).

The lynching of Zachariah Walker is significant because it is atypical. There were no allegations of rape in the case. Walker was actually guilty of killing someone. The event happened outside the old Confederacy. There was no genital mutilation. The episode would not seem to warrant the detail in which I have reported it. Yet it is this very "inappropriateness" that makes the lynching worth considering in detail. Even though it does not fit the specifics of the pattern, it does coincide with the overall pattern interwoven of gender and race, namely that lynching was an affair between men. Recall that mostly young white men participated in the actual burning, and that, like a heterosexual rape, the event functioned to demonstrate to them that they were "men." White manhood in the United States appears to define itself, at least in part, in relation to black manhood, which is widely regarded as superior, more "manly," more masculine, and therefore requiring subjugation. In contrast, the white man seems to himself, evidently, like a wimp, or worse. Lynching in this sense was a defensive and compensatory move made by white men to convince themselves they were not castrated, that they were not the "bitches" they evidently experienced themselves to be vis-à-vis black men. Black men seemed to understand these psychosexual dynamics of homosocial race relations in America, and in prison they would perform them.

2 ❖ TO LIVE *or* DIE *in* DIXIE

I. A Southern Obsession

If lynching was a national crime, it also was a southern obsession.
—W. Fitzhugh Brundage, *Lynching in the New South: Georgia and Virginia, 1880–1930* (1993)

Her [the South's] white citizens are wedded to any method however revolting, any measure however extreme, for the subjugation of the young manhood of the race.
—Ida B. Wells, *Southern Horrors: Lynch Laws in All Its Phases* (1892a/1969)

[T]he practice [of lynching was] a state of liminality where white torture and dismemberment of the black male body allowed for the political reinvigoration of southern masculinity.
—Sandra Gunning, *Race, Rape, and Lynching: The Red Record of American Literature, 1890–1912* (1996)

Why, after all, is the white man in the South so preoccupied with the black man's penis, and with black men "raping" white women?
—Calvin C. Hernton, *Sex and Racism in America* (1965/1988)

During the final days of the Civil War, a slave was lynched for writing a note that offered protection but which white men recoded as at least an instance of being "uppity," at worst as threatening a sexual assault. On Sunday morning, February 19, 1865, Dr. James E. Hix's slave Saxe Joiner wrote a note to Martha Hix, the wife of his white master. While the note has not survived, Saxe allegedly told Mrs. Hix not to "grieve" about the approaching Yankee troops because he had a "safe place" for her. Although Saxe Joiner had expressed himself with unusual directness, his note to Mrs. Hix could have been coded as a sincere gesture from a devoted slave. Dr. Hix and those other white men in Unionville who learned of it interpreted the note in this fashion, and they made no response to it. The problem came when Saxe Joiner also communicated with another white woman in the Hix household, eighteen-year-old Susan Baldwin. On the evening of Sunday, February 19, he sent her a separate note, telling her not to worry because he would "protect" her from the northern troops. It is unclear why Joiner wrote to Hix and Baldwin rather than speaking to them face to face. Such a communication could not have been a matter of public record. But a note could be "evidence," as this one became. Dr. Hix found it, and somehow it became public (quoted in Cashin 1997, 123).

This second message was more likely to be interpreted as a violation of social etiquette, even as a defiance of it, for Susan Baldwin was an unmarried white woman in her teens. Joiner's note to her implied that he regarded himself as equal or even superior to his defeated Confederate masters. After Dr. Hix discovered the note to Susan Baldwin, Saxe Joiner was immediately arrested. Joan E. Cashin (1997) contextualizes the event: "So in the last weeks of the Civil War, with the Confederacy disintegrating around them, Unionville's professionals tried to force Saxe Joiner's case back into court. At first glance the entire business seems perverse, like rearranging deck chairs on the *Titanic*" (123).

After legal jostling, an armed mob of white men wearing disguises and dressed in Confederate uniforms broke into the ground floor of the Union County jail on the night of March 15, 1865. Most of these were not soldiers anymore, but they dressed in gray to perform what they took to be the meaning of the Confederacy, even as it crumbled around them, and to enforce the "proper" hierarchies between the sexes and the races. Many had been drinking, and all of them were enraged by what they judged to be the lenient treatment the law had accorded Saxe Joiner. They knew he had, from their point of view, insulted a white woman, and there was only one punishment appropriate for such misconduct. That spring evening white men lynched Saxe Joiner.

Emancipation did not, of course, mean the end of slavery. In name yes, but not always in fact. Henry Lowry (James Weldon Johnson [1933] spells the name Lowery; see 361), a black man living in Nodena, Arkansas, had been held in virtual peonage for more than two years by a white landowner. His "employer" was not always prompt in paying what he owed his hard-working employee. On Christmas Day, 1920, a frustrated Lowry demanded payment of his back wages. His employer/landlord responded by first cursing then striking him; his son then shot and wounded him. Defending himself, Lowry drew his own gun and in the ensuing struggle killed the landlord and his daughter who had been watching the argument.

Knowing what awaited him, Lowry fled to Texas, where he was arrested. No one less than the governor of Arkansas assured him protection from mob violence and promised him a fair trial. Believing him, Lowry waived whatever rights to which he was entitled regarding interstate extradition. The two Arkansas officers sent to Texas to return him to Arkansas ignored the governor's directives to travel the most direct route to Little Rock. Instead, they traveled by way of New Orleans then Mississippi. At Sardis, Mississippi, a mob—obviously advised of the route—was waiting. They "overpowered" the officers, taking Lowry in their "custody." This news was forwarded to other members of the mob who were dining comfortably at the fashionable Peabody Hotel in Memphis. Local newspapers were informed in time to issue early afternoon "extras" giving full details as to time, place, and other arrangements for the forthcoming lynching (White 1929).

One newspaper which had been informed of the event was the *Memphis Press*, which sent reporter Ralph Roddy to cover the event. His story, appearing in the *Press* of January 27, 1921, bore the headline: "KILL NEGRO BY INCHES." Notice the impersonality, even the exoticism, of the term "Negro" in the first line; clearly he is not quite human. This tone of "objectivity" renders the event surrealistic:

> [M]ore than 500 persons stood by and looked on while the Negro was slowly burned to a crisp. A few women were scattered among the crowd of Arkansas planters, who directed the gruesome work of avenging the death of O. T. Craig and his daughter, Mrs. C. Williamson. Not once did the slayer beg for mercy despite the fact that he suffered one of the most horrible deaths imaginable. With the Negro chained to a log, members of the mob placed a small pile of leaves around his feet. Gasoline was then poured on the leaves, and the carrying out of the death sentence was underway. Inch by inch the Negro was fairly cooked to death. Every few minutes fresh leaves were tossed on the funeral pyre until the blaze had passed the negro's waist. ... Even after the flesh had dropped away from his legs and the flames were leaping toward his face, Lowry remained conscious. Not once did he whimper or beg for mercy. Once or twice he attempted to pick up the hot ashes in his hands and thrust them in his mouth in order to hasten death. Each time the ashes were kicked out of his reach by a member of the mob. ... As the flames were eating away his abdomen, a member of the mob stepped forward and saturated the body with gasoline. It was then only a few minutes until the Negro had been reduced to ashes. (quoted in White 1929, 24)

Writing in the *Nation* on March 23, 1921, William Pickens rendered Lowry more human, although he still uses what sounds to our ears like an objectifying term, "Negro": "[t]he Negro said never a word except when the mob brought his wife and little daughter to see him burning." Despite the fact that the plans for the execution had been widely published hours before the actual event, no effort was made to prevent the lynching. Sheriff Dwight H. Blackwood of Mississippi County, in which Nodena is located, was quoted by the *Press* as saying that "Nearly every man, woman and child in our county wanted the Negro lynched. When public sentiment is that way, there isn't much chance left for the officers" (quoted in White 1929, 24–25).

There tended to be, as one would expect, a considerable variation in journalistic practice between the North and South regarding lynching events. While the pretense at objectivity in the *Memphis Press* report of the Lowry lynching rendered the event surreal, in the following *New York Tribune* coverage of a different lynching it almost functions to confer dignity upon the victims, despite the use, once again, of the abstract concept "Negro," which robs the person of his or her individuality. In contrast to the *Tribune,* the *Vicksburg* (Mississippi) *Evening Post* sensationalizes the event, participating in a kind of necrophiliac titillation. One victim was Luther Holbert, who had killed his (white) opponent in a quarrel; the second was his wife, who played no part whatsoever in the alleged crime. Following is the report of the *New York Tribune* of February 8, 1904:

> Luther Holbert, a Doddsville Negro, and his wife were burned at the stake for the murder of James Eastland, a white planter, and John Carr, a Negro. The planter was killed in a quarrel. ... Holbert and his wife left the plantation but were brought back and burned at the stake in the presence of a thousand people. Two innocent Negroes had been shot previous to this by a posse looking for Holbert. ... There is nothing in the story to indicate that Holbert's wife had any part in the crime. (White 1929, 35)

In contrast, the reporter for the *Vicksburg* (Mississippi) *Evening Post* seems barely able to contain his excitement:

> When the two Negroes were captured, they were tied to trees and while the funeral pyres were being prepared they were forced to suffer the most fiendish tortures. The blacks were forced to hold out their hand while one finger at a time was chopped off. The fingers were distributed as souvenirs. The ears of the murderers were cut off. Holbert was beaten severely, his skull fractured, and one of his eyes, knocked out with a stick, hung by a shred from the socket. ... The most excruciating form of punishment consisted in the use of a large corkscrew in the hands of some of the mob. This instrument was bored into the flesh of the man and woman, in the arms, legs, and body, and then pulled out, the spiral tearing out big pieces of raw, quivering flesh every time it was withdrawn. (quoted in White 1929, 35–36)

These pieces of "quivering flesh" were then thrown to the crowd for souvenirs. Next, the bodies were burned. After cooling, pieces of charred flesh were taken from the ashes and kept as souvenirs. Vicksburg shopkeepers as well as "women of class" shared Holbert's hands, using them as ornamentation in their shops and homes. But before burning, during his torture, his genitals were removed and later pickled, kept as prized souvenirs (Harris 1996). Such events reverberated far beyond themselves, throughout the South. As Jacquelyn Dowd Hall (1983) observed: "A penis cut off and stuffed in a victim's mouth. A crowd of thousands watching a black man scream in pain. Such incidents did not have to occur very often, or be witnessed directly, to be burned indelibly into the mind" (331).

In *Sex and Racism in America*, Calvin C. Hernton tells us that "I have never seen a lynching, never looked upon a black man who has been castrated. I understand, however, and know, that it is a terrible sight." How does he know? He remembers many tales of lynching, including the following story of a lynching as told to him by a young Mississippian:

> I must have been about seven years old. No, I was about nine. ... Anyway, I will never forget it. I can still see him hanging up like that. I was living with my uncle out on his farm. The night of the lynching, my uncle walked up and down the floor, rubbing his hands together, and he made me keep quiet every time I woke up. He tried to make me go back to sleep, but the noise and racket they made kept me woke most of the night too. The next morning my uncle and me and some other colored folks in the county went to look at the man who had been lynched. The man's wife and brother were with us, and they were crying. Everybody was afraid. I wasn't—for I really didn't know what to expect. But maybe I was a little scared just because of all the racket that went on that night. Anyway, when we got there in the woods, everyone started crying and turning their heads away in horror. I looked up at the man. I knew him, yet he was so messed up I could not tell who he was. He was naked, and they had put tar on him and burnt him. He smelled awful. Then I saw what they had done. Even though I was only nine, I knew what they had done was a sin. They had cut out his private and left it laying on the ground. The blood was caked all about his legs and thighs. (quoted in Hernton 1965/1988, 113)

The nightmare was hardly restricted to Mississippi, of course. In nearby Arkansas, John West was lynched near Hope. The *Memphis Commercial Appeal* for July 29, 1922, carried the following story:

> QUARREL OVER BLACK'S RIGHT TO CUP ENDS IN LYNCHING. Texarkana, Ark., July 28—A quarrel over a drinking cup between a white street paving foreman and a negro laborer at Hope, Ark., about 35 miles northeast of Texarkana, was followed this afternoon by the lynching of the negro near Guernsey, four miles southwest of Hope. John West of Emporia, Kan., was the negro lynched. ... This is the second lynching at Hope within the last 18 months; Brownie Tuggles had been hanged here on the night of March 15, 1921, for an alleged attack on a white woman. (quoted in Ginzburg 1962/1988, 165)

Inadvertently bumping into a white person on a sidewalk in the South could cost a young black man his life. Such was the case on March 31, 1916, in Cedar Bluff, Mississippi. According to newspaper reports:

> Jeff Brown was lynched by a mob here late Saturday afternoon. Brown was walking down the street near the car tracks and saw a moving freight going in the direction in which he wanted to go. He started on the run to board the moving train. On the sidewalk was the daughter of a white farmer. Brown accidentally brushed against her and she screamed. A gang

quickly formed and ran after him, jerking him off the moving train. He was beaten into insensibility and then hung to a tree. The sheriff has made no attempt to find out who the members of the mob were. Picture cards of the body are being sold on the streets at five cents apiece. (quoted in Ginzburg 1962/1988, 102)

A white man's cow was the provocation for a black man's lynching. In the March 18, 1906, edition of the *New York Tribune* we read: "IS LYNCHED BY 'ORDERLY' MOB; SUSPECTED OF COW KILLING. Plaquemine, La., March 17—William Carr, Negro, was lynched without ceremony here today. ... He had been accused of killing a white man's cow" (quoted in Ginzburg 1962/1988, 68).

There were occasions when white men ignored the decision of the court; they wanted their man. In the April 10, 1912, issue of the *Montgomery Advertiser* we learn:

> LYNCHED AFTER ACQUITTAL. Shreveport, La., Apr. 9—Tom Miles, a negro, aged 29, was hanged to a tree here and his body filled with bullets early today. He had been tried in police court on the charge of writing insulting notes to a white girl, employed in a department store, but was acquitted for lack of proof. (quoted in Ginzburg 1962/1988, 76)

In this same category, the *Brooklyn Eagle* for December 20, 1925, reported:

> LYNCHED JUST MINUTES AFTER JURY FREES HIM IN MURDER. Clarksdale, Miss., Dec. 19—Lindsay Coleman, negro, was lynched here tonight, a few minutes after a jury in Circuit Court had declared him not guilty of the murder of Grover C. Nicholas, plantation store manager. (quoted in Ginzburg 1962/1988, 174)

On other occasions it became clear soon after the lynching that the mob had murdered the wrong man. The *Indianapolis Recorder* for March 4, 1933, carried a story in this category.

> LYNCHED FOR KILLING BANKER, NEGRO WAS THE WRONG MAN. Ringgold, La., Mar. 1—Nelson Nash, young Negro who was brutally lynched here February 19, was the wrong man. The perpetrator of the crime for which Nash was an unwilling victim may well have been a white man. This was revealed today after careful investigation. ... Protesting and proclaiming his innocence, Nash was taken to the woods outside of town. He asked the mob to spare him a few minutes to pray. The mob told him to open his mouth and stick out his tongue. He did so. The tongue was grasped by a pair of auto pliers and severed by a razor. ... Nash, age 24, was known to be a peaceful young man and had never before been in trouble with the law. (quoted in Ginzburg 1962/1988, 196–197)

In many cases sheriffs were complicit with lynchers. But there were times when a sheriff did do his job and succeeded in protecting his charge. Note that if the mob was unable to strip a black man, they'd settle, at least this night, for a white one. In the April 31, 1916, edition of the *Providence* (Rhode Island) *Bulletin* the following news item appeared:

> SHERIFF NEARLY LYNCHED. Lima, Ohio, Aug. 31—Sheriff Sherman Ely of this county was slashed, kicked and nearly lynched by a mob of 3,000 last night when he refused to divulge the location of a negro prisoner wanted by the mob. The mob descended upon the local jailhouse before dusk and demanded surrender of Charles Daniels, a negro, held for questioning in connection with the assault of Mrs. John Porter, a white woman. The Sheriff refused to surrender him. The mob smashed its way into the jail, searched it cell by cell and realized that the prisoner had been spirited away and hidden elsewhere. The mob seized the Sheriff, stripped him of his clothes, kicked, beat and cut him, dragged him to the principal street corner of this town and tied a noose around his neck threatening to hang him to a trolley pole unless he told where he had hidden the negro. (quoted in Ginzburg 1962/1988, 107)

With blood streaming from a dozen cuts and with two ribs fractured, the sheriff refused. The mob then dispersed (Ginzburg 1962/1988). James Harmon Chadbourn mentions this case in his famous *Lynching and the Law* (1933; see 69).

II. The Yellow Rose of Texas

> *But why the charge of rape as the consolidating moment of lynching's justification? Why this sexualization of blackness as the precondition not only for mob action, but for lynching's broad cultural acceptance and appeal?*
>
> —Robyn Wiegman, *American Anatomies* (1995)

> *We must ask if the ritual of dismemberment and sadistic torture of black bodies is, in fact, a search to expose, and perhaps an attempt to claim, an essence of manhood that is both feared and desired, an essence of the possible which escapes its pursers as the blood pours from their hands and soaks the earth.*
>
> —Hazel Carby, *Race Men* (1998)

Lynchings in the great state of Texas lived up to popular stereotype, at least on occasion. Tortures were especially intense and the crowds who watched were Texas-size. Given its history with and proximity to Mexico, perhaps it is unsurprising that Latinos were sometimes strung up, although here we focus on African Americans, for whom the most explicitly sexualized forms of "punishment" were reserved. For instance, the April 30, 1914, edition of the *Boston Guardian* carried the following headline:

> NEGRO YOUTH MUTILATED FOR KISSING WHITE GIRL. Marshall, Tex., Apr. 29—Because he is alleged to have hugged and kissed

a white girl, daughter of a farmer, Charles Fisher, a negro youth, was recently badly mutilated by a mob near here. According to Sheriff Sanders and County Health Officer Taylor, the mob sheared off the youth's ears, slit his lips and mutilated him in other ways below the belt. (quoted in Ginzburg 1962/1988, 90)

In the May 23, 1902, issue of the *Chicago Record-Herald* the following item appeared:

NEGRO TORTURED TO DEATH BY MOB OF 4,000. Lansing, Tex., May 22—Dudley Morgan, a negro accused of assailing Mrs. McKay, wife of a Section Foreman McKay, was burned to death at an iron stake here today. A crowd of 4,000 men, most of whom were armed, snatched him from the officers on the arrival of the train. Morgan was taken to a large field on the edge of town. An iron stake was driven into the ground and to this he was bound until he could only move his head. Heaps of inflammable material was then piled about him and he was given a few moments for prayer. It was 12:12 when all arrangements were completed. The crowd by this time numbered at least 5,000. ... Then began the torture of the negro. Burning pieces of pine were thrust into his eyes. Then burning timbers were held to his neck, and after his clothes were burned off to other parts of his body. He was tortured in a horrible manner. The crowd clamored continuously for a slow death. The negro, writing and groaning at the stake, begged piteously to be shot. Mrs. McKay was brought to the field in a carriage with four other women, and an unsuccessful effort was made to get her near enough to see the mob's victim. The negro's head finally dropped, and in thirty minutes only the trunk of the body remained. As the fire died down relic hunters started their search for souvenirs. Parts of the skull and body were carried away. ... The last words of the doomed man other than the incoherent mutterings made in prayer were: "Tell my wife good-bye." (quoted in Ginzburg 1962/1988, 46)

On October 12, 1917, in Goose Greek, a suburb of Houston, eight hundred oil-field workers seized Bert Smith. Accusing him of what the newspaper account characterized as "committing an outrage on his employer's wife," the mob "attacked Smith and placed a rope around his neck, hammered his mouth in with a sledge and pierced his body with sharp instruments, and then forced a 10-year-old white lad who carried water around the camp to take a large butcher knife and unsex him. Smith, who was still alive, begged that all his feelings be taken from him." He was then hanged, his body then riddled with bullets and his corpse "horribly mutilated with sledge-hammers and butcher knives after cutting it down. ... He was [then] dragged down the main thoroughfare near the camp houses and viewed by citizens including women" (quoted in Ginzburg 1962/1988, 113–114).

Body parts were often a primary concern for lynchers. Extremities of all kinds—fingers, toes, genitalia—were regularly removed, but on occasion internal organs were also taken as souvenirs. The *New York World-Telegram* for December 8, 1933, reported:

> HEART AND GENITALS CARVED FROM LYNCHED NEGRO'S CORPSE. Kountze, Tex., Dec. 8—David Gregory, a Negro convict accused of attacking and slaying a white woman, was shot to death when he was said to have resisted arrest by a posse and his body later mutilated and burned by a mob which dragged it to a pyre in the Negro section of Kountze early today. ... Members of the mob of approximately 300, cut out the Negro's heart and sexual organs before casting it to the flames. (quoted in Ginzburg 1962/1988, 211–212)

On May 15, 1916, a crowd estimated at 15,000 watched as eighteen-year-old Jesse Washington was lynched in the Waco, Texas, public square (Ginzburg 1962/1988). Not only were lynching mobs "Texas-size" but victims were not single. The *Brooklyn Citizen* for May 6, 1922, carried the following story:

> TRIPLE LYNCHING FOLLOWS THRILLING TEX. MAN-HUNT. Kirvin, Tex., May 6—Three colored men were burned here at dawn for the murder of Eula Ausley, pretty 17 year-old school girl, whose body was found near here yesterday with thirty stab wounds. The three men were tied, one after another, to the seat of a cultivator, driven into the center of the city square and burned before a mob of 500. "Shap" Curry, 26, Mose Jones, 44, and John Cornish, 19, were the victims. All three worked on the huge ranch of John King, the girl's grandfather. Curry was burned first. There was some delay in starting inasmuch as the men maintained their innocence to the last. Third degree burns failed to bring confessions. The men were not shot but their bodies were mutilated prior to burning. Ears, toes and fingers were snipped off. Eyes were gouged out, no organ of the negroes was allowed to remain protruding. ... The lynchings followed one of the most thrilling manhunts in the history of these parts. Farmers and businessmen of the three counties joined together to comb every inch of the territory. Creek bottoms were beaten all day and acres of grassland were flattened. Finally the three men were captured and brought to Fairfield where a mob gathered and took them from the sheriff after storming the jail. (quoted in Ginzburg 1962/1988, 162–163)

A day later in the *New York Call* we learn that:

> SHERIFF HOLDS 2 WHITES IN CRIME THAT 3 BURNED FOR. Fairfield, Tex., May 6—Cliff and Arnie Powell, two white men, were detained today for further questioning in connection with the murder of Eula Ausley, for which three negroes were burned at Kirvin this morning. Sheriff H. M. Mayo declared that tracks leading from the scene of the murder led to the home of the brothers. "The shoes of the Powells fit the tracks," was the terse comment of the Sheriff. (quoted in Ginzburg 1962/1988, 163)

No apology issued, no restitution offered, only an indirect acknowledgment that the lynched black men were innocent.

Political protest, not "rape," would, in the 1960s, provoke white rage. However, the black male body remained the object of white retaliation. In this case, the young man survived. The *Birmingham* (Alabama) *News* carried the story in its March 8, 1960, edition.

> NEGRO IS HANGED BY HEELS, K'S ARE CUT INTO HIS BODY. Houston, Tex., March 8—Four masked white youths hung a Negro man from a tree last night and carved two series of KKK's into his chest and stomach after beating him with chains, allegedly in reprisal for recent sit-in demonstrations by Negro students at Texas Southern University. Felton Turner, 27-year-old unemployed awning worker told police that he was walking near his home in a Negro section at 10:15 last night when a car with four masked white youths pulled up, grabbed him and forced him to come with them. They drove to a wooded area where he was tied and hung from a tree by his heels. The youths beat him with chains, cut off his clothes and, with knives, slashed K's about three inches high into his stomach and chest. One of the white youths said the wounds were in reprisal for sit-ins at lunch counters in Houston by Texas Southern University Negro students. A group of students from the all-Negro university staged their first sit-in Friday at a lunch counter in a supermarket. The sit-ins spread to a drugstore Saturday and a third store yesterday. Police Lt. Breckenridge said Turner's wounds could not have been self-inflicted. (quoted in Ginzburg 1962/1988, 245–246)

Is it any surprise that in the 1960s the struggle for civil rights was widely understood as a struggle for black manhood?

III. Maryland, Missouri, Alabama

> *[C]astration is also an inverted sexual encounter between black men and white men.*
>
> —Robyn Wiegman, "The Anatomy of Lynching" (1993)

Large crowds have hardly been limited to the lone star state, however. The *New York Times* for October 19, 1933, carried the following item; notice the use of a term in the headline ordinarily reserved for sexual events:

> MARYLAND WITNESSES WILDEST LYNCHING ORGY IN HISTORY. Princess Anne, Md., Oct. 18—In the wildest lynching orgy the state has ever witnessed, a frenzied mob of 3,000 men, women and children, sneering at guns and teargas, overpowered 50 state troopers, tore from a prison cell a Negro prisoner [George Armwood, 24 years old] accused of attacking an aged white woman, and lynched him in front of the home of a judge who had tried to placate the mob. ... One boy, apparently about 18 years old, slashed the Negro's ear almost off with a knife. Under the oak tree, despite the presence of women and children, all the victim's clothes were torn from his body and he hung there for some minutes nude. After they had burned the body, the mob members disbanded. (quoted in Ginzburg 1962/1988, 200, 202)

Even after the corpse was buried, lynchers could not leave Armwood's mutilated body alone. The *Birmingham* (Alabama) *News* for November 29, 1933, reported the incident.

> LYNCH VICTIM'S CORPSE MAY HAVE BEEN DUG UP. Princess Anne, Md., Nov. 28—George Armwood, the Negro who was mauled and mutilated before he was lynched here last month and whose body was then burned and further desecrated, appears to have had his grave "tampered with" last Tuesday night, according to a statement by Steve Hopkins, superintendent of Soberest County Almshouse on whose grounds Armwood is buried. Hopkins said yesterday that the turf over Armwood's grave appeared to be churned up and covered with fresh dirt, indicating that whatever fragments of his corpse remained in his coffin may have been dug up. (quoted in Ginzburg 1962/1988, 203)

One might assume that universities were exempt from lynching events; not in the "show me" state. There were very few lynchings reported on college campuses or in university towns, but at the University of Missouri at Columbia students lynched a custodian. The April 20, 1923, edition of the *New York World* carried the story:

> UNIVERSITY STUDENTS HELP MOB LYNCH JANITOR. Columbia, Mo., April 29—A mob that included many University of Missouri students, both male and female, today lynched James T. Scott, a Negro janitor at the University who had been charged with an attempt to assault the fourteen-year-old daughter of the head of the German Department. About 500 citizens broke into the jail, aided by an acetylene torch, and dragged Scott through the streets to the Missouri, Kansas and Texas railroad bridge that spans a deep ravine just outside the university section. Professor H. B. Almstedt, father of the intended assault victim, hearing of the lynching, went to the scene and appealed to the mob to let the law take its course. The students and townspeople laughed and booed him down, crying, "Hang him, too!" Finally, the professor went to his home, and, Pilate-like, washed his hands of the whole matter.
>
> A rope was tied around Scott's neck, the other end secured to the bridge railing. Scott, bareheaded and with shirt torn, repeatedly denied his guilt. "Before God, I swear I am innocent," he cried. ... "I can prove my innocence." The negro's plea brought some hesitation to the mob but then a young man, about 20, stepped forward, lifted Scott to the bridge railing and dumped him over the side. His neck snapped audibly. Scott's body swayed in mid-air for nearly a minute as the mob mutely watched it. (quoted in Ginzburg 1962/1988, 169)

On January 12, 1931, Raymond Gunn, a twenty-seven-year-old black man, was accused of raping and murdering a young white female schoolteacher. Seized by a mob, Gunn was taken to the schoolhouse where the young woman had taught, near Maryville, Missouri. Once there, the young black man asked his captors: "Now what are you going to do with me?" The leader of the mob replied: "Well, nigger, we're going to burn you" (quoted in Raper 1933/1969, 420).

> Using a small ladder, two white men climbed onto the roof of the schoolhouse, pulling Gunn after them. Tearing off pieces of the roof, they passed a chain over Gunn's legs and around under the rafters. They secured his arms in like fashion. A large can of gasoline was sent up, then poured over Gunn and around the roof. Other men drained off gasoline from cars, poured it in through the schoolhouse windows, dousing the walls and floor. Then the leader ordered the crowd to get back, lit a paper and sent it flying through the window. In a flash the interior was in flames. In a moment the roof burst in flames about the victim. For five minutes the flames raged, and then they died down somewhat, as the gasoline had burned out. The clothing quickly burned off the Negro, who writhed about on the roof. He was silent except for one long scream. After eleven minutes he was still. In sixteen minutes the roof fell in. It was 11:30. (Raper 1933/1969, 420–421)

The lynching was quite the event; between 2,000 to 4,000 white men, women and children watched as Raymond Gunn burned to death. Nor did they disperse afterward: "All afternoon, the crowds milled about, poking in the ashes for souvenirs. The charred remains of the victim were divided piece by piece" (Raper 1933/1969, 421). Perhaps the most famous Missouri lynching was that of Cleo Wright; we will read about that in chapter 11.

One of the earliest recorded lynchings in Missouri occurred on July 1859, in Saline County, located in a seven-county area called Little Dixie. There a slave named John was lynched. Thomas Dyer (1997) tells us: "In the grove, John, barefoot and stripped to the waist, was chained to a walnut tree, all the while talking rapidly with his captors. ... While the slave talked, white men gathered dry wood and other combustibles which they piled around John's bare feet at the base of the tree. Only when the mob set fire to the wood did John seem to comprehend that he was to be burned alive" (91). A newspaper (the *Marshall Democrat*) account of the lynching provides several details: "[H]e lived from six to eight minutes from the time the flames wrung the first cry of agony from his lips, the inhalation of the blazing fire suffocating him in a short time. His legs and arms were burnt off, and his body but remained, a charred and shapeless mass." The *St. Louis Democrat* also carried the story. The unendurable pain John suffered as he burned could be seen:

> in the futile attempts of the poor wretch to move his feet. As the flames gathered about his limbs and body, he commenced the most frantic s[h]rieks and appeals for mercy, for death, for water! He seized his chains, they were hot and burned the flesh off his hands. He would drop them and catch at them again and again. Then he would repeat his cries; but all to no purpose. In a few moments he was a charred mass, bones and flesh alike burned into powder. (quoted in Dyer 1997, 91)

Sometimes not even a lynching satisfied white men. Near Dayton, Ohio, a lynching seemed only to intensify white male hatred. In the *New York Herald* for March 9, 1904, was the story:

> NEGRO HATERS FIRE TOWN. Springfield, Ohio, Wednesday—As a result of the murder of a white policeman and the subsequent lynching of Richard Dickerson, a negro, a serious race war is on tonight. One entire square in the levee district inhabited by negroes is in flames and seven companies of the Ohio National Guard are on the scene, holding a crowd of five thousand excited people in check. All yesterday mutterings were heard by the negroes, who, in their determination to revenge the lynching of Dickerson, threatened to kill all the policemen in the city. On the other hand the whites openly announced that they would burn the district during the night. ... [C]rowds gathered in the street, and at nightfall five hundred young men organized at the post office and started for the levee, shouting, "Burn the niggers." (quoted in Ginzburg 1962/1988, 65)

There were many lynchings in Alabama—statistically it ranked fourth in lynchings (Tolnay and Beck 1995)—but probably the most famous case in Alabama involved the "Scottsboro Nine." Nine young black men—thirteen to twenty years of age—had hopped a boxcar on the Chattanooga-to-Memphis freight train at Stevenson, Alabama. A group of white youths, including two women named Ruby Bates and Victoria Price, were aboard the train. A fight ensued. When the train arrived in Paint Rock on March 25, 1931, the nine black men were forcibly removed from the train and charged with rape. Although Ruby Bates later repudiated her claim that the two women had been sexually assaulted, all of the accused were convicted in a hasty trial at Scottsboro, the county seat. All but the youngest were sentenced to the electric chair. The entire episode took sixteen days. Represented by an ill-prepared defense counsel appointed by the local court and tried by an all-white jury in a charged atmosphere of mob violence, the "Scottsboro boys" (as they became known) seemed doomed. Even the N.A.A.C.P. stayed away from the case at first. It was the intervention of the Communist-led International Labor Defense (I.L.D.) that precipitated the court battle which drew in the N.A.A.C.P. and ended in the release of the last prisoner in 1950. The Scottsboro Nine became the period's most celebrated symbols of racial oppression (Carter 1969/1979; Hall 1979; Zangrando 1980). Because the episode discloses the intense rivalry between the C.P.-U.S.A. and the N.A.A.C.P. in the antilynching campaigns of the 1930s, I will report the story in some detail in chapter 12.

IV. Georgia on My Mind

The attempt to justify the lynching of negroes on the plea that lynching for rape committed upon white women is necessary to repress that crime is without support in any respect.

—James Elbert Cutler, *Lynch Law: An Investigation into the History of Lynching in the United States* (1905)

"The sheer scale of mob violence in Georgia alone commands attention," W. Fitzhugh Brundage (1993) observes. "In addition, the long history of mob violence in Georgia reveals fully the pathology of lynching in its various permutations over time and place" (16). The lynching of Sam Holt illustrates Brundage's point. On April 23, 1899, near Newman, Georgia, Sam Holt was lynched before 2,000 onlookers. Holt was first tortured before being covered with oil and burned. "Before the torch was applied to the pyre," the newspaper report tells us,

> the negro was deprived of his ears, fingers and genital parts of his body. He pleaded pitifully for his life while the mutilation was going on, but stood the ordeal of the fire with surprising fortitude. Before the body was cool, it was cut to pieces, the bones were crushed into small bits, and even the tree upon which the wretch met his fate was torn up and disposed of as "souvenirs." The negro's heart was cut into several pieces, as was also his liver. Those unable to obtain the ghastly relics direct paid their more fortunate possessors extravagant sums for them. Small pieces of bones went for 25 cents, and a bit of the liver crisply cooked sold for 10 cents. (quoted in Ginzburg 1962/1988, 12)

The lynching of Sam Holt was horrible enough that news of it reached far north to western Massachusetts. On April 28, 1899, the editorial from the *Springfield Weekly Republican* read:

> The annals of the savage will be searched in vain for anything worse than the exhibition given to the world by the white civilization of the state of Georgia. The best that the devilish ingenuity of man has ever been able to do, in any age or among any people, to make the ordeal of death as excruciating and awful as it could possibly be made, was equaled in the torture and mutilation and burning of the negro Holt. (quoted in Ginzburg 1962/1988, 19)

In June 1921 in Moultrie, Georgia, John Henry Williams was lynched after being convicted of murder by an all-white jury in a trial that took half an hour. The newspaper reports indicates that "not a single colored person was allowed nearer than a block of the courthouse" (Ginzburg 1962/1988, 152–153). "Then Williams," the account continues, surrounded by fifty sheriffs, armed with machine guns, started out of the courthouse door toward the jail.

> Immediately a cracker by the name of Ken Murphy, gave the Confederate yell: "Whoo—whoo—let's get the nigger." Simultaneously five hundred poor pecks rushed on the armed sheriffs, who made no resistance whatever. They tore the Negro's clothing off before he was placed in a waiting automobile. This was done in broad daylight. The Negro was unsexed and made to eat a portion of his anatomy which had been cut away. Another portion was sent by parcel post to Governor Dorsey, whom the people of this section hate bitterly. The Negro was taken to a grove, where each of one of more than five hundred people, in Ku Klux ceremonial [fashion], had placed a pine knot around a stump, making a

> pyramid to the height of ten feet. The Negro was chained to the stump and asked if he had anything to say. Castrated and in indescribable torture, the Negro asked for a cigarette, lit it and blew the smoke in the face of his tormentors. The pyre was lit and a hundred men and women, old and young, grandmothers among them, joined hands and danced around while the Negro burned. A big dance was held in a barn nearby that evening in celebration of the burning, many people coming by automobile from nearby cities to the gala event. (quoted in Ginzburg 1962/1988, 153)

After murdering Williams, the mob burned black churches, terrorized black farmers, and destroyed their property. "A sick woman and her child, who had nothing to do with the matter, were beaten into insensibility and left to die because of the hoodlumism of the mob" (quoted in Ginzburg 1962/1988, 152).

On the last day of January 1930, in a rural community southeast of Ocilla, Irwin County, Georgia, a sixteen-year-old local white girl was found dead, lying in a puddle of water by the side of the road. Circumstantial evidence pointed to James Irwin, a black man who lived nearby. He was seized the next morning and taken to the place where the alleged crime had occurred. Eyewitnesses reported later:

> Upon reaching the place where the body of the girl was found, Irwin was tied to a tree with chains. The tortures began. Approximately a thousand people were present, including women and children on the edge of the crowd. Members of the mob cut off his fingers and toes, joint by joint. Mob leaders carried them off as souvenirs. Next, his teeth were pulled out with wire pliers. Whenever he expressed pain or tried to evade the approaches of his sadistic avengers, he was jabbed in the mouth with a pointed pole. (Raper 1933/1969, 143–144)

There were other "mutilations and tortures" too horrible to describe. "Suffice to say that they were indecent and brutal beyond belief" (Raper 1933/1969, 144).

After more than an hour of mutilation, Irwin's mangled but still living body was hung upon a tree by the arms. Logs and underbrush were piled underneath. Gasoline was added; a match was struck. As the flames engulfed the body, white men shot him. Burned beyond recognition, James Irwin's body hung in the tree by the public road for the remainder of the day. Thousands of white people, including women and children, rode out to see the body. Only after nightfall did county authorities take the body down and bury it (Raper 1933/1969).

Apparently only the "young bucks" were stripped and castrated. Older black men were on occasion lynched, but they suffered less sexually charged punishments. For instance, just after midnight on July 29, 1930, a truck filled with masked white men drove up a farm road, one mile north of Ailey in Montgomery County, Georgia. They drove to the home of S. S. Mincey, a black man prominent in Montgomery County affairs. Forcibly entering the house, they took Mincey, although not without a fight. "A veritable giant and active for his seventy years, Mincey had to be 'quieted' by blows over the head. Then he was thrown into the truck, and taken to points unknown. Early the next afternoon he died of cerebral hemorrhage" (Raper 1933/1969, 172).

Had the seventy-year-old Mincey been accused of raping a white woman? No. Mincey was active and influential in the Republican organizations of the county and state; he had served as a delegate to National Republican Conventions. He was prominent as well in fraternal circles, having been elected secretary and treasurer of the Widows and Orphans Department of the Negro Masonic Lodge of Georgia. At the time of his death he was in the process of opening a Lodge office in Ailey, with a full-time clerk. A number of his friends and associates believed his murder was precipitated by simple envy of his civic accomplishments and personal prosperity, but the most common explanation was that Mincey was "taken for a ride" simply due to his political activities (Raper 1933/1969, 173).

When young black men were victims, their body parts were, on occasion, displayed, as the *Chicago Defender* reported in its February 17, 1923, edition.

> WHITES IN GEORGIA DISPLAY PART OF NEGROES' BODIES. Milledgeville, Ga., Feb. 16—Fingers and ears of two Negroes lynched near this city last week are on display in a large bottle filled with alcohol on the counter of the town's only drug store. An inscription beside the bottle reads: "What's left of the niggers that shot a white man." Lindsay B. Gilmore, a white grocer, was shot when he took after two Negroes, unidentified, who were caught stealing some cheese and cash from Gilmore's store. A number of witnesses have stated that in the chase Gilmore was shot by a local officer whose aim was faulty. The Negroes were lynched, nevertheless. (quoted in Ginzburg 1962/1988, 168)

Lynching mobs often hung signs on the corpse. Sometimes signs displayed a sick morbid humor: a sign placed on the body of John Bailey read "Please Do Not Wake Him." On at least one occasion the corpse was used to advertise goods. In Alexandria, Virginia, a tobacco merchant saw an opportunity for free publicity when Joseph McCoy, a black man charged with rape, was lynched. He attached an advertisement for his products to the lamppost from which the corpse hung. Typically, however, the signs warned that a similar punishment awaited other black men. The mob who lynched Magruder Fletcher, another alleged rapist in Virginia, left such a sign. It proclaimed simply (if falsely) "We protect our mothers, daughters, and sisters. The Committee" (quoted in Brundage 1993, 42).

The spectacle of the dangling corpse, the charred remains of a burned and mutilated body, and stern signs of warning to other blacks invariably attracted white spectators. Typically, local authorities allowed bodies to remain on public display for at least several hours, but sometimes for days. There were occasions when whites tried to preserve the lynching site. John Henry Williams' body had been burned in June 1921; fearing that wild pigs might destroy the charred remains, mob participants protected the smoldering pyre by building a fence around the site. Typically, however, it was not wild animals who posed the greatest threat to the lynching site; it was white spectators seeking souvenirs. Often they would collect pieces of the rope and splinters from the hanging tree, even links of chains used to secure burning victims. Following the lynching of Jim Rhodes near Charlottesville, Virginia, in October 1882, entrepreneurs sold pieces of the rope and tree limb used to hang the man (Brundage 1993).

V. My Old Kentucky Home

> *The Freedmen's Bureau and the Ku Klux Klan wrestled not only for power, but also for differing ideals of justice.*
>
> —Edward L. Ayers, *Vengeance and Justice: Crime and Punishment in the Nineteenth-Century American South* (1984)

> *[T]he transformation from chattel to citizenry is mediated through a complicated process of sexualization and engendering.*
>
> —Robyn Wiegman, "The Anatomy of Lynching" (1993)

In addition to a few lynchings in the North, there were a number of lynchings in the so-called border states such as Kentucky. There, situated in a broader spectrum of violence against African Americans that was both widespread and systematized, lynching became like a sexualized war on African Americans, especially African American men. While the severity and duration—it continues today if more subtly—of the "race war" in the Deep South is well known, the intensity of white racial violence in border states, such as Kentucky, has often escaped scholarly attention. The research of George C. Wright remedies that.

Kentucky had officially remained a state loyal to the union, and that fact, as Wright points out, meant that its citizens were permitted to govern their own affairs to an extent not permitted in the former Confederate states. This misplaced trust worked to the benefit of a large number of former Confederates who returned to their homes in Kentucky after the war. But they were not the only white Kentuckians unhappy at the military outcome of the conflict. Many who had stayed home and who had supported the Union cause were still opposed to the Emancipation Proclamation. Like returning Confederate soldiers, these defeated white men had no intention of losing the peace. No way would freed slaves become equal with whites (G. C. Wright 1990).

Because white Kentuckians responded to the social, political, and economic cataclysms after the war with violence on a scale unprecedented in the state, and because state officials refused to protect African Americans or to prevent white violence, the federal government extended the Freedmen's Bureau to Kentucky in January 1866 (G. C. Wright 1990). During the next five years the Freedmen's Bureau and the Ku Klux Klan fought each other for power, animated by vastly differing ideals of justice. While both organizations disappeared after a few turbulent years, "the South long bore their imprints" (Ayers 1984, 151).

The Freedmen's Bureau maintained courts throughout the South from 1865 to 1868 to adjudicate minor civil and criminal cases involving the freedmen. These courts varied in composition from state to state, but often the local Freedmen's Bureau agent acted alone to protect blacks' legal rights. These individuals were often overwhelmed by the scale of white resistance. Moreover, the weakness of the system drew the wrath of freedpeople. A convention of exslaves in Georgia in 1868 declared that the system was so weak, so infiltrated by rebels "that [our] case is worse than if the Bureau had no agents at all" (quoted in Ayers 1984, 152). Under pressure and threats from southern whites, many agents in fact supported the status quo by masking injustice in the mantle of formal justice. Much depended on the character and conscience of individual agents. Edward L. Ayers (1984) summarizes:

> It seems clear that while the Freedmen's Bureau performed crucial services for the exslaves throughout the south—providing food and clothing to the destitute, supporting schools, furnishing blacks at least some leverage in disputes over contracts with plantation owners—crime and violence against the freedmen remained largely impervious to the Bureau's efforts to stop them. ... The Freedmen's Bureau ... was a well-intentioned experiment that exerted only a temporary and limited influence on the fundamental patterns of postwar southern crime and punishment. (155)

Kentucky was the only slaveholding state that had remained loyal to the Union that also had the Bureau, a fact which seemed to intensify the rage of many embittered whites toward their former slaves. In fact, Wright (1990) tells us that violence was so widespread in Mason County that a number of the freedmen declined to even sign a petition, fearing that their churches and property would be destroyed as a consequence. While the Freedmen's Bureau failed to prevent most of the violence, it did make some difference, and African Americans were worried that the Bureau might be shut down. One black resident of Owensboro explained, "The Bureau is our only protection in Kentucky. The civil laws of the State deprive us of our every right. Every black man is threatened in the State by every rebel ... upon the removal of the Bureau. ... He shall be paid up for daring to assert his manhood before that institution" (quoted in Wright 1990, 2).

The Thirteenth Amendment and the military victories of Yankee soldiers—black and white—was supposed to mean freedom for all black people. But the truth, as Ida B. Wells (1892a/1969) would observe some thirty years later, was that "there [was] little difference between the Antebellum South and the New South" (20). John S. Graham, an agent for the Freedmen's Bureau who traveled throughout northern Kentucky in May 1866, observed that a number of blacks remained in bondage in Boone County. It would take a military force of about thirty men to free these slaves, he estimated in his report. Not all Freedmen's Bureau agents were as responsible as he in reporting such facts. Many of the agents were in fact white supremacists, and they were quickly befriended by other racist Kentuckians who persuaded them they all should work together to solve the "negro problem" (Wright 1990, 22).

Some of these white men joined the Ku Klux Klan; the racial violence committed by the Kentucky Klan equaled that of the Klan anywhere in the old Confederacy. In 1860 African Americans accounted for 20.4 percent of the total population of Kentucky; they reached their lowest point in 1950, when they constituted less than 7 percent of the population. While the exact number is difficult to determine, clearly many African Americans left the state to escape pervasive and continuing white violence (Wright 1990).

That newly freed black people wanted an education outraged many whites who viewed schooling as a step toward equality between the races. To thwart this aspiration, whites destroyed black schools not only in Kentucky but across the old Confederacy. In 1867, when the Freedmen's Bureau and several white northern missionary societies conducted a major drive throughout Kentucky to establish schools for blacks, dozens of buildings were destroyed. One representative reported from Allen County: "The opposition to the education of the freedmen is so great and universal that a school could not exist unless ... protected by an armed force" (quoted in Wright 1990, 34).

This proved to be the case in Louisville, where mobs resorted to arson to stop several white businessmen from leasing their buildings to be used as black schools. As late as 1873, Louisville whites still threatened to destroy any buildings designated for the education of African Americans. After learning that a school would be built at the corner of Sixth and York, area whites wrote letters of protest to the newspaper and held several meetings to halt construction (Wright 1990).

Outraged that schools for blacks should even exist, whites in Kentucky were beside themselves when whites came from the North to teach the former slaves. The experience the following teachers underwent in 1868 was not atypical. One teacher, a young white woman from Cincinnati, had volunteered to teach in the school operated by the Freedmen's Bureau in Bowling Green, but she was unable to find housing. Finally she was offered a room at a boarding house owned by a former Confederate but found herself "severely left alone." Several months later, another teacher in Bowling Green, A. D. Jones, was warned by the Ku Klux Klan to get out of town in ten days or else. A third white teacher in Bowling Green, Mrs. L. A. Baldwin, received the following:

Ku Klux Klans!
Blood! Poison! Powder! Torch!
Leave in five days or hell's your portion!
Rally, rally, watch your chance,
First blood, first premium K.K.K.
If ball, or torch, or poison fails,
The house beneath you shall be blown to hell, or me you.
KKK.
(quoted in Wright 1990, 35)

There were other actions against northerners who came to Kentucky to teach African Americans. Thomas K. Noble, head of the Freedmen's Bureau education program in the state, received the following report in February 1868: "During your absence in Washington, D.C., the Teacher whom you directed me to teach the Freedmen's school at New Castle, Kentucky was mobbed and driven out of Town shortly after reaching his destination, and I believe before beginning to teach" (quoted in Wright 1990, 35–36). A few months later, the teacher at the black school in Crab Orchard just managed to avoid being beaten by a white mob. The report read: "Ever since he has been there, white children have habitually cursed and stoned him in the street as he walked to and from his duty." Things were no better in Danville, where a mob ran the teacher out of town in April 1868, and "it is not deemed safe to reopen the school at present." In early January 1869, Noble wrote a long letter to John W. Alvord, the general superintendent in Washington, citing many occasions when teachers of blacks had been abused by whites. His report also documented the destruction of several black schools toward the end of 1868:

> In Hickman, Fulton County, Miss Jennie Mead (from Ohio) has been insulted many times in the streets and had been threatened with death. One of her pupils has been murdered. At Corydon, the teacher was driven from the town. School houses burned at Rock Springs. At Cadiz, Mr. S. Reeves (white) was beaten while trying to organize a school. School burned in Germantown. The Noble schoolhouse in Shepardsville burned October 1, 1868. Two churches used as schools in Bullitt County were burned. Schoolhouse at Thompkinsville burned. The teacher in Mayfield was driven from the town. Now in other portions of the United States it is not uncommon for houses to be burned, but the motive is usually gain. The remarkable thing about Kentucky arson is the crime is committed from principle; here education is not believed in and schoolhouses are therefore burned ... because instruction is given to ignorant freedmen. (quoted in Wright 1990, 36)

Berea College admitted both white and black students; the institution was attacked periodically for several years after the Civil War. The school was accustomed to white resistance to its project of biracial education. Led by abolitionist John G. Fee on donated land, Berea College had reopened in the late 1850s but closed under pressure from proslavery forces on the eve of the Civil War. When it reopened in 1866, Fee admitted several black soldiers. The daughter of John A. R. Rogers, one of the founders of the school, recalled area whites' response:

> For four years (1867–71) the lives of Mr. Fee and my father were in more or less danger. On several occasions to prevent the school buildings being fired armed pickets patrolled around them all night. For years when my father was away at night my mother had us all sleep on the first floor on cots rather than in our bedroom upstairs so that if the house were fired in the night we could be gotten out quickly. I have heard the bullets sing into our yard to strike the trees several times fired by drunken men at the house. (quoted in Wright 1990, 37)

Nor did things improve in 1871. That year Willard W. Wheeler, an employee of the college, traveled to Lexington to meet with prospective black students. On his way back home, he was ambushed by a mob and almost killed. That same evening, while Wheeler was trying to recover, a group of masked men kidnapped him from his hotel and beat him nearly to death (Wright 1990).

Like lynchers, the white men who burned and blew up black schools and assaulted teachers were rarely prosecuted. State and local officials shared other whites' view that the northern missionaries were nothing more than troublemakers. They declined to apprehend their assailants even when positive identifications were made by Bureau agents. Black witnesses were prohibited by law from testifying in Kentucky courts. They could give evidence in the Bureau's courts, but many of them declined to do so, fearing for their lives. On one occasion, Bureau Agent R. E. Johnson, determined to punish the whites responsible for the destruction of the black school in Midway, insisted that they be arrested and brought before the court. The county attorney declined to participate in the case against the white defendants, so Johnson took the prosecutor's job. He reported that: "I examined a large number of witnesses, both white and black, and I regret to say that I was unable to prove anything against them for the reason that the night was very dark and the witnesses were unable to identify any of the above named party as having committed any such act, and I was unable to prove anything against them. I moved that the prisoners be discharged, and it was accordingly so ordered" (quoted in Wright 1990, 37–38).

Western Kentucky—Wright focuses on Logan County and, in particular, Russellville, the largest town in the county—proved to be especially inhospitable to African Americans. A large number of former Confederate soldiers had returned to the area. Ignoring Appomattox, they remained openly defiant, proudly displaying the "stars and bars" at all public meetings. A number of former slaves who had served in the United States Army also returned to Logan County; they were threatened and told to leave, not just the county but the state. Refusing to leave their homes, a dozen or more black veterans found employment at the Shaker settlement in South Union, Logan County, working there in the woolen and flour mills. They built cabins on the settlement, and for more than two years they worked and lived peacefully in the area. But the mere presence of African Americans irritated area whites. They issued warnings to the Shakers, demanding that they fire all black workers, and expel them from their homes. The Shakers had remained noncombatants during the War; they had no intention of revising their position now, believing that if they were neutral and treated all people with respect they would be left alone. In late August 1868, a mob of white men raided the settlement, burning several of the cabins occupied by black workers. In response the Shakers offered a reward of five hundred dollars for the arrest of those who had destroyed property. This action enraged local whites, who, during the early morning hours of September 2, destroyed not only the cabins where black workers lived, but the mills and entire settlement. The Shakers' property was uninsured; losses totaled nearly seventy thousand dollars (Wright 1990).

Even more than black workers who presumed to live "normal" lives, black veterans were persecuted wherever they tried to settle. Upon returning home to Union County in 1866, a group of black veterans were harassed by former Confederate soldiers. The white men managed to seize the black veterans' weapons, warning them to leave the county immediately. This war against newly freed black people, especially against black veterans, occurred all over Kentucky, as it did throughout the South. One George Rable reported: "Negroes' weapons were seized, including hunting pieces and useless old guns" (quoted in Wright 1990, 40). African Americans in Paducah complained to agents of the Freedmen's Bureau about the ruling of a local judge that permitted former Confederate soldiers to keep their guns, while any white man could disarm any black man he found carrying a weapon. Moreover, white men were entitled to keep any weapon they had confiscated. This ruling encouraged Paducah whites to harass African Americans constantly, disarming them whenever possible. African Americans were told to give up looking for jobs. Any black response was coded as militant, even holding a meeting (Wright 1990).

Given this complete and violent repression, one can imagine how distressed Louisville whites became when a number of local black men started holding military drills (during which they carried firearms) on Saturday evenings at a church. That made the news even in Cincinnati, where the *Cincinnati Commercial* reported: "Steps are being taken to ascertain whether their meetings are of a peaceful character, or warlike character. If the latter, they will be dispersed." In the late 1860s, a congressional report described the desperate situation faced by black veterans living in the remote and mountainous area of eastern Kentucky: "Having served in the Union army, they have been the special objects of persecution, and in hundreds of instances have been driven from their homes" (quoted in Wright 1990, 40). White assaults on the black veterans, the report continued, had precipitated considerable emigration from Kentucky into other states (Wright 1990).

Given the range of postbellum violence aimed at African Americans during Reconstruction, it is unsurprising that many black citizens were murdered by whites in cold-blooded fashion. George Wright points out that few scholars have studied lynchings during Reconstruction, concentrating instead on those occurring after 1880, when the statistical evidence becomes more reliable. One notable exception, Wright observes, is Richard Maxwell Brown (1975), who estimated that from 1868 to 1871, there were over 400 Klan lynchings throughout the South. Wright argues that Brown's figure, horrible as it is, very much undercounts the lynchings that in fact occurred. More than one-third of the total number of lynchings that occurred in Kentucky (117 of 353) took place between 1865 and 1874. But, Wright continues, 117 is too low (so too, he argues, is 400 for the entire South), as that number represents the number of lynchings that can be documented definitively or partially with the names and race of the victims, the dates and places of the lynchings, and the reasons given by the mob for the murders.

The absence of "hard data" for the pre-1880 period is, of course, the major reason students of lynching have not concentrated on Reconstruction-era assaults on African Americans. Focusing on central Kentucky as an example, Wright finds that based on several sources he can estimate that, from 1867 to 1871, as many as 25 lynchings per year occurred in that region, clustered in the rural areas around Danville, Harrodsburg, and Richmond. Because most of these lynchings during these years in this area cannot be documented definitively—in most cases the only known details are newspaper accounts of someone's recollection that a lynching happened in a particular county some years ago—they have been excluded from the total number, leaving the too-low record of 117 (Wright 1990).

Even exercising caution and excluding most anecdotal accounts of lynchings, Wright (1990) found 93 lynchings for Kentucky during the five-year period (1867–1871), with two years—1868 (with 21) and 1870 (with 36)—producing 57. During the zenith of lynching, 1891 and 1895, "only" 64 died at the hands of lynch mobs in Kentucky. While lynching occurred everywhere in Kentucky, it was more likely to occur in western and central Kentucky, the areas of the greatest concentration of African Americans. The fewest number occurred in eastern Kentucky, where relatively few African Americans lived (Wright 1990).

As we have seen, African Americans had little legal recourse. Wright narrates an incident that occurred in Anderson County, Kentucky, to illustrate the point. In April 1874, Mark Rucker, a white man "addicted to drink" (quoted in Wright 1990, 54), went to purchase some liquor at the home of Levi Thompson and Botts Hagerman. No one was home, and so Rucker waited inside the house, where he took a nap. While Rucker was napping, the wives of Thompson and Hagerman returned home and discovered the strange man inside. Alarmed, they began shouting and fled, until several men came running to help. It was by now dark and although they could barely make out Rucker's figure, they fired anyway, killing him instantly. In court, rather than calling Rucker's death an accident, the defendants argued that they had thought they were shooting at a black man. Finding this explanation perfectly reasonable, the court dismissed the charges against the defendants (Wright 1990).

African Americans didn't take all this lying down. On many occasions there were responses to white violence, by any standard rather measured responses. African Americans formed organizations, appealed to state officials, and on occasion armed themselves to protect their property and to prevent lynchings. During the 1870s and again in the early 1900s, black citizens challenged white mobs by arming themselves and guarding jailhouses to protect the lives of those incarcerated and accused of rape or murder. After a lynching in Georgetown in August 1891, African Americans in the area resorted to arson to avenge the victim; whites panicked. On several occasions after a lynching, whites grew so concerned about blacks arming themselves that officials instituted curfews and called out the militia. Black Kentuckians were neither "passive or impotent" (Wright 1990, 11). While not always successful, they did what they could, despite the white supremacist regime, to defend themselves.

Wright tells the story of Elijah Marrs, a former slave, who after being discharged from the Union army moved to Henry County, Kentucky, to teach in the school established for the freed people. Members of the Klan publicly expressed their contempt for the school, reserving their most heated outbursts for this black war veteran who now served as a teacher. In response to Klan provocations, Marrs helped organize the Loyal League to protect African Americans from the Klan. On several occasions, he turned back Klan assaults by firing upon them. In his autobiography, Marrs recalls that for three years he "slept with a pistol under my head, an Enfield rifle at my side, and a corn knife at the door" (quoted in Wright 1990, 58). In 1871, the black residents of Watkinsville, learning that the Klan had murdered one of their own in nearby

Stamping Ground, armed themselves and fired at the first sight of the hooded white men. They too succeeded in turning the white men back, although three African Americans died in the exchange of gunfire. In August and September of that same year, the *Louisville Commercial* reported that African Americans had killed several Klan members who had attacked their homes (Wright 1990).

On occasion African Americans armed themselves to prevent lynchings. In August 1871, the Klan attempted to raid the Danville jail and seize two black men held there. Fearing that very possibility, a group of black men had surrounded the jail; they opened fire when Klansmen neared. They succeeded in driving the white men off. In 1874, a black man named Lewis Franklin, arrested in Versailles and charged with a rape in Nicholasville, feared for his life, as several lynchings had recently occurred in Nicholasville. Black residents armed themselves and guarded Franklin until he could be returned to the city. A mob of approximately fifty white men marched to the jail early in the morning. Who started shooting first is unclear, but one white man was killed, and the others fled. Astonishingly, given the white supremacist judicial system, no charges were brought against any of the black men (Wright 1990).

What did white leaders think of the "race war"—and its most outrageous tactic, lynching—underway throughout Kentucky during the last third of the nineteenth century? For almost fifty years the influential editor of the *Louisville Courier-Journal,* Henry Watterson, seemed to change his mind about lynching. In a June 1894 editorial he lambasted Ida B. Wells and the British press (which she had encouraged—see chapters 7 and 8) for criticizing the South's toleration for lynchings: "The negro woman from Memphis is still stirring up the British over the barbarism of the Southern people in lynching negroes. The British ought to have no indignation for export. They need it all for home consumption. A people which have robbed and murdered more blacks than any other nation on the globe should have nothing to say because the southern whites protect their women by killing their ravishers" (quoted in Wright 1990, 65). Several years later, however, he wrote editorials demanding punishment for those responsible for lynchings in Mayfield and in Graves County. Good men had to take control of the situation, he declared, but not because African Americans were being murdered. As Watterson and many other white leaders saw it, the issue was lawlessness. Even with this deflection of moral outrage, it still represented an improvement in white attitudes (Wright 1990).

In his editorials Watterson pointed out that the identities of the lynchers could not remain disguised, given that there were hundreds of witnesses. Once identified, "if these are brought before the Grand Jury, they can be made to testify and the outlaws can be brought to justice, restoring the good name of Mayfield as a community determined to protect the legal rights of even its meanest citizens. If public sentiment approves the substitution of Judge Lynch for Judge Robbins, nothing will be done and very soon we may be regaled with another story of a victim hung or tortured." Three weeks later a grand jury indicted eight men. Watterson replied in print, praising the actions of the "good citizens of Graves County [who] mean to wipe out the stain cast upon the ... community by a lawless element in its population." Then, in another shift, Watterson finally expressed sympathy for African Americans: "What is worse, this has been done in the case of poor and friendless negroes. It does not appear that well-to-do criminals have suffered at the hands of regulators. The lynchings have been shocking acts not only of lawlessness but of liability and injustice to the class whose rights above all should be shielded by the community, since they cannot protect themselves" (quoted in Wright 1990, 65–66). Wright finds it difficult to know which Watterson was real; I suspect his shifting attitudes reflected those slowly changing attitudes of other influential whites in the state and across the nation.

When investigating lynchings in the early 1900s, Ray Stannard Baker (1905a, 1905b), an "enlightened progressive," blamed African Americans for lynchings. In both the North and the South, he said, "I found that this floating, worthless negro caused most of the trouble." Their crimes were characterized, he said, by an almost "animal-like ferocity" (quoted in Wright 1990, 78). His opposition to lynching, however, was grounded in the link between the mob's vengeance and savagery: "For, if civilization means anything, it means self-restraint; casting away self-restraint the white man becomes as savage as the negro" (quoted in Bederman 1995a, 45). One of Baker's biographers has noted, "Given the enormity of the crime of lynchings, Baker's objectivity and his clear sympathy for lynchers as well as lynched seem now a cruel distortion" (Bannister 1966, 128). In contrast, another white writing at the time, W. D. Sheldon (1906), strongly denounced lynchings under any circumstances and refused to accept the contention that the brutal criminal acts committed by African Americans justified mob violence (Wright 1990).

Black resistance to lynching also took form in print. In his book *Southern Outrages: A Statistical Record of Lawless Doings*, Robert C. O. Benjamin, a black lawyer and newspaper editor who had settled in Lexington in 1897, narrated in detail several of the lynchings that had occurred in the 1890s. He took issue with white rationales for these deadly assaults. Benjamin saw through the rape myth; he argued that lynching functioned to keep African Americans politically and socially subjugated: "It is only since the Negro has become a citizen and a voter that this charge [of rape] has been made. It has come along with the pretended and baseless fear of Negro supremacy. It is an effort to divest the Negro of his friends by giving him a revolting and hateful reputation." The dedication of Benjamin's book read: "To Widows and Orphans of the Murdered Black Men of the SOUTH." Writing just after the turn of the century, Mary Church Terrell agreed with Benjamin that rape was not the actual cause for lynchings in the South. Race hatred, she insisted, "the hatred of a strong people toward a weaker who were once held as slaves," led to lynchings (quoted in Wright 1990, 67). Terrell concluded that rape was only a pretext. Other middle-class black professionals and intellectuals would agree—most notably, as we will see, Ida B. Wells.

Most whites were beyond the reach of rationality. The white press in Kentucky used derogatory and inflammatory terms to depict those black men accused of raping white women. Such phrases as "black fiend," "ape-like," "Darwin's missing link," and "beast" were used repeatedly. The expression "negro brute" seems to have been a particular favorite. Even the *Courier-Journal*, probably the state's most professional white newspaper, ran headlines in bold letters declaring: "A Black Ravisher Receives Proper Attention at the

Hands of Judge Lynch," and "A Black Devil Hanged to a Tree Near Campbellsville: His Crime the Attempted Outrage of a Helpless Young Woman." On one occasion, a journalist used sick humor in his headline: "Blackbird on a Cherry Tree" (quoted in Wright 1990, 80).

The perpetuation of white fantasy occurred everywhere, at all times, including at lynching events themselves. One very public event occurred in September 1897 when the leader of the white male mob about to lynch Raymond Bushrod declared to his audience of hundreds: "Here's the protection we offer our wives and daughters." As at many lynchings, women were present, but positioned at some distance from the "action." The press reported: "During the entire time of the lynching not less than 200 women were on the hill overlooking the public square, and when the negro's dangling form went up their cheers rent the air" (quoted in Wright 1990, 89).

Another very public lynching occurred in Maysville, Kentucky, on December 6, 1899. Described by contemporary observers as the most horrifying lynching in the state's history, the murder of eighteen-year-old Richard Coleman included most elements of the practice: a family member of the victim chose how the young man would die, no one wore a mask, the lynching took place in broad daylight, local citizens were notified well in advance, and local or state officials took no action to prevent it. The husband of the murdered woman, a man named Lashbrook, had settled on burning, and after Coleman was secured on the pyre, Lashbrook started the blaze, to the roar of the large crowd. Afterward, Coleman's corpse was dragged through the streets; participants cut off fingers and toes for souvenirs (Wright 1990).

Thousands of men and hundreds of women and children had watched. The December 7, 1899, edition of the *New York World* carried the story under the headline ROASTED ALIVE. The report tells us that "tortures almost unbelievable were inflicted upon the wretched negro. In all the vast crowd that witnessed the agonies of the man, not one hand was raised in humanity's behalf, nor a single voice heard in the interest of mercy. Instead, when some new torture was inflicted upon the shrieking, burning boy, the crowd cheered and cheered, the shrill voices of women and the piping tones of children sounding high above the roar of men" (quoted in Ginzburg 1962/1988, 24).

There was no fear of retribution, as "not one person in the crowd wore a mask. The leaders of the mob disdained any semblance of any disguise. Every act was done in the open. There was no secrecy" (quoted in Ginzburg 1962/1988, 24). It was quite the event for Maysville and environs, as "the population of the whole city and country for miles around, churchmen and churchwomen, professional and businessmen of eminence, people of distinguished ancestry, formed the mob, and not a single regret for the horrible tragedy can be heard tonight from one end of the town to the other" (quoted in Ginzburg 1962/1988, 24–25). These upstanding citizens and churchpeople were united in their cause:

> The purpose seemed to be to give the wretch the greatest possible amount and duration of torture. The lower part of his clothing was torn away leaving him bare. ... This man has filled a box with cayenne pepper. He stepped close to the shrieking wretch, whose eyes were almost bursting

> from his head with pain and calmly threw the pepper into the eyes of the negro, again and again. The boy writhed and strained at the stout ropes, and his face became horribly distorted with the awfulness of the pain, but the man with the pepper-box kept on deliberately shaking more pepper into his victim's eyes. At least twice, he stopped to press down the eyelids of the negro to make sure that the pepper did its work of agony. ... Relic-hunters visited the scene [afterward] and carried away pieces of flesh and the negro's teeth. Others got pieces of fingers and toes and proudly exhibit the ghastly souvenirs tonight. (Ginzburg 1962/1988, 27–29)

The Coleman lynching also received considerable attention in the white Kentucky press. Headlined "Burned At Stake, Richard Coleman Meets Death at Hands of a Frenzied Mob," the *Courier-Journal* suggested that the lynching would injure the moral character of the citizens of Maysville, especially the youth's: "It was a scene the like of which probably was never witnessed in Kentucky, certainly not since the days of Indian warfare has there been a parallel to the three hours' horrible work of the frenzied mob which tortured and burned the young negro murderer, while thousands of people looked on with mingled exclamation of horror and approbation and others turned away sickened by the awful sight." The *New York Times* was not content to report just the facts, suggesting: "The murder by burning of the negro Coleman at Maysville is an outrage so terrible and so shameful that it can only be explained as an outbreak of delirium" (quoted in Wright 1990, 95). Perhaps this "delirium" was a white male version of the hysteria Freud attributed to (white) women's sexual repression?

Sometimes when black women were lynched, there were explicit links to black men, pregnant with "his" child, for instance, as in the case of Mary Turner. On other occasions, the woman became, in the white male mind, transgendered, as if she were something of a man. In 1904, white men lynched a black woman in Lebanon Junction for the murder of a white farmer. Marie Thompson—described by one reporter as a "negro Amazon"—had merely tried to break up an argument between John Irvin and her son over a missing pair of pliers. She claimed that she had killed Irvin with a razor in self-defense, a statement that, as Wright points out, would have probably saved her life had she been a white woman. The black woman was arrested and charged with murder. A group of black men stood guard to prevent a lynching attempt, but at two o'clock in the morning, a white mob, meeting no opposition from the authorities, took the woman and tried to lynch her from a tree in the jail yard. Thompson would not die without a fight: "The woman was struggling and fighting like a tiger all the time, but the mob was too much for her, and a minute later she was swinging in the air, with her feet several inches above ground. All of a sudden she twisted around and grabbed a man by the collar, jerked a knife from his hands and cut the rope that was choking the life out of her. Dropping to the ground, Thompson started swinging at the men. She eventually broke away but was shot down in a hail of gunfire" (Wright 1990, 116).

The Opera House lynching in Livermore, Kentucky, in 1911 drew national and international attention and in so doing embarrassed state officials to an extent that previous lynchings had not. Accused of shooting a white man, Will Porter was seized by a white mob who took him from the jail to the town theater. Armed men paid an admission fee that entitled them not only to witness the event but permitted them to later fill Porter's body with bullets. The corpse was unrecognizable (Wright 1997).

While the fight against lynching in Kentucky would not gather steam until well into the twentieth century, it began in the middle of the nineteenth. In 1886, John Albert Broadus, a minister and a professor at the Southern Baptist Theological Seminary, wrote a long letter to the *Courier-Journal* in which he discussed lynching as a question of "justice, of fundamental right, of essential civilization, of human welfare." The incidence of lynching was increasing and would prove to be, Broadus worried, destructive of civilization. Unlike most of his contemporaries, he argued that the threat of being lynched was no deterrence to criminals. The problem in the South had to do with the presence of "many ignorant and often degraded white people" and "this mighty mass of colored people." But most unusual for the time, Broadus dispensed with a monolithic picture of African Americans, insisting that not all blacks were alike. In fact, he continued, there were blacks with whom whites could and must cooperate: "There is a goodly number of intelligent Negroes who really take sound and wholesome views of the situation. If we continue to tolerate lynching, we lead these better Negroes to think that we are the enemies of all their race. We alienate the better class from the support of justice and government and civilization." Broadus asked whites to speak out: "I appeal to thoughtful men wherever the *Courier-Journal* is read, will you not come out and condemn this business of lynching? Will you not openly discourage and oppose and stop it? We can stop it. Is not this our duty? Is it not high time?" (quoted in Wright 1990, 159–160).

Wright points out that Broadus's letter was an act of courage, given that his letter was written when the American public often applauded "lynching bees," when the overwhelming majority of whites regarded blacks as proven inferior by science. Unlike the majority of whites of the time, Broadus thought in terms of interracial cooperation, a concept that would not come to organizational form in the founding of the N.A.A.C.P. for another two decades (see chapter 10). Broadus even went so far as to write the word "Negro" with a capital N, a polite and politically provocative gesture that white newspapers and magazines rejected for some time (Wright 1990).

Like Broadus, a number of prominent African Americans spoke out against lynching, demanding that white America do what was necessary to end the practice. Frederick Douglass emphasized that lynching was destroying the moral fabric of the nation. Under no circumstances could a civilized society excuse or defend lynch law because, as he forcefully argued (after Ida B. Wells), by its very nature lynching was a "crime more far-reaching, dangerous, and deadly than the crime it is intended to punish." In his view, northern whites were complicit: "The sin against the negro is both sectional and national, and until the voice of the North shall be heard in emphatic condemnation and withering reproach against these continued ruthless mob-law murders, it will remain equally involved with the South in this common crime" (quoted in Wright 1990, 160).

Legal Lynchings

"An especially pernicious extension of lynchings," Wright (1997) suggests, "was the practice of manipulating the legal system to ensure that blacks accused of rape or murder received the death penalty, the same punishment that would have been meted out by the lynch mob" (251). This practice—often called "legal lynching"—proved popular with the public, especially after resistance to lynching mobilized. The number of death sentences carried out by the state grew rapidly after 1900. Wright quotes Jacquelyn Hall (1979): "The thwarted lynch mob frequently demanded that public officials impose the death sentence in a hasty mockery of a trial. If these 'legal lynchings' were included in the statistics, the death toll would be much higher" (333). Wright observes that Hall recommends that lynchings and legal lynchings should be counted together. Curiously, however, sociologists Stewart E. Tolnay and E. M. Beck (1995) allege that "as yet, little evidence suggests that legal executions served as substitutes for lynching as social control of southern blacks" (81).

What about *this* evidence? The state of Kentucky carried out at least 229 executions between 1872 and 1940, and African Americans, approximately 10 percent of the population, accounted for 57 percent of those the state put to death. Of the 229 people legally executed, 197 were for murder, 31 for rape, and 1 for armed robbery. Given the white fantasy that rape was a "Negro crime," Wright (1997) is amazed that "only 80 percent (25 of 31) of the men put to death for rape were African American" (252). He points out that no one—black or white—died for raping a black woman. In this vein, only a few of the 130 African Americans who died on the gallows or in the electric chair were convicted of killing other African Americans. Wright (1997) also makes the point that no African Americans served on Kentucky juries during these years, so that all of the African Americans put to death during this time were convicted and sentenced by all-white juries. In fact, due to the concerted efforts of the legislature and the courts, not to mention the recalcitrance of the white electorate generally, African Americans were excluded from juries in the Bluegrass State until the late 1930s (Wright 1997).

The Commission for Interracial Cooperation (C.I.C.) established a presence in Kentucky early in the twentieth century. While never ending its fight against lynching, the C.I.C. allowed much of its effort to be taken over by the Association of Southern Women for the Prevention of Lynching (A.S.W.P.L.), an organization that C.I.C. officials helped create in 1930. The C.I.C. planted the seeds of the Kentucky A.S.W.P.L. in December 1923, with the organization of a subcommittee of thirty women, all prominent citizens from communities across the state, all committed to work vigorously in the interests of justice and goodwill between whites and blacks. Nearly all of the women involved in this committee formed by the C.I.C. would become members of the A.S.W.P.L. (Wright 1990).

Board members of the C.I.C. worked with Jessie Daniel Ames, the key figure in the A.S.W.P.L., to establish a branch in Kentucky. In a letter to J. Max Bond, who had become the director of the C.I.C. upon the death of his father, Ames emphasized two points. One was that A.S.W.P.L. would function independently from the C.I.C., thereby "bringing into it many women who may not be sympathetic with the principles of the Commission, but certainly sympathetic with law enforcement." The second was that only white women should be invited to join, a point that Bond, a black man, must have found odd. At the meeting, held on February 26, 1931, Ames spoke at considerable length regarding the work of the organization and the need for a Kentucky branch. The women agreed to establish a Kentucky branch, and, as required of all new affiliates, passed a resolution expressing their opposition to mob violence: "We repudiate the claim that lynching is in defense of the white women in the South, holding that the mob spirit is a greater menace than any other form of crime in the United States, brutalizing the community, men, women and children, where it occurs, discrediting American institutions, and confessing to a breakdown in the government." They further resolved to do all in their power to "eradicate this crime in our State by helping to build up a profounder sense in young and old of law and order and the need therefor" (quoted in Wright 1990, 209).

Members of the Kentucky branch of the A.S.W.P.L. wrote numerous letters to every sheriff in the state, informing them of threats of lynchings and demanding that they do everything possible to prevent them in their communities. "Last year, for the first time since 1929, Kentucky had a lynching," a letter of January 1933 began. "We had thought, when the movement of Southern Women against lynching started, that our State needed no education. Our citizens were committed against this crime. Last year's record shows that we were mistaken." The organization asked sheriffs to help attain their goal of a "Lynchless South in 1933" (quoted in Wright 1990, 209). They also reminded the sheriffs that if a lynching should occur, it would be the responsibility of the sheriffs to arrest the mob members immediately and to prosecute them in court. In 1934, the women asked the sheriffs to sign pledges against lynchings; many sheriffs complied. The Kentucky branch also issued yearly reports noting where lynchings had been prevented in the state (Wright 1990).

More than sheriffs' support was necessary, of course, and so the Kentucky A.S.W.P.L. invited the governor, the attorney general, and numerous local officials to their conferences. Before the governor's race of 1935, it sent a lengthy questionnaire to the leading candidates asking them to state their positions on mob violence and the measures they would adopt to ensure that no additional lynchings disgraced the Commonwealth of Kentucky. The candidates' replies were then released to the public (Wright 1990).

Tension developed between the officers of the Kentucky affiliate and Jessie Daniel Ames regarding the issue of federal antilynching legislation. As we will see (chapter 8, section VI), Jesse Daniel Ames devoted much of her life's work to ending lynchings, but as a southerner she felt that federal intervention in local affairs would infringe on the rights of the states. She also counseled A.S.W.P.L.'s affiliates against working with the N.A.A.C.P. due to its lobbying for a national antilynching law and its vision of a racially integrated American society. By the 1930s in Kentucky, however, nearly all the members of the A.S.W.P.L., as well as leading citizens such as Mark Ethridge, the influential editor of the *Courier-Journal,* had come out in favor of federal antilynching legislation. Nor did the Kentucky A.S.W.P.L. share Ames's view of the

N.A.A.C.P.; members of the Kentucky affiliate appeared on several programs sponsored by the Louisville branch of the N.A.A.C.P. After coming out in favor of federal legislation, Mrs. G. W. Hummel, the president of the Kentucky affiliate and one of its founders, offered her resignation to Ames, who declined to accept it, explaining that consensus on all issues was not a requirement of A.S.W.P.L. membership. Despite the disagreement with Ames over the role of the federal government in ending lynchings, the Kentucky branch continued its efforts to prevent lynchings until the organization was absorbed into the Southern Regional Council in 1942 (Wright 1990).

Slowly white Kentuckians would respond to the appeals of the A.S.W.P.L. and the C.I.C., and lynchings in the state declined. Spokespersons for these two groups promised lynchers that the judicial system would deal harshly with African Americans convicted of rape, murder, and other heinous crimes. Many whites came to realize that they could count on the courts to do legally what they could no longer do extralegally, at least not without increased risk of arrest and prosecution. So many white Kentuckians came to accept the legal execution of black "criminals" in place of that extralegal execution that was lynching. Even antilynchers failed to question the procedures used in many cases, such as why trials were not moved from areas where lynchings were threatened. The fact that African Americans could not serve on Kentucky juries must have seemed as "natural" as the exclusion of blacks from other public spaces. Few whites questioned the fact that nearly all those who were sentenced to death for rape were young, poor, often illiterate. In making his case for the notion of "legal lynching," George Wright (1990) points out:

> Countless numbers of black men were tried in hostile environments; judges and juries were convinced of their guilt before hearing any evidence. To the satisfaction of many "law and order" Kentucky whites, the number of lynchings declined in the twentieth century, but this coincided with a rise in the number of legal lynchings in the state. Indeed, it must be emphasized that a crucial reason for the decline in lynchings was related to how white Kentuckians consistently manipulated the legal system, ensuring that any black accused of certain crimes received the same punishment as that meted out by the lynch mobs. (222)

In contrast, of the nearly one hundred whites executed by the state of Kentucky from 1870 to 1940, not one was so punished for crimes against African Americans. No man—white or black—was executed in Kentucky for the rape of a black woman. It was the black male body that white men wanted. Those black men who were imprisoned but not executed would find ways to exact revenge, as we will see in chapters 16 and 17.

Wright finds support for the legalized lynching thesis in the research of several scholars who also argued that the decline of lynchings, not only in Kentucky but throughout the nation, was due in part to the states taking the place of the lynching mob. Between the period 1930 to 1961 there were 442 convicted rapists who were legally executed in the United States. Ninety percent of them were African American and all but two were executed in either a southern or border state. Were 90 percent of all convicted rapists in the United

States black? No, more than half of them were white. Clearly, convicted black men were likely to receive more severe sentences than were whites (Wolfgang 1958). African Americans were also less likely to be paroled (Von Hentig 1940; R. Brown 1965).

Writing in the 1930s, James Harmon Chadbourn and Arthur Raper found considerable prolynching sentiment among many judicial officials. After a careful study of white justice for blacks, Raper concluded that a legal conviction was little, if any, improvement over extralegal lynchings. Jacquelyn Hall—whose study of Jesse Daniel Ames serves as my sourcebook in chapter 8—was not impressed that the number of lynchings declined in the twentieth century from its high in the 1890s. Many African Americans, particularly men, were put to death in the 1920s, she noted, executed in ways that suggest that they too were victims of (legal) lynchings (Hall 1979; Wright 1990).

Many African Americans had long noticed this fact. Wright notes that Frederick Douglass, for instance, understood that in the South, African Americans would be punished, guilty or innocent. Wright quotes Douglass as saying, "No decent white man in the South will pretend that in that region there could be impaneled a jury, black, white, or mixed, which would in case of proof of the deed allow a guilty negro to escape punishment." Wright also quotes Francis J. Grimké, a contemporary of Douglass, a graduate of the Princeton Theological Seminary and a prominent minister in Washington, D.C. Grimké's wife, Charlotte Forten Grimké (1837–1914), the abolitionist and writer, became close friends with Anna Julia Cooper (Lemert and Bhan 1998). Francis Grimké wrote: "Another effect of this race hatred is seen in the undue severity with which negro criminals are punished by the courts." No mercy was forthcoming, he concluded. Grimké (1899) also questioned the use of rape to legitimate lynching, arguing that so often when the charge of rape was made, the black man and white woman involved had previously had a romantic relationship, a point Ida B. Wells had made nearly a decade earlier.

As Wells knew, when the affair had become public or because the white woman felt spurned, the rape charged was fabricated to save her reputation. Nor did Grimké put any stock in white lynchers' claims that black men usually confessed to their crimes of rape before being killed. There is no reason for the man to confess, he reasoned, for to admit guilt meant certain death anyway. The only point of these "confessions" was to make an excuse for the lynching. "And so, the temptation always is to say, he confessed. Of course, if he confessed, that puts his guilt beyond all doubt, and his execution, though in an unlawful way, doesn't seem quite so bad as lynching an innocent man, or one about whose guilt there is some doubt" (quoted in Wright 1990, 79).

Wright (1990) quotes Mary Church Terrell, who also expressed the view that black defendants had almost no chance of exoneration: "Even those who condone lynching do not pretend to fear the delay or the uncertainty of the law, when a guilty negro is concerned. With the courts of law entirely in the hands of the white man, ... a guilty negro could no more extricate himself from the meshes of the law in the South than he could slide from the devil-fish's embrace or slip from the anaconda's coils. Miscarriage of justice in the South is possible only when white men transgress the law" (quoted in Wright 1990, 224–225).

Underscoring the connection between capital punishment and lynching, the former received considerable publicity in Kentucky and throughout the South (Wright 1990).

Not even all-white racist juries managed to sentence *all* black defendants to death, and so beginning with the end of slavery, the number of African Americans within Kentucky's prison population increased quickly. On January 1, 1868, blacks comprised 38.5 percent of the inmates in the state penitentiary; by the 1880s they became the majority and remained so until the middle of the twentieth century. Black women accounted for 95 percent of the female prison population in Kentucky. When escaping the death sentence, African Americans received longer prison sentences than did whites (Wright 1990).

As early as October 1885, black leaders denounced the discrimination black people faced in court. They noted that the judicial system ignored antiblack white violence. "We are tried in courts controlled entirely by white men," one speaker complained at a convention that year, "and no colored man sits on a Kentucky jury. This seems no mere accident, but a determined effort to exclude us from fair trials and put us at the mercy of our enemies, from the Judge down to the vilest stubborn witness." It was shameful, he declared, that out of the hundreds of lynchings that had occurred since the Civil War not "a single high-handed murderer has been ever brought before a court to answer." Moreover, African Americans were sent to prison mainly due to their race, not due to criminal violations: "The penitentiary is full of our race, who are sent there by wicked and malicious persecutions and unjust sentences, dealt out by Judges who deem a colored criminal fit only for the severest and longest sentences for trivial offenses" (quoted in Wright 1990, 248). Black leaders vowed to protest and work together until these forms of legalized discrimination were ended.

Like speedy trials, public hangings calmed whites' worries that black criminals were not being coddled by the state. Many elements of nineteenth-century lynchings—"the large, frenzied crowds, the vendors selling hot dogs, cotton candy, and souvenirs, and the news reporters writing about every trivial step taken by the condemned man" (Wright 1990, 255)—remained a part of public executions conducted by Kentucky's legal system in the twentieth century. The parallels were not lost on everyone, and a few citizens urged the legislature to eliminate the carnival-like atmosphere, pointing out that it made light of one of the most solemn duties performed by the state. In 1910, a bill was introduced that replaced public hangings with the electric chair, with an additional feature designed to end the circuslike behavior that occurred during executions: "All executions of the death penalty by electrocution shall take place within the walls of the State penitentiary ... and such enclosures as will exclude public view thereof" (quoted in Wright 1990, 256). This bill was signed into law on March 20, 1910, but the white desire to watch the black body die did not disappear, and soon enough the practice of hanging condemned rapists in the county where they had been tried and convicted was reinstituted in Kentucky, despite the law (Wright 1990).

Well into the twentieth century in Kentucky huge, boisterous crowds numbering in the thousands came to watch black men die. In June 1932, Sam Jennings was executed in Hardinsburg for allegedly assaulting a white woman.

A black newspaper reported: "The hanging of the colored man ... attracted such a throng of men, women, and children as might have caused T. Barnum of circus fame to hide his face in shame. It took Jennings seventeen minutes to die, to the delight of the crowd who enjoyed every second of the event" (quoted in Wright 1990, 256–257). The widely reported public hanging of Rainey Bethea in Owensboro on August 14, 1936, was sufficiently gruesome that Wright credits it with ending the practice.

National newspaper accounts characterized those whites watching the hanging as being uncivilized, a rhetorical strategy Ida B. Wells had used with great success during her antilynching crusade in the 1890s (see chapters 7 and 8). Readers across the United States learned, for instance, how white Kentuckians had rushed to the gallows to rip off the dying Rainey Bethea's clothes as well as the hangman's hood, to take home as souvenirs. Editors of small-town Kentucky newspapers sometimes had complaints, as when one in Henderson complained about the hour of Bethea's execution. The hour should have been more convenient—2:00 P.M. would have been much better—so that more people could have attended. Moreover, Bethea's hanging should have been held at the local high school so that everyone "could sit and be comfortable and see the ghastly spectacle" (quoted in Wright 1990, 258). Rainey Bethea's execution focused nationwide attention on Kentucky as the last state in which public hangings were permitted. Not surprisingly, several organizations concerned about the state's image lobbied hard for an end to the practice, among them the A.S.W.P.L. and the *Louisville Courier-Journal* (Wright 1990).

In Kentucky as well as throughout the nation, there were crimes that whites regarded as typically "Negro crimes." Writing in 1910, Gilbert Stephenson pointed out how certain legal statutes, while not naming the black man, "are thought by many to have peculiar application to him." One such law Kentucky had passed in 1904. Popularly called the "chicken-thief law," the ordinance read, "That if any person shall steal chickens, turkey, ducks, or other fowls of the value of two dollars, or more, he shall be confined in the penitentiary not less than one nor more than five years" (quoted in Wright 1990, 290–291). Recall that early in the twentieth century defendants in most minor cases had no lawyers, no public defenders, and that African Americans were usually tried in hostile courtrooms; the chicken-thief law definitely impacted black residents of isolated rural communities. In March 1930, the American Civil Liberties Union wrote to Walter White about a Paris, Kentucky, black man being sentenced to life in prison for allegedly stealing six chickens. The circuit court justified such a lengthy sentence by declaring that the individual was a habitual criminal. As was customary, the national office contacted William Scroggins, a local black leader, and asked him to look into the matter. His intervention made a difference; within a week, the court set aside the verdict and ordered a new trial for the convicted man. In the new trial the defendant was sentenced to four years in jail, still a ridiculous sentence for stealing six chickens, but definitely an improvement on the earlier sentence (Wright 1990). As we see in chapter 16 (section III), sentences for drug consumption and dealing are the contemporary versions of chicken-thief legislation.

Burglary was another crime that whites associated with African Americans, and so when a black man was convicted of burglary, he always faced the possibility of a stiff prison sentence. This possibility became a virtual certainty when the Kentucky legislature passed a statute in 1922 that said, "Every person guilty of burglary shall be punished with death or confinement in the penitentiary for life, in the discretion of the jury" (quoted in Wright 1990, 291). But, of course, for whites, rape was the special black crime, demanding special punishment: first lynching, then state-sanctioned execution, which George Wright (1990) points out was nothing more than legal lynching. Wright summarizes his study of racial violence in Kentucky:

> Legal lynching was only a part of the racial violence experienced by Afro-Americans in Kentucky. Clearly, however, legal lynching, because it made a complete mockery of the law and tended to destroy the respect citizens had for their legal process, proved to be far worse than the horrible acts of the mobs that ran blacks out of town or lynched them. These acts were illegal and no clear-thinking citizens suggested otherwise. On the other hand, the overwhelming majority of white Kentuckians believed that their legal system was fair, that even though blacks were denied equal access to most places in society, they were dealt with fairly in court. Therefore, they simply ignored the omission of blacks from juries and the obvious discrimination they faced in court, whether they were there as the defendant or the victimized party. With such an attitude so firmly embedded in white society, blacks clearly and consistently faced discrimination before the law. (304)

As we will see in chapter 14, today one in every four young black men is somewhere—jail, probation, on trial—in the American judicial system. They have changed form, but legal lynchings of young black men have not ended.

VI. The Sunshine State

> *Consider a white man. Being pure Presence, he is equated with manliness in toto. The manly, or masculine, is in fact a figure of denial, a being who attempts to close all holes and become pure, sealed flesh in search of holes. From the perspective of such a being, all holes are elsewhere; he doesn't even have an anus; when he kisses, nothing enters his mouth—he enters the Other's. In his presence, the black becomes a chasm to* fill. *But the black "man" is a* hole. *Could such a figure seriously accomplish denial by a decision to interpret himself as completely "closed"? Let us look at his primary claim to maleness, if not manhood: his penis.*
>
> —Lewis Gordon, *Bad Faith and Antiblack Racism* (1995)

> *[C]astration [is] the ultimate denouement of the mob's violence.*
>
> —Robyn Wiegman, "The Anatomy of Lynching" (1993)

Like the rest of the South, Florida suffered its highest number of lynchings during the 1890s. While the practice slowly declined over the next five decades, the incidence of lynching remained high enough that during the 1930s, the last phase of the lynching and vigilante era, Florida was the most lynch-prone state in the South. Unlike the remainder of the South, Florida also became known for the lynching of a white man, for political, not racialized or sexual reasons. As we will see, urban vigilantes in Tampa moved to preserve the political status quo in that city by flogging socialist Joseph Shoemaker in 1935. Shoemaker's death from injuries sustained in the vicious attack became for a time a widely embraced *cause célèbre,* thanks mostly to the national agitation by Norman Thomas and the Socialist Party of America (Howard 1995).

The Shoemaker incident notwithstanding, like their counterparts in other southern states, white men in Florida preferred to stalk black men. For instance, a black man from Jasper named Henry Woods was lynched in Hamilton County on June 6, 1932. There was, as usual, torture involved; while he was still alive, his male captors took him "to some secluded spot putting him on a brush heap after slicing the body with knives" (quoted in Howard 1995, 45). After they "got off," they burned him. Walter Howard, on whose study of lynching in Florida I am relying here, is puzzled why the black press and the N.A.A.C.P. were silent about this Woods lynching. He speculates that financial problems combined with internal dissension helps explain the N.A.A.C.P.'s lack of response. As we will see later (chapter 11, section V), there was at this time considerable tension between W. E. B. Du Bois and Walter White, compounded by the Association's absorption in the Scottsboro case in Alabama, which rather completely preoccupied the N.A.A.C.P. during the first years of the Great Depression. Not until 1933 did the N.A.A.C.P. renew its national antilynching drive. In 1932, the fate of Henry Woods fell between the cracks (Howard 1995).

The N.A.A.C.P. was, of course, not alone in the fight against lynching. The Commission on Interracial Cooperation's Southern Commission on the Study of Lynching supported research and education on the subject, one consequence of which was University of North Carolina law professor James H. Chadbourn's well-researched *Lynching and the Law* (1933). Chadbourn surveyed existing legislation relating to lynching, examined court decisions concerning these laws, and proposed a model antilynching statute. In early January 1934 a copy was forwarded to Florida's new governor, David Sholtz; whether he read the book is unknown. Sholtz thanked the S.C.S.L. for the gift and assured them that, as governor, he needed no additional legislation. Antilynching legislation was simply not needed in the great state of Florida, he declared (Howard 1995).

A few days after Governor Sholtz assured the S.C.S.L. and the Association of Southern Women for the Prevention of Lynching (A.S.W.P.L.) that antilynching legislation was superfluous in his state, a lynching occurred in Tampa, the second lynching of 1934. On the 28th of January 1934 Robert Johnson, a black man accused of raping a white woman, was arrested by Tampa police but was soon abducted by "unknown" white men and lynched after midnight on January 30. Antilynching activists were furious. As soon as she learned the news, the A.S.W.P.L.'s Jessie Daniel Ames sternly reminded

Governor Sholtz that he needed no antilynching legislation, that he had, he said, all the legal powers necessary to take action against lynchers. In a telegram she wrote: "Last Thursday you assured a committee headed by Mrs. William Cornell, Chairman of the Florida Council of A.S.W.P.L., that while you are governor of Florida there would be no lynchings" (quoted in Howard 1995, 54). The N.A.A.C.P. also responded quickly; Walter White asked Governor Sholtz to use the Tampa lynching to justify his support of the Costigan-Wagner antilynching bill in Congress. Unsurprisingly, the governor refused, writing to White that: "I am unalterably opposed to lynching and shall use the full powers of my office at all times to bring about the proper punishment of those guilty of this unlawful practice" (quoted in Howard 1995, 55). Sholtz had, presumably, already committed to the agenda of the A.S.W.P.L., which favored antilynching legislation at the state level, not federal (Howard 1995).

We have already read (in chapter 1) of the nightmare that Claude Neal suffered in Marianna in 1934. When Walter White, Will Alexander of the Commission on Interracial Cooperation, and Jane Cornell of the Florida A.S.W.P.L. learned of the impending lynching, they wired Governor Sholtz, demanding that he intervene in the crisis in Jackson County. Sholtz responded by asking Jackson County Sheriff Chambliss if he wanted National Guard units sent to the Marianna area. The sheriff declined the governor's offer for outside help, no surprise given that in all likelihood the sheriff and his staff were in on the lynching. Despite the fact that several hundred cars reached the Cannidy home that night, no deputies were observed anywhere. Chambliss later explained this fact by offering: "I tried to surround Jackson County with deputies, but we never did see the mob" (quoted in Howard 1995, 60). Recall that Neal's body was then dragged by car into Marianna from the Cannidy farm; on the morning of October 27 the mutilated corpse was hung, nude, in the courthouse square. Live-wire photographers were on the scene early to take shots of the remains. The evidently busy Sheriff Chambliss "discovered" Neal's body about 6:00 A.M. on Saturday, when he removed it from public view (Howard 1995, 61).

The vicious flogging "lynching" of Joseph Shoemaker stands apart from other mob actions in the 1930s. First of all, Shoemaker and his two leftist associates—Eugene Poulnot and Sam Rogers, who were also flogged—were white; they were attacked for political reasons. They had come to the attention of the "power elite" as a result of their involvement in Tampa politics in 1935. Tampa policemen and Klansmen responded to their exercise of democracy by assaulting them. Shoemaker, Poulnot, and Rogers and three others were holding a political meeting on November 30, 1935, at 307 East Palm Avenue, a private home. At approximately 9:00 P.M., seven policemen suddenly entered the house without warrants and abruptly broke up the meeting. With guns drawn, three officers came in the front door and four through the back door, where they proceeded to grab papers, and frisk the shocked citizens, who discovered that they were now under arrest. The detained men were taken to police headquarters, where authorities grilled them for hours about their "subversive" activities. When the interrogations concluded, the men were released one at a time, and three of them—Shoemaker, Poulnot, and Rogers—were kidnapped right in front of the police station (Howard 1995).

The three political activists were taken by their white male abductors to a secluded area in the woods approximately ten miles to the east of Tampa. There the kidnappers stripped the three men (why must the clothes always come off when men assault other men?) and began to beat them mercilessly. After Rogers was naked, he was placed over a log, and his hands and feet were held while he was worked over; boiling hot tar was then poured over his abdomen, genitals, and thighs. Poulnot was flogged with a chain and rawhide then tarred and feathered. Shoemaker was beaten to the point of mutilation. Finally, these white male defenders of democracy told the assaulted men: "Get out of town in twenty-four hours or we'll kill you" (quoted in Howard 1995, 82). Somehow Poulnot and Rogers managed to find their way back to town, but the critically injured Shoemaker fell unconscious into a ditch somewhere east of Tampa; there he lay for about seven hours during a chilly night. Worried friends found him the next morning and immediately took him to a local hospital. The attending physician commented on the extent of his injuries: "He was horribly mutilated. I wouldn't beat a hog the way he was whipped. ... He was beaten until he is paralyzed on one side, from blows to the head. ... I doubt if three square feet would cover the total area of bloodshot bruises on his body, not counting the parts injured only by tar" (quoted in Howard 1995, 82). Every effort to save Shoemaker's life failed; he died on December 9 (Howard 1995).

The subsequent investigation concluded that "the entire affair was a well-planned lynching" (Howard 1995, 85). Evidence suggested Ku Klux Klan involvement. Based partly on the Shoemaker lynching, Robert Ingall (1988/1993) argued that class may be a more important factor than race in some vigilante crimes and lynchings. In the Shoemaker incident, a number of Tampa's elite provided crucial support for the accused floggers. For instance, Pat Whitaker, the mayor's brother-in-law, headed up the defense team and several prominent local businessmen posted bail for the defendants, an amount that totaled about $100,000, no small sum in the Depression-era South.

Florida led the nation in lynchings in 1937; this brought considerable if unwanted attention. There was a double lynching in Tallahassee, but even that horror failed to convince Senator Claude Pepper and Governor Fred Cone to support antilynching legislation. In fact, Claude Pepper (who would become known much later as a liberal advocate for the elderly) was quite effective in his opposition to the antilynching cause, figuring prominently in southern efforts to defeat antilynching legislation that came before Congress in 1937 and 1938. The *Christian Century* suggested that the "most ominous item" about the Florida lynchings was that "there was no single arrest, indictment, or conviction" (quoted in Howard 1995, 112). A new governor (Cone) found himself now under considerable pressure, forcing "Old Suwannee," as he was nicknamed, to scramble to keep an increasing number of critics at bay. They correctly perceived that Cone's handling of Florida lynchings was obviously informed "by bigotry and intolerance" (Howard 1995, 113).

The governor's racism surfaced on occasions other than lynching events. At a cabinet meeting early in his administration, he and Florida's secretary of state, Robert A. Gray, argued over the salary of the president of Florida Agricultural and Mechanical College for blacks. At one point Cone thundered: "There's no

Negro on earth worth a thousand dollars a year salary." Gray snapped back: "What is Joe Louis worth?" To which the governor sorted "not a damn, at least by the time he gets tied up with three more Schmelings, he won't be worth a damn." Then Gray informed the chief executive of the Sunshine State that Thomas Edison had once offered a black man fifty thousand dollars a year. Cone was undeterred: "Well, but Mr. Edison also said that there is no God, but just a sort of spiritual something, and a man like that might make that kind of offer" (quoted in Howard 1995, 113). But it was the governor's response to the Shoemaker lynching that generated the most publicity. In a statement that would make national news, Cone declared: "I think a man ought to be hung on a tree if he advocates overthrow of the government" (quoted in Howard 1995, 114).

Many white male Floridians may have applauded the governor's perverted patriotism, but outside the South it made him a pariah. Evidently Cone was oblivious or simply didn't care, but he was shocked when in New York City to visit Florida's exhibit at the World's Fair in 1939, he and the entire Florida delegation were snubbed by Mayor Fiorello La Guardia. The Shoemaker lynching and Cone's apparent defense of it was for most New Yorkers shocking and completely unacceptable. Black spokesmen all over the country were outraged that a governor had actually sanctioned a lynching. Walter White complained that this "was the first time that a governor, even of a southern state, within the last ten or fifteen years, had openly condoned lynching." He added that "Governor Cone has advocated hanging by mobs. In recent years, no governor has made a statement so bold and vicious." The headlines of the *Chicago Defender* on October 30 shouted FLORIDA GOVERNOR APPROVES LYNCHING, and the *Baltimore Afro-American* lamented that "Governor Fred Cone has put his approval upon lynching" (quoted in Howard 1995, 115–116).

During the thirties three different governors failed to stop lynching in Florida. Doyle Carlton (1928–32), David Sholtz (1932–36), and Fred Cone (1936–40) responded in similar ineffectual ways. First, they expressed indignation, followed by an order directed to the "proper authorities" to "thoroughly investigate" the crime in order to bring the guilty parties to justice. But in almost every instance, each governor let the matter die locally when the grand jury or state attorney failed, as they invariably did, to indict any suspects. Despite national outrage and some intrastate pressure, Florida enacted no antilynching statutes. No governor ever took disciplinary action against any law officer who might have behaved inappropriately when a mob of whites came for his black male prisoner (Howard 1995).

Finally, slowly, lynchings did decrease in Florida. Foremost among the reasons, Howard (1995) argues, was the antilynching actions of African Americans themselves. In those rural areas where lynchings were most likely to occur, black residents relied on the time-tested technique of miming and manipulation, pretending to be genial and ingratiating to whites in order to protect themselves and their families. But Florida's urban black citizens began to strike a more militant pose. Many protested lynchings loudly, demanding the arrest, conviction, and punishment of the white men involved. N.A.A.C.P. branches in such places as St. Petersburg, Pensacola, Miami, Jacksonville,

Tampa, and Key West began to join the national office in New York in sustained antilynching protests. Black ministerial alliances in Tampa and Jacksonville denounced lynching directly to local authorities as well as to the governor's office. Additionally, eminent black Floridians such as Mary McCleod Bethune, well-known educator and New Deal official, and J. R. E. Lee, president of the Florida Agricultural and Mechanical College, also expressed their condemnation of lynching. Florida's high lynching rate during the 1930s probably resulted in some migration to the North. Just as an earlier antilynching migration from the South had damaged local economies, this exodus from the Sunshine State also may have inhibited the white male desire to lynch (Howard 1995).

The last recorded lynchings in the United States occurred not in Florida but in Poplarville, Mississippi—"darkest Mississippi" James Weldon Johnson (1933) of the N.A.A.C.P. once called it (310). In 1959, one Mack Charles Parker was accused of raping a young white woman. As was the case in nearly every lynching, the question of Parker's guilt or innocence was never resolved. He never confessed; there were no eyewitnesses other than the alleged rape victim and her daughter. As in most cases of alleged interracial rape, there were two stories: a white one and a black one (Smead 1986). Writing in the late 1920s in the heat of the struggle against lynching, Walter White (1929) understood exactly what was at stake:

> Expectant mothers, children, hopelessly insane, mental defectives, innocent or guilty—American mobs of recent years have drawn the line neither in the choice of their victims nor in the sadism of their deeds of death. One can easily comprehend the truth and depth of James Weldon Johnson's observation to the effect that "lynching in the United States has resolved itself into a problem of saving black America's body and white America's soul." (33)

To us, distracted by all the hype regarding the internet and the new millennium, lynching seems unreal, without relevance to us, to our situation, traveling at warp speed into the twenty-first century. But when we dwell on why lynching occurred, its safe containment in the past begins to fade. The sexual structure of racism contains us still.

3 "AMERICA'S NATIONAL CRIME"

—Ida Wells-Barnett, "Lynching and the Excuse for It" (1901/1977)

I. Origins

It has been said that our country's national crime is lynching. We may be reluctant to admit our peculiarity in this respect and it may seem unpatriotic to do so, but the fact remains that lynching is a criminal practice which is peculiar to the United States.

—James Elbert Cutler, *Lynch Law: An Investigation in the History of Lynching in the United States* (1905)

[B]lackmen did not provoke lynching by raping white women.

—Jacquelyn Dowd Hall, *Revolt Against Chivalry: Jessie Daniel Ames and the Women's Campaign against Lynching* (1979)

Of all the emotional determinants of lynching none is more potent in blocking approach to a solution than sex, and of all the factors, emotional or otherwise, none is less openly and honestly discussed.

—Walter White, *Rope and Faggot: A Biography of Judge Lynch* (1929)

For well over a century in the United States, white men lynched black men. There were exceptions, of course. Among the small number of white persons lynched were several foreigners, such as occurred in New Orleans in late winter 1891, "the worst single incident of white-on-white mob violence" (Beck and Tolnay 1997, 144). Eric Sundquist terms this lynching "the climax of ... anti-Italian feeling" (1993, 261). When a jury failed to convict a group of Italians on trial in 1891 for the murder of a New Orleans police superintendent, allegedly a contract "hit" in response to his effort to bring Mafia members to justice, a rioting mob of several thousand attacked the prison, taking eleven of the suspects. The case created a national controversy; the prosecution complained that it was impossible to get convictions against the Mafia due to their strict code of honor, while politicians and periodicals were quick to defend or attack the mob's murder of the "assassins" and the southern climate of lawlessness and traditions of "bloody duels" that northerners complained had made the lynchings possible (Sundquist 1993; Cutler 1905).

The event ignited a diplomatic crisis when Secretary of State James Blaine declined to grant redress to the families of the victims—some of whom were Italian citizens—or guarantee the indictment of mob members. During this "an exceedingly tense situation" (as Walter White [1929, 198] would describe it) diplomatic exchanges between the two nations ceased. Foreign newspapers and periodicals united in attacking the decision. Outraged Europeans demanded that an indemnity be paid and that the lynchers be brought to justice (Sundquist 1993; Cutler 1905). Finally, President Benjamin Harrison did pay damages of $24,330.90. So severe was the criticism of Louisiana from all around the globe that in 1894 the Louisiana legislature was petitioned in strong language by prominent citizens of the state to pass a law against lynching (Cutler 1905). Nothing was done by the legislature, but the petition was, as White (1929) would point out, significant as one of the first instances where lynching was recognized as a crime that required special legislation to discourage.

White mobs could be vicious with white victims, although no evidence suggests they engaged in sexual mutilation, a practice they evidently reserved for young black men. A case in point concerns George Corvett, a white resident of Crittenden County, Arkansas. Ada Goss of Crawfordsville had been raped and murdered; Corvett was accused of committing the crime. After being interrogated by a mob, Corvett's wife confessed that indeed her husband was guilty. On February 13, 1890, the mob seized George Corvett, took him to the scene of the murder, amputated his arms and legs with a barnyard ax, then decapitated him (Beck and Tolnay 1997).

But that situation was unusual. As noted, in most lynchings the victim was a black man and the lynchers were white men (Raper 1933/1969; Brundage 1993, 1997b). On rare occasions white men were lynched, as were black women. Witnesses reported—and from the event Walter White described (chapter 1, section IV) we can understand—that they never forgot these cross-gender lynchings. The sight of white men hanging a pregnant black woman from a nearby tree, cutting out her fetus, then ripping it apart as the young mother slowly twisted in the evening breeze: such a sight could not easily be excised from memory. Much more common was a mob celebrating the lynching of an alleged black male rapist or murderer (recall that these were the two most common rationales), often mutilating his body, sometimes saving the toes, fingers, and other appendages—such as his penis—as souvenirs. On one occasion a gramophone record was said to have been made of the victim's screams (Ware 1992).

Often the black male victims were not even accused of a crime but, as we have seen, lynched for writing an "improper note" to a white woman, inadvertently bumping into a white woman on the sidewalk, for greeting a white woman inappropriately (Smead 1986; Ginzburg 1962/1988; Brundage 1993). Walter White (1929) likened lynching to addiction: "As the user of the drugs demands increasing quantities of the opiate upon which he relies for excitation, so does the lyncher demand savagery—always the story of physical cruelty is its effect upon those who practice it" (20). The founding president of the National Association of Colored Women, Mary Church Terrell (1904), described lynching "as the aftermath of slavery. ... It is impossible," she wrote, "to comprehend the cause of the ferocity and barbarity which attend the average lynching-bee without taking into account the brutalizing effect of slavery upon the white people of the South" (852). W. E. B. Du Bois (1927) called lynching America's "exciting form of sport" (quoted in Hutchinson 1997, 28). So commonplace were lynchings that Mark Twain sarcastically renamed the country the "United States of Lyncherdom" (quoted in Brundage 1993, 1).

As we have seen, the lynching crowd was comprised mostly of white men. Most were eighteen to twenty-five, although older men often led the group or made suggestions (Raper 1933/1969). White women and children tended to be spectators. While white women were usually bystanders only, on occasion they incited hesitant males to violence, "to do their manly duty" (quoted in Senechal de la Roche 1997, 51). White women were sometimes even present at the forefront of active violence, joining men on attacks on jails to seize alleged offenders, helping to resist authorities sent to suppress crowd violence and, on rare occasion, even inflicting punishment on a suspect, although there is no recorded case of a woman's participation in sexual mutilation. On occasion, even black residents watched as a black man was lynched (Senechal de la Roche 1997).

There were rare occasions when black mobs took matters into their own hands, possibly, Beck and Tolnay (1997) suggest, because they had little confidence in the white-dominated justice system to act appropriately. After all, black victims summoned little white indignation. If this "popular justice" interpretation of black-on-black mob violence is accurate, then a possible reason for black intraracial lynchings is that black-on-black crime then, as now, was a problem African Americans themselves mobilized to punish.

At times, Beck and Tolnay (1997) report, black mobs subjected their victims to considerable suffering, they suggest, in order to send a message to others that such conduct was completely unacceptable. Several lynch victims were burned alive, others after they had been killed by other means. In contrast to white-on-black violence, rarely were victims tortured. Anderson Moreland, lynched in Monroe Country, Georgia, on June 8, 1892, was an exception that proved the rule. Accused of raping a black girl, "he was stripped of his clothes and beaten into insensibility and dropped into a hot tub of salt water" (quoted in Beck and Tolnay 1997, 143–144).

While African Americans rarely felt so, European Americans often felt it their rightful place to assume the roles of both judge and executioner, endowed with the authority to determine life and death. We are good Christian people, as perhaps they assured themselves as they became among the most savage creatures imaginable. White people—especially white men—attempted to disguise their savagery by protestations of righteousness. We were, they insisted, overwhelmed by indignation, shocked by crimes against our pure and endangered white womanhood, our great and civilized "race." During the pursuit and capture of young black men, the feeling among them shifted from serious to festive. Sometimes there was singing. After capture, at the event itself, observers sometimes dressed in their Sunday church clothes; food was brought (Harris 1984). It is easy to imagine these lynchings as Satanic celebrations conducted by good "Christian" white people, southerners mostly, Americans they imagined.

Genesis

The practice, some say, originated in fifteenth- and sixteenth-century England and Ireland. According to one account reported by James Cutler (1905), lynch law owed its name to James Fitzstephen Lynch, mayor and warden of Galway, Ireland. In the council books of Galway there is a report that "James Lynch, mayor of Galway, hanged his own son out of the window for defrauding and killing strangers, without martial or common law, to show a good example to posterity" (quoted in Cutler 1905, 15). This "Galway story" of lynching's origins Cutler dismisses "with but little consideration" (1905, 15). Mayor Lynch was the legally constituted authority and as such resided over the tribunal in which his son had, evidently, a fair trial. By executing his son, Mayor Lynch was merely enforcing the laws of the land, Cutler points out. Lynching, American-style, operated without, even in opposition to, established law.

Etymologically, the word *lynch* has been traced to an old Anglo-Saxon verb *linch*, meaning to "beat severely with a pliable instrument, to chastise or to maltreat" (Cutler 1905, 6), a meaning some say survived into nineteenth-century America. Cutler is unpersuaded; he cannot find any evidence that such a verb "survived" in the United States. Moreover, he reports he was unable to unearth any evidence that such an Anglo-Saxon verb ever existed. He points out that the *Wright's English Dialect Dictionary* (1902) does not contain the word lynch; the *Murray's Oxford Dictionary* (1903) states that the term was original to the United States. In Cutler's (1905) view, mythology aside, the origin of "lynch law" is not to be found in England either.

The first instance of the operation of lynch law in America was, some have suggested, in December 1763 at Paxtang (now Harrisburg), Pennsylvania. Native Americans had been fighting the European settlers, whose appeals to the Quaker government for help had been treated, they judged, unsatisfactorily. Exasperated at the policy of peaceful coexistence pursued by the Quakers toward the Indians, the Scotch-Irish who had settled in Lancaster and Cumberland counties formed several companies of "Rangers" to patrol the borders and provide protection. In a retaliatory mood, on December 27, fifty of these Rangers, under the leadership of Lazarus Stewart, marched to Lancaster, broke open the jail, and with the full fury of a mob massacred every Native American held there, including women and children (Cutler 1905).

Such use of "summary measures" against Native Americans does not, Cutler (1995) insists, mark the beginning of the practice of lynch law in America. In its first expressions, Lynch's law corresponded more closely to what was known as "regulating," a practice which was adopted in frontier areas not served by institutional structures of justice, and on occasion in older, more stable communities well. Cutler (1905) comments: "The Regulation movement in the Carolinas, though stimulated by political dissension, had its origin in frontier conditions" (90). Those who have associated "regulating" with lynch law have suggested it may have derived its name from Lynch's Creek in South Carolina, but Cutler rules out this possibility due to lack of evidence. As an instance of "regulating," Cutler (1905) cites an item reported in the *New York Gazette* for December 18, 1752:

> We hear from *Elizabeth-Town,* that an odd Sect of People have appeared there, who go under the Denomination of *Regulars*: there are near a Dozen of them, who dress themselves in Women's Cloaths, and painting their Faces, go in the Evening to the Houses of such as are reported to have beat their Wives: where one of them entering in first, seizes the Delinquent, whilst the rest follow, strip him, turn up his Posteriors and flog him with Rods most severely, crying out all the Time, *Wo to the Men that beat their Wives.* (quoted in Cutler 1905, 46)

While not lynch law, this early instance of an all-male performance of "justice" does anticipate certain features of late nineteenth-century lynching, namely the employment of "woman"—or at least men's fictionalization of same—to rationalize a homoerotic assault on another man. Note that the offender was stripped, and his ass flogged, by cross-dressed men. Stripping the victim was also a feature in another pre–Revolutionary War instance of "regulating." On the evening of May 18, 1769, in Providence, Rhode Island, Jesse Saville, "a Tidesman belonging to the Custom-House" who was accused of "informing," was seized by local men, stripped naked, covered from head to foot with turpentine and feathers and severely beaten (quoted in Cutler 1905, 63).

The explanation for the origin of the term which Cutler (1905) finds most compelling is also the explanation "most frequently given and which was for years accepted without question" (23). Namely, lynch law originates in the kind of law administered during the latter part of the Revolutionary War by Charles Lynch of Bedford County, Virginia, near what is now Lynchburg, famous for Jack Daniels whiskey (Ware 1992; Cutler 1905). Cutler cites an article (written by someone named "Claverhouse") in the *New York Evening Post* for June 2, 1864: "In America, the term 'Lynch law' was first used in Piedmont, on the western frontier of Virginia. There was no court within the district, and all controversies were referred to the arbitrament of prominent citizens. Among these was a man by the name of Lynch, whose decisions were so impartial that he was known as Judge Lynch, and the system was called 'Lynch law,' and adopted in our pioneer settlements as an inexpensive and speedy method of obtaining justice" (quoted in Cutler 1905, 24, n. 1). Historians seem to agree that the practice of organizing mobs to punish alleged wrongdoers became established during the colonial period (Brundage 1993).

Charles Lynch was born in 1736, at Chestnut Hill, Virginia, his father's estate. His father came to Virginia from Ireland around 1725, where he married the daughter of a planter. Taking over a large tract of land lying between the James and the Staunton rivers, he became a successful tobacco planter. At his death the property on the James was inherited by his eldest son, John. Charles inherited those sections nearer the frontier. Charles' mother, Sarah Lynch, had joined the Quakers in 1750; in the records of this congregation is found the following: "14 of Dec., 1754. Charles Lynch and Anne Terrill published for the first Time their Intentions of marriage" (quoted in Cutler 1905, 25, n. 4). The young couple established their home on the Staunton, in what is now the southwestern part of Campbell County (Cutler 1905).

Charles followed his mother's teachings and became an active member of the Society of Friends; for a time he served as "Clerk of the monthly meetings." Later, however, he decided to ignore the Quaker prohibitions against accepting public office. For that in 1767 he was judged "unsatisfactory" and "disowned for taking solemn oaths, contrary to the order and discipline of Friends" (Cutler 1905, 25, n. 4). In that same year, 1767, he had been elected to the Virginia House of Burgesses, where he held a seat until the War. He was prominent in the earliest organization of Bedford County, formed from Lunenburg County in 1753; he served as a member of the Virginia convention of 1776, which, by sending "Instructions" to the Virginia delegates to the Continental Congress, influenced the movement for independence. Lynch was made a justice of the peace under a commission from Governor Dunmore in 1774, and when the county court was reorganized, according to the ordinance of the convention, passed on July, 3, 1776, he retained the position (Cutler 1905).

At the beginning of the Revolutionary War Lynch's Quaker principles persuaded him to decline active military service. His loyalty to the nation was never doubted, however: "He did not enlist in the army, partly because of his Quaker principles, but chiefly because his presence was imperatively necessary at home. He had to rouse the spirit of his constituents to support the action he had advocated in the convention. He had to raise and equip troops for the army. He had, as it were, to mobilize the forces of his country, and attend to all the duties of a commissary department. In addition, he had to make some provision in the event of an attack from hostile Indians" (church records quoted in Cutler 1905, 25, n. 4). In 1778 the court of Bedford recommended him to the governor for the office of Colonel of Militia for that county. He accepted the commission and organized a regiment, but he did not go to the front until two years later, when the war had shifted to the South and Cornwallis was sent to cooperate with General Philips and Benedict Arnold in the invasion of Virginia (Cutler 1905).

From examination of the records of the court of Bedford County, the minutes of various Quaker meetings, the journals of the Virginia House of Burgesses and of the first Constitutional Convention, as well as family documents, Cutler concludes that Charles Lynch was "a thoroughly and highly respected man, a leader among the men in his community" (25–26, n. 4). At the battle of Guilford Court House, March 15, 1781, he distinguished himself for acts of courage in leading a battalion of riflemen "with much gallantry and ... bringing considerable credit to the Virginia militia" (Cutler, 1905, 26, n. 4). After the War, he voted for the new constitution. Cutler tells us that in the family burial ground on his homestead plantation a tombstone bears the inscription: "In memory of Colonel Charles Lynch, a zealous and active patriot. Died, October 29, 1796, aged 60 years" (Cutler 1905, 26, n. 4). At the time of Cutler's research—the first years of the twentieth century—there were, he reports, many stories still in circulation among the old inhabitants of his environs, all testifying to his character. His name appears in the chorus of a once popular patriotic song:

Hurrah for Colonel Lynch,
Captain Bob and Callaway!
They never turned a Tory loose
Until he shouted "Liberty!"

A slightly different version of the refrain went this way:

Hurrah for Captain Bob,
Colonels Lynch and Callaway!
Who never let a Tory off
Until he cried out "Liberty!"
(Cutler 1905, 26, n. 4)

Strange that the name of such a honorable man would become associated with such a profoundly dishonorable practice.

Enough about Lynch himself; what do we know about the actual practice that became known as "lynching"? Even during the years before the Revolutionary War, there existed, evidently, a state of semiwar between the colonists and the Tories. The conflict was especially heated in that section of Virginia where Lynch lived. Moreover, all colonists were harassed by those who took advantage of the situation to steal horses and other property. The nearest court was two hundred miles away, and was accessible only by frequently impassable and always dangerous roads. In these conditions, then, Lynch and his colonist neighbors decided to create an extralegal court of which Lynch would serve as chief magistrate (Downey and Hyser 1991).

Those accused of a crime—perhaps a Tory soldier or a colonist horse thief—would, after capture, face Lynch and two of his neighbors. The accused was faced by his accusers, permitted to give testimony on his behalf, and even allowed to summon witnesses. In general, then, his rights as a citizen of England were respected. If acquitted, he was set free, with apologies and often with reparation. If found guilty, he was given "thirty-nine lashes on the bare back, and if he did not then shout 'Liberty Forever!'" he was strung up by his thumbs until he did so. During the Revolutionary War the practice of tarring and feathering appeared (Cutler 1905). Only rarely was an accused person sentenced to death (White 1929). Cutler suggests that even after the War—he points to the period 1792–1819—instances of lynch law were "very rare" (1905, 76).

During the Revolutionary War, there were excesses. With the help of a vigilante group he had organized, Lynch hanged a number of Tories captured in the area. Among the officials critical of Lynch at the time was wartime governor Thomas Jefferson (Downey and Hyser 1991). After the War, the Virginia legislature exonerated Lynch for his actions on the grounds that circumstances had been present in which "measures taken ... may not be strictly warranted by law, although justifiable from the imminence of the danger" (quoted in Hall 1979, 130).

James Cutler (1905), among others, has written of the practice's westward migration from Virginia and the neighboring states toward the ever-shifting frontier. Throughout the nineteenth century, frontier elites routinely banded together to form vigilante groups, imposing social order in areas where the population was sparse, officials were few, and the legal machinery primitive: "The weakness and inadequacy of the civil regulations, and the presence of such criminals as the horse-thief, the counterfeiter, the robber, and the desperado, who find the frontier both a retreat from the consequences of past crime and a new theater for the perpetration of crime, gave a constant justification for recourse to lynch-law" (Cutler 1905, 81). Such "establishment violence" (Hall 1979, 131; Hufsmith 1993) became an accepted aspect of American political life.

Curiously, frontier communities were also sites where nineteenth-century men expressed sexual desire for each other, if only because these locations (mining camps, ranches, the prairie) were often inhabited only by men and thereby supported the expression of what has sometimes been termed "situational homosexuality," although we will see from prison research that even the presence of sexually available women does not necessarily depress homosexual desire among men. For example, the writer Charles Warren Stoddard (who clearly preferred the sexual company of men) was drawn toward the bohemian artistic circles of San Francisco in the 1860s, where he met Mark Twain, among others. Interestingly, Twain later employed Stoddard as his secretary in London during a time when Stoddard was actively exploring that city's homosexual subculture. Twain was by no means oblivious, once describing Stoddard as "such a nice girl" (Austen 1991, 39, 65–68; quoted in Looby 1995, 545). In fact, recently Twain scholars have suggested that Twain's relationship with his intimate male friends may well have been sexual (McMillen 1993; Looby 1995). Relying upon Leslie Fiedler (1948/1995; 1966), we will examine Twain's portrait of nineteenth-century interracial male-male relations in chapter 18.

With the exception of the practices specific to the Revolutionary War period, the lynch law that was practiced prior to 1830 occurred primarily on the frontier. Even during the Revolutionary period, Cutler (1905) points out, when war and political instability intensified social disruption sufficiently that lynch law was practiced even in well-settled communities, many of these events might still be characterized as "the frontier type" (90). In remote areas of the colonies a judicial infrastructure had not yet been built, so that to insure the punishment of public offenders recourse "to summary and extralegal methods" was necessary (90). Such "rough-and-ready methods of administering justice" (90) were practiced by many pioneers who moved westward over the Alleghenies into the Mississippi valley. "Before about the year 1830," Cutler summarizes, "lynch law was confined almost entirely to the border settlements, and was generally excused and justified on the ground of necessity. It was not regarded as a serious menace to law and order" (1905, 90–91). In these settings and during these years lynch law was adopted "as a temporary expedient" (91), to be discontinued when the civil government and judiciary structures were established.

After 1830 there was a change in the practice. Antislavery agitation stimulated proslavery apologists to use lynch law, and the practice spread throughout the South. Not only did lynch law continue to be exercised occasionally in the border settlements, but it was revived in well-established communities in order to suppress abolitionism. The early 1830s—especially the years of Jackson's presidency, 1829–1837—saw "an unusual amount of turbulence and violence" (Cutler 1905, 106). The expression "Lynch's law" first appeared in the abolitionist *Liberator* in the issue of September 27, 1834, in an excerpt reprinted from the *Lancaster* (Pa.) *Journal*: "In our quiet village of New Holland, we understand Lynch's law was carried into execution last week, against a stranger who had given some offence to the inhabitants. The man was taken from his domicile, tarred and feathered in the true Yankee style, marched out of town and let run. We have not heard the cause of this summary proceeding" (quoted in Cutler 1905, 97).

As midcentury approached, mob violence became a national phenomenon. In the North, where public disorder often characterized daily urban life, mobs threatened, and in several instances murdered, abolitionists, Mormons, Catholics, immigrants, and African Americans. With the discovery of gold in California, vigilante justice was practiced in mining camps and boomtowns, reaching its zenith in the San Francisco vigilance committees of the 1850s. Frontier lynchings rarely led to the victim's death, although the hanging of a horse thief—the honored guest at a so-called necktie party—was not unknown. In the years 1830–1860, there were occasional episodes of abolitionists and slaves being executed by mobs, as antislavery agitators provoked the rage of defenders of the "peculiar institution" and because slaves and freed blacks were easy targets for southern whites when fears of slave insurrections periodically swept through the region (Brundage 1993; Downey and Hyser 1991; Cutler 1905).

The frequency of lynching events during the antebellum period is indicated in a January 1837 speech Abraham Lincoln made to the Young Men's Lyceum of Springfield, Illinois. Entitled "The Perpetuation of our Political Institutions," Lincoln characterized the times in which he and his listeners lived in the following terms:

> Accounts of outrages committed by mobs form the everyday news of the times. They have pervaded the country from New England to Louisiana; they are neither peculiar to the eternal snows of the former nor the burning sun of the latter; they are not the creatures of climate, neither are they confined to the slaveholding or the non-slave-holding states. Alike they spring up among the pleasure-hunting masters of southern slaves, and the order-loving citizens of the land of steady habits. Whatever then their cause may be, it is common to the whole country. (quoted in Cutler 1905, 111)

Lincoln's statement, Cutler asserts, reflects well the state of affairs at this time. The turbulence of the period, he argues, more than any particular cause, stimulated the practice of lynch law.

Not until after the Civil War did the verb lynch denote the practice of putting to death. However, it is clear that by the end of the Jacksonian period death sometimes accompanied the earlier preference for tar and feathering. To illustrate, Cutler (1905) quotes Philip Hone's diary entry for August 2, 1835: "A terrible system prevails in some of the Southern and Western States, which consists in ... beating, tarring, and feathering, and in some cases hanging the unhappy object of their vengeance, and this is generally called 'Lynch's Law'" (quoted on 117–118). As the War approached, death occurred more frequently.

Whatever its outcome, it is clear that a sexual interest animated the practice of lynching all along, suggested by the ritualistic stripping of the victim. For instance, *The Liberator* for May 2, 1856, prints the following paragraph taken from the *Western Herald*: "Lynch Law in Virginia.—A man named William Hornbeck, living in Lewis County, Virginia, for the alleged ill-treatment of his family, was lynched by the young men in the neighborhood, one night last week.—Stripped of his clothing, rode on a rail, made to run through a briar patch, a stout paddle used to keep him going, and a coat of tar and feathers applied" (quoted in Cutler 1905, 119–120). *The Liberator* for December 4, 1857, reports the fate of an abolitionist lynched in Mississippi: "[A] crowd took him to the woods, told him to strip, carried to a hollow and tied around a tree. He was told what was their intention: to lynch him until he told something. The lashing was commenced by two who used straps fastened to sticks about 10 in. long" (quoted in Cutler 1905, 120).

After the War lynching's victims were overwhelming African American, but from the following editorial, which appeared in the *Liberator,* December 19, 1856, it is clear that before the War many white antislavery activists were also victims: "A record of the cases of 'Lynch Law' in the southern states reveals the startling fact, that within twenty years, over three hundred white persons have been murdered upon the accusation—in most cases unsupported by legal proof—of carrying among slave-holders arguments addressed expressly to their own intellects and consciences, as to the morality and expediency of slavery" (quoted in Cutler 1905, 124). If this figure is accurate, Cutler speculates, then "it is within the truth to say that a considerably larger number of negroes met with summary capital punishment during the various insurrections and excitements which have occurred" (1905, 124).

The summary execution of African Americans did not, however, "become a serious evil previous to the Civil War" (Cutler 1905, 124), probably only due to the economic loss such events would have meant to slaveholders. Still, many enslaved people were murdered prior to the Civil War. It was not common, however, to describe the summary hanging of slaves as lynching. Cutler tells us that such occurrences were not common enough to give the word its modern meaning, even though the execution of slaves has often been designated as lynching. In summary, then, during the antebellum period lynching was not yet a racialized term. Rather, it referred to those acts of lawlessness and summary "justice" which took place primarily in the western and southwestern United

States during the 1850s. These "vigilance committees" were common in those areas at that time; they "often hung desperadoes and horse-thieves, and frequently when such persons were thus executed they were said to have been lynched" (Cutler 1905, 128).

While lynch law prevailed, then, primarily along the frontier, Cutler (1905) points specifically to "the border troubles" (134) accompanying the outbreak of the Civil War. He singles out Kansas as the site of a kind of guerilla warfare that went on "for a number of years," and where "many instances of summary procedure occurred that may be properly classified under lynch law" (Cutler 1905, 134). It was the use of the word lynching in reference to these "summary proceedings against white men of desperate character, the criminals of the frontier region west of the Mississippi, during the period of settlement, that first gave to it its modern meaning of putting to death" (135). It was after the Civil War, when the southern states were being "reconstructed" and whites fantasized being overwhelmed by the freedpeople, "summary practices" became directed toward African Americans. No longer valuable as property, Cutler notes, and regarded "as a dangerous political factor in the community," whites decided that "to take his [the black man's] life was ... the easiest and quickest way to dispose of him" (135). This continuation of the Civil War directed toward the freedpeople gave the term lynching its new meaning.

The formation in May 1866 of the Ku Klux Klan gave organizational form to this war (see chapter 9, section I). Cutler emphasizes that since Reconstruction "to lynch has generally meant to put to death" (1905, 136). But other commentators point to 1880, a slightly later date, to mark when "lynching" had fully taken on its contemporary meaning: "the execution of a criminal or an accused person, usually by hanging or burning, with the victim often suffering perverse torture and mutilation of body parts before succumbing to death" (Downey and Hyser 1991, 3). Whether lynching as we know it began with Reconstruction or after its dissolution, the "blood lust of lynch mobs" (Brundage 1993, 4) was no longer sated by older practices of punishment, such as tarring and feathering and whipping. The lust of postbellum mobs would require new practices, among them torture, sexual mutilation, and burning. Now that young black men were the objects of their disciplining, desiring gaze, many white men became, in fact, consumed by "blood" and "lust."

II. The South

[T]he attribution *to black males of sexual desires toward white women was unequivocal, widespread, and charged with much emotion in the South.*

—Charles Herbert Stember, *Sexual Racism: The Emotional Barrier to an Integrated Society* (1976)

The existence of variations within *the South is less significant than the fact that lynchings occurred* throughout *the South.*

—Adam Fairclough, "Introduction" to *The Star Creek Papers* (1997)

The South ... seemed to be moving against the current of the nineteenth century.

W. Fitzhugh Brundage, *Lynching in the New South: Georgia and Virginia, 1880–1930* (1993)

In the antebellum South, mob violence became explicitly associated with the defense of slavery. Organized vigilance committees continually scrutinized slave behavior, monitored inflammatory abolitionist literature, even unorthodox attitudes among fellow white southerners. When infractions of these extralegal expectations occurred, mobs silenced both real and imaginary abolitionists and savagely suppressed slave uprisings. The *Liberator* of October 1, 1831, reports that a man named Robinson was lashed on the bare back at Petersburg, Virginia, for saying that "black men have, in the abstract, a right to their freedom." After his lashing, Robinson was ordered to leave town and never to return lest he be treated "worser" (quoted in White 1929, 86). By the time of the firing upon Fort Sumter in 1861, the tradition of mob violence was clearly an integral part of southern culture (Brundage 1993).

In 1861, as we have seen, it was still fairly standard practice in the South and along the western frontier to punish crime without an official court hearing. Often the sentence was carried out by a self-constituted court. To be "severely lynched" through the early decades of the nineteenth century meant that an individual (ordinarily a man) might receive as many as one hundred lashes. He might have been whipped, then tarred and feathered. On occasion, a man would be lynched, then hanged. It was during the effort to suppress abolitionist sentiment that lynching took a specifically racial turn. As in Robinson's case, a white man might be whipped for claiming that slaves had a right to freedom, or for subscribing to the *Liberator* (Harris 1984). As young black men became targets, the practice became increasingly sadistic (Zangrando 1980).

African Americans in the South did not die only at the hands of white male mobs. As we learned from George Wright's (1990) research (see chapter 2, section V), they were also "legally" executed in considerable number during the "lynching era." Between 1882 and 1930, 1,977 African Americans were legally executed in ten southern states, according to Tolnay and Beck's count, an average of forty executions a year. During this same period, only 451 whites were legally executed. Clearly, there was an outrageous racial imbalance in southern executions; 81 percent of the legal executions involved a black offender, and 87 percent of the victims of white mobs were black. When combined, the two forms of execution claimed the lives of 4,291 African Americans during the forty-nine-year period. In other words, an African American was put to death somewhere in the South on the average of every four days (Tolnay and Beck 1995).

For Walter White and other important activists and students of lynching in the 1920s and 1930s, such as Arthur Raper, the motives for lynching were primarily, even exclusively, economic. When southern planters became certain that cotton production required large labor pools, Walter White (1929) reckoned, the lyncher functioned as a defender of the slave owners' profits. Many historians have tended to focus upon political and cultural factors, for instance, the code of southern honor, debating, for instance, whether it preceded the development of slavery or was an outgrowth of it. Brundage (1993) points out that this elaborate code of behavior required white men to respond to real or imaginary challenges to their honor by acting outside of the law, and this custom had become widely accepted by the antebellum period. It was also, as we saw in Dennis Downey and Richard Hyser's discussion of it in the context of the lynching of Zachariah Walker, a gendered code that persisted long after the Civil War, even in the North.

Before Emancipation, the lynching of slaves occurred only in exceptional circumstances, as the economic interests of slaveholders ran counter to mob violence. As Eugene Genovese (1976) observed, white planters were reluctant to allow their slaves to be executed summarily as lynching destroyed slave property, questioned the power of planters, and threatened to "open the way for initiatives by the white lower classes that might not remain with racial bounds" (33). Moreover, planters preferred the state to prosecute criminal slaves; many southern states compensated planters for executed slaves (Brundage 1993).

Then in 1860 a "great fear" swept the South. Two years later, in what may have been the largest mass lynching in American history, 171 persons (both black and white) in four counties of central Texas were illegally executed (Hall 1979; Clark 1992). During the War, the practice of lynching in the South began to take on its postwar character. As the conflict dragged on, lynching became intertwined with the violence of the War itself. Mob violence occurred in southern communities where whites feared slave insurrections. Slaves were executed in gruesome public spectacles as increasingly desperate southern whites tried to keep an increasingly restless slave community submissive and loyal. In the backcountry, where allegiances often were divided between the North and the South, partisans often executed their opponents, on occasions ritualistically in ways that resembled lynching (Brundage 1993).

Appomattox and the subsequent end of slavery set the stage for an unprecedented wave of extralegal violence. Many white southerners were embittered, many terrified. Now thoroughly racialized, lynching became common and widespread. The former Mississippi governor, James K. Vardaman, spoke for many southern whites when he declared: "If it is necessary every Negro in the state will be lynched; it will be done to maintain white supremacy" (quoted in Tolnay and Beck 1995, 25). Although individual members of the southern white community may have condemned lynching, there is no doubt that a majority of white southerners supported it throughout the late nineteenth and early twentieth centuries (Tolnay and Beck 1995).

By 1893, the lynching of African Americans in the South had become so taken for granted that Atticus G. Haygood, a prominent Methodist bishop, complained that the murder of African Americans "is not so extraordinary an occurrence to need explanation; it has become so common that it no longer surprises" (quoted in Brundage 1993, 8). With each succeeding decade, the proportionate number of lynchings that occurred in the South increased, rising from 82 percent of all lynchings in the nation during the 1880s to more than 95 percent during the 1920s. Although mob violence has occurred throughout the nation, and while its victims have included whites, Native Americans, Chicanos, and Asians, by the late nineteenth century lynching had become primarily a southern and racialized phenomenon (Brundage 1993).

Table 1. Black Victims of White Lynch Mobs by State, 1882–1930

Deep South		Border South	
Mississippi	462	Florida	212
Georgia	423	Tennessee	174
Louisiana	283	Arkansas	162
Alabama	262	Kentucky	118
South Carolina	143	North Carolina	75
Total	1573	Total	741

Source: Tolnay and Beck, *A Festival of Violence: An Analysis of Southern Lynchings, 1882–1930* (1995)

Black residents of Florida actually bore the highest "per capita hazard" of being victimized by mob violence (Tolnay and Beck 1995, 37). But over the longer period between 1882 and 1952, Mississippi suffered the highest rate of lynching as a proportion of population, with Louisiana second (Fairclough 1995/1999).

Many believe that peculiar mix of sexuality, religion, and politics—quite unlike the mix prevalent in the North—made possible the tragedy of lynching. In his classic study of the practice (dedicated to N.A.A.C.P. colleague James Weldon Johnson), Walter White reserved special invective for the South. He quoted Walter Hines Page who, in an address before the North Carolina Society of New York, declared: "The South, therefore, neither contributes to the Nation's political thought and influence nor receives stimulation from the Nation's thought and influence. Its real patriotism counts for nothing—it is smothered dumb under party systems that have become crimes against the character and the intelligence of the people" (quoted in White 1929, 168).

While the Confederacy was defeated militarily in the Civil War, the South was hardly persuaded by its defeat that its cause was unrighteous. Almost immediately after Appomattox there sprang up a series of legends of a largely fictitious antebellum South, legends "composed of courtly, goateed, mint-julep-imbibing gentlemen, of ravishingly beautiful and virginal women, of stately, porticoed mansions, and faithful, contented, singing 'darkies,' unspoiled by wicked abolitionist notions of any special merits of freedom over slavery" (White 1929, 94). The sound advice of leaders such as General Robert E. Lee had been to accept the verdict of Appomattox and set about rebuilding the South in accordance with the character of the American nation (i.e., the North). Instead, southerners preferred "the opiate of dreams of 'the lost cause' and the direct action of the Ku Klux Klan were adopted. ... For the vast majority of the whites of the late Confederacy—even of those who had owned no slaves—were united in a single cause—to reenslave the Negro as far as was humanly possible" (White 1929, 95).

There was no space for dissent. Speaking of the South after Reconstruction, Douglas Freeman, editor of the *Richmond News-Leader*, concluded: "Forced to think alike politically, many ceased to think at all" (quoted in White 1929, 98).

In *The Martyrdom of Man*, Winwood Reade summarized the South's rejection of cultural integration with the United States: "The history of the South within the Union is that of a people struggling for existence by means of political devices against the spirit of the nation and the spirit of the age" (quoted in White 1929, 14).

Half a century after the War the South remained as stubborn, as inward-looking, and black-obsessed as ever. A passionate defender of slavery and lynching, Winfield Collins (1913), in *The Truth About Lynching*, makes clear the fantasy world many southerners inhabited:

> The Negro, son of a wild and tropical race, content for thousands of years to roam the jungles of Africa, supplied by a bountiful nature with all his heart's desire, failing thus to develop any controlling trait of character, or mental stamina, and although civilizations rose and fell beside him, it meant nothing to him ... and even now in the midst of American civilization he is moved to action, mainly, by gusts of primitive emotion and passion. (quoted in White 1929, 89)

Passing over, Walter White observed, those "gusts of primitive emotion and passion" characteristic of the Ku Klux Klan and those white male mobs that tortured and mutilated human beings, White (1929) notes that Collins was speaking of the African American of his day, some three hundred years removed from "the jungles of Africa" (89). White wonders why the defenders of lynching never noticed the fact that for two hundred years, nearer by a century to Africa than when Collins wrote, Africans in America were not accused of sex crimes to any greater extent than any other of the population groupings of the United States. White men, especially southern white men, were lost inside their own heads, obsessed with the black man, what Frank Tannenbaum (1924) in *Darker Phases of the South* termed "the South's emotional fixation on the Negro" (quoted in White 1929, 16).

On occasion observers almost reached a queer conclusion when pondering white men's sexual mutilation of black male bodies. But evidently that conclusion was unimaginable; note in the following paragraph from the *Baltimore Afro-American* for March 16, 1935, that the queer character of lynching would seem to be acknowledged, but in the last sentence the writer flees for the concept "sublimation."

> LYNCHING TERMED A TYPE OF DIXIE SEX PERVERSION. New York, Mar. 15—The writer once saw a southern white man boastfully display a withered and dried-up right hand of a fourteen-year-old boy whom he had helped to lynch, and this gruesome souvenir was carried around in his pants pocket. In the case of Claude Neal, a mob of Florida sadists tortured him for twenty-four hours, ... castrating their victim, dismembering his genitalia and stuffing them into his mouth to compel him to eat his own flesh. There is no further need of a psychic research or a psychoanalysis to prove that Southern lynchings are caused by sex-urge sublimation. (quoted in Ginzburg 1962/1988, 225–226)

Where's the sublimation?

"Lynching is a peculiarly American tradition," observed Manning Marable (1983, 15). Peculiar indeed; perhaps "queer" is more precise. Lynching was American, if primarily southern. But as in the case of slavery, the North can enjoy little self-righteousness over the issue. There were lynchings in the North and, as we will see, northerners allowed southern politicians to block antilynching legislation for five decades. Despite the intervention of Eleanor Roosevelt, F.D.R. declined to throw his support behind measures which would have mandated federal punishment for lynchers and those who aided them. It would appear to be changed circumstances, cultural, political, and economic, that led to the decline, then the end, of lynching, not northern political and moral leadership. And, of course, the South remained imprisoned in its reactionary politics and racialized culture.

While hardly monolithic, the South has fairly consistently fought against whatever progressives—in whatever walk of American life—have proposed. In education, for instance, only one of the thirty schools in the Progressive Education Association's Eight-Year Study was southern, and that was a small private school in Fairhope, Alabama (on the east side of Mobile Bay), run by a Minnesotan named Marietta Johnson who had fled the harsh winters of her native state (see Pinar et al. 1995, 113). Today the South as a region—again, not monolithically and not only—leads the reactionary gender politics that keeps homosexuality suppressed in education and public life generally. We may not be surprised to learn that the region led the nation in lynching—it was, after all, the site of slavery and segregation—but many have forgotten it also led the fight against women's suffrage as well. Walter White quotes William H. Skaggs (1924) of Alabama who, in *The Southern Oligarchy,* linked gender and race, specifically misogyny and lynching:

> Eight of the states that refused to ratify the amendment for equal suffrage are among the eleven that make up the Solid South. Arkansas, Texas and Tennessee are the three states in the South that ratified the amendment. The eight Southern states which refused to ratify the suffrage amendment are those which have the highest criminal record and the highest percentage of illiteracy. ... "It is for the protection of our mothers, sisters, wives and daughters that we oppose this measure," said some of the political leaders of the South. (quoted in White 1929, 161)

This fantasized identification with women was accomplished by pretending to protect them. It suggests a latent homoerotic dynamic that was expressed, in mangled homicidal fashion, in lynching. It was, as we will see in chapters 7 and 8, women—in particular one black woman—who saw through then led the struggle against this white boys' game.

In general, of course, lynching was a *southern* white boys' game. Still, northern white men were taken in, partly due to racism, partly due to homosocial bonding across region, and partly because southerners have always been rather skillful in manipulating Yankee attitudes, especially when African Americans have been concerned. No one has understood this last point any better than black educator and activist Anna Julia Cooper. Over one hundred years ago Cooper (1892/1998) wrote:

> One of the most singular facts about the unwritten history of this country is the consummate ability with which southern influence, southern ideas and southern ideals, have from the very beginning even up to the present day, dictated to and domineered over the brain and sinew of this nation. Without wealth, without education, without inventions, arts, sciences, or industries, without well-nigh every one of the progressive ideas and impulses which have made this country great, prosperous and happy, personally indolent and practically stupid, poor in everything but bluster and self-esteem, the southerner has nevertheless with Italian finesse and exquisite skill, uniformly and invariably, so manipulated Northern sentiment as to succeed sooner or later in carrying his point and shaping the policy of this government to suit his purposes. (97)

Cooper might well make the same statement today.

III. The Theater of Lynching

> *[T]he masculine space of ritualized white violence (lynching) in which the black body becomes the object of "desire" must logically become the site on which to construct a powerful ideal of white manhood.*
>
> —Sandra Gunning, *Race, Rape, and Lynching: The Red Record of American Literature, 1890–1912* (1996)

> *Lynching plays represent a challenge to the social order of white male supremacy by revealing how the exploitation of black men and women and white women was interdependent and vital to such an order. Additionally, the plays expose the role of white women in maintaining a system of racial oppression.*
>
> —Judith Stephens, *Strange Fruit: Plays on Lynching by American Women* (1998)

Lynching plays represent a distinct subgenre of American drama. Written almost exclusively by American playwrights (one known exception is Jean-Paul Sartre's *The Respectful Prostitute*), lynching drama developed as a cultural and literary form when playwrights moved beyond brief references to lynching in general and focused fully on specific lynching incidents. One of the earliest dramas by a white playwright to include a lynching incident is Thomas Dixon's *The Clansman* (1905/1970) which rationalized lynching as a necessary protection for white women from black men and as a necessary punishment for black men who had (white men imagined) raped white women. In contrast, plays by Angelina Weld Grimké (*Rachel,* 1916) and Ridgely Torrence (*Granny Maumee,* 1914) portrayed the barbarism and injustice of lynching and its devastating impact on black families and communities. Judith Stephens (1998) suggests that these two plays "not only reflect the philosophy and interracial nature of the antilynching movement but also mark the beginning of an antilynching tradition in theater" (4). (Grimké was also a poet whose poetry expressed desire for women [Hammonds 1994].)

That African-American women took the lead in the effort to build an interracial coalition of women in the antilynching movement is reflected in the fact that black women wrote the earliest plays and the largest number of plays. Kathy Perkins underscores the confluence of black female theater and the antilynching campaign: "When black women first picked up the pen as playwrights they chose to speak out against the atrocities of lynching" (quoted in Stephens 1998, 6). Playwrights such as Angelina Grimké and Georgia Douglas Johnson were themselves directly involved in the antilynching movement. Reflecting the interracial character of that movement, plays by May Miller and Ann Seymour were submitted to a contest for one-act plays on the theme of lynching that was sponsored by the Association of Southern Women for the Prevention of Lynching (A.S.W.P.L.). This is the only known organization to have sponsored a contest for plays specifically focusing on lynching and worked to "promote an antilynching spirit throughout the South" (A.S.W.P.L. Papers 1936; quoted in Stephens 1998, 6). Black theater pioneers Randolph Edmonds and Anne Cooke served as contest judges (Stephens 1998).

All lynching plays are structured around a threat or occurrence of lynching and its consequences for the characters. The home is the most common setting for these plays; most of the plays written by black women are set in black homes. Domestic skills such as sewing, ironing, cleaning, and food preparation are performed and become integrated into the action of the plot. By situating their plays domestically and by creating characters whose primary identities are as family members and neighbors, Stephens suggests that these playwrights are portraying "the black home as an important place of education and resistance" (1998, 9). She recalls Jacqueline Jones's argument that black women have historically regarded the "duties of domestic nurturer" (1985, 323) as a means to create a somewhat safe space for their families, relatively insulated from white society. There they might challenge the racialized system of economic exploitation. Black women's lynching dramas reflect black women's valorization of the home and family life. Moreover, Stephens points out, "the juxtaposition of the brutal public act of lynching with the private, intimate atmosphere of the home creates a theater of jarring contrasts and incongruity for those who idealize the 'American home' by equating it with an atmosphere of safety and peace" (1998, 9). Within the home, the repetition of the domestic routine does not represent women's limited and separate sphere but creates a strong dramatic contrast between public and private spheres, heightening the emotional power of the plays. Although a number of community locations such as the church and public workplace provide settings for lynching plays by white women, the home is the most commonly portrayed setting in plays composed by black women (Stephens 1998).

Conversation among characters occurs in multiple forms, including music, poetry, and prayer. These elements—common to lynching plays written by white women too—provide counterpoints to the rhythm embedded in the dialogue. Props and sound effects chosen to heighten emotions—for instance, the Bible, religious paintings, and sounds of birds—are also found in many of the plays. Religious elements not only reveal the influences of Christianity but function to the underline the depth of religious faith in the black community and the religious hypocrisy of whites who tolerated lynching. These elements reflect, Stephens points out, the religious character of much of the women's antilynching movement. In black revival style, the letterhead for Mary Talbert's Antilynching Crusaders advised, "To Your Knees, and Don't Stop Praying" (quoted in Stephens 1998, 10). Indeed, women's church groups were among the supporters of A.S.W.P.L. (Stephens 1998).

In the plays composed by black women, the lynching event is often narrated by a woman, and her communication to the other characters plays an important role in the drama. This structuring of the play acknowledges the key role black women played in the communication of news and knowledge through an oral tradition. Quoting Ida B. Wells's daughter, Stephens suggests that this oral feature also "honors the pioneering efforts of Ida B. Wells who, through her speeches, was 'possibly the first person to publicly recite the horrors of lynching'" (Duster 1970, ix; Stephens 1998, 11). Curiously, white women in the second Klan also used oral traditions, but there to engage in racist politics. This orality may distinguish women's participation in racial politics from men's. Men tended to be focused on genitality, both as a provocation for violence and in the case of black men's bodies, the sites of sexualized violence.

In the composition of antilynching plays, Stephens notes, many white women were publicly accepting the responsibility for racial violence that black women had been explaining to them for decades. That is, white women had allowed themselves to be used by white men as a pretext for racial violence, specifically in that "theater" of white men's minds in which white women were being raped by black men. That many white women—Jesse Daniel Ames most conspicuously—began to appreciate the relationship between southern chivalry, separate spheres (i.e., the idealization and sentimentalization of white women as saintly mothers and asexual wives) and the sexual mutilation of black men is reflected in those plays in which lynching victims had been unjustly accused of attacking white women. The shared subjugation of women, black and white, is further evidenced in the realism of most antilynching plays: lynching is presented as a serious social problem without obvious or immediate resolution (Stephens 1998).

This sober and realistic point of view engendered controversy on occasion. In Angelina Grimké's *Rachel* (1916), for instance, the heroine speaks a truth many African-American mothers have known. Upon learning that her father and brother had been lynched, Rachel shudders at the reality black mothers must face for their newborn sons, and declares, near the end of Act I, "Why it would be more merciful to strangle the little things at birth" (in Perkins and Stephens 1998, 42). Such candid portrayals of white racism's effect upon African Americans did not go unnoticed. The play was first produced in 1916 by the Drama Committee of the Washington, D.C., branch of the N.A.A.C.P. and characterized by Montgomery Gregory as "the first attempt to use the stage for race propaganda in order to enlighten the American people relative to the lamentable condition of ten million colored citizens in this free republic" (quoted in Perkins and Stephens 1998, 23). A minority section of this committee judged the play propagandistic, and left to form the Howard Players organization which favored "folk plays" and a more artistic approach (Perkins and Stephens 1998).

Rachel was also criticized as promoting race suicide, a criticism to which Grimké (1880–1958) responded publicly. The point of the play, she explained, was to show how "a highly strung girl, a dreamer and an idealist" responded to "race prejudice." The play was intended to educate whites, especially white women, whom she regarded as "one of the most conservative elements of society" and "about the worst enemies with which the colored race has to contend." Grimké expressed her hope that "if anything can make all women sisters underneath their skins, it is motherhood." Focusing on motherhood, then, as the most "vulnerable point" in white women's armor, Grimké expressed the hope that *Rachel* might function to bring women, white and black, together: "If, then, the white women of this country could see, feel, understand just what effect their prejudice and the prejudice of their fathers, brothers, husbands, and sons were having on the souls of the colored mothers everywhere, and upon the mothers that are to be, a great power to affect public opinion would be set free and the battle would be half won" (quoted in Perkins and Stephens 1998, 23).

Ridgely Torrence's one-act play *Granny Maumee* (first produced in 1914) also protested lynching, but Angelina Grimké's *Rachel* is the earliest known example of a full-length drama written to protest the practice. Grimké's play revolves around a family, the father and son of which had been lynched. We learn about these events through the speech of the mother. We observe how these lynchings have impacted the lives of all family members and especially Rachel, the daughter. First produced in 1916, the play had been composed in 1914. In 1915 the manuscript was being read for critical response. *Rachel* is the first nonmusical written, produced, and publicly performed by African Americans the script of which still exists (Perkins and Stephens 1998). Of special note is the play's "striking sensitivity to the special way racism and sexism affect the black woman" (Margaret Wilkerson, quoted in Perkins and Stephens 1998, 24).

Mary Burrill (1884–1946) was one of the earliest playwrights to dramatize African Americans fighting whites over lynching. Like her close friend and contemporary Angelina Grimké (other friends included playwrights Georgia Douglas Johnson, Alice Dunbar Nelson, and for nearly twenty-five years her close companion Lucy Diggs Slowe), Burrill was especially concerned about black women. Although she is known to have written other works, only two plays survive. Her first published work, *Aftermath,* appeared in the April 1919 *Liberator*. *Aftermath* illustrates those antilynching plays composed by black women in which characters are lynched for crimes other than rape. In September of 1919, her second play, *They That Sit in Darkness,* was published in *Birth Control Review,* a periodical advocating birth control rights for women. *Birth Control Review* dedicated an issue on "The Negroes' Need for Birth Control, as Seen by Themselves." That issue also included a short story by Grimké. Perkins and Stephens (1998) report that there is no known performance record for *They That Sit in Darkness. Aftermath,* however, was performed in the David Belasco Annual Little Theater Tournament on May 7, 1928, at the Frolic theater in New York City (Perkins and Stephens 1998).

Other black playwrights who wrote antilynching plays include Georgia Douglas Johnson (1877?–1966) and Regina M. Anderson Andrews (1901–1993). Johnson was the most prolific of the antilynching playwrights. Her six known lynching plays are *Safe, Blue-Eyed Black Boy,* two versions of *A Sunday Morning in the South,* and two lost plays—*And Still They Paused* and *A Bill to Be Passed.* Unlike her plays on nonlynching themes, none of her lynching dramas was published or produced in her lifetime. This fact testifies to the controversy of the genre and white men's insistence on their right to lynch black men (Perkins and Stephens 1998). A close friend of Georgia Douglas Johnson and a celebrated and prolific black playwright in her own right, May Miller (1899–1995) wrote fifteen plays, eleven of which were published. Many were staged by numerous little theater groups and at colleges, among them *Nails and Thorns: A Play in One Act* (performed 1933).

Regina Anderson Andrews wrote her first play, *Climbing Jacob's Ladder,* in 1930. The play is significant because it is one of the earliest produced antilynching plays by an African-American woman. Unusually, the action takes place outside of the home, and it does not feature a female lead character. Much of the action occurs in a church and the lynching event is narrated by a young boy. *Climbing Jacob's Ladder* was produced by the Harlem Experimental Theater on April 24, 1931, at St. Philips Parish House, where the group was based. There are no known reviews of the play, but a photograph of the production is featured in the July 1931 issue of the *Crisis* (Perkins and Stephens 1998). Reflecting on her career, Andrews commented: "Before coming to New York, I had been very much influenced by Ida B. Wells Barnett of Chicago. ... When I was a child in Chicago and first heard of lynchings, they were incomprehensible. It's understandable that in my twenties I would have to write a play about lynching" (quoted in Perkins and Stephens 1998, 121).

Written in 1924 by Annie Nathan Meyer (1867–1951), *Black Souls* was not produced until 1932. It is one of the earliest known lynching dramas by a white woman. The play portrays many of the issues Ida B. Wells had articulated in her antilynching crusade, namely that white women sometimes desired black men and that white men often sexually exploited black women. As well, Meyer's play lays bare the hypocrisy of a nation which sent black soldiers overseas to fight for freedom that was denied to them at home, where lynching continued. Letters from Meyer's file at the American Jewish Archives document the long struggle she underwent before finally seeing her play produced. Opening on March 30, 1932, at the Provincetown Playhouse, the play ran only for twelve performances, with New York critics praising the acting but criticizing the play (Perkins and Stephens 1998). Meyer was excoriated for "daring to write a play about Negroes when she had never lived in the South" (quoted in Perkins and Stephens 1998, 135).

Annie Nathan Meyer was born in New York City to a prominent Jewish family. In 1885 she was admitted to Columbia University, where women were not permitted to attend classes. They were permitted to study independently for the same examinations administered to men. Meyer's father warned her that attending the university would probably mean that she would never marry; only a rare man would consider an intelligent woman as a candidate to be his wife. That was, indeed, the case (Filene 1998). Accepting this fate, Meyer committed herself to the struggle for higher education for women and became a founder of Barnard College, serving on its board of trustees for many years. Despite her father's warning, Meyer did marry Dr. Alfred Meyer in 1887, and her marital state, in contrast to say Charlotte Perkins Gilman's, did not dissuade her from pursuing her own literary career, writing novels, plays, short stories, and numerous articles on education, art, and feminism. Her feminism was evidently ambivalent. While she fought for higher education for women and the acceptance of women in all professions, she opposed suffrage for women, and shared her father's estimation of the difficulties women faced when trying to combine marriage with a career (Perkins and Stephens 1998).

Lillian Smith

Known especially for her best-selling novel *Strange Fruit* which was also produced as a Broadway play, Lillian Smith (1897–1966) was the daughter of a prominent Methodist layman (Williamson 1984). She came of age in Jasper, Florida, and in Clayton, Georgia. While a child her parents took in Julie, an orphan girl who had been living with a black family, who became something of a sister to Lillian. One day it was discovered that Julie had some "black blood" and she was suddenly removed from the household. This trauma left the young Smith painfully aware of "the paradox of a culture that teaches hospitality, democracy, and Christian charity at the same time it violently denies the humanity of blacks" (quoted in Perkins and Stephens 1998, 220).

Lillian Smith studied at Piedmont College, Baltimore's Peabody Conservatory of Music, and Columbia University's Teachers College. She spent a year teaching in an isolated mountain community in Georgia and spent three years teaching music at a Methodist Mission school in Huchow, China. Returning to Georgia, Smith directed the Laurel Falls Camp for Girls, which her father had founded at their Georgia home, and a school for girls. At this progressive school, students enjoyed a liberal education, racial and otherwise. In 1936, with her companion, Paula Snelling, Smith established the *North Georgia Review* (later known as *South Today*), a magazine devoted to literary arts and social criticism. Joel Williamson (1984) characterizes the journal as "bold and aggressive" (489). During the 1930s Smith and Snelling began to host biracial gatherings and dinners at the camp where southern intellectuals, artists, and political activists met and discussed the issues of the day (Perkins and Stephens 1998). A recent collection of Smith's letters makes clear the importance of Snelling's companionship to Smith's creativity and writing (Gladney 1993).

In addition to *Strange Fruit* (1944), *Killers of the Dream* (1949/1963) and numerous articles, reviews, and speaking engagements made Smith a national figure, known at once as a southern writer, civil rights activist, and major participant in the civil rights movement in the 1940s and 1950s. During this period she was acknowledged for her courage and creativity with honorary degrees from Oberlin College and Howard University. Although battling cancer, Smith remained active in the civil rights movement in the early 1960s, becoming involved with organizations such as the Congress for Racial Equality

(C.O.R.E.) and the Student Non-Violent Coordinating Committee (S.N.C.C.). On July 4, 1966, she received the Charles S. Johnson Award, named in honor of the distinguished social scientist and former president of Fisk University. Smith died of cancer on September 28, 1966 (Perkins and Stephens 1998).

Published on February 29, 1944, *Strange Fruit* immediately became a best-seller, moving to the top of the best-seller list of the *New York Times Book Review* by May 14. The novel sold a million copies in hardcover and over three million in Smith's lifetime. It was translated into fifteen languages. At the 1993 republication of the novel Alice Walker commented: "The South can hardly be said to recognize itself without this book." In 1944 Smith signed a contract with director José Ferrer and producer Arthur Friend to turn *Strange Fruit* into a play. At the time Smith denied that the novel was about racism and lynchings; it was, she insisted, about "human beings and their relationships with each other." Only two years earlier, however, while still working on the book, she had written to Walter White that her theme was "the effect of the southern concept of race upon not only lives but minds and emotions." By this she meant not only the horrible effects upon African Americans, but as well their effects upon the white mind. She asked European Americans to shift their attention from the so-called "Negro problem" to the white man's "deep-rooted needs that have caused him to seek those strange, regressive satisfactions that are derived from worshipping his own skin color" (quoted in Perkins and Stephens 1998, 222).

As a Broadway play *Strange Fruit* was not successful. The play was as highly controversial as the novel had been. *Strange Fruit* was banned in Boston, a decision upheld by the Massachusetts Supreme Court, which declared the novel to be "obscene, indecent and impure" (quoted in Perkins and Stephens 1998, 222). A ban by the United States Post Office Department, barring the book from the mails, was lifted only after the intervention of President Roosevelt, via the influence of Eleanor. There was also controversy over the title, *Strange Fruit,* which most readers (as well as the book's copyright page) attributed to the 1939 Billie Holiday song about lynching in the South. In her autobiography, Billie Holiday wrote that Lillian Smith had, in fact, confided to her that "the song inspired her to write the novel and the play about a lynching" (quoted in Perkins and Stephens 1998, 223). Smith, however, insisted that her sense of the phrase "Strange Fruit" had to do with the damaged, twisted human beings, both black and white, who are consequence of white racism in America (Perkins and Stephens 1998, 222). It seems to me that the phrase also speaks of the queer character of racial politics, specifically referring to those self-identified "straight" (white) men who imagined themselves protecting the honor of white women while "raping" black men.

The Broadway play was a heavily staged production, involving many large sets (twelve scenes, thirty-four actors, and thirty-five stage hands). Critics applauded designer George Jenkins and the acting. The role of Nonnie Anderson was played by Jane White, daughter of Walter White. Recommended for the role by Paul Robeson, Jane White was widely praised for her performance. Despite their praise for the production, critics panned the play as "episodic" or "too long, too jumbled, too straggling" (quoted in Perkins and Stephens 1998, 222). Robeson demonstrated his support for the play by meeting with the cast backstage and by publicly declaring his hope that "every American could see this moving and prophetic play" (quoted in Perkins and Stephens 1998, 223). Lillian Smith's sister, Esther Smith, observed that the failed Broadway version of the play was not the original version (which was preferred by Lillian), a version that, along with other manuscripts and letters, was destroyed in a 1955 house fire (Perkins and Stephens 1998).

Contemporary Playwrights

Written as part of Endesha Ida Mae Holland's (1944–) master's thesis in American studies at the University of Minnesota during the 1980s, *Miss Ida B. Wells* "powerfully depicts" (Perkins and Stephens 1998, 298) episodes in the life of the antilynching activist, teacher, and journalist. In a series of monologues, the characters "Wells One" and "Wells Two," who are mixtures of historical fact and creative imagination, take the audience through Wells's childhood in Mississippi, her career as a teacher, a journalist, and as a crusader and organizer of the antilynching movement. Also dramatized are Wells's meetings with Susan B. Anthony, her suit against the Chesapeake and Ohio railroad, the lynching of three close friends in Memphis, and her subsequent campaign against the practice. *Miss Ida B. Wells* was first produced in 1982 by At the Foot of the Mountain Theater in Minneapolis, followed by productions at other Minnesota theaters and in the Buffalo, New York, area where Holland later moved (Perkins and Stephens 1998).

Ida B. Wells used the pseudonym "Iola" during her career as a journalist. Michon Boston (1962–) entitled her antilynching play *Iola's Letter* (1994), which received second prize for drama in the Larry Neal Writer's Competition Awards sponsored by the D.C. Commission on the Arts and Humanities in 1994. The first public staged reading of *Iola's Letter* was produced in 1994 by the Source Theater in Washington, D.C. Readings of the play have been sponsored by Playwrights Forum and the Capitol Hill Arts Workshop (Perkins and Stephens 1998)

In the Other Arts

America learned about lynching not only from women playwrights, but from women working in other art forms as well. For instance, visual artists, musicians, and choreographers such as Meta Vaux Warrick Fuller, Lois Malou Jones, Billie Holiday, Nina Simone, Katherine Dunham, and Pearl Primus all testified to the nightmare that was lynching. While white women, such as choreographer Helen Tamaris, used their art in the 1920s and 1930s to fight lynching, it has been African-American women who consistently focused their art on the continuing racial crisis that lynching created and expressed (Perkins 1998). And as Kathy Perkins points out, "these women were participating in the larger social movement initiated in 1892 by Ida B. Wells" (1998, 15).

Possibly the earliest visual artist to protest lynching was Meta Vaux Warrick Fuller, one of the most important sculptors of the Harlem Renaissance. Moved by the lynching of Mary Turner (see chapter 1, section IV), Fuller created *Mary Turner (A Silent Protest)* in 1919. Measuring 15 × 5¼ × 4½", the painted plaster sculpture is of a woman, clutching her pregnant stomach as she gazes into the faces of the mob. A contemporary of Fuller, historian Benjamin Brawley (1921), commented: "Her early work is not delicate or pretty; it is gruesome and terrible, but it is also intense and vital, and from it speaks the very tragedy of the Negro race." "Fuller became a powerful symbol of artistic determination for a generation of Black Artists who came after her" (124; quoted in Perkins 1998, 16). Housed in the Museum of Afro-American History in Boston, *Mary Turner* is one of Fuller's best-known works. Fuller is one of few known artists—visual or literary—to produce a work focused on the lynching of a woman (Perkins 1998).

Another artist who responded to the lynching of Mary Turner was playwright and poet Angelina Grimké. In a short story, "The Creaking" (1920), later retitled "Goldie," Grimké commemorated the horrible event. Nearly half a century would pass before another artist depicted the lynching of black women. In her 1966 *Jubilee,* Margaret Walker portrays two black women lynched for allegedly poisoning their masters' families. Every slave in the county is required to attend the event, which is held on the Fourth of July. While white people are clearly in a holiday mood, the slaves watched silently (Perkins 1998).

The tragedy of lynching was also sung by African Americans. When the blues were prominent during the second decade of the twentieth century, singers such as Ma Rainey, Bessie Smith, and Victoria Spivey sang about the practice, although few of these songs were recorded. "Strange Fruit," made famous by Billie Holiday in 1939, become one of the earliest protest songs to receive national attention (see chapter 1, section II). In 1943 at the same Café Society (an interracial club in New York) where Holiday often sang "Strange Fruit," choreographer Pearl Primus premiered a ballet in protest of lynching performed to the spoken poem "Strange Fruit." Horrified by the vivid images in the song, Primus "created the dance as a solo and interpreted the poem, psychologically, from two perspectives. First she extracted the emotional reactions of one individual following the lynching. Next, she interpreted those emotional reactions through the feelings of a woman; a white woman." Primus has stated, "It dawned on me that if I could isolate a person from a lynch mob, I would have a different character from the brute who participated in the crime. People don't commit horrible crimes like this when they are alone and sober" (quoted in Perkins 1998, 17).

A longtime friend of sculptor Meta Fuller, painter Lois Malou Jones, created *Meditation (Mob Victim)* in 1944. Unlike most works which portray young victims struggling to escape the white male mob, Jones's painting discloses an elderly black man, bound by the hands, quietly looking up to the heavens. In a 1993 interview Jones discussed the origin of the image. On U Street in Washington, D.C., Jones met such a man, and asked him to pose for her. When she asked him to "take the look" of a struggling man with a rope around his neck about to be lynched, the man replied that as a young man he had witnessed an actual lynching in the South (Perkins 1998, 18). It was the memory of this experience that the elderly man performed in his pose for *Meditation (Mob Victim)* (Perkins 1998).

Employing the song "Strange Fruit," choreographer and dancer Katherine Dunham composed the 1953 ballet *Southland,* in which the lynching of a man is performed on stage. Staging the work in Santiago, Chile, Dunham was determined to show the world what white men did to black men in the United States. In a prologue to the ballet, Dunham wrote:

> And although I have not smelled the smell of burning flesh, and have never seen a black body swaying from a southern tree, I have felt these things in spirit, and finally through the creative artist comes the need to show this thing to the world, hoping that by so exposing the ill the conscience of the many will protest and save further destruction and humiliation. ... This is not all of America, it is not all of the south, but it is a living, present part. (quoted in Perkins 1998, 18)

Learning of the event, the U.S. State Department instructed Dunham to delete the scene, but Dunham replied that she would comply only when lynching was no longer practiced in the United States. Her defiance and continued performance of the ballet brought surveillance and harassment by the State Department and the FBI, culminating finally in the collapse of her company in 1965. In a May 14, 1994, interview, Dunham made it clear that she was aware of the penalties of presenting such a piece, but explained that it was necessary for her to expose lynching, as dramatized in *Southland,* to the world. As of 1994, *Southland* had not been performed in the United States, where, Dunham hoped, it might be (Perkins 1998).

Even as lynching died out in the 1950s, representations of the practice in the arts did not. Lynching still shows up in certain contemporary works by African-American visual artists, among them Elizabeth Catlett and Pat Ward Williams. Catlett's 1992 color lithograph *To Marry* portrays a struggling lynch victim next to the kiss of a marrying couple. Williams's most famous piece, *Accused/Blowtorch/Padlock* (1986), presents a series of close-up shots from an actual lynching which appeared in *Life* magazine (Perkins 1998).

In the 1990s, rap artists such as X-Clan, De Lench Mob, Ice T, Sister Solja, Public Enemy, and (as we saw in the introduction) Wise Intelligent reminded their listeners of the nearly forgotten nightmare that was lynching. As well, there have appeared new renditions of the song "Strange Fruit," such as the one by RandB singer Cassandra Wilson. On at least one occasion, lynching as the subject of artistic expression still produced controversy. At the University of Oklahoma, an unidentified woman created a series of quilts that included images of Ku Klux Klan lynchings of black men. The young woman was quoted as saying that she included images of lynchings "to acknowledge a history of social injustice between the races." The quilts were removed from a public foyer at the university because "students could not learn in a setting where they had to pass on their way to class and see how their forefathers had been lynched" (quoted in Perkins 1998, 19).

IV. A Social Science of Lynching?

Mobs, through their rituals and spontaneous behavior, communicated their aims, motivations, and own self-perception.

—W. Fitzhugh Brundage, *Lynching in the New South: Georgia and Virginia, 1880–1930* (1993)

There'll be lynchings as long as white folks and black folks scrounge each other—everybody scrambling for the same penny.

—Lillian Smith, *Strange Fruit* (1944/1972)

Violence figured preeminently in racialized constructions of sexuality.

—Evelyn Brooks Higginbotham, "African-American Women's History and the Metalanguage of Race" (1996)

How, then, do we explain the timing of lynching's peak?

—Edward L. Ayers, *Vengeance and Justice: Crime and Punishment in the Nineteenth Century American South* (1984)

For those scholars writing during the 1920s and 1930s, lynching had multiple causes: lack of education, economics, history, politics, culture. For some it was best understood as an expression of primordial racism. For others, lynchings marked a phase in the economic and social maturation of the South; as the South became increasingly urbanized and industrialized, lynching would no longer be tolerated and the practice finally would disappear (Brundage 1993). Other scholars, such as Dennis Downey and Richard Hyser (1991), characterize such theorizing about lynching "objective." "Rarely," they continue, "have [such studies] come to terms with the subjective element, with that moment of individual choice when persons willfully turn thought into action and engage in the hanging, burning, or mutilation of a human being" (4). In their study of the lynching of Zachariah Walker, as well as in James McGovern's portrait of Claude McNeal's murder, such "subjective elements" are made more visible.

Certainly economics played a role. In his classic study, Walter White (1929) argued that the economic motive was the most powerful, that, after all was said and done, lynching was about maintaining a cheap pool of black labor. "Lynching has always been the means for protection, not of white women, but of profits," he wrote (White 1929, 82). His speculation is supported by recent "empirical" research (Tolnay and Beck 1995), but why did white men choose *this* means to keep wages low? Why not pass legislation protecting white employers and restricting black labor rights? After Reconstruction, that they did. No doubt economics was at work, but there was something else, something that sometimes resulted in castration. Now what could it be?

Predictably, Marxist scholars too insisted on the primacy of economic considerations, arguing that mob violence was a racial means of preventing the solidarity and mobilization of the oppressed. In so doing, it perpetuated the economic and political dominance of the capitalist class. Lynching, they pointed out, intimidated black workers, kept wages of both black and white workers low. When cotton prices declined, these commentators speculated, whites vented their frustrations on the black community. Stewart E. Tolnay and E. M. Beck agree. So did Jesse Daniel Ames. In 1942 she acknowledged that during periods of economic depression, when the price of cotton was low, lynchings increased. "But in 1936," she qualifies, "with the price of cotton still low, lynchings dropped to a new record and, since that year, lynchings have continued to decrease, each year setting a new low record" (Ames 1942, 61).

There was also statistical evidence to suggest that lynchings were more likely to occur in poor counties, although the idea of any causal relationship between lynching and cotton prices subsequently come under challenge and was later revived, as we will see. In demographic terms there did seem to be an inverse correlation between the frequency of lynchings and the total number of black residents in a county; blacks appeared more vulnerable the smaller their proportion in a county's population. In *An American Dilemma,* Gunnar Myrdal (1944/1962) speculated that lynchings dropped as the semi-isolation of southern life ended. Rural electrification and the radio, paved highways and the automobile, motion pictures and educational improvements all contributed to the relative integration of the American South into the American nation, he suggested. And, another commentator speculated, "intercollegiate athletics offered alternatives to traditional beliefs and ritualized behavior" (Zangrando 1980, 11). Were sports, in this instance, a sublimated alternative to ritualized (homo)sexual assault?

More specifically, there is evidence linking lynchings with the business cycle and with poverty. Between 1900 and the Great Depression the number of lynchings declined as economic conditions improved. Returns per acre from cotton production rose from $16.76 in 1902 to $35.14 in 1922. Several classic sociological studies on race relations in the South in the 1930s and early 1940s supported Raper's (1933/1969) view that lynchings were confined largely to the poor rural South. He emphasized economic factors, especially economic frustration. Brundage (1993) summarizes this view succinctly: "The frequency of lynching, in short, was a barometer of the economic frustration of white southerners" (10).

As we saw in George Wright's research on lynching in Kentucky, white southerners fought tooth and nail to prevent the education of African Americans, then used black educational underachievement as incontrovertible proof that blacks were genetically inferior as a race. After "redemption" by the Bourbons in the 1880s (after the old political elite resumed power in the South), some expenditures were equalized. For instance, in 1890, Alabama and North Carolina's per-pupil expenditures for black and white students were equal, but by 1910, Alabama allocated black pupils only 31 cents for each dollar spent on white students. North Carolina was somewhat less discriminatory, spending 54 cents per black student for each dollar spent on white students

(Tolnay and Beck 1995). Well into the third decade of the twentieth century, educational opportunities remain restricted by inadequate investments in facilities and teachers for African-American children. As late as 1930, it was common for southern counties to fund black schools at about one-fifth to one-tenth the level of white schools. Statistically, illiteracy was positively related to outmigration during the early twentieth century, suggesting that African Americans were more likely to abandon southern states (and counties within southern states) in which they had been denied educational opportunities (Tolnay and Beck 1995).

Consider the case of Sumter County, Alabama, the site of several lynchings. According to the 1928 school census, there were 1,899 white children and 10,191 black children of school age in Sumter County. The schools were, of course, segregated. The term for black high schools was 137 days, and for black elementary schools 86 days; white schools were in session 176 days. A white teacher was provided for every thirty-two white children, a black teacher for every 110 black children. In the 1928–1929 scholastic year, the total current expense per school-age white child was $53.75; for the black child it was $2.41. The average Alabama expenditure per white child was $34.89; the expenditure per black child was $9.39. Sumter Country's white teachers received an average annual salary of $1,187; black teachers received an average annual salary of $217. The state average for white teachers was $872; black teachers were paid $368 (Raper 1933/1969).

Irwin County, Georgia was also the site of several lynchings. The expenditures for schools in Irwin County were considerably below the average in Georgia. Less was spent on white schools than was typically the case; the proportion of the county's public funds going to black schools was also below the state average. The figures for 1928 follow: For each white child of school age $29.72 was spent in the county, in contrast to an average for the state of $36.88; for each black child $2.85 in Irwin and $5.07 in the state. In addition to poverty and economic racism, religion was a factor too. The Primitive Baptist denomination—so called because ignorance was considered a virtue—had a strong following in Irwin country. Its ministers boasted that they were unschooled. Among these "Christians" it was considered sinful to use musical instruments in church services (Raper 1933/1969).

Bolivar is the second largest county in Mississippi, known during the first half of the twentieth century as one of the most fertile and most populous counties in the South. Due to its wealth and prestige, it used to be known as "Imperial Bolivar." The title also hinted at its political self-sufficiency. It was, in a sense, "a nation within itself" (Raper 1933/1969, 97). What kind of nation was it?

On its white public schools, Bolivar County expended $45.55 a year for each white child of school age, and $1.08 for each black child. In the academic year 1928–1929, the county board of education received from the state school fund $99,368.24 on account of its 35,708 black children, or $2.78 each. Of this sum, $38,765.64 was spent for black schools. The remainder of this sum, $60,703.60, was diverted to the white schools, which received also all the county's school taxes, amounting to $113,059.10; all special local district taxes, amounting to $92,117.37; and the state funds for the whites, $17,280.48. This means that $283,160.55 was spent for 6,216 white children; $38,765.64 was spent for the 35,708 black children. African Americans comprised 88.2 percent of the school population and received 16.8 percent of public finds; European Americans comprised 11.8 percent of the school population and received 83.2 percent of the public school funds (Raper 1933/1969).

Lynchings were not uncommon in Bolivar County. The white minority felt vigilante justice was necessary to maintain their political control in this so-called black-belt county. These were good "Christian folk," of course; as was typical for southern black-belt counties such as Bolivar, most of the white church members were affiliated with the Southern Baptist and Southern Methodist denominations (Raper 1933/1969). These were, regionally if not genealogically, the grandparents of the same "Christian folk" who felt compelled, in 1997, to boycott Disney due to the company's extension of benefits to partners of gay and lesbian employees.

They were as well the political "grandparents" of those middle- and upper-class whites posing as "tax busters" who opposed late 1990s tax increases to pay for much-needed repairs on Baton Rouge, Louisiana, school buildings. Not since court-ordered busing began some thirty years previously had the white majority electorate passed new taxes to pay for maintenance and new construction. By the late 1990s, many school buildings were in such a state of disrepair that water leaked into classrooms during rainstorms. When taxes to pay for repairs were finally increased in November 1998, they were passed despite the sustained and noisy opposition of conservative and wealthy whites (Hammatt 2000).

There is, of course, a long history of white opposition to black education, especially in the South. At the end of World War I, for instance, Florida spent $11.50 per white children, $2.64 for each black child (N.A.A.C.P. 1919). In Louisiana during the 1936–1937 school year, fifty-eight of Louisiana's sixty-four parishes spent less than the $14.17 it received from Baton Rouge for each black child. Twenty-six parishes spent less than half that amount; St. Martin spent only $2.16. Statewide, the amount reallocated from black to white schoolchildren totaled $991,000 (Fairclough 1995/1999). "The money allocated to the colored children is spent on the education of white children," admitted the school superintendent of a delta cotton parish. "That's unfair, and I know it, but that's the only way we can have decent white schools here" (quoted in Fairclough 1995/1999, 36).

In 1940, the amount allocated for each black child in Louisiana amounted to 24 percent of the amount allocated to whites; black teachers were paid, on average, 64 percent less than white teachers; the average school year in black schools was thirty-seven days shorter than in white schools. "The crowded conditions in these schools is appalling," noted a 1939–40 survey of the Baton Rouge black community. "In many rooms there were more than sixty pupils, all under the direction of one teacher" (quoted in Fairclough 1995/1999, 36). In a 1942 survey, the state was reported as allocating $66 per white child, $15.50 per black. The average salary of white teachers in the state was $1,084, for black teachers $385 (Washburne 1942).

Even in the cities, black high schools were few, and local school boards opposed any expansion, determined that black children would not become trained beyond their "station" and become eligible for "white" jobs. In 1931, the Orleans Parish school board declined to accept a Rosenwald Fund proposal for a black "industrial high school" in New Orleans, despite assurances that it would educate blacks for "negro trades" only. In 1934 the city had one four-year public high school to serve a population of 130,000, "an old brick structure considered unsafe for white children, gloomy rooms, the wooden walls creaky" (quoted in Fairclough 1995/1999, 37). In Hoffman Junior High twenty-six teachers tried to teach 1,250 children. By 1940 the situation had begun to improve, and the number of black high schools in the state increased from four to thirty-nine. There were also eight Catholic high schools (Fairclough 1995/1999).

Even as late as the 1945–1946 school year, these outrageous disparities in school spending persisted throughout the Deep South. That year Mississippi spent $75.29 for each white child's education, but only $14.74 for each African-American child. In Georgia the situation was not much different: $82.57 per white child, $31.14 per black child. And in South Carolina, $100.38 was spent for each white student and $39.64 for each African American (Smith 1949/1963).

Under such circumstances, it seems plausible to think that lynching was only one among many "tools" employed by whites to maintain the racist status quo. Robert Ingalls (1987) certainly thought so, as we have seen, arguing that lynchings were an expression and instrument of "establishment violence" intended to reproduce the reigning social order. Focusing on the history of Tampa, Florida, Ingalls emphasized the collaboration of elites and everyday citizens in the use of lynching to protect the political status quo. In this view, lynching, like other forms of racial violence, is a mechanism of social control that sends a powerful message to an insurgent minority. George Fredrickson also conceived of lynching as a form of social control, writing that lynching was "the ultimate sociological method of racial control and repression, a way to use fear and terror to check 'dangerous' tendencies in a black community considered to be ineffectively regimented or supervised" (1971, 272).

In Marxist terms, lynching was "a preventive measure to deter the black masses from rising up in revolt." As Angela Davis put the matter: "Lynching was undisguised counterinsurgency, a guarantee that black people would not be able to achieve their goals of citizenship and economic equality" (1983, 185). Lynching became racialized after the Civil War due to the "colonization of the southern economy by capitalists from the North" (Davis 1983, 90). If African Americans, by means of terror and violence, could be maintained as the underclass within the swelling ranks of the working class, capitalists could profit doubly: "Extra profits would result from the superexploitation of black labor, and white workers' hostilities toward their employers would be defused" (Davis 1983, 90).

Summarizing various interpretations of lynching, Walter Howard (1995) acknowledges that those who lynched may have, at one time or another, felt what they imagined was frontier spirit, economic frustration, or fear of black threats to the establishment order; on occasion these men may have also been moved by their sense of honor and duty to punish any affront to family and community. Yet none of these causes adds up, Howard rightly concludes, to the nightmare that was lynching. On the verge of saying something new, he retreats to lynching as a form of social control: "That the dissolution of the caste system in the South during the civil rights era prompted a temporary revival of lynching and antiblack violence, strongly suggests that the classical theory of white social control—that blacks were lynched to maintain white supremacy and dominance—may, after all, best explain the phenomenon of southern lynchings" (Howard 1995, 162).

Other interpretations that situate lynching within a historical context point to psychological, social, and cultural tensions that inhered in a biracial and racist society. The brilliant southern journalist W. J. Cash, for example, emphasized psychological considerations, judging the South as "far too much concerned with bald, immediate, unsupported assertion of the ego," with "too great stress on the inviolability of personal whim," and "full of the chip-on-shoulder swagger." Such machismo could easily explode into violence in a region that appears to have imposed few or no restraints upon white male behavior. Machismo plus racism plus poverty equals lynching. In this equation the mob experience crystallized a sense of group belonging for poor, socially fragmented whites; it provided a "safe" outlet for the diffuse but intense frustrations that could not be readily expressed against those responsible, namely other whites more highly placed in the socioeconomic and political hierarchy. For rich whites, lynching not only enacted, in dramatic fashion, the racism of the region but provided a means of deflecting lower-class white anger away from them. In death as well as life, blacks remained central to the psychological, economic, and political life of whites (Zangrando 1980).

The major shortcoming of this interpretation of lynching, contemporary scholars like Fitzhugh Brundage (1993, 1997a, 1997b) argue, is that it rests too completely on causal relationships between racism and ignorance, backwardness and poverty. If lynching, then, was a function of southern backwardness, solutions were predictably intertwined with an explicit championing of "progress" and modernization. In this formula, Brundage points out, there could be little appreciation of the contradictory effects of "progress" on the South, effects that sometimes exaggerated, as well as ameliorated, racial tensions.

Writing in 1927, Will Alexander expressed an early version of what Downey and Hyser (1991) term a psychological approach in the effort to understand lynching. "In the last analysis," Alexander suggested, "[lynching] is a problem of the mass mind ... fear, suspicion, contempt, denial of essential humanity and determination to suppress are still almost universally found in the minds of the masses" (quoted in Downey and Hyser 1991, 5). Downey and Hyser recall Michael Cassity's (1984) novel which emphasized the psychological character of lynching, suggesting that it should be understood as a consequence of those competitive market tensions that accompanied the intrusion of industrial capitalism into a rural, agrarian, "traditional" culture. The social and economic upheaval that followed presumably created the conditions for lynching, namely social and economic displacement and dispossession.

Joel Williamson (1984) is credited by some with pointing to a psychosexual impulse in southern culture in order to think about lynchings. Williamson was clear that somewhere in the constellation of factors associated with lynching was an intense white preoccupation with black male sexuality, and specifically with the potency white men imagined black men possessed. Williamson has been one of the few scholars who emphasizes the fact that sexual mutilation regularly accompanied lynching by whites, linking it with the sexual inhibitions of whites themselves. But most contemporary scholars discount what I insist is the most salient fact of all, namely that, in effect, white men sexually assaulted black men. For instance, Dennis Downey and Richard Hyser (1991) suggest that Williamson and other "proponents of the psychosexual interpretation of lynching have mistaken the reality with the shadow that it casts" (6). They then resort to the umbrella term of white supremacy, a shadowy concept itself attacked by other prominent scholars such as W. Fitzhugh Brundage. Despite the glaring fact of naked black men bleeding from where their penises and testicles once were, Downey and Hyser (1991) are satisfied with saying that lynchings "were a means by which to reassert the ethos of white supremacy; as such, they became moralistic rituals that exposed the extremes to which whites would go to preserve their most cherished beliefs. ... What better sign of a black man's inferior position than the absolute denial of his person through death or castration and other forms of disfigurement?" (6).

Social psychologist Roger Brown too accepts this summary "explanation," writing: "It [lynching] was needed, in sum, to buttress white supremacy" (1965, 748). Murder works in this formula, but how, specifically, does castration? In *The Interpretation of Dreams* Freud understood that "thought is after all nothing but a substitute for a hallucinatory wish ... nothing but a wish can set our mental apparatus at work" (1966, 567). If "white supremacy" had at its center the thought of black men raping white women (who were, after all, fictionalized, banished to a separate sphere), was not white supremacy, at least in part, a recoded and distorted symbolization of white male desire for the black male body?

Frustration-Aggression Theory

John Dollard (1937, 1939) brought psychology to bear upon the study of southern race relations in general and lynching in particular, asking why people apparently "needed" race prejudice. One answer to this question, Dollard suggested, could be found by examining socially accepted channels for aggression in the South. Because day-to-day life continually generated frustrations, Dollard argued, each individual must either turn aggression inward and release it at some future time, or express it at some acceptable target. In the South, social conventions legitimated the expression of white frustrations onto blacks, a politically vulnerable and even defenseless group who were also associated with whites' fears and repressed desires. The apparent irrationality of much white violence against blacks, Dollard argued, reflected a mix of "direct aggression"—rational aggression against the individual or group who "caused" the frustration—as well as previously repressed aggression, which resulted in an irrational release of accumulated rage. The violence of southern race relations, then, followed from the mixing of "free-floating" aggression seeking an outlet combined with the actual frustrations of daily life.

Dollard emphasized the role that lynching and violence played in maintaining a caste system in the South. That all whites shared benefits from the caste system united them in their efforts to preserve white supremacy. Later, scholars influenced by Dollard argued that custom by itself was not enough to keep blacks in their place; only by continual vigilance could whites maintain white superiority. Lynching was in this sense a tool, albeit the most brutal one, to maintain white dominance. By employing mob violence, whites reinforced caste boundaries and their superiority, both to themselves and to blacks. James McGovern (1982) put the matter this way: "whites were conscious of their unlimited power over blacks and were willing to administer it through lynchings because they knew they could do so with impunity" (151).

Dollard's heterosexism surfaces in his speculation that "in relation to this idea I cannot refrain from guessing that the accusations of the Negro man by the white woman may often times be a denial of her own excitation directed toward the Negro" (Dollard 1937, 333). Now why cannot he "refrain" from "guessing?" Once again we see the sexualized structure of the racial relation. The white man relocates his own desire onto the white woman—who has said nothing, who is in fact for him imaginary—where he then can admit that aggression toward the black man represents a "denial" of "excitation"—namely his. When the repressed returns, Jean Laplanche (1999) suggests, it does not return as a copy to the originary trauma; rather, it becomes "dislocated" (104) and forms what he calls a "double inscription" (36).

In his discussion of lynching as displaced aggression, Roger Brown (1965) allows that white motivation was "less rational" than economic competition. Lynchings imply an aggression that has been "displaced." [How about desire relocated?] Citing Dollard et al. (1939), he repeats the psychological "law" that "when an animal or a human being is moving toward a goal, anything that impedes progress toward the goal is said to be a cause of frustration and frustration very often produces aggression" (750). In poor rural counties in the South, there would have been plenty of reasons for a high level of frustration. Economic issues were no doubt at work, Brown acknowledges, but so were factors such as social isolation and the dominance of fundamentalist forms of Protestantism, sects which often disallowed card-playing, dancing and theater attendance, among other pleasures. To Brown's credit, he realizes this is not enough of an explanation, that "the motives we have invoked to account for lynching leave an unexplained residue, the residue of sexual sadism. [And since it's essentially all male, it's homosexual sadism.] It was almost routine in the mob lynching to unsex the victim" (Brown 1965, 751).

Brown (1965) turns to a discussion of lynching and the miscegenation taboo, which he links with incest, missing, however, that the originary biblical act of incest which resulted in the "black race," was Ham's defrocking of his father Noah (Genesis 9:24). The "curse of Ham" became, presumably, the tragedy of dark-skinned peoples. What happened inside Noah's tent that night, that is, the relations among incest, miscegenation, and racism, I hope to explore in volume II of this series. Brown does not stay long in this "tent," but returns to social psychology, concluding that "in panics and riots and lynchings and expressive revelry man [sic] acts out impulses that he usually does not act out" (Brown 1965, 759). Hedging his bets, Brown (1965) allows that "to describe this new thing [that emerges in a mob], this 'emergent,' as a 'group mind' does not seem to be seriously misleading" (Brown 1965, 760). [We review a contemporary instance of "group mind" in chapter 13, in the phenomenon of "beaching."] Evidently trying to formulate a psychological law of collective behavior, Brown hypothesizes that "the outburst will occur because the total set of conditions produces a payoff matrix such that each person can act on his unsocialized impulse and be free of punishment or guilt" (760). The contents of this "unsocialized impulse" remain shrouded in abstraction.

Other scholars appeared to mix Dollard's "frustration-aggression" theory with economic analysis. Colleagues of Dollard's at Yale's Institute of Human Relations (and collaborators with him and others on *Frustration and Aggression*), Carl Hovland and Robert Sears (1940), argued that lynchings were correlated with indices of economic activity such as the per acre value of cotton. The frequency of lynching indicated, then, the economic frustration of white southerners. Poor economic returns bred frustration by "blocking individual goal-directed behavior." This frustration, they argued, found its expression in the lynchings of blacks, rather than in other forms of violence, for two reasons. First, those who in fact personified the frustration—landlords, merchants, and speculators—were powerful; aggression toward them would be ineffective and would be punished. Second, those who were lynched had already been arrested or were being prosecuted for alleged crimes and were thus already embodiments of (noneconomic) frustration for whites.

Alexander Mintz (1946) found Hovland and Sears's study methodologically flawed. By reanalyzing the lynching data using a different measure of association and making other methodological adjustments, Mintz found that the relationship between the value of cotton and black lynchings was still negative but not nearly as strong as reported by Hovland and Sears. In fact, Mintz concluded that the data did not support a linkage between the value of the southern cotton crop and lynching (Tolnay and Beck 1995).

Despite Mintz's findings, the idea that black lynchings were partially a function of swings in the southern economic cycle (primarily the fortunes of cotton) remained appealing to social scientists. Reed and his colleagues (1987) surveyed this literature and found the cotton price–lynching association cited routinely and uncritically as an example of the frustration-aggression process. Characterizing the presumed relationship as "too good to be false," they noted that a definitive study of the form or strength between southern cotton production and black lynchings had yet to be conducted (Tolnay and Beck 1995).

The hypothesized link between temporal swings in the price of cotton and black lynching assumes, Tolnay and Beck (1995) point out, that southern whites converted economic stress into racial violence. Their motives may have been "instrumental," as suggested by Raper, or "emotional" as described in Hovland and Sears's frustration-aggression hypothesis. Is this not too monolithic a view of southern whites, a social segment that were sometimes far from unanimous in their economic interests? Tolnay and Beck cite Bonacich's

(1972, 1975) division of rural southern white society into three major classes: the dominating white planters and employers; a class of white day laborers, sharecroppers, and tenants; and a class of black landless workers. Planters and employers were dependent on the cheap labor that subjugated and exploited African Americans provided, but poor white laborers were threatened by the competition from the cheaper black labor force. Although the economic interests of the two classes of whites diverged in many important respects, Tolnay and Beck (1995) speculate that periods of economic stress may have created a potential for convergence, at least as expressed in racial violence. When cotton profits were low or nonexistent, all whites may have resorted to intensified racial hostility and mob violence (Tolnay and Beck 1995). This is a point well taken, but it still seems too rational a model to explain the sexualized madness that was lynching.

The late nineteenth and early twentieth centuries, Tolnay and Beck point out, were economically depressed years for many southern rural whites. White farm tenancy increased, and black and white labor directly competed for scarce resources. There were some clear cases—here Tolnay and Beck quote Williamson (1984)—when the response of poor whites to financial stress was quite instrumental and driven by a determination to reduce economic competition from blacks. Such a scenario points us to violence—it was common enough in intraracial labor disputes—but why a sexualized violence? Tolnay and Beck (1995) seem incapable of focusing on this point, acknowledging only that "violence in response to economic distress sometimes took an expressive nature as well" (123). But "expressive" is as far as they go, noting that at times poor whites were perhaps reacting out of frustration to the contradiction between their objective economic status (poverty) and the presumed entitlements of white supremacy, while at other times, lynchings were intended as messages to the black community, reminders of its inferior position in white society (Tolnay and Beck 1995). White guys were getting off on the torture and mutilation of black guys; why is that fundamental and essential point so very difficult to name and theorize? Is it because to acknowledge that lynching was in some profound way "queer" makes visible the not-so-latent homoeroticism that many white men felt, and still feel, toward black men?

There were times when the white elite benefited from intensified racial antagonism and the violence that expressed it. These were times when elite whites worried over a possible coalition between black and white labor. Such a coalition was perhaps the greatest threat to the social, economic and political hegemony that the southern white elite enjoyed, as the Populists would discover in the early 1890s. Antagonism and rivalry between black and white men served the interest of the white elite, who on more than a few occasions acted to create conflict between black and white laborers. Tolnay and Beck (1995) quote Raper (1933/1969) on this point: "Lynchings tend to minimize social and class distinctions between white plantation owners and white tenants" (47). They quote Shapiro (1988) as well: "When those committed to racial subordination saw the possibility of blacks and whites coming together for common purposes, their responses most often were to reach for the gun and the rope" (219). The threat of coalition between black and white laborers seemed most real, Tolnay and Beck conclude, when cotton prices were under stress.

The "frustration-aggression" theory has a certain common-sense appeal, which is one reason why it has persisted in many explanations of lynching. Dollard's original work has been subjected to considerable revision in efforts to explain the causal link between frustration and aggression (Bandura 1973; Gilmore 1987). The general argument here is that there is some inherent tendency in human nature toward aggression; all that is necessary is to add frustration to it in order to produce individual or social violence. In this formulation, lynching represents a southern variation of the human condition. It has been revived recently in sociological terms, but Brundage (1993) judges the theory to be tautological. Moreover, he complains that Dollard's theory has had the effect of focusing the study of lynching on some specific, primal cause, thereby obscuring the complexities of mob behavior. In psychoanalytic terms, Elisabeth Young-Bruehl (1996) complains that Dollard's theory "is a rather mechanical version of Freud's claim that experiences of internal or external frustration precipitate neuroses and psychoses" (52).

Probably the most sophisticated theory of "prejudices" is that of Elisabeth Young-Bruehl. In *The Anatomy of Prejudices*, Young-Bruehl (1996) provides an intellectual history of scholarly efforts to understand "prejudice," insisting that no such unitary concept can grasp the historical variability and psychosocial complexity of the various "prejudices," among them racism, anti-Semitism, sexism, and homophobia. Of special interest to us is Young-Bruehl's recognition of the sexualized character of white racism.

White racism may have had its origins in the slave trade and the "conquest of Africa," Young-Bruehl (1996) argues, "but it developed into a sexual sickness" (486). This "sexual sickness" has several imagistic symptoms, among them the hypersexual image of the "black rapist." Young-Bruehl notes that white men also sexualized black women, that is, the image of the "black whore." White women, she suggests—and it is clear white men as well—share an image of the black man as "black stud." There is also, Young-Bruehl adds, an image of the "black mammy or maid," a construction in which black women are de-sexed, fantasized as the "black matriarch," a phallic mother in a commanding position in the black family, an image which surfaced in the Moynihan Report (see chapter 15). These images, collectively, represent the visual symptoms of the "sexual sickness" known as white racism.

Working from Freud's theory of character types associated with the three psychic agencies (id, superego, and ego), Young-Bruehl (1996) develops a typology of "character types and their ideologies of desire" (200 ff.). Of the three basic types—the obsessional, the hysterical, and the narcissistic—the hysterical would seem to be most closely associated with those white men who lynched black men. "Especially in social situations where males are raised for life in the public sphere and females for life in the domestic sphere," Young-Bruehl writes, "hysterical characters ... and their prejudices have quite gender-specific forms" (1996, 226). In such situations, men are socially sanctioned

> to act violently on their prejudices, which implies acting outward and usually targets the sexuality of their victims. Their scope for action accords

> with their tendency to externalize affects, a tendency that is probably reinforced by the externality of their genitals and the ways in which their phalluses become associated with acting, not being acted on. Rather than conversion symptoms on their own bodies, they frequently have their symptoms on their victims' bodies. They do not become impotent if they can diminish the sexuality of the males in their victim group—to the point of castration, emasculation—in order to keep the victims in their place. (Young-Bruehl 1996, 226)

Certainly one discerns the basic pattern of many nineteenth-century lynch mobs in this portrait of the "hysterical" character type. There is the reference to the ideology of separate spheres, which did indeed permit men considerable freedom of action in the public sphere. Women's domesticity and "purity" required men's protection. The very notion of "hysterical" is reminiscent of neurasthenia, a nineteenth-century male version of hysteria, as we will see in chapter 6.

Of particular interest is the focus on the penis, which, however, seems to get symbolized rather quickly into the phallus, associated with "acting" rather than being "acted upon." By castrating the other, Young-Bruehl asserts, the hysterical character type is able to disguise or resist his own impotence, which again gets symbolized as a matter of political supremacy, that is, keeping "the victims in their place," also a reference to white supremacy.

While I confess to suffering an intellectual allergy to typologies, I cannot deny the power of recognition in Young-Bruehl's formulation of hysterical characters and their prejudices. Still, I wonder about what appears to me to be a too-rapid flight to a symbolization of the literal. I do not doubt her analysis, but I do insist that lynchings were not *only* symbolic. They were literal events, as well. Whatever they thought they were doing, white men were sexually assaulting black men. If female victims of lynching had been sexually tortured and mutilated, would there be such a quick flight to the symbolic? Would not we dwell on the fact that women were being sexually assaulted? Why, when the victims were male, must we assume a symbolic meaning? Is there a certain heterosexism at work here? Of course lynching was symbolic, but it was also literal. Already "castrated" by their defeat in the Civil War and further destabilized as "men" by Confederate women's agency (see chapter 4) and by the loss of slaves, southern white men were no doubt "hysterical." Not only were "the white protectors ... associated with the body of the white female victim" (Gunning 1996, 42), these men would seem to have been *identified* with the white female body. Theirs was a convoluted but nonetheless literal homosexual desire. Young-Bruehl (1996) is not unaware of this fact. In her depiction of three subtypes of hysterical characters and their prejudices, one is primarily homoerotic.

A Matter of Culture?

Other scholars have brought anthropology and folklore studies to bear on the subject, suggesting a cultural explanation for lynching. Bruce E. Baker (1997) asserts "we need to think of lynching as a cultural text" (220). Baker has studied lynching ballads, drawing upon G. Malcolm Laws's (1964) definition of a ballad as "a narrative folksong which dramatizes a memorable event" (2, 27, 55; quoted in Baker 1997, 235). Narrowing this broad definition, Baker terms lynching ballads "cultural production[s]" that were "a vital part of the communities' own construction of the meanings of these lynchings" (219). Studying lynching ballads is important, he continues, because it suggests how the social memory of a lynching was constructed.

There is a documentary quality to lynching ballads which functions to preserve the memory of the event as well as allowing those who learn of the lynching to weave its meaning into the local folk culture of the community where the ballad was composed and sung. In lynching ballads, such as "In a Little Country Schoolyard," "Emmet Till," "The Ashland Tragedy," and "The Strayhorn Mob," the victim's name reminds listeners of the event and warns others to avoid a similar fate. Members of the mob remain nameless. "[U]sing the name of the victim while not mentioning the names of the mob," Baker (1997) suggests, "reinforces the power conferred by anonymity" (221). Details of the event—such as dismemberment—underline its nightmarish quality. Lynching ballads were popular musical forms: "The Death of Emma Hartsell" circulated through the late 1920s (Baker 1997).

"The Death of Emma Hartsell"

1) In eighteen hundred and ninety eight
Sweet Emma met with an awful fate.
'Twas on the holy Sabbath day
When her sweet life was snatched away.

2) It set my brain all in a whirl
To think of that poor little girl.
Who rose that morning fair and bright,
And before five was a mangled sight.

3) It caused many a heart to bleed
To think and hear of such a deed.
Her friends, they shed many a tear.
Her throat was cut from ear to ear.

4) Just as the wind did cease to blow,
They caught the men, 'twas Tom and Joe.
The sheriff he drove in such a dash
The howling mob could scarcely pass.

5) They got to town by half past seven
Their necks were broken before eleven.
The people there were a sight to see.
They hung them to a dogwood tree.

6) Fathers and mothers a warning take
Never leave your children for God's sake
But take them with you wherever you go
And always think of Tom and Joe.

7) Kind friends we all must bear in mind
They caught the men who did the crime.
There's not a doubt around the lurk
Tom said he held her while Joe did the work.

8) Sweet Emma has gone to a world of love
Where Tom and Joe dare not to go.
We think they've gone to hell below
For treating poor little Emma so.

9) Dear friends we all remember this
That Emma will be sadly missed.
And one thing more I also know
This world is rid of Tom and Joe.

10) As they stood on death's cold brink
Joe Kizzer [sic] begged the man for drink
No drink no drink the man replied
To Hell to Hell your soul must fly.

11) And one thing more my song does lack
I forgot to say the men were black.
Her friends and neighbors will say the same
And Emma Hartsell was her name.
(quoted in Baker 1997, 222–223)

Baker argues that lynching can be understood as an interruption of the social order. When the social order of a southern community had been disturbed—by actual or imagined black crimes—the community quickly moved to reestablish order, sometimes by silencing the action or statement that was perceived to have provoked the disturbance. Baker observes that such social action qualifies as an instance of Jean-François Lyotard's (1984) definition of "terror," namely "the efficiency gained by eliminating, or threatening to eliminate, a player from the language game one shares with him" (63; quoted in Baker 1997, 238). In addition to the notion of "social control," "power" is a concept that, Baker suggests, helps us understand lynching as cultural text. Embedded in this notion may be the gender of racial politics, as "power [in the United States] was always identified with masculinity, while liberty was perceived as feminine" (Greven 1977, 241).

The stylistics of many lynchings remind Baker of the stylistics of public execution in France as discussed by Michel Foucault in *Discipline and Punish.* Like those public executions, lynching "belongs ... to the ceremonies by which power is manifested." "The public execution," Foucault (1979/1995) suggests, "belongs to a whole series of great rituals in which power is eclipsed and restored." Here Foucault portrays power as a phallus, rising and falling, itself a central object in many lynching rituals. Baker likens the ritual elements of a lynching as "a repertoire of techniques for the creation of meaning in a particular text, like the literary devices of imagery or meter." His use of Foucault's notion of "power" does not move him to a political interpretation however: "lynching becomes a vehicle for the conveyance of meaning, not the expression of some sense of justice, however twisted" (quoted passages on 239). "Its aim," referring here to the French public execution, "is not so much to reestablish a balance as to bring into play, at its extreme point, the dissymetry between the subject who has dared to violate the law and the all-powerful sovereign who displays his strength" (Foucault 1979/1995, 48–49). "It is this surfeit of power," Baker suggests, "which is inscribed as the new message in the text of the body of the lynched man" (1997, 239).

The body of the lynched man, Baker continues, served as the site of the text of lynching, as it is viewed by the pubic. "Mutilation of the corpse, in the forms of wounds, missing fingers or genitalia, bullet holes, and other signs of the mob's work," Baker tells us, "becomes part of the text which is to be viewed the next day by the public" (1997, 239). Not trusting one's fellow citizens' capacity to decode "signs," many lynchers left a particular message at the site, sometimes directly inscribed on the corpse, sometimes scribbled on a sign or placard hung from the victim's neck. In ballads and oral accounts, these messages associated with the lynching were sometimes preserved. Not forever, of course, and lynching ballads themselves have disappeared from the oral tradition. Nearly all the lynchings which provoked ballads occurred before 1920 (Baker 1997).

Others who have read lynching as "cultural text" rely on the work of Clifford Geertz (1973). Occupying the border between collective behavior and ceremonial behavior (Smelser 1963), lynching has been read as a quasi-institutional form of justice, a ritualistic reaffirmation of values (Hall 1979), and a cultural expression of a patriarchal, honor-bound South (Williamson 1984). The central peculiarity of southern culture, these critics have argued, has been the persistence of the notion of honor long after the social conditions which supported it had disappeared. Honor rationalized a range of rituals which functioned to affirm traditional values, among them duels as well as lynchings (Stowe 1987). In this view, the often sexualized mob murders of mostly young black men functioned to confirm culturally inherited attitudes toward blacks, women, and the patriarchal order (Ayers 1984; Wyatt-Brown 1982).

Reading the cultural text of lynching in this anthropological sense, then, one is unsurprised that there were those who suggested that lynching was a "custom" requiring only legalization for legitmation. The *New York World* carried the following story in its December 30, 1900, edition:

> HARVARD PROFESSOR FAVORS LEGALIZED LYNCHINGS. Detroit, Dec. 29. Professor Albert Bushnell Hart, of Harvard College, speaking before the American Historical Association in convention here today, said that if the people of certain States are determined to burn colored men at the stake, those States would better legalize the practice. (Ginzburg 1962/1988, 36)

Was Professor Hart calling southerners' bluff? Or was he a victim of his own culture-relative "logic"?

The Historical Moment

But to look at culture only as structure, some historians have complained, is too static a view; it requires a sense of temporal movement, a feeling for the historical moment (Stowe 1987; Erickson 1975). In other words, "how, then, do we explain the timing of lynching's peak?" After asking this crucial question, Edward L. Ayers (1984) allows that "the triggers of lynching, for all the attention devoted to it by contemporaries, sociologists, and historians, are still not known" (238). He acknowledges that "everyone" agrees on the "obvious causes" of lynching: racism, frustration, poverty, submerged political conflict, irrational white fears, a weak state. But these forces, Ayers continues, were constants in the postwar South. Moreover, these conditions were present to some extent during Reconstruction, and yet lynching had not yet gotten seriously under way, although George Wright's research (1990; see chapter 2, section V) questions this assertion. Ayers also notes that these conditions or "causes" remained after 1900, yet lynching declined during the early twentieth century. "What was it, then, about the early 1890s," he asks again, "that made these few years the time of the most brutal mob violence in southern, indeed, American history?" (Ayers 1984, 238).

To answer that question, many point to the economic crisis that plagued the early years of the decade, but Ayers (1984) looks first to politics, asserting that Populism is "one obvious answer" (239). That political version of miscegenation threatened to unite poor whites and poor blacks, thereby undermining white solidarity and the class rule of the white elite. If the feelings of whites in Whitfield County (Georgia) in the early 1890s were any indication, Populism did indeed whip up white fear. In language that today would be associated with homophobia, one newspaper condemned a Populist meeting as a "huge pile of putrid nastiness and ignorant corruption," a "hermaphrodite" party, "rantankerous bigoted asses who brayed negro supremacy and undertook to array the races against each other" (quoted in Ayers 1984, 239). But white men's gendered indignation over political activism does not "explain" lynching. "Political passions may have helped fuel the lynching crisis of the nineties by creating racial animosity," Ayers (1984) argues, "but overt political motives apparently accounted for little of the bloodshed" (239).

Populism may have contributed to the lynching phenomenon, Ayers allows, but not due to emotions which were expressed over specific elections, but "by upsetting the fragile balance of racial etiquette in the South" (Ayers 1984, 239). Is "racial etiquette" here *only* a reference to a set of social customs and (unstable) political structures? Was not etiquette also a fabrication of white men, and as such a "fantasmatic," a "structuring action" (Laplanche and Pontalis 1973, 317; quoted in Silverman 1992, 425, n. 26) designed to stabilize an already "unbalanced" mind? We will see in chapter 4 how the Civil War destabilized gender arrangements in the South, requiring southern "ladies" to vacate the pedestal on which white men had placed them. After the war they were also required to "see" demolished southern white manhood through "complicated eyes," to throw their lot with their defeated men, in fury at the blacks whose freedom now threatened to take white privilege with them. Ayers

(1984) repeats: "the key to the lynching epidemic in the New South does not lie solely in submerged repercussion of Populism" (239).

"The causes of the epidemic," he tells us, "were both more straightforward and more pathological than politics. Defenders of lynching—and there were many in the white South—repeated the same 'explanation' of lynching like a litany: white men lynched because black men raped" (Ayers 1984, 239–240). Curiously, Ayers moves from repeating the white man's incantation rape, rape, rape to the abstraction "madness," and then to another notorious and gendered instance of North American violence: the persecution of witches. "To deny either the irrationality or rationality of lynching," he writes, "is to miss its essence." And what would that be? "Lynching was madness," he tells us, "but with a method ... not unlike the persecution of witches in colonial New England." In both instances "people"—I believe he means "white men"—"thought they knew what they were doing: combating an elusive but terrible foe" (240). To underline the parallel he quotes lynchers in Maryland: "Before God we believe in the existence of a higher code than that which is dignified by the great seal of a Commonwealth and that the high and holy time to exercise it is when the chastity of our women is ravished by the foul breath of an imp from hell and the sanctity of our homes invaded by a demon" (quoted in Ayers 1984, 240). He concludes: "Defenders of justice in both cases had always to be vigilant for signs of the impending visitation—which had a way of appearing just when people were looking for it" (Ayers 1984, 240).

The point is well taken, but I remain faced with the fact of genital mutilation, with the fact that the "rapes" that moved white men to mutilate were, on the whole, imaginary. Even when other "crimes" "demanded" white men's action, rape was still circulating in their minds. Ayers quotes Edward Leigh Pell's 1898 observation that "while other crimes may renew the lynching fever in the lawless, it is the crime against female virtue that spreads the fever among those who had never had it, thereby not only feeding the ranks of lynchers, but weakening the spirit of many who remain on the side of law and order so that their denunciation of lawlessness encourages the mob by its feebleness." It was in this way that rape, Pell explained, "has a prominence in a lynching epidemic that it does not have in the published statistics" (quoted in Ayers 1984, 240).

Once more Ayers confronts the fact and attempts to theorize it: "The fear of black rape obviously triggered *something deep* within the psyche of the white South. Whites had long associated blacks with sexuality" (240, emphasis added). He is almost there, but he declines to specify that "sexuality," raising again the important question of historical moment: "[w]hy did that association [of blacks with sexuality] suddenly erupt in a wave of lynching in the late 1880s and early 1890s?" (240–241). Rather than Populism, rather than economic crisis, Ayers points to racial estrangement: "In part, that crisis [lynching] developed because a new generation of blacks and whites faced each other across an ever-widening chasm" (241). Without daily encounters, it is true, the imagination operates more freely, more abstractedly; the unconscious "speaks" without the interruption of concrete reality. Even the "best" whites and blacks did not mix, Ayers continues; each side withdrew further into their own neighborhoods and churches. Nor, by 1890, did any man under thirty years old, white or black, have any direct experience of slavery, that is, of racial intermingling, however subjugated the intimacy. With this fact in mind Ayers (1984) suggests: "Since most 'criminals' and most violent men have always been young and nowhere younger than in the postwar South, it is safe to assume that most lynchers and lynching victims came from this new generation. These men, white and black, feared each other with the fear of ignorance. They saw each other dimly, at a distance" (Ayers 1984, 240).

Certainly he is half right, but probably many black men saw white men rather clearly. After all, their lives depended on it. White men saw only an imaginary world they, with the help of white women, had fashioned from military defeat, psychological bitterness, a world compensating for ruined white masculinity. In 1890, most southern white men, whether Confederate veterans or their sons, seemed lost in a narcissistic world of mirrors in which their own images were refracted back at them. Terrified by their own shadows, haunted by their lusts and loves, these white men could only see a world occupied by muscular young black men hell-bent on rape. As Walter White knew: "Having created the Frankenstein monster (and it is no less terrifying because it is largely illusory), the lyncher lives in constant fear of his own creation and, at the same time, has by means of his creation caused more crimes against the women of his race than there would have been in a more safe and normal environment" (1929, 56–57).

Can Ayers be right when he asserts that "the same fear nurtured by unfamiliarity seemed even more intense among white women?" Did white women mimic the fear white men felt, a fear close to paranoia, a pathological condition associated with repressed homosexuality (Freud 1911/1963)? Was the white men's fear also borrowed, a "feminine fear" white women knew from their experience with heavy-drinking, often violent white men? It's not as if white women were trapped in their heads; Ayers notes that well-to-do white women had black servants whom they trusted and imagined they knew. However, they did not know homeless, wandering young black men, "bad niggers" as whites called them. White women's knowledge of this category came from white men, including journalists. At no time before or after, Ayers points out, did white women hear more about black rapists than in the early 1890s. "A person cannot pick up a newspaper without an account of this 'one crime' with all its revolting details," Charles H. Otken reported in 1894. "There is a timidity and dread among the white women of the South, unknown in the days of slavery" (quoted in Ayers 1984, 241).

The *Savannah Morning News* illustrates the point. In 1893, the *News* reported that rapes of white women by black men "are becoming so numerous and bold that accounts of one or more of their crimes appear in the newspapers almost every day. White men living in the country who are distant from neighbors are afraid to leave their wives and daughters unprotected in their homes." *The New York Herald* participated in the hallucination, asking its northern white readers to sympathize with white southern fears, for "the difference between bad citizens who believe in lynch law, and good citizens who abhor lynch law, is largely in the fact that the good citizens live where their wives and daughters are perfectly safe" (quoted in Ayers 1984, 241). Such white solidarity would mean that Ida B. Wells could publish nothing in the white press. As we will see in chapter 8, she would have to go to England to find a white audience ready to listen to a black woman speak on the subject of lynching.

Given "this atmosphere of fear," Ayers (1984) continues, as if this hysteria were like the weather, visited upon inhabitants without their choice, "it is hardly surprising that white women perceived black rapists where they did not in fact exist" (241). Should he not emphasize that this "atmosphere" was imaginary and constructed, a complex sublimation of convoluted white male desire? He is willing to say that "white women in the South, their fears fueled by their white male kin and the press, undoubtedly perceived assault where none existed" (Ayers 1984, 242). As for the "cause" of lynching? "The mysterious recesses of sex and race," Ayers concludes, "provided much of the fuel for the conflagration of the nineties, but not the spark. To some extent, the fires of lynching began by a sort of spontaneous combustion fed by racial and sexual fear" (1984, 243). It will take literary critics, not historians, to improve upon this interpretation. Working in a field straddling the humanities and the social sciences, many historians are drawn to "empirical" not literary research methods in their effort to divine the truth of lynching.

V. "Empirical" Studies of Lynching

Events are complex relational wholes, not analytically isolated facts or aggregates.

—Larry J. Griffin, Paula Clark, and Joanne C. Sandberg, "Narrative and Event: Lynching and Historical Sociology" (1997)

[T]he term lynching embraces a wide variety of mob actions and murders, some of which conform to a model of communal rituals but some of which emphatically do not.

—W. Fitzhugh Brundage, *Lynching and the New South: Georgia and Virginia, 1880–1930* (1993)

Being quantitative social scientists by training, we cannot abandon the habits of decades. We hope that not too much of the human tragedy of lynching is lost amid the statistical analysis.

—Stewart E. Tolnay and E. M. Beck, *A Festival of Violence: An Analysis of Southern Lynhings, 1882–1930* (1995)

Of course, no one approach to the study of lynching is likely to be satisfactory, including my own. W. Fitzhugh Brundage (1993, 1997b) underscores that much about mob violence remains unclear or even unexplored. A historian, he complains that some interpretations of lynching are ahistorical, citing early attempts to discover the socioeconomic causes of lynching, such as Arthur Raper's *The Tragedy of Lynching*. When Raper and his colleagues outlined those economic conditions associated with mob violence, they seemed to assume that the same conditions could be found throughout the history of lynching. Raper had argued that mobs flourished in socially isolated, culturally backward, poor communities like the ones that dotted the vast expanse of south Georgia. That was true. But the contrary was true too; lynching also occurred when the same region was undergoing rapid development and could not be characterized as economically stagnant or backward.

Raper also argued that African Americans were most vulnerable in those areas where they comprised a small minority within the total population. The greater proportion of African Americans in a region, the smaller the threat of lynching. He concluded that, "statistically, per ten thousand population of Negroes are safer from mob deaths in the old Black Belt, where more than half of the population is Negro, than anywhere else in the South." Later, Herbert Blalock, also a sociologist, came to the opposite conclusion, namely that the incidence of "symbolic or ritualistic forms of violence, such as lynching" were directly related to the proportion of the population comprised of African Americans. The more blacks, he argued, the more lynchings. Contrary to Raper, then, Blalock was sure that lynchings would be most frequent in precisely those areas where African Americans comprised the majority of the population, Raper's "old black belt counties" (quoted in Brundage 1993, 103)

The problem in these efforts to explain lynching "empirically" (a problematic if widely used term to refer to the quantification of "variables" in psychosocial and political phenomena; see, for instance, Bauman [1978] for a critique), Brundage argues, has to do with the attempt to isolate specific demographic characteristics or rural conditions to explain what was in fact a multidimensional phenomenon. He reports that efforts to explain lynching as a function of the racial profile of a community have either been marred by methodological difficulties and or have tended to ignore "the symbolic significance of lynchings" (1993, 104), a significance I agree can hardly be measured, although Brundage himself seems to fall victim to the promise of measurement himself, as we will see. For now, he points out that Raper's conclusions, for instance, contradicted what whites and blacks alike have known anecdotally, namely that racial prejudice and oppression were most pronounced in those regions with the largest black populations.

While Blalock correctly predicted that lynchings were in fact most frequent in regions where African Americans comprised a majority of the population, that fact hardly solves the mystery. Even within those counties in coastal Georgia and the Cotton Belt of central Georgia where African Americans dominated demographically, the tone of race relations and the incidence of mob violence differed dramatically. Brundage (1993) suggests that it was the absolute number of lynchings in each area and the fear they created—not the per capita rate—that indexed local race relations. Brundage also rejects those arguments that link mob violence to specific rural conditions. Rural poverty, isolation, and weak legal infrastructure were, he argues, "manifestations of the economic and social foundations of the rural South rather than independent variables themselves. To emphasize these traits in explaining lynching is to mistake the symptom for the disease" (Brundage 1993, 104). As well, there were poor and sparsely populated regions of the South that suffered relatively few lynchings (Brundage 1993).

The southern culture of honor has been invoked to explain the peculiar proclivity to lynch in the South, but what exactly is this code? What is its relation to the gendered nature of racial subjugation, in particular the sexualized character of the master/slave relationship organized around the black body? Brundage (1993) points out that honor did not exist synchronically outside of history anymore than any other element of southern culture. Across the late nineteenth and early twentieth centuries, honor was fading from the culture of the South, but lynchings were at their zenith. Finally, the concept of honor is, Brundage observes, "a very blunt interpretative instrument " (11) which fails to explain the significant geographic variations in the actual numbers of lynchings.

Psychohistorical interpretations of lynching have all tended to be too blunt as well, Brundage judges, if in another way. They have often been flawed by reducing the variegated and contradictory phenomenon of lynchings to simple reflections of individual psychology, as in Dollard's "frustration-aggression" hypothesis. In particular, psychological analyses have failed to provide any convincing explanation for regional variations in lynching or to chart its frequency over time, two prominent features of Brundage's scholarship. Until psychohistorical scholarship addresses fundamental questions about family life, the coming of the age in the South (especially the transition from childhood to adulthood), and sexuality (both white and black) during the postbellum period, psychohistorical interpretations of mob violence will remain insufficient, Brundage judges.

While Brundage's criticisms of extant streams of scholarship on lynching seem sensible, they are also functioning to introduce his own, one characterized by "empirical" methods, that is, the compilation of statistics to show regional and temporal variations in lynching practices. He writes: "No explanation of the butchery of lynch mobs can be entirely satisfactory unless it is sensitive to the historical and regional variations in mob violence" (12). He dismisses out of hand any notion of "lethal racial prejudice." True, such prejudice is evident in lynching but cannot in itself serve as an explanation for the practice. To illustrate his point he cites the work of sociologist Oliver C. Cox. In his pioneering work, *Caste, Class, and Race,* Cox (1948) declared that contemporary race prejudice could not be traced back to "its genesis in some 'social instinct' or antipathy between peoples," that it was not intrinsic to human nature. Instead, Cox argued that racism was historical not "instinctual." Its genesis could be located in the early modern era when Europe began to dominate "weaker ... peoples with subtle theories of racial superiority and racial masterhood" (321–322).

For Cox, then, racial prejudice was a weapon used by Europeans to colonize and exploit politically vulnerable others; it was not an expression of "primordial" racial superiority. Although Cox's scholarship has hardly settled the matter—Ivan Hannaford (1996) and others locate the genesis of contemporary racism in the scientific theories of racial superiority that came into fashion in the last quarter of the nineteenth century—Brundage (1993) credits Cox with pointing out that the concept of racism has too often been applied to a set of ideas and opinions the social context of which is left unelaborated. Cox's observations about the nature of racism are, he suggests, especially helpful in thinking about lynching in the late nineteenth- and early twentieth-century South. For instance, the notion of white supremacy, so often cited as a primary cause of lynching and racism, is finally "a vague folk concept" which is made to do more analytical work than it can handle. An unchanging essentialized notion of "white supremacy" cannot account for such a multifarious and inconsistent phenomenon as lynching (Brundage 1993).

Some scholars, primarily historians, have tried to avoid unchanging abstractions and "theory" in general by writing detailed case studies of notorious lynchings. Providing perceptive, often gripping accounts of the setting, the historical context, and the consequences of specific lynchings, these historians, like good novelists, make names and events come alive, as we have seen in James R. McGovern's (1982) study of the lynching of Claude Neal and the Downey/Hyser account of the lynching of Zachariah Walker (chapter 1). Brundage (1993) criticizes this methodological practice by noting that "few of the case studies have staked out new analytical tracks or have untangled the central questions about the historical evolution of lynching across the nineteenth and early twentieth centuries" (15). True enough perhaps, but will statistical graphs of lynching events "untangle" the "central questions"?

Evidently Brundage thinks so. By studying what he terms "the broad sweep" of lynching, rather than a single event, Brundage (1993) argues that it is possible to grasp the variegated nature of mob behavior. Maybe, but concrete vivid detail will be the casualty. Brundage (1993) continues, asserting: "Not every lynching was an event laden with symbolism. To observe that some lynchings were literally banal is not to deny the obvious significance of the symbolism and ritual evident in other lynchings" (15). He is right; there is, of course, a certain banality of evil. The murders of young black men may have been common enough to lack "originality," to have seemed "trite," but only, I think, to white people. The loss of a son or a husband or a brother was never "banal." Always it was unbelievable, overwhelming, outrageous, inconsolable.

Brundage characterizes his graphs of statistics as "interpretations of mob violence that are broad enough to explain both the rituals of torture administered by huge mobs and the perfunctory murders carried out by secretive bands of whites" (1993, 15). Distinguishing between the sizes of white mobs and the regions where lynchings were concentrated is interesting, and represents no doubt an important contribution to the study of lynching, but can it "explain" white men's sexualized mutilations of young black men?

On December 11, 1940, a group of prominent antilynching leaders met to resolve the definitional issue: what was, after all, lynching? For years, the various organizations that fought mob violence had disagreed over the boundaries of the event: when did an incidence of racial violence become a lynching? As Brundage (1993) notes, this question was more than just definitional hairsplitting: the disagreement had led to controversies concerning the actual toll of mob violence. Furthermore, antilynchers' failure to achieve definitional consensus had played into the hands of southern opponents of antilynching legislation. Southern legislators in Washington argued that proposed statutes would open a Pandora's box of unrestricted judicial jurisdiction for a crime apparently no one could even define. Antilynchers finally agreed upon a definition, stipulating that "there must be legal evidence that a person has been killed, and that he met his death illegally at the hands of a group acting under the pretext of service to justice, race, or tradition" (Ames 1942, 29; quoted in Brundage 1993, 17).

While this definition may have resolved the problem for antilynching reformers, definitional concerns persist among scholars of lynching. In setting up the need for the empirical study of lynching, Brundage reviews several dominant definitions in the literature. Referencing the work of Hall (1979), Harris (1984), and Wyatt-Brown (1982), he observes that lynching has been defined variously as a "communal ritual," a "ritualistic affirmation of white unity," and a "scapegoat ritual." As a social practice, lynching was as well, I trust it is becoming clear, an expression of repressed, mangled desire, a homosexual version of white men's raping of black women.

While the definitions various scholars have used have indeed differed, Brundage points out that there seems little doubt over what constituted a lynching. The ritual of lynching, he continues, summarizing dominant perspectives, both reflected the social and racial cohesion of white southerners and functioned to create that solidarity. Loaded with symbolic representation, lynchings functioned like a text that white southerners read to themselves about southern society. In one specific practice were embedded the racial and gendered values of the society that practiced it: white male dominance, personal honor, and the etiquette of chivalry. An endlessly repeated ritual, performed over and over again, year in year out, lynchings were said to celebrate and reinvigorate essential white southern social values and traditions (Hall 1979; Downey and Hyser 1991; Williamson 1984; Wyatt-Brown 1982). Brundage comments: "While this portrait of lynching has contributed valuable insights into the place of mob violence in the post-bellum South, the sweeping assumptions upon which it rests threaten to obscure the complexities of southern mob violence. Attempts to interpret lynching as a ritualized event thick with the deepest values of white southerners may lead to undue emphasis on the unchanging, ritualized, and mass character of mob violence" (1993, 18). Given the variety of forms that lynch mobs assumed—Brundage will identify four, from small secretive groups to enormous crowds—and given that lynching events were often improvised, he insists that it is a mistake to conclude that mob violence was, quoting Clifford Geertz (1973), a "metasocial commentary ... [for] organizing collective existence" (448; quoted in Brundage 1993, 18).

Skeptical, then, of grand abstractions that have typically served as both descriptors and explanations, Brundage focuses more on what was different about specific lynching events, rather than what as "metasocial" phenomena they might have represented. It was the "the great variations in form" that underline, for Brundage (1993), "the complex and contradictory character of lynching. No single model can describe adequately the great differences in size, organization, and motivation that distinguished mobs" (18). For instance, there were small terrorist mobs whose primary intent seemed to be the intimidation of black sharecroppers, a very different organizational form as well as collective motive from those enormous mobs whose stimulus was, apparently, obtaining revenge and "justice" against alleged criminals.

In his study of lynching in Virginia and Georgia during the period 1880–1930, Brundage (1993) identifies four general categories of lynching mobs, according to size, organization, motives, and the character of ritual. Although the nature of violence associated with each category of mob varied from state to state, the features that typified each category of mob remained consistent across the South. Small mobs (fewer than 50 members) comprise the first two types. The first Brundage characterizes as *terrorist mobs* who "made no pretense of upholding the law" (19). The second type of small mob was the *private* mob who exacted vengeance for a wide variety of alleged offenses. The third type Brundage terms *posses;* these ranged in size from a few to hundreds of participants. While quasilegal in nature, these mobs often ignored the limits of their authorized duties and were themselves responsible for mob violence. The fourth kind, *mass mobs,* numbered from more than fifty to hundreds and sometimes thousands of members. They punished alleged criminals with unspeakable viciousness and, on occasion, great ceremony.

By attending to these variations in the sizes and functions of mobs, Brundage discerns different patterns of violence in Georgia and Virginia. All four forms of mob violence occurred in Georgia, with mass mobs and private mobs murdering the most frequently. Still, terrorist mobs and posses claimed a substantial number of lives; in fact, these two kinds of mobs killed more African Americans in Georgia than the total of all mobs in Virginia. In Virginia, mass mobs and private mobs were responsible for nearly all lynchings; posses and terrorist mobs were insignificant. "Not only was mob violence more frequent in Georgia than in Virginia," Brundage (1993) concludes, "but it also erupted in more diverse ways" (19). Because white violence against blacks took such variable forms with such conflicting motives and methods, lynching was "much more than a simple ritualistic affirmation of white unity" (Brundage 1993, 19).

Terrorist mobs saw themselves as drawing upon traditions of folk justice. These mobs tended to punish individuals whose behavior violated local standards or proper conduct. Outraged whites and sometimes blacks employed extralegal violence as a tool of moral regulation. They punished offenses such as drunkenness, public indecency, prostitution, wife abuse, and laziness. Typically, this type of mob did not intend to kill their victims, but hoped to drive them from the community. The favored mode of punishment was whipping. However, on those occasions when "offenders" refused to comply with their demands or attempted to protect themselves, death could result (Brundage 1993).

Brundage expands the category of lynching to include "whitecapping." During the late nineteenth century, two kinds of stress—federal revenue agents in pursuit of moonshiners coupled with economic depression—produced extensive violence, including whitecapping. Unlike those mobs dedicated, as they might have told themselves, to upholding moral standards, moonshiners meant to murder not just intimidate. United by ties of family, locale and shared economic interests, they organized themselves well. Whitecapping organizations—moonshiners or those whose livelihood depended on the moonshine industry—in north Georgia, Brundage (1993) tells us, marshaled members in counties throughout the region. Moreover, they coordinated the activities of what one would expect to be fiercely local groups. Whitecapping in the defense of moonshining was ordinarily focused on revenue agents and informers, but sometimes it included the punishment of both immoral whites and "suspicious" (a very broad and malleable category) blacks. In communities located in the mountainous upcountry of northern Georgia, whitecapping included "deep-seated fears about the status of blacks as well as economic change" (Brundage 1993, 23). In this regard, Tolnay and Beck (1995) report that early in the 1890s, poor white dirt farmers living in the piney woods of southern Mississippi aggressively engaged in "whitecapping" to intimidate black laborers and tenants of absentee landowning merchants. They quote William F. Holmes who suggested that, in Mississippi, "whitecapping specifically meant the attempt to force a person to abandon his home or property; it meant driving Negroes off land they owned or rented" (quoted in Tolnay and Beck 1995, 24).

In other areas, however, whitecapping seems to have been focused on informers and revenue agents. On rare occasion, black moonshiners employed terrorist violence against black informers. In at least four instances, they murdered blacks for informing. Although white terrorist mobs attacked both white and black "enemies" of moonshining, black whitecappers (also known at the time as "whitecaps" [Tolnay and Beck 1995, 24]) never targeted whites. Although the federal government declined to use its power to prevent lynchings or to prosecute lynchers, it was aggressive in the prosecution of moonshiners (Brundage 1993).

Like terrorist mob violence, lynchings by private mobs cannot easily be explained as communal "repressive justice" or as the nineteenth southern version of cultural rituals such as the Balinese cockfights that Geertz described. Rather, lynchings by private mobs represented a form of private vengeance, accounting for 30 percent of all lynchings in Georgia and 46 percent of all lynchings in Virginia. Like terrorist mobs, private mobs were small, sometimes with as few as four or five participants and rarely as many as fifty. They were closed groups, secretive in nature, and often concealed their identities with masks or disguises. Unlike terrorist mobs, however, they imagined themselves as joining together only to punish the most serious crimes (Brundage 1993).

Mass mobs were the most "spectacular" (Brundage 1993, 36) form of lynching mob; they have received the most scholarly scrutiny. The lynching of Claude Neal falls into in this category, as does the lynching of Zachariah Walker. So does the fictional lynching James Baldwin describes in *Going to Meet the Man*. They are the most memorable because they were meant to be; they were often the most horrible. These events were too important to leave out prominent citizens; as Brundage notes, "there seems no reason to question contemporary news accounts that describe many mass mobs as including 'the best citizens' of the community" (1993, 38). Many watched, and many participated. When shooting was involved, tradition demanded that all fire into the corpse, meaning that large mobs sometimes riddled the bodies with hundreds or even thousands of rounds, leaving the mangled corpses unrecognizable (Brundage 1993). Burning achieved the same purpose: the erasure of individuality and identity. It also erased the site of the white male fixation with black male genitalia.

The pattern of mass violence varied from Deep to Upper South. In Georgia, news accounts suggest that mass mobs tortured and mutilated approximately a quarter of their victims in grisly well-attended ceremonies. In contrast, fewer than one in ten victims were mutilated in Virginia. In Virginia, as in many states outside the Deep South, the crimes (or allegations of crime, or rumors) that provoked lynching were narrowly defined. In contrast, whites in Georgia and elsewhere in the Deep South evidently had a much broader conception of the crimes that justified extralegal punishment, for there blacks guilty of nothing more than eccentric behavior could be lynched (Brundage 1993). The relative absence of lethal terrorist violence in Virginia might at first blush appear to be attributable to a tradition of lower levels of extralegal violence in the border states. The fact is that many border states, including Missouri, Indiana, and Kentucky, also saw "serious and enduring forms of terrorist violence" (Brundage 1993, 20), as we saw in chapter 2.

Recall that homicides and attacks on whites by blacks, whether unprovoked or in self-defense, were the most common "causes" cited by lynching mobs; rapes and allegations of rape were second. In Georgia and throughout the South as a whole, the proportion of lynchings prompted by alleged murders and other violent crimes (excluding alleged rape) increased over time. During the 1880s, alleged murders in Georgia were associated with fewer than 20 percent of all lynchings. During the next four decades, 44 percent of lynchings were associated with murders, a number that peaked at 60 percent between 1910 and 1919. Although black on white murders were rare, when they did occur mob violence was assured (Brundage 1993).

As we will see in the Elaine, Arkansas, case (chapter 11, section V), labor disputes between blacks and whites, which routinely bred frustration, suspicion, and anger on both sides of the color line, on occasion resulted in mob violence. Southern labor relations were predictably racialized and associated with violence. Extending Arthur Raper's research, Stewart E. Tolnay and E. M. Beck (1995) point to the worries of well-to-do whites that black and white laborers might form a coalition against the planters. Racial antagonism reduced that risk. As one white planter put the matter: "when a nigger gets ideas, the best thing to do is to get him under ground as quick as possible" (quoted in Brundage 1993, 73).

Class may have been at work in the composition of some lynching mobs. Roger Brown (1965) reminds us that scholars have distinguished between "Bourbon" (Cantril 1941) or "vigilante" (Myrdal 1944/1962) lynchings. In "vigilante" or "mob lynching" there was little concern with the guilt of the victim; the innocent were not protected, and the leaders were not exactly "respectable" citizens. The Bourbon lynching, by contrast, was led by leading citizens with the knowledge of law enforcement officers and other community leaders. Their objective, presumably, was the punishment of a specific crime, and, also presumably, there typically was some interest in establishing the guilt of the accused, and innocent black men were even sometimes protected (Cantril 1941). The Bourbon lynching was planned and "orderly" and at times so "institutionalized" that Roger Brown (1965) is not sure it belongs in his discussion of collective behavior. In its orderliness and community support such lynchings were directly linked to the lynching practices of Revolutionary and frontier days. I suspect there is some classism at work in this distinction, and that relatively few lynchings could be so neatly categorized. Williamson (1984) suggests that upper-class southern whites were eager to portray lynching as a lower-class phenomenon. Were "Bourbon" lynchings always "orderly," crime-specific and authorized by community support? In what sense could any lynching seem "reasonable"?

The truth is that, regardless of class, there was an element of unpredictability in whites' reactions to alleged black crime. For reasons that are not clear, whites did not interpret every attack by an African American as a provocation for lynching. But even trivial confrontations between white law officers and blacks were volatile, a fact that became clear to all Americans during the 1960s, when southern police officers often responded brutally to black protest, events captured on TV. Even when an African American defended him- or herself, not to mention challenged or attacked an abusive policeman—"the caretaker of the color line and defender of the caste system" (quoted in Brundage 1993, 76)—a furious response was forthcoming. Perhaps only rape of a white woman by a black man could match the power of black disrespect toward white policemen to mobilize whites into lynching mobs. Certainly during (but also beyond) the 1960s in many areas of the South, police brutality enjoyed a degree of (white) community sanction that mob violence no longer could summon (Brundage 1993).

Brundage's sociohistorical research moves the study of lynching toward mainstream social science research, but the work of Stewart E. Tolnay and E. M. Beck appears to complete the journey. Neither is a historian; both are sociologists, the latter having served as head of a center for the study of social and demographic analysis. These intellectual commitments and orientations show through, of course, in their conceptualization of the problem. "[W]e have chosen," they explain, "to scrutinize the general contours of lynchings—especially their distribution over time and across space—to determine whether interpretable patterns emerge. Those patterns may suggest the most useful explanations for lynchings" (Tolnay and Beck 1995, 248). I cannot agree, but for now let us review their main points.

First they criticize the major extant interpretative schema for lynching, stating, for instance: "Our findings are not kind to the popular justice explanation for lynchings, despite its popularity among whites during the lynching era" (Tolnay and Beck 1995, 248). Why? There was no need for "popular justice," they argue, because the southern justice system was more than adequately prepared, even eager, to respond to black criminality, usually in a discriminatory fashion. That interpretation dismissed, Tolnay and Beck (1995) turn to "the historical evidence more carefully to identify the real underlying reasons for the willingness of whites to flaunt the very law they professed to revere in order to punish blacks" (249).

Next they turn to what they take to be "the most common explanation" offered for lynching by earlier generations of scholars and researchers: politics. The argument here has been that whites felt politically threatened by the newly franchised black male population and their proportionately large numbers in many areas of the South. Lynching was simply a form of terrorism designed to neutralize the competition. As George Wright (1990) also noted, "hard data" for lynchings committed during the Reconstruction period do not exist. Consequently, it is not possible to assess the adequacy of the political model in the immediate postwar period when African-American men were assuming some power in the reconstructed southern political system. While a number of scholars have concluded that lynchings during Reconstruction were largely political in nature, Tolnay and Beck can "offer little support for that conclusion. ... [W]e can infer no significant effect of political disenfranchisement on the intensity of black lynchings" (1995, 249).

As an extension of the political explanation for lynching, some scholars have suggested that members of the white supremacist southern Democratic party employed violence to suppress threats to their political domination—for instance, the Populist party during the 1890s. Tolnay and Beck examined the relationship between opposition party strength and lynching across the counties of ten southern states during two key periods of southern political history, the so-called Redemption period after Reconstruction and the Populist Era. They found no statistical evidence to suggest that lynchings were positively related to the strength of the Republican party during either era or to the political threat posed by the Populist party during the latter period. In fact, rather than producing a situation of heightened danger for African Americans, significant political opposition to the southern Democratic party appears to have eased white violence somewhat, at least in statistical terms (Tolnay and Beck 1995).

Nor did statistical evidence support the argument that disenfranchisement had any significant effect on the frequency of lynching. Tolnay and Beck (1995) then suggest a kind of continuum of escalating violence which might explain the lynching phenomenon as a response to black "threat," political or otherwise:

> Any discussion of the use of mob violence to counter perceived threats from the black population would be incomplete without mentioning the wide variety of other social control techniques that could have achieved the same objective. ... [I]t is possible that lethal sanctioning was a last resort to which southern whites turned when the other, less drastic, techniques proved ineffective. These alternative techniques included such practices as political disenfranchisement, economic discrimination, the widespread adoption of Jim Crow laws, and a discriminatory system of criminal justice. (79)

Still, the question remains: why *that* "last resort"? Why strip and sexually mutilate the victim?

Like Walter White, Arthur Raper, and others, Stewart Tolnay and E. M. Beck (1995) turn to economic issues to solve the puzzle of lynching: "[o]ur analysis yields strong support for the conclusion that economic factors were important in motivating lynchings" (251). Acknowledging that this argument "extends back to at least the 1930s," Tolnay and Beck report that statistical evidence indicates that lynchings responded to the economic cycles of cotton production, especially during the nineteenth century. In simple terms, increases in the real price of cotton paid to farmers meant fewer black lynching victims. Increases in inflation, that is, decreases in the "real price" of cotton, meant more black lynch victims. African Americans were, then, less at risk when cotton profits were high and purchasing power was strong. While I do not doubt that economic factors were at play in the phenomenon of lynching, I do resist the tendency here to imply that correlation implies causation. No doubt the price of "real cotton" was a factor, but it hardly explains the precise form lynching took, both in practice and in the white male imagination.

Tolnay and Beck are quick to distinguish their research from its antecedents, noting that Hovland and Sears (1940) would have concluded that this statistical relationship points us to a frustration-aggression explanation, that is, economically stressed whites took out their frustration on a vulnerable minority. Tolnay and Beck (1995) acknowledge Raper's argument that during hard times of economic stress and frustration, struggling whites employed violence to displace black farmers from the best land so that they could use it themselves. "We suspect that Raper's interpretation was correct," they comment, but point out that poorer whites were not the only ones to respond to economic distress by assaulting black men. Economically advantaged whites also had a reason to exploit heightened racial tensions during periods of economic difficulty. There was always, if only in the minds of well-to-do whites, a risk of coalition between black and white laborers, rhetorically hinted at by the Populists of the 1890s. By fostering a climate of racial tension and antagonism, white employers could reduce the likelihood of white/black cooperation.

"Of course," Tolnay and Beck concede, "such interpretations for the linkage between cotton prices and lynching must remain largely speculation. The existence of the linkage, however, is now quite clear" (1995, 251). Perhaps so, but, they acknowledge, "the apparently straightforward evidence demonstrating a linkage between the value of cotton and lynching is far from conclusive" (126). Despite these expressions of caution, with some methodological fine-tuning Tolnay and Beck find "evidence that advances in the constant dollar price of cotton were associated with fewer black lynchings, whereas inflationary shifts in the price of cotton were associated with increased mob violence against blacks" (133).

There was a seasonal cycle of mob violence, which Tolnay and Beck cite as providing further evidence of an economics of lynching, if more broadly understood than cotton prices (although cotton price variation is still a correlative factor, if not straightforwardly). Statistical data suggest that lynchings in cotton-producing regions occurred when the need for labor was greatest. "Through increased terrorism," they conclude, "lynching could also heighten the general level of fear among black workers" (Tolnay and Beck 1995, 251). Agreed. But we are still left wondering why economic terrorism was expressed sexually.

The post–Civil War economy in much of the South had been dominated by cotton. This began to change early in the twentieth century. African Americans were drawn to the northern states to search for job opportunities associated with the war effort. World War I had also meant no more immigrant laborers from southern and eastern Europe. Many southern black families chose to relocate, and soon there was an exodus from the South to fill a growing labor vacuum in the North. Not only dreams of better jobs were at work here; lynching, too, inspired African Americans to leave their homes for the unknown North (Tolnay and Beck 1995).

The "Great Migration"—during the 1920s, the South lost approximately 10 percent of its black population—meant many fewer black laborers for landlords and planters whose economic status was now threatened. Tolnay and Beck suggest that white employers responded "quite rationally" to the reality of a shrinking labor supply. Now it was in their economic interest to reduce the number of lynchings. Their statistical data suggest that those areas that had experienced the greatest losses of black population during the 1910s and the 1920s subsequently had fewer lynchings than areas with lower levels of outmigration. While earlier economic stresses endangered African Americans by increasing the risk of lynching (e.g., reduced cotton prices coupled with competition with poor whites), in the twentieth century such difficulties functioned to protect African Americans from violence, as long as a reduction of racial violence served the interests of the most powerful members of southern society (Tolnay and Beck 1995).

Perhaps the threat to whites was more multidimensional and included "race," another figment of the nineteenth-century white mind. While it is clear that southern whites were preoccupied—obsessed might be more precise—with the integrity of the caste line that split the South by skin color, Tolnay and Beck (1995) find more difficulty in the thesis that threats to caste status may have provoked lynching. While the problem is conceptual—"it is virtually impossible to disentangle the status motives for lynching from the political or economic motives"—their statistical evidence did suggest at least some viability for the status threat model: "With virtually no legitimate claim to economic superiority, poor whites resorted to mob violence in order to shore up the caste line that represented a claim to superiority based on the color of their skin" (quoted passages on 253).

Next, Tolnay and Beck (1995) move to set the limits of major researchers' contributions, namely that of Raper, Williamson, and Ayers. They note that Raper was engaged in political activism when he wrote *The Tragedy of Lynching*. Given his economic emphasis one is unsurprised that the two sociologists praise him: "All subsequent work on lynching owes a heavy intellectual debt to this pioneering book" (Tolnay and Beck 1995, 253). They then deemphasize his economic emphasis and paint Raper as a culturalist, noting that he tended to view mob violence as the consequence of the undereducated, isolated, and backward culture characteristic of many poorer whites and of the unwillingness of the southern power elite to intervene. Raper also argued in classic southern progressive style (ignorant, one suspects, of the work of Ida B. Wells, for instance), that African Americans had a part to play in stopping lynching by taking better advantage of the limited opportunities available to them and by refusing to become involved in criminal activity or to shelter those who do from legal authorities.

Next Tolnay and Beck move to Joel Williamson, whose intellectual power and accomplishment they acknowledge, after a fashion. They note that Williamson has described, "in compelling fashion," the appearance of "radical racism" in the South during the late nineteenth and early twentieth centuries. They acknowledge, too, that Williamson was after more than, say, attitudes; he sought to convey nothing less than "the southern psyche"—perhaps in a way parallel to Cash's notion of the "mind of the South" (of which he is critical). Not only white attitudes but something archetypal of the white southern psyche was expressed in radical racism: "No longer were blacks viewed as the shuffling, obsequious, and harmless 'darkies' who deserved paternalistic protection. Suddenly, they became threatening, atavistic animals who posed a threat to the security of white society, especially to white womanhood. According to Williamson, this psychological transformation was instrumental in the epidemic of mob violence that spread throughout the 1890s and after" (Tolnay and Beck 1995, 254).

Finally, they turn to Edward L. Ayers, who, they allow, "has written extensively and eloquently on the character of the New South, including the shame of mob violence." They note that Ayers suggested that many black victims of lynching were single men looking for work, or simply drifting, without connections to the local community. With fears of black criminality running wild in the white mind by the 1890s, and with no local advocates to turn to for support, these black male strangers to the white community were completely vulnerable to mob "justice," a suggestion perhaps more plausible than data-based, Tolnay and Beck (1995) point out (see 258, n. 27). They quote Ayers' (1992) *The Promise of the New South*: "Lynchings tended to flourish where whites were surrounded by what they called 'strange niggers,' blacks with no whites to vouch for them" (157). Late nineteenth-century lynching contained various ingredients: a paranoid white population, a rootless black population, and white supremacist ideology. In some respects, Tolnay and Beck suggest, "Ayers's framework combines the basic elements of Raper's and Williamson's perspectives. There are many lenses through which to view the phenomenon of lynching," they continue,

> and we do not wish to claim that the conclusions reached by Raper, Williamson, and Ayers are wrong. However, based on our own work, we are willing to say that they are incomplete because they do not do justice to the fundamental role that mob violence played in the maintenance of southern society and economy. Our evidence suggests that lynching was an integral element of an agricultural economy that required a large, cheap, and docile labor force. (Tolnay and Beck 1995, 255)

So, we are basically back where we started, except with the "assurance" of statistics. Certainly they are right on two points: there are many lenses through which to view lynching, and not one of them is complete or definitive. The complex mix of psychosexual dynamics, historical moment, culture, class, and, yes, economics cannot be reduced to any one causal factor or even one explanation, not even homosexual desire.

With the omission of the sexual factor—so clear to African Americans from Ida B. Wells to James Weldon Johnson to Calvin Hernton and even to a white woman, Jessie Daniel Ames—Tolnay and Beck would agree with that string of abstractions in my previous sentence, I think. In one passage in which they position Raper, Williamson, and Ayers as decidedly earlier and more primitive stages (their constructs become not explanations but "manifestations") on the way to the "sophisticated" explanations yielded by statistics, they construct a rather grand abstraction themselves in which their cotton price factor circulates invisibly:

> Thus the story of lynching is much more than uncultured white peckerwoods engaging in drunken carnage, or a shift in the southern psyche that changed the popular image of African Americans, or vulnerable transient workers who may or may not have broken the law. Rather, these were all manifestations of a much grander, more complex, set of social arrangements that saw African Americans at the bottom of a status hierarchy defined by race and class. Only when the status quo was threatened by forces that could not be blunted through the use of violence and terrorism would lynchings begin to disappear. And that is exactly what occurred when African Americans finally had the option to go north. (Tolnay and Beck 1995, 255)

Is this not too rational an explanation, one that positions lynching only as a move in a chess game of class and race? Did the "great migration" play that great a role in the disappearance of lynching?

Conceptual exuberance and complexity aside, Tolnay and Beck return to a humbler tone, in fidelity to their basic economic argument, an argument that leaves unanswered why black men, so often young black men, were victims, why the castrations, why the nearly universal white fantasy that black men were ready to rape white women at every opportunity. These were, if we accept Tolnay and Beck's statistics at face value, evidently fortuitous moves chosen only for their effectiveness in a bottom-line economic game:

> Although we have arrived at our respective destinations by traversing very different terrain, our conclusions overlap significantly with those reached much earlier by White and those described only recently by Brundage. Both investigators describe lynchings, and the terror they created in the African-American community, as crucial mechanisms for assuring perpetuation of the southern status quo, especially the continuation of an exploitative plantation economy. (Tolnay and Beck 1995, 255)

And yet once more: "[e]conomic forces were clearly the most important undercurrent that carried southern society to such outrageous extremes of brutality. Economic forces also turned the tide against mob violence during the 1920s and 1930s, as employers agonized over the exodus of their cheap black workers" (Tolnay and Beck 1995, 257).

I doubt none of this, but it seems so woefully incomplete. Does it speak to the gendered dynamics we sense in Baldwin's fiction, seemingly so much more true to life than numbers in demographic analyses? Statistics seem lifeless indeed compared to the rich and evocative prose of Joel Williamson. For my money, Williamson was much closer to understanding the mystery of lynching than any number cruncher, however circumspect, could possibly be. (I will return to

Williamson in the final chapter.) Finally, it turns out, perhaps Stewart Tolnay and E. M. Beck might themselves agree with me:

> As with all sound bites, the previous paragraph does not do the full story justice. ... This was an extraordinary period of American history, during which ordinary folks did unspeakable things. ... Clearly, they must have been swept along by very strong social forces to feel justified in committing more than two thousand atrocities against their black neighbors. (Tolnay and Beck 1995, 257)

They were "swept along" alright, and not only by "social forces." There is much more to the story, including a "crisis" in white masculinity, the invention of "homosexuality," the appearance of a "new woman," and the continued and bitter mourning of a lost lover, companion, slave. But with that I am ahead of myself. Let us now turn to literary efforts to read the text of lynching.

VI. Literary Research

> *[T]he repeated castrations of lynched black men cries out for serious psychocultural explanation.*
>
> —Cornel West, *Race Matters* (1993)

> *[The] practice of dismemberment enables a* perverse ... *physical intimacy between the white male aggressor and his captive ex-slave.*
>
> —Robyn Wiegman, "The Anatomy of Lynching" (1993)

> *The prevailing concern here is with the* persistency *with which lynching scenes appear across genres and through many generations of black writers.*
>
> —Trudier Harris, *Exorcising Blackness: Historical and Literary Lynching and Burning Rituals* (1984)

> *The fact remains, of course, that men, not women, lynched other men.*
>
> —Edward L. Ayers, *Vengeance and Justice: Crime and Punishment in the Nineteenth Century American South* (1984)

Trudier Harris's (1984) *Exorcising Blackness: Historical and Literary Lynching and Burning Rituals* is a groundbreaking work in the literary research on lynching. Focusing primarily on examples of lynching in American literature, Harris links lynching with the broad spectrum of racial violence and oppression in America: "Lynchings became, then, the final part of an emasculation that was carried out every day in word and deed. Black men were things [like women], not men, and if they dared to claim any privileges of manhood, whether sexual, economic, or political, they risked execution" (1984, x). She observes that African-American writers from Charles Waddell Chestnutt to Sutton Griggs, from Paul Laurence Dunbar to James Weldon Johnson, from Richard Wright to James Baldwin, and from Langston Hughes to Ralph Ellison have all dwelled on lynching. "This tradition [in black literature] of presenting black male characters as powerless and emasculated," Harris explains, "is a counterpart to the works in which black characters are actually deprived of the very power of living and literally emasculated by the specific act of physical castration during lynchings and burnings" (1984, xii).

Among the extraliterary sources upon which Harris draws are Walter White, Richard Maxwell Brown, James Comer, and Gordon W. Allport. She quotes White's observation that lynching became "an almost integral part of our national folkways." We are reminded that as the incidence of lynching increased, the sexualized sadism of the practice intensified: "The nature as well as the quantity of the lynching of Southern Negroes was horrifying, for they came to be regularly subjected to fiendish tortures that had seldom been inflicted on the white victims of lynch law. The lynching of Southern Negroes came to be accompanied routinely by the emasculation of males and the burning of both sexes" (Brown 1971, 105). Harris also quotes James Comer (1972) who observed that "black victims were castrated, tortured, burned and mutilated by white men, women and children in drunken, orgy-like atmospheres" (134). Harris notes that in *The Nature of Prejudice* Allport (1958) understood lynching as a form of projection as well as a group rite of "cleansing," a "process groups undergo when they can project their basest fears and desires onto other groups, including sexual fears and repressions" (Harris 1984, 17).

Harris characterizes white men as the "performers" in the "lynching ritual" (1984, 19), victims of their culture's "imagination" (20). Working heterosexually, Harris suggests that lynching represents "a symbolic transfer of sexual power at the point of executions. The black man is stripped of his prowess, but the very act of stripping brings symbolic power to the white man" (22). True in a sense, but I would argue that the white men's obsession with the black male also functioned to underline the sexual power of the black man, and in prison that, not symbolic power, is what counts. In the next sentence, Harris seems to understand the queer character of lynching. Referring to the white male lyncher she writes: "His actions suggest that, subconsciously, he craves the very thing he is forced to destroy" (22). But this "craving" stays unnamed, and she returns to a view of lynching as power, if sexualized: "Yet he [the white man] destroys it as an indication of the political (sexual) power he has and takes it unto himself in the form of souvenirs as an indication of the kind of the power he would like. In some historical accounts, the lynchers were reputed to have divided pieces of the black man's genitals among themselves" (Harris 1984, 22).

Harris stays with this interpretative thread for only a stitch, and once again, perhaps despite herself, she moves toward the brute fact, believing what she sees. [As Jack Kerouac once said on the "Steve Allen Show" in 1959: "I believed in what I saw."] "From one perspective," she writes, almost gingerly, "[t]here is a communal rape of the black men by the crowd which executes him. [Crowd? Women and children sometimes watched, but the mutilation, as far as we know, was conducted only by the men, white men.] They violated him by exposing the most private parts of his body and by forcing him, finally, into ultimate submission to them" (23). Sounds like sex to me. In the next sentence she's almost there: "Comparable to sexual snuff films, in which the victims participate against their wills, or without knowing what the end of the film will be, and provide pleasure without intending to do so, the lynched black man becomes a source of sexual pleasure to those who kill him. ... Killing the black man, therefore, provides a peculiar kind of satisfaction" (23). Peculiar? Why not say it? Lynching provided a *queer* satisfaction.

Brilliantly I think, Harris turns psychoanalytic at this point, although she does not name it as such. She returns to the primal scene in which the black man is dismembered, and writes that "his death also enables white males to act out a fear of castration even as they are in the process of castrating the black man." Here, situating lynching within the culture of masculinity, she almost deracializes the act: "Perhaps the worst fear any man can have is the fear that someone will cut off his penis; the white man, heir to that fear just as the black man is, designs as the peculiar punishment for black men that which all males fear most." But why focus on black men? Why not Latinos? Why black men and why castration? The white man's "action simultaneously shows his kinship to the black man and denies the connection. He does to the black man what, in his worst nightmares, he perhaps imagines other adversaries doing to him; before he becomes a victim, he victimizes" (all passages are Harris 1984, 23). Because he cannot accept his sexual attraction to him—a position of "castration" as it feminizes him—the white man must lynch the black man?

"Kinship" in that quoted passage reverberates in Lévi-Strauss's patriarchal system of social organization, but I think the sense of "family" relevant here is the one gay men sometimes invoke. The "connection" the white man denies is one of desire, an intolerable, unspeakable homosexual desire that must be denied and heterosexualized. If he is performing on the body of the black man what he "imagines other[s] ... doing to him," does he not imagine the black man all over him, as he in fact will be when the opportunity affords itself, in prison, not a century later? Is not this "fear" inverted desire? Is not the kinship pattern evident in this primal scene of "totem and taboo" a sexualized and racialized father-son relationship, reminiscent of the passages following Genesis 9:24 wherein Noah punishes his son Ham by creating the black race? What had the son done to provoke such paternal rage? There have been biblical commentators who have speculated that the "crime" was Ham's rape of his father (Sollors 1997). At the civilizational genesis of "race" is there incest, the homosexual rape of the father by the son?

Is that why white southerners referred to adult black men as "boy," positioning them as prepubescent children, sons specifically? "Keep in mind," Harris (1984) reminds us, "that it is white man's tradition to call the black man 'boy.' If the black man is indeed a boy, then he can be easily controlled in everyday affairs." Perhaps, but boys, that is, sons, everywhere and always are ready to contest their positionality as "son," knowing, as straight boys do, they are destined to assume the father's seat at the dinner table. Since it is the "father's" idea to call this full-grown man a "boy" perhaps there is effort at sublimation, superimposing a vertical kinship relation on top of a sensory and horizontal encounter in the tent. By repositioning the black man as prepubescent, the white man can deny the sensuality and seductive power he imaged as the black man's own, the attractiveness which he transposed into the black man's desire, now, in a feat of racial and gender alchemy, a "threat" to the white woman the white man has imagined a "lady."

As Freud knew, such identificatory tactics are sublimations of the "negative Oedipus complex" in which the son identifies with the mother and desires the father. Harris too appreciates this sexual subtext to the "boy" fantasy on the part of white men: "Calling him a boy suggests, as well, the strange lens through which the white man must view the black man sexually. 'Boy,' an effort at controlling language and thereby controlling the reality the language is designed to reflect, wipes out the symbolic, sexual implications of the black man as Man" (Harris 1984, 23–24). A man, like his father, to whom "Ham" feels a strange, at times overwhelming, attraction.

Heterosexist critics, even ones as brilliant as Harris, can overlook this imprinting queer element in racial politics. This is evident in Harris's discussion of James Baldwin's *Another Country* (1962), a novel to which we will return briefly in chapter 18 as a "parenthesis" in my summary of Leslie Fielder's analysis of the interracial homoerotic structuring that is, Fielder argued, American civilization. In Harris's commentary on Baldwin's novel, there is no mention of the black character's (Rufus Scott) homosexual affair with a white man. She focuses exclusively on his affair with a white woman (Leona), whom she takes to be the victim in the relationship. In fact, Harris accuses Rufus of "mentally destroying the white woman with whom he has an affair" (1984, 54). Harris then suggests because there were no "legal lynchers" to punish him, "he is so awed by his own violation of taboo and so warped by his tendency to violence that he kills himself" (54). In so doing, the black man assumes the position of the white men in the mob. "During and after his affair with white Leona, he becomes so violent and obsessively self-destructive that it is impossible for him to live a peaceful and healthy life. Consequently, he punishes himself for accomplishing the very destruction—making Leona pay for loving a black man—he has set out as his objective" (Harris 1984, 54).

This rings true, but only within a heterosexist logic; in the novel the narrator suggests that it is Leona who drives Rufus to the edge, although why it is not clear. Harris ignores Rufus's own understanding of his suffering which he ascribes to white society, especially to white men. While locating Rufus's suffering in white society—because the "eyes of whites convey to him that, though he walks with the white woman, he is still a 'nigger' and still barely a grade above animals" (Harris 1984, 54)—Harris argues that Rufus comes to ruin also because he believes his masculinity "is perverted and used against him" (62). One might think Harris is referring to his bisexuality, but again, no mention is ever made of that. Instead she focuses upon the dangers black men face with white women: "It [Rufus's stereotypical black male sexuality] is initially not a burden, and he seduces Leona with all the fire of a young man giving what he knows he is capable of giving. What is not yet a burden, however, is nonetheless a consideration. Rufus believes Leona has come to him because she thinks black males are more sexually endowed than whites" (Harris 1984, 63).

Because Rufus has started his relationship with Leona under the shadow of this stereotype, Harris argues, he is doomed. She suggests that Rufus cannot believe Leona is able to see through the stereotype to his individuality. "[I]n spite of his physical sexual prowess," Harris (1984) continues,

> Rufus is no less emasculated in his relationship with the white woman than are many literary characters who come before and after him. A victim of his own history and his own imagination, Rufus accepts all the notions of what he is as a representative black man and, among those many externally imposed ideas, he has difficulty knowing what he is in reality. As his relationship with Leona goes along, he will find himself acting out more and more the roles which history and custom have assigned to him. He commits suicide as much to escape from those as from the pain which his acceptance has caused. (63)

Rufus's relationship with Leona, then, is a symbolic one, and as such, is not entirely "heterosexual." Harris argues that his seduction of Leona is an expression of racialized rage, a kind of payback—and here Harris cites Eldridge Cleaver's claim in *Soul on the Ice* that his raping of white women was a political act—for all he has suffered as a black man in racist America. Harris reminds us that during their trip from the jazz club where they met to the party where he seduces her, Rufus is thinking not of her but of his boot camp experience in the South, "how he had been beaten into the dirt by a white officer" (63). The black man's desire for the white woman has contained within it, as Michele Wallace (1978/1979) has suggested, desire for the white man, if negatively valorized as "revenge." Rufus, Harris continues, is unable to see Leona as an individual; I would add, as a woman. Rather, as Harris (1984) notes, "she [Leona] becomes one component of that white blob of power, and he sees his opportunity to exert his own power play by subduing her. Poor, timid, previously abused Leona is thus ripe for what Rufus wishes to heap upon her" (63). Harris lays it out:

> Somewhere in the reaches of his mind, the image of himself as a superstud combines with the white-female taboo and makes him evoke the image of the lynch mob. That evocation is a prelude to his loss of confidence, for it has as its center the notion that he is trespassing upon territory forbidden to him even as he tries to convince himself that he can conquer that territory and use it for his own purposes. His cursing of the "milk-white bitch" highlights both his attraction to Leona and the challenge she represents for him; he must not conquer her as mere woman, but as *white* woman. His "thrusting," his thoughts of the "lynch mob," and his use of his penis as a "weapon" are all images tied to violence and destruction, not to making love. With this kind of background for their physical coupling, it is questionable if Leona and Rufus could ever make love with each other. (1984, 64)

That Rufus is being destroyed by a gendered, even sexualized racism—in the world, inside his head, and in the person of Leona as symbol—is evident in conversation with Vivaldo: "How I hate them—all those white sons of bitches out there. They're trying to kill me, you think I don't know. They got the world on a string, man, the miserable white cocksuckers, and they tying that string around my neck, they killing *me.* ... You got to fight with the landlord because the landlord's *white*! You got to fight with the elevator boy because the motherfucker's *white*. Any bum on the Bowery can shit all over you because he can't hear, can't see, can't walk, can't fuck—but he's *white*!" (Baldwin 1965, 62). To Vivaldo's protest that "not everybody's like that" and that Leona loves Rufus, Rufus retorts: "'She loves the colored folks so much ... and sometimes I just can't stand it. You know all that chick knows about me? The only thing she knows?' He put his hand on his sex, brutally, as though he would tear it out, and seemed pleased to see Vivaldo wince. He sat down on the bed again. 'That's all.'" (Baldwin 1965, 62). Harris (1984) comments: "His gesture an indication of his castration, Rufus finds himself aboard a rollercoaster to his destruction" (67). I would suggest that what Harris perceives as his "castration" might also be his frustration at being reduced in the white mind to his sex. So fictionalized, his subjectivity is effaced; he is not "castrated" in a literal sexual sense. Rather, his problem is that he is, in the white mind, (only) a superstud. Yes, Rufus is "unable to separate race from sexuality and stereotype from substance" (67), but is this only *his* failing? Is this not a great problem facing many black men whose racial subjugation by whites is profoundly sexualized?

But Harris concentrates only on Rufus's internal dynamics, suggesting that he is consumed by guilt for abusing Leona: "Rufus strips himself of much more than whites ever could, for even if he were arrested for his treatment of Leona, a jail sentence would perhaps be his severest punishment; left alone, though, he punishes himself mentally and physically" (68). Perhaps, but I see no reason not to believe Rufus when he says that whites are killing him. That includes his white friend Vivaldo as well as Leona and his gay male lover Eric, as even sex mirrors back to him that he is not real, only a figment in the white male mind, a sexual servant in the white homosocial household. Harris will have none of it: "He has tried repeatedly not to be emasculated by Leona, only to discover that he has emasculated himself" (68). This is too simple, I believe, too exclusively heterosexual. "If he had allowed Leona to love him, just as a man, not as a superstud [easier said than done for a subject position that conflates the race and sex], that would have been a denial of one portion of his identity he felt was intact; to be mere man meant to him to be sexually weak, therefore emasculated" (68). Harris continues:

> Since his strongest identification as a black man is with his sexuality, he cannot dissociate himself from it—even when it means reducing himself as a human being. A man at war with himself [as all men are], Rufus cannot afford to be gentle and loving. His refusal to do so indicates that the whites have controlled his mind to such an extent that his entire existence becomes one sustained reaction to them. He cannot exist outside the cage which has been defined for him. Nor does he really believe he has the right to exist outside the cage. (Harris 1984, 68)

The "cage" in which Rufus lives and dies is the prison cell of white men's imagination, materialized into social structures, economic inequalities, sexual practices, and, as Harris emphasizes, internalized subjective spaces.

The "persistency" of lynching as a theme in black, especially black male, fiction does not imply, Harris is at pains to point out, any morbid or "unusual" preoccupation with the practice (70). Nor is it true that European-American writers ignore lynchings. [She mentions Theodore Dreiser and William Faulkner as examples of white writers who do focus upon lynching.] Harris suggests that it is the memory, collective if not personal, of these nightmares that compels black men to write about them. She notes that when white writers treat lynching in their fiction, they "are not inclined to portray gruesome details. Black writers show the ugly details and make history live again, if only for a brief moment, in the works they create" (Harris 1984, 70).

Treatment of the lynching and burning scenes—Harris always makes a distinction—by black writers parallels the statistical incidence of lynchings. Before the South's defeat in the Civil War, she notes, black men were not often lynched, certainly not in the ritualistic manner Baldwin, for instance, described in *Going to Meet the Man.* Early black American literature focused, understandably, more on slavery, the issue at the time. Harris notes that the treatment of lynching in Brown's *Clotel* in 1853 is relatively mild compared to Baldwin's *Going to Meet the Man* published in 1968. Although Brown's portrayal of lynching includes violence, it does not narrate those gruesome details that later works do. After the Civil War, the increased incidence of lynching was accompanied by the increased incidence of lynching scenes in American imaginative literature. Moreover, Harris notes, in these postwar works lynching scenes become more integral to the literary structure.

Perhaps more than any other twentieth-century black writer, Harris (1984) argues, Richard Wright relies on lynching (literal and symbolic) "to shape the basis of his aesthetic vision of the world" (95). Lynching informs both collective and individual character as well as providing the symbolic unifying structure for "Between the World and Me" (1935), "Big Boy Leaves Home" (1938), *Native Son* (1940), and *The Long Dream* (1958). The reality of lynching becomes for Wright's characters the structuring event of their lives. Black men "live, eat, and breathe the threats perpetually hanging over their heads, and the women in their lives are forced to share their anxieties or be dismissed from consideration" (Harris 1984, 95). That one sentence succinctly if partially summarizes the gender of black racial politics in America.

In the rarely anthologized poem "Between the World and Me," Wright introduces "the lynching/burning image" (97) to his work. "The act of burning and mutilating the black youth," writes one student of Wright's work, "is basically an act of sexual revenge. ... The burning of the Negro is a vicarious sexual experience for the women who watch" (Schraufnagel 1973, 22; quoted in Harris 1984, 108). As in prison rape, this critic understands the lynching ritual as a sexual act between men, one which some white women watched. Whether or not women experienced the event "vicariously" is of course speculation, but clearly white women's participation in lynching differed from men's in this respect. There is no evidence of women participating in the sexual torture and mutilation of black men. No doubt gender conventions (and specifically the ideology of separate spheres) were at work here, but if lynching were a finally homosexual event, predictably women would be excluded. Perhaps women wished to be excluded.

Even when castration did not occur during lynching, there was, another student of Wright suggests, still castration. Referring to "Big Boy Leaves Home" in *Uncle Tom's Children*, Blyden Jackson (1976) asserts that the burning of Bobo represents a rite of castration:

> Wright, whether wittingly or not, gathers up the essence of that which he is struggling to express and stores it all into one symbol and its attendant setting. For the spectacle of Bobo aflame at the stake does constitute a symbol. It is a symbol, moreover, the phallic connotations of which cannot be denied. Indeed, the particularity of its detail—the shape of its mass, its coating of tar, the whiteness of the feathers attached to its surface or floating out into the surrounding air—are almost too grossly and gruesomely verisimilar for genteel contemplation. Whether Wright so intended it or not, the lynching of Bobo is symbolically a rite of castration. ... In the lynching of Bobo, thus, all lynchings are explained, and all race prejudice. Both are truly acts of castration. (139–140; quoted in Harris 1984, 109)

And castration, in this context, is a mangled version of homosexual rape, a doubly distorted event. As Fiedler (1966) suggests (see chapter 18), somewhere "behind" the hatred there was love and longing.

Harris thinks of Baldwin's "Going to Meet the Man" at this point, judging Jackson's analysis as "tenable when racial power is viewed in sexual terms" (1984, 109). While unable to decode lynching explicitly as homosexual assault, Harris does make this interpretation a kind of analogy. One step removed from literal reality, she understands lynching in heterosexual binary terms:

> To suppress the black man, in this analogy, is to put him in the feminine position of the [hetero-] sexual act; his manhood is stripped from him [he's a punk in prison parlance]; he is "castrated" (black woman presumably join their men in being powerless and often times submissive, but must suffer additionally from the male-oriented analogy). It is no wonder, continues Jackson, that the grinning, hat-in-hand, bowing and scraping darky so resembles a eunuch. (Harris 1984, 109–110)

In addition to these parentheses, I would underscore that this failed effort to feminize black men was fundamentally defensive and compensatory in character; white men were and remain in a "feminine" position vis-à-vis black men, and the castration of lynching was in this sense a desperate effort to even the gender playing field, as white men imagined it.

In Wright's *Native Son,* Harris (1984) points out, the police take Bigger Thomas to court for what George C. Wright (1990) might characterize a "legal lynching," "justice" almost as "summary" as lynching would have been. Employing the "sexual mythology" of the black men (a mythology, I might add, which makes clear the fundamentally feminine position of the white man),

Noel Schraufnagel (1973) observes that the police encourage the press to paint "vivid images of the bestiality of the already condemned black youth. In the minds of the white bigots, Bigger is the brute Negro incarnate who should be eradicated in any way possible, preferably by lynching" (26; quoted in Harris 1984, 114). As the prosecuting attorney, Buckley is permitted to stir up white emotions toward Bigger just as any leader of a mob might have (a lawyerly tactic we will revisit in chapter 12 in the trials of the Scottsboro Nine). In his summation at the trial, he calls Bigger as a "miserable human fiend" (372), a "half-human black ape" (373), a "black mad dog" (374), a "sly thug" (374), a "subhuman killer" (373), a "hardened black thing" (374), a "rapacious beast" (374), a "beast" (375), and a "piece of human scum" (375; quoted in Harris 1984, 114).

In Wright's *The Long Dream* there is an explicit eroticization of one of the main characters. Throughout the novel, characters comment on Fish's good looks, including a white policeman who arrests him for trespassing at the waterhole during the mud fight. In another incident, Fish and his friends Sam, Zeke, and Tony assault Aggie West, a gay kid in their neighborhood. When he tries to join them in one of their games, they dismiss him as "pansy," "fruit," and "fairy" (38), then join together in beating him until he makes an escape. Harris (1984) comments:

> Still in their pre-teenage and teenage years, the boys have nevertheless formed prejudices as irrational as those whites hold toward them. Aggie is a weaker creature who can be bullied by the "mob" of four players in ways similar to the destructive play white men sometimes direct at black men. ... They feel power over Aggie by virtue of their masculinity, their group solidarity, and their physical prowess, so they do to him together what almost any one of them could have done alone. (Harris 1984, 118)

These comments suggest the homophobia of many teenage boys, themselves struggling to contain the powerful homoeroticism of same-sex friendships (see chapter 13). Unlike white men in lynch mobs, Wright's black characters become ashamed of their conduct. Harris notes that Zeke, one of the older boys, not only experiences guilt, but understands the parallel between their homophobia and white racial violence: "We treat 'im like the white folks treat us," he "mumbles" "with a self-accusative laugh" (39; quoted in Harris 1984, 118). "As [black] boys on their way to becoming men," Harris (1984) notes, using Lacanian language, "they are shown what they lack, forced to desire that lack" (Harris 1984, 119).

In Wright's *The Long Dream,* twenty-four-year-old Chris is lynched and dragged through the streets of Clintonville behind a car, not unlike the lynched body of Cleo Wright in Missouri in 1942 (see chapter 11). One ear is gone, perhaps "eaten away by the friction of asphalt against the side of the head" (76); the "mangled neck ... might've been broken *two* places or more" (76); "the nose is almost gone" (77); "the left cheek has been split by a gun butt" (77); a hole has been kicked through his side to reveal his intestines, and "the *genitalia* are gone" (77; quoted in Harris 1984, 123). Observed by white men while staring at a white girl, Fish faints when one of the police officers opens "a long, gleaming blade," and declares, "Nigger, I'm going to *castrate* you!" (111). For the remainder of the trip to the police station, the policemen enjoy this threat while Fish cringes with memories of "Chris's bloody, broken body" (111; quoted in Harris 1984, 125). Harris (1984) concludes:

> The extent of Wright's preoccupation with lynchings and burnings, both in the metaphorical and literal senses, sets him apart from writers preceding and following him who deal with the subject. His aesthetic concerns are at once unique but also reflective of those shared by other writers in the tradition. Though Baldwin's presentation of the burning in "Going to Meet the Man" is powerful, no writer following Wright would allow the subject such a central place in the corpus of his or her works. Yet, these writers continued to show, through their occasional treatment of lynching, that it had not completely been eradicated from the psyche of the black American writer. (129)

Harris also discusses John Wideman's *The Lynchers,* in which four black men plot the lynching of a white policeman. Littleman (Littleman is the name given the black male character Willie Hall by his fellow plotters) tells us he is "not talking about grabbing just any old body and stringing him up to the nearest lamp post," but that he is calling for a "formal lynching" (60). Such a lynching would have "style" and "power," just like those done by southern white men. Those guys, he continues, did not shy away from "real blood" and "undignified screams and writhing"; rather, there was a "communal hard-on" when the black man was tortured then mutilated (quoted in Harris 1984, 134). Littleman understands the planned lynching as a way of unifying the impoverished and socially fragmented black community in which he lives, but he comes to understand that using white violence as the model for change is unacceptable.

Toni Morrison's *Tar Baby* (1982), Harris (1984) points out, sets us up for an accusation of rape and the summary execution of a black man. A young black man—Son—is discovered in a white woman's bedroom, but, as Harris (1984) notes, the response is surprisingly casual. Son realizes that the white woman's older (white) husband—Valerian—does not fear him: "They are frightened, he thought. All but the old man. The old man knows that whatever I jumped ship for it wasn't because I wanted to rape a woman" (13). I shall again take liberties with Harris's text to insert queer parenthetical supplements to her analysis: "It is perhaps unusual to assume that logic prevails with white men who discover black men in the bedrooms of their wives, but Son's nonchalance suggests that he understands [the gay side of white men] and is reasonably comfortable with Valerian's opinion of [desire for] him" (159). The queer subtext in the white man's response to the black man becomes more direct. Harris (1984) writes:

> He [Son] is so sure of Valerian's attitude he reveals those "dangerous" private parts to Valerian on his first trip to the greenhouse: "[Son] sprayed some of the ant killer on his legs. His kimono came undone at the belt and fell away from his body. Valerian looked at his genitals and the skinny black thighs. 'You can't go round like that in front of the ladies. Leave that alone, and go tell Sydney to give you some clothes. Tell him I said

> so'" (148). Certainly he may be concerned with general propriety [or perhaps he wants the view for himself], but there is no alarm or fear in his observation [why should there be, it's "natural" for a white man to be gazing at the black man's body], nothing to reveal he imagines what he has just seen being used against his wife. (Harris 1984, 159)

Indeed. As we saw in the case of nineteenth-century southern white men, the "wife" was often a pretext for homosexualized assault. Harris seems to understand the gender of lynching; she characterizes it at one point "a male tradition" (1984, 188). Moreover, she appreciates the distinction between men's and women's treatment of the practice: "The sexual component of the lynching and burning rituals presented in this discussion brings up an issue relating to gender: only black male writers include scenes of castration as a part of lynchings and burnings" (Harris 1984, 188). In contrast, "women writers also seem to be less inclined to present graphic details of violence than do black male writers. ... The focus on violence is sustained and unapologetically brutal. It is a rare occasion on which black women writers present violence, either lynchings or otherwise, with the same degree of detail and at the same length" (Harris 1984, 192). There is, of course, an exception to every rule; for this one Harris points to Alice Walker's (1973) depiction of the father cutting off his daughter's breasts in "The Child Who Favored Daughter."

Exorcising Blackness (1984) is a landmark event in the scholarly effort to understand lynching. Trudier Harris understands the practice in profound and nuanced ways that the research methods of mainstream social science cannot support. Perhaps her own racialized and gendered positionality help her intuit what was at stake when black men were burned at the stake. The task now, she says—here she speaks to African Americans and, perhaps, to black men specifically—is to work through the nightmare of the past. As we will see in chapter 14, that working through is, as Harris well understands, no facile matter, as the current "crisis of black masculinity" testifies. Harris concludes:

> To exorcise fear from racial memory is as formidable a task as is attempting to obtain equality for black people in the United States. Yet that is the task black male writers seem to have set for themselves in that long history of engagement with lynchings and burnings in their work. ... The concern with ritualized violence became a baton which each male writer handed to the next in a contest for manhood and civil rights and civil rights bound them to history and to literature, and which made their works simultaneously artistic creations and cultural documents. (1984, 194)

In this respect, fiction portrays a truth to which statistics are blind.

Anatomy of Lynching

One would not be surprised if such an important study as Trudier Harris's stimulated others. Robyn Wiegman's (1993) "Anatomy of Lynching"—revised and reprinted as a chapter in her *American Anatomies: Theorizing Race and Gender* (1995)—may or may not have been stimulated by Harris's work but it is clearly indebted to it. Wiegman will focus on two works that Harris knows—

Ralph Ellison's "The Birthmark" (1940) and Richard Wright's *Native Son* (1940/1968)—to elucidate what she terms "the anatomy of lynching." It is a provocative and important example of the literary research on lynching.

"Above all, lynching is about the law" begins Robyn Wiegman (1993, 445), and as Michael Grossberg (1990) has shown (see chapter 11, section I), the law is preeminently a homosocial site of "men performing masculinity" (Simpson 1994). It is on this institutionalized homoerotic site—a "site of normativity and sanctioned desire" (Wiegman 1995, 81)—that Robyn Wiegman (1993) locates lynching. She characterizes Emancipation—the shift from chattel to citizenry—as a decommodification of the black body. This embodied political process is also one of "sexualization and engendering: not only does lynching enact a grotesquely symbolic—if not literal—sexual encounter between the white mob and its victim, but the increasing utilization of castration as a preferred form of mutilation for African American men demonstrates lynching's connection to the sociosymbolic realm of sexual difference" (Wiegman 1995, 82).

While there was a legal decommodification accompanying "Emancipation," Wiegman (1993, 1995) notes, in the white male mind the black body remained firmly fixed, commodified as "body." Indeed, what I argue in this volume is that the historical throughline from the Middle Passage through slavery to the present is a continuing commodification and de-subjectification of the black body as whites struggle to keep it in its "place," a place in the white imaginary. As Saidiya V. Hartman (1997) shows, racial subjugation means the white occupation of the black body. That body remains commodified today, if remunerated, as athlete, entertainer, laborer, above all, a sexualized body.

Wiegman (1993, 1995) understands that the white male sexual mutilation of the black male body is the key to solving the puzzle of lynching. In the "fusion of castration with lynching," she suggests, white men were attempting to sever the black male from the sphere of the masculine, "interrupting the privilege of the phallus, and thereby reclaiming, through the perversity of dismemberment, the black male's (masculine) potentiality for citizenship" (Wiegman 1995, 83). Certainly the act did communicate to black men that they were not men in a civic sense. And as castration also expressed white men's fascination, compensatory and defensive in nature, with the black phallus, it communicated the black male's status as sexual object, a feminine position vis-à-vis the heterosexually-identified male. Paradoxically, however, by insisting on him as the black "fiend" and "rapist" they also were inscribing upon him "superstud" status. By dismembering and killing him, white men were reinscribing him symbolically as a superman. As Cleaver (1968) would write some seventy years later, in slavery and racism white men relinquished their bodies, their sexuality, indeed their status as "men" in exchange for their administrative, that is, political, triumph over the black body.

In concentrating on black men in the lynching scenario, Wiegman is focusing upon what she terms "the overlay of sexual difference" (1993, 446, n. 1), evident in the primacy of castration events—in the white imagination if not in actual practice—as the ultimate expression of the mob's violence. In doing so, she reminds us, she is hardly ignoring the fact that black women were also lynched. But the white fantasy of the black male as rapist, she points out, was the prerequisite imaginary act that moved whites to violence; this fantasy also communicated the white "negation" of black women through the denial of a "significatory role" for black women in the "psychosexual drama of masculinity" that characterized lynching and specifically the white-male castration of black men (446, n. 1). African-American women were absent from the psychosexual and racial "logic" that defined and sanctioned lynching, but, as we will see, black women's—in particular Ida B. Wells'—pedagogical and political struggle against mob violence during the late nineteenth and early twentieth centuries initiated the half-century-long struggle against lynching.

Wiegman's emphasis upon castration as creating sexual difference works well, if in a heterosexual logic. But like compulsory heterosexuality itself, that logic begins to deconstruct, as when Wiegman (1993) suggests that the white-male "imposition of feminization" upon the black male, performed by the both literal and symbolic castration of the black male body, is rationalized by "an intense masculinization" of that body by imagining the black man "as mythically endowed rapist" (446–447). Wiegman characterizes this paradox, the imposition of feminization producing intense masculinization, by terming it a "double staging of gender," but it is clear that "the hypermasculinized rapist" does not become "feminine through ritualized castration" (447). Rather than becoming feminized (except in a literal sense as castrated, itself a patriarchal pairing), he is now mythologized as sexually dominant and threatening, that is, intensely masculinized. White boys and men carry his body parts around for weeks, months, and years, talismanic souvenirs of their triumph and his resurrection. Through his "crucifixion" the black man becomes a sexual demigod.

Wiegman (1993) continues her provocative and important analysis by examining Ralph Ellison's (1940) little-known story "The Birthmark," published the same year as Richard Wright's *Native Son*. The story starts at the scene of an "accident," as Matt and Clara prepare to identify a body that they have been told has been hit by a car. The body is that of their brother, Willie, who, it is clear, did not encounter metal but other flesh, white flesh, white male flesh. In a passage Weigman quotes to open both the 1993 essay and the 1995 book chapter, Matt and Clara realize that their brother has been mutilated and lynched, his face so disfigured they must seek his birthmark, located beneath the navel, for positive identification. Searching for the birthmark, Matt discovers castration as well:

> When Matt lowered his eyes he noticed the ribs had been caved in. The flesh was bruised and torn. [The birthmark] was just below [Willie's] navel, he thought. Then he gave a start: where it should have been was only a bloody mound of torn flesh and hair. Matt went weak. He felt as though he had been castrated himself. He thought he would fall when Clara stepped up beside him. Swiftly, he tried to push her back ... then Clara was screaming: "He was lynched, Lynched! I'm gonna tell everybody, HE WAS LYNCHED!" (17)

In response to this outburst, the highway patrolman strikes Matt and tells him to "shut this bitch up!" (17).

> *"Goddammit, I said a car hit him! the white man snapped. "We don't have no lynchings in this state no more!"*
>
> Matt pushed [her] to go, feeling hot breath against the hand he held over her mouth.
>
> "Just remember that a car hit 'im, and you'll be all right," the patrolman said. "We don't allow no lynching round here no more. Matt felt Clara's fingers digging into his arm as his eyes flashed swiftly over the face of the towering patrolman, over the badge against the blue shirt, the fingers crooked in the belt above the gun butt. He swallowed hard ... catching sight of Willie between the white men's legs.
>
> "I'll remember," he said bitterly, "he was hit by a car." (Ellison 1940, 17; quoted in Wiegman 1993, 445)

The discovery of the castration—"where it should have been was only a bloody mound of torn flesh and hair"—establishes a link between birthmark and penis that, Wiegman (1993) argues, activates the narrative's symbolic structure. In Ellison's short story, castration becomes "the remedy" (449) for the symbolic birthmark—the penis—that marks black men, a link not unlike that the young Jewish boy, Sorel, suffers in the film *Europa Europa*. There Sorel tries to circumcise himself as his foreskin marks him as a Jew, but, as Wiegman points out, for black men it is the penis itself, not just its foreskin, which is the marker of "difference" in white men's minds. Observing the conflation of race and sex that marks racial politics and violence in America, Wiegman (1995) locates the "remedy" of castration in white men's resistance to black men's movement from enslavement to freedom, "where the measure of the African American's claim to citizenship is precisely his status as man—a status evinced by the penis, but ultimately rewarded in the symbolic exchange between penis and phallus" (89), that symbolic marker of power in Western civilization. Castration interrupts this process of exchange, Wiegman (1995) notes, and "the black male body takes on the 'castrated' determinations of the feminine, becoming the site of both sex and sexual difference" (89). She recalls that in Faulkner's *Light in August* (1932/1968), castration literalized the association of "womanshenegro" (Faulkner 1968, 147), an association that conjoined the racial, sexual, and gendered not only in Joe Christmas' psyche, but in the American "sociosymbolic" itself (Wiegman 1993, 1995).

Within this logic, the missing phallus constitutes the feminine, and therefore castration denies to black men that primary "birthmark" of power in patriarchal society. The threat that white men perceived, Wiegman (1993) suggests, was not so much associated with racial difference as with "the potential for gender sameness" (450), although I would amend "sameness" with "sexual superiority" within a homosocial world of men, the "prison" of American masculinity. Wiegman (1993) argues that within the context of white supremacy, this potential for masculine sameness was experienced by many white men as so unnerving that "only the reassertion of a sexual and gendered difference [through castration and lynching] ... provide[d] the necessary disavowal" (450). But why would gendered sameness be problematic, unless it threatened to reposition the white man as feminine? That would be his fate in prison one hundred years later.

In Ellison's "The Birthmark," Wiegman (1993) notes, the effort to reposition the black man, a civic and sexual subject position, is blatantly portrayed in the story's final image of the body of the castrated black man, bloody and brutalized, "between the white men's legs" (17; quoted in Wiegman 1993, 450). Recalling James Cutler's (1905) observation that "it was not until a time subsequent to the Civil War that the verb lynch came to carry the idea of putting to death" (116; quoted in Wiegman 1993, 454), Robyn Wiegman (1993) reminds us that in the loss of the slave body as property after Emancipation, lynching functioned to convey the continuing "centrality of black corporeality" (455) in the white mind. By casting "blackness" as sexualized and menacing, whites, Wiegman argues, blocked freedpeople's movement toward citizenry. She continues:

> That lynching became during Reconstruction and its aftermath an increasingly routine response to black ... attempts at education, self- and communal government, suffrage, and other indicators of cultural inclusion and equality attests to its powerful disciplinary function. As the most extreme deterritorialization of the body and its subjective boundaries, lynching guaranteed the white mob's privilege of physical and psychic penetration, granted it definitional authority over social space, and encoded the vigilant and violent system of surveillance that underwrote late nineteenth- and early twentieth-century negotiations over race and cultural power. (Wiegman 1995, 94–95)

That analysis underlines why Wiegman began by asserting that lynching is, above all, about the law.

But Wiegman (1993) knows that to say this is not enough, that there remains something else circulating in the groin of the practice that "the law," however homosocial its economy, does not signify. That "something" is sexual, for Wiegman specifically sexual difference, as she argues that the mythology of the black male as rapist represented the use of sexual difference to subjugate African Americans. This use of "rape" to mark sexual difference and to perform racial subjugation is evident "most fully," Wiegman (1993 456 n.) argues, in Richard Wright's *Native Son* (1940).

That novel is American literature's "most compelling" (Wiegman 1993, 456 n.) account of the black man caught in the mythology of the rapist—that death, as Bigger Thomas puts it, "before death came" (1940/1968, 228). In its narration of the fated life of Bigger Thomas, working for a liberal white family, the accidental murder of their daughter Mary, his failed escape and trial, the novel portrays what Wright experienced as the fundamental structure of race relations in the United States. In "How 'Bigger' Was Born," Wright asserts that "any Negro ... knows that times without number he has heard of some Negro boy being picked up ... and carted off to jail and charged with 'rape.' This thing happens so often that to my mind it had become a representative symbol of the Negro's uncertain position in America" (xxviii; quoted passages on 456 n.). In the novel, Weigman notes, such uncertainty is inseparable from black masculinity, especially as black masculinity is intertwined with and distinguished from white masculinity.

The centrality of masculinity as an issue for African-American men is made explicit in the opening scene where Bigger's mother makes economic hardship a failure of his manhood: "We wouldn't have to live in this garbage dump if you had any manhood in you" (12). Bigger feels shame then hatred, followed by a complex mix of guilt and alienation which persists throughout the novel and is, Wiegman suggests, linked to emasculation. When his mother visits him in prison at the novel's end and begs on her knees before Mrs. Dalton for his life, Bigger is "paralyzed with shame; he felt violated" (280). This violation, Wiegman argues, is his symbolic emasculation, the central metaphor in the novel, by which Wright characterized the black man's status in America, a country which, as Wright writes in his autobiography *Black Boy,* "could recognize but part of a man" (1945, 284). This partiality of masculinity signifies for Wright black alienation in general. To illustrate the primacy of this metaphor, Wiegman quotes another passage from the novel. Here Bigger is talking with his friends but his topic is racist America: "Every time I think about it I feel like somebody's poking a red-hot iron down my throat. ... We live here and they live there. ... They got things we ain't. They do things and we can't. It's just like living in jail" (23; quoted in Wiegman 1993, 456–457 n.).

As we will see in chapters 16 and 17, black men in literal jails take revenge for being "punks" in the symbolic prison that is the United States. The homosexualized terms of race relations is evident in that first sentence in the quoted passage, a sentence Wiegman too does not overlook. "In the figure of the red-hot iron," she writes, Wright characterizes Bigger's subjugation in sexualized indeed "phallic" terms, describing segregation, racism, and poverty as "the symbolic phalluses of white masculine power burning in Bigger's throat" (457 n.). Disclosing the conflation of race and gender, Bigger says: "you ain't a man no more ... [white folks] after you so hot and hard ... they kill you before you die" (326–327). Clearly for Bigger the white world, so "hot and hard" against him, is castrating; race relations amount to symbolic rape (Wiegman 1993, 456).

Wiegman does not use that last term but instead a word associated with late nineteenth-century sexology, "inversion," a word which preserves heterosexual coupling as the "natural" sexual order. Weigman (1993) writes: "this castration is also an inverted sexual encounter between black men and white men" (458 n.). To illustrate this point in the context of *Native Son,* she recalls the elaborate scene of chase and capture following the murder. Hiding on the roof of a building, Bigger is trapped by white men wielding a fire hose, "the rushing stream jerked this way and that. ... Then the water hit him. ... He gasped, his mouth open. ... The water left him; he lay gasping, spent. ... The icy water clutched again at his body like a giant hand; the chill of it squeezed him like the circulating coils of a monstrous boa constrictor" (251). Wiegman rightly terms the hose a "monstrous phallic image" which forces the "horrific sexual encounter" (458 n.). In a passage reminiscent of Poe's *Gordon Pym* (see chapter 18), Wiegman quotes Wright again: "He wanted to hold on but could not. His body teetered on the edge; his legs dangled in the air. Then he was falling. He landed on the roof, on his face, in snow, dazed" (252). She comments: "Finally brought down by the monstrosity of white masculine desire for and hatred of the black man, Bigger loses consciousness ... as the violent parody of romantic coupling ends" (Wiegman 1993, 458 n.). I suggest there is no parody here; this is a simple if nightmarish instance of homosexual rape. *That* is the symbolic structure of "race relations" in the United States.

That "race" is in some essential sense "an affair between men" is evident also in two more passages Wiegman (1993) quotes from the novel. In the first it is clear that Bigger understands the murder of Mary as an act between him and "the man," the white man, an act which functions politically as well as sexually in the long history of racial subjugation which imprints his life and compels his fate: "The knowledge that he had killed a white girl they loved and regarded as their symbol of beauty made him feel the equal of them, like a man who had been somehow cheated, but had now evened the score" (155). Because she is a "stand-in" for the white man, by destroying her, "the objectified symbol" of white patriarchal domination (Wiegman 1993, 459 n.), Bigger claims his right to manhood. It is in this historical and political—above all homosocial—context that racialized sexual violence is situated. When Bigger redefines rape he detaches the act from those who suffer it: "Rape was not what one did to women. Rape was what one felt when one's back was against a wall and one had to strike out, whether one wanted to or not. ... It was rape when he cried out in hate deep in his heart as he felt the strain of living day by day" (214). Working heterosexually I think, Wiegman (1993) recodes this statement as a "displacement of the gendered dimensions of sexual violence" (461), but it is clear from the earlier passage that Mary is the medium by which he gets to the white man; her "rape" is not degendered in his definition, but recast as mediated homosexual rape. Wiegman does appreciate that Bigger's definition "points to the gendered inscriptions of black male oppression," and, she adds perceptively, implies that the black woman's [Bessie Mears, Bigger's girlfriend] death "[w]as the ricochet effect of the white woman's pedestaled superiority" (Wiegman 1993, 462 n.).

It is, as Wiegman (1993) points out, very disturbing that Wright depicts rape as "not what one did to women." While indeed disturbing, it is not surprising. As Rosi Braidotti (1994b) summarizes "feminist analyses of the last forty years," "the masculine symbolic rests on a false universalization of the subject position ... and the forceful creation of a set of 'others' among whom the 'second sex'—women—is the most prominent. The relationship between the two poles is postulated in terms of compulsory heterosexuality" (202). Women, black women too, are abstract units in a homosocial economy in which the actors are all male. As we will see in prison, in such an economy sexual desire also circulates, and Bigger becomes, as Wiegman (1993) appreciates, a "*sexual* —and not simply racial—victim" (462 n.). In his erasure of the female body, specifically that of the black woman, in the scenario of sexual violence—an erasure one would expect, given the largely fictional status of women in men's minds—Wiegman (1993) argues that Wright appears to structure racial oppression so that the violation of black masculinity, through literalized castration, effaces the historical fact of the black woman's regularly violated sexuality.

This erasure—not only Wright's, of course, but men's, of black women's history in America, as well as the violating idealization of white women in the rape myth—is, Wiegman (1995) argues, an expression of the "deeper and more culturally complex relation" (97) between black and white men. Here Wiegman quotes Trudier Harris (1984): "The issue really boils down to one between white men and black men and the mythic concept the former have of the latter" (19; quoted in Wiegman 1995, 97). Wiegman quotes as well Frantz Fanon (1967) who knew that "the Negro … has been fixated [at the genital]" (165; quoted in Wiegman 1995, 98). "In reducing the black male to the body and further to the penis itself," Wiegman writes, "white male supremacy … betrays a simultaneous desire for and disavowal of the black male's inscription" (1995, 98). In other words, "the white male creates the image he must castrate, and it is precisely through the mythology of the black male as rapist that he effectively does this" (Wiegman 1995, 98).

This last sentence sounds like classic projection theory, and is no doubt accurate to a point. But like Joel Williamson's and others' employment of the idea, it deemphasizes the cathexis that makes the black man the screen upon which the white man projects in the first place. Not just any "screen" or "scapegoat" will do for European-American men. Why does the white man look at the black man in a frenzy? Is it because, as Wiegman suggests, that in that very look, a look that strips the black man of his manhood, the white man gains power? Again she quotes Trudier Harris (1984): "the black man is stripped of his prowess, but the very act of stripping brings symbolic power to the white man. His actions suggest that, subconsciously, he craves the very thing he is forced to destroy" (23; quoted in Wiegman 1993, 464). Within a heterosexual logic perhaps, but because lynching was a defensive and compensatory act of men in "crisis," it brought symbolic power to the black man, even as he died, as it underscored that every white man is, as Amiri Baraka (1965/1966) will understand half a century later, "a fag" (216).

Wiegman (1995) too seems to find the logic of heterosexuality insufficient: "But while castration may function as a means for enacting a gendered difference at the site of the black male body, it is also the case that such … dismemberment enabled a perverse … physical intimacy between the white male aggressor and his captive ex-slave, pointing to an underlying obsession not simply with gender sameness, but with a broader range of sexuality as well" (99). She quotes Harris's observation that "in some historical accounts, the lynchers were reputed to have divided pieces of the black man's genitals among themselves" (1984, 23), commenting that this fact "allows us to envision the castration scene as more than the perverse sexual encounter offered by the rape metaphor. In the image of white men embracing—with hate, fear, and a chilling form of empowered delight—the same penis they were so overdeterminedly driven to destroy, one encounters a sadistic enactment of the homoerotic at the moment of its most extreme disavowal" (1995, 99).

Now Wiegman has left the logic of "sexual difference" and entered the homosocial world of same-sex desire, recalling Eve Kosofsky Sedgwick's discussion in *Between Men* of nineteenth- and twentieth-century Anglo-American male bonding rituals which used—and use still—the abject image of the homosexual to imagine their bonds free of same-sex desire, thereby normalizing heterosexuality and keeping it compulsory. From such a point of view, Wiegman (1995) writes, "we might understand the lynching scenario and its obsession with the sexual dismemberment of black men to mark the limit of the homosexual/heterosexual binary—that point at which the oppositional relation reveals its inherent and mutual dependence—and the heterosexuality of the black male 'rapist' is transformed into a violent homoerotic exchange" (99). She quotes Sedgwick's depiction of men in the late Renaissance, a characterization, Wiegman (1993) suggests, that also depicts the history of white and black men in America. "The homosociality of this world is not that of brotherhood, but of extreme, compulsory, and intensely volatile mastery and subordination" (Sedgwick 1985, 76; quoted in Wiegman 1993, 466). A nightmarish, involuntary, and queer form of sadomasochism perhaps?

More than any other student of lynching, Robyn Wiegman (1993, 1995) understands the complexity of the practice, how convoluted the white-male cries of "rape" and "revenge" were. She understands precisely the homoerotic current in white men's racism, how desire disguised as "white supremacy" positioned black men as both "rapists" and "studs," two poles of the same binary of desire and its disavowal. It is clear, I trust, that literary research on the subject of lynching, such as Robin Wiegman's—and Trudier Harris's—has yielded rich and provocative theorizations that enable us to understand the practice in far more nuanced and complex ways than do the statistical manipulations of the "empirically" minded.

As we have seen, historians, sociologists, psychologists (including social psychologists), and anthropologists have explained "America's national crime" by emphasizing various developments and events, among them economic depression (and specifically poverty and cotton price fluctuation), the uncertainties of a new industrial economy, southern honor, politics (including Populism) and culture. Feminist historians have tended to emphasize other dynamics, suggesting that the spread of lynching was connected to white southerners' interest in bolstering a besieged male power and authority. LeeAnn Whites (1992) has pointed out that southern white women felt betrayed by their husbands' failure to live up to their antebellum conceptions of manhood. Not only did they fail to "whip the Yankees," they failed to protect and provide for their wives, daughters, and mothers during and after the Civil War. Relying on the research of Drew Gilpin Faust, we will explore the War's impact upon the southern sex/gender system in the next chapter. It does not seem terribly speculative to suggest that many southern white women displaced their anger at white men onto black men.

By accepting the idea of the black male rapist, white women did double duty: they conveyed indirectly their rage over their husbands' humiliation by northern men in the Civil War while at the same time making common cause with those same defeated white men over the issue of racial privilege. Nell Irvin Painter (1988) has argued that lynchings were "pornographic" rituals that functioned to reproduce power relations, keeping black men powerless and exploitable for white men's economic interests. Jacquelyn Dowd Hall (1983)

TWO

The Destabilization of Gender and the "Crisis" of White Masculinity

economic ones, as we see in chapter 6. This was especially the case in the states that had comprised the Old Confederacy. There, the racial, political, and specifically gender legacies of the Civil War were being played out in complex and intersecting ways, converging, however, on the bodies of young black men.

In creating and destroying governments, economies, and societies, the "Civil War necessarily challenged the very foundations of personal identity as well," as Drew Gilpin Faust (1996, 3) observes. Both women and men were profoundly transformed by the circumstances of war. It is easy to imagine how the destabilizing effects of these shifts—political, cultural, gendered—contributed to a "crisis" of masculinity to which many southern white men responded racially. The contemporary conflation of race and sex was also rather complete one hundred thirty years ago; disentangling them altogether is not likely. My ambition here is a limited one, namely, to show—by summarizing the revealing research of Drew Gilpin Faust (1996)—how sharp shifts in gender which accompanied and followed the Civil War "set up" the convoluted unleashing of white (homo)sexual desire which became focused, to a remarkable extent, upon the bodies of young black men.

The Civil War set off what one contemporary newspaper described as a "Stampede from the Patriarchal Relation" that had so firmly fixed white men at the apex of the pyramid that was antebellum southern social structure. Faust asks a series of questions which identify those elements comprising the "stampede." She asks: "What did whiteness mean when it was no longer the all but exclusive color of freedom? What was maleness when it was defeated and impoverished, when men had failed as providers and protectors? What did womanhood involve once the notion of dependence and helplessness became an insupportable luxury?" (4). It is clear that many southerners were quite conscious of at least the magnitude of the shifts these questions specify. "We are passing through a great revolution," a correspondent wrote to the *Montgomery Daily Advertiser* in July of 1864. "The surface of society, like a great ocean, is upheaved, and all of the relations of life are disturbed and out of joint" (quoted in Faust 1996, 4).

The gendered "relations of life" were already, by southern accounts, "out of joint" in the North, as a generation before women's rights activists had begun to challenge conventional understandings of men's and women's roles. In the South in 1861, in contrast, feminism had not yet made an appearance; understandings of womanhood had remained stubbornly and simplistically based on anatomy and were apparently "natural" and unchanging. Many of the South's defenders took note of this contrast, arguing that it was in itself proof of the superiority of southern civilization and indicative of those dangerous tendencies intrinsic to the northern way of life. "There is something wrong," pro-South and proslavery advocate George Fitzhugh warned in 1854, with woman's "condition in free society, and that condition is daily becoming worse." Northern democratization, abolitionism, and feminism all undermined that "natural" hierarchy of gender which, Fitzhugh feared, would result eventually in the destruction of the sacred institution of marriage itself. There was a consistency, some southerners grasped, between abolitionism and feminism. "The people of our Northern States, who hold that domestic slavery is unjust and iniquitous," he declared, "are consistent in their attempts to modify or abolish the marriage relation." Dismissing the feminist struggle for women's rights under way in the North, Fitzhugh proclaimed that in the South "woman ... has but one right and that is the right to protection. The right to protection involves the obligation to obey. A husband, lord and master ... nature designed for every woman" (quoted in Faust 1996, 5–6). He might have added, of course, "as nature had designed for every slave," for the conflation between race and gender hierarchies was, for many, complete (Faust 1996).

Today there are still southerners who still insist the woman's place is a position of "gracious submission," to amend the language of Southern Baptists who tend to cite biblical passages as well as invoke rhetoric of the "natural" to support patriarchy and heterosexism. But evidently the majority even of southern women do not accept their submission as either God-ordained or "natural." One hundred and forty years ago the transformation from antebellum gender relations to the present got under way. It was the Civil War that challenged the South's "peculiar" institutions of racial and gender hierarchy, forcing shifts in traditional "performances" of womanhood and manhood. From the firing on Fort Sumter, the white South's wartime emergency forced an unprecedented reconfiguring of gender, as women were forced to take on unaccustomed responsibilities for the survival of their families and the new nation. From the beginning, many southerners worried, as did the *Milledgeville Confederate Union,* about the "unsexed women" these new responsibilities appeared likely to produce. At first, the War, like any war, promised to reaffirm and even intensify traditional divisions between the masculine and feminine by defining the conflict as the "glorious" and exclusive responsibility of "manly" men. But men's marching off to war quickly produced widespread uncertainty and then distress about gender categories and identities as women now found themselves, as one Texas woman put it, "trying to do a man's business," supporting households and families and managing slaves (quoted phrases in Faust 1996, 6). In the face of the brutal demands of an unexpectedly long and total war, long-cherished fantasies of womanhood and manhood could no longer be supported (Faust 1996).

As white men left for battle, slavery began to disintegrate, and prewar prosperity was only a memory, prerogatives of gender, class and race began to fade, and indeed "all the relations of life" became unclear. Upper-class southern women quickly discovered that their ideals of womanhood had presumed the existence of slaves to perform menial labor, and the presence of white men to force black men and women to do menial tasks. White men were also necessary to provide protection and support for southern "ladies," a term foundational to these women's self-conceptions. "Lady" denoted both whiteness and class privilege as well as gendered refinement; a lady's elite status required the existence of gentlemen, not to mention slaves, black men and women whose daily labor and suffering propped up white delusions of gentility, exclusivity, and civilization (Faust 1996). But the War would change all that. Lucy Buck might have been speaking for all Confederate women when she said: "we shall never ... be the same as we have been" (quoted in Faust 1996, 7).

Before the War, most southern women had accepted as "natural" those gendered divisions between the private and the public, the domestic and the political, that rightfully separated the sphere of women from that of men. But as their knighted gentlemen failed to "whip those Yankees" in the first few weeks, as they had assured their ladies they would, southern white women began to resist being excluded from the ever more total military conflict that threatened to engulf them and their children. One Alabama lady was shocked by the "unexpected proportions" of the Civil War; she was sure most Americans—North and South—had also been caught by surprise. Many southerners had been certain that the North would not have the courage to contest southern secession (Faust 1996). Once the War began, most southern men were sure the conflict would be short and sweet, so much so that a former United States senator from South Carolina, James Chesnut, predicted (with manly swagger) that he would be able to "drink all the blood spilled" in the southern war for independence (quoted in Faust 1996, 12).

No doubt even the most "manly men" of the South had moments of doubt, perhaps even worry, that the North, so much more developed industrially, with so many more soldiers, might not be whipped so quickly and bloodlessly. No doubt some white southern women felt far freer than their men to feel, even admit, such fears. Southern white women did express concern about the War's outcome; they worried especially about the loss of loved ones in battle, fears that masculine pretensions of "honor and courage" would not permit men to express. From the outset this "touch of realism" influenced Confederate women's politics and redirected their patriotism. The gendered conventions of women's private feelings and everyday household obligations counterposed the fantasies of men regarding war, almost always a homosocial affair, as we will note in chapter 13. Soon after the passage of the Ordinance of Secession, one South Carolina lady was unafraid to express her preference of the personal over the political, her privileging of loyalty to family over duty to the state. "I do not approve of this thing," she said with all the confidence of her class. "What do I care for patriotism? My husband is my country. What is country to me if he be killed?" (quoted in Faust 1996, 13). A seventeen-year-old bride was beside herself when she learned her new husband was about to go to war. "Oh Dan! Dan!" she sobbed, "I don't want to be proud of you. I just don't want you to get hurt! ... I don't want fame or glory! I want you!" (quoted in Faust 1996, 16)

The "romance" of military conquest, its intermingling of manhood with "honor, courage, and glory" (Faust 1996, 13), swept away the reluctance many southern women felt in turning over their loved ones to the defense of the new Confederate nation. For many women, the very meaning of manhood had to do with men's willingness to sacrifice their lives in battle. A "man did not deserve the name of man if he did not fight for his country," Kate Cumming declared. And one proud lady of the Shenandoah Valley sent her son off to army camp proclaiming in the columns of the *Winchester Virginian*: "Your country calls. ... I am ready to offer you up in defense of your country's rights and honor; and I offer you, a beardless boy of 17 summers—not with grief, but thanking God that I have a son to offer" (quoted in Faust 1996, 13). Sarah Lawton of Georgia was not alone in welcoming the War as an opportunity for men once again to be men: "I think something was needed to wake them from their effeminate habits and [I] welcome war for that" (quoted in Faust 1996, 15). Of course, not all southern white men were persuaded, at least not immediately. But upon these, pressure could be brought to bear. Mary Vaught refused to speak to those men in her community who had not enlisted; a group of young women in Texas presented hoopskirts and bonnets to all the men in the neighborhood who had declined to volunteer (Faust 1996).

Not only southern men perceived the War to be a test of manhood. Many northern men agreed that the economic success and cultural progress of the North had left some Yankees "soft." The War would be in this respect a suitable antidote. In 1861 the editor of *Harper's Monthly* lured young men to war by promising them that the "discipline of the camp is a wonderful check upon effeminacy and self-indulgence" (quoted in Kimmel 1996, 73). The Civil War was also a gendered event for many black men. Many abolitionists, both white and black, understood the conflict in gendered rather than racial terms. As the governor of Wisconsin put it in 1859, the struggle against slavery was "a question of manhood, not of color" (quoted in Kimmel 1996, 73).

Confederate women came to accept that they could not put their personal preferences above the demands of the new nation. In this moment of crisis, one's country—the Confederate States of America—had to come before husband or son. If the South were to survive, southern ladies had to become patriotic Confederate women, ready to assume many of the political responsibilities hitherto the sole province of men. To put the matter differently, southern women now had to suppress a certain delicacy of feeling associated with being a lady, all for the good of the Cause (Faust 1996). Women must now cultivate a spirit of "self-reliance," must practice "self-denial," wrote Lelia W. in the *Southern Monthly*. The piece, entitled "Woman A Patriot," also advised moderation in these "masculine" virtues, as "we do not mean to say that she should become masculine." The new president of the Confederacy, Jefferson Davis, also felt it necessary to address the question of women's role in the war effort, suggesting to them that they should prefer the empty sleeve of an injured veteran to that of the "muscular arm" of "him who staid at home and grew fat" (quoted in Faust 1996, 17).

One issue, whether to serve or not, became settled in April 1862, when the Confederacy passed the first conscription law in American history. All white men between the ages of eighteen and thirty-five were declared eligible for military draft. By 1865, the legislation had been amended; now all white males from seventeen to fifty were eligible. In the final few months of the War, a desperate Confederacy advised its states to draft black male slaves. During the war years a variety of exemption laws were passed, but even so, Confederate conscription succeeded in mobilizing a very high percentage of available white men. Due to slavery, almost all nonmilitary labor in the South could be assigned to blacks, allowing a very high percentage of white men to be available for army service. As a consequence, three of every four white men of military age served in the Confederate army (Faust 1996).

With so many men leaving home for the battlefield, the Confederate home front became populated almost entirely by white women and black slaves. Louisa Walton complained to her friend Isabella Woodruff that Chester, South Carolina, had by 1862 been "thinned out of men." Margaret Junkin Preston wrote that in Lexington, Virginia, by mid-1862, there were "no men left." Hers was, she lamented, "a world of femininity with a thin line of boys and octogenarians." When Nettie Fondren discussed a friend's wedding plans in December of the same year, she noted that there would be no ushers, "for there is not enough young men around ... to answer the purpose." Not only the composition of wedding parties underwent revolution. As Mary Greenhow Lee of Winchester watched Confederate and Yankee men exchange control of a town full of women, then abandon it altogether in June 1862, she kept her sense of humor, writing in her diary, "I proposed that we shall declare ourselves a separate and independent sovereignty, and elect a Queen to reign over us" (quoted in Faust 1996, 31).

The relocation of white men from households to the military dealt "a devastating blow" (Faust 1996, 32) to the basic structures of the southern society and economy. In nonslaveholding families, the departure of breadwinners brought immediate hardship, requiring many white women to perform, for the first time, hard physical labor in the fields (Faust 1996). For more prosperous women, especially those with slaves, the effects of mass mobilization were more delayed and less obvious at first, but still: "From early in the war the very foundations of the South's paternalistic social order were necessarily imperiled by the departure of men who served as its organizing principle" (Faust 1996, 35).

Many white women had to leave home too, especially when Yankee soldiers approached, making staying too risky. Many refugees wrote despairingly of their experiences, as the circumstances of these women and children, away from their sources of food and shelter, were often very unpleasant. Sarah Morgan reported, in an obvious tone of astonishment, that she found herself "actually sleeping under the same bed clothes with our black, shiny negro nurse!" (quoted in Faust 1996, 43). As slaveholding men left home for battle, white women on farms and plantations across the South were forced to supervise that "peculiar" institution of slavery (Faust 1996).

II. White Women, Black Men

Psychohistories of white racism have always called attention to the tension between the construction of the black male body as danger and the underlying eroticization of that threat that always then imagines that body as a location for transgressive pleasure.

—bell hooks, "Feminism Inside: Toward a Black Body Politic" (1994)

We are "haunted" by our own repressed sexuality projected outwards onto others.

—Paul Hoch, *White Hero, Black Beast: Racism, Sexism, and the Mask of Masculinity* (1979)

Black males have long intrigued the Western imagination.

—Henry Louis Gates, Jr., "Preface" to *Black Male: Representations of Masculinity in Contemporary American Art* (1994)

Before the War white men had enforced slavery; they managed the everyday subjugation and exploitation of millions of African Americans. But as the War emptied southern households of white men, it required white women to assume unaccustomed and often unwelcome power in maintaining order, public as well as private. Slavery was, as Confederate Vice-President Alexander Stephens observed, the "cornerstone" (Faust 1996, 53) of southern society, economy, and politics. Yet the perpetuation of the "peculiar institution" depended less on state policy than on tens of thousands of individual acts of sadism and subjugation performed by white men on black men, women, and children. As the war encouraged slaves to assert their yearning for freedom, the daily battle for social control on hundreds of plantations and farms became more and more intense, and just as critical to the defense of the southern way of life as any military maneuver. Southern ladies, who even in the most placid of times would have declined any invitation to supervise slave labor, were now called to control and manage an increasingly restive and rebellious slave population. These women were, in a real sense, garrisoning a second front in the South's war for independence (Faust 1996).

Public discourse as well as government policy in the Confederacy explicitly acknowledged the gendered character of the Old South's system of subjugation and mastery. Indeed, "the very meaning of mastery itself was rooted in the concepts of masculinity and male power" (Faust 1996, 54). From the beginning, Confederate leaders worried about the transfer of responsibility for slaves to women. After the passage of the first conscription in April 1862, many openly criticized the idea of drafting overseers and other white male supervisors, especially in remote areas with large slave populations. In part this concern was economic, for agricultural productivity and efficiency, white men knew, depended upon the ruthless exploitation, that is, "effective management," of enslaved black men and women. The "truth stares at us in the face," wrote one correspondent to a Georgia newspaper, "slave labor must support this war." "There was," the writer continued, "but one way to do this, and that is, to place the negro under the immediate control and direction of the white man." An Alabama man warned Confederate officials in March 1862 that there already existed "in the negro population ... a disposition to misrule and insubordination occasioned no doubt from the withdrawal of our male population from their midst." The prospect of even fewer white men at home provoked fears of slave revolts, a fantasy of black power and autonomy which merged with a sense of the concrete vulnerability of white women. As Faust points out, "these issues went beyond questions of gender; they represented deep-seated worries about sex" (quoted in Faust 1996, 54–55).

Such worries took political form, and in the fall of 1862 there was palatable support for some official draft exemption for slave managers. The *Macon Daily Telegraph* expressed a concern that was widespread: "Is it possible that Congress thinks ... our women can control the slaves and oversee the farms? Do they suppose that our patriotic mothers, sisters, and daughters can assume and discharge the active duties and drudgery of an overseer? Certainly not. They know better." In October the Confederate Congress demonstrated that it did indeed know better, passing a law exempting from military service one white man on every plantation of twenty or more slaves (Faust 1996). But the soon infamous "Twenty-Nigger Law" provoked widespread resentment, both from nonslaveholders and from smaller slaveholders who were not included (quoted in Faust 1996, 55).

In an effort to contain this threatening eruption of class antagonism among whites and at the same time respond to the military's ever-increasing manpower needs, the Confederate Congress repeatedly amended the conscription policy, each time broadening the age of eligibility and limiting exemptions. A proposal offered by the House early in 1863 would have rescinded the twenty-slave provision altogether, but pressure from the Senate brought about a compromise, a gradual reduction in the scope of the exemption through laws passed in May 1863 and February of 1864. This reduction in overseer exemptions made it much more difficult to find men not subject to military duty who could, in the words of the original bill, "secure the proper police of the country" (quoted in Faust 1996, 55). Women across the Confederacy increasingly found themselves unable to hire white men to run their plantations and farms (Faust 1996).

As war continued and the promise of freedom encouraged growing black restlessness, white women discovered themselves supervising an institution much different from the one their husbands, brothers, fathers, and sons had managed before Fort Sumter. As slaves grew more assertive, white women grew more and more troubled, more fearful, and more resentful of the burdens imposed upon them by the disintegrating institution. Soon these emotions undermined women's enthusiasm for both slavery and the Confederate cause. Throughout the Confederacy the ever-increasing loss of control and consequent diminishing plantation efficiency lowered morale and productivity. Mary Chesnut had never, she said, been afraid of her slaves, but after the War was under way she reconsidered her position, especially when her cousin Betsey Witherspoon was smothered to death. An elderly woman who lived alone with her slaves, Witherspoon was hardly sadistic; indeed, she was well known as "indulgent." Her murder dramatized both the inadequacies and vulnerabilities of white ladies as slave masters; her death was exactly what her South Carolina neighbor Keziah Brevard had feared. Another Carolina widow, Ada Bacot, saw in Witherspoon's death her own fate: "I fear 'twould [sic] take very little to make them put me out of the way" (quoted in Faust 1996, 57).

In 1862, Mrs. Laura B. Comer (who lived near Columbus, Georgia) recorded in her diary that she was suffering periods of intense despair and depression provoked, she writes, by frequent confrontations with "lazy," "obstinate," "willful," and "indolent" slaves. She blamed most of discipline problems she faced upon the lenient treatment her husband (whom she consistently referred to in her diary as "Mr. Comer") had given them before he left to fight the Yankees. She complained as well about the absence of male supervision of the slaves during his lengthy wartime absences. Finally, one cannot help but notice the reference to her husband's practice, at least before their marriage, of evidently sleeping with his slaves:

> I have been able by having no cooking done at all and remaining quietly in my room, to be at peace, but if Mr. Comer lives a few years [longer], I am sure I don't know what anyone can do with his servants about the house, in the field. ... It is a terrible life! Who can appreciate or understand anything about such a life, but a woman who marries a Bachelor who has lived with his negroes as equals, at bed and board. (quoted in Mohr 1986, 224)

Near Stone Mountain, Georgia, in 1863 a black man was accused of attacking an eleven-year-old white girl. He was publicly executed and "his body ... left hanging on the gallows, there to rot, as a monument of warning to others." Usually local tribunals found ways to punish black sexual behavior without destroying valuable chattel. In Bibb County, Georgia, local authorities revived one of the state's more barbaric laws by sentencing the slave Melton to be castrated for attempted rape during the War. When two local doctors carried out the order in February 1864, Melton was "much distressed, and considered the sentence more dreadful than death itself." A local newspaper expressed hope that Melton's punishment would serve as a "terrible warning and example" to other blacks while ensuring that the prisoner himself would commit no further sexual offenses (quoted in Mohr 1986, 220).

Many southern women came to fear their slaves more than they did Yankee soldiers. "I fear the blacks more than I do the Yankees," wrote Mrs. A. Ingraham from besieged Vicksburg, Mississippi. In Virginia, Betty Maury was of much the same mind: "I am afraid of the lawless Yankee soldiers, but that is nothing to my fear of the negroes if they should rise against us." Upon hearing news that a slave revolt was brewing in her own Mississippi county, Susan Sillers Darden found it "dreadful to think of it the danger we are in all the time by the Servants besides the Abolitionists." Living with slavery during wartime was, one Virginia woman wrote, living with "enemies in our own households" (quoted in Faust 1996, 59–60).

The arrival of black Yankee soldiers in parts of the South sometimes turned these fears into near hysteria. Mary Lee of Winchester, Virginia, was "near fainting" when black troops appeared; she felt "more unnerved than by any sight I have seen since the war [began]." These soldiers were three times her enemy: at once men, blacks, and Yankees, her gender, racial, and political opposites, "the quintessential powerful and hostile Other" (Faust 1996, 60). The black Yankee occupation of Winchester so emphasized her vulnerability that she responded with a swoon, that dreaded display of feminine delicacy she had long fought to overcome, but to which she succumbed on numerous occasions during the long years of war (Faust 1996).

Many southern women managed to suppress these fears of racial violence, facing them only in the middle of anxious, sleepless nights. During the days, Constance Cary Harrison remembered, worries about slave violence seemed "preposterous," but at night, "there was the fear ... dark, boding, oppressive, and altogether hateful ... the ghost that refused to be laid." Women sometimes wondered why they did not always, even during the day, feel overwhelmed by fears that were, after all, quite appropriate and rational. Even as Keziah Brevard thought about all the hours she had lain awake wondering if she would be "hacked to death," she asked herself, "Why is it at times I feel safe as if no dangers were in the distance? I wish I could feel as free from it at all times." Catherine Edmondston was amazed that with "eighty-eight negroes immediately around me" and "not a white soul within five miles," she felt "not a sensation of fear" (quoted in Faust 1996, 60).

Some women worried not at all. In fact, some considered their slaves as protectors, trusting in a black loyalty that the many tales of "faithful servants" would later enshrine in Confederate popular culture and, later still, in the myth of the Lost Cause. In such a rewoven remembrance of slavery during the War, Elizabeth Saxon wrote in 1905 that "not an outrage was perpetrated, no house was burned. ... [O]n lonely farms women with little children slept at peace, guarded by a sable crowd, whom they perfectly trusted. ... [I]n no land was ever a people so tender and helpful" (quoted in Faust 1996, 60). The truth was rather different, Faust tells us. White women spent every day of every month of every war year worrying about their lives and the lives of those they loved. This trauma was evidently so profound and pervasive that many white southerners, both during the War and afterward, went into denial, insisting, quite contrary to the truth, that slavery was a benevolent institution appreciated by blacks as well as whites (Faust 1996).

Much of the difficulty of wartime relationships between white women and slaves had to do with white women's increasing dependency upon slaves' labor, competence, and even companionship at the same time when slaves saw freedom just a battle or two away. In other words, white women's reliance upon their slaves intensified just as slaves' psychological independence grew, resulting in a tense and troubled situation. Confused, anxious, ambivalent white women were forced constantly to reassess, to question, and to revise their assumptions about their relationships to their slaves while they struggled alone at night with their fears. No doubt many agreed with Catherine Broun, who complained that by 1863 she was "beginning to lose confidence in the whole race." But other white women turned trustingly to their slaves as the only allies left in an increasingly dangerous world of war and privation. Some slave mistresses, especially those living in remote plantation settings, found that in wartime households emptied of white men, their closest adult companions were female slaves. When the slave Rhoda died in April 1862, her owner Anna Green wrote to her sister: "I feel like I have lost my only friend and I do believe she was the most faithful friend I had [even] if she was a servant." Leila Callaway described the death from smallpox of her slave Susanna similarly: "Next to my own dear family Susanna was my warmest best friend." "I have no one now in your absence," she informed her husband, "to look to for protection" (quoted in Faust 1996, 61). In the War's destruction of the South's hierarchies of gender and race, Leila Callaway had relocated to a black woman those emotions which before had been attached to the person of her husband (Faust 1996).

Kate McClure of South Carolina preferred her slave Jeff to the white men her husband had hired to help manage plantation affairs during his absence at war. McClure thought Jeff more trustworthy and more knowledgeable, not to mention more likely to accept her point of view, than the two white men. Maria Hawkins had bonded with her slave Moses but he had been impressed by the Confederate state government to work ôn coastal fortification. She wrote to Governor Vance in language ordinarily reserved for letters seeking discharge of husbands and sons. Hawkins requested that Moses be returned to her: "He slept in the house, every night while at home, and protected everything in the house and yard and at these perilous times when deserters are committing depredations, on plantations every day, I am really so much frightened every night, that I am up nearly all night" (quoted in Faust 1996, 62). For Hawkins, a black male protector was far preferable to no man at all (Faust 1996).

III. A Subversion of Gender through Curricular Innovation: Confederate Women's Education

[I]f women were once permitted to read Sophocles and work with logarithms, or to nibble at any side of the apple of knowledge, there would be an end forever to their sewing on buttons and embroidering slippers.

—Anna Julia Cooper, "A Voice from the South" (1892/1998)

The training of the schools we need today more than ever—the training of deft hands, quick eyes and ears, and above all the broader, deeper, higher culture of gifted minds and pure hearts.

—W. E. B. Du Bois, *The Souls of Black Folk* (1903)

Antiblack racism is ... intimately connected to misogyny.

—Lewis Gordon, *Bad Faith and Antiblack Racism* (1995)

During the course of everyday life in the Confederacy, most women slaveholders faced neither murderous revolutionaries nor the steadfast loyal happy slaves that would be concocted years later. Most encountered complicated human beings whose yearnings for freedom expressed themselves in ways that changed according to the contingent opportunities that the weakening of slavery brought. As northern military pressure intensified, the "peculiar" institution became even more so. Just as "paternalism" and "mastery" were intertwined with white masculinity, violence too had been gendered as male within the social structure of the Old South. Recourse to physical force to defend male honor and white supremacy was regarded as the prerogative, even the obligation, of each white man, each gentleman, not only within his household and on his plantation, but as well in his community, and with the outbreak of the War, for his new nation (Faust 1996; Stowe 1987).

Southern ladies, now turned slave managers, had inherited a social structure that depended on the threat and use of violence. Throughout the history of the peculiar institution, slave mistresses had on occasion slapped, hit, and even brutally whipped their slaves, especially slave women or children. But white women's relationship to such violence was quite different from that of their men, as no gendered code of honor celebrated women's physical demonstrations of dominance. A contrasting yet parallel code celebrated female sensitivity, frailty, and vulnerability. In the antebellum period, execution of the violence necessary to the enslavement of Africans was overwhelmingly the responsibility and prerogative of European-American men. A white lady disciplined and punished as the master's wife and surrogate. Faust says it succinctly: "rationalized, systematic, autonomous, and instrumental use of violence belonged to men" (1996, 63). When widowed or otherwise without men, ladies sought overseers, male relatives, or neighbors to use violence against slaves, especially slave men (Faust 1996).

Just their ineligibility to bear arms left some Confederate women feeling "useless," so too their reservations about the use of violence, particularly with slave men, left many judging themselves as failures at slave management. Lizzie Neblett described her frustration: "I am so sick of trying to do a man's business when I am nothing but a poor contemptible piece of multiplying human flesh tied to the house by a crying young one, looked upon as belonging to a race of inferior beings." Faust points out that the language she chose to describe her self-loathing is noteworthy, for it is the vocabulary of race as well as gender. Invoking the embodied constraints of biology ("multiplying flesh") as well as the socially fabricated hierarchy of status ("looked upon as belonging to a race of inferior beings") she experienced herself not as a member of the white elite, not as one in whose interest the war was being fought, but as another member of the South's oppressed (quoted in Faust 1996, 65).

Before the War there had been few occupations that "respectable" women could enter and remain "respectable." Such vocations as teaching or shopkeeping, considered quite appropriate for middle-class women in the North, had remained in the South the almost exclusive domain of men (Stowe 1987). The War changed all that, and as women suddenly began to perform jobs only men had performed before, southerners across the Confederacy remarked on the phenomenon with curiosity, even amazement. In 1862 Lila Chunn of Georgia mentioned the development as part of the news from home in a letter to her husband, Willie, stationed at the front: "Ladies keep the stores here now … their husbands having joined the army. It looks funny in Dixie to see a lady behind the counter, but it would be natural if we were in Yankeedom as it has always [been] the custom there, a custom however I do not like. The idea of a lady having to face and transact business with any and everybody. It is alone suited to the North[ern] women of brazen faces. But I say if it's necessary, our ladies ought to shopkeep and do everything else they can to aid in the great struggle for Liberty" (quoted in Faust 1996, 81).

One of the first professions to which women turned was teaching, a vocation that has seemed to many parallel to women's traditional responsibilities as mothers. In the North, a "feminization of teaching" was well under way, but the antebellum South had not yet encouraged women to enter classrooms (Grumet 1988). In North Carolina in 1860, for instance, only 7 percent of teachers were women. During the War, however, this percentage changed significantly, until by 1865 there were as many female as male teachers in the state (Faust 1996).

There was considerable public discussion in the Confederacy devoted to this dramatic shift in perceptions regarding "respectable" vocations for ladies. There was anxiety about what this shift implied about women's intellect and character. The most common and straightforward defenders pointed out that with men at the front, women were needed as teachers. The superintendent of common schools for North Carolina, Calvin Wiley, thought that the two complemented each other, declaring in his annual report for 1862: "Many ladies are compelled by the circumstances of the times, to labor for a living; and there is no employment better suited to the female nature, and none in which ladies can labor more usefully, than in the business of forming the hearts and minds of the young." The *Augusta Daily Constitutionalist* agreed. "Women," the paper informed its readers, "are peculiarly fitted, naturally and morally, for teachers of the young." Be that as it may, the truth of the matter, the editor reminded the more skeptical, was that the War had "swallow[ed] up" all available young men. "We are left no resource but to have female teachers. ... They must of necessity be our teachers, or we shall have to dispense with any" (quoted in Faust 1996, 82–83).

Many others dispensed with arguments of nature and nurture and emphasized the reality of the situation. The *Central Presbyterian* stated that the issue was "eminently a practical question." Announcing that the Female College of Statesville, North Carolina, had recently established a teachers' department, the paper urged, in language reminiscent of military inscription, that "the young ladies of our ... country should volunteer in this service." J. K. Kirkpatrick, president of Davidson College, also saw the parallel between male soldiers and female teachers. He even anticipated some of the same parental resistance to sending daughters to the classroom as they might have felt having sent their sons off to battle. The same war-born patriotism that had succeeded in raising a Confederate army would also advance the cause of education. "It may not be just such a life as you may prefer for your daughter," he acknowledged. Quickly his tone rose: "You have made your son an offering on your country's altar. Would you withhold your daughters from a service, noble in itself and befitting their sex, without which their country must be subjected to a yoke more disgraceful and oppressive than our ruthless enemies would lay upon our necks—the yoke of ignorance and its consequences, vice, and degradation?" To a graduating class of North Carolina women, Kirkpatrick declared, "Our females must engage in the work of teaching. ... [T]here is no other alternative" (quoted in Faust 1996, 83)

Others relied less on calls to Confederate patriotism and more on rational argument. The South, *De Bow's Review* instructed its readers in 1861, must reverse its tradition of "rank[ing] teaching among the menial employments," dismissing it as "socially degrading" or "fit for Yankees only." But more than parental resistance had to be overcome if Confederate schoolchildren were to have teachers. The South had no adequate system of education for young women. Although the southern states had a "vast number" of girls' schools, schools which had no doubt "effected a great amount of good," these institutions had not, observers were pained to admit, "established that high grade of scholarship and literary attainment which ought to characterize Southern women," especially if these women were to be the educators of the new nation's young men (quoted in Faust 1996, 83).

The Confederacy's need for female teachers bred a movement for the reform and upgrading of women's education, which was accompanied by a reconsideration of male assumptions regarding the potential of woman's intellect. Reflecting the "mind-as-muscle" conception of education inherent in nineteenth-century classical curriculum theory (see Pinar et al. 1995, 73), *De Bow's* endorsed strengthening the curriculum in specific areas: mathematics, classics, and natural science. These were the subjects that had been slighted in girls' schooling, but now circumstances required that they be emphasized: "Must she be ever but cut off from the invigorating discipline of mathematics? Must the treasures which lie buried in the Grecian and Roman literature be always hidden from her eyes? Must the immense volume of nature be ever a sealed book?" (quoted in Faust 1996, 84).

The anonymous writer in *De Bow's* just quoted was unafraid to confront the basic if indelicate question embedded in the debates over female teachers. "There is a belief, unexpressed though it may be," s/he began, "that the female mind is ... inferior to the male." While demanding governmental support for women's education, the author hedged about the question of female intellectual potential, allowing that even if women were inferior intellectually to men, they still deserved better schooling than they were receiving. "While then, we would not affirm that there are no original and congenital differences between man and woman, we do believe that the actual difference in the intellectual status of man and woman is mainly due to the different courses of training and development to which custom has subjected the two sexes. ... But we do not go to the length of maintaining an absolute equality in the sexes." "Equivalence," yes; "equality," no, the writer concluded (quoted in Faust 1996, 84). While not insisting on female intellectual parity, the strengthening of the education of women that the writer demanded made any abstract arguments over intellectual potential almost moot (Faust 1996).

The *Southern Field and Fireside* of Augusta entered the discussion, taking a somewhat similar position on educational reform in a piece entitled "Educated Woman—In Peace and War." "It is not proposed here to insist upon her mental equality with man," the journal was careful to point out, "but that whether she is his equal or inferior in mind, she is none the less entitled to all the advantages which mental, moral and physical training can impart to her frail nature." This anonymous (and thereby genderless) writer went beyond strictly practical justifications for improving the education of women by suggesting they are "entitled" to the "advantages" the best educational system can provide (quoted in Faust 1996, 84).

Some men argued in similar terms. Speaking to the "young ladies" of Concord Female College in North Carolina in 1863, Dr. James D. Ramsey denied that men enjoyed any "mental advantage." Any differences in intellectual achievement between men and women was the consequence of inadequate education for women. "No nation," he warned, "has grown great and strong, when women were not strong and great." A professor at Hollins College, Edward Joynes, called for improving the education of women as teachers, declaring the current system "a shallow pretension and a gross outrage." But Joynes was careful to respect the idea of separate spheres, even as he insisted on significant change. An improved curriculum "should be based upon the idea that woman is woman, and not man—nor a butterfly," neither "man's plaything nor his rival." A Confederate education must aspire "to educate neither belles nor bluestockings, but women, for women's sphere." Neither extant southern nor northern models would do. The new nation, born in manly conflict, had very special duties to women, as "they will occupy a larger space not only in relative numbers, but in relative influence" (quoted in Faust 1996, 84–85). In fact, women's progress, Joynes was arguing, will be coextensive with that of the Confederacy itself (Faust 1996).

Joynes had rather concrete ends in mind as he wrote, for he offered as an example of his principles of education and national greatness a detailed plan for the founding of a normal school at Hollins, complete with government-supported scholarships for those students who could not afford to attend. In 1864 he established such a program for the preparation of women teachers, although scholarships were possible only through donations, given the scarcity of public funds. The preeminently practical concerns of Confederate educational reformers were evident elsewhere as well. The catalog of Tuscaloosa Female College in Alabama, for instance, boasted a "prominence in the course of instruction" and listed algebra, geometry, trigonometry, and experimental natural science as central to its curriculum (quoted in Faust 1996, 85).

Despite the efforts of educational reformers to contain the consequences of their proposals for antebellum gender hierarchies, a few, even in wartime, recognized and criticized the subversive implications of these curricular innovations. In the *Southern Illustrated News* in 1862 a writer observed, somewhat acidly, that it had "of late become extremely fashionable to advance women, in the scale of intellect to an equal standard with man." The journal wished to register its objection to this nonsense. When woman "aspires to ambitious situations, she steps out of the sphere allotted her by Nature, and assumes a character which is an outrage upon her feminine delicacy and loveliness" (quoted in Faust 1996, 85).

A number of Confederate women agreed; Jennie Pendleton of Mississippi had resolved not to teach, for she worried "I would lose all my dignity." When she learned of a friend's decision to enter teaching, Emily Perkins was horrified: "Do you know what you are undertaking? ... A life of self-denial and pain." A displaced Louisianian, Sarah Morgan was not exactly enthusiastic as she contemplated teaching, even as an alternative to poverty and homelessness. "I'll work for my living. How, I wonder? I will teach. ... I would rather die than teach. ... My soul revolts from the drudgery" (quoted in Faust 1996, 86). As did other critics of the movement to strengthen female teacher education, she regarded teaching as menial work, undesirable, and probably inappropriate for southern ladies (Faust 1996).

Appropriate or not, the national need was undeniable. In Hunstville, Alabama, Mary Jane Cook Chadick had taken notice of a "mania for teaching" among the "young ladies" of the town and regarded the enthusiasm as "certainly praiseworthy for if the young ladies do not volunteer their services in educating the present generation, to where shall we go for teachers?" (quoted in Faust 1996, 85–86).

As do many women who become teachers today, once on the job, many found good reason for their worries. Caroline Davis faced a classroom of restless boys who made her "wish I did know better how to teach—I feel my inability often enough." When she lost her temper, she felt guilty, then dreamed of fleeing: "I wish at times I could get entirely out of hearing of every child on earth." In Georgia, when a village teacher left for the army, Emma Slade Prescott took his place. "Before I had time to think about it almost—I was teaching." Not quite two months, however, she retired from the profession, noting that "the nervous strain was too much for me" (quoted in Faust 1996, 87).

Other women found teaching a pleasant surprise. Abbie Brooks discovered that she was "enjoying" herself in the classroom "as well as I ever expected to this side of Heaven," even if "it is very hard work." With many students of different ages together in a single classroom, she had to devise strategies for teaching everything "from Natural Philosophy down to cat." Then there was the matter of salary. When she settled her year's board bill, she discovered she had nothing. Her entire salary went to support bare subsistence. Financially pressed parents proved unwilling, often unable, to pay even inadequate salaries. In 1862 Amelia Pinkind recorded that everything in the Confederacy was rising in price except teaching: "That they want for very little, next to nothing" (quoted in Faust 1996, 87–88). Some things never seem to change.

IV. What's a Lady to Do? Desire and Defiance among Southern White Women at War

The cultural constraints under which we operate include not only visible political structures but also the fantasmatic processes by which we eroticize the real.

—Leo Bersani, *Homos* (1995)

[N]orthern and southern men questioned each other's manhood, both on the battlefield and in rhetorical skirmishes.

—Michael Kimmel, *Manhood in America: A Cultural History* (1996)

The man be more of woman, she of man.

—Anna Julia Cooper, "A Voice from the South" (1892/1998)

Confederate ladies found themselves doing more than teaching. As the War progressed, women found themselves working in a variety of hitherto "unladylike" occupations. But it was not only white women who made the Confederate war effort possible: more numerous in number than they were black slaves, male and female, impressed or hired away from their owners, or captured from the enemy. These black women and men worked as cooks, laundresses, and especially as nurses to the wounded. For all their remarkable contributions (all the more remarkable due to their antebellum status as ornaments), it was not the white ladies of the Confederacy but its black slaves who cared for the South's injured soldiers. In nursing as well as in cooking and washing, many Confederate ladies would prove to be much less helpful to their men than the African Americans presumed to be their inferiors (Faust 1996).

Against their will, black people had served white people for two hundred years. It was white women who found their unaccustomed obligations and power unsettling, even more so, at times, than did their men. John Davidson tried to reassure and encourage his wife to rise to the occasion that war forced upon them. "Julia, you must do the best you can. You have to act the Man and Woman both which I fear will go rather hard with you being so timid and reserved, but I am happy to see that a great deal of your timidity is wearing off. You have traveled alone and had to manage for yourself [and] you have become quite a soldier" (quoted in Faust 1996, 123). A woman's independence, at least as John Davidson imagined it, required the transgendering of women into men *and* women, hermaphrodites as soldiers. Despite his encouraging tone, his gender imagery might well have frightened as much as inspired his ladylike wife (Faust 1996).

With their husbands sometimes gone for years at a time, it seems unsurprising that a few white women would have entered into sexual liaisons not only with other white men but with male slaves as well. Testimony before the American Freedmen's Inquiry Commission taken in regions occupied by Union troops contained enough examples of such relationships to warrant an entry in the index of the proceedings under "Intercourse between women and colored men—Instances of" (quoted in Faust 1996, 126). Faust quotes Martha Hodes (1992), who reports that many of these liaisons involved women of the planter class who used their power over slaves to initiate sexual relationships. One former slave, for instance, reported that his forty-year-old white owner had after a year of widowhood "ordered him to sleep with her, and he did so regularly" (235; quoted in Faust 1996, 127).

Many white women did remain faithful to their husbands, sexually at least. Their faith in men's leadership, however, was eroded by the privations of war. Lucy Virginia Smith became disgusted with the entire gender, exclaiming: "I often wonder what men were made for! To keep up the species, I suppose—which is the only thing they are 'always ready' and never slow about doing! For my part I am quite wearied and worn out with their general no-accountability—and wish they were all put into the army where they could kill each other off—the less of them the better!" After hearing that outburst from herself, she mused, "I suppose I am beginning to become embittered by years of hardship, privation, and sorrow." But the moment of detachment was soon over, and once again she found herself complaining over men's foolishness, their weakness for ideas that brought women and children to harm. What was needed was strong men, men able, for instance, to resist the masculine fantasies of military conquest (Faust 1996). "But do such strong men live in reality?" Lucy Smith asked herself. She quickly answered: "No. I expect they only exist in books" (quoted in Faust 1996, 135).

No doubt some women's disgust with their husbands, and with men in general, drove them into the arms of other women. Perhaps the absence of men created a space wherein women could focus freely on other women. Certainly there were "impassioned attachments" between girls at boarding schools. One woman recalled the pleasure of sleeping with her roommate: "We two girls could snuggle up together in each other's arms, and sleep the sleep that only the young can ever know and enjoy" (quoted in Stowe 1987, 140–141). Clara Solomon of New Orleans recorded her crushes as well as those of her older sister, a teacher in Clara's school. The "pleasantest" hour in Clara's day was when she could be alone with her beloved Belle: "I gazed upon those cherry lips and with all the passion of my heart pressed mine to them. When I see her beautiful hair, I think 'how lovely' and when I behold those orbs of 'blue serene' I think 'oh! Nothing can be lovelier,' and when I see that mouth, as ripe and delicious as the fruit just plucked, I say 'oh!' for a lovelier sight do I care not. ... I encircled her waist with my own arm, and though 'Oh, if her heart could only reciprocate the love which mine could yield to her'" (quoted in Faust 1996, 143).

Given the intensity of Clara's desire, it is unsurprising that "the green-eyed monster took possession" of her "when I saw her and M. walk home together." Clara also recorded her sister "courting" a beautiful friend, registered her strong attraction to blondes over brunettes, and described a "tantalizing" dream in which she "lavished ... the fondest kisses and caresses" on an older female student. "But how I enjoyed them," she wrote. "Had they been genuine, my joy could not have been more intense" (quoted in Faust 1996, 143–144). While Clara described her relationships with other young women using language ordinarily associated with heterosexual courtship, clearly the "objects" of her desire are girls, suggesting to us that she is lesbian. But in her time "homosexuality" had not yet been invented; her language and fantasies would not have been regarded "deviant" or even odd. Such language conveyed, in Faust's words, "a sensitivity and authenticity of feeling celebrated in this sentimental mid-Victorian era as appropriate to true friendship as much as true love" (1996, 144).

Certainly many men enjoyed physically intimate friendships with each other. We will focus on the end of nineteenth-century "romantic" friendship in chapter 6. Consider two letters written in 1826 by Thomas Jefferson Withers, then a twenty-two-year-old law student at South Carolina in Columbus (and later to become a judge of the South Carolina Court of Appeals) to his friend James H. Hammond, later to serve as governor, congressman, and senator from South Carolina (and prominent proslavery apologist). Withers tells his friend: "I feel some inclination to learn whether you yet sleep in your Shirt-tail, and whether you yet have the extravagant delight of poking and punching a writhing Bedfellow with your long fleshen pole—the exquisite touches of which I have often had the honor of feeling." There is no self-consciousness here, no concern that he is expressing an "unnatural" sentiment, just playfulness and affection. Withers goes on: "Sir, you roughen the downy Slumbers of your Bedfellow—by such hostile—furious lunges as you are in the habit of making at him—when he is least prepared for defence against the crushing force of a Battering Ram" (quoted in Duberman 1989, 155). These letters suggest, as Christopher Looby (1995) points out, that upper-class white men in the antebellum South enjoyed, as Earl Thorpe (1967) has also argued (if with a different intent), a sexual libertinism not known in the West since ancient Rome and Greece.

Many young Confederate women also shared romantic liaisons with other women, although the extent of genital sexual love that accompanied these intense friendships is, by and large, undocumented. To the women as to the men of the mid-nineteenth century, such questions would have been beside the point. In this pre-Freudian era, neither men nor women would not have identified themselves or their desire according to our rigid binaries of heterosexuality and homosexuality. Intense—to us obviously erotic—female-female friendship (and male-male friendships) coexisted harmoniously with male-female courtship and even marriage. Faust brings the point home nicely:

> If nineteenth-century southerners had more restrictive and unchanging prescriptions of gender roles, it may be that we have more fixed and absolute notions of sexual identities. What we would label as sexual behavior between women may well have been seen in the midnineteenth century as simply a natural extension of already powerful ties of emotional attraction and dependence. (1996, 144)

A poignant instance of the blurring between friendship and sexual liaison appears in the diary of Louise Nichols, a seventeen-year-old Texas schoolgirl. The subject of Nichols' fantasies was her teacher, "Mrs. Rice," with whom she often shared a bed, evidently negotiating with Rice's husband, also a teacher, to plan their calendar. "Mrs. Rice has slept with me every night this week except Monday," Nichols recorded in May 1863. The next day she noted, "I tried a little to get Mr. Rice to exchange tonight for Friday but he would not." On other occasions Nichols took pride in her successes. "Mrs. Rice slept with me Tuesday, Thursday and Friday nights. I bought her of[f] Mr. Rice by writing in my Arithmetics." Nichols' feelings about her teacher were, by any age's standards, strong. "I do love her so much I do not know what I should do without her." The older woman evidently loved her student in reciprocal fashion. When Rice joined the Methodist Church, Nichols was quite disapproving, and Rice was concerned she might have jeopardized the relationship. Borrowing Louise's diary, Mrs. Rice wrote in it: "I wish she would trust me. I love her truly and sincerely, and would do almost anything to make her happy. Louise please take back what you said that you did not care if I never slept with you again. Are you in earnest?" (quoted in Faust 1996, 144–145).

Across the war-torn Confederacy, women found support and comfort in reaching out to each other, sometimes setting up all-female households with relatives and friends. Women worked closely together in hospitals and in women's aid societies. In 1864, with nearly half the white male population of the South wounded or killed, the single life was for many married women inevitable. The young and unmarried, even more explicitly than older married women, turned to one another for more than mere companionship. These relationships were filled with passion and feeling which we today would code as lesbian. Sarah Wadley recorded that she thought of her absent friend Valeria "constantly ... ever lovingly and with a great desire." Such relationships were not just a creation of the War, of course, but the nightmare of total war certainly intensified them. Not everyone approved. "So often lately," Nannie Haskins of Tennessee wrote in 1863, "I have noticed girls carrying on over each other, kissing each other, and so on. I think it looks right foolish sometimes" (quoted in Faust 1996, 145).

War was, women understood, an affair between men. What, after all, did it have to do with us, many southern ladies asked, especially as they learned that Yankee troops were approaching their homes. Like many elite southern women, Mary Lee assumed that her status and gender should and would shield her from any disagreeableness. Before she was an enemy, she reasoned, she was a lady, any gentleman could see that. When Yankees did arrive at her doorstep, Mary Lee started a three-year battle with them, using her status as a lady to camouflage her activities on behalf of the Confederate cause. Many northern soldiers did respect the gender of those they had captured, especially those who seemed to be ladies of the middle or upper class. Union officers did not hesitate to restrain and even punish enlisted men who failed to show the appropriate respect. Even as the "scorched earth" policies of the final years destroyed women's property, there is documentation of very few assaults on their persons. White women, especially elite white women, were rarely victims of rape by Yankee soldiers. Black women were, no doubt, not as fortunate (Faust 1996).

More than a few Confederate ladies were not exactly grateful to their Yankee conquerors for sparing them. Indeed, many took advantage of their sheltered status to express their loyalties to the Confederacy and their contempt for the northern invaders. To do so they employed, as would white women in the second Klan (see chapter 9), what Sarah Morgan of Louisiana called "their woman weapon, the tongue." Suddenly imbued with the same romantic fantasies of war's glories that had earlier inspired their men, southern women seemed filled with, in the words of one Yankee officer, "a theatrical desire to figure as heroines" (quoted in Faust 1996, 202). On occasion they found words insufficient to express this "desire." In Rome, Georgia, students at a ladies' seminary emptied their chamber pots on troops standing unsuspectingly below their windows. A few expressed their desire for heroism, not to mention their fury at Yankee victories, by attempting to become soldiers themselves. From the start, a few women had been envious that their brothers and husbands left boring domestic routines in search of war's glories; a few had, Faust tells us, "fantasies about being men" (1996, 202) and engaging other men in mortal combat. For some inventive women, cross-dressing provided the means to make real the fantasy. As many as four hundred women North and South disguised themselves as men and passed as soldiers (Faust 1996).

When New Orleans, the South's largest city, fell to Union forces in April 1862, Major General Benjamin Butler took on the challenging task of governing a furiously unfriendly civilian population. Not exactly ready to play the role of the defeated and submissive, the residents of New Orleans declined to comply with orders from the newly arrived Yankees. They gathered in unruly mobs, threatening the safety of Butler and his troops. Forced to govern by force and threat of force, Butler reluctantly gave up any effort at conciliation. Crowds refusing to disperse were met by Union artillery. Shopkeepers who refused to do business with the occupying troops found their stores seized and sold. A man destroying a Union flag was sentenced to death. Those pastors who declined to pray for the United States were sent to the North (Faust, 1996). "Very soon," Butler recorded, "there was no uncivil treatment received by our soldiers except from the upper class of women" (quoted in Faust 1996, 209).

The ladies of New Orleans took for granted that they could not be treated in the same harsh ways as New Orleans men had been, and so they continued to treat northern soldiers with contempt. The more mild-mannered among them registered their feelings by immediately and sometimes dramatically fleeing churches or streetcars if Union soldiers entered. Others chose to spit in the faces of northern soldiers struggling to be polite. In countless ways subtle and outrageous, the ladies of New Orleans sought to convey their complete contempt for their conquerors. Butler was uncertain what to do in response to these outrages. The perpetrators were often young, even "pretty and interesting," he noted, frequently socially prominent, the class of ladies who, if treated badly, would immediately become martyrs (Faust 1996). Even so, Butler knew he had to do something, for "a city could hardly be said to be under good government where such things were permitted" (quoted in Faust 1996, 209).

On May 15, Butler issued the infamous General Order No. 28, what Faust characterizes as "an astute invocation of prevailing assumptions about class and gender" (1996, 209) designed to force the ladies of New Orleans to stop their hostilities:

> General Order No. 28
>
> As the officers and soldiers of the United States have been subject to repeated insults from the women (calling themselves ladies) of New Orleans ... it is ordered that hereafter when any female shall, by word, gesture, or movement, insult or show contempt for any officer or soldier of the United States, she shall be regarded and held liable to be treated as a woman of the town plying her avocation. (quoted in Faust 1996, 209)

Butler's order shrewdly exploited the ambiguities in white southern women's identities. "By their behavior shall ye know them," he was saying, not by their categorical pretensions to the privileges and shelters of ladyhood. Those women who acted with the vulgarity of whores would be treated as if they were whores; if they showed no sign of appropriate feminine delicacy and self-restraint, they would see no sign of that masculine protection men accorded true ladies. Unlike many other northern commanders, Butler was determined not to be manipulated by southern ladies simultaneous use and abuse of their feminine status. "I did not carry on war with rose-water," he recorded. Butler rightly predicted that almost all the ladies of New Orleans would want to cling to the title of "lady," and would therefore conform to the day-to-day conduct of civility he wished. The idea that one might be treated as a "woman of the town" was so intolerable, the threatened loss of status so unimaginable, that no Yankee officer ever had to enforce the measure (Faust 1996). As Butler had predicted, the order "executed itself." Horrified at the prospect of being identified as whores, the ladies of New Orleans immediately resumed being "ladies" (quoted in Faust 1996, 209–210).

The ladies of New Orleans may have been tamed, but "chivalrous" men, south and north, were outraged by the news. Not only the southern press described him in less-than-human terms—a "beast" was not an uncommon descriptor applied to the Union officer—even the *New York Times* criticized him. In London, both the press and Parliament were contemptuous of Butler's "intolerable brutality" (quoted phrases in Faust 1996, 210). These criticisms took their toll. After facing additional difficulty in subduing the locals, combined with crises about the rights of foreign nationals in the city, Butler was replaced in December 1862 by Nathaniel Banks. Instructed to conduct a more conciliatory administration of the troublesome city, Banks was immediately challenged by residents who decoded his generosity as weakness. The ladies of New Orleans once again began to insult northern soldiers and to make public declarations of their Confederate patriotism (Faust 1996).

Late in February 1863 southern women's continued resistance created an incident popularly known as the "Battle of the Handkerchiefs." When a group of captured Confederate officers was being shipped to Baton Rouge for a prisoner exchange, New Orleans ladies expressed their continuing allegiance, gathering at the levee to applaud the captured heroes. Union troops tried to control the crowd and silence its treasonous cheering but were met by a mob of women waving parasols and handkerchiefs, daring the soldiers to disband them. Several ladies suffered minor injuries in the melee. A southern newspaper poem celebrated the courage of the ladies and mocked the brutish if inept northern soldiers. Banks had returned to a pre-Butler treatment of southern ladies as existing outside politics, hence invulnerable to military action. The ladies' "victory" in the Battle of the Handkerchiefs was possible only because northern soldiers were unable to engage the enemy (Faust 1996).

The Civil War produced not only ladies acting in such aggressive, even mannish, ways as to be unrecognizable by antebellum standards. Men too seemed forced out of their conventional performances of masculinity, sometimes for tactical reasons, sometimes, well, for fun. Living in an occupied region of Alabama, Rowena Webster reported that women regularly dressed Confederate soldiers "in female attire" when it would help them escape. Moreover, southern soldiers regularly disguised themselves as women in order to spy on northern men. But at times southern men became women for purposes of play as well as for politics. Helen Garner remembered that a Louisiana regiment encamped near her Mississippi home put on theatrical productions for the townspeople of Columbus. Borrowing dresses from local ladies, the soldiers delighted local residents with their passionate performances. The "leading lady," Garner recorded, "had a perceptible moustache" (quoted in Faust 1996, 228–229). The "theater of war," Faust playfully puts it, "offered men an opportunity for experimentation with different gender roles, for play within a play and for seemingly frivolous behavior that had deeper significance" (1996, 229).

The Louisiana soldiers were hardly the only cross-dressed Confederates. Celebrating New Year's Day 1863—and perhaps a new gender identity—young men from a college in Spartanburg, South Carolina, toured the town dressed in ladies' gowns. Faust notes, perhaps with a smile on her face, that this scene was suggestive of "inversion," but she means not sexual inversion, a term that would not become known for another two decades but an acknowledgment of "a world turned upside down" (1996, 229), a notion most appropriate to the disintegrating social order of the slave South as the War wore on. There was, she continues, an additional sense in which "inversion" was an appropriate descriptor for the war-torn Confederacy, however, as "the blurring of homefront and battlefield" had already mounted a serious assault on the antebellum ideology of sharply separate male and female spheres. "The young men," she continues, referring to those revelers in Spartanburg, "must on some level have been commenting on their rather anomalous position in a society where almost all young men had gone off to war. In Texas in 1861 women had sent hoopskirts to men who failed to volunteer for service; these Carolina boys may have been in parallel language expressing their own unconscious ambivalence and guilt about their protected status" (Faust 1996, 229).

Nor was this destabilization of gender occurring below the threshold of southern consciousness. Confederate women spoke openly and frankly of both their pleasure and horror at the War's destruction of conventional sex roles, evident in men's cross-dressing. Men were perhaps less aware, but it is impossible, Faust notes, that the same mix of excitement and dread was not felt. The image of Jefferson Davis, presumably escaping Yankee capture at war's end by cross-dressing, linked visually femininity and defeat. One popular song, "Jeff in Petticoats," recounted the event:

> Jeff Davis was a warrior bold,
> And vowed the Yanks should fall;
> He jumped into his pantaloons
> And swore he'd rule them all.
> But when he saw the Yankees come
> To hang him if they could
> He jumped into a petticoat
> And started for the wood.
>
> (quoted in Kimmel 1996, 77)

By emasculating the Confederate president first as a prepubescent boy, "Jeffie" Davis, and then as a "girl" (the "Belle of Richmond" as another cartoon had it), victorious northern men ridiculed southern manhood, dismissing the defeated southern nation as the "Petticoat Confederacy" (quoted in Kimmel 1996, 77).

Certainly the image of the Confederate president running from Yankee soldiers about to enter his quarters dramatized the humiliation, the loss of status and power, inherent in the destabilization of conventional gender arrangements. But, Faust suggests perceptively, there was perhaps more at stake for southern men than the ruination of their antebellum manhood. Perhaps at some level many may have wished to desert that gendered positionality for the "opposite" one.

> Confederate men may have felt a longing to share certain attributes and shelters of womanhood as well. Most obviously, southern females were protected from military service—neither required nor expected to sacrifice their lives on the field of battle. What was initially seen as a male privilege became an increasing burden and liability as death tolls escalated. ... Jefferson Davis's alleged resort to women's clothes expressed much the same desire for escape from masculine obligations and vulnerabilities. Women were not unique in their new recognition of the constraints and liabilities of traditional gender identities, nor were they alone in employing the language of clothing to express the at once thrilling and terrifying possibilities of changed garments and altered roles. (Faust 1996, 230)

Throughout the War southern men and women performed cross-gendered behavior, Faust argues, "to contain the revolutionary potential of women's new roles and responsibilities" (232). No doubt, for when women acted in newly assertive, powerful, autonomous ways, they transgressed the boundaries of permissible gendered conduct. A Savannah judge made this clear in his statement at the end of a trial of female bread rioters. "When women become rioters," he declared, "they cease to be women" (quoted in Faust 1996, 232). Clearly he thought it impossible that women could or would act in such an unfeminine manner. But in excluding them from the province of women he also unwittingly suggested that their appearance, dresses and hair and all, no longer provided sure evidence of who they were. "Dressed in the clothes and even the bodies of women," these ladies "were nevertheless acting like men" (Faust 1996, 232).

Cross-dressing suggested that southern white men had capitulated, that both their oedipal defeat at the hands of stronger, superior (northern) men, their inability to protect their wives, children, and households, as well the shifts in southern women's identity, all must have meant to some men that the game was up, that they were not just defeated as soldiers, but as men. And if they were no longer entitled to call themselves "men," they were, in some awful, inadmissible but still inescapable sense, women. It is not difficult to imagine the profoundly shattering experience that the Civil War was for southern white men. No longer "gentlemen" who would "whip" those Yankees in a few weeks, "masters" in charge of households filled with children, "ladies," and slaves, including male slaves, whose civic emasculation could not hide their muscular masculinity and physical power, now white men, shells of their former selves, came "home" to shells of plantations and farms, many burned beyond recognition, to the despairing, defeated, and hungry eyes of those loved ones they had sworn, with all their manhood, to protect. Now, in the absence of glory, with the new nation only a lost cause, southern white men must also face newly freed black men, men without chains. Now white men must face black men, man to man. How far are we here from lynching?

Women *did* lose faith in their men, certainly as soldiers and leaders of the new nation they had proclaimed. For many, a residual resentment against the War surfaced, and women's patriotism waned. The War may be lost, the Confederacy just a shattered dream, but give me back my husband! Many married women in the South must have felt as Gertrude Thomas did when she was faced with the grim prospects of a war still on but lost: "Am I willing to give my husband to gain Atlanta for the Confederacy? No, No, No, a thousand times No!" (quoted in Faust 1996, 242). In one sense the erosion of Confederate women's patriotism amounted to a reversion to conventional female concerns, a reassertion of the private and domestic over the public and political. At the same time, Faust argues, these women's vocal disenchantment with the War suggested an assertion of women's rights and identity, of women's self-interest, "strikingly modern" (242) in its implications and consequences.

Confederate women's withdrawal from the public sphere was animated in no minor way by their recognition that in the Confederacy the public interest had not included their own. The "public interest" in fact had killed their loved ones, deprived them of life's basic necessities, not to mention pleasures, and required them to manage restive, increasingly rebellious slaves. A nation founded on radically separate gender spheres had not, naturally, taken women's concerns into account at its birth, and certainly it failed to do so now that it was near death. The "virtual" political representation of women—Faust's clever phrase (242) for the idea that women's interests would be protected by their men—had proved unsatisfactory indeed. Now, as Atlanta burned and the Confederacy faced complete and devastating defeat, southern women began to articulate and defend their own interests apart from those of their husbands and their nation. In crisis and often in despair, women rose up from the rubble to assert themselves as individuals with legitimate interests and rights, not just duties and responsibilities (Faust 1996).

V. Losing the War, Winning the Peace

The South in 1865 was a society without a center, a sense of control, a sense of direction. All certainties had been destroyed.

—Edward L. Ayers, *Vengeance and Justice: Crime and Punishment in the Nineeenth Century American South* (1984)

For southern men, defeat meant a kind of gendered humiliation—the southern gentlemen was discredited as a "real man."

—Michael Kimmel, *Manhod in America: A Cultural History* (1996)

The Civil War was a major turning point for middle-class attitudes toward masculinity.

—Merk C. Carnes and Clyde Griffen, eds., *Meanings for Manood: Constructions of Masculinity in Victorian America* (1990)

[S]outhern white women, betrayed by white men's inability to fulfill their manly responsibility to protect and provide for them after the losses of the Civil War, displaced their anger onto black men. By accepting the idea of the

black male rapist, white women could express their dismay with white men's abdication of their manly responsibilities, while at the same time making common cause with white men over the issue of racial privilege.

—Gail Bederman, *Manliness and Civilization: A Cultural History of Gender and Race in the United States, 1880–1917* (1995a)

The war-provoked transformation in southern white women's self-perception paralleled a much broader shift in American political life during the early and middle years of the nineteenth century, one that many scholars have characterized as a shift from republican to liberal political forms and values, as civic virtue and a sense of community disappeared and in their place appeared factionalism and narrow self-interest. The experience of southern women during the course of the Civil War suggests that shifts in gender both supported and followed from such a broader transformation, for women's changing understanding of their place in society accompanied their discovery of themselves as more than simple appendages to other, presumably more important, social actors, namely men (Faust 1996). But not only the gender of women but that of men underwent significant shifts, and some two decades later there would be widespread acknowledgment of a white "crisis of masculinity." During the last decade of the nineteenth century lynching would be at its apex.

Once the patriarchal order crumbled around them, as they then felt their own needs and desires in the absence of men and in the midst of great emotional and even material deprivations, Confederate women experienced new selves with new interests. It was not, Faust argues, as several studies of women and war have suggested, that new accomplishments (as nurses or teachers or plantation managers) formed the foundations for enhanced self-esteem. Rather, Faust continues, southern women's sense of self arose not from the blush of success but phoenixlike from the rubble of desperation, from the simple need to survive. Confederate women often repeated, "Necessity is the mother of invention," recalling the title of her book, Faust points out. Only "necessity," as Julia Davidson wrote to her husband, John, could "make a different woman of me" (quoted in Faust 1996, 243).

By the final months of the War many women were expressing their new-found self-interest, sometimes boldly. Especially middle- and lower-class women—those who experienced the War's deprivations most severely—were not just keeping husbands and brothers at home; they were forbidding them to join the crumbling Confederate army. Other women were actively urging men already serving the Confederacy to desert. The risk of execution and the certainty of shame must have seemed to these women an acceptable price to pay in the face of almost certain injury, if not death, at the front. Desperate Confederate leaders recognized the influence that Confederate women exercised in persuading soldiers to give up the fight. One military officer recommended to the secretary of war that he censor the mails, for, he insisted, "the source of all the present evils of Toryism and desertion in our country is letter writing to … the army." As a Confederate official in North Carolina declared, "Desertion takes place because desertion is encouraged. ... And although the ladies may not be willing to concede the fact, they are nevertheless responsible ... for the desertion in the army and the dissipation in the country" (quoted in Faust 1996, 243). As war-exhausted southern men fought off complete defeat to the hated Yankees, southern women were busy making their own contributions to just that conclusion to the lost cause (Faust 1996).

Confederate leaders' distress over women's failings as patriots brought more than occasional comment in the press. An 1864 correspondent to the *Montgomery Daily Advertiser* criticized women's fading political commitment. At first "women were rivaling the other sex in patriotic devotion. ... But a change, such a change, has come over the spirit of their dream. The Aid societies have died away; they are a name and nothing more. The self-sacrifice has vanished; wives and maidens now labor only to exempt their husbands and lovers from the perils of service." Starting with a discussion of women's interference with military recruitment and retention, the writer moved to a second indictment of elite ladies' wartime conduct. "Never were parties more numerous. ... Never were the theaters and places of public amusement so resorted to. ... The love of dress, the display of jewelry and costly attire, the extravagance and folly are all the greater for the brief abstinence which has been observed" (quoted in Faust 1996, 243–244).

Indeed, as the end appeared near, elite southern women did respond by throwing parties, not one or two but many, and often extravagant parties. Most memorable perhaps was the party given by Mrs. Robert Stannard, who spent more than $30,000 on entertainment during a winter that saw Confederate troops camped in nearby counties nearly dead from starvation and frozen from inadequate clothing. Mrs. Stannard was hardly alone. Why did elite Confederate women resort to parties while Confederate men fought to their deaths? Faust argues that the reason had to do with upper-class women's greater investment in the antebellum gender system that had conferred upon them their superior status. Their investment had been much greater than their poorer countrywomen and men (Faust 1996). Despite their disillusionment with slavery (following their frustrations at slave management), with the Confederate leadership, and with their individual men, "elite southern women clung to—even reasserted—lingering elements of privilege." Even as the Confederacy breathed its final breaths, "elite white women of the South held fast to the traditional hierarchical social and racial order that had defined their importance. Indeed, their disillusionment with the Confederacy arose chiefly from its failure to protect and preserve that privilege, to serve white female self-interest" (Faust 1996, 246–247).

In that gendered system of the Old South, southern ladies had accepted gender subordination in exchange for class and racial superiority. Yet their appreciation for that contract had changed considerably during the course of the War. Their expectations for male protection had been completely disappointed; suffering and necessity, not a welcomed sense of opportunity, made them, often for the first time, quite clear about both the dangers of dependence and the demands of autonomy. Sometimes overwhelmed by doubts about both themselves and their men, elite southern women faced the postwar world with what Faust characterizes as "a new realism, a deep-seated bitterness, and a frightening sense of isolation" (247). The world they, along with their men, had been determined to preserve, had been utterly destroyed; the ideal of southern masculinity had been proven a fantasy. And yet southern women felt they had insufficient evidence for faith in their own competence or effectiveness; they could not consider replacing male power and authority with their own. In the face of the frightening reality of the South's defeat and destruction, the horror of black emancipation, white women, with reluctance Faust (1996) seems to be saying, came to agree with their exhausted husbands and brothers and sons that the restoration of patriarchy was the route they were still compelled to travel. But how?

After the War southern white women devoted themselves to burying those feelings of bitterness and disappointment and autonomy by commemorating white male courage and wartime heroism through the Daughters of the Confederacy, the Confederate Memorial Society, and other defenders of the Lost Cause. All these activities, Faust (1996) argues, functioned to make what southern white women had accepted as necessary to seem once again real and legitimate. If southern white men were once again to rule the world, southern ladies would have to express sufficient confidence in male superiority that both they and their shattered men could somehow believe that such a patriarchal social order could be again natural and desirable. More than ever before, fantasy, not reality, came to characterize (white) southern history and culture.

Mary Greenhow Lee, the Confederate woman whose frustration with the men's war persuaded her that a Queen might be preferable, left her home in Winchester after the War. She resettled in Baltimore, where she spent the remainder of a long life taking in boarders and dedicating herself to church work. Most of all she labored for the United Daughters of the Confederacy. "Political reconstruction," she wrote late in 1865, "might be unavoidable now, but social reconstruction we hold in our hands and might prevent" (quoted in Faust 1996, 248). Southern white women's determination was, no doubt, highly influential in persuading defeated white men that they once again could be on top. While women's support would reanimate nearly lifeless white men, the journey would have to be men's alone, and band together they did, in the Ku Klux Klan and in other homosocial racist groups. To reach the top, postwar white men increasingly came to believe, they would have to mount the black man.

Black people, newly freed (a fact more fantasy than materially real), figured prominently in the minds of ex-Confederate women too. As Lucy Buck had observed as early as 1862, "We shall never any of us be the same as we have been" (quoted in Faust 1996, 249). For every Confederate woman and man who had been part of the Old South's master class, Appomattox ushered in a new world, one they had never anticipated and never wanted. Perhaps most profoundly, the postwar South was a world without slaves. Loss of the human property that had created the wealth and position of formerly slaveowning families threatened impoverishment and, for the first time for many, physical labor. White women within these formerly elite households were determined to avoid the latter, even if they could not help the former. If they could have no slaves to perform the seemingly endless domestic tasks required to create and maintain a nineteenth-century household, they would have servants. "All the talk, everywhere now," Emma M. wrote just after the War ended, "is servants." Decades later, the "servant problem" continued to preoccupy southern ladies. Asked by a Vanderbilt University social scientist in the early 1890s to name the most significant consequence of the War on the lives of white southern women of her class, a Carolina woman old enough to have memories of "better days" did not hesitate. "From being queens in social life," she said, ladies had become "after the war, in many instances, mere domestic drudges" (quoted in Faust 1996, 249).

Not only household chores occupied white women after the War. Without slave labor generating wealth, many once wealthy families now struggled to make ends meet, often requiring women to work outside the home. Many of these women, no longer able to afford considerations of respectability, turned to teaching. By 1880 the majority of southern schoolteachers would become female for the first time. The necessity for increasing numbers of middle- and upper-class women to find employment prompted southerners to restart the wartime conversation regarding women's education. By the 1890s the president of a southern women's college would observe that nearly a quarter of his graduates now supported themselves. This fact, he explained, moved students to study with far greater earnestness and diligence than had their antebellum predecessors. Several southern state universities introduced coeducation in the 1880s, and women's colleges, such as Sophie Newcomb at Tulane in 1886, were established to offer women educational opportunities nearly equal to those of men. By the 1890s a Vanderbilt researcher found that economic necessity had led to the "growing respectability of self support." Few seemed nostalgic about the loss of the ornamental character of antebellum female life; indeed, one applauded the erosion of prewar beliefs in "the nobility of dependence and helplessness in woman" (quoted in Faust 1996, 251).

In this specific sense some nineteenth-century southern women could be said to be "feminists," but they would not have said so, nor would their northern counterparts necessarily have recognized them as such. As we will see in the disagreement between Ida B. Wells and Frances Willard in chapter 8 and in different form among white female members of the second Klan in chapter 9, women's rights, especially in the South, did not in the postwar period necessarily link up with racial progressivism, as it had among northern feminists in the antebellum period. Many late-nineteenth-century white women in the South found no contradiction at all in working for both, say, female suffrage, and for the Lost Cause (Faust 1996).

The South may have lost the War but it had no intention of losing the peace. The majority of southerners, white women and men, committed themselves very soon, certainly by Reconstruction, to the restoration, to whatever extent possible, of the social and racial order of the Old South. True, legalized slavery might no longer be possible, but slavery by another means—peonage, social hierarchalization—might well be. The much discussed late nineteenth-century "servant problem" amounts, Faust points out, to a postwar expression of southern ladies' commitment to reestablishing the authority and privileges of whiteness. Their husbands and brothers and sons would of course serve as important allies in this cause. This postbellum spilt between feminism and racial progressivism, in Faust's (1996) words, "thus undermined the imperatives and commonalties of gender in the postwar South, separating black and white women, weakening and retarding the development of southern feminism, and subordinating its agenda to the seemingly more pressing concerns of re-establishing class and racial privilege" (254).

There were no Susan B. Anthonys agitating south of the Mason-Dixon line. It was not until the 1890s that a few southern women began to advocate female suffrage, and then they did so in a racist and regionally distinct language. White women in the South argued that they should be given the right to vote, not because they—as women—deserved this basic civil right, or because it would improve the lot of women and children generally, but because it would weaken the power of the black male vote. These southern suffragettes did not seek equality with white men as much as superiority over black men. The letterhead of the Southern States Woman Suffrage Conference expressed its members' sense of their rightful racial and class preeminence, proclaiming "A government is not yet complete that withholds from its most enlightened women what it freely gives to its most benighted men." "Never before," said a speaker at a southern suffrage convention, "in the history of the world have men made former slaves the political masters of their former mistresses" (quoted in Faust 1996, 254). White women in the South thereby sought an alliance with white southern men that would further the interests of both. By so doing southern suffragists emphasized white unity over gender progress and social equality, and feminism in the South became expressed through a shared white supremacist rhetoric. In their racism and elitism, in their complementary concerns with protecting women and rehabilitating men—as we will see, the twin themes of the Women's Christian Temperance Union—the southern suffrage movement and the celebration of the Lost Cause expressed the determination of white southerners to win in peace what they had lost in war, namely the right to live (with blacks) exactly as they saw fit (Faust 1996).

Complicated Eyes

The Civil War experience of southern women left many with profound doubts about themselves and their men. The structure of antebellum sex roles became unraveled in the absence of men, but the opportunities—in teaching, nursing, plantation management—left them questioning the desirability of such freedom and autonomy. It was hard work and many southern women felt they had failed to achieve what they might have. But the bittersweet taste of wartime independence persuaded few to go back, even if they could have, to being gendered ornaments in a male world. In that world they had traded public freedom for male protection; the War taught they could not longer rely on their men for such protection. Their men had failed. Still, they were the only men they had, and so they cast their lot with them once again. This complicated and ambivalent result of the War would influence southern assertions of female power in the late nineteenth and twentieth centuries. As Faust (1996) points out, the "burden of southern history" (Woodward 1960) is also a peculiarly gendered, specifically women's, burden.

The determination and optimism that characterized the movement for women rights elsewhere was not discernible in the South. Many southern women active as leaders in the southern suffrage movement, for instance, expressed a disdain for men and a need to defend the interests of women and children that can only be understood by remembering their wartime experience. As Faust observes:

> Invented from necessity and born of disappointment and desperation, southern female assertiveness grew from different roots than that of their northern sisters. The appeal, the character, and the extent of southern feminism has been shaped by women's sense of their own limitations. Southern women, like their men, had learned to think of success as elusive; their own experience made it difficult for them to identify with the confidence of Susan B. Anthony's much quoted rallying cry, "Failure is impossible." (1996, 256–257)

In this experience, then, is the origin of feminism's very limited appeal in the South, even into the present time, and with a southern popular wisdom that takes for granted a paradox of strength and frailty in white southern women. The pathway, as Faust puts it, "from Altars of Sacrifice to Steel Magnolias" (1996, 257) requires further research, but thanks to her research, and that of other women historians, it is clear that the Civil War left a mark upon southern women, a distinctive and complex mark that remains discernible even today (Faust 1996).

The Civil War left marks of contradiction and ambivalence upon southern white women; it devastated southern white men. Many returned home wounded, many missing limbs, all crushed not only by the utter destruction of the landscape, their homes and cities, but also of their dreams of independence and autonomy. These latter dreams were of course civic and political dreams, but they were, as Faust points out, gendered dreams as well. For in men's eyes, the fortunes of war were very much dependent upon the virility of one's manhood. The battles of the Civil War had demonstrated not only northern military superiority, but northern superiority as men as well. "Johnny Reb" had been sure he was twice the man any "damned Yankee" pretended to be—why the latter's inability to control his women was proof of that. Those northern "poofs" would be put in their place in short order, my darling. And that "darling" was the other object of the white man's gaze: he must demonstrate his manhood not just to the Yankees, to his friends and to himself, he must demonstrate it to his wife, mother, and daughters. He would uphold the antebellum promise of protection in return for the masculine presumption of superiority. When the Confederacy lay in ruins in 1865, it was most literally and blatantly a military defeat, but it was less obviously but perhaps equally profoundly a gendered defeat. Michael Kimmel summarizes:

> Southern soldiers returned to a barren and broken land of untilled farms, broken machinery, gutted and burned buildings, and a valueless currency. Schools, banks, and businesses were closed, unemployment was high, and inflation crippling. For the rest of the century and well into the twentieth

> century, southern manhood would continually attempt to assert itself against debilitating conditions, northern invaders (from carpetbaggers to civil rights workers), and newly freed blacks. The southern rebel, waving the Confederate flag at collegiate football games, is perhaps his most recent incarnation. (Kimmel 1996, 77–78)

The southern white man, if alive, was shattered, often physically, always, I suspect, psychologically. That shattered self was a gendered self, and it was his manhood that had also been the casualty in his inability to establish his independence and defeat those "poofs" from the North. The image of the president of the Confederacy trying to flee in women's clothes delighted northern men—who in their victory felt ever so much more manly—and further crushed southern white men. By the Victorian period that distinctive southern version of manliness evident in studies of the antebellum era had become increasingly unacceptable and had begun to fade (Hughes 1990).

It is clear from Faust's compelling study that southern white women faced their husbands, brothers and sons at war's end with complicated eyes. There must have been thrilled tears at the return of those one loved. But there must have been, maybe only for a moment, in the corner of that eye, disappointment, even resentment, a look southern men had never seen—or noticed—before. It was a look that felt strange, less accommodating, less respectful, less admiring, perhaps even slightly chilly. Southern white men had placed their ladies on pedestals, but when they had looked at them with the pride of possession, they were not looking up, but down. For if their gender subordinates were well placed, they (the white gentlemen of the South) were even higher, and their fall at the hands of Yankee men was all the greater. No wonder this self-shattering trauma lasted, in political terms, for only a year or two, before the support of women and the attempt by the North to "reconstruct" the South in American not Confederate terms swelled the southern phallus once again. He would rise again, the South would rise again, the Yankees would be chased away.

What about the blacks, now freedpeople, those whose slave labor made white southern wealth possible, whose subjugated bodies had been, against their will, sexually available as well as economically profitable. How did southern white women and men regard them? Feeling betrayed by their husbands' inability to perform their manly responsibility to protect and provide for them after the Civil War, many southern white women may have displaced their anger onto black men, as Bederman suggests. By colluding with white men in the fantasy of the black male rapist, white women expressed their contempt for their husbands' failure to perform their manly responsibilities while at the same time making common cause with white men over the issue of racial privilege (Whites 1992; Bederman 1995a). We already know how white men answered the question of their relationship to the newly freedpeople. In 1901 Jane Addams knew, at that time linking lynching in part to "the feeling of the former slave owner to his former slave, whom he is now bidden to regard as his fellow citizen" (quoted in Hall 1983, 344). It was not a civic feeling.

Shifts in the Economy

The end of the Civil War also meant the beginning of an era of unprecedented economic transformation, slowly in the South, rapidly in the North. Between 1870 and 1900 industrial output in the United States would increase by 500 percent. As the trauma of the Civil War faded and the twentieth century approached, both agriculture and industry would be reorganized by what Alan Trachtenberg (1982) terms "the incorporation of America." In 1800 over 80 percent of American men had been farmers; by 1880 only one-half of the nation's labor force earned its living in agriculture. Although four of every five American men were self-employed in the first decades of the century, by 1870 only one-third were self-employed. Large factories, not small shops, now structured the industrial workplace. On the eve of the Civil War, the McCormick factory employed 300 to 400 workers and was the largest factory of its kind in the world. In 1870 Best and Company (which eventually became the Pabst Brewing Company) was the nation's second largest brewery and employed no more than 100 workers. Even in the early 1880s only the railroads and the New England textile mills employed more than 1,000 workers. But by 1884 Best Brewery had 1,400 hundred workers, and by 1899 more than 4,000. Carnegie Steel employed more than 4,000 at its Homestead works alone. Edison Electric, precursor to General Electric, employed 1,000 workers in the early 1880s, 2,400 by 1890, and over 10,000 by 1892 (Kimmel 1996).

As Americans moved from the fields to the factories they moved from the country to the city. In 1830 about one American in fifteen lived in a city over eight thousand. Between 1860 and 1890 the proportion of Americans living in communities with more than two thousand five hundred doubled to about 30 percent; by 1900 one-third of Americans lived in cities of at least eight thousand; by 1910 one-half lived there. In a phrase, Americans found themselves no longer living among extended families on farms but among strangers in urban crowds. Both these developments—the economic shift from farm to factory and the social shift from familial to mass society—were not easy for self-made, self-controlled men. Indeed, mixed with other profound shifts in American society, among them shifts in religion, education, race, and gender, white masculinity went into "crisis" (Kimmel 1996).

Anomie and social dislocation were the least of it in the defeated and devastated South. Nearly every aspect of the antebellum order had been destroyed. As the southern economy struggled to recover and reorganize it would be undermined by weak state governments, lack of industrial experience, reliance on outside expertise, absentee ownership, not to mention competition with long-established northern counterparts. In fact, industrialization and those shifts in social organization it brought in the North failed to occur on the same scale in the postbellum South. Southerners knew they lagged behind the North, and this fact was a constant irritation (Ayers 1992).

As they would so often, southern white men fled to the safety of their imaginations. For decades reports of economic activity would be exaggerated or simply fabricated. By the onset of the twentieth century, one southern trade paper had had enough. "If all the saw mills, cotton mills, tobacco factories, new towns, and other enterprises and undertakings which it has heralded to its advertisers and 'subscribers' as having been started up in the various states of the South, had really been erected and put into operation," the *Southern Lumberman* told its readers in exasperation, "there wouldn't be surface room for them to stand on, water enough under the earthy to supply their boilers, nor room enough in the sky for the smoke from their chimneys" (quoted in Ayers 1992, 104). Defeated on the battlefield and in their homes, southern white men would be economically humiliated as well. For them and for their northern brothers, white masculinity would be contested almost everywhere. Even in church.

5 ✿ CHRISTIAN FEMINISM *and* *the* DESTABILIZATION *of* GENDER *in the* LATE NINETEENTH CENTURY

I. Masculine Fantasies of Anglo-Saxon Superiority: Protestantism, Manifest Destiny, and the Cult of Domesticity

[W]e must consider gender when studying fundamentalism because this phenomenon does not affect men and women in the same way.

—Judy Brink, "Lost Rituals: Sunni Muslim Women in Rural Egypt," in Judy Brink and Joan Mencher (Eds.), *Mixed Blessings: Gender and Religious Fundamentalism Cross Culturally* (1997)

However much then the facts of any particular period may seem to deny it, I for one do not doubt that the source of the vitalizing principle of woman's development and amelioration is the Christian Church, so far as that church is coincident with Christianity.

—Anna Julia Cooper, "A Voice from the South" (1892/1998)

Protestantism in the South stressed the harsher, fatalistic, patriarchal, Old Testament side of the Bible and Christianity, even as northern Protestantism increasingly took on a rational, optimistic, "feminized," New Testament emphasis.

—Edward L. Ayers, *Vengeance and Justice: Crime and Punishment in the Nineteenth Century American South* (1984)

The Civil War punctuated a century of multiple and momentous social and political developments in the United States. After the War's conclusion in 1865 and a brief and failed effort at Reconstruction, once again a united American nation turned its attention toward expansion westward, an expansion accomplished through the genocide of Native Americans and the usurpation of their lands. The nation grew in wealth and power as well as land, and soon a broad white middle class appeared. Each of these historical events were, Carolyn A. Haynes (1998) argues, laced with, sometimes justified by, two separate if interrelated gendered and racialized discourses: manifest destiny and domesticity.

The discourse of manifest destiny declared a divine basis for the expansion of democracy, individualism, capitalism, and American "civilization" across the continent. The discourse of domesticity reassured a restless migrant people that there were "natural" even divinely decreed differences between men and women. These perceived differences legitimated a variety of activist and public roles for men. Women should remain within the private domain of domesticity, wherein piety and purity could be cultivated, safely separate from the tumultuous, predatory, manly world of war, politics, and the marketplace. When women performed their godly roles as devoted daughters, loyal wives, and nurturing mothers, men were free to devote themselves to the divinely ordained political appropriation and economic exploitation of the continent (Haynes 1998).

The relation between domesticity and manifest destiny is illustrated in Ellice Hopkins's 1899 warning: "When shall we learn that whoever touches the higher life and well-being of a family still more vitally affects the wider family of the State, and threatens its disintegration." She continued: "The great question whether the relations of men and women shall be pure lies at the root of all national well-being and progress." In similar terms, Elizabeth Blackwell linked sex, empire, and progress, all dependent upon the family. The family is the "precious center of national welfare," she insisted, and as such requires the instituting of male sexual purity as a "fundamental virtue in a State" (quoted in Hunt 1998, 611).

While the two discourses, domesticity and manifest destiny, were perceived as divine in origin and universal in application, the truth of the matter is that both were rooted in American fantasies of masculine Anglo-Saxon superiority. By the late nineteenth century, perhaps a majority of Americans believed that the divinely ordained triumph of the nation could be achieved only through the removal, acculturation, or containment of nonwhite peoples and, simultaneously, through a careful delineation of sex roles, requiring strict control of white women. Associated with what Haynes (1998) terms "a virulent ethnocentrism and misogyny," these discourses were linked as well "through their reliance on the Protestant belief system and the Church itself" (xii). It is this relationship between Protestantism and the discourses of manifest destiny and domesticity that Haynes's intriguing study explores and which I will summarize in order to establish the broader historical and gendered context in which lynching occurred, a context in white masculinity was in "crisis" even within conservative Christianity.

The relationship between Protestantism and the discourses of manifest destiny and domesticity is not, Haynes will show, a self-evident one. True, nineteenth-century politicians, educators, historians, and ministers claimed that the Bible and Protestantism legitimated territorial expansionism and the separate-spheres bifurcation of gender. To illustrate, Haynes quotes John Quincy Adams, who described the American acquisition of the Oregon Territory in the following terms: "To make the wilderness blossom as the rose, to establish laws, to increase, multiply and subdue the earth, which we are commanded to do by the first behest of God Almighty." The conflation of heterosexuality, military aggression, and oedipal obedience is unmistakable. White Protestants were clear that God demanded his sons to conquer the "dark wilderness" in the name of Christ, their "master." In 1822, a special committee recommended to the Board of the American Baptist Foreign Mission Society "to carry the gospel and the blessing of civilized life to the dark and distant regions of the west, until the rocky mountains shall resound with harmony and praise and the shores of the Pacific shall be the only boundary of this wide sweep of human civilization and Christian benevolence." In 1893, Congregationalist minister Josiah Strong declared "that this race is destined to dispossess many weaker ones, assimilate others, and mould the remainder, until in a very true and important sense, it has Anglo-Saxonized mankind" (quoted in Haynes 1998, xii).

Employing what seems like oedipal language to depict men and women's gendered relationship to God, popular ministers such as George Burnap underscored the proper conduct of women: "The God who made them knew the sphere in which each of them was designed to act, and he fitted them for it by their physical frames, by their intellectual susceptibilities, by their tastes and affections. ... It is enough that she is effeminate and weak; and she does not want another like herself. Just so with man" (quoted in Haynes 1998, xii). Not only was the occupied land suddenly a blank screen upon which American Protestants projected their own racialized fantasies of civilization, religion, and manly conquest: women too were imagined as canvases on which God had painted, a vision men declared themselves uniquely qualified to perceive and interpret (Haynes 1998).

Despite the gendered and racialized exclusionism of these Protestant discourses of manifest destiny and domesticity, the nineteenth century saw an astonishing increase in the conversion of nonwhite people and white women to the Protestant faith. These facts have forced contemporary scholars to confront an apparent contradiction: why were the very peoples who had been the most victimized by Protestantism still drawn to participate in it? To confront this fact, Haynes tells us, requires a reconsideration of the conventional interpretations of the discourses of manifest destiny and domesticity. She cites the work of Reginald Horsman (1981) and Thomas R. Hietala (1985), which suggests that the nineteenth-century view of the United States as a white man's country was expressed in variety of ways and from various sources, each vying for ascendancy and control. Horsman notes that after 1815, the term "Anglo-Saxon" had been ethnically but not ideologically shorn from its origins in pre-1066 Britain and was employed increasingly to represent almost anyone of European descent who perceived it in his or her interest to identify themselves with the phrase. The tone and content of the discourse of manifest destiny shifted during the first half of the nineteenth century, becoming more racialized as the century progressed, as whites, especially white men, imagined themselves increasingly besieged by the sexualized presence and political aggressiveness of non-"Anglo-Saxon" peoples, among them African Americans and "waves" of eastern and southern European immigrants (Haynes 1998).

Many nineteenth-century political activists—including black activists such as Ida B. Wells—were at the same time devout believers. The contemporary tendency to regard Protestantism and the advancement of marginalized peoples as mutually exclusive is mistaken, Haynes believes. Not only does it misrepresent historical facts, assuming an unbridgeable gulf between the two, but the idea blinds historians to the interactive and complex relations between these two phenomena. In so doing, a false hierarchy of secular over religious activism creates "a rigid and binary opposition between Protestant and nondominant groups, falsely compartmentalizes Protestantism as a stable and unified constant, and, in the end, unnecessarily attributes more power to conservative or fundamentalist Protestantism than is probable" (Haynes 1998, xiv). Be that as it may, my interest in Haynes's important research—which this chapter summarizes—is to show how developments within Protestantism helped contribute to a destabilization of gender that had become so profound and pervasive that by the 1890s—the period during which lynching was at its zenith—there was a widespread sense that white masculinity was in "crisis." The two developments, I am suggesting, are not unrelated.

First, some background. Haynes notes that it is possible, as Paul Kleppner (1979) has done, to divide nineteenth-century Protestantism into two broad groups of denominations: the "liturgicals" and the "pietists." The "liturgicals" comprised most members of the older churches, among them the Episcopalians, Lutherans, Presbyterians, Congregationalists. These Christians tended to be more ecclesiastical and ritualistic in their approach to worship. For them, one's faith was interwoven with one's knowledge, worshiping practices, and social upbringing. In contrast, the newer "pietists" (Methodists, Baptists, Quakers) tended to be more "evangelical." Just like their contemporary counterparts—especially, for instance, the Southern Baptists in the 1990s—these Protestants tended to emphasize the New Testament, to be active in parachurch groups, and to stress individual conversion and social reform. For these groups, faith was directly related to one's experience and emotions and had little to do with one's formal education or social background (Haynes 1998).

Haynes quotes historians Paul E. Johnson (1978) and George M. Thomas (1989), whose work showed how these developments within American Protestantism were intimately interwoven with the nation's economic and political transformations. Thomas (1989) points out that nineteenth-century Protestantism "actively used the broad cultural myths of individualism to forge an extremely individualistic Christianity; this 'revival' of 'true' Christianity, however, was not just the revival of the Church, but the reconstituting of the individual and the nation" (11). Acknowledgment of the omnipresent role that Protestantism has played in American history requires us, Haynes argues, to forgo a view of "religion as a uniform, stationary, causal, or autonomous point of origin is problematic at best. The various strands of nineteenth-century Protestantism not only undulated and merged, they also interacted with the social, economic, and political forces of U.S. society" (1998, xviii).

Just as American Protestantism was not monolithic or unchanging, Haynes also notes that no one spiritual state informs an individual's social and political point of view. She insists that, at least in the nineteenth century, believers were at least as, if not more, mercurial than the churches with which they identified. As Ann Douglas (1977) has noted, many ministers during this period publicly changed their religious views, and many laypersons did so as well. Haynes suggests that the fact of such shifts undermines the conservative Christian's claim to a single, stable, and unchanging spiritual truth or Christian identity. Moreover, Haynes continues, by understanding that nineteenth-century Protestantism and its believers were variegated, the right-wing fantasy of one orthodox Christianity is punctured. By appreciating the variegated and perspectival character of American Protestantism, "more cultural possibilities are offered for the constructive use of religion and spirituality. Indeed, one of the goals of this book is to encourage scholars not only to talk about religion as a social and dynamic construction but also to resist automatically accepting religious attributes or effects as necessarily expressive of a conservative interior sentiment" (Haynes 1998, xix). That is a point I have made before, and I reaffirm it here (Pinar 1983/1994/1998).

In addition to showing how nineteenth-century Christianity—in particular Protestantism—was socially and historically constituted and expressed, Haynes (1998) strengthens her point that religion in American culture cannot be severed from other institutional and discursive systems. Nineteenth-century Protestantism functioned as both a generative and structuring force in American life, enabling both women and men to recognize possibilities for social and political action. Haynes acknowledges that it also foreclosed potentialities for many. But many women, white and black, were "both empowered and constrained by Protestantism. ... They appropriated, utilized, and resisted Protestantism in manifold ways, and, more important, often incorporated it to subvert or reject the dominant rhetorics of manifest destiny and domesticity" (Haynes 1998, xix). One form nineteenth-century Protestantism took to "constrain" and "empower" Americans, specifically women, was the advice book.

II. The Advice Book

Religious fundamentalism becomes equated with "radical patriarchalism" because an integral feature of its acknowledged ideology or "traditions" has been support of different roles for, as well as protection of, women within a patriarchal family.

—Janet L. Bauer, "Conclusion: The Mixed Blessings of Women's Fundamentalism" (1997)

It seems hardly a gracious thing to say, but it strikes me as true, that while our men seem thoroughly abreast of the times on almost every other subject, when they strike the woman question they drop back into sixteenth-century logic.

—Anna Julia Cooper, "A Voice from the South" (1892/1998)

To many southern men, piety seemed fine for women and slaves but too confining for a truly masculine personality.

—Edward L. Ayers, *Vengeance and Justice: Crime and Punishment in the Nineteenth Century American South* (1984)

The advice book was the most popular medium employed by conservatives to teach their views concerning the nature and status of women. Advice books proved useful to their political and pedagogical agenda. Haynes quotes Nicole Tonkovich (1995) to suggest that one objective of nineteenth-century advice literature was to "present morally grounded codes of behavior characterized as natural 'law,' and [to] promise that adherence to these 'laws' will smooth otherwise difficult social interactions" (65). Advice literature's constant references to "natural" law and its interest in prescribing a code of moral conduct paralleled the conservative political agenda of ensuring that the United States became a culturally homogeneous, socially harmonious, and "moral" nation. Second, not only was didactic literature immensely popular in the late nineteenth century—we shall see instances of advice books for young men in chapter 6—but Christian advice books as a subgenre were very successful commercially, especially those authored by well-known conservative clergy. These popular books on manners and education proliferated throughout the United States after 1820; they were widely given as gifts and were even included in the curricula of many academies, especially in the South (Haynes 1998; Stowe 1987).

To illustrate this point, Haynes notes that George Burnap, the pastor of a large Baltimore church, wrote more than thirty publications, and according to the *Dictionary of American Biography,* his *The Spheres and Duties of Woman* (1848) enjoyed "a large circulation" (Johnson 1929, vol. 3, 292). Harvey Newcomb's *How to Be a Lady* (1846), an earlier edition of *Christian Character: A Book for Young Ladies,* sold 34,000 copies. Haynes points out that Frances Cogan (1989) has suggested that at midcentury, the *Bibliotheca Americana* listed more titles for advice books than for any other genre. Given that the middle class comprised about 75 percent of the population, advice books—directly written for the middle class—helped set the cultural tone and code of gendered conduct for many middle-class American women and men (Cogan 1989; Haynes 1998).

Large sales, Haynes cautions, do not necessarily mean that these books were studied carefully, approvingly, or even at all. She points out that most of the surviving copies have handwritten inscriptions, suggesting that many were probably given to young women as gifts by protective parents, concerned older siblings, or solicitous local ministers. Because many women did not purchase advice books for themselves, the extent to which they accepted or even read them cannot be known. Haynes notes that annotations, when extant, were minimal. Despite the question concerning how seriously these books were studied, Haynes argues that we can assume that the (intended) readers were probably aware of these books' general content whether they actually studied them or not. Many of the authors of advice books bragged that much of their books' content had already been preached in sermons and public lectures. Given the remarkable consistency of these books' message, it seems reasonable to assume that their advice was well-known to Christian, especially Protestant, women (Haynes 1998).

Who were the students that advice-book writers/teachers had in mind? They were, by and large, young, unmarried or recently married, middle-class, mostly white, women, who regarded themselves as righteous believers, or soon to be. Most advice books made no effort to proselytize to skeptics; they assumed their students had signed up for the class, and so they attempted to guide self-identified, already committed Christian women toward the "moral" conduct of life. That means writers discussed a wide range of practical topics, including fashion, education, courtship, marriage, household economics, friendship, and leisure activities, always using these topics to illustrate the "ideal" woman. As Haynes reminds, the "ideal" woman was a woman in her place, at home, away from men, who were themselves busily at work in a "separate sphere." Nearly every conservative advice book stated this idea within the first few pages of the book's beginning, reminding readers that "man" and "woman" had been divinely created as equally important but strictly complementary creatures, occupying separate, even opposing realms. God's plan required women to stay inside the newly privatized household of the emergent middle class; men, in contrast, were assigned by God to the competitive, often chaotic public world of political struggle and capitalist competition (Haynes 1998).

A rigid binary—Haynes (1998) uses the phrase "strict oppositionality" (82)—characterized the conservative Christians' fantasies of "man" and "woman." He is the public agent, woman his private helpmate, and this divine division not only produced children but united and strengthened the American nation. As Haynes observes, the public-private gender binary was more than a ecclesiastical-political issue, functioning to keep rapidly growing female congregations out of church leadership positions. This rigid division of gender also functioned to support late nineteenth-century American political and economic life. Haynes quotes Rebecca Chopp (1989), who argues that "the public arena ... represent not only individual rights and freedoms, but market exchange. This public, in order for the autonomous individual to exist, depends upon the private sphere in the form of woman's place, not only to take care of procreation, but increasingly to absorb the private values that the bourgeoisie has to deny, things like friendship, tradition, religion and kinship" (113–114; quoted in Haynes 1998, 82). In order for the (male) citizen to fight forcefully and efficiently on the battleground of commerce and politics, private domestic management, child-rearing, and low-level manual domestic labor must never distract him; they must be kept hidden in the domestic sphere (Haynes 1998).

Finally and for us most importantly, the binary tried to stabilize a rapidly changing, beleaguered white manhood.

A steady income, a middle-class house, a virtuous wife, and respectable family slowly replaced courage, physical strength, and property as the markers of American manhood. Whiteness too became a key marker, but we will save that aspect of the story for chapter 6. Keeping women at home made the struggle for that steady income less morally and ethically conflicted, as it kept segregated in the public sphere the ethically questionable practices of industrial capitalism. The private sphere, that domestic domain dominated by the feminine, was constructed as a refuge from the dog-eat-dog world of business. Haynes quotes Betty DeBerg (1990): "Uneasy about the profit motive, about exploiting those less fortunate, about using deceptive means to sell their goods, about ruthless and often unfair competition against other businessmen" (19; quoted in Haynes 1998, 83), white men went home to the peace and succor of comforting wives and adoring children. By remaining at home, women did not threaten masculinity or its predatory performance in the public sphere (Haynes 1998).

As if to compensate women for being banned from the world of work and politics, as well as to heighten the sense of refuge from the vicious world of business, the home and women's indispensability to it were sentimentalized, even glorified. Not only, men said, did "woman" have the power to influence her children and husband while at home; she also had the power to influence indirectly the public sphere from the pivot point that is the home. Haynes quotes William Thayer (1858/1866), who described the "true woman" in terms that still echo in right-wing circles today: "Indeed such is woman's influence, we may add, that she decides social morality. If her standard of excellence is high, the society in which she moves will be elevated. If otherwise, the morals of the community will be loose. Let her treat religion lightly, and the men will rail about it as infidels of the lowest school" (55; quoted in Haynes 1998, 83).

Many have noted that the fantasy of woman as moral exemplar and of man as undisciplined lust-prone sinner (unable to attain righteousness without woman's constraining influence) was widespread during the last quarter of the nineteenth century. As we will see, for women's organizations such as the Women's Christian Temperance Union (W.C.T.U.), drink complicated woman's task of helping men to restrain their animal natures. This is a view somewhat at odds with traditional Christianity's emphasis upon women as descendants from Eve, the deceiver and sexual temptress, and men as morally sound, the spirit and intellect of the species. This alteration was not exactly a feminist revision of Genesis. As Haynes (1998) observes: "[D]espite the conservatives' pronouncement that separate spheres and the ideal of womanhood were divinely ordained, they were in fact constructions that in part served to bolster a growing capitalist economy and a fragile, unstable masculine identity" (84). Conservatives emphasized the power and appeal of woman's role as mother and purveyor of virtue, but they developed a number of other strategies as well to keep women where (they thought) they belonged (Haynes 1998; DeBerg 1990).

Paramount among these strategies was underlining the "naturalness" and divinely ordained character of gendered roles. Those who wrote advice books were quick to invoke their privileged access to God, as they reminded their young female readers that those who accepted God's plan for them as mothers and wives and upholders of morality were to be rewarded, especially in heaven. But those women who rebelled against their moral duties and obligations would face horrible punishments meted out by a God whose fury, as Haynes (1998) nicely puts it, "even the unsparing Jonathan Edwards would admire" (84). And if the threat of God's wrath was not enough to keep woman in her place, conservatives had a back-up plan. Conservatives employed a secular sense of shame, warning young women that if they transgressed their divinely ordained role they would face not only damnation but, perhaps worse for those focused on the present moment, social shame, as their loved ones would go quickly to ruin. Haynes quotes Daniel Wise (1851) whose bridal greetings included this warning: "If you unfit [your husband] for his work by the peevishness of your temper, you cripple his energies, discourage his heart. ... God will curse you in soul and in body, and in all probability both you and he will fail of heaven." If that didn't scare the young bride into "gracious submission" (as Southern Baptists characterized the relation of wife to husband as recently as 1998), perhaps this 1854 advisory from Hubbard Winslow and Mrs. John Sanford would do the trick. Not only would woman's misconduct ruin her husband and children, it would destroy the entire nation: "Countries so unfortunate as to sanction by custom the want of female virtue, become a prey to tyrants and remain in hopeless political slavery" (iv; both passages quoted in Haynes 1998, 84).

While failure to stay at home and lead the virtuous life invited disaster, those women—specifically feminists—who deliberately rejected God's plan faced the worst. Faced by feminists, sweet-tempered conservatives lost their patina of Christian kindness and concern; they hurled at these women every invective from "Amazonian disputants," to "scum and froth of the pot which rise to the surface," to "leprous dregs of corruption" (quoted in Haynes 1998, 84). Haynes quotes the following passage as typical of conservatives' denunciations of feminists:

> Oh how fallen ... is she when, impatient of her proper sphere, she steps forth to assume the duties of the man, and, impelled by false zeal, with conscience misguided, does as even man ought not to do—when forsaking the domestic hearth, her delicate voice is heard from house to house to house, or in social assemblies, rising in harsh unnatural tones of denunciation against civil laws and rulers. ... What a sad wreck of female loveliness is she then! She can hardly conceive how ridiculous she appears in the eyes of all sober, judicious Christian men, or how great the reproach she brings upon her sex. (Winslow and Sanford 1854, 24–25; quoted in Haynes 1998, 86)

Feminists were out-and-out evil, profaning the divine order and defiling middle-class propriety. Most of all, Haynes notes, feminists enraged conservatives whenever they declined to be self-sacrificing servants to men, as

"God" required women to be. Indeed, self-sacrifice was a defining feature of ideal womanhood and the ideology of separate spheres. This "virtue" was, Haynes emphasizes, quite restraining and severe. Not only were women to stay in their place, cheerfully, but they were also instructed to "endure any amount of suffering, of toil, and even of injury ... [and not to] listen to those unthinking women who tell you [that] you will be trampled upon unless you assert your rights, and speak for yourself" (Wise 1851, 122; quoted in Haynes 1998, 86). Advised to "avoid egotism ... [and] to suppress their own claims" (Winslow and Sanford 1854, 11; quoted in Haynes 1998, 86), women were also taught to interpret their heartfelt feelings, even religious feelings, as "spurious ... a delusion of Satan" (Newcomb 1856, 15; quoted in Haynes 1998, 86). In fact, women were to restrain their spiritual enthusiasm, as, like all female emotions, it was "a mere animal fever, ... a wandering of mind, bordering on delirium, which exaggerates realities, and embodies shadows" (Winslow and Sanford 1854, 131; quoted in Haynes 1998, 86).

Again relying on their hotline to heaven, conservatives (mostly men, of course) informed nineteenth-century young women that "true" Christianity required them to conduct themselves rationally, soberly, and, above all, obediently, graciously submissive toward men. That was "God's plan." Rather than dwell on her feelings and experience, even religious experience, the righteous Christian woman should enter fully "into the spirit of her husband's vocation" and focus solely on his salvation: "Then your husband, viewing his crown, radiant with stars, shall gaze upon its brightness, and think, perchance, how much, under Christ, it owes its adornments to you" (Wise 1851, 141). One advice-giver, Haynes tells us, even suggested that women play the role of ventriloquist, thereby erasing herself and her "petty" wishes entirely. Make the husband "appear the sole director; like the statue of the Delphic god, which was thought to give forth its own oracles, whilst the humble priest, who lent his voice, was by the shrine concealed, nor sought a higher glory than supposed obedience to the power he would be thought to serve" (Gould 1857, 241). This was no small task of course, and to succeed the nineteenth-century woman was advised to avoid friendships with other women (indeed, all friendships outside the family) and, of course, to never question or distrust their husbands. Even in those instances where the evidence of wrongdoing or betrayal was irrefutable, the good wife should not only live quietly and acceptingly with this information, but, to protect his reputation, should keep it "from every living soul" (O'Reilly 1881, 113; all passages quoted in Haynes 1998, 86–87).

Like their twentieth-century counterparts, nineteenth-century "Christian" conservatives grounded their insistence on women's self-sacrifice with references to the Bible, preferably to meek biblical women who were "remarkable [for] their strictly feminine deportment. From the wife of Abraham to the wife of Aquilla, there was none who forgot their subordinate station" (Winslow and Sanford 1854, 175–176; quoted in Haynes 1998, 87). When confronted with passages that told of other biblical women who exercised positions of leadership, conservatives changed the subject. One subject they consistently changed was that of women's civil rights, obligated as they were to remain focused on "sacred" matters (like submitting to your husband and covering up his misdeeds). A few women like Georgia Burnap, Haynes tells us, emphatically rejected the idea. For nineteenth-century conservative Christians, it was man who enjoyed the right to full citizenship, including the ownership of property and the right to vote. Christian women were to be content to serve the "common" good, which, despite the inclusive meaning of the word, did not include her. The same "logic" applied to the subject of women's education. Should a woman receive an education, she must remember that its purpose must not be the cultivation of the intellect or preparation for a profession that might afford her economic independence, but the perfection of woman's God-given roles as housekeeper, wife, and mother (Haynes 1998).

Of course, "housekeeper, wife, and mother" were not only "roles." They were jobs, demanding and labor-intensive. As Haynes observes, while Christian conservatives depicted women as helpless, frail, "the lowly vine, which needs support for itself" (O'Reilly 1881, 360) or the poor "bird ... with cropped wings" (Graves 1879, 31) who must remain in "the home with its quiet, its obscurity, its sanctities" (O'Reilly 1881, 359), they did not hesitate to instruct her to take on strenuous domestic tasks. Counseled one female advice-giver: "I know it is hard when there are beautiful, high, and noble thoughts that we would like to enjoy alone than to have to sweep a floor, or mend a gown, or bathe a baby, but the doing of any of these gently and cheerfully is better than thinking high thoughts—it is living them" (Ashmore 1896, 77). Albert Phelps Graves advised: "The greatest evil is that the idea of washtubs, house-cleaning, scrubbing floors, blacking stoves, washing dishes, baking bread, broiling meat, and doing the hardest kind of house work, does not enter into the idea of [woman's] education. But lily fingers loaded with gold rings, pale faces, slender forms tightly laced ... [wrongly] makes up the education" (1879, 37). Jesse Peck (1857) put it this way: "labor here, rest in heaven; [that] is the motto of the true woman in the Church" (307; all passages quoted in Haynes 1998, 88–89).

Upon closer examination, the main points of the true womanhood ideal—domesticity, piety, passivity, and submissiveness—were rhetorical cover-ups for a very different reality. To manage a nineteenth-century household was an ordeal by contemporary standards; most women worked from early morning to bedtime, Monday through Sunday. Nowhere was life more stark than on the farms, where approximately half of American women lived. The typical farmer's wife worked a ten-hour day in the winter and a thirteen-hour day in the summer; among her jobs were carrying water to the house (as late as 1920, only one of three farm families had interior plumbing), then heating it on the stove in order to cook meals or in movable tubs to wash the laundry and bathe the children. Women made their own soap and brooms and clothing, scrubbed the floors, cared for the poultry, cultivated the garden, milked the cows. The preparation of food took considerable time and was often tedious. Urban housewives may have escaped the isolation and loneliness of women on farms but they did not escape the ordeal. Most devoted more than forty hours to housework, a figure that excludes an additional twenty hours of childcare (Filene 1998).

Tolerating "any amount of suffering" (Wise 1851/1987, 122; quoted in Haynes 1998, 86) and overlooking her husband's betrayal and misdeeds do not a virtuous woman make. Nor did the home such a couple might occupy seem so very tranquil. Nodding consent to whatever her husband spouts while suppressing her own feelings, even religious ones, does not a peaceful, contented woman make. Nor do days filled with washing, scrubbing, baking, and so on, seem congruent with the image of the pure, passive woman, too frail to leave the home. Finally, submission in this scheme was—is—not so much to God as to his self-chosen representative, her husband. As Haynes (1998) concludes, "the true womanhood traits served the greater autonomy and power of men than the advancement of women's spiritual state or the glory of an ethereal god" (88).

III. Christian vs. Secular Feminism

> *[D]espite an image for limiting women's options, fundamentalism offers mixed blessings ... for many women.*
>
> —Janet L. Bauer, "Conclusion: The Mixed Blessings of Women's Fundamentalism" (1997)

> *Evangelical Christianity unleashed enormous energy and was particularly significant in providing a context for female participation in the public sphere.*
>
> —Alan Hunt, "The Great Masturbation Panic and the Discourses of Moral Regulation in Nineteenth- and Early Twentieth-Century Britain" (1998)

> *We need women who are so sure of their own social footing that they need not fear leaning to lend a hand to a fallen or falling sister.*
>
> —Anna Julia Cooper, "A Voice from the South" (1892/1998)

Given the profoundly patriarchal character of nineteenth-century conservative Christianity, several questions follow. Haynes (1998) asks: "Did their [women's] conversion serve to thwart or empower them? Was there a way in which nineteenth-century Christianity and women's rights were congruent, at least for certain groups of women? If the two systems of thought were so incompatible, then why was such an inordinate number of active middle-class women so attracted to Protestantism?" (90). Haynes provides us with a series of answers, beginning with the work of Barbara Welter, whose 1965 article "The Feminization of American Religion" represented the first serious effort to examine the crucial role of gender in the history of American Protestantism between 1800 and 1890. For Welter (1976), women, domesticity, religion, family, and anti-intellectualism were inextricably interwoven together. They were also completely severed from the world of men, politics, business, and aggressive competition. Welter argued that there was little interaction between the private and public spheres. Because women lacked access to public power and positions of authority, they were reluctant passive victims of this social-gender binary, forced to dwell on the margins of society, namely the church and the home (Haynes 1998).

Welter did not take into consideration the writings of Protestant women, Haynes (1998) suggests, but limited her investigation to the study of sermons and advice books written by conservative clergymen. As a consequence, Welter's work, Haynes argues, neglects women's experience while privileging the clerical view. Haynes acknowledges that Welter is right to interpret the ministers' injunctions as derogatory and onerous to women, but that she accepts uncritically their fantasy that society was in fact dualistic and that women accepted religion due to their gendered weakness and susceptibility, not from choice. Welter argued that women did not appreciate, when they attended and participated in community revivals, that they were being complicitous with their own devaluation: "Whether in the divine or human order, woman was constantly urged to be swept away by a torrent of energy, not to rely on her own strength which was useless, to sink into the arms of Jesus, to become absorbed and assimilated by the Divine Will—in other words, to relax and enjoy it. The fantasies of rape were nourished by this language and by the kind of physical sensations which a woman expected to receive and did receive in the course of conversion" (Welter 1976, 92–93; quoted in Haynes 1998, 91).

Haynes accepts that Welter's agenda was feminist (i.e., critical of the church as a masculine-controlled institution), but worries that she inadvertently supported the antifeminist fantasy that nineteenth-century women were indeed without agency, "mere putty in the hands of wily clerics" (Haynes 1998, 91), unable to figure out what was happening to them, and in any case lacking the inner strength to do anything about it. Welter's thesis that women were acquiescent in their own victimization by nineteenth-century Protestant men has been developed by other scholars. As an outsider to this debate, to me Haynes seems a little hard on Welter. Recall that in that phase of feminism, emphasizing men's brutality and power was important and necessary work; it was central to many progressive analyses. Once the point was well established, then a second look revealed a more complex picture in which women were in fact only apparently complicit; in many instances they were able to use patriarchal institutions to further their own agenda. The apparently unbridgeable gap between private and public spheres was sometimes traversed.

Something of this movement in feminist historical analysis is evident, Haynes reports, in Nancy Cott's 1977 book, *The Bonds of Womanhood: "Woman's Sphere" in New England, 1780–1835*. Whereas Welter characterized the distinction between private and public spheres as rigid and fixed, Cott (1977) suggests the two domains overlapped in important ways: "The canon of domesticity ... constitut[ed] the home as a redemptive counterpart to the world. Yet the ultimate function of the home was in the world. It was to fit men to pursue their worldly aims in a regulated way. The accent on individual character and self-control in the canon of domesticity simulated and underpinned individual economic struggle, just as women's vocations simulated men's" (98).

Although the domestic or separate-spheres ideology stipulated women and men as well as home and marketplace as irrevocably opposite, they were in fact not so different. In contrast to Welter, Haynes tells us, Cott does not regard women as passive victims of shrewd clerics: "Christian belief had a self-perpetuating force that was not likely to be disrupted by experience that would provide alternative and equally satisfying explanations" (1977, 136; quoted in Haynes 1998, 91). In other words, women's attraction to Protestantism was not only a matter of acquiescence and subjugation, it also provided them opportunities for self-confirmation and power. Cott contends that religious activities, especially Christian women's societies and social reform groups, emboldened women, psychologically and politically. Through a patriarchal institution, then, many nineteenth-century women found ways to fashion relatively autonomous selves through the formation of woman-centered but socially acceptable communities:

> Religion stretched before the convert a lifetime of purposeful struggle, holding out heartening rewards. It provided a way to order one's life and priorities. ... Religious identity also allowed women to assert themselves, both in private and in public ways. It enabled them to rely on an authority beyond the world of men and provided a crucial support to those who stepped beyond accepted bounds—reformers, for example. ... Religious faith also allowed women a sort of holy selfishness, or self-absorption, the result of the self-examination intrinsic to the Calvinist tradition. In contrast to the self-abnegation required of women in their domestic vocation, religious commitment required attention to one's own thoughts, actions and prospects. (Cott 1977, 139–140; quoted in Haynes 1998, 92)

The more clerics insisted on conservative "feminine" values, the more legitimate it became for Protestant women to gather together to question what these men taught regarding God's plan for them (Cott 1977; Haynes 1998). As we will see, several very strong and powerful women—among them Frances Willard and Ida B. Wells—participated in the public sphere through the route of the church and American Protestantism.

Through their engagement in church activities, women who had "previously held no particular avenue of power of their own—no unique defense of their integrity and dignity—found a means of gaining a new sense of self and even a political consciousness" (Cott 1977, 200). Yet paradoxically, Haynes notes, Cott also argues that Protestantism with its doctrine of separate spheres "restrained women's initiative because of its central distinction between womanly self-abnegation and manly self-assertion" (1998, 195). Because separate-spheres doctrine "deprived the sexes of their common ground, [it] opened the door to anti-feminist and misogynist philosophies" (Cott 1977, 195–196; quoted in Haynes 1998, 92). It is in Cott's work, Haynes points out, that the vexed relation between Protestantism and feminism becomes evident. Welter's work had suggested that the force of religion was too overwhelming for women to overcome, and no doubt for some women it was. It was Cott who understood that feminism and Protestantism did at times intersect, inadvertently perhaps, but enough so that "Protestantism formed an advantageous but temporary stage for incipient feminists" (Haynes 1998, 92). Haynes will take this analysis yet another step.

The Protestant doctrine of divinely ordained domesticity functioned to form in some women a sense of group consciousness, even solidarity, to assert women's rights. Still, even for Cott, women must move beyond "the convincing power of evangelical Protestantism" (Cott 1977, 204; quoted in Haynes 1998, 93) to become secular feminists. Cott suggests: "What precipitated some women and not other others to cross the boundaries from 'woman's sphere' to 'woman's rights' is not certain; but it seems that variation or escape from the containment of conventional evangelical Protestantism—whether through Quakerism, Unitarianism, or 'de-conversion'—often led the way" (1977, 204; quoted in Haynes 1998, 92–93).

Haynes will take exception to Cott's sequence of feminist progress, that is, from religious to secular feminism. She declines to position feminist theology as a prerequisite to secular feminism, the more advanced course. She is unconvinced that those women who moved from spirituality to secularism were necessarily superior (politically or otherwise) to those who remained within the confines of Christianity. By establishing a dualistic hierarchy between feminism and secularism, Cott and Welter concluded that the two systems of thought are necessarily always at odds. From Haynes's point of view, such a conclusion ignores not only the intersections of both systems, but the complexities and contradictions internal to each. Finally, Haynes is concerned that the privileging of secular feminism degrades the achievements of those suffragists who never extricated themselves from Christianity. My interest in the late nineteenth-century "crisis" of masculinity prompts me to focus on an implication of Haynes's work that she herself does not make explicit, but which is certainly implicit, namely that because many women worked for women's rights within the church, it was no "safe haven" either for men bent on stable gender roles. From Haynes's research it becomes clear that the "crisis" of white masculinity occurred not just in the marketplace—that is, not just in the secular public sphere—but within the hallowed confines of patriarchal Protestantism as well.

Carolyn Haynes demonstrates that the interplay between and within these presumably strictly segregated spheres was "more fluid and mobile" than many scholars, among them Welter and Cott, have appreciated. By studying advice writing and religious commentaries composed by Protestant feminists (most of whom were women and lifelong Christians), Haynes (1998) argues that through the selective "miming" of a variety of Christian and critical discursive practices—among them, evangelicalism, historical criticism, and liberal individualism—these women formulated a unique and powerful feminist position of their own. While this feminism may not be judged revolutionary by some, it was feminist and Christian at the same time, enabling these women to reach a large audience of churchgoing women that the secular feminists could not (Haynes 1998).

IV. Miming: Domestic Slaves, Secret Rebels

Fundamentalism can clearly provide something for some women in the current climate of economic hardship when gender and gender roles are hotly contested in most societies. We might call it a sense of greater efficacy over their lives or a kind of personal empowerment.

—Janet L. Bauer, "Conclusion: The Mixed Blessings of Women's Fundamentalism" (1997)

Religious feminists may be able to broaden their nascent challenge to celestial patriarchy, raising the crucial questions about power—through either bringing men back to religion ... or questioning the ultimate authority of men to interpret God's wishes.

—Janet L. Bauer, "Conclusion: The Mixed Blessings of Women's Fundamentalism" (1997)

Woman, Mother,—your responsibility is one that might make angels tremble and fear to take hold!

—Anna Julia Cooper, "A Voice from the South" (1892/1998)

What Haynes has in mind by "miming" resembles those indirect forms of black protest we will examine in the chapter 7. Miming is not a simple reiteration of, or subordination to, dominant Protestant discourses but, relying here on the work of Judith Butler (1993), "an insubordination that appears to take place within the very terms of the original and which calls into question the power of origination" (45). Contemporary feminist Rosi Braidotti (1994a) recommends what she terms a "strategic mimesis," "a strategy of deconstruction that also allows for temporary redefinitions, combining the fluidity and dangers of a process of change with a minimum of stability or anchoring" (43). As such, strategic mimesis "does not aim at recovering a lost origin, but rather at bringing about modes of representation that take into account the sort of women whom *we have already become*" (43). As Haynes paraphrases succinctly: "miming repeats the origin only to displace the origin as origin" (1998, 93).

Christian feminists, then, reiterated the conservative rhetoric of true womanhood and separate spheres but reconfigured them in doing so, exposing them as political constructions rather than innate, divinely decreed, "natural" laws. While late nineteenth-century Protestant women may have been positioned to serve as "domestic slaves," within those positions they became "secret rebels." By destabilizing the conservative codes of decidability within the boundaries and discursive rules of Protestant rhetoric, "Christian feminists deferred conservative authority and thereby reconstructed the Church not as the uniform arena that conservatives posited but as a site of multifarious, competing, and unifying discourses or a critical arena of debate and exchange" (quoted in Haynes 1998, 93–94).

Christian feminists were quick to accept conservative men's glorification of woman's integral social role. Lillie Devereux Blake (1883) declared: "The national housekeeping is all out of order for want of that virtue, love of order, and, above all, conscientiousness which woman especially represents" (147).

What allowed the woman to "clean up" the home (and by extension) society? The answer was simple: her devotion to Christ. Frances Willard, president from 1879 to 1898 of the Woman's Christian Temperance Union, the largest organization of women in the nation's history, and, as we will see, adversary of black antilynching activist Ida B. Wells, advised: "Dear girls, CHRIST is the magnet of humanity, and she has found the best vocation, and the highest, who brings most souls diseased within the healing power of His immortal Gospel" (1886/1987, 41; quoted in Haynes 1998, 94). Reiterating the conservatives' discourse of domesticity, Willard (1886/1987) continued: "The home is but the efflorescence of woman's nature under the nurture of Christ's Gospel" (55). In another work she extolled the power of woman's maternal instinct: "Mother-love works magic for humanity. ... Mother-hearted women are called to be the saviors of the race" (quoted in Haynes 1998, 94). As Haynes points out, implicit in Willard's statement is the correct (from the conservative standpoint of separate spheres) conviction that women are aligned with virtue and Christianity, but also the insurrectionary implication that women are divinely positioned to improve those around them, that is, men.

While asserting this potentially radical view that women were pivotal to social progress, Christian feminists also reiterated the conservative view that men and women were different, if complementary. One woman wrote: "The man has more of the material nature, woman more of the moral; he excels in animal life, she excels in the spiritual; he is more coercive, she is more persuasive; he is exterior, she interior; he is self-loving, she loving; he is more theological and speculative, she more religious and practical; he is doctrinal, she devotional; he distrusts, she trusts; he walks by sigh, she by faith; he has more head, she more heart" (quoted in Haynes 1998, 94).

To perform this difference, Christian feminists typically dressed in ways conservatives would approve. For instance, Frances Willard's dresses were "ladylike and fashionable, usually 'black or brown velvet or silk' with 'a blue ribbon or a touch of white or ivory lace at the throat,' and a tasteful bonnet that she removed when she spoke" (Campbell 1989, 130; quoted in Haynes 1998, 95). Willard's and other Christian feminists' conservative appearance was, Haynes argues, key in undermining the conservatives' claim that suffragists were "Amazonian ... [and] were mutilating fair womanhood in order to assume the unnatural armor of men" (quoted in Haynes 1998, 95). Haynes cites Ruth Bordin's (1981, 1986) argument that Willard and other Christian feminists preached and performed a womanliness and domesticity that ostensibly did not challenge patriarchal values. These women's conservative feminine appearance enabled them to more easily gain access to the public sphere and, once there, receive favorable attention. Frances Willard was so successful as a public figure that Nancy Hardesty (1984) has called her, "Woman of the Century" (25; quoted in Haynes 1998, 95). Haynes points out that as lay preachers and lecturers, Elizabeth Oakes Smith, Amanda Berry Smith, Hannah Whitall Smith, and Sojourner Truth often spoke to enthusiastic crowds numbering in the thousands. Among the most skilled and successful public speakers of the nineteenth century, these women often employed conservative religious rhetoric and dress to expand their public following. The question, Haynes reminds us, is whether their conservative exteriors served or undermined their advocacy of women's rights.

Haynes recalls Karlyn Kohrs Campbell's (1989) characterization of Willard's and others' performance as "rhetorical alchemy," or "relabeling ... proposals in ways that transformed them from demands for social change into reaffirmation of traditional arrangements and values" (126; quoted in Haynes 1998, 95). Nancy Hardesty, Haynes points out, suggests the same, arguing that Willard's argument "raises serious theological and sociocultural problems. It is based on and perpetuates cultural stereotypes of women's role as derived from biological differences. ... That concept obviously tends, for the majority of women, to circumscribe their sphere to marriage and maternity within the confines of the home and the nuclear family" (1984, 100–101). Haynes notes Lori D. Ginzberg's (1990) argument that the functions of conservative Protestantism changed with time; while it may have conferred upon some women a personal and "cultural authority" in the postmillennial fervor of the 1830s and 40s, conservative Protestantism had "lost most of its radical potential" after the Civil War. As a consequence, women such as Willard and the W.C.T.U., while employing a discourse of women's indispensability to moral values, Ginzberg asserts, "ended up reinforcing conservativism and lobbying for 'repressive' legislation, among them the 1873 Comstock law, Sunday blue laws, censorship regulations, prohibition, and increased punishment of prostitutes" (206; quoted in Haynes 1998, 96). Certainly this is the case in terms of racial politics, as will be evident in Willard's exchanges with Ida B. Wells over lynching.

Haynes worries that Ginzberg's and Campbell's arguments overstate the case. Acknowledging that many Christian feminists did succumb to an uncritical acceptance of conservative values, some did not. A number of feminists exhibited contradictory views and actions. For instance, Haynes notes that the W.C.T.U. included many chapters across the United States and the world; each had somewhat differing legislative and social goals. Ruth Bordin observes that in addition to "social purity" legislation, Willard's concerns included labor rights for women, a free kindergarten movement, better municipal sanitation, federal aid for education (in part as a way of providing schooling for African Americans), separate correctional institutions for women, Protestant ecumenicism, and, of course, female suffrage. Haynes quotes Bordin's observation that "Willard's journals show her consistent preoccupation with the woman question from her earliest years, but the temperance question is mentioned only rarely" (1986, 69; quoted in Haynes 1998, 96).

Betty DeBerg (1990) suggests, Haynes notes, that because "Willard's rhetoric and strategy used an appeal to 'home protection,' which was an extension and adaptation of the ideology of separate spheres," she smoothed the way for many W.C.T.U. members to enter the public sphere of politics and social reform. Indeed, "many respectable middle-class women were radicalized by their participation in the W.C.T.U." (29; quoted in Haynes 1998, 96). Haynes points out that Bordin (1986) argues likewise: "through the vehicle of a militant temperance organization designed as a vital protection for the home and children, [Willard] permitted women to do whatever they wished in the public sphere and compelled men to praise them for it" (11). Haynes (1998) concludes that "the conservative rhetoric and demeanor may have served as women's 'tickets' into the public sphere of politics" (96).

This may not be as surprising as it might first seem to some secularists. After all, as Haynes observes, after Mark A. Noll (1986), the term "evangelical" has tended to be a somewhat plastic one, connoting different practices and beliefs for various sects. Yet, as Haynes points out, "evangelical" has tended to communicate a core meaning across a broad spectrum of faiths—Catholic, Protestant, independent and denominational, dispensational and antidispensational, mainline and fundamentalist—that includes an insistence on the Bible's divine authority and a belief (based on faith) in "the miraculous birth, death, and resurrection of Jesus to save men [sic] from damnation" (McLoughlin 1968, 6; quoted in Haynes 1998, 98). Evangelicals tend to emphasize the atonement of Jesus and the individual's free will in accepting or rejecting faith in God. In contrast to orthodox Calvinists and Puritans, who experienced God as a merciless king who admits to Heaven only a predestined few, evangelicals felt sure that all individuals shared an underlying moral sensibility and a common consciousness of their freedom to choose. Like teachers, then, evangelical preachers made their cases with the expectation that listeners were capable of responding to them, indeed, capable of learning. As Haynes (1998) puts the matter, anyone, in the evangelical view, can will to accept God and thus be saved. Consequently, the motive of nineteenth-century evangelicalism was to save souls, and its *modus operandi* was persuasion rather than on speculative theology.

Almost all Christian feminists belonged to evangelical churches. Frances Willard was a lifelong member of an evangelical Methodist Church. Born into a family of Quakers, Hannah Whitall Smith converted to a perfectionist strain of Wesleyan Methodism when she met her husband, Robert Pearsall Smith, in the 1860s. Both she and her spouse became prominent and influential evangelists in the Keswick Movement in Britain. Although raised in a strict Calvinist family, Mary Ashton Rice Livermore married an evangelical Universalist minister and adopted his faith as a young woman. Lillie Devereux Blake, the great-great-granddaughter of the legendary Jonathan Edwards, was every much engaged in an evangelical Methodist Episcopal Church. Julia A. J. Foote, Virginia Broughton, and Mary Cook joined the evangelical black Baptist movement. A member of the African Methodist Episcopal Church, Amanda Berry Smith in effect personified evangelical sanctification during her celebrated missionary and preaching career (Haynes 1998).

While evangelicalism strikes many of us as anti-intellectual and patriarchal at best, Haynes shows how a decidedly conservative social phenomenon can be used, especially through miming, to support progressive goals. One reason many women were drawn to evangelicalism, she suggests, was that it undermined the authority of an educated male clergy who then dominated the theology schools and mainline churches. This was due partly to the character of evangelicalism, but partly to the fact that the movement was in its infancy and thus lacked a sufficient number of educated clergy to populate its pulpits. Consequently, mid-nineteenth-century evangelical denominations sanctioned the employment of lay preachers and prayer leaders and supported those individuals, including women, who claimed to be called by the Holy Spirit to minister and evangelize. While traditional conservatives emphasized high educational standards for clergy and a literal reading of the Bible, evangelicals privileged religious experience and divine calling over formal theological knowledge (Dayton 1976; Haynes 1998).

This stress on direct experience and divine calling directly supported the movement of women into leadership roles within the evangelical denominations. While institutions such as Oberlin College, Boston University, and Garrett Biblical Institute were increasingly admitting women to their theological seminaries during the latter part of the nineteenth century, the number of women enrolled in theological institutions overall was still low. By 1900, there were still fewer than 700 clergywomen (Filene 1998). But this disadvantage was neutralized within the evangelical movement: "while women may not always have been able to compete with men in terms of formal education, they could rival them in the realm of experience" (Haynes 1998, 99).

In fact, many Christian feminists suggested that women excelled in the sphere of religious experience, a point elaborated by many Christian feminist advice writers. To illustrate, Haynes quotes Hannah Whitall Smith (1870/1985), who began her book by de-emphasizing formal theological knowledge and privileging direct spiritual experience: "I do not want to change the theological views of a single individual. The truths I have to tell are not theological, but practical. They are, I believe, the fundamental truths of life and experience, the truths that underlie all theologies, and that are in fact their real and vital meaning" (1; quoted in Haynes 1998, 99). Frances Willard (1889/1978) declared the same, if more pointedly: "Men preach a creed; women declare a life. Men deal in formulas, women in facts. Men have always tithed mint and rue and cummin [sic] in their exegesis and their ecclesiasticism, while the world's weary has cried out for compassion, forgiveness, and sympathy. Men's preaching has left hearts hard as nether millstones. ... Men reason in the abstract, women in the concrete. A syllogism symbolizes one, a rule of life the other" (47; quoted in Haynes 1998, 99). Despite the conservative rhetoric, these women were announcing a theology of their own, one that privileged women's experience. By grounding themselves in women's experience rather than in men's theology, they gained access to the most influential evangelical circles. Moreover, by appealing to personal experience as the "true" source of all theological knowledge, Christian feminists such as Willard and Smith were in fact undermining the authority of male theologians and spreading a new woman-centered and experience-based theology of their own (Haynes 1998).

Inadvertently perhaps, evangelicalism functioned to blur public-private boundaries. As well, it prompted attacks on traditional authority. Haynes quotes George M. Thomas (1989) and Paul E. Johnson (1978), who describe how revivalism accompanied and legitimized a new, more horizontal social and economic order. Thomas argued: "Petty capitalists, yeoman farmers and laborers all flocked to revival ... because it articulated new freedoms from local paternalistic institutions" (1989, 87; quoted in Haynes 1998, 100). For evangelicals, reality could only be apprehended according to the level of one's spiritual enthusiasm. The most intense were the "real" Christians; everyone else was a pretender or simply an infidel. This new simple-minded distinction often cut across old gender, class, and race lines; the sense of righteousness it supported sometimes led to civil and social disobedience (Haynes 1998).

Haynes draws on Donald Dayton to show that the *Guide to Holiness* (a nineteenth-century newspaper edited by evangelist Phoebe Palmer) often included within its pages support for women's active participation in the church. Its feminist implications were often explicit, as one issue illustrates: "When the Pentecostal light shines most brightly, women do the bulk of the common-school teaching. They are also principals, professors, college presidents and are admitted to all the learned professions. ... When the light shines clearly, they have equal rights with men, by whose side they labor for God's glory" (quoted in Dayton 1976, 97; in Haynes 1998, 102). Frances Willard (1886/1987) likewise advised the reader to think of herself as "a daughter of God, whose duties are first of all, to her own nature and to Him by whom that nature was endowed" (59; quoted in Haynes 1998, 103). Haynes points out that Willard positioned a woman's loyalty to herself even before her duty to God, suggesting that the two obligations—to self and God—were synergistic.

Indeed, for many Christian feminists these loyalties risked no conflict of interest, for allegiance to God was understood as being pro-woman. For many nineteenth-century evangelical women, Jesus came to supplant their husbands as their "dearest friend, companion, and soul mate" (Haynes 1998, 104). Sojourner Truth (1878/1991) described her relationship to Jesus this way: "'I saw him as a friend, standing between me and God, through whom love flowed as from a fountain" (69; quoted in Haynes 1998, 104). The evangelical image of Jesus as an intimate and loving partner was exciting for many Christian feminists because it offered them an alternative not only to the stern, merciless Calvinist god but also to their sometimes demanding and dominating husbands. Bonded with Jesus, these women could bypass masculinized authority without compromising their Christian womanhood (Haynes 1998).

Evangelical Christianity was not so convenient for men. Not only did it support their wives' greater independence and autonomy, evangelicalism directly required them to deny the most masculine aspects of their own temperaments. For many men, one of the central sources of resistance to the experience of being saved was that it required breaking one's own willfulness and submitting to the will of God. Such submissiveness was in direct violation of their own masculine sense of autonomy and self-direction. Becoming a "bride of Christ" not only implied the breaking of their masculine willfulness, but threatened their very identities as men. Indeed, as Philip Greven (1977) notes, many "evangelicals experienced lifelong difficulties with their sexual identities and their sexuality" (125). Although Greven's research is focused two centuries earlier, it seems to me the psychosexual dynamics of evangelical faith during the colonial period and in the late nineteenth century cannot be entirely different. Certainly by becoming brides of Christ, evangelical men at both times were forced to assume the passive role, the symbolic identity of a woman, in relation to their Savior. In fact, denying one's own masculinity was the only means of being assured of salvation. Only when one's manhood was "broken" could an evangelical male know he was truly subject to Christ's husbandry. "To be *both* manly and impotent," Greven (1977) reports, "was a contradiction to be resolved, for most evangelicals, in favor of impotency" (126).

Evangelical women faced no such identity-threatening choice. Rather than relinquishing the primary measures of conservative true womanhood—piety, purity, submissiveness, and domesticity—many Christian feminists retranslated them in self-affirmative, politically progressive ways. For them being a bride of Christ afforded an alternative to being a wife in total obedience to her husband. Piety for the Christian feminists meant fidelity to a pro-woman God, a god to whom sexism and misogyny were satanic. Haynes quotes Mary Dodge (1868/1972): "A gospel that preaches masculine self-gratification as manly religion, the lowest womanly subserviency to man as the sole womanly way of doing God's service, is not ... to be lightly let slip. Its improbabilities, its inconsistencies, its monstrosities [have] seemed to go down sweetly like the grapes of Beulah" (5; quoted in Haynes 1998, 106). Total submission to God hardly required the devaluation of woman's uniqueness and agency. On this point Elizabeth Oakes Smith (1851/1974) noted: "The individuality of each is a great law of God, and a woman is better when she acts out of her own spontaneity, tenfold, than when she attempts to conform to any theory" (111; quoted in Haynes 1998, 106). Nor did God's affirmation of woman stop at her front door. As evident from Blake's (1883) idea of "national housekeeping" and Willard's (1889) notion of woman purifying the "Stygian pool" of American government, many Christian feminists projected the ideals of domesticity and purity onto the national stage (Haynes 1998).

V. Feminist Hermeneutics

All the advice given by the apostles to the women of their day is [not] applicable to our own intelligent age; nor is there any passage of Scripture making those texts binding upon us.

—Lucretia Mott quoted in Carloyn A. Haynes, *Divine Destiny: Gender and Race in Nineteenth-Century Protestantism* (1998)

So, they [white women] climbed down from the pedestal when no one was looking and explored a bit.

—Lillian Smith, *Killers of the Dream* (1949/1963)

As intriguing as this "retranslation" or "miming" of conservatives discourses of womanhood are, Haynes suggests that it was not the only tactic Christian feminists deployed. Not only did women up the ante in the "holier than thou" game, they also outmaneuvered the men in the game of who knows the Bible better. This issue focused upon the divinely ordained status of women as indicated in specific biblical passages. In contrast to secular feminists such as Elizabeth Cady Stanton who believed the Bible was hopelessly antiwoman, Christian feminists were confident that the Bible could be recoded as profeminist. Mary Cook, an African-American Baptist, pointed out: "As the Bible is an iconoclastic weapon—it is bound to break down images of error that have been raised. As no one studies it so closely as the Baptists, their women shall take the lead" (quoted in Haynes 1998, 106).

In order to recode the Bible as feminist, women needed to outmaneuver men on the playing field of biblical interpretation. Conservative men ignored, of course, hypothetical, metaphorical, or symbolic readings of the Bible, insisting that scriptural passages were equivalent to facts in nature: easily observed (by them), unmistakable. These men insisted: "biblical writers perfectly portrayed what they saw and experienced. Once the modern interpreter understood the established usage of the words in the biblical account, the interpreter was brought into direct contact with the event itself. To read the biblical words was to encounter the biblical thought or deed just as if the interpreter had had direct experience of it" (Rogers and McKim 1979, 291; quoted in Haynes 1998, 106–107). Of course, conservative men's loyalty to literalism was, well, flexible. As Haynes points out, they regularly cited those passages, such as Ephesians 5:22 and 1 Timothy 2:11, that call for women's self-sacrifice, silence, and submission to men, pronouncing them literally and universally true. Somehow they managed to overlook or de-emphasize those passages that indicate otherwise (Haynes 1998).

So Christian feminists set out to show that men's presumably disinterested, literal reading of the Bible was not. This is the reading and research practice well known to students of education, of what in an unrelated context Donna Haraway (1991) characterized as "the god-trick of seeing everything from nowhere" (quoted in Haynes 107). Like contemporary scholarship on this point, nineteenth-century Christian feminists came to insist upon an explicitly situated method of interpretation—in their case, of the Bible. Haynes quotes Lillie Devereux Blake (1883) who declared: "when women interpret the Scriptures they find a very different meaning from that which men ... give to it" (17). Frances Willard (1889/1978) put the matter this way: "The motherheart of God will never be known to the world until translated into terms of speech by mother-hearted women" (46–47). For Willard, biblical exegesis was hardly a universal science but a method of interpretation that necessarily changed over time: "[It is] one of the most time-serving and man-made of all sciences. ... It is in no sense an inspired work, but grows in breadth and accuracy with the general growth of humanity" (23–24; quoted in Haynes 1998, 107).

Still, Christian feminists such as Blake and Willard were not in favor of a radical relativism, or interpretations of scripture according to personal preference. For them, women translators would provide the other side of the story: "We need women commentators to bring out the women's side of the book; we need the stereoscopic view of truth in general, which can only be had when woman's eye and man's together shall discern the perspective of the Bible's full-orbed revelation" (quoted in Haynes 1998, 107). In other words, only women could discern what men could not and thereby women would supplement men's partial reading of divine will (Haynes 1998). Other students of the Bible would come to support these feminist claims, if from nonfeminist grounds.

Haynes refers here to the appearance of historical criticism, which questioned the taken-for-granted idea that the Bible expressed (literally) God's ahistorical, universal, and immutable truth. Haynes suggests that in addition to undermining traditional literalist practices of biblical scholarship, the emergence of historical criticism also challenged orthodox approaches to historical thinking and ideas of self in relation to God and society. She quotes biblical scholar Oscar Wilde (1905), who characterized historical criticism as "part of that complex working toward freedom which may be described as the revolt against authority" (5; in Haynes 1998, 108). She quotes as well contemporary historian Grant Wacker (1982) who called it "the dynamite that ultimately exploded the entire edifice" of late nineteenth-century thought (127; in Haynes 1998, 108). The revolutionary potential of historical criticism, Haynes explains, had to do in part with its reorientation of the focus away from a sovereign (masculine) deity toward the individual believer as the primary agent in the present historical moment:

> historical critics perceived history as an ever-changing progression of time and society that the contemporary individual could rationally understand and manipulate toward subjectively desired ends. In short, rather than succumb to the dictates of an eternal, fixed god as expressed in the completely factual, transhistorical Scriptures, individuals (male or female) could now adjust their behavior to the exigencies of the sociohistorical context according to the intensity of the inner feelings. (Haynes 1998, 108–109)

Christian feminists recognized this historical hermeneutics as the ally it was. First, it consecrated individual action in a secular world; no longer was it incumbent upon one to wait for supernatural intervention or clerical guidance. Christian feminists understood that their engagement in biblical scholarship was thereby divinely driven and legitimated. Their first move was to restore those biblical passages conservative men conveniently forgot or overlooked. As Haynes notes, they became quite fond of Galatians 3:28, suggesting that it "fixes no bounds, names no places, occasions, subjects or duties, but affirms in general and unqualified terms, that there is neither male nor female, but that all are one in Christ Jesus" (Lee 1853/1984, 6–7; quoted in Haynes 1998, 109). In the Old Testament, they fastened upon the prediction (Joel 2:28) that "women's active preaching and prophesying would be a leading feature of the gospel dispensation," to press the point that women ought to play stronger leadership roles in the church (Haynes 1998).

Frances Willard took considerable interest in the politics of biblical interpretation, comparing multiple translations to one another in order to disclose both the masculine bias of male translators as well as simple inaccuracies in previous translations. For instance, Willard noted that while the King James Version of 1 Timothy 2:11 reads, "Let the woman learn in silence with all subjection," the more recent Revised Version reported God's word as: "Let a woman learn in quietness with all subjection" (Willard 1889/1978, 38; quoted in Haynes 1998, 111). The latter translation is considerably gentler than the former. In contrast to Elizabeth Cady Stanton, whose skepticism of the Bible would inspire her to undertake a complete rewriting of the canonical text, many Christian feminists had faith in the latest translation methods to rewrite the Holy Book into a decidedly more pro-woman document (Haynes 1998).

Under the scrutiny of Christian feminists and the influence of historical criticism, the Bible suddenly was no longer a timeless, literal statement of God's dictates. It was now a profoundly historical document. Still regarded as providing insight into the divine, the Bible became seen by many as conveying the thoughts of those human creatures who wrote it, including the limitations of the time in which they wrote. Historical-critical students of the Bible now conceived of their task as separating the "'dross' of the human package from the divine treasure" (Massa 1990, 9; quoted in Haynes 1998, 111). In so doing they began to question the divine authority of some of the most frequently quoted books of the Bible. For these hermeneuts, the Bible's words do not literally record God's message, but, as one nineteenth-century liberal theologian named Andrews Norton noted, they "are only human instruments for the expression of human ideas" (quoted in Haynes 1998, 111). As such, personal biases, historical conditions, not to mention the peculiarities of the language itself made quite problematical the question of God's original intention and message (Haynes 1998).

Realizing, then, that the Bible's words do not always report God's intended revelation, Christian feminists criticized conservative men for their refusal to situate the Bible historically. Haynes quotes Frances Cobbe (1881), who pointed out that those men who accept unquestioningly the Pauline injunction for wifely submission as divine truth should therefore be

> bound to attach the same authority to a parallel passage in another Epistle, wherein the same apostle commands slaves to obey their masters, and actually sends back to his chains a runaway who in our day would have been helped to freedom by every true Christian man or woman in America. ... In our day, men habitually set aside this apostolic teaching, so far as it concerns masters and slaves, despots and subjects, as adapted only to a past epoch. I am at a loss to see by what right, having done so, can claim for its authority, when it happens to refer to husbands and wives. (124–125; quoted in Haynes 1998, 112)

In like fashion, Haynes notes, Frances Willard (1889/1978) complained about ministers who cited Paul when demanding woman's silence in the church, but somehow managed to overlook the apostle's specific exhortations against braided hair, gold, pearls, and expensive attire.

Inspired by historical criticism, Haynes reports, Christian feminists now sought to situate historically specific New Testament verses (such as I Timothy 2:11) that conservative men used to restrict women. Perhaps such verses were not, as conservative men had insisted, precisely God's word and hence universally obligatory; perhaps they were instances of human limitation concocted by the apostles to direct women within a specific sociocultural setting and historical moment. "All the advice given by the apostles to the women of their day," suggested Lucretia Mott, "is [not] applicable to our own intelligent age; nor is there any passage of Scripture making those texts binding upon us" (quoted in Haynes 1998, 112). Specifically in response to Paul's call for women's silence in the church, Willard (1889/1978) observed that "places of worship, in the age of the Apostles, were not built as they are with us, but that the women had a corner of their own, railed off by a close fence reaching above their heads. It was thus made difficult for them to hear, and in their eager, untutored state, wholly unaccustomed to public audiences, they 'chattered' and asked questions" (30; quoted in Haynes 1998, 112).

Furthermore, Paul's demand that women "remain in silence with all subjection" amounted to a political compromise at the time; he was, Willard (1886/1987) argued, trying to head off opposition to women's increased activity in the church: "Paul, who was 'all things to all men that by all means he might save the most,' deemed it expedient for the infant Church, among the many pitfalls in its way, to conform while it endeavored to reform; and that those fateful words 'It is not permitted' and the rest are simple statements of facts as to the customs of that day" (93; quoted in Haynes 1998, 112–113). Without questioning either the integrity of the Bible or of the apostle Paul, Willard reinterpreted biblical passages in a pro-woman light. Haynes (1998) puts the matter this way: "rather than attempt to circumvent the power structure of patriarchal Christianity and the Scriptures, the Christian feminists opted to alter the biblical system within its own boundaries—to perform a similar feat to what Willard claims Paul did in Corinth—that is, 'to conform while [they] endeavor to reform'" (Haynes 1998, 113). In addition, then, to undermining conventional ideals of domesticity, Christian feminists showed there was no biblical support for conservative men's suppression of women's intelligence outside the home, in the public sphere (Haynes 1998).

VI. The Racial Politics of Christian Feminism

> *[Many] continue to accentuate what I call the* metaphor of "reaction." *In this view, religious fundamentalists are characterized as seeing the modern, secular world as morally decadent and as rejecting, fighting or opposing it—as members of the "traditional" or poorer classes or individuals alienated by the pace of change.*
>
> —Janet L. Bauer, "Conclusion: The Mixed Blessings of Women's Fundamentalism" (1997)

> *How is race lived in the modality of sexuality? how gender lived in the modality of race?*
>
> —Judith Butler, *Bodies That Matter: On the Discursive Limits of "Sex"* (1993)

> *[T]he fetishization of the black male body as the object of a white mob's fury divorced the notion of blackness from any association with domesticity.*
>
> —Sandra Gunning, *Race, Rape, and Lynching: The Red Record of American Literature, 1890–1912* (1996)

> *Now the fundamental agency under God in the regeneration, the retraining of the race, as well as the ground work and starting point of its progress upward, must be the black woman.*
>
> —Anna Julia Cooper, "A Voice from the South "(1892/1998)

Relying upon historical criticism and logic as well as the "miming" of conservative and evangelical discourses, Haynes argues, Christian feminists employed a range of tactics to make "gender trouble." As successful as these practices of miming were in undermining the uniformity of religious thought, they also had, Haynes concedes, a disadvantage. In their enthusiasm over using a wide array of successful strategies, a number of Christian feminists used nativist, racist, and elitist sentiments to make their points. To illustrate, Haynes quotes Mary Dodge (1868/1972), who, in arguing for women's right to vote, wrote: "Undoubtedly a very large number of women are by their education unfit to vote; but does the same standard of fitness apply to men? Are American women, as a class, more unfit to vote than Irishmen? Are they less capable of understanding issues involved, of passing judgment upon measures proposed, than negroes who have been slaves for generations?" (87; quoted in Haynes 1998, 115–116).

In the 1880s, Haynes reports, the W.C.T.U. ran a suffrage advertisement with a similar racist logic. The image portrayed a prim, well-dressed, and lily-white Frances Willard encircled by ethically and class-coded examples of three nonvoting groups: idiots, Native Americans, and insane men. The headline read "American Woman and Her Peers," followed by this caption:

> The incongruity of the company Miss Willard is represented as keeping is such to attract and excite wonder, until it is explained that such is the relative political status of American women under the laws of many of our states. No one can fail to be impressed with the absurdity of such a statutory regulation that places women in the legal category with the idiot, the Indian and the insane person. (quoted in Haynes 1998, 115–116)

The point of such visual performances was explicit and, as Haynes notes, laudable: it inverted conservative men's characterization of the politically active woman as the deviant Other. Regrettably the point was made at the expense of other disenfranchised "others" and in nativist and classist language. These ads underscore, Haynes (1998) suggests, the risk of miming. In appropriating reactionary Protestant rhetoric, these women were infected with opprobrious strains of conservative men's thought. The racism of several Christian feminists undermined the antilynching campaign, although, as we will see, Ida B. Wells was able to outmaneuver even the legendary Frances Willard. Given the undertow of racism in Christian feminists: "Why is it that black women aligned themselves more frequently with this group rather than with secular feminists? Even more curiously, why did they seem to follow Protestantism so loyally and fully?" (Haynes 1998, 115).

In last decades of the nineteenth century, African-American Christian feminists were oppressed not only as women but as blacks in an increasingly racist America. Like white Christian feminists, African-American Christian feminists "mimed" conservative rhetoric to engage in what, Haynes notes, Evelyn Brooks Higginbotham (1993) terms a "politics of respectability." Because they faced both racism and misogyny, they had to perform Christian righteousness, in particular those ideals of "pure" womanhood they could tolerate, even more perfectly than their white counterparts. In so doing, Haynes argues, these women moved between apparently opposing positions, that of the secret rebel and the shamed repentant. Because both positions enabled late nineteenth-century black women to perform versions of respectability they could tolerate in a racist, sexist America, these positions were synergistic and empowering. Indeed, Haynes (1998) contends that without having established a socially recognizable identity that the shamed repentant role conferred upon them, black women would not have been able to confront directly the racism and sexism they encountered.

These tactics succeeded at considerable personal cost; the price included hyper-self-vigilance, constant self-regulation. In her study of late nineteenth-century black Baptist women, Higginbotham demonstrates, Haynes suggests, that a politics of respectability "demanded that every individual in the black community assume responsibility for behavioral self-regulation and self-improvement along moral, educational and economic lines" (Higginbotham 1993, 196; quoted in Haynes 1998, 118). To contradict racist stereotypes, these women strongly embraced Victorian sexual morals, temperance, thrift, industriousness, refinement, and piety, evident, for instance, in the life and writings of Anna Julia Cooper, "a race-woman who believed deeply in the unique vocation of black women" (Lemert and Bhan 1998, 2). In fact, one feminist reservation held toward Cooper is that she appeared too comfortable with the white pieties of the true womanhood ideal, specifically those emphasizing a woman's duty to establish the domestic circle. Cooper did create a home—over the years she reared seven children (two foster children when she was young and the five orphans she adopted just shy of her sixtieth year)—and did so on a teacher's salary while commuting to New York City and Paris in pursuit of her doctoral degree, which she received in French from the Sorbonne in 1925. Cooper was "a brilliant teacher" and "an effective school leader" (Lemert and Bhan 1998, 9). While principal of M Street High School in Washington, D.C., from 1901 to 1906, she so strengthened its curriculum in classical subjects that many more of its graduates were accepted to elite colleges such as Harvard. When asked in 1930 to characterize her life's vocation, Cooper answered simply: "The education of neglected people" (quoted Lemert and Bhan 1998, 13).

Higginbotham's findings are evident in the lives and writings of other black evangelical women, Haynes points out. Sojourner Truth (1878/1991), for instance, valued honesty to an astonishing extent. Obeying her mother's injunction to be always honest, Truth

> had educated herself to such a sense of honesty, that, when she had become a mother, she would sometimes whip her child when it cried to her for bread, rather than give it a piece secretly, lest it should learn to take what was not its own! And the writer [Frances Gage, Truth's

> narrator] knows, from personal observation, that the slaveholders of the South feel it to be a religious duty to teach their slaves to be honest, and never to take what is not their own! Oh consistency, art thou not a jewel? Yet Isabella glories in the fact that she was faithful and true to her master; she says "It made me true to my God"—meaning, that it helped to form in her a character that loved truth, and hated a lie, and had saved her from the bitter pains and fears that are sure to flow in the wake of insincerity and hypocrisy. (34; quoted in Haynes 1998, 118)

The employment of honesty in this passage not only illustrates Truth's fidelity to virtue even under difficult circumstances, but, as Haynes points out, her critique of the Christian slaveholders' warped conception of honesty. The white binary of honest white man vs. dishonest black slave is reversed; honesty for white people is what they demand of others, not something they expect from themselves (Haynes 1998).

Many African-American Christian feminists emphasized their virtues as mothers. Haynes cites the case of Harriet Jacobs, who hid in a cramped attic for years in order to watch over and finally rescue her children from slavery. Haynes returns to Sojourner Truth, who, after her son was kidnapped and sent to the South by her former master, went to court to secure his return. Years later, recalling her successful legal case and her abiding love for her son, Truth exclaimed, "Oh, my God! I know'd I'd have him agin. I was sure God would help me to get him. Why, I felt so tall within—I felt as if the power of a nation was with me!" (1878/1991, 45; quoted in Haynes 1998, 119). Embedded within black Christian feminists' self-shaming, Haynes emphasizes, was an implicit shaming of others, specifically whites. If virtuous women like Truth were shameful, so was everyone else. Those who engaged in public shaming—usually whites—warranted more retribution than mere shame (Haynes 1998).

In another speech of Truth's that Haynes quotes, she so masterfully interchanges shaming and being shamed that by the end the distinction between the object and subject of shame is blurred. To make the self-shaming move, Truth asked "Well, if woman upset the world, do that give her a chance to set it right side up again?" But then, in the next question, she redirects the shame, from women to men: "And how came Jesus into the world? Through God who created him and woman who bore him. Man, where is your part?" (quoted in Haynes 1998, 119). By initially accepting the guilt of Eve, Truth "tricks" men into becoming conscious of their own gendered participation in the story of salvation. To emphasize this point, Haynes quotes Eve Kosofsky Sedgwick and Adam Frank (1995), who observed that "shame turns the attention of self and others away from other objects to this most visible residence of self, increases its visibility, and thereby generates the torment of self-consciousness" (136; quoted in Haynes 1998, 119–120).

Despite these brilliant performances of shaming and self-righteousness, black women were still denied the respectability conferred upon white middle-class church women. That ugly fact dissuaded few; many African-American Christian feminists still chose to act out their exemplary piety and trust in God. To express her faith in God's powers, Haynes reports, Amanda Berry Smith took no medicine for over a year. Both Smith and Truth traveled around the country (in Smith's case, the world) without an assured income or lodgings. Wherever they went, these women performed their spiritual powers in public and in dramatic ways. Between January and May 1871, Berry Smith was said to have effected 156 conversions and 112 rededications to the Mount Pisgah A.M.E. congregation. Haynes cites an 1844 camp meeting led by a white woman preacher; when the white worshippers saw a black woman—Sojourner Truth (1878/1991)—cross the stage preparing to speak, they nearly rioted. At first she retreated, but then returned, and under her (she would have said God's) spell, the men quieted (Haynes 1998).

As another means of performing their impeccable piety, African-American Christian feminists acknowledged the racism they suffered during their journeys. Suffering there was plenty of, especially during church and missionary travels across a racist America: "The strain of solitary travel was increased by the rigid segregation of transportation as they traveled on foot through the countryside and by steamer, canal boat, or coach" (Stetson and David 1994, 93; quoted in Haynes 1998, 120–121). To illustrate, Haynes quotes Sojourner Truth's remark to Elizabeth Cady Stanton that she had "been sent into the smoking-car so often she smoked in self-defense—she would rather swallow her own smoke than another's" (quoted in Haynes 1998, 121). Julia Foote, Amanda Berry Smith, and Maria Stewart all endured rude passengers and inadequate lodging, food, and seating. In addition to difficulties in the public world, African-American Christian feminists often faced trouble at home, where they were criticized by family members who wanted them to stay at home. Julia Foote's husband, for instance, threatened to have her committed to an insane asylum if she insisted on continuing with her missionary work (Haynes 1998).

Racism could not, of course, be ignored; its structures were pervasive and corrosive. But these women refused to be dissolved by these structures—institutional, psychosocial and sexual—and, in fact, Haynes argues, learned to construct themselves within them. Here Haynes makes an intriguing discursive move, making use of Judith Butler's brilliant queer theory, in particular Butler's argument that rather than simply setting a limit on identity, constraint impels and sustains it: "an identification always takes place in relation to a law, or, more specifically, a prohibition that works through delivering a threat of punishment. The law, understood here as the demand and threat by and through the symbolic, compels the shape and direction of [identity] through the instillation of fear" (Butler 1993, 105; quoted in Haynes 1998, 121–122). While some might balk at this use of an argument about the contemporary construction of gay and lesbian identities to think about nineteenth-century black female identity, I think Haynes succeeds. Her use of Butler proceeds as follows:

> [P]rompted by the racist derision they encountered, African-American Christian feminists adopted a subservient position but not precisely the one their racist foes had in mind. Instead of being subservient to whites and to men, they retranslated the term to mean utter submission to God. Thus, they may have reiterated the derogatory label assigned to them, but by doing so, they deferred the dominant authority of the label and carved out a new measure of agency. (Haynes 1998, 122)

In Butler's (1993) words, "the force of repetition in language may be the paradoxical condition by which a certain agency—not linked to a fiction of the ego as master of circumstance—is derived from the impossibility of choice" (124; quoted in Haynes 1998, 122).

Not given a choice by racist whites regarding their identity in white society, these women fashioned one for themselves by reiterating or "miming to excess" that true womanhood ideal assigned to and claimed by white Christian women. By "miming in excess," Haynes argues, "they deferred the authority of both the denigrating label assigned to black women as sexualized 'females' and the true womanhood role assigned to Christian women as white, passive, pure, domestic, and pious" (1998, 122). Black Christian men tried something similar—substituting dignity and righteousness for whites' fantasies of them as rapists and beasts—but some secular black men may have remained with the sexualized gaze of white men and simply inverted it. That is, rather than accepting their assigned positions as sexual objects and hence feminized (black masculinity was also, if differently, in crisis), many black men mimed exactly what whites thought of them, but to excess. Many became the "superstud" white men fantasized them to be. In the 1890s, many white men found this excess of masculinity intolerable, especially given their own sense of gendered crisis, stimulated by shifts in the economy, the family, in gender and racial roles, even within the conservative Christian church. For some, this "intolerability" expressed itself in the rape of young black men disguised as "popular justice," that is lynching.

While white women had to construct an identity for themselves out of the abstract and imaginary ideals that white men fashioned for them, formerly enslaved black women faced a heinously sexualized identity, not always imaginary, given white masters propensity for heterosexual as well as homosexual rape. Such women found it particularly difficult to fulfill the "purity" requirement of the true womanhood ideal. Black Christian feminists attempted to compensate for this history by overachieving—performing to excess—other elements of the true womanhood ideal, thereby minimizing the role sexuality played in women's lives. To illustrate this point, Haynes notes that although her narrative spans over four hundred pages, Berry Smith mentions only briefly her relationships with men, including her two marriages. Harriet Jacobs devoted little space in her autobiography to descriptions of her relationship with the father of her children. Nor does Ida B. Wells spend much time in her autobiography narrating her marital relation to Ferdinand Barnett. Haynes points out that Virginia Broughton devoted only one brief chapter, in a narrative of sixteen chapters, to her "private life" and, even in that one chapter, there was no reference to romance. Sojourner Truth was sexually abused, but she provided no details. Haynes suggests that Truth knowingly engaged in a kind of "suppressed interiorization" (1998, 123).

> With the tactical reversal that was her defining strategy, Truth anticipated her audience's fascination with the enslaved woman's life as a secret, enculted, gothic existence, compounded for torture and enforced sex; then between herself and this audience she drew a homespun curtain, around which they could not peek because they were the 'uninitiated,' … as if

they were themselves too simple, too naive, too unschooled to read the horrific book they had written themselves. Perhaps she ... decided that her life was not their fiction. (Stetson and David 1994, 39; quoted in Haynes 1998, 123)

By fashioning their lives as pre-eminently spiritual rather than racial or sexual, African-American Christian feminists refused to succumb to whites' expectations of them. By focusing instead on a broader agenda, one that provided a more equal playing field—that of spirituality and God's grace—black Christian feminists might not have escaped from racist and misogynist oppression, but they did voice criticism of white society and envision a just one. Secular black women, Haynes implies, would have had a much harder time of this without recourse to that legitimization afforded by claimed and experienced relationships to God. She quotes Sojourner Truth's 1853 speech made in New York, a speech highly critical of conservative (white) male preachers, to illustrate the point. These preachers were, Truth declared,

big Greek-crammed, mouthing men, who, for many a long century, had been befogging the world, and getting its affairs into the most terrible snarl and confusion, and then when women came to their assistance, cried "shame on women!" They like the fat and easy work of preaching and entangling too well, not to feel alarmed when woman attempted to set matters aright. [Truth] conceived that women were peculiarly adapted to fill the talking professions, and men should no longer unsex themselves by leaving the plow and the plane, for the pulpit and the platform. She hoped all of her sex would set to work and drag the world right side up, disentangle it from the snarl which men have willfully got it into, and set matters in general right, and then keep them so. They could only do this by being united and resolutely putting their shoulders to the wheel. (quoted in Stetson and David 1994, 211; quoted in Haynes 1998, 123)

Black feminists' "miming to excess," then, functioned not only to negate the highly sexualized white fantasy of the black female. It functioned as well to empower black women, enabling them to criticize white men while linking their concerns with those of white women. Like their white female counterparts, black Christian feminists saw themselves as engaged—in the name of Jesus—in social revolution (Haynes 1998).

VII. Seduction Not Resistance: The Reproduction of Fundamentalism in *The Woman's Bible*

[S]ome associate male-dominated fundamentalism with historical periods when perceived increases in women's independence and changing family relations result in a subsequent backlash against women's participation in the public sphere. This accentuates the portrayal of women as victims of fundamentalist belief systems rather than active participants, even fighters, and ignores the evidence that nonfundamentalist men may also feel this

"challenge" from women but respond in different ways.

Janet L. Bauer, "Conclusion: The Mixed Blessings of Women's Fundamentalism" (1997)

Few white feminists—either secular or Christian—appeared to recognize the conflation of race and sex in gender and racial politics, yet both secular and Christian women aspired to the same: a just and equitable American society. Haynes asks: "If the two groups held the same objective and fell into similar errors, why have scholars differentiated and hierarchized the two feminist coalitions?" (1998, 124). The basic difference between the groups, she notes, is that white and black Christian feminists, in contrast to radical secular feminists, fought for the cause of women without rejecting altogether, or appearing to reject, the doctrine and institution of Christianity. As a consequence, Haynes notes, not only did their feminism seem less threatening to the general public still largely Protestant and powerfully male, but they were able, due to their successful miming of the womanhood ideal, to thwart conservative men's hackneyed accusations of unfemininity or heathenism that were used so effectively to undermine many of the radical feminist causes in nineteenth-century America (Haynes 1998).

In another context (Pinar 1983/1994/1998), I have argued that this tactic amounts to "seduction" (in contrast to a masculinized "resistance"), as one employs the language of the dominant other to engage him reciprocally and relationally. While such "miming" means "laying with" the enemy, and risks being inseminated with the virus of the dominant other, with sufficient inner strength—as we saw in the case of Sojourner Truth, for instance—one can escape more or less intact. But resistance as a masculinized rejection of the "Father" situates one in the position of the heterosexual son, which despite its rage and demands for a more just world, ends up reproducing the same social structure it aspired to transform. Why? In oedipal terms, the defiant son becomes the dominant Father; his position changes at the "dinner table"—now he's at the head—but women remain trapped in subservient roles. It seems to me that Haynes, while not using this schema, is saying much the same in her discussion of Christian and secular feminists. Frances Willard seduced; Elizabeth Cady Stanton resisted.

Elizabeth Cady Stanton is famous today, but in the late nineteenth century the prominence of such Christian feminists as Frances Willard, Catherine Booth, Amanda Berry Smith, and Mary A. Livermore matched and perhaps surpassed hers (Bordin 1986; Haynes 1998). Christian feminism, Haynes suggests, may have been more appealing to large numbers of late nineteenth-century American women, many of whom were involved with the church, than secular feminism. She cites Ellen Carol Du Bois (1987)—a scholar generally unsympathetic to religious feminists—in support of her claim. Haynes also references Betty DeBerg (1990) who argued that the use of Protestant domestic, gendered rhetoric helped to make women's suffrage "more palatable to most Americans" and thus advance the feminist cause (33; quoted in Haynes 1998, 133). In discussing the success of Frances Willard and the W.C.T.U., Ellen Carol Du Bois (1987) suggests it was because they "spoke to women in the language of their domestic realities, ... [women] joined [the movement] in the 1870s and 1880s in enormous numbers" (135; quoted in Haynes 1998, 126). Haynes also cites Ruth Bordin (1986), who speaks to the disparity between the public reception of the secular and Christian feminists:

> Elizabeth Cady Stanton ... most often chose "confrontation and a high moral stance" over political maneuver and compromise. Unlike Willard, Stanton was ... not a politician. She was always forthright in speaking her mind. Willard was an inveterate dissembler and a clever and effective insinuator. She played the role of sweet conciliator whereas Cady Stanton assumed the stance of militant radical. Stanton herself recognized Willard's talent for conciliation. When in March 1888 Willard appeared before a United States committee investigating suffrage as a representative of the International Council of Women, Cady Stanton, who was making the arrangements, scheduled Willard as the final speaker, believing she would leave the committee in a friendly mood. (104–105; quoted in Haynes 1998, 126)

The (religiously) seductive form of Willard's and the Christian feminists' "miming" of conservative language and their performance of the womanhood ideal may have been crucial to their success.

Haynes is not suggesting, because Christian feminists were more favorably received by larger audiences in their own time than were the secular feminists, Christian feminists represent a "better" model for feminists then or now. In terms of effectiveness, neither group was consistently superior. In fact, both strands of late nineteenth-century feminism were, in many ways, interdependent. One of the primary reasons that the Christian feminists could position themselves in the strategically advantaged position of conciliator was that Stanton and her followers so aggressively voiced their views. In comparison, Christian feminists seemed relatively nonthreatening to men, men already in "crisis" over their (white) besieged masculinity (Haynes 1998; Bederman 1995b).

To emphasize her point about the interdependency of secular and Christian feminists in fin-de-siècle America, Haynes quotes Frances Willard, who, in her 1889 autobiography, described herself in the following terms: "I am an eclectic in religious reading, friendship and inspiration. My wide relationships and constant journeys would have made me so had I not had the natural hospitable mind that leads to this estate. But, like the bee that gathers from many fragrant gardens, but flies home with his varied gains to the same friendly and familiar hive, so I fly home to the sweetness and sanctity of the old faith that has been my shelter and solace so long" (627–628; quoted in Haynes 1998, 128). Like the bee Willard described "that gathers from many fragrant gardens," Christian feminists took from others the conservative Christian and radical feminists' flower beds to nurture their own as they cross-pollinated the gardens of others (Haynes 1998). What was unique about Christian feminists was "not as much ... their call for feminine equality or their devotion to Protestantism [but] their utilization of an open, conciliatory, and insurgent method of cultural performance" (Haynes 1998, 128).

The majority of late nineteenth-century feminists were unable to join Elizabeth Cady Stanton and her friend Lucy Coleman in renouncing conservative Christianity's call for women's self-sacrifice. But no matter, Stanton was undeterred. She found herself unable to compromise with an institution that had functioned culturally and politically in such patriarchal, misogynist ways: the "Church has done more to degrade woman than all other adverse influences put together" (Stanton 1894, 12; quoted in Haynes 1998, 130). Such statements cost her support among many younger feminists, many of whom were self-identified Christians. Even some of her oldest friends and allies, including Susan B. Anthony, could not stand with her on this point. In 1896, the National American Woman Suffrage Association (NAWSA) formally censured her ambitious project, *The Woman's Bible,* effectively ending Stanton's participation in that organization (Haynes 1998).

Frustrated by the public's evident lack of enthusiasm for the feminist cause in the last decades of the nineteenth century—the same decades which saw lynchings increase to their highest levels—Stanton decided to take on what she perceived to be the greatest impediment to gender progress: the Holy Bible. Her strategy would be to produce a series of commentaries on biblical passages of special interest to women. Toward this end, she assembled a group of white, middle-class, educated, and mostly American women with whom she could work. The publication of *The Woman's Bible* was greeted derisively at the time, but its reputation has been redeemed in recent years by contemporary feminist scholars. Once censured, the project is now praised widely. It is termed, for instance, as Stanton's "most audacious and outrageous act of independence" (Griffith 1984, 210), "a truly revolutionary deconstruction of patriarchy" (Caraway 1991, 156) and "a radical rejection of the Bible" (Kraditor 1968, 77). Maureen Fitzgerald calls it "an extraordinary document, in part because the questions asked, the topics covered, and the sense of righteous indignation throughout its pages are still resonant today" (1993, xxix). Carolyn De Swarte Gifford points to several problems in *The Woman's Bible,* but her overall evaluation is positive: "As an impassioned call for women's dignity and self-development whose author steadfastly refused to countenance the notion of women's inferiority in the face of powerful institutions and sacred texts which seemed to justify that power, it can be an empowering text for women at all times who struggle for a similar sense of dignity and worth" (1993, 61; all quoted in Haynes 1998, 130).

Other feminists were concerned with other issues, among them suffrage. Susan B. Anthony, as well as many younger feminists born a generation after Stanton and Anthony, were preoccupied with suffrage. Consequently, they downplayed their rejection of Christianity's call for women's subservience, partly in hopes of achieving solidarity with Christian feminists for the sake of winning the vote. (We will attend briefly to the impact of the suffrage campaign on white men's masculinity in the next chapter.) Haynes quotes a letter Susan B. Anthony wrote to Elizabeth Cady Stanton in 1896 to illustrate these different priorities: "Get political rights first and religious bigotry will melt like dew before the morning sun; and each will continue still to believe in and defend the other." In contrast, Stanton considered conservative Christianity to be the bedrock of

American politics and culture, a cord, to change images, around the neck of the American woman. If only that cord could be loosened, all else would be freed:

> here, then, in a fourfold bondage [family, politics, society and religion] so many cords tightly twisted together, strong for men's purpose. To attempt to undo one is to loosen all. ... To my mind, if we had at first bravely untwisted all the strands of this fourfold cord which bound us, and demanded equality in the whole round of the circle, while perhaps we should have had a harder battle to fight, it would have been more effective and far shorter (quoted in Haynes 1998, 131).

Because, for Stanton, women's political and social progress could not proceed without loosening the knotted cord of conservative Christianity, she felt that the sexist strands of the Bible must be untied (Haynes 1998).

The Columbia Exposition of 1893 hosted a World's Parliament of Religions, which included representatives from all the major religions of the world. (I will return to the Columbia Exposition in chapter 8 for a discussion of its racial gendered symbolism.) Influenced by the Exposition's treatment of religions and by comparative theology generally, Stanton and her collaborators compared and contrasted the first creation story in Genesis with Mayan, Yucatan, North American Indian, and Norse creation stories. There are striking similarities. In like fashion, Stanton also emphasized that those stories promoting "love, charity, liberty, justice and equality" as well as the golden rule are hardly unique to Christianity; similar tales can be found in the holy books of all great religions. The Bible could make no claims to uniqueness; it should be treated as any other ancient religious text, compared to other religious writings at the time, scrutinized skeptically to verify names and dates, as well as judged in light of contemporary moral values. Such examination yielded the inescapable conclusion that religious truth cannot be confined to one text like the Bible but is distributed throughout a variety of texts found in all the world's great cultures (Haynes 1998).

So, unlike evangelical Protestants, Stanton did not position the Bible as the ultimate authority; instead, she blurred the previously sharp distinctions between biblical and nonbiblical, sacred and secular. Most importantly, she showed that the Bible was a political document as much as it was a religious one. Stanton employed, Haynes suggests, what feminist theologian Elisabeth Schüssler Fiorenza termed the "hermeneutics of suspicion," which "invites readers to investigate biblical texts and traditions as one would 'search' the place and location where a crime has been committed. It approaches a canonical text as a 'cover-up' for patriarchal murder and oppression" (1993, 11; quoted in Haynes 1998, 142). This tactic was hardly lost on conservative Christian men. One of the founding fathers of American fundamentalism, James H. Brookes, condemned *The Woman's Bible* as "that miserable abortion ... that is only the impudent utterance of infidelity" (quoted in DeBerg 1990, 1; quoted in Haynes 1998, 144). Stanton was not exactly intimidated by the response. When another conservative man dismissed *The Woman's Bible* as "the work of women, and the devil," Stanton returned the favor, addressing him as "His Satanic Majesty." Haynes shrewdly points out:

> Each defined itself by what it deemed the other was not. Despite their differences and animosity the fact that the two sides shares similar binary thinking may not be all that surprising. After all, the dichotomies of the public-private realm and the educated elite-laboring underclass formed the social fabric of nineteenth-century U.S. culture. But binary thinking does not form the only link between Stanton and the fundamentalists. (1998, 144)

Despite her resistance to conservative Protestantism, Stanton's thinking was embedded in—while simultaneously rejecting of—her religious context. Even so, it is clear that *The Woman's Bible* did provide opportunities for women to begin untying those "tangled cords" of conservative Christianity (Haynes 1998).

Because Stanton and her colleagues shared subtle perhaps even unconscious, rhetorical, philosophical, and methodological similarities with their conservative opponents, their message may have seemed somewhat dated to their younger feminist colleagues. Haynes cites Mary Pellauer's point that despite Stanton's exasperation with conservative clergy, she often incorporated Christian rhetoric into her speeches:

> To Stanton the ballot box was a 'holy of holies'; voting was a religious duty to be exercised religiously in more than a debased sense of that word. ... The suffrage cause was religious not because of St. Paul's injunctions or any biblical text, but intrinsically so, on its own grounds. (1991, 39; quoted in Haynes 1998, 144)

Haynes (1998) argues that Stanton turns religious authority on its head; her insistence upon positioning theology according to her feminist theory rather than allowing it to position her represents a significant departure from nineteenth-century biblical scholarship.

Before Stanton and the advent of historical criticism, students of the Bible regarded it as the arbiter of all meaning. Now the frame of reference shifted from the world depicted in the Bible to the world lived outside it, and the point became one of repositioning and reinterpreting the Bible to meet the values of the present day (Frei 1974; Haynes 1998). Stanton was something of a zealot in this regard; she had no interest in collaboration or compromise. Like her fundamentalist opponents, Haynes notes, she believed she was spreading a gospel of her own, her elaboration of truth being "the only safe ground to stand upon" (quoted in Haynes 1998, 144).

Stanton was, Haynes tells us, no historical critic. She had no interest in situating biblical texts historically or culturally, to open up multiple readings of the presumably divinely inspired text. Rather, like the fundamentalists, Stanton emphasized "the external, not the internal, the objective rather than the subjective, the natural over the supernatural, and uniformity over diversity" (Haynes 1998, 148). Neither Stanton nor her opponents had any interest in opening up the sacred text to multiple meanings; both were committed to their own absolute if antithetical positions. Stanton's and the fundamentalists' repudiation of symbolic, figurative, and mythical interpretations ignored or rejected the work of some of the most accomplished and prominent liberal theologians of her time, such as Horace Bushnell, D. F. Strauss, Johann G. Herder, and J. G. Eichhorn. These scholars sought to escape from fundamentalism's insistence on "common sense" and literalism, arguing that the Bible was as much poetry and myth as empirical fact, not a text to be read with blind faith, but with historical and philological knowledge, not to mention a highly developed literary imagination (Haynes 1998).

Many liberal ministers saw in their theological orientations opportunities to support women's campaign for enfranchisement, arguing that if interpreted figuratively or historically, passages that seemed to relegate women to silence and the home could, if interpreted historically and imaginatively, be redeemed. Stanton (1895) wanted none of it; in her introduction she dismissed "liberal translations, interpretations, allegories and symbols" as only serving to enshrine the Bible. On occasion she even appears to endorse the work of conservative exegete Adam Clarke by paraphrasing his criticism of liberal hermeneutics: "if we begin by taking some parts of the Scriptures figuratively we shall soon figure it all away" (quoted in Haynes 1998, 148). Unchanging, fixed, universal meanings served better the purposes of both Stanton and the fundamentalists. If the Bible is acknowledged to have multiple meanings of more or less equal legitimacy, then individuals may be less inclined to accept those truths proclaimed by both Stanton and fundamentalist men as timeless and universal (Haynes 1998).

Haynes's motive for drawing the parallel between Stanton and the fundamentalists is neither to criticize them nor, specifically, to accuse Stanton of hypocrisy. In particular, she does not want to minimize or ignore the vast differences between the two: Stanton sought to remedy the gender inequities in this world, while fundamentalists were concerned with spreading the Christian gospel, which for them entailed gender inequity, presumably an expression of God's will. Instead, Haynes's intent is to show that *The Woman's Bible* does not represent a complete repudiation of or liberation from Christian ways of thinking. Rather, Stanton and her colleagues were only able to express shifts and struggles that were already under way within Protestantism during the last quarter of the nineteenth century. It is clear from Haynes's perceptive analysis that Stanton's thinking was deeply embedded in the varieties of religious thought of her own time. In this sense it illustrates the argument I make against "resistance," a mode of oppositionality that seems to ensure reproduction—in political or, in Stanton's case, conceptual structure—of that which one opposes. The Christian feminists "miming" of orthodox Protestantism and in particular of the pure womanhood ideal represents an instance of "seduction" not resistance (Pinar 1983/1994/1998).

Among the "shifts" and "struggles" in late nineteenth-century Protestantism which Stanton's resistance condemned her to reproduce in her struggle for women's rights was the replacement of postmillennial/evangelical Protestantism with either the more absolutist fundamentalist and dispensationalist movements or with the more secular-oriented social gospel and agnostic (free-thought) movements (Sandeen 1970; Haynes 1998). Between 1870 and 1930—the primary period of lynching in the United States—almost every mainline denomination underwent an inner struggle around issues such as the authority of Scripture, its scientific accuracy, and the supernatural elements in Christ's work or person (Marsden 1980; Haynes 1998). Haynes suggests that all are present in one form or another in *The Woman's Bible:* the social gospel's and freethinkers' concern with social activism, the conservatives' obsession with scientific exactitude, literalism, and "facts," as well as mainline Protestant churches' struggles over scriptural authority.

Finally, Haynes suggests that Stanton's resistance was not to Christianity per se but to the church's conservative influence, especially its inhibition of gender progress. This point is suggested by the fact that despite Stanton's contempt for Protestant clergy and her critics' complaint that she was a "militant anticleric" (Du Bois 1984, 161), on occasion she found them receptive to her and her feminism.

> In 1874, during her speaking tour of Michigan on behalf of a woman suffrage referendum, she [Stanton] enthusiastically noted that ministers of all denominations invited her to speak on suffrage in place of their Sunday sermons. "Sitting Sunday after Sunday in the different pulpits with revered gentlemen ... I could not help thinking of the distance we had come since that period in civilization when Paul's word was law ..." In 1883, after preaching in a London pulpit on the topic, "Has the Christian Religion Done Aught to Elevate Woman?" she admitted privately that, although her sermon had focused on the negative, a strong case could be made for a positive interpretation. (Banner 1988, 149; quoted in Haynes 1998, 149)

In fact, Stanton's opposition to conservative Christianity may have been more tactical than ideological, or so a 1886 letter she wrote to Antoinette Brown Blackwell suggests. In it she is expressing her frustration over the pace of the women's movement: "I feel like making an attack on some new quarter of the enemies [sic] domain. Our politicians are calm and complacent under our fire, but the clergy jump round the minute you aim a pop gun at them like parched peas on a hot shovel" (quoted in Haynes 1998, 150). Haynes comments: "For rhetorical and political reasons, she chose to feature clerical resistance over accommodation and to totalize all of Protestantism as evil; but in actuality, her thinking was in line with much of late-nineteenth-century Protestantism" (1998, 150).

Stanton's resistance to and (unconscious) reproduction of Protestant thought must not, Haynes asks, blind us to her much more conscious alliance with freethinkers who also rejected evangelical visions of supernatural phenomena and fundamentalist theology in favor of rationality and science. But Stanton differed from the freethinkers, Haynes suggests, and in precisely the ways she shares with fundamentalists. First, unlike the freethinkers who wanted to undermine biblical authority altogether, "the discourses engendered by *The Woman's Bible* did not break through their canonical limitations and theological frameworks. Insofar as they restricted their attention to the women's passages of the Bible, they reinforced the discursive boundaries set by the canon. By contesting the authority claims of the women's passages, they reinscribed canonical authority" (Fiorenza 1993, 9; quoted in Haynes 1998, 150). Second, unlike Stanton, who enjoyed the assurance of certainty in her feminist position, the freethinkers were committed to an unrestricted freedom of discussion and diversity of opinion. Rather than entertain a variety of opinions and be willing to be influenced by them as the freethinkers advised, Stanton had no interest in changing her mind. Finally, Haynes points out that Stanton also relied on "common sense" thinking, in contrast to the freethinkers whose faith was in scientific reason and rational inquiry.

Stanton's differences with free thought—Haynes points to her reinscription of canonical authority and absolute truth and her adoption of "common sense" thinking—may have undermined the appeal and political effectiveness of her feminist agenda. Haynes notes that Scottish "common sense" philosophy operates in a contradictory fashion. Its emphasis upon agency and moral judgment as well as its skepticism toward hierarchy and expertise appear to empower the everyday common person, but, Haynes continues, upon closer examination such "empowerment" proves illusory. She argues that "common sense" ends up conveying the sense of the dominant group, whatever that may be. For the conservative Christians, common sense meant accepting the literal veracity of the Bible, a dispensationalist and premillennial view of history, and the absolute divinity of Christ. For Stanton, it meant acknowledging and confronting the fact of the Bible's misogyny and its legitimization of women's subjugation in society (Haynes 1998).

While, then, apparently promoting the individual's cause, "common sense" philosophy subtly persuaded believers to make their convictions coincide with those of the dominant culture (Noll 1986; Haynes 1998). In other words, "common sense" philosophy accepted without reservation the idea of majority rule, consequently aligning itself with dominant modes of patriarchy, liberal individualism, and industrial capitalism. By legitimating a social order founded, presumably, on the individual person/citizen as the basic category and on a work ethic that accepted as fact the faith that honest labor would be justly rewarded, "common sense" simply reproduced the rules and identities of the capitalist marketplace and the social status quo, including male dominance. Haynes quotes Kathryn Kish Sklar (1973) to emphasize the point: common sense philosophy "fostered an energetic moral leadership, yet discouraged assertive, bold, or innovative behavior in the society as a whole" (82–83; quoted in Haynes 1998, 151). Given this conservative undertow, Stanton's employment of "common sense" thinking may have turned away more radical activists and ideas from her cause (Haynes 1998).

Stanton's opposition to liberal theology and method may also have limited the appeal of her feminist agenda. At the end of the nineteenth century, thousands of Christian women were committed to the suffrage movement as well as to the Protestant Church, where they served as ordained, itinerant, and lay preachers as well as board members, deaconesses, missionaries and church members (Zikmund 1982). Perhaps unable to acknowledge her own immersion in (expressed through her resistance to) Protestant thinking or to sympathize let alone respect Christian suffragists, Stanton continually condemned Protestantism or "priestcraft" as rendering women gullible, passive, uneducated victims (Haynes 1998).

Despite its genesis in anti-Protestantism, then, *The Woman's Bible* replicates much of what it was written to reject: there are racist and classist elements; it simply inverts the separate sphere ideology; its value structure is hierarchical; its interpretations are literalist and its readings reductive; its stance, overall, is absolutist. While these limitations of the strategies of resistance demand acknowledgment and critical interrogation, they should not obscure the book's transgressive tactics, among them its opening of the previously male-dominated and elitist field of biblical scholarship; its eagerness to redefine notions of biblical authority and authorship; its comparativist approach to religions; its reading of the Bible as a political as well as spiritual text; and its performance of a more woman-oriented hermeneutic. Not only do such tactics express the creativity, intelligence, and independence of the project's participants, they also demand rereadings of that "traditional, patriarchy-ridden, and multicorded cultural iron: the Bible" (Haynes 1998, 153).

As Carolyn A. Haynes has demonstrated, many fin-de-siècle Christian feminists found ways to live within and even advance the cause of women within misogynistic, patriarchal church culture. How? Haynes points to "miming," a tactic African Americans would use in even more difficult and dangerous circumstances, that of the postbellum South. Just as many "freed" black people appeared to comply with the onerous dictates of white supremacy, many Christian feminists, too, repeated the words and mimed the gestures of conservative Protestant men. But these cultural and gendered performances—this miming—did not represent an enslavement to or uncritical repetition of the original but "an insubordination that appear[ed] to take place within the very terms of the original, and which call[ed] into question the power of the origination" (Butler 1993, 45; quoted in Haynes 1998, 159). Both Christian and secular feminists such as Elizabeth Cady Stanton reiterated Protestant discourses, methods of interpretation, and cultural practices to undermine, not to affirm, conservative and fundamentalist suppositions about women (Haynes 1998). In so doing, they unsettled conservative suppositions about men as well.

Haynes's reading of nineteenth-century women's capacity to employ conservative Christianity for progressive feminist aims appears consonant with contemporary cross-cultural anthropological research on women's participation in fundamentalisms worldwide. Like nineteenth-century Protestantism, contemporary fundamentalisms, as sets of "rules" and religious practices and social support systems, affect women's lives differently, Janet L. Bauer (1997) argues. On occasion such religious participation results in increased social status, even improved standards of living, and an oppositional position vis-à-vis the dominant majority. Bauer acknowledges that in many other circumstances religious fundamentalisms impose new or additional constraints that many women find undermining and limiting. But for many women even patriarchal institutions of religion offer opportunities for self-affirmation, material advancement, political progress, as well as spiritual solace and meaningfulness. As Bauer (1997) observes, "the paradox of women's fundamentalism especially for those who elect it as a way of life may be in the eye of the beholder" (233).

Haynes concludes her study by returning to the present moment, a time she notes, when "a new abject other"—the homosexual—has appeared, demanding not only her/his civil rights but acceptance in the church as well. Haynes notes that a controversy which echoes in major respects the feminist controversies of the late nineteenth century has erupted among conservative and mainline church leaders and gay and lesbian Christians. "My hope in writing this book," Haynes tells us, "is not only to offer insight into the history of nondominant Protestant identity and identity formation but also to provide glimpses into how present and future nondominant identities can be formed and welcomed in Protestant churches and American society without repudiation and exclusion" (1998, 160). Given the responses of, say, Southern Baptists to improvements in the status of women and the civil rights demands of gays and lesbians, that hope would seem to require a strong religious faith.

Haynes's careful research helps us understand why many European-American men went into crisis over their gendered status as men during the last quarter of the nineteenth century. In many respects Christianity was the "last refuge" of besieged manhood, a patriarchal religion structured around the sacrifice of sons, the vengeance, forgiveness, and absolute authority of fathers. When many Christian women mimed the discourses of conservative religion in ways that transformed their "gracious submission" into more complicated positions of relative independence, men's position—so dependent upon their imagined superordinate status vis-à-vis women and blacks—destabilized and deteriorated. Not even in church, not even at home, it seemed to many, could "men be men." This precarious state of white masculinity would be performed, especially by southern white men, in peculiar, shall we say queer, ways. Within the church, many men decided it was time for the remasculinization of religion.

VIII. A Reactionary Reaffirmation of Masculinity

The histories of men and women do not take place in isolation from each other.

—Peter G. Filene, *Him/Her/Self* (1998)

[P]reoccupation with manhood [is] an anxious reaction to the assertiveness and influence of women.

—Mark Carnes and Clyde Griffen, *Meanings for Manhood: Constructions of Masculinity in Victorian America* (1990b)

Hell itself was sometimes associated ... with the vagina.

—Philip Greven, *The Protestant Temperament: Patterns of Child-Rearing, Religious Experience, and the Self in Early America* (1977)

Is fundamentalism a "male" movement or set of practices?

—Janet L. Bauer, "Conclusion: The Mixed Blessings of Women's Fundamentalism" (1997)

What did it mean to be a Christian man in a society where even conservative Christian women seemed to undermine traditional manhood? There was what many men perceived as a "feminization" of boys who came of age in evangelical Christianity, a "problem" at least two centuries old. The libidinal ambivalence of such Christian men is evident, Philip Greven (1977) suggests, in the diary of Michael Wigglesworth. Born in Yorkshire in 1631, Wigglesworth's first nine years were spent as an only child; his sister was born in late 1640. By the time his diary began in 1653, Wigglesworth's feminization is signified by his constant preoccupation with his anguished sense of distance, separation, and rebellion from God, his heavenly Father. He begs this Father to come to him: "Therefore Lord hear my crys, my sighings, my groans bottle thou my tears still prevailing lusts, principally pride and sensuality, want of love to thee and fervent desire after communion with thee" (quoted in Greven 1977, 133).

There is no evidence in his diary, Greven tells us, that Wigglesworth loved his wife, a cousin on his mother's side of the family and sufficiently close to cause concern for incest. There is evidence, however, that he was drawn to several of his young male students at Harvard. One day he reports that he was disturbed by "much distracted thoughts I find arising from too much doting affection," directed (as he then immediately added in shorthand) "to some of my pupils one of whom went to Boston with me today." On another occasion, he records that "I find my spirit so exceeding carried with love to my pupils that I cant tell how to take my rest in God." Several weeks later, he asks his diary, "will the Lord now again return and embrace me in the arms of his dearest love? will he fall upon my neck and kiss me? for he was pleased to give in some secret and silent evidence of his love" (quoted in Greven 1977, 134).

This fantasy of being embraced, kissed, and loved by the Lord may well have been a sublimation of the desire he could not permit himself to name, for on one occasion he records feeling "such filthy lust also flowing from my fond affection to my pupils whiles in their presence on the third day after noon that I confess myself an object of God's loathing" (in Greven 1977, 134). It is clear, Greven notes, Michael Wigglesworth was sufficiently drawn to several of the young men whom he taught that he felt profoundly unsettled by the "filthy lust" their young bodies evoked. Greven continues:

> [F]or Wigglesworth, religious sensibilities, oedipal conflicts, and "feminization" were intimately interconnected, mirroring his persistent conflicts with his own masculinity and his need to see himself in the role of wife rather than husband. The inner conflicts that these tensions and needs produced may well account for his own extraordinary guilt and fear. They almost certainly underlay his need for punishment, articulated so powerfully later in his famous poem on the *Day of Doom,* one of the classics of the fire and brimstone tradition in New England. (1977, 134)

While antedating our story by two centuries, the libidinal politics of nineteenth-century evangelical men may not have been altogether different. In the nineteenth century many (white) boys were instructed to become "Christian Gentlemen," honest and genteel, ambitious and self-reliant. Such a configuration of personality attributes was consistent with the structure of the antebellum economy, especially in the North, comprised as it was of small shops, farms, and factories. This version of manhood was, as we have seen, propped up by evangelical Protestantism. As the American economy became more industrial and domestic culture became more feminized during the last third of the nineteenth century, a new masculine ideal was beginning to become visible (Curtis 1990).

Many of the young men who felt forced to reconstruct American manhood, as the twentieth century dawned, found that, in order to do so, they also needed to reconstruct American Protestantism. That reformulation—a remasculinization—would become known as the social gospel. The social gospel represented, in part, a reaction against the extremes of individual (i.e., manly) responsibility and self-control. By the 1880s and 1890s, Susan Curtis (1990) explains, many young men were increasingly clear that it was difficult to save oneself spiritually and morally while making a success of oneself in an increasingly predatory economy. Feminized versions of Protestantism that were readily available to them comforted some as they struggled to succeed, but such a maternal and feminine religion did not satisfy their longing to emulate, even surpass, their fathers.

Not able or willing to reject feminized Christianity altogether, these men incorporated certain elements of it into a gospel that made an explicit appeal to men, as well as to some women. In 1901 Josiah Strong put the matter in explicitly gendered terms: "There is not enough of effort, of struggle, in the typical church life of today to win young men to the church. A flowery bed of ease does not appeal to a fellow who has any manhood in him. The prevailing religion is too utterly comfortable to attract young men who love the heroic" (quoted in Curtis 1990, 68). Torn between what many experienced as a consuming demand for individualism in industrial America and a contrary influence of feminization in religion, social gospelers at the turn of the century were determined to articulate a version of the Gospel that enabled to them reconstruct their own besieged manliness (Curtis 1990).

Social gospelers tended to be middle-class Protestant men living in rural areas or in small towns. Inspired by the work of older men like Josiah Strong, Washington Gladden, and Lyman Abbott, the movement began to form in the late 1880s and early 1890s. While including the working class as their audience, these men spoke primarily to northern middle-class men. The popularity of the social gospel by the early twentieth century suggests that they had reached their audience, an audience clearly eager to rethink a feminized Christianity in terms of a new masculine ethic, one that was presumably more vigorous and masculine. To show the religious forms this masculine reaction took to the extremes of bourgeois individualism, feminized Protestantism, and an increasingly predatory workplace, Susan Curtis (1990) examines the lives of several men who later became important social gospelers.

What becomes clear is that the social gospel helped affirm masculinity in its time of "crisis." Several of the young men who later became part of the social gospel movement never forgot how the ideal of manly individualism had played out in their lives. As children they had been taught an individualistic religion that emphasized not only personal salvation but the tortures of hell for the unrepentant. Harry Emerson Fosdick recalled "weeping at night for fear of going to hell, with my mystified and baffled mother trying to comfort me." He joined his family's church at the age of seven, an event that, one trusts, allowed the disturbed child to sleep. Francis John McConnell remembered the "almost wholly individualistic" faith of his parents, at a time "when repression was thought to be a mark of genuine religion." McConnell became a member of his father's church in 1881 at the age of ten. Shailer Mathews described his "Puritan" education in a pious community where "hell and devil were very real" and where "the message from the pulpit was essentially for the individual." He underwent a conversion experience at a revival in 1877 led by George C. Needham. Walter Rauschenbusch learned from his father, August Rauschenbusch, a scholar at the Rochester Theological Seminary, that he was headed straight for hell unless he repented immediately. Persuaded, in 1878 young Rauschenbusch repented, declaring, "I want to be a man" (quoted in Curtis 1990, 68–69). Probably this masculinized dynamic was also at work in former Black Panther Eldridge Cleaver's brief flirtation with Rauschenbusch, whose *Social Principles of Jesus* (1916) he read after he returned to the United States in 1975 (Rout 1991).

Perhaps because their fathers were exemplars of industry, discipline, and success, many social gospelers felt deprived of a strong paternal presence during their childhood. This concern over "absent fathers" would surface over and over in American racial and gender politics, most notably, perhaps, in the controversial Moynihan Report issued in 1965, to be discussed in chapter 14. In the late nineteenth century, as in the late twentieth, many fathers played a diminishing role. The simple separation of work from home required fathers to be absent much of the day. No longer did they teach their sons the skills of their craft, as some fathers had before industrialization separated sites of labor and domestic life. Many of the men who became social gospelers experienced this absence even more intensely, for their fathers died or were otherwise gone before the boys reached adolescence. Charles Macfarland, Charles Stelzle, Francis Greenwood Peabody, and Washington Gladden all lost their fathers early. Walter Rauschenbusch and his father were separated by an ocean for much of the boy's childhood (Curtis 1990).

As we know, absence can be felt more powerfully than presence, especially for young men coming of age in a patriarchal culture. These young men were, Curtis (1990) tells us, haunted by memories of successful fathers to whom they felt they must measure up. Both Rauschenbusch and Macfarland idealized their fathers but acknowledged in later years that they hardly knew them. For instance, Rauschenbusch undertook the completion of his father's memoir because he admired him so. These boys may have been dreaming of their dads, but it was their mothers who raised them, whose influence was in fact formative (Curtis 1990). It would be their mothers against whom they would rebel in order to become "men," a psychosexual ritual of gender formation for men around the world (Gilmore 1990).

The relative absence of the father combined with a myriad of social changes undermined the gender stability of many men at this time. Curtis (1990) points to the advent of mass production (and the array of consumer goods it made available), a host of public institutions, increasing vacation and leisure time, and a longing to escape the monotony and degradation of work as developments which functioned to undermine those presumably manly virtues of hard work, self-reliance, delayed gratification, and self-control. These ideals had been embraced by the young social gospelers. They too experienced the tension between those ideals and the realities of the industrial workplace. But soon many concluded that hard work and self-control were no longer guarantees of success. As Henry Atkinson put it, many men "tried as hard as possible" but failed to provide "enough bread for the little ones." Gladden saw "multitudes" of "worthy people" in Columbus, Ohio, who worked and saved and prayed, but who did not succeed in "raising themselves" (quoted phrases in Curtis 1990, 71). For Gladden this broken equation constituted the "labor question" that haunted him and his colleagues for decades, but they were hardly alone (Curtis 1990). The settlement house movement (see chapter 6) was in part a response to the suffering of impoverished urban dwellers.

The social gospelers—among them Rauschenbusch, Mathews, Macfarland, Sheldon, Peabody—came of age in the 1880s when these conditions were becoming increasingly visible. Slowly, they became dissatisfied with what a narrowly individualistic conception of manhood associated with the psychological isolation of their youth. Many began by rejecting the individualistic character of their religious experiences. Fosdick, for instance, confessed to a "hidden anger" at the church due to its "wretched play upon my selfish fears and hopes." In 1888, Rauschenbusch reflected upon his initial conversion experience and judged that "there was a great deal in it that was not really true." At the age of twenty-seven, he underwent a second conversion to "redeem humanity" and to "live again the life of Christ" (quoted in Curtis 1990, 71).

Although these young men came to reject the individualistic religion of their youth, they hardly rejected Christianity itself. Instead they came to formulate a social gospel that would ask Christians to address social problems that undermined moral manhood. Christians, they argued, had a moral obligation to confront the social evils that led to immorality. Both the individual and society at large must shoulder the responsibility for salvation. Like Christian feminists, they attacked the evils of alcohol, prostitution, and gambling, which tempted young men away from righteous living. They responded to poverty by providing soup kitchens, bathing facilities, visiting nurses, industrial training for boys, inexpensive used clothing, and assistance for the unemployed. They bolstered the home and, like Ida B. Wells, created alternatives to street life by organizing social clubs. They persuaded church leaders to allow them to build bowling alleys and gymnasiums on church property (Curtis 1990).

Not only the young were the subjects of their social concern. These men expressed sympathy for the plight of working-class people by evangelizing workers at lunchtime meetings held at factories and shops, by providing nurseries for children of working mothers, and by endorsing the right to collective bargaining. In sum, the social gospelers taught a social not individualistic gospel, one focused on this world not just the hereafter. In order to support their commitments, social gospelers established reform unions, denominational brotherhood organizations, investigative teams, and other social services. Some became affiliated with universities, others with settlement houses, still others with political parties; others formed organizations that required collaboration with other reform groups; few limited their careers to the pulpit. They were surrounded by other men who shared their zeal for social reform, committed to what they took to be the three great laws of the social gospel: service, sacrifice, and love (Curtis 1990). Curiously, many identified excessive individualism with feminization. As Curtis (1990) observes: "These feminine virtues associated with Victorian domesticity were important parts of their disavowal of individualism in work and faith" (72).

The social gospel was no masculine parallel to Christian feminism, but, in part, a reactionary response to it and to the "crisis" of masculinity more generally. The men who came to the movement seemed consumed with the meaning of manhood and, in particular, with the legacy of their fathers, a concern many men at the close of the twentieth century would also share (see chapter 19, section III). They articulated a gospel that recoded the domestic, maternal, even feminine qualities of their reforms into expressions of manly endeavor. Their interest in—obsession with—manhood is most evident in their gendered fantasies of God and Jesus. Jesus, characterized especially as the son and brother, was central to the social gospel; he was construed as an example of cooperative, righteous, and manly behavior. For these men, Jesus was above all a reformer committed to the poor, who labored with others to save humanity. For his social commitment and struggle, Jesus was worthy of emulation. God, the Father, was understood to be present—"indwelling" and "immanent" (Curtis 1990, 72)—but not as an activist or interventionist. As Curtis points out, such a conception of God resembled the social gospelers' memories of their own impressive but absent fathers. For these men, "both Jesus and God in the social gospel served as masculine ideals in industrializing America" (Curtis 1990, 72).

The images of Jesus to which many social gospelers had grown accustomed as Victorian children had been fabricated by sentimental writers. In these images, Jesus was neither masculine nor fully feminine. Popular depictions showed him wearing long white gowns; his hair was long and wavy, his beard a soft brown. Both madonna and man (as Curtis nicely puts it), this Victorian Jesus represented a blend of the separate spheres, of tender nurture and manly endeavor, a blend which helped legitimize a commitment to social service as an acceptable substitute for individual enterprise. Jesus was also imagined as a son, an image which posited him more as a peer rather than a divine personification of authority. Social gospelers rejected any feminized version of Jesus. Rauschenbusch declared that "there was nothing mushy, nothing sweetly effeminate about Jesus." His Jesus was a "man's man," who "turned again and again on the snarling pack of His pious enemies and made them slink away" (quoted in Curtis 1990, 72). Macfarland regretted that he had not been involved with the manly Jesus as a child: "I know it would have been a great help to me in my boyhood and young manhood had I been led to appreciate the manhood of Jesus" (quoted in Curtis 1990, 73).

Between the beginning of the social gospel movement and the 1920s, Jesus became increasingly "butch," although this intensification of his machismo image took variable forms. One thing was sure; no longer was this any gentle or sissy Savior. For some he became a working-class guy, the hard-working carpenter-reformer of Galilee; for white-collar men he was the masterful businessman of Bruce Barton's imagination. In the late nineteenth century, social gospelers were sure that *their* Savior was "robust, muscular, and active," not the "sweet, sad man in flowing gowns" with whom they had grown up (Curtis 1990, 73). Congruent with the trend toward realism in American culture and historical criticism in theology, Jesus' life was made less a divine drama and more a realistic tale. Since Jesus was a Jew who had learned the trade of carpentry from his father and later worked with fishermen, many believers now visualized him "with dark hair and eyes, a well-developed physique, and rough, callused hands ... not unlike the toiling workmen of industrial America" (Curtis 1990, 74). This was no "Miss Jesus" of Paul Monette's (see 1992b, 45) gay imagination.

In *The Call of the Carpenter* (1914), a New York settlement-house worker named Bouck White imagined Jesus as a radical populist who advocated "a social gospel." "His ideal is the civic ideal," White asserted. "Its goal is 'the holy city descending from God out of heaven.' Therefore the Carpenter-Christ is the fit leader of the multitudinous" (quoted in Curtis 1990, 74). "At the same time that Jesus sprouted muscles and a manlier beard and showed a passion for justice," Susan Curtis (1990) points out, "he also became more congenial and social-minded" (74). Some writers characterized Jesus as "the Captain," as an "elder brother," or simply as a friend. Perhaps with a college football player in mind, many men imagined Jesus as more approachable and congenial; maybe he was, they fantasized, a team captain—a leader among equals (Curtis 1990).

Above all Jesus was a "man." Of course he was devoted to "service, sacrifice, and love," but such social commitment did not dissuade him from "manly assertion" (Curtis 1990, 74). Surrounded by his manly disciples, Jesus was clearly a man who could inspire "real" men. In his unsubtly entitled *The Manhood of the Master* (1913), Harry Emerson Fosdick looked his male readers straight in the eye when he said: "The Master appeals to all that is strongest and most military in you" (quoted in Curtis 1990, 74). Jesus performed every one of his manly duties, but, Curtis suggests, he did so rather differently than had the social gospelers' individualistic and absent fathers. Jesus affirmed the social ideal, thereby absolving men from the psychological burden of individual success and salvation. In rejecting earlier models of individualistic manhood (which is not individual at all), Jesus was anything but effeminate. The young men who had failed to live up to the ideals of their fathers in the 1880s now helped to formulate a new set of masculine ideals that tried to re-stabilize a masculinity in "crisis," summarized in the image of a new manly Jesus (Curtis 1990).

Charles Stelzle had organized one of the most effective workingmen's churches in New York City in the early 1900s. From that experience he decided he knew something about building churches; he urged churchmen to appeal to young men through advertising, communicating that churches fostered "the best kind of manhood." In his *Principles of Successful Church Advertising* (1908), Stelzle sketched social reforms that depended upon manly volunteers: "We need the sort of men who can do things," he asserted, "and who do them because they like to do them. Are you that kind of man?" he demanded to know (quoted in Curtis 1990, 75). To any man worth his salt, the question could be answered only in the affirmative (Curtis 1990).

The working-class emphasis of the early social gospel movement faded in the 1910s and 1920s in favor of businessmen's luncheons, business planning, and advertising. While still dedicated to the social gospel and social reform, many younger men were drawn to social efficiency and the businesslike promotion of their religion. This development would seem to parallel the "social efficiency" movement in American curriculum studies (see Pinar et al. 1995). In 1920, for instance, Frederick Anderson spoke about "Jesus and his career" and suggested that "the personality of the Man of Nazareth ... is the power behind Christian history." Burton Easton and Charles Fiske spoke of what they took to be the "real Jesus," who, unsurprisingly, was a man "impressive in appearance and of great physical strength" (quoted phrases in Curtis 1990, 75). As Curtis points out, this new emphasis upon a handsome Jesus and his muscular body had the unintended consequence of de-emphasizing the significance of an abstract, disembodied God.

This remasculinized Jesus was remarkably adaptable to other nonreligious agendas, including racial ones. The Ku Klux Klan (which we survey in chapter 9, focusing there on white women's participation in the second Klan) appropriated "muscular Christianity," invoking the manly Christ, who was "a robust, toil-marked young man" who "purged the temple with a whip," according to Hiram Wesley Evans, a Georgia Imperial Wizard. But even mainstream groups resorted to imagery of racialized sadomasochism when fantasizing about the young muscular son of God. For instance, the Church of Christ in America declared that its members were tempered by "the red blooded and virile" into a "thing of rugged steel ... forged in the terrific stress ... of wresting a continent from savages and from the wilderness" (quoted in Kimmel 1996, 178).

The Reverend Billy Sunday was the most famous of all remasculinized "muscular Christians." A former professional baseball player, Sunday became America's most prominent evangelical preacher. The former right fielder for the Chicago and, later, Pittsburgh baseball teams left his successful career for the ministry not because baseball was immoral but because it was amoral. That was an intolerable state of affairs because," he explained in 1893, "morality was not an essential to success; one may be a consummate rogue and a first class ball player." Like Theodore Roosevelt, Sunday had struggled with being a physically frail child. In fact, he been so sickly that he was scarcely able to walk as a child and had to be carried around on a specially made pillow. But Sunday converted himself into a strong, sinewy specimen whose boundless energy infused his dramatic tent sermons (Kimmel 1996). Sunday, it was said, "brought bleacher-crazy, frenzied aggression to religion"; one journalist reported a Billy Sunday sermon in the following gendered terms: "He stands up like a man in the pulpit and out of it. He speaks like a man. He works like a man. ... He is manly with God and with everyone who comes to hear him. No matter how much you disagree with him, he treats you after a manly fashion. He is not an imitation, but a manly man giving all a square deal" (quoted in Kimmel 1996, 179).

Sunday was the most conspicuous of the remasculinized Christians, but only one among many other men who muscled their way into conflations of the manly and the divine. A prominent Methodist who helped organize the Men and Religion Forward Movement in 1911, Fayette L. Thompson was sure that being a Christian required one to be more of a man now than it had when his father was alive. "If the manhood of this generation does not awake to the fact that in order to be a true disciple of Jesus Christ in these days it must be responsive to a bigger program than any program of the past," he said, "it will fail utterly to realize the glorious opportunity of the present. It will not do merely to measure up to the program of our fathers," he imagined (quoted in Curtis 1990, 77).

Images of Jesus and ideals of manhood evolved together between the 1880s and the 1920s, often in response to, sometimes merging with one another. As Susan Curtis (1990) observes: "Anxieties over their own masculinity prompted social gospelers to look for a manly example, which they now found in Jesus. And as the social gospelers worked through both their identity and their religion, they altered both" (78). The new images and ideals they created inspired other men who also felt besieged as men. The social gospel seems a curious historical footnote today, with evangelical and fundamentalist forms of Protestantism once again emphasizing an extreme individualism of sin and salvation. But one hundred years ago, haunted by their fathers, reacting against their mothers, and threatened by the economy, gender, race, one might say history itself, many white men retreated to a fantasy of a muscular manhood personified in Christ. True, some shifted manliness away from an extreme, aggrandizing, and isolating individualism toward sociality, and in this respect, the social gospel movement mirrored and advanced the cause of Progressivism during the first decades of the century. But by the 1920s these social ideals had, for all practical purposes, disappeared into a capitalistic consumer culture, a culture with a multitude of reactionary elements, including the second Klan. But I am ahead of my story. For now, let us return to the 1890s and the gendered "crisis." I will begin by reviewing the controversy over the term "white masculinity."

6 THE "CRISIS" *of* WHITE MASCULINITY

I. The Complexity of "Crisis"

Were conceptions of masculinity strongly held and deeply satisfying—affirmations of a positive sense of self? Or, at the other extreme, were they compensatory and escapist—ways of evading the realities of class, economics, or gender.

—Mark C. Carnes and Clyde Griffen,
Meanings of Manhood: Constructions of Masculinity in Victorian America (1990)

This fin de siècle crisis of masculinity was a popular theme for critics and experts.

—Michael Kimmel, *Manhood in America: A Cultural History* (1996)

[T]he economy of our sexual drives is a cultural achievement.

—Leo Bersani, *Homos* (1995)

The stern, upright patriarch is perhaps the most memorable image of manhood during the middle of the nineteenth century, the heyday of evangelical Protestantism, but, as Clyde Griffen (1990) makes clear, it was not the only one. As we will see momentarily, the passionate, even effusive, "romantic" abolitionist was another type. Southern men differed according to class, number of slaves owned, but shared, to a considerable extent, a sense of "honor" that bound them to restricted and often violent codes of "manly" conduct. These diverse constructions of manhood faded, especially in the North, during the late nineteenth century, and in their place appeared a more rigidly circumscribed set of gender expectations for middle-class white men, North and

South, especially those who worked in large bureaucratic corporations. Still, considerable differences were discernible according to region, class, and race.

For Griffen (1990), this fact of diversity undermines those historical accounts which emphasize a more generalized concept of "crisis" and a monolithic notion of "masculinity" (Dubbert 1979, 1980; Pugh 1983; Kimmel 1987; Bailey 1988). "The charm of the 'crisis' interpretation," Griffen (1990) says dryly, "has been its combination of simplicity and inclusiveness: everywhere traditional manhood was on the defensive" (183). He cites the "canonical" scholarship of Peter Filene (1998) which argued, when it first appeared in 1974, that at the turn of the century men's sense of themselves as men was under stress, not only at work, but at home, and in terms of sexuality. As women persuaded men that "feminine" values were pertinent for public as well as private life, the male domination of the sphere was eroded. As women complained more loudly about their husbands' conduct away from and at home, the meaning of manhood became less certain. The "crisis" interpretation tends to emphasize broad historical trends and major developments such as the end of the frontier and the disappearing opportunities for economic independence in an era of business bureaucratization. Griffen (1990) is unpersuaded: "The impact of these trends on particular groups within the middle class is arguable and, in any case, not shown" (183–184).

Gail Bederman (1995a) also finds the "crisis" hypothesis mistaken. She has used the term "decline" (Bederman 1995b) to depict the state of white manhood in the 1890s, arguing that "although older meanings of manhood were gradually losing their persuasiveness, masculinity was hardly in crisis" (15). "Men were actively, even enthusiastically, engaging in the process of remaking manhood," yet, she continues, "middle-class men were clearly still convinced that manhood was powerful, that it was part of their identity; and that all beings with healthy male bodies had it" (Bederman 1995a, 15).

Other scholars find the concept of "crisis" compelling, however. In his cultural history of American manhood, sociologist Michael Kimmel (1996) points to several co-extensive phenomena which, he argues, cracked the foundation upon which manhood had been grounded. These included (1) industrialization, (2) the entry into the public sphere of a significant number of women, (3) the Emancipation of blacks, (4) a massive influx of immigrants, and (5) the closing of the frontier. Not for the first time, "the meanings of manhood were again uncertain" (78). More than uncertain, as "the combined impact of these processes led many men to feel frightened, cut loose from the traditional moorings of their identities, adrift in some anomic sea. By the last decades of the century, manhood was widely perceived to be in crisis" (Kimmel 1996, 78). As we have seen in the previous chapters, southern white men fought violently to maintain relations of racial subjugation, but even pious northern churchmen found themselves challenged by Christian feminists.

Literary scholar Scott S. Derrick (1997) also summarizes the historical moment in a way that lends support to the "crisis" thesis, noting that during this period a number of "mechanisms of masculinization" (157) appeared. Among them were the Boy Scouts, muscular Christianity, bodybuilding, institutionalized sports such as a football and baseball, as well as the public modeling of martial aggressivity and imperialism by such public figures as Theodore Roosevelt. In this chapter we will examine these and several others, including rites of initiation into all-male fraternal orders, the gendered character of late Victorian boyhood, the end of "romantic" friendship, and the panic over masturbation. Derrick suggests these developments imply the failure of the "separate spheres" ideology, in which "signs of feminine presences in the masculine psyche" were to be kept carefully contained with female bodies and those practices associated with "true womanhood." "The insistence on specifically masculine virtues," Derrick (1997) continues,

> reflects the success of domestic ideology in producing the feminine as an ongoing and ineradicable challenge to male authority, both intrapsychically and in the material world of social relations. The twin halves of this cultural crisis coincide with the much noted crystallization of homosexuality/homophobia in the late nineteenth and early twentieth centuries. The intense desire for the redeeming stuff of masculinity is shadowed by a growing panic that, experientially, masculine affiliations, enthusiastically cultivated, cannot be separable in kind from erotic desires for other men. Such a threat is in part contained by the casting of the homosexual as a recognizable figure antithetical to normative masculinity, but this defense against homoeroticism paradoxically also intensifies the threat of impermissible, feminizing desires alien to the specular, manifest masculinity of the touchdown run, the heroic charge, or the Western duel. (157)

At the least, it seems to me, one must acknowledge that, if not in actual crisis, white masculinity was in a deeply anxious transitional phase.

Historian Henry Steele Commager (1950) likened the 1890s to a great watershed in American history, a decade in which "the new America came in as on flood tide" (44). While his characterization of the decade does not include gender destabilization or its relation to racial politics, it would seem to imply them. He focuses first on the "passing of the old West" (44), by which he means, in part, the genocide of Native Americans. He means as well the erosion of the frontier line, the decline of the cattle kingdom, the completion of the transcontinental railroad, and the final territorial organization of the West. The decade also "revealed a dangerous acceleration of the exploitation of natural resources" (44), including the seizure of the best forests, minerals, range and farm land by large corporations; these developments helped precipitate the conservation and reclamation movements. The center of economic gravity shifted from country to the city. There was an unprecedented degree of control of manufacturing, transportation, banking, and communication industries in trusts and monopolies. The decade saw the rise of big business, including the emergence of the successful businessman as "hero" (45), and the beginnings of the modern labor movement. Commager mentions mass immigration and "the advent of the New South" (44), although there is no mention that black citizens were being systematically disfranchised state by southern state, that segregation was being institutionalized throughout the region, and that black men's bodies were swinging from southern magnolia trees.

Often omitted in historians' lists of shifts under way during the lynching decade are schools. The schools of the 1890s, Lawrence Cremin (1961) reports, "were a depressing study" (20). The usual problems associated with students, teachers, classrooms, and funding had become "overwhelming" (20). Rural schools, built fifty years earlier, had been allowed to fall into disrepair. Cut off from pedagogical improvements being devised in the universities and undermined by problems of rural decline, rural schools had deteriorated badly. Teachers were forced to concentrate on "the same old drill in the same old readers" (quoted in Cremin 1961, 20). In the cities, problems of skyrocketing enrollments were compounded by a myriad of other problems. School buildings were badly lighted, poorly heated, often unsanitary, and simply overflowing with students, many of whom were young immigrants from a dozen different countries. Some superintendents spoke hopefully of reducing class size to sixty per teacher, but this was, in the main, rhetorical distraction from intolerable classroom conditions. Cremin locates the genesis of the progressive movement in this decade, in part because the schools were in such "crisis."

This educational "crisis" was also an explicitly gendered one, as during the early 1890s the debate over coeducation intensified. Most public school teachers, like those in the National Council of Education, believed that public schools should be coeducational and that the curriculum should be substantially the same for both sexes. During these discussions, the advocates of coeducation sometimes came close to suggesting that the public school might become an institution in which differences of gender might not matter, a view in sharp contrast to the separate sphere ideology dominant in the larger society. Feminists argued that that situation must change, that equal schooling ought not automatically divert women back to the home but should open to them any occupation and activity available to men. Caroline H. Dall observed that a man's right to education gave him the "right to a choice of vocation" (quoted in Tyack and Hansot 1990, 112). The same sequence must become true for women. Former teachers Susan B. Anthony and Elizabeth Cady Stanton demanded coeducation across the nation, and writers like Dall insisted that coeducation was an argument for opening the full range of vocational opportunities for women (Tyack and Hansot 1990).

It seems beyond dispute that the 1890s were a decade of profound tension in many important and intersecting elements of American life. While there is a difference of opinion among historians regarding the appropriateness of the term "crisis" to describe events in the domain of gender (and masculinity in particular), it seems to me this difference may be, at least in part, a matter of emphasis and perhaps of discursive positioning within a politicized academic field. It seems clear there *were* significant shifts in gender formations (for women as well as men) in the late nineteenth century. No one actually disputes that fact. The point of contention seems to concern how dramatic these shifts were, how common they were among different sectors of the population (class, race, region), and what term can be employed to represent these shifts. There is as well some problem with periodization. Bederman's point about men's unchanging belief "that manhood was powerful" does not, in itself, undermine the "crisis" hypothesis in my view, as it is clear from feminist theory and object-relations theory in psychoanalysis that such "belief" is often compensatory, defensive, overdetermined.

Let us say, then, that the concept of a "crisis" of white masculinity is a bit blunt and dramatic, too totalizing, obscuring, perhaps, how historical shifts in manhood worked through and were expressed in various social segments in different locales at different historical moments. Certainly the important collection of essays John Carnes and Clyde Griffen collected and edited—*Meanings for Manhood: Constructions of Masculinity in Victorian America* (and upon which I draw heavily in this chapter)—goes a long way toward correcting that problem. As we will see, for some affluent suburban men masculine domesticity was a reactionary response to "crisis" made possible by job security; for some working-class men, economic crisis exacerbated their sense of gendered difficulty. Other middle-class men became submerged in strange homoerotic initiation rituals into popular fraternal orders, others in a "muscular" Christianity we just examined, still others in aggressive and reactionary politics (against women's suffrage, for black disenfranchisement, a politics of xenophobia, white racism, and homophobia).

The notion of "crisis" does have the virtue, Carnes and Griffen concede, of summarizing evidence of white men's experience of feeling threatened by women's demands, deepening doubts about their own manhood, and stimulating widespread yearnings for a restoration of "virility." But while the word "crisis" presupposes a turning point, it remains unclear when this crisis began, how long it lasted, and when it was resolved, if ever. There is, as we will observe in the final chapter, a "crisis" of masculinity today; how does it differ from and recapitulate this earlier one? Perhaps the main problem with the "crisis" of masculinity thesis for Carnes and Griffen is this matter of its periodization. The turn of the century (1880–1920) is ordinarily identified as the era of "crisis," but, as Carnes and Griffen point out, men and women have worried over the state of American masculinity from time to time over the past one hundred and fifty years. They think of the 1950s in particular, with no obvious challenges from women and no dramatic economic shifts under way. During the 1950s Arthur Schlesinger, Jr., and others (such as Talcott Parsons; see chapter 14) wrote about the "crisis of American masculinity" in which, more than ever before, men and boys were presumably "confused about what they should and should not do to fulfill their masculine roles" (Bailey 1988, 102; quoted in Griffen 1990, 184). For Griffen, "the persistence of anxiety over a long span of time stretches the idea of 'crisis' and makes periodization difficult" (Griffen 1990, 184).

As an alternative to the "crisis of masculinity" thesis, Carnes and Griffen (1990b) prefer to think in terms of "change and continuity" (185) along four major axes of men's gender and gendered relations from the antebellum period to the 1920s. The first of these is style or posture, that is, means of gendered self-presentation: how men communicated their manhood. The second is the separation of male and female spheres; the third the division of labor, and the fourth, male dominance. Carnes and Griffen argue that styles of masculinity varied considerably between groups and over time; that the separation of spheres decreased as gender borders blurred; that labor continued to be divided despite alterations in its rationalization; and that both the extent and reproduction of male domination varied during this period. Their arguments, they acknowledge, are confined almost entirely to the white middle class.

Before the Civil War, Carnes and Griffen argue, there was a wide range of conceptions and styles of masculinity, not only between classes but within them. Included in the working class were southern backcountry white men, engaged in "rough and dangerous" work. These lower-class men valued antebellum homosocial traditions such as honor as much as did men in the planter class, although they tended to defend it even more brutally. Preoccupation with honor and physical prowess was also typical of certain northern urban working-class men, such as immigrant Irish and those native craftsmen and laborers still working in a preindustrial economic sphere. These working-class men found their fantasies of themselves reflected in popular drama and literature, for instance, the tall tales of southwestern humorists, the fiction of northern radical democrats, or the theatrical versions of the Bowery boys, "tough and swaggering." In contrast, as early as the 1840s there were urban workers who had accepted the morality of "self-discipline, sobriety, and seriousness" (quoted phrases in Griffen 1990, 185) associated with nineteenth-century Evangelical Protestantism (Griffen 1990).

There was a range of styles of masculinity in the middle and upper classes as well, Carnes and Griffen continue. They cite Donald Yacovone's (1990) study of the "romantic friendships" of male abolitionists to show that some men "professed undying love for one another, kissed, shed tears, and clasped hands" (Griffen 1990, 185), performing a Christian form of fraternal love known since the Middle Ages. Such expressive male friendships were not limited to racial progressives in the North; as we have seen (in chapter 4), male southern secessionists also became passionately and physically involved with each other. Griffen (1990) remind us that neither group of men experienced their passion for each other as in any way weak, immoral, or what would later be known as "effeminate."

And then Griffen makes a surprising statement, given how careful they have been about generalizing, as in the "crisis" thesis controversy. Referring to those nineteenth-century men who enjoyed "romantic friendships," Griffen (1990) adds: "Nor was there any fear among these celebrants of manly love that their passionate friendships would lead to homosexual acts" (186). To provide "documentation" for this flight of fantasy, they cite studies of English writings on manly love in the same period which have shown, evidently, that fraternal love was, unlike marriage, "purely spiritual," and thereby the "highest" form of love, the opposite, presumably, of what was then dismissed as "beastliness." Even in England, where an urban homosexual "underworld" had been observed since the early eighteenth century, "widespread suspicion of intense same-sex friendships as potentially sexual did not develop until the late nineteenth century" (Griffen 1990, 186). That last development seemed to have helped put an end to "romantic friendship" and certainly could have contributed to the "crisis" of masculinity, however variable its expressions and difficult its periodization.

But Carnes and Griffen do not know—nor do I—whether or not on occasion these "spiritual" unions, which were also expressed physically, did not go "too far," that is, stimulate rather more than one's emotions. Given the prohibition against "beastliness," why on earth would a historian expect to find documentation of sexualized romantic friendship among "respectable" often heterosexually married men? I shouldn't think there would be any. Just as "straight" men today "forget" about such events—what happened after an especially drunken night at the fraternity house, for instance, or that summer hiking expedition with one's best friend—no doubt these men in love were not about to confess if they were, as we say today, "getting it on." Perhaps most were not, although we do not know that. The "crisis" came when people—their wives? other men?—stopped believing that all that effusiveness and physical expressivity ended at the belt line.

To show further the variability of nineteenth-century manhood, Carnes and Griffen point to lawyers, men who confused their profession with their gendered sense of themselves as men. As Michael Grossberg's research (1990; see chapter 11, section I) indicates, early nineteenth-century lawyers came to emphasize competitiveness, physical courage, and political realism. This style of manliness coincided with the emergence, by the 1840 presidential campaign, of the American political parties as forms of male fraternal organizations. Political rallies and processions, often marked by military-style marching groups, became rituals of male homosociality. Election day underlined the homosocial character of electoral politics as voting was conducted in saloons, barbershops, and other places dominated by men (Carnes and Griffen 1990b).

Between the abolitionists' romantic friendship and the "macho" styles of antebellum manliness, there was, Griffen notes, a very influential evangelical conception of Christian manhood. Men's, as well as women's, diaries suggest not only a "prodigious appetite for religion," but as well the persistence of an older, "more submissive" (Griffen 1990, 187) attitude toward God's will. This was mixed with a strong sense of personal responsibility for doing God's work, work it seemed, which was often women's work. Women had constituted the majority of converts throughout the Second Great Awakening and comprised a large majority of all church members. Soon enough (as we have just seen, in chapter 5; see Haynes 1998), women, even conservative Protestant women, would persuade many of their moral superiority, and that the home, the woman's world where men might find respite from a predatory public world, was, next to the church, God's house. Later, these Christian women would argue that "the wider world should be made more like the home" (Griffen 1990, 187). That argument helped persuade many men that women ought to vote and become involved in what before had been an exclusively male domain of governance.

Many Christian women also persuaded many men to convert. Griffen tells us that styles of masculinity among converted, evangelical men varied too. He points out that while abolitionists felt—and were—embattled, small businessmen also struggled to survive, not just political wars but in competitive, unpredictable, unregulated markets as well. Each set of circumstances required somewhat different styles of manhood. Perhaps in part to support each other, abolitionists preached emotional expressivity and commitment to one's fellow man; the businessmen's experience advised suspicion, not trust. Waste not, want not; be wary, keep your plans, and profits, to yourself (Griffen 1990).

Despite these differences in circumstances and styles, and while many businessmen and reformers (some of them clergymen) suffered great anxiety over their individual performances and futures, these turn-of-century middle-class white men suffered no lack of confidence in the power of their religious faith and the superiority of their style of life. Their sense of moral superiority was strengthened when they observed "the abhorrent swaggering rowdiness, heavy drinking, and taste for brutal sports frequent among the antebellum urban working class" (Griffen 1990, 188). Perhaps this relief at the difference between themselves and these lower-class "macho" men helped evangelical men to accept, at least initially, the feminization of their world (Griffen 1990).

Other men were not so accepting. It is possible, Griffen suggests, that concern over what men perceived as a feminization of polite society may have supported an intensifying interest in sports in the 1840s and 1850s among men of the middle and upper classes, religious or not. There was a protracted campaign in the urban press promoting sports as a remedy to softness and vice in the rapidly growing cities. Slowly, the public seemed to accept that a healthy mind and body were related; among educators the mind became perceived as a muscle. By the 1850s, prominent New England men such as Emerson, Edward Everett Hale, and Thomas Wentworth Higginson were promoting a "muscular Christianity" which had appeared earlier in England and which would become popularized in the first decade of the new century as the social gospel (Curtis 1990; see chapter 5, section VIII).

As early as 1859, the *New York Herald* was worrying that "the absence of those athletic and muscle-developing sports so common among the youth of England undoubtedly tended to reduce our young men to effeminacy." By the Civil War, even evangelical men seemed to be thinking of young men's bodies (in terms of morality, of course), as they too joined in the promotion of "innocent" and "rational" recreation (quoted in Griffen 1990, 189). But, Griffen suggests, men were less threatened by a perceived feminization of society and culture than by instabilities of class and ethnicity. The 1890s saw the largest wave of foreign immigration—immigrants from eastern and southern Europe, not England—in American history. And between 1881 and 1905 there were nearly 37,000 strikes, often violent, in which seven million workers (the total work force in 1900 was twenty-nine million) participated. Class war seemed imminent (Bederman 1995a).

"The Civil War," Griffen (1990) asserts, "was a major turning point for middle-class attitudes toward masculinity" (191). I quoted this sentence to open the final section of chapter 4, to suggest that gender shifts among Confederate women—documented so carefully by Drew Faust (1996)—reverberated through Confederate men. But Griffen is thinking more of Yankee men, I believe, as he focuses upon the accommodation of postbellum middle-class men with the emerging world of bureaucratized corporate capitalism. While this economic structure offered many men greater job security, consumer options, and leisure time in more comfortable homes, it also undermined traditional men's sense of independence, the once-dominant fantasy of the "self-made" man. In compensatory fashion, many men now dreamed of male autonomy, adventure, and aggressivity. Carnes and Griffen emphasize that this "new man" did not appear suddenly in the 1890s; rather, the foundations for this new masculinity were being laid in the destabilization and reconstruction of gender that accompanied and followed the Civil War.

The Civil War provoked profound changes in men's sense of themselves as men. In the South, white manhood was defeated, humiliated, and retreated into defensive, often violent racialized and gendered fantasies which functioned, in part, to compensate for Appomattox. But for the victorious as well as the defeated, the Civil War was an ordeal in which men murdered men while in intimate solidarity with men. For that generation, the War was the central event, and it would reverberate for generations. The consequences of the War for national culture, Griffen (1990) writes, "are suggested by the fusion of a previously more pacific evangelical righteousness in the 'Battle Hymn of the Republic' with a martial imagery which would spread everywhere in the Gilded Age, from the Salvation Army to 'captains of industry'" (191). In corporate capitalism camaraderie would become competitive, and the peacetime culture of men became warlike.

Little has been written, Griffen informs us, regarding the influence of the War upon veterans' reentry to civilian life. How pervasive, Carnes and Griffen wonder, was the toughening reported by a young patrician named Oliver Wendell Holmes, Jr., how common was his starker view of life, society, and manliness? Perhaps his antebellum social snobbery was simply strengthened as a result of the War, as after the War he complained about what he perceived as the cowardliness of the lower classes. His conservative social Darwinism had been atypical, but hardly unknown, among postwar men. Clearly within the legal profession the War seems to have hardened an already self-consciously masculinized group (Carnes and Griffen 1990b; Grossberg 1990). In the South, defeat and humiliation shattered some white men's grasp on reality; they retreated into fantasies of muscular young black bucks raping virginal white women (Williamson 1984).

Whether hardening an already "macho" style or toughening what had before been "soft" or leaving men desperate and unhinged, the Civil War functioned to polarize gender. In national politics this gender polarization became explicit; "real" men were presumed to be temperamentally opposite from women. Those who embraced women's domestic values or who spent much time in women's domestic sphere were dismissed by some men as emasculated. Griffen provides two examples of this defensive, compensatory "hypermasculinity," as it functioned in national political campaigns. In 1872, professional politicians ridiculed those patrician reformers who nominated Horace Greeley, and in 1877, Senator Roscoe Conkling went after George William Curtis of *Harper's Weekly,* one of genteel America's favorite writers, dismissing him as one of "the man milliners, the dilettanti, and carpet knights of politics" who "forget that parties are not built up by deportment, or by ladies' magazines, or gush!" Those reformers who were associated with high culture were ridiculed as impractical and ineffectual; for "real" men—which politicians of course claimed to be—"culture is feminine and cultivated men tend to be effeminate" (Griffen 1990, 192).

That philistine and "macho" identification of culture and intellectuality with inadequate masculinization, even feminization, is with us still in this country. One hundred thirty years ago, it extended to the workplace, in a way that has disappeared (as have many working-class occupations) today. For instance, after the Civil War, many men regarded "white collar" work as temporary, required by family hardship, perhaps a business failure. After all, such work was not "manly," especially that white-collar work required in the rapidly expanding federal civil service, the first sexually integrated bureaucracy in America (Carnes and Griffen 1990b). Men's perception of such labor is evident in an 1873 statement which described the government clerk as someone who "has no independence while in office, no manhood. ... He must openly avow his implicit faith in his superior, on pain of dismissal, and must cringe and fawn upon them" (quoted in Griffen 1990, 194).

Such reactionary gender politics could not, as we know, stop the macro-trend toward white-collar work. As Griffen reminds, from boyhood to adulthood, the careers of males over the last quarter of the nineteenth century were characterized by increasing standardization, bureaucratization, and security. But, he believes, reactionary male responses to these long-term trends are insufficient to explain the frequency and intensity of expressions of hypermasculinity from the 1890s to World War I. Long before then, he insists, men and boys of every age sought compensatory excitement and means of escape, vicariously identifying with the exploits and adventures of fictional heroes. Perhaps there is something in men's gender identity development that supports such imaginary identification, resulting in compensatory, defensive, often aggressive styles of self-representation as "men." That is implied in some versions of psychoanalysis, such as object relations theory, as we see in chapters 14 and 15.

The complex and contentious matter of gender formation aside, Carnes and Griffen suggest that more influential than long-term trends in the structure of the workplace were the demands, at the turn of the century, of women, both inside and outside the home. A vocal and visible minority—such as Elizabeth Cady Stanton—explicitly rejected Victorian gender norms and any form of male dominance (Carnes and Griffen 1990b). Some men were shocked, others enraged. Indeed, some men's responses to women's struggle for suffrage became shrill, even hysterical, as we will see later in this chapter. In the South, where women's campaign for suffrage was more muted and racialized, men seemed more focused on other men, especially black men. Hypermasculinity intensified and that male-male "rape" known as lynching reached its zenith in 1892.

In the North, during the Progressive years, hypermasculinity was, Griffen (1990) asserts, "doubly reactive" (200), a response to both long-term change (economic, social, gendered) and to more immediate threats to male dominance such as female suffrage. "There was indeed," he concedes, "anxiety about what seemed to be happening to gender norms and gender relations. But calling it a 'crisis' seems misleading" (200). Why? Carnes and Griffen believe that, in addition to its too summative effect (recall they labor to show the variability of men's masculinity and the ambiguity of its periodization), they offer here that while gender norms and definitions were being revised, they did not end male domination. I'm not sure why Carnes and Griffen think that undermines the "crisis" thesis, as they are here only reminding us that men have lived through "crisis" after "crisis" and somehow managed to retain important and enduring male prerogatives. They further point out that from the 1890s onward many middle-class men were discovering that some initially distressing aspects of women's expanding sphere—as in politics through "municipal housekeeping"—served their own purposes in reforming the public sphere.

Of course, the capacity of men to coopt women's initiatives and rename them as their own hardly refutes the "crisis" hypothesis; it does remind us how resourceful, how compelled, we men are in deflecting, coopting, and reasserting our gendered prerogatives as "men." Still, Carnes and Griffen have succeeded, I believe, in qualifying the "crisis" thesis, requiring its use in quotation marks. But the fact, and Carnes and Griffen do not dispute this, that white men suffered (let us call it for the moment) a gendered anxiety during the last decades of the nineteenth century and the first of the twentieth, conflated as that was for them with racial, political, theological, and economic questions, seems beyond debate. I insist on this point, and I think it clarifies the lynching question by expanding and complicating its historical contextualization.

White men were not only preserving white supremacy, obtaining "summary" or popular justice, responding to deflated cotton prices during off-season lulls in labor; white men were also performing, indirectly, perversely, a kind of gendered breakdown, a "crisis" if you will, in which their own sense of themselves as "men" seemed to be fading before their very eyes, in which a gendered panic, over masturbation and "manhood" itself, set the gender stage for racial terrorism. As Carnes and Griffen seem to think men have done always, they resorted to their fantasy life, and there black men, unacceptable as objects of identification, were the antiheroes in a sadomasochistic (homosexual but heterosexualized) reenactment of their own subjectively experienced "crisis" as "men," albeit in the context of a specific historical moment, in particular regions of the country, in singular circumstances. It was not the case that the black "race" was in retrogression in the late nineteenth century, as white men imagined; it was white men themselves who were regressing. The retrogression was psychosocial and gendered, not racial, and the violence they performed on others reexpressed, I suspect, the violence of their own gender formation as heterosexualized men. This point I explore in theoretical terms in chapter 15.

The OED locates the etymological origins of "crisis" in the Greek "decision" and defines it as a decisive turning point. While a blunt knife, such a definition still cuts through the sedimented layers of "change and continuity" that comprised late nineteenth-century white masculinity. Contemporary views of this "crisis" may be, as Carnes and Griffen (1990) insist, "overblown" (201), but they are not mistaken either. I shall use quotation marks around the term to indicate its tentativeness, to acknowledge historians' difference of opinion regarding its efficacy, but I shall use the term. White men were making a fundamental decision about their identities as men; the decade of the 1890s was, clearly, a "turning point" in the intersecting spheres of gender and "race" in America. Perhaps black men living at that time would understand. In the 1890s, white men's "crisis" meant black men's death.

II. The End of "Romantic" Friendship

> *[I]t appears that a far wider range of male behaviors and gender roles was acceptable during the mid-nineteenth century than a century later.*
>
> —Mark C. Carnes and Clyde Griffen, *Meanings for Manhood: Constructions of Masculinity in Victorian America* (1990)

> *To a surprising degree, mid-nineteenth-century social attitudes permitted great liberty in personal relations, largely untainted by homophobia.*
>
> —Donald Yacovone, "Abolitionists and the 'Language of Fraternal Love'" (1990)

> *The identification of effeminacy with homosexuality was not complete as late as World War I.*
>
> —Mark C. Carnes and Clyde Griffen, *Meanings for Manhood: Constructions of Masculinity in Victorian America* (1990)

Until the "discovery" of "homosexuality" and "heterosexuality" in the late nineteenth century, American men formed intimate friendships with other men, evidently unconcerned about the consequences of these emotionally and often physically intimate relationships for sexual identity. "To be sure," Peter G. Filene (1998) writes, "there were a minority of men, especially in larger cities, who preferred to have sex with other men, behavior that was deemed 'unnatural' and illegal. On the other hand, many men embraced in bed without crossing that line and without shame" (83).

Not only men enjoyed "romantic friendships." Throughout the nineteenth century, a form of female friendship sometimes known as a "Boston marriage" was common. Such a "marriage" involved two women, either living together as a couple or living apart, often each in a marriage, making a vow of fidelity, a declaration that each was for the other the center of her emotional world (Young-Bruehl 1996). As Filene accepts about men in such relationships, Elisabeth Young-Bruehl accepts about women. She writes: "such relationships do not seem to have been sexual (meaning involving genital contact), but they were certainly passionate (as attests the surviving evidence, largely in the form of effusive, unrestrainedly passionate love letters)" (1996, 147). Young-Bruehl also notes that toward the end of the century, when the notion of the "homosexual" became widely accepted, "romantic female friendship virtually ceased, because women in such relationships could not escape the label. They could not be impassioned friends, they had to be lesbians'" (Young-Bruehl 1996, 147). As I wonder about the men, if these were so "innocent," then why did the appearance of the figure of the "lesbian" spell their disappearance?

While the Hungarian physician Karoly Benkert devised the name "homosexual" in 1869, it did take decades before the word came into common usage in America (Young-Bruehl 1996). It was for men, Filene (1998) notes, an indication of middle-class men's intensifying struggle to define what it meant to "be a man." Given the constellation of changes we have chronicled—racial, gendered, socioeconomic—many men found it necessary to draw a more definite boundary line around their gender identity. That would spell the end of physicalized friendships, as "romantic feelings between men became categorized with sexual behavior between men, and both were labeled by doctors and psychologists as signs of degeneracy" (Filene 1998, 83). A man who now felt the need for physical intimacy with another man was deemed an "invert," a woman in the body of a man. During the 1890s, the public began using more colorful and denigrating synonyms—"sissy," "nance," "she-man," and most popular of all, "fairy." Middle-class Victorians had tended to define manliness in contrast to boyishness; now the concept made sense only in contrast to femininity. Beleaguered white men would struggle to fortify their gendered sense of self not only by building their bodies and destroying the bodies of others; they also created a category of person—the homosexual, or "fairy"—to represent their fear of "the woman within" (Filene 1998, 83).

With this "modernization of sex" at the end of the nineteenth century—Freud is, of course, the most memorable name associated with the phenomenon—white men lost that innocence of intimate same-sex relationships they had before enjoyed. (It is an "innocence" Leslie Fielder will examine in the context of black/white male intimacies, work to which we turn in chapter 18.) While Freud was the most important, there were a number of students of sexuality—"sexologists" they were popularly called, such as Havelock Ellis—who detached sexuality from friendship, and thereby made of it a separate sphere of increasing significance for mental health, even "identity." The fundamental shifts in thinking about sex which Freud and others both reflected and instigated were intertwined with other fundamental social, racial, gender, and economic transformations in the West, especially in Great Britain and the United States. Time-honored practices of sexualized friendships were destroyed forever, replaced by modern "sexual liberation" with its emphasis upon sexual experience stripped from friendship and relationship (Yacovone 1998).

Almost overnight, it seems from the point of view of today, sex became key to individual identity, and sexuality became profoundly politicized. "Homosexuals" and "heterosexuals" appeared—although there had evidently been communities of those whose lives were organized around same-sex desire for centuries—and the battle began. What our immersion in the present—including until recently our uncritical acceptance of these categories—obscures is the apparent universality of the yearning to be close to those whose bodies resemble one's own. The suppression of this yearning, intensified by its intermingling racial, economic, and gendered "crisis," was probably a factor in white men's racial politics and violence, including the practice of lynching. The extreme and intense instability of "manhood" as it was narrowed, stylized, and suppressed was expressed variously, including racially. If white men could no longer touch themselves or each other—masturbation as well as intimate physical friendships were suppressed—they could damn well "touch"—that is, castrate and mutilate—black men. In the name, of course, of protecting their "ladies."

Although scholars remain divided over the character and role of "homosexuality" in ancient Greek society (see, for instance, Halperin 1990), Donald Yacovone suggests that Plato's *Symposium* was the first to name the bonds of fraternal love. Serving as a model for centuries to come, the *Symposium* suggested how the intimate relationships of society's "best men" functioned as the homoerotic foundation for Greek culture. Society, Plato argued, was held together by the spiritual, intellectual, and physical bonds between men, bonds more powerful than even those found in "heterosexual" marriage. Male friends became "married by a far nearer tie and have a closer friendship than those who beget mortal children" (quoted in Yacovone 1998, 196). The Romans (Yacovone names Cicero as the key figure) extended Greek ideas of fraternal love, regarding them as spiritual bonds based on moral virtue, expressed in passionate intellectual exchanges as well as in homoerotic relationships (Yacovone 1998).

The next major moment in this (abbreviated) narrative of fraternal love in the West Yacovone names as Christian. Agape, or divinely inspired love, inspired especially the early Christians and, more than any other single factor, he argues, fashioned men's friendships for a millennium: "A spiritual union untainted by carnal desire, the idea of fraternal love helped define personal identity and Christian character" (Yacovone 1998, 196). To illustrate, he points to biblical verses, for instance, 2 Samuel 1:26: "Thy love to me was wonderful, passing the love of women," and 1 John 4:12: "Greater love hath no man than this, that a man lay down his life for his friends." Yacovone finds a strong consistency of language depicting fraternal love in the writings of Americans from the Puritan settlement until the second decade of the twentieth century. Despite age, race, class, geographic location, or occupation, freed of the homosexual/heterosexual binary, American men, Yacovone (1998) argues, felt free to form friendships of emotional intensity and physical affection.

The ideal of fraternal love was no mere passing phase of youth and amounted to "a pervasive cultural ideal." More than the "traditional manly virtues" of independence, force, will, control, and power, fraternal love was, in the nineteenth century, "the true measure of a man." Just as the nineteenth century saw the formation of a sentimentalized ideal of womanhood, there was as well a sentimentalized ideal of manhood, documented in both private and public correspondence and also by lithographers and photographers. In this historical evidence Yacovone finds forms of male-male relations "completely at odds with our understanding of what constitutes a man" (quoted in Yacovone 1998, 197).

To illustrate, Yacovone quotes from correspondence between Virgil Maxy and William Blanding, students at Brown University (classes of 1801 and 1804, respectively). In one letter, Maxy asked his friend: "Do you kick up any dust there or is the ground frozen too hard?" Maxy reports that he met a young woman in Woonsocket, Rhode Island, whom he "squeezed as much as I pleased" and felt "her pretty little legs last night." But Maxy clearly misses his friend, joking with him that he had slept with a stranger the previous evening who told him that "I hugged him all night. I woke up several times and found both my arms right around him." He writes that sleeping alone is no fun as "I get to hug the pillow instead of you." Making explicit the sexual dimension of the friendship, Maxy teases Blanding that "sometimes I think I have got hold of your doodle when in reality I have hold of the bed post" (quoted in Yacovone 1998, 200–201). The custom of sharing beds by members of the same sex, although now raising questions (certainly after pubescence) about one's sexual identity, was, Yacovone asserts, standard behavior among all classes for hundreds of years. Especially for those away from family, such as travelers or craft apprentices, the interest in finding a same-sex bedmate was strong, in part because those who preferred to sleep alone were the ones who raised suspicion (Yacovone 1998).

Denied access to almost all white colleges and universities during the nineteenth century, African-American men established their own schools and learned societies, such as Philadelphia's Banneker Institute, founded in 1854. The friendships formed in these organizations, like those at white institutions, were often long-lasting. Additionally, for African Americans, such bonds helped deflect white racism. "Give my love to everybody," the black abolitionist Parker T. Smith wrote to fellow Banneker Institute member Jacob C. White, Jr., "and consider yourself as entitled to the largest share." Traveling in Canada in 1862, Smith was unembarrassed to communicate his longing for White: "I want to see you so bad that I would almost live upon one meal a day if by that means I could accomplish an end so desirable." White, Smith declared, "is to me a friend, and I shall love him as long as I live" (quoted in Yacovone 1998, 201).

Interracial loving friendships were uncommon during the nineteenth century, but they did exist, including the well-known preference of abolitionist leader William Lloyd Garrison for Boston black men. Frederick Douglass was not timid in expressing his "never failing love" for the New York abolitionist Gerrit Smith. Founder of the Oneida Institute, Beriah Green, extolled the virtues of Amos G. Berman, a future black leader; he had (Green said) "won the confidence, secured the love, and raised the hopes of his affectionate instructors." During the Civil War, African-American soldiers sometimes expressed their appreciation to those whites who helped them in their struggle for equal pay. A black noncommissioned officer in the Fifty-fifth Massachusetts Regiment, James Monroe Trotter, told Edward W. Kinsley, a military advisor to Governor John A. Andrew, that the men of his regiment "all send their love to you." In the famous Fifty-fourth Massachusetts Regiment, acclaimed for its heroism at Battery Wagner, South Carolina, in 1863, it was common practice for an enlisted man to present his white officer with "a bouquet of flowers." During his travels along the California coast, Richard Henry Dana formed close friendships with several Hawaiian sailors that were "such as I never felt before but for a near relative." Dana became especially close to one Hawaiian named Hope. "During the four months that I lived upon the beach, we were continually together, both in work, and in our excursions in the woods, and upon the water." Dana experienced "a strong affection for him, and preferred him to any of my own countrymen" (quoted in Yacovone 1998, 201–202).

The nineteenth century saw not one, but several styles or phases of masculinity, especially as men entered what was experienced by many as a "crisis" of masculinity. Victorian sex roles, Yacovone tells us, "proliferated, not narrowed." For every instance of hypermasculinity, there are many of "gushing sentimentality." For the socially ambitious, the nineteenth-century masculine ideal was far more likely to be the "civilized" gentleman rather than the frontier warrior, and indeed Theodore Roosevelt and others who embraced the West did so, it would seem, to compensate for their effete urban upbringings. For the middle class, "sensitivity and sentiment distinguished the crude and uncultured from the noble and worthy" (quoted in Yacovone 1998, 202). At least since the eighteenth century, the American upper classes had demanded refinement and elegance in both men and women (Yacovone 1998).

For many, one index of manly strength of character was their ability to be affectionate with other (white) men. Nineteenth-century correspondence and photography often reveals the degree of intimacies between same-sexed friends. To illustrate, Yacovone recalls that the early Garrisonian abolitionist, feminist, and Unitarian clergyman, Samuel Joseph May (who, as we will soon see, was also "friends" with Garrison), met his lifelong friend, the naturalist and educator George B. Emerson, while studying at Harvard. When the two discovered they had been born on the same day, their intimacy intensified. In one photograph of the two, May and Emerson reveal their love by their engrossing gaze at each other, not to mention their physical touching. In another case of fraternal love, future president James Buchanan and William R. D. King of Alabama made no secret of their affections for each other. They were well known about Washington as the "Siamese twins" or as "he and she" by those less sympathetic. Lincoln's rival Stephen A. Douglas enjoyed the affections of Urban Linder, who maintained that he loved Douglas "with the love that Jonathan had for David." His openness about the relationship suggests the degree of nineteenth-century acceptance of male emotional and physical intimacy. For Douglas, Linder swooned, [I have a] "love that passeth the love of woman" (quoted in Yacovone 1998, 207). While common to many nineteenth-century men regardless of their politics, romantic friendship seemed especially intense among abolitionist men.

Abolitionist Love

Friendships among male abolitionists were often physically affectionate and, Donald Yacovone (1990) suggests, "nearly identical to the complex reactions of some nineteenth-century women" (85). Might we think of these men as "women-identified"? Was—is—there any relationship between being a racial progressive and a gender progressive? Certainly I do not wish to suggest something monolithic or universal, something opposite to a sexually repressed and politically reactionary "authoritarian personality" (Adorno 1950). Not only racial progressives enjoyed "romantic friendships." As we saw in chapter 4, men in the slaveholding South also enjoyed physical friendships. It is curious, however, that some number of abolitionists and settlement house workers (as we see in the next section) were physically free with their same-sex friends and students. The freedom with which many abolitionists expressed their love and devotion, and the frank, even ritualistic, nature of their relationships, poses intriguing questions about sexuality and politics (Yacovone 1990; Hampden-Turner 1968; Young-Bruehl 1996).

Certainly some racially progressive men were also skeptical of conventional gender arrangements. Recall that abolitionism and feminism had been, until 1866, politically intertwined. For the most committed members of those Boston-based abolitionists allied with William Lloyd Garrison, for instance, the discourse of fraternal love also communicated their rejection of traditional bifurcations of gender, and reflected a notion of Christian social androgyny that sought a fundamental restructuring of American society. Many saw themselves as early Christians, withdrawing from a "corrupt church" to preach an antislavery gospel (Yacovone 1990, 87). The abolitionist newspaper, the *Liberator,* expressed abolitionists' strong sense of fraternal unity, comforting persecuted colleagues. "O! how I long to stand by your side, and the rest of the lion-hearted host that are battling for the rights of man," one man wrote to his "dear and deeply loved Garrison" (quoted in Yacovone 1990, 88). For Garrison, founder of the New England Anti-Slavery Society in 1831 and the American Anti-Slavery Society in 1833 and publisher of the *Liberator*, traditional and aggressive forms of manhood were very much associated with women's subjugation. In his speech to the Fourth Woman's Rights Convention in Cleveland in 1853, Garrison declared: "I believe that man had done this through calculation, accentuated by a spirit of spite, *a desire for domination which has made him degrade woman* in her own eyes, and thereby tend to make her a mere vassal" (quoted in Kimmel 1996, 71, emphasis in original).

Garrison was not the only prominent abolitionist to acknowledge the conflations of race and gender. Frederick Douglass also linked abolitionism to women's struggle for full equality. Critics discerned the betrayal of hegemonic masculinity contained in that stance; they insisted that support of women's rights indicated a failure of manhood. For instance, the Syracuse newspapers dismissed Douglass as an "Aunt Nancy Man" in an editorial the week after his speech at the Seneca Falls Convention, and other pro-women men were ridiculed as "manmilliners" and "Miss-Nancys." The next year the *Syracuse Daily Star* declared:

> The poor creatures who take part in the silly rant of "brawling women" and Aunt Nancy men, are most of the "ismizers" of the rankest stamp, Abolitionists of the most frantic and contemptible kind, and Christian sympathizers with such heretics as Wm. Lloyd Garrison. ... These men are all Woman's Righters, and preachers of such damnable doctrines and accursed heresies, as would make demons of the pit shudder to hear. (quoted in Kimmel 1996, 71)

Just as progressives in the 1950s and 1960s would be dismissed as "pinko commie fags," one hundred years earlier support for women's rights and opposition to slavery also meant one was not a "man." The *New York Daily World* dismissed abolitionist profeminist men as "crack-brained, rheumatic, dyspeptic, henpecked men, vainly striving to achieve the liberty to open their heads in the presence of their wives" (quoted in Kimmel 1996, 72).

Abolitionists declined to take this "lying down." In fact, there were those who tossed the same stones back; Wendell Phillips, for instance, characterized slavery's supporters as "cringing wretches." Garrison declared that it took "a virile Christian manliness" to fight against slavery (quoted phrases in Kimmel 1996, 72). Such an exchange of gendered insults, Kimmel (1996) observes, illustrates a theme that courses throughout American history, namely that when white men declare their support for feminism or civil rights other white men—and some women—judge them as less than manly. It is "as if support for inequality made one *more* of a man" (Kimmel 1996, 72, emphasis in original). Perhaps there *is* something to the notion of an "authoritarian personality."

There were comforts for these beleaguered defenders of women's and African-American rights. These were physical as well as psychological comforts. Abolitionist friends sometimes imagined themselves as nineteenth-century versions of the Bible's David and Jonathan. Isaac T. Hopper, a Quaker abolitionist, knew that he had loved his friend Joseph Whithall since childhood. "I think it will not be extravagant if I say that my soul was knit with his soul, as Jonathan's was to David's." A friend of Lysander Spooner's described Spooner as "delightful to meet and beautiful to look upon." Wendell Phillips communicated his love for New Hampshire abolitionist editor Nathaniel Rogers in the frankest terms. A biblically minded Oliver Johnson described one Garrisonian colleague as embodying "the courage of Paul with the lovingness of John." Within these biblically referenced bonds of abolitionism, men could "look upon one another's countenances, and be glad" (quoted phrases in Yacovone 1990, 88). Antislavery colleagues remarked that Garrison and Rogers seemed as merged, as if Siamese twins (Yacovone 1990).

Perhaps the most visible and celebrated abolitionist friendship was that of Garrison and the Unitarian abolitionist minister Samuel Joseph May. May had joined Garrison at the very beginning of the radical antislavery movement in 1830 and remained close to him until May's death in 1871. Within a few months of having met, they addressed each other as "beloved friend" and "brother." Frederick Douglass saw "something truly admirable in the devotion of Mr. May to Mr. Garrison. Never were two men more dissimilar, yet never was one man, apparently, more devotedly attached to another than is Mr. May to Mr. Garrison" (quoted in Yacovone 1990, 89). In 1852, Garrison expressed his feelings for May in poetic form:

Friend of mankind! For thee I fondly cherish
Th' exuberance of a brother's glowing love
And never in my memory shall perish
Thy name or worth.
(quoted in Yacovone 1990, 89)

Never wanting to be far from the sight of him, Garrison kept May's photograph in his study.

May was not exactly "monogamous," however. He became close with a number of his Harvard classmates. For instance, May spent hours singing with Benjamin Fessenden. "We were wedded to each other not only by a true friendship, but by our mutual love of song. Our voices harmonized perfectly." Another classmate, John D. Wells, was, May said, "pure as distilled water, and affectionate as a woman. I sometimes felt really 'in love with him'" (quoted in Yacovone 1990, 90). May might well serve as an example of a racial progressive who understood that in the struggle for racial equality, gender was key. May strongly supported women's rights; in fact, he was the nation's first minister to advocate the enfranchisement of women (Yacovone 1990).

While the more conservative religious abolitionists may not have become self-conscious gender radicals, they nonetheless seemed to enjoy intimacies with other men, what Yacovone (1990) terms the "'feminized' ritual practices ... of Garrisonian fraternal love" (91). In 1825, the forty-four-year-old British abolitionist Charles Stuart became involved with Theodore Dwight Weld, then fifteen years old. The two exchanged letters expressing their love for each other over many years. On one occasion Stuart told the young man: "You are mine and I am yours. God made us one from the beginning." Their affection simultaneously joined them to one another and to "our Lord, forever" (quoted in Yacovone 1990, 87–88).

After visiting him in 1828, Stuart told Weld: "Adieu, my Theodore, dearer than any ties of blood could make you. ... My soul parts once more to embrace you" (quoted in Yacovone 1990, 91). When Stuart learned that Weld had become an abolitionist, the Englishman's racial politics became intertwined with his passion for Weld. "I long to hear of your being engaged in the sacred cause of Negro emancipation. My soul thirsts after you, beloved Theodore." The feelings were mutual, as Weld confided to his fiancée, Angela Grimké: "I can hardly trust myself to speak or write of him: so is my whole being seized with love and admiration of his most worthy character" (quoted in Yacovone 1990, 92).

Personality conflicts and ideological differences undermined abolitionist unity after 1837. Garrisonian abolitionists advocated women's rights and sought to grant women full membership in abolitionist societies. Conservative abolitionists decried this position as a perversion of women's presumably divinely ordained roles as mother and wife in a separate domestic sphere. Other conservatives insisted that gender had nothing to do with race, and these men bitterly opposed the introduction of such "extraneous" issues into the antislavery movement. Complicating these differences was Garrison's commitment to nonresistance. This position alienated many who were sure that only aggressive political activism would bring about emancipation. Thus the antislavery unity evident at the founding meeting of the American Anti-Slavery Society in 1833 shattered in disagreement. The movement was further splintered, Yacovone (1990) suggests, by the intensity of these men's relationships with each other, meaning that tactical and ideological disputes were merged with felt senses of personal betrayal. In this regard, the intensity and intimacy of male-male abolitionist relationships contributed to the dissolution of the American Anti-Slavery Society in 1840.

The famous Victorian preacher Henry Ward Beecher was also drawn to younger men. As a young man, Beecher had entered into a loving "covenant" with a "Byronic Greek boy" (Yacovone 1990, 93) named Constantine F. Newell. Beecher regarded their relationship as a marriage vow. As an adult, Beecher became involved with the New York editor and reformer Theodore Tilton. Until the famous post–Civil War Beecher-Tilton sex scandal, which destroyed their relationship, the two men were passionately in love with each other. When Beecher traveled to England, Tilton described Beecher's letters as "so many kisses. ... Send me some more! ... I toss you a bushel of flowers and a mouthful of kisses." Tilton regularly and frankly communicated his feeling for Beecher, including how he longed to gaze into Beecher's eyes. The two kissed whenever they met or parted. On one occasion, Tilton's wife Elizabeth discovered Beecher nestled in her husband's lap discussing the Sermon on the Mount. As Elizabeth approached, Beecher rose and greeted her with a kiss, then resumed his position (Yacovone 1990).

The physical and emotional intimacies shared by the liberal clergy, abolitionists, and other men who lived, as Yacovone (1990) puts it, "comfortably at the margins of their culture" (93) gave them strength to carry on. But there is no "progressive personality" here, at least not neat and simple, as the abolitionists' enemies, those antebellum southern intellectuals and defenders of slavery, also became passionately involved with each other. Men's letters to each other were often signed, "Yours lovingly." "Let me hear from you soon and lovingly," William Gilmore Simms begged Nathaniel Beverley Tucker, "for ... [this] sort of nourishment is ... ever necessary to the intellect as well as the affections." Another prominent proslavery southerner, James H. Hammond, confided to Tucker that Tucker's letters were "part of my sustenance" (quoted in Yacovone 1990, 93).

Yacovone asserts that these men were not "getting it on." He insists that when we contextualize these intimacies, we must understand they cannot be, in any contemporary sense, "queer." He points out that nineteenth-century men understood and rejected homosexual acts, even if they did not know the phrase and had no consciousness of a homosexual identity. He reminds us that the concept "homosexual" did not appear until the 1860s, and as late as 1920s, there was no consensus concerning its definition. Sodomy or bestiality were the nineteenth-century terms of choice, and these were not reserved specifically for male-male activity. Yacovone criticizes those who superimpose current conceptions upon a different era. "In their legitimate quest to recover a usable past," he writes, "many historians of gay and lesbian life have distorted our view of pre-modern and pre-Freudian sexuality and culture by mistaking the language of religious ecstasy and sincerity, or agape, for homoeroticism or outright homosexuality" (Yacovone 1990, 94). Moreover, our

> preoccupation with elemental sex says more about the twentieth century than about the nineteenth. The love that bonded antislavery leaders like William Lloyd Garrison and Samuel Joseph May, or Henry Ward Beecher and Theodore Tilton, was not secret or latent homoerotic desire but the expression of a Christian tradition that originated in the "rapturous union of man and God." (Yacovone 1990, 94)

Furthermore, Yacovone (1990) insists that not even those men who were physically intimate with each other can be assumed to have been, in any contemporary sense, "sexual." He points out that nineteenth-century romanticism, a sexually segregated culture, plus the legacy of previous centuries, in which privacy in its contemporary sense simply did not exist for most, rendered emotional intimacy and physical contact "normal." He reminds that from the earliest years of childhood, males shared beds (as they had for centuries) and that they shared beds on through adulthood, "without homoerotic desire or the suspicion of homoerotic intent" (94). Regardless of social class or geographic region, men slept together, especially during illness or personal tragedies. Samuel J. May, Yacovone tells us, tested his nonresistance ideals by sleeping "with a maniac" who had threatened to kill him and his family. After his wife died in 1865, May called upon a neighbor, "Freddy," to serve as "my bedfellow," even though May's daughter and son-in-law already lived in the same house (quoted in Yacovone 1990, 94).

How does Yacovone *know* that men who slept together did so "without homoerotic desire or the suspicion of homoerotic intent"? Certainly he cannot rely on that documentation furnished by the men themselves. Knowing that "bestiality" and "sodomy" were sins guaranteed that respectable men, let alone those committed to what for them were quasireligious causes such as emancipation, would not be forthcoming about their motives. While the concept of homosexuality was not in use, there is a throughline between then and now: men know that genital contact with each other is condemned by many. That hardly stops "straight" men from occasionally "fooling around" today, and I suspect it didn't then. There is an overly fastidious quality to Yacovone's—and Griffen's in the previous section—insistence that these guys were not getting off with each other that stems, I suspect, from a homophobia within the profession. Of course these men were not "homosexual" in any twentieth-century sense. But that hardly guarantees that they did nothing more than sleep when they were in bed together.

The Love of War

Massachusetts congressman Leverett Saltonstall knew what many nineteenth-century Americans valued in a man. While to us his description seems rather gay, for many Victorians it was simply, as we've been told many times, the manly ideal. "I was extremely pleased with him," Saltonstall exclaimed, referring to the Whig vice-presidential candidate Theodore Frelinghuysen. "He is very gentle—manly and interesting." No doubt, congressman. Ralph Waldo Emerson took pleasure in the fact that his friend Charles Newcomb had the face of a girl and the aplomb of a general; he praised Henry James, Sr., as personifying a fusion of womanly qualities and "heroic manners" (quoted in Yacovone 1998, 207). The Transcendentalist Amos Bronson Alcott was clear that he did not like men who failed to remind him "of the graces proper to women." The "Hermaphrodite," Emerson said simply, "is then the symbol of the finished soul" (quoted in Yacovone 1998, 209). In these statements it is clear that many nineteenth-century Americans—not only abolitionists—took for granted what to us today seems like androgyny and/or bisexuality (Yacovone 1998). Then the two states of mind and body were evidently indistinguishable.

Sometimes remembered as coldly intellectual, Ralph Waldo Emerson formed several close relationships with other men; he praised same-sex friendship as a spiritual union. "A good man," he declared, was the "best revelation of God that can be" (quoted in Yacovone 1998, 208). During the 1820s, Ralph Waldo Emerson became infatuated with his Harvard College classmate, Martin Gay. About 1821, Emerson composed a private poem to his beloved (whom, for privacy's sake, he called Malcomb):

> Malcomb, I love thee more than women love
> And pure and warm and equal is [?] the feeling
> Which binds as one our destinies forever
> But there are seasons in the change of times
> When strong excitement kindles up the light
> Of ancient memories.
> (Yacovone 1990, 90)

Recalling both Plato and Swedenborg, Emerson linked friendship with marriage, although he thought friendship the higher bond. "The perceptions of a soul, its wondrous progeny," Emerson held, "are born by the conversation, the marriage of souls." Henry David Thoreau felt similarly. "In his world," Thoreau wrote, "every man would be a poet—love would reign—Beauty would take place—Man and Nature would harmonize" (quoted in Yacovone 1998, 208).

Revered in America as well as in England, the British poet Alfred Tennyson conveyed poetically the androgynous and fraternal ideals of the period. *In Memoriam*, one critic pointed out, is "one of the greatest series of love poems in the English language." Recall that Tennyson's poetry was written about another man. Odd from our point of view that *In Memoriam* was one of the most popular works of poetry in Britain and the United States; Queen Victoria said it was for her second in significance only to the Bible. Such appreciation for bonds between men is unimaginable to us, imprisoned as we are in rigid homophobic gender binaries. But one hundred years ago Tennyson could without hesitation refer to his friend Arthur Hallam as "My Arthur," "Dearest," "My love," the "man I held as half divine," and "mine, mine, for ever mine" (quoted in Yacovone 1998, 208). The domestic imagery he evoked by characterizing their relationship as a marriage was hardly unique, as we will see in chapter 18. Indeed, it was not uncommon for nineteenth-century men to imagine themselves married—to each other, that is—and this fact is narrated in American literature ranging from Herman Melville to Walt Whitman and Mark Twain (Yacovone 1998; Fielder 1966, 1948/1995).

We have seen how during the Civil War, Confederate troops—men's whose manliness was defeated by victorious northern men and by shifting gender roles in the South—explored cross-dressing. On occasion, evidently, so did Union troops. Yacovone narrates an incident at Brandy Station, Virginia, where Yankee troops organized a grand ball. Uninterested in the available women, the men manufactured their own females by cross-dressing their younger comrades—drummer boys were a favorite—as women. "I'll bet you could not tell them from the girls if you did not know them," one soldier wrote home. Some "looked almost good enough to lay with and I guess some of them did get layed with," the soldier mused. "I know I slept with mine," he informed his wife (quoted in Yacovone 1998, 209). Few wives today would receive such news as calmly as evidently this soldier expected his wife to receive his. But then the wife would not understand the event as announcing her husband was gay, only that he was sharing a bed with a younger man. This practice was understood as necessary, not only due to loneliness, but to a shortage of sleeping accommodations during wartime, and, in peacetime, due to cold temperatures (Yacovone 1998).

The Civil War, like any war, was an affair between men, although it is women and children who suffer and die as a consequence of these exercises in hypermasculine madness. Yacovone (1998) declares that "the war did not alter antebellum views of manhood," adding "if anything, it heightened them" (209). From Faust's research (chapter 4), I suspect this is overstatement. Certainly for southern white men, the massive shattering of dreams for (masculine, civic) independence, the shifts in southern white women's roles and experience, and the emancipation of slaves all contributed to a destabilization in gender, and, two decades later, a "crisis" in white masculinity, a phenomenon Yacovone discusses later in his essay. The second half of his statement hints at this point, noting that the horror of war heightened what we might term an androgynous manhood, an intensification due to destabilization I would suggest. To illustrate, Yacovone reproduces a photograph of officers from a Massachusetts regiment which explicitly conveys a physical and emotional intimacy that seems astonishing (see Yacovone 1998).

Correspondence, as well as photography, documents that in war men become close to each other, especially in the face of death. In the Civil War the intensity of wartime friendships is illustrated by the story of Colonel James E. Mallon of the Forty-second New York regiment. Due to the proximity of enemy troops, Mallon was repeatedly warned not to visit a comrade in the nearby Twentieth Massachusetts. A fellow officer begged Mallon to stay put and forget his friend for the night. "No, I cannot stand the suspense," he answered, rising to go. But the moment he left cover, a Confederate bullet struck him down. His friend, Henry Livermore Abbott, was brokenhearted when he learned the news. "I loved him almost as a brother and while his eyes were glazing and he could no longer see me," Abbott wrote, "he told me of his friendship" (quoted passages in Yacovone 1998, 210–211).

Yacovone (1998) also tells the story of Colonel Robert Gould Shaw, the Boston Brahmin who led the Fifty-fourth Massachusetts Regiment, the famed all-black Union army regiment. For members of New England's upper class, Shaw embodied the innate heroism of an aristocratic *noblesse oblige,* calming a "deep-seated anxiety among the members of the cultivated classes about their own ability ... to meet some undefined challenge" (Frederickson 1965, 156; quoted in Kimmel 1996, 74). While hardly fighting fears of effeminacy by going to war, free black men also appreciated the relation between war and manliness, understood that the sublimated phallus of civic manhood was long and hard. "This was the biggest thing that ever happened in my life," confessed one former slave. "I feel like a man with a uniform and a gun in my hand" (quoted in Kimmel 1996, 74).

Before leading the Fifty-fourth, while still a member of the Second Massachusetts, Shaw learned that his dear friend Henry Sturgis Russell had been captured and imprisoned in Richmond. Shaw missed Russell so intensely that he considered surrendering to the Rebels in hopes of being imprisoned with him. "I never knew till now, how much his society had been to me this last year, nor how much I loved him," he recorded. When Shaw came upon the body of another friend struck down at Cedar Mountain, he "stooped down and kiss[ed] him." Shaw was not being exceptionally affectionate. When he served in the Seventh New York at the beginning of the War, his regiment marched down New York's Broadway before leaving for Washington. Evidently a handsome man, Shaw "was seized and kissed by man after man" as he tried to stay in step with his regiment. When he led the Fifty-fourth through Boston before its departure for battles in the South, one of Shaw's uncles broke free from the crowd and reached up for his nephew on his horse. Shaw leaned over "and kissed him before the crowd as naturally as he would have done at home" (quoted in Yacovone 1998, 211).

Shaw was a hit with many men. "He was like a day in June," Henry Lee Higginson wrote of him, "sweet, wholesome, vigorous, breezy." John Chipman Gray, Jr., who disliked Shaw's politics (specifically his abolitionism) nevertheless lamented his death at Battery Wagner. He remembered Shaw as "a very loveable man and ... a great loss." Shaw's field commander, General George Crockett Strong, who later died of wounds sustained at Wagner, took time to write his own sentiments about Shaw to his parents in a letter widely reprinted in the northern press. "I had but little opportunity to be with him," Strong wrote after Shaw's death, "but I already loved him. No man ever went more gallantly into battle. None knew him but to love him" (quoted in Yacovone 1998, 211).

Evidently many women accepted and some even promoted what seems a rather queered version of male-male relations. The black diarist Charlotte Forten was struck by Shaw's feminine virtues. "What purity, what nobleness of soul, what exquisite gentleness in that beautiful face!" she recorded. "As I look at it I think 'the bravest are the tenderest.'" After his death leading the Fifty-fourth Massachusetts Regiment, friends and family were overcome with grief. Lydia Maria Child exclaimed: "So good, so conscientious, so gentle and refined, and withal so brave!" (quoted passages in Yacovone 1998, 211).

By the 1880s men were going into "crisis" over who they were, who women were, what the world was. As Yacovone (1998) puts it: "The last two decades of the century saw vast change in the social construction of gender across the United States and in Europe. Men began to turn away from the fraternal, androgynous ideal" (213). To illustrate, he points to Harvard's Charles Eliot Norton whose intensifying misogyny was accompanied by what today we would call an increasing homophobia, as he published heavily expurgated editions of men's letters stripped of any erotic suggestion. Not exactly "examples of brawny manhood" (Yacovone 1998, 213), George Santayana and Henry James (characteristically universalizing men's experience as that of the "age") helped lead the assault on this "feminine ... nervous, hysterical, challenging, canting age, an age of hollow phrases and false delicacy and exaggerated solicitudes and coddled sensibilities" (quoted in Yacovone 1998, 213–214).

Those generations of American men who came of age in the shadow of the Civil War were sometimes haunted by their elders' heroism and sacrifices, memorialized by the many monuments that punctuated the landscape, and embodied in the empty sleeves and crutches constantly seen on the streets.

Perhaps Theodore Roosevelt symbolized this generation who venerated those men who had fought to restore the union, but he overlooked "their romantic masculinity," and in so doing—in parallel fashion to the pure womanhood ideal—made their fathers imaginary, "marble men," icons of what the younger generation thought it must live up to but knew it could not. Men of Roosevelt's generation were constantly compared—often unfavorably—to those men who had fought in the Civil War. They themselves found their debt unpayable and their manhood wanting. "Our fathers," Roosevelt fantasized in his widely read *The Strenuous Life,* were men with "iron in their blood" who restored the American nation. Their fathers had achieved so much, and Roosevelt urged his generation to prove themselves worthy: "Let us, the children of the men who proved themselves equal to the mighty days, let us, the children of the men who carried the great Civil War to a triumphant conclusion, praise the God of our fathers that the ignoble counsels of peace were rejected ... and the years of strife endured" (quoted in Yacovone 1998, 214).

So in addition to multiple shifts in the public sphere—economic, racial, political—and gendered shifts at home and in the church, young men of the 1880s and 1890s also felt pressure to achieve (despite very different circumstances) the same degree of heroism ascribed to the Civil War generation. They suspected, at least semi-consciously, that nothing they did could ever equal the magnitude of their fathers' accomplishment. Remembering the now mythic Robert Gould Shaw in 1897, William James reminded Americans that "no future problem can be like that problem. No task laid on our children can compare in difficulty with the task with which their fathers have to deal." The memory of the War must inspire American men, "so that we," Roosevelt declared, "may not fall below the level reached by our fathers." The dirty little war that was the Spanish-American imperialist fiasco was meant, however pathetically, as evidence that the sons could be as courageous as their fathers. Those who opposed the War were in a word unmanly, "weaklings unfit," Roosevelt thundered, "to invoke the memories of the stalwart men who fought to a finish the great Civil War" (quoted in Yacovone 1998, 214).

If northern white men compared unfavorably to their mythic predecessors, southern white men no doubt felt even less worthy. After all, they were the sons of defeated men, men who had failed to gain independence, to protect their women, hold onto their property, that is, slaves. Recall from chapter 4 that gendered imagery and language were used to praise Union soldiers for their masculine triumph, while southerners—personified in the president of the Confederacy, Jefferson Davis—were demeaned as not quite men. After all, Davis was a "President in Petticoats" (quoted in O'Leary 1996, 59), a symbol of a defeated and now feminized Confederacy. Numerous songs, cartoons, and newspaper drawings had depicted Davis cross-dressed as a woman fleeing in "feminine fear" before the victorious advance of manly Union soldiers. Nothing could be more insulting to a defeated southern manhood (O'Leary 1996).

Horrified and humiliated, many southern white men rushed to identify with the triumphant United States of America. Even today one finds the most extreme and compensatory expressions of "patriotism" among white southern men. A number of Confederate veterans joined the American army during the Indian wars, as the army pursued a strategy of annihilation toward Plains Indians who declined to be herded onto reservations. Within a month of General Custer's defeat in 1876 at the battle of Little Bighorn, a number of southern veterans volunteered to fight the new common enemy. "As this is the Centennial year of American independence," wrote a former Confederate soldier from Kentucky, "I desire to let the world see that we who were once soldiers of the 'lost cause' are not deficient in patriotism." He asked his congressional representative from Kentucky to offer President Grant the "services of a full regiment, composed exclusively of ex-Confederates to avenge Custer's death" (quoted in O'Leary 1996, 57).

By the time of the Spanish-American War, southern men had nearly completed their disavowal of themselves, fleeing to an imaginary identification with what was now "their" nation once again. When they did speak of the Civil War, they conveniently ignored its treasonous motive and goal, emphasizing instead the courage of Confederate troops. By emphasizing valor and courage, rather than treason, white southerners provided the country with an interpretation of the Civil War that effaced the fact of their assault on the Union and allowed them to imagine themselves as patriotic, as men. The North played along, and in fewer than fifty years, the memory of the Civil War and the tenets of patriotism had been sufficiently revised so that Confederates were now remembered as loyal sons rather than as defeated and demasculinized traitors (O'Leary 1996).

What "caused" the disappearance of "romantic friendship" at the close of the nineteenth century? Yacovone (1990) points to the rise of European imperialism and the aggressive cult of American masculinity during the Gilded Age. Nineteenth-century "feminized male ideals" dissolved in the gender reactionary politics of men determined to remain "men," a determination which stimulated them, among other things, to keep women and African Americans from voting. They were determined to stay "white" and "masculine," via bodybuilding, initiation rituals in misogynist fraternal orders, and a near obsession with sports, especially boxing and football. These gender politics became national politics, evident in President Theodore Roosevelt's emphasis on will, determination, fierce physical activity, and military honor. All functioned to create the illusion, for both southern and northern white men, of a true-blue all-American hypermasculinity. At the center of this gendered Darwinism was a notion of struggle and conquest, a notion with its own racialized and sexualized shadows. Manly honor was to be achieved in honest, strenuous effort. "Far better it is to dare mighty things, to win glorious triumphs, even though checkered by failure," Roosevelt declared, "than to take rank with those poor spirits who neither enjoy much nor suffer much, because they live in the gray twilight that knows not victory nor defeat" (quoted in Yacovone 1998, 214–215). Does "gray twilight" also refer to the ambiguity and androgyny of male-male relations, relations that were now under siege and surveillance? By the beginning of the twentieth century, gendered ambiguity was no longer in fashion, and the very meaning of manhood had changed (Yacovone 1998).

While Christian feminists were "miming" conservative Protestant rhetoric to privilege female moral superiority, men were emphasizing the virility, not the compassion, of Jesus, as a "muscular Christianity" became popular among many white men. The sinewy muscular arms of the Master embodied the cult of the "strenuous life" (popularized by Roosevelt) and the dirty little (imperialist) adventures of the 1890s: all marked a "crisis" of white masculinity and an end to the androgynous ideal. At this same time Freud and the sexologists were discovering "sexuality," a separate and primary domain of desire and relationship which would dictate nothing less than one's identity as a person. Accompanying the disappearance of the language of fraternal love was the discovery of "homosexuality" and "heterosexuality." The concentration of "homosexuals" within the great cities created a visible lesbian and gay culture which provoked public suspicion, not public understanding. Yacovone (1998) quotes Michael Foucault to make this point: "the sodomite had been a temporary aberration, the homosexual was now a species" (quoted passages on 215). Yacovone (1990) summarizes the shifts succinctly:

> Rapid industrialization, massive immigration, profound economic transformation, and dislocation transformed the texture of middle-class life and produced a culture that worshiped muscle and might. Even the children of men who had been some of the greatest exponents of the feminized male ideal censored their parents' published writings or wrote studies glorifying hero worship and the manliness of Christ. (95)

Why would these children want to censor their fathers' loves? Did these gender reactionaries suspect there was more going on than abstract agape love? Otherwise why did they bother to censor? Simple shift in fashion? The response is too strong—"overdetermined" one might say—for it to be a superficial matter.

By the century's end men suddenly stopped openly touching each other, stopping writing frank love letters to each other, and relatively quickly became "homophobic" and "heterosexual." Sexuality was no longer invisible, woven into the seams of fraternal love. Yacovone (1990) cites three developments that brought to an end the "innocence" of romantic friendship: (1) the rise of psychoanalysis, (2) the popularity of the new sexologists, and (3) notorious persecutions of avowed and infamous "sodomites" (or "inverts" and soon to be "homosexuals"), among them John Addington Symonds and Oscar Wilde.

The prosecution of Wilde in particular precipitated a tsunami, waves of what we would now term "homophobia" on both sides of the Atlantic. In 1885, England criminalized "homosexuality" with the Labourchere Amendment. Even the amendment's primary author, W. T. Stead, was shocked and disheartened by the mass hysteria surrounding the Wilde case. "A few more cases like Oscar Wilde's," he wrote to Edward Carpenter, the English author, socialist, and popular sexologist, "and we should find the freedom of comradeship now possible to men seriously impaired to the permanent detriment of the race" (quoted in Yacovone 1990, 95). That "freedom"—open physical intimacy among men—would in fact disappear. No longer did men enjoy in private what they denied in public. The damage that worried Stead was in fact irrevocable and erased the early Victorian era's construction of an "innocent" masculinity that allowed male-male friendship to be "romantic" (Yacovone 1990).

Throughout the nineteenth century, "romantic manhood," echoing classical and Christian conceptions of love, reflected middle-class respectability as it provided a medium for male-male emotional and physical intimacy. By the century's end, white men no longer seemed to know or at least agree over the meaning of manhood, and intimate male-male relationships ended. Indeed, what was once an indication of civilization and refined sentiment now branded one an outcast, as the language of fraternal love gave way to the "gelded men of the Gilded Age" (quoted phrases in Yacovone 1998, 215). For some progressive men, as we will see in the next section, there remained what we might term "romantic" pedagogy.

As Mark Simpson (1994) points out, Foucault understood that the appearance of "homosexuality" as an identity meant the disappearance of intimate male friendships. As "homosexuals," certain men focused upon "desire" often stripped from friendship, while "heterosexual" men struggled to find ways to be close to other men while suppressing their yearning for physical intimacy. As a consequence, the category of "heterosexual" men became an unstable and overdetermined one, homophobia appeared, and the frustration of homosociality slowly turned into the rage of heterosexually identified men. But that story I save for chapter 13. For now, let us return to the late nineteenth century and the emergence of the settlement house movement, a movement in which same-sexed friendships seemed to play, for some, a pedagogical role.

III. The Homoerotic Politics and Pedagogy of the Settlement House Movement

[V]ictorian efforts justif[ied] same-sex desire in terms of classic forms of ideal beauty.

—Scott Derrick, *Monumental Anxieties: Homoerotic Desire and Feminine Influence in Nineteenth-Century U.S. Literature* (1997)

A knowledge disquieting and liberating inhabits my soul.

—Essex Hemphill, *Brother to Brother: Collected Writings by Black Gay Men* (1991)

Settlements originated in England during the 1880s as a response to industrialism. Inspired by the social philosophies of Charles Kingsley, Frederick Denison Maurice, and John Ruskin, a number of university graduates under the leadership of the Reverend Samuel A. Barnett resolved to live as "neighbors of the working poor, sharing their life, thinking out their problems, learning from them the lessons of patience, fellowship, self-sacrifice, and offering in response the help of their own education and friendship" (quoted in Cremin 1961, 59). In 1884 they obtained a building in White

Chapel, an East London slum, and named it Toynbee Hall after Arnold Toynbee, uncle to the historian Arnold J. Toynbee, a friend of Barnett's who had died recently and whose commitment to the cause of the poor had helped inspire the movement (Cremin 1961).

The settlement idea spread quickly, not only through England but to the United States as well. In 1886 a young Amherst College graduate named Stanton Coit, who had lived for two months in Toynbee Hall, established the first American settlement at 146 Forsyth Street on New York City's Lower East Side. The plans of four Smith College alumnae led by Jane Robbins and Jean Fine became New York's College Settlement in the fall of 1889. At almost the same time, Jane Addams and Ellen Gates Starr opened what would become the most famous of the American settlements, Hull House of Chicago. In 1891 Everett Wheeler's East Side House (New York City) and Charles Zueblin's Northwestern University Settlement were established; in 1892 William J. Tucker opened Andover House in Boston with Robert Woods as headworker. There was a Colored Settlement House in Washington, D.C., on whose board of trustees Anna Julia Cooper served, as did Francis Grimké and Mary Church Terrell. Within a few years, then, the half-dozen seminal institutions of the American settlement movement were established (Cremin 1961; Lemert and Bhan 1998).

These young social reformers were convinced that the worst consequences of industrialism lay in its shattering of fundamental human patterns of association. That is not to say these progressive men and women were not aggressive in their attack on what Theodore Roosevelt in 1907 called the "malefactors of great wealth" (quoted in Cremin 1961, 60). But reformers' urgent concern was that industrialism had dissolved the fabric of community, leaving in its place a profound social alienation. It was this social alienation that was, they thought, fundamentally responsible for the deterioration of life in the slums. Such an analysis led them to seek educational as well as political solutions. It also makes intelligible their faith that by sharing their knowledge and ideals with the poor and suffering, they, the poor, could then rebuild their communities and progress socially. While many settlement house workers talked in terms of neighborhood regeneration, their ultimate aspiration concerned the humanization of late nineteenth- and early twentieth-century American industrial civilization. In this ambitious project, education was key (Cremin 1961).

As their work progressed, settlement house residents found themselves concentrating more and more on education. Hull House illustrates this point well. Almost from its inception there were kindergartens for children as well as clubs for older boys and girls, men and women. There was, for instance, an educational program focused on dietetics which, among other things, encouraged women to purchase cheap but nutritious cuts of meat. A Working People's Social Club was founded, as was a Hull House Labor Museum. There were as well drama and choral groups, and a Hull House Music School. Activities for adults were numerous and variable, from English classes for immigrants, a Shakespeare Club, a Plato Club, and a series of courses in cooking, dressmaking, millinery work, child care, and the trades (Cremin 1961).

Jane Addams understood this program of "socialized education" as also a protest against the dominant and narrow conception of the school. She was aggressive in her attacks on the elitism of the monied classes. She was equally critical of the provincialism of many teachers and educational administrators, whose confined conceptions of culture prevented them from acting upon the rich educational possibilities available in the city. "We are impatient with the schools which lay all stress on reading and writing," Addams wrote in *Democracy in Social Ethics* (1902), "suspecting them to rest upon the assumption that all knowledge and interest must be brought to the children through the medium of books. Such an assumption fails to give the child any clue to the life about him, or any power to usefully or intelligently connect himself with it" (quoted in Cremin 1961, 62). To become a force for social progress, Addams knew, the schools would have to engage themselves in the world of affairs, much as the settlement houses had done, and exert their influence toward the humanization of American social and economic systems (Cremin 1961).

Born in 1860 in Cedarville, Illinois, to John and Sarah Addams, Jane Addams was the youngest of eight children. Her father was a mill owner and state senator, one of the most powerful and respected political figures in Illinois. In 1882 Addams graduated from Rockford Seminary for Females to discover that the opportunities for college-educated women to find work in the public sphere were very limited. She spent the next seven years of her life searching for meaningful work. Her search took her to Europe, where in the winter of 1883 she visited Toynbee Hall settlement in the slums of East London. It was there that she saw a role for herself in helping others. She returned to Chicago and, in 1889, at age twenty-nine, with her college classmate Ellen Starr Gates, opened Hull House (Munro 1999b).

Hull House emphasized education as the tool by which the social and economic inequalities of American society could be transformed. Addams's democratic commitment is evident in her assertion that: "We have learned to say that the good must be extended to all of society before it can be held secure by any one person or any one class; but we have not yet learned to add to that statement, that unless all men and all classes contribute to a good, we cannot even be sure that it is worth having" (quoted in Cremin 1961, ix). Addams was involved in numerous organizations and social movements, including the Immigrants Protective League, the National Association for the Advancement of Colored People, the Chicago Woman's Club, the National Women's Trade Union League, the National American Women Suffrage Association, the National Educational Association, and the American Sociology Association. As well, she acted as an arbitrator in several major strikes and worked to establish a juvenile court in Chicago. Under her leadership, Hull House was involved in urban studies, social work, education, politics, public health, debates over the status of women, industrial reform, labor relations, international relations, and the arts (Munro 1999b).

Both Hull House and New York's Henry Street Settlement, led by Lillian Wald, provided sites where educated and committed middle-class women could live and work together for social progress. Lillian Wald, who also participated in the founding of the N.A.A.C.P. (see chapter 10), persuaded the City Health Department to appoint the first school physicians in 1897. Her colleague Elizabeth Farrell started the first classes for handicapped children under Board of Education supervision. Henry Street was also instrumental in establishing the first "practical housekeeping centers" in New York, an experiment that led eventually to a city-wide school-lunch program (Cremin 1961).

Located in urban immigrant neighborhoods, settlement houses provided material assistance as well as educational and cultural programs. Through the settlement house movement, American women developed those political skills and networks that not only influenced the careers of prominent women reformers and politicians, but also served as the blueprint for later welfare policies (Murphy 1998). In addition to reflecting the "separate spheres" ideology (Munro 1999a), the same-sex character of especially the male-run houses suggest that a homoerotic dynamic was circulating among racial and social progressives as well as among reactionaries and racists. This homoerotic dynamic would seem to have been less repressed among the progressives.

Many scholars have pointed out that the majority of American settlement women remained unmarried and formed their primary attachments with one another. The prominence of these same-sexed relationships, or "romantic friendships," has raised a series of predictable questions. Were these relationships sexual? Are such "romantic friendships" appropriate subjects for lesbian history, or is that concept inappropriate for these women, even though those attachments may have been physical? What is the relationship between romantic friendships among women and the political ideologies and social practices of the settlement house movement? Although vigorously debated in the 1970s and 1980s, Kevin Murphy (1998) reports that such questions have receded in more recent scholarly examinations of settlement houses.

Whether or not Jane Addams, for instance, would be considered today a lesbian is less interesting a question for us than the fact that the primacy of same-sexed relationships in her life may well have influenced her assumption—evident in her exchange with Ida B. Wells in *The Independent*—that black men were perhaps guilty of raping white women (see chapter 8, section V). While not understating the racism embedded in that assumption, it is necessary, from the point of view of appreciating the gender of racial politics generally, to note that Addams may well have been skeptical of white men's moral capabilities as well. That generalized view of "men" was clearly a dynamic in Frances Willard's inability to decode her own racism, as we will also see in chapter 8. My point here is that social progressives like Addams and Wald, due to the primacy of same-sex relationships, could not easily take up the cause of black men as, for instance, did Ida B. Wells, whose racial identification as well as family history (her solicitude over her brother, for instance) supported such engagement. The fact that the gender of racial politics was homosocial meant that many white women could not, at first, question the widespread assumption that men, including (especially?) black men, were sexually rapacious and morally weak.

Just as there was a homoerotic dynamic circulating in white women's response to lynching and racial politics generally, there was homoeroticism operative in white men's as well, including progressive white men. Why would only southern white men have formed homoerotic attachments to black men, although given the sexualized character of slavery, the gendered nature of the Civil War, and the "crisis" of late nineteenth-century white masculinity we can understand why southern white men's attachments were more intense, more convoluted and deformed, than were the attachments of many northern white men's. In the North desire circulated in ways that were sometimes racially progressive, as we see in this glimpse into the sexual dynamics of some men's participation in the settlement house movement.

I am not arguing that, for instance, Oswald Garrison Villard was sexually drawn to black men and that this desire provided the impetus for his engagement in racial politics, including the formation of the N.A.A.C.P (see chapter 10). Just as southern white men who lynched black men were not "homosexuals" in any contemporary sense, northern white men thought they were helping a disenfranchised, embattled minority, and they were. But it is clear from Kevin Murphy's study of men's participation in the settlement house movement that homoeroticism and progressive politics were not always unrelated phenomena. The progressive white male self also came to formation and to public expression in "the shadow of the other" (Benjamin 1998).

While women were the leaders in the movement, many men also lived and worked in urban settlement houses. Murphy (1998) focuses on two, Charles B. Stover, head of the University Settlement on New York's Lower East Side (where Eleanor Roosevelt worked when she was 17), and John Lovejoy Elliott of the Hudson Guild, located on Manhattan's West Side. Like the more famous Addams, Stover and Elliott drew on the same intellectual traditions Addams did, embracing social democratic ideas of cross-class "human brotherhood" grounded in humanist ethical theory. Also like Addams, Stover and Elliott became involved in national politics (Murphy 1998).

Like Addams, Wald, and other settlement women, Elliott and Stover included a critique of middle-class gender roles within their ideal of human brotherhood. Jane Addams wrote extensively about the limitations of the "family claim," that is, those limitations that accompanied middle-class marriage and family life, especially those suffered by younger women. Elliott and Stover agreed with Addams that the nuclear family was a problem; that other forms of human organization, associated with what Addams termed "the universal claim," were key if Americans were to achieve social democracy. Also like Addams, Elliott and Stover lived their lives so as to reflect this dissatisfaction with conventional conceptions of family. Like many settlement women, these men created their primary emotional and erotic relationships with members of the same sex. As for Addams and many progressive women, Stover and Elliott saw in settlement houses experiments in fashioning alternative families in which sexuality was not linked to reproduction. In so doing, they performed a cultural and pedagogical politics of same-sex eroticism very different from emerging medical models of homosexual pathology and heterosexual normativity (Murphy 1998).

Despite these choices to live and become involved with other men, settlement men were hardly gender separatists. For instance, Stover enjoyed friendships with such leading settlement figures as Lillian Wald, Jane Addams, and Mary Kingsbury Simkhovitch. Several of these women were sympathetic to

Stover's "peculiarities" and "occasional erratic movements," including his bouts of depression and his occasional sudden disappearances. Simkhovitch, for one, commented that, for all his exuberance, "there was something withdrawn about him, as if he cared only to disclose his activities, while holding shyly and inviolate some core of his personality which was simply his life for all his fellow men." Wald discerned what she took to be "a probable deeper struggle within" the man (quoted in Murphy 1998, 277).

Now what could that struggle be? Consider the clues: friendships not love affairs with women, estrangement from the nuclear family, and a devotion to other men. Then, however, these expressions invoked a model of gender and sexuality only to the knowing, to those who understood this new concept of "homosexuality." Presumed to be an innate quality, such "sexual inversion" occasioned moodiness as well as aberrant sexual behavior. True, the original sexological model did not necessarily stigmatize "the homosexual," although many finding their way through the "crisis" in masculinity quickly decided it should. In fact, there were intellectuals—such as John Addington Symonds and Edward Carpenter in Britain, well-known and highly regarded by many settlement reformers—who argued that this new model provided a unique social role and even inherent superiority to "homosexual" people. Wald took this view seriously, at least in her memorial to Stover. She expressed what was for her a fond memory, her first visit to the book-lined quarters that Stover shared with fellow settlement resident Edward King. She remembered vividly the "frank and instructive" advice that the "unconventional pair" had given her, inspiring her to take up residence in the nearby college settlement with her companion, Mary Brewster. Murphy (1998) points out that Wald's linking of her meeting with Stover and King as a couple to her own relationship with Brewster suggests that she saw a parallel between male and female same-sex relationships. Edward Carpenter had seen the same, theorizing that what he called "homogenic" love be modeled after the relationships of "New Women" (quoted phrases in Murphy 1998, 277–278).

Elliott appeared to suffer less. Like Stover, he structured his life around primary relationships with other men, but he did not experience mood swings. Like Jane Addams, Elliott (and Stover) formulated a critique of the ritualized sexuality of nuclear family life within a progressive vision of a society organized by a cross-class "brotherhood." Both men evoked Platonic models of a society dedicated to a common good; for both Socrates became iconic in teaching about this social dream. But Stover and Elliott also drew upon two nineteenth-century traditions that linked male homoeroticism to specific social ideas and pedagogical practices (Murphy 1998). First was the "social mobility" tradition, best recalled by writer and philanthropist Horatio Alger, and the "democratic comradeship" described and lived by the poet Walt Whitman (quoted phrases in Murphy 1998, 278). [John Dewey once characterized Walt Whitman as the "seer" of democracy (Westbrook 1991, 552). Whitman died in 1892, the year in which lynching was at its height.] In 1866, Horatio Alger had had to flee Brewster, Massachusetts, when his sexual involvements with boys had been exposed (Greenberg 1988). Despite the apparent opposition between them, these two ideas, "social mobility" and "democratic comradeship," intersected in the careers of Stover and Elliott (Murphy 1998).

To describe the "social mobility" model of male homoerotic practice, Murphy (1998) cites the work of literary scholar Michael Moon (1987, 1989, 1995, 1996), which argues that American reform narratives (including nonfiction, as in the case of Children's Aid Society founder Charles Loring Brace, as well as fiction, for instance, Alger's tales of male social ascent) eroticized relationships among working-class boys and older men. While a student at Harvard, Alger had concentrated on the study of Hellenic culture. He wrote popular novels about relationships between middle-class "saviors" and poor youths, depicting the act of "saving" as one of seduction (Murphy 1998). In Alger's stories these narratives of "rescue" involve crossing "seemingly intractable class lines" and end happily in masculine domesticity (quoted phrases in Murphy 1998, 279).

Both Brace and Alger told tales of "descent" (middle-class reformers and benefactors entering working-class slums) and "ascent" (working-class youths escaping their slum homes through bonding with their benefactors), painting an eroticized and masculinized picture of class conflict and cooperation in urban America. In this regard, such narratives intersected with the literary opus of Walt Whitman, especially his *Leaves of Grass,* which includes the highly homoerotic "Calamus" poems. In fact, one of Whitman's early literary efforts, the 1841 short story "The Child's Champion," foreshadowed the plot line of the popular "rags to respectability" stories of Horatio Alger (Murphy 1998).

Whitman quickly abandoned this format in favor of a more democratic vision of male homoerotic attachment. Published in 1855, *Leaves of Grass* suggested a utopia of masculine comradeship that would bind American men together in democratic society. (Whitman lost his job at the U.S. Interior Department when *Leaves of Grass* was published [Greenberg 1988].) In the "Calamus" poem, Whitman sexualized these bonds, making himself, Murphy (1998) suggests, both "the poet of homosexual love and the bard of democracy" (279). Murphy quotes Whitman on the political significance of his "Calamus" poems:

> Important as they are in my purpose as emotional expression for humanity, the special meaning of Calamus cluster of *Leaves of Grass* ... mainly resides in its Political significance. In my opinion it is by a fervent, accepted development of Comradeship, the beautiful and sane affection of man for man, latent in all the young fellows, North and South, East and West—it is by this, I say ... that the United States of the future (I cannot too often repeat), are to be most effectually welded together, intercalated, anneal'd into a Living Union. (quoted in Murphy 1998, 279–280)

For Whitman, as for Brace and Alger, private desire and public politics of interclass solidarity were inextricably intertwined (Murphy 1998).

This comingling of homoerotic desire and class struggle is evident not only in the literary production of Whitman and Alger but in their life histories as well. Both men lived the narratives they composed by becoming involved in eroticized relationships with young working-class men. While Alger was writing his popular tales of success, he worked as a social reformer in the Newsboy's Lodging House established by Brace's Children's Aid Society. Alger "adopted" several young working-class men, who then lived with him, helping him with his work (Murphy 1998). Alger had before been dismissed from a ministerial position for "the abominable and revolting crime of unnatural familiarity" with a young male parishioner; now he expressed his erotic interests as a reformer and writer (quoted in Murphy 1998, 280).

Whitman's primary relationships were with those young working-class men who lived with and worked for him. Whitman "performed" his relationships with these young men in ways that both reflected and supported his commitment to that social leveling and democracy evident in his work. Eschewing the position of philanthropist, Whitman presented himself as a virile man who shared the customs, clothing, and pastimes of the "rough" working-class men whose company he preferred. Performing "the manly virtue of the American yeoman" (Murphy 1998, 280), Whitman tried to make "natural" a "community of desire sharing a sexual, social, and psychological condition" (quoted in Murphy 1998, 280). The democratic ideal embedded in Whitman's expression of "manly" comradeship and desire inspired late nineteenth-century men such as Stover and Elliott who searched for other models of same-sex attachments rather than the dominant ones of pathology and stigmatization. Like Socrates, Whitman, too, became iconic for intellectuals in Europe as well in America who sought to incorporate homoerotics within their politics and pedagogy (Murphy 1998).

Among the intellectuals inspired by Whitman's "manly comradeship" were the British theoreticians of "homogenic" love, John Addington Symonds and Edward Carpenter. Whitman's influence on Symonds and Carpenter reflected an international collaboration in theorizing the relation between homoeroticism and class struggle. In addition to Whitman, Symonds and Carpenter drew upon models of pederasty and pedagogy associated with ancient Greece to formulate a political argument that insisted that homosexual relations were not only moral but socially useful. They challenged the growing suppression of same-sexed relationships by the state. In his 1894 essay "Homogenic Love," Carpenter extended Symonds's earlier arguments to assert that, if not suppressed by the state, homosexuality could prompt a major social transformation. Homosexuality, he argued, could bring "members of the different classes together" (a phrase also used by Jane Addams [Munro 1999a]), and in so doing organize "an advance guard of that great movement that will one day transform the common life by substituting the bond of personal affection and compassion for the monetary, legal and other external forces which now control and confine society" (quoted in Murphy 1998, 281).

These political theories of "homogenic" love promoted by Symonds and Carpenter were well known in socialist intellectual circles in Great Britain, especially at Oxford and Cambridge (where "Greek" love was hardly unfamiliar). But they were institutionalized in London's settlement houses. As the nineteenth century ended, young Carpenter protégés, among them C. R. Ashbee and Frank Llewellyn-Smith, moved into London's Toynbee Hall, where they re-created the familiar all-male world of the university but with a significant difference. Now their primary relationships were forged with "rough" working-class lads, not the sons of England's elite. These reformers did not take tea with their charges; rather they boxed and roughhoused with them, recording these activities in their journals. From these journals we learn that they took their young working-class friends on trips to the countryside where, according to Ashbee, they fell in "eternal love." Murphy quotes historian Seth Koven (1992) who suggested that these young reformers, who learned to speak the sexualized and classed rhetoric of the "rough lad" discernible in London's gay subcultures, aspired to "create nation and community through vertical bonds of comradeship across class lines" (quoted in Murphy 1998, 281).

This politicization of loving cross-class bonds between male friends was not uncommon. In fact, members of turn-of-the-century University Settlement clubs (with names like the Comrade Club, the Spartan Athletic Club, Athenians, and the Young Citizens) took this idea as the very raison d'être of their existence. The constitution of the Promethean Club, Murphy tells us, declared that "conditions exist which are contrary to the ideals of truth, justice and brotherhood. ... We youths do hereby band together to preserve and foster by education of word and deed, and by stimulating friendship, the lofty idealism of youth, to create a sensitive consciousness to conditions about it ... so that youth, when it matures, shall become the strength of the nation to the end that idealism shall govern conduct." The young men in the Promethean and other clubs performed this call to social improvement and nation-building not only by making love; they also participated in mainstream political movements such as labor unionization and tenement house reform (Murphy 1998).

The social and political idealism of many youth club members merged male "friendship" and "fraternity" with a utopian vision of a democratic and classless society. Like many intellectuals and artists of the period (such as John Dewey), they opposed intensifying materialism, the rapidly spreading "selfishness and cynicism" that appeared to accompany the industrialization and urbanization of American society. Of course, these young men were captives of the very class-based society they criticized, living in social settlements supervised by middle- and upper-class reformers, dependent on philanthropic gifts. Within the clubs, both the Alger and Whitman currents flowed, as liberal-capitalist notions of economic improvement and social uplift through education conflicted with more "leveling" ideals of democratic brotherhood. This conflict is discernible in youth club rhetoric, Murphy notes, which speaks of "brotherhood" in the sophisticated language of the privileged and educated. Although the political ideals of these young elite intellectuals may have intersected with those patterns of working-class male camaraderie and solidarity lived in the streets and taverns of New York's tenement house districts, their basic impetus was ameliorative, that is, to "uplift" these young men through education. The life trajectories of many of these young reformers, many of whom later achieved prominence in business, scholarship, and politics, suggest that their commitment to democratic leveling may have been only a youthful ideological flirtation on the way to individual social advancement (Murphy 1998).

This conflict between leveling and uplift was discernible in the careers of Elliott and Stover as well. Their excursion "down" into the immigrant neighborhoods of New York mirrored in many ways those erotic adventures performed by less politically motivated turn-of-the-century New York men. Other prominent New Yorkers, including Charles Parkhurst, Jacob Riis, and

Theodore Roosevelt, were also engaged in reform adventures which combined "doing good" with sexual pleasure. During this same period, middle-class men who could not tolerate living quietly through their "crisis" of masculinity fled their "respectable" homes and families into the bars and streets of immigrant neighborhoods. Many sought sex with working-class women; others explored the burgeoning homosexual subculture; others enjoyed sexual relations with "rough" working-class men whose appearance and masculine style contrasted with their own self-perceived feminization. Like Stover and Elliott, some of these cross-class travelers knew of Whitman, that "prophetic spokesman" for "the manly love of comrades" (quoted in Murphy 1998, 286).

In the careers of Elliott and Stover both erotic and reform models of "descent" blended. Those careers and the tales told about them indicate considerably more "horizontal" commitment than was typical of most middle-class men who went "slumming." After their initial "descent" into working-class immigrant neighborhoods, both men remained there, forming long-term relationships with several young men they met. Like other reformers, they described their work to middle-class readers through reform publications, but they also saw the residents of these poor neighborhoods as their "audience," their constituents. Their Whitman-like efforts to refashion themselves as "simple" men, for example, authenticated them not only with middle-class audiences, but also with those living in the tenement districts, many of whom saw in the absence of middle-class dress coupled with their obvious desire to form close relationships with resident men, signs of personal humility and class solidarity. Moreover, each formulated a politics and pedagogy which, in their advocacy of working-class people, were coded as radical even by other reformers. Stover, for instance, was criticized not only for his effort to construct playing fields in Central Park, but for the campaign he led to open museums to working-class residents on Sundays. Elliott's assistance to convicted criminals from his Chelsea neighborhood and solidarity with neighborhood youths in resisting the draft during World War I sparked considerable controversy (Murphy 1998).

The conflict between vertical and horizontal models of class-based and eroticized male-male relationships is also illustrated by what Murphy (1998) characterizes as the "Socratic role" performed by Elliott and Stover. Like Whitman, Murphy explains, Socrates helped these men theorize their relation to the young immigrant men with whom they worked and lived. The influence of Socrates was not lost on those who observed them; one commented that: "Stover was different—and in the same way—from every other mortal whom I have ever known as was Socrates from all the other Athenians of his day" (quoted in Murphy 1998, 287).

Elliott's colleagues and students knew that Socrates was his "revered hero"; they spoke of "the kind of Socratic probing [Elliott] liked to practice." Elliott performed his version of Socrates with great enthusiasm. His ethics classes were organized as Socratic dialogues, frequently centered around the ancient Greek adoration of the young male body and the crucial role pedagogy played in the development of this body. Elliott told his students stories about "those Greek boys ... each one with his teacher or pedagogue," who

> would start out in the morning about day light and they stayed there until sundown. They would go through the streets in a kind of procession until they came to a place set aside for gymnastic exercises and there, from sunrise until noon, they would exercise and play games in the open air. Think of the tremendous skill and strength they would get—twisting and turning and rolling over in the dirt by the hour. It would really make them strong and skillful. Then they had what they called dancing. They wanted to make their boys wonderfully strong, skillful and beautiful. (Murphy 1998, 287–288)

In other lessons, Elliott described the kinds of male friendships forged in the Greek gymnasia. "Finer, stronger, and more powerful ... than the individual friendship between two men," such a "social friendship" would function to renew "social feeling" in society, overcoming the narrowly economic and psychological self-interest of the bourgeois individual (quoted in Murphy 1998, 288). The creation of this "social friendship," Elliot believed, was the obligation of the social worker (Murphy 1998).

Elliott's mix of democratic "social friendship" and an eroticized Socratic pedagogy did not go unnoticed or unchallenged. Both colleagues and students were sometimes unsettled by the combination. Lucy Mitchell taught with Elliott at the Fieldston School; she once expressed her concern to Felix Adler that Elliott's entire pedagogy was based on "the study of the life and conditions of that man ... the Greek ... the one who took hemlock." She worried that Elliott's obsession with Socrates "had become a joke among the pupils." There was as well, Mitchell confided, something "unspeakable" about Elliott's relationships with his students. When asked to explain, she responded: "Oh dear me, not anything I'd want to tell. ... It was more what the children said and what the children thought and that isn't anything to be repeated." Others who recorded their memories of Elliott after his death were likewise uneasy when asked to discuss the nature of his relationship to his students. One woman, when asked about Mark McCloskey's relationship with Elliott, stammered that it was "a very different kind of relationship ... a very close one" and then told her interviewer, "if you and I were simply talking as people I might tell you things that I haven't today but I can't neglect the purpose of your inquiry" (quoted in Murphy 1998, 288).

It was with Mark McCloskey, to whom Elliott recalled being immediately drawn, that Elliott formed the closest relationship of his life. A "blond haired boy" who was "the first to box," McCloskey was a "handsome and strong boy with a wonderful Irish brogue." As their intimacy deepened, Elliott called him "Marksie" and "Beloved" (quoted in Murphy 1998, 282–283). He paid McCloskey's tuition at Princeton University; afterward he named him his successor as director of the Hudson Guild. As an adult McCloskey played a leading role in several federal programs during the New Deal and World War II. After McCloskey moved on, Elliott formed similar relationships with other good-looking young men from the neighborhood (Murphy 1998).

The distress others experienced concerning Elliott's relationships with his students suggests that the Socratic blend of pedagogy and pederasty was not easily relocated in early twentieth-century America. The eroticized role of the

Socratic pedagogue resonated with early twentieth-century hysteria concerning the sexual corruption of youth. Such fears were common in late-Victorian America and became the impetus for numerous reform crusades. Primarily they concerned older men and young girls, but when these fears focused upon sexual relations between men and boys they became even more intense and more difficult to calm. This was not just a problem of American "Puritanism," as the emergence of a Socratic form of pedagogy at British universities earlier in the nineteenth century had caused similar controversy. Recasting Socrates as a "corrupter of youth" and horrified by the contemporary recovery of "Greek Love," colleagues accused British classicists such as Benjamin Jowett of corrupting youth and promoting "boy love." Although less public, the close association between pederasty and Socratic pedagogy brought criticism of Elliott as well (Murphy 1998).

Kevin Murphy theorizes that the combination of cross-class homoeroticism and the privileged male access to public space meant that Elliott and Stover's careers differed significantly from those of the more prominent woman reformers such as Jane Addams. Settlement house women formed their primary relationships not with their working-class clients, but with each another. Despite this important difference in sexual practices, women reformers shared their male counterpart's view that a reconceptualization of sexuality was a prerequisite for forging interclass solidarity. Indeed, Jane Addams endorsed a class-based analysis of sexuality as key to "human brotherhood." "Tak[ing] a page from the Greeks," Addams suspected that the "fundamental sex susceptibility ... suffused the world with its deepest meaning and beauty." Sexuality had become, she continued, misdirected in industrial society, expressing itself in "vice and enervation" (quoted in Murphy 1998, 289). She attributed this "vice" primarily to the commercialization of street life in working-class neighborhoods and to the "enervation" of the confined middle-class family; both prevented young people from meaningful participation in the formation of a truly democratic society. Recalling Plato's dialogue between Socrates and Diotima, Addams argued that sexuality must be extricated both from species reproduction and from hedonistic sensuality. Reintegrated with "the affairs of the imagination" by people of all classes, the sexual impulse could, she thought, prompt a renaissance of American life (Murphy 1998).

Murphy draws two conclusions regarding the settlement house movement from his study. First, a reconceptualization of sexuality animated settlement house ideology. Both male and female leaders of the settlement house movement argued that a reimagining of sexual desire was key to social reform, specifically to overcoming classism, an idea Herbert Marcuse (1971) would articulate in different terms half a century later. Although they accepted uncritically the white middle-class preoccupation with working-class sexuality, they conferred upon that sexuality considerable significance, that is, as the source of great possibility for the formation of new types of social organization. This reorganization of American society remained a reformer's dream, but women such as Jane Addams and men like Charles Stover and John Elliott forged sexual and pedagogical practices that diverged significantly from the middle-class norms of their day, and transcended the increasingly powerful binary of heterosexuality/homosexuality (Murphy 1998).

Second, Murphy concludes that the settlement house movement was not organized exclusively according to gendered identity. The settlement movement promoted collaboration among men and women who did not perform their gender in congruence with standard norms. Their collaboration was productive and cordial. Elliott and Stover remained friendly with Addams and Wald throughout their lives. The friendship between Elliott and Wald was particularly strong: Wald even asked that "her dear friend John Elliott" speak at her funeral and serve as executor of her will. Correspondence between the two suggests that they well understood and appreciated each other's sexuality; that understanding no doubt supported their friendship. In one 1933 letter, for example, Elliott wrote to Wald praising the controversial film *Maedchen in Uniform*, which portrayed lesbian relationships in a German boarding school. Also that year, Wald wrote to Elliott about her "very, very nice" new companion in playful language which inverted the young woman's gender. "I call her 'Everyman'," she wrote, "and she is very pleasing" (quoted in Murphy 1998, 290). Such exchanges, as Murphy points out, suggest that in addition to the gendered networks of the "female dominion," settlement reformers also developed networks of fluid sexual subjectivity that crisscrossed gender binaries.

It would appear then, that not only bigots were moved to political action due, in part, to sexual desire. Racial and social progressives too evidently experienced social engagement and sexual desire as interlaced. While Murphy's research does not indicate to what extent young black men were the objects of Elliott and Stover's pedagogical affections, immigrant boys were often coded "nonwhite" during this period of immigration dominated by southern and eastern Europeans (Omi and Winant 1983). Certainly Lillian Wald was directly engaged in racial politics, involved from the beginning and for many years with the N.A.A.C.P. Interestingly, those whose desire prompted them to devote their lives to the advancement of black people seemed quite conscious of the relationship between sexuality and social service. Racist southern men, in contrast, were clueless. Even as they danced in a frenzy in front of the naked, tortured, sometimes castrated bodies of young black men, they thought they were protecting their ladies.

As with Donald Yacovone's research on "romantic friendship" among nineteenth-century men suggests, it is not clear that we can apply contemporary terms such as "lesbian" or "queer" to these settlement house reformers. There are scholars who do, of course. Blanche Cook (1977) argued that Wald and Addams, as well as many other politically engaged women of the period, were in fact lesbians, given that they formed their primary attachments to other women. This argument was extended by Adrienne Rich (1980) in her widely read (and debated) essay, "Compulsory Heterosexuality and Lesbian Existence." Robin Muncy (1991) insisted that Jane Addams's companion Mary Rozette Smith played the role of "a Victorian wife" (16). Mina Carson (1990) alludes to Lillian Wald's "crushes" on female residents at Henry Street (93). Other scholars insist that labeling these women "lesbian" amounts to superimposing upon them a contemporary construct that is inappropriate to that time (Murphy 1998). Linda Gordon (1994) has even argued that settlement women and other female reformers involved with other women exhibited a "nuns' sensibility" and dismisses their "sexual activity" as beside the point (79). For those interested in the gender of racial politics and violence, sex is hardly beside the point, but key to disclosing the homoerotics of the white/black binary that structures not only "race" but "sexuality" in America.

IV. Divorce and Domestication

There is no reason at all why men should not sweep and dust, make beds, clean windows, fix the fire, clean the grate, arrange the furniture.

—*American Homes and Gardens* (1905)

Companionate marriage required new roles for both men and women, even if we cannot describe them as egalitarian.

—Margaret Marsh, "Suburban Men and Masculine Domesticity, 1870–1915" (1990)

As women entered the masculine world, men began to enter the sphere assigned to women.

—Margaret Marsh, "Suburban Men and Masculine Domesticity, 1870–1915" (1990)

At least in law, what was significant about nineteenth-century patriarchy was less its decline than its changing shape.

—Robert L. Griswold, "Divorce and the Legal Redefinition of Victorian Manhood" (1990)

The rise of the middle class, the bourgeoisification of American men and women, meant that traditional male prerogatives and behaviors (among them tendencies toward emotional distance, authoritarianism, drinking, gambling, absence from home, and occasional sexual indiscretions) had to be, if not abandoned, reformed. The "rough edges" of manhood needed to be smoothed over if it were to be more congruent with emerging middle-class domestic sensibilities. It was the rise of the middle class and its domestic conception of family authority, not feminist demands for sexual equality per se, that resulted, Robert Griswold (1990) argues, in the reconstruction of nineteenth-century American manhood.

Not that women were passive and complicit with the status quo. Taking advantage of statutory laws and expanded legal interpretations of marital cruelty, nineteenth-century wives went into local courts to lodge a variety of complaints about their husbands, among them charges of insensitivity, domination, sexual indiscretion, and abuse. As wives demanded legal intervention into what had been before strictly private relationships, "courts became a moral theater in which the contours of a new definition of manhood took shape." And that new manhood had to be one "less domineering and forceful and more sensitive and cooperative" (Griswold 1990, 97–98). In fact, as we will see momentarily, certain suburban men became downright domestic.

Robert Griswold (1990) provides a series of examples that illustrate this trend toward domestication among certain middle-class white men. For instance, when displaying insensitivity to their wives' sexual interests or to their special needs during pregnancy, men received sharp rebukes in court. They were almost always well deserved. For instance, in 1869, Ellen Havely testified that her husband's excessive sexual demands had ruined her health. David Savage demonstrated insensitivity in a different way when he insulted his pregnant wife. "I never knew a cow or mare in your condition to eat so much," he had told her (quoted in Griswold 1990, 98). After the birth, he left his wife to struggle with the baby by herself. He simply disappeared, having made no arrangements for a doctor, nurse, or any other assistance.

Not only neglect and abuse of wives came to light in nineteenth-century courts. Fathers' cruelty to and/or neglect of their children were also documented, and such misconduct was regularly punished. Griswold comments: "Courts provided a forum, a ceremony of sorts, for the articulation of a critique of male behavior: the ceremony began when a disgruntled wife sought out a lawyer; the lawyer then drafted a complaint, the clerk copied and filed it, the court commissioner consulted it, the witnesses heard it, and the judge finally assessed it" (1990, 99). Even in the patriarchal domain of the law, white men discovered their status was changing.

Divorce litigation provided a public forum for deliberation over what was and was not appropriate behavior for men in relation to women and children. The vast majority of nineteenth-century divorce cases involved men's cruelty to their wives, a gendered violence that has changed little, as we will see in chapter 13. In two California counties, for instance, women filed over 80 percent of the cruelty suits, and there townspeople's testimony focused specifically on men's misconduct. The articulation of shifting definitions of matrimonial cruelty evolved as the public expanded its conception of what constituted husbands' marital misdeeds. In the process, women's claims to new standards of husbandly conduct were supported socially. The legal definition of cruelty expanded as well, both reflecting and contributing to a larger cultural redefinition of manhood and patriarchy (Griswold 1990).

In the English legal tradition, only violence or threats of violence constituted cruelty, but such a narrow conception would be widened as nineteenth-century Americans sentimentalized and idealized women's domesticity and accepted a more companionate ideal of marriage. What American courts came to accept was a conception of cruelty that both reflected Victorian fantasies of family life and critiqued manhood. In so doing, the courts rewrote traditional English conceptions of cruelty. For instance, in 1883 the Kansas Supreme Court redefined cruelty to include behavior which "grievously wounds the mental feelings of the other" and "so utterly destroys the peace of mind of the other" as to harm bodily health or destroy the high purpose of marriage (quoted in Griswold 1990, 101). Husbandly misconduct that before would have been judged by the courts as insufficiently grievous to end a marriage was now considered sufficient. As a consequence, the "price" of divorce declined in keeping with the new (and for conservative men, "inflated") marital expectations of nineteenth-century American women (Griswold 1990).

Charges of intemperance began to function differently in divorce litigation as jurists tried to interpret new statutes that began to appear as early as the 1830s. Like cruelty petitions, intemperance suits were mainly filed by women; from 1887 to 1906, women received 33,000 divorces due to their spouses' alcohol abuse, men just 3,400. These statistics, Griswold (1990) suggests, actually underrepresent the role that male drunkenness played in marital breakups. A federal study of divorce published in 1909 estimated that male intemperance was a factor in 26 percent of all successful divorce suits filed by wives, although it was the sole cause in only 5 percent (Griswold 1990).

Intemperance was objectionable enough in itself, but when it drew one away from home to one's local saloon rather than ministering to an ailing wife, it was judged outrageous. There are many legal examples of such shifts in public opinion, but the point is that local courts provided a site where sobriety was publicly affirmed as essential to authentic manhood. In nineteenth-century courts, communities across the United States expressed legally their sharpening sense of the interrelationships among temperance, economic respectability, and proper manhood. In these courts, justices underscored the significance of temperate and responsible manhood by releasing women from their bonds to men who were not "manly." To be a man, most nineteenth-century middle-class Americans came to agree, required diligence, frugality, and sobriety. Without these, and in particular without temperance, one surrendered one's claim to manhood (Griswold 1990).

Lawmakers and justices across the country shared these sentiments, and state after state added intemperance clauses during the course of the nineteenth century. By 1900, thirty-eight of forty-six states granted divorces for drunkenness. Griswold (1990) identifies three themes discernible in these legal developments. First, insobriety need not be constant to satisfy statutory definitions of intemperance. Second, like temperance reformers, jurists shared the conviction that alcohol destroyed a man's ability to support his family. This ability was judged as even more important since the emergence of a wage-based economy required men's daily absence from the home. Married women's economic dependence upon their husbands meant that they suffered if their husbands suffered. If a family's suffering was due to a husband's failures at work, and if that failure could be attributed to insobriety, the courts offered redress to wives and children. A 1909 report on divorce estimated that intemperance was present in over 20 percent of successful nonsupport suits filed between 1887 and 1906 (Griswold 1990).

As Frances Willard and her W.C.T.U. colleagues in America and Britain would insist, alcohol was as destructive to the work ethic as it was to family life. Men who drank were not industrious, frugal, and self-denying; indeed, they were often a "reckless, wandering" breed who lacked the ability to hold a steady job. The court's final judgment in an 1892 case from Kentucky was typical of most cases of the time: "While we hold in highest regard the sanctity of the marriage bond and know that courts should be cautious in severing it, we feel that the good of society does not demand or require a wife, without fault in her marital relations, to be bound for life to a drinking, shiftless husband" (quoted in Griswold 1990, 103–104).

Even when alcohol abuse did not destroy a man's ability to support his family, it was held to destroy the emotional bonds that held families together. Drunkenness, many courts ruled, left some men "quarrelsome, profane, profuse in threats of violence." An "amiable and intelligent gentleman" might even become "absolutely crazed and maddened" after drinking, thereby making his presence within the home "repulsive and intolerable" (quoted in Griswold 1990, 104). Of course, in these expanding conceptions of marital incompatibility, there were complaints about husbands' misconduct that were relatively trivial, but in general these grievances were just and often long overdue (Griswold 1990).

While men were forced to relinquish some their patriarchal prerogatives, their retreat did not amount to complete defeat. For instance, despite a declining percentage of divorces granted to both husbands and wives on grounds of adultery, as late as the turn of the century, 28 percent of all divorces granted to men had to do with their wives' adultery. The figure for women was 10 percent, suggesting that men, and the wider culture, still believed in the sexual double standard. Indeed, Griswold tells us that "although courts put forth a vision of manhood congruent with Victorian assumptions about gender, many men resisted this effort to redefine the nature of masculinity, this assault on traditional masculine behaviors" (1990, 109–110). The relative progress made by women in the courts during the nineteenth century was also a factor in the late nineteenth-century "crisis" of white masculinity, a "crisis" that was expressed not only in reactionary gender politics, but in reactionary racial politics as well.

Divorce, declared Susan B. Anthony in 1905, "is just as much a refuge for women married to brutal men as Canada was once a refuge from brutal masters" (quoted in Filene 1998, 53). As did many other feminists, Anthony regarded the rising divorce rate as a sign not of family breakdown, but of progress toward a society where marriage would provide women opportunities for love, respect, and individuality (Filene 1998). This was an optimistic view. Even for those who did escape to "Canada," many difficulties remained. Despite nineteenth-century courts having forged some measure of protection for women, Griswold points out, "relief from misery cannot be equated with autonomy and independence" (1990, 110). Legal limits to patriarchal prerogatives were not equivalent to women's legal, let alone social and political, equality. A fundamental inequality remained.

When men took advantage of adultery, cruelty, or intemperance suits to secure a divorce, they ended their marital troubles and enjoyed the freedom that was so often fantasized as prerequisite to manhood. When women obtained divorces, they were protected from abusive or nonsupportive husbands, but they then enjoyed no freedom from responsibility. With children or without them, divorced women faced a society that refused them the same opportunities for autonomy and independence available to men. As many nineteenth-century feminists understood, more liberal divorce laws and legal interpretations would help, but they were insufficient. Griswold observes: "Such laws might partially refine male gender ideals and curb male excesses, but only feminism could reshape manhood in ways that would foster women's true liberation" (1990, 110). Today it is clear that men must join feminists in working to "reshape manhood," in support of women's "liberation."

A "Healing Domesticity"

Many late nineteenth-century educated women did not bother marrying men in the first place. In public and in private, many "advanced" women, and not just progressives like Jane Addams, rejected the traditional family as a form of slavery, more subtle perhaps, but no less oppressive, they insisted, than the bondage African Americans had suffered. In the name of civil rights and independence, then, a number of women rejected marriage with men. "They would be women of the world," Peter Filene writes, "not angels of the home" (1998, 51). For some, this ideological choice was also a cold one; love and domestic comfort were sacrificed for the sake of gendered self-assertion. For many others, however, such courage did not require the relinquishing of domestic life and emotional intimacy. Many found these with other women. As would be the case for many in the 1970s, these feminists' sense of solidarity went beyond the conventionally political to express itself sexually (Filene 1998).

Just as today the exact extent of same-sex sexual activity cannot be documented, learning how many unmarried women were involved with each other sexually one hundred years ago is also a matter of speculation. That is not to say efforts to learn were not made. Katherine B. Davis's survey in the 1920s of 2,200 college alumnae, ranging in age from twenty-two to sixty-eight, reported that one-third of married women and more than one-half of unmarried women at some point in their lives had entered into intense relationships with other women. For one-half of each group, these relationships involved sexual expression. If one brackets the respondents into age groups, the incidence of reported homosexuality draws a gradual but steady line upward, reaching its peak among unmarried women born in the 1890s and among married women born after 1900. More than one-third of the women surveyed enjoyed homosexual relationships before college, and another third during college; 80 percent pursued them after graduation, in most cases with one other woman (Filene 1998).

Due to problems in her sampling procedures, Davis's study is regarded as not precise; for instance, it disagrees with Kinsey's findings, twenty-five years later, that no more than 10 percent of women born before 1920 had engaged in sexual relationships with other women. Of course, it is certainly possible that, like many men, the women Kinsey surveyed managed to "forget" these episodes; it is certainly possible that homophobia erased them. That is implied by the fact that one-half of Katherine Davis's respondents described their sexual feelings for other women as wrong or abnormal. Many others, however, gratefully acknowledged the "healing domesticity" of same-sex bonds (Filene 1998, 52).

The exact truth will never be known. "The more important truth," Filene asserts, in line with his fellow historians, "is that our modern emphasis on a dichotomy between homosexual and heterosexual identity—and, indeed, our emphasis on sexuality in general—can easily cause us to misunderstand what was happening" (1998, 51). Many professional women at the turn of the century enjoyed romantic friendships with each other, involving physical but not necessarily sexual affection. Given the Victorian custom of effusiveness in words as well as touch, such expressiveness was not unusual. So when Jane Addams asked Ellen Gates Starr (as they founded Hull House) "Let's love each other through thick and thin," we cannot assume the invitation included, in any contemporary sense, sex. But I insist we cannot assume it did not. After Starr moved away, Addams became involved with Mary Rozet Smith; the two women enjoyed a new "healing domesticity" that lasted forty years, until their deaths (Filene 1998, 52).

The "crisis" of white masculinity in the late nineteenth century was stimulated by women's independence, including wives who declined to tolerate husbands' infidelity and other failings, as well as women who declined to tolerate men at all. It was also stimulated, curiously enough, by the appearance of "masculine domesticity" (Marsh 1990, 112).

Domestication

When historians think about American men at the turn of the century, Margaret Marsh reports, among the images that come to mind are that of a bored clerk or middle manager in some cheerless office of a bureaucratic corporation, "pushing papers or counting the company's money, longing nostalgically for a time when a man could find adventure and get rich at the same time by becoming a robber baron or conquering new frontiers" (1990, 111). The primary image remains that of Theodore Roosevelt, "the delicate child who grew up to relish big-game hunting and war, whose open disdain for softness and 'effeminacy' made him the preeminent symbol of rugged masculinity in his own time" (Marsh 1990, 111).

This association of the corporate drone with the flamboyant Rough Rider Marsh (1990) traces back to an influential essay by John Higham, in which he suggested that one of the most significant American cultural developments at the turn of the century was a kind of "cult of masculinity." Beginning in the 1890s, Higham argued, American men experienced an "urge to be young, masculine, and adventurous," rebelling against "the frustrations, the routine, and the sheer dullness of an urban-industrial culture" (1970, 79). For evidence, he pointed to the growing popularity of boxing and football, a disinterest in high culture, and, perhaps most important of all, American imperialism. This research provoked other studies in the historical meaning of masculinity (see, for instance, Rotundo 1983; Filene 1974/1998; McDannell 1986).

While not doubting that widespread anxieties over the meaning of manhood were experienced by "an entire generation of middle-class men—young and middle-aged, married and single, urban, suburban, and rural" (111), Marsh points out that this characterization does not accurately depict a certain social segment of middle-class men who lived in the then just-appearing suburbs. This segment requires us "to supplement the image of the dissatisfied clerk with a picture of a contented suburban father, who enjoyed the security of a regular salary, a predictable rise through the company hierarchy, and greater leisure" (Marsh 1990, 111). Indeed, while the reactionary "cult of masculinity" thesis does explain many elements of male middle-class culture, other elements require a model of "masculine domesticity" (Marsh 1990, 112).

In a period when white manhood seemed to be imperiled and in "crisis," what conditions supported the appearance of "masculine domesticity"? Marsh (1990) points to three: (1) a companionate ideal of marriage that de-emphasized patriarchal authority and the ideology of separate spheres; (2) a period of economic stability which allowed middle-class men to devote more attention to their families; and (3) a physical setting in which the previous two developments could be performed. When the political structure of the middle-class marriage underwent subtle shifts, when the rise of the corporation provided relatively secure jobs with predictable patterns of promotion, and when the suburbs began to be viewed as the appropriate spaces within which to house the companionate family, the emergence of "masculine domesticity" was possible. By the early twentieth century, Marsh tells us, all three of these conditions had been met.

Mid-nineteenth-century male advice writers (excluding the medical advisers who wrote marriage manuals) rarely wrote about the roles of husband and father. Instead, they emphasized economic and social mobility, advising young men to stay sober, be honest, and work hard. This was the formula for economic success. Whether these contributed to a man being a better husband or father was ignored. Most male advice writers had no suggestions for men thinking of marriage or for young fathers who might be wondering about child care. These advice writers warned their male readers against prostitutes, gambling dens, and the tempting but degenerate pleasures of the city, but they offered him no positive advice in building a private life with his wife and children (Marsh 1990).

It was women who persuaded men to rethink their roles as husbands and fathers. This is evident in the publications of female advice writers, who, after a time, stopped paying even lip service to the traditional patriarchal ideal of manly authority and prerogative. By the last decade in the century, many women were insisting that unless they were granted their rights to education and citizenship, they could not be happy in their marriages. As attitudes changed so did the domestic lives of middle-class families. On the surface, the lives of most husbands and wives did not appear to change much; many women, for instance, still did not work outside the home. But as the twentieth century began, wives did choose to leave the home more often and for longer periods of time, whether in mothers' groups or women's clubs, in reform activities, or perhaps shopping in the downtown department stores (Marsh 1990).

Some husbands changed too. As we see in section VII (this chapter), the great age of male fraternal orders had passed by the turn of the century (Carnes and Griffen 1990). Suburban men who commuted to jobs in the city now wanted to relax closer to home, in "field and country" clubs that welcomed the whole family and in social groups that included their wives. For instance, in one Philadelphia suburb, during the first decade of the twentieth century, the Men's (only) Civic Club nearly failed due to lack of interest, and the Women's Sewing Society did disappear in 1903. In contrast, groups whose membership included both men and women (married and single), such as the Penn Literary Society, the Debating Group, and the Natural Science Club, flourished. A new family-oriented tennis club also had no trouble attracting members. Women advice-givers at midcentury had advised women to spend time with *other* women, but by the 1890s a new generation of writers was emphasizing the importance of wives spending time with their husbands. Writing for *Harper's* in 1894, Richard Harding Davis found his married suburban friends boring because they seemed to have no interests beyond each other, their house, and their suburban pastimes. Davis found such conjugal contentment incomprehensible (Marsh 1990).

As certain middle-class men came to feel protected from the economic turbulence that had disrupted the lives of their fathers, some chose to give their families more attention. This economically supported shift, coupled with the arguments of feminists, helped some men appreciate the significance of their own domestic responsibility. During the 1870s, Abby Diaz recalled, many women asked her why, if women needed preparation for motherhood, men did not also need education for fatherhood. Men, she would answer, did indeed need such education, but she was too busy to provide it (Marsh 1990). Harriet Beecher Stowe asserted, "We have heard much said of the importance of training women to be wives." It was past due time, she thought, that "something ... be said on the importance of training men to be husbands" (quoted in Marsh 1990, 120).

By the 1890s, the conversation had changed. Margaret Sangster reported approvingly that she knew a family in which "everyone shared the housework, even the boys," while in another family the son, "a manly young fellow," did the ironing. Martha and Robert Bruere shared the duties of domesticity, insisting that "a knowledge of housekeeping is not a matter of sex, but science." So "all ought to know [it], men and women alike." High schools, they suggested, might well require boys to take home economics courses, since men will someday become "homemakers." In 1905 even the (male) editor of the suburban-oriented magazine *American Homes and Gardens* conceded: "There is no reason at all why men should not sweep and dust, make beds, clean windows, fix the fire, clean the grate, arrange the furniture," and cook. While he was referring to domestic servants, not husbands, he nonetheless was making a point about male involvement in the home. And such involvement was not restricted to servants, as he insisted in his editorial for the following month: "The responsibility for the home is not [the wife's] alone, but equally the husband's" (quoted in Marsh 1990, 120–121).

Readers were taking such assertions to heart. The recently married Helen Sommers, for instance, wrote to her sister in 1909 about the decoration of the house into which she and her husband had just moved: "Harry and I are working every thing out together." Before writing *Rebecca of Sunnybrook Farm*, Kate Wiggin had been a kindergarten teacher, committed, she said, to teaching "the father spirit" in little boys (quoted in Marsh 1990, 121).

These expressions of masculine domesticity, Margaret Marsh argues, became incorporated into middle-class notions of manliness. Not only the role of "husband" was affected; these gender shifts also influenced how men thought of themselves as fathers. These men became convinced that if their sons were to become "manly" in domestic ways, they themselves must become more involved in their sons' upbringing than their fathers had been in theirs. As it will be in the 1950s (see chapter 14), in the first decade of the twentieth century men were advised to abandon the distant, often authoritarian role of the patriarch. Now the stress would be on friendship; fathers were encouraged to be "chums" with their children, particularly with their sons (Marsh 1990).

Accompanying this new domestic definition of fatherhood were new sublimated forms of masculine aggressivity, or, perhaps we should say, new constructions of what was widely assumed to be an "essential" relation between manliness and aggression. On this point, Marsh (1990) appears to accept a somewhat essentialist notion of manliness, suggesting that as men behaved themselves at home their aggressivity shifted to the sphere of fantasy. Of course, for men conditioned to be "manly" men, as many of those Marsh is describing were, such a dynamic may be strictly psycho-historical, not essential to the gendered formation of men. In pointing out that for these men the commitment to masculine domesticity and the necessity of being a "manly" man were complementary not antithetical, Marsh hypothesizes "[t]hat men, as their behavior within the family became less aloof (or patriarchal) and more nurturing and companionable, would develop a fantasy life that was more aggressive. The rage for football and boxing, and the reading of adventure novels, might have provided that vigorous fantasy life, making but not contradicting masculine domesticity; that subject remains to be investigated" (1990, 122–123).

It would seem, then, that the cult of masculinity and masculine domesticity were two sides of the same coin. Consider the case of bodybuilder Bernarr Macfadden. He advocated that husbands be present by their wives' side at childbirth, a far cry of the positions of "self-made men" just decades before. Then a "man's man" like Macfadden would have stressed the virility required by a man's daily economic struggle with other men, not the importance of leaving that struggle in order to be with one's wife and family (Marsh 1990). To be a "man" and a "family man" were no longer antagonistic, at least for these suburban men.

Moreover, Macfadden and advice writers such as Albert Beveridge were among a growing number of Americans in the early twentieth century who regarded city life as a direct threat to family stability. By the turn of the century, many were expressing this fear by moving to the suburbs. In 1909, the American Sociological Society devoted its annual meeting to the family. While there was hardly consensus among the scholars in attendance regarding the character of the changes American families were undergoing, a number of those present agreed that city life and family togetherness had become mutually exclusive. Both advice-givers and academics were in favor of middle-class fathers spending more time with their wives and children in the suburbs rather than with male friends playing in the city. Even architects, ranging from the iconoclastic Frank Lloyd Wright to the conservative Joy Wheeler Dow, designed houses with family togetherness in mind (Marsh 1990).

Many men were persuaded by this chorus of professional opinion. For instance, many suburban men now chose to play golf with their wives rather than with business associates. Of course, husbands and wives did not do everything together, nor did they experience absolute togetherness. But over a relatively brief period of time, during the last quarter or so of the nineteenth century, middle-class, white, suburban husbands and wives did spend much more time together than had the generation before them. For some men, the decline of patriarchy led to a heightened male interest in the home during the first years of the twentieth century (Marsh 1990).

The domestication of white middle-class manliness also represented, Marsh (1990) argues, a reactionary response to the growing feminist movement. Masculine domesticity can be understood as a collective male response to the arguments of Charlotte Perkins Gilman and her followers, who had pronounced the traditional family anachronistic in a modern urban society. Gilman urged women to pursue individual achievement and separate identities, ways of life that had before been reserved for men. While not all middle-class men knew her by name, Gilman's writings and lectures received considerable attention in the popular press of the day, suggesting that most knew the arguments if not the name. Marsh speculates that men's retreat to the suburbs and intensified participation in the family undermined feminist efforts to downplay domesticity, at least for women. In the suburbs men could draw themselves into the domestic circle, where individual needs—including those of their wives—could take second place to the needs of the family. Marsh continues: "Masculine domesticity, in that sense, served as men's rejoinder to those feminists who insisted that women had as much right to seek individual achievement as men. ... would speculate that, intentionally or not, men who espoused masculine domesticity deflected feminist objectives" (1990, 128).

Congruent with Marsh's thesis, middle-class white men's domestication may well have been a response to women's assertive reconfiguration of family structure, informally in relationships and advice manuals, but in the courts as well. As we have seen, women used the courts as public spectacles to force abusive and neglectful husbands to rethink their roles as husbands, fathers, and as men. In addition to deflecting radical feminist objectives as articulated by Gilman and others, the men who fled to the suburbs to play golf with their wives and attend to their children may have been men in retreat from a battle to retain traditional patriarchal prerogatives. The move was one of retreat, not defeat. While these suburban men embraced a more companionate ideal of marriage and responsible fatherhood, they also looked for ways to reassert their own claims to authority and autonomy within this reconfigured family structure. Then as now, the suburbs are not exactly idyllic sites of gender justice.

But then, with the suburb a relatively new development without the nightmarish history of domestic violence it suffers now, fantasies of suburban tranquillity and fulfillment were common and unchecked. The flight to the suburbs was for many men no utopian gesture, however; the flight was also an expression of men's reactionary gender politics. Those who promoted the suburbs in the early twentieth century preached that moving away from the city would both encourage family unity and discourage selfish attention to individual—that is, women's—needs and desires. The suburb would provide the site for what its advocates hoped would be a new form of marriage. Husbands and wives would become companions, not rivals, and the threat of individualistic—that is, women's—demands would retreat in the face of family togetherness (Marsh 1990). Men's demands as men could then be reasserted, disguised as concern for "the family."

V. The Campaign for Women's Suffrage

The white woman could at least plead for her own emancipation; the black woman, doubly enslaved, could but suffer and struggle and be silent.

—Anna Julia Cooper, in Charles Lemert and Esmé Bhan, eds., *The Voice of Anna Julia Cooper* (1998)

Men objected so strenuously to woman suffrage precisely because male power and male identity were both so central to nineteenth-century electoral politics.

—Gail Bederman, *Manliness and Civilization: A Cultural History of Gender and Race in the United States, 1880–1917* (1995a)

Lynching occurred during a period of gender destabilization and reformulation in the United States and was, I am suggesting, very much related to it. As the nineteenth century ended and the twentieth began, white men were experiencing themselves as threatened, as indeed they were, by black political progress, dramatic shifts in the American economy, feminism Christian and secular, and the appearance of "homosexual" men who argued for a restructuring of American society based on homoerotic, cross-class love. Add to this "crisis" of white masculinity women's demands for participation in electoral politics. There can be no doubt that the "crisis" of white masculinity was aggravated by the campaign for women's suffrage. Not only in the church, at home, and at school, but now at the ballot box white men's privileged position was challenged.

Almost as soon as the First Woman's Rights Convention ended in Seneca Falls, New York, in 1848, white men mobilized against those rights, and specifically against women's participation in the public sphere. Unsurprisingly many invoked the "Law of God." Reverend John Todd pointed out that suffrage was a civil right which cannot contravene women's natural right "to be exempted from certain things which men must endure." So understood, woman suffrage is a "rebellion against God's law of the sexes, against marriage … and against the family organization, the holiest thing that is left from Eden." James Long invoked the racial analogue, asking: "How did woman first become subject to man as she now is all over the world? By her nature, her sex, just as the negro is and always will be, to the end of time, inferior to the white race, and therefore, doomed to subjection; but happier than she would be in any other condition, just because it is the law of her nature" (quoted in Kimmel 1996, 57–58). Once again, white women and black men surface together, conjoined in white men's minds.

Support for equal suffrage would come slowly, outrageously slowly. Fifty years after the 1848 Convention, women could vote in only four states, Wyoming, Utah, Idaho, and Colorado, and there they were too outnumbered to make a difference. A half century of committed campaigning—most of the lifetime of suffragists such as Elizabeth Cady Stanton—had encountered defeat after defeat. Indeed, during the lynching decade (the 1890s), opposition intensified, as prestigious civil leaders formed numerous Associations Opposed to Woman Suffrage in order to mobilize those determined to prevent women from voting (Filene 1998).

By 1910, the number of states where women could vote increased by one. Stanton and Anthony died in their eighties deprived of success. But suddenly, it seemed, many men reconsidered. Perhaps the hundreds of campaigns for state referenda and amendments, the thousands of articles and pamphlets, the millions of speeches had finally gotten through. The movement "is actually fashionable now," an astonished Inez Haynes Irwin wrote to her friend Maud Park in 1910. "Altogether, dear Maud Park, the movement which when we got into it had about as much energy as a dying kitten, is now a big, virile, threatening, wonderful thing" (quoted in Filene 1998, 38–39). Over 20,000 suffragists, male and female, could march in New York with only occasional jeers from the bystanders. The National American Woman Suffrage Association (N.A.W.S.A.) claimed 100,000 members. In 1910 only five states permitted women to vote, but during the next seven years ten others would come round, including California and New York (Filene 1998).

In a study of male supporters and opponents of the 1911 California woman suffrage campaign, Eric Dwyce Taylor (1998) connects the scholarship on masculinity with that on the woman suffrage movement, arguing that the woman suffrage campaign prompted men on both sides of the question to articulate their conflicting senses of masculinity. Although much of the suffrage debate obviously focused on the qualities and characteristics of women, concerns over masculinity quickly surfaced and very much influenced the debate and its outcome. As Taylor observes, a "change in the status and role of women engendered a revealing debate about the role of men" (1998, 300).

As the twentieth century began, public life "seemed to be filling with women. After 1890 women push[ed] ahead to perfect the politics of influence, to build organizations of working women, and to bring together the republican claim of female citizenship" (Evans 1989, 142–143). The "new woman" who had emerged during the last decade of nineteenth and first decade of the twentieth centuries challenged the middle-class conventions of separate spheres. No longer were women willing to allow men to dominate the public sphere (however competitive and predatory it was), while they enjoyed, presumably, dominion over domesticity, that private sphere of morality and motherhood. Middle-class heterosexual life in America operated, in no small measure, on the conviction that these "separate spheres" must be kept apart (Taylor 1998).

As the new century dawned, however, the spheres converged, as increasing numbers of women assumed a more prominent place in public life. Colleges, corporations, arts and literature, and urban reform movements offered women opportunities to end the male monopoly of the public domain. "American women," commented Joe Dubbert, "succeeded all too well to suit many American men, who by the late nineteenth century were becoming increasingly fearful of female moral, social, and cultural pre-eminence, to say nothing of growing female interest in politics" (1980, 307). Their masculinity threatened, white men responded to the women's public ascendancy by, among other things, engaging in strenuous physical pursuits, among them bodybuilding and football (Taylor 1998; Kimmel 1990, 1994, 1996; Pronger 1990). And lynching.

Some have argued that the "self-made man" of the nineteenth century gave way to the notion of "passionate manhood" as the twentieth century began. The "self-made man" had been free to pursue his individual interests; his manhood had been measured not only by his success, but by his ability to govern, through reason, his passion. He was quite capable of tenderness and intimacy, often forming close "romantic friendships" with other men, as we have seen. But the fantasy of being "self-made" meant the erasure of white men's bodies as sensual and desirable, as objects of desire. Only women and racial others had bodies.

In a different context, Elizabeth Grosz (1995) has observed: "To sustain this fantasy of auto-production [i.e., as "self-made" man] and pure self-determination in a systematic way, men have had to use women as the delegates of men's materiality. This containment within the (negative) mirror of men's self-reflections strips women of an existence either autonomous from or symmetrical with men's" (122). As women entered the public realm and contested their relegation to the domestic sphere, men's fantasies of themselves as disembodied agents necessarily faded. Moreover, as feminism challenged traditional gender binaries, as work became increasingly bureaucratized, and as African Americans refused to be crushed politically, many white men felt unsettled, even emasculated. Embattled and in "crisis," then, many white men developed a new model of manhood characterized by "ambition," "combativeness" and a cult of toughness (Rotundo 1993; Taylor 1998).

But Eric Taylor's study of the California woman suffrage movement of the late nineteenth and early twentieth centuries discloses a more complex situation than any simple "feminization versus remasculization" binary suggests. As Taylor points out, California men both "reacted to and participated in" women's efforts to become civic agents in the public sphere. The variegated conduct of many men during the suffrage struggle complicates the picture that some hold that white men simply (or only) "reacted with vehemence" to woman suffrage, and that "[f]ew middle-class men were eager to share their power and prerogatives with the opposite sex." While in general the case, not *all* men "strenuously opposed woman suffrage," nor were all men obsessed with "revitalizing manhood by opposing excessive femininity" (quoted in Taylor 1998, 301).

Many men *were* opposed to woman suffrage, of course, many adamantly so. Yet this fact can obscure the fact that the struggle for suffrage engendered an intense debate among men about men, a debate that not only testifies to the internal politics of the "crisis" of masculinity, but also helped shape the woman suffrage movement itself, including its ultimate success (Rotundo 1993). Without understating the centrality of women's efforts and agency in the struggle, the role men played in the suffrage campaign, Taylor (1998) argues, is key to understanding the complexity of gender—in particular the "crisis" of white masculinity—during the late nineteenth and early twentieth centuries.

The suffrage campaign was very highly charged. In the intensity of emotion it stimulated, men's sense of a threatened and changing masculinity becomes evident. At the same time the suffrage campaign functioned to legitimate the male-dominated public sphere as the key site of politics (Munro 1999a). Certainly, after Nancy F. Cott, we must distinguish "between what is exclusively male culture and what is 'public'—the two are not coterminous, although a male viewpoint, past or present, might conflate them. ... To equate the public with the man's sphere is to posit that all women were behind the closed doors of the home" (1990, 207). Clearly the doors had been pushed open and many women were walking—from many men's point of view, marching—outside.

Curiously, one key theme evident in California men's discussions of masculinity was chivalry. As we have seen, chivalry was a term that circulated in the homosocial political and gendered economy of the antebellum South; it was used as an excuse to rape and murder black men in the postbellum South. Astonishingly, chivalric language appeared frequently and proved surprisingly useful to many twentieth-century California men as they tried to make sense of rapidly changing gender roles. Obviously an elastic term, pro- and antisuffrage men both employed elements of "chivalry," including courage, honor, and man's duty to protect women, in their discursive maneuvers either to help or to hinder the cause of woman suffrage. To illustrate, Taylor notes that antisuffrage men insisted that it was their "duty" to "protect" the lady from the "burdens" of the political sphere. Prosuffrage men insisted that chivalry required honorable men to extend to women the right to vote (Taylor 1998).

Whether pro or con, the chivalric sense of masculine duty and honor was at odds with women's full political participation. Although prosuffrage men were factors in the victory of the suffrage campaign, those who acted out of a sense of chivalry undermined the ideal of actual political equality between men and women. "Many pro-suffrage men cracked the chivalric armor of anti-suffrage men in 1911," Taylor notes, "but they never completely abandoned their own sense of knighthood" (1998, 302). He quotes the comments of one prosuffrage male a month before the 1911 California election to illustrate how the concept of chivalry constrained men's capacity to envision a public arena of political equality. "This is as it should be," he announced. "It is the work of the men to give you women the ballot. I am glad that I shall never have to see you women of California going through the streets carrying a banner" (quoted in Taylor 1998, 302).

There were profeminist men who saw in feminist demands for suffrage an expression of deep democratic impulses. It was quite clear to them that equal rights must be extended to women. Some men followed the lead of female social reformers and hoped that feminism would redeem a society submerged in male vice; at the least it should extend to women the same sensual opportunities men enjoyed. Such reasoning, Michael Kimmel (1998) suggests, represented a shift in the rhetorical strategies used by profeminist men in their efforts to support equal rights for women.

There were men who had no doubt been influenced by women's participation in social reform movements, such as temperance and Social Purity. They accepted the argument that only women can serve as the moral reformers of male vice; only women could provide the cure for contemporary social ills. The participation of women in the public sphere, it was argued, would advance the causes of morality, purity, and beauty in the world. Supporters of women's education, for instance, believed that equal educational opportunities would enable women to address the degeneracy and vice that had diseased American culture. For Joseph Sayers, "a liberal, literary, moral and virtuous female education [was] the only detergent remedy for vice, crime, and immorality" (1856, iv). Coeducation was important because men would be refined by it and women would be empowered and "inspired with a higher, nobler ambition" (Buchanan 1851, 49; quoted in Kimmel 1998, 30)

A number of advocates of woman suffrage relied on such reasoning to advance their cause, emphasizing that women were a moralizing force. This, Kimmel suggests, challenged the more simple and abstract morality of individual rights that had characterized earlier discourses on public morality. He quotes Clifford Howard who insisted that "woman should have the ballot, not only for her own benefit, but for the benefit of you and me and every other man who stands for good government and public cleanliness and purity" (Howard 1890, 3). Howard and other like-minded men inverted the antifeminist doctrine of separate spheres and used it to insist that women's participation was imperative precisely *because* women's sphere was the home, a notion of civic housekeeping (Munro 1999a). "The woman's place is the home," Howard allowed, "but today would she serve the home she must go beyond the house. No longer is the house compassed by four walls. Many of its most important duties lie now involved in the bigger family of the city and state" (7). Edward Ward (1900) played with the separate sphere argument when he reasoned that "[w]omen should mind their own business. That is, they would vote in the modern government, for this is their proper sphere, except in its destructive, anti-social, military expression" (7). If women were to honor her natural role as the protector of the home, "she must of necessity interest herself in public affairs and take a part in their management" (Howard 1890, 8; quoted in Kimmel 1998, 30)

Other men agreed. Frederic C. Howe reiterated that social reforms would be enacted only when the domestic sphere of women was extended to the public realm. In "What the Ballot Will Do for Women and for Men," Howe characterized suffrage as the redemption from "the muddle we [men] have made of politics." Only women were capable of ending poverty, hunger, disease, and suffering. Howe continued dreamily:

> I want to live in a world that thinks of its people rather than of business; of consumers rather than producers; of users rather than makers; of tenants rather than owners; in a world where life is more important than property, and human labor more valuable than privilege.

> As women are consumers, users, and tenants rather than producers, makers, and owners, I have hope for a society in which women have and use the ballot.
>
> I want woman suffrage because I believe women will correct many of these law-abiding wrongs that man has made. For women will vote in terms of human life rather than in terms of special privilege. (Howe 1905, 7–8; quoted in Kimmel 1998, 31–32)

It was clear to these men who had participated and/or believed in the Social Purity Movement that women's suffrage was only the social extension of women's natural role as guardian of the home. Only women, they believed, could "save men from the cruelties and excesses that accompanied masculinity in crisis" (Kimmel 1998, 32).

There was, Taylor tells us, another group of men who participated in this contentious debate. These men declined to participate in the inequalities embedded in chivalric discourse and in fact criticized the assumptions upon which the chivalric code rested. They challenged the separate spheres ideology and chivalric fantasy that men were or should be the protectors of women. In an age sometimes characterized as a "crusade for masculinity" (Douglas 1988, 327), these men questioned the obsession with physical strength as an index of masculinity and the bedrock of social order. The presence of these profeminist men, although they were very much a minority, underscores the complexity of the "crisis" of masculinity during the early twentieth century (Taylor 1998). Clearly, there was a small group of men who understood that women's political participation in the public sphere—feminism generally—held profound and welcomed implications for men.

A Village of Progressive Men?

A number of male intellectuals took up the cause of women, including John Dewey, who, probably under the influence of Alice Dewey, became "active in promoting equal education for women and woman's suffrage" (Westbrook 1991, 167). There was also a small group of profeminist men who embraced feminist ideas not only in solidarity with women but also for their potential to liberate men. In the first two decades of the twentieth century, most visibly in New York's Greenwich Village, a group of men linked feminism, psychology (especially psychoanalysis), and socialism. Influenced by Freud and Marx, these profeminist men were committed to women's sexual as well as political autonomy. They enlisted other men to join the feminist cause as they worked to lead lives that were consistent with their beliefs. This new wave of feminism emerged in the 1910s and 1920s, a feminism that was in part "a reaction against an emphasis in the woman movement itself, the stress in nurturant service and moral uplift" (Cott 1977, 37). The woman's movement had promoted social reform and political participation as women's duties; these new feminists promoted women's rights in general and sexual autonomy in particular as their aims. In Floyd Dell's view, feminism was more than "a revolt of women against conditions which hamper their activities; it is also a revolt of women and men against the type of woman created by those conditions" (1921, 349; quoted in Kimmel 1998, 32).

The gender radicals living in Greenwich Village worked to construct new relationships in fidelity to feminist causes. "In this moral health resort," as Dell described it, these men confronted issues of monogamy, women's sexual autonomy, and women's rights to birth control and abortion. Kimmel comments: "Feminism had created a new type of woman" (1998, 33). Such women required "new men" who could not only accept but be excited by women's sexual autonomy, who were outraged at economic and political injustice, and who were committed to bring about a system of sexual equality in both public and private spheres (Kimmel 1998).

Men like the young Max Eastman, Floyd Dell, Hutchins Hapgood, William Sanger, and Randolph Bourne (for a time a protégé of John Dewey; see Westbrook 1991) committed themselves to a democratic revolution in bed as well as on the streets. Eastman was the editor of *The Masses* and secretary and organizer of the Men's League for Woman Suffrage in 1910. Among the officers were Oswald Garrison Villard, grandson of the William Lloyd Garrison and a founder of the N.A.A.C.P. (see chapter 10), John Dewey, and Rabbi Stephen Wise (Kimmel 1996).

Eastman and his wife, Ida Rauh, caused something of a scandal when they posted Rauh's full name on their mailbox in 1911. Their postman refused to deliver their mail; they were forced to go to court to change the law, and in the process started a Village tradition of both spouses' names on mailboxes. Eastman said that he wanted his wife to be "entirely independent of men in every way—to be as free as she was before we were married." He understood that his support for feminism required him to revise his understanding of masculinity. "There was nothing harder for a man who had my mama's boy complex to do than stand up and be counted as a male suffragist," he wrote in the first volume of his autobiography. "It meant not only that I had asserted my manhood, but that I had passed beyond the need of asserting it" (Eastman 1936, 316; quoted in Kimmel 1998, 33–34).

These male gender radicals continued to support feminism because it "is just and right and ... men want to deal fairly and justly by women," as one pamphlet from upstate New York concluded (*Why New York Men Should Give Women the Vote* 1915, 4). A pamphlet printed in San Francisco that same year agreed that there was "no good reason why our women should be treated with less justice" (*The San Francisco Man: A Fable* 1915, 4). Members of the Men's League for Woman Suffrage, the nation's first explicitly profeminist men's organization, tended to employ abstract conceptions of morality and justice to justify their actions. An editorial in *La Follette*'s from May 1911 praised the eighty-five "courageous and convinced men" who had marched in a recent demonstration; one marcher reported that he had found being "booed and hissed down the Avenue a very thrilling experience" and registered his resolve that "if I can help to that end, there shall be a thousand men in line next year." And his estimate wasn't off by far. An editorial in the *New York Times* predicted that eight hundred men would march the next year in a suffrage demonstration, but Eastman counted many more. "Even when the Men's League occupied five blocks, four abreast," he wrote, "the press could see only a grudging thousand of them" (1936, 351; quoted in Kimmel 1998, 34).

For this generation of profeminist men, it was, as Eastman put it, neither "justice as a theoretic ideal, nor feminine virtue as a cure for politics" that inspired them to support feminism. They did "not look to women's votes for the purification and moral elevation of the body politic." It was, instead, a conception of "democratic government as the practical method of human happiness" that animated them (Eastman 1912, 8, 2; quoted in Kimmel 1998, 34). Many of these profeminist men regarded the feminist revolution as the gender complement to the socialist revolution to which they were also committed. Women's assertion of independence was a necessary condition of social change; many men believed that women would assume the leadership in the coming political revolution (Kimmel 1998).

Such political independence required sexual freedom, and many profeminist men supported women's struggles for birth control. William Sanger was arrested in 1915 for distributing his wife Margaret's pamphlet entitled *Family Limitation*. At home he was evidently just as supportive. "You go ahead and finish your writing," she quotes him as saying, "and I'll get the dinner and wash the dishes" (quoted in Kimmel 1998, 34). Kimmel notes that Margaret would draw the curtains to their first-floor kitchen when he did so, worried that passersby would notice this emasculating reversal of sex role expectations. Women's sexual autonomy was key, perhaps even more important than the vote, as Floyd Dell (1913) suggested in his *Women as World Builders*:

> Her development, her freedom, her independence, must come from and through herself. First, by asserting herself as a personality, and not as a sex commodity. Second by refusing the right to anyone over her body; by refusing to bear children unless she wants them; by refusing to be a servant to God, the State, society, the husband, the family, etc.; by making her life simpler, but deeper and richer. That is, by trying to learn the meaning and substance of life in all its complexities, by freeing herself from the fear of public opinion and public condemnation. Only that, and not the ballot, will set woman free, will make her a force hitherto unknown in the world, a force for real love, for peace, for harmony; a force of divine fire, of life giving; a creator of free men and women. (61–62; quoted in Kimmel 1998, 35)

Both Dell and Eastman thought Marx could be married to Freud, that is, interweave their commitments to a socialist political economy with a feminist liberation from sexual repression. In this vein Dell (1914) argued, in "Feminism for Men," that capitalism was antagonistic to feminism because "it wants men with wives and children who are dependent on them for support." Feminism permits men to encounter women as equals, which, he suggested, could happen only in the public sphere, as the home was "a little dull." He continued:

> When you have got a woman in a box, and you pay rent on the box, her relationship to you insensibly changes character. It loses the fine excitement of democracy. It ceases to be companionship, for

> companionship is only possible in a democracy. It is no longer a sharing of life together—it is a breaking of life apart. Half a life—cooking, clothes, and children; half a life—business, politics, and baseball. ... It is in the great world that a man finds his sweetheart, and in that narrow little box outside of the world that he loses her. When she has left that box and gone back into the great world, a citizen and a worker, then with surprise and delight he will discover her again and never let her go. (Dell 1914, 20)

Eastman (1936) devised a similar rationale for supporting feminism. Professing an "unqualified liking for women with brains, character, and independence" (quoted in Kimmel 1998, 35), Eastman was quite certain that feminism held great significance for men as well as women. For these profeminist men of the early twentieth century as for men today, Kimmel suggests,

> [f]eminism is about transformation, both for women and for men. Feminism offers to women a political agenda and a philosophical position that address both women's public sphere experience of discrimination and exclusion and their private experience of powerlessness, pain, and thwarted personal vision. To men it offers the ethical imperative to change as well as the opportunity to change. (1998, 38)

It may well involve changing the structure of "masculinity."

Chivalry

Back on the west coast, California men voted to give California women the vote in 1911. During the nine-month campaign preceding the election, the suffrage debate nearly reached a state of frenzy as men on both sides did everything they could to turn the tide in their favor. Because California voting men were so evenly divided on the issue, both sides fought even more fiercely perhaps, although the issue cut deep across shifting fault lines of a destabilized and changing masculinity. Although women's suffrage was only one of twenty-three issues male voters faced in that October special election, it dominated the press, particularly during the summer and early fall of 1911, the period, back East, during which Zachariah Walker was lynched in Coatesville, Pennsylvania (Taylor 1998).

Women demonstrated extraordinary resolve in forging and advancing this movement toward their own political legitimization, but few men faced the reality that this was a political contest between men and women. As in the case of lynching in particular and racism in general, most men perceived the woman suffrage issue as an affair between men, a matter which men themselves would resolve. To illustrate, Taylor quotes one prosuffrage man who offered that: "The decision rests with the men, and it is among men that the work must be done to get active results" (1998, 306). Legally, of course, only men could confer upon women the right to vote, but the assumption that the suffrage issue was a male matter discloses the narcissism of male homosociality and the imaginary status of women (Taylor 1998).

Allowing women to vote threatened their imaginary status in men's minds, a threat which they coded not so much politically or psychologically but in terms of gender stability. Many antisuffrage men knew that giving women the vote would further "level" the hierarchy of male and female roles. "I am opposing woman suffrage because I do not want to see women made masculine, or men becoming effeminate," declared Maurice Newmark, adding, "I oppose anything which would change the relationship." John Irish predicted in panic that "the ultimate drift of the women's suffrage movement in this state [will] be an attack upon the husband as the legal head of the family." One blunt antisuffrage advertisement expressed what many men believed to be at stake:

> MEN! In the quiet of the election booth
> remember the Quiet *Woman* At Home
> And VOTE NO on Amendment no. 8.
> (quoted in Taylor 1998, 307)

To many men's minds, women were simply biologically ill-suited for public life; they must never leave the private sphere where, it was argued, they belonged. Both Horace Bushnell and Harvard education professor Edward C. Clarke worried that women would grow larger, develop heavier brains and thereby lose their uniquely feminine mannerisms were they to vote or even attend college (Bushnell 1870; Clarke 1873). "I think the great danger of our day is forcing the intellect of woman beyond what her physical organization will possibly bear," wrote the Reverend John Todd (1867, 23; quoted in Kimmel 1998, 30).

For others, feminism signaled a general feminization of American culture, by means of which American manhood had been depleted and unnerved. For these men, women's participation did not spell the end of the world necessarily, as long as separate institutions remained all-male preserves and men could displace women from their control over child rearing, especially the rearing of boys. Such men advocated single-sex schooling and recreation for boys and girls; keeping the sexes strictly separated would maintain manhood and "the mystic attraction of the other sex," that is, fortify men against the threat of effeminacy and homosexuality (Beveridge 1905; McKeever 1913; Macfadden 1900; Kimmel 1998).

Antisuffrage men found the discourse of chivalry useful in expressing their fears about a feminized public sphere filled with masculinized marching women. The primary principle of chivalry states that a man's first obligation is the protection of ladies. In keeping with this axiom, antisuffrage men characterized public politics as a competitive predatory arena in which only men were fit to fight. Chivalry required these men to defend the increasingly untenable notion of separate gender spheres. Antisuffragists insisted that it was man's obligation to protect women from the "dirty pool of politics" and the "burdens of government." Taylor quotes antisuffragist Anthony Cummins to illustrate. Cummins declared that men "in good conscience can not force women to fight the battles of men." Only men, he continued, were "equipped [to] wage political warfare." In like manner, Mr. James C. Woods from northern California made in the *Lake County Bee* an "appeal to men as fathers, husbands, brothers and sons to protect and keep them in their womanly ways and graces."

Mr. Flint of Los Angeles explained his membership in the antisuffrage organization Committee of Fifty; it was, after all, his "duty to give protection to the women, who prefer their homes to the burden of government" (quoted in Taylor 1998, 307).

In a letter to Secretary of State Frank Jordan, California Senator J. B. Sanford employed the discourse of chivalry to argue against the proposed Amendment. In his letter, which he began by guaranteeing that "everything said here is true and I have the data," Sanford declared that "[t]he men are able to run the government and take care of the women." "The courageous, chivalrous, and manly men," he explained, "and the womanly women, the real mothers and home builders of the country, are opposed to this innovation in American political life" (quoted in Taylor 1998, 307). Although Sanford's language implied he believed in an essential "maleness" and "femaleness," it was in fact "historical experience," rather than biology, that for him settled the matter. Like many male antisuffragists who employed the rhetorics of chivalry, Sanford argued that men were "battle-tested" and had thereby earned the privilege of suffering. (Antisuffragists agreed that only men were "fit" to vote but they argued over why; some were sure it was a God-given right while others insisted it was a privilege earned from centuries of physical struggle.) "Do women have to vote in order to receive the protection of man?" asked Sanford. "Why, men have gone to war, endured every privation and death itself in defense of woman. There is no extreme to which he would not go for his mother or sister" (quoted in Taylor 1998, 308).

General George S. Patton was an aggressive antisuffragist, unafraid to charge into debates over the role and meaning of masculinity in politics. Patton, too, used chivalric discourse to make his point, declaring that "the great majority of the women of California do not want the ballot," and it was men's "duty and purpose to protect them" from it. In a September 1911 article entitled "Why Women Should Not Be Given the Vote," Patton expressed his military view of politics: "I submit that the electoral franchise is by its origin, by its evolution, a duty and an obligation, and not a privilege. … Politics is in its final analysis, a struggle, a contest, a combat; [it] is, in fact, merely modified war." Therefore, Patton continued, only real (i.e., fighting) men could claim the right to vote. It was, after all, men who possessed "courage, fortitude, and endurance"; he was the "fighting creature" of the species (quoted in Taylor 1998, 308).

Patton believed that men were "naturally" combative, and as natural-born fighters only men had the right to suffrage: "It is force and force only, fighting, physical brute force, if you will, that stands behind and gives efficacy to the verdict of the majority cast at the polls." Patton found it without historical precedent—not to mention just plain absurd—that women ever demonstrated, or could possibly demonstrate, this ability to wage war. "You cannot have an army of women," he stated. "You cannot have the city of Los Angeles policed by women." To the prosuffrage argument that enfranchised women would ensure a virtuous, middle-class public sphere, that women "could help stamp out the liquor traffic, help pass pure-food laws, abolish child labor, and contribute to other reforms," Patton snorted his skepticism (quoted in Taylor 1998, 308). Moreover, he complained, women resorted to ridiculous comparisons to support their prosuffrage arguments: "Women are prone to compare themselves with men of much inferior education and ability." Continued Patton: "They say: 'My coachman or chauffeur whom I pay can vote. ...' But this is not the true consideration. ... [T]he same chauffeur and the same day laborer can bear arms and may be called upon to bear arms in defense of the laws which they have made" (quoted in Taylor 1998, 309).

Nor did many prosuffrage men hesitate to draw upon the discourses of chivalry in making their case. In contrast to their antisuffrage opponents, these men called upon notions of masculine honor, courage, and a chivalric willingness to assist, not just a simple duty to protect, women. These men fancied themselves the stewards of women's entry into the public political arena. On occasion this "assistance" was painfully condescending, as when one prosuffrage man explained: "The baby doesn't want to be dressed; the child doesn't want to obey, and some women don't want the ballot. But these things are good for them." More often, however, men's condescending discourse was expressed in the language of obligation and honor. Thomas Stevens, for instance, was quite sure that he "owe[d] women this favor" and demanded that other men "stand up and fight for her" (quoted in Taylor 1998, 309).

Other prosuffrage men discussed woman suffrage as a "challenge" to masculinity. But unlike the antisuffragists, these men challenged others to demonstrate their masculinity not by acts of courage and physical prowess, but by supporting woman suffrage. "To take a stand against woman suffrage," suggested C. C. Pierce, "is illogical, unconstitutional and silly—and, worst of all, it is unmanly!" Such men coded support for woman suffrage as an index of masculine honor and courage. On elective eve, for instance, one man appealed to the chivalry of other men by invoking what was at the time racialized imagery. He reminded them that man "has it within his power to help her, or to push her back. Shall he go ahead alone; or shall he extend her a hand; Shall he be a brute; or shall he be a MAN?" (quoted in Taylor 1998, 309–310). For this writer, courage and honor in the service of women expressed authentic masculinity; men could demonstrate that authenticity of manhood by voting for women's suffrage (Taylor 1998).

Chivalry also circulated in the arguments of profeminist men in the woman suffrage debate. However, these prosuffrage men used chivalry not to reject or patronize women's interest in the public political sphere, but to question what they judged to be an old-fashioned view of masculinity and politics. These men challenged the taken-for-granted association of masculinity with politics. Some began to speak of the "domestication of politics." As the state began to assume several of the functions hitherto the province of the domestic sphere, women claimed a right to influence those state policies (Taylor 1998). Indeed, after women achieved the right the vote, "sharp separations between men's and women's participation abated" (Baker 1990, 82).

A number of prosuffrage men supported and contributed to this blurring of what had once been separate spheres. Even these gender progressives employed racialized imagery, as in this statement by San Francisco resident Frederick Baker. "If woman's sphere was restricted to the home, as in the old days," Baker wrote,

> then the argument that there is no necessity for her to share the burden of government would have weight. But, in the face of the economic conditions which have forced her from the home into the arena of the business world, in factory, store, workshop, and the thousand avenues of toil, for man to say he shall have the exclusive right to prescribe the conditions under which she shall labor is to place his co-partner in life's battle in the category of the dumb brute. (quoted in Taylor 1998, 315)

Who might the "dumb brute" be in the white man's imagination? Recall that especially southern white women had argued for their right to vote on racist grounds, namely that if "they" (black men) enjoyed the right to cast ballots, why on earth should they not. No doubt this strategy and its effectiveness—as we will see in chapter 8, Frances Willard was taken in by white southerners' stories—helped drive a wedge between white and black women on this matter. After all, with black men disenfranchised and lynched, women's suffrage must have seemed something of a luxury to some black women. Ida B. Wells found her colleagues in black women's clubs were in fact unenthusiastic. In her autobiography she recalls when the suffrage issue surfaced in Illinois:

> It was about this time [1914] that the Illinois legislature was considering the question of enfranchising the women voters of that state. I had been a member of the Women's Suffrage Association all during my residence in Illinois, but somehow I had not been able to get very much interest among our club women. When I saw that we were likely to have a restricted suffrage, and the white women of the organization were working like beavers to bring it about, I made another effort to get our women interested. (Wells 1970, 345)

In California, some prosuffrage men invoked images of cave men to try to calm antisuffragists' fears of losing their masculinity. One male editorial writer intended to be soothing when he wrote that "barbarous man did not become unsexed when he occasionally left his spear in the hunt and worked with his mate in the field. Woman will not become unsexed when she lays down her distaff and joins her mate in the field of politics." Others were less conciliatory to their reactionary male voters. The secretary of the Citizens' Suffrage League, Charles Borger, snapped: "it would be funny if it were not so serious, to listen to the arguments [of antisuffragists] that 'woman should keep their places and attend the duties God intended her for'" (Taylor 1998, 315) These men, as well as a number of others, recognized and rejected the patriarchal and historically constructed ideology of separate gendered spheres. In the South, after suffrage was granted, white women too would challenge white men's fantasies of who they and black men were. The most prominent of these women, Jessie Daniel Ames, came to her antilynching work through her experience of the suffrage struggle in Texas (see chapter 8, section VI). For now, let us stay with the boys.

VI. Boy Culture During the Lynching Era

On one side lay women's sphere, a world of domesticity and civilization; on the other side, adult control gave way to the rough pleasures of boy culture. ... Some of the most important lessons that a youngster learned from boy culture were those about living a life divided by a boundary between the two spheres.

—E. Anthony Rotundo, "Boy Culture: Middle-Class Boyhood in Nineteenth-Century America" (1990)

As economic and familial conditions permitted, a separate gendered culture of childhood evolved as the nineteenth century closed. Here, relying on the work of E. Anthony Rotundo, we will glimpse this "boy culture" and suggest its relation to the racialized, gendered "crisis" of manhood during the lynching era. Curiously, many nineteenth-century sources described boys as "wild" and "careless," as "primitive savages," full of "animal spirits." They were commonly compared to Indians and African tribesmen. One writer even called them a breed unto themselves—"the race of boys" (quoted phrases in Rotundo 1990, 15).

Before the age of six or so, however, boys were not seen as separate, but integrated in a domestic world comprised of brothers, sisters, and cousins. They rarely strayed from the watchful eyes of parents and other supervisory adults. Mothers were especially vigilant, for most believed that early childhood was an "imprinting" phase during which the foundation was laid for good character. A good mother fashioned early on those intense bonds of love that would crystallize in the form of a strong conscience in later years. More didactic forms of moral instruction were also employed during the early years to ensure that proper language and social understanding developed. For his first five to seven years a boy's adult companions were primarily female, whose care for him was characterized by tender affection and moral instruction. By the time boys reached the age of three or four, however, their mothers were beginning to complain about their rebellious ways. Even so, at this stage little boys were still enmeshed in a domestic world fashioned by women (Rotundo 1990).

During these early years, boys were dressed in the same loose-fitting gowns worn by girls (Greven 1977). Such "girlish" clothing communicated to young boys the message that they were to behave like their sisters; it reminded them of their feminization. Practically, boys' gowns and smocks inhibited the running, climbing, and physical outbursts that so often made boys disagreeable occupants of women's world of domesticity. As psychoanalytic theory would elaborate in later decades, "pre-oedipal" boys—whether they acquiesced or rebelled against their feminine fashion—"were put in a situation where they had to accept or reject a feminine identity in their earliest years" (Rotundo 1990, 16). Even young slave boys had been dressed in girls' outfits; former slave Winger Vanhook recalled that "All de black chillun wore a long shirt. It come down to de middle ob de legs, an' you couldn't tell a gal from a boy." A former slave from Henry County, Tennessee, reported that "when boys got pretty large they wore body breeches. They wore a shirt and nothing else until they got a certain age" (quoted in Parent and Wallace 1993, 384).

All of this changed, however, the moment boys broke away from home and its womanly environment. Suddenly, boys shed their gowns and petticoats and the differences between themselves and their sisters and mothers became emphasized. Like Huck Finn, a boy distanced himself from the "female" which he now experienced as confining; to be "male" meant to be "free," whether on a river raft or a playground (Rotundo 1990). Such freedom was different from the domestic sphere not only in opportunity; it was different in tone and specifically in tranquility. For the world of boys was often a violent one. Rotundo tells us, in fact, that "one of the bonds that held boy culture together was the pain which youngsters inflicted on each other" (1990, 17).

Such violence probably functioned to emphasize the difference between home and away from home, between girls and boys, women and men. It may as well have functioned to suppress, even destroy, the bonds of affection forged in those early years of dependency and ego merging with mothers and other parenting women. Certainly the violence of boy culture kept boys from becoming involved with each other in ways that were unseemly or unmanly. As we saw in section II, nineteenth-century male friendship was intense, often physical. The same held true for very young men. "Friendship," Rotundo tells us, "was certainly the most important relation between boys" (1990, 19). Their friendships have been characterized as "fervent if not enduring" (quoted in Rotundo 1990, 19).

Not all boys enjoyed, as their older brothers and fathers and uncles did, the pleasures of "romantic friendship." Many boys' friendships tended to be "superficial and sudden, however passionate" (Rotundo 1990, 20) they might have been at any given moment. Friendship among nineteenth-century boys was, in Rotundo's words again, "volatile affairs—intense, short-lived, and constantly shifting." Boy culture, then, was not unlike the grown-up world of their fathers, organized around the cult of the isolated (i.e., "free" and male) individual. Although it was a child's culture typified by constant and enthusiastic play, the world of boys was also "a cruel, competitive, uncertain, and even violent world" (Rotundo 1990, 21). Its cohesion, Rotundo suggests, had to do with a common set of values, but I would prefer to call them antivalues, in the sense they functioned as negations, tactics by which they underscored their difference from the women with whom they had, just months earlier, so lovingly and unquestioningly identified.

Certainly boys valued loyalty and physical prowess, but the quality they admired most, Rotundo reports, was courage. Boy courage consisted of two elements, stoicism and daring. Stoicism involved the suppression of "weak" feelings, feelings associated with girls such as fear, pain, or grief. One game, called "soak-about," allowed boys to perform this psychological strategy physically. A group of boys tried to hit another boy in a vulnerable spot with a hard ball, certainly an occasion for stoicism. The boy had to face the pain without flinching, a rehearsal, one might suggest, for a life of feeling denied and suppressed. Having lost the subjective feeling of emotion, these young men in gender training looked for compensation in the objective world around him. "The experience of boy culture," Rotundo writes, "encouraged a male child to become the master, the conqueror, the owner of what was outside him" (1990, 23).

These psychosocial and sexual dynamics of male identity formation are characterized, then, by negation and contradiction. In order to become a young man, a boy had to put behind him, as it were, all that he had been, a mama's boy, a mother-identified infant and child whose relational and feminine world was primary. That world, that relational structure of the ego, had to be negated to support those fantasies of "freedom" and "individuality" so key to nineteenth-century manhood, as many men understood it. Of course, "negated" is not "gone," as psychoanalytic theory emphasizes. The rough and rugged world of boys' play was built upon, and laced with, strong relational bonds, learned at their mothers' sides. The "deeper meaning in some of boys' violence involved their fondness for each other," Rotundo (1990) understands.

> Since boys worked to restrain their tender impulses in each other's presence, they lacked a direct outlet for the natural affection of friends. This warm feeling sometimes found expression in the bonds of the club and of the gang and in the demanding codes of loyalty that bound young comrades tougher. But another avenue of release for these fond impulses came through constant physical exchanges. ... By a certain "boy logic," it made sense to pay one's affections in the coin of physical combat, which served as the social currency of the boys' world. (Rotundo 1990, 24)

We will see this phenomenon repeated, albeit with racial and class differences, in contemporary lower-class black male culture (see chapter 14).

Just as they would for many twentieth-century boys, acts of vandalism provided nineteenth-century boys with opportunities to express their resistance toward male authority, embodied in policemen, constables, not to mention irate property owners. Such "guerrilla warfare" gave boys a chance to contest their presumably submissive roles with men. In acts of vandalism, boys had power, power to disrupt the lives of grown men, power to work for and gain (however illegally and temporarily) the property they wanted. Like today, grown men are, in general, unable to prevent vandalism; then as now they managed to control it enough to make it an exciting transgression for boys (Rotundo 1990). Of course, the son's oedipalized resistance to the father—symbolized in male authority—reproduces patriarchy (Pinar 1983/1994/1998).

Especially at school was there a confrontation between boy culture and male authority that underscored the significance of male authority by virtue of boys' resistance to it. While few boys spent as many hours in school as children do now, those who did seemed compelled to make life difficult for those men who taught. "Men" is actually a misnomer here, since those males who taught were often college students or teenagers. The problem of youthful male pedagogical authority was compounded by students (especially in small-town schools) as old as twenty and as young as three or four (Rotundo 1990).

Why were nineteenth-century boys so compelled to contest their (especially male) teachers' authority? Rotundo (1990) suggests that nineteenth-century boys felt little enthusiasm for school, in no small part because the reward was uncertain. The sequence of courses and grades through which young males progressed into college and onto jobs did not become clearly established until the end of the century. Moreover, the curriculum tended to be abstract, the subjects impractical, the physical confinement unbearable. But that was secondary to a boy culture defined by its repudiation of mothers and resistance to fathers. As Daniel Beard, the founder of the Boy Scouts and a prominent illustrator, suggested in his autobiography, boys as a rule "did not like men," and regarded them as "enemies" who always interfered with "our pleasure" (quoted in Rotundo 1990, 27). Many nineteenth-century boys would seem to have been victims of what a hundred years later would be called "hypermasculinity" (see chapter 14).

Nineteenth-century men and women would try different tactics in responding to "boy culture." Men saw their responsibility as maintaining manly order; women tried to fashion boys into sober, hardworking Christians in a predatory world. As would Leslie Fielder (1966; see chapter 18), E. Anthony Rotundo will refer to Mark Twain to make his point. Rotundo (1990) suggests that Huck Finn perceived this difference between men's and women's parenting orientations when he complained that Aunt Sally wanted to "sivilize" him. Whereas men sought to control boys by "interfering" with their "pleasure," as Daniel Beard phrased it, women were determined to "redeem boys from their barbarism" (Rotundo 1990, 27). In Huck's case, that "barbarism" involved living on a raft with a black man.

This split between a woman's world of relationality and restraint and a man's world of adventure and freedom became structured as a young man's identity. He learned to live as a self divided, in a world divided, a life "with divided loyalties and a divided heart" (Rotundo 1990, 30). Boy culture was a world of separate spheres, very much like the one he would inhabit as an adult, for the clash between boys' culture and women's was only a more tempestuous version of the divide between men's and women's spheres. To know, accept, and live such a conflict as a boy prepared him to live the same conflict as an adult (Rotundo 1990). This is, of course, a somewhat schizoid ego resolution, one that will prepare him to split off what he cannot tolerate within himself as a threat in the world, now imagined as alien and "other." In general, it would seem, the division of the self results in the multiplication of others.

Those boys who were successfully socialized into such bifurcated personalities began, in their midteens, to develop a sexual interest in girls. Now the passionate friendships of boy culture started to lose their appeal, as heteronormative sexuality redirected the passionate intensity of same-sex friendship. Now the young man distanced himself from that world, began to think of marriage, a life's work, and a home of his own. Now, in his eyes as well as those of his significant others, he was becoming a "man," which is to say he was becoming "civilized," maturing out of his "savage" boyhood (Rotundo 1990). He was ready to "tie the knot," not only to a "woman," but around his divided self.

This narrative of "boy-to-man" is hardly unfamiliar to us, partly because there were several developments—each associated with the emergence of a commercial society and a middle-class culture—which influenced the process and which remain, to some extent, in place today. One such development was the psychological isolation of men's world from the home, from the world young boys inhabited. Earlier in the century, many fathers had worked at home, often in fields or in nearby shops and workplaces. Throughout the 1800s,

Rotundo (1990) reminds us, there was a steady shift in the sites of professional and commercial work away from the home. This trend was most obvious in the cities, but it was under way in small towns as well. There the men who comprised small-town elites (men whose sons produced much of the documentation on which Rotundo's research is based) also worked away from home. The work of these men, those occupied with politics and law as well as business, required them to travel, taking them farther and farther away as they pursued the expanding sphere of commerce.

Whether urban or rural, nineteenth-century middle-class white men slowly became more and more isolated from their sons, at first physically then emotionally. In contrast to previous centuries, Rotundo argues, the father-son relationship in the nineteenth century became less familiar, involved less the presence of grandfathers and uncles and older male figures in extended families. Additionally, and here Rotundo's account anticipates Parsons's or Chodorow's (see chapter 14), the father-son relationship was also weakened by the type of work that middle-class men increasingly did. This work tended to be abstract, requiring specialized knowledge and the performance of tasks less accessible to a boy than the crafts and agricultural work through which earlier generations of fathers and sons had come to know each other. Therefore, even when middle-class fathers were at home, their work provided no common ground, little or nothing to share, between the two. As a consequence, middle-class boys grew increasingly alienated from their fathers and from the world they inhabited (Rotundo 1990). This alienation would help contribute to the "crisis" of white masculinity. As the father became a more imaginary figure, mothers figured more prominently in the lives of boys. Focused on domestic tasks, child rearing, and moral uplift, nineteenth-century women's labor and activities intensified her relationships with her children, including her relationships with her sons (Rotundo 1990).

In contrast to the eighteenth century, the middle-class household of the nineteenth century was a private space. It was no longer a site of production for trade or sale, and it was increasingly focused upon child rearing, on moral and spiritual education, on the private life of a nuclear family. More than before, mothers were expected to awaken the soul and stir the conscience of new generations of sons. Boys not only experienced more intense relationships with their mothers, their relationships lasted longer, as most of them lived at home well into their teenage years. This intensity and duration coupled with a relatively estranged relation with their fathers produced tension between women's sphere and boy culture. Not unlike the culture of masculinity today, which we will examine in chapters 13–15, the structure of boys' social sphere in the nineteenth century was in many respects a reaction against the woman's world where they lived (Rotundo 1990).

Given an increasing "normalization" of a homosocial world in an increasingly industrialized society, this masculine rejection of domesticity horrified few parents. After all, if sons were to become "men," to become "masculine," they had to put away pre-oedipal identifications, child's (i.e., female-identified boys') things. Still, in order for patriarchy to be reproduced, resistance must be felt, expressed, then channeled, and the standardization of boyhood by grown-ups helped ensure that that process occurred. During the 1880s and 1890s, adult men formed a number of boys' organizations designed to direct the rejection of their mothers and temper their resistance to their fathers, in other words, to produce "normal" young men. These organizations bore names such as the Boys' Brigades and the Knights of King Arthur; boys' divisions were added to existing organizations like the Y.M.C.A. These organizations attempted to formalize and thereby control many of the traditional games and skills of boy culture blended with their own moral agendas, often Christian, sometimes expressing a nostalgia for rural life. The most important organization formed during this period was the Boy Scouts of America, established during the second decade of the twentieth century (Rotundo 1990).

But for the thousands of boys who had participated in similar organizations before 1900, these organizational experiences meant the end of a boy culture largely unshaped by adults. These organizations exploited many of the homosocial dynamics of that boy culture in order to promulgate a "moral" program designed to standardize gender and identity formation in young men. This didacticism meant the end of boy culture, a didacticism that was hardly limited to these boys' organizations; it was everywhere, of course, in the schools. There was an increase in the duration of schooling for middle-class boys as the nineteenth century closed, meaning that boyhood was less performed in a separate culture unsupervised by adults, but increasingly in institutions designed for political and gender socialization (Rotundo 1990).

Rotundo points to the school's organization around gradedness as "one of the most conspicuous changes that the new system of education brought to boy culture in the late 1800s" (1990, 35). While the school experience hardly ended forms of homoerotic sublimation such as competition and informal peer ranking among boys, gradedness introduced and enforced a new hierarchy of age on their world. This hierarchy created another system of status, one purely fabricated by bureaucratic convenience (despite its educational and developmental rationales), one which undermined the continuity of generations, in which older and younger boys had played freely together and the older taught the younger. Now, younger boys were now just as likely to learn from teachers, recreational leaders, or books (Rotundo 1990). Many would imagine that they pulled themselves up by their bootstraps, a fantasy of "self-made" masculinity hardly new to fin-de-siècle boys (Kimmel 1996).

In her explication of the relation of family and gender to the ascendancy of the middle class, Mary Ryan (1981) has shown how the hardworking and sober clerks and aggressive businessmen of the nineteenth century were, contrary to their fantasy, not "self-made," but had in reality been "cradled" in the evangelical homes of the antebellum era. At home sons learned mothers' lessons of self-sacrifice, industriousness, and temperance; at home they had been protected from the dissipation of tavern and brothel. The slow shift in men's attitudes toward work, leisure, and the family over the nineteenth century is due in large measure to women. While referring to a "family strategy" and to "parental" decisions, it is clear, Ryan argues, that it was women's influence in child rearing that was key. The "revered mother dominated the emotional space of the home," Ryan observes, so much so that the "idea of fatherhood itself seemed almost to wither away as the bond between mother and child assumed a central place in the constellation of family affection. ... In the narrowing home sphere, at least, women had undisputed title to psychological leadership" (1981, 231–232).

As we have seen in Rotundo's analysis of "boy culture," this leadership was regularly rejected by boys determined to escape domesticity and relationality and imagine themselves as separate, individual and free, as "men." Boys' rejection of the former and accomplishment of the latter can, of course, never be fully successful, as object relations theory makes clear (Chodorow 1978). Boys' pre-oedipal symbiotic identification with their mothers may be suppressed but it hardly disappears, however "self-made" men insist themselves to be. In the late nineteenth century, for instance, successful "self-made" men often celebrated their mothers publicly, even while rejecting them privately and embracing the public and homosocial world of business and sport. In autobiographies and at testimonial dinners, these "masculine" and independent men regularly attributed their accomplishments to maternal nurture and influence. These stylized and sentimentalized professions ("I owe it all to my sainted mother") suggest that the earlier phase of matrifocality, now repressed, had resurfaced, if in ritualized and self-dissociated forms. Motherhood becomes symbolic currency in a homosocial economy, "refracted through the haze of distant memory ... [safely removed from] the emotional disposition of ... men" (Carnes 1990, 38). Men relocated their earlier maternal identifications into rhetorical, abstracted, and finally imaginary evocations of those no longer (for them) concretely existing mothers. This particular developmental formation of masculine ego identity characterized by repression and self-splitting can have, as we will see in chapter 13, disastrous consequences, especially for women and children, but also for men, specifically gay men. For now, let us focus on how these processes of repression and self-splitting were expressed in nineteenth-century initiation rites of all-male fraternal orders.

VII. Golden Age of Fraternity

Social change is necessary and a precondition of such change is an attempt to understand masculinity, to make it visible.

—Anthony Easthope, *What a Man's Gotta Do: The Masculine Myth in Popular Culture* (1986)

The fantasmatic not only regulates erotic investment, but it maps out a symbolic position for the subject, the position from which it lives its desire.

—Kaja Silverman, *Male Subjectivity at the Margins* (1992)

In 1897 the *North American Review* proclaimed the last third of the nineteenth century the "Golden Age of Fraternity" (quoted in Carnes 1990, 38). Why? Out of a population of nineteen million American men, five and a half million belonged to fraternal orders, among them the Red Men

(165,000), the Odd Fellows (810,000), the Freemasons (750,000), the Knights of Pythias (475,000) as well as hundreds of smaller orders. Millions more men claimed membership in the Grand Army of the Republic, the Knights of Labor, the Grange, and similar organizations. "The distinguishing feature and central activity of all these organizations," Mark Carnes (1990) concludes, "was the performance of elaborate sequences of initiation rituals" (38). These initiation rituals do more than foreshadow the strange homoerotic activities of contemporary college fraternity initiations; they point specifically to a late nineteenth-century manhood under stress, evidently forced "underground" to perform its most explicitly homoerotic acts of bonding and, on occasion, bondage. Safely contained within these ritualistic initiations, men could fashion for themselves positions from which to perform their (suppressed) desire.

While astonishingly widespread, fraternal ritual was primarily chiefly a practice of white middle-class men. Carnes (1990) suggests that "the rise of rituals coincided with the orders' adoption of middle-class values" (39), gendered values of a racialized manhood characterized, it would seem, by bifurcation and repression. Formerly drinking societies, the Freemasons and Odd Fellows banned alcohol during the third and fourth decades of the nineteenth century. They claimed a moral imperative in membership, even trying to determine the moral character of new members, creating juridical proceedings to expel dissolute or wayward members, and replacing rented tavern rooms with elaborate "temples." Most members were urban middle-class white men (Carnes 1990).

What was the attraction of these orders and elaborate initiations for these men? At the time, a writer for the *North American Review* tried to make sense of it in these sexualized terms: "There is a strange and powerful attraction for some men in the mysticism of the ritual. There is a peculiar fascination in the unreality of the initiation, an allurement about fine 'team' work, a charm of deep potency in the unrestricted, out-of-the-world atmosphere which surrounds the scenes where men are knit together by the closes ties, [and] bound by the most solemn obligations to maintain secrecy." The point of these lodges, presumably, was to meet friends and make "contacts" (for business, right?). But initiation rituals took so much time that members never got to know each other, let alone make friends. Some members developed a sufficiently powerful "craving" for these rituals that they neglected their professions or business. What moved so many men to be "charmed" by and "powerfully attracted" to such rituals? (quoted in Carnes 1990, 39). The writer for the *North American Review* did not say (Carnes 1990).

Certainly there were obvious homoerotic elements in many initiation rituals. Consider aspects of the evolution of the first degree of the Improved Order of Red Men. At one point during the initiation, a council fire was started; in the preparation room the candidate—a "pale face" he was termed—removed his shirt and shoes, replacing the latter with moccasins. A scout rapped at the "inner wicket" and motioned for the candidate to follow him. They moved silently around the lodge room, avoiding an assemblage of "Indians" who were "sleeping" at the far end. Then, "inadvertently," the scout tripped over one of the sleeping "Indians." The startled "Indian" awakens, shouting, "Spies!

Traitors in our Camp!" They capture the candidate; the scout "somehow" escapes. The "Indian" "hunters" then gather around a fire:

> First Brave: This pale face is of a hated nation: let us put him to torture!
> Second Brave: He is a squaw, and cannot bear the torture!
> Third Brave: He fears a Warrior's death!
> Fourth Brave: Let us burn him at the stake! (quoted in Carnes 1990, 41)

The discussion continued along these lines until, at last, the initiate or "pale face" is informed that he will indeed be consumed by fire (Carnes 1990). While the ritual of burning the lynched black man must come to mind here, no doubt the memory of witch burning was also circulating somewhere as well in this misogynistic and racist performance of the white male unconscious.

The "death" of the initiate is not final, of course, as the point of the ritual, ostensibly, was the new life path the initiate has chosen to walk, in the company of his "brothers." At the close of the Adoption Degree these lines were read: "Is our mind with friendship flowing,/Freedom in your pathway showing?/Brothers' love shall never cease" (quoted in Carnes 1990, 43). Here, in secrecy and half-dressed, men could perform their sadomasochistic desire for male-male intimacy. Its inappropriateness to the world outside is implied by its secrecy, but that suggests as well its inner significance. Carnes believes that the rituals had to do with flight from a modern urban industrial society, an escape into what these white men imagined as a primitive past. The Red Men were the most explicit example of this preoccupation, but nearly all fraternal orders assumed that their rituals had some similarity to the rites of so-called primitive men (Carnes 1990). Were these white men newly masculinized "heterosexuals" who had lost "romantic friendships"? Were they, after Leslie Fielder (1966), white men who imagined a redemptive physical intimacy with "primitive" "others"? What *was* the meaning of these initiation rituals?

To explore that question, Mark Carnes turns to the cross-cultural research of cultural anthropologists Whiting, Kluckhohn, and Antony (1958). They determined that male initiation ceremonies were most commonly found in those societies where women exerted a strong influence over male infants and boys, and where men controlled the economic and political resources. This is, of course, a restatement of the "separate spheres" ideology which typified patterns of gender in nineteenth-century America. Not unlike Parsons and Bales's (1955) research on the relatively absent father conducted at about the same time, Whiting and his colleagues hypothesized that in societies where the father is absent or has reduced influence in child rearing, the male infant perceives the mother as all-powerful and comes to envy her and her position. In object relations psychoanalytic terms, this is a consequence of the pre-oedipal phase during which time the child, daughter or son, is identified with the mother.

About five years old, the son begins to notice the world outside the home; he becomes aware, and is made aware, that women control the domestic sphere but that it is men who control the "world." A secondary identification with the masculine role now is constructed and superimposed upon the bedrock foundation of female identification. Like lower-class gangs and college fraternities in contemporary America, initiation ceremonies "serve psychologically to brainwash the primary feminine identity and to establish firmly the secondary male identity" (Burton and Whiting 1961, 90; quoted in Carnes 1990, 46). Initiation rituals were performed in response to this "cross-sex identity conflict." The rituals, by resolving this conflict, presumably promoted the well-being of young men and, as men would have it, of society itself (Carnes 1990). Feminist women would tell a different version of this same story, but it is clear that men themselves—in nineteenth-century America and across cultures—perceive themselves as rising out of the ashes of a primary feminine identification (see Gilmore 1990). Boys are not girls. They *are* girls, of course, but in negation. In a patriarchal heterosexist society, that makes for a somewhat unstable ego identity, to say the least.

Carnes (1990) suggests that the division of gender roles in Victorian America approximated, in general terms, what Whiting described cross-culturally. There was a deep psychological division between Victorian men and women. Confined to the "domestic sphere" of child rearing, many women dutifully devoted themselves to their children. To this "calling" of child rearing, many mothers directed an intensity akin to religious experience. Many held deep the conviction that by inculcating in their children the virtues of Jesus, they could help reconstruct a masculine order that had "fallen" (Carnes 1990). We saw in chapter 5 how Christian feminists employed conservative religious discourses to affirm their moral superiority and in the process destabilizing traditional gender arrangements.

While many women remained mothers, men left home, increasingly preoccupied with work and politics in the public sphere. As we have seen, shifts in the structure of the economy contributed to the separation of men from the home during much of the day. As the distance between home and workplace increased, and the workday itself grew longer, many fathers had little time or energy to parent their children. "Paternal neglect," one observer complained in 1842, had become common (quoted in Carnes 1990, 47). Even when fathers did manage to spend time with their sons, they were often unable to act as meaningful role models to sons who were striking out to make careers for themselves in the new professions and corporations (Carnes 1990). If not in "crisis," many middle-class white men were certainly edgy. In the South, "edgy" isn't quite adequate to depict the violent instability of the masculine gender, a gender still struggling to reconstruct itself in the aftermath of the humiliating defeat at Appomattox and the loss of enslaved black bodies to empower it.

What becomes clear is that these initiation rituals functioned to restabilize a beleaguered male identity, in large part by purging it of its felt female identifications. To emphasize this point, Carnes uses Whiting's terms to frame the 1868 Adoption Degree of the Red Men: (1) "to brainwash the primary feminine identity." Characterized as a "pale face," and also a "squaw," indeed a coward—obviously intersecting if not conflated terms in the minds of the Order—the initiate had to "die." By virtue of his metaphorical death, he was cleansed of his former (female-identified) self. Born again, he was now free to pursue an entirely different life course; and (2) "to establish firmly the secondary male identity." First demeaned, then threatened, then attacked by hostile father figures (the elders), the initiate finally wins their approval and is "adopted" as one of the "children" into the new family of Red Men (quoted phrases in

Carnes 1990, 47). As we will see, the basic pattern holds for college fraternities and lower-class gangs, and even some 1990s "wild men" (Bly 1990). It would seem to be nearly universal (see Gilmore 1990). Boys are made into "men" by suppressing their primary feminine identifications and constructing secondary—necessarily compensatory, overdetermined, and defensive—masculine identities.

In a cautionary note, Carnes reminds us that Whiting's model relies on identification theories which suggest that if fathers are ineffective or absent in child rearing, boys will envy the power of their mothers, imitate their behavioral traits, and identify with the feminine role. (We should be so lucky.) The concept of identification, Carnes acknowledges, involves complexities that make its use in interpreting historical evidence problematical. It is unlikely, he points out as an example, that historians can ever determine whether boys or men, at the core of their being, perceived themselves as "masculine." Moreover, he notes that many contemporary theorists have contested the possibility of any "essential" gender identification, citing Joseph Pleck (1984), insisting that gender roles are socially constructed. The point for Carnes's research is that there is no core masculinity to which a "normal" male initiate aspired.

Given these concerns, Carnes retreats from his use of Whiting's "cross-sex identity conflict" model, replacing it with what he takes to be a less problematic gender-role perspective. The difference, I would suggest, is not significant. Restated in gender-role or social constructivist terms, the dilemma for middle-class white boys in Victorian America was not simply that their fathers were absent, thereby depriving them of psychological models of some "essential" masculinity. The dilemma for Victorian boys was that adult gender roles had been constructed as invariant and rigidly defined, and that they, like their sisters, were mostly taught the sentiments and values associated with women. Certainly by early adolescence, often earlier, boys grasped the gendered divide between women and men, and, as Carnes (1990) nicely phrases it, "fantasized about how they would fit into the world of men" (48). In the absence of fathers and of adult male role models generally, many boys separated themselves into a "boy culture" which in its aggressiveness and competitiveness anticipated what would come to be called hypermasculinity. As young men struggling to internalize heteronormative conceptions of manhood and masculinity, they were drawn to men's secret orders, where they repeatedly performed rituals that presumably bleached from their everyday surface personalities those effusive religious sentiments and intense emotional intimacy associated with the domestic sphere of women (Carnes 1990).

Implied in the initiation rituals was a preconscious appreciation that all boys were mother-identified during important, what we might say "imprinting," phases of childhood. Such matrifocality would later, in the racial politics of the 1960s, be ascribed to black families as a "problem" by the Moynihan Report (see chapter 14), but it would seem to be a developmental fact for all boys, regardless of race or class. Of course, matrifocality is lived and contradicted differentially according to race, class, culture, and the historical moment, but the fact of mother-identification would seem to be universal. In the Order of Red Men male initiates were gendered as female, as "squaws," clearly perceived to be the universal condition among boys before becoming men. (Certainly in prison, as we see in chapters 15 and 16, many men assume they can make "bitches" out of "men.") To move beyond this unacceptable feminine stage of development, to cease being a "squaw," the initiate through "torture" even "death" became a man (Carnes 1990). He had to kill the "woman" he was in order to be a man he was not but would pretend to be.

There were no "short cuts," no detours along the pathway to manhood. Evidently with this notion in mind, fraternal leaders insisted that members experience the entire sequence of initiations provided by their order. Every major order included at least one ritual in which each of the following major themes was performed (bracketed statements are mine; the others are Carnes's):

> 1) The initiate at the outset was portrayed as immature of [or] unmasculine. [The concept of "child" is feminized.] 2) He overcame obstacles as he embarked on a difficult journey through the stages of childhood and adolescence. This journey/ordeal reached a climax when 3) he was killed (or nearly so) by angry father figures. Finally, 4) he was reborn [is that why this verb is used in evangelical Christian circles: one is "reborn" in the empty stare of the loin-clothed man on the cross?] as a man into a new family of approving brethren and patriarchs. In this way the emotional orientations instilled by maternal nurture would give way to the sterner lessons provided by ancient patriarchs, venerable kings, or savage chieftains. (Carnes 1990, 51)

Or perhaps "captains of industry"? After studying the public rhetoric of the orders, some have concluded that they functioned primarily to produce personalities for industrial capitalism (Carnes 1990).

While the orders reflected the homosocial sadomasochism of a predatory capitalism and articulated the racialized masculine values of the emerging middle class, it does not follow, Carnes (1990) argues, that members participated in initiation rituals as a kind of parallel socialization. He points out that middle-class men, or working-class men who aspired to the middle class, did not have to go to the lodge to learn the merits of hard work and self-discipline. In some ways, in fact, the rituals contradicted certain aspects of turn-of-the-century capitalism. To illustrate, Carnes (1990) points to the Adoption Degree, which advised initiates to emulate the "children of the forest," who, it noted, held wealth and property in common (quoted in Carnes 1990, 51). Certainly this value contradicted essential capitalist constructs such as private property.

The fascination for fraternal ritual suggests to Carnes what curriculum theorists appreciate as "resistance," not "reproduction." That is, rather than simplistically reproducing the dominant economic and social order, initiation rituals expressed young men's "resistance" to it. Carnes (1990) puts it this way: "[e]ven as the emerging middle classes were embracing capitalism and bourgeois sensibilities, they were simultaneously creating rituals whose message was largely antithetical to those relationships and values" (51). Such resistance, Carnes understands, did not mean that the orders and their rituals undermined the gender, familial, and economic structures of capitalism. On the contrary:

"By providing solace from the psychic pressures of these new social and institutional relationships, they ensured its survival" (Carnes 1990, 51).

Once again Carnes returns to anthropology to explicate the rituals as a social practice. He recalls the work of Victor Turner (1969), who argued that social life is a dialectical process. On the one hand, individuals are socialized into structures and appropriate roles. However, individuality cannot be completely effaced, and many yearn for a deeper and broader range of experience and meaning. Consequently, even while complying with dominant structures and roles "initiates" are also unconsciously reacting against these structures by participating in liminal rituals whose symbols and practices are in opposition to existing hierarchies and rules. In simpler societies, "antistructure," as Turner termed these liminal states, was often expressed through ceremonies such as initiation rites, in which the ordinary regularities of kinship, law, and custom were replaced by a private domain of secret symbols. Turner believed that no society can function without this dialectical process in which "resistance" ensures "reproduction."

For Carnes, Turner's argument makes intelligible a series of fraternal rituals that otherwise seem "silly, foolish, or downright preposterous" (Carnes 1990, 52). Of course, there was among some a degree of self-consciousness about their practices. Carnes points out that Odd Fellows acknowledged that once they had wrapped themselves in biblical robes and placed masks upon their faces they were indeed odd. Many lawyers, shopkeepers, and industrialists appreciated that it was eccentric to pretend to be Old Testament patriarchs, Roman senators, or medieval knights. From a Turnerian perspective, this peculiar contradictoriness suggests the meaning of the ritual: by conjuring a world very different from the one they inhabited every day, these men sought solace from that life. They sought relief, Carnes notes, from the limited range of personal expression allowed by Victorian gender conventions and by the rigid structures as well as from the discipline of work in a capitalist society. Perhaps solace was achieved, and in so doing, these rituals helped middle-class men to adjust to a new social order that was, curiously, largely of their own making (Carnes 1990).

Fashioned by men but fitting them uncomfortably, the new industrial society was a gendered order in which "masculinity" and an increasingly sexualized identity replaced "manhood," an identity predicated on homosocial honor and for many, "romantic friendship." With the "crisis" of late nineteenth-century white masculinity, stimulated too by the appearance of "heterosexuality" and the segregation and suppression (and creation) of "homosexuality," homoeroticism went underground, as it were, into secret domains where young men were undressed, feminized, made "primitive," then "killed," a not so subtle replication of the developmental formation of the heteronormative male ego. This formation required repudiation of an earlier mother-identified self, the embrace of a split-off identity figured as "primitive"—in the Order of Red Men as Indians—which enabled the "new man" to appear, like a snake shedding its skin. In turn-of-the-century America, for many women, children, African Americans and politically vulnerable others, this new snake was no less deadly than the old one.

VIII. Minds, Muscles, and Masturbation

It's a psychoanalytic commonplace that what we lose in reality we recreate in fantasy. ... American men have been searching for their lost manhood since the middle of the nineteenth century.

—Michael S. Kimmel, "Consuming Manhood: The Feminization of American Culture and the Recreation of the Male Body" (1994)

The cradle of the middle class, and of capitalism, had been rocked by women.

—Mark Carnes, "Middle-Class Men and the Solace of Fraternal Ritual" (1990)

[T]he experience of masturbation [was] a practice that Foucault saw at the very origin of the science of sexuality. What he called the war against onanism during the past two centuries was crucial in constituting the human being as a subject of sexual desire, a constitution that would be gloriously, or ingloriously, crowned by psychoanalysis.

—Leo Bersani, *Homos* (1995)

In this final section on the "crisis" of nineteenth-century white masculinity, I will, relying especially on the work of Gail Bederman and Michael Kimmel, summarize and extend what we have learned thus far. I will focus on what has to now been characterized as something of an addendum, the appearance of "sexuality" as crucial in the formation of identity. As we will see, the gendered and racialized anxiety that accompanied this major historical development became focused, at first, on the adolescent body, particularly the white male adolescent body. In a widespread masturbation panic was signed both the emergence of and suppression of "homosexuality," a figure that was gendered and would become racialized. Homosexuals were widely perceived as "inverts," that is, women in men's bodies or, in the case of lesbians, men in women's bodies. Later, certainly by the mid-twentieth century, especially among some black male intellectuals like Amiri Baraka, there would circulate the assumption that only white men are "fags."

As we have seen, gender became increasingly crucial to middle-class identity during the final decades of the nineteenth century, a point Gail Bederman (1995b) underscores by quoting Mary Ryan (1981): "the American middle class molded its distinctive identity around domestic values and family practices" (15; quoted in Bederman 1995b, 408). White middle-class men celebrated "true" women as pious and maternal, angelic guardians of virtue and domesticity. In contrast were black and working-class women, whose willingness to neglect domestic duties (or so the white middle class imagined) made them appear un-Christian and morally deficient, even unsavory (Bederman 1995b).

Manhood circulated throughout middle-class identity. Middle-class constructions of both manliness and womanliness implied the willful control of sin (Vance 1985). Yet the middle class believed that men, unlike women, who tended to be naturally virtuous (unless ruined by men), were besieged by lust. This "passionate" masculine nature was regarded as the source of men's danger to women and children (and thereby to Christian society) but, if harnessed, the impetus for men's great power to "erect" civilization. Succumbing to emotion or sexual passion would sap a man's strength, indeed his very life force, leaving him weak and degenerate (D'Emilio and Freedman 1983; Kimmel 1996). Given these high stakes, what virtuous middle-class parents could fail to admonish their sons to build a strong, manly "character"?

How could such manly "character" be achieved? Like "mind," manhood was perceived to be a muscle; only through repetitive exercises that strengthened control over licentious impulse could manhood be built up. A man's ability to control powerful passions through strong character and an unwavering will were the primary sources of his strength and authority. By gaining the "manly" strength to control himself, Gail Bederman (1995b) points out, a man was enabled to take on the duty to protect and direct those weaker than himself, including "his" wife, "his" children, and "his" employees. This gendered mix of "manly" power, "honor," and obligation followed from this "self-mastery" and were embedded in the term "manliness."

Late nineteenth-century middle-class white men saw manliness everywhere; it was in some vague but profound way what human (white) life was about. For instance, a man's manhood was evident in how he conducted business. Given the nineteenth-century market economy's unpredictability, a strong character built on high-minded self-restraint was regarded as the rock upon which middle-class men could build their fortunes, indeed their lives. This perception informed nearly every aspect of business practice; middle-class men were, for instance, awarded or denied credit based on others' judgments of the "manly" strength of their characters. Raters like Dun and Bradstreet included in credit reports comments on businessmen's honesty, probity, and family life (Bederman 1995b). Not only did a man's character make for business success; business made for manliness. In *The Strenuous Career* (1908), Madison Peters wrote: "A man's business makes him—it hardens his muscles ... wakes up his inventive genius, puts his wits to work, arouses ambition, makes him feel that he is a man, and must show himself a man by taking a man's part in life" (quoted in Kimmel 1996, 81).

Manly control over impulse and passion very much influenced middle-class family practices. Parents often reminded their sons of the virtues of manly self-restraint, encouraging them to work hard and live abstemiously. Such accomplishments of character would also permit them to amass the capital prerequisite to going into business for themselves, itself a prerequisite to marriage, which ought to be postponed until a man could afford to support a family in proper middle-class fashion (Ryan 1981). By the end of the nineteenth century, Bederman (1995b) emphasizes, such notions of manliness—emphasizing self-mastery and restraint—were foundational to middle-class identity.

Manhood became synonymous with the idea of adulthood; both concepts suggested the opposite of childhood. Likewise, virility was contrapuntal to puerility, not femininity. To be manly implied the acceptance of bourgeois—that is, adult—responsibilities as provider, producer, and protector of the family. As early as the 1830s, Michael S. Kimmel (1994) argues, a new version of masculinity had begun to emerge in the eastern cities. Kimmel terms this new gendered formation "marketplace manhood," as men derived their identities primarily from success in the capitalist marketplace—that is, the accumulation of wealth, power, and capital. "The manhood of the urban entrepreneur, the businessman," Kimmel (1994) tells us, "was restless, agitated, devoted to his work in the homosocial public arena. ... Masculinity became a homosocial enactment, to be proved in the marketplace" (13–14).

To succeed in the market, Kimmel (1994) continues, the American middle-class man had to first gain control over his self. Alcohol was one challenge to self-control since, by contemporary standards, nineteenth-century white men were heavy drinkers. White men would routinely wash down meals with hard cider (or peach brandy in the South); frequent drinks in the workshop or in the farm field "fortified" workers for heavy labor in the cold or in the heat. In the South white men drank constantly, it seemed. Many took a break from work at midmorning for what they called "eleveners," the antebellum version of the coffee break, during which they drank whiskey flavored by berries (Kimmel 1996). White workingmen "liked to drink, at all times of the day, in stupefying quantities" (Johnson and Wilentz 1994, 59). Drink "made them men," they imagined; it "gave them strength" (Sellers 1992, 259; quoted in Kimmel 1996, 48–49). As Michael Kimmel (1996) observes, Americans have always been fond of alcohol; even the Founding Fathers were heavy drinkers.

The Founding Fathers may have been "sots," but white men in America really began to drink during the first decades of the nineteenth century, especially hard liquor. In fact, "alcohol was such an accepted part of American life that in 1829 the secretary of war estimated that three-quarters of the nation's laborers drank daily at least 4 ounces of distilled spirits" (Rorabaugh 1979, 14–15). Americans drank more hard alcoholic beverages between 1790 and 1830 than at any other time in our history or since. This was the "great American whiskey binge" (quoted in Kimmel 1996, 49).

By 1830 hard liquor consumption had climbed to 9.5 gallons a year for every American over fourteen, and over 5 gallons per capita overall. As well, 30.3 gallons of hard cider and other intoxicants were consumed, primarily by white men. This state of continual intoxication can be linked to white men's dreams of wealth, dreams so few realized that the majority of white men were constantly warding off feelings of failure (Rorabaugh 1979). The volatility of the marketplace, dreams (supported by the occasional reality) of fortunes to be won and lost, and the general economic uncertainty of the early Industrial Revolution rendered working white men nervous wrecks. Kimmel quotes Edward Bourne who, at midcentury, suggested, in understated terms, that (white) men's drinking habits "grew out of the anxiety of their condition" (quoted in Rorabaugh 1979, 146; quoted in Kimmel 1996, 49). The "condition" of early nineteenth-century white men was, evidently, very anxious indeed.

This association of drinking with masculine anxiety is hardly limited to the nineteenth century, of course. Paul Hoch has observed that drinking is "one of the most common ways of certifying one's manhood" (1979, 85). As such, it is a homosocial phenomenon; note that most drinking occurs in the company of other men, so-called "drinking buddies." Apart from "its obvious function as an opiate against an oppressive social environment," Hoch continues, alcohol consumption also points to a "retreat to all-male environments as a defense against the 'feminine' elements within. The consumption of alcohol, like the consumption of macho sport and pornography (and indeed like most forms of consumerism generally) is both a 'substitute gratification' and a defense against the repressed" (1979, 85).

The "repressed" must have been gnawing at a number of late nineteenth-century white men. On a typical day in St. Louis, Boston, and the other major cities, half the population stopped by a saloon. Probably one of every fifty men was an alcoholic (Filene 1998). Despite (or due to) the omnipresence of alcohol, some advice manual writers began to promote temperance. In 1826 the American Society for the Promotion of Temperance was founded, primarily by clergymen opposed to Andrew Jackson. Soon writers like Henry Ward Beecher and health reformers like Sylvester Graham began to write about the dangers of drink. Other social reformers joined, among them abolitionists William Lloyd Garrison and Theodore Weld, for whom intemperance and slavery were associated: both, they pointed out, were wasteful and immoral (Kimmel 1996).

Many women knew firsthand the dangers of drink; they and their children had suffered violence and deprivation as a consequence of men's drinking. But this gendered dimension to the controversy made it all the more contentious, especially when women organized to promote temperance. White men's drinking became an expression of masculine protest against feminization (Kimmel 1996). Women were undaunted. "The homes of America," proclaimed one W.C.T.U. resolution, "[h]ave no enemy so relentless as the American saloon" (quoted in Filene 1998, 87). (In the 1880s, the W.C.T.U. wanted the Prohibition Party to be renamed the Prohibition Home Protection Party.). The campaign against drinking was sensationalized, uncompromising, propagandistic, and effective. At the end of the nineteenth century the W.C.T.U. had won prohibition in five states; by 1913 more than half of the nation's counties and seven states were dry (Filene 1998).

Increasingly, a man's self-control meant control of his body, not only control of drinking but as well "its" sexual desires and sensations. In the 1830s and 1840s, a series of advice manuals counseled young men how to do that. The concern for young men's self-control became so widespread, the advice books so popular, the link between economic success and sexual control so explicit, that the phrase "spermatic economy" has been employed to describe the nineteenth-century fusion of sexual and marketplace activities. It became taken for granted that the self-control required by the marketplace required the sexual control of a disciplined body, a body controlled by the will. Specifically, the conservation of sperm signified conservation of energy, to be saved for the marketplace, by and large a homosocial space. "Sturdy manhood," one writer claimed, "loses its energy and bends under too frequent expenditure of this important secretion" (quoted in Kimmel 1994, 15). "Just say no" was not original to the Reagans.

Illustrative of this effort to discipline the young white male body for deployment in the economic sphere was the advice of Sylvester Graham. All desire, Graham wrote, "disrupts and disorders all the function of the system." To control desire, Graham advised a diet of farinaceous foods, properly prepared, like "good bread, made of coarsely ground, unbolted wheat, or rye-meal, and hominy, made of cracked wheat, or rye, or Indian corn" (quoted in Kimmel 1994, 16). Young men ought to avoid full and large suppers, and, most importantly, should eat no animal meat whatsoever, since Graham was convinced that one is more susceptible to the sins of the flesh if one eats another's flesh. This particular piece of advice engendered two attacks on his own flesh by enraged Boston butchers (Kimmel 1994).

Graham was undeterred. He warned parents that allowing boys to become accustomed to bad habits of "luxury, indolence, voluptuousness and sensuality" would lead them to abandon their "nobleness, dignity, honor, and manhood" and become

> the wretched transgressor [who] sinks into a miserable fatuity, and finally becomes a confirmed and degraded idiot, whose deeply sunken and vacant, glossy eyes, and livid shriveled countenance, and ulcerous, toothless gums, and fetid breath, and feeble, broken voice, and emaciated and dwarfish and crooked body, and almost hairless head—covered perhaps with suppurating blisters and running sores—denote a premature old age! a blighted body—and a ruined soul. (quoted in Kimmel 1994, 17)

The gravity of these warnings indicated that, for Graham and for many European Americans at the turn of the century, the very great danger that imperiled young men was the danger of male sexual desire (Kimmel 1994). As we will see in the panic over masturbation, this fear expressed as well the danger of male homosexual desire.

Advice-book writers counseled parents to employ several most "innovative" treatments for sexual intemperance and specifically for the dreaded masturbation. These included the straightjacket, helpful in keeping boys' hands away from private parts, and rope, useful in tying the feet at some distance apart so that the thighs would remain separate. No rubbing those legs together, young man! If these techniques didn't work, students of young men's sexual practices advised a next step: "cork cushions" which could be placed inside the thighs to pry them apart. Finally, if all else fails, there was the very effective "genital cage," a metal truss of silver or tin in which the boy's penis and scrotum were placed and held by springs. Kimmel (1994) tells us that several patents for these devices, including one for a device that sounded an electrical alarm in the event of an erection, were issued at the turn of the century.

Nor were young women exempt from their elders' concerns over autoerotic desire. Priscilla Barker (1888) devised a list of telltale signs by which parents and concerned others would detect girls' practice of the secret vice: their "faces lose their color, and the eyes grew dull, heavy and weak, the hands feel soft and clammy, and often the smell of the feet is unbearable." Masturbation led to self-defloration, "the inroads of self-abuse, [and] leave the citadel of womanhood unprotected and at the mercy of the enemy" (9, 12; quoted in Hunt 1998, 587). Parents could, presumably, see the evidence of masturbation on young people's faces: "one of the most patent signs of his habit in our youth of both sexes today, is the almost universal use of eyeglasses and spectacles" (Hunt

1998, 597). Another "student" of the practice, Joseph Howe (1883), claimed that girls' masturbation left the labia distended and the clitoris elongated; in boys, the opposite problem as it were: the penis of the masturbator was thinner, smaller, and bent, one testicle hanging lower (Hunt 1998).

In an 1893 letter to Fleiss, Freud himself appeared to succumb, it would appear, to the hysteria over masturbation, suggesting to his friend that sexual factors were not simply one among many possible causes of neurasthenia (a peculiarly male nineteenth-century "disease" we will examine momentarily), but that they were the sole cause. "It may be taken as a recognized fact," he wrote, "that neurasthenia is a frequent consequence of an abnormal sex life. The assertion, however, which I wish to make and test by observations, is that neurasthenia actually can *only* be a sexual neurosis" (quoted in Webster 1995, 187). Certain forms of abnormal sexual activity, he speculated, probably produced what he called sexual "noxae," which in turn produced neurological poisoning (Webster 1995). The chief cause of such sexual poisoning was, in Freud's view, masturbation. He expressed his conviction to Fleiss:

> *Neurasthenia* in males is acquired at the age of puberty and becomes manifest when the man is in his twenties. Its source is masturbation, the frequency of which runs completely parallel with the frequency of male neurasthenia. One can observe in the circle of one's acquaintances that (at least in urban populations) those individuals who have been seduced by women at an early age have escaped neurasthenia. When this noxa has operated long and intensely, it turns the person concerned into a sexual neurasthenic, whose potency, too, has been impaired; the intensity of the cause is paralleled by a lifelong persistence of the condition. Further evidence of the casual connection lies in the fact that a sexual neurasthenic is always a general neurasthenic at the same time. (quoted in Webster 1995, 188)

Masturbation, according to Freud's thinking at this time, was the first of the "sexual noxae" which were liable to lead to neurasthenia. The second noxa, which supposedly afflicted men at a later stage in their life, was *onanismus conjugalis,* which Freud defined as "incomplete intercourse in order to prevent conception" and in which he included coitus interruptus, extravaginal intercourse, and intercourse in which a condom was used. A healthy man, Freud thought, might tolerate such practices for quite a long time. But eventually they would take their toll (Webster 1995). "His only advantage over the masturbator," Freud wrote, "is the privilege of a longer latency" (quoted in Webster 1995, 188).

Back in America, R. J. Culverwell invented a chair that served as a kind of douche-bidet for the sexually vulnerable. An armchair was fitted with an open seat, beneath which a pan of cold water, or "medicated refrigerant fluid" would be placed. By means of a pump, a young man could direct this cold water or fluid to his genital area, thus "cooling" his sexual desire, rendering himself more capable of self-control. Kimmel (1994) comments: "This obsessive repression of all things sexual indicates more than sexual prudishness or puritanical repression. It reveals an increasing preoccupation with the body and a correspondingly decreasing interest in the soul" (18). This concern over the young man's body disguises (barely) an obviously intense sexual interest in the male body on the part of those adults who supervised and assisted with this equipment. Prurience and prohibition were intertwined.

When successful, when the young man's semen remained safely within his body, his energy knew no bounds. In fact, it led him outside the confines of the marketplace, for which his body had been prepared, presumably. In fact, these "repressed middle class sexual energies were then channeled into a xenophobic hostility toward the immigrant and the black, then projected into fantasies incorporating the enviable and fully expressed sexuality of these alien groups," as we saw in the case of lynching (Kimmel 1994, 18). They were as well projected onto women, who were imagined either as seductive temptresses, saturated with carnal desires they too were unable to control, or pious asexual angels, for instance, the southern white lady, for whom the merest mention of the body and its desires might precipitate a fainting straightaway. As Kimmel puts it: "Sexual anxieties projected onto blacks, women, and immigrants prompted men to devise social, economic, political, and ideological controls, to keep others out of the way, clearing the field for white, native-born men" (1994, 18). Such hatreds kept men "straight," that is, "men." Curiously, some progressive men, those who yearned to help the immigrant and the poor, men in the settlement house movement, seemed not so sexually "anxious," as we saw in section III of this chapter.

New terms appeared to reflect these shifts in social reality. The notion of "manhood" denoted a certain inner-directedness and autonomy associated with the idea of the capitalist producer. Manhood now gave way to "masculinity," pointing to that set of visible qualities that distinguished one's gender identity. The opposite of masculinity was femininity, those traits associated with being a woman. The opposite of manhood had been childhood; now if one was not a man, one was a woman, or worse, a "sissy." While "manhood was an expression of inner character; masculinity was constantly in need of validation, of demonstration, of proof" (Kimmel 1994, 21). The Boy Scout movement—notorious in the 1990s for its resistance to the inclusion of homosexuals—can be directly traced to the connection established between imperialism (economic, political) and the nation's health, as evidenced in widespread fears of masturbation, degeneration (including homosexuality), and eugenics (Said 1993).

Many men worried over what they perceived to be a widespread feminization of American culture. They identified this deterioration of the nation with the feminization of boyhood, itself perceived to be the consequence of the predominance of women in the lives of young boys, as mothers were left alone at home with their young sons. Women dominated the lives of boys as teachers in both elementary and secondary schools. Many men were alarmed that so many women were teaching young boys. One foresaw only two consequences, the "effeminate babyish boy" and "the bad boy"; he declared that masculine influence "is necessary for the proper development" of young boys. Another, writing in the *Educational Review* in 1914, complained that women teachers had created "a feminized manhood, emotional, illogical, non-combative against public evils." This psychic threat to "masculine nature," he argued, was beginning to "warp the psyches of our boys and young men into femininity" (quoted in Kimmel 1996, 121).

Influential educators such as Edward Clarke of the Harvard Medical School and G. Stanley Hall, expert on adolescence and the president of Clark University, warned that coeducation was dangerous to both boys and girls. Both Clarke and Hall insisted that coeducation distorted and deformed the biological, and therefore "natural," natures of males and females. They suggested that mental, let alone physical, exertion by women would reduce their reproductive and maternal capacities, and that schools with a large number of female students and teachers would, according to Hall and Clarke, "feminize" male students (Tyack and Hansot 1990). Such "a man with feminine traits of character, or with the frame and carriage of a female," warned Dr. Alfred Stillé, president of the American Medical Association, "is despised by both the sex he ostensibly belongs to, and that of which he is at once a caricature and a libel" (quoted in Kimmel 1996, 122).

Even religious leaders spoke out against the danger of "feminization" and its potential for undermining "masculinity." The "predominance of women's influence in our public schools," warned Rabbi Solomon Schindler in 1892, was feminizing American boys; a "vast horde of female teachers" was teaching boys how to become men, was how psychologist J. McKenn Cattell characterized the problem. A British group concerned with the "crisis" concluded in 1904 that the preponderance of women teachers meant that "the boy in America is not being brought up to punch another boy's head; or to stand having his own punched in a healthy and proper manner" (quoted in Kimmel 1994, 23). As we saw in section VI (this chapter), "boy culture" more than compensated for women's influence in young men's lives.

Concurrently, the middle-class, mostly white feminist movement was challenging conventional constructions of manhood by agitating for women's advancement, in both private and public spheres, including, as we have seen, the church and the voting booth. One outraged male clergyman complained that feminists were opposing "the basic facts of womanhood itself. ... We shall gain nothing in the end by displacing manhood by womanhood or the other way around" (quoted in Bederman 1995a, 14). As Gail Bederman (1995a) points out, the "new woman" did "displace manhood by womanhood," if only because her successes undermined male assumptions that education, professional status, and political power were appropriate only for men. In this way the woman's movement intensified the pressure on middle-class white men to reformulate manhood (Bederman 1995a).

Suddenly, it seemed, new words such as "pussyfoot" and "stuffed shirt" were in common usage, as men sought to distinguish themselves from those who had fallen victim to a "moral" and gendered degeneration. Most terrifying to young men of the new century was the horror of becoming a "sissy." The term sissy, Kimmel (1994) tells us, was coined in the 1890s; it came to serve as an umbrella concept for all those qualities "men" were not. A heightened visibility of a growing gay male subculture in many large American cities at the turn of the century intensified heterosexual men's hysterical flight from the horror of not being a "man."

The "crisis" of white masculinity was evidently perceived to be so grave that even breakfast became a crucial site of the struggle to become and remain a "man." Consuming corn flakes for breakfast was promoted by J. H. Kellogg as a massive anaphrodisiac; presumably this cereal could be counted on to temper sexual desire in American men. Kellogg was perhaps the most creative and the most hysterical health reformer of the time. His books, *Man the Masterpiece* (1896) and *Plain Facts for Young and Old* (1888), were best-sellers in the genre of popular self-improvement (Kimmel 1994).

Kellogg was perhaps the preeminent American warrior in the battle against sexual desire. He developed a regime designed to help the righteous "masculine" man in his battle against temptations of all kinds, some too awful to mention in polite company, but which everybody knew, presumably first-hand (as it were). Kellog's advice included:

1. Kneading and pounding on the abdomen each day to promote evacuation before sleep and thus avoiding "irritating" congestions.
2. Drinking hot water, six to eight glasses a day (same end in view).
3. Urinating several times each night (same end in view).
4. Avoiding alcohol, tobacco, and tea because they stimulated lecherous thoughts.
5. Taking cold enemas and hot sitz baths each day.
6. Wearing a wet girdle to bed each night.

(quoted in Kimmel 1994, 28)

Kellog's chief concern, however, was masturbation. In *Plain Facts for Old and Young,* Kellogg demonstrated his creativity by devising a list of home remedies he was certain would solve the problem. He suggested starting with bandaging the genitals. Don't forget to cover the young man's penis with a cage, and, if necessary, tie his hands to the bed. If these tried and true measures still failed, the cereal man knew what to do: circumcision, "without administering an anesthetic, as the brief pain attending the operation will have a salutary effect upon the mind, especially if it be connected with the idea of punishment." But parents of older boys, he acknowledged, may not see results even after circumcision. Not to be alarmed, for his Yankee ingenuity had not yet been spent. Try placing silver sutures over the foreskin of your sons' penises: this should prevent erection. Evidently Kellogg had thought long and hard about this procedure; perhaps he even tested it on a number of young men before promoting it publicly:

> The prepuce, or foreskin, is drawn over the glans, and the needle to which the wire is attached is passed through from one side to the other. After drawing the wire through, the ends are twisted together, and cut off close. It is not impossible for an erection to occur, and the slight irritation thus produced acts as a most powerful means of overcoming the disposition to resort to the practice. (quoted in Kimmel 1994, 28)

"The persistent panic over masturbation," Peter Gay observes, "is far easier to document than to explain. Heavily overdetermined, it was a cultural symptom laden with baffling meanings that reached across nineteenth-century society and down into the buried unconscious core of its most troubling preoccupations" (1984, 309). Was this "unconscious" core that omnipresent homoeroticism which the end of romantic friendship helped drive underground? If so, was the panic over masturbation in part a cover for a deepening homosexual panic? Alan Hunt (1998) answers "perhaps." He cites the earlier work of Vern Bullough and Martha Voght (1973), who argued that the antimasturbation campaign in America assumed an explicit link between masturbation and homosexuality, partly due to a general confusion between the two phenomena. Hunt is not entirely persuaded, although he acknowledges that "there were elements of a deepening homophobia imbricated within the antimasturbation discourses" (605). "The difficulty in addressing this issue," he explains, "is that there was a profound reticence about speaking of homosexuality during the nineteenth century. None of the antimasturbation texts refers explicitly to a link between masturbation and homosexuality" (Hunt 1998, 605). But then, given the general reticence over the sin that dare not speak its name, and a general confusion over auto- and homoeroticism, one would not expect explicit textual links made between the two.

Sylvester Graham (1834/1974) was quite clear that masturbation might lead to sexual relations between men. He was not alone. Carroll Smith-Rosenberg (1978) argues that a number of nineteenth-century health writers worried that masturbation might lead to homosexual activity; many characterized the masturbator as effeminate, a characterization later extended to the figure of the homosexual. Graham worried that masturbation was "taught" boy to boy: it was, he wrote, "communicated from one boy to another; and sometimes a single boy will corrupt many others." Graham claims to "have known boys ... at the age of twelve and thirteen almost entirely ruined ... and many of them went to the still more loathsome and criminal extent of an unnatural commerce with each other!" (42–43; quoted in Derrick 1997, 50). Lord Baden-Powell felt certain his Boy Scouts were at risk. As late as 1908, writing for a mass audience of scouts, Baden-Powell warned them that self-abuse "brings with it weakness of head and heart, and, if persisted in, idiocy and lunacy" (quoted in Hunt 1998, 612). Scout leaders' concern over the sexual identities of the boys in their charge continues today.

By the second decade of the twentieth century, Kimmel (1994) reports, much of this sexual panic had begun to subside, in part, he suggests, due to the popularization of Freudian psychoanalysis. Masturbation was rarely mentioned in public until 1996, when President Clinton found it necessary to dismiss his surgeon general, Joycelyn Elders, for the apparently noncontroversial observation that masturbation is "part of human sexuality" (quoted in Hunt 1998, 577).

The compensatory and racialized character of white masculinity in the early twentieth century is illustrated by three white men who graphically memorialized the premodern west and a masculinity already past: novelist Owen Wister, painter Frederic Remington, and conservationist President Theodore Roosevelt. None was a "real man" in the sense of the phrase they employed. As Kimmel (1994) points out, all three were "effete eastern intellectuals" who spent time on civilized, so-called dude, ranches where, presumably, they rediscovered their manhood. Each spent the rest of their adult lives testifying publicly to their conversion. Theodore Roosevelt organized the Boone and Crockett Club to encourage big-game hunting (see Bederman 1995a). The racialized nature of such "remasculinization" is evident in remarks made by William Kent, a California congressman who linked racial degeneration to the disappearance of the cave man. Kent rejoiced in the savagery of the hunt; after the kill, he declared, "you are barbarian and you're glad of it. It's good to be a barbarian ... and you know that if you are a barbarian, you are at any rate a man" (quoted in Kimmel 1994, 32). Is it any wonder "savage" black men were objects of white men's (repressed) desire?

Jack Johnson

No one, Kimmel (1994) argues, symbolized this cult of "elemental virility" better than John L. Sullivan. Sullivan was, in Kimmel's words, "a walking embodiment of the remasculinization of [white] America." His "manly swagger" and well-waxed mustache signaled the fighter's embodiment of a lost era of "artisanal heroism." And, Kimmel continues, no one symbolized the demise of this momentary return of artisanal manhood better than Jack Johnson, the first black heavyweight boxing champion. Flamboyant and triumphant, Johnson personified "the black specter that haunted white workingmen's sense of manhood since antebellum days—the specter that unskilled free blacks would triumph over skilled white workers in the workplace, the bedroom, and now, in the sporting world they held dearest in their artisanal hearts: the boxing ring" (all quoted in Kimmel 1994, 35). On that classically homosocial site, white and black manhood faced off. Gail Bederman (1995a) tells the story well.

On July 4, 1910, at 2:30 in the afternoon, in Reno, Nevada, as the band played "All Coons Look Alike to Me," Jack Johnson, the first African-American world heavyweight boxing champion, climbed into the ring to defend his title against Jim Jeffries, a popular white former heavyweight champion who had retired undefeated six years before. The event was more than a boxing match, more than a sporting event. The Johnson-Jeffries match was the event of the year. The color of American manhood was at stake. Twenty-thousand men had traveled from across the nation to sit in Reno's hot desert sun and watch the prizefight. Five hundred journalists were on hand to cover it. Every day of the week before the fight, these reporters had wired between 100,000 and 150,000 words; the event was as hyped as much as an event then could be. America's white readership were sure that Jeffries would win. On the day of the fight, American men fled family picnics, ignored patriotic celebrations; they gathered in ballparks, theaters, and auditoriums to hear the wire services' round-by-round reports of the battle. Over 30,000 men stood outside the *New York Times* offices straining to hear the results; 10,000 men gathered outside the *Atlanta Constitution*. The Johnson-Jeffries match was, as Bederman (1995a) observes, "a national sensation."

After Jeffries had first won the heavyweight championship in 1899, he had refused to fight any black challengers. Johnson had challenged him as early as

1901. Jeffries quickly declined, declaring: "When there are no more white men left to fight, I will quit the business. ... I am determined not to take a chance of losing the championship to a negro" (quoted in Bederman 1995a, 1). Jeffries' refusal to risk losing to a black man was hardly unprecedented. Since 1882, when John L. Sullivan had won the title, no white heavyweight champion had accepted a challenge from a black men, although black and white heavyweights had fought before then. Sullivan had announced he would fight all contenders, except black ones: "I will not fight a negro. I never had and never shall" (quoted in Bederman 1995a, 1). It was during this racially nightmarish period marked by lynching and segregation that Jack Johnson had begun his career. He had defeated every fighter, black or white, who dared to face him (Bederman 1995a).

Jeffries refused to fight Johnson for two years, then retired in 1905. The remaining white contenders aroused little interest; the public even began to lose interest in the sport. In 1908, partly to rekindle interest in the sport and partly to win the prize money, the reigning white champion, Tommy Burns, reluctantly agreed to fight Johnson. To the horror of white men everywhere, Johnson easily defeated Burns and won the title. Faced with the unfathomable fact that a black man had been crowned the most powerful man in the world, white men begged Jeffries to return to the ring. "Jeff, just emerge from your alfalfa farm and remove that smile from Johnson's face. Jeff, it's up to you," taunted Jack London in the *New York Herald*. In April 1909, the *Chicago Tribune* printed a drawing of a little blond girl begging the former champion: "Please, Mr. Jeffries, are you going to fight Mr. Johnson?" Across America, white newspapers pleaded with Jeffries to redeem Anglo-Saxon manhood and restore civilization by knocking down the uppity "Negro" (quoted in Bederman 1995a, 2).

The aging Jeffries reluctantly agreed to fight, reportedly saying, "I am going into this fight for the sole purpose of proving that a white man is better than a negro." From its start, then, the Johnson-Jeffries fight was not only a prizefight; it was a symbolic event the outcome of which would determine which "race" had produced the more powerful man. The symbolism was by no means subtle; Jeffries was dubbed the "Hope of the White Race," while Johnson was called "the Negroes' Deliverer." The press hyped the event by focusing nearly exclusively upon the relative manliness of the white and black races. *Current Literature* predicted Jeffries would defeat Johnson because "the black man ... fights emotionally, whereas the white man can use his brain after twenty rounds" (quoted in Bederman 1995a, 2). White men everywhere were supremely confident that Jeffries's highly evolved Anglo-Saxon manhood would mean that he would triumph over the less civilized Negro.

Johnson beat Jeffries badly, bloodily. White men who framed the event as proof of white male supremacy were caught in their own rhetoric. White men had insisted upon seeing the fight as absolute proof that the white man was the superior specimen of virile manhood. Johnson's thrashing of Jeffries gave a unambiguous and unwelcome answer. The black press was not timid in drawing the inevitable and wonderful conclusion; the *Chicago Defender* declared that

Johnson was "the first negro to be admitted the best man in the world" (quoted in Bederman 1995a, 2).

In shock, white men could not accept reality. They rioted. In every southern state, as well as in Illinois, Missouri, New York, Ohio, Pennsylvania, Colorado, and the District of Columbia, white men went crazy, attacking black men wherever they could find them. There were rare instances of black men attacking white men who belittled Johnson, but overwhelmingly the violence was committed by hysterical white men. Everywhere they saw black men celebrating Johnson's victory, they attacked. In Manhattan, the *New York Herald* reported, "one negro was rescued by the police from white men who had a rope around his neck. ... In Eighth Avenue, between Thirty-Seventh and Thirty-Ninth Streets, more than three thousand whites gathered, and all the negroes that appeared were kicked and beaten, some of them into insensibility. ... Three thousand white men took possession of Eighth Avenue and held against police as they attacked every negro that came into sight" (quoted in Bederman 1995a, 3). Nationally, eighteen died; hundreds more were injured (Bederman 1995a).

Soon after white men settled down, an even more horrible nightmare began. After winning the championship, Johnson made public his preference for white women. And many white women certainly preferred Johnson. White men obsessed; was Johnson's success with white women further proof that black men were better men? The spectacle of dozens of white women chasing after Johnson enraged millions of white men. While it turns out that these women tended to be prostitutes, white men imagined—as we will see in the case of the Scottsboro Nine (chapter 12)—*all* white women were considered too "pure" for black men. Nightmare enough that Johnson's first wife was white; those worried over the prospect of miscegenation were relieved when she committed suicide in 1912. When white men discovered Johnson was having an affair with eighteen-year-old blond Lucille Cameron from Minnesota, they went crazy all over again (Bederman 1995a).

Authorities charged him with violating the Mann Act—that is, engaging in white slavery. Whites everywhere were outraged and demanded blood. In Johnson's hometown, Chicago, a man threw an inkwell at him when he tried to transact business at his bank. Effigies of Johnson were hung from trolleys and electric poles all over the city. Wherever white men saw Johnson they screamed "Lynch him! Lynch the nigger!" The fact that Lucille Cameron insisted she was in love with Johnson and soon married him was irrelevant. The fact that she had been a prostitute made no difference either. Nor did it matter that the Mann Act had not been violated and that the original charges had to been dropped. By defeating a white man in the boxing ring and (as white men imagined) in bed, Johnson had violated white men's already beleaguered sense of themselves as men. They demanded revenge (Bederman 1995a).

The National Bureau of Investigation was ordered to find a charge that could not be thrown out of court. After considerable time and money, the Bureau discovered that in the past Johnson had crossed state lines with a white mistress. In the past the government had invoked the Mann Act only to combat commercial prostitution, but officials made an exception in Johnson's case. He was convicted of crossing state lines with his mistress and of giving her money and presents, ordinary activities for many heterosexual American men. The black man who had humiliated white manhood in the boxing ring was, however, sentenced to a year in prison and fined one thousand dollars (Bederman 1995a).

Imprisonment was not enough, however, and government employees suggested to Johnson that he jump bail and leave the country, which he did. For the next seven years, every effort Johnson made to negotiate with the government was rebuffed. Not until 1920 was Johnson, now impoverished and humiliated, permitted to return to the United States to serve his sentence. Photographs of him losing his last championship bout to white fighter Jess Willard in Havana in 1915 hung in many white bars and speakeasies for many years afterward (Bederman 1995a). The white male rage focused on Johnson echoed into the 1960s, when the white actress Jane Alexander, who had starred with James Earl Jones in the Howard Sackler play about Johnson (*The Great White Hope*), was assaulted with hate mail and obscenities when the play opened (Day 1977).

The furor over Jack Johnson, Gail Bederman (1995a) tells us, was "excessive" but "not unique" (4). She sees the symbolization of the Johnson/Jeffries boxing match and the riots that ensued as another indication that "during the decades around the turn of the century, Americans were obsessed with the connection between manhood and racial dominance. This obsession was expressed in a profusion of issues, from debates over lynching, to concern about the white man's imperialistic burden overseas, to discussion of child-rearing" (Bederman 1995a, 4). Bederman is referring to Ida B. Wells's antilynching campaign, and the discourses of "civilization" and "savagery" that were used to rationalize the murder of African Americans as well as the conquest and colonial subjugation of Africans, East Indians, and Native Americans. In the pedagogical and child-rearing views of G. Stanley Hall, these racialized discourses would influence American discussion of child rearing as well (Bederman 1995a).

Between 1890 and 1917, the primary period of lynching, many white middle-class men responded defensively to a myriad of economic, racial, and gendered shifts. In their efforts to reaffirm their wavering status as men, "race became a factor which was crucial to their gender" (Bederman 1995a, 5). No doubt, but I think we can say more. With the end of "romantic friendship" and the heightened visibility of homosexual desire, white men's homoeroticism, long racialized, was no longer free to operate free of surveillance, free-floating in its invisibility. In its repression it intensified and split off as a collective paranoid projection, imagining black men as superstud rapists intent on savaging white women that were in fact stand-ins for white men.

Bederman is of course right when she writes that "the Jack Johnson controversy, then, simply exemplifies one of many ways Progressive Era men used ideas about white supremacy to produce a racially based ideology of male power" (1995a, 5). But she might have added that Johnson's magnificent muscular black body—Bederman (1995a) notes that "late Victorian culture had identified the powerful, large male body of the heavyweight prizefighter (and not the smaller bodies of the middle-weight or welterweight) as the epitome of manhood" (8)—no doubt stimulated a not yet fully repressed homosexual desire. His defeat of Jeffries amounted to a symbolic rape of white men, a form of political revenge that would cease to be only symbolic in mid-twentieth-century American prisons. This sexualized sadomasochism was evident during his fights, when Johnson maintained a steady stream of gendered taunts and insults. "Who told you were a fighter"? he would demand derisively, laughing loudly, exposing his gold-capped teeth. "Who taught you to hit? Your mother? You a woman?" Merciless even in victory, Johnson would rarely offer sportsmanlike praise for his defeated white opponents. "He is the easiest man I ever met," he said of fallen titleholder Tommy Burns in 1908, using an adjective often reserved for seduced women. "I could have put him away quicker, but I wanted to punish him" (quoted in Van Deburg 1997, 92).

Johnson understood well these homosexualized racial politics, it would seem. Certainly he understood that he was positioned by these psychosexual and cultural constructs, because, as Bederman notes, he also actively used them to position himself. He consciously played upon white men's fears of threatened manhood by playing upon these fears in public. During his public sparring matches, well aware that white men were intently watching his muscled black body and specifically his crotch, Johnson wrapped his penis in gauze to enhance its size. Stripped down to his boxing shorts, he would strut about the ring, "flaunting his genital endowment for all to admire, displaying his superior body to demonstrate his superior manhood" (Bederman 1995a, 8). Understanding that homosexual desire was taboo, he fucked white men where they imagined themselves to be vis-à-vis black men, inside white women's bodies. Is that part of the explanation why Johnson physically beat and emotionally maltreated his white wives and mistresses? Bederman notes that he was "implicitly claiming a man's right to dominate women" (1995a, 10), but I suggest he was also, given the conflations operating in the minds of white men, communicating a black man's right to dominate white men sexually, which they would do in prison. By the end of the twentieth century, white men would celebrate black men's athletic accomplishments, so much so that when the line was drawn between a white woman sports reporter and black male athletes, white men expressed no hesitation as to whose bodies they prized (see Disch and Kane 1996).

Hysteric White Men

In the early 1890s—recall that 1892 was the zenith of lynching—both manliness and white middle-class identity were under siege. These gendered and racialized conceptions had been grounded in small-scale, competitive capitalism, forms of economic life which had all but disappeared by the 1890s. Between 1870 and 1910, for instance, the percentage of middle-class men who were self-employed dropped from 67 percent to 37 percent (Bederman 1995a). As the twentieth century began, the national economy and society overall were becoming increasingly bureaucratic and interdependent. Earlier codes of "manly" self-restraint began to appear irrelevant, even quaint. For example, with the proliferation of large-scale corporate entities, the number of middle-class men who could aspire to entrepreneurial independence decreased. A rapid expansion in low-level clerical positions in stores and offices meant that many young men beginning their careers as clerks were unlikely to be promoted to responsible, well-paid management positions, as had clerks in their fathers' generation (Blumin 1989; Bederman 1995b).

Under these rapidly changing conditions in the workplace, manly self-denial and restraint became, well, unprofitable. As middle-class men's career opportunities seemed to disappear, new and multiple opportunities for leisure appeared. The rapid expansion of a consumer culture encouraged many middle-class men already faced with lowered career expectations to locate identity in leisure not work (Erenberg 1981; Kasson 1978). Yet the consumerist culture ethos of hedonism and gratification were in sharp conflict with the ideals of manly self-restraint, further undermining the potency of white middle-class manliness (Bederman 1989, 1995a).

There were other challenges to middle-class male hegemony at the end of the century. Recently arrived immigrant working men were threatening middle-class men's political control of the cities. Laboring men generally were expressing their discontent with working conditions. Beginning with the Great Uprising of 1877, the last quarter of the nineteenth century was filled with labor unrest. Between 1881 and 1905 there were nearly 37,000 strikes, often violent, involving seven million workers, a remarkable number considering that the total work force in 1900 numbered only twenty-nine million. To many, class war seemed inevitable. The visibility of socialist and anarchist movements in the United States and worldwide intensified these concerns. Already concerned about their loss of control in the workplace and at home, now the middle-class feared they were losing control of the country. The potency of manhood, as white middle-class men understood it, meant the power to exercise civic authority, to maintain social order, and to dictate the future of the American nation. Middle-class men's apparent failure to perform these manly obligations and exercise this manly authority, in the face of challenges by working-class and immigrant men, intensified white men's concern about their own manhood (Bederman 1995a).

Also contributing to many men's sense of "crisis" was the rapid entry of women into the work force. Between 1880 and 1900 the number of employed adult women more than doubled; between 1900 and 1910 it increased by another 50 percent, approximately twice the male rate. By the latter year, one of every five women above the age of fifteen was at work. Necessity or misfortune drove most women into the labor market. One-fourth of the female jobholders in 1910 were married, working because their husbands did not earn enough to feed the family (Filene 1998).

Most of these women worked at home sewing dresses, taking in laundry, rolling cigars, accepting boarders; a significant minority left home early each morning to work a textile machine, to clean and cook, to sell candy or clothing, or to engage in some other low-level, tedious task suffered by the lower and lower middle classes. While economic hardship forced these women to supplement their husbands' income, calamity created a crisis for the 15 percent of women who had lost husbands through death or divorce. Widowed and unmarried women constituted three-fifths of the female labor force; most were in their twenties or younger (Filene 1998). One such working girl, a thirteen-year-old employee in an Atlanta pencil plant, was Mary Phagan. Her murder on

Confederate Memorial Day, 1913, created a sensation, for which the Jewish plant manager—Leo Frank—was lynched (Dinnerstein 1968).

Although these political, cultural, and economic developments undermined traditional versions of manliness, white middle-class men continued to promote them, for to acknowledge the disappearance of traditional manliness felt like saying male power itself was lost. As Gail Bederman puts it: "Discourses of manliness were embedded in their very identities. They formed their sons into men by teaching them manliness. Especially in the context of challenges from the Gilded Age woman's movement, abandoning familiar constructs of manliness was an unimaginable option" (1995b, 409). If a man is not a man, then what is he?

Uncomfortably confused about the nature and sources of male power, white middle-class men began somewhat frantically to cast about, searching for new ways to fortify their illusions of manliness. As in the practices of sexual regulation reviewed earlier, Yankee ingenuity was everywhere evident: there were momentary crazes for bodybuilding, then college football, enthusiasms that gave way suddenly to the terror of "neurasthenic breakdowns" among overworked middle-class white men (Pronger 1990; Gorn 1986). Many doctors worried that the newly discovered disease, "neurasthenia," was spreading rapidly throughout the white middle class. Caused, many thought, by the excessive mental labor and nervous strain which professionals and businessmen suffered as they struggled for success in an increasingly competitive economy, the disease led many to fear that white middle-class men as a sex had grown weary, fragile, decadent. Working class, immigrant, and black men seemed to possess a virility and savage vitality which white middle-class men had lost (Bederman 1995a).

Perhaps "neurasthenia" was an "occupational hazard," a risk that accompanied being a man, a white man. In his study of admission (admission made by family members, not physicians) to the Alabama Insane Hospital, John Starrett Hughes (1990) discovered that for many southern men there appeared to be a risk in being "too male." Judging from information collected from admissions forms, Hughes reports that Alabamians almost never imagined that wives, mothers, and sisters had lost their minds due to excessive work or due to trouble resulting from their special varieties of (usually domestic) "business." The caricature of Freud's hysteric woman notwithstanding, evidently many believed that nineteenth-century men—more than women—inhabited a dangerous gendered sphere that demanded discipline and moderation (Hughes 1990).

Not only business was dangerous. Politics was especially so. "Political excitement" was regularly cited as a related reason for committing men to the Alabama hospital. Analysis of all the admissions for the asylum's first five years, 1861–66, show nine were admitted for this reason, eight of whom were men. During these Civil War years, the potential for "political excitement" was of course considerable. Nearly two-thirds of all patients admitted during these years, regardless of diagnoses, were men. But during the postbellum period there were regularly as many women as there were men in the inmate population. Hughes concludes that as the era of dramatic political excitement, even trauma, passed, the proportion of insane men declined and the gender ratio became more nearly equal. Difficulties of secession, war, and Reconstruction obviously put southern white men at risk (Hughes 1990).

Not only the public domains of business and politics could be "maddening." Problems of sexuality were also listed as causes for admission to the hospital. Nearly all commitment descriptions that mentioned masturbation were those of men. Masturbation, Hughes adds, was listed as the disease's "exciting" cause (1990, 57). Like other Victorians, late nineteenth-century Alabamians tended to imagine masculinity and femininity as complementary, almost never as intersecting. Rather than adulthood and character, masculinity became the polar opposite of femininity (Hughes 1990). Very few male inmates were "diagnosed" with any sort of lunacy attributed to "feminine" behavior. One man admitted in 1895 asserted that he was "a woman and that his uncle [had] attempted to ravish him" (quoted in Hughes 1990, 60). The patient's case history reveals that the patient insisted on this point, repeating it again and again. The staff dismissed it as a delusion; the patient, after all, was clearly a man. As Hughes (1990) points out, the staff's gender assumptions were such that they failed to investigate the possibility that the patient had indeed been sexually assaulted, and that his gender confusion originated in an actual event.

As we have seen, nineteenth-century white men drank prodigiously. The Alabama Insane Hospital admitted many victims of alcoholism, and all but a few were men. These men not uncommonly had multiple dependencies that included opium, morphine, or cocaine as well as alcohol. While not heavy drinkers, evidently, Alabama women did acquire serious drug addictions. Early in this period, opium eating was common among women, although a number of men too engaged in this practice. By the 1880s and 1890s, as morphine became less expensive and more available, many women became dependent. This addiction sometimes began under a doctor's care for menstrual pain or postpartum discomfort, as in Mary's case in Eugene O'Neill's (1955/1979) *Long Day's Journey into Night*. Perhaps predictably, the typical history of "feminine" drug abuse was private, sponsored by male physicians, and endured at home. In contrast, "masculine" addictions often began in socially sanctioned nondomestic settings such bars and saloons and underlined men's greater opportunities for experimentation (Hughes 1990).

When men suffered from alcohol and drug dependencies, it was not some strictly inner failing that was to blame, but rather a blend of "inner" and "outer" conditions. The preeminent form of male insanity was judged to be paresis, a partial paralysis that was linked, in the 1872 annual report of the Alabama Insane Hospital, to "habitual intemperance, sexual excesses, overstrain in business. … [Paresis] is especially a disease of *fast life,* and fast business in large cities" (quoted in Hughes 1990, 60). At this moment of nineteenth-century manhood, men's mental derangement resulted not from crossing gender lines, or from becoming "feminine," but from being masculine in excess, without discipline (Hughes 1990).

Not coincidentally, while many doctors were focusing on the health of white men's minds and their often neurasthenic male bodies, other medical and scientific investigators began to study a "new" species of man, the homosexual. The concept of "homosexuality" was not used widely in English until the

1890s, when it was employed by the sexologist Havelock Ellis (Jagose 1996). Many medical experts ceased seeing homosexuality as a punishable act which anybody was liable to commit, and began to see it in terms of identity, as a "third sex," an aberrant and deficient male identity, a case of the male body gone wrong. Medical and scientific attention to this emergent figure of the homosexual man—characterized as an "invert"—was, as Bederman (after Foucault) points out, amounted to a disciplinary normalization of sexuality, which functioned, in part, to manage the wider social, cultural, and economic forces that threatened the hegemony, the civic as well as sexual potency, of white middle-class manhood (Bederman 1995a).

White men began to speak approvingly about something they called "masculinity," a rhetoric that disclosed, despite itself, the fragility of manliness. Although rarely used until the late 1890s, "masculinity" had now become the noun of choice, precisely because it connoted new meanings of maleness different from the more traditional "manliness." Such reformulations were, Bederman (1995b) points out, fragmented and contradictory. For example, increasing numbers of middle-class men frequented urban red-light districts, yet many were ambivalent about such sexual activity. One such district in turn-of-the-century New York, the Bowery, was home to a significant and visible homosexual subculture. According to George Chauncey (1994), "going slumming in the resorts of the Bowery and the Tenderloin was a popular activity among middle-class men (and even some women)" (36). Was such activity the inevitable consequence of naturally explosive masculine passions? Did it represent the sordid and degenerate loss of manly self-control? If yes, could this pervasive moral weakness be counteracted and by whom? By the time Ida B. Wells sailed for England in 1893, Bederman tells us, "middle-class manliness had taken on the character of a beloved but fragile friend, whose weakness must at all costs remain unacknowledged" (1995b, 410).

To compensate for their losses and mythologize what they imagined had made them powerful, now that simply being an anatomical male did not, many middle-class white men began to focus on race. Ah yes, the quality that makes for power and strength and fortitude is that we are ... *"white"* men. The 1890s were a period of virulent racism and racially conceived nativism, a time of lynching, black disenfranchisement, xenophobia, and imperialism (Gossett 1963; Higham 1971; Williamson 1984). The native-born white middle class gazed with distaste, even disgust, upon increasing numbers of eastern and southern European immigrants; they perceived them as cousins of the blacks, that is, masses of inassimilable "races." Their unfamiliar customs and languages were unnerving and their tendency to vote for "machine" Democrats destabilized what had been white political control of American cities. As early as 1849, the president of Middlebury College had wondered whether the new immigrants would be assimilated or prove to be to the Republic what the Goths and Huns had been to the Roman Empire. The answer, he thought, would depend in large measure "upon the wisdom and fidelity of our teachers" (quoted in Cremin 1961, 66). Cultural standardization, itself a gendered phenomenon, would continue to characterize the American school into the twenty-first century (Pinar et al., 1995; Grumet 1988).

A cult of Anglo-Saxonism, fortified with new "scientific" theories of "race," provided incontrovertible "proof" of white middle-class men's supremacy (Stoler 1995). By mythologizing white manhood as racial traits cultivated long ago in the forests of Germany, white men once again knew they were manly men. European Americans could take comfort in the knowledge that the Anglo-Saxon race, as Francis Parkman phrased it, was "peculiarly masculine" (quoted in Gossett 1963, 95; quoted in Bederman 1995b, 410). By virtue of its racial inheritance, Anglo-Saxons were independent, adventurous, strong of will, tenacious of purpose, in a word, manly (Bederman 1995b).

The notion of "the white man" linked manhood to race. When in the 1890s whites spoke of "the white man," they usually contrasted him with "the negro" or "the Indian." As Bederman (1995b) points out, referring to "the black man" or "the red man," the logical parallel construction, might imply that black and red men were also manly, diluting the ideological strength of the phrase "the white man." In 1905 Ray Stannard Baker argued that lynching was unworthy of "the white man" precisely because it rendered him as unmanly as "the negro." Trying to be helpful but simply restating the very assumption Ida B. Wells would challenge while in England, Baker declared: "For if civilization means anything, it means self-restraint; casting away self-restraint the white man becomes as savage as the negro" (quoted in Bederman 1995b, 410). That sentence suggests, Bederman (1995b) notes, that what was most important about "the white man" was how the term worked as a synecdoche. By invoking the notion of "the white man," Americans conflated whiteness with manhood and with "civilization" itself.

Declaring, then, that "civilization" was in fact comprised of manliness and whiteness allowed middle-class white men to reassert their dominance, a dominance fabricated on the ruins of race and gender equality. By creating a binary in which women and blacks were outside the circle of reason, men declared all was right with the world. But "civilization" only disguised the weakness of manliness by repeatedly interweaving manhood and race, by repeating almost frantically that white racial superiority proved white men the most manly in the world. But Ida B. Wells knew the lady doth protest too much. She designed her entire English antilynching tour around this transparent ruse that was the discourse of "civilization," a term Gail Bederman (1995b) helps us understand as she focuses on the 1893 World's Fair in Chicago. Before we go to Chicago, however, let us back up and observe the early stages of black protest against lynching and, in the early 1890s, the emergence of Ida B. Wells.

THREE

Women and Racial Politics

Race relations during the 1880s and 1890s were influenced by the conservatism of the ruling Bourbon Democrats, in power since the close of Reconstruction. During the 1880s, their paternalistic style seemed to pacify those whites increasingly obsessed with the "Negro problem." Henry W. Grady, the editor of the *Atlanta Constitution,* expressed the Bourbons' racial point of view. He had no doubts about the supremacy of the "white race," but pledged that whites would dominate "not through violence, not through party alliance, but through the integrity of the vote and the largeness of its sympathy and justice through which it shall compel the support of the better classes of the colored race." In like tone, Georgia Governor Alfred H. Colquitt explained in 1888: "The people of the southern states are not so foolish as to believe that their peace, prosperity, or even their safety can be assured if a moeity [half] of the population is treated with injustice and denied its rights in the state" (quoted in Brundage 1993, 192). The remarkable progress African Americans had made since slavery buoyed Bourbon hope; many prophesied that, given time and freedom from meddling by northerners, they would serve as architects of a new era of harmonious race relations in the South (Brundage 1993).

Many white newspaper editors embraced the Bourbon point of view; in editorials they asked whites to stop the violence. Lynching, they warned, was not just a problem for blacks; it bred disrespect for the law, disrupted social stability, and risked black revenge. In December 1889, after an unusually violent Christmas holiday period, the *Savannah Morning News* pleaded with white residents to "cultivate the best of feeling between the races, and the best way to do that is for the stronger race to treat the weaker one with absolute fairness and justice." The *Atlanta Constitution* warned that "just so long as a few reckless citizens are allowed to charge around assuming the functions of the courts, the South will be a veritable Poverty Flat, and capital and enterprise will refuse to cross our borders" (quoted in Brundage 1993, 192–193).

However sincere the Bourbons were about improving race relations, their inability to envision aggressive state intervention on behalf of black citizens meant they were unable to protect African Americans from white violence. The Bourbons in Georgia, for instance, inherited an exceedingly weak state government; they succeeded in strengthening it only incrementally before passing it along to their more racially radical successors. Because they suffered an irrational fear of executive authority and centralized power, they had little notion of how to exercise effective leadership. None of the Bourbon governors knew what to do to stop escalating white violence (Brundage 1993).

No doubt black Christian feminists had learned "miming" from the larger black community. Without institutionalized political power, there were few options. Black disenfranchisement would be nearly complete by 1900. But white power in the South had been "redeemed" long before black disenfranchisement. Not long after Reconstruction, certainly by 1880, newly freed black people found themselves surrounded by frenzied, violent white men. Then things got even worse. Between 1895 and 1910 a decisive shift occurred in the tone and substance of discussions among whites throughout much of the old South regarding "race relations." A wave of "radical" racism swept away the Bourbons' pretensions of paternal race relations as whites no longer saw blacks as innocent if primitive children but as beasts, bucks, muscular black studs ready to rape at any moment. White mob violence swelled to record levels. For instance, in Georgia, 154 blacks (and 6 whites) were lynched during these fifteen years. On average, whites executed ten victims a year, and in 1899, the bloodiest year in Georgia state history, mobs murdered twenty-six persons. Several race riots occurred in a number of Georgia cities, including the especially violent white riot of 1906 in Atlanta, a city where the apparent erosion of race lines due to the comparative affluence (what whites fantasized as the profligate decadence) of urban blacks had brought tensions to the breaking point (Brundage 1993).

That racial violence persisted and even intensified after the worst of the Depression of the early 1890s was over suggests the psychosexual depths that lynching expressed. The persistence of the practice confirms John W. Cell's (1982) argument that the agricultural distress of the 1890s does not fully explain such variegated phenomena such as disfranchisement, segregation, and mob violence. As W. Fitzhugh Brundage (1993) observes, there were a number of specific forces in Georgia that "radicalized" whites, among them (1) the rise of a new generation of white extremists, (2) that bitterness that followed Populism, (3) the distress of whites at the training and stationing of black troops in the state during the Spanish-American War, and (4) the rage of southern whites at those small steps toward improved race relations taken by the Republican administrations of William McKinley and Theodore Roosevelt.

Given these steadily deteriorating, horrifying, deadly circumstances, what forms could black activism take during the lynching era? How would one assess the failures and achievements of black antilynching efforts? Through both design and custom, whites rejected black dissent and protest at every turn. When not ignored, black activists were ridiculed or worse. Progressive southern whites were unable or unwilling to organize any resistance against mob violence, a political problem intensified, given that white authorities were often all too sympathetic to what lynch mobs had in mind (Brundage 1993).

Northerners were, by and large, ignorant and indifferent. For instance, after months of travel throughout the South to study the race "question" during the first decade of the twentieth century, the northern journalist Ray Stannard Baker reported naively that "the Negro problem is not unsolvable; it is being solved, here and now, as fast as any human problem can be solved" (quoted in Brundage 1993, 208). As Brundage notes, if there were improvements in race relations before World War I, they occurred at "glacial speed" (1993, 208). In these circumstances, all that was left to African Americans was the sphere of the everyday, where opportunities would have to be found for what Michel de Certeau has called the "guerilla warfare of everyday life" (1980, 7). Except in slavery and some recent labor history, the study of furtive black dissent during the lynching era has only recently been undertaken (Brundage 1997a; Shapiro 1988; Kelley 1994).

Black struggle exhibited a range of expression, from highly public forms of dissent to what Zora Neale Hurston (1935/1990) termed "featherbed resistance" (2). Always vulnerable to the white majority, black struggle was typified, Brundage (1997a) tells us, by "a subtle dialectic of accommodation and confrontation, of restraint and militancy, [which] contravened fundamentally the 'visible' record of black consent, silence, and apathy" (271–

272). Even under impossible circumstances, black protest became, Brundage (1997a) continues, "more than a tactical sleight of hand, something more than merely seizing the possibilities that a moment offered" (1997a, 272). Black protest flowed from—here Brundage quotes George Lipsitz (1988)—"underground streams of resistance from the past" (229). He also quotes Richard Couto, who suggested that "resistance continually emerges because it never stops" (1993, 253). These variegated forms of protest mattered. They expressed and cultivated an ethic of tenacity that would characterize the history of African Americans as "inseparable from though not reducible to victimization" (West 1993, 14).

Conventional wisdom has held that "most blacks responded [to lynchings] by fearfully staying within prescribed social boundaries" and by trying "even more to placate the dominant caste" (McGovern 1982, 11). Others have suggested that during the Jim Crow era African Americans "remained silent ... taking the line of least resistance" (Lamon 1977, 18). But these statements are not accurate, Brundage (1997a) argues, as they accept black behavior at face value and thereby fail to recognize the combination of fear, deception, and pragmatic deference that lay just underneath it. Scholars such as Patricia Schecter, Gail Bederman, Fitzbugh Brundage and others present strong evidence that periodic public displays of submission by blacks cannot be interpreted as genuine acceptance of white supremacy. These displays of "gracious submission" can be decoded, Brundage suggests, only by keeping in mind George Eliot's image of "the roar that lies on the other side of silence" (quoted in Brundage 1997a, 273).

To help make the roar of silence audible, Brundage (1997a) draws upon the work of James C. Scott, who argued that oppressed groups challenge those in politically superior positions by appearing to consent. Having deceived their opponents into believing that they accept the status quo, the subordinate groups then challenge their oppressors by adopting variegated forms of protest, including cultural dissent such as songs, theft, and vandalism. Only rarely does the rage of the politically marginalized and vulnerable become visible in explicit and conventional challenges to ruling elites or their institutions. Rather, through daily acts of insubordination and parody, African Americans engaged in what Scott (1989) termed "infrapolitics," what Evelyn Brooks Higginbotham (1996) termed "micropolitics."

In the American South, blacks struggled against white supremacy in a multiplicity of ways, ranging from infra- to formal politics. Unlike antebellum slaves, African Americans after Emancipation were never entirely silenced or excluded from public life, despite white success at disenfranchisement. Still, southern race relations had little to do with negotiation let alone consensus. They were about domination, often performed in the realm of the everyday, not infrequently through coercion and mob violence. Given southern rage and hysteria and northern indifference, African Americans were completely vulnerable. Only the foolhardy or suicidal would risk direct confrontation with the majority whites. As a consequence, black struggle, and struggle against lynchers in particular, "fell on a continuum somewhere between the poles of outright compliance with white values and brazen rebellion against them" (Brundage 1997a, 274).

At one end of this continuum, then, African Americans asked white leaders to live up to their paternalistic rhetoric by stopping lynching. They struggled to build protest organizations that could bring pressure to bear upon white leaders while they simultaneously appealed to the "best class" of whites to uphold the law and protect them from the mob violence of "white rabble." In public meetings, editorials, sermons, and even in an occasional demonstration, African Americans condemned intensifying white violence. And on rare occasion, African Americans armed themselves to protect alleged criminals threatened by lynching mobs (Brundage 1993).

At the other end of this continuum were indirect, sometimes symbolic, gestures of defiance. Black struggle, Brundage argues, took the form of what he terms "discursive insubordination." Humor became the language of dissent, as African Americans joked about mob violence. After observing such humor during the 1930s, John Dollard remarked: "To take cheerfully a matter of such terrible moment is really to turn the joke back on the white man; some fun is squeezed even out of his warning." Perhaps that is what the aunt of a black man lynched in Alexandria, Virginia, was doing when in 1897 she quipped: "the [white] people killed him, they will have to bury him" (quoted in Brundage 1997a, 274).

African Americans devised a wide range of tactics that allowed them to protest and retaliate while protecting themselves. Ranging from vandalism to arson, symbolic rebellion functioned, in William Faulkner's words, as "one weapon for the preservation of dignity" (1954, 502; quoted in Brundage 1997a, 274). Brundage reports that arson was a common black response to white violence, although exact statistics are not available. Cautious in their responses to white lynchers, African Americans were more direct in their responses to those blacks who aided white mobs. But few African Americans required the threat of black retribution to discourage them from helping white mobs. Most remembered and wanted to honor the tradition of protection and assistance for those in flight that extended back through centuries of slavery. By hiding alleged black criminals and helping them to escape to safety, black communities simultaneously prevented possible lynchings and expressed their contempt for so-called popular justice (Brundage 1997a).

A highly visible expression of black contempt for lynching was emigration; large numbers of black residents fled areas where lynchings occurred. It was clear to white planters and other employers who were suddenly without cheap labor that this was black rebellion. Lynchings were a significant factor in the Great Migration of the early twentieth century, during which the South lost a significant percentage of its black population (Beck and Tolnay 1997). Even rumors of a possible lynching prompted blacks to go into hiding or to flee. For African Americans who lacked, or declined to depend upon, white protectors, flight was one of the few responses to lynching which expressed defiance and yet typically did not provoke retaliation. While black flight did not prevent whites from storming jails or conducting manhunts for their black victims, it did tend to protect escapees from mob violence (Brundage 1997a).

Whites were clear that flight was more than a simple fear reflex. The mass exodus of black farmhands risked a genuine economic problem for white landowners. Following the lynching of Paul Reed and William Cato near Statesboro, Georgia, in 1904, roving bands of rampaging white men indiscriminately attacked blacks across the surrounding countryside. Many black residents fled the area, threatening a labor crisis at the very beginning of the cotton-picking season. White planters were sufficiently worried that they persuaded local officials to issue a public statement demanding that the attacks cease. An extra marshal was hired to help enforce peace. In another instance, blacks declined to leave the area where a lynching had occurred, but they did withhold their labor. Such action could only be understood as a protest. After a lynching in Northumberland County, Virginia, in 1917, blacks refused to work for the leader of the mob. In a panic, he offered them double wages. The protestors held firm. The white elite was persuaded; afterward, the *Norfolk Journal and Guide* warned that future lynchings in the area would depopulate the region, wreaking economic havoc (Brundage 1997a).

Another expression of veiled protest involved the use of what Brundage (1997a) terms a language of dissemblance, a term he associates with Bakhtin's concept of "a doubled-voiced discourse" (Bakhtin 1981, 293–294). Such language undermined the legitimacy of white dominance. Discursive struggle was no rarefied language game for university-based poststructuralists, as neo-Marxists in education have on occasion suggested. Central to the struggle between blacks and whites was the formulation of social meaning—nothing less than social reality itself. In the late nineteenth-century South, whites were determined to prevent blacks from voicing conflicting or subversive alternatives to white supremacy. Whites were determined to control black speech but always failed, as whites and blacks did not internalize the language and ideology of white domination in the same way (Higginbotham 1996). Even while (apparently) speaking the language of white supremacy, African Americans were often conveying skepticism if not outright defiance (Brundage 1997a). Such disguised forms of protest succeeded in keeping hope alive.

The funeral of a mob victim was sometimes a moment of protest as well as mourning. Funerals proceeded with little interference from whites. On at least one occasion, as mentioned, protest took the form of the victim's family refusing to accept the responsibility and cost of burial. Even the strained (if not horrified) atmosphere that followed in the wake of lynchings sometimes did not restrict black ministers' comments to the funeral rites at hand. Ministers knew that criticism of white lynchers risked retaliation. That did not restrain the Reverend William Gaines, who presided at the service for one lynched black man. He was sharply critical of the lynchers, and many whites who learned of his comments were furious. Gaines suffered no penalty, but in other places on other occasions whites were less forgiving. Black ministers whose funeral services and comments were considered impertinent were told to leave the community, or else. In March 1899, for example, following the lynching of four black men in Palmetto, Georgia, an outspoken black minister claimed to have the names of several of the mob members. Whites forced him to leave town immediately (Brundage 1993).

Blacks seized upon any safe opportunity to protest against white violence. If local blacks perceived that certain types of mob violence were not always condoned by whites, they took advantage of the opening in the public space and carefully expressed their accumulated frustration and anger. In 1894, as we see in the next section, following the lynchings of five blacks by a ruthless posse in Brooks County, Georgia, African Americans held a mass meeting and issued a proclamation protesting the failure of law officers and the state to uphold the laws. Still, any protest after a mass lynching required caution because even token criticism under certain circumstances might provoke additional white violence (Brundage 1993).

On other occasions African Americans found white injustice unendurable, and enraged black citizens could not wait for safe opportunities to express dissent. Upon learning of the murder of a black man by his white employer in Greene Country (Georgia) in 1867, over forty neighboring black men "organized themselves into a regular armed company" and marched on the white man's house. "They surrounded the house and, with horrid oaths and vows of vengeance, commenced an indiscriminate fire on the premises, in which Mr. Marchman was severely wounded." These outraged black citizens made no effort at concealment and were soon arrested. "It really seems that the negroes are determined to follow the advice of their Carpet-bag friends from the land of the Puritans," the local newspaper warned, "until it will bring on a war of the races *in earnest*" (quoted in Ayers 1984, 157). Twenty-five years later, this prediction seemed to be coming true.

II. Black Defiance: Brooks County, Georgia, 1894 and the Darien Insurrection

If war ... is the continuation of politics by other means, it requires little imagination to see American life since the abandonment of the Reconstruction as an abrupt reversal of that formula: the continuation of the Civil War by means other than arms.

—Ralph Ellison, *Shadow and Act* (1964/1995)

Confederate veterans refused to accept cultural defeat and sustained a Confederate tradition in spite of the South's reincorporation into the United States.

—Cecilia Elizabeth O'Leary, "'Blood Brotherhod': The Racialization of Patriotism, 1865–1918" (1996)

White men do fear Black men.

—Haki R. Madhubuti, *Black Men* (1990, emphasis in original)

During the Christmas celebrations in Brooks County, Georgia, in 1894, the traditionally festive celebrations were interrupted by violence. Under the pretext of searching for alleged murderers, a white posse ran amok, indiscriminately torturing and murdering African Americans. In Quitman, the county seat, black citizens wired the governor: "We ... are imposed upon by mobbers and we are trying to obtain by the laws of Georgia. What should we do?" (quoted in Brundage 1997a, 276). Elsewhere in the county, skeptical that white authorities could be counted on, black residents sought safety in the dense swamps (Brundage 1997a).

At least at the outset, those who took flight were the prudent ones, as whites took no meaningful action to stop the violence. That is, until white men reached the plantation of Mitchell Brice, one of the county's richest planters. Indignant over the mob's beating of an elderly black woman, Brice warned mob members that he planned to prosecute them. The planter's intervention coupled with the arrival of state militia—the telegram actually produced results—plus the arrest of the alleged black murder suspects, finally ended the slaughter (Brundage 1997a).

Brice was no hero; he was not opposed in principle to either mob violence or extralegal punishment. Brice was indignant that the mob had mistreated his farmhands. One of his neighbors explained: "[His blacks] are just as much his slaves as they were before the war. He don't send them to the chain gang and the negroes are better pleased" (quoted in Brundage 1997a, 276). That Brice responded to the appeal of his black farmhands for protection was, then, no instance of heroism but an expression of his economic interest, not to mention his relative power and their vulnerability. Brice intended to defend his absolute authority over his workers from the reckless actions of rioting whites (Brundage 1997a).

The events in Brooks County suggest both the risk for blacks of accepting white guardianship and the openings that such guardianship made for black protest. By occupying, or appearing to occupy, the "place" the white elite imagined for them, by behaving publicly as if they accepted and believed white paternalism, blacks contributed, knowingly, to white domination in Brooks County. By acquiescing to whippings by white planters and by appealing to them for protection, blacks risked relinquishing any claims upon legal institutions to acknowledge their civil rights. But given black political vulnerability—legal institutions were run, recall, by the same white men—the necessity of relying on whites could not be wished away. In such a setting, no African American could escape the politics of deference (Brundage 1997a). As Oliver Cox suggested: "[The African American] prostrates himself, as it were, before white men in recognition that Negroes enjoy a degree of well-being only by sufferance of their white neighbors" (1948/1970, 564). The politics of deference was a politics of necessity in the Jim Crow South.

Still, African Americans were not defeated. To illustrate, Brundage returns to the idea of the double-voiced discourse of race relations. Without meaningful political alternatives, black residents of Brooks County still found a way to turn the rhetoric of white supremacy to their advantage. Brundage explains: "[B]lacks at once subverted and reconstructed the language of their oppression. By stressing the tenets of white supremacy—that 'good blacks' who 'stayed in their place' would enjoy security of life and property—blacks protested that whites who participated in or condoned mob violence violated the norms by which they justified their own authority" (1997a, 276–277). You can't have it both ways, white boy; you're either my man or you're not.

Blacks often coded their appeals for protection in moral terms; it was the white lynchers who were failing to act properly. Using white concepts of morality or normalcy against whites was a tactic Ida B. Wells would perfect in her campaign to persuade British listeners that white lynchers, not black victims, were unmanly and uncivilized, as we will see in the next chapter. The telegram black residents of Brooks County sent to the governor in 1894 illustrates this point: "We ... are imposed upon by mobbers and we are trying to obtain by the laws of Georgia. What should we do?" (quoted in Brundage 1997a, 277). In other words, victimized blacks were attempting to uphold the law of the great state of Georgia, despite efforts by white "mobbers" to violate them. In performing what we might term a "racial reversal," African Americans manipulated whites by upholding the very racialized norms that structured black subordination. In so doing, they were protesting against white aggression in a fashion that trapped whites into agreeing with them. In like fashion, the deference the blacks performed in front of whites did not necessarily mean acquiescence to the injustice of their situation. Rather, black deference expressed both resignation and indignation (Couto 1993; Brundage 1997a). Playing the politics of public deference testified "to the subtlety, cunning, and ongoing refusal of Brooks County blacks to internalize white ideology, not their craven obedience to it" (Brundage 1997a, 277).

Such a politics of deference anticipates, of course, W. E. B. Du Bois's (1903) notion of "double consciousness" and the African-American oral tradition of "signifying" (Gates 1988). Although blacks' appeals for protection were expressed in a discourse of deference, they were often more strategic than sincere. From antebellum days, blacks had learned to perform in public in ways that whites perceived as submissive, "happily" occupying their "place," but which to black eyes and ears represented an ongoing expression of protest. Once away from the demanding and dangerous gaze of whites, blacks dropped the public face of deference and voiced the rage of those unjustly treated. Revenge, not deference, was what many had in mind for whites. In black social spaces ranging from churches to fraternal lodges, social clubs and barbershops, a dynamic black culture of self-affirmation and political opposition flourished (Kelley 1994; hooks 1990; Brundage 1997a). Whites sometimes suspected that the personae they saw were not the realities blacks lived, and their uneasiness grew in proportion to the degree that blacks successfully fashioned an independent social life. As Brundage (1997a) points out, it is no coincidence that when racial violence erupted, white arsonists and mobs frequently targeted such symbols of black independence and progress as schools, churches, and club buildings.

The refusal to accept the status quo which underlay the public performance of black acquiescence is evident in the antilynching files of the N.A.A.C.P., indeed in the very conduct of that organization, as we will see in chapters 10 and 11. The N.A.A.C.P. organized everywhere it could, and especially in isolated rural areas it functioned as a mechanism of memory and expression for enraged and endangered rural blacks. The N.A.A.C.P.'s files provided a repository for all black citizens to record their individual and collective experience of white repression. Orally and organizationally, African Americans have remembered. The N.A.A.C.P. brought that memory to public notice. By straddling the threshold between micropolitics and formal institutionalized protest, the N.A.A.C.P. and its campaign against lynching would focus a variegated and sometimes indirect campaign of nameless multitudes. It also masculinized what had before been primarily black women's struggle to save black men, most notably the crusade of Ida B. Wells. While fooled "close up and personal" by signifying blacks, white men across the South would soon come to understand precisely the significance of the N.A.A.C.P.'s activities, and they would violently attack the organization and its informers throughout the twentieth century (Brundage 1997a; Zangrando 1980).

As we have see in this chapter, we do not have to wait for the N.A.A.C.P. to be founded in 1909 to observe organized black protest, not only to lynching but to white domination generally. While indirect and furtive protest, cultural and micropolitical, predominated, when the opportunity rose and circumstances warranted, African Americans moved openly and collectively as well. In Jacksonville, Florida, in 1920, outraged blacks canceled their policies with a white life insurance company after several of its agents led a lynch mob. Despite the efforts of the firm, sixteen thousand black customers moved their business to a newly organized black life insurance company. Even during the late nineteenth century, when racism and mob violence were extreme, on occasion African Americans openly repudiated white reality. In Kemper County, Mississippi, in 1888, and in Paducah, Kentucky, in 1892, and elsewhere, blacks mobilized to combat white mobs or to protect those accused of crime while they were in jail. In 1904, African Americans near Norfolk, Virginia, took to the streets to protest a lynching and the apparent complicity of the local police. Unable to silence the crowd, frightened local authorities called for state militia to restore order. Only after several tense days and numerous exchanges between blacks and troops was order restored (Brundage 1997a).

The Darien Insurrection

One of the most memorable instances of defiant black protest in the nineteenth century was "the Darien Insurrection," which, Brundage argues, "exemplifies the protean, unorganized character of such collective actions" (1997a, 278). Apparently without organization or leadership, black residents of McIntosh County, Georgia, mobilized spontaneously to protect one of their own. In August 1899, Henry Denegal was accused of raping a white woman. A group of black residents gathered around the jail in an effort to protect Denegal from lynching. For two days the sheriff made several attempts to transport him to Savannah, allegedly for safekeeping. Those assembled worried that the move was a subterfuge to turn Denegal over to a mob; they refused to let him be moved. Each time the sheriff thought the coast was clear, a sentry rang the bell of a nearby black church. That signal brought hundreds of black residents, many armed, who surrounded the jail. Finally, unnerved white authorities telegraphed the governor and urgently requested the protection of the state militia (Brundage 1997a).

The arrival of soldiers in Darien failed to dislodge those African Americans who had surrounded the jail. Employing that same "racial reversal," they declined to respond to the soldiers' presence as if they constituted a threat. Not only did they allow the white militia access to the jail, they cheered when they—not the local sheriff—placed Denegal on a Savannah-bound train. After the train left the station, the situation quickly deteriorated when two white men were shot while attempting to arrest the alleged ringleaders of the insurrectionists. Black community leaders then met with the white commander of the militia; together they worked out a plan that restored calm. Of course, such explicit black resistance could not go unpunished in nineteenth-century Georgia. While Denegal was acquitted of all charges, twenty-three of the insurrectionists were convicted of rioting and received severe prison terms and fines (Brundage 1997a).

The events in Darien, Brundage (1997a) argues, cannot be dismissed as little more than localized and ephemeral opposition to lynching. He reminds us that local black leaders did not provoke, lead, or control the insurrection; their role was limited to helping end the confrontation and placating local whites. Instead, black residents' spontaneous mobilization and direct action illustrates what Scott (1990) has called an "enabling popular tradition" of protest and the inextricable relationship between private and public protest. The Darien Insurrection also illustrates, as Brundage points out, Gramsci's observation that "spontaneity is the history of the subaltern classes" (1971, 196).

While African Americans' political protest in Darien may have been spontaneous, Brundage notes that it did require a degree of coordination, as demonstrated by the positioning of sentries to watch the jail, the ringing of the church bell, and so on. Such coordination operated through informal networks that traversed the local black institutions of church, family, and community. What Brundage emphasizes is that these networks, foundational to collective action and to the social structuring of the local black community, were largely invisible to white authorities. Because the identities of the actual "insurrectionists" were anonymous, the commander of the white militia had to negotiate with local black officials, who apparently had no role in the action around the jail. While those defiant black citizens who took over Darien in August 1899 to avoid a lynching appear to have acted spontaneously, they were performing collectively what individuals had performed themselves all across the South: rejection of white domination. Such shared, if only occasionally collectivized, black protests kept hope alive during the lynching era and would surface over and over again in the twentieth century (Brundage 1997a).

While the overwhelming majority of violent incidents occurred when white men obsessed over black men, black women played key roles in maintaining and extending traditions of protest, as well as the collective memory of them, "from the cabin table to the church pew" (Brundage 1997a, 279). While educated middle-class black women such as Ida B. Wells were more visible in the struggle against lynching, countless rural black women also fought the white male mutilation of black male bodies. During the Darien "Insurrection" black women protestors outnumbered black men and, according to newspaper accounts at the time, were the most strident and determined sentinels at the jail. Black women in Barnwell, South Carolina, in 1889 were conspicuously outraged by the massacre of eight black prisoners. In Norfolk in 1904, black women openly and aggressively cursed whites in the aftermath of mob violence (Brundage 1997a).

Rural black women, Brundage tells us, worked "independently from but parallel to" (1997a, 280) the efforts of Ida B. Wells and other middle-class black reformers such as Mary Church Terrell and Anna Julia Cooper. Rural and lower-class black women manipulated gender differences in order to contest racial etiquette. Drawing upon Dollard (1937, 1939) and Kelley (1993, 1994), Brundage argues:

> Black women from all walks of life knew that they could commit acts of insubordination that whites would not allow if committed by black men. However dehumanizing prevailing racist stereotypes of black women were, whites still did not assume that black women posed the same threat to white women or men that black men did. Therefore, whites tolerated blatant protests by black women that would have drawn very severe penalties had they been made by black men. (1977a, 280)

Brundage does not elaborate exactly what kind of "threat" black men posed to white men, but I think by now we have an idea.

Black women who contested white domination were by no means immune to punishment. Indeed, black women sometimes suffered severely for their racial insubordination. For example, five women were among the "rioters" arrested following the Darien "Insurrection." In numerous instances whites utilized multiple forms of violence (although only rarely did these include lynching) to silence outspoken black women. While white men bypassed black women to get to black men, Brundage notes that the significance of black women's protests is incalculable. As we will see when we examine Ida B. Wells's "crusade for justice," black women were deft at employing whatever tactics, from the difficult to decode to the unmistakably confrontational, that contributed immeasurably to that collective solidarity which made possible all black protest and struggle (Brundage 1997a).

III. Class Solidarity and Alienation

[It] was virtually a national obsession with the black male body.

—Sandra Gunning, *Race, Rape, and Lynching: The Red Record of American Literature, 1890–1912* (1996)

Only the BLACK WOMAN can say "when and where I enter, in the quiet, undisputed dignity of my womanhood, without violence and without suing or special patronage, then and there the whole Negro race enters with me."

—Anna Julia Cooper, "A Voice from the South" (1892/1998)

Brundage also points to those crusades against lynching conducted by Ida B. Wells while she was editor of the *Memphis Free Speech,* and John Mitchell while he was editor of the *Richmond Planet.* Despite repressive white hegemony, individual African Americans risked everything to register public protest against white barbarism. Their antilynching activities ranged from gathering information on individual lynchings to denouncing mob violence in print and from the lecture podium. Brundage writes that these are suggestive of the central role played by southern black editors in the public struggle against lynching. That acknowledged, Brundage appears to assign to Wells and Mitchell and other black editors and members of the press a lesser role in the struggle against lynching, characterizing (quoting Gunnar Myrdal) their efforts as letting off the steam of boiling black protest. Wells's role was, it seems to me, considerably more powerful and formative than that phrase implies, as later chapters will make clear. In what begins to sound like a kind of Gramscian celebration of the unnamed masses (about which one would be hard pressed to complain), Brundage writes that:

> Against the backdrop of the furtive or spontaneous forms of black protest, it is tempting and perhaps appropriate to assume that the activities of Wells, Mitchell, and others presented a more advanced, more effective, and more important form of black protest. Not only were their protests and those of other southern black editors public, but they were also couched in overtly political language. No translation or interpretation was needed for whites to understand Wells and Mitchell when they denounced white violence and the values that bred it. (1997a, 280)

One cannot help but hear the "but" at the end of the sentence.

Brundage continues that Mitchell and Wells understood that their campaigns of public protest were situated in traditions of black protest that were rarely so public or direct. Both editors (I question the implication of the conjunction that the two were equally important) endorsed violence in the name of self-defense and protection; both were not opposed to black retaliation for white violence. Brundage repeats Wells's oft-quoted advice that "a Winchester rifle should have a place of honor in every black home" (Wells 1892a/1969, 23), and her praise of those black citizens who set fire to Georgetown, Kentucky, in protest of a lynching. "Not until the Negro rises in his might," Wells declared in *Southern Horrors,* and "takes a hand in resenting such cold-blooded murders, if he has to burn up whole towns, will a halt be called in wholesale lynchings." John Mitchell had likewise concluded that: "The best way to secure protection in the South is to own a repeating rifle and a shot-gun and know how and when to use it" (quoted in Brundage 1997a, 281). Not only did both editors encourage black mobilization to protect those threatened by lynchers, on occasion they themselves inspired and led community protests against white violence. Here Brundage is thinking of the famous Memphis lynching "at the curve" in 1892, in response to which Wells called for a black boycott of the Memphis streetcars and black emigration from the city. (The details of the Memphis lynching will be told in section VII, this chapter.)

Both Wells and Mitchell, Brundage points out, focused their antilynching efforts upon the mobilization of middle-class blacks and whites to restrain white southerners. Wells's genius in igniting British public sentiment during her controversial tours of Great Britain in 1892 and 1894 is an example of this strategy—I argue it qualifies as a form of pedagogy—conducted on an international scale. Her pedagogical and political success in redirecting the American discussion of lynching by brilliantly manipulating prevailing white notions of masculinity, femininity, and civilization points, Brundage asserts, to "the common ground that she shared with her white audiences" (1997a, 281), a strange point to make given that it is not entirely true. Wells went to Britain precisely because white middle-class Americans refused to listen to her; her articles on lynching were rejected by white newspapers, for instance. And the "common ground" she shared with British reformers (primarily feminists) was more a gendered relation to dominant imperialist and colonial interests than a bond cemented by class, race, or even gender. (Wells was less interested in the international dimensions of the worldwide racial crisis than she was in lynching back in America.) It is probably more accurate to say that Wells exploited British listeners' unexpressed guilt over their own racism and classism as well as their residual feelings of superiority over their former colonies to ignite indignation over lynching. I amplify this point in the next chapter.

It is true, of course, that "both Wells and Mitchell worked with white allies to suppress mob violence because to do so meshed with their notion of reform flowing from a shared sense of justice as much as from the directed power of blacks" (Brundage 1997a, 281). Mitchell emphasized that concern for social order and sanctity of legal institutions that conservative whites opposed to lynching shared. Mitchell thought primarily in terms of local opposition to lynching and white violence generally (Brundage 1997a). "Despite their inflammatory rhetoric," Brundage again links Mitchell and Wells with a conjunction, saying that both Mitchell and Wells "eventually adopted tactics that relied more on the manipulation of powerful whites than on their fitful attempts to organize blacks" (1997a, 281). Such tactics, Brundage argues, disclose "a gulf that separated many turn-of-the-century black leaders from the communities for which they claimed to speak" (1997a, 281). Brundage has a point, but it seems a somewhat unfair one, especially since Wells remained connected to the African-American community in numerous ways, including, later, the Negro Fellowship League (Munro 1999b; Wells 1970). Not to mention that in a white-dominated society in which racism had become "radical" and black disenfranchisement would soon be almost complete, mobilization of blacks would, at that historical moment, risk genocide. The only tactic—as the character of everyday resistance suggests—involved the shrewd manipulation of a powerful white racist majority.

Given this reality, it seems curious, even if accurate, for Brundage to emphasize that "many other turn-of-the-century black editors in the South, perhaps because of their sense of their own importance as black leaders, virtually ignored everyday resistance" (1997a, 281–282). "At best," Brundage continues, black editors such as Wells and Mitchell "condoned acts of self-defense even while placing little emphasis upon them. Committed as they were to formal and public modes of protest, many editors were little inclined to acknowledge popular forms of protest" (282). To illustrate, Brundage tells us that "the able editor" of the *Savannah Tribune,* one of the South's "best black newspapers," failed to cover the Darien Insurrection. "[E]ven Mitchell," he writes, "eventually seems to have lost interest in celebrating the tradition of informal resistance that had once been so prominent in his newspaper." While he does not doubt "the courage or devotion of such southern black leaders," Brundage concludes that "there is reason to believe that their methods neither articulated nor incorporated the full range of black opposition to white violence" (1997a, 282). What is the point here?

If it is to underscore the growing and continuing gap between the black "underclasses" and the black bourgeoisie, it is unnecessary and probably inappropriate to do so. It is unnecessary because this problem has been sufficiently expressed in both scholarly literature and the public press, and because class-based alienation and antagonism cut across racial lines, and is thereby hardly a dilemma unique to African Americans, then or now. It is probably inappropriate because it could diminish our sense of the courage and genius of leaders like Wells, a figure whose accomplishment, despite significant scholarly attention recently, remains in general underappreciated. But these facts escape Brundage's attention. After raising the issue, he quickly tries to close it: "In time the gap that separated expressions of protest by the black elites and the black masses narrowed" (1997a, 282).

For documentation, Brundage points to Adam Fairclough's (1995/1999) study of Louisiana which describes the N.A.A.C.P.'s effort to forge cross-class alliances during the 1930s and early 1940s. Such alliances encouraged new expressions of black protest. Local leaders devised strategies of protest which mobilized many more black residents than had previous campaigns. Against great odds, American Communists and radical labor activists attacked the American class and racial hierarchy while trying to organize blacks and whites in the South. As we will see, the Communist Party's involvement in the Scottsboro case focused national attention on southern violence. And it would force the N.A.A.C.P. to adopt bolder measures. "Thus," Brundage concludes, "by the beginning of World War II, blacks could tap the resources of a growing array of organizations dedicated to abolishing white supremacy and the violence that undergirded it. Class and ideological divisions among blacks surfaced in subsequent campaigns, but the diversity of participants ensured that organized and ongoing white public protest was never again mobilized by the black elites" (1997a, 282).

I think Brundage moves too quickly here. While he acknowledges that the N.A.A.C.P. becomes bolder, partly as a defensive and competitive response to the C.P.-U.S.A.'s success, he fails to note that the N.A.A.C.P. was comprised of the very middle-class (and upper-class) black leaders he comes close to disparaging in the case of Ida B. Wells. Nor was the C.P.-U.S.A. any closer to the "masses," despite its ideology and rhetoric. What Dan T. Carter's (1969/1979) study of the Scottsboro case makes clear is that the Communists manipulated not only the defendants and their families, but the American public as well in order to convert blacks and whites to the communist cause. Carter's study also makes clear that the N.A.A.C.P., in Alabama at least, did not foster "cross-class alliances," but in fact seemed to work against, or at least in ignorance, of them. Pointing this out is not to diminish the courage and accomplishment of the N.A.A.C.P. in the Scottsboro case; I devote full chapters to its determined efforts in that case and against lynching generally. But it is to acknowledge the centrality of middle-class (and upper-class) intellectuals and leaders such as Ida B. Wells, Anna Julia Cooper, W. E. B. Du Bois, Walter White, and James Weldon Johnson in the formation, direction, and inspiration of mass protest, black and white.

Black efforts to stop white violence were constrained by limited economic and political resources. That African Americans devised methods reflected their prudence in the face of overwhelming white domination. Protest therefore assumed forms that may appear timid and ineffective, given our memory of the 1960s and the aggressive tactics of student groups like S.N.C.C. When the full range of protest to white violence is considered, from everyday cultural politics to heroic efforts by black leaders such as Ida B. Wells to later institutionalized interventions undertaken by the N.A.A.C.P., then the complexities of power relations in the Jim Crow South and of the constant struggle by blacks to contest white supremacy become more audible (Brundage 1997a). The roar of silence *was* deafening.

Black protest was no simple reflex action, a response to the brutal stimulus that was white violence. Since the Middle Passage, blacks had undermined those forms of white supremacy that subjugated them. White supremacy was not fixed or monolithic, but a set of discursive and material relations that had to be defended, propped up, and performed in what was an ongoing power struggle. Perhaps white supremacy was, in part, a compensatory (perhaps subconsciously guilt-ridden) response to white sadism and black insurgency. White domination and black protest were inextricably linked from the outset. Nor did black struggle occur strictly within social and political structures predetermined by white domination. Black protest was ever being reconstructed and performed through everyday life practices, ensuring that white domination and its mystification of reality were being constantly contested. Whites found they had to reassert their fantasies of superiority just as continuously. White domination and black refusal of same, then, were born of the same womb; even while white power worked to reproduce itself and domesticate black power, black protest in turn questioned and destabilized white domination (Brundage 1997a).

IV. The Micropolitics of Everyday Life

[H]owl, yes, howl loudly, until the American people hear our cries.

—John Mitchell, quoted in W. F. Brundage, *Lynching in the New South: Georgia and Virginia, 1880–1930* (1993)

[T]he figuration of silenced womanhood [i]s a crucial component in turn-of-the-century discourses of rape and lynching.

—Sandra Gunning, *Race, Rape, and Lynching: The Red Record of American Literature, 1890–1912* (1996)

The image of black masses cowed by white violence is, obviously, not accurate. A more nuanced portrait reveals an oppressed people creatively experimenting with whatever form of dissent—from private to public—seemed possible. While there were indeed great Americans like Ida B. Wells, we need to remember, or imagine, those millions of African Americans whose names are lost to us but who struggled every day in every way against insurmountable odds to affirm who they were and to undermine what many whites fantasized themselves to be. Acknowledging then the full spectrum of black struggle requires us to imagine the micropolitics of everyday life, in which minor deviations from racial expectation accumulated to support black cultural mobilization; all the while whites insisted that blacks had no culture, no rights, no abilities. To remember requires us not only to acknowledge a black heroic past filled with black heroes and heroines, but as well to imagine those unnamed and unrecorded millions who, without formal education—Munro (1999b) maintains that African Americans educated each other informally in churches, clubs, and at home—or political and economic resources, communicated every day and in every way to each other and to whites that someday we will be free (Brundage 1997a).

The skeptic may question this view. Given the lynchings, the race riots, the daily beatings, continuous intimidation, and general everyday savagery of southern whites ... what could "micropolitics" accomplish? Furtive forms of protest—jokes, flight, arson—would seem too "micro" to have mattered, expressive perhaps for the participants, but inconsequential in terms of presenting a discernible challenge to white domination. Were not these mere substitutes for more meaningful protest? Of course, subtle forms of dissent may well have been too indirect to have been decoded by whites as protest. But this problem has not only to do with the indirectness of subtle protest. Whites could not easily recognize acts of dissent without admitting to themselves the vast scale of black refusal. Recall that southern whites retreated from reality in order to live in denial in their "garden of chattel" (Simpson 1983).

After the War, southern whites retreated farther into the fantasy land of racial superiority; they focused on creating those appearances that would not puncture their hallucinations; they became rabid fundamentalists, writhing in the hands of an angry God, the sinewy muscular arms of their Master (Williamson 1984). Blacks *must,* they thundered, stay in their "place," an imaginary place in the white mind (Frederickson 1971). White southerners desperately needed to keep the large fact of black protest out of public sight (Brundage 1997a). James Scott observes: "The importance of avoiding any public display of insubordination is not simply derived from a strategy of divide and rule; open insubordination represents a dramatic contradiction of the smooth surface of ephemeral power" (1990, 56).

Oblique and disguised protest, however indirect and fleeting it seems to those with mass strikes and street barricades in mind, testified to the continuous refusal of African Americans to accept the legitimacy or inevitability of white supremacy. Such dissent represented an ongoing if veiled renegotiation of power relations in a racist society. Seemingly incidental or minor events in response to white violence which were not savagely repressed redrew the boundaries of what was then permissible; these incidents inspired others to widen that breach, to challenge further white resolve. In this sphere of cultural politics, we are often unable to determine the sources or successes of such action. On some occasions uncontrolled rage, on others courageous self-conscious risk-tasking, and on others rational strategizing enabled African Americans to undermine white supremacy. For Isaac Flowers, a black man in Wayne County, Georgia, the moment came when whites who overheard his praise for a notorious black "desperado" whose "uppityness" had provoked a mass lynching several years earlier demanded that he retract the statement. Flowers refused. Whites became enraged and later murdered him; they then placed his body on the railroad tracks, where passing trains ran over and mangled it beyond recognition. While his murder underlines the savagery of southern white men, it also vividly demonstrates that black citizens like Flowers were quite willing to stand up to white nonsense despite the deadly consequences (Brundage 1997a).

On occasion black protest was public and straightforward; sometimes it yielded public concessions from whites and obviously restrained white violence. John L. Mitchell, Jr., used the *Richmond Planet* to report injustice and, through insistent calls for social justice, strove to mobilize black protest. The masthead of the *Planet,* a drawing of a muscular black arm with a clenched fist, communicated his masculinized determination. Mitchell published letters of protest from readers, reports of sermons against lynching, and news of national organizations devoted to fighting lynching and racism generally. By publishing black eyewitness accounts of lynchings, the newspaper not only communicated black rage, but ensured that white news accounts, which routinely recoded white barbarism as gendered and racial heroism, did not remain the only documentation. In this sense, Mitchell and the *Richmond Planet* helped compile African-American history (Brundage 1993).

In editorials characterized by both passion and sarcasm, Mitchell committed himself "to howl, yes, howl loudly, until the American people hear our cries." His editorials affirmed blacks' experience of white violence, experience left unrecorded in the often legitimating even praising depictions of lynchings published in white newspapers. As we saw in chapters 1 and 2 in the *Chicago Defender*'s accounts of lynching, Mitchell and the *Planet* also lashed out at whites who failed to acknowledge the barbarism of lynch mobs. "Southern white folks have gone to roasting Negroes," he observed contemptuously, "we presume the next step will be to eat them" (quoted in Brundage 1993, 164). Continually and loudly he reproached elected officials for failing to prevent lynchings and prosecute lynchers (Brundage 1993).

White men continued to mutilate black male bodies. Mitchell's frustration led him, like Wells, to advocate that African Americans arm themselves in self-defense against white violence. While always careful to limit his calls to arms as instances of self-defense only, his editorials, given the times, infuriated whites: "You may say what you will, but a Winchester rifle is a mighty convenient thing when two-legged animals are prowling around your house in the dead of night." Every mob, he demanded, should lose "one or more of its members as a silent testimonial to the unerring aim of some Negro" (quoted in Brundage 1993, 164–165).

In 1886, Mitchell received a death threat. A white man assured him that if he were ever to set foot in Prince Edward County, he would be lynched. Mitchell's response was to arm himself and travel openly throughout the county. His widely reported action communicated to whites and blacks alike that Mitchell was, in his own words, a man "who would walk into the jaws of death to serve his race" (quoted in Brundage 1993, 165). Mitchell's courage demonstrated that whites could not intimidate blacks into silence and passivity (Brundage 1993).

In 1893, Isaac Jenkins was accused of arson in Nansemond County. Soon after his arrest, whites tried to lynch him, but the attempt failed. But instead of prosecuting the lynchers, white officials focused on trying Jenkins. Mitchell was outraged; he raised money for the black man's defense while publishing weekly accounts of the case. A jury finally acquitted Jenkins. After his release, Mitchell brought him to Richmond where he organized speaking engagements so that Richmonders could listen to a firsthand account of white violence. In Virginia in the 1890s John Mitchell played a key role in changing white attitudes so that white violence could be contained. His demand that elected officials and concerned whites take responsibility for the protection of black prisoners, that the authority of the state must be invoked to halt lynching, tempered the character and the intensity of white violence in Virginia (Brundage 1993).

On an international stage, Ida B. Wells succeeded in shifting the national debate over lynchings in ways that compelled whites to address at least some of the gendered and economic realities of lynching. By repudiating whites' main rationale for lynching—that black men raped white women—Wells exhibited the will and agency of black intellectuals and activists, and especially of black women, to act outside the parameters of prevailing racist and sexist assumptions. Wells's pedagogical and political interventions invigorated the antilynching campaign, ensuring that it became a site from which black women could denounce both racial and sexual subordination (Brundage 1997a).

The Darien Insurrection left its mark upon white domination. The militancy of black residents of McIntosh County communicated to whites that they would not suffer mob violence without protest. Whites came to accept that violence against blacks could have unintended and even unwelcome consequences. That is evident in the response of white newspaper editors, who, now suddenly interested in at least the perception of tranquil race relations, stressed the importance of maintaining interracial cooperation. As one Savannah newspaper noted, those efforts of prominent blacks in Darien who helped defuse the situation functioned "to cement the peace and harmony which in the past has so signally blessed the relationship between the races in McIntosh County" (quoted in Brundage 1997a, 285). More than one newspaper concluded that the episode taught everyone how important it was that the two races work together to ensure that the "misapprehensions" of either race did not lead to public disorder in the future (Brundage 1997a).

Whites were hardly the only ones to learn lessons from public protest. The Darien Insurrection and countless other such episodes undoubtedly taught African Americans about "the vulnerability of the powerful," "the potential strength of the weak," not to mention "the terrible consequences of failed struggles" (Kelley 1993, 112; quoted in Brundage 1997a, 285). As Brundage nicely summarizes:

> The memory of resistance, which informed the self-definition of blacks and their willingness to take risks, created the social and individual precondition for future resistance. Each time blacks rebuilt a church, a fraternal lodge, or a school burned down by white arsonists, buried a lynching victim with dignity, gave money or information on a lynching to the N.A.A.C.P., sheltered a black threatened with mob violence, and vented resentment against white violence around the kitchen table, they built up a reservoir of shared indignation and collective self-definition that was essential to all forms of black protest. (1997a, 285)

Significantly, this collective self-definition and mobilization was gendered; the struggle for civil rights and emancipation became conflated with the struggle for black manhood.

For much of the lynching era, African Americans prudently limited their public efforts at emancipation and instead retreated into private spaces. There they engaged in forms of protest and self-affirmation that carried the fewest risks of reprisal. As the political and legal structures of white domination in the South eroded during the twentieth century, African Americans increasingly complemented everyday informal struggle with organized protest. As Brundage observes, civil rights activists' success in mobilizing black communities across the South in the 1950s and 1960s was possible "precisely because they tapped into the reservoir of moral anger and power that had been created and sustained by the long history of resistance, both clandestine and public" (1997a, 285). Such private and public traditions of political struggle enabled African Americans, despite the brutality of white oppression, to be "more than the sum of [their] brutalization" (Ellison 1967, 84; quoted in Brundage 1997a, 285).

V. The Southern White Reaction: Radical Racism, Southern Conservatism and Progressivism, and the Beginnings of the Civil Rights Movement

[The] South won in the cultural arena what it had lost on the battlefield.

—Cecilia Elizabeth O'Leary, "'Blood Brotherhood': The Racialization of Patriotism, 1865–1918" (1996)

[A]gitate, complain, protest and keep protesting against the invasion of our manhood rights.

—W. E. B. Du Bois and other delegates,
Equal Rights Convention of 1906,
quoted in W. Fitzbugh Brundage,
Lynching in the New South: Georgia and Virginia, 1880–1930 (1993)

The ritual of lynching, then, seemed to create even firmer ties between "civilized" whites and their class, as well as racial, inferiors.

—Sandra Gunning, *Race, Rape, and Lynching: The Red Record of American Literature, 1890–1912* (1996)

Not all black protest during the lynching era occurred "culturally," that is, outside mainstream political and institutional life, as the work of Ida B. Wells will illustrate. In addition to the popular press, African Americans registered their dissent at local and state conventions. On at least three occasions, black residents of Atlanta organized meetings to protest white attacks; they demanded that state authorities guarantee that lynchers would be prosecuted. In January 1888, led by the Reverend William J. White, editor of the *Augusta Georgia Baptist,* 350 black Georgians assembled in Macon to address the pressing problem of white violence. The convention denounced lynching, and pointed as well as to the problems of underfunded schools and a racist criminal justice system. It called upon the state's black voters to support only those candidates who pledged to reform the criminal justice system, to fight for full civil and political rights, and to pass legislation to end lynching. The Macon convention of 1888 and the various Atlanta meetings encouraged African Americans, especially in Georgia, to continue to press for their rights as American citizens and, in particular, to end white violence (Brundage 1993).

The southern white response was variegated, but, overall, reactionary. Until black Georgians were disenfranchised, some whites seemed somewhat responsive to black concerns, if only out of political expediency. In the intense political battles between Populists and Democrats during the early 1890s, white politicians competed with each other for the black vote. Both the Populist and Democratic parties took stands against lynching in an effort to attract black voters. In 1892, and again in 1894, the two parties assumed similar positions against lynching. In 1894 the Populist Party passed a resolution denouncing the "evil practices of lawless persons taking the law into their own hands," while the Democratic platform condemned "every form and species of mob violence and lynch law" (quoted in Brundage 1993, 194–195).

The bitter political struggles of the 1890s became intensely racialized and gendered. Both Populists and Democrats were guilty of racial demagoguery, despite the Populists' apparent interest in black votes. Democrats were not about to let them get away with it. On one occasion, Senator John B. Gordon, a Confederate war hero and the personification of the Bourbon (conservative, paternalistic) Democrats, charged Tom Watson, the state's prominent Populist, with undermining white civilization and thereby endangering "our spotless, pure and peerless southern womanhood" (quoted in Brundage 1993, 197). At first the Populists had resisted making openly racist appeals, but the invocation of white womanhood was too much. In one instance, during the gubernatorial campaign of 1896, Populists charged Democratic Governor William Y. Atkinson with encouraging black men to rape white women. The evidence, they said, was clear: the governor had pardoned a black man convicted of rape (Brundage 1993). This was a ploy President George Bush would use in modified form against Democratic challenger Michael Dukakis some one hundred years later in the famous Willie Horton incident.

In Georgia, the escalation of racist rhetoric was abetted by a group of right-wing journalists and politicians. Both categories of racists enjoyed large audiences that extended well beyond the boundaries of the state. Among the journalists were Charles E. Smith, better known by his pseudonym Bill Arp, of the *Atlanta Constitution,* Rebecca Latimer Felton of the *Atlanta Journal,* and John Tempe Graves of the *Atlanta News.* The loudest politicians included Governor Hoke Smith, also editor of the *Atlanta Journal,* and the increasingly embittered and racist Tom Watson. Watson had come to rejoice in "popular justice" as a means for taming the black man: "In the South, we have to lynch him [the Negro] occasionally, and flog him, now and then, to keep him from blaspheming the Almighty, by his conduct, on account of his smell and his color. ... Lynch law is a good sign: it shows that a sense of justice yet lives among the people" (quoted in Tolnay and Beck 1995, 18).

Figures such as Felton and Watson were quick to rationalize the barbarism of lynching. They replaced the Bourbon fantasy of blacks as children who required white care with a fantasy of the black as "beast-rapists who needed to be held down by force as he degenerated toward extinction" (Frederickson 1988, 176). The president of the University of North Carolina, George T. Winston, declared in 1901: "The black brute is lurking in the dark, a monstrous beast, crazed with lust. His ferocity is almost demoniacal. A mad bull or tiger could scarcely be more brutal" (quoted in Stember 1976, 23). Convinced of this racial degeneration (which many believed would eventually lead to extinction), many southern whites took for granted that there was an inevitable antipathy between the races. The South, wrote one woman at the end of the nineteenth century, had become "a smoldering volcano, the dark of its quivering night ... pierced through by the cry of some outraged [white] woman" (quoted in Hall 1983, 337).

With whites fantasizing bestial black bucks raping white women, these white journalists and politicians were only doing their "civic duty" in exhorting their fellow white men to take any and all means at their disposal to meet the black "threat." The primary and most intolerable threat was, predictably, rape; black men, white men were sure, were unable to control their overwhelming desire for white women. Abandoning theories of racial degeneration, Leonidas F. Scott argued, in a letter to Rebecca Latimer Felton dated May 30, 1894, that the black rapist was the product of black participation in politics, of vagrancy, and of "free schools with the Boston social equality attachment" (quoted in Brundage 1993, 198). Southern whites would soon find legislative means to block black participation in politics; the Louisiana Constitution of 1898, for instance, stripped black men of all political power. The number of black voters fell from 130,344 to 5,320; by 1904, after the poll tax was enforced, it fell to 1,342. Thereafter the number of Louisiana black voters varied, but the total almost never exceeded 2,000 and in 1940 stood at 886 (Fairclough 1995/1999). To view a photographic blow-up of this nightmare in the postbellum South, let us look for a moment at one incendiary white figure, a white woman named Rebecca Latimer Felton.

Rebecca Latimer Felton

Rebecca Latimer Felton (1835–1930) was a journalist, politician, feminist, prohibitionist, lay leader among Southern Methodists, and the first woman to become a United States senator (in 1922 by appointment upon the death of incumbent Tom Watson). Joel Williamson calls her "one of the most interesting women the South ever produced" (1984, 124). Her father, Charles Latimer, had accompanied his family to central Georgia as a child. Before moving to Georgia, they had lived in Maryland, where they had been successful planters on the lands just across the Potomac River at Mount Vernon. The Latimers were, in fact, related to the Washingtons and the Fairfaxes. In Georgia, Charles Latimer married into a locally prominent family of planters and in so doing, he "married" slaves. Once accustomed to the southern practice, he bought slaves and more land. As well, he opened a store and tavern near what would become Atlanta. Charles Latimer was a very successful businessman; by the time Rebecca was five, he could afford to organize a local school, taught, curiously, by the uncle of Atticus Haygood. Atticus Greene Haygood was one of the first and probably the greatest of those southern churchmen who protested the abandonment of black Christians by whites; he would become president of Emory and write *Our Brother in Black* (Williamson 1984).

When Rebecca Felton's education had progressed beyond what the local school could provide, her father bought a house in Decatur, a hundred years later the site of the second set of trials for the Scottsboro Nine (see chapter 12). There he established a household just so his daughter could continue her studies at "an academy of high grade" (quoted in Williamson 1984, 124). At fifteen, Felton enrolled in the Methodist Female College in Madison, known at the time as the best girls school in Georgia. She completed her studies in 1852 at seventeen, married the commencement speaker, Dr. William H. Felton, at eighteen, and gave birth to their first child at nineteen. The Feltons settled on a plantation near Cartersville, a village on the railroad between Atlanta and Chattanooga. Working closely with his widowed father, William Felton prospered as a planter. In 1860, between them they owned fifty slaves, twenty-eight of whom were "prime hands" (Williamson 1984, 125). Due to ill health, Dr. Felton had given up the practice of medicine; he began to contribute a good deal of his time to the ministry (Williamson 1984).

After the War, the Feltons returned to their plantation near Cartersville, where they began again, having lost everything. Within a few years, they had moved past poverty. But by age thirty-four (in 1873), Rebecca Felton had lost four of her five children. She turned away from domestic tragedy to enter public life. Recall that before 1919 women in the United States could not vote except in scattered and special instances. Despite this fact, women sometimes still entered politics, on occasion through their husbands, at other times as suffragettes and activists fighting for women's rights. Rebecca Felton's political career commenced with her husband, but she soon struck out on her own. Unlike most southern (white) women of her day, she was able to strike out in the public sphere due in part to the support of the men in her life, specifically her father, who had taken pains to see that she was formally educated, and her husband, who supported her ambitions (Williamson 1984).

In 1874, Dr. Felton, a reformer, ran as an independent for Congress and was elected. During the next six years while he served in Congress, Rebecca Felton was his constant companion, helping with his campaigns, and writing to the press in support of his issues and candidacy. She lived with him in a Washington hotel filled with other congressmen, including Alexander Stephens, the former vice president of the Confederacy. She became Stephens' protégé. She moved easily and freely in the Washington social scene; from Stephens, her husband, and others she soon learned the back-door politics of national power. Politically flexible, the Feltons were at various times out-of-party Democrats, Greenbackers, proto-Populists, para-Populists, and allies of Tom Watson. Rebecca Felton promoted her husband's political career aggressively; as he came to be better known, so too did she. Slowly she began to construct a public identity of her own. She published often in the Georgia press, eventually winning a loyal following through her own regular column in Hoke Smith's *Atlanta Journal.* First and foremost, Rebecca Felton fought for women's rights—white women's rights, that is. That commitment, as it did for other women, on occasion led her to take up other reform issues, among them prohibition, prison reform, the industrial education for young white women, especially in the mountainous region of Georgia, and access for women to the pulpit of the Southern Methodist Church. She was, Williamson suggests, a "new southerner," by which he means that she was economically aggressive, supporting industrialization in northeastern Georgia, even buying into mining interests herself (Williamson 1984). But like other southern feminists, Felton was no racial progressive.

In 1890, Rebecca Felton was highly visible in national circles, having been appointed one of the southern representatives on the board of "Lady Managers" of the Chicago World's Fair, to be held in 1893. Her intelligence, apparently endless energy, and strong organizational abilities soon brought her a significant influence in the selection and arrangement of exhibits. Here her reactionary racial views surfaced. As a southern lady, she said, she was offended by a display in honor of Harriet Beecher Stowe, including drawings of Uncle Tom. To counteract such Yankee nonsense, Felton arranged a southern exhibit showing "real colored folks," engaged in real activities such as weaving mats and baskets, spinning and carding cotton, and playing the banjo. Such scenes showed, Rebecca Latimer Felton declared, "the actual life of the slave—not the Uncle Tom sort." The editor of the *Atlanta Constitution,* Clark Howell, agreed to raise the funds necessary to finance the exhibit, and Felton herself recruited two elderly "sober and well behaved" blacks she knew, Aunty Jinny and Uncle Jack, to serve as the living counter-testimony to the fictitious Uncle Tom. The whole point, as Rebecca Felton explained to her husband, was "to show the *ignored* contented darkey—as distinguished from Mrs. Stowe's monstrosities—to illustrate the slave days of the republic" (quoted in Williamson 1984, 127).

After her return to Georgia, Felton became increasingly concerned with racial issues, the primary one the dangers black men posed, especially to white women. Increasingly the picture she saw in her mind was not "the ignored, contented darkey" but the "savage young buck" who lusted after frail white womanhood. In the summer of 1897, Rebecca Felton was given an excellent opportunity to speak to this new threat, and she took to the task with gusto. She had been invited by the State Agricultural Society of Georgia (the largest, wealthiest, and most influential organization of farmers in the state) to address its annual convention which was being held on Tybee Island, a resort near the mouth of the Savannah River. She spoke on strategies farmers might employ to improve farm life. One suggestion she made had to do with the provision of additional security for farmers' wives and daughters. A year later she recalled her speech:

> I warned those representative men of the terrible effects that were already seen in the corruption of the negro vote, their venality, the use of whiskey, the debasement of the ignorant and incitement of evil passion in the vicious. That week there were seven lynchings in Georgia from the fearful crime of rape. I told them that these crimes had grown and increased by reason of the corruption and debasement of the right of suffrage; that it would grow and increase with every election where white men equalized themselves at the polls with an inferior race and controlled their votes by bribery and whiskey. A crime nearly unknown before and during the war had become an almost daily occurrence and mob law had also become omnipotent. (quoted in Williamson 1984, 128)

Her listeners rapt, Felton had raised her voice to as loud a volume as any southern lady might dare, calling upon the good men of Georgia to do their duty. "[I]f it takes lynching to protect women's dearest possession from drunken, ravening human beasts," she cried, "then I say lynch a thousand a week if it becomes necessary" (quoted Williamson 1984, 128)

Of course, few southern white men needed a woman's encouragement to lay their hands on the muscular bodies of young black men, men who (they fantasized in unison) sat in wait each and every day to pounce upon unsuspecting white ladies. To Felton's listeners, her words seemed the gospel truth. Because her speech was reported in the northern press and because she answered northern criticism aggressively, the speech received national publicity. Showing how easily many white women became complicit with white men's fantasies, she concluded an exchange with the editor of the *Boston Transcript* with the charge that people with his liberal attitudes were in fact responsible for inciting the "new Negro" to rape, and "that the black fiend who lays unholy and lustful hands on a white woman in the state of Georgia shall surely die!" (quoted in Williamson 1984, 128).

An instant heroine throughout the South, Rebecca Felton also had her fans in the North. A Chicagoan told her that in regard to lynching many northerners had "long thought *fear* to be the controlling factor in cases of the kind so often occurring" in the South, "and hence largely justifiable." Perhaps a better solution, he speculated, was to "let" blacks lynch their own rapists. One northern woman who had once lived in Florida for ten years admitted to Felton that she "was never free from fear of the negro one moment." She simply could not rid her mind of the image of a muscular young black man; she told Felton, the contemplation of death was tolerable, but "the thought of outrage is worse than that of a thousand deaths." The last sentence in her letter echoed Felton's admonition to her white male listeners: "It is the duty of white men to those whom God has given them, their greatest blessing, to put a *stop* to this awful state of terror and danger in which ample evidence proves we live" (quoted in Williamson 1984, 129).

After her Tybee Island speech, Rebecca Felton, encouraged by her friends John Temple Graves (editor of the *Atlanta Constitution*) and Tom Watson, undertook a crusade to save white women "from the black beast rapist." On lecture platforms and in the press she spoke out passionately on the subject. After the turn of the century she wrote a speech in which she reflected on the race problem at some length. She suggested that there was a "racial antipathy—natural to the Caucasian in every age and country." In the South that antipathy was escalating to an unavoidable conflict. Thirty years of educating black people had only led to a shocking rise in the number of rapes and attempted rapes, now occurring with "appalling frequency." This required keeping all blacks away from the polls because, she speculated, the experience of being on equal footing with white men at the polls duped black men into imagining, evidently, that they could compete in other spheres of American life, with disastrous consequences for vulnerable white women. The North was exacerbating the problem by, of all things, appointing blacks to federal offices and even stationing black troops in the South! "The promoters of Negro equality," she declared, were the ones responsible for the inevitable "revolutionary uprising" and "will either exterminate the blacks or force the white citizens to leave the country" (quoted in Williamson 1984, 129). Felton was confident that whites would emerge victorious, whatever it took (Williamson 1984).

Rebecca Felton was instrumental in both expressing and shaping popular white thought in the South about black people—black men in particular—during the close of the nineteenth century. Concerned above all about the status of women, Felton's racism had a somewhat different origin and destination than did many southern white men's. For her the "fact" that black men were every day raping white women was primarily another index of the abuse white women endured, most of it administered by white men. Felton was quite conscious of (white) women's suffering, and she, like many other (white) southern women, as Drew Gilpin Faust (1996) has shown, came to ascribe responsibility for much of this suffering to the leading men of the South. As Joel Williamson puts it: "Her blows hit southern men at their very roots, in their sense of themselves. The protected charged their self-styled protectors with failure at the crucial juncture" (1984, 130). Quite clearly, Felton and no doubt other white southern women used the fantasy of the raping black beasts—for certain heterosexualized women this fantasy may well have been repressed desire (Munro 1999a)—to get back at their husbands and fathers who had so disappointed them. In doing so, they contributed to the "crisis" of manhood which left white men confused, threatened, and dangerous, especially in the 1890s when lynching was at its zenith.

For a generation after the Civil War, southern white women expressed no greater fear of black men as rapists than they did of white men. What whites did fear, Williamson argues, during the first few years after Emancipation, was black retaliation for slavery. They imagined widespread black revolt, in which former slaves would come looking for their former masters; they fantasized vast numbers of whites—men, women, and children—tortured and murdered, victims of accumulated black rage. White southern guilt conflated with white impotence and rage over losing the War. Two decades later came what Williamson emphasizes was "the new fear, the fear of the Negro as rapist" (1984, 184), a fear Rebecca Latimer Felton articulated and probably intensified. Blacks, not whites, had to fear torture and murder and dismemberment. If we understand slavery as, in part, sexual sadism on the part of white male masters, and Emancipation as a forced divorce from their former subjugated "lovers," is it such a leap to discover white men hunting down their former "spouses" and "raping"—that is, lynching—them?

Many southern white men evidently felt "home" next to the (sexually mutilated) bodies of naked black men. They did not want to soon forget the feeling, evidently, as they would sometimes interrupt the torture "to pose with their victims so that photographs could be taken, or sometimes, stand aside so that the victim could be photographed alone" (Williamson 1984, 188). And, as we saw earlier, participants often wanted a body part as souvenir or to give to friends. A prolynching governor, Cole Blease, was pleased to receive the gift of a finger of a lynched black man in the mail; he planted it in the gubernatorial garden. Even antilynching governors such as William J. Northen regularly received photographs and fragments of victims to remind him who was in fact in charge in the great state of Georgia. Always the white press reported in close detail lynching proceedings, and white readers eagerly consumed the reports. In the 1890s, "a little lynching went a long way" (Williamson 1984, 189). But, horrifyingly, there was not "a little" lynching; there was, as we have seen, a shockingly widespread incidence of it. Some whites opposed it.

The Sledd Case

In the autumn of 1902, in an address to the Society of Friends meeting in New Jersey, black feminist and teacher Anna Julia Cooper (see this chapter, section VII) referred to "a professor in a southern school who in a magazine article condemned the saturnalia of blood and savagery known as lynching arguing that the Negro while inferior, was yet a man and should be according the fundamental rights of man, [who] lost his position for his frankness and fairness" (Cooper, in Lemert and Bhan 1998, 209). Probably Cooper is thinking of Andrew H. Sledd, who in the July 1902 issue of the *Atlantic Monthly* published an article entitled "The Negro: Another View." At the time Sledd was a thirty-two-year-old Virginian living in Atlanta. He had taken a bachelor's degree at Randolph-Macon and a master's at Harvard; he was teaching Latin and Greek at Emory College (later to be Emory University). Sledd was in Williamson's (1984) scheme "a racial conservative," meaning that he believed that blacks were an "inferior race," but that they were human and did have "inalienable rights." Sledd attacked racial "radicals" (in Williamson's scheme) such as Rebecca Latimer Felton, charging that those who tolerated lynching were "blatant demagogues, political shysters, courting favor with the mob; news sheets, flattering the prejudices, and pandering to the passions of their constituency; ignorant youths and loud-voiced men who received their information second hand, and either do not or cannot see." Furthermore, he continued, lynching was not really about the black rapist. On the contrary, only "a very small proportion" of the 1,700 lynching victims in the previous decade were even accused of rape. "Our lynchings," he suggested (not after the facts as we have later learned them), "are the work of our lower and lowest classes" (quoted in Williamson 1984, 260).

Sledd then focused upon the savagery of the mob, suggesting that lynchers used the vulnerability of the black man "to gratify the brute in his own soul, which the thin veneer of his elemental civilization has not been able effectually to conceal." This would seem to be an early and primitive version of projection theory; like Ida B. Wells, his contemporary, he seems to see through the rape ruse. He went on to point out that some lynchings were well-advertised in advanced; on one occasion one of Georgia's leading railroads ran special trains on excursion to the scene: "And two train-loads of men and boys, crowing from cow-catcher to the tops of the coaches, were found to go to see the indescribable and sickening torture and writhing of a fellow human being. And souvenirs of such scenes are sought,—knee caps, and finger bones, and bloody ears. It is the purest savagery" (quoted in Williamson 1984, 260).

At this time the Boston-based *Atlantic Monthly* was not widely read in the South. Several weeks passed before news of Sledd's betrayal of the South reached Atlanta. Late in July, a Georgian living in Washington wrote Rebecca Felton suggesting that she reply. It is clear from her reply that Felton did not realize that Sledd taught at Emory. She suggested that here was another traitor to the South willing to sell out "his people" for a cushy job in the North. Felton then learned that the "enemy" was "within"; a Covington, Georgia, resident wrote at the request of the "good men of our City to let you Know who A. Sledd is" (quoted in Williamson 1984, 260). Soon a chorus of writers echoed Felton's condemnation. Rage flowed loud and uninterrupted; if a voice of moderation appeared, it was immediately inundated (Williamson 1984).

Overwhelmed by a tidal wave of rage, Sledd submitted his resignation to the president of Emory College, James E. Dickey. "I want to get away; I feel alien and wronged," the young man wrote to his father-in-law. "I am cramped and stunted by the atmosphere that prevails. I had thought to be able to bring about a better state of things; but the people and the College will have none of it. Emory College needs regeneration. I had hoped its time had come. But now I believe that I was wrong in such hope" (quoted in Williamson 1984, 260). Sledd's father-in-law was Warren A. Candler, a prominent bishop in the Southern Methodist Church, and, Williamson (1984) notes, the successor to Atticus G. Haygood. Like Haygood, Candler had served as president of Emory and had solved its financial problems, thanks in part to the benevolence of his brother, Asa, soon to achieve fame and fortune (especially the latter) as the founder of the Coca-Cola Company. The resourceful bishop and loyal father-in-law proposed a compromise. Emory would accept Sledd's resignation, but he would be awarded an adjustment in pay enabling him to continue his graduate studies at Yale. Candler's proposal was accepted by the Emory College board of trustees, which sent the young professor away in disgrace to complete his doctorate at Yale aided by a $1,000 "adjustment" in salary to finance the venture (Williamson 1984).

The violence done to academic freedom did not escape everyone. One member of the board tried to reopen the case, worrying that otherwise "every good man will come to believe" that "the College is contemptible." Bishop Candler himself soon thought better of the deal he himself had negotiated; once again approached Emory President Dickey but he was unwilling to up the ante. The bishop flew into a rage and accused his former friend Dickey of acting hastily and irresponsibly. "You let the enemies of the college lynch a capable professor and banish my child from Georgia," he charged, confusing middle-class inconvenience with racial murder (quoted in Williamson 1984, 261). The case was closed.

William J. Northen

Democratic governor of Georgia from 1890 to 1894, William J. Northen was born into the planting gentry of Georgia in 1835. A prominent layman in the Baptist Church, Northen was, as Williamson characterizes him, a racial "conservative, and peripatetic friend of black people." Toward the end of his life he recalled: "I had thirty years' experience with slave service on the part of negroes before the civil war. ... An old negro Mammy nursed me in my babyhood; I grew up with negro slaves in the fields; negroes in the home and negroes all about me" (quoted in Williamson 1984, 288). After graduating from Mercer College in 1853, he became a teacher in and then the principal of an academy, Mt. Zion. After his conversion, also in 1853, Northen served the Baptist Church throughout his life, eventually to hold the offices of president of the Georgia Baptist Convention, the Southern Baptist Convention, and vice president of the American Bible Society (Brundage 1993). He enlisted in the Confederate army as a private, serving in a company of which his father was captain. After the War, he returned to teaching until his health, damaged during the War, began to deteriorate. He retired to farming, but he was not content to accept standard farming practices; he experimented with the diversification of crops, for instance, as well as the production of milk with high butterfat content (Williamson 1984).

Northen entered politics and was elected to the Georgia House and Senate and, in 1886, to the presidency of the Georgia State Agricultural Society. In 1890 he ran for governor with support from both the Society and the Farmers' Alliance. In 1892, when the Populist party was formed and nominated a candidate for governor, Northen expressed concern over the absence of black educational opportunities, voiced strong disapproval of lynching and promised to support antilynching legislation. Many black voters actually voted for

Northen over the Populist candidate W. L. Peek, and he was reelected (Tolnay and Beck 1995). A man who tried to live his faith, he suffered when the depression deepened in 1893, knowing that the mass of Georgians, black and white, were barely surviving (Williamson 1984).

Although his political and economic beliefs were completely conventional, Northen displayed, Brundage (1993) tells us, "a vague understanding of the changes underway in Georgia and a commitment to modest measures to ameliorate the dislocations they caused" (195). By nature conservative, unquestioningly loyal to the Democratic Party, Northen took seriously paternalistic stewardship of hard-pressed rural Georgians. Like Governor O'Ferrall of Virginia, with whom he can be compared, Northen was unpersuaded by those who used "white supremacy" as justification for lynching. That he was troubled by the increasing incidence of mob violence in Georgia was, Brundage suggests, yet another expression of Northen's conservative instincts and paternalistic Christian beliefs.

Northen was far more active than previous governors in working to stop lynching. In 1893 the legislature responded to his request for antilynching legislation by passing a law requiring law officers to summon a posse to prevent lynchings. Sheriffs who failed to follow the law could be charged with a misdemeanor; participants in lynching mobs could be charged with committing a felony, or, if death resulted from their actions, murder. After the passage of the antilynching statute, Northen himself informed (by letter) all Georgia sheriffs of the new law. On one occasion, at his own expense, he had a black man who was threatened by a lynching mob rushed to Atlanta for his safety. He was increasingly opposed to lynchings and warned an obdurate white public that he would call out the militia to disperse mobs if necessary. Northen's actions seem to have had some effect; for the first time, some local authorities began to request troops to prevent lynchings (Brundage 1993).

Neither Northen's public stand nor the antilynching law stopped the practice, of course. The antilynching law was too broadly written and left the prosecution of lynchers and derelict sheriffs to local authorities, who were rarely willing to prosecute. Some legislators recognized these flaws and later in the decade offered various amendments to toughen the legislation, but these attempts failed. Even if these amendments had passed they would have accomplished little, given the blood lust of white men. As Sol C. Johnson, editor of the black weekly the *Savannah Tribune* complained, "negroes in Georgia were lynched before the proclamation, after the proclamation, and will continued to be lynched so long as the State winks at the lawlessness of its citizens" (quoted in Brundage 1993, 196).

All the while governor Northen pursued his career as an influential Baptist layman. For three years, he served as president of the Southern Baptist Convention and, for several years before 1890, he was elected president of the Home Mission Board. During these years, Northen resisted the intensification of racism well under way in Georgia and throughout the South. Elected governor the same year that Tillman took office in South Carolina, Northen, unlike Tillman (who soon accepted lynching as an appropriate response to "the awful crime"), consistently opposed it. During his tenure as governor he stood against lynching, even if he resisted what he took to be British interference in a local matter, as we will see in the next chapter. He was astonished by African Americans' desertion of the Democratic party for the Populist party, complaining in 1892 that "quite a number of colored people of Georgia saw fit to take positions and do active work against me and for the success of a party not at all committed to the interests of the colored people" (quoted passages in Williamson 1984, 288–289).

As the decade came to a close, Northen became thoroughly alarmed at the deteriorating racial situation. In the early nineties, he had been astonished and distressed by the barbarism of white lynch mobs. Toward the end of the decade, he became convinced that white barbarism was being matched by black barbarism. In Boston, in the spring of 1899, he made a nationally reported speech on race relations in which he soundly berated northerners, southerners, and African Americans for their parts in the breakdown of race relations in America. By nature an optimist—Williamson terms him a "progressive person"—Northen became horrified and pessimistic as a result of the increasing frequency of alleged rapes and subsequent lynchings. "Since I returned from Boston," he reported privately to a friend, "there have been more than five assaults, in this State, and practically, in the neighborhood, so to speak, of the fearful and horrible burning that occurred some little time ago. These things amaze me and are not to be accounted for upon any theory with which I have been familiar heretofore. It behooves us all to seriously consider a proper solution of the difficulties that surround us" (quoted passages in Williamson 1984, 289).

In correspondence with Walter Francis Willcox, the Cornell statistician and census expert who predicted black self-destruction and extinction, Northen was especially critical of the eastern press for what he took to be its inflaming of the racial situation in the South. If, indeed, blacks did die out in America, he declared, northern journalists would be to blame. Willcox believed that eventually most blacks would be squeezed out of existence by industrial competition with whites and that those who had managed to survive would be absorbed by the much more numerous lower classes of whites. Torn by events and influenced by "experts," Northen the Christian activist, "high conservative," on occasion sounded like a racial "radical," although he was never one Williamson (1984) suggests. Conservatives had faith, albeit a limited faith, that intelligent white leadership could solve the racial problem. But Northen had grown skeptical of the capacity of both whites and blacks to understand and resolve racial tensions. A race war might in fact occur, not because it was genetically inevitable that blacks would regress to primitivism, but, Northen came to believe, because northern whites would mislead gullible blacks to rash action which would provoke southern whites to seek a final solution (Williamson 1984).

In Georgia the nightmare almost happened, it seemed to Northen, in Atlanta in 1906, and the riot there, as he had worried, was a culmination of "disaster, slaughter and blood." Northen went to work immediately after the riot, determined that it would not happen again. Sponsored at first by the "Business Men's Gospel Union," he spoke throughout rural Georgia, preaching against crime and lawlessness. As he had said in Boston he said throughout

Georgia: both black crime and white mobism must come to an end. Following every speech he asked for a show of hands from those who agreed with him, as well as from those who did not. After speaking in forty-nine counties, he reported with characteristic optimism, "my endeavors were heartily and unanimously endorsed, except by ten adverse votes out of all the multitudes of people I had the honor to address." The ten votes included the mayor of a town, who said he endorsed Tillman's prolynching position—"using Tillman's language." In each county he visited, Northen organized a committee of businessmen to fight against the twin evils of black criminality and lynching. "At every place I have spoken, I pronounced criminal assaults the most villainous iniquity known to the catalogue of crime and I urged the people to remove, as far as may be within their power, the conditions that make such outrages possible." His committees promised to provide local sheriffs with men to form posses to pursue alleged rapists "and to see that the lawless element of the community is entirely excluded from such pursuit." After visiting eighty-five counties, Northen felt sure that "public opinion on law and order is rapidly changing for the better" (quoted passages in Williamson 1984, 289–290).

His civic commitment was no doubt informed by his religious faith, which in turn moved Northen to urge the church to save black souls. In 1909, speaking to the Georgia Baptist Convention, he accused the church of neglecting its mission to African Americans, pointing out that of 3,600 new members who had joined the Baptist Church not a single convert was black. When a Baptist leader told him that blacks did not need the care of the church, Northen responded that ministering to black souls was "a duty upon him by God," and that "he would rather see a million negroes in the South soundly converted than to see the conversion of two million Chinese, Japanese, or savages from some remote island" (quoted in Williamson 1984, 290).

In 1911, Northen turned seventy-six. After twenty years of campaigning for what he took to be racial fairness, he was tired. In his fatigue his optimism waned, and he worried that perhaps, after all, a racial apocalypse was at hand. He was depressed by the apparent physical and moral degeneration of black people, citing for evidence the fantasy of a Macon physician that "they have added to their freedom an almost universal infection from venereal diseases and tuberculosis." Towns, he imagined, were being overrun with professional black prostitutes. "The conditions of the race are pitiable to us of the old South, who can appreciate what the negro had been. His rapid degeneration, physically, mentally, and morally, and his reversion to the barbaric tendencies with all of the added vices of civilization, is appalling" (quoted in Williamson 1984, 290).

Northen was perhaps even more appalled by the intolerance of whites. When he appeared in Boston's Tremont Temple in 1899 to defend the South on the race issue, he was sharply criticized back in Georgia because he had agreed to share the platform with a black spokesman. Such nonsense discouraged him, but he continued to act as if he believed white people could be brought to their senses. After the Atlanta riot, Northen had begun his county-by-county speaking tour supported by the Business Men's Gospel Union. Despite the fact that he had served as president of that organization for several years, he discovered, as he later admitted, a continuing and obstinate opposition to his antilynching work even among his own Christian business colleagues. "I found before I had advanced very far that some of the members of my Committee were not in sympathy with my work, but were in sympathy with the attack made on me by the *Atlanta Journal*," he complained. Since June 1907, he recorded, "I have been practically upon my own resources" (quoted in Williamson 1984, 291).

By 1911, Northen found white racial hatred so intense and widespread that he could not imagine fighting it any longer. "During my recent canvass over the state, in the interest of law and order I was amazed to find scores and hundreds of men who believed the negro to be a brute, without responsibility to God, and his slaughter nothing more than the killing of a dog," he wrote in defeat. Within a few weeks, he declined to do an article for a Baptist home mission journal, telling the editor that he thought it best "to be silent from this time on." He was, he said, very tired. "My nature is sensitive and I have groaned under the burdens I have carried. I now feel I have done my duty and I shall decline to make any moré speeches. ... I deeply deplore the conditions, but I feel that my skirts are clear" (quoted in Williamson 1984, 291).

It was, Williamson tells us, in the nature of racial conservatives like Northen to act as if what ought to be were already true. It demonstrated their strength and their faith to say that things were getting better, and that all would resolve itself in the end. As late as 1907, Northen was declaring in public that honorable Georgia agreed with him. When he gave up in 1911, it was unmistakably clear that Georgia did not agree with him and had not agreed with him on racial issues for at least a dozen years. It was characteristic of the conservative style of leadership that one should begin by chanting: "We're winning, we're winning, we're winning," and end, abruptly, by acknowledging: "We lost" (Williamson 1984, 291). Like their Confederate predecessors, conservative southerners were lost in a dream.

In admitting defeat, some disillusioned conservatives turned on their own kind, racially at least, locating their defeat in the ignorant white masses, the "grits," presumably misled by opportunistic politicians and unscrupulous (often northern) journalists. Many racial conservatives were among the leading intellectuals in the South; they tended to ascribe their defeat to widespread ignorance. The absence of mass education allowed intolerance and close-mindedness, they concluded, smothering the sort of free inquiry and discussion that George Washington Cable and John Spencer Bassett had advocated. This has been, Williamson (1984) suggests, a persisting myth, a "grit thesis" that popular democracy in the South precluded freedom of thought and speech, and that, in race relations, the lower classes were racial extremists while the upper classes were not. If the masses would simply follow the lead of the southern elite, racial peace would follow (Williamson 1984).

In 1932, the influential South Carolina editor and scholar William Watts Ball published *The State That Forgot: South Carolina's Surrender to Democracy*, a condemnation of populist politics. The voice of the people, Ball argued, guarantees mediocrity and corruption. In 1940, North Carolina-born historian Clement Eaton also located the South's "wrong turn" in the antebellum period, but not on slavery. He pointed to Jacksonian democracy. In his *Freedom of Thought in the Old South* he argued that slavery and racism might have been manageable had a vulgar populism not overtaken the South. Before the celebration of the "common man" associated with the Jacksonian era, political leaders had not deigned to "scramble for votes by low appeals to the prejudices of the electorate." But the admission of "large numbers of illiterate or semi-literate men in southern elections tended to intensify intolerance and sectional animosity," and politics deteriorated to "slogans, political workers, and demagogic appeals" (quoted in Williamson 1984, 294). Without freedom of thought and leadership by the elite, a peaceful solution to slavery was not possible (Williamson 1984).

Not only in the South but countrywide, many have subscribed to "the grit thesis" of the origins of segregation, disfranchisement, lynching, and extreme racism. Not until the civil rights movement of the 1960s when, as Williamson (1984) puts it, "the most elegant drawls" in the South were pleading for the closing of schools and defiance of Supreme Court decisions, was the grit thesis seriously undermined. But, writing in the early 1980s at the University of North Carolina, Williamson found that the thesis had returned. This rebirth he regards as "dangerous" (1984, 294), as it remains as fanciful, as false, as it always was. Upper-class southern whites remain, he argues, as unsympathetic to African Americans as lower-class whites have tended to be. Of course, there is and always was a difference between the racism of upper-class southern whites and that of the lower classes, but that difference is one of style, not of one of basic assumptions, attitudes, and practices. Lower-class racism (and hostility toward other "others"—communists, labor organizers, Jews, and Catholics) has been more likely to be expressed in physical violence that compels public attention. Such violence is highly newsworthy. Upper-class racial prejudice, in contrast, is often expressed in more subtle but just as substantive forms of economic, social, psychological, educational, and judicial violence. As Williamson observes, ownership of the land, control of money and credit, of schools and courts, and general domination of the marketplace can be just as violent, if not more widely damaging, than guns, whips, and bombs.

Many upper-class southerners imagined (and some still do) that they understand blacks best, that they know how to talk "them," know how to manage "them," fantasies based on their experience of African Americans as employees, in factories, shops, and as domestics in white homes. Upper-class southern whites can be quite cordial with individual blacks, but, Williamson suggests, they are "often unconscious" of their participation in structural—economic, political—racism. Like white men who relocated their own desire for black men onto imaginary white women, converting it "there" into fear, upper-class whites have often imagined that "others"—lower-class whites, bestial blacks—are responsible for racial "unpleasantness." The truth of the matter is, Williamson asserts, upper- and lower-class whites have worked together to oppress African Americans: "the intermittent, sporadic, open violence of one complementing the steady, pervasive, quiet violence of the other" (Williamson 1984, 295).

As several studies of lynching have demonstrated, upper-class southern whites can be quite physically violent if they are moved to be. Not all of the whipping of and sexual exploitation of slaves on the plantation was done by overseers, imagined in the popular mind as lower-class thugs. Masters and mistresses participated fully in the violence that was done against enslaved men and women. Emancipation hardly changed that fact. As we have seen, the Ku Klux Klan of the Reconstruction era was at first organized and headed by upper-class whites. Turn-of-the-century mobs of lynchers and rioters often included "respectable" even prominent townspeople, sometimes as leaders. When the political subjection of African Americans appeared to be achieved after disenfranchisement, upper-class southerners fantasized themselves as "the even-minded children of light and peace" (Williamson 1984, 295). The myth of a specially vicious attitude toward blacks prevalent among lower-class whites is an upper-class fantasy, a psychological mechanism by which the elite divorced itself from the structural violence it perpetuated, enabling them to imagine a "natural order" with themselves, of course, at the top (Williamson 1984).

Based on their "empirical" data, Stewart Tolnay and E. M. Beck (1995) agree with Williamson that lynching was hardly limited to the lower stratum of southern whites. Nor was it limited to the white elite. Rather, they believe that the lynching era was the combined consequence of proletariat and bourgeois social, political, and economic interests. Their data do not suggest, however, that the various class interests in lynching and racial violence generally were necessarily aligned. During a given period, or in a particular setting, or on a particular occasion, lynchings can usefully be linked to the motives of the white elite. But in a different period or on another occasion, the interests and motives of poor whites might be salient in understanding a specific lynching event (Tolnay and Beck 1995).

While statistics sometimes clarify, at other times they certainly mystify, as in another "finding" of the "empirical" research on lynching reported by Tolnay and Beck, namely that southern politics seem to have no discernible relationship to lynching. They seem to anticipate the reader's skepticism: "Surprisingly, however, the statistical evidence ... offers little support for drawing broader linkages between complex, confusing, and often corrupt southern politics and black lynchings" (Tolnay and Beck 1995, 198). No correlations perhaps, but certainly there were "broader linkages," as Williamson's research makes clear.

Antilynching Sentiment Begins to Build

There were other southern whites besides Northen who were opposed to lynching during its heyday, and these individuals often found themselves the objects of white rage. In 1904, for instance, Georgia Governor James M. Terrell (1903–1907) punished several state militia officers who had failed to prevent the lynching of two black men in Statesboro. At the request of local authorities, the governor had sent militia companies from Savannah to protect Paul Reed and Will Cato. The presence of the militia did allow the trial of the two men to proceed, but at its conclusion a mob stormed the courthouse, overpowered the troops, and seized the prisoners. They were taken just out of town where they were lynched (Brundage 1993).

The mob's obvious contempt for state authority, and the apparent inability of Captain Robert M. Hitch, the militia commander, to prevent the prisoners' seizure, sparked indignation among those serving in the militia and among those white Georgians (such as former Governor Northen) already uneasy over the frequency of lynching events in the state. Governor Terrell appointed a commission to investigate the lynching. In particular, the commission was to determine if Hitch and his subordinate officers should be court-martialed. Prolynching whites were enraged and rallied in support of Captain Hitch. Openly boasting about their participation in the lynching, mob members dared the state to prosecute them. They even raised money to buy Hitch an engraved sword as a token of their esteem (Brundage 1993).

Not only uneducated country boys defended the lynching, as Williamson knew. John Temple Graves and the editors of county weeklies throughout the state rushed to defend Statesboro's "reputation." They lashed out at the governor for misusing state funds to investigate honorable white soldiers; state money ought to be used to capture black rapists, they declared. Terrell should be replaced, editorials demanded, by none other than Hitch himself, that stalwart defender of "popular justice." While Hitch declined to run, there were voters who scratched out Terrell's name on the ballot and substituted Hitch's. Support for Hitch and his officers remained high even after the governor dismissed them from the militia. They retaliated by savaging Terrell in a widely printed letter (Brundage 1993).

In April 1899, following the gruesome lynchings of Sam Holt (see chapter 1) and several others, a group of prominent black residents of Atlanta, including W. E. B. Du Bois, then a professor at Atlanta University (lynching prompted Du Bois to abandon any position of scholarly detachment, observing that "one could not be a calm, cool, and detached scientist while Negroes were lynched, murdered, and starved" [quoted in Howard 1995, 14]), asked Governor Candler to use his influence and authority to stop lynching. His response reveals whites' inability, at least at this time, to imagine an alternative. Despite the deferential tone of the request and its emphasis upon the seemingly noncontroversial issue of preserving law and order, Candler responded by telling Du Bois and the others that the Georgia legislature could do little more than had already been done to prevent mob violence. What was necessary now was for "good negroes" to build up "a sentiment in their race against the diabolical crimes which are always at the back of these lynchings" (quoted in Brundage 1993, 204). The only common cause state authorities and African Americans could share, Candler was saying, was a campaign against black immorality and degeneracy. Such a campaign was of course impossible for Du Bois to share, requiring as it did acceptance of white fantasy as social reality (Brundage 1993).

Slowly, a coalition of groups formed. While not working together they were working at the same time, and finally there appeared to be some progress in the struggle against lynching. White businessmen dedicated to economic progress and Christian social reformers began to focus on lynching; black activists continued to do so. Accompanying this development was what Brundage terms an "intellectual awakening in the South" (1993, 215), most evident on college campuses in North Carolina, Virginia, and Tennessee, but also under way in certain institutions in the Deep South. At the University of Georgia, for instance, Chancellors Walter B. Hill and then David C. Barrow replaced the traditional classical curriculum with a more practical and flexible curriculum; as well they oversaw the rapid expansion of the school's professional and graduate faculties. With administrative support, faculty members began to apply their research to the pressing problems of the day, including the controversial race problem. During Barrow's administration in particular, several faculty members, including R. J. H. DeLoach, Robert Preston Brooks, C. J. Heatwole, as well as Barrow himself, became involved in public initiatives committed to racial reform (Brundage 1993).

Private institutions, at least in Georgia, tended to be more status quo. In Atlanta, Emory College (after 1915, Emory University) remained a liberal but conventional Methodist institution. Under the administrations of Dr. James E. Dickey and Bishop Warren A. Candler, Emory avoided those progressive currents (recall the Sledd case) felt at other Methodist institutions such as Vanderbilt in Tennessee and Trinity (now Duke) in North Carolina. But even conservative campuses in Georgia were not totally immune to new intellectual movements. Faculty everywhere knew of the efforts of regional organizations such as the Southern Sociological Congress (S.S.C.) and the University Commission on Southern Race Questions. These groups demonstrated a new commitment to social welfare in the South, a commitment which included racial reform (Brundage 1993).

Established in Tennessee in 1912, the two organizations attracted considerable attention throughout the literate South, provoking some observers, including Ray Stannard Baker, to announce a "new departure in southern attitudes toward the Negro" (quoted in Brundage 1993, 216). The founding of the organizations reflected changing conditions in Tennessee, evident in the election of the reformer Benjamin W. Hooper as governor. Vanderbilt University became an increasingly independent-minded and secular university. Efforts at urban improvement were perceptible in Nashville. In 1912, hundreds of academics, ministers, and reformers gathered in Nashville for the first meeting of the Southern Sociological Congress. A child of the S.S.C., the University Commission (U.C.) was organized to extend the influence of the Congress to college campuses. It met annually and issued statements concerning lynching as well as other social problems in the South. The U.C. also developed college courses addressed to racial issues (Brundage 1993).

Both the S.S.C. and the University Commission were clear that lynchings were no form of "popular justice" in response to black crimes. In 1916, the University Commission issued a widely read letter that used data supplied by the Tuskegee Institute to show that black "crime"—sometimes trivial, often imaginary, offenses, as we have seen—functions only as pretexts for extralegal violence. Calling upon college students to join the crusade against lynching, the letter stressed that civilization rested upon law and order and that reason and deliberation must overrule impulse and passion, all ideas that Ida B. Wells had used in her earlier campaigns (and which we will discuss in later in this chapter and in chapter 8). Both the S.S.C. and the University Commission accepted that social conditions, specifically illiteracy, poverty, and rural traditionalism, were the causes of mob violence. Only economic development and expanded public education could end lynching and support the formation of a "new" South. Both organizations understood that such a profound social transformation would take time; both accepted that mob violence would persist for a while.

They did, however, ask southern whites to break their silence and publicly repudiate racial injustice (Brundage 1993).

By 1920 the S.S.C. and the University Commission lost momentum and for all practical purposes became moribund. Despite their efforts, neither organization made much headway against the chronic paternalism and racism, not to mention instinctive reactionary conservatism of most southerners. Despite these failures, the sociologist Howard W. Odum pointed to the S.S.C. as one of the most important southern organizations of the period. Brundage judges that "the two organizations played a modest but noteworthy role in the campaign to end lynching by creating a forum for the exchange of ideas" (1993, 218). The organizations provided a kind of apprenticeship for whites who would later work against lynching. In Georgia, these included Thomas J. Woofter, who participated in the University Commission while a student at the University of Georgia; Lily H. Hammond, a prominent Methodist activist in the state; and William W. Alexander, also a Methodist reformer who would later head the Commission on Interracial Cooperation established in Atlanta in 1919 (Brundage 1993; Williamson 1984).

The influence of the S.S.C. was still discernible in the late 1920s and 1930s when a generation of southern academics, primarily sociologists, began to study lynching and racial injustice. Among these was Howard Odum. As a young student at Emory College in 1901 and 1902, Howard Odum studied Latin with Andrew Sledd shortly before Sledd's forced departure for having criticized lynching in the *Atlantic Monthly.* From Emory, Odum moved to Columbia where he took his doctorate; afterward he returned to the South as a professor of sociology at the University of North Carolina. Along with Rupert Vance, he established the Institute for Research in the Social Sciences, and together they brought international visibility to the university as a center for regional studies, specifically southern studies. The institute supported several sociological studies of black life and race relations in the South. Guy B. Johnson, Guion Griffin Johnson, John A. Wooster, and Arthur Raper were among those who made important contributions in these areas (Williamson 1984). In 1933 Raper would publish a study of lynching that would become a classic in the field, entitled *The Tragedy of Lynching.*

Critical southern studies were conducted by Woofter, Rupert Vance, and Arthur Raper. Such research "would have been inconceivable without the precedent established by the S.S.C. and University Commission." According to Josiah Morse, a professor at the University of South Carolina and one of the commission's members, the accomplishment of these southern progressives was "not so much what the commission has actually done, as what it hoped to do, and the spirit in which it has gone about its work" (quoted in Brundage 1993, 218).

Not all antilynching developments were in the secular sphere. The idea that Christianity was not only about legitimating the social status quo—the Bible was often used to justify white supremacy, as Walter White for one complained—but in fact should be an inspiration for social amelioration began to circulate in the South around the turn of the century. One consequence of this incipient social gospel movement was that, beginning around 1900, a growing number of Methodists and Baptists began to apply this social interpretation of the Christian mission toward African Americans. Lily Hardy Hammond was a member of the South Carolina "aristocracy" and became a prominent Methodist reformer. Married to the president of Paine College, a black Methodist college in Augusta, Hammond personified those religiously inspired reformers who interpreted Christianity as calling for social activism. Like other Methodist women, she read a strong social message in John Wesley's teachings. Due to the gender conservatism of the time and region, she was constrained in the enactment of that social message. First limited to women's prayer groups and aid societies, Hammond became the first superintendent of the Methodist Bureau of Social Service in 1899. In part due to her experiences at Paine College, while serving as superintendent she increasingly directed her attention to racial issues (Brundage 1993).

In 1914 Hammond's *In Black and White* expressed her conviction that improved race relations were central to the social gospel. She attacked race prejudice, catalogued those injustices suffered by African Americans, and, referring to her experiences as social worker, explained the primary role that racial discrimination played in perpetuating black poverty. But it was lynching that moved Hammond the most. She believed that many southerners opposed lynching but were too timid or afraid to express that opposition. Unlike some southern progressives, Hammond declined to accept white southern passivity; she castigated her fellow southerners for failing to act together to suppress mob violence. Moreover, Hammond understood that changing attitudes alone was not enough to address racial inequality and violence. She participated in nearly all of the major race reform organizations founded by whites after 1910, including both the S.S.C. and the University Commission. Hammond was also influential in the Southern Publicity Committee, a news service organized to publicize black achievements and the progress of race reform organizations (Brundage 1993).

Not only religiously inspired activists and politicians worked against lynching. Even the white business community slowly became involved, if in incidental ways and for reasons of profit. Big-city as well as those small-town businessmen who populated the Chambers of Commerce, the Kiwanis, the Rotary Clubs, and various other voluntary business groups, formed the core of "the uptown opposition to mob violence" (Brundage 1993, 222). In Georgia, urban dailies such as the *Atlanta Constitution* and *Macon Telegraph* began to make appeals for civic spirit and law and order. Newspaper opposition to lynching intensified after the national and international attention given to the trial and lynching of Leo Frank in 1915. But, as Brundage emphasizes, "the suppression of mob violence, of course, was never a principal, or even major, concern of Georgia's business community" (1993, 222). Nor in Tennessee, apparently, as we glean from this headline in the August 5, 1913, *Memphis Commercial-Appeal:* "LYNCHING BAD FOR BUSINESS" (quoted in Ginzburg 1962/1988, 82). While "business," not black life, was the more important reason, southern newspaper editors thought of several other practical reasons why Georgians should stop lynching black men (among them promoting the image of the city as "safe" and "civilized" and thus suitable for new and expanding businesses), always careful not to provoke a white backlash that could hurt their own business (Brundage 1993).

African Americans, we may surmise, had different motives and concerns. Against all odds, black activists in Georgia and throughout the nation built a fragile network of self-help, religious, and civic institutions during the first two decades of the twentieth century. In addition to the difficulties inherent in such interinstitutional collaboration, African Americans faced shrill, sometimes dangerous, opposition from local whites, nothing less than what W. E. B. Du Bois referred to as the "narrow repression" and "provincialism" of the South itself (quoted in Brundage 1993, 225). All this was no doubt at work in the failure of the Equal Rights Convention of 1906 and during the troubled early years of the N.A.A.C.P. in Georgia (Brundage 1993).

In February 1906 in Macon, William J. White, the editor of the black denominational weekly the *Georgia Baptist,* organized the first Equal Rights Convention. Over four hundred African Americans attended. The meeting marked an increasing militancy among many of Georgia's black leaders and their growing frustration with Booker T. Washington's philosophy of accommodation. White was a strong critic of Washington; directing the convention, he persuaded the collected ministers, teachers, professionals, and farmers to endorse a program of action formulated by W. E. B. Du Bois, John Hope, J. Max Barber, Bishop Henry McNeal Turner, and other black intellectuals and activists. The delegates approved an "Address to the American People" that urged African Americans to "agitate, complain, protest and keep protesting against the invasion of our manhood rights" and to mobilize into "one great fist which shall never cease to pound at the gates of opportunity until they fly open" (quoted in Brundage 1993, 226). A year later, a second meeting took place; plans were made to organize black residents of every county in the state. But conference leaders were ahead of their time; their stirring rhetoric at the convention failed to reach beyond the small number of subscribers to black newspapers. Isolated, the few local branches that were established quickly disbanded. By 1908 the organizers of the 1906 convention decided against holding further statewide meetings (Brundage 1993).

Efforts to start a N.A.A.C.P. chapter in Georgia during the years just before World War I also failed. Hardly unique to Georgia, the failure reflected the problems many black activist organizations faced in the Deep South. After decades of unsuccessful attempts to create a national organization committed to securing the civil rights of black citizens through political lobbying and legal action, a group of intellectuals and reformers, both black and white, founded the N.A.A.C.P. in 1909, a momentous event we will describe in some detail in chapter 9. In 1913, W. R. Scott, founder and owner of the *Atlanta Daily World*, had contacted the national N.A.A.C.P. headquarters about starting a branch in Atlanta, but as late as 1916 nothing had been established. Scott's efforts apparently floundered upon the divisions between supporters and opponents of Booker T. Washington's accommodationist program. Washington's prestige meant that his opposition to the N.A.A.C.P. and its aims, which he dismissed as "nonsense," was influential among many black leaders in the city. Not until his death during World War I did the tensions between pro-

and anti-Washington camps reduce enough to enable the N.A.A.C.P. to take root and expand throughout the state and other states in the South (Brundage 1993).

The failures of the Equal Rights Convention and of early efforts to organize a Georgia chapter of the N.A.A.C.P. did not mean other efforts failed as well. In the late nineteenth and early twentieth centuries a variety of civic, religious, and social organizations were formed. Although none of these groups was principally concerned with lynching—neither had been the Equal Rights Convention nor the N.A.A.C.P.—none found they could not remain silent either. Black civic organizations in Atlanta, Savannah, and Macon regularly condemned lynching while focusing primarily upon basic problems of sanitation, health, and education (Brundage 1993).

In Atlanta, for instance, Lugenia Burns Hope, former resident of Hull House (Munro 1999b; see chapter 6, section III), the wife of the president of Atlanta Baptist (now Morehouse) College, founded the Neighborhood Union. Probably the most notable black reform organization in the state, the Union supported educational, social, and political activities. It served as the training ground for a generation of activist black women. Its activities ranged from improving sanitation to lobbying for recreational facilities for black children. While focused upon the myriad of problems faced by the black residents of Atlanta, the Union was especially concerned about racial violence, especially given the deep scars left by the Atlanta race riot of 1906. Hope and other women active in the organization would go on to play important roles in the interracial opposition to lynching that formed after World War I. Many Union members also belonged to the National Association of Colored Women's Clubs, which in 1897 had fifty thousand members (Carby 1987). The N.A.C.W.C. linked and focused black women's clubs and reform groups throughout the country; its meetings and publications provided forums where racial injustice, including lynching, could be discussed (Brundage 1993).

While the hard work of these various black organizations helped educate and mobilize black public opinion, the incidence of mob violence in the South did not decline. Especially before World War I, whites paid little attention to black activists or to their demands to end the mutilation of black bodies, let alone to their insistence that the civil rights of African Americans be respected. Years later, W. E. B. Du Bois would remember: "Well, it was difficult to do anything as a Negro organization. What influence could we have on white public opinion?" (quoted in Brundage 1993, 227). Despite the political cul-de-sac that massive white racism maintained, these years of institution-building from 1909 through 1920 produced lasting accomplishments. While few in number and limited in their outreach, these organizations taught a small number of activists those grass-roots organizational skills that would help accelerate and intensify protest during the 1920s and 1930s. Without the experience made possible by these various early organizations, black antilynching efforts following World War I almost certainly would have remained tragically undermined by inexperienced leadership and shallow institutional foundations (Brundage 1993).

World War I appears to have been a turning point in the history of racial violence in much of the South, especially in Georgia. The war provoked broad social changes in what had been a static society, changes that challenged the racial status quo. Among these was the Great Migration. In great numbers African Americans fled the South. While the scale of immigration is difficult to determine accurately, in Georgia as many as 250,000 blacks may have left the state between 1917 and 1924. Whereas 90 percent of all African Americans resided in southern states in 1900, that percentage had dropped to 79 by 1930. The percentage of African Americans living in urban areas grew from 17 in 1900 to 33 by 1930, and much of the black urbanization was due to migration. What had been an overwhelmingly southern and rural population became more northern and urban (Tolnay and Beck 1995).

While economic motives were paramount, lynching was a contributing factor. For generations, blacks had fled white violence, ordinarily to nearby areas. After World War I, black southerners fled thousands of miles. Not only was the distance of this flight unprecedented, so was its scale and permanence (Brundage 1993). Ida B. Wells remembers the Christmas of 1917.

> The influx of so many of our people from the South about this time was attracting a great deal of attention. They arrived in Chicago in every conceivable state of unpreparedness, and so great was the confusion at the station, and so many of them were taken advantage of by unscrupulous taxi drivers and lodging-house keepers, that the matter was taken up by our league. We appealed to the ministers' meeting for help, and the result was the appointment of a man of our own race to meet the trains at the Illinois Central Station to see that our people were given proper information and protection. (Wells 1970, 371–372)

Strangely, the Travelers Aid objected to Wells's organization, the Negro Fellowship League, having a representative at the station; the organization even insisted that the police escort the representative out of the station. Wells discovered later that one T. Arnold Hill, head of the recently established Urban League, was behind the Travelers Aid action. "It seemed that the Urban League was brought to Chicago to supplant the activities of the Negro Fellowship League," Wells (1970, 372) concluded.

White Georgians were surprised even shocked by the exodus, but they quickly grasped its implications for the region's labor relations. As train after train left the state filled with African Americans searching for a better life, white Georgians became increasingly worried that an acute labor shortage would destroy the southern economy. During the war years, they aggressively fought black flight, resorting to legal harassment, intimidation, and outright violence, anything in order to slow the self-assertive exodus of those they often before had asked or demanded to leave. This time these techniques of intimidation failed to work. Bitterly, many whites concluded that the war and migration had altered life permanently. White economic fears were, it turns out, by and large exaggerated. While the migration did result in a decline in the overabundance of cheap, unskilled labor, no acute shortage developed across the South. Despite surface changes, it is not at all clear that World War I and the Great Migration resulted in any fundamental changes in the reactionary labor practices of the South (Brundage 1993).

VI. The Emergence of Ida B. Wells

Before leaving the South I had often wondered at the silence of the North. I concluded it was because they did not know the facts and had accepted the southern white man's reason for lynching and burning human beings.

—Ida B. Wells, *Crusade for Justice: The Autobiography f Ida B. Wells* (1970)

The old, subjective, stagnant, indolent and wretched life for woman has gone.

—Anna Julia Cooper, "A Voice from the South" (1892/1998)

Though she argued for the moral capacity of black women, Wells was no pacifist.

—Sandra Gunning, *Race, Rape, and Lynching: The Red Record of American Literature, 1890–1912* (1996)

A number of times in this text I have referred to Ida B. Wells. No description of antilynching activity in the United States is complete without serious attention to Wells. She was a larger-than-life figure in the civil rights movement from the 1890s until her death in 1931. She was the chief architect of the antilynching movement in the nineteenth century, a cause to which she came after a brief but memorable career of militant journalism in the black community. Before working as a journalist, Wells had been a schoolteacher. In my view, Wells remained a teacher, if imagining her classroom more expansively to include the American and British publics. Through her brilliant manipulation of contemporary white assumptions regarding gender, race and civilization, Wells taught European Americans that lynching was barbaric. No small accomplishment for a Memphis schoolteacher who had to battle not only white racism, but misogyny and even occasional envy from her fellow black reformers. John Hope Franklin (1970) summarizes her accomplishment this way:

> Her zeal and energy were matched by her uncompromising and unequivocal stand on every cause that she espoused. She did not hesitate to criticize southern whites even before she left the South, nor northern liberals, or members of her own race when she was convinced that their positions were not in the best interests of all mankind. She did not hesitate to go to the scene of racial disturbances, including riots and lynchings, in order to get an accurate picture of what actually occurred. She did not hesitate to summon to the cause of human dignity anybody and everybody she believed could serve the cause. (x)

And many heard her call, as Wells's solitary and courageous campaign against lynching was joined by such black organizations as the Woman's Loyal Union (1892), the Colored Woman's League of Washington, D.C. (1892), the National Federation of Afro-American Women (1895), and the National Association of Colored Women (1896) (Perkins 1998).

Born a slave in Holly Springs, Mississippi (pop. 3,500), in 1862, Wells was the eldest daughter in a family of eight children. Her father was a skilled carpenter, a man of "considerable ability and much civic concern" (Duster 1970, xv). He served as a member of the first board of trustees of Rust College. At first named Shaw University, Rust was founded in 1866 by Rev. A. C. McDonald, a minister from the North who served as its first president. Rust College offered curricula for students at all levels and grades, including the basic elementary subjects. Both of Wells's parents stressed the importance of securing an education. At Rust the young Wells enjoyed the guidance and instruction of dedicated missionaries and teachers who had come to Holly Springs to help the newly freed people. Her teachers regarded her as an exceedingly able student. On Sundays, her religious parents would permit only the Bible to be read, so Wells read it several times before leaving home to teach in the rural schools of Shelby County, where she worked while studying for the teacher's examination for the city schools of Memphis (Duster 1970).

Wells's life would be abruptly changed when in May 1884, she was forcibly ejected from the train on her way back from her teaching job in Shelby County, Tennessee, about ten miles from her home in Memphis (Washington 1995). Wells had chosen to sit in the women's compartment of a first-class carriage. A guard ordered her to leave. She declined. When the conductor grabbed her arm, she bit him and stayed in her seat. It took two men to dislodge her. They dragged her into the smoking car and (as she recalled in her autobiography) "the white ladies and gentlemen in the car even stood on the seats so that they could get a good view and continued applauding the conductor for his brave stand" (Wells 1970, 18–20). Uninjured, however, she left the train with her ticket intact: "Strangely, I held on to my ticket all this time, and although the sleeves of my linen duster had been torn out and I had been pretty roughly handled, I had not been hurt physically" (Wells 1970, 19). Returning to Memphis, Wells brought suit against the railway company, the Chesapeake, Ohio, and Southwestern Railroad (Higginbotham 1996).

Wells engaged a Black Memphis attorney, Thomas F. Cassels, who had represented Memphis and Shelby County in the Tennessee General Assembly from 1881 to 1883. When the case seemed stalled, she suspected that Cassels had been bought off, noting in her diary that "white men choose men of the race to accomplish the ruin of any young girl" (quoted in Decosta-Willis 1995a, 56). She then hired James M. Greer, a former Union officer, to defend her. When she won her case in December 1884, the *Memphis Daily Appeal* ran a headline: A DARKY DAMSEL OBTAINS A VERDICT FOR DAMAGES AGAINST THE CHESAPEAKE and OHIO RAILROAD—WHAT IT COST TO PUT A COLORED SCHOOL TEACHER IN A SMOKING CAR—VERDICT FOR $500. The railroad, however, appealed to the Supreme Court of Tennessee, and it is this stage of the litigation to which Wells refers in the following diary entry:

> Saturday, April 3, 1887. Nothing of importance to record for the past week. No letter for Charles Morris. Sent him a postal card today in which I reminded him that he owed me a letter. ... The case will come up in the Supreme Court some time this month and a tried friend of mine unfolded

> a conspiracy to me that is on foot to quash the case. I will wait and watch and fear not. (Decosta-Willis 1995a, 57)

The railway company won its appeal. The state Supreme Court of Tennessee ruled that Wells had intended to harass the company and "her persistence was not in good faith to obtain a comfortable seat for a short ride" (quoted in Ware 1992, 179), thereby endorsing both the discrimination and the bodily harm against her. This racist decision, like others of the courts, led to *Plessy* v. *Ferguson* in 1896 and the euphemistic doctrine of "separate but equal" (Higginbotham 1996; Ware 1992).

Before the Court ruled, the Chesapeake and Ohio, through its attorney, had tried to persuade Wells to settle out of court. Despite the financial attractiveness of this option, Wells wanted to make a moral point. She declined: "Before this was done, the railroad's lawyer had tried every means in his power to get me to compromise the case, but I indignantly refused. Had I done so, I would have been a few hundred dollars to the good instead of having to pay out over two hundred dollars in court costs" (Wells 1970, 19).

At first Ida B. Wells had believed that the American legal system might actually protect African-American citizens. After the decision, she was shocked and disappointed, writing in her diary:

> Monday, April 11, 1887. The Supreme Court reversed the decision of the lower court in my behalf, last week. ... I felt so disappointed, because I had hoped such great things from my suit for my people generally. I have firmly believed all along that the law was on our side and would, when we appealed it, give us justice. I feel shorn of that belief and utterly discouraged, and just now if it were possible would gather my race in my arms and fly far away with them. O God is there no redress, no peace, no justice in this land for us? Thou hast always found the battles of the weak and oppressed. Come to my aid at this moment and teach me what to do, for I am sorely, bitterly disappointed. Show us the way, even as Thou led the children of Israel out of bondage into the promised land. (Decosta-Willis 1995b, 140–141)

However crushed Wells felt when she realized that the law was "white," she never wavered in her determination to make the law serve the Constitution and protect the civil rights of African Americans. Later she would abandon her career as a schoolteacher and assume the editorship of the *Free Speech,* the Memphis newspaper in which she had purchased part interest. Then her political commitment would be expressed journalistically. As she turned her attention to lynching, she questioned white male explanations of the phenomenon. In her autobiography she wrote that once she too had "accepted the idea ... that although lynching was irregular and contrary to law and order, unreasoning anger over the terrible crime of rape led to the lynching; that perhaps the brute deserved death anyhow and the mob was justified in taking his life" (quoted in Ware 1992, 179). After one of her best friends was lynched without provocation with the sanction of the white establishment, Wells understood that rape was only a pretext. Lynching was, she concluded, a means of controlling black social and economic life (Ware 1992).

After losing her lawsuit, Ida B. Wells continued to teach in the Memphis schools for several years, but poor working conditions—including the boredom of school routine—left her unhappy. In 1887 she began writing for a church paper, telling the story of her case against the Chesapeake and Ohio railroad and its discouraging results as her first article. Soon her articles appeared in other church papers and then in several of the black weeklies. Increasingly secure in her journalistic abilities, she invested her savings in a small newspaper in Memphis, the *Free Speech and Headlight.* Now part owner as well as editor, Wells did not hesitate to tell the truth as she saw it; her articles criticizing the Memphis board of education for poor conditions in segregated black schools led to her dismissal as a teacher in 1891 (Duster 1970).

Undaunted, Wells threw herself into workings of the newspaper. She abbreviated its name to the *Free Speech,* and was very much engaged with her work and travels for the paper when, on March 9, 1892, "at the curve" (where streetcars turned off Mississippi onto Walker Avenue in Memphis), three young black businessmen—Thomas Moss, Calvin McDowell, and Henry Stewart—were lynched. Wells gives a detailed account of this incident in her autobiography; it was an event that would change her life. The facts were these: three black businessmen—"[t]hree of the best specimens of young since-the-war Afro-American manhood" (Wells 1892a/1969, 18)—were arrested after several white men were wounded in a street fight. Fearing violence, the black community organized protection for the prisoners; a group camped for two nights just outside the jail where they were being held. On the third night, armed white men walked into the jail, took the three prisoners out and lynched them a mile outside the town. One of the Memphis daily newspapers delayed its publication so that it might give a detailed report of the lynching (Ware 1992).

The men who were lynched had recently opened a grocery store in a crowded black suburb of Memphis, threatening the monopoly a white grocer had enjoyed in the neighborhood. The three men were well known and liked in the community; news of their lynching shocked everyone. A crowd gathered outside their shop, the People's Grocery Company, to discuss the incident, but there was no organized protest, no violence. Despite the truth, word soon reached white officials that the "Negroes were massing." Orders were given to the sheriff to take a hundred men and "shoot down on sight any Negro who appears to be making trouble" (quoted in Ware 1992, 180). A white mob broke into the grocery, destroying what they did not eat or drink; black onlookers were forced to watch as they listened to constant abuse. A few days later the shop was closed by creditors; the white grocer then resumed his business without competition (Ware 1992).

During the lynching at least one of the men's bodies had been mutilated: "the fingers of McDowell's right hand had been shot to pieces and his eyes gouged out" (Wells 1970, 51). The lynching shocked, horrified, outraged Wells; it proved to be a key event in her transformation from journalist and teacher to activist (Tucker 1971). Her close friend, Thomas Moss, had pleaded with the murderers to spare him for the sake of his wife and unborn child.

Realizing that his pleas would be ignored, he made his last words these: "Tell my people to go West—there is no justice for them here" (quoted in Wells 1970, 51). In the *Free Speech,* Wells urged readers to take his advice, arguing that there was no protection for black people in Memphis. Within a few weeks a number of black families departed. Those white businesses which relied on blacks suffered. Even the transport system was affected as those who remained preferred to walk in order to save their money for the move west. Distressed executives from the City Railway Company came to the offices of the *Free Speech* and demanded that the black paper use its influence to restore the status quo. Wells published the conversation, then urged her readers to continue to withhold their business. Wells herself traveled west, spending three weeks in Oklahoma. Afterward she reported on the successes of those who had moved west, contradicting fabricated "news" reported in Memphis's white newspapers, stories made up to scare blacks into staying in town (Ware 1992).

Two months later Wells wrote an editorial scathingly critical of the lynching. While the motive for this lynching was probably economic—whites were furious that these black businessmen were opening a grocery store in a black district previously served only by whites—Wells, in her May editorial, hints at noneconomic motives. The headline read: Eight Negroes Lynched Since the Last Issue of the *Free Speech.* "Three were charged," she wrote, "with killing white men and five with raping white women. If southern white men are not careful ... a conclusion will be reached which will be very dangerous to the moral reputation of their women" (Wells 1892a/1969, 4). Shocking enough to hint that white women might desire black men; it was then unthinkable that the bodies of white women might be stand-ins for the bodies of white men.

After writing the editorial, Wells traveled North to cover a conference of the African Methodist Church in Philadelphia, from where she made a short trip to New York before she was to return to Memphis. When Wells arrived in New York she was told that the white establishment in Memphis wanted her dead. Several prominent white businessmen had gathered at the Memphis Cotton Exchange Building to discuss her lynching. They had closed her newspaper; anyone who tried to resume its publication would be killed. The offices of the *Free Speech* were sacked, creditors took possession of what was left, "and the Free Speech was as if it had never been," Ida B. Wells wrote from New York City five months later (quoted in Aptheker 1977, 15). There could be no thought of returning to Memphis, as white men were watching every train. They had been ordered to kill Wells on sight.

While her support of the economic boycott had alarmed the white establishment, it had been that May editorial, which appeared while she was in Philadelphia, that had provoked the mob to destroy her offices, had enraged the white men of Memphis so thoroughly that they published their interest in lynching "her" as well (Ware 1992). I enclose "her" in quotation marks because white men assumed that such a response could have come only from a man, an assumption evident in the pronouns in the following editorial, first printed in the Memphis *Commercial,* then reprinted in *The Evening Scimitar* of same date, which copied the *Commercial*'s editorial with these words added: "Patience under such circumstances is not a virtue. If the negroes themselves do not apply the remedy without delay it will be the duty of those whom he has attacked to tie the wretch who utters these calumnies to a stake at the intersection of Main and Madison Sts., brand him in the forehead with a hot iron and perform upon him a surgical operation with a pair of tailor's shears" (quoted in Wells 1892a/1969, 5; Wells 1970, 66). In response, Wells bought and carried a pistol, vowing "[i]f I could take one lyncher with me, this would even up the score a little bit" (Wells 1970, 62). Clearly, "in an era of growing Jim Crow despotism and black conservatism, Wells was one of the most defiantly militant voices by any standard" (Washington 1995, xvii).

Indeed. This terrible trauma—the lynching "at the curve" followed by the destruction of her newspaper and threats upon her life—dissuaded Ida B. Wells not at all from challenging white fantasies around lynching. Indeed, it only seemed to intensify her resolve. She continued her antilynching efforts at the *New York Age*: "Because I saw the chance to be of more service to the cause by staying in New York than by returning to Memphis, I accepted their advice, took a position on the *New York Age,* and continued my fight against lynching and lynchers" (Wells 1970, 62). It was at this time that she began to lecture. It was from the North that Wells launched what was to become an international crusade against lynching. As news of her "crusade for justice" spread, she received an invitation to speak in England, Scotland, and Wales. In April and May of 1893 she visited England for the first time (Duster 1970).

In the months following the lynchings "at the curve," Ida B. Wells reflected on how the white Memphis establishment had used lynching to prevent black businesses from competing with whites. Not only was the law unable to protect black citizens from intimidation and lynching, but often the highest authorities had been involved in organizing the lynching event. Those outside the South condoned the practice because they believed their white southern friends who insisted that lynchings were spontaneous outbursts of self-righteous revenge against rampaging black rapists. It was clear to Wells that the truth was being actively suppressed, and not just in the Memphis lynching. She decided to investigate reports of lynchings, and she discovered that in nearly every incident in which white women were said to have been assaulted, the facts had been distorted. There was, in effect, no evidence to support the rape theory (Ware 1992).

In those cases where Wells did find that a black man and a white woman had in fact been sexually involved, it had been consensual. In one case, for instance, a sheriff's seventeen-year-old daughter was missing. Finally she was traced to the cabin of one of her father's farmhands, a young black man. Quickly accused of rape, the young man was lynched in order to protect the young woman's reputation. As Ware observes, the facts were nowhere in evidence as the local newspaper reported that "the big burly brute was lynched because he had raped the seven-year-old daughter of the sheriff" (quoted in Ware 1992, 181). In fact, she was seventeen, not seven, and consenting.

Following her exile to the North, Ida B. Wells remained preoccupied with the terrible and "peculiar" practice. She began to see lynching as related to the rape and abuse of black women and girls by white men under slavery. In many cases white men were even more savage toward black men than they were to black women. It was clear to her that most southerners had not recovered from losing the War, from the shock of losing their slaves, from the novelty of seeing freed African Americans. As we know, Emancipation was more a political event between the North and the South than it was a phenomenological event for African Americans (Hartman 1997). After Reconstruction, through a series of legal, political, and psycho-cultural maneuvers (such as racism), southerners made sure black citizens would not be able to work for themselves, would not enjoy their constitutional rights to education, to vote, and hold public office. Given the times, it is unsurprising that Wells would not see the latent homoeroticism of white racism. The reassertion of white privilege in the post-Reconstruction South took, on the surface, hetereosexualized terms, concentrated in a hysterical fear of black male sexuality which made any contact between black men and white women forbidden (Ware 1992). But near the surface was circulating a disavowed, mangled homoeroticism which erupted in the sexual mutilation of black male bodies at lynchings.

As it does today, the North prided itself on its comparative liberalism. Many thought that with the defeat of the South, with Reconstruction and then appeasement, the "problem of the Negro" would be resolved. After the sacrifice of so many sons and brothers and husbands, there was an emotional exhaustion in the North. Yankees did not want to hear any more about the situation in the South, did not want to hear that, in many respects, things had worsened for black citizens. And so it is unsurprising that Ida B. Wells's analysis was received less than enthusiastically in the North. Frustrated, not sure where to turn next, she found herself invited, through Frederick Douglass, to go to Britain. Perhaps in Britain there was hope of receiving a more sympathetic hearing (Ware 1992).

While there, Ida B. Wells was heartened by the progressive activities of English women reformers and their various civic groups. (We examine her work in England in the next chapter.) After returning to the United States, Wells praised the activities of British reformers to New England audiences, urging her American female listeners to become more active in the affairs of their community, city, and nation by organizing civic clubs. Her idea was well received; the first civic club, the Women's Era Club, was organized in Boston, with Mrs. Josephine St. Pierre Ruffin serving as president. Wells inspired the formation of other clubs in New England and in Chicago, where she herself organized the first civic club for Chicago's black women. When Wells returned to England in 1894, this Chicago group named itself in honor of Ida B. Wells (Duster 1970).

Indignation, courage, journalistic competence, pedagogical acumen, and political zeal brought Ida B. Wells to international prominence. Convinced that lynching had little to do with black crime, Wells resolved to reveal the exact details of all lynchings which came to her attention. Long before the statistics were compiled, Wells suspected an "economic motivation behind some lynchings" (quoted in Braxton 1989, 116). She wrote scores of articles, and a half dozen pamphlets, among them *Southern Horrors, A Red Record,* and *Mob Rule in New Orleans.* Insisting that lynching must be challenged as a gendered event, she would focus on exposing the black-man-as-rapist fantasy. This fantasy was more than false; the truth was (she argued to the horror of most white readers) that some white women preferred the company of black men. If you want to talk rape, let's talk about the white man, who, since slavery's inception had systematically and repeatedly raped black women (and, she did not add, men). Performing one of her brilliant reversals of whites' assumptions, Wells suggested that it was white—not black—men who were the rapists in America. Bettina Aptheker (1977) points out: "In defending the integrity of black manhood, the women were able to simultaneously affirm their own virtue. Of necessity, they also defended the independence and integrity of white womanhood. Thus, Ida Wells, and the black women of the antilynching movement, made a basic challenge to both the racist and patriarchal foundations of southern society" (17).

The lynching at the curve and her consequent conversion from journalist to full-time crusader against lynching strengthened her sense of herself as a black woman. Joanne M. Braxton (1989) characterizes Wells as a black woman who did her Christian duty by decrying the evils of lynching and the moral decay at its root. Wells reported that blacks were lynched for wife beating, hog stealing, quarreling, "sassiness," and even for no offense whatsoever. As we have seen, the "offense" was pretext for stripping a young black man naked and having one's way with him.

One of the cases Wells (1892a/1969; 1892c/1969) cites illustrates this point exactly. This was case of Edward McCoy, who was burned alive in Texarkana, Arkansas, on January 1, 1882, after having been accused of assaulting a white woman. Wells writes: "He was tied to a tree, the flesh cut from his body by men and boys, and after coal oil was poured over him, the woman he assaulted gladly set fire to him, and 15,000 persons saw him burn to death." In this case, the woman who started the lynching pyre was known to have been involved with the man for "more than a year previous." As she lighted the blaze, McCoy "asked her if she would burn him after they had 'been sweethearting' so long." That was hardly the end of white hypocrisy in the case, Wells writes, as a "large majority of the 'superior' white men" responsible for the lynching were "reputed fathers of mulatto children" (quoted passages from Braxton 1989, 121; in Wells 1892a/1969, 10). "These are not pleasant facts," Wells (1892a/1969) acknowledges, but facts all the same.

In the lynching story white men told they fantasized about what black men wanted to do with white women; black women were not present in that scenario. Lynching was, it would seem, an affair between men. Of course, black women were involved; there were cases in which black women were lynched, and of course by virtue of being daughters, mothers, sisters and wives of men who were lynched, black women were very much involved. Was it because they were marginal to the lynching scenario in the imagination of white men that black women were able to point how that the emperor had no clothes? While the heterosexism of the time would not permit her to see that lynching was a mangled version of homosexual rape, Ida B. Wells was never fooled by the white male fantasy of big black bucks raping innocent white ladies. Free of white men's imagination (at least in terms of lynching), Ida B. Wells became lynching's most articulate and daring public critic (Schechter 1997).

While lynching may have been "an affair between men," Ida B. Wells's initiatives against the white male practice require one to position as central the role of educated black women in the antilynching protest movement. True, millions of African Americans engaged in indirect protest against lynching, as Brundage points out. But that significant fact must not obscure another significant fact, namely that Wells's critique of the racial-sexual regime in which lynching made sense was pathbreaking—intellectually, politically, and pedagogically. Her international campaign to teach European Americans through British citizens' indignation represented not only a new departure in black women's public activity, but a dazzling display of pedagogical skill. The campaign inspired countless numbers of American women to join local efforts at racial and social reform, where their more radical impulses were rerouted into more domesticated forms of "women's work." Beginning with Anna Julia Cooper in the 1890s, by the 1920s black women's activism against lynching looked rather different from Wells's first efforts at public confrontation. After Wells, black women's efforts to stop lynching were characterized by gendered traditions of female-only organizations, voluntarism, evangelicalism, and a rhetoric of womanhood and maternalism (Schechter 1997).

How did antilynching work become sex-segregated? Given that lynching itself was by and large sex-segregated, perhaps it is little surprise that antilynching efforts followed suit. But specifically what accounts for the political and ideological shifts between the late nineteenth-century work of Wells and those efforts of the black women Anti-Lynching Crusaders of 1922? Was there a certain domestication of black women's antilynching efforts once Wells retired (she never did completely), once the "crusade" became a "campaign" institutionalized by the male-male face-off between the N.A.A.C.P. and Congress?

How, during these years, did black women's agitation against lynching "prepare the way," as Jacquelyn Dowd Hall (1979, 167) put it, for the Association of Southern Women for the Prevention of Lynching (which we will examine in chapter 8). Almost certainly, Patricia A. Schechter (1997) tells us, black women's public protests against lynching over a thirty-five-year period made it acceptable (although still not completely safe) for respectable southern "ladies" to also blow the whistle on this white boys' game. Schechter, on whose research I will rely here, points to Rosalyn Terborg-Penn's (1991) argument to help us think about the scholarly neglect of black women's activism. Tarborg-Penn had argued that because it was devalued as "women's work," the work of Wells and others was ignored in men's narratives, including those of Walter White, Arthur Raper, and other prominent male leaders of the antilynching campaign. I do not doubt that, but I suggest another if related reason: antilynchers, like lynchers, understood that the practice was "between men," a practice in which women were, in men's minds, irrelevant. Lynching was gay sex. Disavowed and therefore horrible and deformed, but sex it was.

VII. Southern Horrors

[L]ynching a black male was seen as a rite of passage for young white males, a ritual in which they asserted their so-called manhood by the public display of vengeful force.

—Judith Stephens, "Lynching Dramas and Women: History and Critical Context" (1998)

T]he queer dream[s] of the mothers' revolt against the fathers.

—Mark Simpson, *Male Impersonators: Men Performing Masculinity* (1994)

The colored woman of to-day occupies, one may say, a unique position in this country. In a period itself transitional and unsettled, her status seems one of the least ascertainable and definitive of all the forces which make for our civilization.

—Anna Julia Cooper, "A Voice from the South" (1892/1998)

Heralding Wells' entrance into what would be a national and finally international anti-lynching campaign, Southern Horrors *is a complex document that functions not only as an early political statement against lynching, but also as Wells' attempt to reaffirm her virtue at the very moment at which the tabooed subject of her speech (the sexual economy behind lynching) threatens to disqualify her from respectability.*

—Sandra Gunning, *Race, Rape, and Lynching: The Red Record of American Literature, 1890–1912* (1996)

Ida B. Wells's first published pamphlet, *Southern Horrors: Lynch Law in All Its Phases* (1892a/1969), has been characterized by Patricia Schechter (1997) as "a point of origin in American critical thought in lynching." This "brief but comprehensive" and "stinging" account challenged taken-for-granted views of southern society as a "white man's country." While the gender critique is there, Wells begins with a definition of lynching her readers could understand, that is, as a chief expression of "opposition … to the progress of the race." But, as Schechter (1997) points out, Wells's creative and novel analysis of the sexuality of racial politics avoided much of taken-for-granted notions of womanhood which played into the white-male fantasy. While she did not confront directly the homoerotic content of white male fantasies regarding the black man, she did, bravely, and to her white readers unbelievably, challenge white women's participation in the sex/gender system.

How? Without hesitation, Wells pointed to the consensual and sometimes illicit sexual contact between white women and black men. She insisted that white women's complicit roles in lynching necessarily undermined any pretensions of "moral purity," the very same concept whites invoked to justify lynching. Moreover, Wells exploited the politics of "true manhood" in the lynching fantasy, declaring it was white men who were uncivilized because they did the lynching. Wells also "linked black men's oppression through lynching to black women's oppression through rape." Schechter argues that Wells's "reformulation of the racialized sex-gender system" resulted in new and heightened authority for black women, who now demanded "that justice be done though the heavens fall" (quoted in Schechter 1997, 293).

The pamphlet's transgressive style underlined its provocative theses. Throughout *Southern Horrors,* Wells used unorthodox punctuation to recode the accounts of lynching she copied from white newspapers. By punctuating these texts with her own quotation and question marks, Wells challenged white journalistic authority, thereby opening a space for her own investigations as well as her rereadings of published articles. For example, Wells (1892a/1969) made a question of the statement America "legally (?) disfranchised the Afro-American" and whether black men "always rape (?) white women" (13, 6). She was openly skeptical of something called "honor" which southerners invoked to justify lynching; she was not especially impressed with what passed for "evidence (?)" of black crime reported in white newspapers. Wells advised her readers to "note the wording" of lynching reports, and in a chapter mockingly entitled "The Black and White of It" (7), she reread a number of such reports. Wells showed that the "facts," white moral platitudes, and racial differences reported in mainstream southern newspapers were journalistic fiction, not facts at all (Schechter 1997).

Consistent with emerging progressive, muckraking trends in journalism, Wells's brilliant analysis of southern racism recoded the assumptions of Christian civilization, bourgeois gender roles, and law and order in an effort to protect African Americans from white violence and to inspire black collectivization and mobilization. Her inversion of taken-for-granted notions of Victorian manhood stimulated European Americans' anxiety over masculinity and morality, especially their conflation of the two. Wells insisted that white male lynchers were far from the chivalrous, manly avengers of white womanhood they claimed to be. In fact, they were "inverts." White men were the true barbarians (Bederman 1995b).

Patricia Schechter (1997) reminds us that Wells also pointed out that "Red Indians and cannibals" had been guilty only of living by their precepts. Unlike white men, they were not hypocrites. While white southern men were professing Christianity, civilization, chivalry and the "majesty of law," they were mutilating the bodies of innocent black men. Wells underscored not only white duplicity, but also the corruption of language inherent in the rape charge, a corruption not limited to language but which extended to all those who degraded themselves by participating in the sexualized practice. By such participation whites became more primitive than the so-called primitive races. By mocking and recoding mainstream press accounts of lynching, Wells attacked the dominant culture's values and ideology from within. Schechter concludes: "Nowhere was the power (and instability) of her rereading strategy more evident than on the issue of gender, which Wells placed at the center of her case for black protection and self-help against lynching" (1997, 294).

As we have seen in chapters 4, 5, and 6, in the late nineteenth century gender had become an unstable but key concept in European-American moral and political life. That gender politics had become intermingled with racial politics was particularly clear to many middle-class African-American women who comprised part of Wells's intended audience. Although lynching was a continuing, even intensifying concern to African Americans everywhere, black awareness and undermining of the race/gender system were especially visible in southern cities and towns, where whites and blacks lived in close proximity. It was in the streets, public accommodations, and the press of the Deep South where these dramas of power, status, and identity were enacted (Schechter 1997; Brundage 1997a).

The post-Reconstruction generation of educated African Americans was determined to enjoy a greater freedom than had their parents. In fact, they did exercise an unprecedented, if circumscribed, autonomy. Many dreamed of black progress and prosperity, dreams they hoped would become reality as African Americans gained respectability. Such fantasies of acceptance were linked to hopes that as Christianity, thrift, sobriety, and adherence to middle-class gender roles spread across the color line, that line would become blurred. Key, then, to middle-class black aspiration was that middle-class Christian values would ease white fear while empowering the entire black community. But black resolve was soon tested. As we have seen, in the 1890s radical racists such as Rebecca Felton conjured up and put into political play white fantasies of black bestiality, innate mental deficiency, and moral degeneracy (Schechter 1997).

During the 1880s, Memphis enjoyed a thriving black community. Hoping to make Memphis the "Chicago of the South," ambitious city boosters pretended to be racially tolerant. Their pretense was not widely shared, evidently, because when black Memphians progressed too quickly or asked that their civil rights be acknowledged, white resistance, even violence, erupted. This is evident in the response to Wells's suit against the Chesapeake and Ohio Railroad and, most dramatically, in the 1892 lynching at the curve and the subsequent destruction of Wells's newspaper. While whites treated her lawsuit as a nuisance, they treated her editorial impugning of white womanhood with brutality and threats of further violence. Once again it is clear that white supremacy was a gendered affair requiring, apparently, terrorism against all African Americans and "special" assaults upon black men and black manhood (Schechter 1997).

As Schechter (1997) points out, during this time the concept of a "manhood" came to represent the entire "race." In *A Voice from the South,* Anna Julia Cooper referred to "the race [being] ... just at the age of ruddy manhood" (61). Part of this was pure patriarchy with its concomitant invisibility of women, and part was simply patriarchy's reflection in the public sphere—that is, those male prerogatives regarding voting, economic independence, and the protection (ownership) of dependents. Thus men and "manhood" came to symbolize an entire community. In this symbolic sense, then, lynching was a political act of white supremacy which insisted on black political submissiveness and civic emasculation. Literally it was the mutilation of individual black men, usually young, sometimes stripped naked and sexually mutilated. The truth of lynching was inadvertently disclosed when whites lied about the source of sexual and violent aggression in the South. "This cry [of rape] has had its effect," complained Wells (1892a/1969) bitterly in *Southern Horrors.* "It has closed the heart, stifled the conscience, warped the judgement and hushed the voice of press and pulpit on the subject of lynch law throughout this 'land of liberty'" (14). Wells was clear that white men were obsessed with the "subjugation of the young manhood of the race" (20). She knew that the so-called "black beast rapist was in reality the innocent victim of both white male blood lust" (Schechter 1997, 295), and a previously unarticulated element, white female sexual desire (Schechter 1997).

For Wells, lynching was about sex and economics. She suggested that "mob spirit has grown with the increasing intelligence of the Afro-American" (Wells 1892a/1969, 15). Citing the annual lynching statistics published in the white press, Wells showed that even according to whites, the rape charge against black men was not the primary cause of lynching. Even when there were accusations of rape, they were often unproven. Wells revised the link between sex and violence which structured the lynching-for-rape story (Schechter 1997). *Southern Horrors* "reduced to plain English" her suspicion that the white man lynched the black man "not because he is always a despoiler of virtue, but because he succumbs to the smiles of white women." In suggesting this "unthinkable" scenario, Wells (1892c/1969) provided a "defense for the Afro-American Sampsons who suffer themselves to be betrayed by white Delilahs" (5).

Before Wells, almost no black commentator on lynching broached these explosive interracial sexual issues. Instead, most antilynching statements focused on issues of law and order. After Wells, few could avoid some reference to black manhood when expressing protest and outrage. Schechter (1997) points to two images of lynchings from the *Richmond Planet* which illustrate how Wells's analysis positioned gender and manhood as central within antilynching discourse among African Americans at the turn of the century and beyond. In one, the image of crucifixion conveys the idea that black men were innocent victims as was Christ. Like Christ's crucifixion, lynching shall be acknowledged on the stage of world history. In another image a black World War I soldier is portrayed as protecting both the black community and American society, exhibiting the restraint of Victorian manhood and a more modern martial manhood. He stands over a map of the old Confederacy, on which the numbers of lynching victims are etched. The caption reads: "Though You have slain mine, yet may you trust me" (quoted in Schechter 1997, 298). Schechter comments: "Echoing *Southern Horrors,* the *Planet* represented black manhood along a continuum of manly sacrifice ranging from innocent victimization to battlefield martyrdom. But unlike Wells, the *Planet* left black women as silent, faceless sufferers or out of the picture altogether" (1997, 298).

In contrast, *Southern Horrors* acknowledged black women's presence in the dynamics of southern lynching and sexualized racism. In fact, the pamphlet is dedicated to: "To the Afro-American women of New York and Brooklyn, whose race love, earnest zeal and unselfish effort at Lyric Hall, in the City of New York, on the night of October 5th, 1892—made possible its publication, this pamphlet is gratefully dedicated by the author" (Wells 1892a/1969, 2). Wells juxtaposed black male lynchings with black female rapes, giving instances of both, including, for example, a savage attack by whites who "legally (?) hung poor little thirteen year old Mildred Brown" (1892a/1969, 24) in Columbia,

South Carolina, in 1890. While she did not make the link between the two explicit—that is, that lynching was a disguised form of rape—Wells did intuit that the two were forms of sexualized racial abuse. While the mutilation of black men was well known, white abuse of black women was not. Wells pointed out whites' ignorance of black women's suffering at the hands of "chivalrous" southern gentlemen, complaining that even if the facts were known, "when the victim is a colored woman it is different" (11). When white men raped black women, whites were silent (Schechter 1997).

Southern Horrors accomplished two goals. First, it vindicated black manhood. Now it was clear that the black male rape of white women was not the cause of lynching. Second, it asserted black women's right to outrage, a response traditionally reserved only for white women. Under white supremacy, black women were "harlots"; they seduced white men but they could not be raped. The clear ringing voice of indignation and rage made unmistakable the black woman's experience of white male tyranny. Additionally, by not commenting on black men's failure to protect black women or themselves, Wells avoided further despoiling of "the race's manhood" and blunted potential criticism from within the black community that she was "rather hard on the young men" of her race, a complaint Wells had evidently heard more than once (quoted in Schechter 1997, 298). Yet the gendered character of racial politics required Wells to frame the imperative for racial struggle against white violence in gendered terms, even if such language might embarrass black men: "Nothing, absolutely nothing," she insisted, "is to be gained by a further sacrifice of manhood and self-respect" (Wells 1892/1991, 42). Perhaps the stakes were higher for black women. By detailing black women's suffering at the hands of white men, Wells disclosed information that was painful and, for many African Americans, shameful (Schechter 1997).

The graphic even sensationalistic nature of Wells's exposé and the profound implications of her arguments for gender, race, and power in America proved to be very upsetting, and not just for whites. Wells would suffer slights at the hands of middle-class black reformers, both women and men. These may be trivial when one recalls that white men wanted to kill her, but they proved painful in the long run. Wells was well ahead of her time: undeterred, brilliant, courageous. Her remarkable self-presentation unsettled her audiences. Her zeal in the pursuit of justice was perhaps loudest in the ears of those who heard her, given the reactionary character of that historical moment. After all, as Schechter observes, it was a time when "(gendered) questions of strategy, authority, and leadership within the black community and the boundaries of sexual discourse in U.S. society were precisely at issue. … Wells' subject matter—law and order, politics, and sexual practices across the color line—was understood by many to be either male terrain or best not breached loudly or publicly" (1997, 299). An examination of what two other African-American intellectuals were saying about these subjects in 1892 shows she was not alone but underlines Wells's originality, courage, and brilliance.

In 1892, the same year that Wells wrote *Southern Horrors,* Anna Julia Cooper published *A Voice from the South,* a collection of speeches Cooper wrote for literary groups and women's clubs in Washington, D.C. Like Wells, Cooper worked as a schoolteacher. The book is dedicated "with profound regard" and "sincere esteem" to Bishop Benjamin W. Arnett of the A.M.E. Church. This dedication and Wells's inclusion in *Southern Horrors* of a letter of endorsement by Frederick Douglass, Patricia Schechter (1997) suggests, signifies the expectation that women, including black women, defer to powerful men. Such deference also served a practical function, as it helped ensure legitimization and distribution. Despite her performance of this deferential expectation, Cooper wrote "a manifesto of possibility for black womanhood" (Schechter 1997, 299).

In her eloquent arguments for an "elevated and trained womanhood," Cooper pointed to the sexual victimization of black women by white men as one of the great problems of the period. To protect single black women vulnerable in a white male world, she proposed the extension of fatherly and brotherly protection: "We need ... men who can be a father, a brother, a friend to every weak, struggling, unshielded girl. We need women ... to lend a hand to a fallen or failing sister." Cooper's moral vision was framed by the family: "A race is but a total of families." Throughout *A Voice,* she emphasized that black women required protection from abuse; unlike Wells, Schechter notes, Cooper never uses the word "rape." Working within a moral discourse of chivalry and Christianity, Cooper shared the widespread view among feminists that women were morally superior. A woman's sheer "pureminded[ness]," she wrote, could cause dangerous "rabble" and "vice" to "slink away" from her path in the street (Cooper 1892/1998, 32–33, 55–56).

A Voice expressed a Christian and patriarchal social order in which strong, chivalrous fathers protected weaker females and, in the spirit of equality before God, welcomed women to equal education with men. Cooper compared the "Colored Girls of the South—that large, bright, promising fatally beautiful class" to "delicate plantlet'[s]," "shivering," before the "fury of tempestuous elements ... so sure of destruction." These girls were "without a father ... often without a stronger brother" to "define their honor with his life's blood. Oh, save them help them, shield ... them!" pleaded Cooper (1892/1998). "Snatch them, in God's name, as brands from the burning!" (24–25; quoted in Schechter 1997, 300). Like Wells, Cooper understood that black women's vulnerability in a violent white male world was a pressing and urgent problem. In so doing, she too rewrote the dominant white stereotype of black woman as sexual temptress (Munro 1999a). But unlike Wells, her heightened moral sense of Christian chivalry allowed her to de-emphasize economic and political issues in racial inequality and she made few references to lynching (Schechter 1997; Lemert and Bhan 1998).

While not focusing upon lynching, Cooper did attend to gendered forms of racism within the women's suffrage and temperance movements. She was one of many black women at this time, among them Frances Harper, Mary Church Terrell, as well as Ida B. Wells, who were unafraid to complain about the racism they found in organizations dominated by white women. Each was quite conscious of their status as currency in the bargain struck between northern and southern white women. Cooper explored this racist regional solidarity to expose the ideological discourse within which white women defended their own class and racial interests (Carby 1987). In one of Cooper's most bitter essays, "Woman versus the Indian," she attacked the racist practices and discourses of white women's organizations which presumed to exist for and address the experiences of "women." Moreover, she insisted that white women exercised a significant influence over racial politics even though they could not hold legislative office. She characterized this influence as an ability to be the "teachers and molders of public sentiment," a sentiment that, she argued, preceded and was the source of "all laws, good or bad" (Cooper, in Lemert and Bhan 1998, 94), including the Jim Crow laws (Carby 1987).

In an 1888 article on "The Model Woman," Wells characterized the ideal African-American woman as one who "hoards and guards ... her virtue and good name," one who "scorns each temptation to sin and guilt," and one who "strives to encourage [black men] in ... all things honest, noble, and manly" (quoted in Gunning 1996, 81). Such rhetoric seems to position Wells safely within the idealized boundaries of nineteenth-century femininity. But as Sandra Gunning points out, Wells's performance of the place and purpose of virtuous black womanhood (as well as the style of "encouragement" she felt it was her duty to render to black men), posed something of a problem. Indeed, "the very conduct of Wells's life seems to fly in the face of any kind of conventional genteel feminism" (Gunning 1996, 81). For instance, *Southern Horrors* and her other antilynching pamphlets were, for the time, quite graphic, a feature that no doubt called into question Wells's claims to feminine gentility (Gunning 1996).

The "elder statesman among African Americans" (Schechter 1997, 300), Frederick Douglass also wrote about the southern racial situation in 1892. In July, he published, in the prestigious *North American Review*, "Lynch Law in the South." Neither Wells nor Cooper could obtain access to white readers at this time. While Douglass, like Wells, understood that white men's rape fantasy was just that, he decoupled gender from lynching, arguing in his essay that lynching was a case of hate destroying law and order. The rape charge against black men was the "best excuse" to disguise and rationalize white resistance to black achievement (Schechter 1997).

While he may have dismissed the rape charge as subterfuge, he knew his white readers would not be so easily persuaded. Douglass used common sense to challenge the rape fantasy. Like Wells, he noted that if black were men by nature "beasts" compelled to rape, how did southern white women and children remain safely on the plantations during the Civil War? (Historian Martha Hodes [1993] observes that while black men were on rare occasion convicted of the rape of white women before and during the Civil War, "Wells and Douglass were correct in their belief that from the Reconstruction era on, white ideas about the dangers of black male sexuality reached an unprecedented level of virulence and brought with them, for the first time, near-inevitable white violence" [Hodes 1993, 416–417].) Disputing white southerners' arguments for "popular justice," Douglass argued that there could be no "rational doubt" that true black criminals would be prosecuted and punished to the fullest extent of the law, especially in southern courts. To end lynching, Douglass argued for education by the "press and the pulpit," a tactic Wells also endorsed. But as Schechter (1997) points out, Wells's list of tactics was a longer one, including boycotts, geographical relocation, and political pressure through voting and lobbying.

Gender laced the critiques and appeals made by Cooper and Douglass. There was now no way to avoid seeing that lynching was "something men did to other men in public—it was publicized aggressively and its victims made a spectacle" (Schechter 1997, 300–301). But rape was "private," something men did to women, usually in private. Consistent with this distinction and with Victorian reticence about sex, Cooper located the problem of the sexual victimization of black women in the black family, a view which enabled her to then appeal to black fathers and brothers to protect women from white men so that the race might progress. Her "feminine" critique delicately identified the problem of rape and sexual assault and kept the solution private and within the family. In contrast, Douglass located lynching in the public world, and his critique was structured by patriarchal conceptions of the public, that is, the importance of social order and institutional authority. Douglass thereby appealed to institutions (press and pulpit) in order to educate whites as to the importance of law and order. Wells's critique, Schechter (1997) points out, traversed the ideological divide between Cooper's and Douglass's analyses.

In *Southern Horrors* Wells connected the "private" crime of rape to the "public" crime of lynching. She did not grasp lynching as a distorted if equally violent homosexual version of heterosexual rape, but she knew both were sexualized forms of racial violence. While Cooper imagined a naturalistic narrative—"tempestuous elements"—for rape and pleaded for help from the fathers and brothers for protection of pure if vulnerable black womanhood, Wells knew there was nothing "natural" or fateful about the two versions of sexual abuse. The remedy for both was the legal restraint of white men, the prosecution of offenders, and the lawful protection of black people. Operating in a heterosexist regime, Wells could only heterosexualize the connection between lynching and rape, and so she pointed to those voluntary and consensual sexual liaisons between white women and black men that sometimes occurred, and the betrayals by white women of black men which on occasion led to lynchings. In so doing, Wells articulated the "private" and gendered character of an issue which Douglass, and most men, could understand only as a failure of public institutions, of law and order. Wells seemed to know that these two were also sedimented forms of white male desire, and as such comprised part of the web of racist sexual politics which raped southern blacks literally and symbolically. In connecting public and private crimes "against the bodies of black people" (Schechter 1997, 301), Wells moved beyond Douglass's and Cooper's critiques of white male violence into an uncharted ideological and theoretical territory (Schechter 1997).

In that territory, boundaries between private violence and public social facts were porous. In *Southern Horrors,* white women were no longer passive or passionless angels but human beings capable of agency, racial hatred, and "even" illicit sexual desire. They were, Wells seemed to be saying, not terribly different from white men. Black women were portrayed not as marginal creatures without will or intellect, but as historical subjects whose subjectivities were violated through sexualized assault. They were, Wells seemed to be saying, much like black men. Both black men and women suffered by virtue of white male sexual desire. Wells mocked the white terror of miscegenation—the supposed "black and white of it"—by underlining the omnipresence of sexual contact across the color line, evidenced by the increasing number of mixed-race southerners (herself included), and to instances when white men committed crimes with "their faces blackened" (quoted in Schechter 1997, 302). By traversing and making porous those boundaries between public/private, male/female, black/white, *Southern Horrors* challenged the conventional narrative of southern lynching, and disclosed the profoundly sexual character of white racism (Schechter 1997).

Wells's blurring of ideological binaries is evident too in the structure of *Southern Horrors.* While the overall structure is the conventional division into chapters, in genre the pamphlet is not easily characterized. It is at once sociological analysis, muckraking journalism, preaching, and a call to arms. (Recall she advised that "a Winchester rifle should have a place of honor in every black home" [Wells 1892a/1969, 23]. On another occasion, when discussing the unequal sentencing practices used against African Americans who stole proportionately less than white criminals, Wells advised black thieves to "steal big" [quoted in Gunning 1996, 81].) In terms of narrative structure, there is little movement toward closure; rather the text is punctuated by numerous questions and commands. "The press is singularly silent," Wells cautioned her readers. "Has it a motive? We owe it to ourselves to find out" (24). As Schechter points out, Wells declines to perform that demurring courtesy praised by men and many nineteenth-century women as "ladylike." Rather, she disrupted the white text of lynching by creative punctuation and the use of asides and sarcasm: "the race was left to the tender mercies of the solid South" (1997, 13). A single tone or voice or monolithic narrative structure could not communicate the complexity of Wells's analysis (Schechter 1997).

In contrast, Frederick Douglass positioned himself within patriarchal notions of masculine authority, a point Deborah McDowell (1993) makes in a different context. The trouble with racism, he and other black men seemed to be saying, was that it did not allow them to be "men," a concept they understood in its civic sense, but which we can see was literal as well. Anna Julia Cooper too seemed to accept dominant notions of womanhood, including the apparent adoption of an essentialist position "woman" which, as Schechter (1997) notes, was a radical discursive move for a black woman to make at the time. In contrast, Wells was defiant in the face of prevalent gender norms. This was no new pose; it is evident in her Memphis diary a decade before, when, for instance, she resisted community expectations that she marry (Decosta-Willis 1995b). (Wells would later marry Chicago attorney Ferdinand L. Barnett.) Given the invisibility of black women in the dominant lynching narrative, Wells's decision to print her name and face on the cover of *Southern Horrors* was striking; her pose is angry, determined, knowing. This gesture qualifies the apparent deference implied by introducing the pamphlet with Douglass's letter (Schechter 1997). On the front page of *Red Record* Wells even lists her street address! It read: "Respectfully submitted to the nineteenth century civilization in 'the Land of the Free and the Home of the Brave.' By Miss Ida B. Wells, 128 Clark Street, Chicago" (Wells 1892b/1969, frontispiece). Who was this woman who was so unafraid to challenge a crime that dare not speak its name?

In *Southern Horrors* Wells identified herself as an exile, and in so doing, claimed the authority of the margins (see Said 1996, for a perceptive discussion of the intellectual as one in exile). As I have suggested, being on the margins is dangerous but at least you can breathe (Pinar 1997). In this instance, one can also "see" through the white male rationalization of lynching as chivalry. In the preface, Wells cited her pen name "Exiled," by which she had signed an earlier newspaper version of the work. A few pages later, she again identified herself as "an exile from home," a reference to being driven from Memphis after her editorial critique of the famous 1892 lynching "at the curve." The exile notion grants her passage between and beyond dominant binaries such as insider/outsider, southerner/northerner, victim/survivor. Schechter (1997) suggests that the ambiguous gender symbolics of the exile metaphor amounts to a retreat from the ideological advance she had made under the category "woman." As exiled, Wells emphasized liminality and intensity over ideology (Schechter 1997).

The exile as victim but survivor resonated powerfully for Wells and for many black women. It spoke of black women's historical experience of sexual victimization during and after slavery. Western literary tradition tends to silence or simply erase the female victim of rape, often through madness or death (Morrison 1992; Brownmiller 1975/1993). In white lynching accounts, too, the "raped" white woman disappears, assumed to be too horrified and humiliated to testify in a court of law. The truth is she never "existed" in most cases. Black women's narratives of victimization tend to stress survival; this emphasis requires a different model of the moral by which women might represent and resist sexual exploitation (Schechter 1997). Think of Harriet Jacobs, for instance, a slave girl who bore two children as a single woman rather than submit to forced concubinage (Brent 1973).

The image of the black woman as victim but survivor contrasted sharply, Schechter (1997) notes perceptively, with that of the black man as victim but victor over lynching. Schechter points to the dramatization of these images in the antilynching cartoons published in the *Richmond Planet,* mentioned earlier. The black soldier's victory has to do in part with his loyalty to the state, a patriarchal authority grounded not only in the political order but, Americans have tended to imagine, in the divine. The black soldier becomes a kind of Christ, tortured by temporal political authorities, but morally authorized and empowered by God. Wells's exile status and gender by definition located her outside such patriarchal institutions as the state, outside even the family. Before her marriage to Chicago attorney Ferdinand Barnett, Wells often depicted herself as "homeless" and an "orphan," a strategy also employed by Sojourner Truth, who named herself "Sojourner" (Munro 1999a). These identities explained (and rationalized) both women's physical mobility/autonomy and their moral claim to political assistance from male members of the African-American community (Schechter 1997).

Wells's analysis both recalled and reformulated black women's historical experience and subjectivity as it reconceptualized the dominant narratives of lynching and southern sexual politics. In revealing that the boundaries between private and public, race and sex, were in fact porous—one hundred years later Henry Louis Gates, Jr. (1996), would declare that "gender and race conflate in a crisis" (84)—Wells broke down binaries, made more sophisticated and accurate our understanding of what was at stake when black men were stripped naked, mutilated, and burned. By juxtaposing lynching and rape she showed that the two events were indeed "connected domains of racial oppression." In a phrase, "Wells rewrote the dominant southern narrative about race relations and female subjectivity in powerfully unsettling terms." Of course many, including more than a few within the black community (her diary narrates several tales of threatened contemporaries), found themselves uncomfortable with such an articulate, undaunted black woman, and they moved to reprimand even silence her. At first, white men could not imagine she even existed. Recall that those in Memphis who destroyed her newspaper office also threatened Wells with a lynching, including castration—"a surgical operation with a pair of tailor's shears" (quoted in Schechter 1997, 303)—since they assumed that the author of such an "uppity" editorial was male (Schechter 1997).

Unfortunately, such white men were not confined to Memphis city limits. Many European Americans could not hear Wells's message of black suffering in the South and, like the white male Memphians, attacked the messenger. White criticism of Wells vividly conveyed how race was mixed up with sex in the 1890s (and beyond). While assertive white women were dismissed as unfeminine or "unsexed" (i.e., "men"), transgressive black women were imagined to be even more female, that is, sexually uncontrolled and always available (Schechter 1997). These two images functioned effectively as male rhetorical moves designed to discredit and control women's speech; they also are examples of the "unconscious speaking," as these are both figments of the white male mind. Transgendered, this equation reads if I'm not a man, I'm a woman, and if I'm a woman, I'm a whore. So when white supremacists vilified anyone who failed to condemn sex across the color line as a dangerous race-mixer, they were also worrying about themselves as "men." Miscegenation and homosexual desire are not unrelated; both require "passing" to escape undetected. But all of this was safely buried in the white unconscious at the close of the nineteenth century. In 1893–1894, southern racists ridiculed Wells—a woman who spoke openly about the love that dare not speak its name (interracial sex)—as a "black harlot" in search of a "white husband," a "strumpet," a "saddle-colored Sappira [sic]," an "adventuress of a decidedly shady character," and "a prostitute bent on miscegenation." Evidently considered news fit to print, *The New York Times* reported that she was a "slanderous and nasty-minded mulatress." But then even northern white women who protested lynching during this period were ridiculed in the South as "the short-haired, strident-voiced sisterhood of Boston" (quoted in Schechter 1997, 305), surely an epithet for lesbians.

In this period characterized by intensified racism and volatile gender politics, few readers, white or black, were comfortable with Wells's analysis (Schechter 1997). In her autobiography, Wells (1970) recalled that a "delegation" of black men in New York City asked her in 1894 to "put the soft pedal on charges against white women and their relations with black men" (220). Apparently, they felt that Wells's analysis complicated and sensationalized lynching, leaving their "real" antilynching efforts even more difficult. There were black women who concluded from Wells's emphasis upon consensual interracial liaisons that interracial sexual intimacy should be made more not less difficult. "The Afro-American shall be taught, that whatever folly a white woman may commit the suspicion of participation in that folly means torture and death for him," declared the Ladies Home Circle of the A.M.E. Church in St. Paul, Minnesota, in 1894 (quoted in Schechter 1997, 305). Black women's disapproval of black men dating white women (or men) has a long history.

Despite these tensions and criticisms, overall the black community welcomed Wells's use of statistics to show that the white male fantasy of black male rape was just that. This time, when lynching was at its zenith, much of the response to *Southern Horrors* did not focus on the issue of stopping racial violence, about which reform-minded readers agreed. Instead, much of the response concentrated on gender politics, made even more volatile when racialized. Wells did not mute the fact that she was a woman. The cover with her photograph and the letter from Frederick Douglass calling her a "Brave woman!" made that fact clear. But neither did she base her authority on an essentialized womanhood which claimed moral superiority over men. While she dedicated *Southern Horrors* to the "Afro-American women of Brooklyn and New York" who supported its publication, she did not evoke widely circulating notions of womanly purity. She was, evidently, a woman, but not Woman. This straightforward, concrete claim of individual self-possession and identity, made all the more remarkable by her exile status and by her apparent calm at all the negative publicity surrounding her crusade, threatened more than a few of those who should have been her closest allies (Schechter 1997).

What is clear from these tensions within the nineteenth-century black community is that the fantasy of "true womanhood" was not limited to the white male mind. Many educated, middle-class African Americans accepted this essentialized and sentimentalized fantasy of what women were meant to be. Women who slipped through the walls of this fantasy were suspect. Julia Coston of Cleveland, Ohio, editor of *Ringwood's Afro-American Journal of Fashion*, spoke for many when she declared that "essentially feminine" women were "not troubled with affairs of State, nor [were they] agents of reform." In 1894, when Coston criticized those black women who would "throw off the veil of modesty, and ... in the name of reform, pose as martyrs, sacrificing themselves to a great work," she might well have been referring to Ida B. Wells (quoted in Schechter 1997, 306).

Others were less hesitant to name names. Clubwoman Fannie Barrier Williams of Chicago complained in 1895 that "the public has been so accustomed to think of Miss Wells' remarkable zeal for the cause of law and order that, I suppose, no one ever reads of a case of lynching without associating with it the indignant protest of our plucky little friend." Clearly submerged in the doctrine of true womanhood and concerned with keeping up appearances, Williams said she worried that Wells's "unique career" opened her private life to unbecoming public scrutiny. Furthermore, Williams asked, feigning sincerity, how could Wells plan to "marry a man while still married to a cause," communicating her (and no doubt her friends') disapproval by raising the specter of polygamy, even promiscuity (Schechter 1997). By suggesting that Wells's wedding to Ferdinand Lee Barnett would become a "topic of national interest and comment," Williams seemed to be calling for, as well as worrying that, such publicity would result in more name-calling, contentiousness, and perhaps even heightened danger for black women generally (quoted in Schechter 1997, 306).

In fairness to Fannie Barrier Williams and other critics, this was not mere pettiness. This was, Patricia Schechter reminds us, a period when middle-class black women were striving to define black womanhood in positive terms, against the grain of white fantasies of black female wantonness and promiscuity. This meant toeing the line, however imaginary the line, and many members of the club movement disapproved of any behavior that seemed unorthodox. This dynamic is evident in the founding conventions of the National Association of Colored Women (N.A.C.W.) in 1895–96, where delegates criticized the "fierce denunciation[s] made by 'mercurial persons' of the race" which they felt did not set the "proper" tone. Along with black male leaders and white women reformers, many black women regarded political speeches and confrontation as unwomanly, dismissing them as tactics of mere "complaint," in contrast to woman's calling to be "actually noble." Public agitation and strong language were clearly at variance with those "genteel standards of decorous ladyhood" to which many clubwomen subscribed (quoted in Schechter 1997, 306). True womanhood was a middle-class, gendered ideal that helped enable clubwomen to refute negative white stereotypes about black females (Schechter 1997). Wells's courageous ignoring of these dynamics, including her refusal to be deterred by her black female critics, demonstrates her courage and determination.

Wells was not without supporters, however. There were those who did not find Wells's aggressive challenge to lynching as evidence of any lack of womanhood. She was a popular public speaker, often in demand, and her success on the lecture platform filled many African Americans, especially women, with pride. A poem was published in 1894 praising Wells as a model for black children. Conscious of gender politics, some Wells supporters recoded her boldness as proof of her femininity. "To our mind, therein lies one of the chief charms of Miss Wells' crusade," the *Indianapolis Freeman* declared, "in that she has not permitted the cares and labors of the same to unsex her. The full blown rose of a blameless womanhood abideth within her." Publicist Monroe Majors allowed that despite her "forcible pen [and] caustic oddness," Wells taught the nation "that sublime lesson of *modesty unchanged* even at the severest test." Others likened Wells to Old Testament heroines Esther, Deborah, and Jael, "mythic women who came forth in times of emergency to lead at moments of 'lost courage' among men" (quoted in Schechter 1997, 307). Such images of moral purity, chastity, and selflessness contradicted criticism that Wells's activism violated traditional femininity (Schechter 1997).

While Wells's supporters were clear that she was very much a woman, they also appreciated that she was trespassing on male terrain: the public sphere of politics. Some understood her as doing a man's job … in his absence. "The hour had come, where was the man?" asked the *Freeman*. "Unfortunately, the man was not forthcoming—but Miss Wells was!" In her analysis of lynching, Wells "handle[d] her subjects more as a man than as a woman," admitted *New York Age* editor T. Thomas Fortune. "We regret we have not a hundred more Ida B.

Wells [sic] to proclaim and defend the truth," lamented the A.M.E. Church's *Christian Recorder*. "But where, oh where are our leading men?" As Schechter (1997) points out, such commentary suggests that publicly representing the community or speaking for "the race" was widely perceived as a man's job. That a woman was doing it was deeply unsettling to some. Defenders of traditional sex roles—the remnants of an European courtly tradition Fielder (1966) will discuss in chapter 18—were outraged that she could possibly defend men, even lynched black men, at the "expense" of white women's moral reputation. Schechter (1997) tells us that two black men complained in the pages of the *New York Times* that it was "dishonorable in the extreme to attempt any defense upon an attack on the virtue of any class of women" (quoted in Schechter 1997, 307). No "gentleman"—that imaginary complement to "lady"—could accept a vindication so unchivalrous as Wells's. After all, not only were white women's reputations destroyed: Wells's aggressive critique threatened the fragile and recently proclaimed image of the black woman as lady. Ida B. Wells was a revolutionary twice over: she ignored both racial and gendered conventions.

The 1890s were, as we have seen, not only a period of extreme or "radical" racism but also a time of reactionary gender politics, the "invention" of "heterosexuality." White men felt their manhood was imperiled; they were determined to retain it, if at the expense of white women and African Americans. Despite these extremely unfavorable conditions, this was also a period of black women's intellectual progress and political initiative, which contributed to flux and debate over women's roles as intellectuals and leaders. By no means did black women occupy an equal place in the arena of racial reform. Anna Julia Cooper, for instance, was not optimistic about men's receptivity to women's political assertiveness, writing that "the average man of our race is less frequently ready to admit the actual need among the sturdier forces of the world for woman's help or influence" (1998, 135). The prestige of the "whole *Negro race*" might become visible in the "quiet, undisputed dignity of [her] womanhood" (31), as Cooper phrased it. Ida B. Wells was not exactly quiet. Dignified she was, but "womanhood" was not her major concern, not while black men were being lynched (Schechter 1997).

Despite her core of supporters, Wells was widely regarded in the educated black community as a usurper of male privilege. Part of this had to do with her violation of the image of womanhood—"quiet, undisputed dignity" as Cooper phrased it—but part of it had to do with the gender dynamics of lynching itself. It was not only black male bodies that were at stake (and sometimes burned at the stake), it was "male power and community prestige (black and white) [that] were at stake in the lynching scenario" (Schechter 1997, 308). When a black woman, among the most marginalized of Americans, intervened in this homosocial political economy, considerable gender anxiety was generated. Patricia Schechter is no doubt right to decode this anxiety as a function of how Wells's antilynching crusade "blurred the boundaries between public and private on issues and responsibilities that were ideally, if not always neatly, coded and divided by gender." Wells's antilynching campaign was upsetting, Schechter continues: "because it destabilized gender dualisms and racial hierarchies and thereby threatened the very terms by which power, order, and legitimacy were understood by many middle-class Americans, black or white, clubwomen or clergy" (1997, 308). Wells left men and women uneasy, so much so that America's most influential woman, Frances E. Willard, publicly criticized Wells, ostensibly for acting contrary to the ideological pillar of white women's reform: female moral purity. About that event we read in chapter 8.

As perceptive as it is, Schechter's analysis remains incomplete, unless we amend it to include men's probably unconscious understanding that lynching had to do with each other. For a woman to blow the whistle on this mangled homosexual liaison called "race relations" was not merely threatening, it was intolerable. While not bringing lynching out of the closet, certainly Wells showed it was not what it appeared to be. Clearly, white supremacy was at stake, and white men were not about to let a woman, especially a black woman, expose its sexualized content, as women's silenced and complicit participation was essential (as is the female sex worker's body in the "money shot"—see chapter 13) to the illusion.

In 1915, the *Chicago Defender* lamented that black men rarely resisted the mobs, which, according to one writer, stripped black men of manhood: "Since there are no men, women came to the front: protect the weaklings that still wear the pants from the lynch mobs." He's close; at least he understands that the event is gendered. But it was not black women who were stripping him of "manhood," it was the white men who raped and mutilated him. Women, too, while not appreciating its explicit (if mangled) homosexual content, knew this was a boy's game, and they wanted no part of it. When a mob looked for a boy in a black neighborhood for a lynching in Louisiana in 1916, the paper reported that "several girls and women of the Race saw the mob coming and they hid the children till things cooled down. They jeered the mob and refused to run. The men were at the mills working" (quoted in Schechter 1997, 308). Finally, of course, gender roles are illusory—historical and cultural constructions—and what was at stake here was human life not masculine pride. As we saw earlier in depictions of indirect protest or micropolitics, when possible, black men and women intervened in white male violence by whatever means were at hand. But once the event was over, the body was buried, and everyday life returned, gender reared its ugly head and divided what should have been a black community united against white violence (Schechter 1997).

This is not to blame black men and complicit black women. After all, dominant white models of gender were profoundly patriarchal, despite fifty years of feminism. Recall that women in the 1890s are still two decades away from being granted the right to vote. And if we are to believe some efforts to retrieve precolonial, West African models of manhood (see chapter 14), patriarchy was by no means a European phenomenon. So we cannot be shocked when, in 1894, the ministers of the powerful A.M.E. Church in Philadelphia denied Wells institutional backing, nastily telling her that the church already "had representative women ... whom they could endorse unhesitatingly." That was just the beginning. For the duration of her activist life Wells was squeezed out of leadership positions in national organizations, including the all-female N.A.C.W., the mostly male Afro-American Council, and later the N.A.A.C.P. When Wells was elected as financial secretary of the Council in 1899—a consolation prize as men condescendingly refused to acknowledge Wells's leadership position in racial politics—men still complained, saying that she would be better placed in "an assignment more in keeping with the popular idea of women's work" (quoted in Schechter 1997, 309). And so she was installed as head of a newly created Anti-Lynching Bureau (Schechter 1997).

The "feminization" of antilynching, which began with the Afro-American Council's patronizing gesture toward Wells, continued during subsequent decades. This process was not linear in any simple sense nor was it completed by the 1920s when the men (primarily men, black and white) of the N.A.A.C.P. assumed leadership of the struggle against lynching. By the end of that decade, white women—Jessie Daniel Ames most prominently—would enter the fight to prevent lynching. As Schechter (1997) points out, black women's protests against lynching (especially Wells's) cannot be neatly categorized as either "feminine" moral influence or "masculine" public politics; they included both. And even during the zenith of Wells's influence in the early 1890s, black and white men opposed to white supremacy also protested lynching. But the potential for shared leadership among black men and women, present in the 1890s, had pretty much disappeared by the 1920s (Schechter 1997).

The feminization of antilynching was marked in the 1920s with the founding of the black women's Anti-Lynching Crusaders, led by N.A.C.W. president Mary Talbert. Working under the aegis of the N.A.A.C.P., the Lady Crusaders organized around the feminine vocations of prayer, networking with white women through letter writing, and fund-raising. The official publication of the N.A.A.C.P., the *Crisis,* applauded their work by characterizing it as "The Ninth Crusade." Their goal was to organize "A Million Women United to Stop Lynching," by which they meant raising money for the N.A.A.C.P.'s lobbying for the Dyer Anti-Lynching Bill. In contrast to Wells's 1890s calls for black mobilization, the Crusaders engaged in a "moral battle" in hopes of encouraging a "new sense of personal responsibility" for lynching among all Americans. Meanwhile, Wells was not sequestered in Chicago; she continued her front-line investigations, fund-raising, and independent agitation against lynching outside the institutional support of the N.A.A.C.P. However, while applauding the work of the Crusaders, W. E. B. Du Bois, Walter White, and other male antilynching activists conspicuously overlooked Wells's efforts and her past accomplishments (Schechter 1997).

Two decades earlier, Ida B. Wells's antilynching lectures were introduced as "the simple story of an eloquent woman." As Patricia Schechter (1997) has shown, Wells's reconceptualization of the dominant lynching narratives proved to be far from simple. No doubt due to the multidimensional and radical character of her critique, she would be repulsed and ignored, despite her eloquence, even by those who shared her outrage. In *Southern Horrors* a black woman named herself in a pamphlet with a picture of her face over the name "Miss IDA B. WELLS;" on the cover of the subsequent *Red Record* she gave her street address. In both pamphlets Wells told stories about lynching while posing questions which challenged taken-for-granted assumptions about race and gender. How readers perceived her face, the stories, and her questions disclosed the complexity and volatility of the times (Schechter 1997).

Ida B. Wells defied easy, quick, traditional categorization. As Schechter notes, she was described by some as unsexed, by others as supersexed; some declared her unladylike, others too feminine, the "man for the job," a "black" woman, and a "mulatress." Wells was undeterred. Contrary to white opinion of the time, Ida B. Wells established that lynching was not an occasional excess committed by fanatics and extremists. Lynching was central to a gendered and racialized system of organized terror. Many southern whites participated in or witnessed lynchings; many insisted, for generations, on the right to do so. As we have seen, lynchings were supported by legal and other authorities, sanctioned by the news media, and ignored (i.e., condoned) by the federal government. The allegation of rape was almost always groundless; the victim often was not even the man charged with the crime. For over a century, African Americans were tortured and burned alive at the stake, the spectacles being advertised days in advance by the local papers and sometimes more widely attended than a county fair (Braxton 1989). Nine years after the last recorded lynching, Eldridge Cleaver would poetically restate, from a heterosexually-identified black man's point of view, the gender dynamics of lynching:

From "To A White Girl"
White is
The skin of Evil.
You're my Moby Dick,
White Witch,
Symbol of the rope and hanging tree,
Of the burning cross.
Loving you thus
And hating you so,
My heart is torn in two.
Crucified.
(Cleaver 1968, 13)

Not identifying with Christ but with the victims, Audre Lorde put it this way:

I was the story of a phantom people
I was the hope of lives never lived
I was a thought-product of the emptiness of space
and the space in the empty bread baskets
I was the hand, reaching toward the sun
the burnt crisp that sought relief ...
And on the tree of mourning they hanged me
the lost emotion of an angry people
hanged me, forgetting how long I was
in dying
how deathlessly I stood
forgetting how easily
I could rise
again.
April 20, 1952.
(Lorde 1982, 118)

Rise again they would, in the American prison.

8 WHITE WOMEN *and the* CAMPAIGN *against* LYNCHING

FRANCES WILLARD, JANE ADDAMS, JESSE DANIEL AMES

I. Chicago's 1893 Columbian Exposition: Civilization/Race/Manhood on Display

Turn-of-the-century black feminists did not advocate a wholehearted embrace of the received conventions of white true womanhood. Rather, like their counterparts earlier in the century, they worked to adapt, supplement, and culturally rewrite these conventions to accommodate black women of all colors, economic stations, and personal histories, who had traditionally been excluded from respectability.

—Sandra Gunning, *Race, Rape, and Lynching: The Red Record of American Literature, 1890–1912* (1996)

The higher fruits of civilization can not be extemporized, neither can they be developed normally, in the brief space of thirty years. It requires the long and painful growth of generations. Yet all through the darkest period of the colored women's oppression in this country her yet unwritten history is full of heroic struggle, a struggle against fearful and overwhelming odds, that often ended in a horrible death, to maintain and protect that which woman holds dearer than life. The painful, patient, and silent toil of mothers to gain a free simple title to the bodies of their daughters, the despairing fight, as of an entrapped tigress, to keep hallowed their own persons, would furnish material for epics.

—Anna Julia Cooper, in Charles Lemert and Esmé Bhan, *The Voice of Anna Julia Cooper* (1998)

By the 1890s, "civilization" had become a racial, not just cultural or educational, concept. Rather than simply meaning "the West" or "industrially advanced societies," "civilization" denoted a precise stage in human evolution, a stage subsequent to more primitive stages characterized by "savagery" and "barbarism." Human races were said to progress in linear historical steps, moving from simple and primitive "savagery" through "barbarism," to advanced and more sophisticated "civilization." In the 1890s, European Americans were sure only they had advanced to the civilized stage. In fact, many believed the state of "civilization" or being "civilized" was itself a racial trait, inherited by all Anglo-Saxons and other "advanced" white races, such as the Germans (Stocking 1987; Hannaford 1996; Bederman 1995b).

Gender was also inseparable from civilization, insofar as extreme sexual difference was seen as a hallmark of civilization's advancement. Savage (that is, nonwhite) men and women were nearly indistinguishable, but in the civilized races pronounced sexual differences had evolved, unsurprisingly the same as celebrated in the middle class's doctrine of "separate spheres." Civilized women were "womanly," that is, spiritual, motherly, domestic; civilized white men were the most "manly" ever evolved: firm of character, self-controlled, dependable protectors of women and children (Bederman 1995b).

Nineteenth-century scientists repeatedly drew analogies between women and so-called primitive races, underscoring their similarities to each other, and the differences of both from white men, measured, presumably, by earlier maturation, prognathism (that is, lower measurements in facial angle), smaller brain volume, and a decreased sensibility to pain. A professor of natural history at the University of Geneva, Carl Vogt, proclaimed in 1864 that "the female European skull resembles much more the Negro skull than that of the European male" (quoted in Meyer 1996, 20). The overwhelming consensus of the scientific study of sex differences was that in the evolutionary development of civilization, women lagged behind men, just as so-called primitive peoples, such as blacks, lagged behind the Europeans (Russett 1989; Meyer 1996).

The power of this gendered concept of "civilization" derived from its racial elements, from the ways it mixed middle-class beliefs about racial and gender hierarchy. "Civilization" naturalized white male power by conflating male dominance, white supremacy, and human evolutionary history and development. Marrying manliness to white supremacy, and celebrating both as essential to human progress, "civilization" temporarily revitalized an exhausted, historically irrelevant concept of middle-class Victorian manliness (Bederman 1995b).

To provide a concrete historical illustration of how the discourse of civilization reiterated the racial power of manliness, Gail Bederman (1995a,b) narrates the tale of Chicago's 1893 Columbian Exposition. The international exposition, as John Willinksy (1998) points out, made a spectacle of the world, rendering it into a lesson on the triumph of advanced "scientific" civilizations, and in particular the wealth of educational and consumer resources appropriated from colonial empires. These were massively attended public events which, Willinsky (1998, 77) suggests, "represented the educational formation" of what Guy Debord describes as "the society of the spectacle," in which "the spectacle is the existing order's uninterrupted discourse about itself, its laudatory monologue" (1977, 24; quoted in Willinsky 1998, 77).

True to form, then, in authorizing the 1893 Exposition, Congress had called for nothing less than "an exhibition of the progress of civilization in the New World" (quoted in Bederman 1995a, 31). Millennial fantasies were embedded in the exposition's rationale, Bederman (1995a) observes. In fact, the exposition would do nothing less than demonstrate American civilization's remarkable progress toward human perfection. In order to exhibit "the progress of civilization," the organizers built a masculinized and racialized idea of civilization; they divided the world's fair into two areas. The section denoting civilization, known as "The White City" (due presumably to the white walls of its buildings, but its racial connotation was lost on no one) celebrated sophisticated, "masculine" technology (Bederman 1995b). For African Americans it was "literally and figuratively a white city" which symbolized "not the material progress of America, but a moral regression—the reconciliation of the North and South at the expense of Negroes." Many black visitors renamed the fair "the great American white elephant" and "the white American's World's Fair" (quoted in Carby 1987, 5).

The focal point of "The White City" was the majestic "Court of Honor," a formal basin stretching a half-mile long, surrounded by huge white *beaux arts* buildings. "Honorable," according to an 1890 dictionary, was a synonym for "manly," and visitors to this world's fair would not have missed the Court's association with manhood (Rydell 1984; Trachtenberg 1982). The Centennial Exhibition that had been held in Philadelphia in 1876 had featured pavilions organized into what were, in effect, racial zones (Willinsky 1998). The 1893 exhibition would blend this racialized symbolism with gender.

The seven huge buildings framing the Court of Honor represented seven aspects of the greatest advancements in human civilization: manufactures, mines, agriculture, art, administration, machinery, and electricity. Each was presented as the domain of civilized white men. In these buildings were exhibited thousands of enormous engines, warships, trains, machines, and armaments. The White City glorified middle-class men's familiar world of commerce, displaying the most advanced products and the most sophisticated manufacturing processes: "dynamos and rock drills, looms and wallpaper." All were housed in magnificent white temples. By celebrating "civilization," the White City celebrated the power, indeed the perfection, of Victorian manhood in America. In the April 26, 1893, edition of the *Chicago Daily Inter-Ocean*, poets hailed it as "A Vision of Strong Manhood and Perfection of Society" (quoted in Bederman 1995b, 411).

Women's place in the "advancement of civilization" was, predictably, more modest, represented in the White City by the smaller, much less formidable Woman's Building. In 1889, over one hundred prominent women including Susan B. Anthony and the wives of three Supreme Court justices had petitioned Congress to name women to the Exposition's governing commission. Congress refused, establishing instead a "Board of Lady Managers," a title many women found ridiculous. Moreover, Congress gave the Board practically no authority, yet through persistent efforts its members were able to make themselves an important part of the Exposition. Led by Bertha Palmer, the Board organized one of the most well-attended exhibits in the White City, the Woman's Building (Bederman 1995a).

Despite the feminist intentions of its lady managers, visitors said they were most impressed by the Woman's Building's softness, in sharp contrast to the masculine dynamos and technological marvels of the rest of the White City. Commented the *New York Times*: "the achievements of man [are] in iron, steel, wood, and the baser and cruder products … [while] in the Woman's Building one can note … more refined avenues of effort which culminate in the home, the hospital, the church, and in personal adornment" (quoted in Bederman 1995b, 411–412). Its location communicated women's position in civilization; not only was the Woman's Building located at the very edge of the manly White City, it was placed just opposite the White City's only exit to the uncivilized Midway. As Bederman (1995b, 412) points out, the Woman's Building was placed between the "civilized" and the "savage" areas of the Exhibition, appropriate, in men's minds, to a "species" less civilized than white men but, admittedly, not as primitive as blacks. This placement of the Woman's Building, Bederman emphasizes, underlined the "manliness" of white male civilization.

In contrast to both the White City and the Woman's Building was the Midway, the Exposition's uncivilized section. Here were displayed spectacles of barbarism: "authentic" villages of Samoans, Egyptians, Dahomans, Turks, and other exotic races. World's Fair guidebooks advised visitors to visit the Midway only after visiting the White City, in order to fully appreciate the differences between the civilized White City and uncivilized native villages. Whereas the White City spread out in all directions from the Court of Honor, underlining the complexity and expansiveness of manly civilization, the Midway's attractions appeared linearly down a broad avenue, teaching a lesson in racial hierarchy. Visitors who visited the Midway from the White City would first pass the German and Irish villages, then proceed past the barbarous Turkish, Arabic, and Chinese villages, and finish this trip backward from civilization by viewing the savage American Indians and Dahomans (Bederman 1995b). "What an opportunity was here afforded to the scientific mind to descend the spiral of evolution," praised the *Chicago Tribune*, "tracing humanity in its highest phases down almost to its animalistic origins" (quoted in Bederman 1995b, 413).

The White City made inescapably clear the manliness of white civilization; the Midway's villages communicated the conspicuous absence of manliness among uncivilized, savage, nonwhite races. In the Persian, Algerian, Turkish, and Egyptian villages, Bederman tells us, dark-skinned men cajoled visitors to suspend manly restraint in order to savor their countrywomen's sensuous dancing. European-American male audiences who stared at scantily clad belly dancers had it both ways, Bederman (1995b, 413) explains, "simultaneously relishing the dances' suggestiveness and basking in their own sense of civilized superiority to the swarthy men hawking tickets outside, unashamedly vending their countrywoman's charms. Those who had just visited the White City would be especially conscious of their own racially superior manliness."

Least civilized, that is to say, least "manly" of all the Midway's denizens, according to many commentators, were the savage Dahomans from Africa. These creatures appeared to their "sophisticated" North American visitors to lack gender differences entirely. The *New York Times* commented: "The

Dahomey gentleman (or perhaps it is a Dahomey lady, for the distinction is not obvious), who may be seen at almost any hour ... clad mainly in a brief grass skirt and capering numbly to the lascivious pleasings of an unseen tom-tom pounded within. ... There are several dozen of them of assorted sexes, as one gradually makes out" (quoted in Bederman 1995b, 413). The columnist ridiculed African-American spectators if they dared imagine themselves more civilized than the Dahomans. As Bederman points out, the Columbian Exposition demonstrated, in a variety of ways, that "nonwhite" and "uncivilized" were "unmanly" and, conversely, that whiteness and civilization were indistinguishable from powerful white manhood.

The gendered and racialized binary of "civilization" and "savagery" was exhibited in the basic division of the Columbian Exposition between the civilized White City and Woman's Building and uncivilized Midway. The contrast would be sharp and unmistakable only if the darkest races were always represented as shockingly savage. The presence of sophisticated black people would blur the distinction and ruin the show; therefore, organizers rebuffed those African Americans who lobbied to gain representation on the White City's organizing bodies. The Exposition's logic of constructing manly white civilization in opposition to savage swarthy barbarism made it impossible for the white organizers to permit the presence of fully civilized African Americans. Despite long and animated objection to their exclusion, there were no African Americans included in the 1893 World's Fair in Chicago (Bederman 1995b).

Women had been invited to participate in the planning of the women's building at the Fair, mostly white women, including southern white women such as Rebecca Latimer Felton. On May 20, 1893, black novelist Frances Ellen Watkins Harper addressed the World's Congress of Representative Women who had assembled as part of the Exposition. Harper encouraged her audience to see themselves standing "on the threshold of woman's era" and asked them to be prepared to received the "responsibility of political power" (quoted in Carby 1987, 3). She challenged her listeners to change a society that permitted "brutal and cowardly men" to "torture, burn and lynch their [defenseless] fellow-men." Moreover, she condemned legislators "born to an inheritance of privileges, who have behind them ages of education, dominion, civilization, and Christianity" but who blocked passage of a national education bill that would grant education "to the children of those who were born under the shadow of institutions which made it a crime to read." Women, Harper declared, should not confine themselves to domestic sphere but should enter the "political estate" (quoted in Carby 1987, 69).

Harper was the last of six black women to address the delegates; on the previous two days Fannie Barrier Williams, Anna Julia Cooper, Fannie Jackson Coppin, Sarah J. Early, and Hallie Quinn Brown had represented black women at this international but overwhelmingly white women's forum. Fannie Jackson Coppin asked that the conference not be "indifferent to the history of the colored women of America," for their fight "could only aid all women in their struggle against oppression" (quoted in Carby 1987, 4). Sarah J. Early and Hallie Quinn Brown gave accounts of the organizations that black women had established (Carby 1987).

Fannie Barrier Williams had been chosen, Charles Lemert and Esmè Bhan (1998) suggest, because she was northern, light-skinned, and affluent. While she gave a temperate speech, it proved controversial for its strong insistence on the unique moral and intellectual importance of black women in American life. Williams spoke of the women "for whom real ability, virtue, and special talents count for nothing when they become applicants for respectable employment" and suggested that black women were increasingly "a part of the social forces that must help to determine the questions that so concern women generally" (quoted in Carby 1987, 3).

Anna Julia Cooper's statement expresses several of the black feminist themes evident in her *Voice from the South*, published the year before the fair. It is striking, however, because the opening lines referred to "the darkest period of the colored women's oppression in this country" (quoted in Lemert and Bhan 1998, 201). Cooper makes clear her commitment to the poorest, most oppressed women:

> I speak for the colored women of the South, because it is there that the millions of blacks in this country have watered the soil with blood and tears, and it is there too that the colored woman of America has made her characteristic history, and there her destiny is evolving. Since emancipation the movement has been at times confused and stormy, so that we could not always tell whether we were going forward or groping in a circle. We hardly knew what we ought to emphasize, whether education or wealth, or civil freedom and recognition. We were utterly destitute. (Cooper, in Lemert and Bhan 1998, 202)

Black women's struggles for sexual autonomy was, as Cooper knew, "a struggle against fearful and overwhelming odds, that often ended in a horrible death." In contrast were white women who "could at least plead for their own emancipation," but the black women of the South would have to "suffer and struggle and be silent." Cooper appealed to the "solidarity of humanity, the oneness of life, and the unnaturalness and injustice of all special favoritisms, whether of sex, race, country, or condition" (quoted in Carby 1987, 3).

Despite the presence of black women, the Columbian Exposition was no occasion for women in general and black women in particular to exert a political influence. In fact, for black women the preparations for the World's Congress had been a distressing experience, and the World's Congress itself proved to be, as Hazel Carby (1987, 4) writes, "a significant moment in the history of the uneasy relations between organized black and white women." Since Emancipation, Carby points out, black women had been engaged within the African-American community in the formation of mutual-aid societies, benevolent associations, local literary societies, and the many organizations of the various black churches. But, Carby continues, black women had also looked toward the nationally organized suffrage and temperance movements, dominated by white women such as Frances Willard, to provide opportunities for the expression of their gendered concerns as women and as feminists. Their white sisters would disappoint them, rebuffing black women's efforts to form interracial associations. In that, the Chicago World's Congress had been no exception. While Harper, Williams. Cooper, Coppin, Early, and Brown were on the women's platform, Ida B. Wells was segregated in the Haitian pavilion with Frederick Douglass, protesting the virtual exclusion of African Americans from the Exposition by circulating the pamphlet she had edited, *The Reason Why the Colored American Is Not in the World's Columbian Exposition* (Carby 1987). Douglass called the Exposition "a whited sepulcher" (quoted in Carby 1987, 5).

The struggle for black representation had been carried to the White House in an effort to persuade Benjamin Harrison to appoint a black member to the National Board of Commissioners for the Exposition. The president's refusal meant that the black community's only hope was the Board of Lady Managers, appointed to be "the channel of communication through which all women may be brought into relation with the exposition, and through which all applications for space for the use of women or their exhibits in the buildings shall be made" (quoted in Carby 1987, 4). Two organizations of black women were formed, the Woman's Columbian Association and the Women's Columbian Auxiliary Association, and both petitioned the Board of Lady Managers to establish opportunities for black representation at the Columbian Exposition (Carby 1987).

While sympathetic sentiments were expressed by a few members of the board, no appointment to the board was made, and in fact several white members of the board threatened to resign rather than serve with a black representative. In fact, most board members were skeptical that black women would be capable of intelligent and organized critique of their committee; they felt certain that a white woman must be behind such "articulate and sustained protests" (quoted in Carby 1987, 5). That six black women eventually addressed the World's Congress was not, as Carby (1987, 5) puts it, "the result of a practice of sisterhood or evidence of a concern to provide a black political presence but part of a discourse of exoticism that pervaded the fair." African Americans would be represented in the Exposition alright, but as part of exhibits with other ethnic groups which underlined mainstream white racist fantasies (Carby 1987).

Ida B. Wells had been outraged by the racist exclusion of African-American citizens from the Fair, an outrage perhaps intensified by her exclusion from the women's planning committee. Attuned to the racial and gender fantasies animating white racism, in her counterattack Wells focused on the main point, namely the Exposition's celebrations of manly white American "civilization." Along with Frederick Douglass, she called for African Americans to fund a pamphlet to be printed in English, German, and Spanish which would explain to the rest of the civilized world why the less-than-civilized Exposition organizers had excluded civilized African-American citizens. Warning organizers that "[t]he absence of colored citizens from participating therein will be construed to their disadvantage by the representatives of the civilized world there assembled," Wells promised that her pamphlet would document "the past and present condition of our people and their relation to American civilization" (quoted in Bederman 1995b, 413). Wells and Douglass's letter was reprinted on page four of the March 25, 1893, edition of *Indianapolis Freeman*, in an article entitled "No 'Nigger Day,' No 'Nigger Pamphlet'!" The *Freeman*'s editor had long been an opponent of Wells; now he accused her of washing American dirty laundry in public, in front of foreign guests, and in so doing embarrassing the entire nation. Wells and Douglass were unable to raise sufficient funds to print full translations into four languages. Only the introduction was translated, and that only into French and German (Bederman 1995b).

In *The Reason Why the Colored American Is Not in the World's Columbian Exposition*, Wells inverted the white organizers' positioning of white manly civilization as the exact opposite of black savagery. Wells argued that the most impressive documentation of America's "moral grandeur" and sophisticated civilization would have been in the exhibition of the phenomenal progress African Americans had made in only twenty-five years after their emancipation from slavery. For centuries, Africans in America had "contributed a large share to American prosperity and civilization" (Wells and Douglass 1893, 3; quoted in Bederman 1995b, 413; in Duster 1970, xx). Moreover, she continued, "the labor of one-half of this country has always been, and is still being done by them. The first credit this country had in its commerce with foreign nations was created by productions resulting from their labor. The wealth created by their industry has afforded to white people of this country the leisure essential to their great progress in education, art, science, industry and invention" (Wells and Douglass 1893, 3; quoted in Duster 1970, xx). Why, then, she demanded to know, was the African American so conspicuously absent from the Columbian Exposition? (Bederman 1995b).

The pamphlet's answer, left implicit so as to defuse a possible confrontation, was that the European American was not the manly and civilized creature he pretended to be. Wells's co-author Frederick Douglass made this point, lamenting how unfortunate it was to be forced to speak frankly of the wrongs and outrages endured "in flagrant contradiction to boasted American Republican liberty and civilization." Indeed, far from embodying a sophisticated civilization, European Americans were guilty of both "barbarism and race hatred." Yet the African American was "manfully resisting" this oppression, and "is now by industry, economy and education wisely raising himself to conditions of civilization and comparative well being." Douglass concluded by reminding his readers that black men were manly: "We are men and our aim is perfect manhood, to be men among men. Our situation demands faith in ourselves, faith in the power of truth, faith in work and faith in the influence of manly character" (quoted in Bederman 1995b, 413).

The remainder of the pamphlet supported Douglass's argument for black manhood. Since Emancipation, African Americans had demonstrated their manly character by making phenomenal strides in education, literature, and the professions. From absolute poverty there were a number who had even succeeded in accumulating wealth. Despite this rapid progress, European Americans continued, perversely, to assault youthful black manliness. Through oppressive legislation, disfranchisement, the convict lease system, and, most horrible of all, through lynching, white men conducted war against black men, women, and children. Finally, the pamphlet pointed out the Exposition organizers' deliberate exclusion of African Americans, except, Douglass complained, "as if to shame the Negro, the Dahomians [sic] are also here to exhibit the Negro as a repulsive savage" (quoted in Bederman 1995b, 414).

What was clear to any sympathetic reader of the Douglass/Wells text was that the exclusion of African Americans from the Columbian Exposition demonstrated European-American barbarism, not civilization (Bederman 1995b).

Wells and Douglass set up headquarters in the White City's small Haitian Building; from there they distributed 10,000 copies of *The Reason Why* during the duration of the Fair. President Benjamin Harrison had appointed Frederick Douglass minister to Haiti in September 1889, a capacity in which he served until July 1891. Douglass "had so won the confidence of this little black republic that it in turn gave him the honor of being in charge of their exhibit. Had it not been for this, Negroes of the United States would have had no part nor lot in any official way in the World's Fair. For the United States government had refused her Negro citizens participation therein" (Wells 1970, 116). Wells heard from readers from England, Germany, France, Russia, and India. Yet Wells's greatest accomplishment in undermining the claims of "manly civilization" and thereby fighting white racism occurred not during her World's Fair protest, but in her 1892–1894 campaigns against lynching in Britain (Bederman 1995b).

II. Ida B. Wells's Crusade for Justice

> *[I]t is not the white woman who is dear to the racist. It is not even the black woman toward whom his real sexual rage is directed. It is the black* man *who is* sacred *to the racist. And this is why he must castrate him.*
>
> —Calvin C. Hernton, *Sex and Racism in America* (1965/1988)

> *Honed in the agony of this slave experience and its aftermath, black women perceived very clearly the connection between the racist imagery of the black woman as whore, and the black man as rapist. Therefore, they placed themselves in the forefront of the struggle against lynching.*
>
> —Bettina Aptheker, Introduction to Addams and Wells, *Lynching and Rape: An Exchange of Views* (1977)

In 1892, as we have seen, Wells had been forced into northern exile by her editorial against lynching, printed in her soon-to-be-destroyed *Memphis Free Speech.* Only thirty, she was already an experienced journalist, teacher, and activist. As a young black single woman in Memphis, Wells had declined to accept conventional views of a woman's destiny, that is, to marry and have children. She would later have four children after marrying Chicago attorney Ferdinand L. Barnett, and she would then suffer criticism by others—most prominently Susan B. Anthony—for abandoning public for private life. For her ambition and independence the young Wells had paid a high price: isolation, criticism, and calumny. Wounded men and jealous women accused her of being "a silly flirt and a heartless coquette" (DeCosta-Willis 1995a, 10) who toyed with men's affections. She became the subject of vicious rumors, among them that, as a girl of sixteen, she had been sexually involved with a white man in

Mississippi, that she and a male teacher were fired for "immoral conduct," and that her sister Lily was in fact her daughter (DeCosta-Willis 1995a). Wells was often hurt but undeterred. Since March 1892, she had spearheaded black Memphis's protest against the lynchings of three respected local businessmen, one of whom had been her close personal friend. It had been white Memphis's violent response to her editorial that had driven Wells into exile; whites had threatened her with mutilation and hanging; her presses had been seized and sold. White men watched her home and the Memphis train station, determined to kill her on sight (Bederman 1995b).

Exiled in the North, Wells devised new tactics appropriate for her new circumstances. While she continued to urge African Americans to boycott, vote, and agitate against white injustice, she knew these tactics by themselves would not stop lynching. Somehow white people, especially northerners, must be persuaded to intervene in white barbarism. She decided, she later recalled, to focus her efforts on "the white press, since it was the medium through which I hoped to reach the white people of the country, who alone could mold public sentiment" (quoted in Bederman 1995b, 414). Yet white newspapers declined to hire African-American writers. To gain a hearing in the white press, Wells realized that she must devise new arguments. Accordingly, Wells began to reflect upon the white middle-class's conflation of manly authority and white racial dominance (Bederman 1995b).

One month after arriving in the North, the *New York Age*, a major black newspaper, published Wells's attack on lynching in the South. It would be reprinted as *Southern Horrors*. As we saw in the previous chapter, in *Southern Horrors* Wells described dozens of lynchings, each incident so horrifying and appalling that any open-minded reader had to conclude that lynching had be stopped immediately. But white people were not open-minded; they tended to shrug off tales of tortured black men as exaggerated or as a necessary deterrent to black crime. Appalled and frustrated but determined, Wells chose to invoke an issue that she knew white men could not so easily shrug off: their anxiety concerning the decline, the "crisis," of white manliness (Bederman 1995b).

Wells was clear that the rationalization for lynching—interracial heterosexual rape—was only that. She began to suspect that inherent in the rationale was a compensatory effort to shore up Victorian manliness. Like the White City in the Columbian Exposition, which had set up black men as unmanly and barbaric so that white men could pose as powerful, manly civilization, the lynching scenario positioned black men as unmanly (i.e., uncontrolled) rapists. White men who lynched could then be said to embody manly self-restraint and defenders of the pure southern white lady. As Jacquelyn Dowd Hall (1979, 148) observed, by constructing black men as "natural" rapists and by resolutely and bravely avenging the (alleged) rape of pure white women, southern white men presented themselves as ideal men: "patriarch, avengers, righteous protectors."

Not only southern white men exploited this false logic. Northern white men were susceptible too, because, Bederman (1995b) suggests, the fantasy of savage black men raping vulnerable and pure white women provided an opportunity to demonstrate the potency of traditional manliness. In this "logic," upright character and sturdy manliness were embodied by the white lynch mobs whose job it was to restrain uncontrolled, that is, unmanly, sexual passion, played by the figure of barbaric black rapist. These fantasies were reported in the northern press whenever stories of southern lynchings were printed. The *Providence Journal*, for instance, in reporting a Louisiana lynching in 1893, praised the "manly restraint" of the white male lynchers: "Three Negroes were lynched in a quiet, determined manner by a mob of white men on Friday night. ... The lynching was one of the coolest that has taken place in this section." Reporting the Memphis lynching of Wells's friends, the *New York Times* pointed out what it praised the "quick and quiet" manner in which the white men had acted. In contrast to their stern, steady and righteous actions were the "shivering negroes" whom they brought to "justice" (quoted in Bederman 1995b, 415). Consistent with the conflation of race and gender, the black male victims were depicted as weak and unmanly, while the white male lynchers embodied the strength of manly self-control (Bederman 1995b)

In *Southern Horrors*, Wells attacked lynching by simple but dramatic inversion. Where whites had depicted black men as unmanly passion incarnate, Wells declared they were the opposite: manliness personified. Those black men who had been lynched for "rape" were innocent victims, often paying with their lives for having been seduced into consensual sexual relations with rapacious white women. In Wells's words these innocent victims were "poor blind Afro-American Samsons who suffer themselves to be betrayed by white Delilahs" (quoted in Bederman 1995b, 415). White men and women (as we will see in the case of Frances Willard) were shocked, then enraged.

Like the biblical Samson, Wells argued, these innocent men had been manly towers of strength until they were trapped, then destroyed, by wicked white women. After using them sexually, these white Delilahs falsely cried "rape" in order to protect their reputations. The truth was, Wells asserted, that it was these white women, not their black male victims, who were the real criminals of lust and carnality. To document her claim, Wells named several white women who willingly had pursued sexual relationships with black men. Only upon the public discovery of these interracial love affairs were they then recoded as "rapes." Several of these women worked as prostitutes; Wells (1892a/1969, 8) had commented with disgust: "'The leading citizens' of Memphis are fending the 'honor' of all white women, *demi-monde* included."

In contrast, then, to white characterizations of white male lynchers as disciplined, manly, and restrained, Wells depicted them as vile, unmanly cowards, disguising their own licentiousness with sanctimonious calls for chastity. They rationalized their savage murders by invoking the honor of white ladies, ladies who were, in some cases, prostitutes. In contrast to whites' characterization of lynchers as righteous defenders of the Christian faith and civilization, Wells argued that it was white southern men, especially those who lynched black men, who were compelled to rape and sexually assault—as long as the victims were black (Bederman 1995b). Far from suppressing lust, "the white man" wallowed in it. Miscegenation laws, Wells (1892a/1969, 6) declared, "only operate against the legitimate union of the races: they leave the white man free to seduce all the colored girls he can," knowing he need neither marry nor support the victims of his sexual aggression.

Southern white men, Wells continued, were "not so desirous of punishing rapists as they pretend." If they were truly committed to protecting women from rape, they would not so readily ignore or forgive the countless white men who raped black women. Here too Wells named names and gave dates, overwhelming her readers with numerous cases of black women and little girls brutally raped by white men, with no effort from their white neighbors to intervene or punish the offenders afterward. Yet these upstanding white citizens of the South—rapists and accessories to rape—mutilated and murdered black men, the vast majority of whom had not even slept with white women. They, she asked, should proclaim themselves defenders of chastity? As Bederman (1995b, 416) tells us, Wells had in mind a different set of descriptors for white men: "Hypocrisy, licentiousness, and unrestrained passion—sexual lust and blood lust—characterized southern white men, as Wells depicted them. Thus, in her account, the southern lynch mob did not embody white manliness *restraining* black lust—it embodied white men's lust running amok, *destroying* true black manliness."

Wells also went after the illusion that lynching demonstrated the potency of white manliness. The only way northern men could demonstrate their manliness would be by stopping lynching. This argumentative strategy, Bederman (1995b) explains, echoed old antislavery debates: just as abolitionists had warned that the slave trade would spread North and undermine free labor, so Wells now warned that southern men's unbridled lust would spread and corrupt northern men's manliness. In fact, she suggested, northern white men had already abrogated their manly duty to restrain vice by allowing white southern men to rape and lynch; such tolerance of vice had already rotted their manly character. Throughout the nation, Wells declared, "men who stand high in the esteem of the public for Christian character, for moral and physical courage, for devotion to the principles of equal and exact justice to all, and for great sagacity, stand as cowards who fear to open their mouths before this great outrage" (quoted in Bederman 1995b, 416).

This was, Bederman observes, not just rhetoric. By refuting the discourse that conflated whiteness and gender in civilization, Wells was refuting white male rationalizations for lynching. Moreover, she was formulating an alternative discourse of race and manhood. Heretofore the dominant discourse of "civilization" had positioned black men as unmanly savages, unable to control their passions through manly will. Accepting this conflation of whiteness, civilization and manhood, northern whites assumed that black men were in fact rapists and they therefore tolerated the southern tradition of lynching (Bederman 1995b). By inverting this logic, Wells, as Hazel Carby (1987) points out, also reformulated the prevailing ideologies of gender to produce an alternative discourse of womanhood. In so doing, Wells's antilynching arguments reformulated dominant discourses of manhood, too, implying connections among lynching, sexuality, and women's rights. The suppression of homosexuality supported both lynching and misogyny, the latter disguised by sentimentalization and idealization, the former not disguised at all.

But in 1892, few white people could appreciate this fact; Wells's pamphlet was by and large ignored. Still, a few scattered antilynching articles in white periodicals borrowed Wells's arguments. On September 24, 1892, Albion

Tourgée, whom Bederman describes as perhaps the most forthright antiracist white of the period, wrote in the *Chicago Daily Inter-Ocean*, "[W]ithin a year half a score of colored men have been lynched for the crime of having a white mistress, while it does not seem to be thought necessary to hang or burn the white woman, nor is the white man who keeps a colored mistress in any danger of violence at the hands of his fellow citizens" (quoted in Bederman 1995b, 417). George C. Rowe (1894), the sole black contributor to an 1894 symposium on lynching in the *Independent*, argued likewise. But Wells was able to publish only in the black press, which few whites read. Despite the rhetorical power and importance of *Southern Horrors*, Wells's strategy to persuade white northerners remained frustrated by segregation (Bederman 1995b).

Even after a year of writing and speaking in the North, Wells remained unable to find journalistic work in the white world. She still had no access to the white press, no way to reach northern white readers. When invited to tour England, Wells eagerly accepted, understanding at once that while the white American press could ignore her, they might not so easily ignore an indignant British public. Although her first tour—in 1893—received almost no American press coverage, it laid the foundation for her 1894 tour. That tour received all the publicity she could have wanted. "When Wells returned," Bederman (1995b, 417) tells us, "she had become notorious; and white Americans had discovered that, due to their tolerance and practice of lynching, the rest of the world's Anglo-Saxons doubted whether white Americans were either manly or civilized." How did Wells accomplish this remarkable turnaround?

Wells planned both campaigns around her reformulation of "civilization." She would demonstrate, by her performance, that is, her speeches, her writings, and her demeanor, that she represented a civilized race. Wells framed her mission as an appeal from one civilized people to another for protection from a violent and barbaric race gone mad. She did not hesitate to flatter her listeners and readers in Britain, appealing to their own highly cultivated sense of cultural superiority. Moreover, Americans, she said seductively, revered the British; whatever the British thought would be most influential in her former colonies. She told one British journalist that if Britain told white America "the roasting of men alive on unproved charges and by a furious mob was a disgrace to the civilization of the United States, then every criminal in America, white or black, would soon be assured of a trial under the proper form of law" (quoted in Bederman 1995b, 417). Wells was quite clear, Bederman (1995b) argues, that she was using her British audiences to convince European Americans that their tolerance of lynching left them perceived as unmanly savages in the eyes of the civilized world.

It was true, of course, and Wells was well aware, that many European Americans felt a pleasurable even prideful sense of kinship with the British. This identification was "racial" as well, especially in the late nineteenth century, when pseudoscientific theories of racial superiority were circulating widely. Presumably Anglo-Saxons were, on both sides of the Atlantic, the most manly and civilized of all races. Wells was determined to form an alliance with British reformers which would destroy this smug and imaginary racial solidarity. She played her cards with precision, telling, for instance, an audience in Birmingham (England):

> America cannot and will not ignore the voice of a nation that is her superior in civilization. ... I believe that the silent indifference with which [Great Britain] has received the intelligence that human beings are burned alive in a "Christian" country, and by "civilized" Anglo-Saxon communities is born of ignorance of the true situation; and that if she really knew she would make the protest long and loud. (quoted in Bederman 1995b, 417)

Of course, many British already knew or had suspected what Wells was telling them, namely that their former colonists were unmanly and uncivilized and very much in need of instruction from their civilized British superiors (Bederman 1995b). A black woman in Britain would persuade them that white men in America were, well, neither "white" nor "men."

III. The Antilynching Campaign in Britain

> *Much work remains to be done in uncovering how white women participated in debates about white supremacist violence, whether as literary figures or as social reformers.*
>
> Sandra Gunning, *Race, Rape, and Lynching: The Red Record of American Literature, 1890–1912* (1996)

> *[T]he debt of gratitude we owe to the English people for their splendid help in that [anti-lynching] movement.*
>
> —Ida B. Wells, *Crusade for Justice: The Autobiography of Ida B. Wells* (1970)

It was in Britain where the first organized public campaign against lynching took place. There and later in the United States, Ida B. Wells led a one-woman campaign against lynching. The last decade of the nineteenth century saw the savage practice at its zenith in the American South, but it was in Britain where publicly organized activity in support of African Americans surfaced. This antilynching work was undertaken and largely led by a few British women who felt keenly the injustice of lynching. In Britain it was a time of preoccupation over the Empire—by what right did Britain rule much of the world?—but these women, who came from different political and social backgrounds, came together in a moment in solidarity with black people across the Atlantic. While the impetus for their labor was the horror they felt when reading and hearing about lynching, Vron Ware (1992) tells us "it was their understanding of the role of white women in justifying the practice that made their involvement so important" (172–173). If white women were imaginary to white men, it would take concerted and aggressive action to make them real. Perhaps if women were real to white men, perhaps black men would become so as well.

In 1894 an Anti-Lynching Committee was formed in London, sponsored by prominent editors, politicians and public figures. Its aim, reported the *Times* for August 1, 1894, was "to obtain reliable information on the subject of lynching and mob outrages in America, to make the facts known, and to give expression to public opinion in condemnation of such outrages in whatever way might best seem calculated to assist the cause of humanity and civilization" (quoted in Ware 1992, 173). The "catalyst for this group," Ware (1992, 173) tells us, was the "young African American journalist" named Ida B. Wells. In 1893 and again the following year Wells traveled about Britain for several months, working to draw attention to the fact that African Americans were being systematically denied the justice and equality guaranteed them in the U.S. Constitution (Ware 1992). There remain fragments from Wells's diary from this time. In her entry for her first day of sailing across the Atlantic we can see that the former Memphis schoolteacher is calm and clear: "First Day Wednesday, April 5, 1893. Sailed for England today. First voyage across the ocean. Day is fine and trip so far enjoyable. Have four traveling companions bound for Africa" (in Decosta-Willis 1995b, 162).

Ida B. Wells was by no means the first black person to visit Britain on behalf of American racial politics. From the 1830s on, an increasing number of African Americans had gone to Britain, first to campaign against slavery and later to raise money for various post-Reconstruction projects. Personal and organizational networks developed, networks which remained in place following the Civil War. A number of friendships that had formed earlier were maintained by younger generations on both sides of the Atlantic. When Frederick Douglass made his last visit to Britain in 1886–1887, it was primarily to see friends rather than to make new political contacts. Still, he was often asked at social gatherings to make public comments regarding the situation of black people in America. At one of these meetings Douglass met Catherine Impey, later to become the primary leader of the antilynching campaign in the Britain. Impey and Douglass met again a few weeks later at the home of Helen Bright Clark, daughter of the radical MP John Bright; she had met Douglass as a child when he was befriended by her father. Catherine Impey describes her second meeting with Frederick Douglass in her diary: "During the evening ... Mr. Douglass gave us a luminous half hour's address on the present conditions of the colored population in America, speaking of the caste barriers that everywhere blocked their way, of the iniquitous truck system, their oppression, and their total inability to protect themselves without the ballot of which they had been deprived by cruel persecution and the fraudulent manipulation of the ballot box" (quoted in Ware 1992, 173–174).

Wells met Impey in Philadelphia. She records her memory of the meeting in her autobiography:

> In Philadelphia I was the guest of William Still, who wrote *The Underground Railroad*. My meeting was attended by many old "war horses." Miss Catherine Impey of Street, Somerset, England, was visiting Quaker relatives of hers in the city and at the same time trying to learn what she could about the color question in this country. She was editor of *Anti-Caste*, a magazine published in England on behalf of the natives of India, and she was therefore interested in the treatment of darker races everywhere.

> She was present at my meeting at the Quaker City and called on me at Mr. Still's home. She was shocked over the lynching stories I had told, also the indifference to conditions which she found among the white people in this country. She was especially hurt that this should be the fact among those of her own sect and kin. We deplored the situation and agreed that there seemed nothing to do but keep plugging away at the evils both of us were fighting.
>
> This interview was held in November 1892 and began what brought about the third great result of that wonderful testimonial in New York the previous month. Although we did not know it at the time, that interview between Miss Impey and myself resulted in an invitation to England and the beginning of a worldwide campaign against lynching. (Wells 1970, 82)

When in March 1894, Ida B. Wells sailed to England to teach about racial violence in the United States, she left a country where lynching was rarely mentioned in the white northern press and where she herself was unknown to most whites, North or South. In June 1894, she returned a celebrity, maligned by some as a "slanderous and nasty-minded mulatress" (*Times* 1894, 4), a "Negro adventuress" (*Memphis Daily Commercial*) by others (Wells 1970, 168), praised by few. As Gail Bederman (1995b) points out, as a result of Wells's campaign in Britain, lynching was no longer the topic that dare not speak its name. Indeed, during the three months she lectured the British on the horrors of "America's national crime" (Wells 1901/1977, 29), lynching became widely discussed as a stain on American civilization.

Wells's success in bringing lynching to the attention of the northern middle class was largely due, Bederman argues, to her shrewd manipulation of the northern middle class's sense that "manhood" was imperiled and in "crisis." By playing on European Americans' anxiety regarding changing patterns of gender, Wells was able to prompt northern middle-class whites to focus on lynching. Before Wells, northern whites had tolerated the practice as a colorful, if somewhat old-fashioned southern custom, illustrated in the *New York Time's* tasteless attempt at humor in 1891: "the friends of order [in Alabama] have been in pursuit of a negro. ... If they catch him they will lynch him, but this incident will not be likely to add to the prevailing excitement" given the more "serious" moonshining problem (quoted in Bederman 1995b, 407).

How did Wells succeed in changing the conversation about lynching? Historians have long acknowledged Wells's success in undermining the myth of the black rapist, but this is only part of the story. What Wells managed to do was to challenge taken-for-granted ideas of gender in the United States, ideas that conflated race, sex, and civilization. As the following line of indignant defensiveness from the August 19, 1894, *New York Times* indicates, Wells had, in Bederman's language, "brilliantly and subversively manipulated dominant middle-class ideas about race, manhood, and civilization in order to force white Americans to address lynching." The *Times* had complained: "All England's congenital meddlers and busybodies are forming societies for civilizing us, and express themselves about our social state in language which Samoan natives would resent" (quoted in Bederman 1995b, 407). Somehow Ida B. Wells had managed to convince heretofore indifferent whites that lynching imperiled American manhood and civilization (Bederman 1995b).

In April 1893, Wells disembarked at Liverpool. In her diary she wrote: "Ninth Day. Woke up this morning to find our ship standing in the middle of the Mersey River opposite Liverpool. Landed about 9:30 am. Went thru the customs office assisted by the baggage master of Bywater Taugery and Co., who directed us to Shaftsbury Hotel where I shall I stay with Miss Patton until she sails Saturday, then go to Miss Impey" (in Decosta-Willis 1995b, 163). After a brief visit to Somerset to recover from the voyage across the Atlantic, Catherine Impey, Isabella Fyvie Mayo (a Scot whose philanthropic interests moved her to welcome visitors from different parts of the world), and Wells settled in Mayo's house in Aberdeen so that the two could plan Wells's speaking engagements. Through Catherine Impey's journalistic contacts and her membership in the Society of Friends, and through Mayo's Scottish connections, meetings and publicity for them were quickly arranged. The two women accompanied Ida B. Wells on a demanding schedule of speeches. A new organization was established called the Society for the Recognition of the Universal Brotherhood of Man (SRUBM). The Society was:

> fundamentally opposed to the system of race separation by which the despised members of a community are cut off from the social, civil and religious life of their fellow man. It regards lynchings and other forms of brutal justice inflicted on the weaker communities of the world as having their root in race prejudice, which is directly fostered by the estrangement, and lack of sympathy consequent on race separation. (quoted in Ware 1992, 175)

Years afterward, Ida B. Wells would describe her trips to Britain in her autobiography, *Crusade for Justice.* She quoted from numerous press clippings, from interviews she had given, and made comments on the various places she had visited and the people she had met. At the time she was employed by the Chicago paper *Inter-Ocean*, making her the first African-American overseas columnist for any U.S. newspaper. In an interview with the *Sun*, a sympathetic American paper, Ida B. Wells described how her British listeners had responded to her lectures:

> Well, you know that the English people are very undemonstrative. At first everything I said was received in absolute silence, but I saw that their interest was intense. ... What I told them about the negro lynchings in the South was received with incredulity. It was news to them, and they could not believe that human beings were hanged, shot, and burned in broad daylight, the legal authorities sometimes looking on. ... They could not believe that these acts were done, not by savages, not by cannibals who at least would have the excuse of providing themselves with something to eat, but by people calling themselves Christian, civilized American citizens. (quoted in Ware 1992, 177)

Anticipating skepticism among her listeners, Ida B. Wells had come with extensive evidence to document that African Americans, primarily in the South, were being systematically murdered. All her clippings came from southern newspapers; no one could accuse her of fabricating the events. To avoid the charge that she was exaggerating the monstrosity of the practice, she had carefully recorded the details of each incident (Ware 1992).

Her audiences consisted "of all classes, from the highest to the lowest." She spoke in churches, social clubs, at political and social reform gatherings, and in drawing-rooms, as requested by "fashionable ladies." In sharp contrast to her experience at home, Wells was surprised to find that many white people in Britain, whatever their class background, were receptive and sympathetic. In the same interview in the *Sun*, Wells was asked if she had often faced racial prejudice in Britain. According to the report she replied "enthusiastically" that:

> No, it was like being born again in a new condition. Everywhere I was received on a perfect equality with the ladies who did so much for me and my cause. In fact, my color gave me some agreeable prominence which I might not otherwise have had. Fancy my feeling when in London I saw the Lady Mayoress taking a negro African Prince about at a garden party and evidently displaying him as the lion of the occasion. (quoted in Ware 1992, 177)

In her autobiography Ida B. Wells remembered the incident; she described her acquaintance with Ogontula Sapara, a young African medical student who volunteered to help with the campaign in 1894. On one occasion he visited her at her hotel in London, accompanied by six fellow students, also from Africa: "Such excitement you never saw, and several of the residents of the hotel said that they had never seen that many black people in their lives before" (Wells 1970, 214). Sapara reported that some of his patients had never seen a black man before and refused to let him touch them. Despite this experience, she reassured him that this was nothing compared to the hatred she had faced in America. Her enthusiasm, Ware reminds us, must be read as an index of the racism in the American South rather than the absence of it in Britain. There resident blacks were well aware of what Catherine Impey called "the dark spirit of Caste, which so often lurks hidden behind the scenes" (quoted in Ware 1992, 178).

The press reports of Wells's lectures and interviews during both visits to Britain testify to her remarkable success in winning audiences to her cause. We are told that she spoke quietly, a mode of self-presentation many British found impressive; she was able to provide anecdotal evidence as well as more abstract analyses of the failure of the American legal system to protect black citizens. On that point she had direct experience, as she had been, as we have seen, the first person to contest newly introduced legislation permitting segregation on the railways.

In many ways, Wells's audiences in Britain were more shocked than those in the American North by her descriptions of racism in the South. She did encounter resistance, even hostility, but these came from those who thought that the British had no right to criticize Americans, especially over what appeared to be a domestic matter of law and order. The *Times* of London took this position when it denounced the Anti-Lynching Committee, which had written to the governor of Alabama asking him to verify certain reports of lynching in that state. The *Times* had obtained a copy of the governor's reply which it printed to illustrate its point. The paper's editorial declared it had no sympathy whatsoever with lynching, but none with "anti-lynching" either, dismissing the committee as "large and well-known Dissenters" who were meddling in what was none of their business:

> Nor do we suppose that those who are responsible for the unfortunate letter have the least suspicion that it was likely to be represented as a piece of officious impertinence. Burning with sympathy for the much trampled on negro, they betray no consciousness of the magnitude and delicacy of the problem in which they are intervening. We should not be surprised if the Anti-Lynching Committee's well-meant letter multiplied the number of negroes who are hanged, shot, and burnt by paraffin, not only in Alabama, but throughout the southern nation. This would be a bitter stroke of irony. But it is the fate which frequently attends a fanatical anxiety to impose our own canons of civilization upon people differently circumstanced. (quoted in Ware 1992, 183)

In an attempt to be humorous, Ware (1992) informs us, the editorial paid almost as much attention to the grammar as it did to the content of the letters, suggesting that the Committee's secretary, Florence Balgarnie, had placed herself in danger of being "lynched by a mob of enraged grammarians." It was much more interested in the governor's reply than in the humanitarian concerns which prompted writing him in the first place. Then, after asserting that this was not the occasion to discuss lynching itself, the *Times* went on to express the same white male fantasies that European-American men used to rationalize their sexual mutilation of black men's bodies. While condemning it as a form of race hatred (since it was primarily blacks who were being lynched), the *Times* declared: "[a]lthough the negro, it must be acknowledged, does something to justify such differential treatment by the frequency and atrocity of his outrages on white women. That is a circumstance which ought to weigh with Miss Balgarnie and the numerous ladies upon the Anti-Lynching Committee" (quoted in Ware 1992, 182).

This was, of course, a matter of misinformation, but misinformation that seemed plausible to the white men in London who, after all, had their own fantasies regarding men of color (Stoler 1995). The Anti-Lynching Committee would not have been at all surprised by this reaction from the *Times*, although they would have ascribed the point of view not to white male fantasies but to the fact that the newspaper represented the most conservative sections of the ruling class. There was another matter at work as well. As Ware (1992) points out, even the facetious tone and arrogant racism of the editorial did not hide the fact that it was hypocritical for British citizens to criticize other countries for their racism when comparable atrocities were not only being carried out in the name of the Empire elsewhere, but on the beautiful isle itself.

Decades before, proslavery agitators had tried to justify the practice to British abolitionists by pointing out that conditions in Britain's growing industrial centers were worse than those on most slave plantations. Now southerners intent on defending their racism pointed to the treatment of many of Britain's colonial subjects. The savage repression of the 1857 uprising in India was a case in point, but there were others. British criticism of the American "race problem" seemed to many Americans to be nothing more than a self-righteous, diversionary extension of Britain's earlier condemnation of slavery in the decades before the Civil War. Many resented both the interference and the tone of moral superiority that accompanied it. In Britain it was easier to express outrage at the way European Americans behaved toward African Americans than it was to challenge those forms of racism that existed within the kingdom and throughout the Empire (Ware 1992).

The simple, ugly fact of free-floating racism was at work as well. As far as the *Times* was concerned, those who defended blacks in America might as well be defending all blacks, whether in the Caribbean, India or Africa. By the late nineteenth century, scientific theories of racism had "proven" that all those with darker skin were biologically different from and inferior to whites. Rebellions in the Caribbean and in India had made these theories plausible to those who believed the British were entitled to their Empire, which at this point existed throughout Africa, Australia, and the Indian subcontinent. Those who actively supported organizations like the Anti-Lynching Committee or the Society for the Recognition of the Universal Brotherhood of Man suffered the epithet "nigger philanthropists" (quoted in Ware 1992, 184), a curious combination spit at them by those who believed science (if not religion) ordained white supremacy. The antilynching campaign launched by Ida B. Wells rallied individuals—many of them women or, as the *Times* editorial condescendingly put it, "numerous ladies"—who came from different class backgrounds and who were increasingly prepared to see the connections between racism at home and abroad. As well, they felt more able to accept what they took to be their own responsibility to challenge it. At the center of this group was the journal *Anti-Caste* and its editor, Catherine Impey (Ware 1992).

Wells's newspaper columns from abroad, published in the white *Chicago Daily Inter-Ocean*, faithfully reported the massive and sympathetic support she received from the most prominent, civilized British dignitaries. Wells carefully detailed both dinners given in her honor by prominent members of Parliament and smaller more intimate gatherings organized by titled aristocrats. Always she made sure her American readers knew how shocked and horrified the British were by accounts of lynching in the United States. Sometimes she shrewdly mentioned the presence at these events of loutish white Americans whose absence of civility further convinced an already persuaded British public of (white) American barbarism. For example, Wells reported that a "swell reception" had been given for her at Princess Christian's Writer's Club, but that "[t]he ubiquitous and (so far as I am concerned) almost invariably rude American was on evidence there. In a strident voice she pronounced my statements false. I found she had never been in the South and was a victim of her own imagination. I heard an Englishwoman remark after the encounter was over that she had seen a side of Mrs.—'s character which she never knew before" (quoted in Bederman 1995b, 418). Carefully inverting the contrast between black and white Americans that whites imagined, Wells always conducted herself with restraint, dignity, and refinement. The strategy clearly worked; nearly all

Britons said she was "a true lady." By presenting herself and performing her mission as the personification of authentic civilization, Wells underlined the barbarism of whites in America (Bederman 1995b).

Always and everywhere Wells hammered away at the white myth of the black rapist. In the context of her reformulation of "civilization," the arguments from *Southern Horrors* were especially incisive. Since civilization, by definition, entailed pure womanliness and righteous manliness, Wells argued that European Americans' lasciviousness and barbarism proved them uncivilized. Barbarous white men mutilated innocent black men, sometimes for the "crime" of consensual relationships with white women, often for "no reason" at all. All the while these white barbarians were brutally and unapologetically raping black women. Lest her British listeners think she herself was a victim of her own imagination, Wells always cited statistics, quoted from the (white) Chicago *Tribune*, to prove that fewer than one-third of all lynching victims had even been *accused* of rape. Wanton white women who took black lovers then watched them dismembered and burned: such creatures were by definition uncivilized and barbaric. Unchastity, unbridled lust: thy name was, Wells declared, the American South: "Why should it be impossible to believe white women guilty of the same crime for which southern white men are notorious?" (quoted in Bederman 1995b, 418). It was easy for her British listeners, horrified by Wells's vivid descriptions, convinced by statistics, to now see their former colonists as depraved and despicable creatures. The sexual crimes of these barbarians had populated the South with mulattos; now their depraved white daughters were seducing, then betraying, their innocent black lovers (Bederman 1995b).

Most unmanly of all, however, were the white men who lynched black men. Wells argued quietly but passionately that by declining to try accused African Americans in a court of law, by subjecting black men to the most horrific of tortures and mutilations, lynch mobs and the (white) Americans who tolerated them showed themselves to be nothing more than savages and barbarians. Writing in the April 28, 1894, edition of the *London Daily Chronicle*, Wells pleaded: "Make your laws as terrible as you like against that class of crime [rape]; devise what tortures you choose; go back to the most barbarous methods of the most barbarous ages; and then my case is just as strong. Prove your man guilty, first; hang him, shoot him, pour coal oil over him and roast him, if you have concluded that civilization demands this; but be sure the man has committed the crime first" (quoted in Bederman 1995b, 418). Only a barbarian could conclude that "civilization demands" that an accused criminal be tortured, sometimes castrated, then burned alive, all without benefit of a trial (Bederman 1995b).

Uncivilized white men in America were, Wells insisted, entirely unmanly. They were not truly interested in the protection of womanhood; they were, the evidence was clear, eager to mutilate the black male body. The victims, Wells reminded, "were caged in their cells, helpless and defenseless; they were at the mercy of 'civilized' white Americans who, armed with shotguns, were there to maintain the majesty of American law." And these "brave and honorable white southerners ... lined themselves up in the most effective manner and poured volley after volley into the bodies of their helpless, pleading victims, who in their bolted prison cells could do nothing but suffer and die" (quoted in Bederman

1995b, 419). Manliness and civilization stood for the rule of law; they guaranteed the defense of the weak, including the protection of womanhood. Neither, Wells taught her British "students," existed in the American South (Bederman 1995b).

Wells's pedagogical tactics worked. The British press and reformers turned lynching into the season's *cause célèbre.* A *Westminister Gazette* writer confessed he could no longer "regard our American cousins as a civilized nation." *The Christian World* was certain that American lynch law "would disgrace a nation of cannibals." The *Birmingham* [England] *Daily Gazette* editorialized, "The American citizen in the South is at heart more a barbarian than the negro whom he regards as a savage. ... Lynch law is fiendishly resorted to as a sort of sport in every possible opportunity, and the negroes are butchered to make a Yankee holiday. ... Either they mistrust their legal institutions or they murder in wantonness and for mere lust of blood" (quoted in Bederman 1995b, 419). Murdering, mutilation, "wantonness," "lusting": it was clear, after hearing Ida B. Wells, that America had degenerated well past any pretense to manliness or civilization (Bederman 1995b).

Realizing that she was succeeding in convincing a large segment of the British public, Wells now called upon the moral forces of Britain to intervene. She asked those gathered to hear her to pass resolutions condemning lynching as uncivilized, resolutions which she would communicate to their former colonies that their tolerance of lynch law was lowering them in the eyes of civilized countries. Wells persuaded the national conventions of the major denominations—Baptists, Methodists, Quakers, Unitarians—to send resolutions back to their counterparts in the United States, resolutions which in no uncertain terms condemned lynching as uncivilized and demanded to know what their Christian brothers and sisters were doing to stop it. Individual churches and reform organizations also sent resolutions to American organizations, politicians, and publications, informing them that the entire civilized world (of which the United States was no longer a part) held all Americans—North and South—responsible for these, as the April 19, 1894, edition of *Christian World* phrased it, "barbarisms" (quoted in Bederman 1995b, 419).

Wells's triumph was nationwide. Liverpool's Unitarian Church wrote to the *Christian Register*, America's leading Unitarian periodical, expressing its "grief and horror" upon learning of "the barbarities of Lynch Law as carried out by white men on some of the coloured citizens of the United States." They demanded to know why American Unitarians did not intervene in such horrific practices of torture and brutality, practices which instilled into white American children the "lust of cruelty and callousness of murder." Shamed, the American Unitarians could nothing but agree that lynching made "the dark deed of the dark ages seem light in comparison" (quoted in Bederman 1995b, 419–420). In a belated protest, the magazine then sent letters of protest to three southern mayors and Governor Northen of Georgia (Bederman 1995b).

Wells shrewdly traded on the British sense of superiority over her former colonies to persuade British reformers that they themselves bore the responsibility of civilizing the United States. As Sir Edward Russell wrote in the *Liverpool Daily Post* (and as Wells quoted to her American readers), Americans were "horrifying the whole of the civilized world." They were very much in need of British uplift, for "when one reflects that [such things] still happen while we in this country are sending missions to the South Sea Islands and other places, they strike to our hearts much more forcibly, and we turn over in our minds whether it were not better to leave the heathen alone for a time and to send the gospel of common humanity across the Atlantic." Soon enough the British made plans to send such "missionaries" to that uncivilized region across the Atlantic known as the American South (quoted in Bederman 1995b, 420). By the time Wells concluded her educational tour, prominent British reformers were busy organizing antilynching societies and preparing to send representatives to the United States to investigate lynching firsthand. Such societies had been formed before to protest Turkish and other atrocities committed by "primitives" and "exotics," but never in the history of Great Britain had citizens been called upon to investigate the barbaric conduct of fellow Anglo-Saxons (Bederman 1995b).

As the volume of British indignation increased, Wells finally got her hearing in the white American press. No longer could she be ignored, not now that she had stirred up the British. After all, the British were fellow Anglo-Saxons, racial equals who understood, perhaps better than anyone, what civilization and manliness were. European-American men felt no choice but reply to their accusations (Bederman 1995b). Heads filled with fantasies of an Old South "gone with the wind," southern white men were especially unhappy with this turn of events. They were, in fact, beside themselves with rage.

The *Memphis Daily Commercial* tried to discredit Wells by libeling her character. Playing on long-standing racist fantasies in which black women were figured as licentious (thereby unwomanly and uncivilized), it accused Wells of being a "negro adventuress" with an unsavory past. When these stories reached Wells in England, she calmly turned them to her advantage. She not only demanded proof of these allegations ... she sued. Her rebuttal, reported in newspapers throughout Great Britain, observing that "so hardened is the [white] southern public mind that it does not object to the coarsest language and most obscene vulgarity in its leading journals so long as it is directed against a negro." Since the *Daily Commercial* was of course unable to deny the barbarism of the South's frequent lynchings, they were, she pointed out, reduced to smearing her character. British papers were as shocked as Wells wanted them to be. Scandalized by these examples of American journalism, the *Liverpool Daily Post* judged the articles as "very coarse in tone, and some of the language is such as could not possibly be reproduced in an English journal" (quoted in Bederman 1995b, 420). The British knew and reminded each other that it was neither manly nor civilized to libel a lady's character; the episode functioned only to reaffirm British opinions of American barbarism (Bederman 1995b).

Southerners were dumbfounded; they responded as if there had been a miscommunication. Southern newspapers reiterated that rape justified lynching and that it was of course "the negro" who was uncivilized. The *Atlanta Constitution* declared that British indignation was pointless and futile, since "the negroes themselves are the only people who can suppress the evil, and the way for them to get rid of it is to cease committing" rape (quoted in Bederman

1995b, 420). The New Orleans *Times-Democrat* pointed out that once Wells left Britain she would no longer be credible, for Americans "know well that the Negro is not a model of virtue and the white man a cruel, bloodthirsty tyrant, as the Wells woman pretends." A southern educator complained that "stigmatizing [southern men] as savages and barbarians" was simply unbelievable; everyone knew that the real problem lay with the Negro, who was "still a semi-savage far below the white man in the science and practice of civilization" (quoted in Bederman 1995b, 421). Imprisoned within their own fantasies, southerners sputtered, unable to defend themselves.

Northerners tended to be less defensive, as they were less traumatized. They tended to experience the event not as a psychotic break with reality but as simply another instance of British smugness and self-delusion. And so they accused the British of hypocrisy, pointing out firmly that British colonists had abused blacks at least as if not more brutally than white southerners had. In response to the British and Foreign Unitarian Association's condemnations, the Democratic *Philadelphia Daily Record* snorted: "John Bull looks at America with one eye and Africa with the other. His hands are bloody with recent African butcheries" (quoted in Bederman 1995b, 421). Of course this criticism was accurate—the British *had* behaved in barbaric fashion in Africa—but the Americans' motive had nothing to do with genuine concern for the Africans. Northerners were simply irritated at this latest instance of the meddlesome and "superior" British (Bederman 1995b).

Many southerners joined northern Democrats in complaining that lynching in America was none of Britain's business. On this point they found allies in Britain, as British conservatives had little sympathy for black people in America nor, for that matter, for their own social reformers. As mentioned, the *London Times* accused British antilynchers of having a "fanatical anxiety to impose our own canons of civilization upon people differently circumstanced." The *New York Times* lost little time in quoting the line, insisting that it represented the point of view of "a big majority of sensible Englishmen, who resent the meddlesome antics of a little and noisy minority." The New York paper approvingly reprinted the entire article. Emboldened, Georgia's Governor Northen—no radical racist as we have seen (indeed, even Wells acknowledged his opposition to lynching in *Southern Horrors* [see Wells 1892a/1969, 20])—expressed his conviction that Wells was funded by nothing less than a syndicate of British and American capitalists who were desperate to stop British immigration to the South (Bederman 1995b).

Wells herself responded in *A Red Record*, acknowledging that "criticism of the movement appealing to the English people for sympathy and support in our crusade against Lynch Law [asserted] that our action was unpatriotic, vindictive, and useless." Wells was not defensive: "It is not a part of the plan of this pamphlet to make any defense for that crusade nor to indict any apology for the motives which led to the presentation of the facts of American lynchings to the world at large. To those who are not willfully blind and unjustly critical, the record of more than a thousand lynchings in ten years is enough to justify any peaceable movement tending to ameliorate the conditions which led to this unprecedented slaughter of human beings" (Wells 1892b/1969, 71). Indeed:

> If Americans would not hear the cry of men, women and children whose dying groans ascended to heaven praying for relief, not only for them but for others who might soon be treated as they, then certainly no fair-minded person can charge disloyalty to those who make an appeal to the civilization of the world for such sympathy and help as it is possible to extend (Wells 1892b/1969, 71).

Nor were British antilynchers deterred by European-American indignation. In September 1894 the London Anti-Lynching Committee sent a small fact-finding delegation to the South. Governor O'Ferrall of Virginia complained, "Things have come to a pretty pass in this country when we are to have a lot of English moralists sticking their noses into our national affairs." Fourteen other governors, North and South, said much the same. Governor Northen accused the British of unmanly hypocrisy and directed the antilynching committee to return to England immediately, where they were needed to "prevent by law the inhuman sale of virtuous girls to lustful men in high places. Hang all such demons as 'Jack, the Ripper'; punish as it deserves the barbarous, wholesale slaughter of negroes in Africa by Englishmen who go there to steal their gold." Governor Turney of Tennessee agreed: "I think they had better purify their own morals before coming among a better people" (quoted in Bederman 1995b, 421).

Governor Turney's self-righteous indignation turned to embarrassment when just several days later six black men were lynched near Memphis. Uncharacteristically, he condemned the murders and even offered a reward of $5,000 for the lynchers' capture. The northern editors of the *Independent* observed: "It is very unfortunate ... that just after Miss Wells's charges had been loudly pronounced false other such atrocious cases should have occurred, as if to justify all that she had said" (quoted in Bederman 1995b, 421). In Memphis, where only two years earlier white leaders had destroyed Wells's presses and driven her north for protesting the lynchings of three black businessmen, Wells's British campaign saw success. Suddenly, Memphis's white leaders reversed themselves; now they piously proclaimed their disapproval of lynch law. The *Memphis Scimitar*—the same newspaper that two years earlier had called for Wells's lynching—now editorialized: "Every one of us is touched with blood-guiltiness in this matter, unless we prove ourselves ready to do our duty as civilized men and citizens who love their country and are jealous of its good name." White merchants now demonstrated their "civilized manliness" by meeting to protest lynchings; they even collected $1,000 for the murdered men's widows and orphans. Thirteen white men were indicted for the lynchings, although never convicted. The Memphis press never again condoned lynch law; no new lynchings occurred there until 1917 when Ell Persons was burned alive, his head severed and left on Beale Street (Tucker 1971; Bederman 1995b).

Not only some southerners were moved to oppose lynching as a result of Wells's British crusade. Now many white northerners objected to lynching more often and more aggressively. In Chicago, Brooklyn, and Santa Cruz, whites were reported as organizing antilynching societies, although these organizations played no discernable roles in ending the practice. While a few northern papers still defended lynching as necessary to deter black rapists, the majority appeared to agree with the *Cleveland Leader* that "[a]cts of barbarism have been committed in this country within the last twenty years by people claiming to be civilized which would scarcely have been credited to the cruelest and most bloodthirsty savages in Africa" (quoted in Bederman 1995b, 422).

Wells's British crusade, in Bederman's (1995b, 422) phrase, "had hit a nerve." With applause still ringing in their ears for the Columbian Exposition, European Americans were shocked to discover that prominent British reformers were describing them as unmanly barbarians. To their astonishment, their United States, surely the zenith of the civilized world, the epitome of evolutionary progress, was now the destination of "missionaries"! Now, finally, Ida B. Wells had the attention of the white American public. By sparking the indignation of British reformers, Wells had forced indifferent, defensive, racist whites to confront the fact of lynching. The *Indianapolis Freeman* was not alone in declaring that Wells's campaign had put an end to white complacency. "For the first time since the commencement of its long debauch of crime, the South has been jerked up to a sudden standstill; it is on the defensive. ... The North has at last realized that the so-called race problem is a matter that concerns not only the South, but the nation" (quoted in Bederman 1995b, 422). While she had not persuaded the majority of European Americans to actively oppose lynching, she had, by 1894, taught them that lynching was unacceptable (Bederman 1995b).

As real and important as Wells's success was, in the long run it was but a step. A large step, but still a step: after all, her British campaign did not stop the lynching. White men in the South continued to mutilate black men until the Civil Rights movement of the 1960s signaled a new era. The frequency of lynchings did decrease after 1892, although most historians credit factors other than Wells's own efforts. Overwhelmed by the vehemence of white Americans' complaints about the London committee's visit, the British antilynching committees canceled further fact-finding tours, limiting their efforts to outraged letter-writing campaigns. In the short term, southern lynchings continued, and Wells continued her struggle against them (Bederman 1995b).

While Wells's campaign had not stopped mob violence, her success in putting American whites on the defensive did, Bederman (1995b) argues, force long-lasting, if subtle, shifts in whites' characterization of lynch law. European Americans could not tolerate being called unmanly and uncivilized by the British. After 1894, most northern newspapers and periodicals stopped treating lynching as if it were a colorful southern folk custom. They dropped the jokes and now piously condemned lynching as "barbarous" (Bederman 1995b, 422–423), although they still pretended to be powerless to intervene. Now few doubted that lynching damaged the country in the eyes of the "civilized world." And Wells's statistics forced the northern press to acknowledge that most lynching victims had *not* been accused of rape, let alone had been found guilty of it. Still, the myth of the lust-driven black male rapist remained widespread. Southern states even began to pass antilynching legislation, legislation which, however, was almost never enforced. Did these small changes actually deter any prospective lynchers? Given the intensification of white racism during the 1890s, it is, as Bederman acknowledges, difficult to know how far-reaching the influence of these changes were. Still, as Bederman (1995b, 422) writes, "they must be seen as modest but definite victories."

To appreciate how shrewdly Ida B. Wells conducted her antilynching campaign, one needs to understand, as Bederman points out, how completely Wells understood the conflation of race, gender, and class in the 1890s. Social, economic, and cultural shifts appeared to threaten white middle-class male dominance. Fearful and uneasy, middle-class white men worried that their identity—their manhood—was imperiled. As a compensatory move to fortify faltering constructs of traditional manly power, white men turned (hardly for the first time, but with renewed intensity) to race. By characterizing themselves as "the white man," whose superior manliness distinguished him from more primitive even savage dark-skinned races, middle-class white men reassured themselves that their identity—their manliness—remained intact. The concept of "civilization" naturalized this conflation of manliness and racial dominance by linking it to human evolutionary progress. Now that they represented "civilization," they celebrated the fact, most visibly at the 1893 Chicago Exposition. There, with African Americans excluded, white women positioned appropriately (in "gracious submission"), and the rest of the world located deferentially, middle-class white men reassured themselves that they were the most powerful creatures ever to inhabit the planet (Bederman 1995b).

Ida B. Wells was fooled by none of it. She knew how fragile this constructed identity was, how easily it might unravel if she only inverted the link between manhood and white supremacy. Whereas whites in the North had imagined that lynching demonstrated white men's superior manliness and civilization by protecting the threatened white lady, Wells inverted the terms of the fantasy. By her logic lynching proved the opposite; black men were far more manly than whites who tolerated lynching. Whites had labored long and hard to construct elaborate pageants like the Columbian Exposition to dramatize their superior manliness and civilization in contrast to the primitive, even savage, nature of the dark-skinned races. Wells pointed out that the emperor had no clothes. Using the term "civilization" to demonstrate that the opposite was true, Wells made it clear that it was "the white man" who was neither manly nor civilized (Bederman 1995b).

Wells's skillful manipulation of manliness and civilization illustrates, as Bederman points out, an important strategy oppressed groups have sometimes employed. Namely, the oppressed use the language of dominant discourse but in subversive ways. Women's and labor historians have described many such cases. Bederman is reminded of those Cleveland unionists who converted their employers' calls for "law and order" into a rationale for a citywide strike (Ross 1985), those young working women in turn-of-the-century New York who parodied upper-class fashions in order to publicly assert their own working-class identities (Peiss 1986), those labor and women's activists who found in Protestantism a rationale for their own political projects; I am reminded of those Christian feminists who used the rhetoric of conservative Protestantism to make gender trouble (Haynes 1998; Gutman 1976; Fones-Wolf and Fones-Wolf 1983; Stanton 1895; Sklar 1973). I think too of Martin Luther King, Jr.'s appropriation of the language of mainstream Christianity to make civil rights activists seem as if they were only taking the moral high ground against the violence and prejudice of southern white infidels. More recently, there has been the political performances of ACT UP which dramatized by inversion the outrageousness of what is taken-for-granted as "normal." Ida B. Wells too inverted the main terms in the discourse of white manly civilization (a discourse which had made lynching seem reasonable to many whites) and in so doing demonstrated that manliness could only be saved, and civilization advanced, by stopping the white male mutilation of black male bodies (Bederman 1995b).

Unlike Christian feminists or unionists in Cleveland or the stylish young working women in New York, who were employing others' beliefs to construct identities for themselves, Wells was working to change her oppressor's beliefs and identities—in a word, to teach. Her effectiveness as a pedagogue derived from the acumen with which she manipulated taken-for-granted middle-class ideologies—that is, conflations of race, gender, and class. Her students were not exactly eager to learn; indeed, these were students who refused to even listen to her until she mobilized those to whom they felt compelled to listen. This ploy was smart enough, but her strategy of playing upon middle-class white men's fears of their own virility and manliness was brilliant. Ida B. Wells knew white people and she knew men; she combined both knowledges to invert binaries key to propping up beleaguered male identities. It was this device—today some would call it "deconstruction"—that made Wells's campaign so effective, her accusations so devastatingly on the mark (Bederman 1995b). How one wishes that uncovering the buried, mangled homoerotic at the center of white racism might have a similar effect.

Let us review briefly Wells's analytic moves. By inverting "civilization" and thereby severing the link between white supremacy and manliness, Wells created an antiracist notion of manhood. She understood clearly that behind middle-class gender lay a fundamental assumption that pure women and manly men were white. To focus upon that one point, as Wells did, was to undermine the entire edifice of white middle-class identity and gender. As Gail Bederman (1995b) so well explains, Victorian ideologies of womanhood marginalized black women by construing them as unwomanly harlots. In sharp contrast were white women. But these were "unreal" women, pedestalized as high-minded and sexually pure. Repudiating these links by insisting on black women's pure womanliness, Wells and other black women reconceptualized womanhood, as documented by Hazel Carby and Vron Ware as well as Gail Bederman. Likewise, middle-class formulations of manliness marginalized black men by fantasizing them as unmanly and lust-driven, rapists whose uncontrolled and wanton sexuality contrasted sharply with the equally imaginary restrained self-mastery and manliness of "the white man." By insisting that it was "the white man," and not the black man, who was lustful and uncivilized, Wells engendered a fundamental "cognitive dissonance" which threatened a restructuring of the European-American male self (Bederman 1995b). And she understood that none of this would be pulled off without the cultural authority of the British:

> Since the crusade against lynching was started, however, governors of states, newspapers, senators and representatives and bishops of churches have all been compelled to take cognizance of the prevalence of this crime

> and to speak in one way or another in the defense of the charge against this barbarism in the United States. This has not been because there was any latent spirit of justice voluntarily asserting itself, especially in those who do the lynching, but because the entire American people now feel, both North and South, that they are objects in the gaze of the civilized world and that for every lynching humanity asks that America render its account to civilization and itself. (Wells 1892b/1969, 72)

The white middle-class conflation of race with gender may seem to some "merely" ideological, but as Bederman points out and Wells recognized, it had crushing material repercussions. White middle-class notions of racialized manliness legitimized both the sexual victimization of black women and the brutal, often sexualized, mutilation of black men. Wells's insistence upon the womanliness of black women and the manliness of black men functioned to dismantle the ideological structure that supported white male violence. By inverting key concepts of whites' racialized discourses of gender, Wells hoped to teach her fellow American citizens how intolerably barbaric racial violence was (Bederman 1995b). By showing that the white male mutilation of black male bodies was in some fundamental sense a snuff film, homosexual desire recoded as chivalry and rape recoded as "popular justice," one hopes to teach contemporary European-American men how to begin to disentangle contemporary versions of similar conflations.

For Wells, critiquing middle-class gender was a tactic, not an endpoint. A theorist, a journalist, a publicist, a committed activist: Ida B. Wells stands today as one of America's greatest teachers. Not a great schoolteacher perhaps, as she disliked teaching in school: "I never cared for teaching" (Wells 1970, 31). But while using all her tactical skills and all her knowledge of the white psyche to end lynching, she was at the same time teaching all Americans to question taken-for-granted assumptions about men, women, race, about "civilization" itself. By disentangling the complexities of middle-class America's race/class/gender system she taught for social change. Sensitive to the subtle dynamics of this system, she was able to invert them to her political and pedagogical ends. Helped by her British friends, her rearticulation of the race/class/gender system shocked middle-class whites out of their denial and forced them to focus upon the fact of racial violence in America. By adeptly reading and decoding conflated discourses of class, race, and gender, Wells was able to teach some of the most resistant students—the white American public—on record. Gail Bederman (1995b, 424–425) concludes by suggesting that Wells's accomplishment makes clear that the deconstruction of dominant discourses of race, gender, and class is not merely an academic exercise, but an important practical and political—I would add "pedagogical"—tactic for those interested in social action and movement. Indeed: today gender is the flash point of American cultural, political, and racial reform, and the "queering" of gender may prove key to reform in each of those intersecting domains.

IV. Frances Willard and the W.C.T.U.

White men all over antebellum America drank a great deal.

—Joan E. Cashin, "A Lynching in Wartime Carolina" (1997)

There is to my mind no grander and surer prophecy of the new era and of woman's place in it, than the work already begun in the waning years of the nineteenth century by the W.C.T.U. in America.

—Anna Julia Cooper, "A Voice from the South" (1892/1998)

The temperance movement, especially under Frances Willard's leadership of the W.C.T.U., progressively widened the range of issues that were deemed to be women's special responsibility based on their role as mothers and guardians of the home. By the 1890s, that expanded responsibility included the community surrounding the home.

—Mark Carnes and Clyde Griffen, *Meanings for Manhood: Constructions of Masculinity in Victorian America* (1990)

The antilynching campaign was initiated and largely sustained by women. In the last decade of the nineteenth century it was the product of collaboration between white English female reformers and an African-American woman who mobilized her British listeners with a coherent and pointed political analysis based on her own research and experience. By addressing issues of sexuality and femininity, the short-lived antilynching movement in England not only forced a division between different kinds of feminism, but actually made possible a radical politics that acknowledged the connection between the mutilation of black men and the subordination of women, black and white (Ware 1992).

British reformers were well ahead of their American compatriots. In this section we see how American reformer Frances Willard, head of the American Women's Christian Temperance Union (W.C.T.U.), resisted Wells's revision of manhood and race. One of the most important American progressives, Jane Addams, was also vulnerable to white fantasies regarding black men and white women, as we will see in her exchange with Wells in 1901. Not until Jesse Daniel Ames do we see a white woman capable of appreciating how southern chivalry is knotted with women's subjugation and black men's mutilation. Ames, however, is limited by her southern (Texas) upbringing which disabled her from supporting federal intervention in southern affairs. The National Association for the Advancement of Colored People (N.A.A.C.P.) understood that only Washington could stop lynching, a story we will read in chapters 10 and 11. That tale, one of (mostly) black men working to persuade white men, illustrates the gendered gridlock that still typifies black/white, and specifically black male/white male, relations.

When Ida B. Wells returned to Britain in 1894, she took with her statistics and arguments that made it clear that white men were deceiving only themselves when they insisted they were mutilating black men's bodies in order to "protect" their ladies. Much of this information was printed in a pamphlet called *United States Atrocities*, published in Britain during her second trip. It was during this second visit she spoke even more assertively regarding southern hypocrisy regarding interracial sex, and in particular about her claims that white women were consensually involved in sexual relationships with black men. It was this point that precipitated the dispute between Ida B. Wells and Frances Willard, the prominent American women's rights advocate (whose Christian feminism was mentioned in chapter 5), which expressed what Vron Ware (1992, 197) describes as the "bitter confusion of ideas about female sexuality and race." Although the argument was over American racial politics, it was, Ware argues, significant that it was first publicly aired in Britain. In this section, relying on Ware's (1992) perceptive account, we learn how the controversy started and how it illustrated the conflation of sex and race in the white mind.

It was pure coincidence that Frances Willard, the world-famous leader of the Women's Christian Temperance Union (W.C.T.U.), was visiting England at the same time as Ida B. Wells. A charismatic speaker and an astute organizer, Willard was there in order to rest from the intense campaigning that had now begun to ruin her health. She was the permanent guest of Lady Henry Somerset, the aristocratic leader of the British Women's Temperance Association; the two women were quite close. Ware observes that their friendship and political alliance was another indication of the extensive networks which existed between different movements in Britain and America.

Frances Willard's views, Ware (1992) points out, were complex and contradictory, reflecting many of the changing ideas regarding women's place in the nineteenth-century Western world. Her influential life and work have been studied by several historians of the period (Epstein 1981; Earhart 1944; Bordin 1986). Like many feminists, Christian and secular, Willard believed that women were by nature more moral than men. Consequently, women's influence in the public world was both politically desirable and morally necessary. As did many of her contemporaries, she ascribed the fact of women's subordination to their capacity to bear children, which led to their general sexual subservience, all of it aggravated by men's propensity for alcohol. Mixing race, sex and booze, Willard summarized her views in the phrase "a white life for two." She advocated sexual abstinence between married couples, which would allow women the time and energy to become independent; men were to become more acquainted with domestic roles. However, as Ware notes, Willard's critique of masculinity only went so far; it did not reject the traditional male-dominated family structure which typified bourgeois society.

The W.C.T.U. was not strictly a feminist organization, as its point was social reform through morality, not specifically to ensure that women enjoyed equal status with men. The temperance movement intersected with other social reform movements of the period, specifically feminism (secular and Christian) and socialism (Epstein 1981; Haynes 1998). Many women who favored suffrage shared the conviction of W.C.T.U. members that women were by nature better prepared than men to reform society. Only by allowing women access to the vote and to public office, these women reasoned, would the interests of the family be represented and an equal balance between the sexes established. In fact, many of the early leaders of the National American Woman Suffrage

Association entered civic work via the W.C.T.U. (Filene 1998). Frances Willard also supported the American labor movement, including proposals for equal pay and employment for men and women. While in England, Lady Henry Somerset introduced her to the Fabian Society, of which she became a member. If she had been ten years younger, Willard is reported to have said, she would have devoted her life to socialism (Ware 1992).

For socialists most of what was wrong in society could be changed by changing the economic system. In the view of the W.C.T.U., all social evils could be linked to the consumption of alcohol. Still, its members tended to sympathize with other social reform movements such as socialism. Under the leadership of Frances Willard the organization broadened its social analysis considerably. She considered the temperance movement the perfect medium to advance her arguments for greater political power for women; using her position as head of the W.C.T.U., she persuaded members that the campaign for women's suffrage must be interwoven with demands for "Home Protection" and social purity (Ware 1992).

Social purity feminism not only affirmed the moral superiority of women, it demanded that men strive for "a virility that was both masculine and pure, 'true manliness'" (Hunt 1998, 613). In Britain, these movements and ideas were, in general, bound up with imperialism with its racist rationale. The racial and imperial "superiority" of the Empire could be maintained only by social and sexual purity. For men this meant a self-denying and self-controlling chivalry which was linked to the biological reproduction of the middle and upper classes within bourgeois marriage. Motherhood was an imperial duty, not a personal choice. Clearly, the strength of the Empire was fragile and depended on the moral rectitude of its citizens who faced, at every turn, the risk of degeneration (Hunt 1998).

As we saw in chapter 6, masturbation—primarily adolescent male but also female—epitomized such degeneration, and this practice became an ideal focus for projects of self-control. To avoid succumbing to the "secret vice," both renunciation and a sustained project of self-surveillance were necessary. The fear of masturbation was also a fear of homosexuality, although that term was not yet in widespread usage. The fear of masturbation brought together issues of gender, race, nation and class in all their complex interrelatedness. The campaign against it was aimed at middle- and upper-class males, felt to be most at risk and most crucial for the maintenance of the Empire. Among the Victorian upper and middle classes, then, there could be said to be a certain alliance between feminism and imperialism, which functioned to reproduce the hegemonic culture, and which was epitomized in the pervasive racism and classism of imperialism (Hunt 1998).

While very much aware of these broader ideas and influences, the agenda of the British temperance movement was more narrow. It was not a cause even especially associated with feminism, although many British feminists did favor the prohibition of alcohol. However, Lady Henry Somerset was entirely won over by Frances Willard's arguments, and together the two women attempted to persuade a resistant membership to take up the suffrage issue as well. The majority of members were, however, quite conservative; they had no interest in participating in public life to any significant extent. Furthermore, they resented what they perceived to be interference from an American. Even those who were engaged in progressive women's politics, such as Helen Bright Clark, who was also a friend of Susan B. Anthony and Elizabeth Cady Stanton, tried to suggest to Frances Willard that she back off (Ware 1992).

Frances Willard was in England for nearly two years, which irritated not only British members of the temperance movement, but American members of the W.C.T.U. as well. During this period she rested little it would seem. Willard lectured extensively and often captivated her audiences. When Ida B. Wells arrived in Britain on her first tour in 1893, many of her listeners were curious to know if Frances Willard, as a prominent American also speaking in Britain on moral issues, had condemned lynching. This was a difficult question for Wells, always eager for allies but committed to the position that silence amounted to consent (Ware 1992). She could not, finally, be silent.

It turns out that Wells had read an interview with Frances Willard in the *New York Voice* in which Willard had nearly condoned lynching. Not having a copy of the paper, Wells could not document the fact, so she never mentioned the temperance organizer's name unless asked specifically about her. On her second visit Wells brought evidence, not so much to "get" Willard—she much preferred to have her on her side—but because she felt Willard's position illustrated how lynching was continually misunderstood by northern liberals. Given in October 1890, the interview was printed on October 23 under the heading: "The Race Problem: Frances Willard on the Political Puzzle of the South." Willard begins by assuring us that she is without even "an atom of race prejudice," having been born an abolitionist. It is, she asserted, the color of the heart not the skin that signaled a person's moral status. But she quickly adopted not a moral but a "practical" argument. Since whites in the South would never consent to real equality with blacks, the sensible solution was to return blacks to Africa: "If I were black and young, no steamer could revolve its wheels fast enough to convey me to the dark continent. I should go where my color was the correct thing, and leave these pale faces to work out their own destiny" (quoted in Ware 1992, 200). Emigration to Africa was not just a white idea, of course; prominent African Americans such as Martin Delany (1860/1969) and, later, Marcus Garvery entertained the possibility.

Wells disagreed with the emigration idea, but what annoyed her, Ware (1992) explains, were the reasons that Frances Willard gave for "the race problem." Rather than giving all men the vote after emancipation, she argued, there should have been an educational qualification. It became clear that, like other Christian feminists (see chapter 5), Willard saw the majority of blacks as illiterate, ignorant alcoholics who multiplied "like the locusts of Egypt" (quoted in Wells 1892b/1969, 59). She felt sympathy for the southerner who, she believed, was most "kindly intentioned toward the colored man," but this was an "immeasurable" problem (quoted phrases in Ware 1992, 200). Moreover, Willard seemed to believe that white women were in fact at risk with black men, especially when black men were drunk: "Better whiskey and more of it is the rallying cry of great, dark-faced mobs. ... The grogshop is the center of power" (Wells 1892b/1969, 59). In that belief—that drunken black men were consumed with desire—she essentially reiterated the same nonsense that southern white men used to justify lynching (Ware 1992; Earhart 1944).

The views Willard articulated in the *New York Voice* interview were not at all unusual; they expressed the standard white northerner's attitude toward what was perceived to be the "special problem" of the South. Many who considered themselves politically progressive thought much the same. Frances Willard's stance was noteworthy, Ware suggests, because her beliefs about white women's safety and black sexuality overlapped with those of several leading American feminists. The early women's rights movement, Ware reminds, had developed alongside the anti-slavery campaign. But after Emancipation, when the vote was given to black men and not to white women, (white) feminism went its separate way. For decades the rights of black slaves and of women had been interconnected, but after the Civil War political pressures forced abolitionists, black and white, male and female, apart. It had been the struggle for the vote that had brought about this bitter division between those who supported universal suffrage and those who had feared that too broad a demand would jeopardize the vote for black men (Ware 1992).

Many younger white feminists who became involved in the movement for women's suffrage in the second half of the nineteenth century were convinced that their rights should come before those of former slaves, that women's interests would only be hindered by being linked to the demands of the recently freed black people. Not only political expediency was at work here. Ware (1992, 200) suggests that "at the heart of this belief was the fear that white women needed protection from black men." She points out that Elizabeth Cady Stanton, formerly a passionate abolitionist, made this very argument during debates over the strategy of demanding votes for both women and blacks. In an article that attacked male abolitionists for failing to support universal suffrage, Stanton argued that just as women had suffered and would continue to suffer despite laws and institutions made by "Saxon" men, it was likely that, once black men were enfranchised, women would suffer even more. To substantiate her fear, she referred to a case in which a young white girl gave birth to a black child and then strangled the infant. Stanton had asked: "With judges and jurors of negroes, remembering the generations of wrong and injustice their daughters have suffered at white men's hands, how will Saxon girls fare in the courts for crimes like this?" (quoted in Ware 1992, 201). "By 1890," Ware tells us, "this quite specific fear of black men's desire for revenge after years of subjugation had become a fundamental aspect of American racism" (1992, 201). By the 1960s, it would become a fundamental aspect of American prison life, but this time the fantasy would be real. Whites would be raped but it would not be "Saxon girls" who were at risk. In prison, the gender of racial politics and violence would become unmistakable. In some fundamental respect, "race" is an affair "between men."

The last decade of the nineteenth century saw not only the "full flower," as Walter White (1929, 101) put it, of lynching, it was a decade in which increasing numbers of non-English-speaking immigrants came to the United States. Ware (1992) reminds us that many middle-class, urban feminists extended their hostility toward black men to a generalized mistrust and hatred of "aliens," a mistrust and hatred they shared with white men. On March 14, 1891, this xenophobia was expressed in the lynching of eleven Italians in New Orleans, noted in chapter 1, yet another instance of male-on-male violence. Is it surprising that many feminists believed that women were morally superior to men? While all male sexuality was potentially threatening, especially if unleashed by alcohol, it was, however, black and working-class men who embodied the threat at its most terrifying.

Frances Willard had repeated in her interview what passed for conventional northern "wisdom" on the subject. She was unaware that her views were based in fantasy not fact, and that in their repetition she was supporting the torture and murder of innocent black men and women. All was done in the name of protecting white women. And, of course, the threat posed by "ignorant and illiterate" men had to do with their consumption of alcohol. Men, she believed, were victims of the liquor trade, the source of most social problems. As Ware points out, on the one hand Willard was probably sincere when in the *Voice* interview she insisted that "neither by voice or by pen have I ever condoned, much less defended any injustice towards the colored people." On the other hand, she did not sense her inconsistency when she argued that it was wrong to give the vote to black men and to "alien illiterates, who rule our cities today with the saloon as their palace, and the toddy stick as their scepter" (quoted in Ware 1992, 202).

Many Americans shared her simplistic response to the cultural complexities of immigration and the fact of a multicultural America. As a social reformer, Willard wanted something done. So under her leadership the W.C.T.U. established numerous departments to focus on specific areas where intervention was needed, among them a department for Temperance Work among Negroes and Foreigners. As far as Ida B. Wells was concerned, the road to hell was paved with good intentions, and it was precisely hell where many African Americans lived and many European Americans were headed. The views Willard had expressed in her interview and the defensive way she would later try to explain herself confirmed Wells's conviction that most northerners were, finally, indifferent to the fate of black people in the South, despite their liberal protestations to the contrary (Ware 1992).

Soon after Wells's return to Britain in 1894, the issue came to a head. This time Wells was able to produce evidence of her allegations against Willard; in fact she published part of the New York interview in *Fraternity*, along with an explanation. The result was immediate: both Willard and Lady Henry Somerset were furious. Somerset threatened to use her influence to stop Wells from giving any more public lectures in Britain. Once again Wells was astonished at the failure of white people to do the right thing; later she would recall the incident in her autobiography: "Here were two prominent white women, each in her own country at the head of a great national organization, with undisputed power and influence in every section of their respective countries, seeming to have joined hands in the effort to crush an insignificant colored woman who had neither money nor influence nor following—nothing but the power of truth to fight her battles" (Wells 1970, 210). Disarmingly humble, Wells sensed her advantage.

Two weeks after this edition of *Fraternity* appeared, the "leading London afternoon daily," as the *Westminister Gazette* called itself, carried a lengthy interview with Frances Willard conducted by her close friend Lady Henry Somerset. As Ware points out, there was no retraction or apology for her remarks made in the American paper; instead Willard repeated the same opinion. She even acknowledged that they were based on what white southerners had told her. Willard declared: "I ought to add that which I had been told by the best people I knew in the South—and I knew a great many ministers, editors and home people—that the safety of women, of children, is menaced in a thousand localities so that the women dare not go beyond the sight of their own roof trees" (quoted in Wells 1892b/1969, 59). This time, Ware notes, Frances Willard added that there was "no crime however heinous [that] can by any possibility excuse the commission of any act of cruelty or the taking of any human life without due course of law" (quoted in Ware 1992, 203). "Because of such utterances," Wells (1970, 152) responds in her autobiography,

> the South is encouraged and justified in its work of disgracing the Nation, and the world is confirmed in the belief that the Negro race is the most degraded on the face of the earth. ... But I do not need here to declare the statement a false one. Honorable Frederick Douglass has already done that. I am only to tell here what truth has compelled me to say as to the words and actions of some of our American Christians and temperance workers, when asked by British friends to do so.

One of the most remarkable features of this interview was the patronizing tone the two white women used when referring to Ida B. Wells. In the introduction, Lady Henry Somerset described Wells as a victim of her own racial bias; to support this assertion she quoted, out of context, a statement Wells had made in another newspaper interview. On that occasion Wells had been asked by the editor about her own racial origins; her reply had been characteristically direct: "Taint, indeed! I tell you, if I have any taint to be ashamed of in myself, it is the taint of *white* blood!" The editor began his interview with Wells's retort, making it clear that it was made in response to a question. Then he went on to do a sympathetic piece condemning lynching on the front and inside pages. Somerset lifted the remark out of context so it could serve as an example of Wells's presumed racism toward whites, and then juxtaposed it with her statement in *Fraternity* that "There was no movement being made by American white Christians toward aiding public sentiment against lynch law in the United States" (quoted in Ware 1992, 203–204).

After this manipulation of Wells's views, Lady Somerset then explained how she sought out Frances Willard's point of view: "I therefore sought the first opportunity of a quiet hour with her under the trees of my garden at Reigate." The conversation began with an attempt at humor to which Wells would refer in her reply. Willard adopted a slightly aggrieved tone when asked about Wells's accusations. Not only was she an innocent and injured party, she was an ally. When she had first heard that Wells was in the country, she had done everything she could to help her, "for I believe in the fraternity of nations and that we ought to help each other to a higher plane by mutual influence." The interview ended with both women agreeing that it was shocking that Wells had "misconstrued" remarks made by Willard in an interview that had "nothing to do with lynching" (quoted in Ware 1992, 203). No doubt, they reassured themselves, British justice would protect Willard's impeccable reputation (Ware 1992).

Ida B. Wells sensed that the way the two influential women had joined forces publicly to denounce her might be put to her advantage. Later she would write that their attack returned like a "boomerang" to Frances Willard. She did not wait long to reply to the interview; she did so in the same paper on the following day. As Ware notes, Wells slices through the condescending, complacent tone of her accusers:

> The interview published in your columns yesterday hardly merits a reply, because of the indifference to suffering manifested. Two ladies are represented as sitting under a tree at Reigate, and, after some preliminary remarks on the terrible subject of lynching, Miss Willard laughingly replies by cracking a joke. And the concluding sentence of the interview shows the object is not to determine best how they may help the Negro who is being hanged, shot and burned, but "to guard Miss Willard's reputation." (Wells 1892b/1969, 85; quoted in Ware 1992, 204)

Ida B. Wells did not spare the famous temperance leader. She ignored Willard's attacks on her own integrity, insisting "with me it is not myself nor my reputation, but the life of my people, which is at stake" (Wells 1892b/1969, 85). It was Frances Willard's record that was at issue, she continued, and specifically her supposed commitment to black people. Particularly damning, Ware suggests, was Wells's observation that Willard had sat in silence when Wells had placed a resolution condemning lynching in front of two national meetings of the British Temperance Association. Even more damaging, Wells offered the following explanation of Willard's silence: "I should say it was because as president of the Women's Christian Temperance Union of America she is timid, because all these unions in the South emphasize the hatred of the negro by excluding him. There is not a single colored woman admitted to the Southern W.C.T.U., but still Miss Willard blames the negro for the defeat of prohibition in the South!" (Wells 1892b/1969, 85; quoted in Ware 1992, 205).

There could be no defense against this charge of segregation practiced by the W.C.T.U. in America. Ida B. Wells later called it a "staggering revelation" which had "stunned the British people," and although this was, Ware suggests, something of an overstatement, Wells did appear to gain support by exposing Frances Willard's apparent hypocrisy. The editor of the *Westminister Gazette* volunteered that she had not expressed any racial bias during his interview with her, thereby undermining the power of that earlier statement which had been quoted out of context. Soon afterwards Wells was invited to both breakfast and dinner in the House of Commons. Wells's greatest triumph, Ware tells us, had to do with the Anti-Lynching Committee, which was established on her last evening in the country. In her autobiography she lists the names of its influential and prestigious members. Among them were MPs such as William Woodall, Dadabhai Naoroji and Alfred Webb; labor leaders like Keir Hardie and the American Samuel Gompers; the editors of the *Manchester Guardian*, the *Liverpool Daily Post*, the *London Daily News*, the *Bradford Observer* and the

Contemporary Review; and leading clergy, including the Archbishop of York. The names of both Lady Henry Somerset and Frances Willard were on the list as well, an accomplishment which Wells judged to be among her greatest. They may have been on the list but, as Ware (1992) observes, the antagonism between the two American women did not end while they were both in London. Afterward, others, on both sides of Atlantic, would join the battle.

The dispute would prove to be long and bitter. At the heart of it, Ware (1992) explains, were several interconnected issues. First was straightforward racial prejudice which included the readiness to believe that it was indeed unsafe for white women in the South due to the licentious and drunken nature of black men. While most members of the W.C.T.U. regarded all men as dangerous to women after the consumption of alcohol, black men were imagined to be especially liable to drunkenness, due to both their race and class. Recall that the last quarter of the nineteenth century saw a proliferation of "scientific" books and articles asserting that there were marked and inherited biological differences between blacks and whites. These identified immorality and bestiality as race traits; they were found most frequently, presumably, in the black population, especially now that "they" were freed from the restraints of slavery.

Frances Willard's claims not to have "an atom of race prejudice" sounded unconvincing when she repeated "what she had been told in the South," namely that blacks multiplied like locusts and that black men in particular threatened the safety of all, including respectable white women. The very language in which she expressed these white male fantasies echoed, Ware points out, the words of one of the South's most well-known academic racists, Phillip Alexander Bruce. In a book called *The Plantation Negro as Freedman* published in 1889, Bruce discussed his theory of "regression." After slavery, with the civilizing influence of whites removed, the black race was condemned to regress, he declared. The most vivid illustration of this regression toward savagery was the increasing frequency of "that most frightful crime," the rape of white women by black men. Bruce wrote:

> Their [black males'] disposition to perpetrate it [rape] has increased in spite of the quick and summary punishment that always follows. ... There is something strangely alluring and seductive to the negro in the appearance of a white woman; they are roused and stimulated by its foreignness to their experience of sexual pleasures, and it moves them to gratify their lust at any cost and in spite of any obstacle. ... Rape, indescribably beastly and loathsome always, is marked, in the instance of its perpetration of by the negro, by a diabolical persistence and a malignant atrocity of detail that have no reflection in the whole extent of the natural history of the most bestial and ferocious animals. (quoted in Tolnay and Beck 1995, 89–90)

White men's fantasies of black men were mistaken for reality.

The second issue Ware identifies was the racial segregation practiced by white women's organizations, a point Hazel Carby (1987) also emphasizes in a different context. Whether or not Frances Willard personally approved, the fact was that the W.C.T.U. permitted segregated sections in some southern states.

Some of their leading white members, women such as Rebecca Latimer Felton (see chapter 7, section V), had been loyal Confederates during the War. These women knew, or should have known, that the fantasy of black male rape was only that, having stayed alone on the plantations with black slaves while their men were fighting for the "lost cause." But their interest in segregation had nothing to do with fact or reason; they were, simply, fiercely opposed to the idea of collaborating with black women (Ware 1992).

Northerners feared losing southern members if they insisted on racial integration, so they refrained from outlawing separate organizations for black and white women. Like many liberals in the North at this time (and later), Frances Willard was sincerely able to profess her belief in the equality of the "races" ... in the abstract. But in the concrete she was also quite willing to turn a blind eye to the reality of segregation and discrimination in those more "distant" parts of the country. By 1897 white racism was widespread, fueled by white male fantasies and supported by female complicity: Recall that Rebecca Latimer Felton had won widespread white support by declaring, "If it takes lynching to protect women's dearest possession from drunken, ravening beasts, then I say lynch a thousand a week if it becomes necessary" (quoted in Ware 1992, 206). Felton linked the figure of the black rapist to that of pandering white politicians, who purchased black votes with liquor. Their passions ignited by ill-gotten whiskey, black men attacked white women in a vain effort "to satisfy their lust for social equality" (Brundage 1993, 198). By linking rape with other social ills such as political corruption and alcohol, Felton fueled the southern fantasy that the black threat was anything but infrequent, isolated crimes committed by aberrant black individuals (Brundage 1993). Encouraged by the enthusiastic white response to her rhetorical aggression, Felton embarked on a crusade for the salvation of white women from the "black fiend" (quoted in Ware 1992, 207).

Cult of (White) Womanhood

There was, Ware suggests, another element that fueled the quarrel between Frances Willard and Ida B. Wells. That was the fact that a black woman was publicly challenging the taken-for-granted, sentimentalized view of white women's sexuality. Wells's insistence that it was white women who sometimes initiated illicit relationships with black men created an intolerable level of "cognitive dissonance" among many in the W.C.T.U., including Frances Willard herself. For them, women were always victims of male lust, never "willing," god forbid "aggressive," partners in interracial sexual relationships. The fantasy of drunken black men—and recall that these women were convinced that men who were "ignorant and illiterate" became doubly dangerous through drink—preying on white women accorded entirely with W.C.T.U. philosophy, as well as with the dominant racial imagery of the day. The very suggestion that white women could conceivably agree to, let alone initiate, an interracial sexual relationship was outrageous and intolerable (Ware 1992).

But, Ware continues, it was not only the idea of women being assertively interested in sex that scandalized so many W.C.T.U. members. It was also that Wells had also raised the taboo topic of miscegenation. It was hardly a secret that black women had been repeatedly raped by white men during two centuries of slavery. (That they probably also raped black men remains beyond documentation.) This fact had been frequently cited and described in abolitionist propaganda, particularly in works of fiction. These women knew that men, white as well as black, would sleep with, well, anybody. But the suggestion that white women might find black men sexually desirable was altogether a different issue. In 1856, the well-known abolitionist Lydia Maria Child lost much of her popular support when she argued against miscegenation laws, citing several happy unions between white women and black men. Even though she dared to speak out (as Hannah Arendt would, with similar consequences, one hundred years later [see Sollors 1997, 316]), risking "the world's mockery" as she put it, Child still felt obliged to distance herself from any such possible desires by asserting that it was only the lowest class of white women who could possibly consider such a union. After all, middle-class women had "taste" (Ware 1992).

Although it was almost forty years later, Ware notes, the racism that Wells encountered both in Britain and in the United States contained the same fantasy that black men smoldered with long-held barely-suppressed desires for white women. Wells constantly dismissed this nonsense by regularly reminding her listeners of those plantation owners who had spent extended periods away from home, leaving wives and families in the hands of trusted slaves: "Do you remember when the American negro had his great opportunity? When his master went into the field openly to fight against his—the negro's—freedom, and left his wife and children to the negro's charge? And what a temptation to vengeance—yet not a man of them betrayed his master's trust" (quoted in Ware 1992, 207). Contemporary historical research corroborates, to a considerable extent, Wells's anecdotally based claims (Faust 1996).

Perhaps Frances Willard was guilty only of believing her colleagues and friends in the South who had assured her that the sexual threat posed by freed black men was real. But this possibility is undermined by evidence that suggests that Willard was not just being sensitive to southerners she believed. It is clear that she was thinking as well of her standing among northern white women who belonged to the W.C.T.U., many of whom, as we have seen, tacitly accepted lynching. Speaking at the 1894 W.C.T.U. convention in Cleveland, Frances Willard attacked Ida B. Wells in her opening address. Perhaps, as Ware suggests, she was hoping to silence her on this issue for once and for all, but she was, no doubt, also reassuring her northern listeners that she had not betrayed their collective fantasies regarding women and men, specifically white women and black men. Willard told the delegates:

> The zeal for her race of Ida B. Wells, a bright young colored woman, has, it seems to me, clouded her perception as to who were her friends and well-wishers in all high-minded and legitimate efforts to banish the abomination of lynching and torture from the land of the free and home of the brave. It is my firm belief that in the statements made by Miss Wells concerning white women having taken the initiative in nameless acts between the races she has put an imputation upon half the white race in this country that is unjust, and, save in the rarest exceptional

> circumstances, wholly without foundation. (quoted in Wells 1892b/1969, 80; in Ware 1992, 208)

It was during this convention that Ida B. Wells finally met Frances Willard. The meeting occurred after Willard had criticized Wells in her speech. In a chapter of *A Red Record*, entitled "Miss Willard's Attitude," Wells reported their conversation, documenting how Willard and other white women tried to silence and dominate their "colored sisters" (quoted in Ware 1992, 208). Wells (1892b/1969, 189) wrote:

> On that same day I had a private talk with Miss Willard and told her she had been unjust to me and the cause in her annual address, and asked that she correct the statement that I had misrepresented the W.C.T.U. or that I had "put an imputation on one-half of the white race in this country." She said that somebody in England told her it was a pity that I attacked the white women of America. "Oh," said I, "then you went out of your way to prejudice me and my cause in your annual address, not upon what you had heard me say, but what somebody had told you I said?" Her reply was that I must not blame her for her rhetorical expressions—that I had my way of expressing things and she had hers. I told her I most assuredly did blame her when those expressions were calculated to do such harm. I waited for an honest and unequivocal retraction of her statements based on "hearsay." Not a word of retraction or explanation was said in the convention and I remained misrepresented before that body through her connivance and consent.

Wells defended herself in public, denying in *A Red Record* that she ever suggested that white women have taken "the initiative in nameless acts between the races." Nor, Wells insisted, could anything she had done in her crusade against lynching possibly be misconstrued as putting "an imputation upon half the white race." Having corrected Willard's mistake, Wells (1892b/1969, 81) now commences to teach:

> What I have said and what I now repeat—in answer to her first charge—is, that colored men have been lynched for assault upon women, when the facts were plain that the relationship between the victim lynched and the alleged victim of his assault was voluntary, clandestine, and illicit. For that very reason we maintain that, in every section of our land, the accused should have a fair, impartial trial, so that a man who is colored shall not be hanged for an offense, which, if he were white, would not be adjudged a crime. Facts cited in another chapter [of *A Red Record*]—"History of Some Cases of Rape"—amply maintain this position. The publication of these facts in defense of the good name of the race casts no "imputation upon half the white race in this country" and no such imputation can be inferred except by persons deliberately determined to be unjust.

Wells was not through with her. In the very next paragraph she suggests that "this is not the only injury which this cause has suffered at the hands of our 'friend and well wisher'" (Wells 1892b/1969, 81). She points out that the

W.C.T.U. had done nothing to stop lynching, and what's worse, had appeared to condone southern attitudes when the organization held its annual convention in Atlanta in October 1890. Wells (1892b/1969, 81) tells us how easily the northerners had been seduced:

> It was the first time in the history of the organization that it had gone south for a national meeting, and met the southerners in their own homes. They were welcomed with open arms. The governor of the state and the legislature gave special audiences in the halls of state legislation to the temperance workers. They set out to capture the northerners to their way of seeing things, and without troubling to hear the Negro side of the question, these temperance people accepted the white man's story of the problem with which he had to deal. State organizers were appointed that year, who had gone through the southern states since then, but in obedience to southern prejudices have confined their work to white persons only. It is only after Negroes are in prison for crimes that efforts of these temperance women are exerted without regard to "race, color, or previous condition." No "ounce of prevention" is used in their case; they are black, and if these women went among the Negroes for this work, the whites would not receive them. Except here and there, are found no temperance workers of the Negro race; "the great dark-faced mobs" are left in the easy prey of the saloonkeepers.

Frances Willard found the southern spell irresistible, as Wells (1892b/1969, 82) reports.

> Said Miss Willard: "Now, as to the 'race problem' in its minified, current meaning. I am a true lover of the southern people—have spoken and worked in, perhaps, 200 of their towns and cities; have been taken into their love and confidence at scores of hospital firesides; have heard them pour out their hearts in the splendid frankness of their impetuous natures. And I have said to them at such times: 'When I go North there will be wafted to you no word from pen or voice that is not loyal to what we are saying here and now.' Going South, a woman, a temperance woman, and a northern temperance woman—three great barriers to their good will—I was received by them with confidence that was one of the most delightful surprises of my life. I think we have wronged the South, though we did not mean to do so. The reason was, in part, that we had irreparably wronged ourselves by putting no safeguards on the ballot box at the North that would sift out alien illiterates. They rule our cities today; the saloon is their palace, and the toddy stick their scepter. It is not fair that they should vote, nor is it fair that a plantation Negro, who can neither read nor write, whose ideas are bounded by the fence of his own field and the price of his own mule, should be entrusted with the ballot. We ought to have put an educational test upon that ballot from the first. The Anglo-Saxon race will never submit to be dominated by the negro so long as his attitude reaches no higher than the personal liberty of the saloon, and the power of appreciating the amount of liquor that a dollar will buy."

It all comes down to liquor, presumably, but we see that there is more than booze in the glass Willard hates. Wells (1892b/1969, 84) is controlled but outraged:

> Here we have Miss Willard's words in full, condoning fraud, violence, murder, at the ballot box; raping, shooting, hanging and burning; for all these things are done and being done now by the southern white people. She does not stop there, but goes a step further to aid them in blackening the good name of an entire race, as shown by the sentences quoted in the paragraph above. These utterances, for which the colored people have never forgiven Miss Willard, and which Frederick Douglass has denounced as false, are to be found in full in the *Voice* of October 23, 1890, a temperance organ published in New York City. (84)

Once again Wells inverts the binaries of the event, and it is she, indeed the "entire race" who are victimized, and Willard is the immoral and complicit party to "fraud, violence, and murder," not to mention, of course, lynching.

The details of this controversy are important, Ware (1992) argues, because they illustrate the various positions that different women took up as they struggled to articulate a political point of view that acknowledged both gender and race. It is also significant that the public quarrel between Frances Willard and Ida B. Wells surfaced first in England, and from there was transported back to the United States where it had originated. That both women were in England at the same was strictly fortuitous, of course; Frances Willard happened to be in Britain when the Society for the Brotherhood of Man was being established. But, as Ware points out, this young, unknown (to whites) black woman would never have been able to attract public support in her own country for her criticism of a figure of Frances Willard's caliber. In London her relative obscurity seemed to add weight to her argument; she had nothing to gain, no ax to grind. Probably the British public felt even more sympathy for her after the two famous temperance leaders threatened to use their influence to silence her (Ware 1992).

It would be mistaken, Ware insists, to attribute Wells's moral victory solely to what Wells perceived as the British sense of fair play. The support Wells enjoyed indicates the presence of substantial anti-imperialist elements in Britain at the time. Because there were British citizens critical of the Empire, especially its racialized rationales, they were quickly able to make sense of and accept Wells's political analysis of racial terror in America, echoing as it did, racial terror worldwide. But Ware wonders to what extent Wells's analysis was accepted *because* it applied to America and not Britain. Would the British have been as receptive to her had they applied her analysis directly to their own British colonies, where segregation and racial subordination were also part of everyday life? Why, Ware asks, did Wells not face more opposition in Britain than she did, since her description of the American South made the South seem uncomfortably close to regions of the British Empire? As she herself often admitted, the most difficult task Wells faced in Britain was convincing her listeners that black men were not "wild beasts after women." When the *Times* demanded that Florence Balgarnie and "the numerous ladies upon the Anti-

Lynching Committee" attend to the "frequency and atrocity of his outrages on white women," the newspaper was not just referring to the black man in America, but to everywhere a man with a darker skin could come into contact with a white woman (quoted in Ware 1992, 213).

This sexualized fantasy was pervasive, not just in America but in Britain and Europe generally. There it was interwoven with the imperial imperative. In Britain, the fantasy attached itself, not so much to the experience of slavery and abolition, but to the uprising of black colonial subjects in India and in the Caribbean (Stoler 1995). In particular, the Indian "mutiny" of 1857 and the Morant Bay uprising of 1865 stimulated the white racist imagination. As Ware (1992) observes, responses to these uprisings cannot be viewed apart from a much more complicated debate about the nature of democracy in Britain as well as the legitimization of imperial rule abroad. Even so, Ware suggests, these rebellions and their suppression remained very much in the British memory of racial dominance when Wells and Willard visited in the 1890s.

British antilynching campaigners did not tend to see the analogies between the racialized character of the Empire and the practice of lynching in the southern states of America. Their opponents in the American South, however, were quick to cite the cruel suppression of the Sepoy rebellion as an example of the barbarity committed by the British, those same British who now, in the 1890s, had the nerve and the hypocrisy to upbraid America for its racial violence. While the "ladies" involved in the Anti-Lynching Committee would have been too young to remember the actual events surrounding those insurrections, they would, Ware believes, have been familiar with how those events circulated in the British racial imagination. Not being Americans, they were not outraged by Wells's remarks about southern white women desiring black men, but they would, Ware (1992) tells us, certainly have been aware of the impact of such arguments had they been made in the context of British imperialism and colonialism.

Like many of her colleagues and friends, Frances Willard believed that society cried out for moral reform, and that the equality of women was justified by their ability to provide moral and spiritual guidance. Equality was not, for Willard and others, an end in itself. Ultimately, as Ware reminds, the W.C.T.U. was a conservative organization, although some of its policies exhibited some degree of radicalism, intersecting as they did with both socialism and feminism. But as the organization reached, for instance, toward feminism, reaction was immediate; the demand for "rights for women" was considered "too strident" by many members. As the nineteenth century came to a close, the movement for social purity was in decline. Victorian ideas on morality suddenly seemed old-fashioned, out of date. Frances Willard died before the new century dawned; her life and her point of view, crystallized in the call for a "white life," quickly became identified with a time that had passed (Ware 1992).

The primary significance of the short-lived British antilynching movement was, Ware argues, that it showed the possibility of an alliance between black and white women. It was an alliance in which white women went beyond a patronizing "sisterly" support for black women. By confronting the complexity of the racist ideology that rationalized lynching, British white women such as Catherine Impey, Florence Balgarnie, and Isabella Fyvie Mayo began to develop a radical analysis of gender relations that intersected with class and race. They were "feminist" because they lived their lives identified with and deeply engaged in the social and political issues of the day. They modeled lives of independence which testified to the proposition that women should be free to choose how and with whom they live and associate themselves—an idea perhaps common enough for us one hundred years later, but an idea which was radical and subversive a century ago. These British white women were able to hear the reasoned authenticity of Wells's case, and in so doing reject the taken-for-granted fantasy of innocent and vulnerable white women which had been promoted by those who supported or ignored lynchings in the United States. As Ware (1992) points out, these women were not only defending the rights of the black population; they were as well claiming a different, more active version of what it might mean to be a woman. As a consequence, they questioned a range of conservative beliefs about both women and black people (beliefs, as we have seen, which were intertwined), beliefs not only held by right-wing reactionaries, but also by those, such as Frances Willard, who considered themselves progressive.

Vron Ware (1992) does not see an obvious difference between the politics of those women who supported Ida B. Wells and those who tried to silence her, but she does make two points. First, whereas Frances Willard and others in the temperance movement saw themselves as representing women's interests and advancing women's causes, both Catherine Impey and Florence Balgarnie also declared themselves to be advocates of human brotherhood. This latter aspiration contained a vision of universal equality across race, class, and gender. The second point Ware makes concerns those who were offended by Wells. These women failed to understand the centrality of racism in misogyny, that is, that racism functioned both to oppress black people and to undermine more progressive ideas about women as well.

That idea points to another significance of the British antilynching movement. It is telling that the fight against lynching was launched by women, and that it would be led primarily by women until the N.A.A.C.P. took up the cause in the second decade of the twentieth century. It is telling that it was an African-American woman who first saw through the lie that white men told so glibly, that their vulnerable, universally desirable white "ladies" were the constant objects of sexually rapacious black men. Black women knew better. They knew black men did not spend their days fantasizing about white women; they knew that white women were not always vulnerable or universally desirable. And they knew that white men were not chivalrous embodiments of manhood, willing to risk life and limb to protect white womanhood. They knew that white men had raped and continued to rape black women. They saw the sexually mutilated bodies of lynched black men. From beginning to end there was not a shred of truth in the white man's fantasy, a fantasy that engaged not only most white men of the time, but more than a few white women. One had to live across the Atlantic in order to be white and be able to see through the collective mystification of social reality that was the American racial order. In the 1890s white women, such as Frances Willard and, as we shall see, even Jane Addams, could not bring themselves to believe that the myth of black rape was only that, probably because, as Ware suggests, it threatened the entire gender order in which they lived their lives as mothers, daughters, wives, and "ladies." For to believe that women were by nature morally superior, that sobriety equaled ethics, meant playing out the other side of the same coin that was the sentimentalized myth of the vulnerable, if morally superior white woman. It would take two decades before a European-American woman would toss the coin aside. It took a woman who had been engaged in the struggle for women's suffrage to begin to appreciate the extent of the white men's self-delusions regarding race and gender. That woman was Jessie Daniel Ames. But before we remember her, let us focus on another white woman who attacked lynching, the great social progressive and activist Jane Addams.

V. The Addams-Wells Exchange

As long as white women were seen to be the property of white men, without power or a voice of their own, their "protectors" could claim to be justified in taking revenge for any alleged insult or attack on them. Whenever the reputation of white women was "tainted" by the suggestion of immoral behavior, it could always be saved by the charge that they had been the victims of black lust.

—Vron Ware, *Beyond the Pale: White Women, Racism and History* (1992)

A careful classification of the offenses which have caused lynchings during the past five years shows that contempt for law and race prejudice constitute the real cause of all lynching.

—Ida B. Wells, "Lynching and the Excuse for It" (1901/1977)

Back in America, Ida B. Wells had an exchange with another white woman, this time not so unpleasant but still indicative of the racial divide over the issue of lynching. This woman was Jane Addams, who did not regard social, including racial, conflict as inevitable, but as a social problem to be solved (Westbrook 1991). Wells admired Jane Addams, calling her at one point "the greatest woman in the United States" (Wells 1970, 259). The estimate, made in Wells's autobiography, is not without merit (Aptheker 1977; Munro, in press).

Jane Addams (1860–1935) is best known for her work in the Settlement House movement, and as the founder of Hull House in Chicago, as we saw in chapter 6 (section III). But Addams was, Bettina Aptheker (1977) points out, considerably more than a social worker in any conventional sense of that term. She was a social activist, a successful organizer, suffragist and civil rights advocate, a courageous opponent of the First World War, and founding president of the Women's International League for Peace and Freedom. She was also a "theorist and intellectual—a thinker of originality and daring," as Christopher Lasch (1965, xv) put it. Both John Dewey and William James were enthusiastic about Addams's work. James, for instance, had written to her shortly after the publication of her *Democracy and Social Ethics* in 1902 (Aptheker 1977). Dewey became her friend during the years he taught at the

University of Chicago; he missed her and Hull House "dearly" when he moved to New York to take up his life-long post at Columbia (Westbrook 1991, 167).

Influenced by both Dewey and James, Addams maintained that the Settlement House was not exclusively, or even primarily, an economic welfare institution (Munro, Smith, and Weiler 1999b). For Addams, the Settlement House was the instrument through which to labor toward realization of an egalitarian social order and an authentic democracy. To be sure, the Settlement House clothed and fed the poor, helped the unemployed to find jobs, fought for protective safety and health legislation for workers and opposed child labor. But "above all else," Aptheker (1977, 2) explains, "it was to provide a cultural, literary and artistic oasis for the slum dweller"

Settlement houses provided educational opportunities for women, immigrants, and migrants. They were also, Munro (1999b, 19) argues, "curricular experiments that contested dominant notions of education." Key to these curricular innovations was the development of community networks across institutional boundaries, networks Munro (1999b) characterizes "as central to enacting democracy as a mode of associated living." The settlement house as well as the women's club movement contested the compartmentalization and instrumental rationality often characteristic of the social efficiency movement in education (Munro 1999b).

Addams argued that the Settlement House movement made "its appeal upon the assumption that the industrial problem is a social one" (Addams 1899, 342) and that "identification with the common lot, which is the essential idea of Democracy becomes the source and expression of social ethics" (Addams 1902, 11). Crucial to Addams's theory was her belief that in cutting itself off from the proletariat, the bourgeoisie impoverished itself (Aptheker 1977). We would see this idea surface over and over again during the twentieth century; certainly it is very evident in the life and art of Pier Paolo Pasolini, for instance (Greene 1990). Identification with the ethics of the poor, Addams insisted, was culturally and morally uplifting, another idea that would receive articulation in a number of twentieth-century movements, in liberation theology, for instance (see Pinar et al. 1995, 643 ff.).

Like Marx, Addams maintained that labor was an essential human function. Estranged from the practical sphere of the production process, the bourgeoisie was necessarily deprived of indispensable cultural and intellectual qualities. This deprivation was especially serious for women of the upper classes, Addams suggested, whose confinement to the home (however opulent its furnishings) was not only assumed, but deemed by men to be the only virtuous activity for a self-respecting lady. These conclusions formed the theoretical basis for the "subjective necessity" (Addams 1893/1969, 2) of philanthropic activity (Aptheker 1977).

Jane Addams was active in the Progressive Party and played an important role in its 1912 National Convention at which Theodore Roosevelt was nominated for president. Aptheker (1977) tells us Addams caused quite a stir as the first woman to deliver a seconding speech for the nomination of a major presidential candidate. She endorsed Roosevelt. "The speech was the entrance of women in national politics in a new sense" (quoted in Aptheker 1977, 4), one observer remarked. Addams's appearance reenergized the movement for woman suffrage (DeWitt 1915; Farrell 1967). The 1912 Convention of the Progressive Party also saw a debate on the role of the black electorate in national politics which, unfortunately, reflected the racism of the period. Addams's role in this controversy suggests both her strengths and weaknesses as a social reformer and practical politician (Aptheker 1977).

Black men were members of integrated delegations to the Progressive Party Convention from Rhode Island, West Virginia, Maryland, Tennessee, and Kentucky. Two delegations, one black, one white, vied for accreditation from Mississippi, as would happen fifty-two years later at the 1964 Democratic Party Convention. Demanding that the Black Mississippians be seated, Addams participated in an all-night debate in the Convention's resolutions committee. She lost that battle; the white delegation was seated. Addams acquiesced in the removal of the black delegates, and later campaigned vigorously for the Progressive Party platform (Aptheker 1977). She rationalized the Convention's action a few months later in an article in the *Crisis*, the official publication of the N.A.A.C.P. It was, she said, a necessary action in order to bring the Progressive Party into the South as the opposition party to the Democrats who controlled the region, "without the bitterness and old hatred evoked by the Republicans" (Addams 1912, 30–31; quoted in Aptheker 1977, 5).

This incident at the Progressive Party convention illustrates Jane Addams's position on "the race question." On the one hand, she was a strong advocate of civil rights. On the other, she was given to compromise. Moreover, certain mainstream assumptions regarding race are evident in her writing. Still, Aptheker (1977, 5) argues, "her procivil rights activities were conspicuous." One such activity involved her support of the club work conducted by African-American women. Addams maintained a working relationship with Ida B. Wells when Wells lived in Chicago, as well as cordial relations with other black leaders and activists such as Mary Church Terrell, Josephine St. Pierre Ruffin, Mary R. Talbert, and others prominent in the leadership of the National Association of Colored Women (N.A.C.W.). Addams's work inspired Settlement House efforts among black women, such as the "White Rose Home for Colored Working Girls" on East 86th Street in New York City, run by the African-American writer Victoria Matthews. When the N.A.C.W. met in convention at Quinn Chapel in Chicago in 1899, Jane Addams extended a luncheon invitation to the officers of the black women's club (Aptheker 1977).

In 1900 a series of articles appeared in the *Chicago Tribune* advocating a segregated public school system in the city. Wells (1970, 274) remembers in her autobiography:

> For a period extending over two weeks interviews were printed, first with parents of children who had struck in one of the schools of Chicago against having a colored teacher. Second, articles were written containing interviews from superintendents of separate school systems in Saint Louis, Baltimore, Washington, D.C., and other places of smaller note. The only places from which there were not interviews on the subject were those in which the mixed school system prevailed. And not a single colored person was quoted on the subject.

Outraged, Wells wrote to the *Tribune* editor, but he ignored it. Not to be silenced, Wells went to his office. She recalls that:

> When Mr. Robert W. Patterson came in I walked up to him and stood waiting for him to finish reading a letter before he entered his private office. He glanced up and said, "I have nothing for you today." I replied that I did not understand what he meant and told him who I was and why I was there. He said, "Oh, I thought you were one of the women from one of the colored churches coming to solicit a contribution, as they very frequently do."
>
> I laughed and said, "It therefore seems natural that whenever you see a colored woman she is begging for her church. I happen to be begging, Mr. Patterson, but not for money." I then said that, not hearing from my letter, I had come down to have a talk with him about the matter. We had quite a chat, in which he let me see that his idea on the subject of racial equality coincided with those of the white people of the South with whom he had been in constant association at his winter home in Thomasville, Georgia. (Wells 1970, 275)

Here she was in the office of one of the most influential men in Chicago, and she discovers his views on "race" have been influenced by southern whites who had gained his ear during times of relaxation. While her tone is calm, Wells must have been horrified:

> He said he did not believe that it was right that ignorant Negroes should have the right to vote and to rule white people because they were in the majority. My reply to him was that I did not think it was any more fair for that type of Negro to rule than it was for that same class of white men in the First Ward flophouses who cast a ruling vote for the Great First War of Chicago. Even so, I was not disposed to condemn all white people because of that situation nor deprive the better class of them of their rights in the premises.
>
> Mr. Patterson further informed me that he did not have time to listen to a lot of colored people on the subject but that he would publish as much of my letter as he could find space for, when they got around to it. I told him that the delegation of Negroes whom I had hoped to bring to him would not waste his time, because they too were busy at their different occupations and could ill afford to waste their time or his own in fruitless discussion. (Wells 1970, 275–276)

"That was as much as I could get out of him," she concludes in a matter-of-fact fashion, and leaves. Her thoughts turn to economic boycott but "I knew that if every Negro in Chicago taking or advertising in the *Tribune* should fail to take it, the result would be so small it would not even be known. Therefore it was up to us to get somebody whose opinion and influence the *Tribune* would respect to interest themselves in our behalf." Now who could that be? "I went to the phone and called up Miss Jane Addams of Hull House and asked if she would see me. When I called upon her and explained the situation I said, 'Miss Addams, there are plenty of people in Chicago who would not sanction such a move if they knew about it. Will you undertake to reach those of influence who would be willing to do for us what we cannot do for ourselves'?" (all passages from Wells 1970, 276).

Addams "very readily agreed" to help, and on "the following Sunday evening there were gathered at Hull House representative men and women of the white race, who listened to my story. There were editors of other daily papers in the city, ministers of the gospel, and social service workers" (Wells 1970, 276). Among those present was a progressive member of the Board of Education. Wells knew she had her chance:

> I stated the case plainly, and told how separate schools always meant inferior schools for Negro children while at the same time making a double tax burden. I also told of my interview with the editor of the *Tribune* and how I had been made to realize that there was absolute indifference to whatever the Negro thought or felt about the matter; that the *Tribune* knew it ran no risk of loss in influence or in financial strength from us; that I had asked Miss Addams to call them together and ask if the influential white citizens of Chicago would do for us what we could not do for ourselves. It was their civic and financial influence which the *Tribune* respected; it was monetary patronage to which it catered. Would they use that power to help us, the weaker brothers, secure in Chicago an equal chance with the children of the white races?
>
> At the conclusion of my talk there was general discussion, the predominant note of which was surprise that there was such a movement on foot. Many expressed doubt as to the gravity of the situation and wondered what they could do. Mrs. Celia Parker Wooley [a Unitarian minister and social activist] especially asked just what I thought they could do about it. I told her that that was not for me to say. I had an abiding faith that it was my duty to bring the situation to them, and I felt sure that they would find a way to help. (Wells 1970, 277)

Following the Hull House meeting, Jane Addams headed a delegation of white citizens who met with the editors of the *Tribune*. Wells (1970, 278) writes: "I do not know what they did or what argument was brought to bear, but I do know that the series of articles ceased and from that day until this there has been no further effort made by the *Chicago Tribune* to separate the schoolchildren on the basis of race."

Addams was an early supporter of W. E. B. Du Bois. It is probable, Aptheker (1977) suggests, that she attended the Atlanta University Conference on the Negro Church in May 1903, which Du Bois had organized. It is also likely that the publication of Addams's *Hull House Papers and Maps* in 1895 influenced Du Bois as he wrote his study of *The Philadelphia Negro* the following year. Addams asked Du Bois to speak at Hull House in February 1907, on the occasion of Lincoln's birthday, a president who had referred to lynching as the "mobocratic spirit" and the "ill-omen amongst us" (quoted in Brundage 1997b, 2).

In February 1908, on the centenary of Lincoln's birth, Jane Addams and Ida B. Wells together organized a mass meeting to be held at Orchestra Hall in Chicago. Du Bois was the featured speaker. The celebration was also a call to action against lynching, peonage, convict-lease systems (see chapter 16, section II), disfranchisement and segregation. A year later Wells and Addams were among the forty signers of the call to found the N.A.A.C.P. Later, Addams was among the American representatives who signed the call in support of the First Universal Races Congress held in London in 1911. Her civil-rights activism earned her the appreciative recognition of N.A.A.C.P. leaders. In 1913, acting on behalf of the National Board of the N.A.A.C.P., Oswald Garrison Villard recommended that Jane Addams be one of fifteen people selected to serve on a National Race Commission to be appointed by President Woodrow Wilson. No friend of African Americans, Wilson refused to appoint such a commission. Instead, he (with the support of his mostly southern cabinet, such as William G. McAdoo) introduced the segregation of federal employees in government offices for the first time in U.S. history (Kellogg 1967; Friedman 1970). "Indeed," Aptheker (1977, 8) points out, "in the context of American politics at the turn of the century and after, Addams's affirmative actions on civil rights were courageous, even radical."

As a social activist and civil-rights advocate, Jane Addams felt compelled to enter the national debate over lynching, a debate which Ida B. Wells had managed to precipitate by stirring up British opinion. In January 1901, Addams's statement on the subject was published in the influential weekly magazine, the *Independent*. Entitled "Respect for the Law," the article condemned lynching not in racial or moral or gendered terms but in Marxist ones. In fact, her analysis indicates, Aptheker (1977, 10) argues, "an extraordinary class understanding of the relationship between crime and punishment." That is, Jane Addams understood lynching as a kind of class warfare; it was that crime committed by so-called "lower" and "inferior" classes against the rich which provoked the most savage punishment. Still, Addams understood that "race" was a factor, even if, from her point of view, it operated within class struggle: "Punishments of this sort rise to unspeakable atrocities when the crimes of the so-called inferior class effect the property and persons of the superiority; and when the situation is complicated by race animosity, as it is at present in the South, by the feeling of the former slave owner to his former slave, whom he is now bidden to regard as his fellow citizen, we have the worst possible situation for attempting this method of punishment" (19; quoted in Aptheker 1977, 10–11).

But her reliance upon class analysis left certain blind spots in her understanding. It is clear, for instance, that Addams felt a certain sympathy for white southerners, writing: "Added to all the difficulties of Reconstruction and the restoration of a country devastated by war, they [present generations of southern men] must deal with that most intricate of all problems—the presence of two alien races" (Addams 1901/1977, 23). It is also clear that she had not questioned the widely held assumption that African Americans exhibited a certain "underdevelopment," by which whites meant that they were primitive, prone to crime, especially to sexual deviations such as rape.

In her 1901 article, Addams (1901/1977, 23) argued forcefully that lynching illustrated the axiom that "brutality begets brutality," and that "one of these time-honored false theories has been that criminality can be suppressed and terrorized by exhibitions of brutal punishment; that crime can be prevented by cruelty." Lynching should stop because "the child who is managed by a system of bullying and terrorizing is almost sure to be the vicious and stupid child" (19). Finally, she concluded "that the bestial in man, that which leads him to pillage and rape, can never be controlled by public cruelty and dramatic punishment, which too often cover fury and revenge" (Addams 1901/1977, 25). Not only does the practice fail to deter black crime, she understood, but it contributes to the self-ignorance and moral degradation of the lynchers themselves (Aptheker 1977).

What illustrates just how widespread was the assumption, how pervasive was the fantasy, of the black male as sexual monster becomes quite clear when the ordinarily perceptive Jane Addams gives the benefit of doubt to the South, writing that we can "assume that they have set aside trial by jury and all processes of law because they have become convinced that this brutal method of theirs is the most efficient ... in dealing with a peculiar class of crime committed by one race against another" (18), namely rape. That an activist and intellectual of such stature and significance as Jane Addams could believe that white southerners were telling the truth, even though she knew how horrible lynching was—"[t]he living victim is sometimes horribly mutilated and his body later exhibited" (Addams 1901/1977, 24) *and* in the face of statistics printed in the *Chicago Tribune*, suggests the grip—even upon independently minded progressive intellectuals—of white racial solidarity in the opening years of the twentieth century.

When Addams turned her attention to the role of women in lynching, she regained her usual perceptiveness. She declared that a woman's virtue could not, should not, be protected by actions that clearly assumed her status as property. Addams (1901, 20) wrote:

> To those who say that most of these hideous and terrorizing acts [of lynching] have been committed in the name of chivalry, in order to make the lives and honor of women safe, perhaps it is women themselves who can best reply that bloodshed and arson and ungoverned rage have never yet controlled lust. ... [T]he woman who is protected by violence allows herself to be protected as the woman of the savage is protected, and she must still be regarded as the possession of man. (quoted in Aptheker 1977, 12)

By arguing against lynching, yet apparently accepting its core and inflammatory rationale, Addams, as Aptheker points out, undermined her own case. Her class analysis allowed her to articulate the symbolic relationship between the alleged property crimes of the so-called "lower classes" and the woman-as-property psychosis that structured not only the compulsory heterosexuality of the day, but the homosocial and misogynistic structure of black/white male relations as well. Yet, the Marxist Aptheker (1977) points out, Addams

> failed to appreciate the dialectics of a racial and sexual oppression with common roots in the ownership of private property which sanctified the lynching of the former slave by maintaining the woman's status as a male

> possession. Furthermore, to concede that rape was the cause of lynching made effective opposition to it impossible because it concealed the real class origins of the racist assaults. (Aptheker 1977, 12)

Both Addams and Aptheker fail to ask the question: even if lynching was a tactic of class/race warfare, why did it so often take the form of sexual assault? The blatantly sexualized character of the mutilation and torture that regularly structured lynching events is a key clue to the puzzle that class or traditional race-relations analysis cannot readily decode.

Despite her admiration for Addams, Ida B. Wells could not allow the *Independent* article to go uncontested. In her reply to Addams, which was published in the *Independent* four months later using her husband's name—Wells had married attorney Ferdinand L. Barnett in 1895, and sometimes used his name as well as her own—Wells appears to start slowly, in an almost chatty way. She underlines her appreciation of Addams's support in the struggle against lynching:

> It was eminently befitting that the *Independent's* first number in the new century should contain a strong protest against lynching. The deepest dyed infamy of the nineteenth century was that which, in its supreme contempt for law, defied all constitutional guaranties of citizenship, and during the last fifteen years of the century put to death two thousand men, women and children, by shooting, hanging and burning alive. Well would it have been if every preacher in every pulpit had made so earnest a plea as that which came from Miss Addams's forceful pen. (Wells 1901/1977, 29).

Still emphasizing her appreciation of Addams, Wells moved to the main point, the problem in the Addams essay and in the white mind: the rape fantasy. At the time, Wells was chairwoman of the Anti-Lynching Bureau of the National Afro-American Council which had been founded in 1887 by T. Thomas Fortune, editor of the most influential black newspaper of its time, the *New York Age*. The Florida-born and Marianna-raised Fortune saw lynching as an "exhibition of barbarity on the part of the South" (quoted in Howard 1995, 14). The Council was in fact the first national civil rights organization in the post–Civil War era (Aptheker 1977). Imagine how easy it would have been for Wells, given what she knew and how she had struggled, to explode. One senses her controlled fury as she writes:

> Appreciating the helpful influences of such a dispassionate and logical argument as that made by the writer referred to, I earnestly desire to say nothing to lessen the force of the appeal. At the same time an unfortunate presumption used as a basis for her argument works so serious, tho[ugh] doubtless unintentional, an injury to the memory of thousands of victims of mob law, that it is only fair to call attention to this phase of the writer's plea. It is unspeakably infamous to put thousands of people to death without a trial by jury; it adds to that infamy to charge that these victims were moral monsters, when in fact, four-fifths of them were not so accused even by the fiends who murdered them. (Wells 1901, 1977, 29)

The truth said, she returns to her praise of Addams. Like a well-prepared teacher, Wells reassures her student before pointing out her error:

> Almost at the beginning of her discussion, the distinguished writer says: "Let us assume that the southern citizens who take part in and abet the lynching of negroes honestly believe that that is the only successful method of dealing with a certain class of crime." It is this assumption, this absolutely unwarrantable assumption, that vitiates every suggestion which it inspires Miss Addams to make. It is the same baseless assumption which influences ninety-nine out of every one hundred persons who discuss this question. Among many thousand editorial clippings I have received in the past five years, ninety-nine per cent discuss the question upon the presumption that lynchings are the desperate effort of the southern people to protect their women from black monsters, and while the large majority condemn lynching, the condemnation is tempered with a plea for the lyncher—that human nature gives way under such awful provocation and that the mob, insane for the moment, must be pitied as well as condemned. It is strange that an intelligent, law-abiding and fair-minded people should so persistently shut their eyes to the facts in the discussion of what the civilized world now concedes to be America's national crime. (Wells 1901/1977, 29–30)

In that last phrase Wells reminds her readers that lynching was no curious southern ritual, no aberration in American national life. Lynching was nothing less than "America's national crime," and the rationalization for it was black male rape. Wells's article was entitled "Lynching and the Excuse for It," and it was precisely this fact—and Jane Addams's repetition of the "excuse"—that she intended to refute, with, as Aptheker (1977, 13) puts it, "tactful vigor." She emphasizes that this fantasy is not only fantasy but a "slander" as well:

> Their almost universal tendency to accept as true the slander which the lynchers offer to civilization as an excuse for their crime might be explained if the true facts were difficult to obtain. But not the slightest difficulty intervenes. The Associated Press dispatches, the press clipping bureau, frequent book publications and the annual summary of a number influential journals give the lynching record every year. This record, easily within the reach of every one who wants it, makes inexcusable the statement and cruelly unwarranted the assumption that negroes are lynched only because of their assaults upon womanhood. (Wells 1901/1977, 30)

If we want to speak about "assaults upon womanhood," Wells pointed out, let us talk about assaults on black womanhood. Wells noted that the lynching statistics published in the *Chicago Tribune* show that "five women have been lynched, put to death with unspeakable savagery, during the past five years." These were no rapists of southern white ladies. And of the men, Wells (1901/1977, 32–33) continues,

> not a few, but hundreds, have been lynched for misdemeanors, while others have suffered death for no offense known to the law, the causes assigned being "mistaken identity," "insult," "bad reputation," "unpopularity," "violating contract," "running quarantine," "giving evidence," "frightening child by shooting at rabbits," etc. Then, strangest of all, the record shows that the sum total of lynchings for these offenses—not crimes—and for the alleged offenses which are only misdemeanors, greatly exceeds the lynchings for the very crime universally declared to be the cause of lynching.

"This table tells its own story," Wells points out, underlining the indisputable character of both the data and their source. "[A]nd [it] shows," she continues, reminding her white readers of the main point, "how false is the excuse which lynchers offer to justify their fiendishness." Here we see again her successful inversion of the series "white/male/civilization." But she does not dwell on this point, returning once again to her figures:

> Instead of being the sole cause of lynching, the crime upon which lynchers build their defense furnishes the least victims for the mob. In 1896 less than thirty-nine per cent of the negroes lynched were charged with this crime; in 1897, less than eighteen percent; in 1898, less than sixteen per cent, and in 1900, less than fifteen per cent were so charged. (Wells 1901/1977, 34)

"No good result can come," she reminds, "from any investigation which refuses to consider the facts." Further, "a conclusion that is based upon a presumption, instead of the best evidence, is unworthy of a moment's consideration." Then she reiterates that the rape fantasy is just that, and concludes by once again breaking up the whiteness/manhood/civilization series:

> The lynching record, as it is compiled from day to day by unbiased, reliable, and responsible public journals, should be the basis of every investigation which seeks to discover the cause and suggest the remedy for lynching. The excuses of lynchers and the specious pleas of their apologists should be considered in the light of the record, which they invariably misrepresent or ignore. The Christian and moral forces of the nation should insist that misrepresentation should have no place in the discussion of this all important question, that the figures of the lynching record should be allowed to plead, trumpet tongued, in defense of the slandered dead, that the silence of concession be broken and that truth, swift-winged and courageous, summon this nation to do its duty to exalt justice and preserve inviolate the sacredness of human life. (Wells 1901/1977, 34)

Aptheker (1977, 14) notes that "the fact that Wells's reply is brief should not belie its significance." What is that significance? Even the Marxist Aptheker suspends the obsession with class analysis for a moment, noting that it is sex that is crucial here: "That she chose to limit her rejoinder to the rape issue suggests how decisive a question this was in the struggle for civil rights. Indeed, Wells's own experiences confirm the point."

Jane Addams might have helped Wells more effectively had she seen through the white male fantasy of black male rape. Still, Wells's estimate of Jane Addams as an outstanding and courageous activist is accurate. Addams possessed a powerful and creative intellect dedicated to social and economic justice in an authentically democratic America. Despite her significance and her stature, this white woman also suffered a grain in her eye which kept her from seeing through to the sexualized fantasies operating in white men's minds. The next white woman we meet—Jesse Daniel Ames—also suffers a limitation, despite her courage, determination and stamina. It will be pinned on the matter of protecting "states rights," white southerners' favorite bugaboo at least since they insisted the Civil War was a war of secession, for states' rights.

VI. Jessie Daniel Ames and the Association of Southern Women for the Prevention of Lynching

Asserting their identity as autonomous citizens, requiring not the paternalism of chivalry but the equal protection of the law, association [A.S.W.P.L.] members resisted the part assigned to them.

—Jacquelyn Dowd Hall, "'The Mind That Burns in Each Body': Women, Rape, and Racial Violence" (1983)

[W]hite women never did ask to be protected from those black men. It was their fathers', husbands', and brothers' idea. [W]hite women were as much victims of the system as black men.

—Beth Day, "The Hidden Fear" (1977)

Finally, white women were publicly accepting the responsibility that black women had been pointing out to them for decades.

—Judith Stephens, "Lynching Dramas and Women: History and Critical Context" (1998)

What the conflation of gender and race meant for white women in the antebellum South, as we have seen, was that the same psychosexual and cultural forces that suppressed indigenous antislavery sentiment also precluded a public advocacy of women's rights. Slavery and the subordination of women were intertwined; as long as there was slavery there could be no organized women's movement in the slave states. The early women's movement, led by Elizabeth Cady Stanton and Susan B. Anthony, understood this. During the antebellum period they called, as we have seen, for both women's and African Americans' equality (Hall 1979).

After the Civil War, the political alliance between racial and gender progressives was broken, as the 1866 meeting the American Equal Rights Association underscored. The failure of the Fifteenth Amendment to secure for women the political privileges it granted to freed black men disillusioned feminists such as Stanton who before had been staunch abolitionists. The subsequent defeats of Reconstruction and, twenty years later, Populism, as well as the nativist response to immigration from eastern and southern Europe, reflected and intensified white racism, indicated by the spread of lynching. A new generation of American women's rights advocates—especially southern white women—were not immune (Hall 1979).

As we have seen, southern feminists and suffragists responded to gender and racial issues differently than their northern sisters. Moderate border-state leaders such as Laura Clay of Kentucky advocated an educational requirement for women's suffrage, the consequence of which would be to eliminate the poor, both black and white, from the voting roles. A minority led by Kate M. Gordon of Louisiana advocated the complete elimination of black voters; she and her allies promoted an independent southern women's movement wed to white supremacy and states rights, a marriage evident, as we will see in the next chapter, in white women's participation in the second Klan (Blee 1991). By 1915, when Texas suffragist Jessie Daniel Ames joined the movement, other southern activists had rejected Gordon's racist position. But like their northern allies, they focused on the political prerogatives of the white middle class. The bargain then struck with southerners involved acquiescing in the disenfranchisement of black voters. Like Frances Willard a generation before, they agreed to ignore "the negro question" for the sake of political expediency (Hall 1979).

Black women in the South enjoyed little access to the newly won franchise. At first, in the first days after the Constitutional Amendment extending the vote to women passed in 1920, African-American women "took the registrars by surprise" in some places, and succeeded in registering to vote. Soon enough, however, white racists in the South refused to register black women, as they refused to register black men. In South Carolina, after a group of black women was turned away from the polls, a legal suit was filed under the Nineteenth Amendment (Hall 1979). These twentieth-century women would soon discover what the still-alive Ida B. Wells had discovered forty years ago—namely the U.S. Constitution is no guarantee of the civil rights of all American citizens.

W. E. B. Du Bois had written insightfully about the women's movement, foreseeing that "southern white women who form one of the most repressed and enslaved groups of modern, civilized women will undoubtedly, at first, help willingly and zealously to disfranchise Negroes." William Pickens of the N.A.A.C.P. asked: "Will the [white] women of the United States who know something at least of disfranchisement tolerate such methods to prevent intelligent [black] women from voting?" (quoted in Hall 1979, 46). As Du Bois had guessed, the answer would be yes (Hall 1979).

A new generation of African Americans had fought for their country in World War I; they experienced racism from fellow (white) American soldiers and tolerance from Europeans. Returning home, they were quickly characterized as the "New Negro." In the North the black arts flourished in what came to be known as the Harlem Renaissance (Bontemps 1947; Baker 1987a, 1987b; Huggins 1971; Hull 1987), a decade-long event I hope to discuss in the next volume. In the South the assertiveness of returning soldiers was coded sexually by whites. The Deep South demonstrated its gratitude to African-American soldiers for helping make the world safe for democracy by lynching ten of them, some while in uniform, during the year 1919; two of the ten were burned alive (White 1929). Only constant vigilance, southerners warned, could prevent these young black men from polluting the white race with "the damned touch of the black." The *Shreveport* [Louisiana] *Times* proclaimed: "We venture to say that fully ninety percent of all the race troubles in the South are the result of the Negro forgetting his place" (quoted in Hall 1979, 61). It was, as we have seen, a place in the imagination of white men.

We can glimpse how a southern white man might have viewed the aftermath of World War I in Lillian Smith's (1944/1972) novel *Strange Fruit.* In one passage that follows the lynching of Henry, an innocent black man, she has a white male character think what might have been rather characteristic thoughts among certain white men in the 1920s. In this passage one discerns allusion not only to the influence of fighting in Europe on young black men, but references to the Great Migration and the subsequent labor shortage as well:

> But a lynching now and then did seem to settle things. ... Bad as it was, and it was bad, it did settle things. And things needed settling. Ever since the war, the nigger had been restless. He'd been dead-set against sending them to France with the A.E.F., said then, they'd get ideas the South would pay high for. God knows, plenty things crawling in their heads without mixing em with the French variety! Well, the Yankees who run things in Washington didn't believe it or didn't care. Goddurn fools promised the nigger the vote if he'd go. And now the cussed idiot expected it. Restless ... swarming North like flies to a dirty pot. Thinking because they'd strutted around in khaki and ogled French women they could eat dinner with a white man. Like as not. Yeah. Thought they had a right now to look at white girls. ... Saw one of them a Saturday on the street staring straight at a bunch of girls down at the drugstore. Bound to be trouble. Just a wonder it hadn't come before. Hands short for the pickin'—short at the still—short everywheres. Some of the towns had stopped letting them buy railroad tickets to the North—turning them back. (Smith 1944/1972, 360–361)

This collective psychosis is what Jessie Daniel Ames faced as a progressive woman working in the South. A proponent of justice for African Americans as well as of equality for all women, Ames's career linked a nineteenth-century tradition of social feminism—recall the British antilynching feminists who helped Ida B. Wells—with the twentieth-century American struggle for civil rights. During the 1920s, Ames headed what was probably the most effective of state interracial councils, councils organized throughout the country in order to improve "race relations." In 1929 she became director of women's work for the region-wide Commission on Interracial Cooperation, and on November 1, 1930, Ames rewrote what had been an amorphous women's program of the Interracial Commission into a well-organized, single-issue crusade against lynching (Hall 1979). This became the Association of Southern Women for the Prevention of Lynching. Hall (1983, 337) notes: "[T]wenty-six white women from six southern states met in Atlanta to form the A.S.W.P.L. ... The association had a central, ideological goal: to break the circuit between the tradition of chivalry and the practice of mob murder."

It was not only Ames's efforts but yet another lynching which precipitated the founding of the A.S.W.P.L. It was only six months after the lynching of George Hughes in Sherman, Texas, in 1930, that a small group of southern white women met in Atlanta, and the Association of Southern Women for the Prevention of Lynching was established. The goal of the organization was simple if immense: to mobilize and focus the moral and social leverage of southern women to prevent lynchings, especially in the rural and small-town South. By challenging the link between racial violence and sexual attitudes, Ames hoped their work might contribute to a new gender and racial order in the South (Hall 1979). Ames's tenacity and the emotional intensity of her campaign derived, Jacqueline Dowd Hall (1983) suggests, from her appreciation that lynching was a women's issue. It was in fact "an insult to white women" (Hall 1983, 338). Key to her campaign was the effort to dissociate the image of the southern white woman from its connotations of sexual vulnerability and retaliatory male-on-male violence. "If lynching held a covert message for white women as well as an overt one for blacks," Hall (1983, 338–339) explains, "then the anti-lynching association represented a woman-centered reply."

There was a certain pedagogical as well as political dynamic in the A.S.W.P.L. Like Ida B. Wells and the progressives who followed her, Ames appreciated that social change is in part a process of education. This view is evident in the pledge taken by Association members:

> We declare lynching is an indefensible crime, destructive of all principles of government, hateful, and hostile to every ideal of religion and humanity, debasing, and degrading to every person involved. Though lynchings are not confined to any one section of the United States, we are aroused by the record which discloses our heavy responsibility for the presence of this crime in our country. We believe that this record has been achieved because public opinion has accepted too easily the claim of lynchers and mobsters that they were acting solely in the defense of womanhood. In the light of facts, we dare no longer permit this claim to pass unchallenged nor allow those bent upon personal revenge and savagery to commit acts of violence and lawlessness in the name of women. We solemnly pledge ourselves to create a new public opinion in the South, which will not condone, for any reason whatsoever, acts of mobs or lynchers. We will teach our children at home, at school and at church a new interpretation of law and religion; we will assist all officials to uphold their oath of office; and finally, we will join with every minister, editor, school teacher and patriotic citizen in a program of education to eradicate lynchings and mobs forever from our land. (quoted in Ames 1942, 64)

The founding of the A.S.W.P.L. in Atlanta in 1930 was, then, also an expression of the new vigor with which many antilynching activists set out to persuade their fellow white southerners to become more racially tolerant. Fitzhugh Brundage (1993, 246) views the organization as "the logical evolution" of previous women's campaigns to address the shared issues of racial and gender discrimination in the South, a reform tradition that he associates with the efforts of Lily Hammond and others. Distressed by the sudden increase in the number of lynchings in the 1930s, white women became convinced that they must repudiate the so-called "code of chivalry" that was "being used as shield which our own men committed cowardly acts of violence against a helpless people" (quoted in Brundage 1993, 247).

Under the vigorous leadership of Jesse Daniel Ames, the A.S.W.P.L. grew to a membership of 43,000 women throughout the South, including border states like Kentucky. Ames had already established herself as one of the South's leading social activists, first as suffragist and then, following World War I, working in the Commission on Interracial Cooperation (C.I.C.) throughout the 1920s. With her "aggressive" and "forthright" (Brundage 1993, 247) personality, Ames masterfully directed the day-to-day operations of the association and its skeleton staff.

In Georgia, prominent A.S.W.P.L. members such as Dorothy Tilly of Atlanta, Julia Collier Harris of Atlanta, Ida-Beall Neel of Forsyth, as well as Ames herself persuaded church and social organizations to support the organization's aims. Elsewhere in the South, state chairwomen such as Bessie C. Alford and Ethel F. Stevens of Mississippi and Kate T. Davis of South Carolina worked against the grain to carry the antilynching message of the A.S.W.P.L. into their states. Brundage (1993) characterizes these women activists as progressives, although regionally distinguishable from their more famous compatriots in the North, such as Jane Addams. The southern version of progressivism combined a yearning for social order and control with a sincere desire to stop mob violence and improve "race relations."

To achieve such a "new" South, these women—like Frances Willard—took for granted the virtues of sobriety, piety, education, industry, and self-restraint, virtues which might be natural to women but which would obviously have to be instilled in the menfolk. In many regards, these white antilynching activists, like their counterparts in the W.C.T.U., had a rather narrow moral vision. Yet, simultaneously, as Brundage (1993) points out, these activists taught a radical lesson to fellow southerners, especially when they challenged white men's fantasies about the world. For all of the limitations of the antilynching campaigns of white southerners during the 1930s—for instance, the inability to accept federal intervention or to challenge segregation—these women still understood the gender of racial politics and violence better than had any previous generation of southerners. In Ames's view the struggle for the vote had been crucial in politicizing southern white women:

> Far-fetched as the statement may appear, the enfranchisement of the women in 1920 has contributed … to a new public opinion on lynching. The South did not accept suffrage for women; it acquired it in spite of the fight-to-the-last-ditch stand taken by both the southern press and southern politicians. That southern women should have been slow to exercise the ballot as weapon in the fight to make the world a better place for children was a natural consequence of the oft-repeated and generally accepted statement that no real lady would degrade herself by participating in politics. But younger women, growing to maturity,

> educated in the increasing numbers of co-educational schools, did not accept the dictum of the manmade society. (Ames 1942, 60)

In establishing the Association of Southern Women for the Prevention of Lynching, Ames dedicated herself to the fight with "extraordinary single-mindedness" (Hall 1979, 127). Lynching was, she knew, a women's issue, laced with cultural assumptions regarding race and gender that were as degrading to white women as they were deadly to black men. What the interracial character of the Association and the Commission on Interracial Cooperation signified, Hall (1979) tells us, was that middle-class white people now appreciated that a black middle class had emerged and would be heard. Linked by this class interest, whites might join with blacks to work on the "race problem," *the* problem of the South it seemed to them. Despite this intention of genuine interracial collaboration, the Interracial Commission was decidedly paternalistic (Hall 1979).

Even so, the Commission on Interracial Cooperation was acknowledged appreciatively by civil rights leaders such as Walter White. In his 1929 study of lynching, White cites the work that the Commission had undertaken on southern college campuses. Courses in race relations were being offered, he observed, and voluntary study groups were organized under the direction of members of the C.I.C. staff. The Commission furnished material that answered those questions that uninformed white southern college students tended to ask. Further, the Commission sponsored distinguished black speakers so that southern white college students could see as well as read about the achievements of African Americans (White 1929). Ames (1942, 60) was heartened by these curricular initiatives:

> Race relations, introduced with misgivings in a few of the colleges as a dangerous experiment in education, became popular courses which have spread in the last ten years to more than 75 white southern colleges. The first students introduced to race relations are today men and women in their middle thirties. They and those who have reached maturity in later years hold opinions on conditions in the South's biracial society which are affecting public opinion on lynching and the causes underlying mob violence. The southern colleges, reaching into more and more homes of the low, middle, and upper middle classes, are inevitably, if occasionally reluctantly, helping to destroy the old mores of the South (60).

The Commission published pamphlets on *Negro Progress and Achievement*, *Popular Fallacies about Race Relations*, and *What the Bible Tells Me about Race Relations* to reach as broad a white audience as possible. In addition to teaching white college students, the Commission worked with southern white women off campus. One of its pamphlets, *Southern White Women on Lynching and Mob Violence*, explained that most white women did not regard lynching as necessary for their protection (White 1929).

Southern white women were not likely candidates for street protests or other forms of mass demonstrations. Such aggressive and public strategies of communicating with fellow citizens seemed, well, unladylike. A "more proper medium," as Ames phrased it, would have to be found. "[B]eing southern born and bred," she explained, southern white women "turned naturally to the one organization with which they were familiar—the church." Not only was the church influential in most southern communities, it was also a safe place, "the one recognized sanctuary for women's undisturbed activities." Echoing the opinion of many of Ida B. Wells's British listeners that it was the American South which needed missionaries, Ames suggests that missionary work, usually directed to foreign lands, might well be conducted "at home." So it was in southern churches and synagogues where "southern women became active in race relations and law observance in their own land while they continued their work to extend the Kingdom of God to foreign lands" (all passages in Ames 1942, 60).

Like Wells, Jessie Daniel Ames began her crusade against lynching by conducting on-the-scene investigations. Like Wells she quickly discovered the disparity between the facts and the reports of lynchings published in the white press. Ames confronted newspaper editors in person, emphasizing how their biased and inflammatory coverage supported the practice. While rebuffed by many newspapermen, she succeeded in winning the support of the influential owner of the *Dallas Morning News.* Men in positions of authority intimidated her not at all; during this early phase of her antilynching campaign Ames also sought the cooperation of county sheriffs. And she lobbied in the state legislature in Austin for a Texas antilynching law (Hall 1979).

One major strategy of antilynching campaigners—a strategy Ida B. Wells had devised in the 1880s and which was used later by the N.A.A.C.P. as well as the A.S.W.P.L.—was to use facts and figures to refute white "rationales" for these often sexualized murders of black men. But what Wells knew and Jessie Daniel Ames and the N.A.A.C.P. soon discovered was that the fear of rape was not easily dispelled; it was mythic, rooted deep in the white imagination. White-male fantasies of muscular black studs raping helpless white ladies occurred far beyond the reach of factual refutation. Whatever these fantasies were—and in the 1920s an explanation informed by queer theory would have occurred to few—clearly they circulated not only at the center of white racism, they had everything to do with white-male attitudes toward white women as well (Hall 1979). Today it is clear that suppressed and mangled homosexual desire—sublimated into everyday homosocial relations—not only mutilates male-male relations, it distorts male-female relations as well (see chapter 15).

White men had no clue. In a regime of compulsory heterosexuality and white supremacy, all they could do was calculate according to the racialized and misogynistic logic they mistook for reality. But theirs was no rational, reasoned point of view they could defend with logic and detachment. Even when the eminently respectable, politically moderate white women associated with the Anti-Lynching Association questioned the contents of their imagination, white men did not respond rationally, let alone gratefully. Not even the fact that these were their beloved and fair and presumably vulnerable white ladies shielded these courageous women from the outraged and vicious responses of many southern white men. Imprisoned within their own fantasy, there was only one explanation they could imagine for this scandalous betrayal of race solidarity, this betrayal of ... them. It must be that these are *not* ladies; it must be these are whores, cheap tramps who want to sleep with black men. "You may have yourself a nigger if you want one, but do not force them on others," wrote one outraged southerner (Hall 1979, 154), saying more about his own repressed desire than about the conscious intentions of his white female audience.

This complete break with the reality of the situation left Ames puzzled. "I have always been curious about the ... white mentality," she wrote, "which as far back as I remember assumes that only segregation and the law against intermarriage keep ... white women from preferring the arms of Negro men" (quoted in Hall 1979, 154). In legal terms, rape had been defined as a transgression not so much against the woman as against the property rights of the man to whom she belonged. As the private sexual property of the white man, "white women became the most potent symbol of white male supremacy" (Hall 1979, 155). True enough, but as we have seen, more is at stake in the rape fantasy than its conscious content, and consequently, much more was at stake in maintaining it. White civilization, wrote Doris Lessing in *The Grass Is Singing* (1976), "will never, never admit that a white person, and most particularly, a white woman, can have a human relationship, whether for good or for evil, with a black person. For once it admits that, it crashes, and nothing can save it" (quoted in Hall 1979, 155). Nor can it admit that the white woman's desire was sometimes not *hers* but *his.*

Like Ida B. Wells, Jesse Daniel Ames knew that white allegations of rape were usually false. It was clear to her and to many of her colleagues that the protection white men offered was a "false chivalry." Like Calvin C. Hernton, Ames knew that "[t]he myth of sacred white womanhood ... was not created by the southern white woman, and it was not propounded by the black woman nor the black man. It was, as it could only have been, the southern white man who invented it" (Hernton 1965/1988, 14). Whatever his motive (Hernton thought it was guilt over the white man's sexual exploitation of black women), it was a white man's fantasy, and Jesse Daniel Ames wanted nothing to do with it. In forming the Association, Ames and her colleagues rejected white men's characterization of them as vulnerable, as requiring protection, and in so doing challenged the whole symbolic economy in which the fantasy of the "southern lady" circulated (Hall 1979). This fantasy was, Ames knew, of no recent origin; it was well in place by early in the nineteenth century. Wilbur J. Cash (1960, 89) quotes a speech made at Georgia's first centennial in the 1830s that brought roars from the crowd: "Woman!!! The center and circumference, diameter and periphery, sine, tangent and scant of all our affections." While she made quite a nice design in white men's minds, she was, evidently, not yet worthy of the right to vote.

In a section of Ames's 1942 monograph entitled "Ladies and Lynchings," Lewis T. Nordyke speaks about the Association, I conclude from his language, "man to man." White man to white man, it would appear. There is a patronizing tone in his characterization of A.S.W.P.L. members as well as the use of the desubjectifying and de-individuating term "Negro." Still, Nordyke is clearly sympathetic to the project of the Association and appreciative of the courage of the women committed to it. He writes: "Mob violence, masquerading as the champion of southern womanhood, is petering out below the Mason and Dixon line." Who is responsible? Government? Men's civic groups? The law? No, "the weaker sex is largely responsible." Perhaps that is primarily a rhetorical ploy, as he continues more respectfully:

> The accomplishments of these southern women are not widely known, even in the South. The women have worked quietly—very quietly in comparison with the notoriety of lynching mobs bent on murder. Through personal effort, pressure on state officials and peace officers, and with the help of the church, social and other organizations, they have greatly affected the South's whole approach to the problem of race relations. (Nordyke in Ames 1942, 63)

In a section entitled "Demolishing the Myth of Mob Chivalry" Nordyke seems clear that this is a gendered as well as racialized movement (in Ames 1942, 63).

How did the movement attempt to demolish the myth and save lives? How did members work? Nordyke tells us: "Then the women started work—talking, writing letters, distributing printed circulars, interviewing officers and state officials, addressing organization meetings—with the ambitious goals of interesting every organization of men and women in every county in the South in the campaign against lynching" (Nordyke in Ames 1942, 65). Like the university, the Association was structured around research, teaching and service. Unlike the professoriate, A.S.W.P.L. members faced constant, explicit, life-threatening resistance from their "students." Nordyke tells us:

> There was ridicule. There were threats. Organizations which had made the terrorizing of Negroes their chief business since the Civil War opposed the women, inspired sinister warnings or sent them under their own official letterheads. In no few communities the women were ordered not to speak. In other communities officials demanded that talks be written and censored locally before the women might speak. (quoted in Ames 1942, 65)

Nordyke quotes Ames, who acknowledged that "many of the women were threatened" (65). Not only were many undeterred, many risked their marriages in order to dispel the myth of southern chivalry and save the lives of African Americans.

> I know women who wouldn't tell their husbands of the threats because they feared their families would insist that the women quit the work. Women went into communities in which there had been lynchings. Many of the people were surly, belligerent. When we take into consideration the fact that some of the lynchings had grown out of politics and crooked business deals, we can understand that the women were by no means safe at all times. They knew of the constant danger, and they didn't forget to pray. (Ames 1942, 65)

Finally, in a section entitled "Mrs. Mullino Prevents a Lynching," we glimpse a concrete instance of how A.S.W.P.L. members worked:

> How do some 40,000 crusading southern women work? On Christmas Day, 1934, Mrs. Ames was preparing for holiday festivities. Her telephone rang. An Associated Press editor informed her that a Negro had killed an officer in Schley County, Georgia, and that a mob was forming. Mrs. Ames rushed to the office. She discovered that the Association had no signatures in Schley County. But in adjoining Macon County lived a member of the Georgia Council of the Association, Mrs. F. M. Mullino of Montezuma. Mrs. Ames telephoned Mrs. Mullino, who stopped preparation of her Christmas dinner and started telephoning everyone she knew in Schley County, urging each to bring pressure on the sheriff to prevent a lynching.
>
> A short time later, Mrs. Mullino was informed that the Negro was in a swamp in her own county. She called the sheriff and his deputies, and a number of ministers and other public-spirited citizens, urging them to aid in preventing mob action. Until midafternoon she stayed at her telephone. Finally the Negro was captured—by officers. That Christmas Day was not blackened by a lynching in Georgia. The law took its course. Had Mrs. Mullino gone to the mob and pleaded for restraint she would have been taunted. She knew that. She knew too, that a sheriff, even though disposed to carelessness in such cases, couldn't afford to take any chances after dozens of influential voters had demanded that every possible precaution be taken to insure a constitutional trial for the accused Negro. (Nordyke in Ames 1942, 66)

The language is paternalistic, the politics limited, but the picture is clear. Inspired by a gendered racial analysis, Jesse Daniel Ames and her associates in the A.S.W.P.L. were determined to, and in fact did, prevent lynchings.

Ida B. Wells had laid the groundwork of a feminist reformulation of gendered identity during the 1890s. Now, thirty years later, Ames and her colleagues knew there was a relationship between homosocial racial violence and heterosexual exploitation, but they came to appreciate and articulate this fact slowly and with ambivalence. Along with black men, black women had long sought the white southern support that the Commission on Interracial Cooperation (C.I.C.) and the A.S.W.P.L. belatedly offered. Decades of black struggle against lynching—initiated and led by Ida B. Wells, often "indirect," and later institutionalized by the N.A.A.C.P.—had influenced the social and political climate to make the founding of the A.S.W.P.L. possible (Hall 1979).

It was in 1910 that the N.A.A.C.P. took up Ida B. Wells's one-woman antilynching crusade. Recall that in 1922 the N.A.A.C.P. formed a women's group called the Anti-Lynching Crusaders to organize support for the Dyer Antilynching Bill. Led by Mary B. Talbert, president of the National Association of Colored Women, the Crusaders mobilized black women to fight for federal legislation to prevent lynching. William Pickens, the N.A.A.C.P. field secretary, characterized their work as "the greatest effort of Negro womanhood in this generation" (quoted in Hall 1979, 165). Ida B. Wells was ignored. The N.A.A.C.P.'s role in the struggle against lynching is described in chapters 10–12.

For southern white women to involve themselves in an issue with such profound psychosexual implications was in itself a sign of significant social change. There had been, evidently, a shift in gender relations. While for black women the struggle against lynching was about race, for white women it was primarily a matter of gender, a rebellion, as Jessie Daniel Ames notes, against "the crown of chivalry which has been pressed like a crown of thorns on our heads" (quoted in Hall 1979, 167). For them, it was white women, not mutilated black men, who figured as the sacrificed savior.

The association between lynching and rape positioned white women as sexual objects, always, presumably, tempting black lust, ever in need of protection and rescue by their white male protectors. But all this was occurring in the fantasy life of white men. White women resented being used as an imaginary object between black and white men, even if they did not yet understand Gayle Rubin's (1975) famous phrase "the traffic in women," a phrase which denotes precisely women's role as symbolic currency in a homosocial economy. Having recently secured the right to vote, Jessie Daniel Ames and her colleagues did know they were autonomous citizens. Secure in their own inner strength and confident about legal protection—black women certainly shared the former but hardly the latter—the women of the A.S.W.P.L. declined to play the role white men fantasized for them. "Public opinion has accepted too easily the claim of lynchers and mobsters that they were acting *solely in the defense of womanhood*," they announced. "Women dare no longer to permit the claim to pass unchallenged nor allow themselves to be the cloak behind which those bent upon personal revenge and savagery commit acts of violence and lawlessness" (quoted in Hall 1979, 194). Such courage inspired other white women in the South; Lillian Smith (1944/1972), novelist and one of the most eloquent white critics in the 1950s of lynching, located herself in a tradition begun by the A.S.W.P.L. (Hall 1979; Loveland 1986; see chapter 3).

Ames and the Association of Southern Women for the Prevention of Lynching were active in protesting the most prominent lynchings of the 1930s, including the Scottsboro Nine and the lynching of Claude Neal. This protest activity did not occur only in the larger cities. Ames did not hesitate to intervene in the locale where the events occurred. "I don't know whether they will get perfectly furious with me or not," Ames wondered, as she fired off a graphic narrative of the slow torture, castration, and murder of Claude Neal to all the women on her mailing list in Jackson County, Florida, where the lynching had occurred (quoted in Hall 1979, 211).

In 1968, sociologist John Shelton Reed found a dramatic decrease in the number of lynching victims in those counties where the Association had made its presence known. Reed concluded that the A.S.W.P.L. had subjected sheriffs to sufficient pressure that they were more inclined to protect their prisoners from lynching mobs. He suggested that A.S.W.P.L. presence forced law enforcement officials to assert a climate of disapproval which discouraged potential lynchers (Hall 1979).

Ames herself was modest about her achievement, at least in her 1942 *The Changing Character of Lynching*. There she credits almost everyone else but herself for the progress made "toward a lynchless America" (Ames 1942, 59). She cites the New Deal, the southern press, southern colleges, and, particularly, the work of those women who comprised the membership of the Association of Southern Women for the Prevention of Lynching. Regarding the New Deal she singles out the Civilian Conservation Corps camps which, she explains, "took the idle, unemployed, and illiterate or near illiterate youth of both races out of their communities and gave them work under supervision. ... The C.C.C. removed these actual and potential lynchers from the environment which favored mob violence" (Ames 1942, 15). After Raper, she notes that in the lynching mobs of 1930 "teen age boys were conspicuously present" (quoted in Ames 1942, 15), rendering the effect of the C.C.C. especially important to the suppression of lynching. "The Works Progress Administration," she adds, "did for adults much the same service that the C.C.C. did for the boys" (Ames 1942, 16).

The largest newspapers of the South, Ames grants, had in recent years criticized lynching on their editorial pages, if with reservation. Relying on Raper's analysis, she points out that even these antilynching papers still allowed that as long "as a certain crime" (15) was committed by black men, lynchings would continue. Such an allowance helped "fix in the public mind that lynchings for some causes were justified" (Ames 1942, 15). Smaller daily newspapers as well as weekly papers tended to support this point of view. Despite this problem, Ames (1942, 15) concludes, "Probably no other public-opinion-forming agency has done more to change the public's attitude toward lynching than has the southern press."

Regarding southern colleges, Ames observed that many southern colleges "began to liberalize their curricula to include sociology, economics, and political science—subjects with current and local applications" (1942, 60). There was as well, she thought, a generational element undermining the practice of lynching: "The young people reaching college age twenty years ago were an awakening group of future citizens. The war had made them restless and disobedient to the mores of the prewar period. In addition, they were the third generation removed from the experiences of Reconstruction and their emotions of sectionalism and race prejudice were not so deep that they were blinded intellectually to the conditions of the present" (Ames 1942, 60).

The women of the A.S.W.P.L. directed their efforts "to exposing the falsity of the claim that lynching is necessary to their protection and to emphasizing the real danger of lynching to all the values of the home and religion" (Ames 1942, 19). Like nineteenth-century Christian feminists, these conservative southern white women invoked Victorian homilies regarding the sanctity of the home to puncture white men's fantasies about the relation between chivalry and race. These women had little interest in social revolution; in general they wanted to preserve the present social structure. But they did want to end lynching, and their role in that, despite certain historians' skepticism, was clear to Ames: "The influence of church women on the lynching situation is not a conjecture" (1942, 61). Ames concludes:

> These—interracial meetings, schools, the church and home, the press and southern women as an organized bloc—are all contributing factors to a changing public opinion in the South toward lynching. To which one is due the most credit depends upon the point of view of the proponents of each. But regardless of credit, lynching is decreasing and disappearing by

> the initiative and support of southern white people. Lynchers are no longer held in esteem and they are beginning to feel it. (Ames 1942, 61)

Jessie Daniel Ames died on February 21, 1972, at the age of eighty-eight. Hall tells us that she had watched the 1960s civil rights movement with "approval and satisfaction." She felt sure that the antilynching campaign had played its part by undermining the white South's obsession with racial oppression. "But," Hall (1979, 255) continues,

> in the shadow, first of the male-dominated liberalism generated by the Depression decade, then of the black-led direct-action assault on segregation, the courage and dedication of her generation of women reformers seemed to shrink to insignificance. Ames's death passed virtually unnoticed; she had not become part of the folklore of southern struggle. With the rebirth of feminism, however, a different climate of opinion emerged ... [and] Jessie Daniel Ames's story could be recovered and the implications of her career better understood.

Ames lived to see the first study of the Interracial Commission published; she resented the condescension and sentimentality with which the southern women's antilynching campaign was treated. "I do hope," she wrote to an interviewer, "that you will confine yourself to facts and not attempt to romanticize the work of southern women in the field of race relations" (quoted in Hall 1979, 262). Lynching may have been primarily about men, but the political struggle against it had been initiated and led by women, black and white. Beginning with the lynching of Zachariah Walker in 1911 and intensifying just after World War I, by the 1920s the male-led N.A.A.C.P. institutionalized the campaign to stop lynching. Before we read about that campaign, let us examine another instance of the complicated and contradictory character of the gender of racial politics: white women's participation in the second Ku Klux Klan. The first Klan, organized fifty years earlier just as Reconstruction of the South failed, had had no female members. It was a group of (mad) men.

9 WHITE WOMEN *in the* KU KLUX KLAN

I. Mad Men: The (First) Ku Klux Klan

It was mostly after slavery that the fear white men had of black men began to take some of its more lascivious forms. It was then that the myth of the black man's sexuality, the myth of the black man as sexual monster, as a threat to pure white womanhood, began to gain force. After the ill-fated Reconstruction period came the rise of the Ku Klux Klan, the thousands of lynchings, and the group effort on the part of white men to sever the black man's penis from his body.

—Michelle Wallace, *Black Macho and the Myth of the Superwoman* (1978)

The terrorization of black men, the abuse of white women of the lower classes, and the conflation of politics and sex were interlocking elements in the broader sexualization of politics in the Reconstruction South.

—Martha Hodes, "The Secularization of Reconstruction Politics" (1993)

The Ku Klux Klan played a crucial role in bringing about the restoration of white southern control.

—Edward L. Ayers, *Vengeance and Justice: Crime and Punishment in the Nineteenth Century South* (1984)

Pictorially, the Klan presents this Return of the Repressed in a stunning manner. White pillow case and sheet ... the face covered ... identity disappears and with it the conscience ... a group stalks in silence through the "darkness" ... a sudden abrupt appearance before the victim ... and finally, the symbolic killing of a black male who, according to this paranoid fantasy, has "raped" a "sacred" white women.

—Lillian Smith, *Killers of the Dream* (1949/1963)

When the phallus becomes erect and is handled like a banana, it is not a "personal hard-on' we see but a tribal erection.

—Gilles Deleuze and Félix Guattari, *A Thousand Plateaus: Capitalism and Schizophrenia* (1987)

Booker T. Washington once observed that the white man could never hold the black man in a ditch without getting in the ditch with him. The Ku Klux Klan, Allen Trelease (1971) argues, illustrates this point perfectly. Beginning as a social fraternity devoted to playing pranks, the all-male group soon became a terrorist organization devoted (so its members imagined) to the preservation of white supremacy. In the context of Reconstruction politics after 1867, the K.K.K. became the militarily defeated but determined South's counterrevolutionary tool by means of which it could fight the Republican party and undermine Congress' Reconstruction policy. For more than four years the K.K.K. whipped, shot, hanged, robbed, and raped, terrifying African Americans and Republicans across the South, all in the name of preserving white "civilization" (Trelease 1971).

The Freedmen's Bureau functioned as a barrier, albeit a weak and unfortunately porous one, between white and black men (see chapter 2, section V). The Ku Klux Klan served as a symbol of white mobilization, solidarity, and contempt for blacks; it also revealed white fear. African Americans had no organization such as the Klan, but they did band together when white authorities did not obey the law, as we saw in chapter 7. In the old plantation regions of the so-called black belt, the Klan was really a testimony to black assertion and autonomy, not to black powerlessness. In the mountainous northwestern corner of Georgia, however, freedpeople offered whites no political challenge and little economic competition or resistance. Yet the Klan in the area was vicious and brutal (Ayers 1984).

The Klan could have not been active, of course, without public support in those areas where it dominated. Throughout the Reconstruction South, there was a large element—perhaps a majority of the population—who were both repelled and attracted by the Klan. Writing in the first years of the twentieth century, James Cutler (1905, 154) put the matter this way: "It is true that the extreme measures taken under Ku-Klux disguises never received the approval of the mass of the southern people, but, on the other hand, few determined efforts were made by the civil authorities in the southern states to bring Ku-Klux offenders to justice." Klan membership included all classes of southern white men, but the leaders were often well-to-do. For instance, the former Confederate general Nathan Bedford Forrest (who would later insist that the Klan "had no political purpose" [quoted in Hodes 1993, 414]) became the Klan's leader, or Grand Wizard, and state leaders included lawyers, businessmen, journalists, former governors, and future U.S. senators (Hodes 1993). Much of its membership, however, was drawn from middle-class white men who longed for a return to traditional standards of "moral" conformity (Brundage 1993), meaning a social order in which white men were "on top" and blacks stayed in their "place," which was "on bottom." The two years between Appomattox and Reconstruction allowed the South to recover psychologically from its defeat, enough so that all its energies could be mobilized to serve the only cause that was not lost, that of race. The South, as it has been observed, may have lost the War, but it would win the peace (Trelease 1971; Lacy 1972; Hartman 1997).

At first, as we saw in the final section of chapter 4, southern men sunk into defeat, military and gendered. Some were physically mutilated; many were injured; no man returned to the life he had led before the War. James Cutler (1905, 142) writes: "At the close of the war, when the young men of the South who had escaped death on the battlefield returned to their homes, they passed through a period of enforced inactivity." Cutler points out that the southern economy had been destroyed; men were unable to resume or start businesses or professional pursuits. For many, four years of war and suffering had destroyed their capacity for self-sacrifice and work. Few had capital to start up mercantile or agricultural enterprises. Moreover, there were no amusements and social diversions to distract shattered southern white men from their misery and defeat. When a few Confederate veterans in Pulaski, Tennessee, suggested commemorating their deceased comrades, "the reaction ... was intense" (Cutler 1905, 142).

Hardly an issue arose after the War that did not involve "the race question," directly or indirectly. The issue was overdetermined because it carried psycho-political freight for which the South had no other conveyance. But it was not only or even primarily a symbol for other inexpressible sentiments; those southerners who had owned slaves missed them. Like jilted lovers, if they could not have them, no one would have them. But the eroticized character of white bitterness in the South was always masked by race rhetoric. For instance, the Louisiana Democratic party platform of 1865 proclaimed: "That we hold this to be a Government of white people, made and to be perpetuated for the exclusive benefit of the white race; and ... that people of African descent cannot be considered as citizens of the United States, and that there can, in no event, nor under any circumstances, be any equality between the white and other races" (quoted in Trelease 1971, xv).

"Race" was the question whites could not stop asking. White men in the South generally agreed that freed blacks behaved well after the War. For many this was a relief, even a pleasant surprise, as they had assumed that slavery alone could keep them in check. Most freed black people were as submissive and deferential to whites as slavery had required them to be before the War. African Americans committed fewer murders than whites in proportion to their number, and most of these were crimes of passion in which other blacks were the victims, as remains the case today. As we have observed in reference to lynching, black men were more often the victims than the perpetrators of interracial violence (Trelease 1971).

But this fact would not matter to southern whites; the occasional act of black violence would function only to confirm the stubborn white fantasy that Anglo-Saxon "civilization" was in peril. As early as 1868—some twenty years before the zenith of lynching—the white imagination grew restive. The *Fayetteville* (Tennessee) *Observer* spoke for most of its readers when it condoned the lynching of an alleged black rapist in 1868: "The community said amen to the act—it was just and right. We know not who did it, whether Ku Klux Klan or the immediate neighbors, but we feel that they were only the instruments of Divine vengeance in carrying out His holy and immutable decrees" (quoted in Trelease 1971, xxi). As they had in reference to slavery, southerners continued to claim an especially close and privileged relationship to God on a number of social issues. Today these are abortion and homosexuality; then it was "race."

The Old South had never tolerated rational discussions of slavery, and it had no intention of beginning now. Instead, the South wallowed in bitterness in having lost the War. After all, no one less than the president of the Confederacy had made it clear that dissent on slavery—or on "race"—was unacceptable and should be met with harsh penalties. Before the War Jefferson Davis told a New York audience that those northerners who proclaimed a higher law than the Constitution, that is, those who had condemned slavery on moral grounds, "*should be tarred and feathered, and whipped.* ... The man who ... preaches treason to the Constitution and the dictates of all human society, is a fit object for a Lynch law that would be higher than any he could urge" (quoted in Trelease 1971, xli). It was this defensive self-righteousness that prompted southerners to take their revenge on the formerly enslaved. Speaking of southern officials, observers reported to Congress: "These regulators shoot freedmen without provocation, drive them from plantations without pay, and commit other crimes" (quoted Trelease 1971, xlvi). Similar reports came from almost every southern state during the first two years after the War, the interim before Reconstruction governments were established (Trelease 1971).

The Report of the Congressional Commission of 1872 recorded federal investigation of Klan activities. The Report fills thirteen volumes, each volume approximately six hundred pages in length. Two statistics give some sense of the situation. In Alabama, for instance, there were 107 lynchings within a two-year period. Within a few weeks in 1868 more than two thousand persons were murdered, assassinated, or "handled" by mobs in Louisiana. In Bossier Parish the bodies of 120 African Americans were found following a "nigger hunt" (White 1929, 95). Who were these murderers and terrorists?

They were men, white men. At first they came together in informal, roving bands, but soon enough several of these became sufficiently organized to adopt a certain ceremony and ritual, and to assume such names as (in Alabama) the Black Calvary and the Men of Justice. Most of these early groups lost these separate identities (at least to outsiders) in 1868 when the Ku Klux Klan became famous. While most chose to become part of the Klan, several carried on as before, and one, the Knights of the White Camellia in Louisiana, was large enough to become well-known in its own right (Trelease 1971).

The Ku Klux Klan reached its Reconstruction zenith only with the advent of black suffrage. Organizing first in Tennessee, it spread quickly throughout the South. The testimony of its victims makes its central purpose clear: the intimidation and punishment of Republican voters and officeholders, which is to say, mostly freed black men. Klansmen repeatedly attacked the recently emancipated for no other stated offense than voting, or intending to vote, the Republican ticket. Few Democrats in the South were willing to acknowledge the Klan's explicit political and racial purpose at the time. Northern Democrats too evidently felt compelled to join their southern colleagues in denying the obvious (Trelease 1971).

While the Ku Klux Klan was a mass movement with several objectives, all of them had something to do with white supremacy. (The only exception to this rule was in several mountain counties of Georgia and North Carolina, where the Klan protected moonshiners.) The Klan evolved out of white folk beliefs and practices of the Old South, focused and intensified by the chaotic conditions of Reconstruction. It provided a new form of collectivization, a new social medium for white outrage which many conservatives felt. Like group rape (see chapter 13), the Klan freed its members to commit atrocities which they might not have committed as individuals (Trelease 1971).

The Ku Klux Klan was born in the law office of Judge Thomas M. Jones in Pulaski, Tennessee. The date is uncertain. In later years, when the founders were willing to discuss their paternity, memories had dimmed and details were vague. Each of the six founders were young Confederate veterans, "hungering and thirsting" (Trelease 1971, 3) for amusement, as one of them later put it, after the excitement of wartime had given way once again to the boredom of small-town life. They were Captain John C. Lester, Major James R. Crowe, John B. Kennedy, Calvin Jones, Richard R. Reed, and Frank O. McCord. All were said to come from "good" families and were, given the time and the place, well educated (Trelease 1971). All were white men.

The organization of the new society took form at successive meetings, with the membership growing to eight to ten from the beginning. Two committees were chosen, one to select a name and the other to decide upon rules and rituals. They settled on the name first, choosing "Ku Klux Klan" due to its novelty, its alliteration, and its unclear meaning. Quite likely, as Lester and Wilson themselves later speculated, the name itself had something to do with the group's survival and expansion. The derivation of the name was relatively simple. "Ku Klux" was merely a corruption of the Greek *kuklos*, meaning circle or band. "Klan" was redundant but it alliterated (Trelease 1971). This was an age of the classical curriculum and faculty psychology, and Greek was the machine by which the muscle that was the mind was hardened (see Pinar et al. 1995, chapter 2).

The proliferation of academic and social fraternities in American colleges (beginning with Phi Beta Kappa in 1776) drew heavily on Greek to devise names (not to mention rituals). In the South the best known of these organizations was the social fraternity Kuklos Adelphon or "old Kappa Alpha," founded at the University of North Carolina in 1812. By midcentury it had spread throughout the South, not only to college campuses but to cities and towns where there were college alumni. The society began to dissolve in the 1850s and disappeared altogether by Reconstruction, but most educated southerners in 1866 were familiar with it, including no doubt the founders of the Ku Klux Klan. One of the founders indicated that the Klan's ritual was closely patterned after college fraternity rites; almost certainly Kuklos Adelphon served as the model. Modeled after Kuklos Adelphon's, the initiation ritual for new Klan members was rather elaborate. The actual process of induction combined false solemnity with practical jokes and hazing. Allen Trelease (1971, 5) comments: "The whole process would be familiar to anyone who has gone through college fraternity initiations, formal and informal." In chapter 13, we will read what those are like. Frank McCord was elected the first Grand Cyclops (Trelease 1971).

The Klan was limited to Tennessee and a few counties of north Alabama before 1868. Probably it was never as popular elsewhere as in the state of its birth. The first four months of 1868 saw a horrifying expansion of the Ku Klux Klan, from half a dozen or so counties in middle Tennessee to every southern state between the Potomac and the Rio Grande, plus Kentucky. At its Reconstruction zenith, it had 550,000 members across the South and more than 40,000 in Tennessee. Most of this expansion occurred suddenly during the time when "radical" state governments were being organized under the Congressional Reconstruction Acts of 1867. This timing points to its political genesis, and the Klan's activities confirm it. As in Tennessee, the Klan's purpose was to fight every aspect of Radical Reconstruction, especially the idea of racial equality—which southern whites transposed into "negro domination" (Trelease 1971). The phrase resonates sexually as well as politically.

African Americans as well as the small Unionist element were subject to continual harassment and violence. The responsibility for this state of terrorism throughout the South lay, Trelease (1971) tells us, with the entire community. While members of the dominant class, the old planters and politicians, complained loudly about the influx of outlaws from the "outside," they made no effort to provide the police protection necessary to discourage them. Law officers were either incompetent or involved in the violence themselves. Blacks faced a double standard; crimes against whites were seldom punished (unless committed by blacks) and crimes against freedmen went wholly unnoticed. Trelease comments: "Bullying Negroes was an established pastime with a sizeable portion of southern white manhood, and the inclination increased with Emancipation" (Trelease 1971, 11). "Bullying" and "manhood" indeed.

The fate of Henry Lowther, a married freedman in central Georgia, illustrates the conflation of white male rage and sexuality. Twenty disguised Klansmen had surrounded the Lowther home one night, but Lowther wasn't there. "They said I had taken too great a stand against them in the republican party," Lowther recalled later. "I worked for my money and carried on a shop. They all got broke and did not pay me, and I sued them." Lowther continued: "They have been working at me ever since I have been free. I had too much money." At first Lowther was jailed on charges of conspiring to murder another black man but was denied a trial. Then he was warned by a white man of coming trouble; he asked Lowther if he was "willing to give up your stones to save your life," meaning was he willing to allow himself to be castrated. As Lowther remembered the scene, almost two hundred Klansmen arrived in the middle of the night. Twenty of them forced him into a swamp. "The moon was shining bright," and I could see them," Lowther recalled (quoted in Hodes 1993, 407). There the Klansmen castrated him (Hodes 1993, 407). Lowther was by no means alone; in North Carolina, for example, Klansmen forced a black man to mutilate his own sexual organs with a knife. They were angry over a labor dispute (Hodes 1993). As we will see, women who participated in the second Klan fifty years later were guilty of much, but they did not genitally mutilate other women, or men.

Although the Reconstruction-era Klan excluded white women from membership, there is evidence that white women played a part in Klan activities. Female relatives of Klansmen sewed costumes, either voluntarily or by force; some women loaned their clothing as disguises. There is evidence too that other women urged their husbands not to participate in raids, probably primarily due to concern for their safety. As a specifically male-only organization, one of the Klan's stated purposes was that "females, friends, widows, and their households shall ever be special objects of our regard and protection" (quoted in Hodes 1993, 409). Such "chivalry" applied, of course, to white women only. In addition to sexually assaulting black men, Klansmen also assaulted and raped black women (Hodes 1993).

Not only black women were excluded from white male "protection." "[Lower-class] white women," Martha Hodes (1993, 410) reports, "could not count upon white ideology about white female purity and black male aggression to absolve them of illicit sexual activity." Such women, judged by Klansmen and their sympathizers as "impure," were subject to abuse ranging from insults to rape. On at least one occasion white male Klansmen sexually mutilated a Georgia white woman who was living with a black man. After castrating the black man, a witness reported later, Klansmen "took the woman, laid her down on the ground, then cut a slit on each side of her orifice, put a large padlock in it, locked it up, and threw away the key, and then turned her loose" (quoted in Hodes 1993, 410). "For white southern men," Hodes writes, "the threat of black men's political power and its link to sexual transgressions with white women indicates the conflation, in the minds of Klansmen and their supporters, of sexual immorality and party politics" (1993, 412).

Lynching cannot be blamed on the Ku Klux Klan, but Klan members were often instrumental in precipitating lynchings, and they were often present at lynching events. Who were these madmen? In the first version of the Klan—that we see today, in contrast, are tired, misshapen old white men—the great majority were young white men. They were strong young men, physically able to perform long night riding necessary to capture the fleeing, hidden "game." These were young white men who found such "work" appealing. "I believe that very frequently young men—boys and youth—are deluded into this thing by its novelty and mystery and secrecy," the attorney general of Mississippi testified in 1871; "there is a sort of a charm in this respect to young men, and they go into it frequently without realizing the extent of their wrong-doing" (quoted in Trelease 1971, 52).

The Klan was a madman's adventure, in part an effort to escape the tedium of rural life; as such it was intertwined with male fantasies of "action" and risk. It was also a "patriotic" venture which, like military service in wartime, enjoyed the support of ex-Confederate public opinion. Men for centuries have murdered other men in the name of the fatherland. Charles Stearns, a Republican born in the North who maintained a cotton plantation in Columbia County, Georgia, where he had had several years' experience contending with the K.K.K., said that the Klan was composed of men who "are neither better nor worse, than the average of the population; but simply young men, with plenty of leisure on their hands, and with great love of adventure in their souls, and intensely rebel in their proclivities" (quoted in Trelease 1971, 52).

There were Klansmen who appeared to understand, at least at some subliminal level, that their activity had content beyond its self-declared honoring of the memory of Confederate war dead (thus the sheets, conjuring up their spirits or ghosts roaming the southern countryside), content in addition to the protection of white womanhood and southern honor. This "understanding" was in evidence near Monticello, Arkansas, where the Klan decided to punish a local sheriff who, they decided, had been too sympathetic to blacks. A band of about fifteen disguised Klansmen took Deputy Sheriff William Dollar from his home one night and tied a rope to his neck. They tied a black man named Fred Reeves, to the other end, then shot the two to death. Then they intertwined the two bodies together in an embrace and deposited them in the road, where the couple "remained as an object of attraction to the curious for two days" (Trelease 1971, 150).

An ancient practice in the Scottish highlands, the burning of crosses was evidently introduced to the South by Thomas Dixon, a turn-of-the-century novelist and preacher. His 1905 novel *The Clansmen* and its film version, *The Birth of a Nation*, did more than anything else to create a national fantasy of the Klan as heroically southern. If the post-Reconstruction Klan had not burned crosses, it did comparable nonsense; individuals were sometimes awakened in the morning to find gallows or miniature coffins placed in front of their houses (Trelease 1971).

One of the fervent admirers of *The Birth of a Nation* was William J. Simmons of Atlanta. Simmons's father had belonged to the Klan and had filled his son's ears with tales of southern glory throughout his boyhood. In 1900, at the age of twenty, Simmons had a sudden nocturnal vision of white-robed Klansmen passing across the wall of his room; thereupon, as he later recalled, he vowed to "found a fraternal organization which would be a memorial to the Ku Klux Klan" (quoted in Trelease 1971, 421). While a memorial to the past, the reborn K.K.K. was to be as well "a new fraternal organization dedicated to the everlasting exaltation of southern heroism, chivalry, and Anglo-Saxon splendor; an organization that would work for the revival of rural, Protestant culture; an organization which shunned the alien, put the Negro in his place, and elevated the Anglo-Saxon American to his rightfully superior niche in American society" (Dinnerstein 1968, 149).

In 1915, doubtless inspired by *The Birth of a Nation*, Simmons founded such an organization. Perhaps the movie would not have been enough, but he had a ready-made group: the thirty-three members of the Knights of Mary Phagan, named after the thirteen-year-old girl who had been murdered in a pencil factory in Atlanta, Georgia, on Confederate Memorial Day, 1913. The plant's superintendent and part owner, Leo Frank, had been tried in a mob atmosphere of virulent anti-Semitism. After the governor of Georgia had commuted his death sentence, the Knights of Mary Phagan formed to carry out lynch law. Leo Frank was lynched on August 16, 1915. In the autumn of 1915

Simmons led thirty-three of the Knights of Mary Phagan to the top of Stone Mountain, where they burned a cross on Thanksgiving night. With this act of confused symbolism the second Ku Klux Klan was born (Trelease 1971; Dinnerstein 1968).

During the First World War the new Klan won attention as a group of superpatriots. In the early 1920s it grew rapidly across the country, far exceeding the membership and geographical range of the Reconstruction Klan. The new order shared the virulent antiblack racism of the old, but its list of hates and fears was not limited to African Americans. Catholics, Jews, immigrants, radicals, organized labor, and other groups (such as homosexuals) were also imagined as posing a threat to the nation's integrity and survival. There was another significant difference; this second Klan recruited women members into an allied but separate organization, the W.K.K.K. This second Klan also promoted financial schemes which made a few of its leaders rich. While this financial preoccupation had not been present in the Reconstruction Klan, the reborn K.K.K., as a vigilante organization practicing intimidation and violence, and wielding considerable political power on behalf of intolerance and hatred, bore a striking resemblance to its predecessor (Trelease 1971). The women's Klan did not.

II. Ordinary People: White Women of the (Second) Ku Klux Klan

The exact size of the women's Klan in Indiana cannot be determined. Historians estimate that a quarter-million women joined the W.K.K.K. during the 1920s, or 32 percent of the entire native-born female population of the state. Many women were members only for short periods, making membership estimates at any specific date lower than cumulative totals.

—Katherine M. Blee, *Women of the Klan: Racism and Gender in the 1920s* (1991)

The expansion of the [second] Klan had resulted from its ability to tap all of the prejudices that surged up in American society in the wake of World War I.

—Elisabeth Young-Bruehl, *The Anatomy of Prejudices* (1996)

White women's participation in the second Klan occurs in conjunction with white men's participation in the Klan, and, more broadly, within the history of racial politics and violence in the United States. As we have seen, American racial politics and violence are profoundly gendered. To suggest why so many white women found the racist program of the second Klan attractive, let us, for a moment, examine the state of gender in the 1920s, the conditions under which women lived as women, and men as men.

In the 1920s, most women spent between forty-three and fifty hours each week cooking, cleaning, mending, and shopping. If they lived in cities, they spent somewhat less; if they lived on farms, somewhat more. If they had children, the number of hours committed to domestic labor increased sharply. Then the average workweek was fifty-six hours: an eight-hour day, Monday through Sunday. For those women with children who lived on farms, the hours were even longer: ten hours in winter, thirteen in summer. Moreover, despite the mass production of labor-saving appliances, many women lived in primitive circumstances. One-quarter of the homes in Cleveland, for instance, had neither running water nor stationary laundry tubs; two-thirds in Indianapolis; and nine-tenths in Atlanta. Nationwide, one home of every six had no kitchen sink, one-fifth were without flush toilets, and three-quarters were without electric washing machines. While the use of electric irons and sewing machines increased, middle-class mothers were no better off, having lost their full-time servants. While middle-class and white housewives and mothers were at the privileged end of all these averages, they did not escape the life-defining labor suggested by these statistics. At home, American women were doing a job that made their husbands' seem, in contrast, rather manageable (Filene 1998).

In what condition were their husbands? Many American men returned home from the Great War wounded and shell-shocked. The war had been widely characterized as occasion for men to prove they were "men," and many had failed the test. The return to "normalcy" promised by the Republicans in the 1920 presidential campaign was not just a political promise, but, as well, a racial and gendered one. Despite the election of a "family man" from Marion, Ohio, the promise of "normalcy" would not, could not, be kept.

Those men who made it home came home from World War I not to the domestic sphere they might have been taught by their fathers to expect. Many came home to find that women were sometimes no longer there. At war's end, women continued to enter the workforce in record numbers. The passage of women's suffrage in 1920 accelerated women's entry into the public sphere. By 1920 about one-half of all college students and one-third of all employed Americans were women. The "new woman" of the 1920s was not only more assertive in civic senses; she was more aggressive sexually. The "flapper" threatened many men's fantasy of the sexually pure, stay-at-home mother devoted to her children and to her husband (Kimmel 1996).

When there was a home, it turned out to be, in gendered terms, something of a battlefront itself. This time "manhood," not democracy, was threatened, specifically the manhood of America's sons. In J. B. Watson's influential *Psychological Care of the Infant and Child* (1928), mother's role was positioned as pivotal. This apparent compliment contained, it soon became obvious, unwanted liabilities. In a chapter entitled "The Dangers of Too Much Mother Love," Watson cautioned readers that a "heart is full of love which she [the mother] must express in some way. She expresses it by showering love and kisses" upon her devoted sons, but this is all wrong, as it threatens their independence and mental health, and reduces potentially virile young men into whining, dependent mama's boys. "Mother love is a dangerous instrument," he announced. Mothers must guard against their own impulses in loving their sons overmuch; they must be careful to treat their sons differently from their daughters. "Never hug [boys] and kiss them, never let them sit on your lap," Watson counseled (quoted in Kimmel 1996, 203).

In the 1920s, "homosexuality hovered like a specter over anxious parents," writes Michael Kimmel (1996, 203). Anxiously parents looked for signs of effeminacy in their young sons; they were told that these foreshadowed adult male homosexuality. Almost a third of Joseph Collins's *The Doctor Looks at Love and Life* (1926), one of the decade's best-selling advice books to parents, focused on male homosexuality. The homosexual was effeminate and unmanly, he warned, a "man of broad hips and mincing gait, who vocalizes like a lady and articulates like a chatterbox, who likes to sew and knit, to ornament his clothing and decorate his face" (quoted in Kimmel 1996, 203). Clement Wood's advice book *Manhood* (1924) tried to reassure anxious parents and their sons that homosexuality was a stage of development out of which they would soon (gratefully) pass. Wood informed his readers that a twelve-year-old boy's preferences were 40 percent autosexual, 50 percent homosexual, and 10 percent heterosexual; by puberty the percentages would shifted to 20, 30, and 50 percent, respectively (Kimmel 1996). Many anxious parents were not exactly soothed by these figures.

The failure of the nation to return to "normalcy" was evident also in the decade's divorce statistics. In 1920 there were 7.7 divorces per one thousand marriages. As the decade unfolded, the number increased; between 1922 and 1926 there was one divorce for every seven marriages, and by 1927 there was one for every six, sixteen times the rate for the 1870s. One ongoing source of stress was men's continuing concern about their status as men, specifically their ability to balance their roles as fathers and breadwinners. This concern was intensified by the practice of mocking fathers and husbands, a practice which found its way into the popular press of the 1920s, even in new comic strips like *Blondie*. Dagwood Bumstead, Blondie's bumbling, incompetent, hopeless husband, parodied 1920s "patriarchs" as inept fools without the intelligence and common sense of their superior and patient wives (Kimmel 1996).

Conservatives were not pleased. Many American women expressed their displeasure by joining their husbands and brothers and sons in an organization opposed not only to changes in the sphere of gender, but in "race relations" as well. Relying on the ethnographic and historical research of Katherine M. Blee (1991), we can glimpse the complex relation between racial and gender politics in the 1920s as they became institutionalized in the formation of the Women's Ku Klux Klan. We have seen how racial and gender politics have been conflated; here they pull apart somewhat, as white women used reactionary racial politics to make gender progress, a move late nineteenth-century white southern suffragists and temperance advocates had employed as well. Like their southern predecessors, few participants in the second Klan seemed self-conscious of their bifurcated agenda.

An elderly white Protestant woman from rural northern Indiana, for instance, remembered her participation in the Ku Klux Klan movement of the 1920s quite unself-consciously. It was, she said, "just a celebration ... a way of growing up." The Klan had blended into her daily life easily, as it did for many white Protestants in Indiana in the 1920s. For many women it had been an especially memorable period in an otherwise ordinary and uneventful life. Interviewed by Katherine Blee (1991), this former Klanswoman expressed little remorse over the cruelty of the Klan's crusade against Catholics, Jews, immigrants, and African Americans. What she expressed, with pride and without remorse, was her pleasure in the social and cultural life of the Klan; the Klan was "a way to get together and enjoy" (quoted in Blee 1991, 1).

Thousands of native-born white Protestant women like the one Blee interviewed found the women's Klan of the 1920s to be more than a political tool by means of which they could support the racist, anti-Semitic, and xenophobic agenda of the men's Klan. The women's Klan was also a social group in which they could enjoy each other, including their own racial and religious prejudices and privileges. These former Klan members recalled their participation not in terms of racial prejudice and hatred, but rather as a time of friendship and solidarity among like-minded women. In other words, white women's participation in the Klan—Katherine Blee focuses on Indiana women participants, many of whom she interviewed—was not solely or even preeminently an expression of racism, anti-Semitism, and nativism. As was the case in nineteenth-century Protestantism and in fundamentalist religions worldwide (Bauer 1997), the Second Klan offered contradictory opportunities for women. For instance, in an effort to recruit members among women newly enfranchised in the 1920s, the Klan promoted itself as the best guarantor of white Protestant women's rights. A women's Klan, the men declared, could safeguard women's suffrage and secure additional legal rights within a framework of white Protestant supremacy (Blee 1991).

"All the better people," Blee's informant assured her, were in the Klan. Bristling at the suggestion that there was any resemblance between the Klan of the 1980s and "her" Klan, Blee's informant insisted that hers was "different." In her day women joined to defend themselves, their families, and their communities against what they perceived to be spreading corruption and immorality: "Store owners, teachers, farmers ... the good people all belonged to the Klan. ... They were going to clean up government, and they were going to improve the school books [that] were loaded with Catholicism. The pope was dictating what was being taught to the children, and therefore they were being impressed with the wrong things" (quoted in Blee 1991, 2).

More than half a million white Protestant women in the 1920s joined the Women of the Ku Klux Klan (W.K.K.K.). In several states, women constituted nearly half of the Klan membership; in many others women were a significant minority. And the truth is, despite Blee's informant's claim that women's participation was defensive, that women were responsible for some of the Klan's most vicious and destructive campaigns. That fact has been overlooked, Blee argues, in the voluminous scholarship on the Ku Klux Klan (K.K.K.). Many historians who have studied the Klan treated Klanswomen as incidental to the movement, as smokescreens behind which men pursued the political objectives of the K.K.K. Both popular and scholarly treatments of the Klan emphasize that it was white men, not women, who carried out that organization's campaigns of hatred and destruction (Blee 1991).

Certainly it is true, as we have seen, that men dominated the first Klan, organized in 1868. And it is also true that men started the second Klan in 1915. But the history of the second Klan in the 1920s is incomplete without serious attention to the participation of Klanswomen. Women constituted a significant fraction of the Klan's membership, and they were no carbon copies of their male counterparts. Both their activities and ideologies differed sufficiently from those of most Klansmen that an examination of the women's Klan changes our interpretation not only of the second Klan, but of white women's participation in that affair between men known as racism. Many of the men's activities—electoral corruption, night riding, and gang terrorism—require us to conclude that often the Klan's campaign against Catholics, Jews, African Americans, and others was a failure. When we consider the less public and less examined efforts of Klanswomen—the "poison squads" that slandered targeted individuals and organized consumer boycotts which brought down various businesses—that judgment changes. Klanswomen's campaigns complemented those of their male counterparts, and their successes made the Klan's destructiveness both more extensive and more deadly than the men's activities alone would have (Blee 1991). Still, Klanswomen did not castrate black men. That act of homosexual rape was strictly a preoccupation of white men.

Instead of torture and mutilation, Klanswomen worked in social ways to achieve their aims. They drew on familial and community ties and rituals, including traditions of church suppers, family reunions, and social occasions, to communicate the Klan's message of racial and religious bigotry. Hatred circulated through neighborhoods, families, and friendships. "The Klan's power," Blee observes, "was devastating precisely because it was so well integrated into the normal everyday life of white Protestants" (1991, 3).

While Klanswomen shared the men's reactionary views on race, nationality, and religion, they did not share their male counterparts' views on gender. On that subject Klanswomen's views were neither consistently reactionary nor progressive. A number of the women Blee (1991) interviewed had been active in progressive politics, working for peace and women's equality in the decades after the Klan collapsed. As self-styled progressives, they saw their participation in the Klan as an effort to contain the reactionary forces of Catholicism, Judaism, and rural southern black culture. That very strange mix of what was progressive and what was reactionary seemed to these women completely consistent with campaigns to extend Social Security benefits or promote equal pay for men and women. Blee (1991, 6) reports her own surprise:

> These former Klansmembers were not the "other," with strange, incomprehensible ways of understanding the world, as I had earlier assumed. On some level, many were sympathetic persons. Even more disturbing, some Klanswomen had a facile ability to fold bitter racial and religious bigotry into progressive politics. One former Klanswomen, for example, insisted that she saw no inconsistency between participation in the 1920s Klan and her support of economic redistribution and feminism. (6)

It is clear from Blee's intriguing research that the popular stereotype of the Klan members as ignorant, brutal, and naïve is not entirely accurate, at least when we focus upon the W.K.K.K. An accurate account of white women's participation in the 1920s Klan movement requires those of us committed to a more just and egalitarian society to acknowledge the apparent ease with which racism and bigotry appealed and still appeal to mainstream American citizens. In

Blee's judgment, the Klan exaggerated but certainly did not fabricate what was in fact a rather widespread notion that white Protestants were the apex of a religious and racial chain of being. Astonishingly, even those living in racially and religiously monolithic settings, in no way "besieged" by the presence of those whose cultural and religious practices differed from their own, still managed to feel threatened, still could accept the Klan's paranoid and racist interpretation of contemporary events, and could thereby join an organization designed to protect and perpetuate their already considerable political advantages (Blee 1991).

The 1920s Klan was comprised, then, by white Protestant women and men who loved and worried about their families and who could be generous to neighbors and friends. Often living in racially and religiously segregated communities (communities overwhelming populated by white Protestants), they had been blinded by generations of invisible privilege to the facts concerning those who did not enjoy that same privilege of being in the majority. These "others"—Blee extends the list to include African Americans, Catholics, Jews, immigrants, Mormons, labor radicals, bootleggers, moonshiners, theater owners, dance hall operators, radical feminists, and conservative oppressors of women—became enemies because their lives were so distant (and hence so easily imaginary) from the privileged white Protestant majority. Imagined as incomprehensible "others," they became excellent candidates for the category of the "enemy" of ordinary upright and God-fearing women and men. Blee (1991, 7) points out that

> [t]he mainstay of the 1920s Klan was not the pathological individual; rather, Klan promoters effectively tapped a pathological vein of racism, intolerance, and bigotry deep within white Protestant communities. In this sense, the history of the 1920s Klan, although distant in time, is frighteningly close in spirit to the pervasive strands of racism and unacknowledged privilege that exist among dominant groups in the United States today.

In his 1929 study of lynching, Walter White was clear about the relationship between Protestantism and racial violence. Living in Louisiana, I too am acutely aware of the "pathological vein of racism, intolerance, and bigotry deep within white Christian communities." Hidden under a thin patina of "southern hospitality," the vicious hatred that has never been fully worked through psychologically surfaces at any time, even in college classrooms.

III. Gender and Sexuality in the Ku Klux Klan

[H]ow do we integrate the study of gender within the framing of racialized culture?

—Sandra Gunning, *Race, Rape, and Lynching: The Red Record of American Literature, 1890–1912* (1996)

[B]ourgeois sexuality and racialized sexuality [are] not ... distinct kinds ... but ... dependent constructs in a unified field.

—Ann Laura Stoler, *Race and the Education of Desire: Foucault's History of Sexuality and the Colonial Order of Things* (1995)

Gender and sexuality were primary symbols in the two largest waves of the Ku Klux Klan, those of the late 1860s and the 1920s. The post–Civil War all-male Klan's agenda of racial terrorism operated in very different circumstances than did those racist, nativist men and women who joined the second Klan in the early twentieth century. Still, both Klans emphasized gender and sexuality. Each fantasized white men as the protectors of vulnerable white womanhood and white female purity. A myriad of complicated social, economic, and racial issues disappeared into fantasies of white womanhood, sexual virtue, and black male hypersexuality (Blee 1991).

In the first Klan, Blee suggests, fantasies of imperiled womanhood substituted for white men's own paranoid sense of assault by newly freed African Americans. No doubt that is true, but it is incomplete. As we have seen, fantasies of white women also stood for white men's denied and relocated desire for black men's bodies. Fantasies of imperiled white womanhood enabled white men not only to disclaim their own homoerotic interests, but they functioned also as a rationale to act on those interests, as occasions to strip, torture and sexually mutilate the black male bodies they desired but could not allow themselves to love. The second Klan, Blee argues, also imagined white womanhood as a symbol for threatened religious, national, and racial supremacy. But newly won female enfranchisement and women's political experience left women less willing to accept their imaginary and symbolic status. Now even many conservative women thought they might exist outside men's imaginations (Blee 1991).

For the first K.K.K., black men were the primary site around which circulated fantasies of white masculinity and vulnerable white femininity. When the K.K.K. was organized in Tennessee soon after the Civil War, it summoned defeated Confederate soldiers, and the ghosts of dead ones, to defend white womanhood and southern "civilization" against carpetbaggers, scalawags, and, always, black men. As the Klan quickly evolved from a prankish fraternity to a loosely organized and highly secret terrorist organization operating with the support of the larger community, the Klan came to personify convoluted fantasies of sexual menace and racial and political danger (Blee 1991; Trelease 1971).

During the late 1860s the Klan faced little opposition. Gangs of Klansmen threatened, flogged, and murdered countless newly freed people. But the Klan's violence was not arbitrary. The Klan's terrorism was designed, presumably, to rescue the crumbling and quickly disappearing "Lost Cause" as the South was brought back into the union. In addition to African Americans, Republicans, and northern whites who came to help with Reconstruction—schoolteachers, revenue collectors, election officials, among others, all working to dismantle the racist southern state—were regularly victims of Klan violence. The first Klan seemed especially drawn to sexual assault and brutality. White-male mobs humiliated white southern Republicans ("scalawags") by sexually abusing them, routinely raping and sexually torturing women, especially black women, during "kluxing" raids on their households, and of course sexually mutilating—lynching—thousands of young black men (Blee 1991).

As we saw, the secret and juvenile rituals of the First Klan drew upon the tradition of male college fraternities, a fact that will not be so surprising when we review fraternities' hazing practices in chapter 13. Southern white men declared their allegiance to one another over issues of race, gender, and a determination to avenge military defeat upon those least able to protect themselves. Although the 1920s Klan become rabidly anti-Catholic, the first K.K.K. created a culture whose costumes and secret ritual mimicked the symbolism and rites of the male-controlled hierarchy of the Roman Catholic Church. It barred white women (and, of course, all nonwhites) from membership, just as the Confederacy had barred women and nonwhites from political participation. If the stalking and rape of recently freedpeople underscored their imagined racial superiority, the exclusion of white women functioned to underline the gender of racial politics, which, as we have seen, was profoundly and regrettably masculine (Blee 1991).

Supported by the physical absence of women in the first K.K.K., the omnipresence of the fantasy of "white womanhood" was a crucial rallying point for Reconstruction Klan violence. Klansmen were certain that white women loved their place in the white male imagination; women were, of course, rarely consulted on this matter. In an appearance in 1871 before the U.S. Senate, Nathan Bedford Forrest, the first Grand Wizard, testified that the Klan was very much necessary, as white southerners—especially young ladies—faced great insecurity in a society where slaves had been freed (Blee 1991). He spoke dramatically of a chaotic situation in which "ladies were ravished by some of these negroes, who were tried and put in the penitentiary, but were turned out in a few days afterward" (quoted in Blee 1991, 13). From the beginning, white men imagined black men naked, having their way with vulnerable young ladies, imaginary stand-ins for themselves.

This fantasy of imperiled southern white womanhood was made real by repetition; it is evident throughout the writings of the first Klan and its apologists. White women, especially frail widows living alone on isolated plantations, were cited hysterically as "proof" of the terrible risk white women faced. Through the image of the lonely white lady the Klan aroused public fears that black men were busily taking their revenge against their former white masters by sexually exploiting white daughters, wives, and mothers. Without the Klan, members declared, white women were completely helpless when faced by the frightful and evidently limitless sexual energies of newly freed black men (Blee 1991).

All histories of the first Klan emphasize, Blee points out, that these images of rape and miscegenation between white women and black men were used very successfully. Accounts that lack a feminist-informed analysis, she suggests, miss some of the political significance of the obsession over rape and miscegenation. Blee cites Wyn Craig Wade's argument that slavery corrupted sexual relations between white men and white women. Made almost holy in antebellum southern society, white women became, Wade (1987, 20) suggests, "like statues in bed," sexually inaccessible to white men. Sexually rebuffed, white men turned to powerless black slaves, to "release the passion they were unable to experience with their wives." As the Confederacy crumbled, white men feared that black men would avenge themselves in like manner. A feminist analysis, Blee argues, understands these images of rape, gender, and sexuality somewhat differently.

Modern feminist scholarship, Blee summarizes, characterizes rape as preeminently a matter of power, not sexual desire. In this regard, Blee interprets the Klan's call to defend white women against rape by black men as a declaration of their power over black men *and* white women, and only incidentally having to do with the (after all) relatively rare black-on-white rape. The Klan's emphasis on the rape threat functioned, then, to remind white women that rape was always a possibility. In this sense, the obsession with rape was a compensatory response to a sense of threatened sexual and racial privileges. According to Catherine MacKinnon (1983), "the definitive element of rape centers around male-defined loss, not coincidentally also upon the way men define loss of exclusive access" (30; quoted in Blee 1991, 15). The loss of exclusive access to white women? Not entirely, I should think. What I suspect white men found intolerable after their military humiliation was the loss of access to black bodies, female and male.

The Klan and countless other white southern men claimed to be horrified by miscegenation, but they practiced it daily, as had antebellum white plantation masters. Blee suggests that Klan members experienced a kind of parallel between rape and their gendered humiliation and disempowerment after the Confederacy's defeat. But, Blee cautions, "we cannot reduce this complex symbolic layering of race, sexuality, and gender in the language and the political practice of the Ku Klux Klan to a collective manifestation of psychosexual frustration, repression, and fear by white southern men. Rather, we must analyze the massive social movement of the first K.K.K. in the context of long-standing cleavages underlying southern society" (1991, 16).

Blee argues that freed black men threatened white men's sexual access to women (both black and white), and perhaps that is so. But black men also simply threatened white men, as "men." Those muscular black bodies had before been available for white use, economic, psychological, and sexual; now that these bodies were free, in the civic sense they were "men." Suddenly it seemed, white men feared (and wanted?) bondage. "Negro domination" was a rallying cry for decades in the postbellum South; never a real political possibility, it probably was a stand-in for other fears of (and unconscious desires for) domination, sexual and psychological. In this logic, white men were making preemptive strikes, attacking before they could be mastered. And what form did their attacks take? Blee puts the matter this way: "Sexual torture and emasculation of black men by mobs of Klansmen validated the claim that masculinity ('real manhood') was the exclusive prerogative of white men" (1991, 16). She suggests, perceptively, that even the rape of black women by white Klansmen operated in a homosocial economy,

> as symbolic emasculation of black men through violating "their" women while affirming the use of male sexuality as a weapon of power against women. Southern women, white and black, occupied a symbolic terrain on which white men defended their racial privileges. The symbols of white female vulnerability and white masculine potency took power equally from beliefs in masculine and in white supremacy. (Blee 1991, 16)

The first Klan movement collapsed quickly, despite an elaborate organizational hierarchy. Perhaps living so completely in the imagination, Klan members were bound to lack a sustainable sense of realpolitik. By the late 1860s many local Klan units had become chaotic unorganized gangs, bands of roving terrorists. In response, the federal government tried to assert its military and political control of the southern states. In 1870 the Grand Wizard ordered the organization dissolved, claiming that Klan atrocities were in fact committed by nonmembers. The remaining remnants of the first K.K.K. disappeared by the mid-1870s (Blee 1991).

As noted earlier, the second Ku Klux Klan was established in 1915 in the aftermath of the lynching of Leo Frank. By the mid-1920s approximately four million women and men had joined. Why did so many Americans, and not only southerners, find the K.K.K. so appealing in the second decade of the twentieth century? Blee points to declining agricultural prices which caused widespread hardship among farmers and agricultural laborers. Economically crippled, these rural whites were susceptible to Klan propaganda about "Jewish bankers" and "foreign interests" controlling the U.S. economy. Blee points as well to especially rapid technological and social changes, including high rates of immigration from abroad not to mention the Great Migration of African Americans from South to North, events which contributed to rapid urbanization. Suddenly the nation white Protestants identified as their own was decidedly more complex (Blee 1991). I point to the state of gender in the 1920s, an impressionistic review of which opened this chapter. The state of "race" was crucial too, but I save that part of the story for chapters 10 and 11.

While the factors she lists are important, Blee too appreciates that they do not explain the extent of the second Klan's success. Racist, nativist, and reactionary sentiments, as she points out, were hardly unique to the 1920s. Nor are economic explanations definitive: while some communities where the Klan flourished were economically depressed, others were not. Indeed, in some places the Klan was popular among the prosperous. While some joined in response to sweeping changes in their lives, others led stable, predictable lives. The Klan was especially popular among populations whose supremacy was never challenged and in areas characterized by almost no racial and religious diversity. For these, Klan membership was not defensive in origin or function; it merely celebrated and affirmed long-held privileges (Blee 1991).

For Blee, the second Klan becomes more intelligible when it is considered within (rather than as an aberration from) those ideas and values that informed white Protestant life in the early twentieth century, ideas and values that supported religious fundamentalism and prohibitionism as well as the Klan. Contextualized in white Protestantism, then, the virulently racist program and whites-only membership policy of the second Klan movement become remarkable primarily for their resort to violence. The Klan's underlying ideas of racial separation and white Protestant supremacy, Blee insists, were widely shared throughout white society in the 1920s. Whether or not it came from Klan members, racial and religious hatred informed political maneuverings in many communities. Few white-controlled institutions or organizations in the United States—including the U.S. Congress and the Supreme Court, as we will see—either practiced or espoused racial integration or equality, allowing the Klan to insist, with accuracy, that its policies were consistent with the sentiments of many whites. A 1924 defense of the Klan's policy of racial exclusivity, Blee points out, correctly noted that many fraternal lodges practiced exactly the same policy.

IV. Simmons, Tyler, Clarke, and Evans: Internal Tensions and the Birth of the W.K.K.K.

The knot that bound subversion to perversion could only be undone if people themselves believed in the sexual codes of the moralizing state, if personal affect and sentiments could be harnessed to national projects and priorities for racial regeneration.

—Ann Laura Stoler, *Race and the Education of Desire: Foucault's History of Sexuality and the Colonial Order of Things* (1995)

In the language of Freudianism, the Klan is essentially a defense mechanism against evils which are more imaginary than real.

—Elisabeth Young-Bruehl, *The Anatomy of Prejudices* (1996)

If, then, all the ingredients for the Klan were present in white Protestant America, making the Klan unnecessary in a certain sense, why did the organization enjoy such a widespread resurgence in the 1920s? The omnipresence of white supremacist, anti-Catholic, and anti-Semitic ideas as well as the state of gender and race after the war provided the ground for the Klan's appeal, but Blee argues that its recruiting success had little to do with ideology and politics. She argues that it was financial opportunism and a sophisticated marketing system that fueled the phenomenal growth of the 1920s Klan.

The originator of the second Klan, William J. Simmons, drew upon his past careers as a circuit-riding minister, unsuccessful itinerant salesman, and fraternal society organizer. Mystically inspired, he claimed, Simmons devoted himself to the unification of foreign-born Protestant men in battle against the heathen forces of "aliens," "commodity madness," political corruption, excessive taxation, and religious infidelity that were, he had no doubt, destroying America. Like the Klan leaders who would soon replace him, Simmons traveled a "hell and brimstone" revival circuit, preaching sermons with titles like "Red Heads, Dead Heads and No Heads," "Women, Weddings, and Wives," and "Kinship of Kourtship and Kissing." Crowds responded enthusiastically to such alliteration, cheering him as he defended traditional sexual morality against the demon forces of "ungodly modernism." Like his Reconstruction-era predecessors, Simmons often invoked imperiled white womanhood as a symbol of white Protestant values in need of protection against imminent destruction. But the specific conceptions of gender that would characterize the second Klan would prove to be somewhat different from those either Simmons or his predecessors had in mind (Blee 1991).

Simmons's bizarre and rambling writings testify that the Klan was also responding to the continuing "crisis" of a white masculinity threatened in the 1920s by overly affectionate mothers who raised mama's boys and homosexuals, not red-blooded all-American "men." The Klan would remedy that condition by declaring itself a fraternity for "real American manhood," men of mental toughness and moral dedication. "No man," Simmons declared, "is wanted in this Order who hasn't manhood enough to assume a real OATH with serious purpose to keep the same inviolate" (quoted in Blee 1991, 19). To mobilize his white male listeners, Simmons repeated a successful tactic of the first Klan, declaring that the threat of black rapists and miscegenation endangered white civilization. Simmons often compared himself to Jesus Christ, a prophet victimized by the devils and infidels who surrounded him and controlled the nation. In this convoluted fantasy, Simmons imagined his Klansmembers as his children with himself, the Christ figure, as (strangely enough) not the father but the mother. This transgendered fantasy communicated a sense of womanhood and motherhood as strength and power as well as racial and sexual vulnerability. Simmons's imaginative description of the Klan's birth, composed to rationalize and defend his supremacy in the organization, illustrates his internal gender ambiguity:

> I was [the K.K.K.'s] sole parent, author and founder; it was MY creation—MY CHILD, if you please, MY first born. I, ALONE, am responsible for ITS borning and being. ... No devoted mother ever endured for her babe more mental anguish and gave more constant attention, through many sleepless nights and troubled days. ... Every dime I earned was earned to preserve its life and promote its development. (quoted in Blee 1991, 19)

For Simmons "woman" remained imaginary, but here a fantasy not split off, dissociated from himself. Claiming the imaginary lady in danger as himself shifted his sense of manhood, as one might expect. The explicitly violent masculinity of the first Klan had become "kinder and gentler" now characterized as a loving fraternity of brothers. Simmons instructed Klansmen to live on a higher ethical plane than that of the "alien" (non-Klan) men: they were to respect fellow Klansmen, avoid sexual debauchery, especially sexual relations with nonwhite women. As Blee points out, Simmons's ethical code was, like everything else he believed, fantasy, not reality. Probably few Klansmen obeyed his instructions. Blee's point is that it discloses a changed meaning of masculinity, one I would suggest, that was more explicitly homoerotic. Come on guys, let's just love one another.

And perhaps they did, although the K.K.K.'s strict policy of secrecy will leave us forever wondering. That policy coupled with Simmons's allergy to publicity functioned to keep the fledging Klan from reaching many potential recruits. Simmons was, Blee surmises, an incompetent leader. His unhappy "children" began to complain about him, alleging he was "a man of weakness and vice [whose thoughts] run to women and liquor" (quoted in Blee 1991, 19). They didn't just run there, as Simmons fantasized too about Klan-written history texts, a banking and trust institution to help farmers, a free house for every newly married Klan couple, a national full employment policy, a program of support for Klan orphans, several medical research centers, and a chain of hospitals. These remained imaginary (Blee 1991).

In 1920 the Klan's fortunes would change with the arrival of Elizabeth Tyler and Edward Clarke and their Southern Publicity Association. The first major female leader of the 1920s Klan, Tyler had worked earlier as a volunteer hygiene worker visiting tenements as part of the "better babies" movement of the 1910s. At an Atlanta harvest festival (she sponsored a better babies parade), Tyler met Clarke, the festival organizer. Clarke's career as an itinerant promoter had not been very successful, but by the time of the Atlanta festival his luck had changed. Now introducing himself as a "doctor of sick towns," Clarke had devised a lucrative scheme arranging festivals and other publicity events for ambitious if incautious communities all over the South (Blee 1991).

Together Tyler and Clarke organized the Southern Publicity Association. They marketed their talents in promotion and publicity to groups as diverse as the Anti-Saloon League, Salvation Army, and Red Cross. When Tyler's son-in-law joined the K.K.K., the Southern Publicity Association found, as Blee puts it, the "perfect client" (1991, 20). Under Simmons's dreamy leadership, membership in the Klan had not increased and its financial condition stayed uncertain. While rather different from, say, the Salvation Army, the Klan was much like fraternal organizations such as the Woodmen of the World with which Tyler and Clarke had experience. Tyler, for example, had been a member of the Daughters of America, an auxiliary of the Junior Order of United American Mechanics (Blee 1991).

Clarke and Tyler persuaded Simmons to create a Propagation Department by means of which they would publicize and recruit for the Klan in exchange for a percentage of the Klan's $10 initiation fee. They refashioned Simmons's image into that of a sincere and hardworking civic leader. Although Simmons had hired Tyler and Clarke to work only as publicity agents, their phenomenal success in promoting the Klan soon gave them additional authority. In time, Simmons became increasingly peripheral. During the first six months of Clarke and Tyler's association with the K.K.K., 85,000 new members (paying $850,000 in dues) joined. By 1922 Simmons told a *New York Times* interviewer that 3,500 new members were joining each day and that the Klan's total membership exceeded five million in all forty-eight states plus Alaska and the Canal Zone. Simmons was probably exaggerating, but under Tyler and Clarke the Klan had become a national phenomenon (Blee 1991).

Key to Tyler and Clarke's strategy, Blee informs, was their decision to expand the list of enemies. No longer were African Americans the sole objects of Klan hatred, although blacks would retain a special place in the Klan imagination. Tyler and Clarke added Catholics, Jews, nonwhites, Bolsheviks, and immigrants, new enemies that proved very popular, especially in northern states. They also discovered that an especially successful strategy involved focusing on local minorities. Kleagles (paid organizers) were instructed to study their territories, identify the sources of anxiety among native-born Protestant whites, and presto: the Klan was in business. Tyler published a weekly newsletter where she helped kleagles identify local "enemies," among them the Mormons in Utah, union radicals in the Northwest, and Asian Americans on the West Coast (Blee 1991).

Using skills sharpened by organizing festivals and parades, Tyler and Clarke promoted the Klan with modern marketing and advertising techniques. They instructed kleagles to recruit members by soliciting their friends, and their friends' friends, as potential recruits and following all contacts with application blanks, Klan "information," and a request for dues. Kleagles often approached local Protestant ministers, asking them to join and/or to help, openly or covertly, with Klan recruiting efforts. The national offices of the Klan directed and complemented kleagles' efforts, dispatching lecturers (who were often ministers) throughout the country to mobilize Protestants to the cause of the Klan (Blee 1991, 21).

In addition to the publicity generated by Tyler and Clarke's promotional machine, the *New York World* inadvertently drew additional members to the Klan with an exposé that exaggerated the size of its membership and strength. But the *World*'s coverage in 1921 also triggered Tyler and Clarke's downfall. The newspaper questioned their financial dealings and their sexual propriety, citing their 1919 arrest for disorderly conduct in a house owned by Tyler in a morally "questionable" district of Atlanta. The police had been alerted by Clarke's wife, May Clarke, who had earlier sued him for divorce on the grounds of desertion. Clarke and Tyler denied the charge but seemed disinclined to hide the fact that they were sexually involved with each other, despite the Klan's emphasis upon "family values" (Blee 1991).

Tensions began to develop within the Klan; these had surfaced in testimony that same year before the U.S. House Committee on Rules. The precipitating matter was the role of Elizabeth Tyler in the Klan's rapid growth. Unhappy Klansmen charged that Tyler was the actual head of the Klan and that Simmons, and even Clarke, were mere figureheads, hiding the fact that a woman ran things. Despite repeated denials from Klan officials, this allegation provoked widespread discontent among men who joined what they had been told would be a male fraternal preserve. Tension converted to conflict when the congressional investigation concluded that Tyler was in fact in charge of the Klan. This public portrait—the all-male Klan organized and dominated by a woman—was humiliating for many Klansmen (Blee 1991).

Disgruntled Klan members were not soothed when Simmons, in a move calculated to reestablish his authority in the Klan, appointed Tyler to head up planning for a women's organization. Tyler did not plan long; soon she announced plans to induct into the Klan five hundred prominent women from all over the country. Tyler claimed that women were already drawn to the Klan, due to the Klan's opposition to Jews, Catholics, African Americans, socialists and other political radicals (Blee 1991). Well aware of many Klansmen's gender grumblings, Tyler declared nonetheless that the new women's organization would not be a "dependent auxiliary of the Knights of the Ku Klux Klan" but an equal partner with the men (quoted in Blee 1991, 22).

Apparently cooperating with Simmons, Tyler conspired with Clarke to bring Simmons down. They persuaded Simmons to take an extended vacation and while he was gone restructured the Klan hierarchy, conferring upon Simmons the exalted title of lifetime imperial emperor but without any real power in the organization. Actual power went to a Texas dentist, Hiram Evans, who quickly moved to consolidate his power in the Klan, with Tyler and Clarke as allies. He arranged to have his leadership ratified at the November 1922 K.K.K. Klonvokation in Atlanta, a gathering that also lavished praise on Tyler as "a model of American womanhood" (quoted in Blee 1991, 22). But Tyler's power would quickly fade, the victim of internal Klan controversies. Charges of sexual immorality and financial mismanagement continued to mount; four regional Klan leaders filed suit against Tyler and Clarke (Blee 1991).

Evans turned against Tyler and Clarke. As soon as he was appointed Imperial Wizard, Evans directed Clarke to return Tyler's share of the funds generated by the Propagation Department contract. On his return from vacation Simmons tried to block this move, but it was too late. Now charged with mishandling church funds, misuse of the mails, transportation of liquor, and under indictment by a federal grand jury for violation of the Mann Act's prohibition against "white slavery," Clarke fled the country. Powerless, Tyler resigned and died in 1924 (Blee 1991).

The sudden departure of Tyler and Clarke and the conflict between Evans and Simmons wracked the Klan. Leaders called upon members to be "real men" and remain loyal to the Klan. This seemed to work, so Klan officials reiterated that the current "problems" simply underlined the significance of strong, masculine men. Only "true manhood" could meet and resolve the current crises (Blee 1991). One Grand Dragon challenged Klansmen to convert the organization's problems into opportunities for expanded membership: "Never before in the history of our great movement have the hearts and souls of manly men been thrilled with such emotion for our righteous cause. ... The spirit of Klankraft is bringing untold thousands of big, manly men into the fellowship" (quoted in Blee 1991, 23).

The Klan's call upon manhood and masculinity expressed as loyalty proved effective; membership swelled. Evans disguised racism and nativism as science. Recall this was a time when eugenics, presumably the science of genetics, was widespread; even the National Education Association (N.E.A.) formed a Committee on Racial Well-Being in 1916 (Pinar et al. 1995, 94). Evans drew upon this popular acceptance of genetic superiority and inferiority to rearticulate, in "scientific" terms, the Klan's oldest and most vicious symbols. The Klan's opposition to miscegenation, he explained, was based not in moral outrage over the degeneracy of interracial sex (as Simmons and the first Klan argued) but in science. Scientific research, he said, had conclusively shown that the children of "race-mixing" were genetically unstable. In like manner, Evans phrased his demand to restrict immigration and his anti-Semitism and anti-Catholicism as scientifically grounded. After all, how else could we (white Protestants) ensure the development of a biologically and genetically "good stock of Americans" (Blee 1991, 23).

Internal tensions, including the protracted leadership struggle, created an opening for women to enter the organization. As Simmons and Evans fought for power between themselves and together against increasingly powerful regional Klan leaders, each embraced the idea of a female Klan in hopes of improving their respective positions. Despite the controversy associated with Tyler's participation, Evans and Simmons hoped that Klansmen would accept women as members, even if unenthusiastically. Perhaps the civic concern evidenced by women's aggressive campaign for temperance and suffrage would spill over into concern for the issues the Klan saw as primary (Blee 1991).

There were precedents to support this speculation. As early as 1922, the *Fiery Cross*, a Klan newspaper, published letters to the editor from women who were distressed over their exclusion from the Klan. Blee points out there is no way to validate the authenticity of these letters (which may in fact have been written by Klansmen), but at the very least they raised the issue of women's participation in the "Invisible Empire." These 1922 letters contrasted women's new right to vote with their continuing exclusion from the Klan. In pioneer days, said one, men justly excluded women from many undertakings in order to protect them from the possibility of physical injury. In these "new days of freedom," however, that rationale was no longer relevant. Now women wanted to "stand alongside our men and help with the protecting," not be "patted on the head and told not to worry." In another letter, signed the "unhappy wife," a woman complained about her husband, active in the Klan. While he is out and about saving America, she was left at home with the children, like any domestic servant. Why should white native-born Protestant women be excluded from the Klan, she demanded to know, no different, apparently from other excluded groups such as the "Knights of Columbus, Jews or negroes?" (quoted in Blee 1991, 24)

In fact some women had participated in the Klan, if not as full members, but in informal K.K.K. auxiliaries and women's patriotic societies. Tyler had been a member of the Ladies of the Invisible Eye, a women's secret society closely linked with the Klan. Several women's patriotic societies and auxiliaries recruited broadly and made their work public, but many groups had adopted the secrecy and exclusionary practices of the Klan. The Dixie Protestant Women's Political League, for instance, paraded openly through downtown Atlanta while members hid their identities by wearing hoods, masks, and costumes very much like those of the Klan (Blee 1991).

The immediate predecessor to a national women's Klan was the Ladies of the Invisible Empire (L.O.T.I.E.). Many L.O.T.I.E. chapters had large memberships. The chapter in Portland, Oregon, for instance, accepted more than one thousand new members into the order in a single month in 1922. Typical of L.O.T.I.E. membership requirements were those of the Baltimore chapter, which required potential members to report their religion, family, and politics, then swear allegiance to Christianity (as the Klan interpreted it) and to "pure Americanism" (Blee 1991, 26).

Unlike the later women's Klan, L.O.T.I.E.s seemed to have no political agenda of their own, no goals to improve the status of women. Instead, these women seemed to prefer a role as "chosen messengers of men." Certain

L.O.T.I.E. chapters did devote time to learning the art of politics, but overall these women directed their efforts toward installing the Bible in the public school curriculum, advocating strict immigration restrictions, opposing racial equality and interracial marriage, and working, as the Shreveport and Vivian, Louisiana, L.O.T.I.E. chapters (organized in January 1923 with 150 charter members) phrased it, to "cleanse and purify the civil, political and ecclesiastical atmosphere" of the nation (Blee 1991, 26).

Eager to draw upon existing networks but fearing that these groups might undermine men's efforts to organize a women's Klan, the K.K.K. considered the idea of a women's auxiliary. At the 1922 Imperial Klonvokation in Atlanta, Klansmen debated whether they should negotiate with women' secret societies; a committee was organized to make recommendations to the Imperial Wizard and the Imperial Kloncilium (council). The committee quickly concluded that a women's Klan should be established. Evans agreed and asked the Exalted Cyclops (Head of Klan realms) to elect two delegates to a convention. Along with the Grand Dragons and Great Titans of organized realms and the King Kleagles of unorganized states and two representatives of growing Klans, these delegates would formulate K.K.K. policy regarding the women's organizations. Then, in June 1923, the men summoned representatives of all the major women's patriotic groups and informal Klan auxiliaries to a conference in Washington, D.C. (Blee 1991).

Conflict and tension within the leadership of the K.K.K. slowed organizing efforts. In March 1923, three months before the Klonvokation was scheduled to meet and establish a women's Klan, Simmons announced that he was setting up a competing group, the Kamelia, a move calculated to strengthen his deteriorating position vis-à-vis Evans. Simmons declared that the Kamelia would be a "great women's organization adhering to the same principles" as the K.K.K. Like the L.O.T.I.E., Kamelia would assume a very limited view of women's role in politics, seeking mainly to "educate women in the science of government and history of the United States and to contribute funds to orphanages and similar deserving institutions" (quoted in Blee 1991, 26).

During Evans's absence from Klan headquarters, Simmons called the Imperial Kloncilium into sessions and persuaded members to support his women's auxiliary. Furious, Evans alleged that Simmons organized the Kamelia for his own financial gain only. Evans warned his men to have nothing to do with Kamelia but Simmons proceeded anyway. By June he had established Kamelia chapters in twenty states, several of which were already sponsoring public parades of white-robed women. Simmons, Blee tells us, had staked his future in the Klan on power of his women's organization, declaring that the Kamelia was "as much my child" as the men's Klan was (Blee 1991, 27).

A second women's group, the Queens of the Golden Mask (Q.G.M.), had been organized by D. C. Stephenson, a powerful regional Klan leader (he controlled the Klan newspaper, the *Fiery Cross*) based in Indiana. Stephenson chose Daisy Douglas Barr, a well-known evangelist, as head. The Q.G.M. attracted mainly the wives, mothers, and daughters of Klansmen and recruited women "in the interest of cleaner local politics and a more moral community" (quoted in Blee 1991, 27). The Q.G.M. would be folded into the Women of the Ku Klux Klan and Barr would ally herself with Hiram Evans against Stephenson (Blee 1991).

In June 1923 Evans directed the Imperial Kloncilium to establish the Women of the Ku Klux Klan (W.K.K.K.), a group he fully expected to absorb Simmons's Kamelia and Stephenson's Q.G.M. At once the battle began. Acting like "poison squads" of one, Stephenson and Evans each spread shocking stories about the other's improprieties with women, escalating to a "ceaseless wagging of tongues" (Blee 1991, 27) in the Klan. While the forces of Evans and Stephenson traded verbal blows, Evans and Simmons met in the courtroom. Evans had petitioned the Fulton County (Georgia) Superior Court to dissolve all competing women's organizations and appoint a commission to take administrative control of the entire Klan organization. The court approved Evans's petition, but Simmons then countersued for an injunction against the W.K.K.K. or any other women's group using the name of the Klan. Simmons's suit failed. In February 1924 the court ordered Simmons to relinquish his rights, title, and interest in the Kamelia and the Ku Klux Klan. In exchange he received a $145,000 cash settlement to replace the $1,000 per month annuity he had been receiving from the Klan. Then Simmons left the K.K.K. (Blee 1991).

On June 10, 1923, Judge R. M. Mann of the second division circuit court in Little Rock, Arkansas, officially chartered the Women of the Ku Klux Klan. In a three-room office in the Ancient Order of United Workmen Hall in Little Rock, the W.K.K.K. set up shop. Blee (1991) tells us that Little Rock was chosen in part because its distance from the male Klan's Atlanta headquarters underlined its purported independence from its male counterpart. Perhaps so, but with the exception of gender, membership requirements paralleled the men's organization. Members of the W.K.K.K. would be white Gentile female native-born citizens over eighteen years of age who owed no allegiance to any foreign government or sect, which to the K.K.K. meant that they were not Catholic, socialist, Communist, and so on. To reduce the possibility of infiltration by spies, applicants for membership were required to have been a resident in a Klan jurisdiction for at least six months and to be endorsed by at least two Klanswomen or a W.K.K.K. kleagle or Imperial Commander. Klanswomen were instructed to investigate "carefully and personally" (Blee 1991, 28) the qualifications and background of every candidate they endorsed. Dues were ten dollars and bought not only membership but one robe and a helmet. The national offices of the W.K.K.K. were lavish, drawing generously upon a portion of all dues, an Imperial Tax (a per capita assessment), profits from the sale of regalia, uniforms, stationery, jewelry, and costumes, and by interest and profits from investments (Blee 1991).

In part to distinguish itself from Simmons's Kamelia, the W.K.K.K. declared itself an organization "by women, for women, and of women [that] no man is exploiting for his individual gain" (quoted in Blee 1991, 28). The structure of the new women's Klan, worked out in a meeting of W.K.K.K. leaders in Asheville, North Carolina, would follow specific functions; each function would have a corresponding task department. The major functions of the W.K.K.K. included Americanism, education, public amusements, legislation, child welfare and delinquency, citizenship, civics, law enforcement, disarmament, peace, and politics (Blee 1991).

Women representing chapters from Texas, Oregon, Arkansas, Indiana, Iowa, and Wyoming were appointed as the officers of the new W.K.K.K.. Lulu Markwell of Arkansas, described by the K.K.K. as "well-known in Protestant American women's organization work" (Blee 1991, 28), became the W.K.K.K.'s first Imperial Commander. Born Lulu Boyers, Markwell was fifty seven years old when she was appointed to head the national women's Klan. A native of Indiana, Markwell lived in Little Rock in the 1920s and was married to a local physician. She had been involved in the W.C.T.U. and had worked for women's suffrage (Blee 1991).

V. The Miming of Men's Words

One must assume the feminine role deliberately. Which means already to convert a form of subordination into an affirmation, and thus to begin to thwart it.

—Luce Irigaray, *This Sex Which Is Not One* (1985)

As Evans had hoped, the W.K.K.K. soon absorbed many women's secret societies and nativistic leagues, including the L.O.T.I.E.s, League of Protestant Women, Ladies of the Cu Clux Clan, Ladies of the Gold Mask, Order of American Women, Ladies of the Golden Den, Hooded Ladies of the Mystic Den, and Puritan Daughters of America. The charter membership of the new W.K.K.K. included 125,000 women, most of whom lived in the Midwest, Northwest, and Ozarks region, strongholds of the K.K.K. Eager to expand the membership base from wives, sisters, lovers, and mothers of Klansmen, Markwell embarked on a recruiting trip throughout the West and Northwest, where she succeeded in drawing many women to the Klan. Markwell also hired female field agents and kleagles to collaborate with K.K.K. kleagles. Often the wives and sisters of the K.K.K. officers, W.K.K.K. kleagles worked on a commission basis, keeping a percentage of the initiation dues collected from each new member. Organizers used techniques proven effective in the men's Klan: they relied heavily on personal, family, and work contacts and held highly publicized open meetings to reach politically inactive women and women not associated with Klan men. W.K.K.K. kleagles also recruited women from existing organizations, especially nativist and patriotic societies (Blee 1991).

All this worked amazingly, disconcertingly, horrifyingly well. Within four months, the W.K.K.K. membership had doubled to 250,000, or so the organization reported. By November 1923 thirty-six states had chapters of the Women of the Ku Klux Klan. Throughout 1924 the W.K.K.K. exploded, as the organization now accepted women over sixteen years old. Over fifty new locals a week were chartered in 1924. The following year a critic of the Klan complained that at least three million women now belonged. His figure was too high; scholars estimate the entire 1920s Klan, male and female, to have enrolled no more than three to five million members. Still, that is a frightening number, and the W.K.K.K. represented no small fraction of it (Blee 1991).

National W.K.K.K. klonvokations occurred irregularly. The first meeting was held in 1923 in Asheville; in 1926 one thousand women delegates from the W.K.K.K. met in Washington, D.C., at the same time, but separately from, the men's Klan. The following year five hundred Klanswomen delegates, representing every state plus the Canal Zone and Alaska, met in St. Louis for a two-day klonvokation to discuss uniform marriage laws, Prohibition, and "threats to the sanctity of the home" (Blee 1991, 31). A second W.K.K.K. klonvokation in that year convened in Indianapolis where 1,600 candidates heard speeches attacking New York governor and presidential candidate Al Smith for his support of liquor. In October 1928 a much reduced W.K.K.K. met in Dallas (Blee 1991).

In chartering the women's Klan, the K.K.K. underlined women's obligation to help Klansmen. Women's cooperation and assistance were needed, the men insisted, to ensure that the K.K.K.'s political struggle was successful. The K.K.K. press talked often of the W.K.K.K. as its "women's auxiliary," and declared that the men's Klan had created the W.K.K.K. as God had created Eve from Adam, from the same flesh as its male counterpart. But many Klansmen wondered what Klan membership would mean for women. While women would be useful in strengthening the Klan, the terms of their actual political participation was another matter. An early advertisement designed to solicit members for an organization of Klanswomen discloses the men's ambivalence. Although it was a recruitment pitch for the W.K.K.K., the advertisement inadvertently revealed the men's anxiety that political involvement might masculinize their women. The ad acknowledged that many men worried "giving [women] the ballot would foster masculine boldness and restless independence, which might detract from the modesty and virtue of womanhood" (quoted in Blee 1991, 31).

To soothe this anxiety, the K.K.K. advised the establishment of a separate organization for Klanswomen. The W.K.K.K. would allow women to be politically active without "sacrifice of that womanly dignity and modesty we all admire" (quoted in Blee 1991, 31). What would prevent masculinization was a "feminine" acquiescence—seventy plus years later Southern Baptists would call it "gracious submission"—to the political agenda of Klansmen. By coming together under men's leadership to serve the sacred cause of white Protestantism, the English language, public schools, the Bible, and immigration restrictions (it reads like a list of conservative causes from the late not early twentieth century), women could exercise their newly granted enfranchisement without being forced to demonstrate "masculine" traits of political judgment and strategizing (Blee 1991).

From the beginning, there were indications that leaders of the fledgling women's Klan did not completely share this view of women's limited role. A recruiting notice for the W.K.K.K. noted pointedly that men no longer exercised "exclusive dominion" in American society. Whether working in the home as a housewife or working in the business world, the ad went on, a woman could support 100 percent American womanhood by joining the W.K.K.K. Markwell herself was even more ambitious, seeing in the W.K.K.K.

numerous opportunities for women to advance the cause of women. Women's interest in politics, latent until legitimized by the Nineteenth Amendment granting women the vote, would now express itself. Now, Markwell declared, women will understand that it is their duty to work "in the maintenance of that amendment" (quoted in Blee 1991, 32)

The W.K.K.K. emphasized its interest in advancing the cause of white womanhood in recruiting for new members. Its Washington chapter, for instance, reminded white Protestant native-born women that they had common political interests. These common interests could be more effectively pursued if they were politically organized. The Washington recruitment advertisement posed these questions for women to consider:

> Are you interested in the welfare of our Nation?
> As an enfranchised woman are you interested in Better Government?
> Do you now wish for the protection of Pure Womanhood?
> Shall we uphold the sanctity of the American home?
> Should we not interest ourselves in Better Education for our children?
> Do we not want American teachers in our American schools?
> (quoted in Blee 1991, 33)

Many white native-born Protestant women found themselves unable to answer "no" to these. These "patriotic women"—those who answered the questions affirmatively—"must" join the women's Klan. Protestant white women, the W.K.K.K. declared, shared a special concern and sacred obligation for their children's education and the welfare of the country. It was nothing less than the "duty of the American Mother" to stamp out vice and immorality and restore the nation to its Christian past (quoted in Blee 1991, 33). Joining the Klan allowed white Protestant women to do just that (Blee 1991).

Blee points out that when Klanswomen swore to uphold the "sanctity of the home and chastity of womanhood" they spoke the words, but not necessarily the sentiments, of their male Klan counterparts. This miming of men's words is reminiscent of late nineteenth-century Christian feminists, who agreed with their husbands and clergy that "woman" was sacred and belonged in the home but in so agreeing elevated their own moral and political status (Haynes 1998). Simply comparing the lists of W.K.K.K. and K.K.K. principles and rituals would suggest that there was little difference between the two organizations, but Blee underscores that we must remember the same words were interpreted differently by each gender.

Certainly many principles of the new women's Klan were identical to the racist and xenophobic politics of the first and second men's Klans. The W.K.K.K. endorsed patriotism, militarism, national quotas for immigration, racial segregation, and antimiscegenation laws. Klanswomen declared their solemn obligation to safeguard the "eternal supremacy" of the white race against a "rising tide of color." They deplored Catholic and Jewish influence in politics, the schools, the media, and in the economy. Markwell articulated the mission of the women's Klan as "fighting for the same principles as the Knights of the Ku Klux Klan," although she was quick to point out that the W.K.K.K. had a special interest in "work peculiar to women's organization, such as a social welfare [and] the prevention of juvenile delinquency" (quoted in Blee 1991, 34).

The W.K.K.K. also employed the men's political rhetoric to advance its agenda of nativism and racial hatred. Women too called for separation of church from state when railing against Roman Catholic political influence, for free public schools in hopes of destroying parochial schools, and for the purity of "race" when demanding racial segregation and restricted immigration. In the public sphere or the private, the racial hatred of the W.K.K.K. was just as vicious as that of the K.K.K., illustrated by the W.K.K.K.'s condemnation of "mulatto leaders forced to remain members of the negro group [who] aspire to white association because of their white blood [thus] boldly preaching racial equality" (quoted in Blee 1991, 34)

While many of the W.K.K.K.'s basic principles and practices coincided with the men's, the two groups did not always share a common perception of which problems required Klan action. Klansmen of the 1920s denounced interracial marriage for its destructive genetic outcomes; their Klan forefathers, Blee suggests, fought interracial sexuality to perpetuate white men's sexual access to both white and black women. As we have seen, the nineteenth-century white woman functioned as an imaginary stand-in for white men in the rape scenario, and so antimiscegenation fears can be decoded, in part, as disguised homosexual panic. And, as I will argue in the next volume, fear of miscegenation was also related to incest, specifically homosexual incest. Twentieth-century Klanswomen, however, emphasized a different danger in miscegenation: the destruction of white marriages by cheating white men who "betray their own kind" (quoted Blee 1991, 34).

Katherine Blee argues that on many occasions women and men in the Klan heard different messages while speaking the same words. Klansmen praised womanhood to underline the legitimacy of male supremacy while Klanswomen agreed in order to point out the inequities that women suffered in society and politics. Klansmen sought political inspiration in the "great achievements" of white American Protestantism, but Klanswomen read this history somewhat differently. To many, the men's praise for "true American women" was hollow; the W.K.K.K. did not hesitate to complain that historically women had been excluded from public politics, even though "our mothers have ever been Klanswomen at heart, sharing with our fathers the progress and development of our country" (quoted in Blee 1991, 35). Klanswomen endorsed the K.K.K.'s racist, anti-Catholic, and anti-Semitic agenda and the men's idealization of American womanhood, but they used these issues to argue for the cause for white Protestant women. This cause was intelligible not only racially, religiously, ethnically, but in terms of gender as well (Blee 1991). At some level, then, the W.K.K.K. appeared to understand that their "enemies" were also white men.

In general, the W.K.K.K. adopted the militaristic hierarchical organizational structure of the K.K.K.. An Excellent Commander served at the top, with a four-year term of office and responsibility for issuing, suspending, and revoking the charters of locals and realms (state organizations). Second in the chain of command was the klaliff, who acted as presiding officer of the Imperial Klonvokation; the klokard (lecturer) was responsible for disseminating Klankraft and the kludd (chaplain) presided over Klan ritual. Other major officers included the kligrapp (secretary), bonded for $25,000 to handle minor Klan funds; the Klabee (treasurer), bonded for $50,000 to handle major Klan funds; and the officers of Klan ritual and ceremony, including the kladd (conductors), klagoro (inner guard), night hawk (in charge of candidates), klokan (investigator and auditor), and kourier (messenger) (Blee 1991).

Like their male counterparts, Klanswomen wore white robes with masks and helmets, although there were chapters which preferred red robes. While hiding the identity of Klanswomen in public, the W.K.K.K. insisted that masks had only a symbolic function. The mask indicated that the individuality and identity of Klanswomen were secondary, performing the Klan motto "not for self, but for others." The robes were said to symbolize the same: self-effacement and devotion to others, although "others" was of course racially and religiously boundaried. Officers' robes had more colors and accouterments, but the official line was that the costumes indicated the equality of all women within Klankraft. Robes set Klanswomen apart from the unjust world of social class distinctions expressed in fashion, setting right the injustice so pervasive in alien society (Blee 1991). "As we look upon a body of women robed in white we realize that we are on a common level of sisterhood and fraternal union" (quoted in Blee 1991, 36).

Once assembled, officers were quizzed about the seven sacred symbols of Klankraft in a ritualized catechism apparently (if strangely, given the W.K.K.K.'s anti-Catholicism) patterned after the catechism ritual of the Roman Catholic Church. Each officer declared, reverentially, the sacred symbols: The Bible (God), fiery cross (sacrifice and service), flag (U.S. Constitution), sword (law enforcement and national defense), water (purity of life and unity of purpose), mask (secrecy, unselfishness, banishment of individuality), and robe (purity and equality). To punctuate these declarations of Klan doctrine, the audience and officers sang a Christian hymn (Blee 1991).

It is difficult to compare the political practices of the W.K.K.K. and the K.K.K. These varied considerably across the country and over time but, Blee points out, the national agendas of each organization suggest the differences. The political practices of the K.K.K. ranged from infiltration into legislative and judicial politics on the state, municipal, and county level to acts of violence and terrorism against Jews, Catholics, and African Americans. Many Klansmen, however, were not particularly active politically; they used the K.K.K. as a male fraternity, a social club of like-minded white Protestant men (Blee 1991).

Women also participated in a range of activities and practices. Nationally, the women's Klan pledged allegiance to the K.K.K., agreeing with the men's program of violence and terrorism. The national office published and distributed a detailed guide to the proper display of the American flag as well as pocket-sized version of the U.S. Constitution. It printed a card reminding Protestants to attend church faithfully; each item prominently displayed the W.K.K.K. logo. The W.K.K.K. tried to influence national legislative politics, but without much success. Curiously, given right-wing policies recently, the W.K.K.K. actively supported the establishment of a federal Department of Education to bolster public schools. That move was, not incidentally, calculated to undermine parochial education. Consistent with contemporary right-wing points of view regarding the United Nations, the W.K.K.K. opposed U.S. membership in the World Court. Although it pledged itself to the protection of white Protestant children and the home, the women opposed a 1924 bill outlawing child labor on the grounds that it was "a Communistic, Bolshevistic scheme" (quoted in Blee 1991, 39). That same year the women worked hard to block efforts by anti-Klan forces to introduce a plank in the national Democratic party platform condemning the Ku Klux Klan (Blee 1991).

Despite its willingness to tolerate the economic exploitation of children, the W.K.K.K. sometimes sought to promote itself as an organization fundamentally committed to social work and social welfare. One national W.K.K.K. speaker announced that she left social work for the "broader field of Klankraft" because the Klan was so committed to the promotion of morality and public welfare (quoted phrase in Blee 1991, 40). Many chapters claimed to collect food and money for the needy, but these donations typically went to Klan families, often to families of Klan members arrested for terrorism and vigilante violence. A powerful Florida W.K.K.K. chapter operated a free day nursery because, it charged angrily, the presence of Catholic teachers made the local public schools toxic to Protestant children (Blee 1991).

Significantly, Klanswomen tended not to engage in physical violence and rioting, although there were exceptions. After a 1924 Klan riot in Wilkinsburg, Pennsylvania, Mamie H. Bittner, a thirty-nine-year-old mother of three children and member of the Homestead, Pennsylvania, W.K.K.K. testified that she (and thousands of her fellow Klanswomen) had paraded through town, carrying heavy maple riot clubs. Bittner further testified that the W.K.K.K. had instructed its members to kill to advance the cause of the Klan (Blee 1991). As in lynchings, women participated in reactionary racial politics, but, even considering the Wilkinsburg incident, they did not use torture and mutilation to express their desire.

While the political practices of the women's Klan were in sync with the political policies of the men's Klan, the W.K.K.K. cannot be understood only as a dependent auxiliary of the men's order. Blee emphasizes that Klanswomen created a distinctive ideology and political agenda that blended the Klan's racist and nativist objectives with aspirations for equality between white Protestant women and men. The ideology and politics of the W.K.K.K. and the K.K.K. were not identical, although on most points they were close. "But," Blee (1991) points out, "women and men of the Klan movement sometimes found themselves in contention as women changed from symbols to actors in the Klan" (41). The imaginary white "lady" of the nineteenth century was becoming, however gradually, "real."

VI. A Womanless Family: Manliness and Womanhood in the K.K.K.

The "woman question" was, in fact, also a question about men. For one thing, in a wholly female world there would have been nothing to ask—any more than in a wholly black world would there have been a Negro question. The pedestal had, after all, been built by male hands.

—Peter G. Filene, *Him/Her/Self* (1998)

> *Klan rhetoric was soaked with masculine imagery.*
>
> —Michael Kimmel, *Manhood in America: A Cultural History* (1996)

The differences that existed between the women's and men's Klan, Katherine Blee argues, became most visible in the symbology of white womanhood. By keeping women imaginary—that is, by employing their fantasies of feminine virtue as political symbols—the men affirmed the K.K.K.'s masculine identity as an organization of "real men." As Blee notes, this masculinization of racial politics was entirely in keeping with the original Klan, as well as an effective recruitment strategy for the second one. But in the 1920s financial and political expediency (the latter having to do with the recent enfranchisement of women) prompted the Klan to accept female members, a move which threatened that identity organized around symbols of masculine exclusivity and supremacy. For Klansmen, defending white womanhood meant safeguarding white male Protestant supremacy, but many women decoded the equation differently. The W.K.K.K. agreed that they were racially and religiously superior, but—on this point, like Jessie Daniel Ames and the A.S.W.P.L.—they rejected the subtext of white female vulnerability. In its place Klanswomen substituted support for women's rights and a challenge to white men's political and economic supremacy (Blee 1991).

One site of these conflicting codings was the idea and meaning of the term "Klanswoman." For women the term represented a synthesis of women's rights with the men's xenophobic, anti-Semitic, racist politics. For the men the first thesis was irrelevant. In fact, Klansmen were hostile to the idea. The men had assumed that the women would serve deferentially the cause of the K.K.K., but many women resisted. Even a few W.K.K.K. klaverns (chapters) sought to separate from the male Klan. Underscoring that racial politics was in some essential sense a boys' game, even anti-Klan activists focused on the existence of Klanswomen, using it to ridicule Klansmen as effeminate and degenerate (Blee 1991).

In its early years, the second Klan's images of masculinity, femininity, and appropriate sex roles were consistent with those of its predecessor. For men in both Klans, masculinity and K.K.K. membership were synonymous. Klansmen were "true men," "real men," "100 percent men," "all-American men." Because the Klan claimed to admit only men whose masculinity was beyond question, "the very act of joining the Klan conferred manhood" (Blee 1991, 43). As we will see in chapter 13, the very idea of being a "man" seems to confer "rights" to violence.

While the men were clear who they were (!), the concept of Klan femininity was softer and fuzzier. That had much to do with the soil on the men's lens of perception. During the early 1920s K.K.K., women were in fact invisible. Only the men acted politically; only men knew how to function in a man's world. Like children (who were also idealized), white women tended to exist in the white male imagination. There they were possessions or symbols on whose behalf "real men" acted and for whom men fought one another. Of course, in a man's world there is no place for women, not even as Klansmembers. How could there be? Those ideals Klansmembers claimed coincided with those very same ideals (male) society defined as inherently masculine: aggressiveness, bravery, and toughness. These were the exact opposite of the men's fantasies of a gentle, accommodating femininity (Blee 1991).

Klan propaganda always emphasized the manliness of its fraternal union. The K.K.K. stood for those principles Klansmen thought any white Protestant man worthy of the name should espouse: defense of his possessions (including wife and children) from outside interference and principled conduct toward like-minded white Protestant men. An often-reprinted poetic call for real men to join the Klan made this clear:

> God Give Us Men! The Invisible Empire demands strong
> Minds, great hearts, true faith and ready hands,
> Men whom lust of office does not kill;
> Men whom the spoils of office cannot buy.
> (quoted in Blee 1991, 44)

The Klan's call for a masculinity of individualism, courage, self-possession, and vigilance was strangely out of sync with the 1920s. The second Klan mimicked its predecessor's use of masculinity to symbolize and affirm the righteousness of white male supremacy, but unlike the postbellum South, there were in the 1920s, at most, remnants remaining of this supremacy. The klannish fantasy of manhood exalted the exercise of physical violence decades after the middle and working classes from which the Klan drew much of its membership had abandoned such aggression as socially inappropriate. Its exaggerated images of autonomy, absolute male privilege, and fraternal camaraderie were lost in a time long past. Nineteenth-century norms of patriarchal autonomy and artisanal society had long ago been erased by industrial capitalist production and the imposition of market values on human relations, not to mention the advent of feminism and the political progress of women and African Americans, all producing that "crisis of masculinity" Ida B. Wells had so successfully exploited (Blee 1991).

The image of masculinity promoted in the K.K.K. was not only past, it was contradictory. These "all-American" men, presumably fearless and in charge of their own destinies, were constantly told by Klan leaders that they must act now if they hoped to defend home and nation against imminent peril, a theme the right wing seems to use regardless of time and place. (Interesting in this context too is Freud's famous formula: paranoia = repressed homosexual desire.) Passionate, even "hysterical," commitment rather than cool rationality typified true Klansmen, even while the "passionate natures" of Jewish, black, and immigrant men relegated them (in the minds of the K.K.K.) to the category of nonmen. Finally, not only were the individualism and self-possession that manly Klansman claimed not possible in the bureaucratic workplace or the companionate family, they were also fantasies within the militaristic hierarchical Klan itself (Blee 1991).

The appeal of klannish masculinity, Blee tells us, had to do with the multiple layers of meaning within this complex, convoluted symbol. In the nationalism and racism of the Klan was one such message. When the second Klan evoked the masculinity of the Reconstruction-era Klan, it underscored (if inadvertently) the extent to which white male privileges had disappeared during those fifty years. When the Klan demanded restoration of "real" American values, male recruits decoded it to mean that "real" manhood needed restoration as well (Blee 1991).

The moralism of Klan rhetoric could not hide the fact that the K.K.K. was committed to violent vigilantism and male camaraderie. Clearly, given the size of the second Klan, these images of hypermasculinity were very appealing to many "proper, God-fearing" men whom the Klan targeted as recruits. Independence and self-determination, fantasies only in the increasingly bureaucratized world of work, lingered as hallmarks of masculinity in the early twentieth century. The extralegal violence of the Klan permitted "little men" (Reich 1970) to act "big," unrestrained by middle-class norms. But the promise of release from restraints and obligations—surely only a negative version of autonomy and self-determination—was coupled with the fantasy of solidarity, an end to individual isolation. The K.K.K. heralded the collectivity of "true men." Sure, white Protestant masculinity meant, presumably, tough-minded and individualistic exercise of personal judgments, but the reality was that individual Klansmen were wedded to a common cause and to one another. In this way, the contradiction between fantasies of self-determination and the reality of the Klan's organizational hierarchy dissolved. Evidently, self-possession and independence translated into obedience to freely chosen (male) authority (Blee 1991).

Another masculinized appeal of the K.K.K. was its characterization of Protestant religion as manly. By converting the gentleness of the Christ figure into a weapon of terror and political manipulation, the K.K.K. sought to "transgender" the softer countenance of twentieth-century religion into, as one Illinois pastor put it, "the masculine part of Protestantism." Predictably, while K.K.K. membership conferred masculinity, ineligibility must mean failure to be "men," and so Klan opponents, including priests and other non-Protestant clergy, were ridiculed as effeminate. On this point the Klan was expropriating a tactic common among fundamentalist Protestant ministers such as Billy Sunday, who used a falsetto voice to mimic the "effeminate" oratory of "modernist" ministers (Blee 1991; see chapter 5, section VIII). Catholic priests and Jewish rabbis, the Klan insisted, were the more appropriate targets of such ridicule: "Why burlesque the Protestant minister and hold him up as a weak sister, an effeminate fellow, a proper subject for ridicule, and let the priest and the rabbi go 'scot free'? I tell you, the Ku Klux Klan is opposed, to the death, to such partiality and favoritism" (quoted in Blee 1991, 45).

Particularly during its early years, the male Klan held two contradictory images of femininity and womanhood, one imaginary, and one a concession to the reality of concretely existing people. In their imagination, white Protestant women (femininity applied only to these) were innocent, virtuous creatures whose *raison d'être* was to support and serve men. In turn, men would protect these vulnerable sexually appealing ladies from those sexually rapacious demons (i.e., black men) who could not help but desire them. The image of actual wives, mothers, and lovers could not so easily remain on the plane of imagination (Blee 1991).

As symbols, white Protestant women were perfect; the Klan pledged undying respect and adoration for these lovely creatures of white womanhood. The *Klansman's Manual* declared that (white, Protestant) womanhood was "all that is best, and noblest in life" and warned that "no race, or society, or country, can rise higher than its womanhood." The Klan's very existence had to do, presumably, with the "sacred duty" of "real men" to protect (white, Protestant) womanhood. Echoing the Reconstruction-era Klan, the second Klan declared that the "degradation of woman is a violation of the sacredness of human personality, a sin against the race, a crime against society, a menace to our country, and a prostitution." An Illinois Klan minister-lecturer knew the drill: "After God created man and saw him so desolate he created woman, the most beautiful, the most perfect, and the greatest creation God ever made, for man to cherish and protect" (quoted in Blee 1991, 46).

For the Klan, the epitome of white womanhood was motherhood. In his address to the first meeting of Grand Dragons, James Comer declared that good mothers were key to men's success. Officers and kleagles throughout the K.K.K. hierarchy emphasized the critical role of motherhood in perpetuating a white Protestant manly nation. A directive from the Indiana K.K.K. Department of Propaganda and Education to all state exalted cyclops and kligrapps on the occasion of Mother's Day 1925, for instance, instructed Klansmen to honor their "glorious mothers as the only reliable source of counsel, sympathy, and courage in a man's life" (quoted in Blee 1991, 46).

The Klan's idealization of motherhood was inextricably linked to another symbol: the home. The K.K.K. insisted that "the American home is fundamental to all that is best in life, in society, in church, and in the nation." The *Klansman's Manual* directed members to protect the home by "promoting whatever would make for its stability, its betterment, its safety, and its inviolability." Before he resigned, Simmons proclaimed the American home as the "veritable rockbottom of our national well-being" and warned that if homes were to fall apart "all our wealth and material achievement is naught but poverty and trash." In propaganda, songs, poems, and rituals the K.K.K. fantasized the sanctity of "the home":

> Home, home, country and home,
> Klansmen we'll all live and die
> For our country and home.
> (quoted in Blee 1991, 46)

As we will see in chapter 13, the home is the primary site of violence against women, more dangerous for women than urban streets at night. Ignoring reality, Klansmen fantasized that the home stood for nothing less than Americanism (itself a convoluted term compacting race, gender, class, and religion), including the protection of American "values" from aliens' "corrosive" influence. The Grand Dragon of the Realm of Colorado warned Klansmen that they must be zealous when guarding the home, telling them that "all the forces of evil which attack the American home strike at the life of the nation, for when the home is broken, all pretext of government vanishes" (quoted in Blee 1991, 47). Home ownership—an idea which was not strictly economic—gave "real Americans" a stake in the nation's future plus a stability that the nomadic, ever-increasing mass of immigrants could, presumably, never know (Blee 1991).

Klansmen knew, they said, that the home represented women's dreams and identity. By guarding the home, the men were protecting their women. Such a fantasy is not contained within gender arrangements; it "bled" into the nation as a whole. White Protestant homes symbolized the future of the nation. Home life of the kind the Klan imagined was a prerequisite to the patriotism and other klannish values upon which the nation depended. When the Roman Catholic Church required marriage contracts to contain the promise to raise children as Catholics, it was, the K.K.K. insisted, assaulting the very basis of the American home and, through the home, the foundation of American Protestant nationhood (Blee 1991).

Even as the K.K.K. glorified symbols of home, mothers, and white womanhood, how these men treated the concretely existing women they knew is less clear. At the very least, a certain ambivalence toward wives is detectable. In rallies and meetings Klansmen sang songs and told tales depicting the perils of marriage to demanding bossy women. One such ditty suggested that the K.K.K. functioned as an escape for abused husbands:

> Oh, Barney Google he belongs to the Ku Klux Klan
> Barney's wife was big and fat,
> She knocked him out from under his hat,
> Because poor Barney he joined the Ku Klux Klan.
> (quoted in Blee 1991, 47)

These men feared that their wives (or lovers) had nearly limitless influence over them. That wasn't all surprising, since, the men reassured each other, everyone knows that real men are nearly helpless in the gaze of attractive women. It was the job of the wife to maintain a man's moral character, a responsibility that underlined the power men imagined women had over them.

> A many a night have I went away from home
> And left my dear wife a weeping
> I'd get drunk and fight and stay out all night
> When I ought to be down home sleeping.
> Now those days have past and I quiet at last,
> And better days now I am keeping.
> Most any time about the hour of nine
> You can find me right down home sleeping.
> (quoted in Blee 1991, 47)

The Klan's ambivalence toward actual women extended to women as mothers. Actual mothers (as opposed to their fantasy of motherhood) exercised, Klansmen worried, frightening power over men. Unchecked by men, women's child-rearing practices could well undermine the "building of manly character" essential for Klansmen (Blee 1991, 48), a pervasive fear during the 1920s as we saw in the paragraphs introducing the second section of this chapter. The presence and ultimate authority of fathers was key to the proper development of Klan children, especially Klan boys, a misogynist view we will encounter again in chapter 14. There it takes the form of the so-called matrifocality thesis, which argues that the "crisis" of black masculinity has to do with the absence of strong fathers in the home. Evidently, in a patriarchal society where masculinity is violent, even more powerful men are needed to temper young manhood into sublimated, socially acceptable forms.

Nearly every piece of Klan propaganda from the early 1920s instructed Klansmen to protect the virtue of white womanhood. But in this literature, Blee informs us, "the Klan's ambivalence toward flesh-and-blood women was apparent." The American womanhood Klansmen swore to protect was, of course, sexually monogamous and premaritally chaste. Men never seemed to forget to remind women of these obligations, insisting that "the purity and moral integrity demanded of women have proven of priceless value to the race" (quoted in Blee 1991, 48). According to a prominent Klan minister, chastity in women (but evidently not in men) was a prerequisite to the preservation of marriage, the home, and the government. This line is reminiscent of the Reconstruction-era Klan's obsession with women's purity and chastity, then in relation to what they imagined to be the sexual powers and proclivities of hypermasculine black men. The second Klan sought to protect pure womanhood less from sexually rapacious black men and more from unladylike conduct by the women themselves (Blee 1991).

A Certain Bifocality

There was, then, a certain bifocality of Klansmen's perception of women. On the one hand they idealized women, especially as they imagined them as the personifications of home life. On the other, clearly women were untrustworthy, easily manipulative, undermining, finally mysterious. This bifocal perception evidently structured gender for many men, and it strengthened the appeal of the Klan fraternity as a substitute family for Klansmen. The K.K.K. was a womanless family where concretely existing women could not jeopardize men's fantasies. God was the collective father and all Klansmen were brothers. Women were superfluous in this spiritual household where men doubled as "brides of Christ" (Greven 1977). These brothers and brides were sworn by The Oath of Allegiance to fraternal "klannishness," which prohibited defaming, defrauding, creating, or deluding other Klansmen or their families. Local K.K.K. klaverns were, then, men's clubs, sponsoring speakers, social hours, group prayers, homosocial groupings that underlined men's sense of solidarity with themselves. Women and children were excluded (Blee 1991).

When K.K.K. leaders competed with one another to enlist women in the Invisible Empire, their decision threatened the gender exclusivity of the Klan. Men's interest in women members, you recall, was hardly ideological but financial and political; the reality of women as members contradicted the Klan's image of itself as an organization of and for manly men. In the Klan press and in countless speeches K.K.K. leaders tried to solve this dilemma: how could the Klan support a political role for women that kept them both appropriately subordinate to men and allowed them to serve as activists for the Klan cause?

How could the Klan maintain itself as an exclusively male fraternity with a masculine image in the face of this feminine presence? (Blee 1991).

Blee explains that the decision to create the W.K.K.K. as a distinct organization for women was in part an attempt to solve this dilemma. As a separate but affiliated organization, the women could support the Klan's efforts without directly encountering men in the organization. A national Klan minister-lecturer expressed the convoluted sentiments of many Klansmen when he demanded separate groups for men and women. While women are not inferior, evidently there are some things only a man can do: "It isn't because women can't keep a secret. We know they can. It was Adam, not Eve, who did the talking. We will never admit women because they can not do some of the work we have to do" (quoted in Blee 1991, 49).

This bifocality allowed the K.K.K. to define women's political role as separate and subordinate to that of men while they supported women's legal and political rights, issues that would appeal to potential female members. The *Fiery Cross* reported favorably on the launching of the National Women's Party campaign for women in the U.S. Congress, characterizing it as a search for justice for women. The paper also applauded a movement for women's equal representation in the legislative bodies of the Presbyterian church. Another Klan publication, the *Fellowship Forum*, endorsed the actions of a woman who obtained a passport in her own, rather than her husband's, name. It also published a regular feature entitled "The American Woman," a page that reported on women's rights' but included recipes and fashion news as well (Blee 1991).

The K.K.K.'s official attitudes toward women reflected this bifocality. The Ku Klux Klan Katechism asked Klansmen: "What is the attitude of the Klan toward women?" They were to reply: "The Klan believes in the purity of womanhood and in the fullest measure of freedom compatible with the highest type of womanhood including the suffrage" (quoted in Blee 1991, 49). The K.K.K. officially endorsed the political rights of white Protestant women, but it maintained, stubbornly, its male fantasy of white womanhood as racially and sexually pure and subordinate, requiring manly protection (Blee 1991).

Klanswomen answered the question of women's status differently than the men did. While always agreeing with them that home life was key, the W.K.K.K. dissented from their fantasy of home and family which allowed men to segregate themselves as men, away from that same home and family to which they had pledged allegiance. Without spectacles that altered their vision, Klanswomen were not hesitant to describe the home as a place of labor, the site of "monotonous and grinding toil and sacrifice." The life of a homemaker, the W.K.K.K. complained, was held in "low esteem" by the larger society (i.e., men) and women were insufficiently appreciated for their efforts. Nor were Klanswomen able to participate fully in the men's fantasy of marriage. While acknowledging the sacred state as women's "crowning glory," women also were quick to point out that it was also a burden they bore. Nor was this burden recently acquired, as one Klanswoman's comment indicates: "Pilgrim mothers not only endured the hardships of the Pilgrim fathers, but what was a greater burden they had to endure the Pilgrim fathers" (quoted in Blee 1991, 51).

Whether in the mothering of children or the nurturance of a nation, the W.K.K.K. did not hesitate to emphasize that motherhood was women's *work*. Klansmen heralded child-rearing as women's "glorious mission," but for many whose "mission" it was, "burden" was the more apt descriptor (Blee 1991). In a description of a well-attended W.K.K.K. celebration of Mother's Day we can detect both the pride and resentment associated with motherhood:

> Throwing off her hood to reveal a modish bob, and employing a brogue ... the leader of the feminine hosts in the realm of New Jersey cried "I'm glad to be here to speak today with all these girls present, because the girls of today are the mothers of tomorrow! ... When you see a lady that acts a little peculiar don't ridicule her. Just remember she's somebody's mother, and she's working 24 hours a day while you're working 8." (quoted in Blee 1991, 51–52)

There were women's Klan leaders who proposed that Klanswomen act together to change not the rhetoric but the reality of motherhood. One kleagle encouraged Klanswomen mothers to organize a campaign demanding an eight-hour day for the job of mothering. Like the New Jersey leader quoted above, she complained that women work twenty-four hours a day while men have to work only one-third that much. The only hope for Klanswomen was political action. By protecting the privileges of all white native-born Protestants, the W.K.K.K. insisted, white Protestant women could achieve more equitable working conditions in the home, more acknowledgment of their importance as wives and mothers. Like most Klan propaganda, there was no "action plan," no outline of steps to be taken (Blee 1991).

Klanswomen characterized their support for white Protestant women's political and legal rights in different terms than Klansmen did. The men's position was direct and simple; we must harden the political muscle of white Protestant men. Female followers can help. The W.K.K.K., in contrast, saw a more crucial role for women. Women needed the vote for two interrelated reasons: to maintain a moral white Protestant nation and to promote women's rights. Even while burdened by never-ending family responsibilities, it was women who kept the "spiritual fire of the nation burning" and who acted as the "conscience-keeper of the race." It was women who inspired "every moral law, every law regarding sanitation, prison reform, child labor, and control of liquor." Klanswomen worried they could not count on men to support women's rights and so they urged women to "hold fast" to the franchise (quoted in Blee 1991, 52). Only in never-ending struggle could women hope to improve upon their unequal status with men (Blee 1991).

The speeches of W.K.K.K. Imperial Commander Robbie Gill suggest the evolution of the W.K.K.K.'s position on equal rights. Soon after taking office in 1924, she addressed a K.K.K. Klonvokation on "American Women," an address reprinted widely in the Klan press. Gill appropriated the Christian emphasis of the Klan to legitimate women's rights (Blee 1991). "It has never been the purpose of God," Gill declared, "that women should be the slave of man." Like Christian feminists the century before, Gill insisted that women's subordination was a misunderstanding of God's will associated with "primitive" theologies.

Gill argued that in a Protestant nation women (i.e., white Protestant women) were entitled to "education, refinement, and honor" (quoted in Blee 1991, 52).

Gill's statement makes it clear that many Klanswomen did not share Klansmen's fantasies of helpless ladies, fantasies which animated men's own racism, nationalism, and anti-Semitism. Until women had gained the right to vote, Gill reminded her listeners, they had been forced to exercise political power by influencing men emotionally, indirectly, in private. Thank goodness, she said, women have been and continue to be quite capable of that. "The greatest strength of woman's power," Gill reminded, "lies in the way in which men depend upon her and are for the most part absolutely, or nearly so, helpless without her" (quoted in Blee 1991, 53).

But women's enfranchisement gave women political power that was public, direct, and independent of men. Using one's "charms" to influence men's political behavior was now an option. Furthermore, women constituted a numerical majority of voters; if women would vote together they could take over. Evidently Gill thought it not implausible that white Protestant women might vote as a bloc, given that their obligation—here there are echoes of the W.C.T.U.—to curb the excesses of men bound them in common cause: "She knows who will suffer most if her husband or son or brother or sweetheart becomes a drunkard or a drug addict ... if gambling grips the life of her loved one ... if some silly, irresponsible 'affinity' breaks up her home" (quoted in Blee 1991, 53).

But Gill did not mirror the attitudes of all Klanswomen. Many accepted their subordinate status; many saw in socially constructed gender arrangements the judgment of God. These contradictions and ambiguities of gender ideology were never resolved within the W.K.K.K., just as the men's Klan never resolved its gender tensions. But it is important to emphasize, as Blee does, that contrary to expectation, many women were attracted to the women's Klan *because* it supported women's rights as well as white and Protestant supremacy. Klanswomen worked for women's equality in society both inside and out of the Invisible Empire, contradicting the traditional Klan's beliefs in Christian progress and female helplessness. However, Klanswomen were never willing to endorse any political agenda that appeared to link them with what they took to be feminist "extremists." Klansmen's reactionary gender, racial, and religious politics tempered Klanswomen's full endorsement of women's equality. Klanswomen sought protection and promotion of their rights in politics, the economy, marriage, and the law, but they could not imagine full equality between white Protestant women and men (Blee 1991).

The Gender of Anti-Klan Politics

It was not only within the Klan that the presence of women caused tension. Anti-Klan forces exploited the existence of Klanswomen to ridicule Klansmen. While the men of the second Klan struggled to maintain their gender fantasies while accommodating a changed gender reality, anti-Klan Progressives did not hesitate to express their own misogyny, rationalized, presumably, because it was directed at the hated K.K.K. As early as 1922 opponents ridiculed Klansmen by suggesting that Elizabeth Tyler was their true leader, hinting that they could hardly be men if led by a woman. After the W.K.K.K. was established, anti-Klan forces pointed to Klanswomen as the definitive proof of the moral degeneracy of the Ku Klux Klan (Blee 1991).

Exploiting the widely held misogynistic binary of women as either virgins or whores, Klan opponents saw Klanswomen in two predictable ways. Either these women were politically innocent and naive and had been seduced by the political and sexual enticements of Klansmen, or Klanswomen were political shrewd and sexually licentious women who manipulated sexually starved Klansmen for their own purposes. Whichever was true, anti-Klan forces declared, Klan meetings provided the occasions and Klan meeting halls the locations for "assignation purposes" between Klanswomen and Klansmen (Blee 1991, 66). Not only the right wing resorted to sexual fantasies of the "other."

The gender of racial politics is evident in the struggles of two major anti-Klan figures, George Dale of Muncie, Indiana, and Ben Lindsey of Denver, Colorado. Their tactics illustrate how anti-Klan activists used women to attack the K.K.K. This was no mere ideological chess game; both Dale and Lindsey suffered personal assaults by the K.K.K. for their anti-Klan activity. But revealingly, each man focused upon the image of violent Klanswomen to direct his efforts at revenge (Blee 1991).

The publisher of the *Muncie Post-Democrat*, George Dale fought the Klan in the Klan stronghold of Muncie, Indiana. Dale was sure that Klan members dominated the Delaware County courts and that the city administration of Muncie accommodated Klan interests. His newspaper published lists of those reputed to be Muncie Klansmen, and those lists named many of the city's officials and business leaders. As horrified as he was by the Klan's infiltration of county and city government, Dale became outraged when he learned that the Delaware County Klan was recruiting women and children into the organization. Klan parades through Muncie in 1923 gave women a prominent, even provocative, role in the battle between pro- and anti-Klan men. As Klanswomen passed by, if male bystanders did not remove their hats in respect they were physically threatened by Klansmen. Dale thundered: "All men who have a spark of manhood left in their veins" should refuse to salute (quoted in Blee 1991, 66). Already unpopular with the Klan due to those lists, Dale was now targeted by the Klan. Soon he and his family were assaulted. When he did not stop publishing editorials against the Klan, Dale found himself arrested by a Klan-dominated police and held in contempt of its judiciary (Blee 1991).

While it had been Klansmen in the municipal administration that had caused most of his legal troubles, Dale did not choose to focus on them. Instead, he obsessed over Klanswomen who had functioned as pawns in this affair between men. In an editorial entitled "Bloodthirsty Women," Dale characterized the audience of Klanswomen at his 1923 trial as "bob-haired Amazons" demanding the death penalty. "Amazons" of course is a homophobic synonym for lesbians, hardly an appropriate image for the vulnerable ladies in deference to whom Klansmen had demanded all men tip their hats. But Dale did not stop there. Not only did he impugn the femininity of Klanswomen, he also assailed the masculinity of Klansmen and the husbands of Klanswomen. In new editorials Dale ridiculed men who stayed at home taking care of the children while their wives were out cavorting with sister Klanswomen. Klan wives, he was suggesting, had become the real heads-of-household: "It is real fun to see men waiting with autos at the Kamelia [W.K.K.K.] meetings, to take the boss home. It sure takes a fat head Koo to wait around for hours with a machine full of kids waiting till midnight to take Ma home" (quoted in Blee 1991, 67).

Benjamin B. Lindsey was a Denver judge internationally recognized as an authority on juvenile court systems. Lindsey came under attack from the Denver Klan for his support of companionate marriage, lenient divorce laws, and birth control, but mostly because he was critical of the K.K.K. A Klan candidate lost a close judicial election to Lindsey, then filed for a recount of the votes, claiming electoral fraud in a mostly Jewish district in Denver. The Klan candidate lost the recount but refused to accept the outcome. He appealed the decision through the courts and, in 1927, he was awarded the judicial post by the Colorado Supreme Court. But the Klansman had committed suicide two years earlier. Contemptuous both of the court's decision and the Klan's tactics, Lindsey burned the records of his court in a "shame bonfire" and moved out of state (Blee 1991, 68).

While obviously a matter between men, Lindsey's account of his battle with the Klan, like Dale's, focused on Klanswomen. The antagonism shown him by the women's Klan, while more emotional than legal or political, had infuriated Lindsey. Perhaps he could not imagine opposition from women, given his support for judicial and legislative issues to protect women and children. "Like screaming furies," Lindsey wrote, women of the Klan had led the assault. Evidently imagining himself an aristocrat he wrote: "The conduct of the women at meetings cannot be likened to anything but that of women before the Tribunal at the French Revolution, demanding the blood of their victims." From 1789 he returned to the 1920s, remembering vividly that one woman screamed in his face at an anti-Klan meeting, addressing him as "you cur, your dirty cur ... you are not 100 percent American, you are against the Klan" (quoted in Blee 1991, 68).

Like Dale and others who fought the Klan during the 1920s, Lindsey focused upon the presence of women in the Klan. Perhaps they were an easy target; perhaps they, like white women in the nineteenth century, represented a symbol for displaced desire. Whatever the complex conflation of motive, the result was that once again the "traffic" was in women (Rubin 1975). The actual presence of concretely existing women collided with those imaginary figures who were supposed to stay in their place, a place in the white male imagination. Women's physical presence distressed many Klansmen, but many men outside the Klan also had trouble accepting an active and assertive role for women in politics. Was it not a man's world? Women who transgressed the traditional boundaries of feminine involvement in politics also threatened the boundaries of traditional gender arrangements. Suddenly the issue was not fascist tactics or anti-Semitism or white racism; suddenly what was horrible about the Klan to anti-Klan activists was the fundamental corruption and degeneracy of a movement filled with aggressive "Amazonian" women and henpecked, effeminate men. As Blee observes: "The symbolism of womanhood had power for the second Ku Klux Klan, as it had in the original Klan. But the Klan's decision to admit women as Klan members changed the terms for discussing gender issues. *The abstraction of white womanhood gave way to the reality of actual women*, whose political agenda in the Klan did not always correspond to those of Klansmen" (1991, 68, emphasis added).

Morality

The first and second Klans differed considerably in their definition and use of the term "morality." Like its immediate successors, such as the Guardians of Liberty, the first Klan linked sexual morality to the danger of miscegenation, a "horror" that justified the lynching of black men with their insatiable sexual appetites for virginal white women. In the first Klan, gender structured the concept of morality: white women were the sexual victims of immoral black bucks. In the second Klan, morality remained tied to gender and specifically to the ideal of white womanhood. But in the 1920s men were forced to incorporate ideas and rhetoric from women's rights in defining the term. Torn between traditional and modern views of women's rights, Klansmen played on both in an effort to promote themselves as agents of morality.

To do so, Klansmen stayed focused on the bodies of young black men. But they also ranted against the victimization of white Protestant women by unscrupulous Jewish businessmen and sexually sadistic Catholic priests. At the same time, Klansmen promised to honor marital monogamy, punish wife abuse, and restrict alcohol, gambling and other vices, all favorite pastimes of many white Protestant husbands. The second Klan used its predecessor's imagery of women's victimization by immoral and alien forces to inflame white Protestant men's political passions, but when speaking to potential female dues-payers, the story shifted. Now the K.K.K. spoke in a language of women's rights, arguing that vice and immorality dishonored white Protestant women, hindered their cause, and that women had the right, indeed the duty, to act (Blee 1991).

The Klan's morality campaigns succeeded in aggravating existing fears and distrust of "others." When the second Klan attacked blacks, Jews, and Catholics, it did so by portraying them (especially black men) as "ruthless beasts" (Blee 1991, 71) who were ignorant and/or contemptuous of the moral code that made civilized life possible. Such tactics allowed the Klan to intensify white Protestant suspicions that nonwhites and non-Protestants were strange, alien, and threatening. Disguising a viciously racist, anti-Semitic, and anti-Catholic rampage as a moral crusade was especially effective in homogeneous white Protestant communities in which racial and religious minorities were inconsequential economically or socially (Blee 1991). Without concrete-existing persons to puncture the caricatures, white fantasies swelled.

Young white women, as usual, were precious images in the white male imagination. The K.K.K. press operated within this imaginary and intensified public fear with a steady stream of suggestions of a vast sexual traffic in young white women. Klan "journalists" reported that tens of thousands of girls each year were kidnapped from their homes into a sexual netherworld. The northern Indiana Klan attempted to stop a scheduled boxing match near Chicago on the grounds that Jack Johnson (the flamboyant, interracially married black champion about whom we read in the final section of chapter 7) was a professed "negro white slaver" (Blee 1991). Working with these same fantasies, a Klan pamphlet posed this chilling question to potential recruits: "Do you know that annually there are 50,000 girls, from approximately 50,000 American homes, whose virtue is sacrificed upon the altar of vice? [That] there are thousands of girls of foreign birth who were once sent to this country's shores and sold as slaves to the godless passions of men?" (quoted in Blee 1991, 84).

The Klan reserved a special place in its imagination for young black men, especially those it fantasized or knew to be "involved with" white women. To the Klan of the 1920s, dating and marriage across racial or even ethnic lines evoked the same mix of rage and desire that fueled the Reconstruction-era Klan. Nonwhite, foreign-born, and non-Protestant men who were caught with white women faced whipping, beating, kidnapping, and even lynching. This Klan, aware to some extent of female agency, was able to understand that certain white women chose to be involved with black men. Such women, even those who dated Jewish or immigrant men, were at risk from reprisals of some kind from the Klan. In Muncie, Indiana, an especially imaginative Klanswoman accused blacks and Catholics of a conspiracy, claiming that Catholics had concocted a powder that would bleach the skin of black men so that they could then secretly marry white girls (Blee 1991).

VII. The Indiana Klan

Purity and wild oats formed a contradictory masculine mythology.
—Peter G. Filene, *Him/Her/Self* (1998)

In white supremacist thinking black women are invisible and their experience of lynching and rape completely denied.
—Sanda Gunning, *Race, Rape, and Lynching: The Red Record of American Literature, 1890–1912* (1996)

Like the national K.K.K., the Indiana Klan presented itself as a movement for moral reform. Of course, not unlike right-wing groups such as the so-called Christian Coalition today, "morality" is a code word for intolerance and white Protestant supremacy. The contemporary right wing has learned its media lessons well, but the second Klan was hardly as smooth. At the same time as it proclaimed itself the force of morality and sexual purity, the Indiana Klan spent a good deal of time fantasizing about female sexual enslavement. For the Indiana K.K.K., black men were not the only, at times even the primary objects of these fantasies. The Indiana Klan was certain that Catholic priests and Jews were busy kidnapping fair young white maidens, an odd fantasy for contemporary readers, given the present association between priests and altar boys (Blee 1991).

Perhaps the most obsessive day dreams (which were translated into powerful anti-Catholic allegations) of the Indiana Klan concerned the sexual practices of priests and nuns. Here the fantasies turned homosexual, lesbian to be precise. Klan publications and lecturers reported the existence of an international network of convent prisons populated by enslaved young Protestant girls. Not unlike white men's fantasies of prison life with black men, these 1920s Klansmembers visualized these convent prisons as S&M torture chambers where lovely young white girls were forced to perform whatever the demanding nuns required, including sex. As if in a trance, these girls would later emerge back into society, now compliant Catholic adults. According to the W.K.K.K., Catholics preyed upon innocent Protestant couples, fooling them into signing over their children to the Catholic Church. Occasionally, boys entered the fantasy life of Indiana Klansmen, as in the tale of fifty-two boys snatched from a Methodist Episcopal orphanage by a Catholic-incited police raid and placed in Catholic homes from which they desperately tried to escape. But in the main, Indiana Klansmen dreamt of Protestant girls, always innocent and always in danger of being kidnapped by perverted Catholic institutions. In this dream, the Klan was the hero, as it announced to the world that its job was the safeguarding of the virtue of 100 percent American girls (Blee 1991).

One of the most successful Klan propagandists was Helen Jackson, billed as "an escaped nun." Jackson traveled across the country, regaling her sex-segregated audiences with tales of sexual nightmares behind convent walls. In small towns of the West and Midwest, she brought looks of terror upon the faces of thousands of avid listeners. Catholics were, she said (confirming their own fantasies), sadomasochistic maniacs. She herself had suffered a cross burned onto her naked back. Jackson's autobiography, *Convent Cruelties*, sold well at Klan rallies. It was also advertised in Klan publications, with a suggestive drawing of a girl being whipped by aroused nuns. Helen Jackson frequently traveled with L. J. King, who also presented himself as an "ex-Romanist." King made money for years on the anti-Catholic lecture circuit, claiming to be a former priest. Like other anti-Catholic evangelists of the 1910s, King specialized in highly charged, hysterical harangues. With his audiences segregated by sex, King horrified his listeners with lurid tales of Catholic sexual tortures devised by priests and nuns from at least the time of the European Inquisition. In modern times, King thundered, these same unspeakable perversions continued every day in convents and churches all over the world, led by priests whose "unnatural" pledge of celibacy drove them into depravity and degeneracy (Blee 1991).

L. J. King had enlisted in the K.K.K. in the early 1920s, accompanying Helen Jackson on the Klan lecture circuit. King's harangues on the consequences of the unmarried clergy—namely unending sexual exploitation of fair young Protestant maidens—was ideal for the Klan's anti-Catholic agenda. His grisly portraits of alien, perverted clergy fed white Protestant fantasies. "Every priest and nun connected with the [school] system," he said, "is chained to a life of celibacy in defiance of nature and clad in strange, unsanitary costume" (Blee 1991, 90). Small-town Indiana Protestants were breathless.

Not only young Protestant women suffered at the hands of demented Catholic clergy. King and Jackson also described (in vivid terms, of course) the grotesque tortures which nuns suffered for the sexual gratification of priests, including tales of nuns confined in coffins filled with human excrement. A favorite fiction narrated by the pair was the tale of Maria Monk and the nunnery of the Hotel-Dieu in Montreal, a famous anti-Catholic diatribe dating to the early nineteenth century. Nearly all of Blee's respondents (now old women) recalled owning a copy of Maria Monk's story, and most could still recount its "awful disclosures" of convent life, including the murder of innocent infants inadvertently conceived during priests' sexual rampages (Blee 1991, 90).

A major theme of the Klan's anti-Catholic campaign was that of a church under foreign leadership, an idea which would persist long after the second Klan had disappeared, showing up in the 1960 presidential campaign of John F. Kennedy. Catholics in the United States (whether they were citizens or immigrants was irrelevant) were assumed to be spies for the Vatican. Of course, this horrible fact was covered up, in part because the police forces of the major cities (the Klan confided to its horrified members) were under the control of Catholics, who themselves were under the control of the pope in Rome. Like contemporary right-wing opposition to the United Nations and to "the new world order," the second Klan's opposition to the World Court was based on the certainty that the Vatican would manipulate the World Court as a tool for "romancing" America and forcing "papist aliens" into the United States (Blee 1991, 92). Overlooking its own hierarchical structure, the Klan denounced the strict lines of authority within the Catholic Church, declaring such an organizational structure as antithetical to democracy and individual freedom. Furthermore, the Klan alleged, Catholics were not only alien but lower-class monsters devoted to destroying America having come from the lower classes and criminal elements of Europe. Impoverished and imprisoned, the price of their immigration to the United States had been their pledge to do the bidding of the pope (Blee 1991).

During this writing, the U.S. House of Representatives voted to impeach President Clinton. Republicans' indignation over Clinton's indiscretion created a climate in which sexual indiscretions by Rep. Henry Hyde (R.-Ill.), chair of the committee voting to impeach, and by Rep. Bob Livingston (R.-La.) came to light. Likewise, in the 1920s, the Klan's success in making morality a major topic of public discussion in Indiana also inadvertently turned that public's attention to the sexual practices of Klan leaders themselves, "an attention that the Klan could ill afford" (Blee 1991, 93). Evidently the right wing, victim of its own psychological self-division, never quite understands that the subject of one's indignation is often oneself. The case of D. C. Stephenson, whose downfall brought down the Indiana Klan itself, illustrates this point.

As a leader Stephenson was horrifyingly successful. He built the Indiana K.K.K. into the most powerful state Klan in the country. Through his influential Klan paper *Fiery Cross* he influenced the national Klan. Locally, he dictated Indiana state politics. "The ultimate demagogue" (Blee 1991, 94), Stephenson spoke to and intensified Indiana Protestants' xenophobia and hatred of minorities. Mindful of the Great Migration, Stephenson told his small-town listeners that a tidal wave of black labor would sweep up from the South to work for a dollar a day. Not only would they take away white jobs, these subhuman creatures would live in squalor and commit unspeakable crimes against "our" daughters and sisters and mothers. Not satisfied with daydreaming about muscular black bucks, he declared that Catholics were slaves of the pope, a maniacal dictator determined to take over the world. Not content thinking about old men in robes, Stephenson turned his attention to Jews who, he alleged, had an international banking conspiracy against the interests of Protestant American businessmen and farmers (Blee 1991). Not exactly an archangel of moral righteousness, Stephenson attracted constant allegations of sexual impropriety. Married and divorced several times, Stephenson had deserted wives and children in various states. Long before Hiram Evans recruited him as a K.K.K. kleagle for Indiana, Stephenson was well-known for many of the sins of which he would accuse others.

After leading the Klan to stunning electoral victories in Indiana in 1924, Stephenson felt all-powerful. He decided that he no longer needed to take orders from Evans, and began to ignore all Klan directives. Evans was furious and went for the jugular, telling anyone who would listen that Stephenson was a lecher and a drunkard. Local klaverns added their own fantasies to multiply these rumors. The Evansville K.K.K., Stephenson's home klavern, brought charges against Stephenson for "gross dereliction" in the attempted rape of a local "virtuous young woman" (Blee 1991, 94). They also charged Stephenson with numerous other immoralities, alleged to have occurred in Columbus (Ohio), Columbus (Indiana), and Atlanta. Secretly tried on the charges with the Klan, Stephenson was found guilty and officially thrown out. In fact, he remained. His fall would not come until the following year (Blee 1991).

That year a twenty-eight-year-old social worker, Madge Oberholtzer, was invited to Stephenson's mansion. There she was drugged and forced to accompany Stephenson on a train to Chicago. On board the train, Stephenson raped Oberholtzer. He also brutalized her, chewing and biting her tongue, breasts, back, legs, and ankles. Near Chicago she was taken off the train and installed in a hotel but received no medical treatment. She managed to escape the hotel room long enough to go to a drugstore, purchase bichloride of mercury tablets, and swallow them. When Stephenson realized that Oberholtzer had attempted to kill herself, he rushed her back to his Indianapolis mansion where he still declined to provide the dying woman any medical treatment. Finally she was released to her parents; her narration of the events resulted in Stephenson's arrest for mayhem, rape, kidnapping, and conspiracy. A few weeks later, due to the combined effects of injuries and poison, Madge Oberholtzer died. The charges against Stephenson were upgraded to second-degree murder (Blee 1991).

Stephenson was convicted, sentenced to life imprisonment, and served twenty-five years in the Indiana state penitentiary. Once the strongest in the Invisible Empire, the Indiana Klan collapsed precipitously. By 1928 only four thousand in Indiana claimed Klan membership, down from a high of almost half a million. Klansmembers loyal to Stephenson mounted petition campaigns demanding his release. Many suspected that Stephenson's lengthy sentence was simply a way to silence a man who knew too much about the Klan's major role in Indiana politics. Some in fact disputed the murder charge, arguing that his actions amounted to nothing more than "drunk and disorderly" conduct. In 1956, on the condition that he leave the state, Stephenson was pardoned. In 1961 he was again arrested in Indiana, this time for attempting to force a sixteen-year-old girl into his car. D. C. Stephenson was sent back to prison (Blee 1991).

Once the most powerful man in Indiana and among the most influential on the national Klan scene, D. C. Stephenson and his Klan movement were destroyed by the publicity that surrounded his sexual crimes. Blee suggests that "it was ironic, but perhaps inevitable" that the same tactics that built the Indiana Klan also destroyed it. Those who once listened rapt to pro-Klan pornographic tales by an "escaped nun" and a "converted priest" were just as wide-eyed over Stephenson's arrest and trial for manslaughter. Even Oberholtzer's suicide attempt echoed the alleged fate of Protestant girls forced into sexual slavery in Catholic convents (Blee 1991, 96).

VIII. The Complexities of Motive: Women's Participation in Racial Politics

> *The real issues that divided men from women and parents from children in the Midwest of the 1920s—issues of women's rights and families shattered by geographic mobility, for example—could be forgotten or ignored in the common white Protestant reaction to strange and remote sexual crimes.*
>
> —Katherine M. Blee, *Women of the Klan: Racism and Gender in the 1920s* (1991)

Hundreds of thousands of women joined the W.K.K.K. in the mid-1920s. What persuaded them that the Klansmen's agenda of racial and religious hatred should be their own? Part of the answer, Katherine Blee argues, has to do with the Klan's explicit appeal to women through the symbols of home, and family, not to mention their apparent endorsement of women's rights. But, Blee continues, this answer is incomplete. Not all white Protestant women accepted the "party line" regarding white and Protestant supremacy. Like Christian feminists thirty years earlier, Klanswomen mimed men's messages to suit their own purposes. To understand the complexities of motive, Blee (1991) examines the lives of individual members, both leaders and rank and file, before the W.K.K.K. was organized. What were these women's lives like in the 1920s and earlier? By what organizational or political routes did they find their way to the Ku Klux Klan? To answer such questions, Blee examined the life histories of more than one hundred members of the Indiana women's Klan. By such life history research she shows us the complexities of motive, the specifics of recruitment, and furthers our understanding of the gender of racial politics.

The most commonly traveled route to the Indiana W.K.K.K., Blee discovered, was the temperance movement. Many rank-and-file Klanswomen, and some of the W.K.K.K.'s most prominent spokeswomen, had worked in the Women's Christian Temperance Union, the same organization which Frances Willard headed when she clashed with Ida B. Wells in the 1890s. To illustrate, Blee focuses on one W.K.K.K. member who had been a temperance activist, Quaker minister, and clubwoman who, in the 1920s, would mobilize midwestern Klanswomen to attack Catholics, Jews, blacks, and immigrants. This Klanswoman—Daisy Douglas Barr—evidently experienced no discontinuity in moving from temperance to Klanwork. Her career as a temperance activist as well as a Republican party stalwart and active clubwoman overlapped—in ideology and in personal networks—with the Indiana Ku Klux Klan (Blee 1991).

The political careers of women like Daisy Barr become more intelligible when situated within the temperance movement of the late nineteenth century. W.C.T.U. historian Ruth Bordin (1981) suggests that temperance in the United States was "a 'safe' women's movement," one that did little to challenge existing gender or racial arrangements, as we saw in Frances Willard's acceptance of white southerners' fantasies regarding black men. The W.C.T.U. provided women an organizational means through which they could express grievances against abuse and mistreatment by drunken husbands, but the movement did not require that women challenge the constraints of women's "separate sphere." It attacked alcohol as a threat to that separate sphere—that is, the home and family—and drew heavily on women's church networks. The Klan-dominated paper *Fellowship Forum* employed this tactic, reporting that the group "believes in women's rights but isn't feminist" (quoted in Blee 1991, 104).

While hardly racial progressives, the W.C.T.U. did not share the vicious bigotry that characterized the later Klan movement. Indeed, the W.C.T.U. had a few black members and was willing to work, to some extent, with immigrants and ethnic minorities. Frances Willard did not perform her dispute with Ida B. Wells in a hateful way, although she was defensive and instrumental, always careful not to jeopardize her status with the white majority. As Bordin (1981, 9) concludes, the W.C.T.U. "could not really rise above its white Protestant middle class origins." As early the 1890s the W.C.T.U. bowed to increasingly widespread nativist sentiment and began seeing connections among Catholics, immigrants, and alcohol (Blee 1991).

In some states, antiliquor forces like the W.C.T.U. wielded a great amount of political power and enjoyed considerable electoral and legislative success. For many, especially midwestern Protestants, Prohibition was the single most important issue of the day, determining both party alignment and voting patterns. Among the groups lobbying for Prohibition in Indiana was the Anti-Saloon League (A.S.L.). This powerful national organization was built on a network of evangelist as well as mainstream Protestant churches; it claimed responsibility for the enactment of the Wright Bone Dry Law in Indiana. That measure made it a felony to have liquor in a car; judges were unable to suspend the sentences of those convicted. Despite its denials, the Indiana A.S.L. had strong ties with the Klan. Many who joined the A.S.L. soon entered the K.K.K. and the W.K.K.K. (Blee 1991).

Religious evangelism was the dominant influence for Barr and other Klanswomen of the 1920s. In the Protestant-dominated Midwest of the 1920s, the transition from religious to political zealotry was easy. Religion nearly always determined politics, and politics often determined religion. As one Indiana historian observed, "religion was the fundamental source of political conflict in the Midwest ... [forming] the issues and the rhetoric of politics" (quoted in Blee 1991, 104). As Walter White (1929) observed, Protestantism and lynching were related, as the former built up a convoluted mix of desire and resentment disguised as righteousness and love.

Closely intertwined with religion, politics provided another path to the 1920s women's Klan in Indiana. In the postwar, post-Bolshevik Revolution era of "red scares" and hysterical nativism in the United States, political leaders, civic associations, and even some women's rights groups spoke in terms that were repressively patriotic and xenophobic. This was, Blee tells us, especially the case in Indiana where women's organizations had a history of militant antiradicalism and isolationism. In early 1923, before the Klan had gathered full force, a number of state women's associations, including the Business and Professional Women and the League of Women Voters, cooperated with the Indiana Bar Association to fight radicalism in the state. There was, as one might guess, precious little of it in the state of Indiana, but local women's clubs regularly sponsored speeches about the racial dangers of unlimited immigration, including the threat to Prohibition posed by the presumably heavy-drinking foreign-born. A frequent Bible lesson at women's church and missionary meetings involved prayers to the Almighty, as well as reassurances to themselves, that "true" Americans might survive the onslaught of foreigners and blacks. Speakers spoke of threatening, mysterious outsiders—an early version of the "invasion of the body snatchers" theme—as they begged listeners to defend the "real American home," the "real American women," and "true citizenship" (quoted in Blee 1991, 113). After listening to this nonsense for years, the W.K.K.K.'s call for preservation of 100 percent Americans did not sound extraordinary (Blee 1991).

Other women entered the W.K.K.K. through nonelectoral political experience, such as racist nativist movements, women's suffrage, and even progressive politics. How? Blee supplies two answers. Recall that some of those involved in the women's suffrage movement used nativist and racist rhetoric when demanding the vote for white women. Were not white women as worthy of suffrage as black and immigrant men? Indeed, did not white men need the votes of white women to counter the corruption of Catholics, Jews, and blacks? Second, the Klan represented a kind of right-wing populism (a political ideology well known in Louisiana, for instance), expressing its right-wing political agenda in language which demanded the rights of the "common" man and woman. Due to this ideological miscegenation, the Klan appealed to women with very different political points of view (Blee 1991).

The life histories of leaders such as Daisy Barr suggest that involvement in temperance, religious evangelism, electoral politics, or even women's suffrage were all avenues into the 1920s women's Klan in Indiana. But, Blee asks, were these routes only for women who achieved prominence and leadership positions within the W.K.K.K.? To answer that question, Blee set out to investigate the life histories of anonymous rank-and-file members of the W.K.K.K.. She found a total of 118 Indiana Klanswomen with significant biographical information which, when added to data already profiled in published biographies, allowed her to analyze several common assumptions about why women joined the W.K.K.K. in Indiana.

Many Klan historians have taken for granted that women joined the Klan in the 1920s only through and due to their husbands' Klan membership. Blee's study of Klanswomen in Indiana suggests that this was not the case. Of 118 women Blee studied, 19 (16 percent) were clearly identified as single and had never married by the time of their deaths in the mid-1920s; 7 women (6 percent) were clearly identified as widowed. The marital status of the remaining 92 women is less obvious, as they were identified as "Mrs.," a term used for currently married but also widowed and even divorced women. Even under the extremely conservative assumption that every women identified as "Mrs." was married and residing with a husband who was a Klansman, only 78 percent of the women Blee studied had the possibility of joining the W.K.K.K. due to their husbands' K.K.K. membership.

Other evidence affirms that all women did not follow husbands into the Klan. For instance, one woman was described, derogatorily, by the *Post-Democrat* of Muncie as busily campaigning for the W.K.K.K. in Michigan while her hapless husband was stuck at home in Indiana doing the housekeeping. There were men who followed women into the Klan, as well as women who followed their men. An Indiana K.K.K. kleagle recorded that the "ladies' organization" was responsible for two men who joined his klavern during the past week "because their wives preached K.K.K. to them from morn' to night" (quoted in Blee 1991, 120).

The second issue Blee considers concerns the class status of W.K.K.K. members. Contrary to the popular view that Klansmembers were subproletarian "white trash," Blee concludes (cautiously, given such a small number of cases) that most Klanswomen probably were middle or working class. Data from Indiana rank-and-file Klanswomen and W.K.K.K. leaders suggest that Klanswomen, like Klansmen, were not economically or socially marginal members of society. For twenty-four of the Klanswomen Blee studied, information was available on the occupations of their husbands (who were not necessarily themselves in the Klan) in the mid-1920s. Eight of these husbands (33 percent) had business or professional positions, among them fire chief, physician, and town mayor. Two owned farms, two were in the military, three were salesmen, two had skilled occupations, six were semiskilled or unskilled workers, and one, evidently unmindful of the temperance-Klan connection, was a bootlegger (Blee 1991).

As Walter White found in regard to lynching, Blee found in regard to the W.K.K.K.: religious involvement was a major avenue for women into the Klan. "Virtually all women" whose church affiliation was recorded were described as "active churchwomen," very much involved in various church activities. There were only two Quakers in the Indiana W.K.K.K.; the most common affiliations were Methodist, Baptist, Christian, and Methodist Episcopal, a finding Blee acknowledges as consistent with extant scholarship on the religious membership of Klansmen (Blee 1991). Given the relation between institutionalized religion—Protestantism in particular—and anti-democratic, racist, homophobic, and anti-Semitic movements, it is time to rethink the privileged position churches and religious groups enjoy in American society.

Recall that church and state were hardly separated—damn the Constitution—for many Protestants. (They still are not, especially for many Protestants in the South.) The connection between religious and civic involvement was intimate; the lives of W.K.K.K. members that Blee studied point to the continuity of Klan philosophy with the political culture and attitudes of many Indiana women in the early 1920s. Blee notes that city and rural county newspapers of the time were full of notices for meetings of women to discuss immigration restrictions, Protestantism, Prohibition, patriotism, declining public morality, the "godlessness" of the public school curriculum, and the growing threat posed by immigrating radicals. The main question, for many of these "concerned citizens," was how to exercise their recently granted voting rights in patriotic,· God-fearing ways. In some sense, Blee (1991) concludes, the W.K.K.K. introduced few, if any, new political ideas. Instead, the W.K.K.K. consolidated and made exciting a reactionary political ideology that was already very much present in the earlier movements for women's suffrage, temperance, and civic improvement.

Political actions by Klanswomen did not tend to involve physical violence, but they were often pointed. W.K.K.K. chapters in Indiana bombarded public schools with protests, demanding reform of a public school system that Klanswomen charged was laced with foreign, Catholic, and even Bolshevik influences. Klanswomen demanded that Catholic encyclopedias be removed from public school libraries, campaigned against the teaching of the German language in the wake of World War I, and constantly pressured for a cabinet-level Department of Education to upgrade public education as a federal priority. The agenda here was less, say, the democratization of specialized knowledge through upgraded public schools, but the undermining of Catholic schools. Women of the Klan in many Indiana counties met with township trustees demanding compulsory Bible reading in public schools (Blee 1991).

Klanswomen in Indiana also were aggressive in their efforts to "cleanse" public schools of the corrupting influence of non-Protestants. The innocent minds of Protestant children, Klanswomen declared, were being tainted with Catholic propaganda. A number of Indiana's W.K.K.K. klaverns lobbied to have teachers, even superintendents, who were Catholic fired. The Anderson W.K.K.K., for example, doggedly fought to have two Catholic teachers fired. The School Board was hardly the only target of this effort: after being bombarded with letters from the W.K.K.K. demanding her resignation, one teacher left town. The other teacher resigned after "several other small incidents happened" (quoted in Blee 1991, 145), but she refused to move from her home. In Muncie the Klan tried but failed to have a Catholic teacher with thirty-seven years' experience fired (Blee 1991).

The political highpoint of the Indiana Klan occurred in 1924. Klan-backed candidates won the governorship, many mayoral elections, including those in Indianapolis, Evansville, and Kokomo, and numerous local offices of sheriffs, district attorneys, and so on. In the legislature, many Klan-backed candidates were elected. But success here was marred by intra-Klan battles. Many Klansmen (or Klan-backed candidates) in the state legislature fought one another as much as they fought Klan enemies. Still, several threatening bills were proposed, for instance, an "Americanization" program to ban religious officials and parochial school graduates from teaching in public schools, mandated state-selected textbooks and Bible reading in the public schools, the granting of college credit for Bible study outside schools, and mandatory release for students from school to attend Bible education classes. Fortunately, the only bill that passed was a relatively innocuous one which required all students to study the U.S. Constitution (Blee 1991).

In addition to the Klan's electoral success in Indiana, its other political tactics like the boycott were even more effective. This strategy drew upon women's traditional role as homemaker. A boycott recoded the act of shopping as a tactic in the Klan's struggle for racial and religious supremacy. Ordinary and daily tasks associated with women's familial responsibilities were now organized as political weapons. Acting individually but with a collective impact, Klanswomen could and did force Jews, Catholics, and African Americans out of business and out of their communities. Indiana Klanswomen were quite effective in using the boycott (Blee 1991).

Daisy Barr directed the W.K.K.K.'s "crusade of selective shopping" in her weekly addresses to Indianapolis Klanswomen. At each meeting, attended by as many as fifteen hundred women, Barr read the list of Indianapolis W.K.K.K. and K.K.K. members who were also local businessmen. Members were directed to shop at these businesses only. Any business or service provider not listed were assumed to be "Catholic or Jew" (or "alien") and was to be avoided. Barr was particularly aggressive about "Jew-owned" stores, complaining that "Jews had 75 percent of the money of the United States." This situation would change, however, "when the women should be as strongly organized as the men." Then, she raged, "they [Klanswomen] would have the power and then God help block [Jewish businessman] and his slacker son. There will be no Jewish business left in Indianapolis" (quoted in Blee 1991, 147). Barr's directives had immediate and powerful consequences. Businesses owned or operated by Jews, whether these were large department stores or small shops or professional services (including medical or legal), went bankrupt throughout Indiana. In droves, Jewish professionals and business owners were forced to move out of communities where they had lived for decades, sometimes for generations (Blee 1991).

Barr's list of approved businesses was disseminated through a shadowy network of Klanswomen and Klan sympathizers. Informal conversations among women, often dismissed as "gossip" by men and Klan historians, became one of the Klan's most powerful weapons. Rumor did not spread by accident; the W.K.K.K. used tightly organized bands of Klanswomen which guaranteed dissemination throughout the entire state. The economic power of this "poison squad of whispering women" was profound, as Vivian Wheatcraft (one of the organizers of the W.K.K.K. in Indiana) has pointed out. Within twenty-four hours women's poison squads could spread stories to every small town and rural corner of the state. Even when anti-Semitic, anti-Catholic, anti-black stories were proven to be false, doubts lingered. One of Blee's informants in central Indiana put it this way: "Many of the rumors possibly had a degree of truth in them so you could not deny it all but it was not the truth as it was told" (quoted in Blee 1991, 148).

This tactic of "klannishness" functioned to discriminate against workers as well as merchants and professionals. Employers sympathetic to the Klan, or those who feared Klan reprisals if they failed to cooperate, advertised for 100 percent American employees and refused to hire Catholics, Jews, African

Americans, new immigrants, or people of "poor character." For its own members, the Klan functioned as an quasi-employment service. The state headquarters sent directives to all field officers of the K.K.K. and W.K.K.K. in Indiana, listing employment opportunities for "100 percent American" women and men. Like commercial newspapers, the Klan's *Fiery Cross* carried notices of "Situation Wanted" or "Employees Wanted" separately for women and men. Not only applicants were affected: longtime loyal employees who were Catholic, Jewish, or suspected of anti-Klan leanings were suddenly fired from their jobs (Blee 1991).

The Klan in Indiana performed its power not via boycotts, but through physical violence and terrorism. Both men and women used threats and intimidation, but, as in the case of lynching, it was men who sought out the bodies of other men. Unlike the first Klan, the Indiana Klan in the 1920s used physical violence only sporadically. Even so, these men did kidnap, beat, and even lynch those who aroused them. Blee argues that the women, not the men, were more effective during the 1920s, due to the more subtle destructiveness of rumor, gossip, and other demonstrations of political strength. She notes that these political tactics have typically been overlooked in the scholarship on the Klan movement. But it was via these tactics that the second Klan wielded its power, and Klanswomen's participation was key (Blee 1991).

Commitment to the Klan or other extremist right-wing movements is often understood as aberrant behavior, radically discontinuous from mainstream American life. Participants are dismissed as fundamentally alien, different from "everyone else." Traditional histories of the Klan seem to take this tact: "When a man joins the K.K.K., a sensation seems to come over him as definite as falling in love. He simply drops out of society and enters a new world" (quoted Blee 1991, 154). As Blee points out, this was not the case in the Indiana Klan in the 1920s. Continuity, not divergence, characterized the relations between Klan and mainstream society. The Klan succeeded in recruiting approximately one-third of Indiana's eligible women and men precisely because it articulated the fears and hopes of many white Protestants. The Klan did not create racism, anti-Semitism, or anti-Catholicism out of the Indiana air, nor did these did disappear with the demise of the 1920s Klan. The truth is, as Blee (1991, 154) observes, that "the Klan nested within the institutions and assumptions of ordinary life of many in the majority population."

The culture of the Klan was key to its success in converting private hatreds into an influential political movement. Through the efforts of women, the Klan politicized daily life on behalf of white Protestant supremacy. How? First, as Blee notes, the culture of the Klan, with its rituals of exclusivity, became the core of a new Klan society, if in embryonic form. Klannish political culture provided a way of life, a social purpose, and a worldview that converted ordinary white racism and Protestant intolerance into a compelling political mission necessary for the survival of the nation. Second, Blee continues, klannish culture remained mobilized, always in a state of alert as Klan enemies continued their efforts to destroy the racist organization. Through these twin dynamics of self-affirmation (white Protestantism as superior) and mobilization (white Protestantism as imperiled), the Klan socialized new members and youngsters into the K.K.K. Through the appropriation of everyday rituals, the Klan taught its political creed across generations. The parties, weddings, and parades that comprised much of Klan life in the 1920s were, Blee underscores, hardly frivolous or apolitical. These performances of klannish culture were intensely and consciously political. And Klanswomen were central figures in the political culture of the Ku Klux Klan (Blee 1991).

How comprehensive was Klan culture? Work, play, marriage, funerals, and even children were all woven into Klan ritual and ideology. The children and teenagers' auxiliaries were patterned after the children's orders of patriotic societies; they introduced klannish values to children during their earliest years. These groups provided the Klan with a never-ending supply of new members as well as access to their parents. Not only were Klan children recruited from families of Klan members, they were also seduced by public announcements and probably peer pressure. Klanswomen and Klansmen visited Protestant churches to announce the formation of new children's chapters, emphasizing to parents the Klan's ability to help children remain loyal to parental—Protestant—values (Blee 1991).

Is it a surprise that an organization for teenage boys, the Junior Ku Klux Klan, was the first children's auxiliary? Plans for the junior order were considered at a 1923 meeting of Grand Dragons, and within a few months the adult Klan wrote a tentative constitution, a set of bylaws, and a ritual for the boys to follow. A central office was set up in Atlanta to oversee the new organization. A magazine was designed for the new order, entitled the *Junior Klansmen Weekly*, published by Milton Elrod, editor of the *Fiery Cross*. Boys in the Junior K.K.K. elected their own officers but a K.K.K. or W.K.K.K. chapter supervised every activity. Adult kleagles even prepared a boys' ritual modeled after the men's but dropped it when K.K.K. officers complained that the phraseology was so esoteric and complicated that boys would have no clue what it meant and would find it boring anyway. By 1924 fifteen states, mostly in the Midwest, had chapters of the new boys' order. Only native-born white Protestant boys between the ages of twelve and eighteen who could demonstrate "an understanding of the meaning of the Constitution" and who would pay the three-dollar membership fee were permitted to join. Like the K.K.K., the boys' order was organized along a military chain of command (Blee 1991).

Soon a separate junior order for girls (the Tri-K Klub) was organized under the direction of the W.K.K.K. The Tri-K Klub had its own set of robes, hierarchical organizational structure, and ritual modeled after the W.K.K.K. Like the women, the girls pledged themselves to the seven sacred symbols of the Invisible Empire: the fiery cross, water, mask, robe, Bible, sword, and flag. They memorized and repeated the Klan catechism of loyalty, obedience, selflessness, and Christian patriotism. The close supervision of the teen orders, as well as their integration with the adult orders, was especially appealing to Klan parents. For instance, the Junior K.K.K. and the Tri-K.K.K. Klubs of South Bend were so active, the *Fellowship Forum* reported, because "parents of the young people are happy to be able to have whole families of 100 percenters interested" (quoted in Blee 1991, 159). Former Klanswomen who had been members of the Indiana's children's orders remembered vividly the sense of excitement of being a part of Klan familial culture, where, one told Blee, "you were junior Klan members and that was big stuff" (quoted in Blee 1991, 160).

The Klan also sought to expand its ideological reach with the formation of a Klan university to educate young men and women. In 1923 the Klan donated a substantial sum to Lanier University in Atlanta, citing its full agreement with the principles of the university. Although not exclusively Klan-run, Lanier University advertised itself as an institution dedicated to the teaching of "pure Americanism" and claimed to admit only the sons and daughters of "real" Americans. Two years later, the Ku Klux Klan tried to purchase Valparaiso University in northern Indiana to become a Klan university but the marriage was never consummated. Blocked in its effort to influence young adults, the Klan looked the other direction, organizing a cradle roll to enlist youngsters from birth through age twelve in the Klan's crusade. Parents made little Klan costumes for their children, complete with hoods and masks (Blee 1991).

Klan weddings were an important feature of Klan life, cementing the "God-given" and "natural" union between a white Protestant man and his white Protestant bride. Always eager to dramatize its ideology through event, the Klan organized large-scale public Klan weddings in Indiana. These succeeded in attracting additional recruits, but they also provoked public mockery from anti-Klan forces. As the Klan reveled in the publicity accompanying a public wedding of fifty Klan couples in Muncie, for instance, the *Muncie Post-Democrat* insisted that the event proved that "marriage [is] a joke" to the Ku Klux Klan (quoted in Blee 1991, 163).

A second rite of passage important in the lives of Klansmembers was birth observances. W.K.K.K. klaverns sponsored both public and private christening ceremonies to acknowledge the births of infants to sister Klanswomen. Open-air baptisms of groups of babies and small children performed by Klan ministers were widely reported in the Indiana press, and these events too brought new recruits to the Klan. Secret Klan baptisms inducted newborns into the Christian fellowship of the K.K.K. The *Fellowship Forum* reported on a typical Klan christening in South Bend, Indiana: "Klan no. 10 recently dedicated three very small babies at a regular meeting [of the W.K.K.K.]. Each baby was presented with a Holy Bible by a Klanswoman" (quoted in Blee 1991, 164).

Perhaps the most elaborate Klan ritual was that reserved for the final rite of passage for Klansmembers. W.K.K.K. funerals featured Klanswomen in full regalia serving as pallbearers, eulogists, and bodyguards; klanswomen also led the graveside services for their departed sisters. The Klan published a guide to proper Klan funerals, with intricate instructions for the procession, the graveside hymn, the Exalted Cyclops's sermon, the kludd's readings, and the placement of Klan regalia on the casket, not to mention the procedure for formal presentation of floral offerings and sealed communications to the family. In some states Klan orders staged large-scale "lodges of sorrow" to commemorate those Klan members who had died in the year preceding (Blee 1991).

Most popular of Klan events, however, were the rallies. In Martin County, a rural south central Indiana county with five hundred W.K.K.K. and five hundred K.K.K. members, the Klan organized, in 1924, a march through the county involving more than 2,000 members. Every detail was carefully planned to ensure the march's effectiveness. As marchers reached a town, for instance, street lights were turned off to highlight burning and electrically lighted crosses. An airplane flew overhead dropping paper "bombs" that "exploded" into American flags suspended by tiny parachutes. Nor was Klan spectacle limited to parades and marches. Anticipating Nazi night rallies in the decade to follow, formations of Klanswomen created living fiery crosses by holding burning torches aloft. On other occasions, huge wooden crosses were wrapped in burlap, doused in coal oil, and set on fire, lighting up the night sky. During daylight, Klan balloonists soared overhead in huge decorated balloons. Blee's (1991) informants remembered the heyday of the Klan as a time of great fun and striking spectacle. When Blee asked one informant, a woman from northern Indiana, to recall the feeling of being present at a cross burning, she told her: "Oh, it was fun. And, the way they wrapped it in gunny sacks and soaked it in oil and then those guys lit it, and it was just a fun thing to do" (quoted in Blee 1991, 167).

While these people seem stark raving mad to us, in most small-town and rural communities of Indiana the Klan conferred considerable legitimacy, partly due to fear, but also partly because so many Indianians were involved. Local newspapers, for instance, did not hesitate to publicize the routes Klan marches would take; they willingly reprinted Klan-supplied lists of expected delegations and featured entertainment. Town mayors issued parade permits; city police and county sheriffs' departments sent officers, at public expense, to assist with those traffic and parking problems that a march or rally created. Not exactly news, still newspapers reprinted the details of impending Klan events using, without editorial revision, publicity material mailed out by the Klan itself. Did the following report in the *Kokomo Daily Tribune* qualify as "journalism"?

> Nathan Hall Klan No. 11 and Kourt No. 2 of the Women of the Ku Klux Klan, the two local Klan organizations, are preparing for a big local celebration to be held in this city October 11 afternoon and evening. The plans contemplate a huge open air meeting at Foster Park and a big parade at night. State speakers of both the men's and women's organizations will be present. The local drum corps will be in action, and out-of-town bands will probably be there. (quoted in Blee 1991, 168)

This was, simply, free publicity.

Local newspapers also sent reporters to cover Klan events, including public speeches, parades, even social events, as they would, presumably, any other event taking place in the environs. The *Kokomo Daily Tribune* announced upcoming events of the Klan not separately but along with other planned events in town, in the daily front page column, "What's Doing in Kokomo." The *North Manchester News Journal* made only one editorial comment regarding a cross burning by the local Klan: it expressed the hope that future cross-lightings would not be marred by excessive wind. Both Kokomo newspapers characterized as "eloquent" a Klan speech that denounced black population growth, demanded the end of Catholic education, and deplored Jews' control over the motion picture industry. Local city directories (which preceded phone books) listed Klan chapters under the heading "lodges and churches" or "miscellaneous societies," as if these were legitimate societies; they even provided information regarding local Klan headquarters, meeting places, and meeting times (Blee 1991).

This "apparent normalcy" (as Blee puts it) conferred upon the Klan in Indiana resulted in rather odd sights and strange alliances. A Jewish man in Muncie recalled that his father took him as a child to Klan parades, just to see the spectacle. Probably a black father did not enjoy that option. In an exercise in apparent self-contradiction, the Klan organized a unit for foreign-born Protestants. Protestantism was good but being foreign born was not. The resolution was that these "American Krusaders" (as they were called) were barred from full Klan membership. Quasi-klanners perhaps. If not something for the Protestant foreign-born, what about something for the native-born and Protestant but black? Yes, the Klan tried to organize an order of black Protestants, what the Klan called its "colored division." There were even assurances to potential black recruits that the new order would have "all the rights of membership" of the white Klan, but privately much preparation went into guaranteeing that white supremacy would be preserved as the Klan was focusing on expanding its dues-paying base. The black group could not, of course, wear the sacred white robe. Instead, these black members were to wear red robes and blue masks. As a consolation prize, these Klansmembers were permitted to wear white caps. But black members were prohibited from being seen in public with white Klansmen or handling any membership funds (Blee 1991).

There was organized resistance to the Klan in areas of Indiana, but it was sporadic and not very effective. The vastness of the Invisible Empire made a direct assault impossible, although there were notable efforts. The American Unity League in Chicago and in Marion County, Indiana, focused upon "outing" Klansmembers by publishing their names. There were local Indiana officials who passed municipal antimask ordinances or simply refused to issue parade permits to the Klan. Tales of other anti-Klan activities circulated throughout Indiana, creating moments of hope and encouragement to those enraged and victimized by the Ku Klux Klan. One such tale told of an Indiana mayor who waited until just before the Klan parade began (he had been unsuccessful in denying a permit to march), and then dispatched fire engines to false alarms in order to disrupt the event. From other communities came stories of heroic individuals who physically blocked Klan parades: one thinks of the image of the lone Chinese protestor standing quietly but defiantly before a tank in Tiananmen Square. There were of course violent confrontations between Klansmembers and organized anti-Klan groups, and those opposed to the K.K.K. told over and over again tales of temporary triumph, when white robed men fled back into the night (Blee 1991).

But the horrible fact is that in the Indiana of the 1920s it was, in general, respectable to be a member of the Ku Klux Klan. What a Brown County Klanswoman told Katherine Blee was true not only for many Indianians, but for many European Americans: "it was considered the thing to do to join the Klan in the 1920s" (quoted in Blee 1991, 171–172). Why? As Blee points out, Klanswomen and Klansmen did not differ significantly from other white Protestant Indianians in background, values, ideologies, and even politics. Far from the popular media image today of strange and disfigured creatures with obvious defects of character and temperament and intellect, the Klanswomen and Klansmen of the 1920s were more often, possibly more chillingly, mainstream. They were ordinary looking women and men who evidently loved their families, often acted kindly and sympathetically to other people like themselves, and even held progressive views on selected issues such as women's rights (Blee 1991).

In acknowledging that Indiana Klanswomen and Klansmen were "mainstream" does not, of course, imply that they were not racist, anti-Semitic, anti-Catholic, xenophobic, violent, hateful creatures. In a ploy Klansman David Duke would perfect seventy years later, public speakers for the Klan often denied that the Klan was "anti-anything or anti-anybody," coding their hatred and bigotry in calls for "a stronger America" or a more muscular Christianity. Yet claims that the Klan was little more than a Protestant advocacy group were and are ridiculous. Behind the closed doors of meeting halls and at Klan rallies, the true point of the Klan was unmistakable and embraced by its adherents. In Whitley County the crowd applauded wildly as a Klan speaker wished out loud: "I want to put all the Catholics, Jews, and Negroes on a raft in the middle of the ocean and then sink the raft" (quoted in Blee 1991, 172).

There was no mystery whatsoever regarding the Klan's agenda throughout white Protestant Indiana. When D. C. Stephenson told Fort Wayne Klanswomen to "whisper" the proper message into the ears of their political leaders, "everybody" (as Klansmembers universalized themselves) knew what message to whisper. State Klan officials counseled members that "you can't make it too strong against the Jew and the Catholic in a closed meeting—give them hell" (quoted in Blee 1991, 172). Advocates obliged, warning anyone who would listen that Jews, Catholics, and blacks were secretly organizing to murder white Protestant children ... and their parents. Jews as "Christ-killers" was tempered language for Klansmen who spoken openly of Jews amassing vast fortunes through the sexualized exploitation of Christian labor. Blacks were inherently stupid, the K.K.K. insisted, forever socially inferior, and, at best, should be returned Africa. The racist film *Birth of a Nation*—still in the memories of millions who viewed it in the Teens—was widely shown at Klan rallies. Klan speakers horrified audiences when they announced in pained, indignant voices that the Catholics controlled New York City, New York State, Chicago, and other major cities; that most criminals were Catholics; and that 50 percent of the teachers in public schools were practicing Catholics, busily seducing innocent naive Protestant youth into the degenerate ways of Rome (Blee 1991).

Obviously the truth meant nothing to these demagogues. Nothing was "off limits" if it meant that the enemies of the Klan were routed. And, Klansmen reminded themselves, deeds not words were required in times of peril and crisis. In several cities in Indiana, Klan organizers and officers were arrested for burning school buildings, fires they set but which they blamed on foreigners, Jews, or blacks. The arrest of a Klansman, especially a Klan leader, was a rare event in Indiana, a state where law enforcement officers often owed their positions to the Klan or to Klan politicians. But if arrested, conviction was even rarer. Just as black men had no chance before southern white juries, white men took no risk facing juries comprised of Klan sympathizers, or of non-Klansmen who were terrified of angering the Klan. Even when the evidence was incontrovertible, Klansmembers were rarely convicted (Blee 1991).

White Protestantism in the 1920s meant racism, intolerance, and xenophobia, certainly in Indiana but in many other states as well. While northern states had no laws mandating racial segregation, cities and towns practiced strict racial segregation of social life, schooling, and housing. Newspapers ran separate columns or pages for news for and about local blacks, reserving the newspaper as a whole for what was considered "normal," indeed universal: the white experience. While less sharply segregated, Catholics and Protestants did not tend to mix, nor did Christians and Jews. In such a highly segregated, "imaginary" social fantasmatic, "the Klan movement of the 1920s was eerily unremarkable for many white native-born Protestants" (Blee 1991, 173).

Once vast and powerful, the second Klan collapsed almost overnight. By 1928 membership had fallen dramatically to several hundred thousand. By 1930 fewer than fifty thousand women and men claimed to be subjects of the Invisible Empire. Vicious, bitter battles between contending leadership factions, continuing disclosures of widespread corruption, as well as public exposure of Klan atrocities, undermined the Klan. Finally, public authorities began to intervene in the Klan's manipulation of everyday life (Blee 1991).

Although African Americans continued to move north in great numbers, the vast foreign immigration of 1890–1920 was over, reduced to a trickle by World War I. The number of foreign-born residents in the United States also declined dramatically as new immigration laws took effect. Slowly the nationalist fervor associated with World War I diminished, until the threat of a second world war whipped American emotion back into a frenzy. The economic depression of the 1930s brought an end to a decade of Republican rule, and a relatively left-wing president undertook the economic and social revitalization of the nation. Of course, racism, anti-Semitism, and anti-Catholicism hardly disappeared with the election of Franklin D. Roosevelt, but by the early 1930s most white Protestants no longer perceived the Klan as the appropriate medium for expressing their religious intolerance and racial hatred. From its zenith in the mid-1920s, by the early 1930s the Klan had fallen into public disgrace and political inconsequentiality (Blee 1991).

Between 1930 and the end of Word War II, the Ku Klux Klan was small and southern. In this fragment of the 1920s Klan, women played no significant role. Like the first Klan, white men dominated, and white men continued their terrorism against the bodies of other men, men in organized labor, men who worked in New Deal programs, men who worked as Communistic party organizers, and, of course, always, black men. Like the first Klan, these men imagined white women's and white children's sexual vulnerability to rationalize its virulent anti-Bolshevik, anti-Semitic, and antiblack violence (Blee 1991).

The third major Ku Klux Klan emerged in the 1950s, fueled by federal intervention in the racially desegregating South. Now Klansmen (not women) bombed schools and homes, rioted, lynched blacks and murdered those (mostly northern) whites who supported racial integration. This third Klan found support among some white southerners, but not enough to successfully stop the black civil rights movement. Worse, from the Klan's point of view, local anti-Klan activity increased, and slowly changing racial attitudes among many whites eventually resulted in a backlash. Federal investigations and arrests, together with state and local ordinances against its parades or charters and general public opposition forced the K.K.K. into the background in the 1970s (Blee 1991).

The Klan Today

The fourth and current Klan movement Blee (1991) dates to the early 1980s. It is largely based in the South, but with some presence in the Far West and Midwest. The primary obsession remains black men, with Jews, Mexican Americans, gay men and lesbians, Communists, and Southeast Asian immigrants also targeted and victimized. Although relatively small compared to the 1920s Klan (Blee estimates approximately ten thousand members), the current Klan appears stronger through its alliances with other extralegal terrorist and paramilitary groups. Some Klansmembers have joined with self-proclaimed Nazis and right-wing survivalists and tax evaders in a secret national network known as the Aryan Nations. Violently antiblack and anti-Semitic, the Aryan Nations has created a terrorist organization, The Order, whose members are linked through a computer bulletin board, which promises to assassinate anyone who interferes with its goal of world supremacy (Blee 1991).

Women have joined the current Klan and Aryan Nations (though perhaps not The Order), but in general women play mostly supporting roles in the fourth Klan. Certainly there is no separate women's organization with its own reading of Klan dogma. Women's rights are anathema to the current Klan, which regards conventional gender roles as the only correct ones for God-fearing Christians. Also like others on the right, such as the so-called Christian Coalition, the current Klan opposed affirmative action programs on the grounds that these undermine the rights of white men (Blee 1991).

What happened to those 1920s Klanswomen after the collapse of the second Klan? Blee speculates that the majority of Klanswomen, like their male counterparts, withdrew from politics after the collapse of the Klan. Among those few who remained politically active, some continued in right-wing nationalistic and patriotic politics; others worked for women's equality. Some, Blee reports, even worked for economic justice. As Blee's research makes clear, the racial politics of gender intersected with the gender of racial politics in the 1920s, making the second Klan more difficult to categorize than the first Klan, indeed more difficult to characterize than most contemporary right-wing movements. The W.K.K.K.'s promotion of women's rights resembled nativist strands of earlier women's suffrage and temperance campaigns, excluding nonwhite and non-Protestant women from their struggles for full citizenship and the reconstruction of the social order. But unlike these earlier movements, the W.K.K.K. used its agenda of women's rights in a vicious and brutal campaign against African Americans, Catholics, Jews, immigrants, and political radicals (Blee 1991).

In the early twentieth century the currents of the American political and social life flowed rapidly. They did not slow after World War I into the congealed alliances of social class and party that would emerge after World War

II. Under the chaotic conditions of the 1920s political movements incorporated what seem to us today contradictory ideologies and political agendas. Currents within the temperance movement endorsed female suffrage, but many social reformers worked to discipline "unruly" immigrants, and some strands of the women's rights movement split off, obsessed with nativism and racism. In this turbulent political stream, it was possible for the W.K.K.K. to float on currents that were neither purely reactionary nor fully progressive. Indeed, the W.K.K.K. was, as Blee puts it, "a reactionary, hate-based movement with progressive moments" (1991, 177).

The impact of the W.K.K.K. on early twentieth-century society and politics was enormous. The women's order brought the men's agenda of bigotry and hatred into the heart of white Protestant communities, into schools, homes, leisure activities, and key rituals such as births, weddings, and funerals. While the men focused on political corruption and vigilante violence, the women's "poison" (Blee 1991, 178) spilled throughout the fabric of everyday life, including social networks of family and friendship, as well as the everyday and usually women's work of shopping and child care. The participation of women (and children) in the second Klan extended the order's influence in another and highly significant way. Klanswomen, Klan teens, and Klan babies contributed to the "normalization" of the Ku Klux Klan. Important as well as innocuous family events became Klan occasions, underscoring the disingenuous claim that the Klan was just another way for "good folks" to get together and enjoy themselves. The perfunctory manner in which former Klanswomen discussed their involvement with Katherine M. Blee makes clear the Klan's success in integrating itself into ordinary white Protestant life. The racist, nativist venom of Klan politics flowed easily, unremarkably, through the veins of these ordinary European Americans (Blee 1991).

The history of the W.K.K.K. requires us, Blee argues, to complicate our models of political ideology. The widely shared expectation that women in right-wing reactionary movements are inevitably antifeminist blinds us to the complexity of relations among gender, race, economics, and nationalism. As Blee points out, these phenomena are not unrelated, but neither are they consistently or logically related. Support for gender equality, in the 1920s at least, did not guarantee other progressive political views. But a number of political movements of the late twentieth century have also exhibited similar contradictory combinations of gender politics with the politics of race, religion, and class. Blee reminds us, for instance, that women were very much engaged in the black civil rights, anti-Vietnam War, and new left movements of the 1950s to the 1970s. But when women asserted common interests as women they were often met with ridicule and defensive hostility from male leaders and participants. In the feminist movement of the 1970s and 1980s, in contrast, the commonality of women's experiences were primary in setting the political agenda. Yet any expectation that women's heightened awareness of their common gender interests would lead them to progressive views on race and social class was disappointed. True, a commitment to women's rights and gender equality led many, maybe most, feminists to a radical examination of national inequities of class and race, but commitment to gender equality also took the liberal form of speeding women's access to the ranks of the economic and political elite. As well, feminist political rhetoric stressing independence, autonomy, and self-direction left many working-class, poor, and minority women dismissing the women's rights movement as a white, middle-class phenomenon (Blee 1991).

Today there are many women, although disinclined to identify themselves with organized feminist politics, who strongly support gender equality and women's rights in the home, workplace, and the public sphere generally. A minority, however, especially right-wing women who identify themselves ideologically as homemakers, mothers, and wives rather than as wage-earners, frames their common interests as women in opposition to feminist causes like abortion and the Equal Rights Amendment. Blee speculates that the feminist movement's failure to find a way to honor women's individuality without implicitly denigrating traditional roles in the family and at home may have pushed some women to the political right during the late 1970s and early 1980s. "Just as the second Klan used images of white masculine supremacy and womanhood to charge a political effort to restore lost privileges," Blee writes, "so, too, the new right wields a rhetoric of morality and nuclear families to create a momentum of support for the existing social order against threats to change it, by feminists or by political progressives" (1991, 179).

But, Blee points out, the apparently consistent ideology of antifeminism and conservative economic and racial politics on the right is apparent only. In fact, the right, especially right-wing women, live out some of the same contradictions faced by their predecessors in the W.K.K.K. The "new right" demands that traditional home and family life be women's primary sphere and obligation, yet it promulgates this nineteenth-century agenda with aggressive spokeswomen like Phyllis Schlafly whose life has hardly been confined to the home. Indeed, her public employment and political engagement, and maternal loyalty to a gay son all contradict and complicate a simplistic agenda of reaction and intolerance. Also like the 1920s Klan, the contemporary new-right movement has framed its political agenda around issues of "morality." As in the 1920s, this political exploitation of morality was at first quite successful, allowing the Republican Party and its right-wing splinter groups to enlist thousands of women and men to confront school boards, politicians, feminist activists, and the courts. The scandals that later erupted among the leaders of these morality crusades—particularly around religious fundamentalist preachers such as Jimmy Swaggart and political leaders such as U.S. Representatives Newt Gingrich and Bob Livingston—have undermined the new right's integrity and effectiveness (Blee 1991).

Both the 1920s Ku Klux Klan and the contemporary new-right movement and antifeminist movements demonstrate that the racial politics of sexuality and gender as well as the gender of racial politics are very complex, often convoluted. Morality, sexuality, and women's roles are powerful symbols for reactionary political movements determined to turn back the clock, often a clock that never told time in the first place, an imaginary, nostalgic impulse expressed as hatred and longing. But if gender and sex are potent tools for political mobilizing, they are internally inconsistent, and perhaps unconscious impulses make mockery of expectations and political agendas that become impossible to sustain over time. The second Klan collapsed almost overnight, done in by its own contradictions of political moralism. When the W.K.K.K. disappeared, the convoluted ideological merger of women's rights with racism and nativism also nearly disappeared from the American political landscape (Blee 1991).

For progressives, the short life of the 1920s K.K.K. and W.K.K.K. allows one to hope that mass movements based on extreme racist, religious, and nativist views are necessarily fragile, perhaps even inherently self-destructing. But it also provides yet another warning regarding the appeal of reactionary politics based on imaginary fears that are mixed with or are in fact disguised desires. Those white Protestant women who joined one of the most vicious political campaigns in U.S. history shared men's fantasies of white supremacy. But it is necessary to note, as Blee underscores, that the Klan's appeal to women of the 1920s also lay outside its reactionary nativism, anti-Semitism, and racism. In its ambivalent support for women's rights it offered collective friendship and sociability among like-minded women that became an effective political power (Blee 1991).

Perhaps white women who participated in the second Klan "adopted" white men's racism in order to keep them at bay, to affirm and make horizontal the bonds of gendered relations, then worked within that "safety" of solidarity to further their position as women. In this sense (and to a limited extent), women in the second Klan "mimed" the rhetoric of the men's Klan. Of course, they did more than that, as they closed down Jewish businesses through their gossip networks and provided psychological support for their violent husbands, sons, and brothers. They did more than "adopt"—they believed. But they didn't lynch. They didn't sexualize their hatreds as white men did. They didn't obsess over black women's genitalia, as white men did over black men's. There seems to be no repressed overwhelming homoerotic at work in white women's racial politics, at least not to the extent and the ways that it is obvious in white men's. In prisons some white women will choose black lovers, but those associations appear to be more voluntary than forced, in sharp contrast to the nature of the interracial relations among imprisoned men, as we will see in chapters 16 and 17.

For some white women, "race" was evidently more crucial than "gender," although the two were always mixed. But for many white women, as Blee's perceptive analysis makes clear, racial politics was more about them and their children than it was about African Americans, Jews, Catholics, and immigrants. It was perhaps a relocation of their unconscious hatred of their husbands onto imaginary others. In this sense their complaints about foreign-born American citizens were also complaints about their own subjugation within male-dominated marriages and families. Perhaps their children were the subtext of the rhetoric of an "endangered" white race which symbolized the destruction of their own "innocent" selves in the patriarchy of Protestant marriage and family. One can never know; one can never forgive. My point is that Blee's analysis suggests that for many Klanswomen in Indiana in the 1920s, racial politics functioned to further, as had conservative Christianity for many nineteenth-century women, their own cause—and that of their children—within a powerful and racialized patriarchy. But for men, racial politics was more narrowly about power, precisely in the sense that rape can be said to be about power.

FOUR

Men and Racial Politics

10 THE N.A.A.C.P. *and the* STRUGGLE *for* ANTILYNCHING LEGISLATION, 1897–1917

I. Du Bois, Washington, and the Niagara Movement

The most persistent, systematic, and organized attack upon lynching has been waged by the National Association for the Advancement of Colored People.

—Walter White, *Rope and Faggot: A Biography of Judge Lynch* (1929)

This movement [the N.A.A.C.P.], which has lasted longer than almost any other movement of its kind in our country, has fallen far short of the expectation of its founders.

—Ida B. Wells, *Crusade for Justice: The Autobiograhy of Ida B. Wells* (1970)

The conceptual structure of Du Bois's genealogy of race and nation has, at its center, the dilemma of the formation of black manhood.

—Hazel Carby, *Race Men* (1998)

In 1897, W. E. B. Du Bois (1868–1963) first expressed the revolutionary idea that the black experience in America was not only different from that of the white, but that it was inevitably and beautifully different. Du Bois suggested that every people was blessed by God with a distinct genius. Throughout their history each people struggled, often in confusion and at times even in opposition to themselves, to realize their unique essence. Different peoples achieved self-realization to greater or lesser extents at different moments in human history. African Americans, so recently freed, were, Du Bois suggested, at a child's stage, only then awakening to self-understanding and realization. There had been pain and suffering, but in time "the true nature of black soul" would be more and more revealed (Williamson 1984).

Even in 1897, Du Bois declared, while still a "child," it was clear that African Americans were an especially spiritual people, living in the midst of increasingly materialistic European Americans. Blacks were also an artistic people, especially sensitive to music, to colors, and to language. In time, by virtue of their own striving, the genius of black people would become unmistakable, and they would then find themselves in close harmony with God, and, presumably, with nature. The path of progress, therefore, the way to harmony and perfection, lay in the pursuit of blackness not whiteness, in black people seeking communion with black people, not with white. Self-realization would not be achieved one person at a time, but altogether, as a community, or not at all. Consequently, a certain black exclusiveness, a certain voluntary separation from whites, a certain confederation in all-black endeavors: these were key to black self-realization (Williamson 1984).

While Du Bois's racial politics differed fundamentally from Booker T. Washington's (1856–1915), the difference was not at first obvious. The two men agreed that black people must come together as a collective. Washington's agenda emphasized race pride, solidarity and self-help. Du Bois was hardly opposed to these. Du Bois shared Washington's commitment to the economic improvement of African Americans. Du Bois regarded industrial education as legitimate, and he applauded the growth of black businesses not dependent on white patronage, but growing thanks to the support of black patrons. Du Bois agreed with Washington that black people must organize themselves if they were to pursue their interests in a hostile white America. Finally, both wanted full political and civil rights for African Americans, although they quickly disagreed as to how these could be achieved. Early on, Du Bois could accept gradualism. During the last years of the nineteenth century, he, along with nearly every other influential black leader in the South, applauded Washington's program and leadership. Washington recognized Du Bois's talents and acknowledged his support. On three occasions he offered the young Atlanta University professor appointments at Tuskegee Institute. On each occasion Du Bois declined the offer, reluctantly (Williamson 1984).

There is a gendered subtext to Du Bois's understanding of racial politics in America, a subtext Hazel Carby makes explicit: "Du Bois described and challenged the hegemony of the national and racial formations in the United States at the dawn of a new century, but he did so in ways that both assumed and privileged a discourse of black masculinity." That is, the "problem" of being black was, for Du Bois, "an issue of both commonality and exceptionalism; it was not just about learning that he was black but also about learning how to *become* a black man" (Carby 1998, 31). Because he conflated "race" with black masculinity, Du Bois failed to incorporate black women into the sphere of intellectual equality and racial leadership. His failure "is not merely the result of the sexism of Du Bois's historical moment," Carby continues, but it is specific to him, resulting from his "complete failure to imagine black women as intellectuals and race leaders" (1998, quoted passages on 10).

The break between Washington and Du Bois had nothing to do with gender politics. It was a function, Joel Williamson (1984) suggests, of the shift in the racial and political environment in which they lived and worked. In effect, those white people with whom Washington had negotiated a racial pact in 1895 were, by 1900, rapidly losing power to white people who had very different ideas about the proper state and structure of race relations. In the black belts of the South, whites who had accepted accommodation were being replaced in positions of authority by whites whose racial attitudes rejected any accommodation. These whites were intent on bloody aggression. Whereas conservative whites could tolerate blacks as long as they accepted their subordinate position, the "radical racists" could accept black people only in a position of "supersubordination" (Williamson 1984, 75).

As "radical racists" gained political control, they moved to turn back the clock in American race relations. Washington steadfastly maintained an overt posture of accommodation; perhaps he was psychologically incapable of changing. He would try for what he wanted, but he would take what he could get. Even as his political posture became less appropriate to the changing circumstances, his power with the black community increased. By 1902 his control over black politics in the South was nearly complete. While he used his power to hold white racists at bay, he did so secretly, indirectly, and with only occasional success. Joel Williamson paints the picture vividly: "Under Washington and with accommodation, black resistance began from a kneeling position to face an on-rushing, powerful, and fanatical foe bent upon nothing less than rendering black people prostrate" (1984, 75). The sexualized subtext here is, I trust, clear.

Du Bois was the first black leader to criticize Washington's leadership. According to Du Bois (1901), an increasingly significant group of black intellectuals declined Booker T. Washington's leadership and vision, arguing against a narrow vocationalism and for "self-development and self-realization in all lines of human endeavor which they believe will eventually place the Negro beside other races" (quoted in Kellogg 1967, 5). Du Bois extended his critique in *The Souls of Black Folk*, published in April 1903. The book stimulated considerable controversy. In her autobiography Ida B. Wells recalls a discussion of the book at the home of Mrs. Celia Parker Wooley, a Unitarian minister active in racial causes:

> Mrs. Wooley had a gathering of the literati at her home near the university to discuss it. Again there were only six colored persons present whom she knew. And we were given the privilege of opening the discussion. Most of it centered around that chapter [chapter 3 is entitled "Of Mr. Booker T. Washington and Others"] which arraigns Mr. Booker T. Washington's methods.
>
> Most of those present, including four of the six colored persons, united in condemning Mr. Du Bois's views. The Barnetts [recall that Wells had married Ferdinand Barnett and sometimes used his name] stood almost alone in approving them and proceeded to show why. We saw, as perhaps never before, that Mr. Washington's views on industrial education had become an obsession with the white people of this country. We thought it was up to us to show them the sophistry of the reasoning that any one system of education could fit the needs of an entire race; that to sneer at and discourage higher education would mean to rob the race of

> leaders which it so badly needed; and that all the industrial education in the world could not take the place of manhood. We had a warm session but came way feeling that we had given them an entirely new view of the situation. (Wells 1970, 280–281)

We do not know exactly what was said that night, but from Wells's remembrance the discussion seems to have circulated around education.

Hazel Carby (1998) points to another issue at work in *The Souls of Black Folk* and in Du Bois's critique of Washington specifically. In his conflation of "race" with manhood, Du Bois characterized Washington's racial politics as not only inappropriate but in some way "unmanly." Du Bois accused Washington of being a sycophant, of selling out to commercialism. These positions were blameworthy in practical terms, but they were also, Du Bois argued, evidence of a stunted or deformed manhood: his policies were "bound to sap the manhood of any race" (Du Bois 1903, 88; quoted in Carby 1998, 40). "Because Du Bois makes his narrative of the transition from male adolescence and immaturity to full manhood and maturity so entirely dependent upon being an intellectual," Carby (1998, 38) observes, "Washington's standing as an intellectual and as a race leader is challenged at the same time as his masculinity is undermined."

In 1905 Du Bois organized the so-called Niagara Falls Conference, a meeting which included twenty-nine black leaders, only five of whom were from the South. There, "radical racists" had rendered black people powerless. In the South, any black assertion was met by "galloping violence, rope and faggot, and expatriation." Given this state of affairs, it was clear that any explicit and public struggle for racial equality would have to be made from the North. The Niagara Conference was frank in facing this situation; it asked African Americans to acknowledge the desperation of black people in the South and to meet the white enemy fully "erect and armed." Conferees resolved that black people should protest aggressively against political, civil, and economic inequality, an implicit attack upon Washington's philosophy of accommodationism. In language Washington had to take personally, the conferees denied that "the Negro-American assents to inferiority," or "is submissive under oppression and apologetic before insult." Moreover, for ourselves, "we do not hesitate to complain and to complain loudly and insistently" (quoted in Williamson 1984, 75).

The Niagara Movement convened each year. At its peak, approximately four hundred activists belonged. It sufficiently unnerved Booker T. Washington that he resorted to spying upon the group, denying funds to some of its members, and undermining the movement through the words and actions of his agents. Du Bois and his fellow militants were enraged. Between 1907 and 1910 they sponsored a newspaper in the District of Columbia that attacked "King Booker" and his pretense of absolute authority, charging him with accepting Jim Crow and remaining "dumb as an oyster as to peonage," believing, evidently, "that colored people can better afford to be lynched than the white people can afford to lynch them" (quoted in Williamson 1984, 76). In 1909 the members of the Niagara Movement would come together with northern white racial liberals to form a permanent organization, the National Association for the Advancement of Colored People. Booker T. Washington would try to undermine the new organization, but this alliance of black and white leaders would prove both effective and long-lasting (Williamson 1984).

II. The Committee on the Negro

The black man is not a saint, neither can he be reduced to an algebraic formula.

—Anna Julia Cooper quoted in Charles Lemert and Esmé Bhan, *The Voice of Anna Julia Cooper* (1998)

[T]he [race] problem is becoming a question of mental attitudes toward the Negro rather than of his actual condition.

—James Weldon Johnson, *Along This Way* (1933)

The black male body, hypersexualized and criminalized, has always functioned as a crucial and heavily overdetermined metaphor in an evolving national discourse on the nature of a multiethnic, multiracial American society.

—Sandra Gunning, *Race, Rape, and Lynching: The Red Record of American Literature, 1890–1912* (1996)

During the first decade of the twentieth century most white racial progressives were just becoming aware of the rift between Washington and Du Bois; most whites accepted Washington's more visible, and for many more commonsensical, program of vocational education as the medium for social and economic improvement for African Americans. Among those who took seriously Booker T. Washington and his work, but were becoming increasingly interested in Du Bois's point of view, was the Garrison family of Boston. For generations the Garrisons had been racial progressives. They objected to the reactionary racial politics dominant in the North at this time; they were shocked at and discouraged by what they perceived as the retreat from New England "enlightenment." The daughter of the abolitionist William Lloyd Garrison, Fanny Garrison Villard was stunned by the "wave of passion and hatred toward the race to whom opportunity has been denied." There were, it seemed to her, no white friends of black folk as there had been during the antislavery struggle. Her brother, the second William Lloyd Garrison, was more cynical and less shocked; he felt sure that there had never been a white majority in support of African Americans in the North, except for a brief period at the moment of Emancipation in 1863. From the struggle for abolition to the present day, Garrison saw no basic shift of feeling in the North regarding African Americans. Like the South, the North intended to keep blacks at the lowest social and economic levels, even if the northern agenda was expressed "more by subtle action, and less by war cries" (quoted in Kellogg 1967, 5).

The third generation of the Garrison family continued to fight for the civil rights of African Americans. Grandson of the famous abolitionist, son of Fanny

Garrison Villard, and nephew of William Lloyd Garrison, Jr., Oswald Garrison Villard took great pride in his abolitionist ancestry. His first opportunity to speak in public on behalf of civil rights for African Americans came in 1903, although he had remarked, in an earlier address to a conference on education held at the governor's mansion in Richmond, that changed conditions made it possible for him "to speak where [his] grandfather would so cheerfully and happily been hanged" (quoted in Kellogg 1967, 5).

Villard was also opposed to the prevailing policy and mood of American imperialism. When the United States declared war in 1898 he had been "utterly miserable mentally" (Kellogg 1967, 5); he had protested the injustice of what he termed the iniquitous war with Spain. He was appreciative that the *New York Evening Post*, which was eventually to come under his management, had not been swept away by the majority mood. He looked forward to the day when he would take over the paper and make it a worthy successor to his grandfather's *The Liberator*. The *Evening Post* was one of the few newspapers that reported the news concerning African Americans, and sympathetically. In 1926 Mary White Ovington was to write: "Long before there was a N.A.A.C.P., there was a Garrison in New York setting forth in his larger *Liberator* the wrongs of the Negro Race" (quoted in Kellogg 1967, 6). Ovington was a social worker who would become associated with Villard during the early years of the N.A.A.C.P. She knew from experience how seldom African Americans were reported fairly in the white press. Even the muckraking *McClure's Magazine* had declined to print an article of hers in which African Americans had been depicted honestly and favorably (Kellogg 1967).

Despite the important role Ovington would play in the N.A.A.C.P., Ida B. Wells was not enthusiastic about her. Wells's main criticism of Ovington appeared to be that she never moved outside the circle of middle-class black men in which she found herself. Wells (1970, 327–328) complained:

> It is impossible for her [Ovington] to visualize the situation in its entirety and to have the executive ability to seize any of the given situations which have occurred in a truly big way. She has basked in the sunlight of the adoration of the few college-bred Negroes who have surrounded her, but has made little effort to know the soul of the black woman; and to that extent she has fallen far short of helping a race which has suffered as no white woman has ever been called upon to suffer or to understand.

Another Bostonian would also become important during the early phases of the N.A.A.C.P. Moorfield Storey's views on race had been influenced by his early association with the abolitionist Charles Sumner. He was convinced that racial progress was possible only if the solid South could be broken up and the Fifteenth Amendment federally enforced. Certainly he disagreed that "the race problem" should be left to southerners to solve; he insisted that the civil rights of the African Americans had to be protected by concerned whites from other parts of the country. Like Oswald Garrison Villard, Storey was opposed to American imperialism; he served as president of the Anti-Imperialist League. When Du Bois congratulated Storey on his persuasive pamphlet concerning United States policy in the Philippines and on the atrocities committed there by

American soldiers, he learned that Storey was familiar with and appreciative of his own work. In fact, Storey was eager to meet Du Bois so they might discuss their shared concerns over imperialism and racial politics (Kellogg 1967).

Just as the first decade of the twentieth century was ending, these three men—Oswald Garrison Villard, Moorfield Storey, and W. E. B. Du Bois—would join together to form an organization dedicated not only to the abolition of what some called the "new slavery," but to the securing for African Americans of first-class citizenship. The series of events that was to bring them together was started by two days of bloody racial rioting, not in the Deep South, but in Abraham Lincoln's Springfield, Illinois. It was on the fourteenth of August 1908 that rioting broke out in Springfield; white mobs raged throughout the black district, burning black homes and then interfering with the efforts of firemen. It took two days before 4,200 militiamen brought the rioting whites under control; by that time two blacks had been lynched, six had been killed, and over fifty wounded. More than 2,000 African Americans fled the city, and hundreds took shelter in the camps of the militia (Kellogg 1967). Ida B. Wells (1970, 299) recalls that she had "such a feeling of impotency through the whole matter."

Lynchings and race riots in the city where Lincoln had lived and was buried outraged Oswald Garrison Villard. In the *New York Evening Post*, of which he was now president, Villard condemned Springfield whites, calling the riot the climax of a wave of white crime and mobbism that had set back racial progress by decades. The *Post* was not alone in its reaction; the liberal periodical the *Independent* was also shocked that such antiblack violence could occur in the North. "Springfield," the editor pointed out, "will have to carry a heavier burden of shame than does Atlanta, for Illinois was never a slave state." Horrified at the possibility that race riots might occur in other cities, the *Independent* urged its black readers, if attacked, first to seek protection from the police and other officials. If that failed, African Americans should defend themselves however they could, making sure rioting whites "would be sorry that they came and be slow to come again." Booker T. Washington too issued a statement that was sharply critical of lynching, although it did not mention the Springfield riot. A black periodical often critical of Washington, the *Horizon*, praised his statement as the clearest and strongest and most courageous he had ever spoken. In the main, then, northern newspapers had responded satisfactorily, Villard judged, but he remained very much concerned over what he called "the southern attitude in the press" (quoted passages in Kellogg 1967, 9–10).

Neither Villard's outrage over white mobs nor Washington's indictment of lynching contained any concrete program to combat intensifying white racism. That was provided by William English Walling in his article "The Race War in the North" (1908), which appeared the following month in the *Independent*. A wealthy southerner from a former slave-owning Kentucky family, Walling was a writer, settlement house worker, and a "renegade socialist" (Westbrook 1991, 190). Once a factory inspector in Illinois, Walling had decided to devote his life to the labor movement. In 1903, he had joined Jane Addams, Lillian Wald, and others in founding the National Women's Trade Union League (Kellogg 1967).

Even before John Dewey himself fully appreciated this point, Walling linked pragmatism to a socialism that, as Dewey would understand later, was not state socialism. In the second volume of his major study of socialist thought and politics, *The Larger Aspects of Socialism* (1913), Walling argued that "pragmatism is socialism, if taken in what seems to me to be its most able and consistent interpretation, that of Professor John Dewey" (quoted in Westbrook 1991, 190). Walling appreciated the significance of Dewey's educational theory for libertarian socialists like himself, as the "new education," he knew, was intended as schooling for participation in a democratic society. By the eve of World War I, Dewey came to accept that the democratic reconstruction of American society he imagined could not take place by virtue of a revolution in the classroom alone—that, in fact, there would be no revolution in the classroom until the students' parents took up the cause of radical democracy (Westbrook 1991).

Walling was married to Anna Strunsky, a Jew who, in her youth, had been imprisoned in her native Russia for revolutionary activities. The Wallings traveled from New York to Springfield to investigate the riots. There they became convinced that America's treatment of African Americans was even worse than Russia's treatment of Russian Jews. In his article, Walling blamed the local press for inflaming white opinion against African Americans. As would any perceptive observer of the media today, Walling showed how newspapers linked crime with the race. Today imprisonment is proffered as the solution; in 1908 the Springfield press suggested to its readers that the South knew how to deal effectively with such "racial problems." Walling argued that the white public refused to acknowledge that war had been declared on black citizens, and that this war was modeled in all respects on the war against blacks conducted in the South. The small black population in Springfield could mount no real challenge to white supremacy; Walling criticized the belief among many white northerners that there were "mitigating circumstances," perhaps not for mob violence but at least for antiblack prejudice. Equally shocking to Walling was Springfield's lack of shame. In general, white people approved what the mobs had done; they were not timid in saying they hoped all blacks would leave. Prevailing opinion in Springfield, Walling wrote, was expressed by the *Illinois State Journal*, which called the riot inevitable and ascribed responsibility for the event not to white hatred but to blacks' "misconduct, general inferiority, or unfitness for free institutions" (quoted in Kellogg 1967, 10).

After the riot, Walling reported, whites had organized a political and business boycott designed to drive out of Springfield those African Americans who had not already fled, a boycott which the local white press had declined to criticize. Walling regarded this action as an even more serious attack upon black citizens than the riot. If this kind of attack, conceived and performed not in moments of passion but in rational deliberation, were permitted, whites would take over black property, jobs, and businesses, thereby rewarding, not punishing, the white rioters. Racists and those who used "race" to their own political advantage would not only dominate Springfield, he warned, but other northern towns and cities as well. Political democracy would disappear, Walling wrote, and American civilization with it. He concluded: "Who realizes the seriousness of the situation? What large and powerful body of citizens is ready to come to [the Negro's] aid?" (quoted in Kellogg 1967, 11).

One of the readers of Walling's article in the *Independent* was Mary White Ovington. A Unitarian, a socialist, the descendant of an abolitionist, and a social worker of independent means, Ovington's life was already dedicated to the socially and racially marginalized. She had spent nearly four years gathering material for a study of black New Yorkers; at the time Walling's article appeared she was living in a black tenement. Walling's questions spoke to her directly; they so moved her that she composed a reply as soon as she had finished reading (Kellogg 1967).

When Walling had asked "what large and powerful body" could fight for civil rights, he had in mind an answer. He had already imagined a national biracial organization of "fair-minded whites and intelligent blacks" (quoted in Kellogg 1967, 11) that would fight for the civil rights of African Americans. Upon returning from Springfield he confided his idea to his close friend, Charles Edward Russell, and then to other sympathetic members of the Liberal Club in New York. There was much enthusiasm at that time in the Liberal Club and in other left-wing organizations regarding the cause of the African American, but there was little concrete or firsthand knowledge upon which to construct a course of action. Several weeks later, Mary White Ovington attended a lecture on Russia given by Walling at Cooper Union. In the course of that talk Walling expressed his view that the race situation in America was worse than what Jews suffered in Russia. After the lecture, Ovington spoke to him, proposing that they undertake at once to form an organization like the one he had in mind. But it was not until she wrote him after reading his article that Walling agreed to organize a meeting at his New York apartment for the first week of the year 1909 (Kellogg 1967).

The meeting was to have included Walling's friend Charles Russell, a writer and fellow socialist, whose father had been an abolitionist editor of a small newspaper in Iowa, but Russell was unable to be attend. In his place was Dr. Henry Moskowitz, a social worker among new immigrants to New York; Ovington, Moskowitz, and Walling shared a commitment to civil rights but came from widely varied backgrounds. Ovington would later reminisce that "one was a descendent of an old-time abolitionist, the second a Jew, and the third a southerner." All were white. At this informal gathering in Walling's apartment in January 1909, two "next steps" were agreed upon. First, the group chose Lincoln's birthday to mark the opening of a campaign to secure the support of a large and powerful body of citizens, and second, those present agreed that Oswald Garrison Villard should be invited to become the fifth member of the group. Thirty years later Villard would write that "no greater compliment has ever been paid to me" (quoted in Kellogg 1967, 12).

Soon after that first meeting, the group was further expanded and made biracial at Ovington's initiative. Two prominent black clergymen, Bishop Alexander Walters of the African Methodist Episcopal Zion Church and Rev. William Henry Brooks, minister of St. Mark's Methodist Episcopal Church of New York, were invited to join the five. Walling then invited Lillian Wald (whom we met in chapter 6, section III) and Florence Kelley, one of the first women graduates of Cornell University. On the staff at Hull House in Chicago,

Kelley had become a close friend of Jane Addams and Julia Lathrop. Instrumental in securing the passage of a factory inspection law in Illinois, Kelley had afterward been appointed chief inspector in 1893. It was probably during this time that she met Walling. After becoming general secretary of the National Consumers' League, Kelley took up residence at Lillian Wald's Nurses' Settlement on Henry Street in New York (Kellogg 1967).

Villard joined the group in sending out a call for a conference on the race problem. He had already come to the conclusion that the organization should be focused on the advancement—political and civic more than economic (this prioritizing would set the agenda of the organization for decades to come)—of African Americans. In reply to a letter from Booker T. Washington, suggesting that there should be a test case against peonage in Alabama, Villard wrote: "This is precisely the kind of case for which I want my endowed 'Committee for the Advancement of the Negro Race.' With such a body we could 'instantly handle any similar discrimination against the negro, and carry the case, if necessary, to the higher court. Sooner or later we must get that committee going" (quoted in Kellogg 1967, 13). Years later, Villard recalled that from the start his vision of the new organization was that "it should be aggressive, a watchdog of Negro liberties, and should allow no wrong to take place without a protest and a bringing to bear of all the pressure that it could muster" (quoted in Kellogg 1967, 14).

Villard's vision was reflected in the "Call" (for a conference) which was issued by the group on Lincoln's Birthday, and which Villard sometimes referred to as the "manifesto." Signed by sixty prominent African and European Americans, the call acknowledged the disfranchisement of black citizens. The signatories declared that the Supreme Court had sidestepped several opportunities to pass judgment squarely upon this disfranchisement; that taxation without representation was the fate of millions of African Americans; that the Supreme Court in the Berea College case had upheld the right of a state to criminalize any assembly of whites and blacks together for any purpose; that Jim Crow was being practiced in public transportation and elsewhere; that many states were failing to fulfill their basic responsibilities in educating black children; and, finally, that the wave of white mobs attacking African Americans across the country could not be tolerated. The call closed with an appeal to all who believed in democracy to stop their silence, which amounted to complicity; to end the indifference of the North, which had also played a significant role in racially undermining the principles of democracy; to end racial discrimination; and to join in a national conference to discuss present problems, to voice protests, and to the renew the historical struggle for full civil and political rights for all Americans (Kellogg 1967).

In spite of his considerable efforts to publicize the "manifesto," Villard failed to interest the New York press. At first, this indifference discouraged him, but not for long. Even the black press, for instance, the *New York Age*, paid little attention. A brief item had appeared in the February 18 issue, reporting that a call had been issued for a conference "for discussion of the present state of the Negro" (quoted in Kellogg 1967, 15). During this time, the founders of what was eventually to become known as the National Association for the

Advancement of Colored People continued to meet at Walling's apartment, due to its central location. The number who attended varied. One afternoon in March, five were present. On other occasions there were as many as eight. Rabbi Stephen S. Wise of the Free Synagogue and Miss Leonore O'Reilly, a teacher in the Manhattan Trade School for Girls, joined the original group during these early meetings (Kellogg 1967).

Slowly the group expanded. Walling's apartment became too small to accommodate those who wanted to attend, and the group moved to the Liberal Club at 103 East 19th Street. It was here where the first meeting for which minutes are extant was held. The exact date was not recorded, but Kellogg (1967) suggests it took place in mid-March. Fifteen attended and it was recorded as "the first meeting of all the members of the Committee on the Negro" (quoted in Kellogg 1967, 16). At this meeting plans were formulated for the conference, which had been scheduled for May 31 and June 1 at the Charity Organization Hall in New York (Kellogg 1967).

It took three meetings to plan the conference. At one meeting Walling was chair, at another, Charles Russell. Mary White Ovington served as recording secretary and Walling as treasurer. Walling was also to direct the conference with the title of secretary. The members discussed who should lead the organization; they were unclear what its name should be, an issue they would debate for some time. At first, they called themselves the "Committee on the Negro," then the "Committee on the Status of the Negro." Villard made constant references to the "advancement" of the race, and this term would eventually find its way in the name. Over one thousand invitations to attend "A Conference on the Status of the Negro" were mailed, and about 150 persons agreed to sponsor the meeting. One such sponsor was Moorfield Storey of Boston. As noted, a constitutional lawyer, anti-imperialist, and onetime secretary to Senator Charles Sumner of Massachusetts, Storey would be unable to attend the conference, but he was to play a significant role in the early history of the organization (Kellogg 1967).

To link this new abolition movement with the earlier one, Villard asked his uncle, William Lloyd Garrison, Jr., to preside at the conference. Garrison was too ill to attend (he would die a short time later) but he composed a letter to conference registrants, urging them to confront the intensifying racism head-on. The danger today, he suggested, was that (white) social reformers had lost interest in problems of African Americans. Reformers committed to the solution of social problems, while claiming to be friends of black people, had acquiesced in black disenfranchisement; they had also accepted separate schools. Villard was very moved by this "last bugle blast" of his uncle, an echo of the elder Garrison (Kellogg 1967, 17).

Perhaps it was Villard's own movement toward a more aggressive racial politics that precipitated a rift between him and Booker T. Washington. Perhaps there was a more "political" reason as well. Villard's growing involvement in this more "radical" group made him realize that Washington could have little influence with those men and women likely to attend the conference. Although Villard never broke with Washington completely, he came to see that Washington would come to be "simply disregarded as a man who is lost for the righting of any of the spiritual, or civil, or legal wrongs of his people" (quoted in Kellogg 1967, 18). Despite this perception, Villard was determined that the divisiveness of the two factions among African Americans engaged in racial politics—one headed by Booker T. Washington, the other by Du Bois—would not undermine the conference nor the formation of a permanent organization (Kellogg 1967).

It was during these deliberations that he wrote a candid but cordial letter to Washington, inviting him to the conference, but tactfully hinting that Washington might decline. The conference would not bear the Washington or the Du Bois stamp, he explained. The conference would initiate a movement, formalized by the establishment of an organization, aggressive enough to fight for the civil rights of African Americans. Due to Washington's prominence and influence, Villard was keenly aware of the delicacy of his position. Washington would be invited to attend the conference, but his absence must not be misinterpreted. In declining the invitation, Washington displayed an insight into the situation that apparently he would decide to ignore later: "I fear that my presence might restrict freedom of discussion and might, also, tend to make the conference go in directions which it would not like to go." Four days before the conference opened, Villard's uncle volunteered that he suspected that Washington's influence was diminishing. He expressed relief that he would not attend. "It seems strange to have a Negro conference without B.T.W.," he wrote to his nephew, "but I fear he would be much too politic in his utterance" (quoted in Kellogg 1967, 19).

III. *"[E]qual justice ... man as man."*

—quoted in C. F. Kellogg, *NAACP: A History of the National Association for the Advancement of Colored People* (1967)

I saw them [African Americans] hedged for centuries by prejudice, intolerance, and brutality; hobbled by their own ignorance, poverty, and helplessness; yet, notwithstanding, still brave and unvanquished. ... The situation in which they were might have seemed hopeless, but they themselves were not without hope.

—James Weldon Johnson, *Along This Way* (1933)

On Monday and Tuesday, May 31 and June 1, 1909, in New York's Charity Organization Hall, the National Negro Conference was held. The evening mass meetings were held at Cooper Union, attended by some 300 African and European American men and women. William Hayes Ward, editor of the *Independent*, delivered the keynote address. "The purpose of this conference," said Ward, "is to re-emphasize in word, and so far as possible, in act, the principle that equal justice should be done to man as man, and particularly to the Negro, without regard to race, color or previous condition of servitude." After abolition and the legal and nominal granting of suffrage and equal rights, he reminded his listeners, northern interest in the plight of African Americans had waned. The fervor of the original abolitionist generation had central legal bureau with the ablest counsel possible to prosecute those white men "who kill and call it law" (quoted in Kellogg 1967, 21). A political and civil rights bureau should lobby for the enforcement of the Fourteenth and Fifteenth Amendments and to obtain court decisions reversing disfranchisement and other discriminatory legislation (Kellogg 1967).

Villard also envisaged an education department in the new organization which would advise black educational institutions, assisting them in raising standards, in coordinating fund-raising campaigns, and in devising more efficient uses of funds; if resources permitted, the department would make grants. There would also be an industrial bureau to work on labor problems, including the problem of white racism within the labor movement, the problem of housing and land ownership, and the mass migration of southern blacks to the North, which was well under way in 1909. If necessary, Villard continued, the new organization should be empowered to purchase land in large quantities for resale at reasonable prices to interested black buyers. Finally, Villard argued that the association's leadership must find ways to identify and educate exceptional young black people and to place them where they could be of the greatest possible service to the black community. He added that two extant political groups formed to fight for civil rights, the Niagara Movement and the Constitution League, had indicated that they were willing to cooperate with or incorporate within the proposed new organization (Kellogg 1967).

The final sessions of the two-day conference were "stormy" (Kellogg 1967, 21) and lasted until midnight, but next steps were finally taken. By the time the conference adjourned, a Committee of Forty on Permanent Organization had been formed, the incorporation of a National Committee for the Advancement of the Negro Race had been ordered, and a series of resolutions were passed which demanded equal civil and educational rights, the right to work, and protection from violence, murder, and intimidation. As well, a resolution passed criticizing President Taft for his failure to enforce the Fifteenth Amendment. Those who drew up the list of members of the Committee of Forty on Permanent Organization were concerned that without Booker T. Washington's name the organization would have difficulty obtaining grants from white philanthropists. Moreover, Washington's followers would not participate in the new organization unless Washington publicly gave it his seal of approval. But Washington would not be involved: "The whole colored crowd was bitterly anti-Washington," wrote Villard to his uncle (quoted in Kellogg 1967, 22).

The nominating committee took a middle course which left many unhappy. The compromise they reached meant not only Washington and supporters were omitted, but also were his critics, among them William Monroe Trotter, like Du Bois a graduate of Harvard and now editor of the *Boston Guardian* as well as president of the National Independent Political League. Also omitted, unbelievably, was Ida B. Wells (now Wells-Barnett). Neither was pleased at being left out. J. Milton Waldron, president of the National Negro Political League of Washington, D.C., was another prominent African American unhappy at not being appointed. Not content to allow events to take their course, Ida B. Wells complained to Charles Russell after the meeting. Illegally been followed by a "cooling sympathy" (quoted in Kellogg 1967, 19 while the white elite in the South kept presumably "freedpeople" in rationalizing this inhumanity on the widely accepted argument that bl essentially inferior, not fully human, half beast, incapable of becoming The theme of the conference, then, involved the refutation of such namely that African Americans were physically and mentally inferior 1967).

Leading scientists of the day spoke at the conference, amo anthropologist Livingston Farrand of Columbia University and neurol zoologist Burt G. Wilder of Cornell University, both of whom detailed scientific evidence disproving the white fantasy that bla inherently inferior due to differences in brain structure. They cite showing conclusively that while there were significant differences bet brains of humans and apes, there were no significant differences in the black and white people. They characterized "race" as an indeterminat used loosely as an umbrella term to designate physical differences i Another Columbia professor, Edwin R. A. Seligman, applied his theory of history to the development of the Negro, showing that conditions and policies had undermined black advancement, n inherited inferiority. John Dewey declared that with democrat conditions each individual, regardless of color, would be able to r potential. Celia Parker Wooley of the Frederick Douglass Center in linked racial politics with other social problems of the day, such as rights, specifically suffrage, and the right of working people to (Kellogg 1967).

No doubt with Washington in mind, W. E. B. Du Bois insisted problem of "race" in America was as political as it was economic. Elimi African-American voters also eliminated African Americans as w industry. There would be no solution of the race problem unti Americans in the South could cast a free and intelligent vote. Disfrancl restricted access to education (vocational education only), the loss freedoms generally: these were all parts of a systematic effort to instit white racism, to kill black self-respect, and to force black people int slavery." Other speakers proposed solutions to these problems: chan attitudes, work for federal legislation to stop lynching, lobby for red representation of southern states where Negroes were disfranchised, sta aid to education, and, finally, establish a new organization to worl realization of these aims (Kellogg 1967).

On this last point all were agreed. Then Villard communicated h he wanted an association national in scope, incorporated, and devoted large amounts of money. He believed that African Americans would su organization's program as soon as they were persuaded that its founc sincere, free of factional conflict, efficient, and committed to all education for African Americans. One of its chief functions, Villard s should be a campaign of education to inform the public about the achi of African Americans. A publicity bureau with a press section head competent journalist should investigate lynchings and other racial outr distribute its findings widely. In addition, the organization needed but wisely (according to Mary White Ovington), her name was quickly added to the committee (Kellogg 1967).

A black weekly controlled by Booker T. Washington, the *New York Age,* was predictably critical of the conference. Whites who had attended were characterized as "able, distinguished, earnest friends of the Negro," but the *Age* had little regard for those African Americans who had been present. Other protest groups populated by the same people had failed in the past, and the *Age* predicted failure for this latest attempt. In Chicago, the Equal Opportunity League had been torn apart by an inability to cooperate. The Niagara Movement, which, according to the *Age*, looked very much like an earlier version of the recent New York conference, had fallen victim to inadequate leadership. The Constitution League and Trotter's National Political League were both fading fast. African Americans must solve their problems by work and thrift, reminded the *Age*, and by solidarity: "as doers, not as talkers" (quoted in Kellogg 1967, 23).

Though acidic in tone, the *New York Age* was right about the other organizations dedicated to advance the cause of African Americans. The Equal Opportunity League and the National Political League enjoyed very limited influence and seemed destined to extinction. The Constitution League had been founded and was almost wholly supported and financed by John Milholland, a wealthy New Yorker, an anti-imperialist, a former newspaper man, now active in the Republican Party. The Niagara Movement was an early effort to stop disenfranchisement and the general assault on the political and civil rights for African Americans. Organized in 1905 by Du Bois, it was comprised of those blacks whom he considered the "talented tenth," those with sufficient ability and education to assume leadership. Through "publicized agitation" Du Bois and his colleagues tried to arouse the black population to protest and to enlist the support of sympathetic whites. The platform called for restoration of "manhood suffrage" and condemned the loss of civil rights, the denial of equal opportunities in the economic sphere, the Jim Crow railroad car, the discriminatory treatment of black soldiers, and "recent attitudes of the church." A major theme was that "manly agitation was the way to liberty" (quoted in Kellogg 1967, 23–24).

The *New York Age* pointed out that the two black periodicals, the *Moon* and the *Horizon*, both edited and published by Du Bois, had also failed to make a go of it. From 1907 to 1910 Du Bois, together with F. H. M Murray, and L. M. Hershaw, published the *Horizon*, a small periodical which served as the publication for the Niagara Movement. The Niagara Movement had failed to gain momentum, and by 1909 the *Horizon*, as well as the Niagara Movement appeared to be on the verge of collapse. What confidence, therefore, could black readers of the *New York Age* have in the prospects of this latest effort, asked an unsympathetic *Age* (Kellogg 1967).

The *Age*'s pessimism aside, the conference had kindled excitement and optimism, both of which were reflected in an article Du Bois wrote for the *Survey.* He wrote that the conference was the consequence of a long-term deliberation over increasingly serious racial problems. Some participants had worried that the group would prove too radical, that it would provoke a conservative reaction, not to mention intraracial competitiveness and bitterness.

But Du Bois judged that the white leaders had inspired confidence and provided a sense of stability to the group, an interesting acknowledgment in light of his later interest in removing whites from N.A.A.C.P. leadership (Kellogg 1967). At the heart of the race problem was, Du Bois suggested, this (gendered) question: "From the standpoint of modern science, are Negroes men?" (quoted in Kellogg 1967, 24). As Hazel Carby's (1998) analysis makes clear, Du Bois conflated manhood and "race." The racial question was, for him, a question of the male gender.

To Du Bois the last session of the conference had been highly significant, as the "black mass moved forward ... to take charge." There was throughout the room a strong commitment to present the problem to the public "without compromise and quibbling." There was at the same time considerable uncertainty as to what practical steps were appropriate and possible. And finally there was profound black suspicion regarding "the white hands stretched out in brotherhood" (quoted in Kellogg 1967, 24). Despite this suspicion, Du Bois observed that most African Americans in attendance did have confidence in the grandson of William Lloyd Garrison; they voted to endorse his vision of a national organization devoted to the advancement of black people. Writing in the *Horizon* five months later, Du Bois judged the conference to be the most important event of 1909 (Kellogg 1967).

In the same *Horizon* article, Du Bois identified an important problem, the splitting off of the problems of African Americans from other social problems, and their consequent neglect. The problems African Americans faced were not and could not be segregated from other social problems and reform movements—that is, women's rights, consumer leagues, prison reform, social settlements, world peace. Many white social reformers were uniformly ignorant of the problems blacks faced; many refused to even acknowledge their existence. Most African Americans also regarded their own problems as radically distinct from other social problems, subject to their own specific remedies. The New York Conference on the Negro represented, Du Bois suggested, an "awakening" from this fallacious reasoning. The social workers who organized the conference realized that all social problems in America involved African Americans, and those African Americans who had attended the conference became aware that their problems were also problems of property, ignorance, suffrage, women's rights, distribution of wealth, law and order. A concerted effort to solve these problems demanded close cooperation in parallel spheres. It was not, Du Bois wrote, simply a matter of "millionaires and almsgiving." It was, he said, a "human problem" demanding "human methods" (quoted in Kellogg 1967, 25).

The segregation of the "race question" from the other social problems and social reform movements of the time was a post–Civil War phenomenon. In antebellum days the movement for the emancipation of women had been, as we have seen, closely linked with other reform activities, including the temperance (as we saw in chapter 8) and abolition of slavery movements. For many there were parallels between the status of women and the status of African Americans. Women too were held to be inferior to men in most respects, and the so-called scientific arguments used to defend that point bore a striking resemblance to those used to suggest the inferiority of Negroes. Both blacks and women had a place in society, a subordinate place. By keeping women and Negroes in their "place"—a place in the white male imagination—white men were sure they were acting in the best interests of these "inferior" groups (Kellogg 1967).

The abolition and temperance movements had served as training grounds for leaders of the feminist movement in the twentieth century. Feminists had been supported by such abolitionists as William Lloyd Garrison and Wendell Phillips. The Civil War and the passage of the Fourteenth and Fifteenth Amendments (which pertained only to males) ended the alliance between the feminist movement and the black civil rights movement. By 1903, the two movements had drifted so far apart that only a few progressives, black and white, thought to link the two causes. Villard associated the two, as had his father and grandfather before him. His mother, Fanny Garrison Villard, was active both in the suffrage movement and in the struggle for black civil rights (Kellogg 1967).

Along with his plans for the Committee for the Advancement of the Negro, Villard had for some time envisioned a men's club to support the cause of woman suffrage. Perhaps, he thought, it should be a "paper organization for use on special occasions." By the end of 1909, as we saw in chapter 6 (section V), his "Men's League for Woman Suffrage" had been launched, and in 1911 he was one of eighty-four men who had been booed and hissed as they marched in a suffragist parade down Fifth Avenue. Intimidated not at all, Villard regarded the incident as a "thrilling and inspiring experience" (quoted in Kellogg 1967, 26).

Most white suffragists were indifferent, even hostile, to the cause of black people in America. A single event will illustrate. In 1916, a bitter dispute occurred at the funeral of Mrs. Inez Milholland Boissevain, daughter of John E. Milholland, attorney, suffragist leader, and champion of black civil rights. On this occasion suffragists snubbed black women delegates and even tried to prevent them from speaking at the service. In spite of Du Bois's prophecy that the 1909 Conference on the Negro would signal a turning point in American race relations, any realization that "race" was not a separate question but interrelated with other social problems and social reform movements was still decades off. Even now, a relative few discern the link between feminism and racial politics. This is in sharp contrast to the founding moment of the N.A.A.C.P., when women played a conspicuous role. Approximately one-third of the signers of the "Call" were women, including two prominent black feminists, Mrs. Mary Church Terrell and Ida B. Wells-Barnett. Both women were appointed to the Committee of Forty that was established after the 1909 Conference (Kellogg 1967). That Committee would face opposition on several fronts.

IV. Oppositions

Can the subject ... ever evade the dominant discourse?

—Roger Célestin, *From Cannibals to Radicals: Figures and Limits of Exoticism* (1996)

Nothing tempers the fact of black-on-black violence.

—Charles Johnson and John McCluskey, Jr., *Black Men Speaking* (1997)

Among those who neither responded to the "Call" nor participated in the first conference was Charles Waddell Chesnutt, one of the best-known black intellectuals of the day. He declined the invitation to speak at the Cooper Union mass meeting, but privately gave approval to the principles which were elaborated there. He made no public statement nor endorsed nor disapproved the resolutions passed at the conference, including the proposal to form a permanent organization. Although he disagreed with much of Booker T. Washington's view of racial politics, Chesnutt remained on good terms with him. Chesnutt did take exception to Washington's subordination of civil and political rights to economic gradualism, and to his failure to endorse higher education for the mass of African Americans. But he made it clear to the radicals, specifically Monroe Trotter and Du Bois, that he did not share their hostility to Washington. He had stated this view to Trotter as early as 1901, declining to be drawn into the acrimonious personal quarrels in which Trotter (James Weldon Johnson would later characterize Trotter as "zealous to the point of fanaticism" [1933, 314]) had engaged in the *Guardian* (Kellogg 1967).

Villard realized that Washington probably could not support the new movement, but he hoped he could prevent Washington's open opposition. Two days after the close of the conference, Villard wrote Washington, thanking him for his "friendly spirit" and sending copies of his own address, the resolutions, and the names of those appointed to the Committee of Forty. He was hopeful, even confident, Washington would not oppose the new organization. But Washington was not mollified. A week later Villard learned from his uncle Francis Garrison that Washington had criticized the conference in a public address, arguing that the vote was less important than earning and accumulating wealth. Garrison wrote his nephew that he worried that Washington might "chill and prevent the interest of a good many people who ought to be with us" (quoted in Kellogg 1967, 28).

William E. Walling had no interest, evidently, in trying to appease Washington. Walling attacked Washington's views in the *Independent* one week later. Washington's policies in the North, he argued, only functioned to postpone the day when African Americans would experience that political and social equality consistently denied them by southern whites. The battle was on. T. Thomas Fortune, editor of the *New York Age*, answered for Washington. Fortune said Walling was merely a southerner expressing the usual southern prejudices. Walling had confused social privileges with civil rights, a mistake that would only mislead African Americans, a time-honored practice among southern whites "with whom the madness is method designed." Fortune further discredited Walling by observing that he was a socialist, "whatever that may be" (quoted in Kellogg 1967, 28). These exchanges marked phase one of a long period of antagonism between Washington, his allies, and the new movement (Kellogg 1967).

Washington could not slow the growing momentum for the new organization. On May 5, 1910, the Preliminary Committee's report recommended that the new organization be called "The National Association for the Advancement of Colored People; its object to be equal rights and opportunities for all" (quoted in Kellogg 1967, 41). The last word "all" was taken quite seriously; from the very beginning, the Association aligned itself with other oppressed minority groups. For instance, in the so-called Russian Resolution of the 1910 conference N.A.A.C.P. members protested and condemned the expulsion of Jews from Kiev (Kellogg 1967).

Around this time the new organization persuaded Du Bois to leave Atlanta University to become director of publicity and research. He would become as well the editor the N.A.A.C.P.'s monthly magazine, the *Crisis.* Ida B. Wells (1970, 327) recalls the meeting at which the periodical was born:

> At the meeting of the executive committee the discussion came up as to whether we should try to have articles representing our cause appear in periodicals already established, since to attempt a publication would be expensive, to say the least. Miss Addams was very much in favor of the opinion that the former was the better plan. When asked for my views I said that by all means I favored establishing our own organ, for then we could publish whatever we chose whenever we wished; whereas if we sent articles to other magazines we should have to depend upon their good will to say nothing of the disposition to change our views to suit their own ideas. This view prevailed, and the *Crisis* was born almost immediately.

Recall that the first conference had concerned itself with the scientific refutation of racist beliefs and stereotypes. The theme of the second was disfranchisement. Delegates advocated the use of the black vote only for those candidates who would champion the cause; no longer would there be blind devotion to one party, the Republicans. Delegates also endorsed: (1) making aggressive efforts to reduce southern representation in Congress in retaliation for violations of the Fourteenth and Fifteenth Amendments, (2) systematic study of the consequences of disfranchisement on segregated schooling in the South, and (3) study of the relationship between disfranchisement and lynching (Kellogg 1967).

The N.A.A.C.P. had been founded in response to the Springfield, Illinois, riots of 1908. The crusade against mob violence, specifically lynching, continued to be a primary motive behind the Association's work. The *Crisis* published the lynching toll annually, although accurate statistics were difficult to obtain, as recent research indicates (Tolnay and Beck 1995). Even the conservative Booker T. Washington would work quietly against lynching until his death in 1915. He was more outspoken on this subject than on any other aspect of American racial politics (Kellogg 1967).

As we have seen, lynching and white mob violence continued in the North, witness the August 1911 lynching of Zachariah Walker in Coatesville, Pennsylvania. Northern lynchings were even less tolerable than those that occurred in the South, and as we have seen, the N.A.A.C.P. Executive Committee at once began a prolonged and costly investigation of the lynching, including the use, for the first time, of professional detectives in the hope of providing evidence for a conviction. A conviction was never achieved in the lynching of Zachariah Walker, but the Association kept a close watch over the investigation and legal proceedings. Recall that on the first anniversary of the Coatesville lynching, John Jay Chapman, grandson of an abolitionist, and himself a civil rights advocate, held a prayer meeting of three in a vacant store in Coatesville. When Francis Garrison learned that no resident of Coatesville had attended the prayer meeting, he exclaimed that "the earth should yawn and swallow the whole community" (quoted in Kellogg 1967, 213).

Conditions that contributed to heightened racial tensions were also on the N.A.A.C.P. agenda. On June 11, 1917, for instance, the director of publications and research, W. E. B. Du Bois, reported to the Board that he planned to go to East St. Louis, Illinois, to study conditions in a city typical of those to which many southern blacks were migrating in large numbers. Not quite a month later, a riot occurred in that "typical" city, during which hundreds of African Americans were shot or burned alive in their homes. Much property was destroyed, and nearly 6,000 were left homeless. Politicians and the white press blamed blacks for the outbreak; a number of black residents were even charged with inciting to riot and with murder (Kellogg 1967).

Booker T. Washington had long urged southern blacks to remain in the country and on the farm. True, white southern businessmen were hurt by the mass migration. But they were hardly the only southerners to suffer; black professionals and black business, such as insurance companies, were also hurt. Nothing, however, not even the advice of the influential Booker T. Washington, could stop the flood, which peaked in 1916. The *Crisis* took issue with Washington and other black leaders who were urging Negroes to remain in the South. Du Bois and others urged southern blacks to flee their homes as a protest against lynching and disfranchisement in a "devilish country" (quoted in Kellogg 1967, 222).

To provide the N.A.A.C.P. with reliable information regarding the migration, Du Bois visited six southern states. Additionally, he obtained additional information through N.A.A.C.P. associates throughout the South. To the surprise of the N.A.A.C.P. Board, the data showed the migration to be much larger than they had imagined. Du Bois estimated that 250,000 black southerners had moved North, and prophesied, correctly, that the United States would undergo a significant social change as a result. Du Bois was right, but much of this change was not positive, at least not initially. Those who moved north found no "promised land" but yet another site of white resistance and racism. Many industries would hire Africans Americans only when they could not find other labor. Frequently white employers used newly arrived blacks as strikebreakers, which earned them the enmity of white workers who saw in the new arrivals scabs as well as competitors for jobs. Finally, the number of jobs available did not begin to equal the number of migrants flooding the cities. Unemployed African Americans began to concentrate in impoverished areas neglected by municipal governments; these areas soon became slums. All these developments functioned to intensify white racism and create "powderkeg" situations in the overcrowded and often impoverished northern black ghettoes (Kellogg 1967).

The violence that erupted in East St. Louis on July 2, 1917, did not come as a complete surprise to N.A.A.C.P. officials. Southern in its racial attitudes, the city was heavily industrialized, serving as a major railroad junction as well as the home of stockyards and meatpacking plants. Most workers lived in slums near the factories. During 1916, the owners had waged war against unionization, using black labor to undermine efforts to unionize workers. Public opinion became inflamed by tales of black crime and by specific allegations made by the local Democratic machine that the Republicans had imported southern blacks to vote in the 1916 election (Kellogg 1967).

After learning of the riot, Ida B. Wells called a meeting of her Negro Fellowship League to protest against this "outrage." Reporters for the Chicago newspapers were present and published "our speeches of condemnation and our resolutions" (Wells 1970, 383). At the meeting "it was moved that a representative from the meeting be sent to deliver the resolutions to Governor Lowden in person, and I was asked to be that person. I told them that I had no objection to going, but it seemed to me that someone ought to go to East Saint Louis and get the facts, and that then we would have something to present to the governor" (Wells 1970, 384). The next day Wells left for East Saint Louis.

As her train arrived in the city on the morning of July 5, Wells was warned by the conductor that she would be in "great danger" should she get off the train. In fact, he continued, train personnel had been locking the porters in the coaches as the train ran through East Saint Louis, for their protection, given how riotous whites had been. The conductor begged her to travel on to Saint Louis, just across the river. "But," Wells told the worried conductor, "the papers say that Governor Lowden made a patriotic speech in East Saint Louis yesterday, and that there are eleven companies of militia there, and that all the workers who had been driven out by the mob two days ago have been invited to return and have been assured of their safety" (Wells 1970, 384). Wells got off the train. In her autobiography she remembers that:

> It was seven o'clock in the morning, and as I walked up to the front of the train where the train conductor was standing ready to signal the engineer, I seemed to be the only person getting off. The conductor gave a second look at me and yelled, "Get back on that train!" I said, "Why should I? This is the station where I wanted to get off." "Have you been reading the paper?" I said, "Oh, yes. They tell me that the governor and the militia are here, and I want to see him." The conductor shrugged his shoulders, turned and waved to the engineer and hopped on the train. It pulled out and left me standing there. (Wells 1970, 384)

Undaunted, as usual, Wells "walked over to a khaki-clad youth who was standing there with a gun and asked him what the situation was." He replied, "'Bad'—a Negro had killed two white men the night before. I didn't believe him and I suppose my look showed as much. So I asked him if the governor was in town and he said, 'No, he left last night'" (Wells 1970, 384–385). Still undaunted, and even though "I saw not another colored person, I sauntered up the main street as if everything was all right." Upon reaching city hall where the militia was encamped, she discovered that Adjutant General Frank S. Dickson was not present. Determined to speak with him about the situation, "I talked with him on the phone and went over to see him" (Wells 1970, 385).

Over the telephone Dickson was "courteous," and assured Wells that he would do all he could to help her "to find out conditions first-hand." Unlike the train personnel, he felt certain that the danger was over and those who were responsible for "the slaughter" would be apprehended and punished. Wells returned to city hall to wait for General Dickson to arrive. She had left her bag there with the only African American "I had seen up to that time." Employed as a janitor at the City Hall building, the man told Wells that his wife was coming with breakfast and she might share it with them. She had refused to sleep in East Saint Louis since the riot, but traveled here each morning "to see that he was safe and to do what she could for him" (all passages in Wells 1970, 385). When Wells returned to the city hall she saw "numbers of colored women all making for the same point. Each of them was accompanied by a soldier carrying a gun and many rounds of ammunition. These women had on the clothes in which they were when they had run out of their homes two days before, and they had come back on the assurances of the morning papers that it would be safe for them to return to see what, if anything, was left of their belongings" (Wells 1970, 385–386). Wells (1970) continues: "We went to the homes of these women and found many of them looted. The things that had not been stolen and carried away had been demolished—pianos, furniture, and bedding. Windows were broken, doors torn from their hinges, and several places had been burned" (386).

Wells returned to Chicago the next day where she learned that "a delegation of our leading citizens" had already visited Governor Lowden and advised him to disregard the resolutions of the Negro Fellowship League which had been published in the daily papers, "that the Barnetts were radicals, and that they knew that Governor Lowden had done all he could do for the citizens" (Wells 1970, 388). Wells made her report on conditions in East St. Louis "to a crowded meeting at Bethel A.M.E. Church, at which the names of these gentlemen were hissed. Another delegation was appointed to wait on Governor Lowden with my report and to urge that something be done. We went to Springfield that night, but the governor had early been made to feel that we were a lot of sensation hunters and therefore little attention was paid to our report" (Wells 1970, 388–389).

The governor was evidently rather selective in the information to which he chose to attend, as Wells learned that a delegation from East Saint Louis itself had met with him a month before, informing him of the labor troubles brewing. The group was sure that efforts would be made by whites to terrorize black workers, who were being hired by local industries. The group ended by pleading with him to act in advance in order to protect black lives. Governor Lowden declined to do so. At Wells's meeting with Governor Lowden she spoke plainly:

> [W]hen we told him of the soldier standing by and permitting the men to attack and murder helpless Negroes, he said that if we could get him facts upon which to work and could find people who were willing to appear and

> testify, he would see what might be done; that a sweeping investigation was to be made into the whole matter. Accompanied by Mrs. Fallow, we returned to Saint Louis and tried our best to find persons who could and would so testify. (Wells 1970, 389)

But Wells and her colleagues soon learned that the black residents of East St. Louis had fled the city; "hundreds of thousands of Negroes left by every train going in other directions." Nor did she find that the citizens of Saint Louis seemed very curious to investigate the riot: "there seemed a strange disinclination to hold any meeting by which we could get the facts. There seemed a feeling present that we wanted to start something" (Wells 1970, 389). Wells's presence in St. Louis evidently sparked the local N.A.A.C.P. representative to contact the national office: "Dr. Du Bois ... was sent for. An investigation was set on foot, the result of which centered strangely on the colored men who had organized for their own protection. It was a delegation from their group which had gone to see the governor a month before the riot and urged him to throw the power of the state in an effort to prevent the outbreak which they feared" (Wells 1970, 389–390). Realizing that no protection was forthcoming, it had been this group that had stored ammunition with which to defend themselves in case of attack. "On Sunday evening July 1, at about eleven o'clock, a large touring car drove through the Negro district out in the suburbs. The inmates of the car shot right and left into the homes of the colored residents. ... When the men responded and this same big black touring car came rushing by, firing as it went, that handful of colored men fired in return" (Wells 1970, 390).

The riot originated, it was now being claimed, with the self-protective firing of local black residents: "When the investigation was held afterward it centered mostly on tracing the movements of the colored men who were trying to protect themselves and their neighborhood. The result was that fifteen men were arrested and jailed and these fifteen men afterward bore the brunt of all the investigation about that terrible riot. ... [They] each received sentences of fifteen years" (Wells 1970, 390). Wells reports that approximately seventy-five white men and women were also tried, receiving much lighter sentences, ranging from a few days in jail up to five years. Wells continues:

> Only ten of the sixty-five white persons convicted received as long a sentence as five years. ... It will thus be seen that the Negroes, who acted in self-defense and tried to protect their homes and their lives when refused protection elsewhere, received the brunt of the punishment. The white rioters and labor union agitators who murdered over 150 Negroes and destroyed a million dollars worth of property received a very light punishment comparatively. (Wells 1970, 391)

Wells could not have been surprised.

V. John R. Shillady

Lynching is, of course, a relic of slavery.

—James Weldon Johnson, "The Practice of Lynching: A Picture, the Problem and What Shall Be Done About It" (1927)

The legal protection that N.A.A.C.P. branches attempted to provide for black criminals also posed a direct challenge to mob violence. By exposing the trumped-up charges that blacks routinely faced, the N.A.A.C.P. called into question the justifications of lynching that stressed the pervasiveness of serious black crime.

—W. Fitzhugh Brundage, *Lynching in the New South: Georgia and Virginia, 1880–1930* (1993)

Racisms are never pure and unencumbered.

—Ann Laura Stoler, *Race and the Education of Desire: Foucault's History of Sexuality and the Colonial Order of Things* (1995)

John R. Shillady was a handsome young white social worker who worked in the Department of Charities and Corrections in Westchester County, New York. On January 7, 1918, the Board voted to hire Shillady as secretary. (At that same meeting it hired as assistant secretary Walter White, an active member of the Atlanta branch who had worked for an insurance company.) Shillady's job involved raising money for the association. At the first board meeting he attended he brought plans for a membership drive—the Moorfield Storey drive—which turned out to be very effective. James Weldon Johnson (1933) would later write of Shillady's great ability as an organizer (329), and Mary White Ovington would commend his contribution as well (Kellogg 1967)

Johnson (1933) also credits Shillady with conducting the "first adequate statistical study" of lynching (329). Shillady sent two research workers to the Congressional Library at Washington; there they studied newspaper accounts of every lynching for a period of thirty years. They recorded the names, sex, and age of the victims; the place, date, and manner of each lynching; and the charge upon which each victim was lynched. Shillady compiled, tabulated, and published these data in a monograph of over a hundred pages, entitled *Thirty Years of Lynching in the United States.* "The most startling fact revealed," writes Johnson in his autobiography, "was that the common opinion that Negroes were lynched only for rape was without foundation." The evidence indicated that of the more than three thousand African Americans lynched in the thirty-year period, not quite 17 percent had even been charged with rape (Johnson 1933, 329).

Lynchings continued. Shillady worked to make sure the federal government knew when lynchings occurred. When Jim McIllheron was tortured with red-hot irons and burned alive on Lincoln's birthday in 1918 at Estill Springs, Tennessee, Shillady sent a telegram to President Wilson. The president's secretary referred the telegram to the attorney general, who told the N.A.A.C.P. that the federal government had no jurisdiction given that the crime had nothing to do with the war effort. Frustrated but not finished, Shillady wrote Wilson again, asking him to make a public statement condemning the lynching. He suggested that while not directly related to the war effort, such a public statement by the president would help the morale of those African Americans fighting to the make the world "safe for democracy" (Kellogg 1967).

Despite Shillady's messages, those around Wilson had chosen not to inform him of the Estill Springs lynching. He did not learn of it until James Weldon Johnson mentioned it during a conversation with the president at the White House. Earlier, the association had failed to persuade Wilson to mention lynching in his second inaugural address, but when Johnson pressed the point during their meeting, Wilson relented, promising that he would "seek an opportunity" to say something on the subject (quoted in Kellogg 1967, 227). Wilson was no friend of African Americans (Friedman 1970).

Shillady also worked to bring the harsh glare of publicity upon Governor Hugh M. Dorsey and the state of Georgia following a five-day "orgy" of violence in Brooks and Lowndes Counties during which eight African Americans were lynched. The white reign of terror began with the fatal shooting of a white landlord and the wounding of his wife by a black man they had held in peonage and whose (very minimal) wages they had declined to pay. Whites rioted, resulting in the deaths of several innocent African Americans, one of whom was Haynes Turner. Walter White describes the scene in his 1929 study of lynching entitled *Rope and Faggot* (see chapter 1). In terms close to White's, Mary White Ovington also described the scene: "His wife Mary, after her husband's death, mourned and loudly proclaimed his innocence. For this she was slowly burned to death, watched by a crowd of men and women. She was pregnant, and as she burned, the infant fell to the ground and was trampled under a white man's heel" (quoted in Kellogg 1967, 229).

James Weldon Johnson and Walter White carried out separate investigations for the association, the findings from which Shillady sent to Governor Dorsey. The N.A.A.C.P. had discovered the identities of the two ringleaders and fifteen other participants in the murders. Dorsey had risen to the governorship of Georgia as the result of his prosecution of Leo Frank, whose trial had been marked by anti-Semitism and a white mob (Dinnerstein 1968). Dorsey replied to Shillady perfunctorily, informing him and the association the state of Georgia had been unable to apprehend the guilty parties. Nor, it appeared, had they tried (Kellogg 1967).

Other N.A.A.C.P. efforts to force public officials to perform their duties responsibly were more effective. Governor Stanley of Kentucky personally defied a mob at Murray, Kentucky, and saved from lynching a black man who was later legally tried and condemned to death—what George C. Wright (1990), in his study of mob violence in Kentucky, terms "legal lynchings" (see chapter 2, section V). The N.A.A.C.P. Anti-Lynching Committee hired a writer from the *Louisville Courier-Journal* to write a detailed report of the incident, which was later published in the *Independent*. The constitution of Kentucky was later amended to permit the removal from office of any sheriff, jailer, constable or peace officer who neglected his duty to protect prisoners. Of course, border and southern states were not the only targets of N.A.A.C.P. vigilance and protest. The lynching of Edward Woodson at Green River, Wyoming, in December 1918 prompted publicized N.A.A.C.P. protests to the governor against the lynching and the subsequent driving from their homes of black residents of the community. The protest paid off; in 1919, Wyoming enacted a law against mob violence (Kellogg 1967).

The Anti-Lynching Committee tried to organize a conference of southern leaders on lynching but failed. At the end of 1918 the committee changed tactics and decided to work for a national conference, calling upon "the most substantial and influential leaders of public opinion" to endorse it (quoted in Kellogg 1967, 232). They hoped to persuade a number of state governors, including governors of southern states, to attend the conference, as the number of lynchings was increasing. But the call fell on deaf ears in the South, where the organization was at this time called the Advancement Association, or Negro Advancement Society. In response to an inquiry by the association concerning the lynching of Eugene Green at Belzoni, Mississippi, Governor Bilbo's indifference was evident in his inappropriately playful response: "He was 'advanced' alright from the end of a rope, and in order to save burial expenses his body was thrown into the Yazoo River" (quoted Kellogg 1967, 233).

Despite such resistance in the South, the Anti-Lynching Conference found support elsewhere. The conference convened at Carnegie Hall with an attendance of 2,500. Charles Evans Hughes, Governor Emmet O'Neal, Anna Howard Shaw of the woman's suffrage movement, Brigadier General John H. Sherburne of the 92nd (black) Division, and James Weldon Johnson were among the speakers. Later Walter White would describe the astonishment that rippled across the faces of several white liberals seated on the platform when Johnson expressed his conviction that "the race question involves the saving of black America's body and white America's soul" (Johnson 1933, 318; Kellogg 1967).

Astonishment aside, the conference participants agreed on three points: (1) lynching must be made a federal crime, (2) the N.A.A.C.P. should organize state committees to create a climate inhospitable to lynching and work for antilynching legislation at the state level, and (3) the Anti-Lynching Committee should initiate a systematic fund-raising and ad campaign against lynching. Even though N.A.A.C.P. officials were disappointed that few New York lawyers attended the session conducted by Storey on the legal aspect of lynching, the session bore fruit, as the New York City Bar Association soon adopted resolutions calling for a congressional investigation of lynching and federal legislation to criminalize the practice (Kellogg 1967).

Following the Anti-Lynching Conference, Shillady and the Anti-Lynching Committee composed "An Address to the Nation on Lynching," signed by 130 prominent citizens including those who had signed the call and several prominent new sponsors, among them former President William Howard Taft, novelist William Dean Howells, President John Grier Hibben of Princeton University, Theodore D. Bratton, Episcopal bishop of Mississippi, and the governor of Tennessee. The manifesto drew public attention to the problem and helped the N.A.A.C.P. exert additional pressure for a congressional action (Kellogg 1967).

In 1919, the N.A.A.C.P. sent Herbert Seligmann to Tennessee and Mississippi to investigate intensified racial tension. From these talks with leading blacks and whites, Seligmann learned that the shortage of cheap labor in rural regions of the South, caused by massive black migration north (in part to escape lynching), was deeply resented by the white plantation owners. Southern whites were also resentful that the drafting of African Americans into the army had tended to equalize relations with white men. An additional resentment was the widespread white male fantasy that black soldiers were "recognized on equal terms by white women in France." There was some basis for this, of course, but white southern males, as always, tended to transpose fact into fantasy, and then become obsessed with it. Du Bois called this "the sex motive, the brutal sadism into which race hate always falls" (quoted in Kellogg 1967, 235).

After the war, blacks soldiers were lynched in Georgia and Mississippi for appearing on the streets in uniform. One politician, a candidate for the Louisiana State Legislature, told Seligmann that lynching was very necessary, and that no black should ever be allowed to vote or acquire an education. Why, asked the N.A.A.C.P. representative? The Louisianian snorted back (as if everybody knew): because education made confidence men of the males and prostitutes of the females (Kellogg 1967).

"The Red Summer of 1919 broke in fury," remembers James Weldon Johnson (1933, 341). There were several violent race riots during the summer and fall of 1919. The war was a factor; many African Americans were now inclined to fight not flee when rampaging white men came their way. Johnson tells us: "The colored people throughout the country were disheartened and dismayed. The great majority had trustingly felt that, because they had cheerfully done their bit in the war, conditions for them would be better. The reverse seemed to be true. There was one case, at least, in which a returned Negro soldier was *lynch[ed] because of the fact* that he wore the uniform of a United States soldier" (341). But "in the popular mind of the white South in the decades after World War I," Joel Williamson (1984, 7) notes, "there was no race problem, no black history, and no history of race relations if the Yankees and Communists, Catholics and Jews, outsiders and aliens would simply leave black people alone."

The intransigence of whites, the fighting spirit of the new abolitionism, plus black men's wartime experiences with European allies: all were probably factors in the explosions that occurred in Washington, Chicago, Omaha, Knoxville, Indianapolis, and in Phillips County, Arkansas. The riot at Longview, Texas, in June, between whites and returning black soldiers cost a number of lives, black and white. The clash suggested that African Americans were in no mood to submit to white supremacy. "Negroes are not planning anything," reported an Associated Press report in a Longview newspaper, "but will defend themselves if attacked" (quoted in Kellogg 1967, 236)

The N.A.A.C.P.'s investigations and the more aggressive mood among many African Americans intensified white reaction, which was sometimes focused on the association. Early in August 1919, the Austin, Texas, branch informed the national office that the state attorney general had subpoenaed the branch president to bring all N.A.A.C.P. records to court. The state of Texas was acting to shut down all branches operating in the state on the grounds that the N.A.A.C.P. was not chartered to do business in Texas. The national office reminded the Austin branch that the N.A.A.C.P. was not a business but a membership corporation, whose purposes were not economic but civic and educational. If Texas succeeded in shutting down the N.A.A.C.P. within its borders, other southern states would no doubt follow its lead. In 1919 there were 31 branches and 7,046 members in Texas. According to Mary White Ovington, the subpoena had been issued because copies of the *Crisis*, reporting resolutions adopted at the 1919 annual conference demanding the end of segregation in public transportation, had come to the attention of Texas officials (Kellogg 1967).

John Shillady wired Governor Hobby and the Texas attorney general asking for a meeting so that he might explain to them the aims and purposes of the association. In Austin, both the governor and the attorney general refused to see him. He did manage to speak with the acting attorney general and tried to explain, in response to questions, that the N.A.A.C.P. was in no way working to provoke black attacks on whites. When Shillady left the attorney general's office, he was hauled before a secret session of what was purported to be a court of inquiry. There the county attorney asked Shillady insulting questions regarding his private life. The following morning Shillady was attacked and beaten unconscious by a group of men who had been seen loitering about the building the night before. Six to eight men took part in the assault, while "an auto full of tough-looking men" (quoted in Kellogg 1967, 239) stood by. Among the assailants were a judge and a constable, both of whom later bragged about their part in the attack, claiming that Shillady was inciting blacks against whites and had been warned to leave Austin (Kellogg 1967).

N.A.A.C.P. officials in the national office in New York learned through an Associated Press dispatch that Shillady had been attacked. Immediately, officials fired off a telegram to Governor Hobby demanding that the assailants be punished. Hobby replied that the only offender had been Shillady and that he had already been punished. When Mary White Ovington wrote to police officials at Austin, the deputy sheriff answered that Shillady had been "received by red-blooded white men," who would not tolerate "Negro-loving white men" in Texas. They were returning him to New York: "We attend to our own affairs down here, and suggest that you do the same up there" (quoted in Kellogg 1967, 240).

In the face of such intransigence, the N.A.A.C.P. conducted its own investigation. James Weldon Johnson learned that a prominent black clergyman in Austin had been involved in the attack on Shillady; he had told a Texas ranger that the N.A.A.C.P. was coming to town in order to excite sedition and start race riots. Johnson exposed the clergyman in the black press and demanded the severest, most complete ostracism possible as punishment. At about the same time Richard Carroll, a black lecturer from Columbia, South Carolina, complained in the *New York Age* that "fully half the outrages and lynchings and brutality were caused by 'Judas Iscariots' among Negroes" (quoted in Kellogg 1967, 240). There may well have been "Judas Iscariots" at work in lynchings and other acts of mob violence, but there were Romans—whites—as well. Whites, not frightened disloyal blacks, merit our scorn today.

At a special meeting of the board, an appeal was sent to President Wilson asking him to appoint a "responsible commission" to investigate the attack on Shillady. Resolutions were drafted demanding a congressional investigation, given that the governor of Texas had approved and defended a criminal assault by public officials. The board demanded that Governor Hobby remove from office the judge who participated in the assault, and the governor of New York was urged to demand protection for citizens of New York who might visit Texas. Mass meetings were held across the country, including one in New York, to protest the attack on Shillady. A team of lawyers—Moorfield Storey, Arthur B. Spingarn, Charles Studin, George Crawford, Butler Wilson—looked into the legal aspects of the case. They agreed that if Shillady were to return to Austin to testify, he must first be given guarantees by the governor of protection from physical violence (Kellogg 1967).

Shillady suffered serious physical and psychological effects from the assault. Johnson met him when he returned to New York: "I met Mr. Shillady when he arrived at Pennsylvania Station. His face and body were badly bruised; moreover, he was broken in spirit. I don't think he was ever able to realize how such a thing could happen in the United States to an American, free, white, and twenty-one. He never fully recovered spiritually from the experience" (Johnson 1933, 343). He would soon resign his post at the N.A.A.C.P.

Johnson may have been understanding of Shillady's condition, but others were not. Arthur B. Spingarn suggested that the secretary lacked courage and left the association out of fear of returning to Austin. Like Johnson, Walter White was more sympathetic. Mary White Ovington likened Shillady to a shell-shocked soldier. By November the secretary's health was so obviously broken that he was given a vacation with full pay for six weeks in order to recuperate. The board agreed to reimburse him for medical and other expenses related to the attack. Shillady returned to his duties as executive secretary of the association for a time, but he resigned in August 1920, an act which erased the possibility of a trial in Austin. It is unlikely that there would ever have been a trial, as the N.A.A.C.P. was unable to secure a local lawyer willing to argue the case. In his letter of resignation, Shillady wrote: "I am less confident than heretofore of the speedy success of the Association's full program, and of the probability of overcoming, within a reasonable period, the forces opposed to Negro equality by the means and methods which are within the Association's power to employ" (quoted in Kellogg 1967, 241).

W. E. B. Du Bois found Shillady's disillusionment "old news." African Americans had known for a long time that racial hatred would disappear no time soon, that many whites were either vehemently opposed or indifferent to racial equality, and that the legal means available to the N.A.A.C.P. for changing the situation were quite limited. But white people, warned Du Bois, especially white social workers, must accept the fact that white racism cannot be sidestepped. The 90,000 members of the association had banded together to confront it. Shillady had tried to speak quietly and reasonably to Texas officials but "the haters of black folk beat him and maltreated him and scarred him like a dog" (Kellogg 1967, 241). If peaceful, legal, and reasonable means were inadequate to the task, what, asked Du Bois, did whites propose? (Kellogg 1967) The question would reverberate for decades.

VI. The Great War

National culture, never just a point of fixed identity allegiance, reflected changing relations of power.

—Cecilia Elizabeth O'Leary, "'Blood Brotherhood': The Racialization of Patriotism, 1865–1918" (1996)

It is the white man's civilization and the white man's government which are on trial.

—Ida B. Wells, quoted in Gail Bederman, "'Civilization,' the Decline of Middle-Class Manliness, and Ida B. Wells' Antilynching Campaign (1892–94)" (1995b)

Not quite fifty years after the bloodiest civil war of the nineteenth century, white Union and Confederate veterans declared themselves "brothers" once again. The unification of the nation came at the cost of abandoning Reconstruction and "forgetting" the link between the Civil War and the struggle for racial equality. Organized veterans also seemed to "forget" the republic's early definition of patriotism, with its focus on citizen virtue and moral behavior. In the second decade of the twentieth century, American patriotism meant the celebration of male warrior heroism. Although the discourse of patriotism continued to allude to democracy and equality, the glorification of battlefield heroism facilitated the reincorporation of the treasonous Confederates. By the 1913 anniversary of the Battle of Gettysburg and the Emancipation Proclamation, Cecilia Elizabeth O'Leary (1996, 54) observes, "the racist terms of reconciliation were complete."

The racist terms of the reconciliation were made explicit on July 4. When Woodrow Wilson arrived to give the keynote address that commemorative year, a Confederate veteran carrying the Stars and Bars and a Union veteran carrying the Stars and Stripes formed his honor guard. In his Gettysburg address, President Wilson congratulated "the Blue and the Gray" on having "found one another again as brothers and comrades, in arms, enemies no longer." Without any mention of sedition or slavery or the Emancipation Proclamation, Wilson praised the "blood and sacrifice of multitudes of unknown men" in their battle "to make a nation" (quoted in O'Leary 1996, 54). The celebration of Confederate veterans as patriots in the "national brotherhood," however, had not always been assumed. As long as Reconstruction held, freed black people were the primary participants in patriotic celebrations in the South. During that brief moment of opportunity, those white and black patriots committed to racial justice had secured a significant voice in debates over the moral character of postbellum America (O'Leary 1996).

In World War I northern and southern white men were to fight side by side in a racialized alliance. African-American men would be expected to risk their lives in Europe even while they continued to face inequality and racial violence in the United States. While black brothers continued to be lynched back home, black soldiers faced racism from their fellow Americans on the battlefields of France. African Americans, O'Leary points out, fought World War I on two fronts: proving their loyalty in Europe while on the home front linking the Wilson administration's demand "to make the world safe for democracy" with black citizens' demand "to make America safe for the Negro." Reflecting intensifying black indignation, the *Chicago Defender* featured a graphic of the Statue of Liberty that offered "Liberty, Protection, Opportunity, Happiness, For all White Men" and "Humiliation, Segregation, Lynching, For all Black Men" (quoted in O'Leary 1996, 79).

When Congress had declared war on the German Empire in April 1917, American public opinion had been split. Recall that Randolph Bourne broke with John Dewey over Dewey's support for American intervention. Prowar advocates used the opportunity to suspend civil liberties, even at universities. Columbia University president Nicholas Murray Butler declared that Columbia would not tolerate those "who are not with whole heart and mind and strength committed to fight with us to make the world safe for democracy." He told the faculty that "what had been tolerated before becomes intolerable now. What had been wrongheadedness was now sedition. What had been folly was now treason" (quoted in Westbrook 1991, 210). An old friend and colleague of Dewey's who had been instrumental in bringing him to Columbia, James McKeen Cattell, was fired for sending a letter to Congress asking support for an antiwar bill. The faculty committee designed to deal with such matters, on which Dewey sat, was bypassed, resulting in Dewey's resignation from the committee and his condemnation of the Trustees' action: "For the time being the conservative upholders of the Constitution are on the side of moral mob rule and psychological lynch law" (quoted in Westbrook 1991, 211).

The board of the N.A.A.C.P. was also split, although the majority opposed American intervention. Association attorney George Crawford warned Joel Spingarn that he should, if possible, prevent the board from taking any public stand on the war due to the strong pacifist opinions of important board members and their "violent adherence to peace" (quoted in Kellogg 1967, 249). He feared that bitter dissension would cripple the board and draw public retribution. Among the influential board members who were adamantly opposed to American participation in the war were Villard, Lillian Wald, Jane Addams, Unitarian minister John Haynes Holmes, and Mary White Ovington (Kellogg 1967).

Not only university faculty suffered as a consequence of wartime hysteria. Such groups as the Non-Partisan League, the Industrial Workers of the World, German Americans, socialists, pacifists, aliens, and African Americans were considered by the right-wing majority as potentially seditious. Under the espionage acts, the Department of Justice was authorized to deport anyone judged a traitor or subversive. Rumors were rampant that there was "widespread sedition" among blacks. The *New York Tribune* reported that German agents were persuading African Americans to slip into Mexico to join the Germans there in preparation for an invasion of the United States. The N.A.A.C.P. protested to the managing editor of the *Tribune*, and urged black editors to challenge publicly all such nonsense (Kellogg 1967).

The *Crisis* came under the scrutiny of the Department of Justice, which said that the "tone" of some of its articles was questionable, potentially "un-American." When passage of the Sedition Act appeared inevitable, Du Bois emphasized to the board that caution would be required when discussing the war. The board asked attorney Charles Studin to join the *Crisis* committee so that he could monitor, from a legal point of view, all *Crisis* material before publication. The committee agreed to restrict the *Crisis* to facts and constructive criticism for the duration of the war (Kellogg 1967).

A conference of black editors was called by the War Department to discuss how African Americans could contribute to winning the war. Representing the *Crisis*, Du Bois took the lead in drafting resolutions which were then adopted unanimously by the thirty-one editors in attendance. Resolutions pointed to such problems as lynching, mob violence, and the refusal to employ African Americans as Red Cross nurses and as war correspondents. The War Department was not able (or inclined) to solve these, but at least the conference succeeded in uniting the black press in support of the war. Du Bois came out in favor of the war in an editorial in the July *Crisis*, urging African Americans to suspend their skepticism and "close ranks" with their fellow white citizens and the nation's allies in the war effort (Kellogg 1967).

The Second Universal Races Congress, scheduled to meet in Paris in 1915, was canceled due to the war. The N.A.A.C.P. had been represented by four delegates to the first Congress held in London in 1911. When the war broke out in Europe, Du Bois tried to have the second meeting relocated to New York to avoid its cancellation, but he was not successful. Toward the end of the war, the League of Small and Subject Nationalities invited the N.A.A.C.P. to take a seat on its council, which was to look after the interests of Africa and black people worldwide. Du Bois was eager for the N.A.A.C.P. Board to align itself with the league and to contribute toward its expenses, but the board hesitated. Two months later Du Bois announced that he had, without authorization, been sitting on the league's council as the representative of the N.A.A.C.P. The board voted not to become affiliated with other organizations. It did, however, vote to allow staff members, such as Du Bois, to accept appointments or take part in other movements on their own. Du Bois was not satisfied, and in September 1918, he urged the board to take action concerning the future of Africa. He himself was seeking ways to persuade the Wilson administration to ensure that the rights of colonized African peoples would be recognized at the coming Peace Conference (Kellogg 1967).

Representatives of other black protest organizations announced plans to lobby at the Peace Conference, competing with the N.A.A.C.P. to represent African Americans. W. H. Jernagin of Washington planned to lobby for the National Race Congress, the largest of the new organizations, and William Monroe Trotter of Boston would represent the older National Equal Rights League. Their purpose, they said, was not only to represent African Americans, but the interests of blacks throughout the world. These moves and pronouncements by rival leaders and organizations strengthened Du Bois's resolve to go to France to appeal to the Peace Conference on behalf of the blacks peoples of Africa and the world (Kellogg 1967).

The Pan-African Movement

At the December 1918 meeting of the board, Mary White Ovington explained to the other members that, although Du Bois's primary reason for going to Europe was to collect material for a history of black soldiers in the war, he would also take part in a Pan-African Congress in Paris. This meeting had been called to discuss the internationalization of Africa and promote self-determination for the former German colonies. Du Bois's prior interest in and growing preoccupation with a Pan-African Congress soon pushed the black soldier project into the background. The indirectness with which he presented his interest in attending the Congress perhaps prompted him to write years later that the association "did not adopt the Pan-African movement on its official program, but it allowed me on my own initiative to promote the effort." However, the N.A.A.C.P. Annual Report for 1918, published shortly after that meeting, reports that Du Bois was sent to France in a three-fold capacity: (1) as special representative of the *Crisis* to report on the Peace Conference, (2) as historian to collect material for a history of black soldiers' participation in the war, and (3) "as representative of the N.A.A.C.P. to summon a Pan-African Congress" (quoted in Kellogg 1967, 279).

The idea of a Pan-African Congress originated at the turn of the century in London. A young black barrister from the West Indies practicing in London, H. Sylvester-Williams, is generally credited with the idea. Several years later, when Booker T. Washington proposed holding a conference on Africa, T. Thomas Fortune claimed he had been the originator of the idea. Fortune claimed that Williams had stolen his proposal and issued as his own the call for the first Pan-African Congress, held in Westminster Hall, London, in July 1900 to coincide with the Methodist Ecumenical Congress and the Paris Exposition. Approximately thirty delegates attended that meeting, including Du Bois, who was elected a vice-president. Kellogg tells us that Du Bois's later assertion that the movement went dormant for a generation is not completely accurate. In 1906, Kellogg points out, the Pan-African Association was still extant, with Bishop Alexander Walters serving as president. Additionally, J. Max Barber, head of the Pan-African League Department of the Du Bois–led Niagara Movement, was in touch with at least one prominent African, A. K. Soga, concerning the prospects of a Pan-African movement (Kellogg 1967).

Booker T. Washington convened an "International Conference on the Negro," in April 1912, at Tuskegee Institute. This was a far larger and more representative gathering than the 1919 Pan-African Congress in Paris. Those in attendance at Tuskegee studied how the methods employed by the Tuskegee and Hampton Institutes might be employed in Africa, the West Indies, and South America. Some claimed that the Tuskegee conference had for the first time brought together blacks from all parts of the world and that it gave new impetus to the idea of an African nationality or "personality," anticipating later conceptions of "blackness" and "*négritude*." Registrants decided that the conference should become a triennial event and, moreover, that Booker T. Washington should travel to South Africa to try to persuade the white majority there that the aspirations of blacks were just. Before a second conference could be held, World War I began, and a year later Washington died. Given these events, one must agree with Kellogg (1967, 280) that "Du Bois's claim that he was the founder and convenor of the First Pan-African Congress is something of an exaggeration."

The cause of the African peoples was not only on Du Bois's mind. In January 1919, John Shillady proposed that the theme of the annual conference should be "Africa in the World Democracy." Archibald Grimké, however, cautioned the board that the association must not be diverted from its primary purpose, the advancement of African Americans. Walling and Mary White Ovington countered that no disproportionate amount of time would be devoted to Africa, but that the African question was very timely and that its inclusion on the agenda would result in much valuable publicity for the N.A.A.C.P., which in turn would help to promote the primary cause, that of African Americans (Kellogg 1967).

The idea of a Pan-African Congress in Paris in 1919 was not without its difficulties. Lengthy negotiations had to be held with the French government before permission was finally granted to hold the Congress in Paris. Then the United States and the colonial powers refused to issue passports to those who wished to attend, jeopardizing the event. Finally, the N.A.A.C.P. intervened to save the conference. It was an N.A.A.C.P.-sponsored Congress that opened in Paris on February 19, 1919. Only fifteen countries were represented; nine were African, with twelve delegates out of the total of fifty-seven. Twenty-one represented the West Indies, sixteen the United States. Blaise Diagne, a member of the Chamber of Deputies from Senegal, was elected president; Du Bois was elected secretary. Other N.A.A.C.P. members who attended included John Hope, Mrs. W. A. Hunton, Joel Spingarn, Walling, and Charles Edward Russell (Kellogg 1967).

One of the welcomed consequences of the Pan-African Congress, Du Bois argued, was the idea for the Mandates Commission of the League of Nations. The Commission, Du Bois suggested, was a direct response to the Congress's request for an international organization for the administration and supervision of the former German colonies. Other resolutions adopted by the Congress concerned such African issues as natural resources, concessions, investment of capital, labor, education, and the participation of the indigenous people in government. The *New York Evening Globe* reported that the Pan-African Congress would appeal to the Peace Conference to grant black Africans the freedom to develop the continent unhampered by Europeans and other colonial interests. The Paris edition of the *New York Herald* judged it a reasonable request, in particular the Congress's call for the creation of a permanent bureau attached to the League of Nations to ensure observance in Africa of an international code of law. This bureau would aim to protect Africans from European exploitation and support Africans' political and economic interests (Kellogg 1967).

Du Bois had wanted to stop over in Haiti on his return from Europe, but could not. Representing the N.A.A.C.P., he had hoped to investigate reports of intolerable conditions there. Such reports had been filtering into the association since 1915, when the United States had taken control of Haitian finances. This move had been followed in 1916 by American military occupation of the country. The N.A.A.C.P. was concerned because Haiti, as Du Bois put it, was "a continuing symbol of Negro revolt against slavery and oppression, and [of] capacity for self-rule" (quoted in Kellogg 1967, 284). Many of the civilian and military personnel the Wilson administration had stationed in Haiti were known to the association to be racist southern whites. In 1915, on behalf of the N.A.A.C.P., Villard pressed the Wilson administration to establish a commission to visit Haiti. In letters and private conversations with Joseph Tumulty, Secretary of State Robert Lansing, and other Wilson administration officials, he urged that the Haitian problem be resolved not only politically and economically, but also from the point of view of social justice (Kellogg 1967).

Lansing was unenthusiastic. Indeed, nothing was done by the Wilson administration concerning the commission, and reports of intolerable conditions continued to reach the New York office despite tight government control. The news of American atrocities in Haiti combined with reports of the military expedition sent by Wilson to Mexico to suppress Francisco "Pancho" Villa enraged both Storey and Villard, both strongly anti-imperialist as well as antiracist activists. No relief was in sight, however, as reports of the mistreatment of Haitians and American suppression of self-rule continued during the war years. In 1918 the board authorized James Weldon Johnson to travel to Haiti to investigate, as soon as funds became available. The board declined to allow Du Bois to make the trip. Kellogg speculates the reason might have had to do with Johnson's previous diplomatic experience in Latin America, which in some board members' minds made him more qualified than Du Bois. Johnson did not make the trip to Haiti until 1920; his revealing report prompted the N.A.A.C.P. to lobby intensively on behalf of the Haitians during the 1920s. The association's efforts were largely responsible for the evacuation of American troops from Haiti and the end of U.S. financial control (Kellogg 1967).

VII. Commission on Interracial Cooperation (C.I.C.)

It [C.I.C.] functioned as the principal vehicle of southern liberalism during the interwar period.

—Adam Fairclough, *Race and Democracy: The Civil Rights Struggle in Louisiana, 1915–1972* (1999)

The decline of lynchings during the 1920s and 1930s reflects the effectiveness of antilynching activists.

—W. Fitzhugh Brundage, *Lynching in the New South: Georgia and Virginia, 1880–1930* (1993)

The Atlanta-based Commission on Interracial Cooperation (C.I.C.) had been founded in 1919 to rally influential white moderates and carefully chosen blacks for its campaign against mob violence. A decade later, it would sponsor the Southern Commission on the Study of Lynching, which published its findings in *The Tragedy of Lynching* (Raper 1933/1969). As well, the commission encouraged the establishment of the Association of Southern Women for the Prevention of Lynching (A.S.W.P.L.), and lobbied politically to stop the "peculiar" practice. In 1944, the Interracial Commission dissolved into the Southern Regional Council, an organization with much broader interests. While the council as such was not an activist group, members often were active as individuals and pressed the organization to take direct action, especially in the struggle against segregation. After World War II, the council became an important collector and dispenser of material concerning African Americans and race relations in the South and in the nation (Williamson 1984; Zangrando 1980).

The Commission on Interracial Cooperation (C.I.C.) was founded by a group of prominent white ministers, educators, and social workers in Atlanta. The organization had some of its roots in the "Reconstruction" work that followed the Atlanta riot of 1906. Unlike the N.A.A.C.P., the C.I.C. was an entirely southern and largely white organization. It grew to include local and state interracial committees, but only by carefully avoiding any appearance of challenging segregation and white supremacy. The commission declared that it was "absolutely loyal ... to the principle of racial integrity." Despite these compromises, the organization was, Brundage (1993) judges, "enduring and effective" in the campaigning against lynching (quoted passages on 234).

The founding of the C.I.C. represented a certain culmination of the interracial movement in Atlanta, reinvigorated at the time of World War I, in part to respond to the rapid changes engendered by the war. Beginning in 1916, several white ministers in Atlanta, calling themselves the Committee on Church Cooperation, had periodically met with black ministers to discuss racial problems, especially those associated with urban areas. After two years of informal meetings, these encounters were formalized as meetings of the Christian Councils, comprised of representatives from both races and officials of the Y.M.C.A., Y.W.C.A., and the Salvation Army. The hope was to stimulate communication between racially segregated congregations (Brundage 1993; Williamson 1984).

In January 1919, several members of the Committee on Church Cooperation were concerned that readjustment to peace after the war might be complicated by racial friction, a legitimate concern given that black soldiers were being lynched in uniform upon their return from Europe. These concerned members organized what they called the Atlanta Commission on Interracial Cooperation, the immediate forerunner of the C.I.C. Under the leadership of John J. Eagan, a prominent Atlanta manufacturer, and Plato Durham, former dean of the Candler School of Theology at Emory University, the commission brought together a number of prominent Atlanta citizens who had long expressed an interest in "developing better conditions in the South" (quoted in Brundage 1993, 234).

Among the founders were M. Ashby Jones; Cary B. Wilmer, rector of St. Luke's Episcopal Church; Richard T. Flynn, a Presbyterian minister; Will A. Alexander, a 1912 graduate of Vanderbilt's divinity school and for some years a practicing minister in Tennessee as well as a member of the War Work Council of the Y.M.C.A.; and Richard H. King, executive director of the Southeastern Department of the Y.M.C.A. War Work Council. During the remainder of 1919, Jones, Eagan, and especially Alexander ("for whom the interracial campaign became a crusade" [Brundage 1993, 234–235]) searched for sufficient financial backing to expand the Atlanta program throughout the South. Finally, in January 1920, funding was secured from the Laura Spelman Rockefeller Memorial and the Commission on Interracial Cooperation was founded, with Alexander as its executive secretary. For the most part, the commission would function as an organization for investigation, study, and publication toward the improvement of race relations (Brundage 1993; Williamson 1984).

The C.I.C.'s most important achievements, Adam Fairclough (1999) suggests, were in the promotion of black education. Functioning as a conduit for northern philanthropy, the commission helped to establish Dillard University in New Orleans, a merger of two older black colleges. (Dillard's first president would be Will Alexander.) The C.I.C. also supported the building of thousands of black schools with money from the Julius Rosenwald Fund, a Chicago-based charity founded with profits from the Sears, Roebuck Company. To a remarkable extent, Fairclough (1997) tells us, the "Rosenwald schools" became embedded in the fabric of rural black communities, a fact that their very name—implying that they were outright gifts of northern white philanthropy—tends to disguise.

The truth of the matter was that Rosenwald money furnished less than half of the necessary funding required to build Rosenwald schools. The greater portion came from state government and from the local citizens themselves. Their contribution was made in the form of money, materials, and labor, a direct involvement in the project that made these schools more than mere buildings. Drives to build Rosenwald schools, encouraged by state agents employed by the fund, provided opportunities for disenfranchised African Americans to mobilize around a common purpose and to achieve a sense of community progress at a time when white violence, including lynching, continued unabated. In rural Louisiana, the Rosenwald Fund helped fund 372 schools, a quarter of all black schools, a third of the total enrollment, and a half of all the teachers. Throughout the South, the fund financed 5,000 schools between 1914 and 1922 (Fairclough 1997, 1999).

As a representative of the Rosenwald Fund, Horace Mann Bond and his wife Julia Washington Bond traveled to Washington Parish in southeastern Louisiana in 1934. Horace Mann Bond was at that time in the early years of a distinguished career as a historian, curriculum theorist, and university president (Urban 1992). At age twenty-nine he was a professor at Fisk University with an impressive list of scholarly publications; his expertise as an authority on black education made him attractive to officials of the Rosenwald Fund who asked him and his wife to live in the small Louisiana farming community to study the operation of the local black schools there. As Adam Fairclough (1997) quips, today the two would be called "participant-observers," but in 1934 they were most certainly "explorers" (xvii). This experience, Horace Mann Bond would later write, "proved one of the most valuable of our lives" (quoted in Fairclough 1997, xvii).

For three months in late 1934 the Bonds, who had married in 1929 and had as yet no children (their son Julian would figure prominently in the 1960s civil rights movement), lived in a wooden cabin in a district known as Star Creek. Describing Star Creek, the Bonds reported:

> Immediately after the War, when the price of cotton gave economic security to the community that it has never since enjoyed, the members of the community obtained a Rosenwald grant-in-aid. They then rented a saw mill, bought some timber ... and cut the trees, sawed the timber, and hauled it to the site of the school where they erected the structure. This community experience is recalled with pride. ... They speak of the school as "our school" in a sense that transcends the ordinary use of that term. Teachers have come and gone, but the memory of that united community and of their contribution centers the life of all in the institution. (quoted in Fairclough 1997, xix)

So important was the school that it, not the church, functioned as the center of the black community (Fairclough 1997). The lynching of Jerome Wilson (see section V of chapter 11) precipitated the Bonds' premature departure (Bond and Bond 1997).

Unlike the enthusiasm these school-focused groups enjoyed, the C.I.C.'s local committees started with a zeal that often could not be sustained. While local committees located outside the main cities of the South often failed to survive, in Georgia, local committees not only survived but flourished. No doubt the easy access to and constant attention from the C.I.C. headquarters' staff in Atlanta helped sustain Georgia's local committees. The state committee enjoyed the skilled leadership of Thomas J. Woofter, Jr., a recent doctoral graduate in sociology from Columbia University; Clark H. Foreman, the grandson of the founder of the *Atlanta Constitution*; and Arthur F. Raper, a product of Howard Odum's sociology program at the University of North Carolina at Chapel Hill. In probably no other southern states was the combination of talent and resources more favorable (Brundage 1993).

By the 1930s antilynching activists went about their work with an intensified sense of urgency. C.I.C. members routinely urged prominent whites in communities where lynchings might occur to use their influence, specifically to remind sheriffs and other local law enforcement officers of their legal obligation to protect prisoners. When commission members were unable to prevent a lynching, they investigated the incident and, when possible, secured indictments against the mob leaders (Brundage 1993). Also in 1930, the C.I.C. took an important step toward activism when it employed Jessie Daniel Ames to organize the A.S.W.P.L. As we have seen (see chapter 8, section VI), Jessie Daniel Ames traveled from state to state, persuading women's clubs and other women's groups which had been successful before in the fight for suffrage to concentrate now on the fight against lynching. When a crime occurred that might result in a lynching, local A.S.W.P.L. members would pressure local officials to take whatever actions were necessary to prevent it. Joel Williamson (1984, 485) regards Ames as "a personality much like Rebecca Felton, but she delivered a message to white men that was precisely opposite to that of the fire-eating Georgian. She was a very strong woman who labored to maintain a household and rear three children after her husband's early death, and she was not very respectful toward men as men. She was forceful, a superb organizer, and highly effective."

Such activism was especially appreciated by the N.A.A.C.P., and Walter White and other N.A.A.C.P. officials watched with hope what appeared to be an increasing resistance to lynching across the South. This resistance seemed fairly widespread, but White looked in particular to Will Alexander and the C.I.C. Both the C.I.C. and A.S.W.P.L. sought to discredit those myths—especially the rape myth—which white men used to justify the practice. The effort involved research and publicity, community education, as well as the political work of the A.S.W.P.L. Robert Eleazer and C.I.C. secretaries in the several states implemented the overall program, while Jessie Daniel Ames organized women locally and regionally (Zangrando 1980; Hall 1979).

Alexander began to feel confident that lynching was nearly played out, and said so. The *New York Times* for January 12, 1930, reported his prediction: "*FORESEES END OF LYNCHING.* Atlanta, Ga., Jan. 11—Lynching will be a lost crime by 1940—something for scientists to study and the rest of us to remember with unbelief—and it will be wiped out by radio, good roads and the newspapers, according to Will W. Alexander, director of the Commission on Interracial Cooperation" (quoted in Ginzburg 1962/1988, 181). Alexander would be too optimistic by twenty years, as the last recognized lynching occurred in Mississippi in 1959 (see the final section of chapter 2).

Also in 1930 Will Alexander proposed that the organization conduct detailed investigations of each lynching in hopes of understanding the specific causes of mob violence. The C.I.C. had already committed itself to the investigation of lynchings, as had the N.A.A.C.P. What distinguished the new campaign, named the Southern Commission on the Study of Lynching, was the prestige of those involved. Among the participants were the Pulitzer Prize–winning journalist Julian Harris of the *Atlanta Constitution*, John Hope, the president of Atlanta University, and B. F. Hubert, president of Georgia State College in Savannah. Other members included Howard W. Odum of the University of North Carolina, Dallas attorney Alex Spence, Nashville's W. King, Methodist Episcopal Church, South, President W. J. McGlothlin of Furman University, and such major black figures as R. R. Moton and Monroe N. Work of the Tuskegee Institute, and sociologist Charles S. Johnson of Fisk University. Alexander recruited the young editor of the *Chattanooga News*, George Fort Milton, to chair the commission (Zangrando 1980; Brundage 1993).

Research on each lynching was to be conducted by two social scientists: Arthur Raper, a young white sociologist educated at the University of North Carolina, the emerging center of southern white liberalism, and Walter R. Chivers, a black sociologist from Morehouse College in Atlanta (Brundage 1993; Howard 1995). In November 1931, the commission published its first findings in an eight-page pamphlet, "Lynchings and What They Mean." In

1933, the commission issued its full report in two volumes published by the University of North Carolina Press: *The Tragedy of Lynching*, by Arthur F. Raper, and James Harmon Chadbourn's *Lynching and the Law* (Zangrando 1980; Raper 1933/1969; Chadbourn 1933).

These publications communicated the conclusions of southern white liberals and antilynching activists concerning the causes of lynching and how the practice might be stopped. Brundage (1993) suggests there was not much new in Raper's analysis of lynching; Walter White (1929) had reached similar conclusions just a few years before. But, perhaps due to their scholarly, methodical and the scientific tone, the commission's findings became the definitive contemporary analysis of lynching, at least as far as southern whites were concerned. What was newsworthy about Raper's book was that it provided, as the *Chattanooga News* put it, "all the necessary facts concerning the malady which has made the South a synonym for barbarity in other countries" (quoted in Brundage 1993, 246). Ida B. Wells had seen to that.

From Raper's point of view, the evidence concerning the lynchings of 1930 was unmistakable; illiteracy, poverty, and cultural stagnation were the root causes of mob violence. Unpersuaded by the conventional catch-all concept, white supremacy, Raper insisted that lynchings could not be understood apart from the South's profound social and economic problems. Only the modernization of the southern economy would eradicate those causes which erupted, all too often, in the white male mutilation of black men. Such modernization would not happen overnight. In the meantime, the commission urged influential southern whites to become engaged in the struggle against the practice, as "the primary responsibility for the lessening of crime and eradication of the lynching rests upon that portion of the white population which controls political, social, and economic conditions" (quoted in Brundage 1993, 246). Raper was not content to conduct research on lynching; he spoke to civic clubs, churches, and similar groups throughout the South. The S.C.S.L. sent his book to educational institutions and libraries (Howard 1995).

The Raper study was reissued in 1969. A sober and scholarly study, it merits reading today. The appearance of *The Tragedy of Lynching* as well as an increasing opposition to mob violence encouraged southern liberals and progressives to combat the practice. But southern liberals' position has always been an awkward one. In their public opposition to lynching they seemed too "radical" to their neighbors, but the fact was that they always trailed an increasingly national condemnation of the phenomenon. A character in Lillian Smith's novel of interracial love and lynching, *Strange Fruit,* personifies the problem of the southern liberal.

> Prentiss Reid, editor of *The Maxwell Press*, sat late in his office. Yellow sheets of paper lay in front of him, covered with pencil marks. The town's religious skeptic, the admirer of Tom Paine, the man who fought Prohibition, who had dared raise questions in 1917 about the persecution of aliens, had drawn a blank for tomorrow's editorial. Anything you say now will do more harm than good. That's the trouble. Always the trouble! Say what you think, make a gesture, you stir up a mare's nest. Make things worse that they were before—So they say.

> He lit a cigarette; stared at the bookshelf above his desk. *Holy Bible, Common Sense, Age of Reason, Rights of Man.* Four books worn from handling. Pages marked, words underlined, comments scribbled in the margins. There was no man in Maxwell who could with so much ease cite Holy Writ in an argument as could the town's infidel; and none who could quote whole pages from Tom Paine as casually as if from a talk with a friend (Smith 1972/1944, 364–365).

What will he say about the lynching of an innocent black man? Reid talks himself into accepting the crime. Instead of criticizing his fellow southerners, he blames the North.

> Prentiss Reid lit another cigarette; stared into the wall, shrugged, wrote rapidly for a few minutes. "... [B]ut what's done now is done. Bad, yes. Lawlessness and violence are always bad. And this particular form smacks of the Dark Ages. It hurts business, it hurts the town, it hurts the county, it hurts everybody in it. But it's time now to get our minds on our work, get back to our jobs, quit this talking. Those who participated in the lynching were a lawless bunch of hoodlums. We don't know who they are. They ought to be punished. But who are they? No one seems to know. ... As for northern criticism. There will be plenty. All we can say is: if the damyankees can handle these folks better than we who've had more than two hundred years' practice, let them try it. Lord knows, they're welcome to try it. Up there. And we might ask them how about their own gangsters? And how about East St. Louis and Chicago? (Smith 1944/1972, 367)

These are, of course, references to the famous East St. Louis and Chicago race riots. With southern progressives stymied, is it any wonder that nationally, Americans felt decreasing patience for southerners to solve the problem themselves, and an increased sentiment for federal legislation? (Zangrando 1980).

The C.I.C. served as a clearinghouse of information on lynching. For instance, in 1921, at the urging of Will Alexander, Governor Hugh M. Dorsey (1917–1921) used C.I.C. records to write a speech and a pamphlet that described 135 incidents of mistreatment of African Americans in Georgia, including lynchings and violent intimidation. While hardly an antilynching activist, Dorsey was nonetheless heartened by the work of the C.I.C. in light of the social and economic tensions aggravated by the Great Migration after World War I. Racial violence in Georgia had reached a point, Dorsey decided, where "to me it seems that we stand indicted as a people before the world" (quoted in Brundage 1993, 236). The pamphlet attracted national attention. In it Dorsey called for a comprehensive state antilynching law, including the creation of a state police force controlled by the governor's office. The Georgia C.I.C. drew up an antilynching statute which was introduced into the 1926 legislature by Alexander R. Lawton, a C.I.C. member from Savannah, but the bill, as had previous bills, failed to pass (Brundage 1993).

To what extent the campaigns of the N.A.A.C.P. and the C.I.C. influenced public attitudes toward lynching is difficult to determine. Steven Tolnay and E. M. Beck, two sociologists whose research on lynching we examined in chapter 3, are skeptical, pointing instead to "larger" social and economic shifts in the South. Fitzhugh Brundage, a historian sympathetic to the "empirical" study of lynching whose research we also examined in that chapter, is somewhat more appreciative: the "two organizations almost certainly contributed significantly to the growing intolerance of Georgians toward lynching." He recalls the assessment of another sociologist, Howard Odum, who in 1936 suggested that "the value of the C. I. C. has come from ... [its] continuous, uninterrupted major effort constantly under the same management and motivation. ... It has modified that culture in vigorous and constructive ways" (quoted in Brundage 1993, 238).

VIII. James Weldon Johnson

[James Weldon] Johnson situates the black male body at the center of what he perceives as a national crisis, a crisis conceived in the dual terms of black body and white soul.

—Hazel Carby, *Reconstructing Womanhood: The Emergence of the Afro-American Novelist* (1987)

At the forefront of the quickening crusade against lynching was the newly invigorated N.A.A.C.P.

—W. Fitzhugh Brundage, *Lynching in the New South: Georgia and Virginia, 1880–1930* (1993)

Despite the importance of southern-based groups such as the C.I.C., Robert Zangrando (1980) argues that it was organized pressure from outside the South that contributed most to lynching's decline. The most visible and concerted pressure was exerted by the N.A.A.C.P. Ida B. Wells had ended the white silence on lynching in the late nineteenth century, and in the early twentieth, the N.A.A.C.P. undertook to end the official governmental silence. The N.A.A.C.P. worked long and hard to force elected officials (who were almost all white men) to face the fact of the illegal and obscene violence against black men in the South. As early as 1916, black academician William Pickens (1969) had argued that white acknowledgment of southern sadism would be a necessary precondition to ending the practice. In like fashion, Walter White argued that the N.A.A.C.P.'s investigations, exposés, and campaigns for a federal antilynching legislation were absolutely necessary in order to provoke public concern, force a national political dialogue on the subject, and prod the South into reflecting on its most vicious form of racist aggression and violence. Writing just after the peak of the association's congressional lobbying efforts, students of American racial relations as diverse as Hortense Powdermaker

(1939) and Gunnar Myrdal (1944/1962) endorsed White's analysis (Zangrando 1980).

Walter White knew that the struggle to secure federal legislation against lynching would be difficult. He knew something of the history of black resistance to lynching, and he knew everything about the depth of black dismay over federal inaction. He was aware that in 1898, prompted by such atrocities as the lynching of Frazier B. Baker, a black postmaster in South Carolina, and the riot in Wilmington, North Carolina, Ida B. Wells and Bishop Alexander Walters of the A.M.E. Zion Church, among others, had organized an Afro-American Council to focus national attention on lynching and other forms of racial hatred. A mass meeting had been held in Chicago at which resolutions were adopted demanding the arrest and prosecution of Baker's killers, indemnities for his survivors, and a federal antilynching law. Wells had delivered the appeals to Washington herself. Accompanied by a delegation of Illinois congressmen, she presented these resolutions to President William McKinley. Wells (1970) remembered: "President McKinley received us very courteously, listened to my plea, accepted the resolutions which had been sent by the citizens of Chicago, and told me to report back home that they had already placed some of the finest of their secret service agents in the effort to discover and prosecute the lynchers of that black postmaster" (Wells 1970, 253).

Wells spent five weeks in Washington; she went daily to the Capitol in the effort to help Congressman George E. White, the lone African-American congressman in the House of Representatives at that time, pass a bill to provide indemnity for the widow and children of the lynched black postmaster. Congressman White told Wells that he had reduced the amount in the original bill from fifty thousand to one thousand dollars in hopes that this lower amount would permit southern congressmen not to oppose the legislation. Wells (1970) knew better: "Whereupon my reply to him was that he did not know the South as well as I had hoped for; if he did, he would know that they would object to the compensation of five dollars not because of the amount, but because of the principle of the thing" (253).

During this time Congress declared war upon Spain, and Congressman William E. Lorimer from Chicago advised her that the war would destroy any chance of action on the bill. Wells returned home (Wells 1970). A federal court failed to convict any of those arrested in the postmaster's death (Zangrando 1980). Despite White's knowledge of Wells's centrality to the antilynching struggle, he did not acknowledge her significance. As Schechter (1997) has observed, by the 1920s the struggle against lynching had become "feminized," women antilynching activists segregated in traditional feminine spheres such as the church. The big boys would go at each other where it counted, in Congress.

The biggest boys of all—those who occupied the White House—had proven themselves undependable allies in the fight against lynching. Benjamin Harrison had been the first president to advocate a federal law against the practice. While he said he opposed violence against African Americans, he acted only in response to official embarrassment over the lynching of eleven Italians in New Orleans in 1891. As would his successors, Harrison emphasized the "limitations" of federal power in interracial matters, a tactical retreat which allowed him to maintain political support from the South. As governor of Ohio,

William McKinley had opposed vigilantism; he had supported the state's 1896 antilynching law. In his first presidential inaugural address he had said that: "Lynchings must not be tolerated in a great civilized country like the United States. ... Equality of rights must prevail" (quoted in Zangrando 1980, 15).

Despite such rhetoric, mobs of southern white men encountered no federal interference in their pursuit of black male bodies. President Theodore Roosevelt encouraged others to denounce lynching but continued to associate it with rape when he spoke of it publicly. William Howard Taft preferred to leave the problem to the states (Zangrando 1980). As we saw in the case of Claude Neal, even Franklin Delano Roosevelt, hardly a states' rights advocate, could not bring himself to intervene, even after Eleanor asked him herself to do so. Lynching was, evidently, a male-male matter.

Key N.A.A.C.P. leaders such as Walter White and James Weldon Johnson knew that the rape rationale was sheer fantasy. They knew that lynchers were not exactly white knights on horseback; they themselves had faced firsthand incidents of mob violence. Lynchers were not, as Ida B. Wells had shrewdly driven home to her British listeners, civilized men. And both White and Johnson knew that every African American alive knew of someone—a family member, a friend, an acquaintance, a friend of a friend—who had been mutilated and murdered by a mob of white men. There could be no question whatsoever that federal intervention was justified (Zangrando 1980).

While the campaign against lynching was sincere, White and Johnson and the N.A.A.C.P. also used the issue to draw attention to other forms of racial violence and inequality. While determined to end lynching, White and Johnson viewed the practice in two ways: each murder justified a continued struggle against the practice, *and* the association used each incident to educate European Americans regarding the necessity for federal protection of the civil rights of African Americans generally (Zangrando 1980). Decades later, in the 1960s, this linkage between gender and civil rights would become explicit; what moderate civil rights workers as well as black revolutionaries said they were fighting for was ... manhood.

As we will see, Congress never would enact antilynching legislation. The closest it had come, long before the N.A.A.C.P. began its lobbying efforts, was in segments of those civil rights statutes passed during the Reconstruction period, specifically in the so-called Enforcement Act of 1870 and the Ku Klux Klan Act of 1871. After the Supreme Court nullified portions of these laws, residual elements were incorporated into sections 51 and 52, later 241 and 242, of Title 18 of the United States Code. As interpreted in the judicial system and implemented by law-enforcement officials, however, these did not justify federal intervention against lynching. With intense N.A.A.C.P. lobbying, the U.S. House passed antilynching legislation on three occasions, 1922, 1937, and 1940, but on each occasion a filibuster or the threat of a filibuster in the Senate prevented the law from reaching the White House. Congress did finally pass five civil rights measures from 1957 to 1968, the last of which established fines and jail sentences for anyone who injured or killed a person seeking to exercise a wide range of federally protected civil rights. This was the closest Congress ever came to passing national antilynching legislation (Zangrando 1980).

A decade after the Baker lynching in South Carolina, which had prompted the formation of the Afro-American Council and Ida B. Wells's trip to the White House, another lynching event had sparked another organized response. As we saw earlier, in mid-August 1908, in Springfield, Illinois, two men had been lynched and 2,000 other African Americans were forced to flee the city. Over 4,000 militia had been required to reestablish order. Recall that it had been this racially motivated riot that led directly to the founding of the N.A.A.C.P. The fact that such brutality had occurred in a northern city—indeed, in the capital of Illinois so closely associated with the memory of Abraham Lincoln—mobilized black leaders to organize their resistance against lynching (Zangrando 1980).

Recall too that among those involved in the founding of the N.A.A.C.P. had been W. E. B. Du Bois, the legendary black scholar-activist, whose 1903 *The Souls of Black Folk* had startled readers with its attack on Booker T. Washington's accommodationism. Du Bois would settle for nothing less than absolute equality in political, educational, and civil matters. Not fooled by America's contrived ignorance of racial injustice, Du Bois had spoken of the veil separating the races. He argued, memorably, that "the problem of the twentieth century is the problem of the color-line" (23, 41, 87). When Du Bois agreed to leave Atlanta University in 1910 to become the association's first director of publications and research as well as editor of its magazine, the *Crisis*, Mary White Ovington had observed, "we nailed our banner to the mast. … From that time onward, no one doubted where we stood" (quoted Zangrando 1980, 24).

Two intervening developments influenced the N.A.A.C.P.'s struggle against lynching. First was the addition to the national staff of James Weldon Johnson in late 1916 and, in early 1918, Walter Francis White. As had Ida B. Wells, and Jessie Daniel Ames would be, White soon became involved in firsthand investigations of mob violence. As noted earlier, his 1929 book, *Rope and Faggot: A Biography of Judge Lynch* (dedicated to his colleague James Weldon Johnson), remains today an important study of the phenomenon. White denounced lynching as an instance of the larger economic and political exploitation of African Americans rationalized by the ideology of white supremacy. He argued that lynching functioned for southern whites as a diversion from their otherwise dull and empty lives, that lynchers were a product of a reactionary southern white culture that rejected new ideas, and that fundamentalist religion aggravated those sexual repressions and ambivalences that surfaced in the sadism of the mobs.

The second development which influenced N.A.A.C.P. antilynching tactics was America's involvement in World War I, which in disrupting traditional social arrangements—black soldiers had been treated with more respect by the French and English than they received at home—greatly increased racial tension and violence. N.A.A.C.P. membership had risen from 329 in 1912 to over 8,700 in 1916, and it would jump to almost 44,000 over the course of the next few years. The circulation of the monthly *Crisis* exceeded 37,000 by the middle of 1916. In its first half-dozen years, the N.A.A.C.P. staff was small in number and sometimes part-time. Board members were forced to divide their energies among personal, business or professional matters and the association's work. There were occasional tensions, for instance, when Du Bois objected to the presence of too many whites in major staff positions (Zangrando 1980)—an issue that would surface again fifty years later in radical student organizations such as the Student Nonviolent Coordinating Committee (Carson 1981).

James Weldon Johnson

James Weldon Johnson became field secretary of the N.A.A.C.P. in December 1916, acting secretary in 1917 and again in September 1920, then executive secretary in December 1920. As an African American and a native of Florida, where more lynchings occurred per black population than in any other state, Johnson had lived through the nightmare that was lynching. In fact, he had himself almost been lynched. After a particularly devastating fire in Jacksonville, Florida, Johnson's hometown, a white woman reporter from New York traveled to Jacksonville to write about the impact of the fire upon the local black population. She asked Johnson to read and critique her article; he agreed to meet her in a park (Johnson 1933).

The white streetcar conductor who saw him get off the car to greet a (white) woman reported the "incident" to the local military authority, who sent "eight or ten militiamen in khaki with rifles and bayonets" to arrest Johnson and the unsuspecting reporter. Johnson was beaten while the men in uniform shouted "Kill the damned nigger!" Though the "misunderstanding" was eventually cleared up, the incident haunted Johnson: "For weeks and months the episode with all of its implications preyed on my mind and disturbed my sleep. I would wake often in the night-time, after living through again those few frightful seconds, exhausted by the nightmare of a struggle with a band of murderous, bloodthirsty men in khaki, with loaded rifles and fixed bayonets. It was not until twenty years after, through work I was then engaged in, that I was able to liberate myself completely from this horror complex" (Johnson 1933, 170; quoted in Harris 1984, 205 n. 3).

The memory of this near lynching no doubt strengthened Johnson's resolve to fight the white male practice during his N.A.A.C.P. days. His (1912/1960) *The Autobiography of an Ex-Colored Man*, first published in 1912 and reissued during the height of the Harlem Renaissance in 1927, remains today one of the best-known literary studies of the mulatto and the problems of "passing," a phenomenon that is at once racialized and gendered (Starke 1971; Clarke 1995; Harper 1996). The tragic death in an auto-train collision in early summer 1938 of this novelist, activist, autobiographer—Trudier Harris (1984, 190) adds "songwriter, lawyer, and diplomat"—cut short a remarkable career of activism, public service, and literary achievement (Zangrando 1980).

Johnson proved himself a very able organizer, and his leadership and influence did much to invigorate the N.A.A.C.P. The N.A.A.C.P.'s rapid growth in membership during the war was reflected in the establishment of new branches throughout the South. For instance, by 1920 branches had been organized in all the important Georgia cities; in fact that state boasted the second largest number of branches in the nation. For much of this success in organizing new branches Brundage (1993) credits Johnson, and specifically his tour of the South made during January 1917.

In Virginia, in 1914, students and faculty at Virginia Union University in Richmond had organized the first branch of the N.A.A.C.P. in the state, but black interest in starting branches elsewhere was limited. The turning point for the organization in Virginia came in 1917, when James Weldon Johnson spoke at mass meetings in Richmond and Norfolk. Later, he would think of his tour as not being "overwhelmingly successful," but that, at the very least, it had demonstrated that "everywhere there was a rise in the level of the Negro's morale" (quoted in Brundage 1993, 184).

After Johnson's visit, black residents of Norfolk and Richmond established N.A.A.C.P. branches in 1917. The "quickening effect" that Johnson perceived among black southerners increased during the war years, the organization attracted new members, and branches were established in many of Virginia's most important cities and towns. By the end of 1918, branches had been chartered in the smaller cities of Charlottesville, Danville, Lynchburg, Portsmouth, Roanoke, and Salem, and soon after branches opened in Alexandria, Graham, Louisa County, Martinsville, and Petersburg. Although enthusiasm seemed to wane in the immediate postwar period, black residents of Arlington, City Point, Leesburg, Newport News, and Staunton had established branches in their communities by 1921 (Brundage 1993).

As the initial enthusiasm for the N.A.A.C.P. in Virginia dissipated in the 1920s, many branches disappeared due to apathy, ineffective leadership, and white hostility. In Norfolk, for instance, after the initial excitement surrounding its founding faded, the local branch fell dormant. After several failed attempts, the branch was finally revived in 1926. In nearby Portsmouth, branch president David Harrell grew bitter over the resistance he encountered in his decade-long struggle to sustain the organization. After its founding in 1918, the Portsmouth branch had to be revived and reorganized in 1927 and then again in 1933. The same pattern of initial enthusiasm and later disintegration was visible in the Leesburg, Martinsville, Salem, and Staunton branches. Despite the struggles, the Lynchburg, Roanoke, Richmond, and Norfolk (after 1926) branches survived and would later play important roles in mobilizing and expressing black anger over racial violence in Virginia (Brundage 1993).

The establishment of N.A.A.C.P. branches in Virginia did not mark a dramatic departure from earlier traditions of black protest against mob violence. A staunch defender of law and order, the organization was circumspect, not confrontational. Its strategy was to pressure white officials into preventing and punishing mob violence, in part by providing legal representation for alleged black criminals, in part by publicizing injustices. The decline of mob violence in Virginia during the early twentieth century allowed local branches to turn their attention from lynching to other pressing problems, among them poverty, education, and other forms of racial discrimination. Soon enough, residential segregation, not lynching, became the preeminent concern of most branches of the N.A.A.C.P. in Virginia (Brundage 1993).

The New Orleans branch of the N.A.A.C.P. was founded in 1915. Outside New Orleans, the association had a tenuous existence. A branch had been organized in Shreveport as early as 1914, the first in the Deep South, but after ten years of occasional activity it lapsed into silence. "The N.A.A.C.P. is thoroughly hated in this section," the branch president, Dr. Claude Hudson, reported in 1923 (quoted in Fairclough 1999, 20). The previous year, angry newspaper editorials and threats from city officials persuaded branch officials to cancel a visit from field secretary William Pickens. An earlier attempt, in 1920, to band the branches together into a state organization came to nothing (Fairclough 1995/1999).

When Johnson visited Georgia, he met with a group of black citizens in Atlanta who were eager to become involved. This group was led by Walter White, a recent graduate of Atlanta University and a cashier with the Standard Life Insurance Company, a prominent black insurance firm, by Harry Pace, an executive of Standard Life, and by Herman Perry, the founder of the firm, who had founded an Atlanta branch of the N.A.A.C.P. in December 1916. The "quickening effect" that Johnson perceived was "especially noticeable" in Atlanta (quoted phrases in Brundage 1993, 230). It was hardly confined to that city, however. In 1916 there had been sixty-eight N.A.A.C.P. branches in northern and western cities, and only three branches in southern cities: New Orleans, Shreveport (Louisiana), and Key West (Florida). Southern membership totaled 348. In 1919, there were 310 branches, 131 of them in the South (Johnson 1933).

At the time of his visit, the all-male Atlanta branch (the only N.A.A.C.P. branch segregated by gender [Johnson 1933, 316]) was already campaigning to improve public education facilities for black children. In Atlanta and throughout the state, Johnson inspired increased activism (Brundage 1993). While in Atlanta he was struck by "a very young man who acted as secretary of the conference. ... I saw him several times and was impressed with the degree of mental and physical energy he seemed to be able to bring into play and center on the job at hand. I did not need to guess that the representative conference and the extraordinary mass meeting were largely results of his efforts. I left Atlanta having made a strong mental note about him" (Johnson 1933, 316). That man was Walter White.

Back in New York, Johnson nominated White for a position in the national office. The board hesitated, worrying about his youth, his inexperience, and his southern upbringing. Johnson pressed his case and was finally authorized to offer White the position of assistant executive secretary (Zangrando 1980; Johnson 1933). White, Johnson (1933, 316–317) reports in his autobiography, "hesitated for a while, and I could not blame him, for he had a position and a promising outlook with an insurance company; and the salary that we offered him was very small. However, in the end he wrote that he would accept the offer." At the beginning of 1918, both White and John R. Shillady, the newly elected secretary, assumed their new positions.

James Weldon Johnson traveled extensively for the association. One trip took him to Memphis, where Ell Persons had been lynched in the spring of 1917. This lynching was widely publicized, including a photograph of the victim's severed head. Below the photograph in the *Chicago Defender* for September 8, 1917, was the following explanation:

> GRIM REMINDER. Above is the head of Ell Persons, Negro, who was burned to death in Memphis, Tenn., on May 18th. His head was cut off the body and is seen here on the pavement of Beale Street, the principal

> business street of the Negro section. Both ears have been severed from the head by souvenir hunters, along with the lower lip and nose. Copies of this photograph are sold in Memphis for a quarter apiece. (quoted in Ginzburg 1962/1988, 112–113)

Johnson investigated the charges that Persons had been an "ax murderer." After ten days in Tennessee talking with journalists, the sheriff, several white and many black citizens, he found no conclusive evidence confirming Persons's guilt. His investigation persuaded black residents to establish a local chapter of the N.A.A.C.P. He returned to New York to attend a rally in Harlem organized to denounce Persons's murder (Zangrando 1980). Later, Johnson published his findings in a widely read pamphlet (Johnson 1933).

Such shocking, seemingly unintelligible brutality suggested to James Weldon Johnson that there was more to racism than "prejudice." It suggested to him that there was more to lynching than economics. "Through it all," Johnson (1933, 170) wrote in his autobiography,

> I discerned one clear and certain truth: in the core of the heart of the American race problem the sex factor is rooted, rooted so deeply that it is not always recognized when it shows at the surface. Other factors are obvious and are the ones we dare to deal with; but regardless of how we deal with these, the race situation will continue to be acute as long as the sex factor persists. ... It may be innate; I do not know. But I do know it is strong and bitter.

Now what could that "sex factor" be?

After fourteen years of service with the association, James Weldon Johnson resigned as executive secretary. He was elected to membership on the board of directors and made a vice-president. The Rosenwald Fund awarded him a fellowship which allowed him to revise *The Book of American Negro Poetry* he had published earlier and to begin work on his autobiography. He was awarded the Adam K. Spence Chair of Creative Literature at Fisk University. In the spring of 1931, a committee of his friends, headed by staff members of the association, gave him a farewell dinner at the Hotel Pennsylvania in New York. Three hundred persons attended the dinner, and, Johnson (1933, 408) reports, "I experienced the ordeal of hearing one's friends say extremely nice and generous things about one before a large company." Among the speakers were Walter White, W. E. B. Du Bois, J. E. Spingarn, Mary White Ovington, Robert W. Bagnall, Heywood Broun, M. Dantes Bellegarde, the Haitian Minister to the United States, Mary McLeod Bethune, and Carl van Doren. Arthur B. Spingarn was toastmaster; a letter of tribute from Wilbur J. Carr, First Assistant Secretary of State, was read, and Countee Cullen contributed an original poem. Before the speeches began, his brother Rosamond—with whom he collaborated on a number of songs, including what later became known as the "Negro National Anthem"—played and sang a number of their old Broadway songs (Johnson 1933).

IX. The War Ends … Another Begins

Eternal vigilance is the price of liberty.

—Ida B. Wells, echoing Thomas Jefferson, *Crusade for Justice: The Autobiography of Ida B. Wells* (1970)

Lynching did not make for southern hospitality, at least as far as African Americans were concerned. In droves they fled the eleven states of the old Confederacy. During the lynching decade—1890 to 1900—approximately 242,400 black men and women moved north. Over 216,300 moved during the period 1900 to 1910; 478,800 from 1910 to 1920; and 768,600 from 1920 to 1930. The North, as we have seen, was not exactly the promised land. First, it was cold, often very cold. Most refugees from Dixie arrived with very few personal possessions, no coats, few sweaters, few savings accounts. Many were greeted with icy hostility, especially from northern white workers who were threatened by this new source of cheap labor (Zangrando 1980).

As we have seen, on July 2, 1917, white labor in East St. Louis, Missouri, started one of the most vicious race riots in American history. This was the city which Du Bois had proposed to study as a "typical" city affected by the "great migration" and whose schools Jonathan Kozol (1991) later described so vividly in *Savage Inequalities.* Nearly 6,000 African Americans had been driven from their homes; between 150–200 had been murdered. Ida B. Wells went to investigate. In New York, thousands marched down Fifth Avenue in protest on July 28, 1917 (Lemelle 1995; Rudwick 1964). James Weldon Johnson (1933) estimated that nine or ten thousand marched; (white) newspaper accounts placed the figure considerably lower. Protestors marched in silence; the only sound was muffled drums. The procession was headed by children, some of them not older than six, all dressed in white. These were followed by women also dressed in white, followed by men dressed in dark clothes. They carried banners, some of which read:

> MOTHER, DO LYNCHERS GO TO HEAVEN?
> GIVE ME A CHANCE TO LIVE.
> TREAT US SO THAT WE MAY LOVE OUR COUNTRY.
> MR. PRESIDENT, WHY NOT MAKE AMERICA SAFE FOR DEMOCRACY?
>
> (quoted in Johnson 1933, 321)

In front of the man who carried the American flag stretched a streamer half across the street that read: YOUR HANDS ARE FULL OF BLOOD (quoted in Johnson 1933, 321).

"The streets of New York," Johnson (1933) comments, "have witnessed many strange sights, but, I judge, never one stranger than this; certainly, never one more impressive. The parade moved in silence and was watched in silence" (321). There were those who watched with tears in their eyes. Black Boy Scouts distributed to those lined along the sidewalks printed circulars which explained why black New Yorkers were marching:

> We march because by the Grace of God and the force of truth, the dangerous, hampering walls of prejudice and inhuman injustices must fall.
>
> We march because we want to make impossible a repetition of Waco, Memphis, and East St. Louis, by rousing the conscience of the country and bringing the murderers of our brothers, sisters, and innocent children to justice.
>
> We march because we deem it a crime to be silent in the face of such barbaric acts.
>
> We march because we are thoroughly opposed to Jim-Crow Cars, Segregation, Discrimination, Disfranchisement, LYNCHING, and the host of evils that are forced on us. It is time that the Spirit of Christ should be manifested in the making and execution of laws.
>
> We march because we want our children to live in a better land and enjoy fairer conditions than have fallen to our lot.
>
> (quoted in Johnson 1933, 321)

Something of the power and majesty that characterized the parade made it into the press accounts. The July 29th edition of the *New York World* reported:

> NEW YORK NEGROES STAGE SILENT PARADE OF PROTEST. Leaders among the negroes of New York City decided that a silent parade would be the most dramatic and effective way to make felt the protest of their race against injustice and inhumanity growing out of lynch law. And this silent parade was staged with real impressiveness and dignity and with an indefinable appeal to the heart in Fifth Avenue yesterday afternoon. From the time that the 3,500 or 4,000 men, women and children marchers left Fifty-sixth Street shortly after 1 o'clock until they were completing their dispersal in Twenty-fourth Street about 3 no note of discord was struck. ... Of the many printed signs prepared by the marchers, [Police] Inspector Morris doubted the good taste of only one. It showed a colored mother crouching protectively over two cowering children with the caption, "East St. Louis." And then it showed a photograph of President Wilson and his assertion that the world must be made safe for democracy. (quoted in Ginzburg 1962/1988, 104)

That last comment leaves one wondering: how can matters of "taste" be relevant when thousands of black citizens were driven from their homes by frenzied racist white men?

The association achieved some success in changing white opinion, at least enough to alter the matter of the long-standing presidential resistance to speaking out against lynching and mob violence. Presidential statements, however, came neither quickly nor easily. For instance, Woodrow Wilson (in the words of one observer) remained "inexcusably slow" (quoted in Zangrando 1980, 40) in using his authority against lynching. Wilson worried that an intense debate over race in America would jeopardize his political support among southern leaders. He was also concerned such a debate would endanger the nation's wartime unity. And his southern upbringing had left him imprinted with a southern hostility toward African Americans (Friedman 1970). On July 26, 1918, Wilson did finally issue his much-anticipated, much-quoted denunciation of those who participate in mob action. Even so, the respected *Survey* magazine, in an editorial entitled "Democracy Versus Demo-n-Cracy," judged the message ineffective, as Wilson had failed to deal specifically with lynching (Zangrando 1980).

Like Ida B. Wells, the leaders of the N.A.A.C.P. combated lynching by questioning the myths southern whites used to rationalize the practice—in particular the rape myth. In April 1919, the N.A.A.C.P. had published—under Shillady's supervision—*Thirty Years of Lynching in the United States, 1889–1918.* Recall that one important point made in the report was that the rape myth was precisely that. Fewer than 20 percent of the more than 2,500 black people lynched during that thirty-year period had been accused, let alone tried and convicted, of rape. Along with the annual supplements that the N.A.A.C.P. published, *Thirty Years of Lynching* helped puncture the fantasy that lynching had anything to do with the protection of southern white women (Zangrando 1980).

When World War I began in 1914, upwards of nearly a million European immigrants were coming to America each year. When the U.S. entered the war in 1917, Charles S. Johnson (of Fisk University, formerly the editor of *Opportunity: A Journal of Negro Life*) put the matter this way: "the cities of the North, stern, impersonal and enchanting, needed men of brawny muscles, which Europe, suddenly flaming with war, had ceased to supply, [then] the black hordes came on from the South like a silent, encroaching shadow" (quoted in White 1929, 189). Nearly a million and a half African Americans moved northward between 1916 and 1928. At first, Walter White reports, the migration north was greeted "with joy" in the South. He reports that more than a few southerners said: "Now that we're getting rid of the niggers we'll have nothing but peace." Soon enough white southerners felt a not so peaceful, joyous feeling when they discovered that a maid or a cook could not be hired "with the old ease and at the old wages." Surprise gave way to consternation when "vast areas, especially after a lynching, were depopulated overnight" (quoted in White 1929, 190).

In 1918 the Great War ended. Restrictive immigration legislation further limited the flow of European migrants and opportunities for African-American migrants continued in the North (Tolnay and Beck 1995). Due partly to their experience of the war and its aftermath, black men and women adopted a less accommodationist view, a transformation of black political attitudes also enabled by the mass migration to the North and Midwest. These demographic shifts had not only depopulated the South but had also established important black constituencies for political action. Chicago was one such important center; the following editorial in the black *Chicago Defender* for February 12, 1916, illustrates the coming new mood in its demand:

> HOW MUCH LONGER? In four weeks the intelligent and cultured citizens of the commonwealth of Georgia have lynched sixteen colored people, which is a record. ... As ghastly as are the horrors of the European

war, man's inhumanity to man is not confined to our brethren across the sea. We have this same hideous story every year. Are we ever going to do anything about it? (quoted in Ginzburg 1962/1988, 101–102)

Perhaps it is no surprise, then, that an attempt to enact federal law against lynching was made in April 1918. In that month both Leonidas Dyer (R-Missouri) and Merrill Moores (R-Indiana) introduced an antilynching bill. Dyer's (H.R. 11279) became the prototype for subsequent N.A.A.C.P.-sponsored legislation. These bills failed, as we shall see, but the N.A.A.C.P.'s intensive lobbying drive from 1919 to 1923 was a portent of more aggressive civil rights activism in the future (Zangrando 1980; Van Deburg 1997).

Despite the aggressiveness of the N.A.A.C.P.'s efforts, its visibility, particularly within African-American communities, was not as great as it is today. While thousands joined the association's interracial coalition to fight lynching and secure basic civil rights protections for African Americans, millions endorsed Marcus Garvey's black-nationalist, back-to-Africa movement: the Universal Negro Improvement Association, founded in Jamaica in 1914. Based in Harlem after 1916, Garvey pointed out that lynching and racial discrimination occurred only in nations where African peoples did not control their own governments (Zangrando 1980).

Meanwhile, a heightened self-consciousness among intellectuals of the worldwide black community inspired Du Bois to organize the first of several postwar Pan-African Congresses. Fifty-seven delegates from sixteen nations had attended the Paris meeting in February 1919. Recalling Du Bois's and Ida B. Wells's campaigns of the mid-1890s, William Monroe Trotter traveled to Paris in May 1919 to register international protests against lynching as well as other forms of racial violence. That same month a Du Bois (1919) editorial in the *Crisis* expressed the new tone. African-American soldiers had fought for the United States in World War I, he pointed out, but when these men returned "home" they still faced lynching, job discrimination, unequal educational opportunities, disfranchisement, and general insult. Things, he warned, must change: "But by the God of Heaven, we are cowards and jackasses if now that that war is over, we do not marshal every ounce of our brain and brawn to fight the sterner, longer, more unbending battle against the forces of hell in our own land." He concluded:

> We return.
> We return from fighting.
> We return fighting.
> Make way for Democracy!
> We saved it in France,
> and by the Great Jehovah,
> we will save it in the United States of America,
> or know the reason why.
>
> (13–14; quoted in Zangrando 1980, 53–54)

The editorial proved upsetting, especially to southerners and to many in Congress. Might not blacks return to prewar Jim Crow patterns of racial subservience? Recall that the Bolshevik Revolution had established the Soviet Union in Russia in 1917, and in 1919 the first wave of communism-phobia swept across the U.S. This "Red Scare" was used by the right wing to suspend the civil rights of political opponents in the name of national security (Zangrando 1980). The right wing, primarily through the Republican Party, would again use fear of communism to suspend Americans' civil rights during the early 1950s when Senator Joseph McCarthy (R-Wisconsin) conducted his own Senate-based witch-hunt. It would occur again a decade later when F.B.I. Director J. Edgar Hoover used the agency to undermine the civil rights and anti–Vietnam War movements (Churchill and Wall 1988).

In this first Red Scare in 1919, postal authorities were directed to withhold the May edition of the *Crisis* from the mails for seven days. In earlier *Crisis* articles discussing the treatment of black soldiers in France, Du Bois had attacked the Wilson administration. Recall that the Justice Department had warned the N.A.A.C.P. the year before concerning the "tone" of some of its articles. Mary White Ovington had given strict orders that Du Bois must submit his editorials to the *Crisis* committee before publishing them. Despite these precautions, Du Bois's attacks on the Wilson administration continued. Finally, the Post Office Department was directed to hold up the May 1919 issue of the *Crisis*. No reason was given (Kellogg 1967, 286).

The May issue inflamed conservative Democrats. In addition to the poem, the issue reproduced official documents showing prejudice and discrimination in the army, including attempts to influence French attitudes and behavior toward African-American troops. The League of Nations, wrote Du Bois, was absolutely necessary to the salvation of black peoples everywhere. Only an international organization could intervene in racist nations such as the United States and South Africa. Unless such an agency is established, he warned, "we are doomed eventually to *fight* for our rights." Only such an organization could counteract the barbarism of the white ruling classes in the American South. Peace for the Negro was not only peace in Europe, but prevention of a Great War of Races, which Du Bois argued was absolutely inevitable unless "the selfish nations of white civilization are curbed by a Great World Congress in which black and white and yellow sit and speak and act" (quoted in Kellogg 1967, 286–287).

Given postwar hysteria, specifically the fear of communism in America, it was perhaps unsurprising that Du Bois's words, hardly outrageous by today's standards, provoked many whites, including, for instance, Representative James F. Byrnes of South Carolina. Byrnes claimed that the black press, not white mobs, was responsible for the wave of race riots that swept the nation in the summer of 1919. Du Bois was undaunted; in the October *Crisis,* Du Bois replied that it was Byrnes and white men like him, white men who had supported and sometimes participated in fifty years of lynching and had enforced ignorance on three million American citizens and disfranchised half that number, who were primarily responsible for the riots (Kellogg 1967).

The Post Office's delaying of delivery of the *Crisis* verged on censorship, but that was hardly the only form of political repression in the land. Once again, white men hunted down and mutilated black men. There had been sixty lynchings in 1918 and seventy-six in 1919. There were twenty-five race riots. In late September, a mob of several thousand whites, among whom were numerous returning servicemen in uniform, burned a black man to death across the street from the federal courthouse in Omaha. The mob very nearly lynched Mayor Edward Smith when he refused to assist them. Desperate, municipal and state authorities requested and received army troops to restore order (Zangrando 1980), but not before the prisoner had been lynched. Twenty-four hours later Mayor Smith died from injuries sustained while fighting the mob (Ginzburg 1962/1988).

Predictably, the situation was even worse in the South. One army veteran was lynched for refusing to take off his uniform, a decision that was evidently financial as well as patriotic. The *Chicago Defender* for April 5, 1919, carried the story:

> NEGRO VETERAN LYNCHED FOR REFUSING TO DOFF UNIFORM. Blakely, Ga., Apr. 4—When Private William Little, a Negro soldier returning from the war, arrived at the railroad station here several weeks ago, he was encountered by a band of whites. The whites ordered him to doff his Army uniform and walk home in his underwear. Several other whites prevailed upon the hoodlums to leave Little alone and he was permitted to walk home unmolested. Little continued to wear his uniform over the next few weeks, as he had no other clothing. Anonymous notes were sent him warning him not to wear his Army uniform "too long" and advising him to leave town if he wished to "sport around in khaki." Little ignored the notes. Yesterday, Private Little was found dead on the outskirts of this city, apparently beaten by a mob. He was wearing his Army uniform. (quoted in Ginzburg 1962/1988, 118)

The annual N.A.A.C.P. conference was held in Cleveland in 1919, and delegates were in no mood to pander to right-wing paranoia. To make sure that the Wilson administration and the American public understood the seriousness of their commitment to equal rights, delegates prefaced their resolutions with a warning that Bolshevism ought not be rejected out of hand, that in fact it offered an attractive political program to disenchanted African Americans. The inference was unmistakable that the two major parties could only counter this threat by demanding full citizenship and integration of African Americans (Kellogg 1967).

When Attorney General A. Mitchell Palmer's report on radical propaganda in the United States was released in November 1919, James Weldon Johnson, on behalf of the N.A.A.C.P., immediately took exception to the section entitled "Radicalism and Sedition Among Negroes as Reflected in Their Publications." Specifically, he demanded proof for the allegation that there was "a well-concerted movement" among certain black intellectual leaders to set themselves up as "a determined and persistent source of radical opposition to the

Government, and to the established rule of law and order" (quoted in Kellogg 1967, 288–289).

Following release of the attorney general's report were two bills introduced into Congress early in 1920, the Sterling Bill (S. 3317) and the Graham Bill (H.R. 11430). These legislative proposals denied postal privileges to all books, magazines, newspapers and communications of any kind which could conceivably contribute to the heightening of racial tensions. N.A.A.C.P. officials correctly interpreted these bills as efforts to restrict and possibly suppress the *Crisis* and other black publications. If these bills passed Congress, any protest against lynching and mob violence generally could be interpreted by the southern-dominated Wilson administration as appealing to racial prejudice and inciting to riot. Consequently, the N.A.A.C.P. and the black press waged war against the passage of these bills, a war they won (Kellogg 1967).

At the state level things were different. Mississippi passed legislation forbidding the sale of any publication "tending to disturb relations between the races," resulting in the arrest of a *Crisis* agent in April 1920. Not merely arrested, the agent was badly beaten, heavily fined, and sentenced to six months' imprisonment for simply selling the magazine. The lawyer retained by the black community to defend the agent was threatened by mob violence. When the N.A.A.C.P. wired Governor Lee M. Russell asking protection for the attorney, the lieutenant governor answered that, should the *Crisis* editors visit Mississippi, "we would make an example of them that would be a lasting benefit to the colored people of the South and would not soon be forgotten" (quoted in Kellogg 1967, 290). The N.A.A.C.P. repeated its request for protection to the governor, who replied that he shared the sentiments of his lieutenant governor (Kellogg 1967).

The North was hardly free of the postwar Red Scare. In the report of the so-called Lusk Committee, New York State, presumably worried over the role African Americans might play in revolutionary radicalism, listed several *Crisis* editorials as dangerous and attributed the N.A.A.C.P.'s "decidedly radical stand" (quoted in Kellogg 1967, 290) to certain board members who were sympathetic to socialism, namely, John Haynes Holmes, Archibald Grimké and Mary White Ovington. It was this report that provoked Joseph C. Manning, editor of the *Southern American* and formerly a member of the Alabama Legislature, to publish a vitriolic attack on the N.A.A.C.P. Such attacks combined with legislative efforts to silence the black press, not to mention increased racial violence, led to heightened interest in both the *Crisis* and the N.A.A.C.P. At no time since has the *Crisis* enjoyed as many readers as it did during the frightening opening of the 1920s (Kellogg 1967).

The year 1919 was important to the association not only due to attacks from outside the organization. The year also marked a turning point in its internal history. By this time a number of the "old guard" had departed the organization due to death or retirement. Their departure marked the end of the abolitionist tradition within the association. No longer would the N.A.A.C.P. be referred to as the "new abolition movement." This meant the beginning of the end of white leadership and control of the N.A.A.C.P. From the beginning the association had sought African Americans to serve on local and national levels. Since 1915 suggestions had been surfacing that it was now time for an African American to become the executive head of the organization. By 1919, the local branches no longer operated under the scrutiny of advisory committees, committees which had been populated, by and large, by white liberals. Fewer whites were asking to serve as officers and members of the local branches. By 1919 only on the national board did white leadership still predominate, but white influence was on the wane as more and more of the actual direction of the association's affairs was assumed by the secretary and the executive committee, composed primarily of African Americans. In 1920, James Weldon Johnson became the first black secretary, succeeding John R. Shillady, who had effectively organized the national office but whose nearly fatal beating in Austin, Texas, had left him no longer able and willing to participate (Kellogg 1967).

The year 1919 also saw an expanded thematic emphasis at its annual convention. Still under Shillady's leadership, for the first time the N.A.A.C.P. concerned itself with the problem of black workers and the organized labor movement. Partly this was acknowledgment of the increased visibility of "class" due to the Bolshevik revolution in Russia and to the "Red Scare" in the United States. But partly this was acknowledgment of the association's enlarged membership. The number of members had increased dramatically in 1918; afterward most of the support of the association no longer came from a few wealthy (often white) members and friends, but from the (black) membership at large. Income reached a peak in 1919, but the Great Depression a decade later would be felt severely by African Americans and N.A.A.C.P. income would fall precipitously (Kellogg 1967).

Finally, 1919 was noteworthy because for the first time membership in the South outnumbered that in the North. The conference in Cleveland disclosed a heightened militancy among delegates, and an end of the former domination of the association by philanthropically minded whites. In Cleveland blacks dominated discussions regarding what should be done for African Americans. Black delegates had begun to take the association into their own hands. Although the N.A.A.C.P. had from its inception been considered by many whites militant and radical, after 1919 the organization had an even more clearly defined public identity. The N.A.A.C.P. stood for militancy but biracialism too, in contrast to what was perceived as the extremism and racial separatism of Marcus Garvey's Universal Negro Improvement Association, with its racial chauvinism and Back-to-Africa movement. Militant but committed to working within the judicial system, the N.A.A.C.P. continued to rely upon legal measures to achieve its aims. Only through law, N.A.A.C.P. officials believed, could one "fix beyond question the status of the American citizen of Negro descent" (quoted in Kellogg 1967, 293). Key to the association's efforts, then, was an ongoing struggle to secure the repeal and to prevent passage of discriminatory legislation on local, state, and national levels and to promote and pass new civil rights legislation (Kellogg 1967).

The end of the association's first decade also saw its participation in international affairs. The N.A.A.C.P.-sponsored Pan-African Congress held at Paris in 1919 and the Pan-African theme at the 1919 annual convention were protests directed to both international and national levels against continued imperialism and exploitation of blacks in Africa. They proclaimed that the association was concerned with the fate of blacks everywhere, if most especially in the United States. During the war African Americans' attention had been drawn to the American occupation of the black republic of Haiti. In 1920 an N.A.A.C.P. investigation of the American occupation marked the beginning of prolonged agitation for the restoration of Haitian independence, which was finally achieved in 1934. N.A.A.C.P. intervention in Haiti's fate marked a transition from strictly domestic protest to effective international action (Kellogg 1967).

With its powerful southern segregationist wing, the Democratic Party was not exactly out in front on racial issues in 1919. The grandchildren and great-grandchildren of this reactionary segment later switched parties; today they form the southern political base of the Republican Party. These southern whites remain an influential force against racial and gender progress, including gay/lesbian civil rights. Those leaders of the Southern Baptist Convention who called for a boycott of the Disney Corporation to protest that company's extension of family benefits to its gay employees and later demanded that women "graciously submit" to their husbands are in spirit, if not in genealogy, the descendants of those same segregationists and white supremacists who lynched black men in the 1920s. Then as now, they quote scripture to justify their hatreds.

In the 1920s the party of Lincoln was difficult to distinguish from the Democrats on racial matters. Despite this fact, the N.A.A.C.P. sent James Weldon Johnson to the 1920 Republican National Convention, where he conferred with party chairman Will Hays, Senator James Watson of Indiana who chaired the Resolutions Committee, and Harry Daughtery, Warren Harding's campaign manager and the future attorney general. Johnson and other black advocates were given just twenty minutes before the Resolutions Committee. Johnson used the opportunity to stress the need for a plank against lynching (Zangrando 1980). Johnson achieved some success; the GOP platform did "urge Congress to consider the most effective means to end lynching." He came away, however, with the feeling that "the Republican Party desires, more and more, to get rid of the Negro" (quoted in Zangrando 1980, 56).

Johnson was not finished lobbying the Republicans. On August 9, he and Harry E. Davis, a Cleveland resident and member of the N.A.A.C.P. board of directors, visited candidate Warren G. Harding at his home in Marion, Ohio. They asked Harding to make several preelection statements on racial issues, including voting rights, the problem of segregation in federal departments, passage of a federal antilynching law, an investigation into the American occupation of Haiti, federal aid to education, equal opportunity in the armed services, and Jim Crow restrictions in interstate travel. Harding expressed concern over each but declined to make a campaign issue of any, except Wilson's decision to occupy Haiti, and specifically charges that American marines had killed, without provocation, three thousand Haitians. Only that issue might embarrass the Democratic administration in the national election (Zangrando 1980). Johnson reported later that "Mr. Harding's handsome face was a study while I talked with him. Despite his occasional grave and cautious protestations, I could see that he looked upon the Haitian matter as a gift right off the Christmas tree. He could not conceal his delight" (Johnson 1933, 359).

After the meeting, Johnson investigated the Haitian occupation further, writing four articles that were published in the *Nation*, articles for several other publications, and a lecture on "Self-Determining Haiti" (Johnson 1933). His estimate of the number of Haitians murdered was soon confirmed by the U.S. military. In a published report the number of "indiscriminate killings of Haitians" was calculated to be 3,250, the number of Haitians wounded "impossible to estimate" (quoted in Johnson 1933, 359 n. 1). Harding and G.O.P. strategists used the facts Johnson uncovered to good advantage in the party's successful campaign. Indeed, the scandal "struck Washington like a bombshell" (Johnson 1933, 359). Later, the new president thanked Johnson for his help (Zangrando 1980). But Johnson's labor was not remunerated, financially or politically.

On January 15, 1921, Johnson returned to Marion to discuss a governmental inquiry into conditions facing African Americans, including federal appointments, voting rights, the Ku Klux Klan, and lynching. Harding was cordial but, predictably, even less willing to promise action than he had been the summer before his election. The president-elect, Johnson said later, while an "average, decent American citizen," was really "a man of very little imagination and seemingly of very little human sympathy." He met with Harding once more, on April 4. Johnson asked: would the president in his first message to Congress ask for the passage of federal antilynching legislation? Harding declined to do that, but he did tell Congress that we "ought to wipe the stain of barbaric lynching from the banners of a free and orderly representative democracy." The *New York Times* reported that the president's remarks on the subject drew "applause and then silence" from House and Senate members (quoted in Zangrando 1980, 57). Was the applause automatic and the silence an expression of disapproval following the listeners' awareness of what he had said? Subsequent events would suggest so.

The spread of lynching and mob violence mobilized African Americans across a broad political spectrum. When Jake Brooks was lynched in Oklahoma in 1922, editor Roscoe G. Dungee of the Oklahoma City *Black Dispatch* sent reports to President Harding and to Representative Dyer for distribution to members of Congress. Early that summer, on June 14, the black community in Washington demonstrated its concern. Headed by Shelby J. Davidson of the N.A.A.C.P., some five thousand black people picketed the White House and the Capitol. STOP LYNCHING NOW and PASS THE DYER BILL were the signs and sentiments of the day (Zangrando 1980).

The black nationalists of Marcus Garvey's Universal Negro Improvement Association flirted with the idea of supporting federal legislation against lynching. In early summer 1919, Garvey's weekly *Negro World* had dismissed the N.A.A.C.P.'s antilynching drive as fundamentally mistaken. The proper response to the threat of lynching was not fund-raising, the paper declared; it was self-defense. Despite his differences with the N.A.A.C.P., lynching was too important an issue for Garvey to ignore. Early in 1922 he wired Congress his support of the Dyer bill. When it was passed by the House by a vote of 230 to 119, he took some credit for its success (Zangrando 1980).

Especially during the nineteenth and early twentieth centuries, the law was not just another occupation; it was a distinctively gendered one. That gender was masculine. Embedded in American legal consciousness, Michael Grossberg (1990) argues, has been the notion that the bar is a masculine domain. That is less so today, but for much of the history of the American bar "masculinity was so fundamental to the profession's consciousness that ... it acted as an unarticulated first principle" (Grossberg 1990, 134). By examining what Grossberg terms the "institutionalization of masculinity in the bar" (134), we can glimpse links between the public and private sides of men's lives in nineteenth-century America, gendered sides that became visible in the congressional struggles over antilynching legislation.

After the Revolutionary War, Grossberg tells us, lawyers occupied a powerful position in the new nation, suggested in part by their rapidly increasing numbers. Those practicing law in the new nation increased almost four times as fast as the population. The United States became "the most lawyer-ridden nation" (Grossberg 1990, 134) in the West. As the number of men practicing the profession increased, so did the sense that the lawyer's job was a masculine one. As a masculinist and homosocial community, the bar influenced in gendered ways how lawyers performed institutional roles and formulated public policies (Grossberg 1990).

The profession's distinctive institutionalization of masculinity took shape in the opening decades of the nineteenth century. Grossberg points to a gradual disjunction between law and letters that illustrates how masculinity helped shape the bar's professional consciousness. In colonial America, the law had been a sideline for merchants, farmers, and planters. At the time lawyers were assumed to be men of letters broadly educated and conversant in all branches of knowledge. As practitioners of an ancient and learned profession, these men were assumed to be wordsmiths, skilled at composing not only legal briefs, but philosophical essays, political satire, even fiction. During the revolutionary era, though, this marriage between law and letters began to dissolve as lawyers took up new professional roles. As the full-time professional replaced the part-time amateur, literary pursuits (specifically novels and poetry) were no longer perceived as appropriate lawyerly avocations (Grossberg 1990). Conflicting conceptions of the profession, summarized in phrases such as "visionary versus practical" and "passion versus utility" (quoted in Grossberg 1990, 135), seemed to require lawyers to choose. Either lawyers were men of letters or they were men of action.

The pressure to choose grew as lawyers increasingly defined their vocation as a masculine, public profession. Henry Wadsworth Longfellow experienced this pressure in 1825. Unhappy over being forced to study law in his father's office, he asked Theophilus Parsons, Jr., editor of the *United States Literary Gazette*, for a job with the journal. Longfellow communicated to Parsons his interest in leaving the law in order to write poetry. Parsons replied with a candor that underlines the profession's intensifying masculinization: "There is a stage in the progress of a bright mind, when the boy has thrown away his toys and marbles, but the young man is still so far a child as to value things more by their elegance and power of amusing than by their usefulness. He plays with his books and thinks he is working when he is only playing hard. ... Get through your present delusion as soon as you can; and then you will see how wise it will be for you to devote yourself to the law" (Grossberg 1990, 135–136). Though such advice did not dissuade Longfellow or lawyers like Washington Irving, Richard Dana, or Herman Melville, such antiliterary prejudice did persuade men like John Quincy Adams, Daniel Webster, and probably many other young men away from "frivolous" life of letters and to the more "manly" professions of law and politics (Grossberg 1990).

This growing professional aversion to a life of letters expressed a new and gendered sense of the successful lawyer as "a man of action and cunning, not a scholar" (Grossberg 1990, 137). It replaced a colonial and early postrevolutionary notion of lawyers as educated gentlemen who were engaged with ideas as well as commerce. The emerging ideal of the lawyer as a man uniquely capable of solving the practical problems of the contentious society had been present from the beginning, and it would become explicit as the nineteenth-century bar's affinity for politics intensified (Grossberg 1990).

Especially in the South lawyers comprised a significant percentage of state legislators and won great wealth and respect through their profession. Even a man like Andrew Jackson, who turned so eagerly to violence when "honor" was invoked, spent much of his life as a lawyer. Jurors tended to be feminized in that they were acted upon rather than being the agents of action. Jurors were characterized as "gullible, ignorant men, who, if not susceptible to bribes, were easily swayed by subtle misrepresentation, sensationalism, and demagoguery." Moreover, "Public opinion, stirred to excitement by gossip and newspapers, was quick to condemn the innocent or to justify the guilty without adequate evidence" (quoted in Ayers 1984, 33). During the antebellum era American fiction portrayed all American justice as ineffectual (Ayers 1984).

Increasingly a man's admission to the bar and professional success afterward depended on his conformity with dominant masculine values. These values are suggested in the obituaries of antebellum lawyers, who tended to be characterized as "fearless," "manly," and "independent" (quoted in Grossberg 1990, 138). These qualities represented a lawyerly version of what Grossberg (1990, 138) terms "responsible manhood." It was a time of unprecedented opportunity for American men, and unprecedented failure, captured most repeatedly in the image of drunken husbands guzzling family wages in dimly lit barrooms. Lawyers themselves aggressively promoted the image of the lawyer carefully reasoning his way—"our" way—through complex and momentous problems, soberly addressing complexities of political life, courageously defending the victimized in court, and acting as an independent crusader for moral right in society (Grossberg 1990). Many, perhaps most, men believed their own fantasies. Moses B. Butterfield did. In 1852, in a letter to his wife, he "describes" the "manly" qualities of the young men practicing law in Racine, Wisconsin, in a letter to his wife: "The bar of Wisconsin are fine looking men, as fine as I ever saw anywhere—but one or two ordinary looking men. But as a general thing, I should say not too much given to hard study. Some appear to have spent much time in study but most appear to enjoy sport and pleasure and are apt to try and live by their wits" (quoted in Grossberg 1990, 137).

In such a homosocial and, it would seem, homoerotic sphere, splits between desire and friendship, indeed masculine and feminine, were inevitable. Law and literature became split, underscoring a growing masculinization of the bar. Public and private patriarchy became split; the judiciary became public patriarchs, the law converting, as lawyers Abraham Lincoln and Joseph Story put it, into the nation's civil religion. In this secular religion judges were becoming the republic's priestly class; unsurprisingly, perhaps, the public image of the judge became intertwined with the "mystique of the robe" (Grossberg 1990, 140). Men may have been in skirts, but the script was explicitly masculine: "If the courtroom can be termed a theater—as it surely was in nineteenth-century America—then the judges performed in a series of one-act plays, donning different persona for each performance, with each pose a version of responsible manhood" (Grossberg 1990, 142).

As the nineteenth century drew to a close, the most destabilizing change was the rise of the corporate lawyer and corporate law firm. The corporate lawyer indicated the dramatic and continuing shift in the attorney's role from advocate to counselor. For many lawyers, this new role provoked fears of lost professional autonomy: the independent man turned hired hand. Debates raged within the bar over the meaning of professionalism, often phrased in terms of manliness. Would the bar cease to be a profession and become a business; would lawyers stop being "men" (Grossberg 1990)?

One site of this struggle for the "manhood" of the profession was curricular and pedagogical, that is, the case method of teaching law. Replacing the lecture method, the case method was, presumably, more masculine. Its "virility," as Harvard law professor James Barr Ames phrased it, contrasted favorably with the old law-school dependence upon lecturing, which had failed as "a virile system," for it regarded the student "not as a man, but as a school boy reciting his lines" (quoted in Grossberg 1990, 144). In the era of lynching and besieged white manhood, even the classroom became a battlefield, especially formative for those seeking to practice law. Increasingly, the law school came to dominate legal education (Grossberg 1990).

Many resisted this institutionalization of reading for the bar. "What our profession needs," one Iowa lawyer declared, "is moral stamina, sterling integrity, and recognized noble manhood" (quoted in Grossberg 1990, 144). What he meant was old-time lawyering, legal education, and manhood, conflated elements in his mind and in the minds of many. Proponents of the new professional standards responded to such defenses of traditionalism by appealing to the racism of many practitioners, combining anti-immigrant hysteria with industrial-era formulas for competence. The influx of southern and eastern European immigrants during the 1890s threatened elite "Anglo-Saxon" standards. Writing in his diary in 1874, patrician attorney George Templeton Strong praised Columbia Law School's decision to employ admission tests. The requirement of a college diploma, or an examination including Latin, he thought would "keep out the little scrubs (German jew boys mostly) whom the School now promotes from the grocery-counters ... to be 'gentlemen of the Bar'" (quoted in Grossberg 1990, 145). Such anti-Semitism mixed freely with the racism of the time, embedded in a "crisis" of white masculinity.

A feminist challenge to the bar intensified the profession's gender crisis. In the last decades of the century a few women demanded a place in the masculine and homosocial community of lawyers. Barred from the profession by custom and statute, these women were forced to mount campaigns in order to receive a legal education. They lobbied legislators and filed suits, on occasion with success. "Their challenge," Grossberg (1990, 145) tells us, "stirred a particularly telling mixture of resistance and support that adds another perspective on the role of masculinity in defining the nineteenth-century legal community."

The general reaction of practicing male lawyers to the prospect of female colleagues appears to have been one of disbelief, punctuated at times with "horror and disgust." Many male legislators, judges, and lawyers echoed the views of a California lawmaker who spoke against a bill that would end gender bias in the legal profession: "The sphere of women is infinitely more important than that of men, and that sphere is the home" (quoted in Grossberg 1990, 145). It was as if women failed to understand the nature of things. That is the only explanation for Wisconsin Chief Justice Edward Ryan's conduct. When he denied R. Lavinia Goodell the right to practice law, he felt compelled to remind her of the proper gender roles. "[N]ature has tempered women as little for the juridical conflicts of the courtroom," he explained, "as for the physical conflicts of the battlefield." Ryan was sure that the use of masculine pronouns in statutes regulating the bar communicated a legislative intent to limit the bar to men (Grossberg 1990).

In fact, the chief justice rejected the very possibility of reading "persons" in a gender-free fashion: "If we should follow that authority in ignoring the distinction of sex, we do not perceive why it should not emasculate the constitution itself and include females in the constitutional right of male suffrage and male qualification. Such a rule would be one of judicial revolution, not of judicial construction" (quoted in Grossberg 1990, 146). Judges like Ryan reproduced dominant gender roles, such as the ideology of "separate spheres," by restating them jurisprudentially. The legal statutes they interpreted were presumably indeterminate and flexible, but their interpretations were hardly declarations of fixed rules. They were expressions of the bar's fantasies of responsible manhood (Grossberg 1990).

In 1880 there were exactly 75 female lawyers; thirty years later, despite the proliferation of women's colleges and the woman's rights movement, there were only 1,341. Some states still forbade women to practice law; scores of the leading law schools excluded them from studying it (Filene 1998). Slowly women were admitted to the bar. Their presence resulted in the creation of a female sphere in the law as part of the profession's new hierarchy, but it did not change its gender prejudices. Within that separate sphere women created alternative professional institutions, among them the Woman's International Bar Association, founded in 1888, the Equite Club, a correspondence club of women lawyers also founded in the 1880s, and the *Women Lawyers Journal*, established in 1911 (Grossberg 1990).

For women, as for "ethnic" and black men, prejudice plus legal specialization resulted in professional segregation. While male Jewish lawyers found themselves restricted to criminal work and personal-injury cases, women found themselves kept out of the courtroom, restricted to processing paperwork, working in secretarial pools, and doing research at libraries (Grossberg 1990). Yet the presence of women in the legal community, like that of "ethnics," blacks, and lower-class whites, provoked professional battles and debates that would eventually change the American legal profession. But not immediately: when a woman challenged her exclusion from Hastings College of Law by pointing out that an Asian student had been accepted, the lawyer representing the California school retorted that "the Chinaman" had been thrown out too (quoted in Grossberg 1990, 149).

Not all professions were closed to women, of course. Teaching was increasingly feminized, while remaining "pedagogy for patriarchy" (Grumet 1988; Tyack and Hansot 1990). Medicine too provides a gendered contrast to the bar. The barriers to a medical career, though several, were less impassable than those blocking women's entry to the bar. In this regard Barbara Harris (1978) notes: "Female doctors could claim that their careers were natural extensions of women's nurturant, healing role in the home and that they protected feminine modesty by ministering to members of their own sex. By contrast, women lawyers were clearly intruding on the public domain explicitly reserved for men" (110; quoted in Grossberg 1990, 149).

Clarence Darrow—memorable for us not only for the Scopes curriculum trial but for the Scottsboro case (see chapters 1 and 12) articulated the consequences of what segregating women lawyers to the fringe of the profession might mean. In an early twentieth-century speech to Chicago women lawyers, Darrow reminded his listeners what most of his male colleagues believed: "You can't be shining lights at the bar because you are too kind. You can never be corporate lawyers because you are not cold-blooded. You have not a high grade of intellect." Wondering whether women could ever command the fees male attorneys demanded, Darrow questioned whether women could "ever make a living" at the law. He did think women could become successful divorce lawyers. Then Darrow thought of "another field you can have solely for your own. You can't make a living at it, but it's worthwhile and you'll have no competition. This is the free defense of criminals" (quoted in Grossberg 1990, 149). "Real work, commercial practice," Grossberg tells us, "remained adversarial and thus a male responsibility." In such professional segregation, "[m]asculinity found new forms of professional definition" (Grossberg 1990, 150).

The nineteenth-century bar had been strictly a man's profession. Manhood, and later masculinity, was profoundly embedded in lawyers' professional consciousness and community membership. Patriarchal values helped position the lawyer politically in American society and legitimated his power by making it appear natural, if not preordained. Because judges and lawyers operated in a relatively autonomous professional realm, their versions of responsible manhood became "law." As Grossberg (1990, 151) concludes, "Institutionalized masculinity had become part of American legal consciousness." In becoming so, the law, even well into the twentieth century, was a man's world, and exchanges within law enforcement and lawmaking must be understood as exchanges in a male homosocial economy. It was a man's world that was being constructed and enforced, and struggles over legal issues, in Congress over constitutionality, were also struggles among men over the nature of manhood. As we will see in the following sections, U.S. congressmen—white men, almost all of them—used legalistic issues, such as "states' rights" and "constitutionality" to wage war over the right of access to black men's bodies.

II. "[A] Very Important Prerogative Reserved for the States?"

—quoted in Claudine L. Ferrell, *Nightmare and Dream: Antilynching in Congress, 1917–1922* (1986)

The negro has many fine qualities; he is joyous, lighthearted and aisily [sic] lynched.

—quoted in Claudine L. Ferrell, *Nightmare and Dream: Antilynching in Congress, 1917–1922* (1986)

"Damn the law; we want the n[i]gger."

—quoted in Claudine L. Ferrell, *Nightmare and Dream: Antilynching in Congress, 1917–1922* (1986)

The politicians have dished out most of the racial hog slop but preacher and editor have done their full share, too.

—Lillian Smith, *Killers of the Dream* (1949/1963)

In 1961, in response to right-wing warnings that federal civil rights legislation would fail to legislate morality, Martin Luther King, Jr., asserted that "the law may not be able to make a man love me, but it can keep him from lynching me" (quoted in Ferrell 1986, 1). Forty years earlier, "the law" did not even try to keep white men from lynching black men. During 1917 and 1918, while 300,000 black soldiers served their country, a tenth of them in Europe, lynch mobs murdered over 100 African Americans at home. The contradiction between American idealism and the daily reality of lynching became intolerable for many who became more determined than ever that the federal government must be made to intervene in the "peculiar" practice (Ferrell 1986).

Along with its friends, allies, and a handful of northern congressmen, the N.A.A.C.P. refused to accept the indifference with which most Americans regarded the practice of lynching. Reformulating their earlier antilynching strategies in the face of resistant states and localities and rejecting the unspoken but widespread belief that racial justice and constitutional federalism were mutually exclusive, a coalition of African and European Americans began a thirty-year effort to persuade Congress to pass antilynching legislation. Although they never succeeded, national indifference to lynching slowly changed, as did the crime for which the antilynchers wanted federal intervention. Not until 1952 did the United States record its first lynch-free year in seventy-five years. By the 1950s lynching was no longer a national issue, but by 1950 no longer did the federal government imagine itself unable to do what the states had long refused to do, namely, try to protect black men from white (Ferrell 1986).

Southerners may have lost the argument for "states' rights" during the first half of the nineteenth century, but they succeeded during the second half, and the first half of the twentieth century as well. Northerners who were once willing to fight and die to preserve "the Union" seemed, after their victory, quite willing to concede the point, seduced by doctrines of "federalism," especially when "race" was concerned. Northern capitulation to southern arguments for "states' rights" and federalism was so complete that on occasion certain southern congressmen actually referred to an "inalienable right" to lynching. Constitutionally sanctioned "equal protection" and "due process of law" were clearly secondary to local prerogatives. They indicate that European Americans, North and South, perceived a conflict, perhaps inevitable and unsolvable, between a multicultural America and an egalitarian America. The Emancipation Proclamation was just that, and rhetoric it would remain, as reformer Archibald Grimké put it, a "national contradiction between profession and practice, promise and performance" (quoted in Ferrell 1986, 4).

In December 1921, only days before the House of Representatives turned its attention to the Dyer antilynching bill, the *Greensboro* (N.C.) *Daily News* characterized the measure as: "[a]nother invasion of State's rights by the Federal government; but the Federal Government is justified in this instance, because none of the States had made an honest effort to prevent lynchings by making examples of those who indulge in them" (quoted in Ferrell 1986, 5). The *Nashville* (Tenn.) *Banner* informed its readers that: "[t]his anti-lynching law would overthrow a very important prerogative reserved for the states, and would be a dangerous encroachment on the right of local self-government—the principle of federation, the groundwork on which the Union is built" (quoted in Ferrell 1986, 5). Odd to hear the grandchildren of Confederate soldiers speaking about "the groundwork on which the Union is built," but then that phrase was, in the context of debate over antilynching legislation, only a recoding of the white southern male desire to mutilate the black male body.

Of course, not only southerners were involved in the ruse. Perhaps some actually believed, as some do today, that we Americans actually are endangered by our federal government. Democrat Clarence Lea of California, for instance, declared that the Dyer bill was not only unconstitutional, it would convert the federal government into "a colossus with a club over the State," asserting "the superior virtue of a superman" and dictating "standards of virtue." Republican Edward C. Little of Kansas City was not seduced by the oedipalized fears of his California colleague. The Dyer bill was quite constitutional, although he did allow, dryly, that measure would deprive the states of "the alleged power ... of allowing their citizens to burn people occasionally without any interference by the Federal Government" (quoted in Ferrell 1986, 6). And so the rather concrete issue of white men mutilating black men's bodies was sublimated into a constitutional question of states' rights and the role of the federal government in local affairs. While not doubting the sincerity of some of those who participated in these debates, it is difficult to believe that these white men had a clue what they were saying.

President Wilson would help not at all. Arguing that "constitutional law … must look forward, not backward," Wilson praised both "conservative change" and "conservative progress." He suggested that courts should continue to "'make' law for their own day," but he insisted that judges and legislators should never "wilfully [sic] seek to find in the phrases of the Constitution remedies for evils which the federal government was never intended to deal with." When the federal government intervened in "moral and social questions originally left to the several States for settlement," the strangulation of state and local "vitality" occurred. As sociologist William Graham Sumner had argued in *Folkways* (1913), Wilson was convinced that legislating morality would not change "vital habits or methods of life unless sustained by local opinion and purpose" (quoted in Ferrell 1986, 70–71).

However much they relied on constitutional arguments, southerners were never content with them. Sooner or later God would have to be brought in, as when Florida Representative Frank Clark explained to Congress in 1908:

> If God Almighty had intended these two races to be equal, He would have so created them. He made the Caucasian of handsome figure, straight hair, regular features, high brow, and superior intelligence. He created the negro, giving him a black skin, kinky hair, thick lips, flat nose, low brow, low order of intelligence, and repulsive features. I do not believe that these differences were the result of either accident or mistake on the part of the Creator. I believe He knew what He was doing, and I believe He did just what He wanted to do. (quoted in Ferrell 1986, 82)

Others saw racial relations more, well, erotically. Lester Frank Ward, extolled by a few educational theorists as "the architect of environmentalism in American education" (Pinar et al. 1995, 104), was sure that something instinctive moved the black man "to seek a higher race with which to mate" (Ferrell 1986, 85). Of course, this was sociologically speaking, only. While some at the time believed interracial mating was conceivable (others argued that fertile offspring could not be produced by such unions), it was still "unnatural." After all, white men explained, "the black penis [is] too large for the white woman's uterine canal and the mulatto children produced [are] mentally superior but physically inferior to the Negro" (quoted in Ferrell 1986, 85). One must not tamper with the black body, unless of course that body be male and had entered the body of a white female. Then, as southern apologist Winfield Collins "explained" after World War I: "As the world is to be made safe for democracy, so ought the South to be made safe for white women" (quoted in Ferrell 1986, 86). To fight that war required lynching, white men insisted. Lynching was, Washington University historian Roland G. Usher explained in 1919, "nothing more nor less than the old self-help" (quoted in Ferrell 1986, 87). Lynching was not a violation of the law but its execution (Ferrell 1986).

In the wake of the East St. Louis riot, Wilson had assured black leaders that he was doing his "utmost" to protect "the interest of the colored people," but at the same time he was instructing Attorney General Thomas Watt Gregory that "we cannot under the existing law extend our jurisdiction [to the riot], as much as we should like to." Then Wilson told Missouri Congressman Dyer, to whose St. Louis district many East St. Louis blacks had fled, that, after "a great deal of thought," he felt obligated to say "in candor" that there was no constitutional authorization for federal action other than "[a]id to the state authorities in their efforts to restore tranquility and guard against further outbreak" (quoted in Ferrell 1986, 94–95). Claudine L. Ferrell (1986) informs us that Justice Department memoranda on the riot as well as precedents for employing federal troops to aid state authorities in other riot situations indicate otherwise. The federal government did have constitutional jurisdiction to protect the lives of black citizens, a fact that Wilson declined to acknowledge.

The East St. Louis riot had its roots, as we have seen, in municipal corruption, irresponsible and erroneous press reports, not to mention labor tension, but the committee appointed by the U.S. House of Representatives concluded that it had to do only with "bitter race feelings." East St. Louis whites were enraged when southern blacks took what they perceived as "their" jobs; there was the matter of increasing crime and reports of stolen elections. A corrupt police force had done little to stop the riot. In fact, many policemen "shared the lust of the mob for negro blood, and encouraged the rioters by their conduct, which was sympathetic when it was not cowardly" (quoted in Ferrell 1986, 98). The state militia had also failed to perform its duty properly (Ferrell 1986).

The war had intensified racial tensions. Having experienced something akin to respect in Europe, returning black soldiers felt bitterness and resentment at their subjugated status at home, feelings that intensified as most white southerners demonstrated to returning black soldiers "that a uniform changed nothing." In appraising the situation in early 1919, N.A.A.C.P. president Moorfield Storey, who once served as Charles Sumner's private secretary, described "a deliberate purpose … gradually taking form in the South to prevent the negroes from claiming any further consideration on account of their service in the war. The negroes will come back feeling like men, and not disposed to accept the treatment to which they have been subjected. The South will be afraid that with arms in their hands they will be a dangerous element, and the attempt will made to disarm and intimidate them" (quoted in Ferrell 1986, 99).

The black press had noticed the change too, of course. The *Chicago Defender* wondered: "With tens of thousands of our Race fighting for civilization in France under the American flag, how much longer are the American people to tolerate lynching" and render America unsafe for African Americans? The nation should, the paper continued, "[i]nsist that charity begins at home and that the Prussianism which infests the south, and to a great extent the north, first be wiped out by the men who call us to colors." Antilynching protestors had marched silently in 1917 with placards declaring that "No land that loves to lynch 'niggers' can lead the hosts of Almighty God" (quoted in Ferrell 1986, 100).

Concerned that black dissatisfaction and protest might undermine the war effort, an officer in military intelligence, Major Joel E. Spingarn, also a board member of the N.A.A.C.P., proposed to his superior officers a general program to counteract enemy propaganda. He recommended that President Wilson issue an antilynching statement, that Congress pass antilynching legislation, and that in order to initiate dialogue with cooperative black leaders, a "conference of thirty or forty colored editors, and race leaders" be convened immediately. Spingarn's idea for the June 1918 conference followed from the "constant complaints from Intelligence Officers and others ... that the colored press was spreading dissatisfaction from negroes." Addressed by Secretary of War Newton Baker, George Creel of the Committee on Public Information, Assistant Secretary of the Navy Franklin D. Roosevelt, and various French officials, the conference in Washington encouraged the black representatives to "let off steam" about racial injustice and to communicate to military and governmental officials that there was indeed "great unrest" among African Americans. "[T]he unwillingness or inability of the federal government to protect colored people against lynching seemed the paramount grievance," Spingarn concluded from the meeting (quoted in Ferrell 1986, 102–103).

Not quite a month after the conference, Secretary of War Baker again took Spingarn's advice, this time regarding a presidential statement on lynching. The secretary of war told Wilson "that there has never been so much unrest among the colored people as at the present time, and that the main source of this unrest is the prevalence of lynching." Profoundly distressed by "the numerous outrages," African Americans' low morale was "interfering in some measure with the prosecution of the war." Therefore, he recommended that Wilson tell the American people "that the military, by necessity no less than justice and humanity, demands the immediate cessation of lynching." Baker argued that "an utterance from you would have more effect ... than anything else that could be done" (quoted in Ferrell 1986, 103). Baker's appeal succeeded, for one week later, on July 26, Wilson publicly denounced mob violence. Three days after that, however, Baker rejected Spingarn's recommendation for a war-powers antilynching bill, deciding to focus on the problem of military, not both military and civilian, morale (Ferrell 1986).

A year later the war ended but concern in Washington over black unrest continued, aggravated by the Red Scare and disillusionment over the terms of peace, as well as by economic and labor disruptions. On August 15, 1919, a memorandum was directed to the director of military intelligence and forwarded to the Justice Department, written by James Cutler, "a recognized expert" (quoted in Ferrell 1986, 103) on racial violence on whose work I relied in chapter 3. A University of Michigan professor of political economy during the early 1900s, Cutler was one of the first social scientists to study lynching behavior. Among those who subscribed to the "substitution" model of social control, he believed that African Americans existed on a different moral and ethical plane than did whites. Lynchings, Cutler argued, were reserved for "unusually brutal and atrocious crimes" (quoted in Tolnay and Beck 1995, 102), but, as we have seen, that was not the case. Formal and legal executions, Cutler hoped, would satisfy that savage desire for vengeance among southern white men that was lynching (Tolnay and Beck 1995).

Almost twenty years later, Cutler now warned the army that political radicals were "daily winning new converts among negroes, particularly among the young and more irresponsible element." He worried that N.A.A.C.P.

"propaganda" in favor of racial equality and advocating the use of force when "necessary" was "bearing abundant fruit" among the "new negro." Those black citizens who had been "led to expect a modification, or possibly removal, of some of the discrimination" were increasingly disappointed and bitter over the continuation of lynching and segregation. "'Fight for your rights'" was the black postwar slogan; arms purchases and claims by some black activists that blacks had triumphed in certain race riots indicated to Cutler that the internal security of the nation was potentially jeopardized by the deterioration of race relations in 1919 (quoted in Ferrell 1986, 103).

Until Cutler's memorandum, few in Washington had been persuaded there was a racial crisis brewing. The Justice Department, for instance, considered it not "a very serious matter." "[A]t first" the Department "paid little attention to propaganda among the negroes," but when Cutler's report arrived, the Department took an interest. Its investigative branch assigned "a negro man as a special agent" in the District of Columbia and gave instructions to field agents to gather information regarding the situation by "employ[ing] reliable negroes" (quoted in Ferrell 1986, 104). For a time the Justice Department worried that black discontent was more than a few editorials, random riots, and silent protest marches, that it might indeed pose a threat to the (white) nation. But Wilson was never persuaded; the "black threat" never won the president's attention or concern (Ferrell 1986).

Wilson even resisted meeting with black representatives. Deluged with letters and petitions from black citizens who hoped a presidential denunciation of lynching would end or at least sharply curtail the practice, Wilson, taking Baker's and Spingarn's advice, did issue a statement, as noted. But Wilson, single-minded in, if not obsessed with, his dream of establishing democracy and order throughout the world, framed his statement around that goal:

> "[M]ob spirit … has recently … very frequently shown its head … in many and widely separated parts of the country. There have been many lynchings, and every one of them had been a blow at the heart of ordered law and humane justice. No man who loves America … or who is truly loyal to her institutions, can justify mob action while the courts of justice are open. …
>
> We proudly claim to be the champions of democracy. If we really are, in deed and truth, let us see to it that we do not discredit our own. I say plainly that every American who takes part in the action of the mob or gives any sort of countenance is not a true son of this democracy, but its betrayer. …
>
> I, therefore, … beg that the Governors of the all the States, the law officers of every community and, above all, the men and women of every community in the United States … will cooperate—not passively merely, but actively and watchfully—to make an end of this disgraceful evil. It cannot live where the community does not countenance it. (quoted in Ferrell 1986, 105)

Although black reaction to this general statement was initially favorable, the continuation of lynching, on occasion of black veterans in uniform, persuaded activists that a stronger presidential statement on lynching as well as federal intervention in the matter were absolutely essential. Wilson never seemed to find the right "occasion" to make such a statement. The truth of the matter is that Woodrow Wilson was not terribly concerned by the fact that white men hunted down and murdered black men. Lynchings were, for him and for many other European Americans, "a regrettable social malady to be treated with cautious and calculated neglect," as activist Kelly Miller phrased it. Wilson continued to believe that the "Negro question" occupied a place well down the list of national priorities (quoted phrases in Ferrell 1986, 106).

For many black leaders and activists, as well as for ordinary black citizens who sent sometimes pleading, often patriotic, dignified, and on occasion desperate letters to the White House, Wilson's refusal to act proved that he was "out of sympathy with them, and ... indifferent to their fate as a people." He was, James Stemons of Philadelphia put it, perhaps the greatest "exponent of abstract justice" the American nation had produced; however, "the verdict of the masses ... has long been that while you were vigorously preaching one thing you were, when expediency demanded it, as vigorously practicing the direct opposite" (quoted in Ferrell 1986, 106).

Wilson was, many complained, even worse than his Republican predecessors, a strong criticism given that William Howard Taft had hardly acknowledged that African Americans even existed, and Theodore Roosevelt, often fondly called "our president" by many black citizens, finally had been "no more than a child of his age and a politician of the *real-politick* school" (Ferrell 1986, 106). Taft had believed that lynching was a state matter; he had even imagined that southern whites were black people's "best friend." While, as you recall, Roosevelt had criticized Coatesville residents for their lynching of Zachariah Walker, on other occasions he linked lynching to black rapists. Perhaps because he had mixed feelings on the issue, finally he left the antilynching cause to others (Ferrell 1986).

One consequence of the disappointment in Wilson was a growing belief among black voters that African Americans had to be free agents, politically speaking. If not disfranchised, as in the South, the black voter must support whichever party best listened and responded to black needs. Black voters should, A. D. Coles of New York said, "get together and support the most friendly Party, not because we are indebted to the Party, but in order to make that Party feel indebted to us." Chandler Owen, an editor of the black *Messenger*, argued that "we Negroes can make lynching an issue. We can question each candidate running on lynching and make him take some position or else knife him at the polls, be he spineless Republican or spineless Democrat" (quoted in Ferrell 1986, 107).

In the election of 1920 the majority of black voters remained loyal to the Republicans. Like whites, black citizens were weary of war and world involvement; they too were concerned with what appeared to be increasing lawlessness, and the threat of communism. They were also, as most white voters were not, concerned over a resurrected Ku Klux Klan, about which we read in chapter 9. It all added up to voting for Warren G. Harding and the Republicans to replace the Democrats. For black leaders, the primary issue was not membership in the League of Nations but "The Race Question—and

Continued Lynchings." Would Harding simply continue the tradition of nonaction of which Roosevelt, Taft, and Wilson were guilty, or would he find the will to enforce the long-ignored Reconstruction amendments? Harding had, evidently, some interest in civil rights and even made occasional statements which could be read as calling for action. But few whites in 1920 listened for or responded to such calls, and blacks soon found Harding's "flattering assurances and evasive replies" little else but. The president's April 12, 1921, statement that "Congress ought to wipe the stain of barbaric lynching from the banners of a free and orderly representative democracy" (quoted in Ferrell 1986, 107) secured Harding an antilynching reputation, but the statement, which the N.A.A.C.P. had recommended in an April 4 meeting, asked only for a general investigating committee and for Congress to take antilynching steps. In his speech in Birmingham, Alabama, six months later, Harding ignored lynching in favor of general statements supporting black political equality and educational opportunity (Ferrell 1986).

Always, for whites, there were reasons not to act, but constitutional reasons were evidently among the most convenient. James Weldon Johnson seemed to see through this ruse; he knew that the N.A.A.C.P. had more to do than simply convince Congress, through the use of lynching statistics, of the need for federal action, given the states' failure to do so. The association had to demonstrate "that there are constitutional grounds on which the federal government may proceed" (quoted in Ferrell 1986, 111). If that argument could be won, whites would be left with no excuse why the federal government could not provide basic protection of life and liberty for black citizens.

Missouri Congressman Dyer had been very much distressed by the racial violence in East St. Louis, partly because fleeing blacks had settled in his St. Louis district. The House declined to act on his proposal for a joint Senate-House investigating committee, just as Wilson had ignored his request for use of federal jurisdiction over the riot area. But when he proposed antilynching legislation in 1918 he was not brushed aside; hearings did begin. True, the focus of congressional hearings was not Dyer's Fourteenth Amendment bill but rather the issue of war powers; true, no report ever came out of the investigation. But lynching as an issue did receive a public hearing and, in Claudine Ferrell's words, "the federal antilynching crusade was launched" (1986, 111).

The N.A.A.C.P. communicated with Wilson's assistant attorney general William G. Fitts regarding the constitutionality of antilynching legislation. On February 16, 1918, Fitts told the N.A.A.C.P. that the administration's position was, after review of pertinent Supreme Court decisions, that the federal government had no jurisdiction over lynching. Fitts added, "nor are they connected with the war in any way as to justify the action of the Federal Government under the war powers" (quoted in Ferrell 1986, 112). While the constitutional issues and arguments were complex, the war powers act was not. It seemed obvious to many that the government's war powers could easily be extended to lynching. Clearly, draft-age black men as well as black soldiers worried that their loved ones were endangered while they fought for America, enough so that black loyalty was understandably undermined. It was this fact that had led to the proposal made by Major Joel Spingarn and Captain George S. Hornblower, both of the Army's General Staff, Military Intelligence (Ferrell 1986).

Spingarn and Hornblower attended the congressional hearings with the permission of their supervisors. While Hornblower wrote the proposed statute, the bill was the brainchild of Spingarn, the N.A.A.C.P.'s "new abolitionist" chairman of the board. Transferred from the infantry to military intelligence while he recovered from ulcer surgery, Spingarn, a former Columbia University professor of comparative literature, used this unexpected and at first unwanted home-front assignment to carry on his civil rights work. He hoped that he could use his position in military intelligence to formulate a "constructive [race] program" while he "look[ed] into this question of negro subversion" in an effort to counter German propaganda and improve black morale. His longtime association with black and white activists animated him as he set about devising a plan to respond to growing black bitterness. That very discernible state of affairs had already prompted the appointment of a black man, Emmett Scott, as special adviser to Secretary of War Baker on black military affairs. Spingarn worked with Scott on how best to reassure black soldiers and civilians. On June 10 he outlined a plan to counter "Negro subversion," a plan which included not only "Intelligence" activities, such as the conference of black editors, but also "counter propaganda." To "offset [the] chief causes of colored dissatisfaction," Spingarn proposed that General John J. Pershing issue a statement on the equitable treatment of black troops in Europe, the reassignment of Colonel Charles Young, who until his forced retirement (presumably for health reasons) had been the ranking black army officer, a presidential proclamation condemning lynching, and antilynching legislation based on Congress's war powers (quoted in Ferrell 1986, 112).

Like any ruse, I suppose, the constitutional question did not always work—Hornblower examined it in some detail in a July 19 brief—and the committee of eleven Democrats and ten Republicans chaired by North Carolina's Edwin Y. Webb did in fact discuss the real question, lynching itself. Several committee members questioned why blacks were lynched, whether lynchers had concentrated on uniformed black men during the war, and how the states would respond if the federal government intervened in what had been an area—crime—in which it had before exercised no jurisdiction. While Spingarn and Hornblower were stressing the significance of responding to black insecurity and bitterness that, at least potentially, undermined recruitment, congressmen seemed more focused on what would prove to be two critical issues in postwar antilynching debates (Ferrell 1986).

Thinking about the future allowed them to return to the ruse, and so they wondered about the basic question of constitutionality. Congressmen wondered about the need to provide special protection for *one* group when states presumably protected all groups. Even as they had been authorizing federal intervention into areas traditionally reserved for the states, wartime legislators were now suddenly very sensitive to even the slightest encroachment into the sovereign states. Southerners were still quite willing to express their conviction that "a [black] man who is guilty of rape should be lynched" (Ferrell 1986, 116), but it was clear they understood they had more at stake than lynching if the Spingarn-Hornblower bill were to pass. Southerners shared the N.A.A.C.P.'s conviction (with different affect, of course) that a war powers bill might accustom the nation to federal antilynching jurisdiction, which then might set the stage for further gains, even a challenge to segregation itself. With different feelings, white southerners and N.A.A.C.P. officials appreciated that an antilynching bill grounded constitutionally would echo far and wide (Ferrell 1986).

Southern and conservative resistance generally was, however, formidable. Once the link between a temporary war powers antilynching measure and a postwar federal bill was established, almost no congressmen agreed with the Hornblower-Springarn legislation. Even within the military, policymakers quickly concluded that the usefulness of a war measure was not worth a full-blown congressional struggle. Within six weeks after Hornblower's presentation, the War Department ended its support of the bill. But not only racial reactionaries lost interest in a wartime bill; Dyer himself doubted the point of a temporary wartime measure (Ferrell 1986).

III. The Dyer Bill

> *"To protect citizens ... against lynching in default of protection by States."*
>
> —quoted in Claudine L. Ferrell, *Nightmare and Dream: Antilynching in Congress, 1917–1922* (1986)

> *And yet politics, and surely American politics, is hardly a school for great minds.*
>
> —Anna Julia Cooper, "A Voice from the South" (1892/1998)

Dyer had begun communicating with the N.A.A.C.P. in early April 1918, informing association officials of his interest in sponsoring a federal antilynching bill and requesting "all the facts you have with reference" to recent lynchings (quoted in Ferrell 1986, 119). His strategy, he explained, was to show his congressional colleagues that a federal law was necessary, given that state laws had failed to end the practice. Later Dyer would insist that his interest in civil rights was not a recent one, that it had not suddenly materialized after black residents of East St. Louis flooded his district after the riot in 1917. First elected to Congress in 1911, the Missouri Republican explained that he had waited until 1918 to introduce a bill because he had wanted to be certain that "such a Bill would be constitutional and stand the test of the Courts" (quoted in Ferrell 1986, 120). The scenario, he hoped, would be that once he introduced the proposal the public would demand its passage, and that this public response would lead to a hearing by the House Judiciary Committee, of which he was also a member (Ferrell 1986).

Claudine Ferrell (1986) is skeptical of Dyer's claims. She points out that his bill, so "carefully drawn" and refined over the many years, was actually the same bill Albert Pillsbury framed in 1901. Pillsbury had written the proposal for

Representative, later Supreme Court Justice, William H. Moody of Massachusetts; George Frisbie Hoar, also of Massachusetts, had sponsored the legislation in the Senate. Hoar was also an anti-imperialist; as White (1929, 207) tells us, he "fought valiantly against American imperialism in the Philippines." On January 13, 1902, a bill was introduced in the U.S. House of Representatives by Indiana Representative Crumpacker, legislation designed to provide federal protection against lynching for alien residents of the country, a bill designed to prevent another diplomatic embarrassment like the one the 1891 New Orleans event had created. Jurisdiction over such offenses was to be given to the federal courts, and those who were convicted would be ineligible to serve as jurors (Cutler 1905).

While insignificant in number compared to the numbers of black men lynched, from time to time in various parts of the country mobs had lynched Italians, Chinese, Japanese, Bohemians, Mexicans, even citizens of Great Britain and Switzerland (who, presumably, would have been viewed as fellow "Anglo-Saxons"). While never a dime was paid to the survivors of black men who were lynched, in response to these lynchings the United States Government paid, between 1887 and 1901, a total of $475,499.90 in indemnities to the governments of China, Italy, Great Britain, and Mexico. In 1903 an additional $5,000 was paid to Italy for yet another lynching of an Italian citizen, this time in Mississippi. No action was taken on the bill introduced in Congress in 1902; Walter White (1929) emphasizes that the legislation was designed to protect aliens only; it did not even address the question of the lynching of American citizens.

Dyer acted as if he were ignorant of this history. Not only did he fail to acknowledge the true author of H.R. 11279, Dyer also failed to reveal that the Senate Judiciary Committee, chaired by Hoar, had returned an adverse oral report on the 1901 bill precisely due to doubts regarding its constitutionality. Dyer's May 7, 1918, speech basically plagiarized the work of Pillsbury, which he had read when the N.A.A.C.P. had responded to his earlier request for information. Among the documents the association had forwarded was a copy of Pillsbury's 1902 *Harvard Law Review* article, "A Brief Inquiry into a Federal Remedy for Lynching." Written to support the Moody-Hoar bill, the essay was largely an appeal to the Fourteenth Amendment. So was Dyer's speech (quoted phrases in Ferrell 1986, 120).

Because Dyer substituted Pillsbury's bill for his own, Ferrell suggests, he adopted a strategy doomed from the start. Given the rules of the ruse, a Fourteenth Amendment attack on lynching would not succeed, given the widespread view that both Congress and the Supreme Court would reject such an approach. Additionally, Ferrell points out, Dyer seemed incapable of grasping the complexities of such an argument. His command of the Fourteenth Amendment was, Ferrell writes, "rather weak and loose" (Ferrell 1986, 121), which became painfully obvious in his public defense of the bill. Save for those he "borrowed" from Pillsbury's article, Dyer's speeches, she suggests, were "simplistic and dominated by faulty analogies" (120). Not only did he fail to add contemporary cases to Pillsbury's 1902 list when he made his May 1918 defense, but he even referred to sections 19 and 20 by their pre-1909 section numbers (Ferrell 1986).

As a member of the Judiciary Committee, his questions, asides, and contributions were, Ferrell reports, often off the point, seldom substantive, and on occasion insensitive or frivolous. While his understanding of the relevant issues had changed over time, his grasp of case law, constitutional arguments, and logic remained faulty. Ferrell speculates that perhaps Dyer's legal preparation—by the apprentice method, with only brief contact with law schools—may have been partially to blame, but then she points out that Dyer's legal education was little different from most other members of Congress. Moreover, he had been practicing law for several years before he entered Congress in 1911. Of course, probably few of the cases brought to him by the citizens of St. Louis required constitutional expertise, but by 1918—and certainly by 1928—Dyer had opportunity to study such questions by virtue of his responsibilities as a member of Congress, where, among other activities, he authored antilynching bills for a decade and gave his name to the interstate auto-theft law. Perhaps, Ferrell continues to speculate, "Dyer simply lacked the mind of a constitutional lawyer" (121). But then, why did he not consult others who had such minds and expertise? While constitutional experts would probably have not been more successful than he in convincing a stubborn racist Congress to pass an antilynching statute, the Missouri Republican's ineptitude rendered the arguments of lynching's defenders more effective. Even as principal sponsor of the legislation, he promoted his bill with "superficial, illogical, and irrelevant arguments" (Ferrell 1986, 122).

Despite Dyer's failures as a constitutional lawyer and as a congressman, his sincerity has, evidently, never been at issue. From the start Dyer wanted a long-range solution to the problem, a commitment which contributed to, if not explained, his response to the military intelligence bill. Despite his ambivalence over the Spingarn-Hornblower proposal, Dyer supported it before the Judiciary Committee since it could "form a good foundation" for asserting the necessity of his H.R. 11279, the subject officially before the committee. The war powers measure might, he allowed, function as the foundation for antilynching legislation "for all time to come" (quoted in Ferrell 1986, 122).

Leonidas Dyer was not the only congressmen in 1918 concerned about lynching, nor was he the only who was thinking about the postwar period. By his count there had been 4,210 lynchings since 1885; Indiana Representative Merrill Moores, a Republican, felt certain that those states which had withheld the protection of the law in the past would continue to do so after World War I. On April 19, just two weeks after Dyer introduced his bill, Rep. Moores asked the House to consider H.R. 1154. Dyer's bill, based on the Fourteenth Amendment, read: "To protect citizens ... against lynching in default of protection by States." Arguing somewhat along the same lines, Moores's bill read: "To assure to persons within the jurisdiction of every State the equal protection of the laws; and to punish the crime of lynching" (quoted in Ferrell 1986, 122). As these titles suggest, there were differences and similarities between the two bills, differences some backers and opponents considered significant (Ferrell 1986, 122).

Moores's bill promised protection for all persons, the first proposal to cast such a wide net since an 1897 bill by Alexander Stewart of Wisconsin. Dyer's bill limited protection only to citizens. Procedurally, Dyer's bill gave federal district and circuit courts jurisdiction over the lynching crimes; Moores's gave such authority to the district courts only. Counties in which lynchings took place faced a $5,000 to $10,000 fine under Dyer's plan; they were liable for $10,000 under Moores's. In addition, Moores's measure provided forfeiture for those counties through which mobs transported victims, an idea the Indiana congressman had borrowed from antilynching legislation in South Carolina and Ohio. (As Ida B. Wells [1892a/1969, 23] understood: "The appeal to the white man's pocket has ever been more effectual than all the appeals ever made to his conscience.") Perhaps the greatest difference between the two bills, other than the citizen-person distinction, were the seven sections Moores, an 1880 graduate of Central Law School, included for the prevention of lynching. These sections, written to broaden the civil rights removal statute, Section 641, specified the procedures to be used by "every man who may have cause to think that his life is in danger from the mob" (quoted in Ferrell 1986, 123).

Both Moores's and Dyer's bills owed much to Pillsbury's 1901 measure. Recalling the Fourteenth Amendment's guarantee of equal protection of the laws, both measures defined a lynching as a killing by three or more persons in concert, in violation of state law, and in default of protection by the state or its officials. For both the mob's action amounted to a state denial of equal protection and a violation of "the peace of the United States" (Ferrell 1986, 124). Consequently, lynchers were guilty of a federal offense and subject to prosecution in federal court for murder. Counties in which mob killings took place faced forfeitures recoverable by the dependent family of the victim or, if none, by the United States, all through legal actions in the name of the latter and conducted by federal attorneys (Ferrell 1986).

Advised by its lawyer-president Moorfield Storey and by Pillsbury, the N.A.A.C.P. doubted that either Moores's or Dyer's rationales was sufficiently dissociated from "race" to slip past southern congressmen. In deliberations over whether to support one of the bills and to send witnesses to Judiciary Committee hearings, the association focused on two considerations, constitutionality and the politics of backing a specific measure, thereby underscoring that antilynching was primarily a racial issue. Dyer requested N.A.A.C.P. support for his proposal, and the N.A.A.C.P.'s Anti-Lynching Committee, headed by the association's co-founder William English Walling, considered the matter. On May 13 the committee recommended that the association should "actively" support one of the two bills, "whichever ... seemed most likely to accomplish the purpose the association had in mind and to have some chance of passage." Regarding the political issue, the committee decided that "favorable publicity" would follow from even failure, and that too justified the N.A.A.C.P.'s "participation in public hearings" (quoted in Ferrell 1986, 127). The committee's conclusion, however, still left unanswered questions, including which bill to support and whether to spearhead the congressional drive for the chosen proposal (Ferrell 1986).

To answer these questions the association consulted Moorfield Storey, still a practicing attorney in Boston and, as we have seen, a longtime supporter of the association. Citing the Dyer's bill dependency upon the doctrine of "the peace of the United States" (128) and on the Fourteenth Amendment's guarantee of equal protection and due process, Storey advised the association not to support the Missourian's bill. Nor could he recommend Moores's bill. Instead, he supported both the chances of enactment and the constitutionality of the military intelligence proposal. While he doubted that the Supreme Court would allow federal coverage of soldiers' relatives, Storey did believe that Hornblower's general approach was sound. Since the proposal only "suggested" (130) that its aim was the protection of African Americans, it had, Storey thought, a better chance of passage. Based on Storey's opinion, the association declined to take part in any antilynching hearings in 1918 and only supported the Spingarn-Hornblower proposal from behind the scenes. No association attorney or witness ever appeared at any committee hearings, although the organization did quietly provide Dyer all the information it had collected on lynching (Ferrell 1986).

The N.A.A.C.P.'s refusal to become publicly involved with the antilynching struggle of 1918 was not the only reason the Dyer and Moores bills failed to move forward. Other events contributed to their fate. The War Department's decision to drop Spingarn's antilynching program and Dyer's dedication to a Fourteenth Amendment–based bill (which left the legislation vulnerable constitutionally) also undermined the proposed legislation. With the armistice of November 1918, the wartime foundation of Spingarn's bill had disappeared. Lynching did not disappear, of course, despite Wilson's July 26 antilynching statement; in fact, as we have seen, postwar racial tensions intensified across the country, a country over which the national government declined to claim jurisdiction. The Justice Department's position was simple and was repeated without variation to the numerous letter writers who demanded that the attorney general use federal power to end lynching: it did not have jurisdiction (Ferrell 1986).

By 1919 Pillsbury had come to believe that the Fourteenth Amendment's national citizenship clause might function as the foundation for antilynching legislation: "[A]s the government has a direct interest in the lives of its citizens, the United States has the same power to protect them in their lives in the states that it has in all other parts of the world" (quoted in Ferrell 1986, 133). State failure to protect its citizens was an additional, although not foundational, basis for federal action. Dyer pressed on, his bill little changed. On January 29, 1920, the House Judiciary Committee, chaired by Andrew J. Volstead of Minnesota, conducted hearings on three bills introduced in 1919: one by Dyer, another by Moores, and a third by Frederick W. Dallinger of Massachusetts, whose bill was, he acknowledged, "almost identical" to Dyer's (Ferrell 1986, 138). This time, Ferrell tells us, the committee studied in greater detail the statistical reasons for lynching and the constitutional basis of a general federal antilynching bill than its successor had in 1918 hearings.

Testimony by Dallinger and Moores and by several N.A.A.C.P. officials raised a number of constitutional questions while also demonstrating that the nation did have a problem with lynching and state nonaction. The N.A.A.C.P.'s presence at the hearings and the evidence it introduced on lynching's racialized character publicly and formally linked the postwar congressional antilynching effort with the broader struggle for civil rights. Ignoring or minimizing its racial character had not succeeded, and the N.A.A.C.P., especially Storey, was coming to admit the futility of pursuing remedies short of federal criminal statutes. From now on, the racialized nature of lynching was an unmistakable fact and would provide a subtext to all discussions, as would the fact that once again the sponsors of the antilynching bills were Republicans. How southerners and conservatives responded to these facts would be evident in the committee's minority report (Ferrell 1986).

Support of the 1918 war-powers bill and the 1920 majority report implied that antilynching legislators understood the complexities of the constitutional issues embedded in antilynching legislation, but they did not. In fact, as Ferrell (1986) puts it, "they plunged into deep constitutional waters aware that it was critical to know how to swim but unaware that they would have to swim so hard. As a result, their efforts against the current of constitutional interpretation was only a treading of water" (149). Familiar with the Fourteenth Amendment's operational meaning, congressmen were clear that the federal government's intervention into a traditional state domain could be only a limited and closely defined one, but they were less clear exactly what those limits were. Immersed, then, in federal limitations, state nonaction, and private discrimination, and unappreciative of the constitutional distinction between the murder of a black man and the denial of his civil rights through murder, congressional antilynchers naively attacked both lynchers and the states in 1920. The subtly of these issues "caught the antilynchers in a swirl of constitutional whirlpools" (149). But they knew as long as lynchings continued, they must continue, and continue they would (Ferrell 1986).

There were antilynching activists who thought from the start that the effort was doomed in Congress. Philanthropist George Foster Peabody advocated an educational campaign against lynching; he told Walter White that, in his estimation, it was "a waste of energy to try to deal with the [lynching] issue through congressional legislation." Without "a courageous leader," the "moral issue" would be obscured, "tangled up in the great issue of the liberty of the individual." The latter issue, he implied, would always win. Congressman Anthony Griffin, a New York Democrat who represented black Harlem, watched as Peabody's fears became reality in the House of Representatives in 1921. He reported: "The prolonged argument on the bill ... actually degenerated into a quasiconstitutional defense of the inalienable right to resort to lynching." Across the House floor, Kansas Republican Edward Little watched the same nightmare, as fellow congressmen defended vigorously "the constitutional right to burn ... fellow citizens alive" (quoted in Ferrell 1986, 150). Griffin was not fooled; he commented bitterly that Americans become reverent toward their Constitution only "when some impending law threatens to tread on our prejudices" (quoted in Ferrell 1986, 151). The Dyer bill of 1921 did so tread, unleashing racial prejudices so naked that constitutional arguments did not always succeed as "camouflage" (Ferrell 1986).

The fact that there were very few legal experts on lynching did not simplify matters for the House Judiciary Committee. Although the N.A.A.C.P.'s volunteer attorneys and the legal experts whom the association consulted were familiar with many of the constitutional issues, Albert Pillsbury was basically accurate when he said, in late 1921, that there were fewer than "half a dozen competent lawyers in the country who have given the subject serious consideration or have any definite idea of what ought to go into the bill or ought to be left out of it" (quoted in Ferrell 1986, 151). The N.A.A.C.P.'s preliminary investigation into "what should go into the bill" yielded mostly questions. No wonder why the white men who served on the Judiciary Committee, some of whom were indifferent to the fate of black men and all of whom were without much experience in constitutional law, found agreement so difficult to reach. Attorneys Moorfield Storey, Pillsbury, and George Wickersham agreed on what Wickersham called "the public situation" and on the need for federal action, but after studying the Constitution's operational meaning in 1921, they were not optimistic. It would be nothing short of a miracle if meaningful antilynching legislation passed the Congress and then survive the courts (Ferrell 1986, 151).

If one of the "two great [constitutional] problems" facing the United States during the late nineteenth and early twentieth centuries had to do with the limits of the Fourteenth Amendment, the Judiciary Committee's consideration of the Dyer antilynching bill in the summer of 1921 suggested why. While the committee's deliberations ended favorably, there was no reason to celebrate. A reluctant if not obstinate House and a filibustering Senate awaited the bill, and the hearings that preceded the committee's favorable report had clarified few of the constitutional ambiguities and complexities embedded in any federal intervention to stop lynching. The committee presented its amended bill on October 31; Dyer had introduced his original version on April 11; the intervening months had brought no more clarity regarding the scope of the federal government's jurisdictional powers. The doctrine of federalism seemed more sacrosanct that human life itself (Ferrell 1986, 187).

In their speeches the antilynchers tended to overlook the fact that the N.A.A.C.P. supported the bill; they spoke in generalities: "The time has passed to apologize for lynching, or even to explain it. It must be stamped out" (quoted from the *Congressional Record* in Ferrell 1986, 188). But their critics frequently reminded them and the American public of the fact. Southerners and conservatives complained loudly about the lobbying pressures of "race agitators and Negro organizations of the North," that is, the N.A.A.C.P. which was "responsible" for the dreaded Dyer bill. These "foolish Negro agitators" used such "vicious" vehicles as the N.A.A.C.P.'s *Crisis* and the *Chicago Defender* to incite "sentimental hysteria," provoke Republican promises, and upset the social order (quoted in Ferrell 1986, 193).

Behind the scenes antilynching congressmen were hardly unaware of the N.A.A.C.P.'s involvement. Several representatives, whose districts had significant black voter blocs, wanted the fact well publicized by the association before the fall elections, just as their opponents had charged they did. For itself, the N.A.A.C.P. had made it clear that it would work to deny the black vote to those who did not support the Dyer bill. Walter White acknowledged that the organization was "straining every nerve to bring pressure to bear on Congress." In February 1922 the *Crisis* told its readers: "If your congressman votes against the Dyer Bill mark him down as your betrayer in the hour of trial and defeat him by every legitimate means when he asks your suffrage next fall. In the same way, reward those who met the tests without flinching" (quoted in Ferrell 1986, 193).

IV. The Southern Response

"Ah well, the South must be left to manage the Negro. She is most directly concerned and must understand her problem better than outsiders. We must not meddle. The Negro is not worth a feud between brothers and sisters."

—Anna Julia Cooper, "A Voice from the South" (1892/1998)

Southern tradition, segregation, states' rights *have soaked up the fears of our people; little private fantasies of childhood have crept there for hiding, unacknowledged arsenals of hate have been stored there, and a loyalty covering up a lack of self-criticism has glazed the words over with sanctity. No wonder the saying of them aloud can stir anxieties until there are times when it seems we have lost our grasp on reality.*

—Lillian Smith, *Killers of the Dream* (1949/1963)

Fantasy in politics is a subject that has been insufficiently explored.

—Elizabeth Wright, "Review of Renata Salecl's *The Spoils of Freedom: Psychoanalysis and Feminism after the Fall of Socialism*" (1996)

The arguments against lynching held sufficient rhetorical power that some southerners no longer felt they could defend the practice. The Dyer bill must be defeated, but, they reasoned, they must offer some solution of their own. The main point, they insisted, was that federal interference was not the way to end lynching. The solution—surprise surprise—had to be a local one; public opinion had to change. One could not legislate morality. Public opinion was key they argued, and if the federal government participated in the lynching debate with "blanket indictment and gratuitous insult to conscientious State officials everywhere," local resentment would grow and localities would be unable to stop mob violence. Only "race strife, race conflict, race riots, and lawlessness" would follow if the North (which would, of course, "do the same thing" if it suffered "the Negroes in New England") attacked the South without appreciating the unique and difficult situation (white) southerners faced (quoted in Ferrell 1986, 197).

Gathering steam, other southerners complained that the black was "the most favored race protégé ever coddled and petted by the sentimental sacrifice of an indulgent people." Moreover, they warned, "to treat one [race] as helpless infants requiring Federal aid [was] ... a mistake." Federal protection would encourage the black, whom the southerner knew as no outsider could possibly know him, to expect charity and to demand social equality even though he remained a "slave to his appetite," had "but little moral restraint," and demonstrated a "trend toward cruelty, which is seen in the merciless and frequent abuse and beating of his children." Yankees must understand there is no "race problem" between whites and "good" blacks, not now at least. But passage of the Dyer bill would convert contented and docile blacks into "uncontrollable brutes" loudly demanding all the foolishness long promised them by ignorant Yankee do-gooders. Already good (white) southern people were faced with this new type—"arrogant, swaggering"—which will eventually only force righteous southern white men to resort to violence to protect their women. Keep in mind, southern congressmen drawled, the South will allow social equality only when "the stars ... cease[d] to shine and the heavens ... rolled up as a scroll" (quoted in Ferrell 1986, 197–198)

This racist nonsense—the convoluted contents of white male fantasy—intertwined with presumably rational theories of states' (i.e., white male) rights, culminated in a southern insistence that racial issues were and must remain a "purely local" problem. Southerners had used this argument successfully since Reconstruction, and they would continue to use it until the present day. Lynching was not the issue, southerners would insist as they condemned the bill. Why, southerners were of course opposed to lynching, southerners with their "unflagging friendship for the Negro." Why, it was black rights that were jeopardized by the bill, as its passage would inflame white violence on a scale never seen before. Any fool could see that southern speeches substantiated rather than disproved "Yankee" charges that the South had a "peculiar" problem it was unwilling to eliminate (quoted phrases in Ferrell 1986, 198).

The contradictions inherent in such rhetoric were most obvious when, relying on the imaginary link between rape and lynching, southern congressmen pleaded for the safety of white women. "[Y]ou are buying black votes with the safety of white women in the South," one southerner thundered. Passage of the Dyer bill would give black men the "incentive and a license" to commit such crimes [rape] and expect flowers and gifts afterward from the family of his raped victim. Mississippian Thomas Sisson declared that he "would rather the whole black race of this world were lynched than for one of the fair daughters of the South to be ravished and torn by one of these black brutes." Minority leader Finis Garrett, who represented northeastern Tennessee, summarized these sentiments when he asserted that H.R. 13 be renamed "A bill to encourage rape." Outraged that lynched black men but not their female white rape victims were the subjects of sympathy, Georgia Democrat William C. Lankford demanded that African Americans and white northerners "quit howling about lynchings and begin preaching against rape." North Carolinian Edward W. Pou knew the solution to the problem; blacks themselves could end lynching by ending black crime. Joining this chorus of hysterical southern Democrats, several northerners urged that the South must be left alone, as only it knew how to deal with rape, that "legacy" of Emancipation and the only cause of lynching (quoted in Ferrell 1986, 198–199).

For these southern white men rape was the only reason for lynching, and rape was the reason why the Dyer bill must be defeated. South Carolina Senator Benjamin Tillman delivered one of the most emotionally charged statements of the debates, one which conveys the general southern response to the antilynching proposal. The Dyer bill, Tillman warned his congressional colleagues, would do nothing less than eliminate the states as separate entities and "substitute for the starry banner of the Republic, a black flag of tyrannical centralized government, a black flag indeed, black as melted midnight, black as the dust on the hinges to the gates of hell, black as the face and heart of the rapist ... who deflowered and killed [the young white girl]" (quoted in Ferrell 1986, 199). How many times, one wonders, had he visualized the awful act? I am reminded of the more contemporary tale of U.S. Senator Jesse Helms who, during his battle against the National Endowment for the Arts, carried around one of Robert Mapplethorpe's black male nudes folded up in his back pocket. Rather obsessively Helms is said to have unfolded and displayed the "shocking" image to anyone he could detain, in order, *of course*, to prove his point about the moral necessity to ban such "obscene" images (Alexander 1996). The lady doth protest too much.

Clueless, southern congressman (then and now), even while disclosing the contents of their queer and racist unconscious, refused to acknowledge that they were "prejudiced." Lynching was not a race question, they went on. Was it a matter of sex? No, of course, it was a matter, simply, of "states' rights." But the construction of their protestations exposed them for what they were. As the horrified Democratic representative of Harlem, Anthony Griffin, muttered, "They do not believe in lynching, but ... they do not believe in stopping it [either]." Other northern congressmen tried (not very shrewdly) to make it easier for southerners to support the bill by suggesting that one could not conclude from the fact that southerners were prejudiced that they supported lynchings. Southerners explained that the black man who got the "wrong idea of his relation to the white man"—and that's the relationship that matters isn't it, not the one to the imaginary white woman—faced a fate of his own making: "A few of the worst Negroes will be lynched. The Negro in the South who commits rape knows what is coming. He simply commits suicide, that is all" (quoted in Ferrell 1986, 199–200). Southern white men were themselves a rather "peculiar" institution, were they not? Strange fruit, one might say.

Finally, southerners argued that there were more important national issues facing the Congress, "so many things that worry [them] more than the occasional lynching of a criminal." Fed up with the debate, Tillman threw up his hands, saying he could not be worried over "the burning of an occasional ravisher," particularly when the Dyer bill was delaying congressional consideration of the "important" issues of currency, tariff, and the veterans' bonus (quoted in Ferrell 1986, 200). Louisiana representative John Sandlin pleaded with Congress to turn its attention to the truly significant problems of railroad rates, unemployment, and trade imbalances (Ferrell 1986).

Antilynchers either did not see through this ruse or declined to call southerners on it. Nor did northern congressman exploit southerners' explicit and implied admissions of racism. For instance, antilynching Republican Richard E. Bird of Kansas said little during the debates, finally distancing himself from the issue by relocating it as "largely a question of the South and the colored man" (quoted in Ferrell 1986, 200). Southerners would have had none of it anyway, arguing, as did Finis Garrett, that the Republican interest in the so-called race question disguised the real issue, federalism under attack. Some

Republicans saw through that one and said so, as when Missourian Edgar Ellis snorted that he would listen not one minute more to arguments based on "the old pestiferous bugaboo of states' rights" (quoted in Ferrell 1986, 202). Southerners were undeterred; they continued to wail that the hallowed principle of states' rights would become extinct if the Dyer bill passed. Doggedly, antilynchers argued otherwise (Ferrell 1986).

Something in the race question (what could it be?) sparked the discussion of federalism, that is, diverted the debate away from the brute fact of white men mutilating black men. Throughout the debates, Ferrell (1986) tells us, "race led debaters from secondary topics to issues of constitutionality and federalism and vice versa." In lynching we have seen how homoerotic desire gets relocated; in the congressional debates about lynching, white men still could not face up to the facts. Instead, they screamed at each other over federalism (the southern white man's "right" to the black male body?) insisting that the Dyer bill invaded the states' domain, explicit in the provision to allow the federal government to "tax" counties, punish common murderers, and prescribe the duties of state officials. Such federal intervention in local affairs would lead to nothing less than the complete destruction of the states. By stripping states of their "sovereignty" and reducing them to "governmental vassalage," Congress would "out Herod Herod" and shock "even Alexander Hamilton" with the "super-government" it established. Therefore, the southerners continued, as if the Confederacy—oops, Union—itself were at stake, the honorable defenders of "liberty and self-government" must pledge to do everything to protect "the last defensive ditch around the citadel of states' rights." Referring one supposes to racist judicial decisions like *Plessy* v. *Ferguson* which had legitimated racial segregation, southerners recalled wistfully the "strong and brave judges" who had once resisted the "fanaticism" that threatened to create "the 'medieval fogs' of Federal imperialism and [to destroy] the 'sunlight of human freedom'." Congress must, they droned on and on, resist Dyer's "act to assassinate states' rights; to nullify the constitutions of the several States" (quoted in Ferrell 1986, 202–203).

With the "stakes" so high, southerners would stop at nothing. When antilynchers argued that the bill must be passed even with doubts about its constitutionality, southerners responded, holding their noses no doubt, by conjuring up the ghost of no one less than Abraham Lincoln himself. "'No man,'" southerners quoted in grave tones, "'who has sworn to support the Constitution can conscientiously vote for what he understands to be an unconstitutional measure, however expedient he may think it.'" Next, shaking their heads in disbelief, southerners sermonized in sorrowful tones over the Republicans' willingness to violate "the integrity of their oaths," to avoid their solemn responsibility by passing it onto the courts, and, most unbelievably to me, to "lynch" the Constitution. The same Constitution that meant so little to their grandfathers in 1860 now was extolled as no mere "scrap of paper" that could be torn up and discarded. But that was what the antilynchers were doing when they insisted on passing the Dyer bill. In fact, southerners said to (no doubt incredulous) northern ears, supporters of the measure had become like the very lynchers they so righteously denounced: "you each get ropes and they go after the criminal and you go after the Constitution" (quoted in Ferrell 1986, 203).

Despite this outrageous southern recalcitrance, the Dyer bill passed the House. A major accomplishment, it would mean nothing, of course, unless the Senate did the same. Many in Washington were less than jubilant, worrying that there had been "a lot of pretty good oratory and pretty bad law about this constitutional question." On both sides, emotionalism and fantasy rather than rationality characterized the discussion of what some observers dismissed as "constitutional nothings" and "legalistic quibbling." Lawmakers with limited knowledge of constitutional complexities had turned to "friends" for solutions to their dilemmas and reiterated pat phrases and made clichés out of decontextualized judicial one-liners. Legislators oversimplified and generalized as they brought up every possibility, relevancy and tangential issue. Ferrell (1986) puts it this way: "'The world, the flesh, and the devil' all received attention when the representatives opened the Pandora's boxes which both lynching and antilynching presented the nation" (quoted passages on 234).

The majority of Americans, that is, whites, worried over economic and labor unrest; they responded with indifference to a bill that seemed to directly affect so few, and the long-term implications of which seemed distant and hypothetical. The Dyer bill was reported, when it was mentioned at all, on newspapers' back pages, where most of the sixty-three lynchings that occurred that year (1921) were also noted. Only the N.A.A.C.P. took a moment to celebrate. Apathetic legislators had responded appropriately to the nightmare that was lynching, not to mention to the rapidly increasing number of black votes. Whether or not the House had solved the constitutional dilemma was of secondary importance. Now was the time to focus on the Senate. For Storey the significance of House passage was political as well as legislative. He told Dyer, "I think the contest in the House was in itself of great value to the cause for it helped to clarify public opinion. It indicated to the southern representatives that we are in earnest" (quoted in Ferrell 1986, 234). As the debate in the Senate loomed, the N.A.A.C.P. marshaled its energies to fight yet another campaign. In the House, there was an audible sigh of relief that the thing was over (Ferrell 1986).

The more optimistic had hope that the Senate too would do the right thing. Dyer told a mass meeting at New York's Town Hall on March 1, 1922, that the Senate would, after careful and no doubt contentious conflict, approve the legislation. A filibuster was not finally a threat, as "the Senate can make its own rules and can consider and vote upon legislation they see fit to do." On an even more optimistic day, he told Storey that passage was practically inevitable. Many in Illinois were confident; in his reelection campaign tour, Chicago Representative Martin Madden relayed the words of President Harding: "'If the Senate of the United States passes the Dyer anti-lynching bill, it won't be in the White House three minutes before I'll sign it; and having signed it, I'll enforce it'" (quoted in Ferrell 1986, 236). But before the Senate could send the bill to Harding, it had to survive scrutiny by an inhospitable Senate Judiciary Committee (Ferrell 1986).

Borah's Betrayal

The most influential member of a five-man Judiciary subcommittee to study the Dyer bill was the influential Idaho Republican William E. Borah. It was the conservative Borah who quickly became the major barrier to Senate action. But he was only the most prominent member of the Judiciary Committee who came to the bill with, at best, skepticism, at worst, a determination to bury it. Of the committee's ten Republicans and six Democrats, not a one was an "N.A.A.C.P. man." Four senators were from southern or border states and none of the other twelve represented states with significant numbers of black voters. Not one committee member, Borah included, had expressed any prior interest in civil rights issues, except for Kentucky Republican Richard Ernst and Lee Slater Overman, a four-term North Carolina Democrat whose interest took the form of "open hostility" (quoted in Ferrell 1986, 237).

Borah said he abhorred lynching. Promising Moorfield Storey and others that he would consider the bill sympathetically, Borah also emphasized that he could vote for H.R. 13 only if he found no constitutional difficulties. He declined to leave what he took to be Congress's duty to the courts: "[I] have never been able to satisfy myself that I ought to do that" (quoted in Ferrell 1986, 241). Borah had not yet begun his study of H.R. 13's constitutionality, but he was, he said, hopeful. On May 19, after six weeks of studying the measure, Borah announced he could find not "even a shred of a principle upon which to hang this measure under the Constitution." There was "no authority whatever for the law" (quoted in Ferrell 1986, 243). Horrified, Storey pleaded with the senator: "Is there no remedy?" (quoted in Ferrell 1986, 236). Borah replied, sounding suddenly rather southern, that any congressman who voted for the bill while doubting its constitutionality and any activist who supported that vote were "lawless brothers of those who ... take the law into their own hands and join the mob" (quoted in Ferrell 1986, 254).

"Why," Claudine Ferrell (1986, 244) asks, "did Borah equate, to whatever degree, a vote for the Dyer bill with a prostitution of his responsibility as a lawmaker and representative of the people?" (244). Why indeed? In a June 8 *Boston Transcript* letter to the editor Borah summarized his concerns. The central problem, he thought, was the bill's doubtful constitutionality, but there were additional problems of effectiveness and applicability (Ferrell 1986). Why didn't the federal government have jurisdiction over its citizens? Why could no legal means be devised which would keep white men's hands off black men's bodies? What did "constitutionality" symbolize? Can it be read as a displaced, not altogether "straight"forward argument over the structure of male-male relations, specifically white/black male relations, the public sphere, which had been until very recently an entirely male sphere?

The N.A.A.C.P. accepted the debate literally. Walter White followed "the procedure" the association had used in the House fight and, "pounding away as hard as we can," senators received figures concerning custodial lynchings (quoted phrases in Ferrell 1986, 268). They learned that only 92 of 212 lynching victims from 1919 through 1921 had been taken from custody. They received newspaper accounts of lynchings, copies of *Thirty Years of Lynching*, "An American Lynching," and other N.A.A.C.P. publications. They were informed that Belgian, French, and Czechoslovakian newspapers printed accounts of American lynchings. In an August 11 press release, the American Bar Association announced its endorsement of federal antilynching action. But the "inside word" was not encouraging; indeed one friend told N.A.A.C.P. officials: "The Dyer Anti-Lynching Bill is dead; long live the next antilynching bill!" (quoted in Ferrell 1986, 254)

"The Shame of America"

The N.A.A.C.P. was not ready to accept defeat. Even if the bill were dead, the struggle in the Senate must be used to intensify antilynching feeling among Republican senators, a majority of whom "assured" the N.A.A.C.P. of their support (Ferrell 1986, 255). To strengthen that support, the N.A.A.C.P. bought a one-page ad in nine major daily newspapers with the headline "The Shame of America." The ad listed the legal-constitutional supporters of the Dyer bill and urged readers to "telegraph your Senators today." There must be "an avalanche of telegrams on the Senate which will give supporters of the Dyer Bill sufficient backbone to offset the well organized filibuster opponents." The association had "to arouse the great mass of Americans who are ignorant and apathetic" (quoted in Ferrell 1986, 276–277).

As defeat appeared inevitable, *Crisis* editor W. E. B. Du Bois became so enraged that he wrote a vituperative editorial that James Johnson asked him to revise. The N.A.A.C.P. secretary suggested that Du Bois not declare that "the Republicans did not *intend* to pass the Dyer Bill." Wouldn't, Johnson suggested, "they were not willing to put up the fight necessary" be a more temperate choice of words? Additionally, Johnson suggested that Du Bois write that the Republicans "wished to ignore us" rather than it was "a great political party filled with men who despised us, hated us." Finally, Johnson pointed out, calling Harding a "jelly-fish" indicated disrespect for the office as well for the man who temporarily occupied it (quoted in Ferrell 1986, 282). Johnson's revision did not mean that he felt any less angry than did Du Bois about the Republican "betrayal," as he labeled it, just less willing to burn political bridges than the more volatile intellectual and activist. Kansas Republican Edward Little had warned the N.A.A.C.P. that the antilynching fight in Congress would be no less acrimonious than abolitionism had been eighty years earlier. Passing federal antilynching legislation would be "a matter of long delays, repeated failures and ultimate success" (quoted in Ferrell 1986, 301). While Little's remarks accurately described the antilynching campaign in general, he was, of course, mistaken regarding the "ultimate success" of struggle (Ferrell 1986).

Failure on the national level would continue, mitigated by some success on the local, during the remainder of the decade. The N.A.A.C.P. did not drop federal legislative action from its agenda, but it de-emphasized it until the 1930s, concentrating instead on state and local action. That several states adopted antilynching and antimob laws during the 1920s and early 1930s indicates that the N.A.A.C.P.'s strategy was not wrongheaded, especially given the overwhelming resistance in the Senate. However, at no time did antilynching legislation disappear from congressional consideration; Dyer continued to propose bills, all essentially identical to H.R. 13 and all less successful than their predecessor. N.A.A.C.P. officials and representatives continued to appear before Judiciary Committees to testify in favor of federal legislation. But the N.A.A.C.P.'s emphasis, as well as the nation's attention, was elsewhere (Ferrell 1986).

Despite abandoning H.R. 13, Republicans continued to appeal to and win the black bloc vote. In his first annual address after assuming the presidency in 1923, Calvin Coolidge indicated he would continue past presidential policy. Congress, he said, should "exercise all its power of prevention and ... punishment against ... lynching, ... for which [African Americans] ... furnish a majority of victims." Congress ignored the statement. Nor were Republican legislators persuaded when their party's 1924 platform "urge[d] the Congress to enact at the earliest possible date a federal antilynching law so that the full influence of the federal government may be wielded to exterminate this hideous crime. ... The President has recommended the creation of a commission for the investigation of social and economic conditions [which cause lynching] and the promotion of mutual understanding and confidence" (quoted in Ferrell 1986, 301–302).

By 1928 the party's rhetoric seemed empty, although Republicans still called for antilynching legislation. But by 1932 the party's platform did no more than promise to continue being "the friend of the American Negro" and the supporter of "equal opportunity and rights" (quoted in Ferrell 1986, 302). It was not until the 1936 election that the mass of African-American voters gave up on the Republicans and voted for Franklin D. Roosevelt. Roosevelt was hardly adequate in his support for civil rights generally, and against lynching specifically, as we have seen in the case of Claude Neal and will see in the case of the Scottsboro Nine.

But we are ahead of ourselves. In the early 1920s, black hope that Republicans would deliver on their promises remained alive. Alfred C. Bradshaw asked Coolidge, as other black leaders had once asked Wilson, to become a twentieth-century Lincoln and "free the colored race from the most horrid and brutal death through mob violence and lynching." J. G. Robinson, editor of the A.M.E. *Church Review*, pleaded with the Republican president to "issue a pronouncement—a specific one—[on] the horrors of lynching." So too did the N.A.A.C.P. In 1927 James Weldon Johnson and Mary White Ovington took their eyes off the states to ask Coolidge for a "public utterance" of condemnation and a call to Congress for an antilynching bill (quoted in Ferrell 1986, 302).

No president until Harry Truman in 1947 would exercise any leadership in the antilynching campaign, and by then it was no longer the national issue that it was in pre–World War II years. Despite congressional and presidential recalcitrance, lynching declined during every twentieth–century president's administration, including Harding's and Coolidge's. There were 57 lynchings in 1922, 33 in 1923, 16 in 1927, and "only" 8 in 1932. Some lynching experts and observers, including Johnson and scholar James Chadbourn, credited the drop in part to the southern fear that a continuing high incidence of lynching would force federal action. Others, including the *New York Times*, the *New Republic*, and N.A.A.C.P. director Mary White Ovington, gave the credit to publicity and education campaigns as well as more determined law enforcement efforts. The numbers rose briefly during the Depression—the high for the decade was 28 in 1933—and southerners were right: new campaigns would be launched to secure federal legislation (Ferrell 1986).

V. Antilynching in the 1920s and 1930s

By the end of the 1930s, the demise of lynching was irreversible. During the decade, the combination of the continued efforts of antilynching activists and profound changes in the southern economy delivered the decisive blows to the tradition of mob violence.

—W. Fitzhugh Brundage, *Lynching in the New South: Georgia and Virginia, 1880–1930* (1993)

The remainder of the 1920s would prove less and less hospitable to civil rights legislation; not for a decade would it seem politically feasible to once again lobby for antilynching legislation in Congress. There was, as noted, a gradual decline in the number of reported lynchings over the course of the decade; this fact served both sides. While the decline consoled those who fought lynching, it also gave credence to conservatives who argued that the states themselves could handle the problem without federal intervention. The N.A.A.C.P. knew better; its staff knew that the basic issues had not been resolved. They were pleased, therefore, with Congressman Dyer's willingness to reintroduce his measure session after session, despite the fact that enactment was unlikely (Zangrando 1980).

The political struggle against lynching drew support from nonblack communities as well, such as the Association of Southern Women for the Prevention of Lynching (A.S.W.P.L.) led by Jessie Daniel Ames. Leaders of the Jewish community also joined the N.A.A.C.P. in the fight. A common concern for justice, a shared sense of suffering as beleaguered minorities outside the dominant Anglo-Saxon culture, and a mutual abhorrence of violence (whether lynching or pogroms) provided bonds for an alliance (Zangrando 1980).

There were white racists who believed that miscegenation explained Jewish-black political partnerships. In the March 1926 issue of the *Forum*, Lothrop Stoddard produced a series of sketches he called a "gallery of Jewish types." A description of the article written later by the National States Rights Party claims that it demonstrates that "a Negroid strain undoubtedly exists in Jewry." This "explains why Jews support and finance the N.A.A.C.P." (quoted passages in Stember 1976, 51).

Jewish leaders such as Henry Moskowitz, Stephen Wise, and the Spingarn brothers had played important roles in the N.A.A.C.P.'s founding years; Martha Gruening worked on antilynching matters for the N.A.A.C.P. staff; her brother Ernest, a journalist, assisted the association in various ways. Louis Marshall of the American Jewish Committee provided legal assistance, and his son-in-law, Jacob Billikopf, introduced Walter White to various Jewish contributors to civil rights funds, such as Julius Rosenwald. As a gesture of the association's appreciation for Marshall's help, Johnson served as an honorary pallbearer at Marshall's funeral. James Weldon Johnson (1933, 407) characterized him as "one of the most valuable and active members of the Legal Committee of the Association." The Council of Jewish Women supported the antilynching drive of the early 1920s. Louis Brandeis, Felix Frankfurter, Herbert Lehman, Jacob Schiff, and others contributed goodwill, public support, and financial backing for various N.A.A.C.P. campaigns (Zangrando 1980).

Walter White did not confine his activities to fund-raising. As noted earlier, he too investigated lynching events firsthand. For instance, when black farmers in Elaine (Phillips County), Arkansas, had attempted to organize and improve working conditions in the fall of 1919, whites responded predictably, murdering over two hundred black men, women, and children in retaliation. White investigated and was himself very nearly lynched. The prosecution behaved predictably too: seventy-nine black sharecroppers were charged for starting the violence in which one white man had died. Local authorities conducted a sham court trial. Black witnesses were whipped until they consented to testify against the defendants, and an all-white jury listened to the proceedings while a mob threatened lynchings if no convictions ensued. The defendants' court-appointed counsel asked for no change of venue, called no witnesses, and asked no defendants to take the stand. The "trial" lasted less than an hour. Five minutes later the jury voted a dozen black men guilty of murder in the first degree. The twelve were sentenced to death; sixty-seven others received long prison terms (Zangrando 1980).

As key as Walter White and the association were in the case, they did not act alone. They *tried* to act alone, it appears, as we learn from Ida B. Wells's autobiography. Now a married woman and mother of four living in Chicago, the events in Arkansas outraged Wells:

> A letter of mine had already appeared in the *Chicago Defender* calling attention to the fact that the riot [Elaine, Arkansas] had been precipitated by the refusal of colored men to sell their cotton below the market price because they had an organization which advised them so to do. I appealed to the colored people of the country to use their influence and money for those twelve men, who had been found guilty of murder in the first degree and then sentenced to be electrocuted.
>
> This letter ... had a widespread response. Many people all over the country sent in contributions to assist in securing legal talent. One of the letters received came from one of the twelve men who said that they were so glad to see "the piece that the people of Chicago had spoke for them in the *Defender*." They thanked us for what had been said and done, and said it was the first word or offer of help they had from their own people. The letter ended by saying that if I had anything that I wanted them to know to send the reply to a certain address in Little Rock. For after scores of helpless Negroes were killed, scores more of them were herded into prison in Helena, Arkansas, where the mob tried to lynch them and where they were shocked by electricity, beaten, and tortured to make them confess they had a conspiracy to kill white folks. After the mockery of a trial, twelve of them were sentenced to be electrocuted. (Wells 1970, 398–399)

Wells offered a resolution at that Sunday's meeting of the People's Movement. She pointed out that thousands of African Americans had fled Arkansas due to white violence; many of these were now living in Chicago: "we pledge ourselves that if those twelve men were electrocuted we would use our influence to bring thousands more away from Arkansas, which needed Negro labor. There were about a thousand persons in that meeting that afternoon, and the resolution was unanimously adopted" (Wells 1970, 399).

The resolution was sent to Arkansas Governor Brough; Wells notes that it was the only one of several resolutions of protest he received and to which he paid any attention. In an interview he announced he would ignore the resolutions sent by the N.A.A.C.P. and the National Equal Rights League. "But when he got our resolution," Wells (1970) adds, "he said he was going to let his own people there in Arkansas decide the matter. Our pledge in it was one that he could not very well ignore" (399). Money began accumulating in Chicago to donate to the legal defense of the "rioters" and Wells made a list of those who had donated to be published in the *Defender*. The paper declined to publish the list, as:

> [t]he N.A.A.C.P. objected to the *Defender*'s permitting me to start a subscription list in its column because the N.A.A.C.P. was already doing all the work necessary in the matter.
>
> The manager ended his letter by suggesting that I turn over to the N.A.A.C.P. all money that had been received by me to date. I protested to the *Defender* for its course because they should have published that list as a matter of news. ... I prepared a circular letter and sent it to them [the contributors], not only explaining why the information was not given in the *Defender*, but asking permission to use the money sent to make an investigation and find out just what the N.A.A.C.P. had done. (Wells 1970, 401)

Wells would conduct that investigation herself. For the first time since the Memphis lynching in 1892, a sixty-year-old Ida B. Wells returned to the South. It must have been a momentous journey for her, but in the autobiography we hear nothing of that, only a simple acknowledgment that it was indeed her first trip back:

> I took the train for Little Rock in January 1922, arrived there Sunday morning, and went directly to the address that had been given me in the letter sent me by one of the twelve men. I found the wives and mothers preparing to go up to the penitentiary on a visit to their sons and husbands. I made myself look as inconspicuous as possible, joined them, and thus had no trouble whatsoever in gaining entrance to the prison. It was my first return to the South since I had been banished thirty years before. (Wells 1970, 401)

This fact acknowledged, Wells returns to the business at hand. Fearlessly, she proceeds incognito to death row:

> When we came into the building in which these twelve men were incarcerated, we were readily admitted. Mrs. Moore, the leading spirit among the wives, who was well known because of her frequent visits, said, "Boys, come and shake hands with my cousin who has come from Saint Louis to see me." The iron bars were wide enough apart to enable us to shake hands. The one guard on duty sat about fifty feet away reading the Sunday paper. When he looked up, he saw only a group of insignificant looking colored women who had been there many times before, so he went on reading his newspaper.
>
> When we got up close to the bars, Mrs. Moore whispered, "This is Mrs. Barnett from Chicago." An expression of joy spread over their faces, but I put my finger to my lips and cautioned them not to let on, and immediately a mask seemed to drop over the features of each one. I talked to them about their experiences, asked them to write down everything they could recollect about the rioting, and what befell each of them.
>
> I asked them also to tell me the number of acres of land they had tilled during the year, how much cotton and corn they had raised, and how many heads of cattle and hogs they owned, and be sure to say what had become of it all. They told me that since they had been moved to Little Rock they had been treated with a good deal of fairness and consideration, but that while they were in jail in Helena they were in constant torment. First a mob tried to get into the jail to lynch them. Then they were beaten, given electric, and in every possible way terrorized in an effort to force them to confess that their organization was a conspiracy for the purpose of murdering white people and confiscating their property. (Wells 1970, 401–402)

Having obtained the information she required, it was time to relax, lest the prison officials becomes suspicious. For the first time, evidently, the accused men felt something like hope:

> Then Mrs. Moore said, "Boys, don't you want to sing for my cousin?" Whereupon they sang a song of their own composition and many others. The warden of the penitentiary heard them singing from outside, and came in and stood with his hands in his pockets listening to them. I sat on a bench a few feet behind him and said to myself, "There is something in that singing which has never been there before. You don't know what it is, but I do."
>
> It was the note of hope which they were voicing for the first time, because in me they seemed to see somebody who had come to help them in their trouble. ... I listened to those men sing and pray and give testimony from their overburdened hearts, and sometimes the women would take up the refrain. They shed tears and they got "happy," and the burden of their talk and their prayers was of the hereafter.
>
> Finally I got up and walked close to the bars and said to them in a low tone, "I have been listening to you for nearly two hours. You have talked and sung and prayed about dying, and forgiving your enemies, and of feeling sure that you are going to be received in the New Jerusalem because your God knows that you are innocent of the offense for which

> you expect to be electrocuted. But why don't you pray to live and ask to be freed? The God you serve is the God of Paul and Silas who opened their prison gates, and if you have all the faith you say you have, you ought to believe that he will open your prison doors too.
>
> "That is all I've got to say. Quit talking about dying; if you believe your God is all powerful, believe he is powerful enough to open these prison doors, and say so. Dying is the last thing you ought to even think about, much less talk about. Pray to live and believe you are going to get out." (Wells 1970, 402–403)

After leaving the prison, Wells (1970) "spent nearly all night writing down the experiences of the women who were also put in prison in Helena, and within two days I had written statements of each one of those twelve men of the facts I had requested." What she learned amounted to "a terrible indictment of white civilization and Christianity." What she had discovered was that Arkansas whites had done precisely what they had accused their black neighbors of doing, namely murdering them and stealing their crops, their stock, and their household goods. After committing these crimes, including the rearrangement of the facts, local whites used the judicial process "to put the seal of approval on their deeds by legally (?) executing those twelve men who were found guilty after six minutes' deliberation" (quoted passages on 403).

A local black attorney, Scipio Africanus Jones, upon learning that Wells was in town, asked for a meeting. At that meeting Wells reports Jones's acknowledgment of her role: "Well, Mrs. Barnett, we have to give you credit for starting this whole movement. When the matter was first broached, I didn't believe that we had a ghost of a chance. Since then a new trial has been granted, colored people of the state themselves are organized, and they are raising money all over the United States to help in this case." "I know," he said, "you want to see these prisoners. I'll get you a permit and have Mrs. Jones drive you out" (quoted in Wells 1970, 403–404). Wells had a small surprise for him:

> When I told him I had already seen them and had spent nearly all day Sunday with them, he was a very surprised man. I copied what I wanted of the brief which he had prepared, visited the committee which had been organized to receive funds and complimented them that they had at last gotten a move on themselves in the effort to defend and protect innocent men of the race, and said that all the world admired those who fought for the rights of the weak.
>
> Having assured myself that they were doing all they could to raise the needed funds, I offered to cooperate with them by publishing facts I had gathered and helping them to circulate them. I came back to Chicago, wrote my pamphlet about the Elaine rioters, raised the money to print a thousand copies, and circulated almost the entire edition in Arkansas, but received no help, no communication from that committee. (Wells 1970, 404)

The pamphlet was entitled *The Arkansas Race Riot* (Sterling 1995).

While the N.A.A.C.P. had evidently muscled her out, Wells found her reward on earth, indeed at her front door.

> The following winter I came home one Sunday evening and knocked on the door for admittance. A strange young man opened it. He said,
>
> "Good evening, Mrs. Barnett. Do you know who I am?"
>
> "I do not," I said.
>
> He said, "I am one of them twelve men that you came down to Arkansas about last year."
>
> He was well dressed and had been living in Chicago for three months; he said he had been looking for me all that time. He wanted to tell me how much he felt indebted for my efforts.
>
> When my family came in to be introduced, he said, "Mrs. Barnett told us to quit talking about dying, that if we really had faith in the God we worshiped we ought to pray to him to open our prison doors, like he did for Paul and Silas. After that," he said, "we never talked about dying any more, but did as she told us, and now every last one of us is out and enjoying his freedom." (Wells 1970, 404)

The N.A.A.C.P. and Ida B. Wells won freedom for all seventy-nine defendants. Working through its Arkansas branch and two lawyers in the region, a white man named U. S. Bratton and Scipio Jones, the N.A.A.C.P. succeeded in bringing the case to the U.S. Supreme Court. Oliver Wendell Holmes, Jr., who had written the dissent in the Leo Frank case, spoke for the majority on February 12, 1923, in *Moore* v. *Dempsey.* Moorfield Storey credited Walter White with the association's success in the case; James Weldon Johnson commented on the intelligence and skill with which White had conducted the original investigations and his subsequent work on the cases at the national office. Such praise helped create a strong appreciation for White, and no doubt led to his selection as Johnson's successor as secretary of the association. White's and Wells's and Storey's determination paid off. On January 14, 1925, Scipio Jones wired the national office that the six-year fight to save the lives of the twelve men condemned to death and to reduce the sentences of the sixty-seven men serving life imprisonment or very long prison terms had come to an end. The last of the prisoners had been released. Jubilant N.A.A.C.P. officials called the victory the greatest of its kind ever won (Zangrando 1980; Kellogg 1967).

In addition to freedom for the defendants, this case had other consequences. A few days after the Supreme Court decision, the association received a substantial check from Louis Marshall, who had previously failed to secure a favorable ruling from the Supreme Court in the case of Leo Frank (Dinnerstein 1968). It was the *Moore* v. *Dempsey* decision that persuaded Marshall to join the N.A.A.C.P. legal committee. The case also brought the N.A.A.C.P. considerable attention in both the white and black press. Nine years later, when the Supreme Court in *Powell* v. *Alabama*, 287 U.S. 45 (1932), reversed the death sentences in the Scottsboro case and granted the defendants a new trial, White declared that *Powell* reaffirmed the association's earlier work in *Moore.* In competition with the International Labor Defense and its sponsor, the Communist Party-U.S.A. (see chapter 12), White's strong sense of public relations proved useful to the association and its work (Zangrando 1980).

In his thirty-seven-year career with the N.A.A.C.P., Walter White would investigate forty-one lynchings and eight race riots. He wrote two books on lynching. As a colleague and protégé of James Weldon Johnson, who had written the novel *The Autobiography of an Ex-Colored Man*, White was eager to participate in the Harlem Renaissance. He also wrote a novel, *The Fire in the Film*, published in 1924, which told the story of a northern-trained black physician who returned to Georgia to help his people. Because he showed too much support for them, he was lynched. White's examination of lynching was published in 1929. A scholarly study rooted in his own N.A.A.C.P. work, the writing of the book was supported by a Guggenheim Foundation fellowship award in 1926. *Rope and Faggot: The Biography of Judge Lynch* drew considerable attention when it appeared and has remained a standard work in the field since. In addition, White enjoyed a national audience through his articles in black newspapers. In these writings, too, he drew attention regularly to the nightmare that was lynching (Zangrando 1980).

While White and the N.A.A.C.P. were perhaps the most visible opponents of lynching, there were others. In *Rope and Faggot* White cites newspapers whose editorial stances and reporting practices contested lynching. In the South he judged the *Columbus* (Georgia) *Enquirer-Sun* the "most notable instance of courage in the new press" (1929, 174). Edited by Julian Harris, son of the late Joel Chandler Harris, and "his brilliant wife" (174), Julia Collier Harris, the *Enquirer-Sun*'s antilynching position was met with advertisers' boycotts, loss of readers, financial difficulties, not to mention threats against the editors' lives. Against these odds the Chandlers and their paper "militantly and brilliantly" (175) combated lynching, the Ku Klux Klan, opponents of evolutionists, and, as White (1929, 175) nicely sums up the southern right wing, "every other emblem or manifestation of racial or intellectual bigotry." When the *Enquirer-Sun* took on the Klan, that movement, White tells us, dominated the state of Georgia. Even the governor was a Klansman.

While the *Enquirer-Sun* stood alone in White's eyes, there were other southern newspapers that deserved acknowledgment for taking stands against lynching. Among these were the *Atlanta Constitution*, the *Columbia* (South Carolina) *Record*, and the *State* of the same city, the *Charleston* (South Carolina) *News and Courier*, the *Greensboro* (North Carolina) *Daily News*, the *Chattanooga Times*, the *Birmingham News*, the *Houston Post*, the *San Antonio Express*, and perhaps half a dozen others (White 1929).

Also helping to influence white as well as black public opinion were African-American newspapers and magazines. White (1929) estimated that perhaps 250 black newspapers worked against lynching, but he named three monthly magazines as most important: the *Crisis*, the *Opportunity*, and the *Messenger*. The first was the official magazine of the N.A.A.C.P., the second of the National Urban League. As well, White acknowledged the northern white press, most notably the *New York World*. Among (white) magazines, the *Nation* he judged to be the most aggressive in combating lynching. Finally, White was not afraid to name those states which were the most hospitable to lynching: these were, in the 1920s, Mississippi, Arkansas, Florida, and South Carolina.

The N.A.A.C.P. was not the only player on the field of racial politics in the 1920s. Three other groups were prominent, groups whose views of race relations differed sharply both from the association's and from each other's. Among black nationalists, Marcus Garvey and his Universal Negro

Improvement Association (U.N.I.A.) were most visible and vocal; on the far Right, the racist white supremacists of the Ku Klux Klan were all too visible, as we saw in chapter 9; and on the Left, the Communist Party-U.S.A. was invariably critical of the N.A.A.C.P.'s tactics and positions. Garvey accused the N.A.A.C.P. of undermining racial pride and jeopardizing racial solidarity. The Klan condemned the association's interracial objectives as threatening segregation and white dominance. The C.P.-U.S.A. argued that the "lynching of black men and women was one of the extra-legal terrorist devices used to secure and maintain ruling class hegemony" (Aptheker 1977, 9). From such a Marxist perspective, the N.A.A.C.P.'s legal-judicial efforts amounted to accommodationism, avoiding any fundamental, structural changes in an exploitative, capitalist economy. Indicative of the central role of lynching in the racial politics of the period, each organization found it necessary to formulate its own position on the subject (Zangrando 1980).

From Jamaica, Garvey had come to the United States in 1916, where he found an enthusiastic audience among black urban dwellers. The U.N.I.A. siphoned off members from other black activist groups, including the N.A.A.C.P. The differences between the two organizations were never resolved. Garvey was sure that African Americans could never achieve justice in the United States, while Du Bois, Johnson, White, and their European-American allies pressed for reforms within the system. During the spring and summer of 1922, when the U.N.I.A. endorsed the Dyer bill, Garveyites attempted to negotiate a peaceful coexistence with the N.A.A.C.P., but Du Bois and N.A.A.C.P. field secretary William Pickens declined to negotiate (Zangrando 1980; Van Deburg 1997).

While always suspicious of the U.N.I.A., what outraged the N.A.A.C.P. was Garvey's trip to Atlanta in 1922 to meet with Edward Young Clarke, Imperial Kleagle of the Ku Klux Klan. Convinced that all whites were racists and that lynchings and mob violence would never end, Garvey had two motives in meeting with Clarke: (1) to forestall Klan harassment of U.N.I.A., and (2) to see if Clarke would endorse his program for relocation to Africa. From the N.A.A.C.P.'s point of view, *any* dealings with the hated K.K.K. were unthinkable. The meeting mobilized Garvey's critics and enemies, but Garvey and his followers were not discouraged. In mid-1922, Assistant Secretary General Robert L. Poston assured U.N.I.A.'s annual convention that the Dyer bill was a poor alternative to black people's best hope, that is, the establishment of an independent state in Africa (Zangrando 1980; Lewis 1979/1997).

Probably competition between the N.A.A.C.P. and the U.N.I.A. played a role in the N.A.A.C.P.'s decision to intensify its struggle for a federal antilynching law, precisely at the time of Garvey's greatest public success. This was a secondary motive, given that Garvey's trial and conviction in 1927 did not result in any relaxation of the association's efforts. Association personnel were involved in Garvey's downfall, and the N.A.A.C.P. suffered less competition afterward. "But," Robert Zangrando (1980, 91–92) tells us,

> the nature of its interracial visions and legal-judicial programs and the realities of racist violence, not Marcus Garvey, had launched the N.A.A.C.P.'s federal campaigns. The inability to secure passage of the

Dyer bill in 1922 and the unlikelihood of doing so throughout the rest of the decade, not Garvey's removal, caused the Association to temper its drive for a federal law—until renewed violence and a changed political climate in 1933 forced a reconsideration of priorities.

The disagreement with the U.N.I.A. over Garvey's meeting with the Klan was no minor point. The interracial, reformist N.A.A.C.P. could never reconcile itself to that antiblack, anti-Jewish, anti-Catholic, anti-immigrant organization that had been reorganized in its "modern" form by William J. Simmons in Atlanta in 1915, following the lynching of Leo Frank, and expanded by Edward Young Clarke and Elizabeth Tyler in 1920 (Dinnerstein 1968; see chapter 9). During the war, the association had pressed federal officials to take "immediate and strong action" against the Klan (quoted in Zangrando 1980, 92). During the early 1920s N.A.A.C.P. branches worked to undermine the K.K.K. locals. Congressional inquiries into Klan activities were heartening to association members, as was the *New York World*'s 1921 exposé of the Invisible Empire, to which N.A.A.C.P. officials had contributed information (Zangrando 1980).

A dramatic example of the N.A.A.C.P.'s war on the Klan occurred in the fall of 1926. A white mob had seized three black people: Demon Lowman, age twenty-two; Clarence Lowman, fifteen; and Bertha Lowman, twenty-seven, from the Aiken, South Carolina, jail. A mile and a half from town the three were lynched. They had been falsely accused of murder, then sentenced to death in a courtroom crowded by armed Klansmen. When the state supreme court reversed the convictions, and when developments at the retrial indicated the three might go free, whites intervened, lynching them (Zangrando 1980). "Death at the hands of parties unknown," the Aiken, South Carolina, coroner's jury concluded (quoted in White 1929, 32).

Under cover of a press card from the *New York World*, Walter White joined the paper's star reporter, Oliver H. B. Garrett, to investigate firsthand. On October 28, White wrote a public letter to South Carolina Governor Thomas McLeod, in which he detailed the conduct of the Klan in the Aiken lynchings. White advised the governor that he was returning to New York, which "will allow some forty-eight hours before any of the material I have gathered will be published" (quoted in Zangrando 1980, 92).

White's investigations had provided documentation of the premeditated nature of the mob violence, including the collusion of prison officials. White knew the identity (including addresses and occupations) of prominent mob participants, among whom were a bonded constable from the courthouse, a magistrate's constable, two deputy sheriffs, a captain of the chain gang, the town's superintendent of streets, two of the governor's special state constables, two policemen (one of whom wore his uniform to the lynching), a local attorney, a three-time member of the state legislature, a constable from the neighboring community, the town jailer, the town traffic policeman, and the sheriff of the county. Also in his letter White mentioned that three cousins of Governor McLeod were among the spectators. The governor, however, was unimpressed (Zangrando 1980).

For thirty days the *New York World* featured the story on its front page. Other newspapers, including several in South Carolina led by R. Charlton

Wright of the *Columbia Record*, campaigned daily for indictments and convictions. The incoming governor, John G. Richards, promised action. In January 1927, despite the evidence, a grand jury refused to return indictments. Governor Richards denounced the verdict as "a travesty upon justice" (quoted in White 1929, 33) and launched a vigorous campaign—against playing golf on Sunday! Justice was never obtained in the case (Zangrando 1980).

The association never allowed such injustice to undermine its determination to fight lynching, which also meant fighting the Klan. Among its informational publications, the N.A.A.C.P. prepared and distributed a pamphlet entitled "The Recent Record of the Ku Klux Klan—As Set Forth by 2 Alabama Editors," which denounced the sadistic and murderous practices of the Klan. White himself gave considerable attention to the Klan in *Rope and Faggot.* By the late 1920s the Klan was in a state of decline, and the number of reported lynchings decreased (Zangrando 1980).

Still, the N.A.A.C.P. did not stop pressing for federal intervention in the American system of racial injustice. It asked President Herbert Hoover's Law Observance and Enforcement Commission to study lawlessness against African Americans, including lynching, disfranchisement, peonage, mob violence, as well as discrimination in schools, places of public accommodation, and residential occupancy. James Weldon Johnson submitted a brief to the commission chair, George W. Wickersham, with whom the association had discussed the Dyer bill in 1918. Predictably, the Wickersham Commission declined to deal with lynching and racial lawlessness, attending instead to crimes associated with bootleg alcohol and gangland activities (Zangrando 1980). At least it left golf alone.

With Garvey and the U.N.I.A. no longer a factor, it would seem that the N.A.A.C.P. had the playing field to itself. Not so. On its left was the Communist Party-U.S.A., which by mid-decade would denounce the association for allegedly exploiting the antilynching campaign for its own ends. In 1925 the Communists had established the American Negro Labor Congress. A thirty-one-page pamphlet, entitled "Lynching Justice at Work," written by B. D. Amis, followed. The N.A.A.C.P. and the National Urban League were condemned as "the misleaders of the Negro masses" and "the agents of the white ruling class" (quoted in Zangrando 1980, 94); the American Negro Labor Congress's drive against lynching was praised. In general, however, black citizens were unpersuaded (Zangrando 1980).

By 1930 the nearly dormant A.N.L.C. had been renamed the League of Struggle for Negro Rights. Among its positions included the requirement of mandatory death penalties for those convicted of violence against black citizens. The party had also formed a legal unit, the International Labor Defense, to wage "a persistent and militant struggle against lynchings and the entire lynch law system" (quoted in Zangrando 1980, 94). In the spring of 1930, the I.L.D. held a meeting in New York at which lynching was condemned. On the agenda were plans for mass protests, the distribution of one-half million antilynching pamphlets, and an I.L.D. membership drive. The C.P.-U.S.A. accused White and other reformists of misunderstanding the phenomenon of lynching, which, it insisted, could only be comprehended as a consequence of class conflict under capitalism. In 1933, the Communist's Party League of Struggle for Negro Rights called on black people to abandon the N.A.A.C.P., comparing its officials to Booker T. Washington, now in general disrepute as an accommodationist (Zangrando 1980).

The Great Depression provided Communists with new opportunities. Despite a high turnover rate (black involvement rarely exceeded 7 or 8 percent of the party's membership during this period), the C.P.-U.S.A. recruited African Africans vigorously in the early 1930s. The *cause célèbre* of this period, the Scottsboro affair, underscored the competition between the two organizations. The Communist Party's International Labor Defense and the N.A.A.C.P. soon engaged in a heated public struggle over who would represent the defendants. We will examine in detail the legal efforts to rescue the Scottsboro Nine in chapter 12. Zangrando judges the N.A.A.C.P. the victor, but, as we will see, the N.A.A.C.P. blundered more than once in combating the I.L.D. for the right to represent the nine young black men. That battle, during a period when there was an increased number of black delegates, often in positions of leadership, at C.P.-U.S.A. conventions, party training schools, and party-sponsored unemployed councils left the N.A.A.C.P. worried. Who, finally, would represent the majority of African Americans?

The Great Depression

Let us take a moment to step back from racial politics to its gendered and economic concomitants. The Depression was not only an economic nightmare for many Americans, it was a gendered nightmare, especially for working men and women, including those middle-class white men who were unaccustomed to hardship. As it had been the case in the 1890s, white men's suffering would mean black men's suffering, as the incidence of lynching increased in the 1930s. How was white men's economic hardship gendered and racialized?

During the Depression many men suffered psychological breakdown; some committed suicide; some deserted their families and others joined the tramps who wandered from town to town, campfire to campfire, not unlike those who figured prominently in the Scottsboro case. Many men stood in bread or job lines day after day, but most went nowhere. With nothing to do, many of these shocked and traumatized men did nothing but stay home. Inside their "castles" where they were no longer "kings," men hid from the glance of anyone who had known them as they used to be. Safe from the gaze of other men, these imprisoned souls were now more exposed to the family. The older children, especially if they had jobs, often lost respect for their fathers (Filene 1998). "How can you be glad to see your wife and children when you come home," asked a New Haven man, "when you see debts all around you and that's almost all you can talk about? And every time you think of them you know they cry to heaven that you're a failure. The wife may not say so, but she knows it the same as you do" (quoted in Filene 1998, 165).

During the three years following the Crash the marriage rate dropped precipitously, lower than in any period before or since. This reluctance to go to the altar was particularly prevalent among those aged sixteen to twenty-four. As Filene (1998, 169) notes, "a young man dared not take responsibility for a wife when he could not support himself." For those whose manhood was defined by his ability to provide, they were no longer "men," and so the entire wedding scenario was unimaginable. For those who were married, the rate of sexual intercourse decreased sharply and, in a few cases, ceased altogether. Between 1925 and 1945, young women had a below average birthrate of first children (except during the period 1935–1939). Many husbands withdrew into passivity and silence, sitting for hours in isolation in the kitchen or bedroom, slowly disappearing into a deep psychological depression (Filene 1998).

As millions lost jobs and millions of others feared their turn was next, men became defensive and embattled. Many wives tried to help, offering to seek employment; such generosity was often met by male rage. Women lost confidence in men, even women who had embraced conventional ideas of patriarchy. In a national poll taken by the *Ladies' Home Journal* during the Depression, 60 percent of women objected to the word "obey" in the marriage ceremony, 75 percent declared that men and women should make important decisions together, and 80 percent had no problem with an unemployed husband doing housework if the wife worked. There were, of course, limits to this gendered assertiveness: 60 percent admitted that they would lose respect for their husbands if the wife were to earn more than the man, and 90 percent declared that the woman should give up her job if her husband preferred her to stay home (Filene 1998).

The phrase "the forgotten men" indicates how most Americans gendered the Depression. Bread must come first: gender equity and racial justice would come later, much later. And the breadwinner was, of course, assumed to be male. Married women workers, declared a Chicago civic group, "are holding jobs that rightfully belong to the God-intended providers of the household." Congresswoman Florence Kahn asserted that "woman's place is not out in the business world competing with men who have families to support" (quoted in Filene 1998, 160). The city council of Akron, Ohio, agreed, as did 82 percent of Americans in a Gallup poll of 1937 (Filene 1998).

Opinions expressed became actions taken. Many banks and factories dismissed married women; the mayor of Northampton, Massachusetts, fired eight wives working in city hall; three of every four cities across the nation excluded married women from teaching positions; and eight legislatures adopted laws making them ineligible for state jobs. In Washington, Congress ruled that two married persons could not both work for the government. Although in such cases the "person" who must then resign could be, in principle, either male or female, in fact four-fifths of those fired were wives. The National Federation of Business and Professional Women's Clubs, the editors of the *Ladies' Home Journal* and *Woman's Home Companion*, the director of the United States Women's Bureau, and even the First Lady, Eleanor Roosevelt, all protested loudly against this outrageous discrimination. Congress did repeal its law in 1938, but across the nation many would continue to blame working women for men's unemployment (Filene 1998).

Not only white women lost their jobs to white men during the Depression, so did black women and men. The New Orleans city government, for instance, tried to restrict municipal and public works jobs to "qualified voters," thereby eliminating nearly all black employees. Only a federal injunction plus opposition from the Board of Trade and Steamship Association stopped an effort, endorsed by the white longshoremen's union, to exclude blacks from the municipal wharves in New Orleans. Nationally, the New Deal too often turned out to be the same old deal for black citizens. For instance, the Farm Security Administration had been designed to assist small farmers; its resettlement program created a number of new communities of family-sized farms on land purchased by the government. Under leadership of Will Alexander, the F.S.A. made an effort to avoid racial discrimination, and black farms comprised almost a third of its resettlement units in Louisiana, for example, some 791 farms. Never a major program, however, the F.S.A. did little to alleviate rural poverty. Moreover, Alexander's attempt to prevent racial discrimination within the F.S.A. bureaucracy was undermined by the New Deal's tacit acceptance of segregation (Fairclough 1995/1999).

Internal Tensions

The economic deprivations of the Great Depression were felt throughout the N.A.A.C.P. Branches that had struggled to stay alive during the 1920s fell silent as economic conditions deteriorated. Often the national office simply lost contact with branches; by 1933 the New Orleans branch had grown so quiet that officials in the New York office assumed that it had disappeared. The fortunes of the association slowly improved as economic activity increased toward the end of the decade. The New Orleans branch showed signs of life in 1934 and, under the leadership of James E. Gayle, expanded its members to 750. New branches appeared in Jennings (1935), Plaquemines (1935), and Lake Charles (1936). Long dormant branches in Shreveport (1936) and Lake Providence (1938) were reorganized and made active. By 1940 the Baton Rouge branch had 800 members (Fairclough 1995/1999).

Economic hardship, political complexity, and the gendered intensity of racial struggle in 1930s America required a mobilized N.A.A.C.P. The association stayed mobilized, but, of course, any organization undergoes internal tensions, perhaps aggravated by the gendered and racialized Depression. In 1934, the N.A.A.C.P. faced what Zangrando characterizes as an "ominous staff problem," a problem involving no one less than W. E. B. Du Bois. There had been for some time tension between Du Bois, "the aloof and senior scholar of black protest," and Walter White, "the flamboyant, energetic, vain younger staff officer" (Zangrando 1980, 107). A persisting question had been how much autonomy Du Bois should enjoy as editor of the *Crisis*. The journal had lost money since 1929. Along with other N.A.A.C.P. officers, White argued that the Depression would not allow the organization to subsidize the journal indefinitely. At the end of 1932, the board organized the Crisis Publishing Company, a legal maneuver designed to limit the association's liability for the magazine's future debts. This event, coupled with the influence that White increasingly exercised through the *Crisis* editorial board, irritated Du Bois (Zangrando 1980).

In an action that would foreshadow another such move in the Student Nonviolent Coordinating Committee (S.N.C.C.) some thirty years later,

Du Bois asked for a reorganization of the N.A.A.C.P. hierarchy, a reorganization that would replace whites with blacks. In a series of *Crisis* editorials, starting in January 1934, he advocated a program of self-help and economic autonomy. Many association leaders interpreted this as an endorsement of segregation. After Du Bois alleged in the April *Crisis* that N.A.A.C.P. programs were ineffective and that Walter White's "white" features shielded him from a full appreciation of racial oppression, the board responded. It disavowed all unauthorized public disclosures of internal matters, declaring that no salaried officer could use the journal to criticize the "policy, the work, or officers of the association" (quoted in Zangrando 1980, 107–108). Du Bois submitted his resignation in June 1934. Twenty years earlier, in a similar but less serious dispute, Mary White Ovington had sided with Du Bois. This time she felt differently, given "all that White had gone through ... since the Depression Du Bois has made it infinitely harder. ... Now we are rid of our octopus, for of late he has been draining our strength, I hope we shall do better work" (quoted in Zangrando 1980, 108).

Scholars have long noted that Du Bois was, himself, often in bitter conflict with the parent organization of his magazine. The conflict was not superficial; it had to do with the fact that Du Bois was no assimilationist or gradualist. For the early N.A.A.C.P., an ideal society would be one in which color held no practical significance. Far from eradicating race consciousness, Du Bois thought it essential that it be supported, developed, and refined. In insisting that blacks were innately different from whites, Du Bois took a position that was nearly opposite from the integrationist, assimilationist stance of the N.A.A.C.P. Inevitably, the difference caused a breach. When in the early 1930s Du Bois came out for black people voluntarily segregating themselves from whites, his N.A.A.C.P. colleagues were horrified. After separating from the association, Du Bois went his own way. He became a Marxist and settled in Africa, where he lived the remainder of his life (Williamson 1984).

Du Bois was a radical and a revolutionary, articulating views well in advance of their acceptance among black activists generally. Before Du Bois, no influential black intellectual or leader, or any white leader for that matter, argued that black people were ordained by God to be essentially different from white people, and forever and wonderfully so. In the 1930s among black African intellectuals, this idea would be developed into a theory of *négritude*, that blackness was essential and eternal and, to anticipate the language of American racial politics in the 1960s, beautiful. But in the first decades of the twentieth century, Du Bois was virtually alone. Certainly he was isolated on the N.A.A.C.P. staff. Placed along a continuum of assimilation versus separatism, the N.A.A.C.P. and Booker T. Washington occupied one end and Du Bois the other. The N.A.A.C.P. was committed to the assimilation side, Washington and his associates were as well, but closer to the center of the continuum. Du Bois sat at the end of the other side (Williamson 1984).

For a time, practical racial politics required Du Bois to accept assimilationist rhetoric, but only for a time. For him, blackness was hallowed, to be protected and perfected, never merged with, of all things, whiteness. If there were to be assimilation for Du Bois, it would be transcendental. Black people had contributed and would contribute to a total American culture that was simultaneously black and white, each pursuing its own identity by means of which it would know itself and God. Through God social harmony might be achieved (Williamson 1984).

Du Bois's vision was more sophisticated and comprehensive than any other. One index of these qualities was his position toward Africa, which contrasted with Washington's and that of the N.A.A.C.P. Before Du Bois, most African-American leaders had exhibited little interest in Africa, and much of the interest shown was in Africa as an opportunity for missionaries, not as the sacred homeland of a displaced people. Washington had almost no interest in Africa. Nor, in its first years, did the N.A.A.C.P. exhibit much. Probably most educated African Americans would have shared Charles Chesnutt's attitude: he was "not greatly concerned about Africa except as an interesting foreign country [sic]" (quoted in Williamson 1984, 77). But Du Bois, as early as 1899, was interested in the idea of Pan-Africanism. His interest in blackness was not limited to national boundaries.

As Joel Williamson (1984) puts the matter, Washington allowed black people to join with him if they were industrious and "good" blacks. The N.A.A.C.P. allowed blacks to join if they were "good" Americans. Du Bois allowed them to join him if they were, simply, black. Washington's position as the spokesman for African Americans was brief, from about 1895 to about 1907, and then diminishing until his death in 1915. The N.A.A.C.P. would be dominant for over half a century. In the 1960s, Du Bois's ideas would prove to be the most influential of the three, attracting many, regardless of class or region. Black power would affirm that "black is beautiful," and Du Bois might well have recognized himself in the radical civil rights movement three decades after his participation in the N.A.A.C.P. (Williamson 1984).

Depression-Era Antilynching Activism

Its internal crisis resolved, the association's attention turned once again to the passage of antilynching legislation in Congress. At one point the N.A.A.C.P. decided that chances for passage would be improved if a southern congressman sponsored the bill. No southern congressman would, however. The association turned to Senators Robert Wagner (D-New York) and Edward Costigan (D-Colorado). Referring to what he termed a "shocking reversion to primitive brutality," Wagner condemned the inaction of elected officials. He also criticized those law-enforcement officers who condoned and colluded with the lynchers. Long an advocate of liberal measures, and since Roosevelt's election in 1932 a major sponsor of New Deal legislation, Wagner insisted to his colleagues that circumstances justified federal intervention. He declared that "the most painfully won previous gain in mankind's long march from savagery to civilization has been the subordination of mob rule to constituted authority and the guarantee that constituted authority will dispense equal justice to every race, creed, and individual" (quoted in Zangrando 1980, 111). In Wagner's wording we hear echoes of Wells's 1894 rhetoric, as well as the legal emphasis of Jane Addams's 1901 condemnation of the practice in the *Independent*.

Not as nationally visible as Wagner but no less committed to liberal and humanitarian reforms, Costigan brought impressive credentials to his sponsorship of the antilynching measure. He had successfully defended seventy-nine miners indicted for conspiracy in the Ludlow massacre of April 1914. Over the course of his career Costigan had supported federal and state work projects; the child-labor amendment; accident, sickness, old-age, and unemployment insurance programs; increased tax levies on the wealthy; the National Labor Relations Board; the regulation of holding companies; an independently functioning tariff commission and reciprocal tariff agreements; and revised banking legislation to increase federal control over credit and currency (Zangrando 1980).

Walter White was eager to promote the new campaign. Drawing upon the numerous friendships he and Johnson and others enjoyed in literary and journalistic circles, White and his colleagues organized the Writers' League Against Lynching. Among those who joined were Sherwood Anderson, Dorothy Parker, and Drew Pearson. These were impressive and influential names, but they were not likely to frighten southern sheriffs and magistrates into protecting black men. Still, they proved helpful in drawing attention both to lynching and to the campaign against it. The league sent, for instance, a message to Franklin Roosevelt urging his support of the Costigan-Wagner bill and one to California Governor James Rolph, demanding that he retract his defense of lynching (Zangrando 1980; Ginzburg 1962/1988).

Once again the occupant of the White House proved unreliable. In 1933, the association twice sought, without success, to meet with the new president. Not until the end of the year did its appeals appear to be heard. Still, Roosevelt kept his distance from the antilynching campaign. He did address the Federal Council of Churches in December on the subject, and in his January message to Congress, Roosevelt expressed his opposition against "organized banditry, cold-blooded shooting, lynching and kidnapping" (Zangrando 1980).

In January 1934, journalist Mark Ethridge of the *Washington Post* reported that Senator Bryon (Pat) Harrison (D-Mississippi) had predicted in confidence that Roosevelt would not back the Costigan-Wagner proposal. Ethridge also reported that the N.A.A.C.P. "does not expect—really does not care for—the bill to get through, but is rather using it for the moral effect." Such "news" was very distressing to Walter White, James Weldon Johnson, and other N.A.A.C.P. officials and workers. The N.A.A.C.P. redoubled its efforts, persuading Eleanor Roosevelt to arrange a face-to-face meeting between her husband and White. Their conversation was cordial, but F.D.R. did nothing, and the bill went nowhere in the Senate (Zangrando 1980).

The 1934 Costigan-Wagner bill was, more or less, a copy of the earlier Dyer measure. It was written to disturb southern complacency by making lynching too hazardous for southerners to tolerate or practice. The bill was written to "assure persons within [the] jurisdiction of every State the equal protection of the laws, and ... punish the crime of lynching" (quoted in Zangrando 1980, 114). Still, the Costigan-Wagner bill involved no federal retribution against lynchers themselves; it was aimed at law-enforcement officers who, by indifference or collusion, allowed lynching, and at those counties in which lynchings occurred. The measure was criticized by the Left and the Right. Communists denounced the measure for its failure to impose a mandatory death sentence upon lynchers, while conservatives and strict constitutionalists were outraged by federal intervention in what they insisted was the prerogative of the individual states. The N.A.A.C.P. considered the bill wisely drafted. From its own investigations it was clear that lynchings were carried off only because local officials and citizens looked the other way. The Southern Commission on the Study of Lynching agreed (Zangrando 1980).

Walter White was, overall, a shrewd player on the field of racial politics. He understood, for example, the potential power of radio broadcasting. Thanks in no small measure to his efforts, the 1934 Costigan-Wagner proceedings made radio history. For the first time a Senate committee hearing was broadcast nationwide. But, it turned out, not all the broadcasts had been transmitted "live." For instance, all references to segregation, lynchings, and riots, and to the Dyer and Costigan-Wagner bills, were deleted from Joel Spingarn's radio speech on February 11. Both the N.A.A.C.P. and the A.C.L.U. protested; N.B.C. production manager John F. Royal insisted that the network intended no censorship. N.B.C. offered the N.A.A.C.P. fifteen minutes of prime air time during which any speaker could say anything he or she chose about lynching and the association. "In all this," Zangrando (1980, 120) tells us, "White stole the limelight from his competitors, especially those in the C.P.-U.S.A., and provided himself and his colleagues with vital lobbying and public relations experiences that would later benefit the N.A.A.C.P. in its support of a wide range of socioeconomic, New Deal and Fair Deal legislation valuable to black Americans."

Victory remained elusive, however. In January 1935, former Congressman and still ally Leonidas Dyer warned the N.A.A.C.P. that a Democratic Congress would never enact meaningful antilynching legislation. The political structure within Congress did suggest that position, dominated as it was by entrenched senior Democrats from the South. The disproportionate influence of southern senators would undermine the civil rights movement for another thirty years. Senate rules protecting unlimited debate meant that reformist measures could be delayed by filibusters indefinitely. A divided, indifferent European-American public had not faced its own racism; we still have not. Finally, F.D.R. refused to jeopardize his economic and social programs by supporting federal antilynching legislation. As late as March 1936, a president known worldwide for his activist federal government still avoided facing the lynching issue head-on. Instead, Roosevelt sought refuge in pieties about local remedies. Clearly, a double standard prevailed in racial matters. Worse, the more vigorously Walter White lobbied to secure White House support, the more hostile presidential staff members, such as Stephen Early, became (Zangrando 1980).

As we saw in chapter 1, the lynching of Claude Neal in 1934 drew considerable attention to the issue across the nation. In an eight-page pamphlet entitled "The Lynching of Claude Neal," the association summarized the pertinent points: (1) the intentions to lynch, (2) the news media's contribution, (3) local officials' knowledge of the planned lynching, and (4) the totally inadequate protection provided the prisoner. Because the mob had seized Neal in Alabama then taken him across the state line to Florida, the association tried to invoke federal jurisdiction under the so-called Lindbergh Kidnapping Act. The Lindbergh Act had been passed in 1932 after the kidnapping and murder of Anne Morrow and Charles Lindbergh's infant son. Only five months before Neal's death, Congress had broadened the law to provide punishment in those cases where victims were "held for ransom or reward or otherwise." It would seem an open-and-shut case. The association asked Franklin Roosevelt and United States Attorney Homer S. Cummings to begin proceedings against Neal's lynchers. Additionally, N.A.A.C.P. staff approached several legislators and legal scholars regarding the applicability of the Act, as amended; most, although not all, agreed that the lynching of Claude Neal was a federal matter (Zangrando 1980; Howard 1995).

Cummings, however, declined to cooperate; he insisted that the Lindbergh Law did not apply to the Neal lynching because the kidnapping of Neal did not involve "ransom or reward." Walter White and the N.A.A.C.P. disagreed. White made the argument that this interpretation was in error, pointing out that in May 1934, the Lindbergh kidnapping law had been amended to read, "ransom, reward, or otherwise." White obtained confirmation from the amendment's authors, Senators Royal Copeland (N.Y.), Arthur Vandenberg (Mich.), and Lewis Murphy (Iowa), that they had in fact intended the amendment to give the federal government power to act in any interstate kidnapping. Still, the Justice Department, under Cummings, declined to involve itself in the Neal case (Howard 1995).

Walter White used the Neal lynching to promote the national antilynching cause. Although he was sickened by the details of the nightmarish event, he knew that its gruesome nature might stir national sentiment. The N.A.A.C.P. leader asked Howard Kester, a liberal white southerner, to investigate the Neal case at the scene in Jackson County, Florida. As we read in chapter 1, Kester dutifully reported the horrifying tale of the torture, mutilation, and castration of Neal. His work proved invaluable in helping White and the N.A.A.C.P. shock the nation into awareness that federal antilynching legislation was necessary. He and the N.A.A.C.P. circulated one series of five thousand copies of the Kester Report, then a second series of ten thousand copies as hundreds of requests flooded the association's offices (Howard 1995).

Not quite a month after Neal had been lynched, on October 27, Eleanor Roosevelt informed White of her conversation with her husband regarding the Neal lynching: "He hopes very much to get the Costigan-Wagner Bill passed in the coming session." She regretted that the Justice Department did not see the legitimacy of federal authority in the matter, adding hopefully, "I think possibly they will." That hope was short-lived. Five days later, in a memorandum to Assistant Solicitor General Angus MacLean, the attorney general stated his opinion. He began by observing that there had been many appeals to the federal government in the matter of lynching. He worried that an attempt at too wide an application of existing federal laws would have little effect and could, by provoking a conservative reaction, undermine the department's overall program against crime. Cummings doubted that Congress ever intended for the kidnapping statute to apply to lynching: "It must be remembered that the same Congress declined to pass a law dealing with the general subject of lynching. It is difficult for me to believe that the Congress inadvertently passed an antilynching statute where kidnapping and interstate commerce were involved" (quoted in Zangrando 1980, 123). He warned F.D.R. that if the Justice Department tried to prosecute lynchers, political repercussions would follow. New Dealers were politically dependent upon southern Democrats. As a consequence, as Zangrando (1980, 123) puts it, "citizen Claude Neal and other black Americans from the Deep South would have to find their justice in heaven or in hell, or in some less ethereal setting, like Florida or Alabama."

In spite of these setbacks, White kept interest in the Neal episode alive. He devoted the entire January 1935 issue of the *Crisis* to the subject of lynching; he was also instrumental in arranging, through the cooperation of the College Art Association, the "Art Commentary on Lynching" at the Arthur V. Newton Gallery in New York City from February 15 to March 2, 1935. However, it had to be relocated at the last minute when the designated gallery withdrew its invitation, allegedly because "political, economic, and social pressures had been brought to bear" (quoted in Zangrando 1980, 125). Several other art dealers telephoned the national office to offer space; from these the staff chose the Arthur U. Newton Galleries on East Fifty-seventh Street (Zangrando 1980).

The exhibit featured the work of more than three dozen artists, including Peggy Bacon, Thomas Hart Benton, Reginald Marsh, Hale Woodruff, and George Bellows's "The Law Is Too Slow." Pearl Buck spoke at the show's opening; Sherwood Anderson joined Erskine Caldwell in writing forewords for the catalog. The exhibit was attended by more than two thousand people; White praised the event as a "phenomenal success." Further, the visitors' registration list included the names of more than 800 people whom the staff hoped might take an interest in the association's work. Eleanor Roosevelt accepted White's invitation to view the exhibit, although she did so without the media attention White had wanted (Zangrando 1980).

The exhibit also fared well in its brief road tour, but an extended cross-country showing proved impossible. Charles Houston (a member, along with Thurgood Marshall, of the association's legal team) informed White from Washington that Elizabeth Eastman had tried without success to get the Phillips Gallery, but the management judged the show too grisly (Zangrando 1980; Howard 1995). Houston added acidly that perhaps "lynching should be nice and tidy." Despite the limited tour, the N.A.A.C.P. raised money from the Art Commentary during March, the *Baltimore Sun* praised the exhibit, and the *New York World-Telegram* exclaimed: "It ... tears the heart and chills the blood. If it upsets your complacency on the subject, it will have been successful" (quoted in Zangrando 1980, 126).

The Lynching of Jerome Wilson

Claude Neal was not the only black man lynched in 1934, of course. The lynching of Jerome Wilson provided Walter White with additional "ammunition" in his battle for antilynching legislation, and illustrates how local officials and even, in this instance, a U.S. senator, declined to intervene in white men's "blood lust." The story is a familiar one, but it is worth telling not only to provide concrete detail in this impressionistic history of racial politics in the

1930s, but to honor the murdered man as well as his family, which was completely destroyed by the event.

John and Tempie Wilson were prosperous landowners with five sons and three daughters, all living at home near Franklinton in Washington Parish in southeast Louisiana. The parish bordering on Washington to the west had earned the name of "Bloody Tangipahoa" (Bond and Bond 1997, 9). On July 21, 1934, a white stock inspector named Joe Magee came to the Wilson farm and told Jerome, John Wilson's twenty-eight-year-old son, that one of their mules had not yet been dipped under the tick eradication law. Jerome knew otherwise and told the inspector that he would have to wait for his father to return from Franklinton. Unhappy at being told what to do by a young black man, Magee became argumentative, threatening to seize the mule there and then. Not intimidated, Jerome ordered Magee off the farm and promised to shoot him if he touched the animal (Fairclough 1995/1999).

When the enraged Magee returned an hour or two later with Deputy Sheriff Delos C. Wood and two other deputies, Jerome Wilson appreciated his situation and offered to surrender the mule. But Wood wanted more than the mule. "Go with me, boy," he told Wilson, and walked toward him to place him under arrest. Wilson refused to comply and, with his brother Moise, demanded to see a warrant. When the deputy sheriff tried to force Jerome to come with him, a fight ensued, with Moise Wilson and Wood wrestling over Wood's pistol. Wood managed to pull his arm free and shot Moise in the stomach; either Wood or another deputy shot Jerome in the thigh. Jerome stumbled back to the house, picked up his shotgun, and fired at Wood, hitting him in the head. With the deputy sheriff dead, the other deputies arrested the Wilsons, although not before shooting two other brothers, including a twelve-year-old boy, as they left. Within hours the entire family was in jail, including the mother, the sisters, an uncle, and—even though he had not been present—John Wilson. His son Moise died of his wounds later that day. A mob gathered outside the jail each night threatening to lynch the prisoners. Only repeated promises of a speedy trial and swift punishment kept the mob at bay (Fairclough 1995/1999).

On July 24, Jerome Wilson, his brother Luther, and their mother Tempie were all charged with the murder of Delos C. Wood. John Wilson and four of his other children were kept in jail as material witnesses. The lawyer appointed by the trial judge to defend them was given only three days to prepare his case; a second attorney had only two days. The fact that Jerome Wilson was seriously wounded, and that the entire Wilson family was in jail, each in a separate cell, seriously impeded preparations for the defense. Moreover, no one was told until the morning of the trial whether the three defendants were to be tried together or separately (Fairclough 1995/1999).

The trial of Jerome Wilson began on July 30 in Franklinton just nine days after the incident that sparked it. Still recovering from his gunshot wound, the young man had to be carried into the courtroom in a chair. In the courtroom it was standing room only, and some observers were perched on the window sills outside. There was only one black person in the room, the defendant. A relative of the Wilsons had tried to enter the room only to flee when whites attacked him. The selection of a jury took most of the day; the trial itself did not begin until late afternoon. The defense pointed out that Jerome had resorted to his firearm only after Wood had shot Moise. Magee and Deputy McCain testified that the black man had gone for his gun before any shots had been fired. When the jury finally returned at 9:30 P.M. on July 31, the white men surrounding the courthouse were visibly impatient. Spotting Jerome Wilson being carried back to jail, someone shouted, "Get him!" and the crowd surged toward the prisoner. From inside the courthouse, the jury could hear Sheriff J. L. Brock pleading with the mob "to give the jury a chance" (quoted in Fairclough 1999, 28). The next day Jerome Wilson was found guilty, and the day following Judge C. Ellis Ott rejected the defense lawyers' motion for a new trial. On August 6 Ott sentenced Wilson to death by hanging (Fairclough 1995/1999).

In Chicago, Percival L. Prattis of the American Negro Press news agency had been following the trial. On August 3 he alerted Roy Wilkins, a member of the N.A.A.C.P.'s national staff and an experienced journalist, to the travesty of justice under way in southeast Louisiana. "It's as clear as crystal that convictions in these cases cannot stand," Prattis wrote. The speed of the trial, the lynch-mob atmosphere, the facts of the shooting made it "a case in which you cannot lose and which will enable you to sensationally contrast the association's methods with those of the I.L.D" (quoted in Fairclough 1995/1999, 28). As we will see in chapter 12, the aggressive defense of the Scottsboro Nine by the International Defense League (I.L.D.) was making the N.A.A.C.P. appear inept and timid. Earlier that year (1934), the I.L.D. had made its appearance in Louisiana by publicizing the lynching of Freddie Moore (Fairclough 1995/1999).

At the direction of Walter White, the New Orleans branch retained a white criminal lawyer, G. Wray Gill, to appeal Jerome Wilson's sentence and to prepare the defense of Tempie and Luther Wilson. When the state asked for a continuance in the case of Tempie Wilson on November 5, it was obvious that the prosecution was losing confidence. Two days later the Louisiana Supreme Court ordered a new trial for Jerome Wilson on the grounds that the defense had been given inadequate time to prepare the case. "It is only natural that there should be public indignation when it might appear that a foul and brutal killing took place," the court ruled, "but it should not be permitted to interfere with the orderly process of justice in such a way as to deprive the accused of his constitutional rights and guaranties" (quoted in Fairclough 1995/1999, 28). On January 11, Walter White received a letter from James E. Gayle, president of the New Orleans branch, informing him that the appeal had succeeded (Fairclough 1995/1999).

Jerome Wilson was not tried a second time. Earlier that day, in the first hours of the morning, a group of white men entered the Washington Parish jail in Franklinton. They lynched him, leaving his naked and barely recognizable body in a ditch: "You couldn't tell that it was him except for his mouth" (quoted in Bond and Bond 1997, 80). The reaction of Sheriff J. L. Brock, who gave the reporters an account of how Wilson met his death, was typical of southern intransigence: "There wasn't any lynching. There wasn't any mob either. ... They were just about six or eight men who were going about their business" (quoted in Fairclough 1995/1999, 28–29). As Adam Fairclough points out, this local sheriff not only ignored the civil rights of Jerome Wilson, he flouted the highest judicial tribunal in the state of Louisiana (Fairclough 1995/1999).

With the Costigan-Wagner antilynching bill before Congress, the lynching of Jerome Wilson provided the N.A.A.C.P. with more "ammunition" in its struggle against the South on Capitol Hill. In an angry letter to President Roosevelt describing the case in detail, Walter White restated his demand for the president to intervene in the struggle against lynching. The Writers League Against Lynching, whose letterhead read like a who's who of the literary world, also protested Jerome Wilson's death. And on January 30 in New Orleans, sixty-two community organizations sponsored an antilynching rally at the Pythian Temple (Fairclough 1995/1999).

In a telegram to Huey Long, now a U.S. senator, Walter White observed that "it is widely reported ... that you are virtual dictator of State of Louisiana and that you are able to accomplish anything you choose to attempt in State." If so, White asked, would Long prove the truth of his recent statement, delivered in opposition to the Costigan-Wagner bill, that the southern states would themselves wipe out lynching? In a conversation with Roy Wilkins of the N.A.A.C.P. the day after the lynching, Huey Long was unmoved. It was "too bad," he said distractedly, "but those slips will happen." Still, he offered, "that nigger was guilty of cold-blooded murder." Wilkins reminded Long that the Louisiana Supreme Court had just granted Jerome Wilson a new trial, but the senator was unimpressed. "This nigger got hold of a smart lawyer somewhere and proved a technicality. He was guilty as hell." The N.A.A.C.P. ought to back off, Long continued. If they went after the lynchers "it might cause a hundred more niggers to be killed. You wouldn't want that, would you?" (quoted in Fairclough 1995/1999, 29).

Defeat

Despite these outrages, Walter White's campaign to move the Costigan-Wagner bill through the Senate in 1935 would prove unsuccessful. That year marked the beginning of that phase which would later be classified as the second New Deal or the "Second Hundred Days." From January to late August 1935, Congress passed such important measures as the Emergency Relief Appropriation Act (which established the Works Progress Administration), the Resettlement Administration, the Rural Electrification Administration, the National Resources Committee, the National Youth Administration, the Farm Mortgage Moratorium Act, and the tax-provision Revenue Act. During the same period, while the Costigan-Wagner bill was being blocked for the second consecutive year, New Deal forces were starting their own successful campaigns for the passage of four major laws: the Social Security Act, the National Labor Relations Act, the new Banking Act, and the Public Utilities Holding Company Act (Zangrando 1980).

With such an important series of legislative initiatives preoccupying them, neither the White House nor the Democratic majority in Congress intended to allow the business of the Senate to be delayed indefinitely over the antilynching bill. The Costigan-Wagner measure would meet the same fate as the earlier Dyer bill and for the same reasons. Southerners made passage too expensive politically and northerners capitulated, deciding there were higher national priorities than protecting the bodies of black men. In exasperation Walter White resigned from the Advisory Council for the government of the Virgin Islands on May 6: "It is a matter of great disappointment that you as President did not see your way clear to make a public pronouncement … giving your open endorsement to the antilynching bill and your condemnation of the shameless filibuster by a willful group of obstructionists. … [I]n justice to the cause I serve I cannot continue to remain even a small part of your official family" (quoted in Zangrando 1980, 129). The breach between the N.A.A.C.P. and the New Deal would not prove permanent, however (Zangrando 1980).

Jesse Daniel Ames was not pleased with the Costigan-Wagner Act, despite the fact that it spoke directly to the chief legal weakness in the antilynching efforts of southern activists like herself, namely their inability to bring lynchers to trial or to punish colluding officials. The measure required federal trials for lynchers when local authorities refused to act, fines or jail terms for law-enforcement officers who failed to discharge their duties, and damage claims against those counties where lynchings occurred. Like other southern liberals, Ames preferred state action. Despite her objections to the bill, she did decide to make no public criticism of it (Hall 1979).

Still, Ames's position was no secret within the civil rights community, especially after she wrote to her old friend and then Senator Tom Connally, a letter that was leaked to the press. In that communication she expressed to him her faith that the "South can and will stop lynchings." Roy Wilkins of the N.A.A.C.P. responded angrily, but Ames was unapologetic. In fact, she reiterated her opposition to federal legislation in a long letter to Mary McLeod Bethune, a letter in which she defended her own sincerity and integrity. Her letter to Senator Connally had been, she pointed out, "private and personal." She had written to encourage him to make good on his claims that the southern states "could and would stop lynching." Bethune believed Ames. In her reply, she reassured her that southern black women would continue to support her and the A.S.W.P.L.: "Enough said. I understand you thoroughly. We should all press forward, doing our best. I have unswerving confidence in your interest and cooperation and sincerity" (quoted in Hall 1979, 247–248).

Why had Ames failed to support what was so obviously needed, federal legislation against lynching? In addition to the contradictions inherent in the southern liberal position, there were, her biographer Jacquelyn Dowd Hall tells us, more personal reasons, reasons rooted in her life history. The possibility that Congress, not Ames's own laboriously built association, might succeed in stopping lynching "posed an intolerable personal threat." She worried, Hall speculates, that her position would be undermined, that "she would lapse into the obscurity that had marked her childhood and her married life." Furthermore, Hall tells us,

> she lacked the flexibility to change her mind. Provided with such psychological space neither by her private experience as a woman or by a society which recognized her abilities and supported her aspirations, she could not supply the imaginative leadership demanded by changing times. The necessity of "fighting every step of the way" meant, in the end, that

> she could never risk an admission of error or a moment of deference. Under her leadership, the practice of the A.S.W.P.L. remained static, a force for social order but not for fundamental social change. (1979, 253)

Despite the outright opposition of conservative southerners and the absence of support from southern liberals, in 1937 there seemed new momentum for Costigan-Wagner. Ames herself would concede that passage was imminent. There was talk of disbanding the A.S.W.P.L. once a federal law went into effect, although Ames preferred that the group redirect its program "to make the law effective" (quoted in Zangrando 1980, 137). Despite their differences, the A.S.W.P.L. and the N.A.A.C.P. could agree that the fight for a federal antilynching law served a major purpose in the overall scheme of improved race relations (Zangrando 1980).

The momentum did not last long. Once again southerners filibustered, stalling all business in the Senate in their opposition to Costigan-Wagner. Southerners not only opposed the legislation, they denounced it. Why couldn't Yankees understand? Senator Theodore Bilbo tried to explain:

> Mr. President, I may inquire, what Senator ... will not understand that the underlying motive of the Ethiopian who has inspired this proposed legislation, the antilynching bill, and desires its enactment into law with a zeal and frenzy equal if not paramount to the lust and lasciviousness of the rape fiend in his diabolical effort to despoil the womanhood of the Caucasian race, is to realize the consummation of his dream and ever-abiding hope and most fervent prayer to become socially and politically equal to the white man. (quoted in Zangrando 1980, 150)

Southern white "good ole boys" could not, even in the face of facts, give up their fantasy of muscular black bucks "despoiling" their fair "womanhood." It was, obviously, a zealously loved, zealously guarded fantasy they would not relinquish.

The filibuster continued; southern reactionaries continued to control the tone, substance, and direction of debate. Louisiana's Allen J. Ellender, for instance, spoke for twenty-seven hours, holding the floor for a record six days. During the course of his "speech," Ellender not only openly disparaged African Americans but advocated repeal of the Fifteenth Amendment, and demanded federal legislation to ban interracial marriages as well (Fairclough 1995/1999). Dismay settled over the N.A.A.C.P. On January 15, 1938, Roy Wilkins complained to Charles Houston about the "the one-sided harangue which is going on in Washington." The *New York Daily News*, which had once endorsed the measure, now reversed itself in deference to southern opposition. The *News* now advised Congress to drop the bill. While acknowledging the noble purpose of the Act, Nebraska's George Norris worried that the racial bitterness surfacing in the debate would prove a higher price than the Senate wished to pay. Wilkins understood that these developments meant defeat: "we have plenty of friends in the Senate who are willing to argue at length and effectively on the question. ... We have few men who are willing to go down the line in a nasty discussion involving the race question" (quoted in Zangrando 1980, 150). There was, as we saw, even opposition to the antilynching bill among southern reformers such as Jessie Daniel Ames. In addition to their allegiance to states' rights, they feared an antilynching bill would retard the spread of liberalism in the region. The fact that twenty southern newspapers had responded favorably to the bill did not weaken the opposition to it in the South overall (Zangrando 1980).

Wagner had been ill during the early phases of the debate, but on February 3 he took the floor to make a lengthy and comprehensive defense. Relying on materials provided by the N.A.A.C.P., Wagner made his points tellingly. But it was clear there was insufficient political will in the Senate to break the filibuster and win passage. On March 28, 1938, the antilynching bill was displaced, and, in effect, buried (Zangrando 1980). The effect was, of course, devastating, not only on African Americans generally but specifically on those who had fought long and hard for the legislation. But, somehow, those opposed to lynching, while defeated, found the psychological strength and moral courage to continue.

While Roosevelt, as we have seen, declined to intervene personally in the antilynching campaign, he did encourage southern liberals to challenge southern stubbornness. In 1938 he cautiously supported the formation of the Southern Conference for Human Welfare (S.C.H.W.), an interracial coalition of liberals and radicals that held its first meeting in Birmingham, Alabama. In 1939 he created the Civil Rights Section of the Justice Department, which instigated F.B.I. investigations of lynchings and allowed the first federal prosecution of a police brutality case. At the least, the existence of the section encouraged southern officials. When Clinton Clark, an organizer for the Louisiana Farmers Union, was detained in a Natchitoches jail in July 1940, state attorney general Eugene Stanley phoned the local district attorney and advised him to protect the prisoner (Fairclough 1995/1999). "We've got to be careful," Stanley said. "The State is on the spot. We can't afford that kind of thing with the federal government like it is. Remember now, no lynching!" (quoted in Fairclough 1999, 31).

Within days of Stanley's warning, the *Louisiana Weekly* reported a legal decision that, Fairclough (1990) points out, gave pause to those many southern sheriffs fond of saying, "I *am* the law around here." This case had followed the lynching in October 1933 of Freddie Moore, accused of murdering Annie Mae LaRose, a seventeen-year-old white girl. After the lynching, the girl's stepfather confessed to the crime. Moore's parents sued Sheriff Lezin H. Himel for $10,000 in criminal damages, arguing that two of his deputies had assisted the lynchers. Their attorney (Johnson Armstrong) managed to move the case to a federal court on the basis that the action involved an interstate dispute, Moore's father being a native of Arkansas. An all-white jury awarded the Moores $2,500 in a judgment against the sheriff, an award that took four years to collect (Fairclough 1999).

In 1940 a final bipartisan effort to pass federal antilynching legislation got under way. On January 10, 1940—for the second time in three years, the third time in eighteen years, and the last time ever—an antilynching bill passed the House of Representatives. This time the margin was 252 to 131. The Senate, still dominated by southerners and conservatives, once again proved to be the problem. Committee hearings ended in mid-March. During those hearings, association witnesses repeated the nightmarish stories, the same compelling reasons for federal legislation to stop the mob rape of black men (Zangrando 1980).

This time there was an effort to relate lynching and racism to the world situation, a strategy sanctioned by the N.A.A.C.P. board in 1938. White began to suggest that antidemocratic forces around the world, on both the Right and the Left, opposed the antilynching bill in hopes that its defeat would alienate African Americans sufficiently that they would then withhold their allegiance from America. In his testimony, Arthur Spingarn emphasized the international theme with references to newspaper articles from Germany, Italy, Japan, the Soviet Union, and several Latin American nations that reported lynchings in the United States. Among those he cited was a piece from the January 28, 1938, issue of *Voelkischer Beobachter*, the Nazi party publication, which judged American treatment of its black citizens as worse than Germany's own conduct toward its Jews. In 1940, the idea that the United States must reform its racial customs for the sake of its image abroad was new and, for most whites, unconvincing. This argument would become more convincing during the war against Nazi Germany and more convincing still in the post-1945 era of cold war tensions and Third World decolonization (Zangrando 1980).

While the bill was being battered in the Senate, N.A.A.C.P. executives renewed their efforts to persuade the White House to intervene. There, however, secretary Edwin M. Watson kept them at arm's length from a president immersed in a rapidly escalating world war. Finally, on February 7, White and Arthur Spingarn were permitted to meet with Roosevelt, but once again the president declined to intervene. Spring and summer passed, and by the fall of 1940, the full Senate still had done nothing about the antilynching bill, even though the Judiciary Committee had judged the measure favorably on March 25. In October the Senate moved into executive session and laid the antilynching bill to rest (Zangrando 1980).

The death of the antilynching bill in October meant, once again, that the issue of federal protection for African Americans still had little priority in Washington. Once again the Democrats refused to risk party unity, and 1940 was a presidential election year. The Republicans too were disinclined to risk their alliance with conservative southern Democrats whom they needed to fight against other liberal reform initiatives. That both major parties could dismiss the bill only a month before Franklin Roosevelt's bid for an unprecedented third term—a bid strongly contested by Republican Wendell Wilkie—underscored both parties' assumption that, no matter what, black voters would support the Democrats. There would be one more sustained push for federal legislation during the postwar period (1947 to 1950), but the most intense phase of the fight against lynching had ended. During 1882 to 1933, 61 antilynching bills had been introduced to Congress; from 1934 to 1940, 130; from 1941 to 1951, 66. When the seventy-seventh Congress opened in 1941, six members (Gavagan of New York, Arthur Mitchell of Illinois, U. S. Guyer of Kansas, Lee E. Geyer of California, Bartlett Jonkman of Michigan, and Louis Ludlow of Indiana) sponsored antilynching measures. Nothing came of any of them. No antilynching bill was successfully reported from committee in either 1941 or

1942. It was, as Robert Zangrando (1980, 165) concludes, "an idea whose time had gone."

In 1940, the South enjoyed its first twelve-month period without a lynching. That fact made the news. The May 10, 1940, edition of the *New York Times* reported that the:

> SOUTH GOES WHOLE YEAR WITHOUT SINGLE LYNCHING. Atlanta, May 9—The modern South ended its first year without a lynching last midnight, and today a foe of mob rule credited this new record to effective education, plus swift work of police radio patrols. Mrs. Jessie Daniel Ames, executive secretary of the Association of Southern Women for the Prevention of Lynching, said midnight marked the close of the first twelve-month lynchless period since tabulations were started in 1882. ... The association, representing 41,000 southern women and now in its tenth year, Mrs. Ames said, campaigned especially against public opinion that has "accepted too easily the claim of lynchers that they acted solely in the defense of women." (quoted in Ginzburg 1962/1988, 234–235)

During the 1940s the N.A.A.C.P.'s agenda broadened; federal antilynching legislation ceased to be the organization's primary legislative objective. In organizational terms, however, whatever protest momentum, political contacts, public visibility, community support, and staff competence the association could boast were owed, in part, to the antilynching campaigns of the previous decades. Walter White continued to argue that lynching, the threat of mob violence, and physical intimidation in general was embedded in every form of racial subjugation, whether it be illiteracy, education, disenfranchisement, job discrimination, housing segregation, or the segregated transportation system. Years later a former colleague commented on White's commitment to the issue, recalling that, "regardless of the topic, Walter would eventually steer it around to the fight against lynching" (quoted in Zangrando 1980, 166).

VI. World War II

> *Beginning in the 1930s, when black lawyers began to provide competent—indeed, superb—representation for black defendants, the courtroom became the setting for rituals that called into question in profound ways white notions of black inferiority.*
>
> —W. Fitzhugh Brundage, *Lynching in the New South: Georgia and Virginia, 1880–1930* (1993)

> *[T]he Second World War never developed the intense psychic meaning that the Great War had. Although it lasted three years longer and drafted six times as many young males, it did not become a crucible of masculinity. Most men served with patriotic loyalty but felt surprisingly little personal commitment.*
>
> —Peter G. Filene, *Him/Her/Self* (1998)

Our moral position in international relations is seriously compromised by the reflection that the United States is the only country on the face of the globe pretending to civilization, where human beings, in the presence of men, women and children, can be burned alive at the stake or done to death in defiance of the courts and with the connivance or actual assistance of officers sworn to uphold the laws and protect the public peace.

—James Weldon Johnson, "The Practice of Lynching: A Picture, the Problem and What Shall Be Done about It" (1927)

The outbreak of World War II in 1939 provided a new opportunity for African Americans to press for their civil rights. A Committee on the Participation of Negroes in the National Defense Program had been formed in 1940, but it failed to gain meaningful concessions. Public statements by the president in general opposition to segregation were ignored locally, especially in the South. So was the vague antidiscrimination language in the Draft Act. As we have seen, it was not until just before the election of 1940 that President Roosevelt was even willing to even see a delegation of black leaders, and on that occasion they were rebuffed. Representatives of the N.A.A.C.P., the Urban League, and the Sleeping Car Porters asked for integration of the armed forces and the removal of all racial barriers within them; but the War Department, with the president's approval, simply reiterated its policy of keeping African Americans segregated in all-black regiments (Lacy 1972).

In these frustrating circumstances, A. Philip Randolph, who had been one of the rebuffed spokesmen in that 1940 meeting with the president, decided in late January 1941 to organize a mass public demonstration against racial injustice. He envisioned this as taking the form of a march on Washington in which 10,000 African Americans (an estimate later raised to 100,000) would come to the capital to declare before the president and Congress their demands for equal treatment in the armed forces and in war industry. It was in his union newspaper, the *Black Worker*, that Randolph issued a call for African Americans to march on the capital, an event to take place July 1. White and the N.A.A.C.P. staff kept in touch with Randolph as they watched support for the idea spread (Lacy 1972; Zangrando 1980).

By early May, the momentum was palpable. By mid-June, anxious administration officials, including the president himself, were meeting with Randolph and White in order to stop the march. F.D.R. and his advisors became increasingly distressed. It was clear that to ignore or deny black demands would be more disruptive of the war effort than to concede them. When various public statements about equality and nondiscrimination failed to persuade the sponsors of the march, the president moved. In a tense atmosphere, on June 25, 1941 (a week before the march was to begin), Roosevelt signed a long-sought Executive Order (E.O. 8802) forbidding racial discrimination by defense contractors and by agencies of the federal government. The Order also established a Committee on Fair Employment Practice (F.E.P.C.) within the Office of Production Management to oversee its execution. In spite of the fact that nothing had been gained in the fight against discrimination in the armed services, the march was called off—officially it was "postponed"—and the black community awaited the results of the Executive Order (Zangrando 1980; Lacy 1972).

The results were noteworthy but unsatisfying. Many who had been excited by Randolph's success found themselves disappointed. The Executive Order did not, for instance, apply to the everyday racism black soldiers faced from their white comrades. The White House had promised reforms in employment but could not fully deliver. The order lacked enforcement powers, as there were no penalties for noncompliance. F.E.P.C. was in many respects a paper tiger (Zangrando 1980). But for hundreds of thousands of African Americans who were helped to better jobs, even the limited achievements of F.E.P.C. were important. In the long run, Executive Order 8802 established a precedent which would prove useful for future protest. For the first time the equitable treatment of African Americans in employment had been articulated as a national policy matter. Prior to 1940, almost no white, even those who worried over unjust employment policies, would have accepted as legal or proper federal regulation of the hiring practices of private employers, even those with federal contracts. For the first time, then, discrimination in private employment—even if restricted to private employment in the fulfillment of government contracts—was defined as illegal, remediable by government action (Lacy 1972). Twenty years later Randolph would once again propose a march on Washington, a march that would not be stopped, despite the efforts of another Democratic president. This time substantial federal legislation would follow.

The Lynching of Cleo Wright

Despite the gains suggested by E.O. 8802, lynchings continued. Not two months after the bombing of Pearl Harbor, a lynching took take place that was not easily ignored. The N.A.A.C.P.'s response to the event mobilized public, especially black, opinion, and forced a war-focused administration to once again confront the fact that white men were still going after the bodies of black men.

Early in the dark, wintry morning of January 25, 1942, on the southeast edge of Sikeston, Missouri, an unknown black man entered the home of Grace Sturgeon at approximately 1:30 A.M. After attacking her with a knife, the assailant fled into the night. Thirty minutes later and within a short distance of the Sunset Addition, where most black citizens lived, Cleo Wright stood before the headlights of a police car. He was covered in blood. Arrested and placed in the vehicle, he soon took a hidden knife and stabbed Night Marshal Hess Perrigan in the lower jaw. Point-blank gunshots riddled Wright's body in response to this assault on an officer; Wright began to bleed profusely.

Cleo Wright, Officer Perrigan, and Grace Sturgeon all received treatment at the small Sikeston General Hospital, soon the site of a death watch as residents gathered. News of the assaults had traveled quickly through the small community. Dominic J. Capeci, Jr. (1998, 1), characterizes the white response: "Already anxious over the recent bombing of Pearl Harbor and U.S. entry into World War II, they grasped for resolution to the black brutalities that rubbed raw their white nerves. Some believed that it lay in still more bloodletting. How could public order be restored abroad, if not first at home?"

After receiving medical treatment for his gunshot wounds, Wright was taken from the hospital to his home, then back to city hall by policemen. During this time white men organized a lynch mob. As he lay semiconscious in a jail cell, having already confessed to the crimes, small groups of curiosity-seekers became larger crowds. White men grew increasingly impatient. At noon on Sunday, January 26, these men became lynchers. The mob entered the jail and took the unconscious Wright from his cell. Capeci reconstructs the scene:

> [O]ne of the mob tossed the battered prisoner into the hallway, then climbed atop the broken door, jumped down on his chest, and kicked him several times. ... [F]our others dragged their prey back down the corridor and through the entrance, enveloped by the multitude and spurred on by shouts: "Let's take him to Sunset and burn him." Under the portico of City Hall, with its graceful white columns framing their brutality, ringleaders paused while others kicked Wright. They quickly pulled him feet first, arms overhead and skull bouncing down seven concrete steps amid the kind of cheering that follow "a ninety-nine yard touchdown" run. Once beyond the sidewalk, members of the mob first jammed him into the trunk of a Ford idling in Center Street, then changed their minds and pulled him out, hooked his legs behind the car bumper, and drove off to the blasts of honking horns. (Capeci 1998, 21)

Witnesses later reported their astonishment at seeing "a near-naked body being hauled behind the lead car and armed men riding the running boards of several vehicles that followed it" (Capeci 1998, 22). The young black man, still unconscious and now dying, was moments away from the same fate thousands of other black men had met in "the land of the free and the home of the brave." Capeci (1998, 22–23) tells us:

> The mob halted on Maude, near the schoolhouse and within view of both Smith Chapel and the First Baptist Church. ... [A] middle-aged man in coveralls doused the victim with five gallons of gasoline brought from a nearby service station and a younger inebriated man unsuccessfully tried to set him ablaze. From behind the county prosecutor someone flipped a lighted match onto the saturated ground, which sent flames racing up Wright's naked body and caused him to cry out once. Blanton [an observer] became nauseated as fire and smoke engulfed the victim, whose arms contracted in the heat and reached skyward as if pleading for a mercy that did not come. Cleo Wright perished. ...

Wright had been burned in the Sunset Addition, within full view of black church services. Many churchgoers just going home came upon what more nearly resembled "a roast pig" than a human being: "body naked, charred, and drawn up; human features mocked by a cigarette inserted between the lips and a match placed in the nose. [Many] left the barbaric scene quickly, some became ill, and few ever forgot the sight and smell of Wright's burnt carcass" (Capeci 1998, 24).

News of the lynching was communicated quickly via radio broadcasts and newspaper copy. State and national reporters, including representatives of the Associated Press, Associate Negro Press, and Southern News Service, soon traveled to Sikeston to question local officials, newsmen, and residents for information. Occurring so soon after Pearl Harbor, the lynching of Cleo Wright would attract international attention, a federal investigation, and a strong response from the N.A.A.C.P. (Capeci 1998).

As soon as black Missourians heard the broadcasts and read the news reports, they called on officials to investigate the lynching. Groups as ideologically disparate as the Communist Party of Missouri and the St. Louis Urban League condemned Wright's death as "an act of vicious Hitlerism" which endangered national unity, sabotaged war preparations, and created distrust among nonwhite allies, thereby giving "hope to Hitler and his Axis partners." The lynching of Cleo Wright, declared the St. Louis Y.W.C.A. Public Affairs Committee, should make white Missourians "feel ashamed and degraded, and fearful of the future" (quoted in Capeci 1998, 38). Black leaders, especially from St. Louis and Kansas City, quickly organized protests, assisted by the N.A.A.C.P. (Capeci 1998).

St. Louis resident Sidney R. Redmond led the way. Probably it was Redmond who provided the N.A.A.C.P.'s national office with its earliest information. After speaking with Walter White several times via telephone, Redmond called members of his chapter together within forty-eight hours of the lynching. They scheduled a meeting with Missouri Governor Donnell for Thursday, and planned a mass rally to take place on Sunday. Redmond broadened the base of protest by drawing on eight N.A.A.C.P. chapters and several business and civil groups to meet with the governor. On January 29, Redmond arrived in Jefferson City with more than eighty persons whose names read like a Who's Who of Missouri's black elite. On Sunday, February 1, 3,500 attended the N.A.A.C.P. mass rally in St. Louis (Capeci 1998).

During this time Walter White was busy on several fronts. He had telegraphed Roosevelt on January 26, immediately upon hearing of Wright's death. Nothing short of "positive, affirmative action"—specifically, enactment of antilynching legislation—would assure "citizens of all races" that democracy "applies inside as well as outside of the United States," the telegram read (quoted in Capeci 1998, 43). White released the telegram to the press and after speaking once again with Redmond, he arrived in St. Louis the following day. In a series of phone conversations, he and Redmond had planned the meeting with Governor Donnell scheduled for Thursday and the mass meeting to be held on Sunday (Capeci 1998).

Before these events could occur, White asked Redmond if he could send a "competent investigator" into Sikeston (quoted in Capeci 1998, 43). The question was, of course, rooted in both long-standing N.A.A.C.P. policy and White's own experience as the association's lynching authority, one who had investigated mob violence firsthand. White recommended to Redmond that Mary Taussig Tompkins, a white St. Louis resident who knew southeast Missouri, investigate. She and her husband, L. Benoist Tompkins, visited Sikeston on January 29 and 30, viewed the lynching site and interviewed several black and white residents. In a series of press releases between the date of the lynching and early February, White linked Cleo Wright's lynching in Sikeston to the brutal attacks on black soldiers in Alexandria, Louisiana, and both incidents to the issue of America's democratic war aims. A pamphlet was planned, to be distributed to congressmen, senators, and other influential citizens. Within two weeks of Wright's death, White's battle cry, which quickly caught on around the country, became "Remember Pearl Harbor ... and Sikeston, Missouri!" While it is unclear whether White or association staff members came up with the powerful slogan, it caught on, and many others arrived at it independently (Capeci 1998).

Within white Missouri, the reaction was mixed. Now practicing attorney Leonidas Dyer who, as we have seen, introduced antilynching bills in the U.S. House of Representatives in the 1920s and 1930s, wrote that "burning a human being at the stake" proved the presence of lawlessness in the state and the need for federal legislation to restore racial justice (quoted in Capeci 1998, 45). The *St. Louis Post-Dispatch* was perhaps the most outspoken, demanding the prosecution of those guilty of Cleo Wright's murder. Sikeston residents, including some who opposed the lynching, were dismayed by all the attention. Why, they wondered (as Coatesville residents had in 1911), did the press coverage have to "go on and on" (quoted in Capeci 1998, 46).

Press coverage had to go "on and on" because the nation, entering a world war on two fronts, was in no mood for southern nonsense. Opposition to the lynching was widespread in the national press, ranging from eastern liberal dailies to more moderate publications elsewhere. "It was," declared the *Washington Post*, referring to the lynching, "an act on par with the diabolical murders perpetrated by Nazi and Japanese gangsters." The event raised questions, asserted the *Tampa Daily Times* of Florida, about "what kind of democracy we claim to be fighting for" (quoted in Capeci 1998, 47).

For over three weeks there was a nationwide outcry. Through his attorney general, Francis Biddle, President Roosevelt reacted as he had not reacted before. Politics, public opinion, black protest, and war diplomacy all combined to make Biddle "vitally interested in this case" (quoted in Capeci 1998, 49). Especially distressed by Japanese propaganda depicting Wright's death as an indication of what East Indians might expect if the U.S. won the war, on February 10 Biddle ordered an F.B.I. probe into the incident (Capeci 1998).

Biddle was also disturbed by the lynching's impact on black military morale and support for the war. In addition to national unity issues, Capeci tells us, Biddle was also moved by his own liberal sensibilities. He understood that Wright's murder had delivered, in Walter White's words, "the most crushing blow to Negroes." More than racial discrimination in the defense industries or segregation in the armed services, the lynching of Cleo Wright blunted the very point of citizenship, the right to live in peace. A Harvard-trained Philadelphia lawyer from a distinguished family committed to the New Deal, Biddle considered this denial of basic constitutional rights "a tragic mockery" and a threat to victory (quoted phrases in Capeci 1998, 49–50).

Biddle realized, as did most liberals, that the presence on American soil of Nazi-style racism during what was being billed as a war for democracy brought into question "the moral integrity of America." Wright's was the first lynching after the bombing of Pearl Harbor; it demanded a federal response. Consequently, Biddle concluded that some action from the office of the attorney general (within very carefully drawn parameters) would be appropriate. He knew that Roosevelt would not support renewed calls for antilynching legislation, as he continued to fear alienating powerful southern Democrats whose votes he needed to pass New Deal programs. Given the compromise politics and programmatic priorities of Roosevelt, who concentrated on the Depression and the war rather than on race relations in either decade, Biddle focused on legal moves within his department under existing legislation (Capeci 1998).

The lynching of Cleo Wright is noteworthy, then, in the history of racial politics and violence in America. For the first time the F.B.I. investigated the lynching and, even more extraordinary, the Civil Rights Section of the Department of Justice brought charges against members of the lynch mob. These and other protest events illustrate both the N.A.A.C.P.'s political responsiveness as well as how lynching played out in the context of World War II. Because Wright was lynched not two months after Pearl Harbor, the nation was still in shock and in the midst of intense mobilization. Under these extraordinary conditions, modest federal intervention was possible (Capeci 1998).

The War Ends

N.A.A.C.P. records showed six lynching victims during 1942. White wrote to Senator Wagner asking him to once again propose a federal statute. In the midst of world war, White knew that winning congressional approval was unlikely (Zangrando 1980). But with black men still hanging naked and mutilated in southern trees while clothed black men risked their lives in Europe and in the Pacific for the nation's survival, the effort had to be made.

In the spring of 1943, Walter White testified before the Senate Military Affairs Committee. He complained about the government's failure to protect black soldiers from psychological harassment, physical intimidation, and, on occasion, death at the hands of white racists. White recalled for his listeners the November 1942 murder of an on-duty black M.P. by a Louisiana state policeman. Such occurrences—and this one too had gone unpunished—made it impossible for the N.A.A.C.P. to endorse the compulsory military service legislation that the committee was considering. On September 30, 1944, White, Mary McLeod Bethune (of the National Council of Negro Women and a presidential advisor on minorities), and Channing H. Tobias (of the N.A.A.C.P. and Y.M.C.A.) met with a war-weary Roosevelt to ask his help in the passage of two measures: S. 2048, to make F.E.P.C. a permanent governmental agency, and S. 1227, to provide federal protection "from assault or killing of persons in the uniform of the government" (quoted in Zangrando 1980, 169). Neither bill would pass.

As the war drew to an end, N.A.A.C.P. officials became quite conscious of the link between their struggle for racial justice in the United States with the racial situation globally, a complex situation characterized by decolonization. The board rehired W. E. B. Du Bois in 1944, this time as director of special research. Soon after, he and other staff members started to explore an internationalist position for the association. In late February 1945, Du Bois represented the N.A.A.C.P. at a meeting of 106 organizations assembled in Washington to discuss international monetary stabilization and those economic development plans formulated at the Bretton Woods conference which had been held the previous summer. In April, Du Bois, Walter White, and Mary McLeod Bethune attended the founding conference of the United Nations in San Francisco; they were invited by the secretary of state to consult with the official American delegation. This acknowledgment of the importance of racial issues contrasted sharply with Du Bois's and William Monroe Trotter's inability to get a hearing at Versailles twenty-six years before. In late spring White met with President Truman to protest the American government's support of the British and French, instead of the Soviet and Chinese, position on colonial independence. Du Bois helped organized the fifth Pan-African Congress, which met in England during October 1945 (Zangrando 1980).

Internationalization of the N.A.A.C.P. agenda did not, of course, bring racial justice to postwar America. Racial violence persisted. But by the mid-1940s the poll tax, not lynching, had become the legislative issue most vigorously pursued by civil rights groups. Through use of a discharge petition, the antipoll tax bill had reached the House floor, where it passed on June 12, 1945, in a 251–105 roll-call vote. The bill died in the Senate thirteen months later for lack of cloture, once again the victim of southern and conservative obstinacy (Zangrando 1980).

For decades southerners had insisted that the region would solve the problem of lynching. Indifferent northern and western whites showed little skepticism. The facts indicated otherwise. Mid-decade two blacks were lynched in Columbia, Tennessee; the N.A.A.C.P. made the incident a cause in 1946. Still serving as legal counsel for the association, Thurgood Marshall went to investigate. He was nearly lynched himself when four white men kidnapped him; they represented themselves as acting on behalf of the law and falsely accused Marshall of drunk driving. There can be little doubt that the good sense shown by his colleagues—following the "arrest" vehicle closely, as it sped along secondary country roads—saved Marshall's life (Zangrando 1980). Marshall would later become the first black member of the U.S. Supreme Court.

The incident was not an isolated one. On July 25, 1946, two black men and their wives were lynched in Walton County, Georgia. The N.A.A.C.P. investigated immediately. It then submitted its findings to the F.B.I. White urged President Truman to reconvene Congress in order to enact federal antilynching legislation and the association announced rewards totaling $10,000 for information leading to the arrest and conviction of the lynchers. Near Gordon, Georgia, black worker John J. Gilbert was murdered on August 3, apparently having made white enemies by participating in an effort to unionize workers at the local chalk mines. In Athens, Tennessee, a black man was murdered for attempting to vote. There were assaults on black veterans in Alabama, where whites seemed determined that ex-service personnel "must not expect or demand any change in their status from that which existed before they went overseas" (quoted in Zangrando 1980, 174).

The Lynching of John C. Jones

On August 7, a black veteran named John C. Jones was lynched near Minden, Louisiana. The lynching of Jones was, Adam Fairclough writes, "a typical southern horror story, but it is a tale worth telling" (1995/1999, 113). Jones was a twenty-eight-year-old veteran who had survived the Battle of the Bulge and who had been promoted to the rank of corporal. Webster Parish, his home, was no typical agricultural area; a gigantic shell-loading plant had been built near Minden, and numerous oil wells dotted the surrounding countryside. Jones's own grandfather owned oil-producing land; he had been tricked into signing leases with the Premier Oil Company at absurdly low prices. In 1946 he was earning just $1.50 a month for the remaining active well (Fairclough 1995/1999).

After his discharge from the army, Jones was hired by Premier where he raised questions about the leases. Fairclough tells us that, in contrast to many black southerners at the time, Jones was quite able to say "no" to a white man. When a white neighbor expressed interest in his German pistol, for instance, Jones told him he'd give it up only "over my dead body" (quoted in Fairclough 1995/1999, 113). On August 9, 1946, fishermen pulled Jones's body out of Dorcheat Bayou, about three miles north of Minden. Not until August 16, however, the day after Jones's burial, when the local newspaper reported the verdict of the local coroner's jury, did reports of Jones's death travel beyond Webster Parish. N.A.A.C.P. member Dan Bryd, in Bogalusa at the time, suspected that this was a lynching. After picking up A. Tureaud (Fairclough describes Tureaud and Byrd as N.A.A.C.P. "stalwarts" [p. 19]) in New Orleans, he drove the three hundred miles to Minden, stopping only for gas. Accompanying the pair were three black journalists, John E. Rousseau, editor of the *New Orleans Sentinel*, and two reporters from the *Pittsburgh Courier* (Fairclough 1995/1999).

The following day, having "covered territory in Louisiana that we seriously doubt is on the map" (quoted in Fairclough 1995/1999, 114), Byrd wired Walter White in New York, providing him with the names of three white men suspected of the lynching. Bryd had also learned gruesome details that the N.A.A.C.P. used to gain the attention of the white press. According to the local embalmer, Jones had not only been beaten but mutilated and burned. Although subsequent testimony questioned the embalmer's allegations, the N.A.A.C.P.'s news releases reported that Jones had been tortured with a blowtorch and hacked with a meat cleaver. R. L. Williams, the director of the Shreveport N.A.A.C.P., learned the names of six more possible participants in the lynching. Williams's main informant, a black café owner, claimed that the white men, who included two sheriff's deputies, had come to his barroom to celebrate immediately after the lynching (Fairclough 1995/1999).

The main witness to the lynching, however, had disappeared, and the N.A.A.C.P. spent a week trying to find him, worrying that if they did not, the lynchers or the Webster Parish sheriff would. Albert Harris, Jr., Jones's seventeen-year-old cousin, had been beaten alongside Jones, but had somehow managed to escape, fleeing first to Texarkana with his father. When the N.A.A.C.P. discovered where they were, Walter White tried to move them to

Washington or New York. A Justice Department official suggested that the local sheriff take Harris into protective custody, but White could not agree, knowing, as he did, that a man had been lynched in Texarkana just four years earlier. An Arkansas N.A.A.C.P. official put them on an eastbound plane on August 19, but the Harrises failed to appear. Four days later the pair showed up in Muskegon, a small town in Michigan, where they went to the local N.A.A.C.P. office to ask for help. After having the younger Harris examined by a physician, who made note of the scars and abrasions about the young man's head and body, the Detroit branch flew the two to New York, where they appeared beside Walter White at a dramatic press conference (Fairclough 1995/1999).

The Harrises told a tale at once unique and nightmarishly familiar. On July 31, two white sheriff's deputies, Oscar Haynes and Charles Edwards, arrested the young Harris, who was known by the nickname "Sonnyman." On the way to jail, they stopped by the home of Sam Maddry, Jr., who alleged that Harris had planned to rape his young and pregnant wife. After letting him sit in jail for two anxious days, Deputy Haynes, son of the sheriff, took Harris to a waiting car. Its white occupants drove him into the woods, tied him to an oil rig, placed a gunny sack over his head, then beat and tortured him. In unendurable pain and in fear for his life, Harris told the white men what they had evidently wanted to hear all along, that he had acted as a scout for Jones. Yes, the bleeding young man "confessed," it was Jones who plotted to rape Maddry's wife. Somehow the badly beaten Harris staggered home and collapsed on the floor; his father drove him to Henderson, across the Texas state line (Fairclough 1995/1999).

The following day, Saturday, August 4, Deputies Haynes and Edwards returned to the Harris home only to find "Sonnyman" gone. Furious that the elder Harris was reluctant to tell them his son's whereabouts, Edward struck him across the face. Learning that the young black man was safe across the Texas line, the policemen demanded that he be returned at once. Harris and his wife complied; on August 5 they delivered their son to Haynes at the Minden jail, where he was placed in a cell across from Jones. On August 8, at approximately 8:30 in the evening, Haynes turned the two over to a group of approximately ten white men who had come for them; Jones tried to escape but was violently thrown into one of two cars. Taken from the vehicles about three miles north of Minden, the two young black men were stripped and beaten, in Jones's case fatally (Fairclough 1995/1999).

Predictably, the Webster Parish grand jury declined to return any indictments. In Washington, the Department of Justice instructed the U.S. attorney for the Western District of Louisiana, Malcolm Lafargue, to start federal proceedings under Sections 51 and 52, Title 18, of the U.S. Criminal Code. This Reconstruction-era statute specified penalties of up to ten years' imprisonment for conspiracy to deprive American citizens of their civil rights. The trial took place in Shreveport during the last week of February and the first few days of March 1947. This was not the first time the Justice Department had brought alleged lynchers to trial; there had been several such cases since 1942. But it was the first time in Louisiana. It was the first time, too, that a Louisiana lynching had been investigated by the F.B.I., a fact that enraged local whites. It was also a fact that irritated the director of the F.B.I., J. Edgar Hoover, whose foot-dragging in the case brought angry criticism from the N.A.A.C.P.'s Thurgood Marshall (Fairclough 1995/1999).

Hoover was completely opposed to F.B.I. involvement in civil rights cases. After being ordered to investigate the Minden lynching, he asked Tom Clark, the U.S. attorney general, to review the policy of using the F.B.I. in civil rights matters. "Rushing pell-mell" into these cases at the insistence of "vociferous minority groups," Hoover complained, only discouraged state action and embarrassed the Justice Department when the prosecution failed (quoted in Fairclough 1995/1999, 116). Clark knew Hoover was expressing his politics, not genuine concern for the Justice Department; he overruled him, directing him to investigate any and all civil rights complaints regardless of the prospects of successful prosecution. "Hoover swallowed his defeat but liked it not one whit" (Fairclough 1995/1999, 116).

Hoover was even less happy when the F.B.I.'s performance in this area was criticized by Thurgood Marshall. Marshall complained about the F.B.I.'s record in civil rights cases to Tom Clark and Robert Carr, chief counsel to the President's Committee on Civil Rights, observing that "the F.B.I. has established for itself an incomparable record for ferreting out persons violating our federal laws," from spies and kidnappers to "nondescript hoodlums who steal automobiles and drive them across state lines" (quoted in Fairclough 1995/1999, 116). But somehow, he continued, this laudable capacity for catching criminals vanished when it came to cases where African Americans were the victims. In such cases, Marshall pointed out, the Bureau had been unable to identify or bring to trial a single person. He pointed specifically to the Minden case of John C. Jones (Fairclough 1995/1999).

Upon learning of Marshall's complaint, Hoover went into a rage, complaining to Walter White that Marshall only wanted to "embarrass" and "discredit" the F.B.I. It was hardly the Bureau's fault if southern juries failed to indict or convict, he replied indignantly. Not wanting to alienate the director of the F.B.I., Walter White asked Marshall to draft a "temperate and documented reply" in preparation for a meeting with Hoover at which, hopefully, the powerful man might be, at least to a degree, placated (quoted in Fairclough 1995/1999, 116). Hoover was not about to be placated, however. While agreeing to meet White, Hoover refused to see Marshall, whom he accused of "gross misstatements and unfounded accusations." Marshall was not intimidated. "I ... have no faith in Mr. Hoover or his investigators," he told White, "and there is no use in my saying so" (quoted in Fairclough 1995/1999, 117).

The U.S. attorney in the Minden case, Malcolm Lafargue, faced widespread white resistance. The venue, Shreveport, was the least favorable in Louisiana, described by Fairclough (1995/1999, 8) as "conservative even by the standards of the South[.] Shreveport's planter-business elite enforced white supremacy with an iron fist." He notes that between 1900 and 1931, at least nineteen African Americans were lynched in Caddo Parish, more than in any other Louisiana parish. In 1931, when organizing the A.S.W.P.L., Jesse Daniel Ames enjoyed little success in north Louisiana. "I failed utterly in securing someone to represent this part of the state," reported her Shreveport contact (quoted in Fairclough 1995/1999, 13).

In 1946, in the lynching case of war veteran John C. Jones, little had changed. The defense lawyers used their right of peremptory challenge to eliminate the only African American on the jury panel. They tried to discredit Harris's testimony by accusing him of having murdered Jones himself and by linking him with the N.A.A.C.P. Jones had deserved his fate, they continued, because he tried to rape the defenseless and pregnant Mrs. Maddry. As proof of his intention, they told jurors that he had been carrying "lewd pictures and obscene poetry" in his wallet (quoted in Fairclough 1995/1999, 117). Additionally, the defense fueled indignation over the F.B.I.'s participation in the case, declaring that witnesses had been intimidated by overzealous F.B.I. agents. Finally, the defense dismissed the prosecution's case as politically motivated federal meddling in local affairs that threatened the very basis of "white civilization" in north Louisiana. While Judge Gaston Porterie was "a model of fairness" (Fairclough 1995/1999, 117), the outcome was predictable. In their summation, the four defense lawyers instructed the jurors as to their duty. As southern white men, they were reminded, they must teach the N.A.A.C.P. and the government a lesson. The jury acquitted all five defendants (Fairclough 1995/1999).

The Campaign against Lynching Ends

John C. Jones was one among a number of black veterans who were "rewarded" for their military service to the nation by being lynched by southern white men. The case of Isaac Woodward was reported internationally. Three hours after his discharge at a military demobilization center, this young black veteran was dragged from a bus at Batesburg, South Carolina, and brutally assaulted by two white policemen. As he lay semiconscious on the ground, the two law-enforcement officials gouged out both his eyes with the blunt end of a blackjack. They then threw him into jail where, denied medical attention, he suffered all night long. Using press releases, interviews, radio announcements, conferences with federal officials, branch communiqués, and other information outlets, the N.A.A.C.P. brought the story to national and international attention. Plans were made to reopen the campaign for an antilynching law. The events of 1945–1946 made it clear that black male bodies were still imprisoned in a violent white male gaze (Zangrando 1980).

The number of lynchings declined to one in 1947, then increased to two in 1948. Maybe the worst was over. There would be three in 1949, two in 1950, one in 1951, and none at all for the next three years. As noted in chapter 1, the last reported lynching occurred in 1959 in Mississippi. Started by the colonists as a political tactic against the British in the eighteenth century and evolving into a racialized and gendered practice fifty years later, lynching remains today a key clue to the complex mystery that is white racism. While whites fought to end what was primarily but not exclusively a southern phenomenon, it was African Americans who led the fight. Beginning with Ida B. Wells in the final quarter of the nineteenth century and continuing in the twentieth century with the N.A.A.C.P., African Americans fought the sexualized mutilations of black bodies. The high points of the campaign occurred from 1918 to 1923, 1934 to 1940, and 1946 to 1950. The U.S. House of Representatives passed an antilynching measure in 1922, 1937, and 1940, but the Senate—dominated by southerners, conservatives, white heterosexual men—declined to even vote on the measure. This unbelievable refusal to act underscores the centrality of lynching to the American experience, "an almost integral part of our national folkways" as Walter White (1929, viii) characterized it. It was "America's national crime," as Ida B. Wells well understood (1901/1977, 30). Many African Americans knew that lynching was no eccentric southern distraction from the main problems of racial justice in the United States. Understanding lynching is key to understanding the problem of "race" in America (Zangrando 1980).

Nationally, the political struggle against lynching always took a backseat to "larger" public imperatives, such as the G.O.P.'s legislative agenda for 1922–1923, the New Deal's economic initiatives in 1937 and 1938, and those cold war issues with which Washington officials became obsessed by the late 1940s. Regionally, the Commission on Interracial Cooperation of the 1920s and the Association of Southern Women for the Prevention of Lynching throughout the 1930s seemed, finally, more concerned about their white neighbors' sensibilities and sectional autonomy than about the bodies of black men. The modernizing influences of federal interventions—such as the Tennessee Valley Authority—undermined only slightly southern loyalties to states' rights and regionalism. In the 1940s anti-Communist hysteria as well as their own hesitations slowed reformers associated with the Southern Conference for Human Welfare and the Southern Regional Council. Zangrando (1980, 213) blames American liberalism.

> Overall, there existed no greater index to the inelasticity of twentieth-century American liberalism than the unwillingness of its adherents to stand and make a fight for black people's security against unchecked mobs or select committees sworn to execute their victims without public notoriety. When it came to the protection of black rights, most liberals, North and South, scored higher on professions of concern than they did on actual performance.

In the 1960s, liberalism would once again be shown to be inadequate. This time American liberals would not quickly recover from their failure to deliver on their promises.

While the N.A.A.C.P. was hardly alone in its condemnation of and struggle against lynching, in the twentieth century the association did lead the fight. It fought with a perseverance and intensity unmatched by any other organization in American society. In doing so, the association played a singularly important role in changing white attitudes as well as public policies toward African Americans. As much as—perhaps more than—the N.A.A.C.P. campaigns, historians suggest, fundamental demographic, political, economic, and gender shifts (including the heightened visibility of "homosexuality") brought about the extinction of lynching. Black migrations from the rural South to the urban North during the first half of the century and African Americans' subsequently intensified participation in urban and national politics, plus nonagricultural economic developments within the South, all contributed to the creation of national and regional climates inhospitable to lynching. This is, of course, hindsight, and very general. At the time no one could be absolutely certain that white men would not someday re-experience the desire to strip, torture, and mutilate a young black man, as the lynching of Emmett Till in 1955 dramatically indicated. But the N.A.A.C.P. was intent upon ending more than lynching. Johnson, White, Wilkins and their colleagues were determined to bring to an end all forms of racial violence, subjugation, and discrimination (Zangrando 1980).

In 1940, a Texas congressman named Lyndon B. Johnson opposed the antilynching bill. Twenty-four years later, as president, Johnson negotiated the Omnibus Civil Rights bill into law. That same year—1964—he commanded the federal forces at his disposal to locate the bodies of three missing civil rights workers in Mississippi, and then to prosecute their murderers. For many Americans, the connection between those presidential actions in the 1960s—and the massive and complicated civil rights campaigns and black power movements then under way—and the antilynching campaign headed by James Weldon Johnson, W. E. B. Du Bois, Walter White, Jessie Daniel Ames, and Ida B. Wells decades earlier may not be obvious. For those who know the history, the connection is unmistakable (Zangrando 1980).

But this too is hindsight and very general. In the midst of the battle against lynching, it was not clear which organization would finally emerge as the primary engine of civil rights progress. During the Depression the N.A.A.C.P. became involved in what was perhaps the most famous "legal-lynching" case of all, the Scottsboro Nine. To conclude this review of "America's national crime," I turn now to the *cause célèbre* of the early 1930s. The battle to rescue the Scottsboro Nine engaged, in what seems like a death match, the competing commitments of the Communist Party-U.S.A. (through its International Labor Defense or I.L.D.) and the National Association for the Advancement of Colored People. Here we will see—in my summary of Dan T. Carter's riveting account of the Scottsboro trials—not only the painful and still shocking miscarriage of American justice in the South, but the political maneuvering, even exploitation, of nine young black men who were, finally, not so much victims of circumstance as they were of the white male imagination.

northeastern tip of Mississippi and back into Tennessee. When the train made one of its Alabama stops, at Paint Rock, the local sheriff—a white man named Charles Latham—was ready. He had been told that nine young black men had gang raped two white women (Carter 1969/1979).

The nine young black men who stood before Latham that day looked rather ragged. Although the day had warmed up to sixty degrees, they were dressed for the cool Tennessee mountain nights. Only one of the men, Charles Weems, was not a teenager; he was twenty. Latham reported later that Weems looked "mean" with his soot-black complexion, shaded eyelids, and long, narrow face. Ozie Powell and Clarence Norris were strapping young men in their late teens, muscular and healthy. Olen Montgomery was blind in his left eye and through his right one he saw poorly. His drooping eyelids gave him a "sleepy-eyed" appearance as he stood quietly with the others. Willie Roberson had contracted syphilis and gonorrhea the year before. Without medical attention his condition had deteriorated, and now he walked with a cane. Weems, Powell, Norris, Montgomery, and Roberson were all from Georgia; they told Latham they did not know each other (Carter 1969/1979).

The other four black men told the Alabama sheriff that they were from Chattanooga, on their way to Memphis to look for work. Haywood Patterson was nineteen and acted as spokesman for the four. Eugene Williams was only thirteen. Short and slender, with dark complexion, "he was," Dan Carter (1969/1979, 6) tells us, "the most handsome of the nine." Andrew and Leroy Wright were brothers, and they stayed by each other's side. Andy (as he was called) was nineteen; he tried to reassure his thirteen-year-old brother, but Roy (as he was called) was plainly frightened and could not hide his fear. While Deputy Sheriff Charles Latham tied the nine together with a length of plow line, the two white women who had presumably just been gang raped sat under a sweet gum tree, chatting with several other white women who had gathered at the station. One woman, Ruby Bates, told Latham the tale of how she and her friend, Victoria Price, had been brutally raped by the nine black men (Carter 1969/1979).

In the days that followed the arrest of the young black men only one subject occupied the conversation of Jackson County, Alabama, citizens: the "nigger rape case" (quoted in Carter 1969/1979, 12). It would come to occupy the conversation of the nation. More than the lynching of Claude Neal, the matter of the "Scottsboro Nine" would engage the passions, loyalties, and resources of various groups, among them the Communist Party-U.S.A., the N.A.A.C.P., as well as various Alabama officials and agencies. I will follow Dan Carter's reconstruction of this struggle in order to create, in the context of this study of the gender of racial politics and violence, a kind of photographic blow-up of the gendered politics of lynching in the early 1930s, in particular the rivalry between the C.P.-U.S.A. and the N.A.A.C.P.

From Jackson County, Alabama, word soon reached Chattanooga, some sixty miles away. There one of the city's leading black citizens read with increasing concern about the charges against the nine young men. Dr. A. Stephens was a well-known physician and president of the Laymen's association of the East Tennessee Conference of the Northern Methodist Episcopal Church.

When he learned that the young men had been charged with raping white women and that four of the accused were from Chattanooga, he called a meeting of the Interdenominational Colored Ministers' Alliance. When the group learned that Mrs. Ada Wright, mother of two of the accused, attended one of the churches in the Alliance, they decided to take action. By nightfall of the day after the arrest, $50.08 had been raised for the defense of the nine young men (Carter 1969/1979).

Even in the midst of the Great Depression fifty dollars was a small retainer with which to approach any attorney, but Dr. Stephens knew one lawyer who might be willing to take the case. Stephen R. Roddy was a white man who practiced law in Chattanooga; he spent most of his time checking real estate titles and doing minor police court work. On occasion, Roddy had taken on cases for African Americans. Unfortunately, Roddy's legal abilities were modest. This limitation wasn't helped by his inability to stay sober. Typically, local police officials overlooked his binges, but he had been jailed in June 1930 on a charge of public drunkenness. The chairman of the Chattanooga Commission on Interracial Cooperation judged Roddy adequate—when sober. But sobriety seemed to elude him much of the time, despite several hospitalizations in efforts to recover from the disease. When Dr. Stephens called him, Roddy was not enthusiastic, but soon he was persuaded to take the case for a total fee of $120 (Carter 1969/1979).

A fair trial was, let us say, unlikely. The nine had already been tried, found guilty, and sentenced to death by the local news media. The *Chattanooga News* demanded that the Jackson County grand jury return indictments immediately, declaring: "We still have savages abroad in the land, it seems. Let us have the solace of knowing that at least we have risen above the justice of the savages." The alleged victims' hometown newspaper, the *Huntsville Daily Times*, characterized the rape as "the most atrocious ever recorded in this part of the country, a wholesale debauching of society ... so horrible in its details that all of the facts can never be printed." It "savored of the jungle" and the "meanest African corruption." The white men of the South, the Huntsville newspaper proclaimed, "will not stand for such acts." The "nine brutes" had been protected by the law since their arrest, but as soon as the machinery of justice had gone through its motions, "this newspaper joins with the public and the duly constituted authorities in seeing that the law is carried out to the letter." Swift and final justice was the only answer to such a "heinous and unspeakable crime" (quoted in Carter 1969/1979, 20).

Roddy soon discovered that at least one of the alleged victims was not exactly the ideal of southern womanhood. His strategy would become to impugn the reputation of Victoria Price and thereby undermine the integrity of her accusations. The court, however, quickly made it clear that it would not tolerate this strategy. On the stand, Victoria Price admitted that she had been married twice and that she was separated from her second husband, and that she had always gone by her maiden name, even when she was married. But when Roddy asked her how long she had "known" her husband before she married him, the local prosecutor—a white man named Bailey—objected and the judge—a white man named Hawkins—sustained the objection. Roddy asked if she had ever been in jail. Again the judge sustained an objection by the prosecution. The defense attorney was stymied, said he thought that was all, and shortly after 3 P.M., after less than fifty minutes of testimony, Victoria Price stepped down from the witness chair (Carter 1969/1979).

The state of Alabama was not content to rest its case solely on the testimony of Victoria Price. Solicitor Bailey called to the stand Dr. R. R. Bridges, one of the two physicians who examined the two women within an hour and thirty minutes after the alleged rape. The pertinent finding he disclosed at the outset: Victoria Price had indeed participated in heterosexual intercourse at some time previous to his examination. Even more damaging was that he found "a great amount" of semen in the vagina of Ruby Bates. But he went on to say that it did not appear, contrary to her allegation, that she had been physically assaulted. There were small bruises about the top of her hips and a few "short scratches" on the left arm, but Dr. Bridges emphasized that these were minor. He found neither bruises nor tears in or around her vagina. The semen, he added, was "non-motile." Moreover, he told the jury that "Victoria Price was not hysterical at all at the time." Despite these facts which undermined any allegation of gang rape, Bridges replied to Solicitor Bailey's direct question that it was "possible" that six men, one right after the other, could have had intercourse with her without lacerations or other discernible damage (quoted in Carter 1969/1979, 27–28).

In his examination of Victoria Price, defense attorney Roddy tried to show she had fabricated the story by asking her multiple and sometimes contradictory questions. She did waver on certain details, but one thing of which she was certain was that Haywood Patterson was one of the defendants whose "private parts penetrated my private parts." Roddy again tried to attack Victoria Price's reputation, but the state successfully lodged objections. Still, on occasion, Price insisted on answering Roddy's insinuations. When Roddy asked her if she had ever practiced prostitution, she retorted: "I don't know what you're talking about. I do not know what prostitution means. I have not made it a practice to have intercourse with other men" (quoted in Carter 1969/1979, 36).

Bailey called Ruby Bates to the stand to confirm Victoria Price's charge that she had been raped by Patterson, but, Bates said, she wasn't sure. In fact, she had to admit that she "could not be sure about the boys that had intercourse with Victoria Price" (quoted in Carter 1969/1979, 36). Quickly it became clear that if Haywood Patterson was to be convicted it would have to be on the testimony of Victoria Price and not on that of Ruby Bates. A moment after Bates stepped down from the witness chair, the bailiff stepped up to the bench and whispered to Judge Hawkins that the jury in the cases of Norris and Weems—tried just before Patterson's—had reached a verdict: "We find the defendants guilty of rape and fix their sentence at death in ..." (quoted in Carter 1969/1979, 37). His last words were drowned out when a roar went up from those in the court. Many leaped to their feet, rushing through the doors to tell those who had not been able to squeeze into the courtroom. The crowd, over fifteen hundred in number, shouted its approval while inside, Judge Hawkins pounded the bench for order (Carter 1969/1979).

Haywood Patterson would also be found guilty by the all-white male jury and also condemned to death. In the trial of Willie Roberson Judge Hawkins still struggled to maintain order, as spectators made fun of the defendant, referring to him loudly as "that ape nigger." Roberson had begun hoboing at age fifteen. Early in 1930, he had contracted syphilis and gonorrhea and had gone to Atlanta's Grady Hospital in an effort to receive treatment. Hospital officials declined to treat him since he was not a resident. Since he had lived for several months in Memphis the year before, he had boarded the train that day to go there in hopes of receiving medical treatment. He too would be found guilty (Carter 1969/1979).

From the outset both the N.A.A.C.P. and the Communist Party-U.S.A. took great interest in this example of southern justice. The C.P.-U.S.A.'s official organ, the *New York Daily Worker*, reported the trials at Scottsboro. They were, in the language of the party, the latest instances of "capitalist atrocity." Soon it became clear that the cases held an appeal for readers that surprised party leaders. Charles Dirba, the International Labor Defense's assistant secretary and a member of the Communist Party's Central Committee, recognized that the case could dramatize the plight of African Americans throughout the South. Not long after he learned of the arrest and that there had been an attempted lynching of the nine black men (from the *New York Times*), Dirba telegraphed Lowell Wakefield in Birmingham (one of the few representatives of the Communist Party in the South at this time), and asked him to investigate the case himself. Accompanied by Douglas McKenzie, a black man who worked for the League of Struggle for Negro Rights, Wakefield attended the trial in Scottsboro (Carter 1969/1979).

After observing the first day's proceedings Wakefield cabled Dirba that it was another Sacco-Vanzetti case. [Recall that these two Italian anarchists had been executed on August 23, 1927, for allegedly murdering the paymaster and guard of a shoe factory during a hold-up in Massachusetts. While they denied any involvement in the crime and none of the $16,000 taken was ever traced to them, they were, nonetheless, convicted. Their execution illustrated how strong anti-immigrant feeling was in the U.S. during the 1920s.] Without a doubt, Wakefield said, Alabama authorities planned a "neck-tie party" for the nine young men. With Wakefield's telegram, Dirba persuaded the Central Committee of the party to publish its lengthy statement analyzing the historical "significance" of the Scottsboro Case and hinting at a more active role for the Communist Party in the defense of the accused (Carter 1969/1979).

Walter White followed the affair in the newspapers, but the N.A.A.C.P. remained, at first, uninvolved, partly due to a lack of local information. During this period the N.A.A.C.P. depended primarily upon its branches for accurate information and advice regarding local incidents. The nearest chapter had been in Chattanooga but it had collapsed in 1930; the only information to which White had access came from southern newspapers which reported incorrectly that able council—the occasionally sober Roddy—represented the nine young black men. Two days before the first trial opened in Scottsboro, A. Stephens had communicated with White from Chattanooga, informing him of the Ministers' Alliance action, and asking if the N.A.A.C.P. planned to help the defense effort in any way. On the day that Judge Hawkins sentenced the nine young men to death, White's special assistant, William T. Andrews, replied to Stephens, wondering if the case might be similar to the Elaine (Arkansas) riot trials.

Stephens was asked for his judgment of the facts, but he was circumspect and cautious. Clearly he did not know if the men were guilty or not. Given that N.A.A.C.P. officials were protective of their organization's reputation, they were fearful of identifying the association with a gang of mass rapists. Unless they could be reasonably certain the men were innocent or that their constitutional rights had been abridged, the N.A.A.C.P. would stay out of it (Carter 1969/1979).

The next day the N.A.A.C.P.'s central office in New York received inquires from eight individuals, six branches, four other organizations, and the editor of the *Nation*. In fact, the office telephone began to ring without pause. Late that afternoon, White received a call from Clarence Darrow, the distinguished and famous criminal lawyer who had defended the high-school teacher (John Thomas Scopes) who had agreed to test the Tennessee law banning the teaching of evolution. At this time Darrow—about whose near-death experience in Mobile we read in chapter one—was a member of the N.A.A.C.P.'s Board of Directors. Darrow told White that he had been contacted by the International Labor Defense's chief lawyer, Joseph Brodsky, who had asked him to serve as chief counsel in an appeal to the Supreme Court. White advised Darrow against helping the Communists. "I have no objection to the I.L.D. because it is a Communist organization," he insisted. "On the other hand, it has been our experience that it is impossible to cooperate with them in any legal case" (quoted in Carter 1969/1979, 53). The problem, he said, was that their main goal seemed to be propaganda not justice. He told Darrow that the N.A.A.C.P. had the matter well in hand (Carter 1969/1979).

That conversation marked the beginning of the N.A.A.C.P.'s involvement in the affair. An impromptu statement to Darrow meant that White now had to act, to demonstrate that, in fact, the association had the matter well in hand. And fast, given that the I.L.D. was already engaged in planning an appeal. Through Andrews (White's assistant), he telegraphed Stephens, asking him to airmail the transcripts as soon as possible. When they had not arrived four days later, White called again; Stephens reported that the court stenographer had yet not completed the transcripts. Finally, on April 22, White learned that they had never been ordered. The Ministers' Alliance had no funds and Roddy declined to guarantee payment to the court stenographer. White immediately sent a check for twenty-four dollars, but precious time had been wasted. Carter (1969/1979) observes that while it was standard procedure for the N.A.A.C.P. to rely on local contacts, in this instance the reliance on Stephens and the Chattanooga Ministers' Alliance cost the organization valuable time. "This was," Carter (1969/1979, 53) tells us, "the first of a number of costly hesitations and miscalculations by White."

Like the N.A.A.C.P., the International Labor Defense depended upon its field representatives for information and advice. But when the I.L.D. Executive Committee voted to defend the Scottsboro Nine, George Maurer dispatched Allan Taub, one of his most able attorneys, to Chattanooga to coordinate activities. Taub's first and immediate task was to take complete control of the defense. Although the *Daily Worker* had dismissed Roddy as a "tool of the reformist traitors" (quoted in Carter 1969/1979, 54), Wakefield (who was on the scene) advised the I.L.D. to try to work through him, at least initially. Taub promised Roddy that he would become a national figure, on the scale of Clarence Darrow. But when Taub explained that the money for his salary would be raised by holding mass meetings of African Americans, the southern white man found the prospect distasteful and declined the offer (Carter 1969/1979).

Perceived as only a temporary setback, the two I.L.D. representatives requested permission to speak to an April 18th meeting of the Chattanooga Negro Ministers' Alliance. Accompanied by Joseph Brodsky, they promised the group that the I.L.D. would assume the financial burdens of the case. The three men impressed the ministers with their eloquence and progressive racial politics. Although nothing was put into writing, Wakefield wired Maurer in New York that things were well in hand. The Chattanoogans wanted to find a way to keep Roddy, he said, "but we will eliminate [him] somehow" (quoted in Carter 1969/1979, 54).

The I.L.D. proposed a successor to Roddy, a "southern gentleman" who had once served as attorney general of Hamilton County (Chattanooga), Tennessee. George W. Chamlee, Sr., was the grandson of a decorated Confederate soldier and his family was highly regarded in Tennessee social circles. He was, Carter tells us, an unusual, even eccentric, figure in southern politics. In 1926, in an article published in *Forum*, he had defended lynching under certain circumstances. Despite this reactionary and racist position, a coalition of trade unionists and African Americans had helped elect him county solicitor. He was one of the few Chattanooga lawyers willing to defend Communists and other political radicals. Just three weeks before he was approached by the I.L.D., he had defended three leaflet-distributing Communists who had been arrested on trumped-up vagrancy charges by the Chattanooga police. When the prosecution thundered that the Communists favored overthrowing the government, Chamlee quietly reminded the court that all their grandfathers had tried very hard to overthrow the federal government and had, in fact, sworn allegiance to the Confederate States of America (Carter 1969/1979).

For the relatively modest fee of $1,000 Chalmee agreed to serve as attorney for the nine young black men accused of gang raping the two white women. The news of Chamlee's acceptance of the case raised eyebrows all round. Will Alexander of the Commission on Interracial Cooperation acknowledged that for "once, our Communist friends seem to have been more successful in their selection of an attorney" (quoted in Carter 1969/1979, 55). Even those dumbfounded by Chamlee's decision agreed that he was one of the best lawyers in southern Tennessee and far superior to Roddy (Carter 1969/1979).

On April 20 Joseph Brodsky boarded the train for Birmingham. The next day he interviewed the nine defendants who were being held in the Birmingham jail. The young men must have thought the short and disheveled Brodsky strange—they knew nothing about him—but they liked what they heard. He dismissed the defense they had received in Scottsboro as halfhearted, promising them nothing but the best lawyers in the country. What was more important, he continued, they were not alone. Indeed, they would have the support of "thousands of black and white workers across the nation" (quoted in Carter 1969/1979, 56). He asked them to sign an affidavit which assigned the case to the I.L.D. Andy Wright signed his name; the others made their marks on the paper (Carter 1969/1979).

The swift and decisive actions of the I.L.D. caught the N.A.A.C.P. off guard. Walter White did not even know that Taub and Wakefield were in Chattanooga until he read about it in the *New York Times* on April 20. In a letter composed too late he wrote to Stephens asking him to "communicate with the ... boys ... [and] urge them that they sign no agreement as to their defense or commit themselves in any way, pending opportunity by us to examine the transcript of the testimony and to determine what action we shall be able to take in this matter." White included with his letter information regarding the I.L.D., emphasizing that it was not just another civil rights group, or even a radical political organization, but the legal arm of the Communist Party. As it often would in the United States, this "red-baiting" worked. Stephens quickly convened a meeting of the Ministers' Alliance and told them of the I.L.D.'s "Communist leanings" (quoted in Carter 1969/1979, 56). At Stephens's request, Roddy drove to Birmingham and persuaded the now-confused young men that the I.L.D. radicals were a millstone around their necks. They readily signed a statement prepared by Roddy asking the Communists to "lay off" (quoted in Carter 1969/1979, 57).

The Rev. L. Whitten, a prominent black minister in Chattanooga, released the statement to the press. He assured those assembled that "Negro preachers of the South and Negroes in general, are not in sympathy with intervention in the case by the International Labor Defense." The New York–based radicals—anti-Semitism now mingled with anti-Communism—wanted only to promote Communism, he offered; they had no "sincere interest in helping these condemned Negroes." The chain reaction continued and one week later the Ministers' Alliance formally censured the I.L.D. and accused it of being "communistic in its doctrine and the principles which it advocates." According to its statement, the Alliance allowed that the I.L.D.'s commitment to "justice and fair play to all mankind, regardless of race or previous condition" was laudatory, but the ministers believed that this meant nothing "without a due regard for the principles which are fundamental to the common good of all mankind as embodied in the Constitution of the United States" (quoted in Carter 1969/1979, 57). Walter White was relieved; he reassured N.A.A.C.P. supporters that things were well in hand (Carter 1969/1979).

White "could not have been more mistaken," for the red-baiting only inspired the I.L.D. to work harder to save the case from "the bosses and the N.A.A.C.P." Working as a team, the I.L.D. men in New York and in the South would make a two-pronged counterattack: first they would regain the support of the defendants, and second, they would discredit the N.A.A.C.P. and its friends. As an attorney, Taub knew the affidavit the young men had signed was meaningless; the nine were minors. Legally, it was their parents' responsibility to select legal representation. He and Brodsky spoke to as many parents as they could find in Chattanooga and explained what they planned to do if they were selected to defend their sons. For Claude and Janie Patterson, Ada Wright, and Mamie Williams Wilcox "it was an exhilarating experience. For the first time in their lives, white men were not telling them what to do, but asking their support, on the basis of complete equality" (quoted in Carter 1969/1979, 57).

The contrast with the Ministers' Alliance was clear; neither Roddy nor Stephens had bothered to contact them. The parents readily signed a statement which read in part: "We are the parents of Haywood Patterson, Andy Wright, Roy Wright and Eugene Williams. ... Although our sons are minors, we were never consulted as to the retainer of Steve Roddy." They agreed that their sons should be represented by the I.L.D. The next day Mrs. Patterson wrote to her son, Haywood, telling him that the parents had agreed that the International Labor Defense should represent all nine. "I don't want Roddy to have nothing to do with you," she wrote. All he wanted, she said, was money. She continued: "Don't let nobody turn you around from what Mama says." Haywood's father was even more directive: "You will burn sure if you don't let them preachers alone and trust in the International Labor Defense to handle the case" (quoted in Carter 1969/1979, 58).

Brodsky and Taub worried the nine young men might not do as their parents had instructed. So they arranged a visit. On the morning of April 24 Mrs. Williams, Mrs. Wright, and Mr. Patterson arrived at the Birmingham jail, driven there by a car hired by Brodsky and Taub. Accompanied by Wakefield and Chamlee, the three parents saw their sons for the first time since they had been arrested at Paint Rock, Alabama. The reunion was "tearful" and the sons "enthusiastically endorsed" the I.L.D. once again. They suggested that they did not "understand" the affidavit they had signed for Roddy on April 23: "This statement was obtained without the consent or advice of our parents and we had no way of knowing what to do," the boys alleged in an affidavit they signed for Wakefield. "We completely repudiate that statement and brand those who obtained it as betrayers of our case." As they turned to leave, Haywood's parents advised: "Listen son, this our bunch. You stay by them" (quoted in Carter 1969/1979, 58).

Its first initiative successful, the I.L.D. turned to the second phase of its counterattack: discrediting the N.A.A.C.P. and positioning the I.L.D. as the only group competent and aggressive enough to defend the young men. The I.L.D. quickly captured public attention by bringing Mrs. Janie Patterson to New York to speak at a "mass rally" in Harlem. On Saturday afternoon, April 25, Mrs. Patterson spoke to a small but supportive crowd at the corner of Lenox Avenue and 140th Street. To strong applause she told how the "Alabama boss-lynchers" had framed her son and eight others for a crime they had not committed. She asked all those who believed in justice and fair play to flood Alabama state officials with telegrams, demanding a new trial. New York police stood quietly by as Mrs. Patterson spoke. But when I.L.D. speaker Frank Alexander got on the platform, things changed. Alexander began shouting that the death sentences the nine had received in Scottsboro were nothing less than a "railroading" unheard of in the history of the country, engineered "by capitalists against children of the working class." The crowd of two hundred cheered angrily. Then, shouting defiantly at the nervous policemen, he led the crowd in a fast march down Lenox Avenue through the center of Harlem, waving banners and placards: "Death to Lynch Law," "Smash the Scottsboro Frame-up," "Legal Lynching." Between 139th and 138th Streets the parade met a phalanx of policemen. As the crowd marched on, the police began to beat them with nightsticks, concentrating their blows on those who held the banners and placards. The crowd fought back, screaming and striking the policemen. At first, the police spared women, but when a woman marcher drove her heel into the face of a prone policemen, northern chivalry evaporated. After four arrests and numerous injuries, the crowd dispersed. The next day the *Times* headlined: "Police Clubs Rout 200 Defiant Reds Who Attacked 'Lynch Law' in Alabama" (quoted in Carter 1969/1979, 59). No one now doubted that the I.L.D. was involved in the case of the Scottsboro Nine (Carter 1969/1979).

The *Daily Worker* embarrassed the N.A.A.C.P. on April 24 when it reprinted on its front page a photostatic copy of a letter from William Pickens, the N.A.A.C.P.'s field secretary in Kansas City. A former academic dean at Morgan College in Baltimore, Pickens had left the college in 1920 to become director of branches for the N.A.A.C.P. He was an accomplished orator and enjoyed a large following. In his letter to the *Daily Worker*, Pickens praised the activities of the I.L.D., noting that the I.L.D. had moved "more speedily and effectively than all other agencies put together." He admonished "every Negro who has the intelligence enough to read, to send aid to you [the *Worker*] and to the I.L.D." Just before Pickens's letter appeared on the *Daily Worker*'s front page, Walter White and other N.A.A.C.P. officials had assured everyone that it had things under control. Now, to the association's great embarrassment, it was obvious that the N.A.A.C.P.'s field secretary was not even aware of his organization's activity in the case. "It was," Dan Carter (1969/1979) observes, "a stunning setback for the Association" (quoted passages on 60).

Despite the fact that it was the New York office's failure to inform Pickens of events in the case that was to blame, the committee on administration (chaired by Mary White Ovington) unanimously reprimanded Pickens for the "unwisdom—and what might be construed as the disloyalty—of his action" (quoted in Carter 1969/1979, 60). Pickens apologized for his mistake, emphasizing that he knew nothing of the national office's activities. Nor had he imagined that his letter would be used by the *Daily Worker*. Carter (1969/1979) tells us that Ovington replied "acidly" (60) that the damage had been done and no apology could undo it. In these first decisive weeks of the struggle between the two organizations, the I.L.D. used Pickens's letter to sway reluctant observers to support their efforts. While there was, Carter (1969/1979, 61) allows, "a certain Machiavellian touch" to their use of Pickens's letter, the C.P.-U.S.A.'s campaign to discredit the N.A.A.C.P. was not, in general, duplicitous. It had in fact, as one black columnist observed, all the finesse and subtlety of a thundering rhinoceros.

II. "[T]he Communists have the N.A.A.C.P. people licked."

—quoted in Dan Carter, *Scottsboro: A Tragedy of the American South* (1969/1979)

To many Americans, progressivism was for whites only.

—William L. Van Deburg, *Slavery and Race in American Popular Culture* (1984)

For the Communist Party of the 1930s, May Day was the focal point of all public mass demonstrations. Under directives from the Central Committee, demands for the release of the Scottsboro Nine became the key theme for the 1931 celebrations throughout the country. At rallies from San Francisco to Boston, "the speakers all dwelt on the Scottsboro Case, exposing its vicious frame-up nature and calling upon the workers to join the fight to save the boys," reported the *Daily Worker*. Street-wide banners denounced "N.A.A.C.P. Bourgeois Reformists" and "Murderers of Negro and White Workers." In a long editorial the *Daily Worker* accused Walter White and his colleagues of almost every crime imaginable. The N.A.A.C.P., declared the *Worker*, took more seriously the "'respectability' of this organization in the eyes of the liberal white millionaires and upper class people" than "saving the lives of nine children being murdered in Alabama." Furthermore, the "cowardly" N.A.A.C.P. was fearful of offending the "'dignity' of the southern white ruling class court which has just heartlessly railroaded these children to death" (quoted in Carter 1969/1979, 61–62).

The sporadic criticisms of the N.A.A.C.P. by the C.P.-U.S.A. and its affiliated organizations during the late 1920s had not prepared White and his fellow officers for the intensity of the attack they now were undergoing. Given the ideological character of American communism in the spring of 1931, the attacks on the N.A.A.C.P. were predictable. Carter quotes the southern sociologist, Guy Johnson, who summarized in 1937 the rather different ideology of the N.A.A.C.P. The N.A.A.C.P., Johnson argued, was characterized by a "bread-and-butter philosophy of gradualism, good will, and conciliation" (quoted in Carter 1969/1979, 62). The association was no revolutionary organization; indeed, it accepted the status quo for the most part, focusing on specific goals and problems. N.A.A.C.P. officials expected no racial revolution; they perceived no shortcuts to racial equality. It was this commitment and vision that was "radical" about the association, but these were sometimes understated in order to achieve short-term objectives. There was, for example, little or no opposition to American capitalism on the part of N.A.A.C.P. leaders, except in the case of Du Bois, at this time still the editor of the *Crisis*. Du Bois could readily accept the Communists' call for a coalition of white and black workers. But the brilliant and shrewd Du Bois knew this was a fantasy, for it "is intelligent white labor that today keeps Negroes out of the trades, refuses them decent homes to live in and helps nullify their vote." Given the racism of white workers, Du Bois found himself in agreement with the general view of the association that African Americans must work with white capitalists who were "willing to curb this blood lust when it interferes with their profits" (quoted in Carter 1969/1979, 63).

With its commitment to revolution, the Communist Party had contempt for the tactics of gradualism. The party's official position on the race question was more complicated, however, than the term "radical" suggests. In 1922, the Fourth Comintern Congress, meeting in Moscow, discussed America's race problem for the first time. The final report focused instead on Africa and emphasized the black African's role in the struggle for liberation from their colonial masters. Party leaders made little effort to formulate a broad and popular program which might have enlisted the allegiance of America's black masses. In general, the party simply adopted the old Socialist Party's position on race, a position which declared that the misfortunes of African Americans were only another instance of capitalism's class exploitation, redress of which would occur when existing economic order was overthrown. The Communist-created American Negro Labor Congress convened in Chicago in October of 1925; party leaders hailed it as the start of an "unprecedented mass organization" (quoted in Carter 1969/1979, 63). The fact of the matter was it never amounted to more than a paper organization which was laid to rest in 1930 (Carter 1969/1979).

In 1932, the C.P.-U.S.A. ran James W. Ford, an African American, for vice president of the United States; it would do so again in 1936 and 1940. The major parties have yet to match that accomplishment. The party became increasingly engaged in issues that were once presumed to be the province of the N.A.A.C.P. Early in the summer of 1933 the I.L.D. announced that it had sent its own antilynching bill to Washington: a "Bill of Civil Rights for the Negro People," sponsored by the League of Struggle for Negro Rights, endorsed by the National Scottsboro Action Committee, and transmitted to the president and Congress by the Free the Scottsboro Boys Marchers. This drive against lynching as well as the I.L.D.'s fight for racial justice generally gained the attention of the American Fund for Public Service: the 1934 annual résumé of A.F.P.S. gifts listed $10,000 to the N.A.A.C.P. for its program of court cases; $35,361 had been donated to the International Labor Defense (Zangrando 1980).

Many African Americans began to lose patience with the N.A.A.C.P. over the Scottsboro case. When the *Pittsburgh Courier*, a strong supporter, defended the organization's refusal to cooperate with the I.L.D. and remarked that Secretary White would announce his plans in "due time," the *Courier*'s readers were skeptical. The *Chicago Defender*, America's largest black weekly, was less patient. The paper charged that the N.A.A.C.P. had unnecessarily dragged its feet in the case. It urged African Americans everywhere "to put aside division and bickering and join the effort" for a new trial under the leadership of the I.L.D., "an organization distinguished for its love of justice, though unpopular among the wealth and power of the land" (quoted in Carter 1969/1979, 68). The *Florida Sentinel*, another black weekly, acknowledged that often the Communists' words were "ill-timed and carelessly hurled," but it judged that "the men seem to be sincere and wholehearted" in their efforts to defend the

Scottsboro Nine and "all workers without regard to color" (quoted in Carter 1969/1979, 68).

The influential *Baltimore Afro-American* declined to endorse the I.L.D., but criticized the N.A.A.C.P. for attacking those who were trying to defend the jailed black men. Roy Wilkins was at the time editor of the *Kansas City Call.* A loyal supporter of the N.A.A.C.P., he wrote White expressing his exasperation, not over the association's refusal to join with the Communists, but its failure to defend itself and explain to the nation its position. As a result of its inaction, Wilkins warned, the N.A.A.C.P. stood a good chance of losing the support of the black press (Carter 1969/1979).

Wilkins's letter was, evidently, persuasive. White began to issue periodic reports to the press on the case. He remained resolved that the N.A.A.C.P. must gain undisputed control of the matter and then mobilize the support of prominent white southerners. With this strategy in mind, White decided that he must hire a first-rate attorney for the nine young men. The first name considered was George Huddleston, considered by many Alabamians as "a fiery left-winger." When approached, Huddleston exclaimed that he did not care "whether they [the defendants] are innocent or guilty." The fact that the nine black men were riding on the same freight car with two white women was enough for him: "You can't understand how we southern gentlemen feel about this question of relationship between negro men and white women" (quoted in Carter 1969/1979, 70). So much for "fiery left-wingers" in 1930s Alabama.

White then consulted Charles A. J. McPherson, the head of Birmingham's N.A.A.C.P. chapter, who suggested that a more likely candidate would be Roderick Beddow. The N.A.A.C.P.'s executive committee agreed. White moved quickly. On Wednesday, May 13, he traveled to Birmingham where he found Beddow and the other members of the firm Fort, Beddow, and Ray friendly, but noncommittal. Beddow reminded White that there was still some question as to who controlled the case. They could hardly commit themselves unless it was clear that the Communists were no longer involved. White was certain he could persuade the nine young men to go with the N.A.A.C.P. After a lengthy interview with several local black ministers, he visited the nine defendants in Kilby Prison in Montgomery. The Communists were using the case for propaganda purposes only, he told them. Their best hope lay with the N.A.A.C.P., he continued. His organization would hire the best attorney in Alabama and would take their case to the United States Supreme Court if necessary. Willie Roberson, Ozie Powell, Clarence Norris, and Charley Weems signed the affidavit he presented, but Andy Wright and Haywood Patterson told him they wished to write their parents before switching sides. Olen Montgomery and Eugene Williams remained loyal to the I.L.D. With the signed affidavit in hand, White went once again to Beddow, who assured him that he would give the matter careful consideration after he had a chance to read the trial transcripts (Carter 1969/1979).

Back in New York, White now issued his first lengthy public statement regarding the case. Acknowledging that several of the parents seemed committed to the I.L.D., he said: "It should be remembered that the boys and their parents are humble folk and have had few opportunities for knowledge. They have been confused by the conflicting statements made to them" (quoted in Carter 1969/1979, 72). His condescension would not wear well with the parents, whose support he would later have to enlist. Not twenty-four hours after White issued his statement, the I.L.D. rushed the young men's relatives to Kilby Prison. Once again, they succeeded in persuading all nine against the N.A.A.C.P. and for the I.L.D. The parents then attacked White and the N.A.A.C.P. for trying to "persuade our children to disregard our advice in this matter." As they left, they warned their children "against the methods of Walter White and his preachers and Ku Klux Lawyer allies." Carter (1969/1979) comments: "Once again, the N.A.A.C.P. was cast in the role of defender with no one to defend" (quoted passages on 73).

Discouraged but not defeated, White now sent William Pickens (by now having regained the confidence of the national office) to both Chattanooga and Birmingham. On May 31, Pickens and Beddow, who still had not accepted the case, traveled to Kilby prison. There Beddow told the defendants: "If I thought you were guilty I would not for anything take your cases." But having read the records carefully and after speaking with the young men, "I frankly believe you innocent. I will appear in court for those who want me to defend them," Beddow told the defendants (quoted in Carter 1969/1979, 74). Despite misgivings that he could win an appeal, Beddow decided to enter the case. White and Pickens were elated ... for a time. But even with Fort, Beddow, and Ray in charge of the case, even after the Birmingham firm had accepted a retainer of $500, Beddow and his colleagues maintained a low profile, leaving the lower court proceedings to the unreliable Roddy and Moody (Carter 1969/1979).

In asking for a new trial, both the I.L.D. and the N.A.A.C.P. attorneys pointed out that the trial, conducted with a menacing mob just outside the courthouse, deprived the defendants of their rights under the due process clause of the Fourteenth Amendment to the Constitution. It was Roddy, during the trials at Scottsboro, who had managed to have included in the court record that Patterson's jury overheard the loud victory celebration when the first jury brought in its guilty verdict. Chamlee questioned the integrity of the third jury's deliberations, arguing that their convictions against five of the defendants had been influenced by the mob-like atmosphere. Members of the jury admitted hearing some "hollering," and "clapping of hands" (quoted in Carter 1969/1979, 78), but, to a man, they insisted that this had in no way affected their judgment. Judge Hawkins refused to allow Chamlee to ask the jurors if they thought racial prejudice had been a factor in their decision (Carter 1969/1979).

In addition, Chamlee and Brodsky submitted a sheaf of affidavits in support of their motion for a new trial. Hawkins quickly glanced through the statements, but he did not read them aloud; their contents were known by nearly everyone. They were statements questioning the character of Ruby Bates and Victoria Price, signed by ten black residents of Chattanooga. All alleged that both Ruby Bates and Victoria Price were promiscuous; both liked black men. During the trials at Scottsboro the state's attorney had characterized the two women as representatives of "the flower of southern womanhood." As these allegations against Bates and Price became known through the little town, anger intensified against the "scalawag" Chamlee and his "Jewish carpetbagger" associate, Joseph Brodsky (quoted in Carter 1969/1979, 80).

When Judge Hawkins adjourned the hearings shortly after 11:30 A.M., Brodsky gathered up his papers and stored them into his briefcase. As he turned to leave the courtroom, a spectator walked to within a foot of him, saying, "It's about time you left town, or it might not stay too healthy for you." Brodsky was not intimidated: "Tell it to the Judge," he replied. Outside, nearly fifty "hard-eyed" men formed a circle around the two lawyers as they tried to leave. One "grizzled" mountaineer reached out and touched Brodsky's shoulder, saying: "The best thing you can do is to get up the road right away" (quoted in Carter 1969/1979, 80). Then Brodsky and Chamlee were permitted to leave. A few hours later, Brodsky confided that he had never been more frightened in his life (Carter 1969/1979).

Not only black residents of Chattanooga knew Ruby Bates and Victoria Price. The A.C.L.U. had hired an investigator—Miss Hollace Ransdell—to check on the two women's reputation elsewhere. In Hunstville, Alabama, Deputy Sheriff Walter Sanders told Ransdell that he knew the women well. In particular Victoria Price was a "quiet prostitute" (Carter 1969/1979, 83); both women appeared to accept sexual intercourse with whites or blacks as part of their routine of life. When the A.C.L.U. issued Ransdell's report in May of 1931, readers were shocked. But southerners (and particularly Alabamians) refused to believe the report, dismissing it as the product of radicals and outsiders who knew nothing of the South. But a series of reports issued by the Commission on Interracial Cooperation during May and June were more difficult to dismiss. Using private detectives the C.I.C. confirmed the findings of Ransdell and the A.C.L.U. Ruby Bates and Victoria Price had indeed worked as prostitutes (Carter 1969/1979).

The N.A.A.C.P. continued to undermine the position of the I.L.D., especially among southerners. But White and Pickens grew frustrated; they gained little in the standing of southern whites by attacking the I.L.D. as a Communist front. No matter what the N.A.A.C.P. said, most white southerners distrusted both organizations. Even a southern progressive like George Fort Milton, the chairman of the Southern Commission on the Study of Lynching, took the position that only the "liberal white people of the South" should handle the case. Especially given that the N.A.A.C.P. and the I.L.D. seemed "engaged in a joint battle to secure the exploiting possibilities of the case rather than to defend the boys themselves," southerners should decide the fate of the nine young men by themselves. The Birmingham *Age-Herald* expressed this suspicion of the New York–based organizations this way: "It is now clear that these darkies do not mean a tinker's dame [sic] to the organizations which have supposedly been moving heaven and earth in their behalf." The whole mess was a "nauseating struggle between the Communist group and the negro society, not so much that justice may be done as that selfish interests may be advanced through the capitalization of the episode" (quoted in Carter 1969/1979, 87).

Dan Carter (1969/1979) argues that Walter White not only misjudged white southern progressives but the temper of the black community as well. Even during the "Red Scare" of the early 1920s, there had been few militant black "anti-Communists." While America's black masses had not rallied to the red flag (as the Communists had hoped), African Americans in general did not share the virulent anti-Communism to which the majority of European Americans were susceptible. Carl Murphy of the *Baltimore Afro-American*, for example, reminded his readers that, unlike the Democrats or the Republicans, the Communists were "the only party going our way." Since the abolitionists had disappeared after the Civil War, he pointed out, "no white group of national prominence has openly advocated the economic, political and social equality of black folks" (quoted in Carter 1969/1979, 89).

Even a more circumspect member of the black press like B. Young of the *Norfolk Journal and Guide* suggested that African Americans ought not dismiss communism as a complete evil. The C.P.-U.S.A. was, he wrote, simply another political organization which could help blacks to achieve greater economic and legal equality. Why shouldn't African Americans look favorably on communism? asked William H. (Kid) Kelley of Harlem's *Amsterdam News*. What had capitalism given blacks? "Oppressed on every hand, denied equal educational facilities, discriminated against in public places and in employment, Jim-Crowed on street cars and railroad trains ... even lynched, it would seem that any program—Communistic or Socialistic—should readily find converts among America Negroes." Did it make sense to "go to war with the Communist Party," asked the *Chicago Defender*, "when it was the one organization in white America that practiced complete political, economic, and social equality?" (quoted in Carter 1969/1979, 89).

Frustrated in their efforts to gain widespread support for the N.A.A.C.P. by criticizing the I.L.D., the officers of the association continued to try to gain complete control of the case. But, Carter (1969/1979) suggests, "the condescending attitude" (Carter 1969/1979, 90) of both Pickens and White, detectable in their public remarks, proved to be a grave tactical error. The I.L.D. national office in New York carefully clipped their condescending remarks and sent them to the parents, further alienating them from the N.A.A.C.P. The kindness and respect of the I.L.D. officials contrasted sharply with the condescension of the N.A.A.C.P. White's mishandling of the case did not go unnoticed by the black press. In midsummer 1931, editor Carl Murphy of the *Baltimore Afro-American* observed: "It may be treasonable to say it," [but] "as the Scottsboro Case stands today the Communists have the N.A.A.C.P. people licked" (Carter 1969/1979, 97). The I.L.D. had won the backing of the parents and the majority of their sons, noted Murphy. It seemed that the N.A.A.C.P. was in court without clients (Carter 1969/1979).

With the N.A.A.C.P. near defeat, Walter White turned to Clarence Darrow. "We had hoped that it would not be necessary for us to call on you in the now famous Scottsboro cases," White told Darrow, "but we are frankly right up against what is probably the most delicate and difficult situation of our history." He asked the aging Darrow if he would be willing to argue the case as far as the Supreme Court. Darrow was conflicted. At seventy-four, he had been in semi-retirement since 1926. His health was deteriorating. On the other hand, he worried that the I.L.D. was jeopardizing any chance for the release of the defendants. Moreover, in the midst of the Great Depression, the $5,000 fee was no doubt attractive. Darrow told White that he would be willing to take on partial responsibility for the case. Due to his health, he explained, he did not have the physical strength to take responsibility for preparing the appeal, "but I would be willing to make one of the oral arguments before the Supreme Court" (quoted in Carter 1969/1979, 97). As Beddow was ready to leave the case, White went to him to tell him that Darrow had taken on the case. As he had hoped, the possibility of being associated with the distinguished attorney persuaded the Birmingham law firm to remain on the case (Carter 1969/1979).

Collaboration with the I.L.D. proved impossible, as the Communists demanded that Darrow repudiate the N.A.A.C.P. When newsmen interviewed Darrow as he left Birmingham, he explained that he had decided to withdraw not because he feared involvement with the Communists, but because the I.L.D. had made two intolerable demands. In addition to requiring him to repudiate the N.A.A.C.P., the I.L.D. had insisted that he agree to abide by their decisions. "I have no objection to any man's politics," Darrow told the press, "but you can't mix politics with law." If these cases were to be won, they would have to be won in Alabama, "not in Russia or New York" (quoted in Carter 1969/1979, 101–102). Soon after, the N.A.A.C.P. National Board of Directors announced that the association had decided to withdraw from the case (Carter 1969/1979).

Despite the temporary embarrassment over the Darrow episode, the International Labor Defense was jubilant when word came that the N.A.A.C.P. had officially withdrawn. George Maurer credited the I.L.D.'s victory to its bold and aggressive tactics. No doubt the I.L.D.'s aggressiveness had paid off, but Dan Carter credits the organization's successes to the weaknesses of the N.A.A.C.P. He points to the lethargy of the association's initial actions, as well as its reliance on local representatives. "What they [White and his associates] failed to understand," Carter (1969/1979, 103) argues, "was that there had been dramatic changes during the first two years of the Depression, changes which demanded new tactics and a new strategy. For better or worse, the politics of the nation had shifted to the left; the N.A.A.C.P. had not."

III. "[T]he old way of the rope was better than the new way of the law."

—quoted in Dan T. Carter, *Scottsboro: A Tragedy of the American South* (1969/1979)

[H]ow do we pursue the question of sexuality and the law, where the law is not only that which represses sexuality, but a prohibition that generates sexuality or, at least, compels its directionality?

—Judith Butler, *Bodies That Matter: On the Discursive Limits of "Sex"* (1993)

Three years before the publication of *An American Dilemma*, Gunnar Myrdal suggested that the South was an "exception in Western nonfascist civilization since the Enlightenment in that *it lacks nearly every trace of radical thought*." No radical thought, but there was a tradition, however uninfluential, of self-criticism of the region. In the 1920s, for instance, three southern newspaper editors had won the Pulitzer Prize for coverage critical of the Ku Klux Klan. Editorial prizes had also been awarded to the *Charleston News and Courier* for an editorial on the decline of southern statesmanship and to the *Norfolk Pilot* for its campaign against lynching. But without exception, Carter (1969/1979) points out, these journalists critiqued southern problems from a conservative point of view. Not a one of them could by any stretch of the imagination be termed "radical." A handful of liberals, as noted earlier, primarily located around academic institutions such as the University of North Carolina in Chapel Hill, were tolerated and even grudgingly respected due to their national prominence. But southern progressives remained such a minority that they became, as Myrdal put it, "inclined to stress the need for patience and to exalt the cautious approach, the slow change, the organic nature of social growth" (quoted in Carter 1969/1979, 116–117).

The problems faced by the Interracial Commission as it contemplated a role in the Scottsboro case illustrate the situation southern progressives faced. After the controversy between the I.L.D. and the N.A.A.C.P. became intense, the Commission kept its distance from the case. Any consideration of a future role was enough to solicit angry responses from its membership. "I have always been the negro's friend," began Jesse B. Hearin of Mobile. "But I believe there is a line beyond which we cannot go." Should the Interracial Commission participate in any way in the defense of the Scottsboro Nine, "I will thank you to tender my resignation as a member of the Commission." Dean of the Auburn University School of Education, Zebulon Judd reflected the mood in Alabama when he expressed complete satisfaction with the trial and conviction. "The whole state seems satisfied not only that justice was meted out, but that it was done in an orderly legal fashion," he declared. The only difficulties were caused by the "pestiferous interferences from the outside world that knows little or nothing about the case." As to the pace of the Alabama judiciary: "All sensible men will agree that the surest way to prevent heat and extralegal measures is to give speedy trials" (quoted in Carter 1969/1979, 118–119). Another member of the Commission, a prominent Methodist layman in Alabama, insisted that any appeal of the conviction would communicate approval of black men raping white women (Carter 1969/1979).

Even the small minority who favored a retrial shared with the majority of Alabamians the conviction that the communists had become involved in the Scottsboro case for purely mercenary motives. For instance, the Alabama Interracial Commission charged that there was "brilliant leadership, sleepless energy, and apparently unlimited money behind the malevolent [Communist] activity." These "apostles of revolution" faked friendship for southern blacks, but this pretense was only a means to achieve their nefarious ends. The Commission even alleged that one of the I.L.D.'s defense lawyers had quipped that the defendants would be more valuable executed than alive. Without a doubt, concluded the Commission, "race hatred, race discord, murder, rape [and] lynchings" were the Communists' "immediate object." Even Will Alexander charged the I.L.D. with participation in the case only as "an opportunity to make propaganda." The Communists had fomented a "world-wide agitation under the assumption that it [the case] was part of the class struggle," when in fact there was no element of class conflict "and the interference of the Communists ... injects into the case elements which make it very difficult to get adequate defense for the boys" (quoted in Carter 1969/1979, 121).

Alexander may have been right about the difficulties of mounting an "adequate defense" for the nine young black men, but that was hardly a function of communist ideology. No organization would have found defending the nine easygoing. And certainly Alexander overstated his case regarding class: had the nine been college-educated, upper-class African Americans things might well have gone a bit easier for them. But, as usual, American liberals overreacted to the far left. In fact, the C.P.-U.S.A.'s contention that the Scottsboro Nine were victims of "class war" proved disturbing for American liberals, who responded defensively. The *World Tomorrow*, a Protestant-Socialist publication, protested: "Communist doctrine makes it inevitable that the fate of the boys will be made subservient to the case of dramatizing the class struggle in America." The Communists' characterization of the condemned youths as "victims of capitalist injustice" was both pathetic and ominous, argued the *Christian Century*. The class struggle thesis provoked not reasoned discussion but "unreasonable prejudice," concluded the *New Republic* (quoted in Carter 1969/1979, 139). Along with the *Nation* and the *New Republic*, many others demanded that the Communists turn over the defense efforts to a non-radical group. Otherwise, American liberals charged, the main issue—the guilt or innocence of the defendants—would remain only a tool in the Communist Party's struggle for proletarian revolution (Carter 1969/1979).

The Scottsboro case was not only a prominent public controversy in the United States. The C.P.-U.S.A. as well as mainstream news coverage produced international interest in the case, including international protests of the death sentences. On one occasion organized protest led to violence. Young Communists in Dresden, Germany, marched on the American consulate. When American officials refused to accept their petition, they threw bottles through several windows. Inside each had been written: "Down with American murder and imperialism. For the brotherhood of black and white young proletarians. An end to the bloody lynching of our Negro co-workers." The Dresden incident was reported on the front page of the *New York Times*, and the news set off a rash of stonings and bottle throwing throughout Europe. Demonstrators damaged the American consulates in Berlin, Leipzig, and Geneva during the summer of 1931. Nor was the protest limited to Europe: in Havana, a mob of Communists carried red banners condemning "Yankee Imperialism" and the Scottsboro verdicts (quoted in Carter 1969/1979, 142). The marchers then attacked the Galiano Street Branch of the National City Bank of New York, shattering the plate glass window with stones (Carter 1969/1979).

Back home, the I.L.D. and the C.P.-U.S.A. organized fund-raising and political events at which the mothers of the Scottsboro Nine spoke. At first, the women were timid about public speaking, but as they gained confidence and enjoyed the warmth of the crowds they became more at ease on the platform. Mrs. Patterson, in particular, became a fiery orator. "They tried to tell me that the I.L.D. was [sic] low-down whites and Reds," she told a rally in New Haven, Connecticut. "I haven't got no schooling, but I have five senses and I know that Negroes can't win by themselves." The I.L.D. had saved her son, she continued, "and I have faith that they will free him if we all is united behind them." As to the skittishness about ideology: "I don't care whether they are Reds, Greens or Blues. They are the only ones who put up a fight to save these boys and I am with them to the end" (quoted in Carter 1969/1979, 144).

Widespread interest in hearing the Scottsboro mothers waned in 1932. During one spring trip that year, collections barely covered expenses. While a failure at fund-raising, the tours were successes in keeping the case before the public, even when there were no significant new developments. After every speech a stream of petitions, protests, and demands poured into the office of Governor Miller in Alabama and President Hoover in Washington. Of course, no meeting protesting the Scottsboro verdict was complete without a plea for letters to Alabama officials. Through the summer of 1931, Governor Miller received countless thousands of communications from around the world, some going on for pages, some pleading eloquently for pardon. Most, however, were "brief, abusive, and to the point" (Carter 1969/1979, 145). At one point, the attorney general of Alabama became so enraged at the intensity of insult and threats expressed in most communiqués that he refused to accept any more, demanding that the telegraph company cease delivery (Carter 1969/1979).

The I.L.D. and other C.P.-U.S.A. organizations encouraged letters from all concerned persons, but of course the names of prominent Americans were specifically solicited. Many famous Americans complied, among them Theodore Dreiser, Lincoln Steffens, Upton Sinclair, John Dos Passos, Clifton Fadiman, Hubert C. Herring, and the distinguished symphony conductor Leopold Stokowski. All wrote to Alabama officials demanding justice. In Germany, former Argentine Professor Alfonso Goldschmidt, an eminent lawyer, organized a committee among whose members were Albert Einstein, Thomas Mann, and three hundred other German intellectuals. The group petitioned President Hoover and Governor Miller "in the name of humanity and justice" to pardon the nine young men. From England came a petition signed by H. G. Wells and thirty-three members of Parliament demanding a reversal of the "inhuman" death sentences (quoted phrases in Carter 1969/1979, 146). Langston Hughes was amazed and disgusted at the apparent apathy of many black students and educators. When a handful of students at Hampton Institute tried to march silently to protest the case, the administration prevented them, declaring: "That is not Hampton's way. We educate, not protest" (quoted in Carter 1969/1979, 154).

When the Alabama Supreme Court began, on January 21, 1932, to hear the appeal for a retrial, Chief Justice John C. Anderson issued an unprecedented statement regarding the mail he and his colleagues had received. "These messages are highly improper, inflammatory and revolutionary in their nature," he complained. They were "sent with the evident intent to bulldoze this court" (quoted in Carter 1969/1979, 156). Chamlee assured the court that the I.L.D. had nothing to do with the mail, but the icy glare of the justices betrayed a certain skepticism. But Chamlee was not the major attorney in the case; Joseph

Brodsky was. Even the hostile *Montgomery Advertiser* acknowledged his eloquent performance in the courtroom. Attorney General Thomas G. Knight, the son of one of the court's associate justices, replied to the defense brief, while six guards monitored the courtroom audience in order to discourage a threatened demonstration. On March 24, by a vote of six to one, the Alabama Supreme Court upheld the conviction of all but one of the defendants. Eugene Williams was granted a new trial on the grounds that he was a juvenile at the time of his conviction (Carter 1969/1979).

Predictably, the *Daily Worker* attacked the majority decision, but unpredictably the newspaper also criticized Chief Justice Anderson's dissent as well as the court's decision to grant a new trial for Eugene Williams. These were, the paper complained, "fake gestures" intended to conceal "the bestial oppression of the Negro masses." Nor could the nation's workers place any hope in the United States Supreme Court, the paper continued. These judicial machinations amounted to nothing more than moving from "one capitalist court to another capitalist court, and the same hatred toward the Negro masses and the working class will govern whatever actions are taken by the United States Supreme Court" (quoted in Carter 1969/1979, 160). Despite this contempt for the American legal system, I.L.D. officials retained Walter Pollak, one of the nation's most eminent constitutional attorneys when, after a preliminary hearing on May 27, the Supreme Court agreed to hear the case (Carter 1969/1979).

Just before 11 A.M. on November 7, 1932, Chief Justice Charles Evans Hughes nodded to Justice George Sutherland, one of the most conservative members of the court. After briefly summarizing the history of the case, Sutherland focused upon the main point of the decision. The court had restricted itself to one question, he reminded, "whether the defendants were in substance denied the right of counsel, and if so, whether such denial infringes on the due process clause of the Fourteenth Amendment." After quoting at length from the Scottsboro transcript, Sutherland judged the appointment of counsel as unacceptably casual. Judge Hawkins's naming of all members of the Jackson County bar to defend the nine young men was an "expansive gesture" which functioned to diffuse the final responsibility for the defendants' case (quoted in Carter 1969/1979, 161). At this point, it was clear that the U.S. Supreme Court would reverse the lower court's verdict on the grounds of inadequate counsel. Justices Pierce Butler and James C. McReynolds, two of the most conservative members of the court, dissented from the majority view, arguing that the defendants had received a completely adequate and fair trial. But the force of their criticism had been muted by Hughes's success in persuading the conservative Sutherland to write the majority opinion (Carter 1969/1979).

The *New York Times* hailed *Powell* v. *Alabama* as an important moment in American jurisprudence. The Supreme Court's decision "ought to abate the rancor of extreme radicals while confirming the faith of the American people in the soundness of their institutions and especially the integrity of the courts." It proved false the Communist claim that "a spirit of wicked class prejudice pervades the United States and that here no justice can be had for the poor and ignorant." The *New Republic*, the *Nation*, and *Christian Century* joined the

Times in praising the court's decision. The Communists were willing to conclude only that the case indicated only that "mass organization and militant struggle outside the legal forms of capitalist 'democracy' is the most effective method for all oppressed" (quoted in Carter 1969/1979, 165).

Back in Alabama, Olen Montgomery wrote the I.L.D. for all nine defendants. "Since the Supreme Court have granted we boys a new trial I thank [sic] it is my rite to express thanks and appreciation to the whole party for their care." All of the accused were "so happy over it," he wrote. "I myself feels like I have been born again from the worrying ... I have had" (quoted in Carter 1969/1979, 165). The eighteen months since their conviction had not exactly been easy for the nine young men. In addition to the discomforts and dangers of prison life, they had faced (several times) what had been an agonizing decision over whether to accept the I.L.D. or the N.A.A.C.P. Once that decision had been made, there had been a brief period of hope and expectation as the prisoners received well-wishers on weekends and money every day in letters from supporters. Even on death row, they were able to buy special food, candy, and cigarettes, all of which helped make prison life slightly more tolerable. And they took some solace from the fact that they were world celebrities, a development that followed in part from the devoted attention of the Communist press. Even the Russian novelist Maxim Gorky commented on the case in the Soviet newspaper *Pravda* (Carter 1969/1979).

But these amounted, in the end, to nothing more than temporary distractions for the imprisoned men. Late in January 1932, black poet Langston Hughes was speaking at Tuskegee Institute when a local minister suggested that a reading of his poems might cheer the Scottsboro Nine. On a Sunday afternoon, January 24, Hughes visited death row of Kilby Prison. He found the men dressed in their gray prison uniforms, at the end of a long corridor in small grilled cells. Not far away was the steel door leading to the electric chair, a constant reminder to prisoners that death was close by. The eight youths were sitting or laying listlessly in their bunks. They had not heard of Langston Hughes, nor were they enthusiastic about the visitor. After the minister introduced him, only Andy came over to the bars and shook his hand. Hughes read humorous poems to them in hopes of cheering them. He mentioned not once their case or the racism of the South. "I said nothing of any seriousness," he said later, "except my hope that their appeals would end well and they would soon be free" (quoted in Carter 1969/1979, 166–167). After reading his poems, the minister prayed, but still there was no movement among eight of the young men. Only Andy thanked them and said good-bye. Hughes looked back: the men were unchanged, unmoving, dozing or simply staring at the walls (Carter 1969/1979).

Never supportive, after the Supreme Court's decision Alabama public opinion crystallized hard against the defendants. As always, Chamlee remained hopeful, but he warned I.L.D. officials that acquittal would require an impeccable defense. Establishing "reasonable doubt" would be insufficient, he continued; the I.L.D. defense team would need to prove beyond question the innocence of the defendants. Persuaded by Chamlee's advice, the I.L.D.'s William L. Patterson turned to a New York lawyer, born in Rumania: Samuel

Leibowitz. With the retirement of Clarence Darrow in the early 1930s, Leibowitz had become one of the leading criminal attorneys in the United States (Carter 1969/1979).

Leibowitz did not exactly jump at the invitation. First, there would be no fee. But no fee meant also that the I.L.D. would be in no position to influence his social, economic, and political views, which did not coincide with those of the C.P.-U.S.A. Despite his differences with the party, Leibowitz agreed to take on the case. And the I.L.D. accepted Leibowitz. Carter (1969/1979, 183) comments: "From the outset, however, the relationship between Leibowitz and the I.L.D. was a marriage of convenience, never of preference."

The retaining of a brilliant attorney did not necessarily improve the prospects. *New York Times* reporters in Scottsboro reported that many citizens were disgusted by the retrial. They did not hesitate to "declare ... that the old way of the rope was better than the new way of the law" (quoted in Carter 1969/1979, 183). But that was just the beginning of problems for the defense. From the Huntsville police Alabama Attorney General Knight received word that Ruby Bates was missing, one of his star witnesses. A conference with Sheriff Ben Giles proved shocking. Giles had been monitoring Bates for the state; she had told him she had been offered a large sum of money if she would disappear before the second trial. This was not the first hint of trouble with Bates. From the start Bates had felt in competition with Victoria Price, annoyed because she had taken center stage. As early as June 1931, Bates had hinted that she had "important" information for the defense. On January 5, Huntsville police discovered a letter which caused consternation all around. Addressed to a boyfriend, Ruby Bates had written:

> dearest Earl
> I want to make a statement to you Mary Sanders is a goddam lie about those negroes jassing me those police man made me tell a lie. ... those negroes did not touch me. ... i hope you will believe me the law don i love you beteor [better] than Mary does are any Body else. ... i know it was wrong too let those negroes die on account of me ... i was jaze But those white Boys jazed me i wished those negroes are not burnt on account of me. ... (quoted in Carter 1969/1979, 186–187)

Upon investigation, a friend reported that Bates was "drunk as she could be when she wrote the letter." In fact, getting Bates drunk had been, presumably, part of Chamlee's plan in order to get her to write the letter. After questioning by the police, Ruby signed an affidavit agreeing with this version of events: "I was so drunk that I did not know what I was doing." Chamlee declared the affidavit an "absolute falsehood" (quoted in Carter 1969/1979, 187). A subsequent investigation by the Bar Association would find that Chamlee had been only peripherally involved in the incident and that there was no proof that Ruby Bates had been bribed. The charges against Chamlee were dropped. Knight hoped that this embarrassing turn of events would deter the defense from trying to contact either of the two women again. He directed all state and local officials to find Bates and to take her into custody (Carter 1969/1979).

IV. "My God, Doctor, is this whole thing a horrible mistake[?]"

—Judge Horton, quoted in Dan T. Carter, *Scottsboro: A Tragedy of the American South* (1969/1979)

The law is the shadow toward which every gesture necessarily advances; it is itself the shadow of the advancing gesture.

—Michel Foucault, "Maurice Blanchot: The Thought from Outside" (1987)

I.L.D. attorneys were successful this time in obtaining a change of venue, but given attitudes toward the trial throughout Alabama the victory seemed pointless. The trial would take place in Decatur, situated in northern Alabama on the south bank of the Tennessee River. "Southern to the core" (Carter 1969/1979, 189), Decatur had been a center of the Ku Klux Klan in both the Reconstruction period and during the 1920s. The position of African Americans was much the same as it was in Scottsboro. Only a handful bothered to vote; white hegemony was nearly complete. After mingling with the townspeople, Leibowitz told reporters, "The people impress me as being honest, God fearing people who want to see justice done" (quoted in Carter 1969/1979, 192). They seemed, he said, genuinely friendly. He would, soon enough, change his mind. As would many other northerners, he would find "southern hospitality" less than an inch deep.

Leibowtiz's first impression of southerners was not contradicted right away. He seemed to expect a certain resistance, even from the judge. He focused at first on the issue of the all-white jury. But Judge Horton would have none of it: "The motion to quash is overruled," Horton snapped. "I respectfully except," replied Leibowitz, whose good humor remained in tact for a while (quoted in Carter 1969/1979, 199). Judge Horton's decision came so suddenly and unexpectedly that many reporters were caught napping; they had to inquire about it at the press table. Leibowitz, evidently, had not expected Horton to do otherwise. He was simply making certain he had the fact of an all-white jury in the transcript in case an appeal became necessary. The exclusion of African Americans from jury duty was not a class issue. As the columnist Mary Heaton Vorse observed, those called by the defense were all men of importance—doctors, ministers, and businessmen. "Almost all have college degrees—some more than one" (quoted in Carter 1969/1979, 210). Of course none had ever been called to jury service; none of Knight's fiery questions on minor points obscured that fact (Carter 1969/1979). Women, white or black, were simply unimaginable as jury members at this time. The gender of the law was masculine.

When the testimony on the quashing motion resumed the following morning, the atmosphere deteriorated rapidly. There had been no open threats, but throughout the town there had been expressions of rage over Leibowitz's attack on the jury system. Attending the trial for the Interracial Commission, Robert Burns Eleazer reported to Will Alexander that Leibowitz had "handled the case remarkably well" and "with fine courtesy." But Eleazer also told Alexander that he had "prejudiced unfavorably his chance for acquittal by his fight on the jury system." Raymond Daniell of the *New York Times* observed an intensification of white anger. Leibowitz's insistence on referring to black witnesses as "Mr." had annoyed the white spectators, but when he questioned the integrity of (white) jury commissioner Tidwell, "row upon row of rough-faced unshaven countrymen in blue denim overall" set their faces in "hard, unsympathetic lines." Leibowtiz concluded his arguments on the motion shortly before noon on Friday, and Judge Horton, almost as abruptly as he had done in the case of the earlier motion, denied the motion. Horton also ruled that the defense had established a prima facie case of exclusion, a decision which allowed Leibowitz confidence that no conviction could now stand before a higher court. But he responded only with "I respectfully except" (quoted in Carter 1969/1979, 202).

In his effort to raise questions regarding the character and credibility of Victoria Price, Leibowitz offered in evidence records from the Hunstville, Alabama, city court showing that she had been found guilty of adultery and fornication on January 26, 1931. Along with her boyfriend, L. J. (Jack) Tiller, who was married, she had been fined and sentenced to serve time in the city jail. Perhaps the news of her "reputation" helped alter Price's conduct, for at the Scottsboro trails she had been "colorful and inventive" (Carter 1969/1979, 206), describing in lurid detail even the most insignificant events. At Decatur her mood was different; she stuck to a plain, unembroidered story. There were few details. In an effort to draw her out, Leibowitz noted sympathetically that it must have been a nightmare, pinned, semi-nude, to the jagged floor, with nine young black men writhing on top of her "like brutes." No response. "Was your back bleeding when you got to the doctor?" he asked. "I couldn't say," replied Price. "When you got to the jail did you find any blood on your back?" A little, maybe she allowed, but quickly added: "I ain't sure, that has been two years ago." Well, Leibowitz continued, "when you got to the doctor's office, were you not crying in any way?" "I had just hushed crying, the best I remember I was crying—I won't say, I ain't positive" the now elusive witness replied (quoted in Carter 1969/1979, 206–207). Finally Leibowitz extracted a statement from her which he knew the examining physician would contradict (Carter 1969/1979).

At another point Leibowitz succeeded in showing that her testimony was self-contradictory, clearly inaccurate. Then Price's demeanor changed. Now enraged, she screamed at Leibowitz: "That's some of Ruby Bates's dope." She added defiantly, "I do know one thing, those negroes and this Haywood Patterson raped me." Leibowitz did not reply; he stood and stared at her for a minute. You are a "little bit of an actress," he said with quiet intensity. Victoria Price replied quickly: "You're a pretty good actor yourself" (quoted in Carter 1969/1979, 207). To any impartial observer it was that clear that Leibowitz had established that Victoria Price was not a reliable witness. But Leibowitz himself knew that a sympathetic jury might discount this and dismiss her errors as forgetfulness or confusion (Carter 1969/1979).

Leibowitz did not know that his strategy—self-evident in its reasonableness, or so it seemed to him, perhaps to any northerner—had to backfire. This was the Deep South and he was a northerner. Moreover, he was a Jew, as the locals (Protestants to a man) well knew, and attacking a white woman—whatever her reputation—in order to defend black men. If Leibowitz read southern newspapers he would have known. "One possessed of that old southern chivalry cannot read the trial now in progress in Decatur ... and publish an opinion and keep within the law," complained the *Sylacauga News.* The "brutal manner" in which Leibowitz cross-examined Mrs. Price "makes one feel like reaching for his gun while his blood boils to the nth degree." Leibowitz had made a "fatal mistake" when he treated Victoria Price as he might a man, and proceeded to discredit her as, simply, a prostitute. He was "not accustomed to addressing southern juries," reported Robert Eleazer to the C.I.C. (quoted in Carter 1969/1979, 210). Too late the chief defense attorney would realize that Victoria Price was nothing less than a symbol of white southern womanhood (Carter 1969/1979).

The last witness for the state on the first day of the trial was Dr. R. R. Bridges, the physician whose testimony, along with that of his colleague, Dr. Lynch, had worked well for the state's case at Scottsboro. Under direct examination, he repeated almost word for word the same story he had told at Scottsboro two years earlier. Under cross examination, however, Samuel Leibowitz managed to turn the doctor's testimony into evidence supporting the defense. Less than one hour and thirty minutes after the alleged rape, the two women were, Bridges acknowledged, "composed and calm." Their pupils were not dilated nor were their pulse and respiration abnormal. In response to Leibowitz's questions, Bridges repeated that the semen was completely non-motile, and he was quick to agree that this was curious since the spermatozoa normally remained active in the vagina for twelve hours to two days. "In other words," Leibowitz emphasized, "you were not able to discover any single [living] spermatozoa [sic] from this woman who claimed she had been raped by six men" not an hour before. "Yes, sir, that is right," he replied. It was curious too, Bridges acknowledged under questioning, that although Victoria Price had supposedly been raped six times, only with great difficulty did he and Dr. Lynch find enough semen to make a smear slide. Despite her claim that she was bleeding from her vagina and had been cut "a little bit" on her forehead, the Scottsboro physician admitted he had seen no blood. Then he volunteered that while in general she was calm, after the examination Victoria Price "seemed a bit cross with us and didn't want to cooperate" (quoted in Carter 1969/1979, 213–214).

Leibowitz's skill in converting the doctors' testimony from supporting the state's case to favoring the defense gave the first day of the trial to the defense, or so Robert Burns Eleazer of the Interracial Commission reported to Will Alexander. Nor had there been any "injection of the Communist issue yet." Joseph Brodsky had been at the defense table, "but [he] hasn't said a word." In the southern press, however, the first day went to Attorney General Knight. The *Birmingham Age-Herald* reported that Mrs. Price had been "unshaken," and neither it nor the *Chattanooga Daily Times* reported more than a hint of Dr. Bridges's damaging testimony (quoted in Carter 1969/1979, 214). In the Deep South, such talk of anatomy and of bodily fluids simply wasn't done (Carter 1969/1979).

Bridges returned to the witness chair on Tuesday morning and after a brief cross-examination that yielded no new information, Leibowitz told the court he had no further questions. Dr. Marvin Lynch, the second Scottsboro physician who had examined the two women, was the next scheduled witness. Before he could take the stand, Attorney General Knight asked if he could speak privately with Judge Horton. During the brief recess, the judge, Dr. Lynch, and the state's attorneys assembled in a smaller courthouse room. Knight explained that Lynch could only reiterate Dr. Bridges's testimony and the state wished him excused. Judge Horton agreed. As Knight and the other lawyers for the state were walking into the courtroom, Lynch asked Horton if they could have a word. The only unoccupied room they could find was one of the courthouse restrooms and, with the bailiff standing outside the door, the two talked. The young doctor appeared uneasy and distressed. He blurted out that contrary to Knight's statement, his testimony would not be a repetition of Dr. Bridges's, because he did not believe the two women had been raped. From the very beginning, Lynch told Horton, he was sure the two were lying. To an astonished Judge Horton, he offered that even Dr. Bridges had admitted that the two women were "not even red" (quoted in Carter 1969/1979, 216).

It took a moment for the judge to recover. "My God, Doctor, is this whole thing a horrible mistake[?]" Horton asked, clearly stunned. "Judge," Lynch said quietly, "I looked at both women and told them they were lying, that they knew they had not been raped ... and they just laughed at me." Now thoroughly shaken, Horton told Lynch he must testify, but the young physician, now looking even more distressed, replied, "Judge, God knows I want to, but I can't." The situation in Scottsboro was frightening, he said. "If I testified for those boys I'd never be able to go back into Jackson County" (quoted in Carter 1969/1979, 215). He had graduated from medical school not four years before, his practice was just getting established, and he did not want to start over again, he said. The other white man understood (Carter 1969/1979).

By the time Judge Horton returned to the bench, he had managed to compose himself, but inwardly he remained in shock. Before the trial, Horton thought that the men had probably raped Ruby Bates and Victoria Price. The only thing keeping the case alive was all this outside interference. He had even instructed his court reporter to be very careful as he wanted no technical errors in the record. But the evasive and contradictory testimony of Victoria Price and the statements of Dr. Bridges had left him wondering. Now Lynch's statements made the black men's guilt even less likely. None of his alternatives was appealing. Horton could force Lynch to take the stand or he could himself end the trial. Either would mean that Lynch would never practice medicine again, not in this region, perhaps not anywhere in the South. He was, the judge considered, an honest man who had taken a courageous step in even speaking to him. And perhaps Lynch was mistaken. Then Judge Horton considered the twelve jurors who sat on his left. Despite Leibowitz's misgivings about an all-white jury, Horton was convinced they were good men. He knew many of them personally and he had faith that the evidence presented by the defense would convince them that Patterson was innocent. He decided to allow the trial to continue (Carter 1969/1979).

The chief lawyer for the defense, Samuel Leibowitz, had now become aware that his tactics had uncovered considerable white hostility, but he was slow to change his conduct. He had even received a number of threatening letters, but these he dismissed as the ravings of "cranks." Once again he would underestimate the ill will of the local citizens. During his cross-examination of Victoria Price his miscalculation became clear. During the second day of the trial, Mary Heaton Vorse overhead one man whisper to another, "It'll be a wonder if ever he leaves town alive." During a recess she spoke with a "handsomely dressed and obviously well-educated young man" who told her casually that he would be surprised if "they" let him finish the trial. "Do you mean there's a movement on foot to railroad him out of town?" she asked him. "They were not advertising or making speeches," he told the astonished reporter, "but they'll know what to do when the times comes" (quoted in Carter 1969/1979, 223).

As the afternoon session prepared to resume, a grim-faced Judge Horton ordered the jury to leave the courtroom. His voice filled with emotion, he said, "The Court wishes to make an announcement." He had been told, on good authority, that concerned citizens were planning to take an "undescribed action" against the defendants and/or their counsel. The guilt or innocence of Haywood Patterson and his companions was, the judge said sternly, for the jury alone to decide. "Any man on the outside who has not heard the testimony, and would try the case from rumor ... has no right to say whether or not they are guilty or innocent." He wanted it known that as far as he was concerned any "man who would engage in anything that would cause the death of any of these prisoners is a murderer; he is not only a murderer, but a cowardly murderer." Any man, he continued, who attempted to take the law into his own hands "may expect that his own life be forfeited, or the guards that guard them must forfeit their lives. I am speaking with feeling, and I know it, because I am feeling it," Judge Horton said to the astonished courtroom. For the first time in the trials he now raised his voice so that he was almost shouting: "I absolutely have no patience with mob spirit. ... Your very civilization depends upon the carrying out of your laws in an orderly manner," he lectured. "I believe I am as gentle as any man; I don't believe I would harm anyone wrongfully" but, he emphasized, he would have no mob violence. A meeting had taken place on Tuesday night, he announced, and the men who participated should be ashamed: "they are unworthy citizens of your town." He looked into the spectators' eyes: "Now gentlemen, I have spoken ... harsh words, but every word I say is true, and I hope we will have no more of such conduct. Let the jury return" (quoted in Carter 1969/1979, 223–224).

During a brief recess later in the afternoon, reporters rushed over to city jail to interview Captain Joseph Burleson, in charge of the National Guard unit. Somewhat reluctantly, Burleson admitted that an undercover man in the community had attended a meeting on Tuesday night. Over two hundred white men had assembled in "protest against the manner in which Mr. Leibowitz had examined the state's witness" (Carter 1969/1979, 224). He admitted that several men at the meeting proposed that they ride the New York lawyer out of town on a rail and then lynch the nine black men (Carter 1969/1979).

Back in the courtroom, Leibowitz called to the stand Dr. Edward A. Reisman, a forty-eight-year-old Chattanooga gynecologist. Reisman had been born in Alabama but had spent all his adult life in Tennessee. To an attentive jury he gave a technical description of the female anatomy. Then Leibowitz asked a series of hypothetical questions. If six young, healthy men had raped a woman, would an examiner expect to find only a trace of semen ninety minutes later? He replied: "To my mind it would be quite inconceivable that six men would have intercourse with one woman and not leave telltale traces of their presence in considerable quantities in the vagina" (quoted in Carter 1969/1979, 227). Moreover, he found it difficult to believe that respiration, pulse, and pupil dilation would be normal not two hours after a savage serial rape by six men. Outward emotional expression is unpredictable, he said; he is not surprised by descriptions of the women's calm. But these three factors cannot easily be controlled. The implication was clear: the women had not been raped. Reisman's testimony, Leibowitz hoped, would be definitive. It should be enough, in itself, to bring an acquittal. But once again Leibowitz miscalculated the local mood. A Decatur resident summed up the attitude of the jury as well as the spectators when he told a reporter: "When a nigger has expert witnesses, we have a right to ask who is paying for them" (quoted in Carter 1969/1979, 228).

On the fourth day of the trials, just before ten in the morning, Leibowitz called to the stand Lester Carter. The twenty-three-year-old, wearing a new suit and a large flowered tie, would be, Leibowitz hoped, his insurance. He could complete the story Leibowitz was telling the jury. In January 1931, he acknowledged, he had been convicted of vagrancy and sentenced to a term in the Hunstville (Alabama) jail. There he had met Victoria Price and her boyfriend Jack Tiller, serving time for adultery. When they were released, Tiller invited him to stay with them in Hunstville for few days. Victoria promised Lester she would set him up with her friend Ruby Bates. The next night, March 23, the four met and walked together to the hobo jungles of Huntsville. "What occurred in the jungles that night?" Leibowitz asked him. "I had intercourse with Ruby Bates and Jack Tiller had intercourse with Victoria Price," he answered. When it began to rain, the four left the honeysuckle bushes where they had had sex and climbed into an empty box car pulled onto a sidetrack. During that night, March 24, Carter testified he and Ruby Bates had had sex once again. The next day, they continued traveling together, boarding the Huntsville-bound freight first on a tank car. Due to strong winds, they moved to a gondola when the train stopped at Stevenson. This was not the story Victoria Price had told (Carter 1969/1979).

Carter's testimony seemed reliable, but both the jury and the spectators were obviously skeptical. His apparent eagerness to testify, his dramatic gestures, and his immaculate appearance all gave the impression to the locals, Eleazer reported, that he had been "carefully schooled" by the I.L.D. lawyers. No doubt the most incriminating mannerism, by the locals' point of view, was Carter's insistence on saying "Negro," instead of the common southern pronunciation, "Nigra." In cross-examination, Solicitor Wright first tried to rattle the young man into contradicting himself. When he failed in this, he implied through questioning that Carter had fabricated his story thanks to payoffs from the I.L.D. Carter did admit, in response to questioning, that Joseph Brodsky had paid his room and board for almost a month and yes, had also paid for the new eleven-dollar suit he was wearing (Carter 1969/1979).

Leibowitz had, it turns out, a star witness. He waited for the most dramatic moment before signaling the guardsmen. They opened the back doors of the courtroom and in walked a heavy-set, matronly woman in her forties. This turned out to be May Jones, a social worker from the Birmingham Church of the Advent. Behind her—from the spectators there was "first an audible gasp and then excited murmurs" (Carter 1969/1979, 231)—walked, slowly, Ruby Bates. She stared at the floor. Once seated in the witness stand, Leibowitz asked: "Did you have intercourse with Lester Carter [on the night of March 23, 1933]?" "I certainly did," Bates replied softly. "Did Victoria Price have intercourse with Jack Tiller ... in your presence?" he asked next. "She certainly did," came the reply. At this point Leibowitz asked that Victoria Price be brought in for identification. Charles Edmundson of the *Birmingham Post* reported that "Victoria's eyes fell and she flushed noticeably" when she first saw her old friend. She quickly recovered, however, and became so angry she began to pant. Attorney General Knight stepped in front of her and directed her: "Keep your temper, you hear" (quoted in Carter 1969/1979, 232).

Leibowitz now asked her: Did any rape take place on the freight train travelling from Chattanooga to Hunstville? Not that she knew of, Ruby Bates replied, and she had never left Victoria Price's side once during the trip. The main points made, Leibowitz ended his questions. Now Knight rose slowly and stared intently at Ruby, who sat with her eyes downcast. "Where did you get that coat?" he demanded. She bit her lips, hesitated for a moment, and then answered in a near-whisper, still not able to look him in the eyes. "I bought it." "Who gave you the money to buy it?" Knight demanded again. Somewhat hesitantly, evasively it seemed, she stammered, "Well, I don't know" (quoted in Carter 1969/1979, 233). Heartened no doubt by his success in intimidating her, Knight continued to ask about the cost of the coat. Finally she mumbled something about loans from her employer in New York, but it was unlikely anyone in the courtroom believed her (Carter 1969/1979).

Ruby Bates's performance deteriorated rapidly. Her evasiveness was so obvious at one point that several spectators began to laugh loudly. Horrified at the unraveling of his star witness, Leibowitz became enraged. Pointing at one of the loudest offenders, he declared: "Your honor I ask that you bring that man ... before the Bar. It is discourteous to these men in the jury box for these people to be snickering and laughing, these rooters for the blood of this negro" (quoted in Carter 1969/1979, 234). Horton reprimanded those who had been laughing, but the incident made it clear that Ruby Bates's testimony had made little impression on the jury (Carter 1969/1979).

There were a few more witnesses called by both sides, but the main drama of the trial ended when Ruby Bates stepped down from the witness stand. Her testimony provoked an "immediate and bitter reaction among the residents of ... [Morgan] and neighboring counties," reported Raymond Daniell. People had no doubt that Bates had been bribed by the defense. Although Attorney General Knight had dismissed the danger of "mob spirit" before, now he admitted there was a real danger of violence (quoted in Carter 1969/1979, 234). After consultations with Judge Horton, Knight had Ruby Bates taken by National Guardsmen to a secret location. Nine soldiers holding riot guns were stationed outside the courtroom (Carter 1969/1979).

When Morgan County Solicitor Wade Wright began his summation the next afternoon he expressed many of the fears and hatreds of the local residents. He began calmly, but within a few minutes he was waving his arms and shouting at the top of his lungs, as if he were a man possessed. He went on and on about the "fancy New York clothes" of the defense's chief witnesses, Lester Carter and Ruby Bates, as Leibowitz sat at the defense table with a look of stunned disbelief on his face. Across the way Attorney General Knight stared at a place in the floor, his face flushed with embarrassment, but he was hardly surprised. At one point Leibowitz objected to an anti-Semitic slur; Horton reprimanded the solicitor, but Wright went on shouting, lost in his frenzied state. Now, with his finger pointed at the counsel table where Leibowitz and Brodsky sat, he thundered: the evil East had sold slaves at a profit and then, when they were ready, had taken them away. "Show them," he paused with electricity in the air, "show them that Alabama justice cannot be bought and sold with Jew money from New York." Shocked, horrified, enraged, Leibowitz leaped to his feet, pounding the defense table with his fist. "I move for a mistrial," he shouted. "I submit a conviction in this case won't be worth a pinch of snuff in view of what this man just said." Judge Horton reprimanded Wright for his "improper" statements, but he declined to end the trial (quoted in Carter 1969/1979, 235–236). Several of the jurors sat stony-faced, without expression, but one reporter observed that several were clearly excited by Wright's performance (Carter 1969/1979).

Now it was Leibowitz's turn. First, he had to restore some semblance of calm to a "feverish" courtroom. He began his remarks late in the afternoon, then continued for another hour the following morning. A "powerful blend of logic and emotion" (Carter 1969/1979, 236), Leibowitz's summation made acquittal inevitable, or a rational mind might conclude. Late in the morning he ended, wearily taking his seat at the defense table. Now Attorney General Knight began the final statements on behalf of the prosecution. Victoria Price might not be the ideal instance of southern womanhood, he acknowledged, but she deserved the full protection of the laws of the Great State of Alabama. Referring contemptuously to the nearly forgotten defendant as "that thing," he warned the jury: "If you acquit this negro, put a garland of roses around his neck, give him a supper and send him to New York City." There, he said, "[he will be] dressed up in a high hat and morning coat, gray-striped trousers and spats." The defense had "framed" its testimony to create a false impression, he told them (quoted in Carter 1969/1979, 237). They knew, as he knew, that there was only one possible verdict in this case: death in the electric chair (Carter 1969/1979).

At 10 A.M. on Sunday word came that the jury had reached a verdict. Judge Horton arrived at 11 A.M. Due to competition with church services perhaps, the courtroom was only half full. "Have you agreed upon a verdict?" Horton asked the foreman. He replied, "We have, your honor," and handed a slip of paper to the bailiff who laid it on the judge's bench. Horton read the large pencilled letters: "We find the defendant guilty as charged and fix the punishment as death in the electric chair." No one made a sound; several spectators strained to see Leibowitz. The chief defense attorney was "white and drawn from lack of sleep"; as Horton read the verdict he looked as if "he had been struck" (quoted in Carter 1969/1979, 239). He slumped back in his chair. Patterson's face disclosed no emotion. Leibowitz learned later that the jury had taken the first ballot less than five minutes after the judge gave them the case; the vote was: guilty—12; not guilty—0. On the next ballot, eleven jurors voted to send Patterson to the electric chair; foreman Eugene D. Bailey, Jr., a draftsman, had held out for life imprisonment. They argued for twelve hours before he gave in. One of the jurors admitted that the star witness for the defense—Ruby Bates—was not even discussed (Carter 1969/1979).

The prosecution's victory had everything to do with Wright's and Knight's success in stimulating the latent desire (via disavowal and denial "inverted" into fear and hatred) of twelve southern white men. Reporters at the trial observed that Wade Wright's anti-Semitic summation was the single most effective statement made by the prosecution. Until he invoked local fears and hatred of Jews, many of the newspapermen felt there was an outside chance for a hung jury. That hope disappeared as Wade Wright, in the words of John Hammond of the *Nation*, "registered to perfection the repressed feelings and prejudices of the twelve good men" (quoted in Carter 1969/1979, 240).

Carter argues that anti-Semitism, disguised ordinarily as fear of "outside agitation," provoked the death sentence against Haywood Patterson. To understand the verdict, he argues, one must remember that nothing had really changed from the first trials in Scottsboro. The same fears and antipathies which dominated those trials informed everything that happened in Decatur. To illustrate, Carter (1969/1979) quotes one old-timer who said without emotion after Victoria Price stepped down from the witness stand: "Any man would have to [convict] after hearin' her say that niggers raped her." The medical testimony—indeed, all the defense testimony—"don't count a mite with the jury." Throughout the trial, rumors circulated that an acquittal would be used as a legal precedent toward forcing "social equality" between blacks and whites in Alabama. Leibowitz's attacks on Alabama's all-white jury system only seemed to legitimate these fears. Journalists gave voice to the rumors: "Leibowitz in the Scottsboro Case has thrown down the challenge to the Democratic Party to maintain white supremacy in the South," declared the *Alabama Wiregrass Journal*. Unless this "Russianized northern element" was run out of the state there could be no peace in Alabama. While the defense had "the triple disadvantage of being radical, Jewish, and 'northern'," even a local defense probably could not have gained a compromise such as life imprisonment (quoted in Carter 1969/1979, 241–242). Whether Haywood Patterson was guilty or innocent was, for most white men in Alabama in the 1930s, an incidental question (Carter 1969/1979).

In New York City, William H. (Kid) Davis, publisher of Harlem's *Amsterdam News*, posted the news of the jury's decision. On the same bulletin board outside the *News's* office, he issued a statement calling on the residents of Harlem to march to Washington to protest this outrageous travesty of justice.

By that evening, twenty thousand African Americans had signed a petition promising to take part in the Washington demonstration. Bitter and angry, protestors began to gather in such numbers on the corner of Seventh Avenue and 135th Street that traffic was stopped. The next day Leibowitz arrived from Alabama; more than three thousand African Americans filled the concourses of Pennsylvania Station to greet him. When Leibowitz stepped down from the car, the cheering throng nearly trampled him; only by lifting him over the heads of the crushing crowd were friends able to get him out of the station and into a taxi. Police had refused the crowd permission to assemble outside the train station. When more than five hundred disobeyed the order and began walking up Broadway toward Harlem, mounted policemen and additional riot personnel dispersed them (Carter 1969/1979).

Expressions of indignation and determination continued throughout the week. One night Leibowitz addressed four thousand African Americans in Harlem's Salem Methodist Episcopal Church. Hailed by some as a "new Moses," Leibowitz brought the assembly to its feet with a promise to "sell his house and home" if that became necessary. "I promise you citizens of Harlem that I will fight with every drop of blood in my body, and with the help of God ... these Scottsboro boys shall be free" (quoted in Carter 1969/1979, 244). The following night, ten thousand met in Union Square to hear Janie Patterson and I.L.D. officials ask listeners to never give up the struggle against the oppression of the southern blacks. At another rally on Sunday, April 16, four thousand came to hear New York Mayor John O'Brien and a number of other Democratic political leaders. All demanded justice in Alabama (Carter 1969/1979).

Shared outrage over the Decatur verdict stimulated the rivalry between the N.A.A.C.P. and the I.L.D. The association's Board of Directors could not refrain from criticizing the International Labor Defense. The only remaining hope for the defendants was to "remove from the overwhelming prejudices which militate against them the additional burden of communism." In response, the I.L.D. accused the N.A.A.C.P. of "gloating" over Patterson's death sentence. The organization, the I.L.D. alleged, had made an "effort to do what the white lynch gangs have tried to do and failed—eliminate the one organization, the International Labor Defense, which has thus far prevented the murder of these innocent victims." Even as the two groups exchanged charges, they were meeting privately with Leibowitz to negotiate some kind of agreement of cooperation. The N.A.A.C.P. had decided, despite its public rhetoric, that its differences with the I.L.D. would have to be suspended in the interest of the Scottsboro Nine. "Time will tell who has the best philosophy on the so-called race problem," explained Walter White, "but the Scottsboro boys cannot wait" (quoted in Carter 1969/1979, 247). The N.A.A.C.P. offered to help pay the expense of Patterson's appeal and any future appeals (Carter 1969/1979).

The I.L.D. did not accept the offer with enthusiasm. Only reluctantly did C.P.-U.S.A. leaders agree to cooperate with the N.A.A.C.P. While the N.A.A.C.P. and the I.L.D. were working out an agreement to work together, plans were well under way for William Davis's "March on Washington." Davis soon learned that for the C.P.-U.S.A. "united front" meant that the

Communists marched in the front and that non-party members followed behind them. When the planning committee met, it was dominated by C.P. and I.L.D. members. Even though the origin of the march was Davis's idea, C.P.-U.S.A. leader Patterson took over, expanding the agenda to include the party's current civil rights agenda: an end to discrimination in voting, jury service, schools, transportation, housing, public accommodations, labor unions, the army and navy, and stiff penalties against lynching (Carter 1969/1979).

A mass rally was held on Friday evening, May 5, as a send off for the march on Washington. At St. Nicholas Arena in New York, Leibowitz and Chamlee spoke briefly to a crowd of at least five thousand, but the main event of the evening was an appearance by Lester Carter and Ruby Bates. Bates told her listeners that she had lied at Scottsboro because "I was excited and frightened by the ruling class of white people of Scottsboro and other towns" (quoted in Carter 1969/1979, 249). If she had refused to participate in the fabrication of the rape story, the ruling class of the South would have had her lynched. Only later, she continued, had her conscience plagued her, resulting in her decision to "go back to the Decatur Courthouse and tell the truth on the nine innocent Scottsboro boys" (quoted in Carter 1969/1979, 250). As she left the platform she was rushed by several hundred persons who wanted to shake her hand (Carter 1969/1979).

Just before noon on Sunday, demonstrators from New York, Philadelphia, Baltimore, and other eastern cities began to assemble outside the White House. C.P.-U.S.A. leader Patterson, accompanied by Janie Patterson and Ruby Bates, asked to see the president, but Louis Howe refused, saying that the president was busy conferring with Dr. Hjalmar Schact, a special German envoy. The three rejoined the crowd of three thousand and together they marched to the Capitol. Speaker of the House Henry T. Rainey and Vice-President John Nance Garner did receive representatives of the group, but they could do nothing, they insisted, except refer the civil rights petition to the proper committee. As for the Scottsboro case, said Rainey, "that is a matter for the courts. Congress has no authority to direct the release of men charged with a crime" (Carter 1969/1979, 250–251). In a cold rain, the crowd dispersed, discouraged. The March on Washington was supposed to have been the beginning of a nationwide "united front" for justice; instead it represented the high-water mark of national protests during the spring of 1933. Many African Americans worried the I.L.D. was "polishing up the electric chair" (Carter 1969/1979, 251) for the Scottsboro Nine by insisting on linking their case with the overall program of the C.P.-U.S.A. (Carter 1969/1979).

Not long afterward Judge Horton decided that Haywood Patterson must be tried again, a decision that did not sit well with Alabama officials. In mid-October Will Alexander learned through confidential sources that Attorney General Knight had pressured Chief Justice Anderson to remove Horton from the case. Alexander hurried to Montgomery in an effort to intervene, but he was too late. Anderson, he discovered, had already succumbed to Knight's pressure and had written Horton, asking him to withdraw voluntarily from the case. The conscience-stricken Horton had reluctantly agreed. Clearly state officials were determined that the "honor" of Alabama would be upheld by the conviction of the Scottsboro Nine. Now that the cases were no longer under the jurisdiction of Horton but to be tried by Judge William Washington Callahan, the second judge of the district, "honor" was well in sight (Carter 1969/1979).

Knight made this final arguments in the retrial on Thanksgiving Day, demanding once again the death penalty. "There is no middle ground in this case," he shouted at the jury. A death penalty would not avenge the suffering of Victoria Price. "What has been done to her cannot be undone." But what "you can do is to see that it doesn't happen to some other woman." Jumping to his feet, Leibowitz protested: "That's an appeal to passion and prejudice." Knight whirled around and faced Leibowitz, trembling with rage. "It certainly is. It's an appeal to passion!" Leibowitz demanded a mistrial, but Judge Callahan refused and Knight continued, still agitated. "We all have a passion, all the men in this courtroom and that is to protect the womanhood of the state of Alabama." Just outside Victoria Price sat on a stool peering in through the partly opened door, occasionally leaning over to a nearby spittoon. Beside her stood Jack Tiller, her lover, or, as she preferred to call him, her "bodyguard" (quoted in Carter 1969/1979, 296).

When word reached the courtroom that the jury had reached a verdict, the scene seemed little different than that of the spring, except this time Haywood Patterson stood beside Leibowitz to face the jury while Court Clerk John Green read the verdict: "We find the defendant guilty as charged in the indictment and fix his punishment at death" (Carter 1969/1979, 300). Patterson had been standing with a forced smile while the jury took their places, but as the verdict was read, he suddenly grimaced and his right arm came upward as if in disbelief. The trial of Clarence Norris followed. Even though Leibowitz knew the chances for acquittal were nil, he grimly argued the case. In his cross-examination of Victoria Price, he exposed her lying over and over again. As the trial continued and Judge Callahan limited his examination of Price, Leibowitz became embittered over what was clearly a parody of courtroom procedure. His disagreements with the judge became less civil (Carter 1969/1979).

Each time Leibowitz and Brodsky left the courtroom they were heavily guarded by three special deputies as well as two personal bodyguards. Throughout the week rumors had been flying that armed men planned to shoot Leibowitz when he came across the courthouse lawn and that the defendants would then be lynched. During the trials there had been lynchings elsewhere, intensifying the fears that it could happen here. For four consecutive days beginning on November 27, the headlines of *Decatur Daily* had to do with lynchings or near lynchings (Carter 1969/1979).

V. "I'd rather die than spend another day in jail for something I didn't do."

—Haywood Patterson, quoted in Dan T. Carter, *Scottsboro: A Tragedy of the American South* (1969/1979)

Racial hatred, then, is carnal hatred. It is sexualized hatred.

—Calvin C. Hernton, *Sex and Racism in America* (1965/1988)

Once again the verdicts had been guilty, the sentence death. Appeals for a new trial continued throughout the winter. On Thursday, June 28, the Alabama Supreme Court unanimously denied the defense motion for new trials. The execution date was for August 31. During the brief break in the appeals, Leibowitz and his wife took time off for a holiday in Europe. Exhausted by the strenuous appeals (he had lost ten pounds during the trials before Callahan), Leibowitz had been persuaded by his wife that a rest was necessary. Soon after he returned, he faced an unexpected development: two I.L.D. attorneys had been caught trying to bribe Victoria Price (Carter 1969/1979).

This was the final straw. From the outset, relations between Leibowitz and the I.L.D. had been strained; now Leibowitz issued a statement announcing that he would withdraw as counsel for the defendants "unless all Communists are removed from the defense." The Scottsboro Nine are innocent, he said. They hardly needed the kind of help offered by the two I.L.D. men arrested in Nashville for attempting to bribe Victoria Price. The following day Patterson announced that Leibowitz had been dropped as chief attorney due to his inexperience in constitutional appeals, an explanation few believed. Patterson and Brodsky did not understand how committed to the case Leibowitz was, however. His response was to try to achieve what the N.A.A.C.P. had failed to achieve: oust the I.L.D. completely from the case. At his request, several Harlem ministers traveled south and persuaded Norris and Patterson to sign an affidavit turning the case over to Leibowitz and dismissing the I.L.D. On the way back to New York they also visited Mrs. Ada Wright and Mr. and Mrs. Patterson, persuading them too that they should repudiate the I.L.D. The statement the three Scottsboro parents signed demanded that the I.L.D. and all its "agents, servants, representatives, and employees" stop taking "any actions or steps with reference to these cases" (quoted in Carter 1969/1979, 312). With these affidavits in hand, Leibowitz publicly called upon Brodsky to turn over all records in the case within forty-eight hours (Carter 1969/1979).

The next day the *Daily Worker* reported that "Leibowitz ... aided by a certain group of bootlicking Harlem preachers and other reactionary white and Negro misleaders, had secured statements from two of the boys ... giving him full power to carry on their further legal defense." Reluctantly Brodsky agreed to cooperate, turning over to Leibowitz all I.L.D. documents concerning the case: "We will not do anything to jeopardize the defense" (quoted in Carter 1969/1979, 313). In the meantime, I.L.D. officials were in the prison, persuading the nine men to return to them. When Leibowitz learned of this turn of events, he sent a representative to the prison the following week. Once again the nine signed an affidavit pledging undying support to Leibowitz (Carter 1969/1979).

As the struggle for the right to defend the Scottsboro Nine continued, Leibowitz moved to consolidate his support. When news of the bribery attempt first broke, Leibowitz knew he had a chance to oust the I.L.D.; he hoped the N.A.A.C.P. would replace the Communists. Of course, he must remain chief counsel. After all, as he assured Walter White, the nine young men would do "anything I tell them" (Carter 1969/1979, 315). But White and other N.A.A.C.P. officials were reluctant to become involved again, especially given that the allegiance of the defendants and their parents remained so uncertain. All White would do was promise Leibowitz that the N.A.A.C.P. would continue to take a deep interest in the case, but that it could not become directly involved (Carter 1969/1979).

On October 11, Leibowitz secured public support from the New York Interdenominational Association of Preachers, an organization representing the pastors of Harlem's twenty largest churches. But Leibowitz needed more. On October 17 a group of New Yorkers met in his office to form the "American Scottsboro Committee." The American Scottsboro Committee remained in existence for more than year, but it managed to raise few funds. In the South, for instance, little had changed. Leibowitz had hoped that by dissociating himself from the Communists some of the resentment against him in Alabama would disappear. This turned out to be wishful thinking, however. In fact, the continued presence of Leibowitz as chief counsel undermined any effort to build support for the American Scottsboro Committee among southern progressives (Carter 1969/1979).

The I.L.D. did not exactly roll over and play dead. It continued to try to attract public support for its defense of the Scottsboro Nine while the American Scottsboro Committee struggled. While their respective public campaigns went on, the two groups continued to fight each other for the allegiance of the defendants. During the months of October and November, the nine changed sides five times. Despite the continuous switching of allegiance, Haywood tended to favor the I.L.D. while Norris tended to prefer Leibowitz. Finally, both Leibowitz and the I.L.D. lawyers realized that continued bickering could only undermine the case. When the Supreme Court agreed to review the cases in early 1935, Leibowitz decided to meet with other I.L.D. attorneys to negotiate an agreement. Leibowitz and Chamlee (who had also disclaimed the I.L.D.) would defend Norris, while Fraenkel and Pollak would represent Patterson (Carter 1969/1979).

In mid-afternoon February 14, 1935, Samuel Leibowitz, who had never argued a case before the Supreme Court, made the case for a retrial before the eight highest judges of the American judicial system. On April 1, he learned how he had done. On that day Chief Justice Charles Evans Hughes delivered the Court's opinion in *Norris* v. *Alabama*. There was, he noted, "no controversy as to the principle involved" (quoted in Carter 1969/1979, 324). The exclusion of African Americans from jury service deprived a black defendant of his right to the equal protection of laws guaranteed by the Fourteenth Amendment. Without actually ordering a new trial, the Supreme Court's decision to send the case back to the Alabama high court required it to order a new trial. If the lower court failed to act, the highest Court would, it was clear, intervene (Carter 1969/1979).

Throughout the North, public response was favorable, in places jubilant. Throughout the South, the mood was rather different. The *Charleston News and Courier* said defiantly that racially mixed juries were "out of the question." The Supreme Court decision "can and will be evaded" (quoted in Carter 1969/1979, 326). But the Alabama Supreme Court had no choice; on May 16, it quashed the existing indictments. But, the court made clear, this was only the first step leading to reindictment and retrial. With white public opinion throughout the state hostile, with the unyielding Callahan still on the bench, and with the defense sharply divided, "the Scottsboro defendants faced a bleak and unpromising future" (Carter 1969/1979, 329). Indeed, for the first time the I.L.D. indicated it was willing to withdraw into the background if a graceful exit could be arranged (Carter 1969/1979).

Several organizations met to assess the situation, among them the I.L.D., the N.A.A.C.P., the A.S.C., the A.C.L.U., and the League for Industrial Democracy. They agreed from the start that the main problem was Samuel Leibowitz. The A.C.L.U. opposed him because it seemed clear that the defendants would never be freed as long as the New York attorney remained the chief defense council. After considerable consultation with prominent southern supporters, the N.A.A.C.P. agreed. But Leibowitz did not agree; indeed, he had no intention of withdrawing. White was, not for the first time, frustrated: "We may form a score of united fronts, but if the defendants stick to Leibowitz and he sticks to his present attitude, the united front would be on the outside looking in with no real authority." And any more public fighting over who would represent the men would "further confuse the public mind, which God knows, is confused enough already" (quoted in Carter 1969/1979, 334).

An agreement was finally reached. In early December, Leibowitz agreed to remain in the background at the next trial, and the A.C.L.U., the N.A.A.C.P., and the I.L.D. would allow him to remain as chief counsel. But most of the visible courtroom work would be handled by a first-rate southern lawyer. On December 19, 1935, representatives of the N.A.A.C.P., the I.L.D., the A.C.L.U., and the Methodist Federation for Social Service signed an agreement establishing a "Scottsboro Defense Committee." On Christmas Eve, 1935, the A.S.C. officially disbanded and turned all its files over to the S.D.C. But even at this early date, there was "suspicion and misunderstanding" (Carter 1969/1979, 337) between the Committee and moderate Alabamians. Even southern progressives like Will Alexander found it hard to believe that the I.L.D. had actually relinquished control of the case (Carter 1969/1979).

Predictably, the Alabama system of "justice" did not wait for its Yankee adversaries to work things out. By the time the S.D.C. was officially established in December, the judicial machinery was moving quickly. On November 13, a Jackson County grand jury of thirteen whites and one African American returned a new indictment against the nine black men. The trials would open in Judge Callahan's court on January 20, 1936. Concerned, in early December, Leibowitz wrote Horton to ask for his advice. Horton had paid a price for his apparent disloyalty to white Alabama; he had been defeated in the 1934 election, a victim of white backlash. Now an attorney for the Tennessee Valley Authority, the former judge gave Leibowitz the name of a Huntsville lawyer who might be willing to take the case. The "Scottsboro Judge," as Horton came to be called, also advised Leibowitz to refrain from any verbal outbursts at the next trial, no matter how outrageous the provocation. No doubt remembering his private conversation with Dr. Lynch, he recommended almost complete reliance on the medical evidence to show that the two women had not even had sexual intercourse while on the train (Carter 1969/1979).

As agreed, Leibowitz kept a low profile in the 1936 trial of Haywood Patterson. With great reluctance Clarence Watts, the Huntsville attorney recommended by Judge Horton, had accepted the S.D.C.'s offer to join the new defense team. A graduate of the University of Alabama law school, Watts came from one of the Alabama's "better families." His views on race relations were, at best, paternalistic. As one staff member of the S.D.C. observed, "outside of his belief in the innocence of the boys he certainly has a point of view that is most objectionable" (quoted in Carter 1969/1979, 340). But the fact that he believed firmly, and was willing to state publicly, that Victoria Price had never been raped compensated for his objectionable racial views generally. Watt's participation had required some courage, of course. His Huntsville neighbors were horrified. Watts was to receive a substantial fee of $5,000 for the first trial and $500 for all subsequent proceedings. This generous amount was intended to offset the expected loss of numerous Hunstville clients (Carter 1969/1979).

The defense rested its case after Patterson and several of the other Scottsboro defendants testified they never saw any women on the train. Melvin Hutson, who had replaced Wade Wright as the Morgan County solicitor, began the summary statement for the state. The courtroom was silent as he dropped his cud of tobacco into a spittoon, then combed his hair, and smoothed his small black bow tie. Now he began to speak. Alternately shouting and speaking in a low intimate voice, he reminded the jurors that they would have to go home and face their neighbors. His voice rose to a crescendo, and once he choked back a sob as he praised the martyrdom of Victoria Price. "She fights for the rights of the womanhood of Alabama," he thundered. Whether "in overall or furs" the women of the state must be protected from rape, the vilest of all crimes. He pleaded with the jurors to "protect the sacred secret parts of the female," otherwise the fine womanhood—he meant white women of course—of the great state of Alabama, "this glorious state," would have "to buckle six-shooters about their middles." A local leader of the Methodist church, Hutson concluded with his voice almost intolerably loud. "Don't go out and quibble over the evidence," he roared at the drawn jurors. "Say to yourselves, 'We're tired of this job' and put it behind you. Get it done quick and protect the fair womanhood of his great State" (quoted in Carter 1969/1979, 344–345).

For the defense Watts's strategy was different. He spoke in a quiet, confidential tone, never raising his voice once during the summation. He characterized himself as a "friend and neighbor" from Madison County and gently pointed out that the Mrs. Price's testimony had been refuted by the state's own witnesses. As well, it had been "contradicted by the physical facts in this case." He could not help wondering why the state had left it for the defense to present medical testimony which was in its hands. In response to Hutson's histrionic pleas for the protection of womanhood, Watts quietly appealed for "protection of the innocent." Looking tired and strained, he said softly, "It takes courage to do the right thing in the face of public clamor for the wrong thing." But "when justice is not administered fairly," he worried, "governments disintegrate and there is no protection for anyone, man or woman, black or white" (quoted in Carter 1969/1979, 345).

It was suppertime when the summations ended. After a recess, the jury returned to hear Judge Callahan's charge. It lasted for almost two hours and was identical to his statement in the earlier Patterson trial. He repeated his statement that there was a strong legal presumption that a white woman, whatever her station in life, would never consent voluntarily to sexual intercourse with a black man. As well Judge Callahan went on at some length on how the jury might find the defendant guilty of conspiracy. At this point the defense protested that the new grand jury indictment had not charged conspiracy on the part of the defendant, but the judge ignored this point. Finally, at the insistence of the defense, Callahan made several supplementary charges to the jury, but he would decline to retract his instructions on conspiracy or his statement that intercourse between a white woman and a black man was necessarily rape (Carter 1969/1979).

The defense lawyers and their supporters gave up hope. Covering the trials for the *Nation*, Carleton Beals was certain that Judge Callahan's attitude alone was enough to insure a death sentence. The case might be free from reversible errors, "but no one who was not present can realize the inflections of the court and the subtly changed meanings that were put upon the words." When charging the jury, Beals continued, "Judge Callahan said that if such and such things were true, in a tone implying they probably were, then the defendant was a 'rapist' and should be convicted." As he spoke these words, Beals reported, "he glared over at the defendant in fury, his lips drawn back in a snarl, and he rolled out the word 'r-r-rapist' in a horrendous tone." The record would not show these inflections, "but continue them hour after hour and day after day in an already prejudiced courtroom, and the sum total weights upon the minds of the jurors" (quoted in Carter 1969/1979, 346). All day Thursday the jury deliberated Patterson's fate; the court commenced the task of selecting a jury to try Clarence Norris (Carter 1969/1979).

Then word came that a verdict had been reached. As the men filed into the courtroom, the hitherto silent Leibowitz whispered to Patterson to prepare himself for the sentence that everyone expected. The clerk read the slip of folded paper: "We, the jury, find the defendant Haywood Patterson guilty as charged and fix his punishment at seventy-five years in prison." Shocked silence spread throughout the courtroom. Lieutenant Governor Knight and especially Solicitor Melvin Hutson were visibly stunned by the jury's decision. The two people who were most clearly disappointed by the verdict were Haywood Patterson and Victoria Price. Afterward, Patterson told newsmen he had assumed it would be the electric chair and that in fact he preferred that. "I'd rather die," he explained, "than spend another day in jail for something I didn't do." Laughing and talking in the courthouse corridors while waiting for the verdict, Victoria

Price was now reduced to repeating over and over to anyone who would listen that it "wasn't fair" (quoted in Carter 1969/1979, 347).

Samuel Leibowitz expressed extreme disappointment over the result and pledged that the fight would go on until all nine defendants were free. As unjust as the verdict seemed to the defense, as unjust as it *was*, the sentence amounted, in 1930s Alabama, to a victory of sorts. The astonished *Birmingham Age-Herald* observed that the jury's decision "represents probably the first time in the history of the South that a Negro has been convicted of a charge of rape upon a white woman and has been given less than a death sentence." The *New Republic*'s correspondent in Decatur acknowledged that it was difficult for northern readers to conceive of how a verdict of seventy-five years represented a "victory" for the defense. "But when one realizes that the state in its plea never suggested an alternative for the death penalty ... and that the Judge broadly hinted as to the necessity of the extreme penalty, the compromise becomes all the more remarkable" (quoted in Carter 1969/1979, 347).

State officials, particularly Lieutenant Governor Thomas E. Knight, Jr., were furious. These Yankee meddlers would not, he pledged, succeed in releasing these black despoilers of white womanhood. He had a chance, he thought, to make a point, when he obtained a piece of secret correspondence between the Alabama Scottsboro Fair Trial Committee and Files Crenshaw, Sr., president of the Alabama Bar Association. No radical organization, the Alabama Scottsboro Fair Trial Committee, while insisting on the right to express interest in the case in any way it saw fit, did declare that it had no commitment to the innocence of the Scottsboro Nine. Its only goal was an unprejudiced trial. The piece of secret correspondence Knight had obtained recorded the committee's interest in finding a lawyer who would be suitable to replace Leibowitz, in order to eliminate the "Yankee meddler" problem. This interest needed to be kept completely confidential, as if it were made public it would be extremely embarrassing to the S.D.C., for Leibowitz knew nothing of negotiations. After deliberately releasing the correspondence to the press—he was sure it would amount to a "bombshell"—Knight "sat back and gleefully waited for the feathers to fly" (quoted Carter 1969/1979, 357). Knight was confident that public reaction would destroy the recently established Alabama committee (Carter 1969/1979).

At first Knight's plan seemed to work. Leibowitz knew vaguely that something was being negotiated with the Alabamians, but when he learned it was his position on the defense team that was the negotiating chip, he was indignant. The head of the S.D.C., Allan Chalmers, managed to calm Leibowitz by assuring him he would have the right to approve any Alabama counsel. By the time the meeting ended, the diplomatic Chalmers had even persuaded Leibowitz to remain in New York for the next trials if a southern lawyer of national stature could be found to defend the nine black men (Carter 1969/1979).

Back in Alabama, the lieutenant governor's press release produced a contrary result. Henry Edmonds, head of the Alabama Committee, was well known as a "fighter," and Knight's "unwarranted and ungentlemanly action" (as Edmonds characterized it) only intensified his determination. Between June 11 and 15, the Birmingham minister suspended almost all of his pastoral duties and traveled throughout the state, reassuring all those who had been intimidated by Knight's move. By June 16, he was able to write Chalmers, "We are making very definite and rapid strides in the direction of our goal." Now there were welcome rumors that Callahan would be replaced for the next trial due to his deteriorating health. Knight's removal was the next goal, but that would not be easy; however, "we feel that through a little judicious editorial pressure from newspapers throughout the state some change in the prosecution can be effected" (quoted in Carter 1969/1979, 358). Perhaps the best news, reported Edmonds, the Alabama Committee had succeeded in retaining Archibald Hill Carmichael, congressman from Alabama's eighth congressional district. A representative from the northwestern corner of the state, Carmichael had racial views not unlike those of Clarence Watts. Despite his racial paternalism, he believed that Judge Horton's opinion as well as the transcripts proved, as they had to the Huntsville attorney, that the defendants were innocent. Carmichael was prepared, he said, to fight until the nine young black men were released (Carter 1969/1979).

Not two weeks later Edmonds's rosy scenario faded. Yes, Representative Carmichael was indeed willing to serve. But as the secretary of the Scottsboro Defense Committee, Morris Shapiro, learned, Carmichael required ten thousand dollars for the first trial and an additional five thousand for each subsequent trial, sums completely beyond the financial resources of the S.D.C. The bad news wasn't over. Contrary to the rumors, there was no evidence that either Callahan or Knight was about to withdraw. Finally, on June 30, 1936, Leibowitz wrote Clarence Watts to inform him that he could no longer consider remaining in New York during the next trials. "Frankly, I am disappointed at what has been accomplished up to the present by the Alabama Scottsboro Committee," wrote Leibowitz. "It was my impression that they represented so influential a section of the South that they could properly effect the withdrawal of Lieutenant Governor Knight from the prosecution and likewise be influential in having another judge appointed as trial judge in the cases." Reluctantly, Leibowitz, continued, he had come to the conclusion that despite the "good intentions of the gentlemen who constitute the Alabama Committee," their effectiveness had been "exactly zero." Under the circumstances, "I can not help but feel that for me to step out of the picture would constitute a desertion of the Scottsboro boys, and such an act I never have and never will voluntarily commit" (quoted in Carter 1969/1979, 359). The Alabama Scottsboro Fair Trial Committee remained in existence for another six months, but a lack of funds and an inability to unite various factions on a common policy proved Leibowitz's assessment to be accurate (Carter 1969/1979).

VI. "Providing only 50 per cent protection for the 'flower of southern womanhood'."

—Morris Shapiro, quoted in Dan T. Carter, *Scottsboro: A Tragedy of the American South* (1969/1979)

The Negro still hopes that some day the United States will become as great intellectually and morally as she is materially.

—Ida B. Wells, *Crusade for Justice: The Autobiography of Ida B. Wells* (1970)

Alabama "justice" was not confined to the courtroom, unsurprisingly. The Scottsboro Nine were being kept in solitary confinement, the strain of which began to show. In August 1936, Chalmers asked the Alabama Committee if it would use its influence to have the boys returned to the regular cellblock. "Much as we deplore the fact that the boys are being kept in solitary confinement," replied Waights Taylor for the Committee, "it has been the general contention of our committee all along that our work will be more effective if it is confined to the effort of securing a fair and impartial trial" (quoted in Carter 1969/1979, 361). Members of the national committee were astonished when the Alabama Committee refused to intervene, even privately. Chalmers began to suspect that the solitary confinement was intentional, designed to effect a punishment the courts had been prevented from enforcing. On December 8, Chalmers wrote Governor Graves complaining that the defendants had no chance to exercise, or even to read, while in solitary confinement (Carter 1969/1979).

Five days before Judge Callahan announced resumption of the trials in July, Thomas Knight, Jr., suddenly died. The Alabama attorney general was the one figure most closely associated with the prosecution, and with his death the chances for the defense brightened. Things looked even brighter when, on June 12, Grover Cleveland Hall came out editorially for a compromise solution to the case. Hill had used the columns of the *Montgomery Advertiser* to attack the Scottsboro Nine and their supporters; now he decided that nothing could be gained by continuing the prosecution. The state of Alabama had been denounced throughout the world. The good name of the state, Hill argued, was worth far more—trading racism for misogyny it would seem—than the honor of two "hook-wormy Magdalenes." "Nothing can be gained by demanding the final pound of flesh," he advised his readers, "and the *Advertiser* has reason to believe, even to know, that it is not the wish of the State to exact the final pound of flesh." The editorial concluded: "Throw this body of death [the Scottsboro case] away from Alabama" (quoted in Carter 1969/1979, 365–366).

Grover Cleveland Hill was not alone. On June 14 the Alabama Supreme Court upheld Patterson's guilty verdict, but other Alabama newspapers continued to report that a compromise was imminent. The *Birmingham Post* strongly endorsed these efforts, finally admitting that the evidence overwhelmingly indicated the defendants were not guilty. But nothing materialized as the trial date approached and Samuel Leibowitz, now tired and discouraged, prepared to defend the Scottsboro Nine for the fifth time in five years (Carter 1969/1979).

This time the defense tried something new. Rather than themselves attacking the character of Victoria Price, something the court interrupted anyway (an unendurable assault as that was on "southern womanhood"), now the defense called witnesses who did the job for them. Richard S. Watson was a former Huntsville deputy sheriff; he told the court: "I would not believe her [Mrs. Price] under oath." When Clarence Watts asked Watson about Mrs. Price's reputation, he said, simply enough, that it was "bad." Sol Wallace still served as a Madison County deputy; he was unable to dispute Watson's characterization of the state's chief witness. "She is completely untrustworthy," Wallace testified. "I would not believe anything she said." But, as Leibowitz worried, attacks on southern "ladies" meant "not a snap" to the twelve jurors. On the following day, only two hours and thirty minutes after the jury received the Norris case a decision was reached. In the hot summer courtroom the clerk read the verdict: "We the jury find the defendant guilty and fix his punishment at death" (quoted in Carter 1969/1979, 370).

Before the trial of Andy Wright could commence, Clarence Watts arose from his seat and, swaying slightly, told the judge he was too ill to continue. The long hours and the sweltering courtroom were more than he could endure. Callahan was reluctant to halt the proceedings, but the assistant attorney general intervened, remarking that it was plain to see Mr. Watts was not well and that he would prefer to have a recess. Callahan postponed the trial for one week. Carter (1969/1979) tells us that the pressure, not the heat, had done Watts in. Not the pressure of the courtroom but that of his hometown friends and neighbors. Despite the courage and forthrightness he had shown in the court—much to the satisfaction, even surprise, of the S.D.C.—he found the unrelenting hostility of lifelong friends unendurable. And when, in spite of his best efforts, the jury perfunctorily condemned his client to death, it was more than he could take. As Leibowitz confided to Morris Shapiro, Watts's collapse was not physical, but emotional; he had completely "lost his nerve" (quoted in Carter 1969/1979, 371).

There were further indications of a possible compromise in 1937. One hint came the following morning when the state announced at the start of Andy Wright's trial that it would not ask for the death penalty. But hints were all there were. With Watts gone from the case (he left for an extended vacation), Leibowitz carried on doggedly, as if he thought the jury might actually acquit his client. But during his summation the following day, his true frame of mind—fatigue and disgust—became visible. After Jackson County's solicitor, H. G. Bailey, had delivered a thundering attack on New York City in general and Lester Carter in particular, Leibowitz replied that he was growing weary of listening to attacks on his home. This extraneous issue was introduced, he pointed out, at the close of every trial as a "knockout punch for the defense" delivered by a frenzied preacher/prosecutor. Leibowitz shook his head with disgust: "I can't fight this kind of thing. I'm entitled to an acquittal in this case and I ask you men in all seriousness to do what you swore at the outset you would do" (quoted in Carter 1969/1979, 372–373). The following day, just one hour and fifteen minutes after receiving the case, the jury reached a verdict: guilty and a sentence of ninety-nine years (Carter 1969/1979).

When the trial of Charley Weems began, Leibowitz's mood was changed. Disgusted he may have been, but there was no sign of weariness or dejection. Now he was fighting mad. Indignant at his complete inability to break through the racism of the court, he abandoned any pretense of politeness as he cross-examined Victoria Price. Unintimidated, she responded venomously and defiantly, shouting her answers at the distinguished attorney. Leibowitz soon regained control, but Price lost her composure completely. Beside herself with rage, she quickly became trapped in a maze of contradictions. As Leibowitz pressed her about her testimony regarding the injuries she claimed to have suffered, Judge Callahan interrupted: "It is not too late for the court to enforce its order," he warned Leibowitz. "Your manner is going to lead to trouble ... and you might as well get ready for it." Leibowitz softened the tone of his voice and changed the subject, but he continued to cross-examine Victoria Price mercilessly. Now that she was completely confused and nearly speechless, Leibowitz asked that the jury be dismissed from the courtroom. The chief defense lawyer turned to Judge Callahan: "I move the testimony of Victoria Price be stricken from the record on the ground that ... [it] is so rampant with perjury that the court is constrained." Here the judge, his face red with rage, cut Leibowitz off: "Motion denied; bring the jurors back into the room" (quoted in Carter 1969/1979, 373).

Leibowitz used his summation to express his contempt for Alabama justice. It had become clear, after five years, that he had no chance at all of convincing a white jury that a black man accused by a white woman could be innocent. In a voice trembling with rage and fatigue he declared, "I'm sick and tired of this sanctimonious hypocrisy. It isn't Charley Weems on trial in this case, it's a Jew lawyer and New York State put on trial here by the inflammatory remarks of Mr. Bailey." The state witnesses, he continued, were nothing more than "trained seals" and "performers in a flea circus." Now he expressed what he had known but had kept to himself: Bailey and the officials of Jackson County were guilty of suppressing evidence favorable to the defense. Gasps from the spectators could not constrain him now, now that he was finally expelling from his system all the anger and frustration which had been accumulating for five years. The state's insistence that African Americans received the same justice as whites in an Alabama courtroom was, his voice overcome with contempt, so much "poppycock" (quoted in Carter 1969/1979, 374). He had examined more than one thousand prospective jurors from Morgan County, he told the courtroom, and he had found not one person who would admit prejudice against blacks or would acknowledge he would treat them any differently from white men. Outside the courtroom, on the streets of Decatur, white men told him in no uncertain terms that a black man under these circumstances was dead on arrival (Carter 1969/1979).

The jury deliberated for two hours and twenty-five minutes in the Weems case before returning with a verdict of guilty. The sentence was seventy-five years in the state penitentiary. As soon as Judge Callahan pronounced the sentence on Weems, Sheriff Sandlin brought Ozie Powell into the courtroom. Something odd was underfoot. Thomas Lawson announced that the charge of rape had been dropped. In its place was an indictment of assaulting Deputy Blalock, clearly a substitute and lesser charge. The judge explained to Ozie that he could plead guilty or not guilty. "Don't plead guilty unless you are guilty," advised Leibowitz, who was running to keep abreast of events. "I'm guilty of cutting the deputy," Powell replied, entering a plea of guilty. Since the state had dropped the rape charge, Hutson told the court he would insist on the maximum penalty for assault, twenty years. Leibowitz pleaded with the judge to take into consideration the more than six years Powell had already served, but Callahan replied, "had not the State dropped the other charge against him, I would have given him fifteen years. As it is, I will have to sentence him to twenty years in the penitentiary" (quoted in Carter 1969/1979, 375).

Suddenly, four of the defendants were released, presumably on the same evidence that had convicted four others. As Morris Shapiro observed, the compromise left Alabama in the "anomalous position of providing only 50 per cent protection for the 'flower of southern womanhood.'" There was a defensive tone in the prosecution's "explanatory statement" underscoring the strange logic the state employed in its effort to extricate itself from the Scottsboro case. The state announced that it was "convinced beyond any question of a doubt ... that the defendants that have been tried are guilty of raping Mrs. Victoria Price." However, "after careful consideration of all the testimony, every lawyer connected with prosecution is convinced that the defendants Willie Roberson and Olden Montgomery are not guilty." The severe case of venereal disease of Willie Roberson and the relative blindness of Olen Montgomery made it unlikely that those two would have been involved. Additionally, the "two men were seen in a box car by a disinterested witness." It was true that Victoria Price still insisted that the two men raped her, but "we feel it is a case of mistaken identity." As for Eugene Williams and Roy Wright, a careful investigation had disclosed that, "at the time of the actual commission of this crime, one of these juveniles was 12 years old and the other was 13." Given the fact that the two had been in jail for "six and a half years, the state thinks that the ends of justice would be met at this time by releasing these two juveniles on the condition that they leave the State, never to return" (quoted in Carter 1969/1979, 376–377).

Among those who had known all along that the Scottsboro Nine were innocent, the state's explanation for its release of four defendants provoked outrage. If, as the state now confessed, Olen Montgomery and Willie Roberson were clearly innocent, why had they been imprisoned for six long years? "The State would indemnify a farmer ... for damages he sustained if a State ran down and killed his mule," Leibowitz pointed out. But now the state of Alabama admits that "for nearly seven years it caged four innocent Negro boys without any evidence against them." Would it not be appropriate, said Leibowitz, if state officials provided "some measure of compensation for the injuries it has inflicted" (quoted in Carter 1969/1979, 377). Moreover, if Victoria Price was "mistaken" in her identification of Willie Roberson and Olen Montgomery, how could the state defend sending four others to death and long prison sentences on her discredited testimony? (Carter 1969/1979, 377)

The *New York Times* agreed: either all were guilty or none was guilty. Alabama had released the four for the sake of expediency, accused the *Times*.

Perhaps, the paper continued, the state was coming to its senses and would "do more complete justice later on." Below the Mason-Dixon line, the *Richmond Times-Dispatch* was even more blunt: the dropping of charges against the four "serves as a virtual clincher to the argument that all nine of the Negroes are innocent" (quoted in Carter 1969/1979, 377). Even the *Montgomery Advertiser* suggested that all of the defendants should now be released (Carter 1969/1979).

Intensifying indignation over the compromise was overtaken by events. On October 26, 1937, the United States Supreme Court declined to review the seventy-five-year conviction of Haywood Patterson. Defense lawyers knew that the state's case against Norris, Weems, and Wright was no different than it had been against Patterson. In New York, Chalmers acknowledged that the Supreme Court's decision "apparently closes out further legal action in the case of Haywood Patterson" (quoted in Carter 1969/1979, 379). This did not mean, however, that the Scottsboro Defense Committee was prepared to accept the continued imprisonment of the remaining defendants. Now Chalmers appealed directly to Governor Bibb Graves to use his pardoning power (Carter 1969/1979).

Graves was not exactly a progressive governor. As the *New York Times* noted, Graves had "venerated and been venerated" by the Alabama Ku Klux Klan during his first term in office from 1927 to 1931 (quoted in Carter 1969/1979, 379). He had directly intervened in the state legislature to defeat an anti-Klan bill and when the Alabama attorney general began investigation of several Klan crimes, Graves moved to stop funding of the attorney general's office. So Chalmers could not have been shocked when Graves replied that he could take no action at the present time. His excuse was he was powerless as long as the appeals for Norris, Wright, and Weems were still pending in the courts, but, he promised, when they had been decided he would act "quickly and definitely." In a private meeting he confided: "I cannot make any promise which would look like a deal. I have already stated my feeling that the position of the State is untenable with half out and half in on the same charges and evidence." He continued, "My mind is clear on the action required to remedy this impossible position" (quoted in Carter 1969/1979, 381). Chalmers felt sure that Graves had definitely set the date for the pardoning of the remaining Scottsboro defendants (Carter 1969/1979).

The governor *had* set a date for the release of the four remaining men; it was October 31, 1938, at 11 A.M. But on Saturday, October 29, while seated in a barber's chair in the University Club in New York, S.D.C. chairman Chalmers was handed a telegram from Governor Bibb Graves. It read: "Please defer Mondays engagement until further notice. Am not ready to act. Please acknowledge receipt" (quoted Carter 1969/1979, 389). Chalmers hurriedly telephoned Grover Hall, but the Montgomery publisher had no idea what had happened. Hall promised to meet with Graves as soon as possible. Horrified then depressed over this sudden turn of events, Chalmers cancelled the limousine he had rented to meet the defendants. Suddenly, the weekend became even longer (Carter 1969/1979).

It turned out to be five days long, as that is how much time passed before the S.D.C. chairman learned what had happened. A special delivery letter from

Grover Hall read in part: "I had a long and intimate talk with Governor Graves late this afternoon. I found him adamant and passionate in his resolve not to parole the Scottsboro defendants." Graves told Hall the following story: Norris had come into the executive office still in a rage over an earlier quarrel with Patterson, a dispute that officials at the Atmore Prison Farm said revolved around a mutual homosexual friend. (In her discussion of the Scottsboro case, Susan Brownmiller [1975/1993, 261 reports that "Patterson had stated forthrightly that by taking a gal-boy he preserved his stature as a man.") Disturbed, the governor questioned Norris about his threats to kill Patterson; the handcuffed prisoner looked Graves in the eye and snapped, "Yes, I'll kill him! I never furgits!" Moreover, when security guards had searched Patterson before accompanying him into the governor's office, they found a knife made from a file hidden in the fly of his pants. Graves told Hall that from this incident it was clear to him that the release of the defendants would be a nightmare. "They will humiliate you, Grover, they will humiliate Dr. Chalmers and Mr. Shapiro, they will humiliate Comer and Johnston and all other decent sponsors. They are anti-social, they are bestial, they are unbelievably stupid and I do not believe they can be rehabilitated in freedom," the governor exclaimed (quoted in Carter 1969/1979, 390).

At Chalmer's urgings, Hall asked Graves to postpone a public announcement of his decision. Reluctantly the governor complied; he also agreed to meet Chalmers on November 10. Despite the grim outlook, Chalmers tried to express optimism to his Alabama friends as he outlined his strategy for his meeting with the governor. He would begin by conceding that the boys were "cocky," had caused trouble in the prison, and some had even developed homosexual "tendencies." But he would point out to Graves there had been "no indication of any homosexual characteristics in any of them before their incarceration." It was "well known that personality maladjustment is almost inevitable in the very nature of prison life," assuming that it had been revulsion at homosexuality that, in part, had persuaded Graves to renege on his promise to release. Furthermore, Chalmers would tell the governor, psychiatric reports on the nine had shown that the four already freed had been the least suited for rehabilitation and yet they had caused no serious trouble after their release. Finally, he planned to explain to Graves that the S.D.C. had made elaborate preparations for the training of Patterson, Norris, Wright, and Weems after their release so that one could be assured that they would find jobs. Chalmers's last words before the meeting were: "I am confident we can win" (quoted passages in Carter 1969/1979, 391).

Accompanied by Grover Hall, Chalmers met with the governor on November 10. His optimism vanished. The governor, Chalmers reported later, was a "weary, defensive man," adamant now that he would never release the defendants. Grover Hall was completely discouraged; he felt that the long battle was over. They had been defeated. Despite his dismay, he suggested to Chalmers that they make one more effort and "call out the reserves, including That Man and Eleanor," referring to President and Mrs. Franklin D. Roosevelt (quoted in Carter 1969/1979, 391). The idea of asking the president to intervene appealed to Chalmers; he knew that Graves was devoted to F.D.R.

Moreover, he knew that the president had before expressed an interest in the Scottsboro affair. On November 11, at the request of Chalmers, Walter White met with Eleanor Roosevelt at the White House. She agreed to ask her husband if he would use his influence in some way to change Governor Graves's mind. That evening, after Eleanor Roosevelt spoke with him, F.D.R. decided to invite Graves to visit the summer White House in Warm Springs, Georgia, over the Thanksgiving holiday. There perhaps he could persuade the man to release the remaining defendants (Carter 1969/1979).

Roosevelt did invite Graves to Warm Springs, as promised to Eleanor, but Graves declined, using the excuse that he had too much work and could not leave Montgomery. Then Graves's press secretary read a brief statement to several reporters acknowledging that the governor had decided to deny the pardon applications of the five Scottsboro prisoners. With no legal avenues left open and the governor's mind apparently made up, the issue seemed to be settled. On December 7, 1938, Franklin D. Roosevelt wrote a letter to the governor of Alabama. "Dear Bibb," he began, "I am sorry indeed not to have seen you while I was at Warm Springs because I wanted to give you a purely personal, and not in any way official, suggestion." He flattered the governor: "You have been such a grand Governor and have done so much for the cause of liberalism in the State of Alabama that I want you to go out of office without the loss of the many friends you have made throughout the nation." Frankly, confided the president, there was a "real feeling in very wide circles that you said definitely and positively that you were going to commute the sentences of the remainder of the Scottsboro boys." Many "warm friends of yours all over the United States relied on what they thought was a definite promise." Roosevelt added that there was no point in rehashing the details of the case and that he was certain the defendants did not have a best record in prison. But he expressed his hope that the remaining men could be taken "away from the State of Alabama ... with a guarantee on their part that they would not turn up again." He finished by saying, "As I said before, I am writing this only as a very old and warm friend of yours, and I hope you will take it in the spirit it is said" (quoted in Carter 1969/1979, 394).

Graves's use of Norris's death threat against his brother and the prisoners' reputed homosexuality was, it turns out, diversionary. Dan Carter tells us that "the governor had simply got cold feet." What dissuaded him from making good on his promise to release was that his mail was running heavily against the Scottsboro defendants. Former Senator Tom Heflin had visited the governor's office warning him that he was committing political suicide should he release the defendants. Apparently Graves had not caved in to Heflin, but when an unofficial group of politicians also told the governor he was through politically if he went through with the pardons, Graves collapsed. Evidently, this was the background of his statement to Chalmers, "I ... know very well what they can do" (quoted in Carter 1969/1979, 396).

One of the top news stories of the 1930s, the Scottsboro case never made the headlines after 1939. Although there was an occasional one-paragraph story, Governor Graves's refusal to pardon the remaining five defendants was for the media the final chapter of the Scottsboro story. For Allan Knight Chalmers it was the end of nothing. In fact, it was beginning of eleven years of continuing struggle and frustration. The governor's failure to keep his promise only foreshadowed a frustrating series of negotiations, agreements, and then retractions. As Chalmers would learn over and over again, freedom for the five Scottsboro prisoners—now approaching middle age—was in the hands of Alabama officials who were politically motivated if not just plain malevolent. On December 17, 1942, Chalmers wrote the five men, communicating his frank and honest appraisal of the situation. He admitted there was little hope for their immediate release due to the tense racial situation in the South. Chalmers urged the five to make a good record in prison, even though this was hard when they knew they were innocent and there was little hope for immediate release. He promised them he would never give up (Carter 1969/1979).

As films like "Fortune and Men's Eyes" (Hart 1971) and research makes clear (see chapters 16 and 17), prison life is, at best, extremely difficult. In the South it was much worse. And during the 1930s Alabama's prison system was one of the worst anywhere. Carter (1969/1979, 407) characterizes it as "a human refuse heap where the inmates were overworked and often brutally mistreated." By 1939, Andy Wright showed signs of "prison psychosis" (Carter 1969/1979, 410). Of the five men, only Patterson had "adjusted" to prison life. He had learned to be cooperative, even submissive, with prison officials and to "Uncle Tom" (as he put it) with skill. Over the years Patterson had become an aggressive homosexual. Most of the "trouble" he had "caused" had had to do with homosexual jealousies and the "bank system." Under this arrangement, prisoners borrowed from loan sharks within the prison at a rate of interest as high as 50 or 100 per cent per week. In August 1945, for instance, Patterson became involved in a fight over a four-dollar loan. As punishment, he was thrown into Class C for fighting where he could receive neither letters or money. By the time he had worked his way out of Class C two months later, interest on his debt had increased the sum from $4.00 to $39.50 (Carter 1969/1979).

The first break came on November 17, 1943. After months of quiet negotiations, the Alabama Board of Pardons and Paroles agreed to release Weems. The Board declined to release Norris and Wright, despite Chalmers's assurances that they would move immediately "up North." The N.A.A.C.P.'s Roy Wilkins had secured jobs for them in Cleveland, working at a smelting plant for forty dollars a week. Finally, in January, the Board agreed to release the two, but only if they worked at a lumber company near Montgomery. Living in a room eight feet by ten feet and forced to sleep in the same small bed, the two men worked irregular hours for only thirteen dollars a week. Andy Wright said it was "no different than prison" (quoted in Carter 1969/1979, 411). As Chalmers had worried, the two soon despaired and fled northward, leaving the state they now passionately hated. Chalmers managed to persuade Wright and Norris to return on a promise from the pardon board that they would be given another chance. But it was a setup, and the Board sent both men back to prison (Carter 1969/1979).

The Scottsboro Defense Committee disbanded in 1944. A discouraged Chalmers continued his negotiations with the Alabama authorities, thanks now in part to the financial assistance of the N.A.A.C.P. Finally, his commitment and his patience paid off. In late 1946, the Board released Ozie Powell and granted Clarence Norris another parole. Haywood Patterson was another story. Given that he had been described to members of the Pardon and Parole Board as "sullen, vicious and incorrigible" (Carter 1969/1979, 412), there seemed little chance for his release. On a hot summer day in 1948, Patterson took matters into his own hands, slipping away from his work gang into the nearby sugar cane fields. For almost a week, prison dogs and search planes looked for him, but he escaped first to Atlanta and from there to his sister's home in Detroit. For two years he remained in hiding, assisted by officials of the Civil Rights Congress, the organization which had succeeded the International Labor Defense. When F.B.I. agents arrested him, Michigan's Governor G. Mennen Williams refused to sign extradition papers. Only at that point did Alabama authorities announce that they would no longer seek to have him returned to the state penitentiary (Carter 1969/1979).

There was one of the original Scottsboro Nine still in prison. In May 1950, the Alabama Pardon and Parole Board voted unanimously to grant another parole to Andrew Wright. On June 9, 1950, nineteen years and two months after he was taken from a train in Paint Rock, Alabama, Andy Wright walked through the gates of Kilby Prison a free man. Chalmers had arranged a job for Wright, working as an orderly in an Albany, New York, hospital. His parole "salary" amounted to $13.45. One of the reporters who greeted him outside the gate asked how he felt. "I have no hard feelings toward anyone," Wright replied, in a barely audible voice. Someone asked about Victoria Price, "I'm not mad because the girl lied about me," he said. "If she's still living, I feel sorry for her because I don't guess she sleeps much at night" (quoted in Carter 1969/1979, 413). Without waiting for any additional questions, Andrew Wright turned and walked away. The last of the Scottsboro Nine was free (Carter 1969/1979).

Certainly there were "villains"—as Carter (1969/1979, 462) puts it—in the Scottsboro case, men like Alabama Attorney General Thomas Knight, Jr., who manipulated the racism of his fellow Alabamians, knowing full well that the nine young men were innocent. His assistants, Wade Wright and Melvin Hutson, also warrant this category, using the anti-Semitism and provincialism of the jury to make an implausible case "plausible." Nor would I exempt Dr. Lynch or Judge Horton, although Carter seems to, as well-meaning men, "victims" of time and circumstance. To save his practice, Lynch declined to speak up; to save his political career (which failed in any case), Horton declined to speak up. Both are villains, not victims. Finally, one must judge harshly both the I.L.D. and the N.A.A.C.P., the latter of which had withdrawn from the case in 1932. The former was guilty of using the Scottsboro Nine for ideological purposes, and the latter was too slow in acting, too concerned about respectability. In 1930s Alabama white men still obsessed over black men's bodies. In some way black bodies "belonged" to them, they felt, and "outside interference" only intensified their determination to "dispose" of those nine black male bodies as they wished. This time white women were not imaginary, although they were nonetheless used as symbolic currency in a homosocial economy of power, lust, and sadism. Carter quotes Will Campbell, director of the Committee of Southern Churchmen, who summed up what more than a few white southerners finally came to realize, namely that nine young black men, with their lives in front of them, were, on white men's whim, converted to "nine captured, caged, tortured, broken, battered and destroyed human beings" (1969/1979, 462).

Why did white men's whim so often settle on black men's bodies? Is there something about the culture of white masculinity that requires the presence of the black man, if as a mythic, imaginary highly sexualized creature? Why in the U.S. is gender, and specifically masculinity, so racialized? What are the racial politics of masculinity? How have they affected black men? What is the state of "men"—white, black—in contemporary American society? How does the present state of "men" follow from their racialized past? To explore these questions, to discern the traces of the gender of racial politics in contemporary constructions of "manhood," we turn in the next section to studies of "men" and "masculinity." First, let us briefly review the Scottsboro case from a feminist point of view, the terms of which will transport us to the culture and racial politics of "masculinity."

VII. "[I]s interracial rape ... a national obsession"?

—Susan Brownmiller, *Against Our Will: Men, Women, and Rape* (1975/1993)

[T]he poor reputations of a certain class of white women render[s] their rape a lesser crime even if their rapists are black.

—Susan Brownmiller, *Against Our Will: Men, Women, and Rape* (1975/1993)

If only we could rise up against the killers of man's dreams. But, sometimes, that killer of dreams is in us and we do not know how to rid ourselves of it.

—Lillian Smith, *Killers of the Dream* (1949/1963)

When Susan Brownmiller's *Against Our Will: Men, Women, and Rape* appeared in 1975, it was widely praised. In 1976 *Time* magazine selected Brownmiller as one of its "women of the year," describing the book as "[t]he most rigorous and provocative piece of scholarship that has yet emerged from the feminist movement" (quoted in Davis 1983, 178). Others criticized the book, arguing that Brownmiller sacrificed race for gender, and in so doing, as Angela Davis charged, resuscitated "the old racist myth of the Black rapist" (1983, 178). Davis also charged that Brownmiller's study disregarded African-American women's pioneering efforts in the antilynching movement: "While Brownmiller rightfully praises Jesse Daniel Ames and the A.S.W.P.L., she makes not so much as a passing mention of Ida B. Wells, Mary Church Terrell or Mary Talbert and the Anti-Lynching Crusaders" (Davis 1983, 195).

While I can appreciate how Angela Davis might decode Brownmiller's sometimes excessive defense of poor southern white women who participated (on occasion actively, usually passively) in southern white men's obsession with black men, I think the charge that Brownmiller participated in the myth of the black rapist is also excessive. Neither Brownmiller nor Davis notices the buried homoerotic at work in the white male subjugation of the black man, but that is not my main point here. There *was* a certain excessive devaluation of Ruby Bates and Victoria Price during the Scottsboro nightmare, a devaluation Brownmiller attempts to repair, but also, I think, to excess.

Brownmiller begins her discussion of the Scottsboro affair by recalling the publication, in the midst of Communist Party's rivalry with the N.A.A.C.P., of the party's official policy on lynching. Published in 1932 by International Publishers, the pamphlet focused on N.A.A.C.P. leaders W. E. B. Du Bois and Walter White, although Clarence Darrow was attacked as well, all for their "dastardly evasion of the real cause of lynching." "International Pamphlet No. 25" denounced the N.A.A.C.P. for suggesting that lynching might be an isolated phenomenon, a problem of lawlessness, involving mostly uneducated poor whites. Predictably the Communists asserted: "Lynchings defend profits! Lynchings are a warning to the Negro toilers. Lynching is one of the weapons with which the white ruling class enforces its national oppression of the Negro people and tries to maintain division between the white workers and the Negro toilers" (quoted in Brownmiller 1975/1993, 227).

"The rhetoric was terrible, the attack on Du Bois and the others was patently unfair," Brownmiller (1975/1993, 227) comments, "but the germ of the idea was sound." By that she means that the idea became fused with mainstream American thinking, so that in 1947 the President's Committee on Civil Rights issued a famous report, *To Secure These Rights*, which concluded, "Lynching is the ultimate threat by which his inferior status is driven home to the Negro. As a terrorist device, it reinforces all the other disabilities placed upon him" (quoted in Brownmiller 1975/1993, 227). This 1947 statement would seem to focus more on white supremacy than class struggle, but this is incidental to where Brownmiller is going.

"International Pamphlet No. 25" also focused on rape, the crime most associated with lynching. Rape, Brownmiller points out, was never written as rape but always in quotation marks as "rape" and sometimes as the phrase "the capitalist rape lie."

> The "Rape" Lie
>
> To incite the white workers against the Negroes and to further build the myth of "white superiority," the white ruling class has coined the poisonous and insane lie that Negroes are "rapists." ... The cry of "rape" is raised whenever any Negro worker begins to rise from his knees. (Brownmiller 1975/1993, 227–228)

Skepticism regarding cries of rape have long been embedded in "male logic," Brownmiller (1975/1993, 228) observes; she cites "the days when men first allowed a limited concept of criminal rape into their law." The male leaders of the Communist Party did not bother to question this logic although, she points out acidly, they had aggressively challenged other aspects of property law. She recalls Wilbur J. Cash's description of "the rape complex" of the South; he had written of "neurotic old maids and wives, hysterical young girls." She links that characterization of southern white women with the work of John Dollard (see chapter 3), the Yale professor of psychology whose *Caste and Class in a Southern Town* was widely read. In it Dollard quoted verbatim the views of Helen Deutsch, views he acknowledged he had found "illuminating." Deutsch, Dollard reported, had analyzed several white southern women in which she had found "marked sexual attraction to Negro men and masochistic fantasies connected with this attraction." Deutsch's conclusion: "The fact that the white men believe so readily the hysterical and masochistic fantasies and lies of the white women, who claim they have been assaulted and raped by Negroes, is related to the fact that they (the men) sense the unconscious wishes of the women, the psychic reality of these declarations, and react emotionally to them as if they were real. The social situation permits them to discharge this emotion upon the Negroes" (quoted in Brownmiller 1975/1993, 229). Overlooked in Deutsch's comment is that *men* fabricated these crimes; women, in general, did not. It's not women's "unconscious wishes" white men were expressing; it was their own.

In her two-volume *Psychology of Women*, Deutsch remained convinced that "hysterical" women were to blame for the epidemic of rape charges in the post-bellum South. "Rape fantasies," Deutsch wrote, "often have such irresistible verisimilitude that even the most experienced judges are misled in trials of innocent men accused of rape by hysterical women. My own experience of accounts by white women of rape by Negroes (who are often subjected to terrible penalties as a result of these accusations) has convinced me that many fantastic stories are produced by the masochistic yearnings of these women" (quoted in Brownmiller 1975/1993, 229–230). Trapped in her own heterosexism, Deutsch cannot discern how these women were exploited by the white men who were pretending to protect them. Never mind. With the Deutsch passage Brownmiller has prepared us for her discussion of the Scottsboro Nine.

"If one case convinced the American public—and international opinion—that lying, scheming white women who cried rape were directly responsible for the terrible penalties inflicted on black men, the name of that case was Scottsboro." So Brownmiller begins her discussion of the case itself, a case, she acknowledges, "remains an ugly blot on American history and southern jurisprudence." But, she adds, the case of the Scottsboro Nine was also "damning proof to liberals everywhere that Eve Incarnate and the concept of Original Sin was a no-good, promiscuous woman who rode a freight train through Alabama." She moves to establish the innocence of the two white women, reminding us that Ruby Bates was seventeen and Victoria Price was in her mid-twenties, "rootless young people riding the rails" (Brownmiller 1975/1993, 230). Brownmiller repeats the facts of the morning of March 27, 1931, that somewhere past Stevenson a fistfight broke out between black and white men on the train, that the black men won and had forced the white youths off the train. News of the racial encounter was telegraphed ahead to Paint Rock along with the information, volunteered by the defeated white boys, that the two white girls were still aboard the train and were no doubt in serious trouble. When the train arrived at the Paint Rock station, cries of rape were everywhere. An armed posse of seventy-five men, supplemented by an angry crowd, was waiting. "Ruby," she tells us, dropping her last name for familiarity's sake, "was the one who first answered this question with a faltering yes" (Brownmiller 1975/1993, 231).

The first set of trials held at Scottsboro were quick affairs, Brownmiller (1975/1993, 231) reminds us, "farcical" except for the fact that eight of the nine defendants were sentenced to death. Bates and Price were kept in jail on possible vagrancy and/or prostitution charges and required to testify for the prosecution. Here Brownmiller's identification with victimized women permits her to imagine the choices faced by these two young women:

> The singular opportunity afforded Price and Bates should be appreciated by every woman. From languishing in a jail cell as the lowest of the low, vagrant women who stole rides on freight cars, it was a short step to the witness stand where dignity of a sort could be reclaimed by charging that they had been pathetic, innocent victims of rape. (Victoria Price could never get herself to admit in court that she had spent a night at a Chattanooga hobo jungle. No, she stubbornly insisted in trial after trail, she had stayed in the home of a respectable lady.) Operating from precisely the same motivation—to save their own skins—some of the black defendants tried to exculpate themselves in court by swearing they had seen the others do the raping. (Brownmiller 1975/1993, 231–232)

Whether Price could not "get herself to admit" or simply refused to admit that she spent the night before in the hobo section is not clear from Carter's study of the trials.

After the case of the Scottsboro Nine received international attention through worldwide agitation from the Communist movement—"the Communists must be credited with keeping the youths alive"—and a million dollars had been raised on their behalf, a new series of trials began. Hired by the International Labor Defense to represent the defendants, Samuel Leibowitz made legal history by persuading the Supreme Court to acknowledge that black men had been systematically excluded from serving on Alabama juries. Later, Leibowitz pronounced this the proudest accomplishment of his life. After reviewing these facts, Brownmiller (1975/1993, 231) reminds us:

> [A]nd yet a feminist looking at the Scottsboro case today must note that while every person who ever served on a Scottsboro jury and voted to convict was white, he was also male, and no one, no political grouping, no appellate lawyer, no Scottsboro pamphlet ever raised the question of the exclusion of women from the jury rolls of Alabama, although many a pamphlet charged that Victoria Price was a prostitute.

(According to Carter's account, it was the Huntsville sheriff who first reported that Price was a prostitute.) Women, Brownmiller points out, did not win the right to sit on Alabama juries until 1966.

Next Brownmiller asks: "Would a fair number of women, white and black, have made a difference on a Scottsboro jury?" "Maybe so," she answers, especially at that moment when the prosecuting attorney went into his frenzied "protection of southern womanhood" speech. Brownmiller remembers that the Association of Southern Women for the Prevention of Lynching had been organized to contest this southern male nonsense, and just maybe there might have been female jurors who might have seen through the ruse. Brownmiller (1975/1993, 232) continues:

> Would women sitting on those juries have been able to understand the predicament faced by Victoria Price and Ruby Bates? Perhaps. Might they have been able to distinguish a false rape story from a true one? Would they have been quicker to understand the import of dead, nonmotile sperm in Victoria Price's vagina to the exclusion of living sperm, which the defense vainly argued was proof that whatever recent intercourse Victoria Price had experienced had occurred in Huntsville or in the hobo jungle but not on the train?

Perhaps Alabama white women could have resisted the racist, misogynist spell cast by the prosecution. Perhaps not. The fact remains, Brownmiller underscores, that no woman ever served on a jury of the Scottsboro Nine. Each and every vote to convict was cast by a white man. She reminds us that *all* the forces of the law faced by the black defendants—judge, prosecution, defense and jury—were white *and* all male. "It was a white man's game that was played out in the Scottsboro trials," Brownmiller (1975/1993, 232–233) concludes, "with black men and white women as movable pawns." But she stops short of a strong gender analysis like that of Gayle Rubin (1975) or Monique Wittig (1992). Instead, Brownmiller (1975/1993, 233) makes a Marxist move: "white men judged interracial rape according to their own particular property code." Perhaps it is her own heterosexism at work here. At any rate, this move will buy her little sympathy from Angela Davis, as we will see momentarily.

Leibowitz once remarked that if Victoria Price and Ruby Bates had walked into a New York City police station and charged nine black men with rape, after five minutes of questioning they would have been "tossed out of the precinct and that would have been the end of the whole affair. Even the dumbest cop on the force would have spotted those two as tramps and liars" (quoted in Brownmiller 1975/1993, 233). Brownmiller will not concede the point (however grossly made), only that "this may have been a fair assessment of the stereotypic northern cop mentality" (233). Leibowitz, she suggests, "deliberately missed an essential point" (233). Price and Bates did not walk into a police station at all. They were surrounded by a posse of frenzied white men who already "knew" a rape had taken place. Probably Brownmiller is right: "Confused and fearful, they fell into line" (1975/1993, 233).

This fact, Brownmiller emphasizes, "is a critical truth about Scottsboro" (233). She recalls that Hollace Ransdell, the white woman sent south by the American Civil Liberties Union to conduct a private investigation of the Scottsboro case, reported that George Chamlee, the I.L.D. attorney from Chattanooga who followed the case from the very beginning, was certain "that when the two girls were taken from the train at Paint Rock they made no charges against the Negroes until they were taken into custody; that their charges were made after they had found out the spirit of the armed men that came to meet the train and catch the Negroes, and that they were swept into making wholesale accusations against the Negroes merely by assenting to the charges as presented by the men who seized the nine Negroes." Writing in the *New Republic* in 1933, Mary Heaton Vorse said much the same: "The girls, fearing a vagrancy charge, then accused the Negro boys of assault" (quoted in Brownmiller 1975/1993, 233–234). This plausible explanation of the origin of the rape complaint, Brownmiller is right to point out, was buried in the avalanche of Scottsboro publicity. But Angela Davis (1983, 198) is also right to point out: "No one can deny that the women were manipulated by Alabama racists. However, it is wrong to portray the women as innocent pawns, absolved of the responsibility of having collaborated with the forces of racism."

To strengthen her case that these were intimidated young women, Brownmiller reminds us that Hollace Ransdell conducted personal interviews with both Bates and Price, their mothers, neighbors and local social workers. (Their fathers had abandoned them.) Ransdell observed that the quick-witted Victoria Price prided herself on being able to perform as the prosecution wished; she quickly became the star witness, while the less articulate Ruby Bates receded into the background where she grew resentful. Two years later Ruby Bates wrote her letter (Brownmiller 1975/1993).

Despite Ruby Bates's dramatic recantation in the second trial of "ringleader" Haywood Patterson—Victoria Price determinedly stuck to her original story and even embellished upon it—a new jury of twelve white men still voted a sentence of death. It was then that Judge James E. Horton, the "good" judge who knew Dr. Lynch's skepticism regarding the rape charge, set aside Patterson's conviction and ordered a third trial, a decision that cost him his judicial career. Brownmiller notes that Judge Horton did not confront the jury; rather he had faith that his "white brothers" would do the right thing, would not convict a black man for rape and sentence him to death on insubstantial evidence. Nor did he intervene in "the uncorroborated, improbable testimony of the prosecutrix" (quoted in Brownmiller 1975/1993, 234).

Horton, Brownmiller asserts, "had a grander theme, one that reached back to man's oldest suspicions" (1975/1993, 234). That suspicion is of "woman," well, not all women but those who are not "ladies."

> History, sacred and profane and the common experience of mankind teaches that women of the character shown in this case are prone for selfish reasons to make false accusations both of rape and of insult upon the slightest provocation, or even without provocation for ulterior purposes. ... The tendency on the part of the women shows they are predisposed to make false accusations upon any occasion whereby their selfish ends may be gained. (Horton, quoted in Brownmiller 1975/1993, 234)

Brownmiller is right, of course, to make visible Horton's mix of misogyny and classism. She is perhaps a bit bitter in alleging that "blaming Scottsboro on the predisposition of a certain class of woman to make false accusations was an easy handle for the liberal mentality to grasp." But she speaks in excess when she then declares: "Trouble was a white woman of murky virtue—the root of all evil—how neatly everything fell into place, how cleanly white men were absolved of guilt" (Brownmiller 1975/1993, 234). What white men? Southern white men, indeed, but Brownmiller is really after the Yankees. How are they "absolved of guilt"?

Brownmiller argues that northern liberals, from a feminist perspective, are the opposite side of the same coin as southern white men. She quotes a study of penalties for rape in Louisiana from 1900 to 1950 which indicates that thirty-seven black men and only two white men had been executed by the state during the same fifty-year period. Another study of executions for rape or attempted rape, this time of Virginia during the years 1908 to 1963, reveals that fifty-six black men and not one white man had been given the maximum penalty. Brownmiller (1975/1993, 234–235) comments: "As southern white men continued to round up black men, lynching them or trying them in a courtroom and giving them the maximum sentence for the holy purpose of 'protecting their women,' northern liberals looking at the ghastly pattern through an inverted prism saw the picture of a lynching white woman crying rape-rape-rape."

It is probably true all white men engaged in the Scottsboro case tended to accept uncritically the masculinist binary of women as either "ladies" or "whores." The southern white men involved stubbornly insisted that Ruby Bates and Victoria Price were the former, while northern white men, on evidence, saw these two as the latter. Probably none of the defense attorneys and staff was free of misogyny—no man is—but when Leibowitz goes after Victoria Price it is partly the frustration of the racist Alabama courtroom that animates him. In part it was knowing that Price was collaborating with—lying for—the prosecution. And it was probably some free-floating misogyny as well. I have no interest in exonerating white—or black—men from charges of misogyny, but I do want to suggest that Brownmiller overstates her case.

Overstatement is evident too in Brownmiller's conclusion to her discussion of the Scottsboro case. "The left," she charges, "was more at ease [in the Scottsboro case] politicizing rape as 'rape,' a fantasy charge designed to kill black men. ... In its mass-protest campaigns to save the lives of convicted black rapists, the left employed all these tactics, and more, against white women with a virulence that bordered on hate" (Brownmiller 1975/1993, 236, 238). While overstating her case, she is not entirely mistaken. White liberal men sometimes did occupy the other side of the same coin as southern white men; they revalorized the bodies of black men as positive. Today, white men will sometimes sacrifice white women for the sake of black men. That dynamic is clearly at work in the Lisa Olson episode (see Disch and Kane 1996). In her study of rape and women, Brownmiller's primary commitment is to women. That commitment does seem to blunt her sensitivity to the plight of black men. Angela Davis goes further: "Brownmiller's provocative distortion of such historical cases as the Scottsboro Nine ... are designed to dissipate any sympathy for black men who are victims of fraudulent rape charges" (Davis 1983, 197). That racial divide within American feminism I hope to elucidate in volume two. For now, let us focus on men.

For both southern and northern white men involved in the Scottsboro case, Ruby Bates and Victoria Price *were* irrelevant, pawns moved in a man's chess game, as Brownmiller notes. As we have seen, the law itself has been a gendered site in which masculinity has been constructed and defended and destroyed. There is an important sense in which the Scottsboro case was yet one more instance in which white men fought over the bodies of black men. Once again southern men insisted they had the right—again invoking the fantasy of "southern womanhood"—to do what they chose with the bodies of black men. Northern white men insisted that their motives were justice and freedom, that all they wanted was to set these innocent young men free. Both sets of men were no doubt sincere, but both were blind to the subtext of racialized homosexual desire, a subtext which rendered women imaginary and expendable. In such a homosocial universe women were, and are, often victims. Who are these creatures who pretend to be drawn to women but instead draw women as fictional characters in a homosocial, homoerotic economy in which men's bodies get mutilated? To begin to sketch an answer to that question let us leave lynching, antilynching, and turn to contemporary discourses on a previously invisible subject, but one that is now what widely regarded as a major social problem: "men."

FIVE

The Culture and Racial Politics of Masculinity

Should Stoltenberg have modified his noun with "heterosexual"? Who, as Delease Wear (1999) asks, are these creatures who mutilated the bodies of young black men? In section one of this study, the historical specificity of the phenomenon was uppermost: names, dates, who, when and where. Then we turned to the scholarly study of lynching to underline how complex, and, unless a queer analysis is included, how mysterious and elusive lynching is. If we appreciate that lynching was—in addition to being an expression of popular justice, white supremacy, social control, and frustration-turned-aggression aggravated by seasonal and economic cycles, specifically the price of cotton—a maniacal and distorted form of homosexual rape during a period in which white masculinity was widely experienced to be in "crisis," the practice comes into sharper focus. What becomes clear is that racial politics in the United States has tended to be sexual politics, and vice versa. From the early alliance of feminists and abolitionists to British female reformers and the antilynching campaign and well into the twentieth century, many women seemed to have understood that gender and race were intertwined. Specifically, women understood that they had been used in racial politics, in the case of lynching as an excuse for white men to do what they wanted to do with black men. Even when white women chose to participate in the racist politics of the second Ku Klux Klan, they were not willing to mutilate black bodies. In contrast to their male counterparts, women in the second Klan used the movement, yes to hate others, but also to affirm themselves as women.

When lynching is studied primarily as a subset of racial violence, its queer aspects recede into mystery. In this section let us focus on the gender of those primarily involved in lynching: men. White men were in "crisis" as men during the late nineteenth century, a crisis precipitated by profound shifts in the workplace, in the domestic sphere (as more women resisted the separate spheres ideology), in the church where women "mimed" conservative theology to advance their cause, in school where "co-education" threatened (many men worried) to "feminize" boys, and in the racial sphere as African Americans inched out of the "prison" whites had fashioned for them after "Emancipation." As well, "heterosexuality" was being invented, as had "homosexuality," and opportunities for what historians have termed "romantic" friendships receded into anxieties over "masculinity" and heterosexual manhood. White men performed their gendered "crisis" politically and racially, and many "others"—in the 1890s many black men—died. There was a tiny minority of "progressive" men, as we have seen, who fought for racial, economic, and gender justice, but the majority of white men in America continued to resist, until the second decade of the twentieth century, even white women's right to vote. Those same men who disenfranchised black men during the 1890s also lynched them in record numbers. The civic and the sexual conflated in politics and violence.

Who *are* these people? What is there about white "men" (or is it heterosexually identified white men) that seems so interwoven with violence, especially racialized and gendered violence? Of course, "white men" are hardly all the same; "white straight masculinity" is no "single, monolithic, absolute evil against which an interminable struggle for turf and power must be waged" (Pfeil 1995, xii). And yet the fact that racial and other forms of gendered violence has and remains, as we will see momentarily, very much associated with "white straight masculinity" does require us to view that violence, not as exceptional to the category, but instead as profoundly expressive of its difficulties.

What about black men? If lynching, and by extension racial violence, has been in some sense "queer," if black men have experienced their oppression in the United States as a kind of rape (civic and sexual), what shape would we expect to find black men in today? Would there be a "crisis" of black masculinity, akin to those victims of male-male rape who wonder if perhaps the event was somehow their fault, that perhaps they are not quite "men," that there is something about them that the rapist discerned and took advantage of? Is there a racialized culture of compensatory masculinity in the United States that reproduces a certain tendency toward sexualized violence? Is there something about heterosexually identified "masculinity" and "manhood"—white and black—that makes these unstable and socially disruptive, a threat especially to women and children, but to other men as well? The power of patriarchy makes these questions seem odd, if not crazy, unless one has read some of the burgeoning literature on "men." In this section let us impressionistically review some of this work, and in so doing, perceive lynching and the gender of racial politics in the context of "men."

Terribly important in itself, lynching is like a loose thread. If I pull at it, I find the fabric of white patriarchal civilization comes apart, the queer under pattern of its composition revealed. Laced throughout is homosexual desire—disavowed, denied, recoded, but laced throughout. Men practice other sexualized rites of male torture and murder besides lynching. Let us survey for a moment statistics that are not often situated in the history of racial violence. Let us think about the family, about stalking, rape, and torture. We won't forget murder. Lynching is the loose thread in a male fabric, a fabric "colored," on the surface at least, heterosexual. Unlike lynching, most heterosexual male violence, such as rape, is intraracial. But heterosexual male violence, like "manhood" and "masculinity," is no unchanging, essential concept. All are culturally variable and historically specific. But acknowledging the variability of its expression, male violence—on men, on women, on children—seems a constant. Are "straight" men at war? If so, what on earth are they fighting? What could it be?

"'Men' are now on the political agenda," Jeff Hearn (1998, 1) writes, "and about time too!" Of course, men have always been there, in the sense that the political sphere has been conducted by men, by groups of men, for centuries. We saw that fact in men's battles over other men's bodies in the antilynching efforts in Congress (chapters 10 and 11) and in the struggles between the N.A.A.C.P. and the C.P.-U.S.A. over the Scottsboro Nine. That fact requires us to ask: why not study men? Have not they written the "curriculum"—school, political, sexual—for centuries? What Hearn means when he suggests it is now important for men to think about men, is that studying men at this historical conjuncture represents a questioning of the "species." In fact, "men" have become recognized as problematic to an extent not appreciated before, thanks in no small part to feminism and feminist theory. Now that "men" are problematic they are indeed on the political agenda (Hearn 1998). As many women have understood for a very long time, men are a problem.

Acknowledging that, "men" become a topic for scholarly study and theoretical critique because the concept is no longer coherent, certain, known, safely invisible in its claims of universality. The location of "men" on political agendas, Hearn argues, both solidifies and decenters it, contributing to its problematization. These political agendas are also, he adds, personal, popular, theoretical, and professional. They are important for us, not in order to dehistoricize the concept, but to theorize it, to help us understand what it means to say that the gender of racial politics and violence in America is masculine.

The contemporary scholarly interest in "men," this simultaneous "solidification" and dereification (Hearn likes the phrase "falling away") of "men," functions differently for women and men. For men to focus on "men" feels peculiar; for many straight men it feels downright uncomfortable. There are of course women for whom focusing on men is uncomfortable, at least in the detached, skeptical way that scholarly understanding requires. For feminist women, it has always been clear that the problematization of "men" is important for gender progress, for the advancement of women, the protection of children, and the increased self-consciousness of men. For men, the solidifying moment by itself might appeal as a means to further power, illustrated, Hearn suggests, by the contemporary male backlash against feminism, a phenomenon we will visit briefly in chapter 19. With understatement he observes: "The falling away is for men more difficult" (Hearn 1998, 1).

Hearn, who has written widely on the subject of men's violence, will provide my source material to introduce the subject of "men." I choose him in part because he is, as he phrases it, "unreservedly, unapologetically, pro-feminist" (1998, 2). Hearn is mindful of the "impossibility of men in feminism" (Heath 1987), that is, that feminism is, or more accurately, feminisms are theories and practices by women for women. Men can express support for and solidarity with feminism by undertaking the study and transformation of men, including ourselves. He adds: "It is not [men's] task to try to change women; they can do that themselves if they wish" (Hearn 1998, 2). Certain feminists seem to agree, for instance, Kaja Silverman (1992).

Men changing men is certainly a different matter. There would seem to be something profoundly reactionary simply in the structure of hegemonic masculinity, as women who have tried to change men well know. Men tend to appear opaque to themselves, taken-for-granted, not a text to be rewritten but a text that demands a loyalty oath, unchanging, inviolate, something for which to do and die. In Hearn's (1998, 3) words, "men have been all too visible yet invisible to critical analysis and change. ... To put this bluntly, men need to be named as men." To do so, he suggests, requires situating men socially and in terms of their power relations to women. I agree, but I add that "men" need to be situated historically, and, especially racially. Lynching helps us do that.

While I have devoted separate chapters to white and black men, by the titles I trust it is clear I see the two masculinities as relational, in part constructed in opposition to each other, but still resembling each other. While historically and culturally different, these two orders of American men are locked in an often tortured embrace. Both white and black men's identities tend to accept uncritically some version of a basic power relation to women. The hierarchy of "difference" between the two—white men to black, all men to all women—has tended to be coded as superior to inferior. This sense of masculine superiority, as Hearn notes, appears to accompany the process of male socialization, the process of affirming oneself as a boy and then a man. While Hearn specifies taken-for-granted acceptance of that hierarchical power relation to women as a "common aspect of men's identity," it is clear there are noteworthy variations, racially, culturally, in terms of class and in terms of politics, as he himself acknowledges (1998, 4). And probably Hearn is thinking of straight men, not that gay men are automatically profeminist. Hardly. One "important aspect of men's power and sense of power" that is more identified with heterosexual than with homosexual men is the use, potential use or threat, of violence. "Men's violence," he observes rightly, "remains a major and pressing problem" (Hearn 1998, 4). But he should have said "heterosexual men's violence," for few if any gay-identified men rape women, stalk women, or murder female lovers. Moreover, it is mostly heterosexually identified men who rape other men, as we will see.

The violence of men, mainly heterosexually identified men, may be expressed not only toward women, but to children, young people, each other, animals, and to the planet itself. Hearn prefers the term "men's violences" to "male violence" for two reasons. First, he regards it as more precise in that it attributes the violence to the social construction "men" rather to some biological category for whom violence is inevitable. As well, the term acknowledges the plurality of men's violences. Likewise, Hearn prefers "men's violence or sexualities towards young people" (219) rather than the problematic term "child abuse." Hearn is right; study after study makes it clear that 90 percent of all incidents of "child abuse" and "molestation" are committed by heterosexual men on girls, the majority of the victims being relatives of the victimizers (Young-Bruehl 1996).

Singular or plural, it is the constancy of men's violence to women that staggers one, as one appreciates how the phenomenon cuts across culture and time (Dworkin 1974). Robert Jenson (1998, 105) prefers the construct "patriarchal sex system." He observes that "[t]he result of the patriarchal sex system is widespread violence, sexualized violence, and violence-by-sex against women and children. This includes physical assault, emotional abuse, and rape by family members and acquaintances as well as strangers. Along with the experience of violence, women and children live with the knowledge that they are always targets."

Yes, the sex/gender system is patriarchal, but that phrase hides the fact that it is heterosexual men who commit nearly all the violence against women and children, and much of it against other men. I am not trying to position gay men as morally superior; after all, they *are* men. They are often guilty of racism and misogyny, among other things. But Matthew Sheperd's (1998, 191) comment that "[f]requently ... gay men have attitudes toward women and feminism that are as misogynist as the worst heterosexual men's attitudes" is misleading. True, gay men can be misogynist in attitude—and that *must* change—but it is not gay men who rape women, fail to support, and sometimes abuse, their children. Nor it is gay men who rape other men. The gender of violence is, to a staggering extent, masculine and heterosexual.

"If dominance, force, and control are crucial aspects of even the most standard scripts of heterosexual interaction," Michael Awkward (1995, 99) asks, "how do we participate in the experience of heterosexuality in ways that do not mark our enactments of sexual desire as socially transgressive?" Perhaps one doesn't, unless one abandons the heterosexual position—that is, positioning oneself as "straight," as "the man"—and becomes, for instance, a "girl" in a "lesbian" relationship, the "fem" one at that. Then one *might* avoid being "socially transgressive," might avoid seeing "the female body's figurations as site of recreational phallic desire" (Awkward 1995, 107). Better yet, be gay. Play the "straight" guy to a "fem" guy's "girl" if one *must* experience "heterosexuality" as "phallic desire." Then women might be safe, at least within relationships. For it is in relationships, as Hearn understands, that men's violence to women becomes sexualized.

In fact, men's (straight men's) violences toward women tend to occur in "intimate," usually sexual, that is, heterosexual relationships: "Estimates based on national and regional surveys ... show that ten to twenty-five percent of British women have, at some time, during their life, been the victim of violence from a male partner" (Dobash et al. 1996, 2). Hearn is quick to add that such figures tend to underreport verbal, psychological violence and abuse, and rape, especially coerced sex within the context of ongoing intimate relationships. Women are most at risk with the man with whom they are in closest relationship. Why, Hearn asks, is it that men are most dangerous to the women with whom they are the most intimate? As he understands, "this effectively raises the question of the relationship of men's violence to women and men's heterosexuality and heterosexual relations" (Hearn 1998, 5).

To pursue this question requires for men to cultivate a critical relation to "men," to stop taking the category for granted, as if it were somehow "natural," and in fact to become skeptical of the primary modes of masculinity, especially compulsory heterosexuality. Hearn (1998, 6) puts the matter this way: "For men to do this [to challenge the taken-for-granted notion of "men"] involves a challenge to the way we are; it involves a critique of ourselves, that is, first, personally; second, in terms of other men we are in contact within our personal or public lives; and *also*, third, more generally and socially, towards men as a powerful social category, a powerful social grouping." I shall focus on his second element, the relation of men to other men, especially white men to black men. The relation of misogyny to homophobia, and the relation of those to violence, including racial violence, will, I hope, become somewhat clearer.

In the next section I will survey, impressionistically, the violence of men, focusing on rape and war. In Hearn's study, focusing as it does on British heterosexual men, the following violences are reported: "rape fantasies; sexual wrestling; long-term verbal abuse; restraining, holding, blocking; throwing against the wall; slapping, hitting, striking, punching, beating up, attempted murder; murder; the use of sticks, knives and other objects and weapons; rape; abduction; torture, throwing and smashing things, for example, bottles, damaging property, houses, furniture, cars" (Hearn 1998, 12). Many men, in this instance straight men, seem quite ready to destroy pretty much anything and anybody. Why would that be?

Hearn reviews the research on the biochemical bases of masculinized behaviors, noting that in some animal studies, surges in testosterone appear to be followed by increased aggression toward sexual partners and to food, as well as greater vigilance regarding potential territorial infringement by other males. Hearn also notes that some animal studies indicate that victory in struggles for dominance tends to increase testosterone levels, while defeat tends to decrease them. In studies of human males, surges in testosterone often occurred at puberty, as well as during sexual arousal. But testosterone levels were also found to increase in a variety of other situations, such as winning in sports, after successful athletic or other physical accomplishments, even with nonphysical achievements and social celebrations. However, Hearn underscores, the relation between testosterone and dominance is no simple one. For instance, increases in testosterone have been detected following *decisive* victories, such as winning tennis matches *decisively* (Mazur and Lamb 1980). Similar results were found in wrestling matches (Elias 1981). Hearn (1998) summarizes these studies: (1) men who had committed violent crimes at a younger age were found to have higher testosterone levels (Kreuz and Rose 1972); (2) men who committed violent crimes were found to have higher levels than other convicts (Dabbs et al. 1987); (3) prisoners who were rated "tougher" by other inmates were found to have higher levels (Dabbs et al. 1987); and (4) men who committed violent crimes and prisoners who enjoyed high status within the institution both had higher levels than other prisoners (Ehrenkranz, Bliss, and Sheard 1974).

In order to make sense of such findings, Kemper (1990) has argued for the establishment of a field of sociopsychoendocrinology, in order to study reciprocal links among testosterone, aggression, dominance/eminence, social structure, and sexual behavior. Hearn also acknowledges biologically based studies of aggression and violence that focus upon human intervention in the biochemical sphere, such as in studies of steroids (Haupt and Rovere 1984). These studies, Hearn notes, also underscore the need for additional social and biological research.

Hearn (1998) reviews psychological and psychoanalytic research on masculinity, starting with the work of I. D. Suttie (1935), who argued in *The Origins of Love and Hate* that it was the "taboo" on tenderness imposed on boys that prompted their differentiation from women, a differentiation sufficiently violent as to stimulate and direct their development toward violence. This theme is echoed in Jukes's (1993) *When Men Hate Women*, in which the conflicted complexity of boys' relations with their mothers is seen as remaining a potential, and, for him, an almost inescapable source, of hate and violence well into adult life (Hearn 1998).

Acknowledging the complexity of dependency, and specifically the psychodynamics of male gender identity formation, Hearn cites Nancy Chodorow's (1978) *The Reproduction of Mothering* (to which we will return in the context of matrifocality; see chapter 14) and Jessica Benjamin's (1988) *The Bonds of Love* and *In the Shadow of the Other* (1998). For Benjamin, Hearn notes, domination begins with efforts to deny dependency; in fact the origin of domination may reside in the breakdown of the inevitable tension between self and other. Domination and its related forms of violence tend to be the consequences of the complex dynamics of self-differentiation and fusion, specifically, the exaggerated maintenance of difference. In Hearn's (1998, 22) words: "Domination and desire are not ... opposites: domination does not repress desire; rather domination and violence use and transform desire—the bonds of love."

Another important strand of research on men's violence Hearn cites is "reactive" theory, a theory which resembles, it seems to me, Dollard's (1937, 1939) frustration/aggression theory of lynching and racial violence. Evidently influential in thinking about both child abuse and men's violence to women (Straus, Gelles, and Steinmetz 1980), this approach points out factors such as low income, unemployment, part-time employment and a greater number of children as associated with men's violence toward children and "between spouses." A somewhat similar logic is sometimes found in explanations of men's violence to women as associated with men's alcohol use/abuse. While acknowledging that there appears to be association between the two, Horsfall (1991) points to some of the difficulties in conceptualizing alcohol as a direct cause of men's violence, among them the possibility that both may have a similar etiology through other individual, social or structural conditions and circumstances. Horsfall concludes: "If their [men's] gender identification is positional, their self-esteem shaky, work or sport are closed to them or work is a frustration in itself, then drinking with the 'boys' may make them feel like 'men.' Behaving in an authoritarian way at home may also provide a similar opportunity" (1991, 85; quoted in Hearn 1998, 28). For Frances Willard and her colleagues in the W.C.T.U., such distinctions would have seemed overdrawn.

As Hearn points out, such interpretation fails to answer why it is that so many men respond to these situations in violent ways, and why the social structuring of "boys" and "men" takes these violent rather than more pacific forms. Hearn criticizes reactive approaches for employing degendered terminology, such as "spouse," "marital," "parent," terms which deemphasize the gendered character of violence. He also dislikes how stress is conceptualized as a separate causal factor in stress-based theory, whereas in fact stress—he uses the more broad and vague term "change"—is a constant feature of "family life." Left unanswered in stress theories, he repeats, is why stress prompts men to be violent and not women, at least not to the same physicalized extent.

The problem of terminology is important, Hearn insists. He critiques the widely used notion of "domestic violence," as well as well-known phrases such as "conjugal violence," "marital violence" and "family violence." Such constructs, he points out, take the family or the conjugal or marital relationship as their empirical focus, conceptual assumption, and theoretical framework. In doing so, they relocate the political problem away from men. Hearn acknowledges that some family focused approaches draw attention to the relational context of violence, but they also tend to divert attention from who does what to whom, and thereby fail to name and acknowledge the omnipresence of straight men's violence.

True, gender and gendered violence is relational, Hearn notes, but it is also true that all violence is not a function of "the relationship," but of the man in relation to others, usually women and children. Unfortunately this fact has not always been pinpointed in family violence or family therapy studies. More often, Hearn continues, violence has been located in the family "as a whole," that is, as a system or a structure. The mistake here resides in the implication that it is "the family" that does the violence, when in fact "the family" does not "do violence." "[V]iolence," Hearn (1998, 29) reminds, "is done by people, usually men, albeit within violating relationships, including those of families," but above all, by heterosexually identified men.

Hearn argues that family violence, and specifically men's violences to women, must be situated in the context of the analysis of men, rather than within the context of violence or "domestic violence." This requires us to understand the social construction of men and masculinities, not just violence itself, as if it were a degendered phenomenon (Newburn and Stanko 1994; Collier 1995). Others have argued that violence and masculinity are interwoven. For instance, Messerschmidt (1993) insisted that crime, including violence, functions as a resource in the making of masculinity, at least in specific forms of masculinity. The production and reproduction of masculinities is discussed by Miedzian (1992) in her description of the functions of violence in the upbringing of boys and sons (see also Jackson 1990). Both Miedzian and Jackson emphasize that the socialization of boys, that is, the construction of masculinity, occurs within broader society and is inextricably interconnected with violence. Stanko (1994) has examined the masculinity/violence link in order to explicate the power of violence in negotiating masculinities. While this approach is important in considering men's violence to each other, such a "simultaneous but negotiated" analysis, Hearn (1998) argues, must be extended to men's reproduction of violence/masculinity in relation to women. But if, as I have argued, men's violences to women are in part a function of their deformed relations to one another, the two *are* very much interconnected (Pinar 1983/1994/1998).

Hearn acknowledges that all men are not violent all the time, nor it is only men who are violent. But it is men who dominate the business of violence, men who seem to specialize in violence. Moreover, "all men can be violent" (Hearn 1998, 36–37), and in fact "some men simply enjoy violence, or at least say they do." The reproduction of men's violences to women, and to themselves, occurs generationally, and, evidently, across class, race, culture (at least the dominant cultures). The performance of violence seems key to the performance of masculinity, at least heterosexual masculinity. (The case of gay men's sadomasochistic sexual practices is another story; see Bersani [1995, 79 ff.].) But Hearn forgets to add that adjective and says simply: "Being violent is an accepted, if not always acceptable, way of being a man. Doing violence is, that is, available as, a resource for demonstrating and showing a person is man." He is thinking not only of rape and of abuse in the home, but as well of quite public performances of masculinity in the public sphere: "The connections between violence and masculinity are everywhere—in the media, sport, film, representations of physical action, fantasy, and elsewhere" (Hearn 1998, 37).

That acknowledged, Hearn returns to the primary and inescapable fact that it is not gay men who are raping women, refusing to pay child support: "[t]he more general question to what extent heterosexual relations are necessarily harassing" (Hearn 1998, 37). This acknowledgment—he does not seem eager to make it; it is as if he is reminded of an unpleasant fact—is automatic when focusing on the genre of violence, which is his specialization, that violence which occurs in the context of intimate, often marital, relations (see Delphy and Leonard 1992). Hearn is interested, then, in what he terms the question of "known-ness" and intimacy in all their multiple forms and expressions. Intimacy and intimate relations, he points out, typically involve confidences, trust, "care," psychological and physical closeness, conversation as well as silence shared together. Intimacy may or may not involve sex (Hearn 1998).

Because many of the violences that men perform occur within intimate relations with women (heterosexual men do not tend to have self-consciously intimate relations with each other), the closest relationship women experience with a man is often the most dangerous (or potentially dangerous) for them and/or their children. This paradoxical relation of danger and closeness is further complicated by the intermingling of "pleasure and danger" in both men's and women's sexuality (see MacCannell and MacCannell 1993). Sometimes sexualized violence occurs during the couple's closest moment, and, as Hearn (1998) notes, "the violence itself may be intimate, intricate, detailed, variegated, and based on intimate knowledge and knowledge of intimacy." Such violence "is predominantly violence in the context of *heterosexual* relations and relationships" (quoted in Hearn 1998, 38; emphasis in original). Hearn prefers to regard heterosexuality and violence as "linked in an intimate nexus—the sexuality/violence nexus—within particular forms of heterosexuality, than to see one as 'causing' the other" (159).

If heterosexuality, at least contemporary compulsory forms of it, seem inextricably bound up with the performance and achievement of masculinity, then I am not so sure Hearn's preference is appropriate. In one sense such heterosexuality is not about women at all, but about demonstrating virility to oneself and to other men. This is the well-known instance of the "traffic in women," in which women circulate as symbols or currency in a homosocial political economy. In a psychoanalytic and specifically object-relations sense, heterosexual men cannot finally escape the echoes of their earlier rejection of the preoedipal symbiotic identification with the mother. In this scenario, adult male heterosexuality recapitulates, or threatens to recapitulate (especially when coupled with psychological intimacy) the earlier (and no doubt forgotten) struggle of disentangling self from the other, from the "phallic" or "engulfing" mother. In this regard, it is not insignificant that Hearn found that "in the text of violence, men (apart from a deliberately threatening minority) generally locate their *violent self as somewhere else*" (Hearn 1998, 106). It is a self long repressed, a developmental moment long forgotten, in which the boy's identification with the mother had to be broken and suppressed. In those acts of intrapsychic "rape" and violence, the contemporary heterosexual man is born.

War

Are straight men—as a category, not every individual—in some sense always at war? Certainly war would seem to be a boy's game ... I mean a *man*'s game. But why? What are the gendered attractions of war? J. Glenn Gray (1996, 47, 49) suggests one answer: "the delight in seeing, the delight in comradeship, the delight in destruction." "War," he suggests, is a spectacle, "something to see." There is, he says, "in all of us" what the Bible characterized as "the lust of the eye," a phrase, like the universality of his claim, "at once precise and of the widest connotation." It is not "beauty," not in any ordinary sense, that appeals to men in such spectacles of destruction: "it is the fascination that manifestation of power [the phallus?] and magnitude hold for the human spirit." Staring at men all day every day: is that the "lust of the eye"? Gods and monsters.

Comradeship is involved in the "pleasure" of war, although, Gray (1996, 52) acknowledges, "men can live in the same room and share the same suffering without any sense of belonging together. They can live past each other and be irresponsible toward each other, even when their welfare is clearly dependent on co-operation." For many soldiers, at least since ancient Greece, being comrades has meant being lovers (Bérubé 1990; Percy 1996). For some men, then, the attraction of war has to do with its sense of spectacle and power, for others some dimly perceived sense of being together as comrades, and yet for others it has meant sex and, on occasion, love. But for most war is about death. And not only death of men. It has been estimated that in the twentieth century, women and children constituted 80 percent of the casualties of modern warfare (Clatterbaugh 1996).

It seems to me that Margaret Atwood (1994, 3) understands war. If you add "straight" before "men" in the following passage, the picture becomes even clearer:

> The history of war is a history of bodies. That's what war is: bodies killing other bodies, bodies being killed. Some of the killed bodies are those of women and children, as a side effect you might say. Fallout, shrapnel, napalm, rape and skewering, anti-personnel devices. But most of the killed bodies are men. So are most of those doing the killing. Why do men want to kill the bodies of other men? Women don't want to kill the bodies of other women. By and large. As far as we know.

Could it be we murder what we cannot bear to experience as objects of desire? Atwood's title is "alien territory." Is that where straight men live, estranged from their (homosexual) desire? Is that what makes them edgy, and not so very happy? Enough whiskey consumed and someone might be raped. In prison no whiskey is required.

War is a homosocial affair among men. Michael Kimmel quotes an army general who insists that what every soldier fears is "losing the one thing he is likely to value more than life—his reputation as *a man among other men*" (quoted in Kimmel 1996, 7). Understanding war as a homosocial communication suggests it is a point men make to other men, a point about honor, about power, about sex. Consider the story Slavoj Zizek (1995) tells of heterosexual rape during the Bosnian War. He tells of soldiers' eyes locked into the eyes of the father of the girl they are serially raping. That's male bonding, homosocial desire (Sedgwick 1985); that is trafficking in women (Rubin 1975). Stoltenberg (1989/1990, 86) is clear: "When male combat troops do aggress against the territorial rights of other men, their actual military strategy often involves heterosexual rape of women belonging to those men (for example, American soldiers in Vietnam). But the aggression men fear, and the fear upon which their 'national defense' is predicated, is aggression from other men—that is, homosexual attack." Is that the subtext of the fear of invasion?

If homosexual desire and fear circulate among men in the military, would it be unsurprising if it surfaced racially? If lynching was rape, is all racial violence gendered violence? Was the experience of the first African American admitted to West Point what we would term "hazing"? On April 17, 1880, James Webster Smith, the first black cadet in the history of West Point, was "taken from his bed, gagged, bound, and severely beaten, and then his ears were slit." Webster was unable to identify his assailants. The other (white) cadets claimed that he did it to himself (Ginzburg 1962/1988, 9). A twentieth-century student of male-male rape asserts: "[M]ilitary culture, not sexual orientation, is in fact the predominant influence on the same-sex rape behavior of servicemen" (Scarce 1997, 46).

Ah, for God and sodomy. In ancient days, victorious soldiers sometimes sodomized prisoners of war before killing them. For instance, the Ancient Egyptians, when victorious in battle, had a "ceremonial custom of buggering defeated troops, thereby asserting sexual and political mastery over them" (Woods 1987, 53). In 1990 the *New York Times* reported that ethnic tensions among the soldiers of the crumbling Soviet army had erupted in murder and male-male rape. Also in 1990, the *Washington Times* reported the rape of Kuwaiti men by Iraqis soldiers as part of the Iraqi invasion (Scarce 1997). Not all sex in the military is forced of course; one famous (and controversial) survey found that 40 percent of men enjoyed at least incidental homosexual relations while in the American armed services (Kinsey, Pomeroy, and Martin 1948). But to desublimate the homosociality of the military, as Clinton's 1993 pledge to end the Pentagon's ban on lesbians and gays in the military threatened to do, endangers "national security." We shall focus briefly on that event in chapter 19 (section III).

In his study of homoerotic desire and feminine influence in nineteenth-century American fiction, Scott S. Derrick argued that because overt homosexuality was not generally narratable as itself—recall it was not popularized as a concept until the early twentieth century—it surfaced as a fictional obsession with "the plot of death and disaster, which authorizes a violent and genocidal penetration of the male body, and which also produces emergencies that authorize the expression of tenderness and the giving of care. The most culturally acceptable culmination of desire between men involves the annihilation or near annihilation of one of the parties" (1997, 90). This dynamic is evident in Stephen Crane's novel of the Civil War, *Red Badge of Courage*, in which Crane is fascinated with a "queer kind of hurt" (quoted in Derrick 1997, 182).

Is this "kind of hurt" related to nostalgia, that nostalgia which seems to accompany combat and militancy generally? Kim Michasiw (1994, 156) links the two, defining "nostalgia [as] a gentrified keeping buried of loss, [and] militancy [as] an ordered regime of misdirection understood as a cause or a code." That cause may be nationalism or patriotism but in its gendered mobilization, Michasiw continues, "militancy is a skewed fixing of the subject's affective position, an assertive, even manic manliness ... pinned and sentimentalized by the nostalgia." Is that nostalgia for the male body? "Militancy," Michasiw continues, "allows the subject to go on about its business of appearing to search while averting its gaze from anything that might give the lie to its aboriginality. ... The latter [nostalgia] assures the subject that what is lost [homosexual desire] will stay that way while the former [militancy] ensures that the subject will make its way without stumbling across what it marches in search of" (1994, 156).

In the twentieth century (about which Paul Monette [1992a, 2] declares bitterly but correctly: "Genocide is still the national sport of straight men, especially in this century of nightmares"), what the subject is "in search of" becomes clearer as homosexuality is more overt. So is the sexual symbolism of certain "military" practices. Consider, for instance, the military dictatorship in Argentina some two decades ago, during which time thousands were murdered or simply disappeared. These Argentine "patriots" used, among others, the following technique of torture: rats were placed inside a tube plugged on one side that was then inserted open ended into the victim's anus or vagina. Slowly, painfully, the rats tore away at the victims' internal organs, finally killing them (Simon 1996).

Did these men actually believe patriotism was involved? This was about fucking, rats substituting for men's dicks. As Susan Brownmiller (1975/1993) discovered during her research into wartime rape, the ramming of a stick, a bottle or some other object into a woman's vagina is not uncommon. Police department m.o. sheets in Los Angeles and Denver provide blanks to be checked off next to "inserts object in vagina." The Denver form also lists "inserts foreign object into rectum" (quoted in Brownmiller 1975/1993, 195). Brownmiller notes: "Castration, the traditional coup de grace of a lynching, has its counterpart in the gratuitous acts of defilement that often accompany a rape, the stick rammed up the vagina, the attempt to annihilate the sexual core" (1975/1993, 255).

This capacity for violation and torture is not rare among men. The National Institute of Mental Health has estimated that those in the United States with antisocial personality disorder is 3 percent of men but fewer than 1 percent of women. Antisocial personality disorder is most commonly diagnosed in the 26- to 40-year-old age group; thereafter, the incidence decreases (Simon 1996). Are younger men more dangerous than older ones? Is that because they are so determined to be "men"? Remembering himself as a university student Goebbels (A&E 1997) mused: "I wanted to become a man." Perhaps we should fear those who want to become "men." How does one become a "man" in most cultures? One must take a wife, then have "kids." Ah, the family, which Foucault (1978, 109) judges to be "the most active site of sexuality." If the statistics that follow are not misleading, the family is also the most active site of violence.

Family Values

Twenty to fifty percent of all murders occur within the family. The most common predictor of stalking is domestic violence. Where domestic violence exists, approximately 60 percent of children are physically or sexually abused. During 1997, approximately 2,000 children died as a consequence of child abuse (CNN 1998). Approximately 30 percent of women who suffer physical injury by spousal abuse are eventually murdered by their husbands. The F.B.I. estimates that one in four women who are murdered are killed by husbands or live-in partners. Every physician in America, regardless of specialty or location of his or her practice, has seen a battered woman in his or her office in the last two weeks (Simon 1996).

Such statistics prompted former Surgeon General Antonia Novella to launch the American Medical Association's (A.M.A.) *Campaign Against Family Violence* in 1991 by suggesting that the home is actually a more dangerous place for American women than city streets. The U.S. Public Health Service, the C.D.C., the American College of Obstetricians and Gynecologists, the American Nurses Association, and the A.M.A. have all agreed that family violence constitutes the number one health threat to American women. In other words: "The safest place for men is at home; the home is, by contrast, the least safe place for women" (Edwards 1989, 214). Dobash and Dobash (1992, 2; quoted in Hearn 1998, 4) comment: "It is now well known that violence in the home is commonplace, that women are its usual victims and men its usual perpetrators. It is also known that the family is filled with many different forms of violence and aggression, including physical, sexual, and emotional, and that violence is perpetrated by young and old alike." Conclusion? "Home can be a very dangerous place—even more dangerous than a dark city alley at night" (Simon 1996, 51). In the early 1990s many Republicans insisted that we need a Defense of Family Act. How about a Defense of People Trapped in Families Act?

Nor is men's violences upon women and children within the family a recent phenomenon, as the work of Elizabeth Pleck (1987) makes clear. During the years from 1874 to 1890, for instance, in response to a number of highly publicized cases of assault on children, concerned citizens created organizations to intervene in the pandemic of family violence. It is possible, given the publicity and the efforts of law enforcement agencies, that the incidence of child abuse might actually be lower now than during earlier periods when such violence was less likely to be reported, and more than likely covered up.

Heterosexually identified women are not the only ones at risk from angry male partners. David Island and Patrick Letellier (1991) estimate that some 5,000 gay men are victims of domestic violence every year. The National Coalition of Anti-Gay Violence Programs released a 1996 report which indicated domestic violence may be no less common among gay male couples than heterosexual couples, but the victims receive even less sympathy when seeking protection and support they need (Scarce 1997). Even butch *gay* guys are headed straight to hell.

Those men who support the "gracious submission" of women say they represent God. The church is God's family on earth. Right. Between 1984 and 1992, 400 Catholic priests in North America were reported to have molested children. The Catholic Church has paid out $400 million in victim settlements, legal fees, and bills for medical care of the errant priests. It is estimated that in a few years' time, the tab may reach $1 billion (Simon 1996).

Priests are hardly the only category of men who use their professional power to sexually aggress against the less powerful. Between 20 percent and 30 percent of all female graduate students have been sexually approached by their professors. Quasi- and nonprofessionals are active too. Thousands of children are killed each year by abusive caretakers, not just nannies but mothers' boyfriends and teenaged babysitters. Tens of thousands are the victims of sexual abuse. The current estimate is that between 100,000 and 300,000 children are sexually abused each year. Approximately 6 percent of men and 15 percent of women had been abused as children, one-third of them before age 9. Other surveys set the percentages of abuse at 9 percent for men and 19 percent for women. Males were 94 percent of the abusers in one study. Another study concluded that 50 percent of the abusers were relatives and that 80 percent of abuse is at the hands of either a parent or legal guardian (Simon 1996).

If women try to escape their gendered positions of "gracious submission," more than a few men go after them. Stalking is recognized today as a major social problem. Approximately 200,000 stalkers are said to be stalking at any given moment in the United States. At some time during her life, one out of every twenty women will be pursued by a former boyfriend, an ex-husband, or a stranger. Most stalkings are associated with domestic violence, often when the woman attempts to leave the relationship. In 1992, 29 percent of all women who were murdered were killed by their husbands or boyfriends. The Centers for Disease Control and Prevention reports that domestic abuse is responsible for more injuries to women each year than the combined total caused by minor automobile accidents, rapes, and muggings. Nearly all stalkers are men who have been rejected by women (Simon 1996). Stalking is nothing less than "psychological terrorism" (Simon 1996, 63). Heterosexuality can be dangerous for women. And to black men.

BMOC: Big Man on Campus

A single event sometimes expresses something essential about men, in this case a heterosexual man who felt threatened by feminism. On December 6, 1989, Marc Lepine mounted a well-planned aggressive armed assault at the School of Engineering (Ecole Polytechnique) at the University of Montreal. Expressing his rage against women, he killed or injured fourteen people with a rifle. After one wounded victim screamed for help, Lepine pulled out his knife and stabbed her repeatedly in the chest until she was dead. Finally he put the muzzle of the rifle against his head, said "Oh shit," and shot himself. It was the worst mass murder and hate crime against women in Canadian history. Lepine left a suicide note that said:

> Please note that if I kill myself today 12/06/89 it is not for economic reasons (because I waited until I used up all my financial means even refusing jobs) but for political reasons. Because I decided to send Ad Patres [meaning gathered to the fathers, or simply, dead] the feminists who have always ruined my life. For seven years my life has brought me no joy, and, being utterly weary of the world, I have decided to stop those shrews dead in their tracks. (quoted in Simon 1996, 248)

Six months later, Lepine claimed his last victim. One Sarto Blais, an engineer who had been at the same school and who could not rid himself of his memories of the killings of his classmates and friends, hanged himself. Then his parents, seeing no reason to go on living, committed suicide as well (Simon 1996).

While spectacular, the event was not entirely unique. Violence on campus is not uncommon. In 1993, students and faculty on college campuses were victims of 1,353 robberies, 3,224 aggravated assaults, 7,350 motor vehicle thefts, 21,478 burglaries, 466 rapes, and 17 murders. This violence was gendered, much of it directed toward women and racial and sexual minorities. Twenty-one percent of lesbian and gay students, compared to 5 percent of the total student body, report having been physically attacked (Comstock 1991).

Thirty years ago Edgar Friedenberg described what he called the "vanishing adolescent." Perhaps today, adolescents in "crisis" would be an more apt phrase. There has been a 300 percent increase in teenage suicides in recent decades and shocking incidence of juvenile crime, homicide, illegitimate pregnancies, drug use, venereal disease, and HIV/AIDS. In a study of antiblack and anti-Semitic assaults, vandalism, and harassment, the New York City Police Department found that approximately 78 percent of those arrested on bias charges in 1985 were nineteen years old and younger, half of them younger than sixteen (Comstock 1991).

Indeed, near every report on prejudice involving vandalism (against property) and violence (against people) records that those most frequently involved are aged fifteen to twenty-five. Elisabeth Young-Bruehl (1996, 299) reports: "The case literature for studying the origins and developments of the various prejudice types suggests that adolescence is the key period for the conversion of incipient prejudices into fully articulated prejudices and acts of discrimination or violence." The Ku Klux Klan targets adolescents in its recruitment drives (Young-Bruehl 1996). The majority of lynchers—and lynching victims—were also young (Ayers 1984).

In one study of "young people," Gary David Comstock reports, we learn that many teenaged boys characterize their favorite activities as "rough sports," the most popular of these being football. One respondent reported he likes "mauling people, and hurting 'em so they're afraid to come again." (Of course, in an athletic context, by "people" he means other boys.) That is important, the respondent continued, because "I want others to know about me. ... If you hurt someone, or shoot an animal in hunting, you know you are somebody. ... The pain on the face of the adversary or the lifeless carcass are witness to your awful power" (quoted in Comstock 1991, 104). Football and other team sports fail to excite many gay men, Mark Simpson points out. Why? "It might be argued," he suggests, "that with their homosexuality completely (or mostly) desublimated they have no need for them; for gay men team sports are experienced not as sexualized aggression, just aggression" (Simpson 1994, 90).

It is the very brutality of the game of football, Simpson (1994) contends, that makes permissible the obvious homoerotic moments: the hugs, the slaps on the butt, boys piling on top of boys, a sublimated version of gang rape in uniform. "In this masculine universe, Simpson (1994, 71, 73) observes, "there can be no loveliness without horror; pleasure is circumscribed by pain, gain by loss, love by hate; each goal scored and game won, each and every joy attained, is wrung from the despair of other men." That violence makes the experience of homoeroticism permissible. Of course, all such desire must be focused upon the game. Again Simpson understands exactly: "[I]nterest in men is permitted, indeed encouraged, but must always be expressed through the game. A man's love for football is a love of and for manhood, composed of a condensation of introjected (turned inwards) homoerotic desire."

In the *Three Essays on Sexuality* (1905/1953/1995), Freud argued that adolescence is the stage in which the libidinal developments and the oedipal configurations of childhood are reactivated and recapitulated, including homoerotic feelings for the father. A colleague of Anna Freud, Peter Blos (1979, 68) observed that one of the features of the adolescent revival of the Oedipus complex is that "polarities of masculinity and femininity reign supreme." Unlike most prelatency children, American teenagers, especially boys, cannot tolerate feeling homosexual desire, cannot enjoy it in the mode that Freud once called "polymorphous perversity," pleasure in all the erogenous zones and any and all sexes of objects (quoted in Young-Bruehl 1996, 316).

Blos argued that the negative Oedipus complex (or boys' desire for the father) waits for adolescence for its resolution. To become a "man" requires destroying this same-sex object relation; to do so many adolescents employ what Blos calls the "oedipal defense." That defense involves the use of "heterosexual fantasies and behaviors defensively, to cover or to block the original homosexual object relation or whatever substitutes for the original have come from ties to other same-sex adults or peers" (Young-Bruehl 1996, 317). According to Blos (1979, 68; quoted in Young-Bruehl 1996, 317), "since the resolution of the negative Oedipus complex is the task of adolescence, the coming to terms with the homosexual component of pubertal sexuality is an implicit developmental task of adolescence." Is that why fraternity brothers and athletes and just plain "buds" obsess over "women" while "hanging" with each other? Is that why intense homosocial bonds can suddenly explode into violence, oedipal competition mixed with homosexual suppression?

While going a long way toward explaining the explosiveness of especially male adolescence in America, the fact of pandemic male violence is still a mystery, at least to me. How to explain the following? In Olivehurst, California, Eric Huston returned to his old high school and killed four people to take revenge on those he held responsible for preparing him for such a "lousy job" with Hewlett-Packard, from which he had been fired (quoted in Simon 1996, 249). Boys murdered other students and teachers in 1997 in Pearl, Mississippi, and West Paducah, Kentucky, in 1998 in Arkansas and Oregon, and in 1999 in Littleton, Colorado, and Conyers, Georgia. During 1993, 39 percent of urban school districts reported a shooting or a knifing, 23 percent had a drive-by shooting, and 15 percent reported at least one rape. Most violence in the workplace is committed by white men (Simon 1996). If the shootings mentioned above are any indication, it appears most violence in schools is committed by white boys.

Approximately 40 percent of the boys (and 12 percent of the girls) in South Carolina's public schools reported carrying a weapon to school in the preceding 30 days; knives were the weapon carried most frequently, except that black males were more likely to have carried guns (Valois et al. 1993). College students are only slightly less likely to carry guns or other weapons. Approximately 14 percent of male college students carry a weapon on campus; 5 percent carry a gun (Douglas et al. 1997).

One form of gendered violence is bullying, which remains a problem in many schools. In Minnesota a third-grade student reported that he was at first bullied, then sexually harassed by other boys at school over a period of several months. Jonathan Harms, a student in the Sauk Rapids-Rice School District, was at first ignored, not only by school officials but as well by a regional office of O.C.R. [Office of Civil Rights, Department of Education], which at first refused to investigate. Finally, Harms taped his verbal harassment by concealing a small tape recorder. What became clear is that the boy had been sexually taunted over a period of months by about a dozen of his male classmates in the third grade. Harassment became sexual assault when the boys pulled Harms's pants and underwear down to below his knees (Stein 1995).

What we need, many insist, is "discipline" in our schools and colleges. Safety yes, but sometimes school discipline can be a bit too strict, even when practiced at home. A 30-year-old model police officer with numerous commendations, one Henry Hubbard, was the last man police would have suspected as a predawn rapist. A psychological evaluation later revealed that Hubbard's father had regularly humiliated and abused him. During the week his father was a sober, respected school administrator and teacher. As the week ended, he became a monster. The son, too, followed this Dr. Jekyll and Mr. Hyde routine. He pled either guilty or no contest to numerous counts of kidnapping, robbery, rape, and attempted murder; he received a prison sentence of 56 years (Simon 1996).

Hubbard is hardly the only police officer guilty of desublimating his official position. Susan Brownmiller (1975/1993) reports the case of James J. Farley, a New York City police detective assigned to the robbery squad and the recipient of four citations in six outstanding years of service. In October 1972, officer Farley was quietly suspended from the force when he was arrested and charged with raping a fifteen-year-old girl in nearby Suffolk County the previous June. A small item about his arrest and suspension appeared in the newspapers and Brownmiller filed it. In February 1974, another small news item caught her eye. James Farley had been sentenced to fifteen years in prison when he confessed to the rape at gunpoint of two women on the West Side of Manhattan. In addition, Farley had received a twelve-year sentence in another jurisdiction for three other rapes in the borough of Queens and his Suffolk County case was still pending. Farley's career as a rapist, Brownmiller learned, had occurred while he was a member in good standing of the New York police department. In the course of monitoring New York newspapers over a four-year period, Brownmiller reports that one new police rapist per year had been apprehended, that is, one new case per year in which the evidence against a policeman was sufficient to warrant his arrest and department suspension that was announced to the public. Nor is tendency to rape restricted to New York City policemen; on Thanksgiving Day, 1973, three Detroit policemen were suspended from the force and charged with rape and sodomy (Brownmiller 1975/1993). Is desire the call of the law?

Serial Murderers

While there have been notable serial sexual murderers overseas—Dennis Nilsen killed 15 men who visited his London flat; Chikatilo killed at least 52 victims at various sites all over Russia—the United States produces more serial sexual murderers than any other country: 75 percent. Probably less sophisticated crime detection techniques in other less industrialized countries contribute to some underreporting of serial sexual killers outside the United States. That acknowledged, the United States still leads the world in serial murderers. Fewer than 5 percent of serial killers are women. Serial killers can appear as quite ordinary and indistinguishable from other men (Simon 1996). Is freedom, for men, just "another word for nothing left to kill?" (Gitlin 1992, 30).

Even in the face of such massive violence, somehow conservative men insist on the antiquated "right to bear arms," even when this means emergency room personnel are the ones bearing arms, and legs, and other bullet-riddled body parts. The number of individuals killed each year by handguns in the United States was 400 times that in Great Britain and 220 times that in Japan (*F.B.I. Uniform Crime Reports* 1992). In 1994 alone, more Americans were killed with firearms than died in the Korean War. Firearms kill more people between the ages of 15 and 24 than all natural causes combined, and the most important predictor of carrying a weapon among college-age students is the male gender (National Center for Health Statistics 1994). Approximately six out of 10 homicide victims in the United States are killed with firearms; nine out of 10 are killed with a weapon of some type (knife, gun, etc.) (Center for Disease Control 1986). Males between the ages of 15 and 34 are at the highest risk of death from suicides and homicide in which guns are the weapons used. Who *are* these people?

Freud knew, or appeared to. In a discussion of sadism in the *Three Essays on Sexuality*, Freud observed that "the sexuality of most male human beings contains an element of aggressiveness—a desire to subjugate" (1905/1953/1995, 157–158; quoted in Silverman 1992, 187). Aggression, even a tendency toward sadism, would seem to typify heteronormative masculinity. Not only men know this about men; women know it, very well.

II. Straight Men Rape Women

[T]he exclusive sexual interest felt by men for women is also a problem that needs elucidating and is not a self-evident fact based upon an attraction that is ultimately of a chemical nature.

—Sigmund Freud, *The Ego and the Id* (1923/1977)

Violence sublimates same-sex desire and reinforces paranoid distances between men. At the same time, it terrorizes and subjugates women, who are necessary to establish the heterosexuality of the masculine order.

—Scott S. Derrick, *Monumental Anxieties: Homoerotic Desire and Feminine Influence in Nineteenth-Century U.S. Literature* (1997)

[T]he ethics of male sexual identity are essentially rapist.

—John Stoltenberg, *Refuing to Be a Man* (1989/1990)

Don't you mean *heterosexual* male identity, John? Even in male-on-male rapes the aggressors tend to be "straight." Gay men do not tend to rape women, now do they? During the last decade in the United States, rape has increased four times as fast as the overall crime rate. In 1992, 683,000 women reported being raped. More recently, nearly 18 percent of women in the United States reported having been raped or having been the victims of attempted rape at some point during their lives. In 1998 that translated into 17.7 million American women. More than half of the rape victims were under 17 when first raped. More than half of women reported that at one time in their lives they had been physically assaulted, ranging from slaps and punches to gun violence (Associated Press 1998). In another rape study, the National Women's Study, 20 percent of rapists were described as friends. Husbands committed 16 percent of rapes, boyfriends committed 14 percent, and 9 percent were committed by nonrelatives such as handymen, coworkers, neighbors. Estimates are that 1,871 women are raped in the United States every day, one every 1.3 minutes. Almost one-fifth of the victims are between the ages of 12 and 15. One out of every four women will be raped at some point during her lifetime, but fewer than 10 percent will report the assault (Simon 1996).

Possibly half of all women will be physically hurt by an intimate partner at least once in her lifetime (Walker 1979). Long-term intimacy is not a prerequisite for heterosexual male violence; at least 20 percent of dating relationships contain some physical violence (Hong 1998). No, this is not a two-way street; men commit 95 percent of all assaults on spouses (U.S. Department of Justice 1983). Nor is all this violence spontaneous, under the influence of alcohol or drugs or work stress; one-third of all women with injuries who enter a hospital emergency room are the victims of deliberate, premeditated acts of violence committed by intimate male partners. In fact, battering by a male partner accounts for more female injuries requiring medical attention than rapes, automobile accidents, and muggings combined (Hong 1998). An estimated 25–30 percent of pregnant women have experienced physical abuse just prior to and during pregnancy. Thirty percent of all female homicide victims were killed by husbands, boyfriends, ex-husbands, or ex-boyfriends (N.C.H.S. 1994/1996).

Fewer than 5 percent of the accused offenders will go to jail. Fifty-one percent of rapists are white, 42 percent black, and 6 percent have other racial or ethnic backgrounds. Power, not the joy of (hetero)sex, appears to be the major motivation for rape. Seventy-one percent of arrested rapists have prior criminal records: these prior crimes tend to be assault, robbery, and homicide. Fewer than 1 percent of all rapes and attempted rapes result in arrest and convictions. Those rapists who have been studied do not appear to be very different from other men. Rape fantasies are, it appears, rather common among the general male population (Simon 1996). The straight male population, that is.

Of course, many men do not consider violent sex fantasies instances of rape. A rape myth is defined as a "prejudice, stereotyped or false belief about rape, rape victims, and rapists" (Burt 1991, 26). Examples of rape myths include: "all women fantasize about being raped"; "a woman who doesn't want to be raped can't be raped"; "women who lead men on deserve to be raped"; "a woman who gets drunk is looking for sex"; and "men who rape are sexually deprived." These myths function to rationalize heterosexual men's sexually aggressive behaviors by blaming the victims for being raped (Calhoun and Townsley 1991; Bostwick, DeLucia-Waack, and Watson 1995). Moreover, these myths diminish the seriousness of acquaintance rapes, suggesting that they are not in fact "real rapes" (Burt 1991).

Another myth is that "real rapes" happen only at night, in dark, secluded alleys. A stranger disguised in a ski mask wielding a long dagger ravishes innocent young woman. The reality is that rape happens anywhere and everywhere, and it is often committed by husbands, boyfriends, acquaintances. As W.C.T.U. members knew one hundred years ago, alcohol can be a factor in male sexual assault. For instance, Antonia Abbey (1991a) found that while drinking on the part of the rapist tended to mitigate his guilt, drinking on the part of the victim tended to increase her responsibility in provoking the rape. She also found that men and women differed significantly in their perceptions of sexual intent on the basis of touch, friendliness, or flirtatious behavior. In general, men perceived higher levels of sexual interest from women than the women reported or intended. Whereas men (and women) readily identified types of clothing (e.g., low-cut blouse, slit skirt, high heels) that indicated a sexual invitation on the part of women in their eyes, neither men nor women could identify a comparable style of dress for men (Abbey 1991b).

Several studies have found that a strong belief in rape-related myths and stereotypes results in restricted definitions of rape, "not guilty" verdicts in mock rape trails (Burt and Albin 1981), a minimization of perceived injury to the victim (Calhoun, Selby, and Warring 1976), and even blaming rape victims for their victimization (Jones and Aronson 1973). Acceptance of men's rape myths is also a strong predictor of men's self-reported likelihood of raping.

Both males and females are socialized to believe rape myths from an early age. In a 1988 study of adolescent youth, 56 percent of girls and 76 percent of boys said that forced sex is acceptable under certain circumstances. For instance, if "he spends a lot of money on her" during a date, 39 percent of the males and 12 percent of the females said forced sex would be justified. Similarly, if "she's led him on" sexually, 54 percent of boys and 27 percent of girls believed forced sex was acceptable (Goodchilds et al. 1988, as cited by White and Humphrey 1991). A survey of 1,700 11–14 year olds conducted by the Rhode Island Rape Crisis Center in 1988 found that 31 percent of the boys and 32 percent of girls said it was okay for a man to rape a woman who had past sexual experiences, while 65 percent of the boys and 47 percent of the girls believed it was okay for a man to rape a woman if they had been dating for more than six months (White and Humphrey 1991). As Lynn Higgins and Brenda Silver (1991, 3) understand: "rape and rapability are central to the very construction of gender identity," namely heterosexual identity. Patti Lather and Chris Smithies (1997) remind us that, as Cindy Patton (1994) has pointed out, heterosexuality has always been dangerous for women, given the statistics on rape, domestic violence, and sexually transmitted diseases. AIDS raises the ante, as straight men often refuse to wear condoms, despite safer sex educational efforts to shift the focus from risk groups to risk behaviors.

There are two settings (one physical, one social) in which heterosexual male sexual aggression is heightened. First, straight men who live together in groups seem to experience aggravated levels of sexual tension. (Go figure.) Second, men whose primary social affiliation is with other men also tend to exhibit greater sexual aggressivity specifically, and exaggerated conformity to traditional male norms generally. Examples of such "fraternal" settings, include: campus fraternities (Sanday 1990; Sandler and Ehrhar 1985; O'Sullivan 1991, 1993; Martin and Hummer 1989; Hirsch 1990); intercollegiate and professional athletic teams, primarily football, basketball, lacrosse, and ice hockey, which are considered high contact sports (Sanday 1990; Messner 1992; Eskenazi 1991; Crosset and McDonald 1995); and military combat units, especially in times of war (Brownmiller 1975/1993; Pope 1993; Herman 1989; O'Sullivan 1992). Like fraternities and athletic teams, sectors of the U.S. military are typified by a culture of violence, as well, as in the Tailhook incident in September 1991 (Pope 1993).

Because straight-male (traditionally straight at least) groups such as fraternities, intercollegiate athletic teams, and soldiers tend to be involved in a disproportionate number of gang rape incidents, Chris O'Sullivan (1993) opposes campus fraternities and athletic teams. (What to do about the military—"Be all that you can be" promise the army ads—remains a puzzle.) If Indiana University's famed basketball coach is at all representative, universities cannot act fast enough in scaling down or closing altogether big-time, media-promoted team sports. Knight is reported to have placed sanitary napkins in the lockers of his players to shame them as "wusses" in order to make them play more aggressively. Once when asked by a television reporter how he handled stress, Knight responded, "I think if rape is inevitable, relax and enjoy it" (quoted in Kimmel 1996, 298).

With such a culture of hypermasculinity structuring homosocial groups such as sports teams, is it any surprise that studies have shown that members of fraternities and sports teams are not only more likely to commit sexual assaults as a group, but that studies also show that group members are more likely to perpetrate individual acts such as acquaintance rapes? O'Sullivan (1993, 25) is clear that "combined with male socialization in our society and the connotations of masculinity in our culture, fraternal cultures at schools and colleges breed a propensity to abuse women sexually, along a continuum of behaviors." They also abuse gay men (Comstock 1991).

Even nonviolent heterosexual relationships may be exploitative. A young man may have sex with a young woman to prove his manhood. And a young woman may use a young man to prove her womanhood. Moreover:

> Each may, unconsciously, also be borrowing a location for forbidden desires—he can put his feminine dimension in his girlfriend, and she can put her masculine dimension in her boyfriend. Similarly, each may be unconsciously taking on the other's desired characteristics—he may be against his conscious wishes taking on her femininity, and she may be against her conscious wishes taking on his phallic power. But these unconscious processes go on behind the scenes of proof of manhood or proof of womanhood. (Young-Bruehl 1996, 317)

This would seem to be a paradigmatic instance of the relocation of desire.

Campus Rape

Compared to sexual assault, less data is available on domestic, or courtship, violence on the college campuses. But we know that going out on "dates" can be risky; date rape is only one kind of acquaintance rape that occurs (Schwartz and DeKeseredy 1997). Coeds might keep in mind when they accept that date that over one-third of college men report that they would rape if they were sure they would not get caught. Approximately 15 percent of college women report having been raped (Candib and Schmitt 1996).

That figure may be too low. A study of campus rape sponsored by the National Institute of Mental Heath suggests so. Quantitative descriptive data regarding assaults, victims, and the social context of date rape were obtained from surveys administered to a nationally representative sample of 3,187 women and 2,972 men at undergraduate institutions across the U.S. Among the key findings were that 25 percent of women surveyed had an experience that met the legal definition of rape or attempted rape, 84 percent of those raped knew their attacker, and one in 12 college males surveyed had committed acts that met the legal definition of rape or attempted rape (Koss, Gidycz, and Wisniewski 1987).

If rape is understood at the end of a continuum of sexually aggressive behaviors, then one understands that the event is not exceptional. The potential for rape is present always, apparently, at least for heterosexually identified males. For instance, of 261 undergraduate psychology and business students interviewed at Auburn, 17 percent reported having committed both sexually and physically aggressive acts against their female partners (Hannan and Burkhart 1993). Rapes tend to occur in social settings, such as fraternities, which support rape-tolerant beliefs and condition members to adhere to them. Male assumptions regarding masculine sex roles were the most reliable predictors of college men's acceptance, even endorsement, of rape myths (Good et al. 1995).

The F.B.I. defines *group rape* as rape committed by three or more offenders. Twenty percent of all rapes are group or "multiple" rapes (Simon 1996). Is gang rape a growing fad, not only among street gangs, but in fraternity houses as well? Ten men rape an unconscious woman, not privately but surrounded by their male friends. Some of the terms used to describe these rapes include "beaching," the woman being likened to a "beached whale," and "spectoring," to emphasize how integral a role those who watch play (Bordo 1993, 275). In street language, gang rape is known as "running a train" (White and Cones 1999, 159). Is this simply a "safe" (i.e., "heterosexual") way for men to watch other men with erections? Certainly the term "spectoring" implies that. Marla Morris (1999, 99) points out that "the horde mentality allows defense mechanisms to vanish, unleashing all sorts of hatreds. Freud suggests that group ties are bound by thanatos and eros. Freud claims that, at bottom, group ties are sexual." *Homo*sexual?

Susan Brownmiller (1975/1993) reports a study of gang rape by a California group psychologist, W. H. Blanchard. Blanchard had focused on two sets of youthful gangs, one white and one black. While he did not indicate their ages, he called them "boys" and mentioned their placement in a juvenile custodial institution. Cautiously Blanchard suggests that gang rape is only ostensibly heterosexual: "The idea of 'sharing the girl among us fellows,' congregating around a common sexual object, and being sexually stimulated together as a group certainly have their homosexual implications." After discussing the dynamics among the boys, Blanchard concludes that Harry's admiration of Keith's machismo was "almost masochistic" and an "eroticized attachment ... so strong that it is just short of being overtly homosexual in its content." Two other gang members, Peter and Keith, were, as leaders, sexually stimulated by the presence of the other guys; as leaders they were able to stimulate the group, but, Blanchard concludes, Keith's feeling was "not as obviously homosexual" as Peter's (quoted in Brownmiller 1975/1993, 192–193).

Blanchard concludes that: "It is felt that the most interesting and unique aspect of the group examination is the degree to which sexual feelings in the leader are stimulated by the presence of the [male] group, his feeling that he must perform for them, and, in a sense, 'exhibit himself.' The degree to which the leader channels, crystallizes, and directs the attention of the group to sexual matters seems to be of primary importance in the development of a group rape" (quoted in Brownmiller 1975/1993, 193). Brownmiller scoffs at this point: "I don't think we need to go as far afield as Blanchard to gain some understanding of the group-rape phenomenon. Homosexuality, overt or latent, may be present in a variety of innocuous situations, such as Friday-night bowling 'with the boys,' and so what? (It may so be present in a Tuesday-night consciousness raising session with the women, and so what?) The Freudian approach to latent homosexuality, or ambivalence about homosexuality, has always been to sniff it out as a dangerous, causative factor, and this I believe is dangerous" (193). Her reading of Freud is of course overly simple, but it is more interesting to note how she uses her apparent concern over Blanchard's characterization of homosexuality in order to reject it altogether. In the next sentence, in fact, she becomes rather flippant, making the customary crack about prison:

> Harry may indeed have had a crush on Keith, and Peter, if he continued his life of crime, may today be happily raping other men in Soledad prison, but the reinforced sadistic impulses of both gangs, stemming from a need to find or prove their masculinity—a far cry from the need to either hide or "act out" their homosexuality—is much more central to the rape of women. ... Male bonding stems from a contempt for women, bolstered by distrust, and it is not, per se, homosexual. ... "Sharing the girl among us fellows" strengthens the notion of group masculinity and power. (Brownmiller 1975/1993, 193–194)

Not per se, perhaps, but certainly latently so.

Curiously, Brownmiller fails to see that heteronormative masculinity is built not only on contempt of women but on homosexual repression as well. Her fantasy about Soledad hints that somewhere she knows gang rape is not only about the woman, but in her commitment to female rape victims, she cannot acknowledge it. Like several other heterosexual feminists, Brownmiller tends toward heterosexism. She seems to conflate "sexuality" with "heterosexuality." She tends to assume that when men have sex with women, they aren't also having sex with each other.

Gang rapes committed by college males, in particular, by members of fraternities, typically follow a "script." The victim is selected by one of the fraternity brothers before the party or soon after she arrives. She is then "seduced" by that fraternity brother and led to a room where the other fraternity brothers are waiting. She is assaulted upon entering the room. Typically, alcohol is plentiful at such social events, alcohol which can render the victims helpless, sometimes unconscious (Hirsch 1990). How can this event be about her, or rather, *only* about her? It is also about them, just as lynching was. Certainly Brownmiller (1975/1993, 254) appreciates the parallel: "Women have been raped by men, most often by gangs of men, for many of the same reasons that blacks were lynched by gangs of whites."

The culture of rape is embedded, Kathleen Hirsch (1990) argues, in fraternity culture, especially in its language and its rituals. The gang rape event functions as a bonding ritual for its members, confirming their "macho masculinity." Because fraternities often attract men who tend to be insecure about their manhood, the brotherhood of the fraternity becomes a compensatory and powerful influence. Fraternities demand conformity and solidarity. Conformity is compelled by men bonding together against women (Hirsch 1990).

One is reminded of Anthony Rotundo's (1990; see chapter 6) research on late nineteenth-century "boy culture," where such conformity and solidarity—Nancy Cott (1990, 210) terms it "herding"—supported the formation of an "individual" and masculine identity by belonging to and being "like" a certain group, and unlike other groups. Boy culture was then and perhaps is now as much created by domesticity as restricted by it; determined to "prove" they are "men," boys and young men concentrate on distinguishing themselves from their "home," that is, mother and women, and from their fathers and other adult men (Cott 1990). The effort sometimes turns violent.

Significantly, sorority hazing is more psychological than physical. Fraternity hazing is both, especially physical and often sexualized (20/20 1999). Unlike sororities, since the early 1970s most fraternities have not been required to have adult supervision. Without supervision, the culture of rape may develop more easily. Certainly the sexual objectification of women remains a primary element of fraternity life; it is sometimes evident in fraternity serenades. In 1992, the UCLA-based feminist magazine *Together* (now called *FEM*) received an anonymous copy of the Phi Kappa Psi songbook in which one song—"S&M Man"—contained lyrics depicting female genital mutilation. Four male undergraduates at Cornell University posted on the Internet the "Top 75 reasons why women (bitches) should not have freedom of speech." Reason #20: "This is my dick. I'm gonna fuck you. No more stupid questions" (quoted in Jensen 1998, 99).

Some college males are unwilling to participate in such misogynistic performances. A Duke University student organization called Men Acting for Change (M.A.C.) is one of several men's groups at colleges and universities across the United States and Canada, such as Men Against Violence organized at Louisiana State University and elsewhere (Hong 1998). Besides meeting regularly to discuss men's issues, these groups present programs to fraternities and other campus groups about gender and sexuality, focusing on sexual violence and homophobia. M.A.C. members were interviewed about pornography on the A.B.C. newsmagazine program 20/20. On January 28, 1993, these college men described the negative effects of pornography on their (hetereo)sex lives and their relationships with women (Stoltenberg 1998). But these organizations represent a small fraction of college and university students.

Rape can be conceptualized as a consequence of sociocultural conditions that tend to conflate violence and sexuality. Therefore, it is difficult to differentiate rape from "normal," heterosexual relations, argues Dianne F. Herman (1989, 22), because "the image of heterosexual intercourse is based on a rape model of sexuality." This conflation of violence and lovemaking in the sexed subject position of the male heterosexual is suggested by the fact that many rapists do not regard their actions as rape. Many evidently imagine themselves as terrific lovers. Not only nineteenth-century white men had no clue what they were doing.

Consistent with this "sociocultural" interpretation of rape, men who rape tend to exhibit normal personality characteristics, physical appearances, intelligence, and social behavior. They cannot easily be construed as deviants in a broad social sense; indeed, they see themselves as conforming to the traditional, mainstream ideal of manhood. Understood in this way, rape is one means for a heterosexual man to prove this masculinity (Herman 1989). Some straight guys evidently have to prove it over and over again. Take athletes, for instance.

A star tailback on the nationally ranked Louisiana State University football team, Cecil Collins was arrested on June 25, 1998, on a felony charge of unauthorized entry and sexual battery. Two Oregon State football players, Jason Dandridge and Calvin Carlyle, were arrested the same day as Collins and charged with sexual assault and sodomy and unlawful sexual penetration. Sometimes these young men get lucky. A Queens, New York, jury acquitted three members of the St. John's University lacrosse team, Andrew Draghi, Walter Gabrinowitz, and Matthew Grandinetti. The three men had been accused of plying a woman with alcohol and making her perform oral sex on them; the teammates alternately used force and took advantage of her intoxicated state. Although the defendants were acquitted, St. John's University did the right thing: it expelled the three on the grounds that each of them was guilty of "conduct adversely affecting his suitability as a member of the academic community of St. John's" (quoted in Bohmer and Parrot 1993, 30).

These were not isolated cases. A recent report by E.S.P.N. SportsZone indicated 145 college athletes were arrested in 1998 for 134 alleged crimes. Other studies suggest the same. For instance, using information from 30 N.C.A.A. Division I schools, a study conducted during 1990–1993 by Northeastern University and the University of Massachusetts showed that of the reports received by campus administrators, male athletes were connected to 19 percent of sexual assaults (Thompson 1998). Another report, based on information from an F.B.I. survey, indicated that police had 38 percent more complaints of sexual assault by basketball and football players at N.C.A.A. colleges than the average for the combined number of males on college campuses (Bohmer and Parrot 1993). Another study suggests that male student-athletes are six times as likely as their nonathlete peers to be reported for sexual assault to campus judicial affairs (Crosset, Benedict, and McDonald 1995). Is there something in "male team sport culture [that] somehow *encourages* this sort of behavior" (Katz 1995, 173)? Now what could that something be?

III. Straight Men Rape Men

Ten girls are molested for every one boy.

—Susan Brownmiller, *Against Our Will: Men, Women, and Rape* (1975/1993)

[T]he incidence of gay men raping heterosexual men is relatively low.

—Michael Scarce, *Male on Male Rape* (1997)

The straight mind valorizes difference.

—Leo Bersani, *Homos* (1995)

Rapes of boys and men are significantly underreported. Male-male rape is more violent than that male-male assault called "bagging," wherein heterosexual men, often at the workplace, strike other men's genital area (20/20 1997). Recently, the U.S. Supreme Court ruled that men can sue for such sexual harassment. "Perhaps," Mark Ledbetter (1996, 65) speculates, "man's own tendency to 'sever' his own body (by reducing himself to his penis) for self-definition suggests to him a right to do this to others." Bagging?

The rape of men, Michael Scarce (1997) suggests, is perhaps the most unaddressed violent crime in contemporary America. He points out that much has been written regarding the sexual molestation of boys, but that adult male victims of rape are often silenced and overlooked. Perhaps male-male rape is somehow unmentionable. Why? Perhaps when men rape other men the fragility of traditional, that is, heterosexual, conceptions of masculinity and manhood is made explicit. Perhaps it is unmentionable, too, because homosexuality is criminalized in nearly 20 states. The male rape survivor faces the additional burden of fearing that he himself will be charged with sodomy. In cases of "date rape," gay male complainants may well encounter responses like those women have typically endured: a sense that the gay man "must have wanted it." This response is made more likely by homophobic stereotypes concerning gay male promiscuity (Rubenstein 1997; Scarce 1997).

Most men who rape other men are *not* self-identified as homosexual. In fact, the sexual orientation of most men who rape other men is heterosexual. Those who are raped by other men tend to be in their late teens or late 20s at the time of assault. Gay men have been raped at much higher rates than heterosexual men (Scarce 1997; Groth 1979). According to the Department of Justice, an estimated 123,000 men were the victims of rape attempts between 1973 and 1982 (Simon 1996). In 1994, 15,000 men reported they had been victims of rape or attempted rape, but this number represents only the reported cases. The true number of men raped each year is unknown. Most victims are gay but the great majority of the rapists themselves are heterosexual. Thirty-five percent of male rapists report being victims of sexual abuse, according to the National Organization on Male Sexual Victimization in St. Paul, Minnesota (Asika 1997). Women commit less than 20 percent of sex abuse against underaged boys.

Male on male rape is sometimes politically motivated. In August 1985, police in Iowa City noticed a pattern of male rapes committed against gay and black men. Ku Klux Klan involvement was considered likely. Those who rape men sometimes sexually assault gay men to punish them for their "sin," a punishment which the self-righteous evidently find pleasurable. On two occasions in August 1993, gay men were kidnapped as they left gay bars in Salt Lake City and then gang-raped. One man was abducted and raped repeatedly for three days. Local community leaders learned later that these gang rapes were politically motivated; the rapists were straight men who hated homosexuals (Scarce 1997). Not in bed, apparently.

Most rapes occur without rationale. In December 1995, Baton Rouge police arrested a 58-year-old apartment complex security guard for allegedly raping an 18-year-old man after offering him a ride home from a local laundry. The guard drove the young man to a parking lot where he raped him at knife point. A police officer commended the rape survivor for stepping forward and reporting the crime, acknowledging that adult male rape may be the most underreported of violent crimes (Scarce 1997).

There is evidence that same-sex rape in military organizations is not uncommon. Military psychiatrists Peter Goyer and Henry Eddleman (1984) reviewed cases of Navy and Marine Corps men who reported sexual assault to a military outpatient psychiatric clinic. More than half of the those men who had been assaulted asked to be discharged. Many reported symptoms associated with rape trauma syndrome, including fear of living in close quarters with men, depression, and sleep disorders. Rape in the military mirrors rape in prison in several respects, including denial (not only among participants and observers but officials as well), abuse of power, and a refusal on the public's part to acknowledge the problem (Scarce 1997).

In August 1995, there were reports of a court-martial case of a chief warrant officer charged with training abuses at Camp Lejeune. One witness, a first lieutenant, told the court he observed an incident wherein a Marine was held down by a number of other Marines and threatened with sodomy. One of the assailants rubbed a mini-flashlight across the Marine's rectum. The first lieutenant insisted that he had informed the chief warrant officer of this and other such incidents, but the Marines continued to employ these practices as part of their training exercises. A four-officer military jury found the warrant officer innocent of all charges, including that he poured Tabasco sauce on a Marine's genitals (Zeeland 1996).

In 1987, the *New York Times* reported on rituals of brutality within the ranks of the British Army. As part of initiation ceremonies conducted by members of several regiments, multiple beatings and sexual assaults were reported. Initiation rites included forcing naked recruits to perform anal intercourse in public. Four men were accused of assaulting a 20-year-old private by burning his genitals, penetrating him with a broomstick, and forcing him to march in place with string that secured his genitals to his ankles. With apt imagery Scarce (1997, 47) comments, "Beyond the establishment of a totem pole, top-down governance, military training, and initiations are notorious for 'making men out of boys'."

Military hazing is perhaps a worse problem than fraternity hazing. In a segment entitled "Hell Night" that aired on A.B.C.'s news program Primetime Live in 1992, Sam Donaldson reported on a pattern of sexual abuse in the U.S. Marine Corps. While inducting men into an elite drill team, leaders of the group commanded the junior Marines to strip. Once naked the young men were forced to stand stationary as the leaders painted a tarlike, military shoe polish called "edge" dressing on the men's genitals. The young men were later treated for painful chemical burns. The edge dressing contains toluene, a substance that, in sufficient dosage, has been associated with birth defects and impairment of the central nervous system. In addition to being physically assaulted with fists and rifles, one Marine reported the edge dressing dabber had been inserted into his anus. Two Marines became so distressed after the initiation that they went A.W.O.L. They then contacted their congressmen for assistance (Scarce 1997).

Homosexual desire also surfaces (if in deformed ways) in military programs ostensibly designed to prepare young soldiers for worst-case scenarios during which, as prisoners of war, they might be subjected to sexual abuse. One such program was S.E.R.E, an acronym for Survival, Evasion, Resistance and Escape, which included a "sexual exploitation scenario." Ordered by the Department of

Defense, approximately 2,000 cadets at the Air Force Academy had witnessed, been briefed or taken part in it since 1993 (Palmer 1995). One of the participants was Christian Polintan.

> Polintan was a 6-foot-1-inch honor student from Arizona and an outstanding high-school wrestler, varsity football player and Eagle Scout. He'd been accepted by all the service academies, but chose the Air Force. Polintan, then 19, never expected his training to include parading around S.E.R.E as "the executive officer's sex toy," wearing a laundry-bag skirt and makeup. "They made me act like a girl, curtsy and sit on his lap," Polintan says. Later, an N.C.O. groped his buttocks, and he was tied face down and groped again, he says. "Then they brought in another cadet, a 'prisoner' like me, and told him to take off his clothes, get on top of me and act like he was having sex." Polintan says the cadet protested, but stripped to his underwear and mounted him. Polintan, who left the Academy after his second year, told his story on "20/20" in April [1995]. (Palmer 1995, 24)

This "spilling over" (as it were) of desire in programs designed to prepare young people for "worst-case scenarios" is not limited to the military. The specter of sexual assault behind bars (which we examine in some detail in chapters 16 and 17) is sometimes used by prison officials who wish to instill fear in "at-risk" young men. Like S.E.R.E., this "scared-straight" pedagogy teaches more than its instructors planned. At an experimental boot camp for juvenile offenders in Florida, simulations of prison rape were performed as a method of rehabilitation for teenaged boys. The *St. Petersburg Times* reported:

> [Drill Instructor] Venis grabbed a pudgy 14-year-old named Jason for a vivid demonstration of prison rape. The 55 year-old [Drill Instructor] stood directly behind Jason and began gently, rhythmically raising his knee, pressing it into the boy's rump, to simulate an assault. "That's how they do it when you get to prison!" Venis yelled. The fear of homosexual rape quickly became a powerful lever of intimidation. The [Drill Instructors] made sure recruits knew just what happens in prison, subtlety be damned. One told Veysey: "You don't change, they'll be sticking things up your butt, son. Right up your butt!" (quoted in Scarce 1997, 43)

After this report appeared in the press, the practice was discontinued.

In February 1997, Texas corrections officials suspended a sergeant and four prison guards after learning of their allegedly inappropriate behavior during a "scared straight" field trip to Eastham prison. During the visit, the guards allegedly permitted inmates to fondle five of the teenage boys. A spokesperson for the Department of Criminal Justice in Texas reported that the prisoners had admitted fondling the boys but that their actions had not been sexual in nature. The point was strictly pedagogical, a lesson to show the young men what awaited them in prison if they failed to "go straight" (Scarce 1997). As Foucault (1979/1995, 111) observed, prison officials have long imagined that "[m]en as well as boys should be taken to the [prisons] and contemplate the frightful fate of these outlaws." Deterrence only, of course.

Homosexual desire surfaces also in homophobic, heterosexist school athletics, albeit in mangled form. In 1992 a junior teammate of the Johnson Creek High School wrestling team in Wisconsin filed a lawsuit alleging that his fellow wrestlers had beaten then raped him by shoving a mop handle into his rectum. He was punished for missing practice, his teammates said. The athletic director of the high school found the young man blindfolded and naked on an exercise mat. His legs, hands, and head were bound with tape. During the resulting trial a teammate testified that other school athletes had also been threatened with "getting the mop." Those accused were acquitted of the rape charges due to insufficient evidence. Because the young man had been blindfolded he was unable to identify who had assaulted him, although he knew that at least six of his teammates had held him down while he was taped. The assistant wrestling coach testified that "taping" was not uncommon among wrestling teams, particularly in college athletics (Scarce 1997).

Five students at Waynesville High School in Ohio were suspended in 1988 for allegedly staging a locker room hazing event. Freshmen players were forced to masturbate and fondle each other's genitals. A similar incident occurred a year later at a high school football training camp in Pennsylvania. There a high school sophomore was allegedly forced to insert his finger into the anus of another sophomore while 20 to 30 teammates watched. In 1990 the *Boston Globe* reported that eight new members of the local Brockton High School track team had been hazed: "According to one anonymous student, the eight new team members were stripped to their underwear and pushed halfway out the back door of the [school] bus. Some of them had their underwear ripped off them, and some were made to choose between eating pubic hair and being beaten up. Some were forced to rub their genitals" (Bloom 1990, 22; quoted in Scarce 1997, 50). Hazing in high schools continues to become more violent (Jacobs 2000).

A national survey published in 1999 reported that 80 percent of college athletes have been hazed at some point in their careers. The National Survey of Initiation Rites and Athletics, a yearlong study conducted by Alfred (N.Y.) University in cooperation with the N.C.A.A., found almost 80 percent of the 10,000 student-athletes at various Division I to Division III colleges and universities had been hazed. Sixty percent of the athletes who responded said they had engaged in criminal, dangerous, and/or alcohol-related hazing. The study found that men were more at risk than women, and that the sports most associated with hazing are swimming and diving, lacrosse, soccer, football, and ice hockey. Hazing was also more likely in the East or South, and on rural or residential campuses. Sports with significantly fewer reports of hazing were track, fencing, and golf (White 1999). Among the milder activities typifying the practice was being forced to wear "embarrassing" (Duncan 1999, D-6) clothes. Nor is this male-male sado-masochism limited to non-professional sports. In 1998 New Orleans tight end Cam Cleeland was injured in a well-publicized incident at training camp (Duncan 1999).

The town of Smithfield, a small Utah farming community, blamed the victim when in 1993 a member of the local high school football team was taken naked from the shower by ten of his teammates, then bound by his genitals with tape to a towel rack. Approximately twenty of his male and female schoolmates watched. High school sports were so popular in the community that when the victim reported this event *he* received telephone threats. The national media reported the story; later the young man appeared on the television talk show *Phil Donahue*. From his point of view, "The humiliation I suffered was tons worse than the physical injury" (Plummer and Johnson 1993, 52; quoted in Scarce 1997, 51).

Clearly, "hazing" is an indirect, disavowed form of homosexual rape. Sometimes it is not so indirect. In January 1997, Sheldon Kennedy, a hockey player with the Boston Bruins of the National Hockey League, alleged that a former coach had sexually assaulted him more than 300 times over the course of eleven years. Kennedy was fourteen when the coach first approached him; he was twenty-six when the "relationship" ended. The events included forced oral sex and masturbation. The coach was found guilty on two counts of sexual assault against Kennedy and another unnamed man, who alleged he had been assaulted approximately fifty times in four years. The coach was sentenced to 3½ years in prison. Kennedy reported in a newspaper interview with the *Toronto Star* that the coach had used a variety of tactics to maintain control over him, from verbal abuse to a shotgun. On January 17, Reuters newswire reported that "Mick Mitrovic, president of the eastern region of the Canadian Professional Hockey School, said he was not surprised when he heard about the conviction because there had been cases and rumors about problems with players and coaches before" (Blinch 1997; quoted in Scarce 1997, 51). If "sport" is sublimated sex, should we be shocked if on occasion desublimation occurs?

The "Greeks"

After prisons and military bases, the U.S. Bureau of Justice reports that more alleged rapes occur within the property lines of Greek-letter houses than any other location. The initiation rites of young men into fraternities are notorious for their symbolic and literal (homo)sexual assault. Anthony M. Scacco (1975, 85) reports: "One such fraternity makes the pledges strip naked, then bend over after having greased a nail which is handed to a senior member of the fraternity standing behind them. Although the nail is never delivered to the buttocks, the pledge gets the idea that he has subjected himself to another male in this manner." Here the homosociality of fraternity life almost dissolves into homosexuality.

Reminiscent of a nineteenth-century K.K.K. incident (see chapter 9, section I), a University of Minnesota fraternity allegedly forced two Kappa Sigma pledges to strip. Their "brothers" then taped them together while fraternity members photographed the unhappy couple. The Delta Kappa Epsilon fraternity at Tulane University was banished from campus in 1984 after a series of hazing incidents. Neighbors of the D.K.E. house reported that pledges had cords tied to their genitals and bricks tied to the other end. In 1988, two fraternity pledges at the University of Colorado were forced to spread their legs while their drunken fraternity brothers threw darts near their genitals. In 1990 the Sigma Nu chapter at the University of Texas was expelled from campus for hazing that allegedly included sexual abuse. At the University of Florida, one-fourth of the fraternities faced disciplinary action in 1992 for alcohol abuse and hazing. Illustrative of hazing activities was Kappa Sigma, whose members forced pledges to ride around campus nude while chained to a pickup truck. During another hazing episode a pledge of Delta Tau Delta lost a testicle (Scarce 1997).

Nineteen-year-old Gavin Fugate, a 1996 pledge to Sigma Alpha Epsilon at Louisiana State University, reports he was beaten, then forced "to scoot across the floor covered with broken glass" (Varney 1997, 1). The result was "severely lacerated elbows and butt." However, Fugate reports, "one brother was nice enough to treat the cuts with a traditional Louisiana topping, Tabasco sauce." Fugate recounted how fraternity brothers tried to sodomize him with a bar of soap, beat him, all the while forcing him to drink liquor until he vomited blood. When his parents visited one weekend, "the Fugates saw their son muddy and nearly naked, his body bruised and his spirit broken" (17).

At one fraternity at a large midwestern university, hazing resembled the verbal harassment evident in many prisons. Rush participants were called "girls," and "wusses," during a week of intense hazing. During this time they were compelled to perform in exaggerated female stereotypes. Finally, they were directed to "do to women what we did to you to get your manhood back" (Funk 1994, 17; quoted in Scarce 1997, 54). Comparing fraternities and prison Scacco (1975, 85) remarks: "The inmate in prison, chosen as the victim, is not so lucky. The attacker not only makes sure he completes the act of sodomy, but usually invites his friends to share his punk, thereby making the act even more humiliating and 'demaling' for the victim."

Hazing is not limited to predominantly white fraternities, if we can take film as "data." In the conflict between the frat boys and the "fellas" in Spike Lee's *School Daze*, verbal fag-bashing becomes the tactic of preference in the competition for male domination: "When I say Gamma, you say Fag. Gamma. Fag. Gamma. Fag." As black gay artist Marlon Riggs (1991b, 227) complains, Lee's movie not only reflects homophobia among black men, it "glorifies it." Black manhood is the subject of the next chapter.

Since 1978, 36 states have passed laws prohibiting hazing. A study commissioned by the president of Rutgers University concluded that "fraternities 'demean human dignity' and are hostile toward women, minority-group members and homosexuals" (quoted in Comstock 1991, 108). Since the early 1990s, prestigious colleges such as Trinity, Middlebury, and Bowdoin Colleges have abolished the Greek system (Twardowski 1997). All universities would be well advised to follow their lead.

IV. Homophobia

> *Nothing seems more certain than that homosexuality is contagious.*
>
> —Willard Waller, *The Sociology of Teaching* (1932)

Can it be that we are all repressed homosexuals?

—Paul Hoch, *White Hero, Black Beast: Racism, Sexism and the Mask of Masculinity* (1979)

Homophobic virulence in America has increased in direct proportion to the wider acceptance of homosexuals.

—Leo Bersani, *Homos* (1995)

Occasionally, gay bashing incidents include forcible rape, either oral or anal.

—Joseph Harry, *Hate Crimes: Confronting Violence against Lesbians and Gay Men* (1992)

The homophobes have *invented the homosexuals.*

—Elisabeth Young-Bruehl, *The Anatomy of Prejudices* (1996)

Although an accurate and useful term to depict an irrational preference for heterosexuality, "heterosexism" does not express the negative side of "compulsory heterosexuality" (Rich 1980, 637) that "homophobia" does. "Heterosexism" is appropriate for describing why nearly all television couples are straight, why marriage and joint tax returns are reserved for heterosexuals, why openly lesbian or gay candidates face great odds in being elected to office, or why often only heterosexuals can adopt children or be foster parents. But "heterosexism," Patrick Hopkins (1996) points out, while still technically accurate, does not seem to describe the scene of ten Texas teenage boys beating a gay man with nail-studded boards, then stabbing him to death. "The blood pooling up on the ground beneath that dying body," Hopkins (1996, 99) observes, "is evidence for something more than the protection of heterosexual privilege. It is evidence for a radical kind of evil."

The episode to which Hopkins refers was the murder of Paul Broussard in Houston, Texas. The homicide provoked outrage in Houston's queer community over antigay violence and police indifference. To "quell the recent uproar," Houston police undertook an undercover operation in which officers posed as gay men in a well-known gay district. Police had been skeptical of gay men's claims regarding the frequency of violence, but within one hour of posing as gay men, undercover officers had been sprayed with mace and attacked by young men wielding baseball bats (Yang 1991; Hopkins 1996, 114 n. 15).

Houston is no isolated example. In a Philadelphia study, 24 percent of gay men and 10 percent of lesbians reported that they had been physically attacked: a rate twice as high for lesbians and four times as high for gay men than for heterosexual women and men in the city. According to the New York City Gay and Lesbian Anti-Violence Project, there were 2,064 antigay incidents recorded in nine United States cities in 1994, up 2 percent from the year before (Dunlap 1995). Another study of violence against lesbians and gay men reported by Gary Comstock (1991) yields the following facts: (1) 94 percent of all attackers were male; (2) 99 percent of perpetrators who attacked gay men were male, while 83 percent of those who attacked lesbians were male; and (3) while 15 percent of attacks on lesbians were made by women, only 1 percent of attacks on gay men were made by women. Regardless of the gender or race of the victim, those who engage in homophobic heterosexist violence are most likely to be white (67 percent). Hopkins (1996, 110) concludes: "Homophobic violence seems to be predominantly a male activity." It would seem to be a white heterosexual male activity.

Is "homophobia" one thing? "Do lesbians," Elizabeth Grosz (1995, 211) asks, "experience the same forms of homophobia as gay men?" Grosz poses other questions as well. While those who attack both lesbians and gay men seem to share a subject position—white, male, young—is there a shared experience of oppression for both lesbians and gays? Can we assume that homophobia takes on universal forms across cultures? Does the fact that they are women and men (however one chooses to define these terms) change the forms of homophobia each experiences? Finally, Grosz (1995, 211) asks, "does the very category of sex/sexuality differ sexually, that is, according to the sex of the subject under question?" These questions suggest that the notion is undertheorized; they also suggest that it might need to be made plural: homophobias, a view shared by Elisabeth Young-Bruehl (1996).

Homophobia may be plural, but definitions, however totalizing, still seem possible. For instance, Grosz (1995, 226) offers: "Homophobia is an attempt to separate being from doing, existence from action." This would seem to locate it within the Western system of binarization and self-splitting which tends to accompany heteronormative formations of "masculinity." Michael Kimmel (1993, 127) too suggests a definition based in gender binaries: "Homophobia (which I understand as more than the fear of homosexual men; it's also the fear of other men) keeps men acting like men, keeps men exaggerating their adherence to traditional norms, so that no other men will get the idea that we might really be that dreaded person: the sissy."

Those guilty of antigay/lesbian violence have been known to rationalize their actions by referring to parental expectations, religious teachers, even everyday social standards. Moreover, the same disapproval typically expressed against crime has not been forthcoming after homophobic/heterosexist violence toward lesbians and gay men. Summed up with a "boys will be boys" attitude, "permission" has been granted in the form of: (1) familial, church, and community "values" which exclude, condemn, and are antagonistic to lesbians and gay men; (2) the failure or refusal of educators to protect lesbians and gay students who are harassed and/or assaulted on school grounds; (3) the failure or refusal of educators to defend harassed sexual "others" and teach the full range of human sexualities; (4) the tendency of the police to respond slowly or not at all to reports of antigay/lesbian violence and/or to release perpetrators and apprehend victims; and (5) the practice of judges and juries to acquit or sentence lightly those who are found guilty of assaulting or killing lesbians and gay men (Comstock 1991).

Those who assault lesbians and gay men tend to be not only male and white, but middle class as well. When they are high school students, most have been found to be doing well in their classes; they are often involved in school and community activities, organizations, and athletics; they are characterized by fellow students and teachers as popular, friendly, and sociable; generally they are enrolled in college-preparatory programs in high school or enrolled in college; and/or in the military (Comstock 1991). Perhaps these are kids who have been taught to hate, or to rationalize their hatred, whose assaults are in some fundamental sense ideological as well as psychologically compensatory and defensive, shoring up fragile even endangered heterosexual egos. Over half a century ago John Dollard and his colleagues (1939, 72) observed that early adolescence can be a period of sexual identity confusion: "Some children [adolescent males] experience a renewed appearance of strong homosexual instigation and find it variously met by social patterns, though always inhibited in overt form."

Studies of criminal and rebellious behavior by teenagers make clear that acts of physical violence are committed with greater frequency by young men than by young women. Studies of gender-role socialization suggest that males—if they are to be "men," that is, heterosexual, a "man's man"—are expected and taught to be socially and physically aggressive and sexually dominant. Qualities such as warmth, emotional expressivity, as well as capacities to be sensitive, supporting, nurturing, noncompetitive, and not dominant are often regarded as positive traits for women. This socialization process toward heteronormativity begins at birth and is firmly imprinted by early childhood (Comstock 1991). Mark Simpson (1994, 190) says it succinctly: "Teenage boys are required to confront the feminine [in themselves] or else jeopardize their successful graduation into manhood."

Despite this terrorist regime of compulsory heterosexuality, not everyone succumbs, although the number of heterosexually married gay men and lesbians is no doubt high. Nor does the regime "work" for all "straight" kids, especially young men. Perhaps it is the matrifocality of pre-oedipal identifications, but young men often emerge with overdetermined—that is, compensatory and defensive—gender identifications. Because the heterosexual object choice is unstable, these kids cannot tolerate instances of "deviance" in the social field, as that information threatens the fragile ego system they are determined to congeal and strengthen. Given this narrative, can one be surprised when surveys indicate that young "men tend to react more strongly than women to sex-role 'violations'," that penalties for gender-role "violations" are "most strongly administered by men," and that recognizing and conforming to mainstream stereotypes of masculinity is much more important for high "self-esteem" in young men than is the counterpart for young women (quoted in Comstock 1991, 107)?

That "homosexual activity" and antigay/lesbian violence tend to occur more frequently among adolescent males than among any other age or gender group may not be fortuitous. Comstock (1991, 116) suggests: "[S]ome teenage males may attempt to resolve a conflict between their sexual experiences [experimenting with gay sex] and the social expectations placed upon them by attacking lesbians and gay men. ... The greater frequency of antigay over antilesbian violence (and perhaps especially of antigay rape) may reflect the preferred targeting of the gender more closely associated with the feelings and interests that are in conflict with the social norm."

As Christopher Lane has observed, conservatives sometimes find such conflict and the attendant absence of social cohesion intolerable. At least this tension is a cause for complaint, but for some, it is also an excuse to take the law into one's own hands, "to transform oneself psychotically *into* Law by acting on fantasies of religious prophecy, racial retribution, or sexual 'correction'" (Lane 1996, 115). To illustrate, Lane recalls a Colorado organization named "STRAIGHT (Society to Remove All Immoral Godless Homosexual Trash)." STRAIGHT reminded its members and others that the "Death Penalty for Homosexuals is prescribed in the Bible," and invited the submission of material for the group's journal thus: "Wanted: All Criminals Protecting, Promoting, or Practicing Homosexual Perversion." Lane (1996, 115) understands such language as "an American manifestation of fantasies operating in 'ethnic cleansing,' this time as the projected erasure of homosexuality not only from society, but also *from private fantasy*, where it is clearly more disturbing."

So far this seems to be the same dynamic that is at work in sexually threatened white boys. But Lane (1996, 115) moves to focus on the injunction *"wanted"* in the call for materials. What, he asks, are "the psychic terms and pressure" of this injunction? He focuses upon the internal dynamics of right-wing groups such as STRAIGHT, whose psychosexual and social cohesion is not as stable as they would like to believe. He points out that cohesion is achieved:

> either by vitriolic negation (as in the above example) or by elements of psychotic foreclosure, in which the Right attributes social—and perhaps even global—collapse to individual "degeneracy" and "pathology." But although these conservative forces are clearly misguided—even deluded—in fundamental ways, they realize that their vision of social "integration" is partly compatible with fundamental principles of psychic life; the Right offers an expression of jouissance that is often missing in radical-Left account of social alienation; this is the "enjoyment" of Fundamentalism. (Lane 1996, 115)

So were those Nazi soldiers who tortured gay men as well as straight Jews getting off? Before being gassed, many men were in fact sexually tortured, although not necessarily castrated as were thousands of African-American men in America. In the camps, many were made to perform meaningless and humiliating tasks before going to their deaths. Heinz Heger (1980, 35), whose memoirs were made into the 1979 play *Bent* by Martin Sherman, recalls that death camp tortures "resulted in many suicides, as men would run into electrified fences or throw themselves in front of carts filled with rocks and clay" and "human bodies were flying through the air, and limbs would be crushed to pulp." Not only were gay men subject to brutalities such as these, but they were also "treated with contempt by their fellow prisoners" (Muller 1980, 3). Pierre Seel (1997, 91) comments that after liberation, he "returned as a ghost." Unlike their fellow prisoners who were freed after the war, gay men never felt liberated. Pierre Seel remarked that "liberation was for others" (88). Gay men were treated as criminals not only in Germany but also in France. In Germany Paragraph 175 was not repealed until 1969 (Plant 1986), and in France homosexuality did not become legal until 1982. Because gay Holocaust survivors were considered criminals, they did not receive restitution from West Germany after the war (Morris 1999).

In the United States, antigay/lesbian violence by members of organized neo-Nazi, religious right-wing, and various hate groups continue, with the F.B.I. reporting that at least 9,000 hate crimes are committed every year (Marshall 1999). A gay newspaper reported in 1978 that more than 100 teenaged men organized Ku Klux Klan chapters in two Oklahoma City high schools. One member declared: "We are not just against blacks, like the old Klan. We are against gays and the clubs that support them and are going to try to shut them down because this activity is morally and socially wrong." Members are reported to have vandalized cars near gay bars and to have attacked bar patrons with baseball bats. In 1988, the *New York Times* reported that neo-Nazi activity among U.S. young is increasing and that lesbian-gay people are high on their enemies list (Comstock 1991).

Two lesbian respondents, an interracial couple living in rural upstate New York, reported that they have been the "victims of a KKK cross-burning" (quoted in Comstock 1991, 62). In Ohio in 1981, a nineteen-year-old lesbian was kidnapped by her father and subjected to "deprogamming from lesbian mind control," a process that included rape as well as food and sleep deprivation. The parents paid $8,000 for the "treatment" and were aware of the methods to be employed (quoted phrases in Comstock 1991, 70). All was done in the name of "morality," of course.

On October 27, 1992, the badly beaten body of 22-year-old Seaman Alan Schindler was found in a park toilet near the U.S. Naval base at Sasebo in southern Japan. Schindler had been murdered—his body so badly disfigured that his mother could identify him only by his tattoos. Letters Schindler had written before his death indicated that he had been subjected to vicious harassment for his homosexuality; complaints to his superiors, including his chaplain, brought no response. While there is no evidence that his superior officers were involved in his killing, their apparent indifference to the homophobic attacks on him communicated a clear signal to Schindler's murderers (Simpson 1994).

Scott Amedure's crush on another man evidently cost him his life. Three days after disclosing that he was drawn to Jonathan Schmitz during a taping of "The Jenny Jones Show," Amedure was killed at his home near Detroit. Schmitz was charged with murder. Presumably acting on behalf of the murdered, the prosecutor was quoted as saying that the [Jenny Jones] program had "ambushed" Mr. Schmitz "with humiliation" (Dunlap 1995, 16E). Homosexual desire, not murder, was the crime.

If not a crime, perhaps a disease? The National Association for Research and Therapy of Homosexuality treats homosexuality as if it were a disorder. Its president, Dr. Charles W. Socarides, faulted both the media and the gay rights movement for the Jenny Jones murder. "To turn the world upside down and say it doesn't matter if we are homosexual or heterosexual is folly," he said. "We can ask for tolerance, but to ask for total acceptance and enthusiastic approval of homosexuality as a normal and valuable psychosexual institution is truly tempting social and personal disaster" (quoted in Dunlap 1995, 16E). Could the "disaster" be the exposure of "straight" men? That the queen has no clothes? As Essex Hemphill (1991) reports: "I discovered that any man can be seduced—even if the price is humiliation or death for the seducer" (xxviii). Jeffrey D. Turner (1995) says it simply: "All men are gay."

A gay man's glance in the locker-room shower annoys some straight men, disgusts others, leaves a few unmoved. Possibly it even flatters a few. A research psychologist at the University of California at Davis, Gregory M. Herek, suggests that the object of the glance might speculate: "If a gay man finds me attractive, I must somehow have some hint of homosexuality in myself. So maybe the one thing I can do to prove that's not true is physically attack that person." Herek continues: "Society says that homosexual behavior is such an awful thing that practically anything is better. Even the notion of murdering someone might be preferable to being labeled a homosexual" (quoted in Dunlap 1995, 16E).

After a night in the Vieux Carré, be careful not to be appear too friendly with your drinking buddy. In 1995 New Orleans jurors convicted Ronald Graves, 25, of first-degree murder for the 1993 Quarter stabbing death of a man he mistakenly believed was gay. Witnesses testified that he and three others attacked and killed 22-year-old Joseph Balog because they thought he was a homosexual. The victim's father testified that the men were not gay (Loh 1995).

Comparisons with national crime statistics about perpetrators of all violent crimes indicate that perpetrators of antigay/lesbian violence tend to be younger and that a greater percentage is male. Also in contrast to violent crime in general, perpetrators of antigay/lesbian crime tend to be unknown to their victims. A greater percentage of lesbians and gay men of color experience homophobic/heterosexist violence from whites than do victims of color in general. Antigay/lesbian attackers are more likely to attack in groups with weapons (Comstock 1991).

Is it significant that most gay bashers tend to be white kids? Is white adolescent heterosexual masculinity so tenuous, so fraught with internal contradictions, that "straight" "white" "kids" must attack lesbian and gay people to preserve their beleaguered sense of who they are? Is there a historical throughline from the white men whose masculinity was in "crisis" one hundred years ago with those white kids who attack lesbian and gay men today? This testimony of rock pioneer "Little Richard" suggests so:

> I went through a lot when I was a boy. They called me sissy, punk, freak, and faggot. If I ever went to friends' houses on my own, the guys would try to catch me, about eight or twenty of them together. They would run after me. I never knew I could run so fast, but I was scared. They would jump on me, you know, 'cos they didn't like my action. ... Sometimes white men would pick me up in their car and take me to the woods and try to get me to suck them. A whole lot of black people have had to do that. It happened to me and my friend, Hester. I ran off into the woods. My friend, he didn't. ... (quoted in Julien and Mercer 1991, 167)

One hundred years ago in the South, sex and race conflated in "white supremacy," an umbrella concept that included white sexual exploitation of black men and women. Serve the white man? Little Richard muses: "A whole lot of black people have had to do that."

Lynching was a performance of white men's obsession with the black male body, a body they had once owned, had their way with, and would have their way with again. "Charles Johnson reminds us," Laurence Goldstein (1994, xi) writes, introducing Johnson's essay in *The Male Body*, "how the black body has been stereotyped as a phallus to suit the needs of a racist society." How does the "black body" as phallic "suit the needs" of racism? The white man has obsessed over the black man's penis from the earliest slave days, examining genitalia to determine breeding potential, presumably. Right. And with his obsession with the black male body, the white man has remained stunningly ignorant of the black man's subjectivity, his inner self. Who is the black man? The white man has not a clue. Nor, in general, does he appear interested in finding out. As we have seen, white men grow very attached to their fantasies. For many white men—straight and gay—black men remain firmly planted in their "place," inside the white man's head, a fragment of his (often eroticized) imagination.

If white racism is in some fundamental sense an affair between men, if white racism is in part a recoding of a white male fascination with the black male body, what would an alien visitor to planet earth find among black men? Would the alien find black men concerned about ... "manhood," as if they had been cultural victims of an assault that was somehow also—if unacknowledged, disguised, recoded—sexual? Would the alien find that the white man has little clue who he is, consumed as he is with making the world conform to his fantasies? Who is the white man? He hasn't a clue. Who is the black man? To find out, perhaps the white man should look first inside his head, in the "place" he left "him," the black man, that imaginary construct with a material body. Would the alien be surprised to hear black men snarl at "the man": "you don't even know who I am?"

14 ❖ BLACK MEN

YOU DON'T EVEN KNOW WHO I AM

I. A "Crisis" of Black Masculinity?

It is because the nation, the entire nation, has spent a hundred years avoiding the question of the place of the black man in it.

—James Baldwin, *The Price of the Ticket* (1985)

[A]merica has not made the black woman its universal bogeyman. The black man is.

—Earl Ofari Hutchinson, *The Assassination of the Black Male Image* (1997)

[O]ne realizes that the much discussed crisis of the black male is no idle fiction.

—Henry Louis Gates, Jr., "Preface" to Thelma Golden, ed., *Black Male: Representations of Masculinity in Contemporary American Art* (1994)

[B]lack manhood generally is … in desperate trouble.

—Michael Awkward, "A Black Man's Place(s) in Black Feminist Criticism" (1996)

The blood of young black men runs curbside in a steady flow.

—Essex Hemphill, "Introduction,"
Brother to Brother: Collected Writings by Black Gay Men (1991)

As nightmarish, as evil, as wantonly destructive as white men's sexual, political, and economic exploitation of black women has been, the oppression of black men contains one additional element. There was a specific if unnamed psychosexual exploitation as the white man obsessed over the black man's sexuality, his body, his phallus, "his" alleged desire for the white "lady." While both black women and men were sexually violated by white men, the black man's subjugation was, by definition, homosexual. That is to say, in addition to assaulting his dignity as a human being, his civic status as male citizen, his stature as father and husband, the white-male sexual subjugation of black men necessarily threatened his sexual identity. True, not until the late nineteenth century did sexual identity—the binary notions of "heterosexuality" and "homosexuality"—assume a form recognizable to us today. It is clear that pre-twentieth-century forms of male-male "friendship" included erotic elements, and that these appeared not to threaten the (white) man's sense of himself as a man, at least not until the "crisis" of white masculinity intensified during that same decade that lynching was at its zenith. Moreover, "homosexual" assaults do not tend to threaten a woman's sense of herself as a heterosexual woman to the extent that homosexual rape did and does threaten men's identity as "men," that is, heterosexual men.

In the epigraph, Baldwin reminds us that the (white) American nation has avoided the question of the place of the black man in it. I submit that the political question has been avoided in part because the black man already had a place: in the white man's imagination. Because he existed civically as the white man imagined him sexually, he was left (against his will) in a homoerotic, if not explicitly homosexual, position, socially, politically, erotically. This position, in an increasingly heterosexist, homophobic twentieth century has necessarily meant for black masculinity an ongoing, at times explosive, crisis: sexual, political, social. (Although there are contradictory movements and indications, overall I am accepting Foucault's general thesis that increased visibility of sexual minorities has been in the service of surveillance, that "repressive tolerance" has required a certain "outing.") While, as Du Bois knew, black men were an "oasis" in relation to the "desert" that was unself-knowing, predatory, desperate white masculinity, black men were trapped in the "social reality" white men imagined, then enforced, by law, institution, and culture.

I submit that the "crisis" of black masculinity—a black not white diagnosis, as we will see—becomes fully intelligible only in a gendered and historical context that underlines lynching as *the* imprinting instance of white male racism. Both black women and men were rape victims; both suffered as bodies and souls caught in the vicious grip of white men's minds. For black men this has meant that the struggle for civil rights, and racial politics generally, has been inextricably and homoerotically gendered: "I AM A MAN" read the signs in many a civil rights march. Laced through all of this has been an effort to extricate himself from the white man's mind and discover—and assert—his own subjectivity, apart from white folks' fantasies of him. "You don't even know who I am," the black man might say to the white, but finally it does not matter. It's the white man's loss, and you don't need him. From the beginning, it has been he who has needed you.

The Trace Today

The United States suffers higher rates of violent crime than any other industrialized nation. Media sensationalism tends to racialize crime, creating the impression that African Americans, especially black men, are "dangerous" (Haymes 1995)—white people beware. Statistics tell a different story. Yes, black men, like white men, are dangerous, but violent crime is primarily *intra*racial. For example, the F.B.I. reports that in 1992, 94 percent of African-American murder victims were killed by African Americans; 83 percent of European-American murder victims were killed by European Americans. Criminal victimization surveys confirm the intraracial nature of interpersonal violence by analyzing the self-reports of assault, robbery, and rape victims (Oliver 1994). In the 1960s one category of crime, however, was significantly interracial: The staff report of the National Commission on the Causes and Prevention of Violence discussed interracial aspects of other crimes that the F.B.I.'s Uniform Crime Reports avoid. In a 1967 seventeen-city survey National Commission on the Causes and Prevention of Violence estimated that seventeen reported robberies were cases of "younger black males robbing older white males" (Brownmiller 1975/1993, 214 n). But in general, violence is expressed intraracially. As one black man, John A. Williams (1995/1996), quipped: "It is still eat, drink and be murderous, for tomorrow I may be among the murdered" (776).

African Americans represent 12 percent of the population but they are disproportionately represented among persons arrested for violent crimes. For example, in 1992 African Americans represented 55 percent of the persons arrested for murder, 39 percent for aggravated assault, 34 percent for misdemeanor assault, and 61 percent for robbery. Moreover, African Americans represented 50 percent of the 23,760 murder victims known to the police in 1990. But these are not African Americans in general; all of the major sources of data on violent crime consistently report that African-American violence is a social problem in which black males are most likely to be both the perpetrators and victims. This disproportionate representation of black males among perpetrators and victims of violent crime is evident in arrest statistics, criminal victimization surveys, mortality reports, and numerous local studies of homicide and assault (Oliver 1994).

Every forty-six seconds of the school day, a black child drops out of school, every ninety-five seconds a black baby is born into poverty, and every four hours of every day a black young adult, age twenty to twenty-four, is murdered (Gates 1994). As one black man observed: "I see far too many young black men take rides in what I call the 'macho man cabs.' One is a police car and the other is an ambulance"(Michael O'Neal, in Johnson and McCluskey 1997, 154).

A 1990 study showed that, on any given day in 1989, 1 in 4 black men from the ages of 20 to 29 were either in prison, on parole, or on probation. By mid-decade, this figure had risen to 1 in 3. In 1995, 827,440 black men in their twenties were in prison or jail or on probation or parole (30 percent of this group, compared to 7 percent for whites and 18 percent for Hispanics), many of them for drug violations. In 1995, African Americans accounted for 13 percent of monthly drug users, 35 percent of drug arrests, 55 percent of drug convictions, and 74 percent of those sentenced for drug violations (Johnson and McCluskey 1997; Lather and Smithies 1997; Oliver 1994).

A young dealer who works steadily can easily earn $40,000 a year tax-free. In Washington, D.C., a 1990 Rand Corporation report estimated that young black men brought in $354 million a year from drug sales, which is equal to one-fourth of the $1.2 billion earned by young black men working at legitimate jobs (Johnson and McCluskey 1997). Adam Walinksy (1995) predicts that of young black males in Washington, D.C., "70 percent ... [will] be arrested before the age of thirty-five, and ... 85 percent [will] be arrested at some point in their lives" (quoted in Johnson and McCluskey 1997, xii). In California, 39 percent of black men in their twenties are in prison, in jail, or on probation. The leading cause of death for black men aged 15–34 is homicide (Johnson and McCluskey 1997; Mills 1996). For slightly older black men, ages 25–44, AIDS is the leading cause of death for black men, as of 1996. African Americans are infected by the AIDS virus at six times the rate of whites (Johnson and McCluskey 1997; Lather and Smithies 1997; Oliver 1994).

For white men in the age group 20–29, one in 16 (6.2 percent) is under the control of the criminal justice system. Latino males fall between two groups, with one in 10 (10.4 percent) held within the criminal justice system on any given day. Direct criminal justice costs for these 609,690 black men are $2.5 billion a year. The number of young black men who are under the control of the criminal justice system is greater than the total number all black men of all ages in colleges and universities (Sbarbaro and Keller 1995; Mauer 1990).

There continues a higher-than-average threat of HIV in American prisons. At year's end 1993, 21,538 of the 880,101 inmates held in U.S. prisons—2.4 percent of federal and state prison inmates—were known to be infected with the human immunodeficiency virus (HIV) that causes AIDS. In state prisons 18,218 male and 1,796 female inmates were infected with HIV at year's end 1993. In local jails, on June 30, 1993, 6,711 inmates were infected with HIV, and of these, 1,888 had AIDS and 1,200 had some symptoms (Brien 1995). Although only about 1 percent of individuals diagnosed with AIDS between 1993 and 1994 were between 13 and 19 years old, many youths engage in high-risk behavior that puts them in danger of contracting HIV and STDs (National Institute of Justice 1996). Respondents to a survey conducted by the National Institute of Justice reported a total of 60 juveniles with AIDS (50 boys and 10 girls, 54 in state systems and 6 in city/county systems out of a total 73 systems responding) (National Institute of Justice 1996).

While the HIV rate behind bars was 2.3 percent, there were spikes as high as 14 percent in New York State. The overall rate of AIDS cases in prison is almost seven times what it is outside prison. Despite the obvious risk, only sixteen states test inmates for HIV upon entering the system, the largest of which are Georgia, Missouri, and Michigan. Two states' penal systems distribute condoms—Vermont and Mississippi—the latter selling them for 25 cents apiece in its prison commissaries. But in most states, condoms are contraband, and their possession is a serious, punishable offense (Hodges 1998). Outside of prison not only black men suffer disproportionately from HIV/AIDS; AIDS is a leading killer of black women and their children in impoverished areas (Higginbotham 1996).

Homicide rates among black men are generally six to seven times the rates among white men. In 1987 alone, more young black men were killed within the United States in a single year than had been killed in Southeast Asia during the entire nine years of the Vietnam War. Black on black violence, primarily black male on black male violence, is pandemic. According to the N.A.A.C.P. Legal Defense and Educational Fund, on an average day in the United States, thirty-one African Americans are murdered, one person every forty-six minutes. More black men are murdered every six weeks in the United States than were lynched during the last 110 years. Put another way, black men in America are less likely to live to the age of sixty-five than men in Bangladesh (Johnson and McCluskey 1997; Dyson 1995/1996). "In their night march, statistics can be terrorists of the soul" (Johnson and McCluskey 1997, xv).

Suicide, too, is increasing, ranking as the third leading cause of death among young black men. Since 1960, the number of black men who have committed suicide has tripled (Dyson 1995/1996). More than a few whites think black guys are just plain crazy, and they have (of course) looked not to themselves but to, for instance, the black family, for explanations (Moynihan 1965). African-American scholars who have studied black men tend to conclude that it is "difficult to view the black male condition as the product primarily of black cultural failure" (Dyson 1995, 168). "From the plantation to the postindustrial city," Michael Eric Dyson continues, "black males have been seen as brutishly behaved, morally flawed, uniquely ugly, and fatally oversexed" (168–169). Black men have been imprisoned in the white man's imagination.

Why are men—black and white—so violent? Why is there so much violence among men, between white and black men, and among black men specifically? Interpretations of violence associated with Foucault were expressed in somewhat different form decades before by black intellectuals as varied as Richard Wright, Frantz Fanon, Eldridge Cleaver, and Cedric J. Robinson. It was Fanon (1967, 1968) who theorized that internalized violence, first expressed by the colonists to the colonized, would reverberate, reexpressed by the colonized against themselves, but someday, inevitably, reexpressed by the dominated against those who dominate. Eldridge Cleaver (1968) first "practiced" rape against black women. When his rape techniques had been "mastered," he raped white women, in revenge, he said, against white men.

There seems a consensus among many black scholars, intellectuals, and activists that there is today a "crisis" in black masculinity, evidenced, in part, by the crime statistics just surveyed. One prominent African-American intellectual expresses his sense of the "crisis" this way:

> The pain is in the eyes. Young black men in their late twenties or early thirties living in urban America, lost and abandoned, aimlessly walking and hawking the streets with nothing behind their eyes but anger, confusion, disappointment and pain. These men, running the streets, occupying

> corners, often are beaten beyond recognition, with scars both visible and internal. These men, black men—sons of Afrika, once strong and full of the hope that America lied about—are now knee-less, voice-broken, homeless, forgotten and terrorized into becoming beggars, thieves or ultra-dependents on a system that considers them less than human and treats them with less dignity and respect than dead dogs. I am among these men. (Madhubuti 1990, frontispiece)

There has been little acknowledgment of this crisis among whites. Not only is he imprisoned in the white imagination, the black man is also imprisoned in the white man's jails. He has been variously described as "black beast with bull-sized genitals" (Day 1977, 198), as some kind of "walking phallus" (Hernton 1965/1988, 38), an animalistic satyr driven by insatiable sexual appetites, a sexual athlete gifted with extraordinary sexual prowess. His reputation among many whites is as a "super-stud" (Blackwell 1977, 226), "America's fearsome sex symbol" (Poussaint 1972, 114). As James Blackwell (1977, 226) observes, dryly: "There was, and is, of course, a certain amount of projection and fantasy in these perceptions of the black male." Fanon declared: "The black man is locked into his body" (quoted in Johnson 1994, 123), seen by whites "predominantly in genital terms" (Hernton 1965/1988, 38). These fantasies do not appear to cluster around the black *female* body in quite the same way as they do around the black *male* body (Johnson 1994).

African-American men, Haki Madhubuti observes, are without power, land, and money in a country where European-American manhood is measured by such possessions. "Black young men," he continues, "are quickly becoming an illiterate, nonverbal, directionless, unattached, nonresponsible, uncreative, jobless problem" (Madhubuti 1990, 78). He quotes Hannibal Tirus Afrik who, Madhubuti argues, has a forceful analysis of the black male problem: "The glorification of the 'phallic power,' hustling, conning and strong-arm techniques against our own people is rewarded with materialistic trinkets and false ego-tripping. The best way to build a 'rep' in the neighborhood is through getting over on black folks" (quoted in Madhubuti 1990, 79). "I might add," Madhubuti continues, "that the impregnation of sisters adds 'positively' to the 'reputation' of young Black men" (79).

The white image of the black male, Ronald L. Taylor (1977) summarizes, would seem to have three basic elements: (1) the black male has been emasculated by white society, (2) the emasculation process has prevented him from coming to full emotional maturity, and (3) as a result of these psychocultural processes, the black male tends to be a poor husband and unreliable father. These elements of black manhood follow, presumably, from the experience of slavery, segregation, and the multitude of forms, including sexual, white racism has taken. History may be past but it is not gone; its residual effects further undermine black men in the contemporary situation in which so-called macrostructural forces make black manhood elusive and unstable. Many commentators, both black and white, point to "certain socialization practices which tend to convey a view of masculinity that is essentially 'deviant,' or 'psychopathological' in extreme" (Taylor 1977, 1). Was this always so?

II. Precolonial West African Manhood

In patriarchal societies—as most West African communities were—males were privileged as the more valuable of the two sexes.

—Daniel Black, *Dismantling Black Manhood: An Historical and Literary Analysis of the Legacy of Slavery* (1997)

[O]ne must maintain a skeptical attitude toward claims that many contemporary social or cultural forms represent direct continuities from the African homelands.

—Stanley Mintz and Richard Price, *The Birth of African-American Culture* (1976/1992)

As his Americanization became more and more total, he [the black man] was conditioned to define his rebellion in terms of the white nightmare. He accepted as appropriate the white man's emphasis upon his sexuality. And accepted as sincere the white man's reasons for trying to abort his sexuality.

—Michelle Wallace, *Black Macho and the Myth of the Superwoman* (1978)

There is no slavery without sexual depravity.

—Gilberto Freyre, *The Masters and the Slaves* (1946)

The sense of black manhood imperiled or lost is sufficiently powerful today that studies have been undertaken to attempt to retrieve precolonial, pre-American, meanings of black manhood. In one such study Daniel Black (1997) argues that black manhood was "dismantled" by slavery. He works to establish the meaning of black manhood in precolonial West Africa (the region from which many enslaved Africans were stolen) in an effort, apparently, to help contemporary black men remember who they are, or were, before Europeans and European Americans had their way with them. Prior to subjugation by the Europeans, Black asserts, "the concept of manhood throughout West African communities was quite unlike the notion possessed by black males in the United States today. ... [P]roverbs and folktales suggest that manhood was inextricably linked to a male's ability to support others, whatever that entailed" (11).

To become a man in precolonial West Africa, boys passed through four consecutive stages: (1) boyhood rites of passage, (2) demonstrations of physical prowess as adolescents, (3) husbandhood, and (4) fatherhood. Only after a male had achieved the maturational goals associated with these four stages did the community consider him a man: "one who could fend for himself and procreate like other men of the village" (Black 1997, 12). This identificatory direction seems not unlike that suggested by contemporary object relations theory. Both young boys and girls spent their childhood with their mothers. Later, sexed segregation occurred, as boys were put through a number of tests, at least one of which sounds like hazing: "In one place, boys were shaven and made to walk between double rows of older boys of the previous initiation group as the latter flogged them severely" (Black 1997, 13–14). If a boy wept during this initiation, or showed any fear or even timidity, he was frowned upon by all and, on occasion, beaten. Circumcision was often an aspect of this second stage of initiation. While the procedure was very painful, boys were expected to endure the process without screaming or weeping (Black 1997).

Other phases of initiation into precolonial West African manhood also disclose a certain resemblance to hazing. Black (1997) reports that "initiation boys are required to take a pebble in their mouths. Each boy is then given two severe blows and he must afterward spit out the pebble into a hole in the ground. If the boy writhes and cries he loses the pebble and is disgraced" (quoted on 15). In Nigeria, at a certain point in the third stage of initiation, boys performed plays which they wrote and directed. One is reminded of Paulo Freire's pedagogical use of theater and Judith Butler's elaboration of gender as performativity, although the three are by no means equivalents. The young African men disguised themselves with self-made masks and costumes and produced a masquerade. Black (1997) quotes Ottenberg (1989) to elaborate: "Masquerading is an aesthetic device, with all its complex symbolism, to separate the growing boy from his mother, who is now on the other side of the fence, as it were. Here art and aesthetic act in the service of boyhood maturation, whatever else they do" (77; quoted in Black 1997, 17).

Females were excluded from these rites, which functioned for the boys as a kind of "weaning" from their mothers. Homosociality now established, the young men are said to now appreciate "the importance of secrecy as a male quality" (Black 1997, 17). Black explains that initiation ceremonies often took place outside the village limits; he repeated that "boys were never to discuss their experiences with others. ... Fathers told sons, 'You are just small boys and still sleep near your mothers. Now we will take you to sleep with us in the men's house'" (35). Perhaps object relations theory is not limited to contemporary white middle-class settings, as David Gilmore's (1990) review of cross-cultural research on manhood suggests.

Now weaned from their mothers, young African men sought nothing more "than the applause of their fathers, which they received freely if their performance in boyhood rites was meritorious. Consequently, initiation ceremonies were times of great excitement for most boys as they moved closer to being their father's ultimate joy and, in the process, closer to manhood" (Black 1997, 19). Key to these ceremonies, especially for those between ages 13 and 18, was the display of physical prowess. Such prowess appears to be equivalent to virility, a quality teenage males were expected to demonstrate in order to receive the respect and admiration not only of male initiators but everyone in the community (Black 1997).

Physical strength was most often displayed through wrestling matches. Perhaps because wrestling in precolonial West Africa was both competitive and combative, it was "developed to an extent which makes it comparable with the Olympic games" (quoted in Black 1997, 19). We are told: "Wrestling was a test of manhood and thus a means of courting" (Baker and Morgan 1987, 29). Most wrestlers were between 16 and 20, during which time they were expected to abstain from sexual intercourse. So idolized were these muscular young men that when a wrestling champion entered the ring, trumpets were sounded. They were compared to warriors. Black tells us: "Like great wrestlers, famed warriors brought immeasurable honor and prestige to their communities. To capture one's war enemies and take them back to one's home community resulted in untempered praise of the warrior-captor, who, in turn, often kept the captives as slaves" (1997, 27). Not only the young man's peers appreciated his physical accomplishments; Alexander Falconbridge's 1788 diary reports that West African men were "extremely athletic and muscular and very expert in the water and could swim for many miles" (quoted in Black 1997, 28).

In most groups, Black (1997, 29) tells us, "until a son married, his father still functioned as his head," which is to say as a kind of "husband." In Ghana, sons were advised, "When you walk behind your father, you learn to walk like him" (quoted in Black 1997, 33). The structural parallel between "husband" and "father" is further suggested when we learn that "wives were expected to treat their husbands with great honor and reverence. Some women walked behind their husbands in public" (29). Both fathers and husbands structured not only each other's lives but women's lives as well: "[i]t was within the husband's bounds to dictate his wife's public and private character. She was never to disagree with him publicly nor was she to refuse any of his requests" (30).

No doubt realizing how this reads today, Black (1997, 30) is quick to add that "this is not to suggest that husbands manipulated wives much like one would a robot, but to illustrate that the husband was the head of the household, as defined by precolonial West Africans, and wives usually allowed husbands such authority." The disclaimer does not seem to me to be very successful. Black senses that, perhaps, as he continues: "[b]oys were taught to honor and respect women. ... Young husbands were told 'A good wife is more precious than gold'" (30), but the commodification of "woman" here only reiterates, not humanizes, the position of women in precolonial Africa. Indeed: "A husband who could not control his own wife was never honored as a man among those who questioned his ability to rule his own compound." But, Black adds, the privilege of power is not without its responsibilities: "Along with being the head of the family, the husband was also the provider" (quoted passages on 31). Such a mix of authority and responsibility might have required divine authorization. Indeed, religion was important in traditional West African culture; the father was also a religious figure (Black 1997).

Black's apparent interest in idealizing this lost past of West African manhood conflicts with his apparent concern over how patriarchal African manhood "reads" to contemporary American readers, who are well aware of the present politicization of sex roles and gender generally. So, Black argues, defensively it seems to me, that as patriarchal as West African culture might appear to contemporary readers, it is still not as patriarchal as European culture: "To be sure, African men were patriarchal long before they ever left home. This is why they assumed the captor's notions of manhood so readily. White men were definitely more destructively and tyrannically patriarchal than most African men had probably ever been; yet the ideas of male dominance, power, and control were well-established aspects of West African concept of manhood centuries before the Europeans ever arrived in Africa" (Black 1997, 100).

Black assures us that "[i]t is a misconception to think that African women were simply 'kept' by African men." But in the next sentence we learn that African women's career options were, let us say, limited: "Quite the contrary, wives spent their days cooking, weaving baskets, molding pottery, tending to children, and working alongside their husbands in the fields. Even when pregnant, wives were expected to fulfill their traditional roles." Women were, then, confined to domestic duties; they provided for their husbands and families through a daily regimen of disciplined labor, even when pregnant: "In short, husbands were expected to rule wives and to provide for them" (quoted passages in Black 1997, 31–32). Indeed, the thoroughly domesticated status of the precolonial West African women Black describes is evident in his comment on polygamy, a marital arrangement at least one contemporary theorist of black manhood has endorsed and which precolonial African men were permitted:

> The implication here is that polygamy is a direct result of the male desire for large numbers of children. Whether or not this is so, I cannot determine. However, if a wife was found barren, she was sometimes dismissed from her husband's household and returned to her own family. ... Children composed more than 65% of most village populations and brought great pride to fathers who could boast having conceived many of them. (Black 1997, 33)

Fathers and mothers could easily lose their children to the usual childhood diseases and accidents, and after the sixteenth century, to white men. This danger became sufficiently common that the Ashanti of Ghana were known to warn young male initiates: "A man who moves about alone is met on the road and seized as a slave" (quoted in Black 1997, 18). If seized, he was taken across the Atlantic to the Americas.

Middle Passage

The long horrible trip to America became known as the Middle Passage. The first stage was the Long March when captives traveled from their home villages to the slave vessels on the coast, where they started the three-to-eight-month journey across the Atlantic to the "new world." Before they were herded aboard slave vessels, captors branded them with hot irons and attached numbers inscribed on leaden tags. The Middle Passage was characterized by sexual abuse which, along with "[c]hains and irons [,] robbed the African male of his virility and began the annihilation of his concept of manhood" (Black 1997, 47). John Newton described how naked black bodies were bonded to each other: "Their [slaves'] lodging rooms below the deck ... were sometimes no more than five feet high and sometimes less, and this height was divided toward the middle for the slaves to lie in two rows, one above the other, on each side of the ship, close to each other like books upon a shelf. [Slave ships] resembled a 'slaughter house'" (quoted in Black 1997, 48). Because members of one tribe or cultural grouping were often split up, they spoke different languages and were, therefore, unable to communicate. Black (1997, 49) imagines: "Yet even for those who shared a common tongue, what was there to say? For the trauma known to men throughout the Middle Passage leads me to believe that conversation would have soothed few woes."

Enslaved Africans did fight back, as best they could under the circumstances. The most widely employed form of resistance during the Middle Passage was mutiny, perhaps the best known instance of which involved the *Amistad.* The second most common form of resistance was suicide. Throughout the Middle Passage, African bodies were jettisoned whenever white overseers deemed it necessary. In fact, so common was the practice that historians still disagree as to the total number of African bodies thrown overboard. When those enslaved males who were still alive finally reached the Americas, Black tells us, "they were already enraged, culturally displaced, dehumanized, and probably convinced that manhood, as they understood it, would never be theirs again" (Black 1997, 56). Who can doubt the catastrophe of personhood that enslavement meant, but Black here seems to superimpose "manhood" on everything, making gender identity the omnipresent and final reality. Like several other black male intellectuals, Black suggests that black men suffered more than black women: "Certainly women and womanhood, too, underwent a certain level of displacement; yet possibly the displacement of African manhood could have been more severe" (57).

Enslavement

Replacing his father in the West African village of his birth and upbringing and maturation is the white man, his "master" who becomes "the Man" (Black 1997, 63). Enslaved, the black male was totally dependent upon the whims of the white man, a situation of oppression that all but destroyed what remained of African manhood (Black 1997). Black quotes controversial slave historian Stanley Elkins (1959): "He could now look to none but his master, the one to whom the system had committed his entire being: the man upon whose will depended his food, his shelter, his sexual connections, whatever moral instruction he might be offered, whatever 'success' was possible within the system, his very security—in short, everything" (Elkins 1959, 102; quoted in Black 1997, 59). As Hartman (1997) has shown, the white master occupied the enslaved black body, even sexually, always as an extension of his capacity to labor. Any signs of resistance to this "occupation" could be met with flogging or worse. To illustrate Black quotes from such a scene of subjugation from a narrative written by the slave Henry Bibb. Trying to escape, Bibb is captured by Whitfield the overseer. Back on the plantation he is punished; he recalls the ordeal:

> My clothing was stripped off and I was compelled to lie down to the ground with my face to the earth. Four stakes were driven in the ground, to which my hands and feet were tied. Then the overseer stood over me with the lash and laid on according to the Deacon's order. ... After I was marked from my neck to my heels, the Deacon took the gory lash, and said he thought there was a spot on my back yet where he could put in a few more. He wanted to give me something to remember him by, he said. (quoted in Black 1997, 105)

Despite such sadism, Black (1997, 80) suggests that "the destruction of African male virility via physical abuse was only the first stage in the annihilation of the West African concept of manhood. The second stage was the displacement of enslaved African men from the home, particularly as husbands." It was a tragic loss as black fathers were no longer able to "usher sons into manhood" (85). Black (1997, 90) concludes: "West African men arrived in America with a very explicit idea of what it meant to be a man, and when enslavement forced them to exist outside of that cultural standard, they suffered a degradation only they could understand." And when the first generation of enslaved men died, "the West African concept of manhood, in its purest form, expired in America, too" (Black 1997, 92).

Students of the family structure and sex roles within the slave communities suggest that when monogamous family relationships existed, there was a tendency toward some degree of male domination. Clarence Mohr (1986) reasons that black men were not unaffected by the overwhelmingly patriarchal orientation of white society and that they probably tended to define their roles as husbands and fathers within a social framework that mimicked their white masters. The significance of chattel slavery was "doubly ironic," Mohr (1986, 222) suggests, "for while the slave system encouraged and reinforced a male-dominated, patriarchal family structure in white society, it acted to prevent the full development of corresponding sets of relationships in slave families by stripping black men of the capacity for autonomous action in domestic matters. At the same time, of course, slavery also placed white women in a position of dominance over all black men."

Perhaps not surprisingly, under such circumstances, more than a few male slaves "vowed early in life never to marry. They did not want to marry a woman and be forced to watch as she was beaten, insulted, raped, overworked, or starved without being able to protect her" (Rose 1982, 40; quoted in Black 1997, 119). "Marriage," Black (1997) argues, "ceased being a lifestyle to which black males aspired enthusiastically, and husbandhood lost most of its glory. This means, of course, that the family was ascribed a new place in the black male psyche" (Black 1997, 119).

By the end of enslavement, Black (1997) continues, the West African formation of manhood was no longer recognizable. Enslaved black men had not been able to either demonstrate their physical prowess in self-defense nor provide for and protect wives and children. Still, Black implies, the need for manhood remained. Consequently, black men searched for standard of manhood they could achieve within political and socioeconomic constraints. "They found one," Black tells us. "The new concept of manhood"—sounding here (inadvertently) like Judith Butler—"was also rooted in male performance, but not as provider and protector," but "upon one's sexual virility" (quoted passages in Black 1997, 126). This seems logical to Black, "for a black man's penis was the only aspect of his maleness which the captor had not usurped." In fact it was admired by slavetraders and masters alike, presumably as an indicator of breeding potential.

After Emancipation, in fact, the white man "took" it, that is, castration during lynching. Now Black (1997) himself seems to succumb to racial fantasy, not a solitary sin as we will see, since Robert Staples (1977, 1982) will as well. "Sexual performance," Black tells us, "provided black men an arena in which they could be the guaranteed victor, never being forced to relinquish their title to any one. And, without doubt, white captors contributed to this idea." No doubt. So concludes Black's tale of a pure (and patriarchal) precolonial West African manhood emasculated by enslavement to a contemporary concept of black manhood "disproportionately tied to his sexual abilities" (quoted passages in Black 1997, 126). To summarize he quotes bell hooks (1992):

> [W]ith the emergence of a fierce phallocentrism [during the latter years of enslavement], a man was no longer a man because he provided care for his family, he was a man simply because he had a penis. Furthermore, his ability to use that penis in the arena of sexual conquest could bring him as much status as being a wage earner and provider. A sexually defined masculinity ideal rooted in physical domination and sexual possession of women could be accessible to all men. Hence, even unemployed [or enslaved] black men could gain status, could be seen as the embodiment of masculinity, within a phallocentric framework. (94; quoted in Black 1997, 126–127)

Black adds that black men did not willingly embrace this phallocentric idea of manhood voluntarily or even consciously. In fact, Black speculates that black men at first rejected the role as "stud," regarding it as another means of white male exploitation of black bodies.

Still, this was a way black men could have their manhood unquestioned and uncontested. Stereotypes of "studs" and "bucks" began during enslavement as white men obsessed over laboring and procreating black male bodies. "Over time," Black (1997, 127) suggests, "black men began to participate in that celebration [of studliness], to the extent that they even constructed myths and folkloric tales about the length of their penises and the extent to which they could 'go all night'." From enslavement, then, black male heterosexuality would seem to have been circulating in a white male system of desire. Black (1997, 170) sees the historical throughline from West Africa to contemporary America as he concludes: "Yet black men still struggle for manhood to a degree no less severe than their forefathers. It is critical that the black community continue to wrestle with this phenomenon, for our success in reconceptualizing the notion of black manhood could be the answer we have long awaited concerning the current dilemma of the African American male."

Black's study probably tells us as much about the current black male fascination with "manhood" as much as it does about any throughlines from West Central Africa to the present. There is no mention, for instance, of homosexuality in Africa. Both male homosexuals and lesbians had culturally sanctioned roles in a number of tribes (Sweet 1996). Moreover, anthropological research questions any culturally monolithic view of the Africans who were enslaved. Enslaved individuals on the same ship often came from different language and cultural groupings. As awful as the Middle Passage and slavery were, they were not only destructive, as African peoples found moments of self-affirmation and cultural creation despite the nightmare of enslavement.

Anthropological research suggests that African-American culture is hybridized, that "pure" and identifiable retentions of African culture are more fantasy than reality (Mintz and Price 1976/1992).

Consider, for a moment, the Middle Passage. Black's view is that the Middle Passage was, after the Long March, the second phase of the complete destruction of West African manhood. No doubt that is accurate as far as it goes. But anthropologists Sidney Mintz and Richard Price provide a more complicated view of the birth of African-American culture. This birth begins in the traumata of capture, enslavement, and transport. As pure African cultures were destroyed, the beginnings of what would later develop into "African-American cultures" occurred in those very earliest interactions of newly enslaved men and women on the African continent itself. On the Long March they were shackled together in the coffles, packed into filthy "factory" dungeons, literally squeezed together between the decks of stinking ships, separated often from their kin and even from speakers of the same language. They were

> left bewildered about their present and their future, stripped of all prerogatives of status or rank (at least, so far as the masters were concerned), and homogenized by a dehumanizing system that viewed them as faceless and largely interchangeable. Yet we know that even in such utterly abject circumstances, these people were not simply passive victims. In the present context, we are thinking less of the many individual acts of heroism and resistance which occurred during this period than of certain simple but significant *cooperative* efforts which, in retrospect, may be viewed as the true beginnings of African-American culture and society. (Mintz and Price 1976/1992, 42–43; emphasis in original)

Significant for us is that these cooperative efforts which comprised the birth of African-American culture were primarily homosocial. Not homosocial in Sedgwick's (1985) sense or in Gayle Rubin's (1975), as these formations of "homosocial" depend upon the subjugation and commodification of women. Enslaved men were stripped, as Black documents, of such patriarchal prerogatives. They were themselves commodified, and not just in economic terms, but in sexual ones, as they were made to stand naked before slave traders, their muscles fingered, their genitals "examined," their very bodies locked in the gaze of white male (economic, political, sexual) desire. When these tormented, injured, suffering young black men came to each other, it was in need—psychological, sexual?—not in triumph after the passage of manhood initiation rites nor as patriarchs ready to exchange female property. Due to their enslavement, black men came to each other on different terms:

> Various shreds of evidence suggest that some of the earliest social bonds to develop in the coffles ... especially, during the long Middle Passage were of a dyadic (two-person) nature. Partly, perhaps, because of the general policy of keeping men and women separate, they were usually between members of the same sex. The bond between shipmates, those who shared passage on the same slaver, is the most striking example. In widely scattered parts of Afro-America, the "shipmate" relationship became a

> major principle of social organization and continued for decades or even centuries to shape ongoing social relations. (Mintz and Price 1976/1992, 43)

In the experience of enslavement was the intensification of black male bonding.

The sex-role structure of African Americans has sometimes been ascribed to enslavement and to European and European-American influence generally. Certainly the picture Black (1997) presents of precolonial West African tribal life suggests sharply differentiated sex roles structured patriarchally. One segment of laboring life would appear to support the allegation that European cultures distorted a pristine patriarchal African manhood. During slavery both men and women worked plantation grounds; both worked long hours in the fields under the unrelenting southern sun. Upon Emancipation, men took over agricultural production in all of its facets. Did this male takeover of agriculture represent an adaptation to the sex-role expectations of the dominant white society? Or did smart women want to escape the dirt, heat, and hardship of the fields? Is there some other explanation (Mintz and Price 1976/1992)?

The Saramaka Maroons of Suriname suggest that the European explanation for black patriarchy may not be sufficient. Though Saramaka women were in many respects strongly dependent economically on men, and had been for centuries, a man's masculinity or status was not tied to his wife's dependence (or lack of it). Nor was this association evident among African peoples elsewhere in the Caribbean. Since the original New World ancestors of the Saramaka spent relatively little time as slaves, we must be skeptical that their sex-role structures were a consequence of the plantation experience or of intermingling with Europeans generally. If this is the case, then, in sex-role formation perhaps certain fundamental West and Central African traditions of appropriate male and female behavior were still being performed. Somewhat in contrast to Daniel Black, Mintz and Price (1976/1992) argue that not enough is known about seventeenth- and eighteenth-century West or Central African societies to be certain about this point. Again, the hybridity hypothesis is probably the most sound one in thinking about African-American culture, including the African American culture of masculinity.

Contemporary popular efforts to reclaim a lost African past can prove psychologically effective, however mythic and removed that past is. Its largely imaginary status today leaves some adherents in gender conservative positions, presumably in the service of loyalty to a precolonial period. For instance, in Joseph L. White and James H. Cones III's (1999) *Black Man Emerging*, we are told that "boys [in precolonial Africa] were taught their responsibilities as husbands and fathers, proper care of the body, and appropriate sexual behavior" (20). Moreover, "in pre-colonial Africa, gender role identity followed a patriarchal pattern in community and family life" (White and Cones 1999, 20), a statement that would, one would think, disqualify that culture and time as models for the present. Instead, the accolades continue: "African existence is deeply spiritual" (21). In their chapter (6) entitled "masculine alternatives," there is not one word about homosexuality.

In *Coming of Age: African American Male Rites-of-Passage*—another example of present uses of an imaginary past—Paul Hill, Jr. (1992, 69), declares that "Africentric Rites-Of-Passage is a transformational process that functions as a prelude to a metamorphosis, to manhood, to adulthood, to wholeness. Wholeness reflects self-knowledge, personal mastery, and an Africentric locus of control. The Africentric locus of control places descendants of Africans in the center. It proceeds on the basis of the question, 'Is it in the best interest of the African people?'" Presumably, answers to this question require an unquestioning acceptance of precolonial West African gender formation, indicated in one of the major objectives: "to help a youth realize and achieve masculine and/or feminine roles that are satisfying, responsible, and consistent with acceptable cultural norms and values" (Hill 1992, 91). One suspects precolonial African homosexual practices are not included (Sweet 1996).

III. In the Old Northwest

For then, the Negro's body was exploited as amorally as the soil and climate.
—Ralph Ellison, *Shadow and Act* (1964/1995)

What the dark man wants then is merely to live his own life, in his own world, with his own chosen companions, in whatever of comfort, luxury, or emoluments his talent or his money can in an impartial market secure.
—Anna Julia Cooper, "A Voice from the South" (1892/1998)

Most of all, black couples wanted to be let alone to live in peace.
—Joan E. Cashin, "A Northwest Passage: Gender, Race, and the Family in the Early Nineteenth Century" (1998)

Slavery subjugated black men in every sense, including sexually. But what about those black men who escaped the sadism of white male masters, who escaped to the North, to what was in the early nineteenth century termed the "Old Northwest," what now we would refer to as simply the Midwest. Joan E. Cashin (1998) has studied this question, introducing it by reminding us of one of the most memorable incidents in American literature. That incident occurs in Harriet Beecher Stowe's *Uncle Tom's Cabin* and involves a slave woman's courageous escape to the Old Northwest. Eliza Harris leaps across the Ohio River clutching her infant son, jumping from one teetering ice floe to another until she reaches the Ohio shore, where she and her child are free. Soon she is reunited with her husband, George Harris, who fled the South because "slavery threatened to destroy his family as well as his self-respect as a man" (Cashin 1998, 222). While the scene of a brave mother taking her infant to freedom celebrates maternal devotion and women's bravery, Mrs. Harris's trials do not end there, as she endures a wild carriage ride through Ohio which includes a gunfight with slave-catchers. To disguise herself, she cuts her hair, cross-dresses as a man (and her son as a girl), and succeeds in sailing with her family across Lake Erie. The Harris family settles in Montreal, where they live happily ever after, in a fantasy of safety and domesticity shared by many in the white northern middle class during the time Stowe was writing (Cashin 1998).

The Harrises were fictive, but as Joan Cashin points out, there were many factual versions of them. Many black women and men exhibited astonishing courage and intelligence to escape bondage. Like black women, black men fled to protect their families and to find freedom for themselves, but many black men also risked death in order "to preserve ... their sense of masculinity" (Cashin 1998, 222). Unlike the fictive Harrises, most African Americans did not travel all the way to Canada but settled in the Old Northwest. While "free," most of these refugees still had to contend with legalized discrimination, bigotry, poverty, and the constant threat of recapture. They had to face on a daily basis multiple dangers that other (white) families in the Northwest never knew. Living in a besieged state, many were forced to diverge from white, middle-class gender norms. Their experiences, Cashin writes, "remind us how malleable gender roles can be and how dramatically they may change over time and geographic space" (223). Relying on legal records, census returns, registers for free blacks, memoirs, and postbellum interviews with reformers and fugitive slaves, Cashin tells us about black families in the Old Northwest from the beginning of the nineteenth century through the 1850s.

The states and territories of the Old Northwest did not provide full legal equality for black settlers, and those rights they did provide they gave grudgingly. Both Illinois and Indiana periodically barred free blacks from entering, and Indiana once appropriated funds to expel its black residents, although it never in fact did. In Ohio, Indiana, and the Michigan territory, black settlers were forced to register with local officials, prove their free status, and give bond for good behavior, a practice which the slave states already required of free black residents. Only a few African Americans living in the Old Northwest were permitted to vote in school elections; black children could not attend public schools in Indiana, Michigan, or Wisconsin. In 1849 Ohio's legislature finally allowed black students to enroll in its public schools, but in 1850 and again in 1859 the state courts overruled the statehouse. Segregation in other public facilities, such as hospitals and orphanages, was the universal practice, even though all the states in the Old Northwest taxed black residents to support those white-only facilities (Cashin 1998).

Many whites were not exactly welcoming to black refugees. Not all whites were racist; a few even became the friends and allies of their embattled black neighbors. Some even became abolitionists, but the racial prejudice that Alexis de Tocqueville observed in the free states was very much visible in the Old Northwest. Most whites took for granted that they were superior to all people of color. In 1827, the Ohio governor spoke for many when he declared that blacks constituted a "degraded race." That state's legislators once pronounced African Americans a "serious political and moral evil." Like European Americans elsewhere, whites went crazy periodically, a deranged state that often took the form of mobs, as we have seen. Mobs savaged black neighborhoods in Cincinnati, Portsmouth, and other Ohio towns, and a white mob once shut down a private school for black children in Zanesville. A gang of whites in Jeffersonville, Indiana, publicly whipped two black men who, it was alleged, were involved sexually with white women. Black abolitionists seemed to summon a special fury; whites beat Frederick Douglass after a speaking engagement in Pendleton, Indiana, in 1843, and stoned Martin Delany in Marseilles, Ohio, in 1848. One white Quaker remarked, with staggering understatement, that Indiana was a "hard state for a colored man to live in" (quoted in Cashin 1998, 224). So was the entire Northwest, for black women and men, that is (Cashin 1998).

Because daily life required a state of constant alertness, black men and women could hardly afford the luxury of observing ordinary or taken-for-granted gender conventions. Of course, the slave experience had required, as Cashin notes, "adaptability from both sexes; the chief gender convention for men and women in these circumstances was flexibility." But "freedom" afforded little opportunity to perform gender ideals, which, in the case of white men, allowed considerable flexibility anyway. Cashin quotes J. W. Loguen who described his mother as both "feminine" and "masculine," a devoted nurturant mother who also fought ferociously to protect herself from an abusive white master. She quotes as well Daniel Shaw, who recorded that his mother taught him to cook and sew in case he had to run a household by himself one day. According to Shaw's biographer, his mother knew he needed to be gender flexible, so that he could do whatever a slave might "have to do" (quoted passages in Cashin 1998, 225).

During their escape from the South, both male and female runaways sometimes cross-dressed to disguise themselves, a tactic that turned out to be remarkably effective. Like the Harrises in *Uncle Tom's Cabin*, Mom and Dad as well as children sometimes changed gender identities several times on their way to the North. Some slaves planned their changes in costume while making their plans to escape; others decided to change genders on the run, on their own initiative or at the suggestion of black and white "conductors" on the Underground Railroad. A few went beyond mere costume-changing and tried to "pass" as whites; one black man cross-dressed, powdered his face, and passed successfully as a white woman. Such gendered creativity and flexibility would continue to be required of both women and men in their new homes in the Old Northwest (Cashin 1998).

Slaveowners' rights were codified in the Constitution (Article IV, Section 2), the Fugitive Slave Law of 1793, and the Northwest Ordinance's sixth clause, which legalized the capture of escaped slaves in the region. Personal liberty and other due-process legislation in practice proved of little help to black fugitives. Nor were free-born African Americans safe, for slave-catchers sometimes took them by mistake or, rather than return south empty-handed, by design. The legal records indicate, Cashin reports, that slave-hunters divided many black families, destroyed countless marriages, sometimes many years after the couple had escaped bondage. One white slave-hunter discovered a former slave nineteen years after his escape and returned him to the South, leaving his distraught wife behind (Cashin 1998).

The apprenticeship system in the Northwest broke up many black families, separating children from their parents. More than a few whites manipulated the system to extend servitude for blacks, much as white southerners exploited it to enslave free blacks below the Mason-Dixon line. The legal codes in territorial

Indiana permitted long-term indentures of blacks and mulattos; terms of ten, twenty, and forty years were not uncommon. One sixteen-year-old named Jacob was indentured for ninety years. In other sections of the Northwest, black children were apprenticed to pay for the unfulfilled indentures of their parents, while others were forced into apprenticeships by migrating slaveholders who were determined to profit from their labor (Cashin 1998).

African-American families in the nineteenth-century Northwest not only lived in constant fear of capture; they lived only a day or so away from absolute destitution, as economic opportunities were few. This combination of circumstances, Cashin (1998, 229) reports, had a powerful effect on gender roles: "parallel roles emerged for the sexes, revolving around family duty, political activism, and physical combat against slave-catchers." By all accounts, black men felt outraged that slavery prevented them from exercising the rights and responsibilities of fatherhood. One runaway from Kentucky testified that slaves felt "no security for their family ties." Contrary to proslavery propaganda which depicted black men as uncaring husbands and fathers, much like racist propaganda today, most black men believed that their obligations as fathers and husbands constituted the foundation of masculinity. For most nineteenth-century black men, the most important gender convention was the exercise of familial responsibilities. White men, especially slaveholders and slave-hunters, seemed intent on disrupting the black family and in so doing wounded the masculinity of black men throughout this period. One runaway declared that slavery prevented a man from "being a man," by which he meant, in part, that black men were unable to plan for his children's future. Many vowed that their children would be raised in freedom. One freed black man named Charles Ball was determined to somehow "safeguard" his family still enslaved in Maryland; he tried several times to rescue his wife and children and felt "tormented" by the separation (quoted passages in Cashin 1998, 229–230).

Such struggles for manhood continued when black men reached the Old Northwest and set up their own households. Many men went to considerable lengths to find or create opportunities for their children, only to be undermined or blocked by their white neighbors. One black father placed his daughter in an academy at Massillon, Ohio, despite opposition from local whites. When the principal expelled all the black pupils, he refused to accept the situation. He moved his family to Canada. Many black men and women generously opened their homes to children that were not their own, a tradition Hortense Powdermaker would find still operative in twentieth-century Mississippi, as we see later in this chapter (Cashin 1998).

In 1850, a quarter of the eighty-eight two-parent households in the Old Northwest included children with surnames different from that of the man of the house. These were not servants, as all of these households were poor. They were poor, in part, *because* they supported orphans and runaway children. Most public orphanages in the Old Northwest refused to admit black children, and many black men understood how easily children could lose their parents to slave-hunters. Black fathers also went to great lengths to recover their own children despite nearly overwhelming odds. When slave-hunters snatched Lewis Williamson's children from his Ohio farm, probably with the collusion of his white neighbors, and sold them down the Mississippi River, the horrified father searched unceasingly for six years before locating his children enslaved on a Louisiana plantation. Williamson proved their free status and brought them home (Cashin 1998).

Another gender convention changed for black men in the Northwest, one without precedent under slavery: political activism. Although individual enslaved men surfaced as quasi-political figures in many plantation communities, only in the free states could men work openly for political progress. In the Old Northwest such men as John Mercer Langston, William Howard Day, John Sella Martin, and Henry Bibb rose to prominence. As the abolitionist movement intensified in the 1830s, black men found and made more opportunities to act in solidarity, organizing reform societies and fraternal orders across the region to agitate for the rights of citizenship. Black men used petitions, referenda, court challenges, and protest meetings to make their case. They tended to perceive these civic and political rights in gendered terms, just as white men conflated politics, race, and gender. Martin Delany called on black men to reclaim the "manhood" that subjugation had taken from them. Other men described their yearning for political equality in gendered language. In a complaint that echoes still today, one nine-year resident of Indiana complained that whites did not treat him like "a man." Another left Indiana for Canada where he imagined he would enjoy "every right that every man has" (quoted in Cashin 1998, 231).

It took time and resources to become political activists; few black men had both. But all black men had to protect themselves and their families against slave-hunters. The traffic in recaptured slaves did not become heavy until the 1830s, but it was an element of African-American life throughout the period. Proslavery apologists declared that all black men were helpless cowards, but that was another white man's fantasy. Most black men fought ferociously to avoid being returned to slavery. When a fugitive in Indiana named Sam believed that his master had found him, he grabbed a butcher knife and prepared himself for a hard fight, preparing to "sell his life or liberty as dearly as possible." When Horatio Washington and two nephews realized that a man had turned them over to the Ohio authorities, they ambushed him and managed to escape. As John Parker went about daily life in Ripley, Ohio, he found it necessary to carry a pistol, a knife, and blackjack on his person. This was not his paranoia; he did in fact have to use these weapons more than once both to help runaways and to defend himself from assault (Cashin 1998).

Sometimes black men acted in groups, unable to wait until abolitionists settled their ongoing debate regarding the ethics of using physical force. In Detroit in 1833, a group of black men surrounded the sheriff and prevented him from returning a fugitive to Kentucky. In 1849, several hundred armed black men from Michigan swept into South Bend, Indiana, to free a group of recaptured slaves. These were not only political activities, they were gendered ones as well. William Newman of Cleveland made the link to masculinity explicit when he pleaded for black men to take up arms in order to resist the detested Fugitive Slave Law of 1850. It was absolutely necessary, he said, to "show yourself a MAN" (quoted in Cashin 1998, 231). This particular conflation of masculinity with political activism was specific to black men in the

Northwest, as white men rarely, if ever, had to defend themselves or their families from kidnappers (Cashin 1998).

In the War of 1812, black men in the Old Northwest took the opportunity to fight in uniform. Routinely excluded from military service since the Revolution, federal law had closed militia duty to them in the 1790s. Many whites were either ignorant of or had forgotten about black participation in the Revolutionary War; many believed that African Americans would not fight if given the chance. During this second war against the British, however, a number of African Americans served in combat or in support units. On Lake Erie approximately one hundred black men served with Oliver Perry; two regiments helped Andrew Jackson fight the Battle of New Orleans, and a black company defended Detroit from British attack. A number of black men were so appreciative that Commodore Perry had accepted them into his forces that many named their sons after him (Cashin 1998).

Black women were eager to participate as equal partners in political causes; some black male journalists were critical of them for wanting to do so. Other black men, most prominently Frederick Douglass, became a strong supporter of the woman's rights movement. Cashin cites the work of Rosalyn Terborg-Penn (1978) which suggests that many black men accepted black women as reformers more readily than white men. Many white men could barely tolerate white female reformers, let alone black. Cashin notes that many black men in the Northwest witnessed firsthand the courage many black women exhibited, not only in escaping slavery but in surviving in a hostile Northwest. The ideals of pure womanhood emerging in the white, middle class—among them passivity—would be in these circumstances inappropriate, even irresponsible (Cashin 1998).

Like black men, black women were forced to fight to protect themselves and their children from harm. Court cases from the Jeffersonian and Jacksonian eras indicate that many black women defended themselves with physical force when slave-catchers tried to take them back. One Michigan woman ran into a cornfield after her white master suddenly appeared, turned to face him, and proceeded to give him a "terrible pounding" (quoted in Cashin 1998, 235). Many black women succeeded not only in protecting themselves but their children, husbands, and other relatives from kidnapping. Such feats of physical and psychological courage were peculiar to the Northwest, for unlike slave women or free black southerners these women could fight back without the certainty of swift, deadly retaliation. The Northwest offered its black residents both danger and opportunity (Cashin 1998).

How did black women and men feel about this combination and the unstable gender roles it forced upon them? Most men and women in the Northwest appear to have accepted this gender instability as necessary, recalling their experiences in a matter-of-fact tone, without apology or embarrassment, despite, from white standards, their departure from conventional conduct. Did blacks find white, northern, middle-class gender roles desirable? Cashin asks. A few black women commented on these roles, and Sojourner Truth, no doubt the most famous of the region's female activists, attacked them directly. A young black woman named Sophia Snowden lived in a small town in Ohio during this period; she felt ambivalently about white gender conventions. She kept a scrapbook of newspaper stories, poems, and lyrics; some of these praised white, middle-class femininity, while others questioned or subtly criticized the construct. Neither Truth nor Snowden ever married as free women; their attitudes may not represent those black women who did (Cashin 1998).

IV. Black Masculinity Today

An entire generation of black youth is being destroyed before our eyes.

—Essex Hemphill, "Introduction" to *Brother to Brother: Collected Writings by Black Gay Men* (1991)

I found little of value in the black masculinist discourse of the time, which spoke ceaselessly of Afro-American male dehumanization and castration by white men and black women (our central social narrative for too long).

—Michael Awkward, "A Black Man's Place(s) in Black Feminist Criticism" (1996)

There is no one black masculinity, no essential "subject."

—Thelma Golden, "My Brother" in *Black Male: Representations of Masculinity in Contemporary American Art* (1994)

Will the real black man please stand up?

—Nathan Hare, "Will the Real Black Man Please Stand Up?" in *Black Scholar* 2 (10) (1971)

Slavery did not support the institution of heterosexual marriage; as property, black families were regularly split up. White men raped black women, and probably many black men, at will. As John Blassingame (1979, 172) observed: "Under such a regime slave fathers had little to no authority." Given the nearly absolute power of the white master, Orlando Patterson (1967, 167) declared that "slavery abolished any real social distinctions between males and females." While an exaggeration, structurally speaking both black men and women were white men's "wives." Not those idealized, sentimentalized fantasies in whose "defense" white men would later sexually mutilate black men, but "wives" in the sense of being sexually vulnerable, available whenever and however the white master desired. This structural position led sociologist Robert Park (1950, 280) to assert in the 1920s that "the Negro is the lady of the races."

In the beginning century of slavery, black men greatly outnumbered black women; not until 1840 was there an equal ratio (Staples 1977). In addition to this purely numerical pressure toward male homosexuality, there was a history of homosexuality in Africa, including the prominence of transvested homosexuals in African religion (Sweet 1996). Then there was the sexual vulnerability of the enslaved, part of what Michael Eric Dyson (1995/1996, 159) has characterized as "the pernicious commodification of the black body during slavery." Not only black women were at risk for sexual exploitation; as Saidiya Hartman (1997, 81) observes: "enslaved men were no less vulnerable to the wanton abuses of their owners, although the extent of their sexual exploitation will probably never be known."

In her well-known autobiographical narrative, Harriet Jacobs makes it clear that the subjugation of enslaved black men was sometimes explicitly sexualized. Near the end of *Incidents in the Life of a Slave Girl*, Jacobs (1861/1987) recalls a fugitive slave named Luke, whom she met in a New York street soon after his escape; she warned him about the slave-catchers who might seize him there. Luke's master, Jacobs tell us, was riddled with unspecified "vices" that reduced him, "by excessive dissipation," to a "mere degraded wreck of manhood," whose whim it was to keep Luke naked except for a shirt, "in order to be in readiness to be flogged." The bedridden young master "took into his head the strangest freaks of despotisms," Jacobs continues; "some of these freaks were of a nature too filthy to be repeated" (192). From another slave narrative, *The History of Mary Prince, A West Indian Slave, Related by Herself* (1831) we learn: "Both my master and mistress seemed to think that they had a right to ill-use [the slave boys] at their pleasure (quoted in Alexander 1994, 98; see also Ferguson 1987).

As Christopher Looby (1995) points out, such horrified evocations of homosexuality by tropes of unnameability—"the sin that cannot be named," "the unmentionable vice," and "the love that dare not speak its name"—suggest that Jacobs was intimating that Luke's master abused him sexually. Other "tips of the iceberg" flow to us living nearly a century and a half later. Looby points to the letter of a Confederate private written to his sister in 1865 wherein he reports that his fellow soldiers "rode one of our company on a rail last night for leaving the company and going to sleep with Captain Lowry's black man" (Lowry 1994, 112; quoted in Looby 1995, 544). Looby (1995, 544) acknowledges that while the phrase "sleep with" is not necessarily equivalent to sexual activity in 1865, clearly "what was being punished was taboo physical intimacy—though it seems that the race (and perhaps the social class) rather than the gender of the participants was what made this intimacy punishable."

Slavery in the new world, Taylor (1977, 1) argues, imposed additional responsibilities upon black women, granting to black women "an 'unnatural' superiority over black men." Moreover, he continues, the dual position of husband/father was institutionally erased, thereby denying to black men a legitimate role and function in the slave family. "[T]he black male," Taylor (1977, 2) summarizes, "was put in a predicament in which conformity to masculine norms was all but impossible." The subservient position in which he was cast—docile, humble, and responsible only to his white master—compromised, some black commentators say severely damaged, his masculinity. While ambivalent on that issue, Taylor does say that the role black men came to perform with skill was itself "an adaptive device purchased at considerable psychic cost. Hence, the process of emasculation begun under slavery was compounded and intensified by the relationship to women it imposed, and a somewhat similar set of circumstances produced the same effects on subsequent generations of black men" (1977, 2).

What Taylor (1977, 2) characterizes as "the often antagonistic relationship between black husbands and wives" is assumed to influence black children. Consequently, girls may, he says, come to hold "an exaggerated view of female self-sufficiency," while boys may become more sensitive to their "marginal status and the difficulties involved in assuming a self-satisfying masculine posture." Black boys' difficulties are said to be compounded should the father leave the home, as boys reared in fatherless families are reported to be less socially responsible, less achievement-oriented, and more susceptible to delinquency than young men raised with fathers (Moynihan 1965). This is a view that has been contested (Spillers 1987), but it remains widespread, especially among men. "These days," Haki Madhubuti (1990, 191) writes, "most black boys learn to be fathers by watching the wind (i.e., spaces reserved for missing fathers)." Fifty-three percent of all black families are single mothered, in contrast to 18 percent of white families (20/20 November 4, 1998). "The upshot," Mark Simpson (1994, 3) explains, "of both usages of the absent father formula was the same: families without men at their heads will produce unsuccessfully masculinized men and thus the ruin of society."

Certainly many researchers seem to believe that. Black boys raised without fathers are said to experience "greater difficulty in differentiating the roles of the sexes" (Taylor 1977, 3). They may struggle more over issues of dependency and autonomy; some say they are less mature at any given age. In the absence of the father, Taylor (1977) writes, "the black male child may identify too closely with the mother, the results of which are expressed in ambivalence over sexual identity and overt homosexuality." Writing in a homophobic and heterosexist mode, Haki Madhubuti (1990, 74) blames white society for trying to turn black men "into so-called 'women,' in which case homosexual and bisexual activity becomes the norm rather than the exception." Whether due to the relative absence of a father and/or emasculation by a racist white society, Ulf Hannerz (1977, 56) reports that he found "a kind of fascination with sexual deviation" in the language of many of the black boys he studied. While "faggot" was infrequently used as a term of abuse, "sissy" and "punk" were. As we will see, "punk" is common parlance in prisons where a disproportionate percentage of lower-class black men reside. It does not tend to refer to them.

Given the strong societal prohibitions against homosexuality, black male "confusion over [heterosexual] sexual identity is thought to be compensated for in the form of exaggerated masculinity (e.g., toughness and strong language), or various defense mechanisms (e.g., aggressive independence)" (Taylor 1977, 3). Black male youth tend to develop manhood largely outside the home and under the supervision of his peers, who, according to this heterosexist and patriarchal narrative of black male socialization, tend to present a model of masculinity often at variance with dominant white models. Moreover, Taylor continues, peer-supervised socialization tends to reflect the generalized relationship between the sexes, not a highly individuated one. "[T]he peer group," Hannerz (1977, 35) writes, "is a necessary institution, [but] it is only a poor substitute for family security and stability. Yet without this group, the self-doubts and insecurity of the male would be even stronger and more crippling; in the peer group they can be shared by the frightened and confused little boys and the tough but embattled 'mama's men' they grow into."

But "mama's men" is exactly who many, especially lower-class, young black men do not want to be. On the streets the men they encounter exhibit what Hannerz (1977) terms "ghetto-specific" hypermasculinity; there is a tendency for many boys to be more strongly exposed to this version of masculinity than to any other as they start to spend much of their lives away from the household. Away from their mothers, they share a lived space with men who also are in flight from the home. Hannerz terms this "the reaction formation view" which understands street corner socialization as a backward-looking ritual: in order to arrive at a "normal" male identity, the boys have to purge themselves of identificatory errors made in early childhood. In other words, "peer group formation is seen to be simply a response to the discovery that the identification with mother is all wrong; the boys get together to enhance their masculinity" (Hannerz 1977, 45). A black policeman named David Lemieux told Haki Madhubuti (1990): "We think we're men once we start screwing. Our young men become sexually active possibly earlier than other groups of young men" (quoted in Madhubuti 1990, 42–43).

Hannerz suggests we must also entertain the other possibility—are they mutually exclusive?—that these young men are looking forward to adulthood, and life in a community sharply divided between males and females, whose relationships to each other are often characterized by conflicts and ambivalence. Lemieux put it this way: "There is such a hellacious disrespect for black women among black men" (interviewed in Madhubuti 1990, 47). Forwards or backwards, "[i]t appears that the peer group is born again and again, like a Phoenix arising from those ashes of mother identification perhaps not completely burned to the end, out of a sheer psychological need for a place where masculinity can be celebrated" (Hannerz 1977, 46).

While he cautions against psychological reductionism in accounting for the existence of male peer groups, Hannerz and other students of black masculinity have difficulty escaping some form of object relations theory to account for the social production of black manhood. While reflecting on "joning"—bragging about sexual prowess while degrading the other's mother or sister—Hannerz (1977, 53) suggests:

> The boys have supposedly just found out that they have identified with the wrong person, the mother. Now they must do their utmost to ridicule her and thus convince everybody and themselves—but particularly themselves—of their independence. (Only since they are not yet daring enough to attack their own mothers, they attack somebody else's instead, thus setting the stage for him to go to work on his own.)

Hannerz (1977) draws an analogy between "joning," which he terms "the dozens," and brainwashing; Abrahams (1962) suggests that joning may be a way of working through an unsatisfactory sense of sex identity. Abrahams (1964, 63) interpreted most of the lore he gathered in terms of matrifocality, the battle of the sexes, and the plight of the disadvantaged, dispossessed black male. He argued that verbal contest skills, "good-talking," and word control in general enabled a man to perform his aggressivity and in so doing "achieve a kind of precarious masculine identity for himself and his group in a basically hostile environment." It represents a masculine struggle against the feminine domination of the "stable" respectable world of the family. In this regard, joning or playing "the dozens" may be understood as a collective ritual cleansing in which the young men point out each other's weaknesses, an assaultive process from which, presumably, they can finally all emerge as men (Hannerz 1977).

The Housing Project residents Schulz (1977) interviewed reported that boys there begin to play the dozens when they are about eleven years old; girls about a half a year later. While the game is played by both boys and girls, it is preeminently a male activity in which the mother becomes the target of ridicule and satire. Even when girls play, the imagery still expresses images of masculine virility, as indicated in this rhyme given by a six-year-old girl:

> I was walking through the jungle
> With my dick in my hand
> I was the baddest motherfucker
> In the jungle land.
> I looked up the tree
> And what did I see
> Your little black mama
> Trying to piss on me.
> I picked up a rock
> and hit her in the cock
> and knocked that bitch
> A half a block.
>
> (quoted in Schulz 1977, 15)

In this imagistic scenario, the "phallic mother" is relocated away from the child who is evidently desperate to differentiate herself from what she perceives to be the all-powerful mother. Abrahams (1962) too acknowledged that "one occasionally finds girls making dozen-type remarks, but for the most part not in the organized fashion of the boys" (quoted in Schulz 1977, 15). While one function of the dozens common to both sexes is training in verbal ability, which becomes a necessary element in the male-female interchange of the late teens and early adulthood, it is not the primary function (Schulz 1977).

Like other students of lower-class black masculinity, David A. Schulz (1977, 15) argues that for the boy entering puberty the dozens has a most important and specific function: "It enables him to break free from the world of the mother and enter the world of the man, expressed in its earliest forms in the project of the 'gang'." This would seem to be a version of object relations theory in which masculinity represents an overdetermined repudiation of the pre-oedipal identification with the mother. Given these psychodynamics, such masculinity would seem to be inherently misogynistic, and thereby effaces not only the subjectivity of the male, but his individuality. Like white and black middle-class fraternity members, he becomes a member of a "gang," an outward badge of conformity which mirrors that inner violence by means of which he enforces upon himself standardization of masculinized conduct and thought.

In playing the dozens the boy can subject the mother, who is often the chief source of love and care as well as discipline and authority, to criticism and even abuse within the boundaries of a specifically defined rhythmic game. These boundaries prevent this volatile activity from getting out of hand. Playing the dozens occurs at the point when the boy is about to enter puberty and undergo a traumatic final separation from his mother as a consequence of becoming a "man." Playing the dozens enables him to develop a defense against feeling his rejection of her, as well as her possible retaliatory rejection of him, while providing a vehicle for his transition into the male world of the street dominated by those masculine values epitomized in gang life (Schulz 1977).

The consequences of this traumatized split with the mother, Schulz (1977, 15) suggests, are considerable. By the end of adolescence, he argues, "an incipient mistrust between the sexes has become an overt and central aspect of a way of life for both men and women. The dozens is thus a 'ritualized exorcism' enabling the combatants to break away from the family dominated by the mother and to establish their own image of male superiority celebrated in street life." In object relations terms, the exorcism is an effort to expel the "mother" or "woman" within, and in so doing achieve "manhood."

While the feminine role is associated with respectability, dependability, the family, and the home, masculinity, especially in lower-class settings, is more often associated with the reverse of these, Schulz (1977) reports. The locus of lower-class black manhood tends to be the street. According to this narrative, a young black man strives to achieve a "rep" on the street because he perceives that he does not have much status in the home. The assertion of his masculinity is always against the grain, he feels. His father may occupy his "place," but it is an unattractive location, not only in society but in the family. It is his mother who is the pillar of the family and supporter of the church; it is she who sees to it that he at least makes an effort in school. If the young black man is in his late teens, Schulz (1977, 7) writes, "he has seen in himself what he feared he saw all along in this father—a person ill-prepared to 'go it alone.' He sees himself more destined for the dependence of welfare than the independence of manhood. Coming up as a boy in the ghetto is thus a most difficult process indeed." Given this scenario, is it any surprise that:

> [b]oys become problems at an earlier age in the eyes of project residents. They are more difficult to manage, engage in such activities as dropping bottles out of windows (sometimes aimed at persons below), stealing, playing hooky from school, smoking cigarettes, drinking to get drunk, marijuana, and engaging in homosexual activities at an earlier age than girls. They are not seen, however, as engaging in most heterosexual activities at an earlier age. (Schulz 1977, 16)

In the group of teenagers he studied, Schulz (1977) found that 61 percent of the boys had police records, 29 percent of the girls, or 48 percent of the total teenage population.

Growing up with such "macho" conception of masculinity, is it any great surprise that, as Anthony J. Lemelle, Jr. (1995, 22), notes, black men pose a threat to white men in so-called masculinized arenas, that is, as laborers, entertainers, sports competitors, sexual competitors, and in the military? "The interest of white men," he writes, "favors a peculiar form of dehumanization and subjugation directed toward black males." It is an "interest" alright, but only "peculiar" if it is not decoded. Once its homoerotic aspects are discerned, it makes perfect if nightmarish sense. Racism is, in this sense, a distorted and repressed form of homosexuality. We might even say racism is a mangled and somewhat sublimated form of gay S&M.

Such sexualized dynamics lace American culture, including the youth culture. Many students, Lemelle (1995, 23) asserts, understand that money has become "the omnipotent cultural production," and that efforts to justify the system morally are only transparent "rationalizations committed to the perpetuation of master-slave relationship." In black culture, Lemelle argues, a persisting theme of liberation, particularly among black youth, has "developed as a 'pop hedonism' exposing the inherent contradictions in reason—not just technological society but a revolt against reason" (23). This "revolt against reason" is not limited, he thinks, to black youth or black culture generally; rather it is endemic to white society as well. In the primary rituals of culture—marriage and family, schooling, working, and dying—he sees "deep-rooted protest and resistance" (23). Are these signs of cultural revolution or familial breakdown or both?

The nuclear family is, in Lemelle's judgment, no longer a model for black families. The decline in black nuclear families, he suggests, is not simply due to the fact that African Americans are financially unable to support what he characterizes as "the luxury of marriage and family." The decline is also due, he continues, to "a gradual disenchantment with the ideology of the nuclear family since 1925" (Lemelle 1995, 23). Male-present black households were, Lemelle asserts, the norm only between 1880 and 1925, curiously enough, roughly the period when lynching was at its zenith (Brundage 1993). Many African Americans have now rejected the ideology of the nuclear family, Lemelle says. And the rejection doesn't stop with the nuclear family: "It is likely that the rejection of the nuclear family is in fact a deeper rejection of capitalist economic organization" (Lemelle 1995, 24). That seems hopeful, doesn't it, too hopeful I think, too simple. Black feminist thought (Collins 1991, 1993; Christian 1980, 1985, 1990; Wallace 1978/1979, 1990) would point to other dynamics at work within the black family.

Black culture also has tended to reject European-American education, Lemelle (1995) believes, a view a number of other black scholars (see for instance, Taliaferro 1998; Guillory 1999) would dispute. Many of the most successful and famous African Americans are often among the least or most poorly educated. This tends to be the case, Lemelle continues, even among the self-employed business persons and high-profile entertainers. Young black males have not failed to make this observation. Is this always a rejection of education, or making virtue out of necessity after having been rejected by a European-American educational system? (see Lomotey and Rivers 1998).

It seems to me that Lemelle (1995) oversimplifies what is a more complicated situation, but clearly he does understand key elements of racial politics. He knows that, generally speaking, many black men have shown a consistent estrangement from the American social system, a system shaped by and identified with white men. The strongest evidence of this estrangement, in his view, is the high homicide and suicide rate among black men. As we saw at the beginning of this chapter, the highest death rate from accidents and violence is found among black men. Mainstream (white) popular media have consistently failed to address these symptoms of what Lemelle (1995, 25) terms "systemic fraud." Rather than appreciating black male violence as symptomatic of white racism and a continuing American cultural crisis, politicians, preachers, and commentators moralize over teenage pregnancy and the use of drugs.

Under such conditions it does not seem unreasonable that there are black men who "are oblivious to the full significance of their development of masculinity" (Lemelle 1995, 39). So, I would argue, are many white men "oblivious," and in particular unaware of the ways their own manhood is intertwined culturally and psychosocially with black men. But being "oblivious" for the white man does not involve the risk it does for many black men. For many black males, for instance, the choice of career paths appears to be, as Lemelle (1995) puts it, either "ball" or "time." Such a situation produces what he terms a cultural form of ambivalence toward masculinity. He cites a passage in Claude Brown's *Manchild in the Promised Land* (1965) that illustrates:

> The first time I heard the expression baby used by one cat to address another was up at Warwick in 1951. Gus Jackson used it. The term had a hip ring to it, a real colored ring. The first time I heard it, I knew right away I had to start using it. It was like saying, "Man, look at me. I've got masculinity to spare." It was saying at the same time to the world, "I'm one of the hippest cats, one of the most uninhibited cats on the scene." I can say "baby" to another cat, and he say "baby" to me, and we can say it with strength in our voices. (quoted in Lemelle 1995, 39)

Brown's point, Lemelle (1995) asserts, should be discerned with care. Cultural constraint in black masculine socialization is not a simple fear of being called a "sissy." Unlike white men, many lower-class black men do not tend to obsess over homosexuality. Black men are more concerned about being exploited by peers, officials, justice and educational systems, or specific situations. Being a "sissy" is a problem because they know that "sissies" are fair game for exploitation, as are their sisters. Homosexuality for many black males would appear to be a matter of power not identity. The prison research I review in chapters 16 and 17 supports that view.

Many black males, Lemelle argues, rely on the myth of the player, hustler, or playboy as models for self-presentation. More than a few white men, including white policemen and teachers, view these styles of self-presentation as offensive displays of virility. Each role, in Lemelle's judgment, is fundamentally a labor market orientation. Because, he says, many black males experience insecurity about their labor market roles, they compensate by converting insecurity into aggression. Those black men involved in pimping and pandering, drug dealing, robberies, or prostitution, occasionally or regularly, often rely on "the trickster mode" to accomplish the exchange. The ideal trickster is an apparently magnanimous man whose intentions are in fact malicious (Lemelle 1995). It may be labor, but it is also the labor of gender formation and expression. One would expect those under covert homosexual assault to respond with a compensatory masculinity. I am not your bitch, bitch.

Harry Edwards, famous for organizing the 1968 Olympic boycott, has elaborated the definition and process of what he terms the "macho hustle." Edwards argues that black masculinity is "hustled by the white patriarchy" (quoted in Lemelle 1995, 49). For instance, black athletes, he argued, are "20th century gladiators for white America" (Edwards 1973). This subjugated relationship to the white man transforms the fundamental labor and social roles of the black man into that of a prostitute to masculinized systems, such as athletics, the military, and prisons. Here macho is the drill by means of which one passes through the forms (Lemelle 1995). Does Dennis Rodman parody this form of black machismo?

If the black man tends to be a "defense mechanism," the neurosis is not indigenous to black culture. It is not, in Dyson's phrase (1995), a failure of black culture. Lemelle (1995) points to Frantz Fanon's contextualization of black neuroses socially, politically, racially, in colonialism. Lemelle notes that Fanon's work on colonialism found its way to 1960s America, when there were several major spokespersons for the concept of internalized colonialism. Lemelle lists Eldridge Cleaver, Stokely Carmichael, Tom Hayden, Huey Newton, and Bobby Seale, all major players in the 1960s civil rights and anti–Vietnam War struggles, all of whom I hope to pursue in an examination of Cleaver, later in this series (Pinar 2000).

The nuclear family is a form of colonialism, Lemelle argues, in which the interests of the father, the colonizer in the analogy, are accommodated in exchange for his "protection." He writes: "As in Fanon's work, the concern of such a perspective is the resistance of a personality struggling against social and cultural inequality" (Lemelle 1995, 70). In Fanon's work, especially in *Black Skin, White Masks* (1967), we see that the black man's struggle is against the internalized "other," the white man who has "entered" him culturally. Racism, Fanon well understood, is sexualized.

Black socialization includes the strategies of "getting around old master," knowledge which is, Lemelle (1995, 139) asserts, "present in the remote goals and ambivalent moral moods of African-American culture." As Lemelle argues, the history of black men in the United States reveals that their status in civil society has been essentially constructed as criminal. Du Bois pointed out that the true test of a democracy is always found in an examination of a nation's criminal and penal systems. I would add that the true test of a nation's sexuality is also found there. Black men are imprisoned in disproportionate numbers; white men obsess over what will happen to them (white men) if they (white men) go. Rarely is it the black man who, in the white man's fantasy, is going to be "the bitch."

Who is the black man? Don't bother asking white men. Partly due to that ignorance which accrues from cultural segregation, partly due to the dual consciousness of black men in which their subjectivities are kept concealed from whites, and partly due to the active fantasy life of white men regarding black men (as criminals, rapists, studs), white men haven't a clue. In a later volume I will, with help from Leigh Gilmore (1994) and others, propose an autobiographical process for European-American men in which their racialized selves can be explored, bracketed, reconfigured. Such a project presses up against the blocks, those repressive structures white men have constructed, in many more than one lifetime ("present in the remote goals and ambivalent moral moods of European-American culture" as Lemelle might have phrased it), to defend against their mangled and repressed desire for the black man, their split-off, projective fantasy of what a black man is.

Such autobiography is a process of self-reclamation, of self-analysis, hopefully of self-reconfiguration. In one sense I ask the white man to give up being "white," abandon the pretense of being a "man." Then it might become easier, should he choose, for the black man to give up being a black man, at least those self-undermining forms of black masculinity that white desire, guilt, and aggression have made, apparently, seem so inevitable. To help the white guy in this way is to declare solidarity with black men, and with black and white women, who are often the victims of contemporary configurations of masculinity, white and black. To help the white man, I turn to autobiography, and not for the first time (Pinar 1994). Not to those traditional autobiographical forms white men devised to boast of their triumphs and to disguise their dependencies, but to forms of autobiographical theory and practice which are rooted in the social, in the political, in the racial, and in the gendered struggles of our victims: an autobiographics of alterity. That I will elaborate in volume III of this series.

Cool

Being male and being black, we are told, has meant feeling "psychologically castrated," rendered impotent in those economic, political, and social arenas where white men have historically dominated (Majors and Billson 1992, 1). There is a "war" going on between black and white men: a war over a specific piece of cultural terrain: manhood. Black guys are determined to win. Majors and Billson suggest that it is commitment to masculine toughness that channels so many young black men into military duty: "they need to prove their manhood" (18).

Historically, Richard Majors (1995/1996) suggests, "coolness" was key to the culture of masculinity in several ancient African civilizations. Like Daniel Black, Majors too looks to precolonial Africa for the origins of black masculinity. He cites the Yorubas of Western Nigeria (900 B.C.E. to 200 C.E.) as an example of an African civilization where "cool" was interwoven throughout the social fabric of the community. Performances of cool ranged from the way a young man carried himself before his peers to his efforts to impress his elders during initiation rituals. Coolness functioned, then, to build character and pride in precolonial African settings. After being uprooted from Africa by enslavement, cool became detached from its indigenous cultural setting and but re-emerged as a survival mechanism (Majors 1995/1996).

Since slavery, African-American men have employed "coolness" to express a range of attitudes and feelings without risking punishment from white men. "Playing it cool," Majors and Billson (1992, 27) explain, "becomes a routinized, stylized method for expressing the aggressive masculinity that pervades black life." While the hard facade associated with the cool pose may be a signature of black masculinity, it is, they assert, "one-dimensional. If it fails, masculinity fails. [It is only a] mask that provides outer calm in the midst of inner turmoil" (Majors and Billson 1992, 28). That is suggested in Paul Laurence Dunbar's (1920) poem "We Wear the Mask."

We wear the mask that grins and lies,
It hides our cheeks and shades our eyes,
This debt we pay to human guile,
With torn and bleeding hearts we smile,
And mouth with myriad subtleties

Why should the world be overwise
In counting all our tears and sighs?
Nay, only let them see us while
We wear the mask

We smile, but oh great Christ our cries
To thee from tortured souls arise
We sing, but oh the clay is vile
beneath our feet and long the mile

But let the world dream otherwise
We wear the mask. (17)

"Cool" would seem to be one version of what Du Bois (1903) termed "double consciousness." He wrote:

> It is a peculiar sensation, this double-consciousness, this sense of always looking at one's self through the eyes of others, of measuring one's soul by the tape of a world that looks on in amused contempt and pity. One ever feels his twoness,—an American, a Negro; two souls, two thoughts, two unreconciled strivings; two warring ideals in one dark body; whose dogged strength alone keeps it from being torn asunder. (Du Bois 1995/1996, 36)

Two souls in one dark *male* body one might amend, given the conflation of "American African" (in Du Bois's day "Negro" was the term of choice) and "black man" (see Carby 1998). The historic struggle for civil rights in America, for the black man particularly, has been a gendered struggle:

> The history of the American negro is the history of this strife,—this longing to attain self-conscious manhood, to merge his double self into a better and truer self. He would not Africanize America, for America has too much to teach the world and Africa. He would not bleach his Negro

> soul in a flood of white Americanism, for he knows that Negro blood has a message for the world. He simply wishes to make it possible for a man to be both a Negro and an American without being cursed and spit upon by his fellows, without having the door of Opportunity closed roughly in his face. (Du Bois 1995/1996, 36)

Is there a parallel here with the "glass ceiling" women, black and white, have encountered? Is there not also a parallel between the struggle of black man as Du Bois depicts it and the problem faced by the hyperfeminized white woman who internalized what the "man" wants her to be, the "place" he wants her to occupy, a place in his imagination?

The hyperfeminized white woman and the hypermasculinized black man may be structurally parallel subject positions vis-à-vis the white man, itself an imaginary subject position. Well, imaginary in any monolithic discursive sense, but this fact seems irrelevant when being raped or beaten or lynched. Then that second soul comes to the surface, as one's life may depend upon being what the white man demands one to be. As Majors and Billson (1992) point out, in this regard, that even while being beaten by a white cop, the young black man stays "cool." Recall Claude Neal in the midst of his torture: "kind gentlemen" he said to the white men as they were carving out bits of his flesh. Cool affirms black male dignity while expressing a contempt the white man misses, a version, perhaps, of miming (see chapters 5 and 7).

Playing it cool is an important aspect of what Rainwater (1967) has called "the expressive life style." This survival technique is an attempt to "make yourself interesting and attractive to others so that you are better able to manipulate their behavior along lines that will provide some immediate gratification." When a person "loses his cool," he has become victimized by this strategy or "put in a trick." Playing it cool is in this sense a defense against exploitation. "Learning to lie effectively," Schulz tells us, "is central to the notion of 'cool' and the expressive life style" (quoted passages in Schulz 1977, 24). The following definition of cool is offered by Robert H. DeCoy (1967, 30): "Cool—In control, wise, aloof, detached. A state of being in admirable possession of one's wit and emotions." Does this amount to a socially useful form of self-dissociation?

Often an effective expressive weapon, being "cool" can also be part of a pattern of what Majors and Billson and others also term "compulsive masculinity," in which so-called masculine values become a prescription for "toughness, sexual promiscuity, manipulation, thrill-seeking, and a willingness to use violence to resolve interpersonal conflict. These values, perpetuated through male-to-male transmission in a tightly knit street culture, lead toward smoking, drug and alcohol abuse, fighting, sexual conquest, dominance, and crime" (Majors and Billson 1992, 34).

In a statement they say is "worthy of Fanon," Majors and Billson (1992) quote William Faulkner, who observed: "No white man understood [blacks] and never would so long as the white man compelled the black man to be first a [black] and only then a man, since this, the impenetrable dividing wall, was the black man's only defense and protection for survival" (quoted in Majors and Billson 1992, 42). You don't even know who I am.

There are others who testify to "dual" or "double consciousness," to the mask, to flying under radar. Richard Wright once admitted: "[W]e are not what we seem" (quoted in Rajiv 1992, 1). It is this distinctly racialized experience that lies beyond the perception or comprehension of most whites. Fanon conceived of this difference as "cultural estrangement" (quoted in Rajiv 1992, 10). A form of suffering and oppression, did such estrangement also permit African Americans to be, in Langston Hughes's words, "free within ourselves" (quoted in Rajiv 1992, 17)? (See Pinar [1997] for a discussion of the psychodynamics of marginality.) For Malcolm X, "Negro" was nothing more than a false identity imposed on the black man by the white civilization to justify the various myths that go into the making of the "white collective unconscious" (quoted in Rajiv 1992, 23).

Since slavery the mask has functioned as a coping style common to many black men and women. The purpose of "styling" is to paint a self-portrait in colorful and vivid strokes that makes the black person—here we are focused upon the male—"somebody" (Majors and Billson 1992, 84). [In 1952 Fanon asserted: "The greatness of a man is to be found not in his acts but in his style" (quoted in Lionnet 1993, 113).] Among some black men, however, such coping leads to what Majors and Billson term an insult war: "accusations of cowardice, homosexuality, or stupidity are common" (Majors and Billson 1992, 92). One commentator went so far as to suggest:

> An American Negro isn't a man—he's a walking defense mechanism. (Frank Yerby, quoted in Majors and Billson 1992, 105)

What can scholars do? "[E]xpand the study of masculinity" advise Majors and Billson (1992, 110). Indeed.

So, we see that slavery displaced African men from their position as patriarchs. Slave women were often the victims of white rape; both men and women were required to be loyal and deferent to their white masters. Post-Emancipation racism continued the work of slavery, and, especially in lower-class settings, black children often grow up without fathers, leaving mothers as the dominant figure in the lives of black boys and girls. The preoedipal identification with the mother that object-relations theory postulates for all children would not seem to lead to the usual heterosexual oedipal resolution in many black families. The primacy of the black mother, commentators suggest, risks leading young black men to become more feminine, perhaps, they suggest, even homosexual. "Very casual observations in the ghetto," Ulf Hannerz (1977, 34) writes, "also lead one to believe that male homosexuality is not particularly infrequent in the community." Given compulsory heterosexuality, it is at an early age that "small ghetto boys are well aware of what a 'faggot' is" (34). Remarkably, maternal identification has been cited as a contributing cause of schizophrenia among black mental patients, which Hannerz observes, homophobically, "sometimes occurring in conjunction with homosexuality" (34). Most students of black masculinity, however, see as the final consequence of this early identification with the mother "a compulsively masculine reaction" (Hannerz 1977, 34; Oliver 1994).

V. The Matrifocality Thesis

[T]he black American male embodies the only *American community of males which has had the specific occasion to learn* who *the female is within itself.*

—Hortense J. Spillers, "Mama's Baby, Papa's Maybe" (1987)

[T]he current panic about the absence of fathers is really about the presence of homosexuality—if the boy has no father to love and introject how will he be successfully masculinized? What, in other words, is to prevent them from being/remaining a queer?

—Mark Simpson, *Male Impersonators: Men Performing Masculinity* (1994)

I mean, part of the cult of masculinity is "faggot this, faggot that."

—Larry, 24-year-old black gay man, quoted in Darrell Dawsey, ed., *Living to Tell About It: Young Black Men in America Speak Their Piece* (1996)

[4]0 percent of ... children will live a major portion of their childhood without their fathers.

—E. J. Dionne, Jr., *They Only Look Dead: Why Progressives Will Dominate the Next Political Era* (1996)

Are we to believe the matrifocality thesis? Does the research on black men amount to "the fine art of black male bashing" (Hutchinson 1997, 32)? Or is it a variant of the time-honored practice of blaming the mother? Is it simple racism, blaming the victims themselves for the socially disintegrative consequences of white racism? Each of these questions, I suggest, can be answered in the affirmative. Still, while never free of political undertow, notions of "matrifocality" can help us to understand the social production of gender and sexual identity, including masculinity, white and black.

Efforts to shift the discussion away from the black family and black masculinity—that is, defensive responses attempting to relocate the problems of African Americans away from black society and culture—have, as we will see, not entirely succeeded, in part because they involve rejection of the matrifocality thesis. As they have critiqued the psychoanalytic paradigm in which the matrifocality thesis is situated, several commentators have retreated to defiant affirmations of what they call, simply, black culture. Some even return to the psychoanalytic paradigm they have apparently rejected. Can the matrifocality thesis and the problematization of black masculine identity be rescued from racist political uses in order to shed light on the queer character of racism? I think so.

In its simplest terms, the matrifocality thesis posits the mother as the key "object" in the process of social development and, more specifically, of gender identity formation. Due to the symbiotic relationship that the fetus and, after birth, the infant enjoys with the mother, both sons and daughters are matrifocal—that is, identified with and oriented toward the mother. Only gradually and incrementally during infancy does it dawn on the infant that s/he is not She. During the oedipal phase boys reject this fetal and infantile identification with the mother in order to become "men" while daughters retain an identification with the mother mediated by the father and the public sphere generally, and/or language (Chodorow 1978).

Due to the rejection and subsequent loss of the maternal identification, boys lose (relatively speaking) access to emotion, intuition, and relational potential. Due to the compensatory nature of their identification with a relatively (or in single mother homes, completely) absent father (or father-figures), boys become "excessively" masculine in an effort to bleach any remaining feminine elements or features from their "all-man" identity. Due to this bifurcation of sex roles in "men" and "women," men become more violent, re-enacting the intrapsychic violence of their identificatory separation from the mother and compulsory, if imaginary, identification with the father. The violence of this process is intensified, presumably, in father-absent homes, a fact that various commentators have seized upon in attempting to explain the high incidence of black "hypermasculinity" and black-male violence. This narrative has also been employed in theorizing gender identity formation cross-culturally (see Gilmore 1990).

The release of the Moynihan Report in 1965 provoked a storm of controversy, as it seemed (especially to black activists and intellectuals) to "blame the victim," that is, the black family, for the problems African Americans faced trying to live in a racist America. Entitled *The Negro Family: A Case Study for National Action*, the report decried black "family pathology—divorce, separation, desertion, female family head[s], children in broken homes, and illegitimacy" (Moynihan 1965, 19). In fact, the lower-class black family was judged to be a "tangle of pathology," a phrase borrowed from Kenneth Clark (Young-Bruehl 1996, 92). When men were present at all, they tended to be derelict, emasculated characters, forcing mothers to act as heads of household. Black sons suffered a lack of discipline and male role models and were therefore at risk for delinquency. The document conflated the "American" family with the white, middle-class, nuclear, patriarchal fantasy of "normalcy" and "stability." The effect was to stigmatize the lower-class African-American "matriarchy" (Young-Bruehl 1996).

Stigmatization was not Moynihan's intention. In the report, he acknowledges that 300 hundred years of slavery coupled with 100 years of postslavery racism had, understandably, negatively impacted black family life. However, as Elisabeth Young-Bruehl (1996, 92) points out, Moynihan "showed no appreciation whatsoever for the strength and resilience in Negro families by speaking only of distortions." Nor did he acknowledge positive facts about black families, such as, for instance, the fact that child molestation is much less frequent in African-American households than in white ones. While blaming slavery and postslavery institutions for black family "pathology," Moynihan went on to claim that the problem had become self-perpetuating. Throughout his report Moynihan spoke of racism as a virus—also a common image for homosexuality among gender reactionaries—which implies that, once contracted, the racist viral infection has a course of its own. The virus and pathology metaphors located "the disease" in black, not white, people (Young-Bruehl 1996).

As Young-Bruehl (1996) points out, the distortions lacing the Moynihan Report circulated widely. For instance, the Coleman Report employed the same fantasy of white, middle-class family "normalcy" to claim that black children failed in schools due to their home and family environments. There was no acknowledgment of racism in the schools, or in the society in which those home and family environments were located. Despite their authors' antiracist intentions, both the Moynihan and Coleman reports were easily co-opted by conservatives who argued that the federal government was wasting money on programs for compensatory education, like Project Head Start, which assumed that intelligence is not based on heredity or race. In 1969, psychologist Arthur Jensen argued just the opposite, that differences in I.Q. scores between black and white children were based in heredity. Such racist nonsense about I.Q. inheritability has surfaced in every white backlash against compensatory education and affirmative action, most recently in Richard Herrnstein and Charles Murray's *The Bell Curve* (1994; see Kincheloe, Steinberg, and Gresson 1996).

In her discussion of the Moynihan Report twenty-two years later, Hortense Spillers (1987, 65) points out that in certain societies, a child's identity is determined through the line of the mother, "but the United States, from at least one author's point of view, is not one of them." She quotes Moynihan: "In essence, the Negro community has been forced into a matriarchal structure which, because it is so far out of line with the rest of American society, seriously retards the progress of the group as a whole, and imposes a crushing burden on the Negro male and, in consequence, on a great many Negro women as well" (Moynihan 1965, 75; Spillers 1987, 65). From the point of view of object relations theory too, a child's identity is determined through the mother.

This analysis, Spillers observes, declared that the "Negro Family" had no Father and, moreover, that this "crushing" fact is "the fault of the Daughter, or the female line." There is in this "logic" a "stunning reversal of the castration thematic, displacing the Name of the Law of the Father to the territory of the Mother and Daughter." In this displacement, the black woman is misnamed: "For Daughters and Fathers are here made to manifest the very same rhetorical symptoms of absence and denial, to embody the double and contrastive agencies of a prescribed internecine degradation. 'Sapphire' enacts her 'Old Man' in drag, just as her 'Old Man' becomes 'Sapphire' in outrageous caricature" (Spillers 1987, 66). Spillers understands well the machinations of the white man's mind.

Moynihan's fantasy of a "tangle of pathology" sets up the fourth chapter, which suggests that "underachievement" in lower-class black males is primarily the fault of black females, partly because they overachieve and thus, presumably, undermine their brothers' egos. Spillers quotes Moynihan: "Ours is a society which presumes male leadership in private and public affairs. ... A subculture, such as that of the Negro American, in which this is not the pattern, is placed at a distinct disadvantage" (75; quoted in Spillers 1987, 66). Dressed in liberal drag, Moynihan was repeating the white man's historical (and defensive) aside to the black that "you're not a real man, I am." Trapped in a "matriarchal" prison, Moynihan asserted, African Americans are caught in a state of social "pathology" (Spillers 1987).

Moynihan's "Negro Family," Spillers points out, reproduced a series of historical associations around the enslaved. She asks us to recall that under conditions of captivity, children did not "belong" to their mothers. Despite this fact, African peoples enslaved in the "new world" still maintained powerful bonds among parents and children. The fact that the "black family" survived against all (white) odds represents, as Spillers (1987, 74) notes, "one of the supreme social achievements of African Americans under conditions of enslavement." This achievement of affiliation and affection is in no minor way the black woman's doing, but as Spillers notes, this achievement, her "dominance" and "strength," came to be recoded by later generations—by both black and white—as a "pathology," as threats of castration.

Embracing matrifocality as a psychological achievement against historical enslavement and racism, Spillers argues that "the African-American male has been touched, therefore, by the mother, handled by her in ways that he cannot escape, and in ways that the white American male is allowed to temporize by a fatherly reprieve" (1987, 80). Because the black male slave was stripped of his rights to his children and his spouse, the only parental relation the slave child might experience was that of the mother. This brutal fact of American slavery points, Spillers reminds, to that "inexorable difference" among American women, namely that the black woman, due to slavery, "becomes historically the powerful and shadowy evocation of a cultural synthesis long evaporated—the law of the Mother" (80). Understood matrifocally, then, Moynihan's fantasy of "illegitimacy" evaporates. For African-American males, Spillers continues, this fact means that black men embody "the only American community of males which has had the specific occasion to learn who the female is within itself, the infant child who bears the life against the could-be-fateful gamble, against the odds of pulverization and murder, including her own. It is the heritage of the mother that that the African-American male must regain as an aspect of his own personhood—the power of 'yes' to the 'female' within" (80).

Given the gender of racial politics in America, however, Moynihan and other white men appear able to focus only upon the absence of the father, an absence white men themselves demanded during enslavement and homoerotically invited afterward. Effacing the past, blind to the affirmative meaning of matrifocality, white men focused instead on black men. If only the black family (headed by a responsible patriarch like me, white men asserted) could get itself together, then African Americans could get on track and succeed in this country where, after all, anyone can prosper if they only try. Among many whites, the perception that blacks (and black family dysfunctionality) are responsible for black poverty and social struggle has never disappeared, as this excerpt from the August 30, 1993, edition of *Newsweek* indicates:

> Behind the electric clippers, a muscular black man is trimming hedges with the intensity of a barber sculpting a face; nearby, his wife empties groceries from the car. In most quarters, they might elicit barely a nod. But in this

> largely black, working-class community, the couple is one of the few intact families on the block. All too common are the five young women who suddenly turn into view, every one of them pushing a baby stroller, not one of them married. Resigned, Caballero says with a sigh, "Where are the men?" (Chideya 1993, p 17; quoted in Blount and Cunningham 1996, ix)

Marcellus Blount and George Cunningham (1996) not only point out the historical throughline between the 1965 Moynihan Report and the 1993 *Newsweek* article, but they also bring to our attention how this persisting white fantasy erases much of what has occurred in the meantime, specifically the women's movement, as well as the gay and lesbian movements. While this white fantasy is about "race" it is also, then, about "gender." They write:

> Behind the racial veil, conventional gender and sexual norms are the saviors from the chaos of the "world without fathers." The collapsing of the time that separates the "Moynihan Report" and the *Newsweek* essay neatly elides, or rather squeezes out, all of the discussion of gender that has taken place in the last three decades. A world without fathers projects as its salvation for blacks (and, by implication, for all of American society) a world without feminism, without gays and lesbians. Most importantly, while the "Moynihan Report" was soundly condemned by African Americans in the 1960s, its normative premises and prescriptions have insinuated themselves in contemporary racial discourse, returning to us in the *Newsweek* article in a black voice. (Blount and Cunningham 1996, xi)

Students of African-American life and of black masculinity more specifically have tended to reject the Moynihan thesis. No doubt they are right to reject its political function in the national debate over "race." They are right to reject those elements which "blame the victim," right to denounce how it erases white racism—individual, institutional, historical, cultural—right to decry how it undermines individuals, ignores the heroism of black mothers and fathers as it impugns black family life (Pinar 1996). Blount and Cunningham are certainly right, and rare, in pointing to the conservative gender politics embedded in such a view, including its heterosexism. Some white critics have tried to reduce the racism of the report, often by affirming multiculturalism and eschewing "ethnocentrism." Other whites have joined black critics in rejecting the report in toto. Critics white and black have also dismissed the matrifocality thesis which gets associated with the report. These writers have worried that the matrifocality thesis reduces black masculinity to a compensatory denial of the black mother's influence. But, as we will see, this matrifocal narrative of masculinity production is not restricted to black families, nor does it necessarily "blame the victim." In fact, it might point to a way out of gendered racial violence.

Illustrative of the effort to reject the matrifocality thesis is Charles Keil's (1977, 74) argument that Freudian and neo-Freudian ideas suffer from "oversimplification and ethnocentrism." "Clearly," he points out, affirming cultural difference, "lower-class Negro culture includes a concept of manhood that differs in kind from the white middle-class definitions of a man as a head of a household, who holds down a steady job and sends his kids to college" (77).

Black forms of masculinity have to be understood and respected as culturally different, he insists, not as culturally inferior to European-American manhood rituals. Rejecting those who have employed psychoanalytic interpretations to suggest greater sexual ambivalence among African-American men, Kiel acknowledges: "This is not to say that there are no ambivalent men in the Negro community or that Negro homosexuality shouldn't be studied—quite the contrary" (79). In dated language he adds:

> The nature of Negro homosexuality is a problem that needs to be explored in depth. A typology of faggots and lesbians, coupled with the types of familial organization that tend to promote deviance, might go far in clearing the haze of illusion and controversy that surrounds Negro sexuality. I suspect that a surprising number of lower-class Negro men and women are ambisexual, homo-, or hetero- according to circumstances. I might add that I have noticed a high tolerance of sexual deviancy in some Chicago blues bars. (Keil 1977, 84 n. 57)

Kiel tries to reject psychoanalytic and quasi-psychoanalytic ideas of black masculinity production, but in this paragraph he has inadvertently provided anecdotal data in support of them.

In this regard, Keil is not alone. For instance, Ulf Hannerz (1977, 35) has this to say: "In the face of a lot of evidence, this [matrifocal] view of male identity development cannot easily be rejected altogether. There are points in the story, however, where modifications may be suggested, question marks inserted, and alternative interpretations proposed." First he points out that the problem of identification and reidentification are not unique to the boy in the black ghetto matrifocal family. It is a widely accepted tenet of psychoanalytic theory that infants, black and white, first identify with the mother. Later, boys reconstruct their identification to copy the father or any other significant male "other." The psychosocial necessity of boys' reconstruction of their pre-oedipal identities with their mothers is, then, hardly peculiar to the ghetto; what may be unusual, he acknowledges, is the problems boys experience in fatherless homes in finding that significant male other with whom to reidentify.

But these problems in gender identity associated with the absence or relative absence of fathers and/or father figures are hardly unique to the black ghetto either. Studies of European-American boys whose fathers were absent from family life during World War II, as well as studies of Norwegian sailors' sons, found that these boys were more immature, submissive, dependent, and effeminate than other boys. Hannerz (1977) points out that these Norwegian boys may have had very different relationships to their mothers than many ghetto boys in matrifocal families have. Additionally, there are no doubt historical as well as cultural factors at work here.

Allowing for such differences, theorists from Parsons (1942; Parsons and Bales 1955) to Chodorow (1978, 1989, 1994, 1996) have argued that matrifocality influences gender and sexual identity development across class and race and culture. Norwegian sailors' sons, black ghetto children, and middle-class white children are all so influenced. Both Parsons in the 1940s and Chodorow thirty years later make this point, focusing especially upon those middle-class homes where, typically, the father works all day and sometimes at night. Talcott Parsons (Parsons and Bales 1955) suggested that when fathers are mostly absent during child rearing, sons are deprived of those identificatory processes that forge masculine connections to society; conversely, excessive maternal affection discourages sons from entering into the instrumental world inhabited by men. When Parsons studied this phenomenon, fewer mothers worked outside the home than when Chodorow studied the same phenomenon in the 1970s. Both argued, however, that the traditional nuclear family supports girls' initiation into a female role from an early age, precisely because mothers are usually the ones to perform child care and home maintenance tasks which are visible and meaningful to the children. Typically, fathers are absent from home at work so that their performance of "the masculine" is to a large extent invisible, inaccessible, and relatively unknown, so that white and black middle-class sons, as well as lower-class fatherless black boys, have to undergo the labor of an imaginary reidentification.

Fatherhood in the 1950s

To put this gendered narrative of the American family in historical perspective, let us return for a moment to the 1950s, which were, argues Jessica Weiss (1998, 350), "a flash point for fatherhood." The postwar moment, for all its euphoria, was also a time of masculine dissolution, a "crisis" attributable to World War II, a war which had followed, of course, the Great Depression, another period of gendered and racialized as well as economic difficulty (Kimmel 1996). These "historical traumata" left American manhood "castrated." (Interestingly, Elaine Showalter [1987] has suggested that war trauma is finally a form of hysteria, and as such, a protest against masculinity.) Kaja Silverman shows how Hollywood tried to come to the rescue, creating films—in particular *Pride of the Marines* (1945), *It's a Wonderful Life* (1946), and most especially *The Guilt of Janet Ames* (1947)—in which women were called "to disavow the male subject's castration, and, by looking at him with her imagination rather than with her eyes, to confer upon him a phallic sufficiency" (Silverman 1992, 8). American women were accustomed to this ploy, having in all likelihood employed it in the South after the Civil War, nationwide during the last decade of the nineteenth century, and after World War I.

Besides the inevitable trauma of battle, military service during World War II subverted conventional gender definitions in another, quite unintended, way by giving gay men and lesbians opportunities to meet more easily and in greater numbers (Bérubé 1990). But the war brought more than gay men and lesbians together; it made, if only for short periods, gay men and lesbians out of "straights." When soldiers and sailors and airmen were shipped out to the South Pacific or Europe, they were forced into various kinds of intimacies. Some army and navy outfits, for instance, instituted a "buddy system," under which pairs of men were responsible for each other's safety. Purely pragmatic relationships sometimes deepened into emotional and sexual ones:

> In the confines of a navy carrier and the stress of danger, buddy relationships often evolved into romantic ones, sometimes sexual,

> sometimes affectionate. While watching movies at night on the deck of an LST in the Pacific, men held hands, kissed, hugged—not all of them gay men. In other words, the war reopened the continuum that Victorians had enjoyed before the barrier of "homosexuality" was raised. The war, one might say, proved to be a large-scale coming-out event. (Filene 1998, 174)

Despite the experimentation, most American men returned, in 1945, to their "rightful" place in the family. During the baby boom years, 1946–1964, many Americans fled the past by embracing "the family." Marriage license bureaus did more business in 1946 than in any single year before or since (Filene 1998). "Togetherness" became a kind of slogan for the postwar emphasis upon family sharing and companionship. Especially for the white middle class, the postwar period stood in sharp contrast with that deprivation associated with the Great Depression (Weiss 1998).

Most Americans fled into traditional gender roles not only to compensate for the economic deprivation and gender destabilization associated with the Great Depression and World War II but, Elaine Tyler May (1988) argues, to flee the anxieties associated with the Cold War, anxieties that were also gendered. During this decade the United States worriedly sought "containment" of the Soviet threat. Government spokesmen as well as social scientists promoted the nuclear family as the cornerstone of American society and security. The American family was, presumably, nothing less than "a psychological fortress" (May 1988, 11) on the home front (Filene 1998).

The economic and ideological stage was set for a revitalized American family. But it was to be a restructured middle-class family in which, experts hoped, men would play a greater role. Not only women were encouraged to become immersed in child rearing and "homemaking," men too were encouraged to make contributions to home life in addition to financial support. In so doing, they did the preliminary transitional work that would enable many fathers, a generation later, to become more fully involved in family life. But for 1950s fathers, these calls for intensified parenting posed a dilemma, especially for middle-class men caught between work and home demands (Weiss 1998).

Those family experts in the 1950s who encouraged fathers to become more involved with their children than their fathers might have been with them were not the first to focus on the topic. In fact, as early as the turn of the century, characterized by a widespread "crisis" in masculinity, many had focused on the role of fathers. Declining family size, suburbanization, and a reduced workweek had functioned to restructure family life for middle-class Americans, whose increased income and leisure made spending more time with the family a realistic goal for many middle-class men. Even then, some sixty years before the publication of the Moynihan Report, experts were concerned about men's (in this instance mostly white men's) daily absence from family life. There were many who advised turn-of-the-century fathers to become more engaged and involved fathers (Weiss 1998; Bederman 1995a; Marsh 1990).

After World War II, many professionals committed to improving family life listed fatherhood near the top of their reform agendas. They encouraged fathers to be more than the agents of discipline in the home; they asked them to be companions and role models for their children. Psychologists linked fathers to the development of sexual identity and gender roles in their offspring, adding a certain tension to the issue of men's role in rearing children. Despite these calls for increased participation at home, few challenged the central role men continued to play as breadwinners. Added to that continuing demand on men's time and energy, recall that the middle-class family was perhaps at its most "nuclear" at this time. Suburban housing spread rapidly in the 1950s. Young couples may have been pleased to escape the crowded urban housing conditions that typified the war years, but they were not always eager to leave behind an extended family and community that had long been, in many cases, a source of advice and support. Postwar men and women married younger, had children sooner after marriage, and had more of them in a shorter span of time, all of which led to the baby boom (Weiss 1998).

Isolated from parents who had traditionally offered advice concerning child rearing, young parents sought alternative, "expert" sources of authority and advice. A veritable army of experts sought to capture their attention, chief among them the "calming voice" (Weiss 1998, 352) of pediatrician Dr. Benjamin Spock. Spock's 1946 *Common Sense Book of Baby and Child Care* was a best-seller; it was revised the first of five times in 1957. His advice brought letters of thanks from suburban parents, one of whom exclaimed: "I've got a copy in the living room, a copy in the bedroom, a copy in the kitchen, a copy in the bathroom" (quoted in Weiss 1998, 353). Spock's book was only one, albeit the most popular, volume in a barrage of how-to books that rushed to instruct insecure baby-boom parents (Weiss 1998).

Not only did most of these agree that fathers should spend more time with their children, many argued that fathers offered contributions to child rearing that mothers could not. Comforting a crying baby had different consequences when it was a man's arms holding the infant: "Father's arms are strong and the child who experiences the security they give him grows up with a warm regard for the some of the best qualities of masculinity—tenderness, protection, and strength" (quoted in Weiss 1998, 354). By using such language, experts characterized tenderness and nurturing as male qualities, redefining the meaning of the phrase "real men" and, they hoped, setting the stage for a rather different masculinity in the next generation. With fathers more involved, a certain balance between mothers and fathers would be struck, one that some experts theorized would make more likely that children would learn appropriate sex roles (Weiss 1998).

"Appropriate sex roles" were of particular concern during the 1950s. Many men who had been deeply involved with other men during the war returned to their wives and girlfriends. Many women who had enjoyed intimacy with other women returned to homes where such love dare not speak its name. Many gay and lesbian veterans married and had children, suppressing their sexual identities, sometimes quietly engaging in homosexual affairs, unable to find social support to "come out," living lives of quiet desperation. In fact, during the 1950s, "in Cold War culture, there was room only for straight gender identity—straight and narrow" (Filene 1998, 180).

Feeling threatened by communist gains in Eastern Europe and Asia, many American officials undertook a witch-hunt at home, but the "witches" turned out to be not only communists but homosexuals as well. Homosexuals who worked for the government were condemned as "security risks" because, presumably, they were susceptible to blackmail by Soviet spies. One Republican party national chairman in 1948 warned that "sexual perverts ... have infiltrated our Government in recent years," and they were "perhaps as dangerous as the actual Communists." Two years later, a Senate committee concluded that even "one homosexual can pollute a Government office" (quoted in Filene 1998, 179). Once again, white men—straight white men—made their fantasies social reality.

Gay federal employees were being fired in increasing numbers: five per month between 1947 and 1950, sixty a month between 1950 and 1953. Across the nation, F.B.I. agents were instructed to gather information about gay bars, the post office conducted surveillance on subscribers to gay erotic materials, and local police arrested lesbians and gay men in bars, public restrooms, parks, and beaches. In Philadelphia, for instance, there were a hundred arrests per month during the 1950s. On a single night in 1956 in San Francisco, thirty-six lesbians were arrested at the Alamo Club, and that suspension of civil rights was repeated over and over again across the country. After a sensational murder case, the county attorney in Sioux City invoked Iowa's sexual psychopath law and committed twenty-nine local gay men to mental institutions (Filene 1998). Clearly, there was only one place for American men during the 1950s: in the family.

Not only was the American man supposed to be above all suspicion, a "family man," he was also supposed to be a parenting man. If husbands resisted increased participation in parenting, many suggested, women should make sure they encouraged them to try. Experts worried that many women mistakenly assumed that child rearing was solely their responsibility and subtly (or not) excluded fathers in shared responsibility for parenthood. Experts advised wives to encourage and guide their husbands' interest in the children, as husbands were presumed not to know how to proceed. Jessica Weiss (1998) argues that despite this rhetorical emphasis upon fathers and fatherhood during the 1950s, it was still women who were finally responsible for child rearing, even when that included the additional duty of regulating their husbands' sometimes blundering efforts. In this respect the emphasis upon fatherhood was a set-up for mothers: if Dad turned out to be less than a great father and/or if their children were in some way disappointing, she could only look to herself to explain the failure of the family (Weiss 1998).

The ideal postwar father worked a day with more than 24 hours in it. While allowing for class, ethnic and regional variations, middle-class fathers worked eight-hour (or longer) days (don't forget the commute to and from the suburbs), came home to read advice books with his wife, then "bounced up" from the dinner table to help out with the occasional diaper or bottle, not to mention playing and conversing with the children until their bedtime. Shared care for children, the experts taught, should be subordinated to having fun and enjoying each other's companionship, but how much energy could middle-class men have available after an exhausting day at the office? Experts urged fathers to make the most out of the few hours they had available after work and commuting demands. While the experts left undisturbed the division of labor in the middle-class nuclear family, their advice did help blur the boundaries. In practice, Weiss tells us, many middle-class men and women did make efforts to find space between the demands of work and family to perform the prescriptive ideals of mothering and fathering. Many more did not, as frustrated and exhausted men, despite their wives' encouragement to spend more time with the kids, remained focused on the financial rewards their hard work brought the family. Indeed, for most fathers of baby boomers, providing remained the cornerstone of fatherhood. They devoted themselves to work and hoped that the financial rewards their labor brought would compensate for their absence from the home (Weiss 1998).

So, contrary to the implication of the Moynihan Report, it was not only lower-class black fathers who were absent from their wives and children. White middle-class fathers of the 1950s were unable to escape the demands of work, driven by their financial and professional ambition. Despite the advice of experts, the encouragement of wives, and their own professed interest in spending more time with their children, middle-class men were by and large absentee dads. As a consequence, by the early 1970s, their children grown, most men found themselves psychologically isolated, retiring from the work which had preoccupied them, strangers to those wives and children for whom the work had presumably been about. Weiss (1998, 360) concludes: "Two decades of career commitment and limited involvement with now teenaged or grown children left hopes for fatherly intimacy stillborn."

The 1950s fatherhood ideal, which experts so eagerly taught, lacked the material conditions for it to be realized. The postwar workplace made few concessions to men's family lives; indeed American corporate culture prevented men from being the fathers many hoped they would be. Sincerely interested in doing more for their children than their Depression-era fathers had been able to do for them, postwar dads aspired to take a more active interest in their children. Weiss suggests that not only did work demands undermine this interest, the very character of the interest dissuaded some men from making the effort. How, many bottom-lined focused working men asked, does one measure success in parenthood? How does one count the benefits of affection and emotional intimacy? In contrast, success in the breadwinning role was easily measurable, in dollars and cents. Those postwar dads who had suffered the Great Depression as boys were determined that their children, set to go to college in record numbers, would not suffer as they had, and many experienced deep satisfactions from their financial contribution to their children's achievements. Few were willing to risk failure as providers in exchange for the "intangible" benefits of engaged child rearing (Weiss 1998). In blaming the black family for the effects of white racism, were white men, in part, displacing their own sense of failure as fathers onto black men? Both sets of men had been absent from home, but the Moynihan Report focused on only absent black fathers.

Mama's Boys

Given the postwar structure of the American family (mother present, father absent), Parsons (1947) suggested that sex-role socialization allowed for more than observation for girls. In a traditional two-parent family, daughters helped their mothers with domestic activities and thereby underwent sex-role training firsthand. Not only could boys not observe what their fathers did in order to be "men," they could not help him at work, partly because work tended to be away from the home, and partly because many middle-class male jobs were, and are, abstract, specialized, and not easily learned. Hannerz (1977) points out that Parsons viewed white male peer groups quite similarly to how other commentators have perceived the peer groups of boys from black matrifocal families. For both sets of young men, peer groups tend to be regarded as both source and focus of "compulsive" or "hypermasculinity." It is in the all-male group where boys reinforce one another's reaction formations, that is, overdetermined repudiations of the mother. These rituals of manhood formation involve exaggerated enactments of male sex roles, such as acting tough, playing the "dozens," or in the suburbs shoplifting or drugs. Hannerz (1977, 35) concludes that "the gap between white mainstream and ghetto matrifocality thus appears to have narrowed down even more as far as the socialization experience of boys are concerned."

Despite, or is it due to, the pervasiveness and explanatory power of psychoanalytic, and quasi-psychoanalytic, interpretations of black masculinity, many commentators, including those who employ it (such as Hannerz), also resist it. They resist it by inflating even more the importance of the son's identification with the mother, then cry reductionism, as Hannerz (1977, 56) does when he declares: "It is questionable, however, whether they [sex-role problems in the black ghetto] can all be laid at the door of matrifocality." Of course, one must agree; so would Parsons and Chodorow. One also agrees with him when he asserts: "If the kind of argument about male growth which has been questioned here is carried too far, it lends itself to facile judgments about 'solving the masculinity crisis' which are more than a little bizarre" (Hannerz 1977, 58). They are bizarre because they fail to take into account the history of black masculinity in the United States, and specifically the complicated, convoluted, eroticized relations between black and white men.

Being a sociologist, Hannerz suffers the weakness of his discipline, a too-exclusive focus upon the structures of contemporary society. He focuses on social structure in order to avoid overreliance on the psychoanalytic explanation. He refers to rather vague but recognizable social factors, but the same pathologization of the black family and problematization of the lower-class black masculinity gets reintroduced:

> It would seem rather likely that sex role deviations, and a concern with such deviations, could occur rather frequently in a community where ambivalent and conflict-ridden relationships between the sexes are understood to be prevalent, where one of the alternative male roles is difficult to live up to because of severe macrostructural constraints, and

> the other alternative is as personally demanding as the ghetto-specific role may be to some. (Hannerz 1977, 56)

That conceded, Hannerz still insists that his main point is "not to pose an alternative explanation of a 'pathology,' but to throw in doubt the existence of much of it" (57). He works hard to "normalize" masculinity production in the black ghetto, arguing, a bit painfully I think, that

> the ghetto-specific male role is dependent on macrostructural factors not just because these make males disappear from the arena where they should be role models, but because these factors have forced ghetto men to redefine their sex role in a ghetto-specific way. After this role has been defined in accordance with circumstances, however, the man may well be the father of the child, in a socializing sense—that is, the role modeling process is at work. (Hannerz 1977, 57)

Perhaps it is not a problem that the father or some other significant male "other" is absent. Perhaps the young man identifies with an imaginary, absent father, omnipresent in a patriarchal society. Perhaps he identifies with the men he watches on television, sees at school, meets on the streets. Perhaps mother is not "the" problem at all.

"Matriarchal and Elastic"

In *After Freedom*, Hortense Powdermaker (1939) described a Mississippi town where single black mothers often worked outside the home. Even when these mothers were home, they were very busy with their own domestic duties. There was little time or energy to focus exclusively upon child rearing, no time to read experts' books on the significance of the father. Powdermaker observed that many unmarried women had male lovers; they had no need to make the children, especially the sons, emotional substitutes for a husband (Powdermaker 1939, 197), another worry students of the "fatherless" family have articulated.

Given the state of race relations in Mississippi in the early 1930s (about the same or worse as we observed them to be in 1930s Alabama; see chapter 12), it was impossible for Hortense Powdermaker, a white woman, to interview black men. Accordingly her informants were mainly black women. Since, however, the black family in "Cottonville" (where she lived for a year during the course of the study) was in general matriarchal, and given the impossibility of obtaining "material of equal intimacy" from both men and women, she did not regard this to be "a serious handicap" (quoted phrases in Powdermaker 1939, xii).

In the structures of marriage, family life, and sexual behavior, Powdermaker found that the black middle class differed strikingly from the classes above and below it. Most middle-class marriages were of the common-law type, "easily entered and easily dissolved." Both premarital and extramarital relations were common, although they tended to be pursued in secrecy or attempted secrecy. Given the relatively informality of the marriage union, indicated too by the customariness of sexual relations outside it, Powdermaker characterized middle-class black family life as one of "instability," although "fluidity" might have been a more appropriately neutral term. This contrasted sharply with what she calls the "Puritanism" associated with the black upper class, clearly a conceptual superimposition. As well, the middle class contrasted with the lower class, which "makes no pretense of monogamy and attempts no secrecy in its sexual life" (quoted passages on 68). Female prostitutes were identified as members of the lower class (Powdermaker 1939).

For Powdermaker, the structure of most white families of "Cottonville" mirrored the structure of families generally in "western cultures," typically understood to be "the primary biological group consisting of father, mother, and children." This described nearly all white families in Cottonville and as a rule, a family constitutes a household (things may be different, she allows, in the surrounding countryside). Among the black residents of Cottonville, household and family were generally considered synonymous; but, she reports, there were more instances in which "the household exceeds the family, and the family itself is far more elastic." In most of the black households she observed, grandparents, nieces, nephews, adopted children, as well as unrelated persons often comprised part of the family group. Indeed, members of the biological family were often absent. Sharecroppers and renters who lived in town during the winter months often stayed with relatives and shared household expenses; they were usually included in the family group. Temporary boarders who rented rooms were not, however, considered part of the family proper. The structure of these black households in Cottonville was hardly unprecedented, Powdermaker notes. "It is by now," she tells us, "a well-established generalization that the typical Negro family throughout the South is matriarchal and elastic, in striking contrast to the more rigid and patriarchal family organization of occidental white culture" (quoted passages on 143).

Powdermaker suggests that the matriarchal structure of many black families can be traced to the difference in the position of male and female slaves. She suggests that the woman had a greater economic value, which "may well have bred in her a greater self-esteem." That more women than men were house slaves may also have advantaged black women, both in terms of social status as well as training. Additionally, Powdermaker continues, the black man "sexually was at a disadvantage." By that she means that "the white master"—"enjoying complete monopoly of a wife" propped up by "protections and taboos"—also had unlimited access to any black woman he desired. (In all likelihood, the "white master" took sexual advantage of black men as well.) In an odd sentence, Powdermaker muses that "the Negro woman at least reaped certain compensations for her availability," but perhaps "vulnerability" would have been a more accurate word choice. Her point is that black men "had no compensation and no redress." Consequently, she perceived black men as "less confident and less effective" than black women, thereby contributing, inadvertently, "psychological support to the matriarchal family form" (quoted passages on 145).

What does Powdermaker mean by "matriarchal family form"? First, she found that the black women often contributed the larger share of the income and assumed the larger share of responsibility in the black families she observed. This economic difference was greater in town, where employment was more available to women than to men. But the matriarchal structure of black family life was equally evident on the plantations. In many cases women were the sole provider for the household. Often there was no man in the household at all. In a number of instances, elderly women in their seventies and their middle-aged daughters, with or without children but often without husbands, comprised one household with the elderly woman as the head (Powdermaker 1939).

Members of these matriarchal families were "variable" and "even casual," including stepchildren, "illegitimate" children, adopted children, as well the biological children of the mother. "No matter how small or how crowded the home is," Powdermaker reports, "there is always room for a stray child, an elderly grandmother, an indigent man, a homeless friend." Perhaps, she speculates, the "already crowded conditions" support this "hospitality." Among the lower and lower middle classes, especially, she found little privacy and comfort, meaning that the addition of a new member made little perceptible difference, far less, she continues, than it would in those households where each member had his own room but there was no spare room; and where each had enough to eat but there was none left over. But the pattern of "flexibility"—"expanding and contracting the household according to need"—was not limited to the poorer or more crowded households (quoted passages on 146).

Powdermaker found three structures of heterosexual cohabitation: licensed marriage, acknowledged by a ceremony, usually in a church; common-law marriage; and temporary association, not considered a marriage. For the large majority of black households in Cottonville, common-law marriage was the norm. It was a legal form of heterosexual union in Mississippi in the 1930s. For a minority, temporary liaisons were more numerous than licensed marriages, most of the latter found in the upper and upper middle class. Temporary unions were "easily countenanced" in the lower class, but were by no means uncommon in the middle class. Indeed, a licensed marriage in the lower or lower middle class was quite rare, just as a common-law marriage was in the upper class. In the black upper class, by contrast, for a woman and a man to live together with no pretense of licensed marriage would have been considered "shocking" (quoted phrases on 149).

In the upper class, chastity for the unmarried girl was an "absolute requirement." But for everyone else, chastity was "neither very common nor very highly prized." This sharp contrast in expectation and practice meant, given the frequent contact between social classes, that the parents of young girls in the black upper classes were "beset with anxieties." Often they decided that for safety's sake they must send their daughters away to some small denominational seminary or college, of which there were a large number in Mississippi at that time. Supported by church and missionary funds, such residential schools were "strict" in demanding church standards of conduct among the students (quoted phrases on 151).

Those few licensed marriages in the middle class functioned chiefly to enhance social status. They occurred almost entirely in the upper segment of the middle class; they were occasion for great pride. "Yet," Powdermaker (1939, 152) notes, "in neither the upper nor the lower middle class is there a feeling that to live together without a marriage license is sinful." Because it was the norm, common-law marriage did not connote instability, she notes (without revising her choice of terms). The marriage license was considered "an ornament of rare glamour" (153). Those couples she found trying to conceal a common-law marriage to give the impression that they had a license had social, not moral, pretensions. Consequently, "permanence in marriage ties and legalized divorce have barely penetrated below the upper class" (157). She found that it was not regarded as immoral to remarry without securing a divorce, since the marriage license has more to do with social status than with moral belief. Divorce proceedings were not only expensive, but they involved dealings with a white court, which African Americans in 1930s Mississippi preferred to avoid. Consequently, a legal divorce was something of "a luxury," connoting "pretensions and extravagance" (quoted phrases in Powdermaker 1939, 156).

Most black unions, then, dissolved when the husband and/or wife simply left the household. In some instances, Powdermaker found that husbands were not sure whether their wives had "divorced" them "or merely gone on a visit." In Powdermaker's study, most husbands who left their wives did so in order to live with another woman. Most wives left their husbands in response to discovering that they were "running around with other women" (quoted phrases in Powdermaker 1939, 157). Sometimes, however, women left because their husbands beat them; sometimes they left men because the men were economic liabilities, but these reasons were less common. Any couple known to be faithful to each other was pointed out to Powdermaker as exceptional. Broken marriages and infidelity were the norm, considered by many black women in 1930s Mississippi as natural (Powdermaker 1939). The fact that these social patterns were considered "natural" by the participants failed to persuade Powdermaker to abandon the language of "broken homes" and "infidelity."

Powdermaker found that a very large number of black women apparently experienced little difficulty in accepting "infidelity" on the part of their husbands or in practicing it themselves. It was not unusual, she found, for wives to enjoy extramarital affairs without feelings of guilt or regret, while at the same time convinced that they loved their husband best. When discussing this issue, one woman shrugged her shoulders and said: "When the men go hunting the women go fishing" (quoted in Powdermaker 1939, 160). Still, self-respecting women of the middle class tried to hide their extramarital relations from public view. Whatever "disgrace" was connected with adultery had to do with others knowing about it. One way in which middle-class women attempted to protect themselves from gossip was by working in pairs. One woman used the house of her confidante; her friend pretended innocence and warned her if she was in danger of being exposed. Then the second woman used her ally's house. Powdermaker (1939, 164) found that such "confidants may have quarrels but they never really 'fall out,' because each one knows too much about the other."

Ministers, Powdermaker (1939, 162) found, were "notorious violators of the seventh commandment," despite their weekly tirades against adultery from the pulpits. Their inability to "practice what they preach" was one reason why they had lost influence with young educated African Americans, who, Powdermaker reports, "openly sneer" (162) at the preachers' apparent helplessness before temptations of the flesh. Powdermaker speculates that ministers' well-known failings may also have been one of the reasons that religious precepts seem to have had little influence on church members who were regularly promiscuous. Only in the black upper classes was adultery viewed as a serious sin. Many of the most enthusiastic churchgoers in the middle and lower classes enjoyed great sexual freedom, and experienced no apparent conflict when attending weekly church services (Powdermaker 1939).

There was, Powdermaker reports, a high level of violence, both within black households, in black communities, and in Mississippi generally. Domestic violence tended to be absorbed by black women quietly. Only rarely did a woman have a man called into court for beating her, and when she did, other women criticized her for taking action. Powdermaker found that most men, black and white, carried guns, and many of them also carried knives. Unsurprisingly, she points out, Mississippi suffered a high homicide rate, and most crimes occurred within black communities. In 1933 the rate for the total population of the United States was 9.3 per 100,000; in Mississippi the rate was 20.5 (Powdermaker 1939).

The attitude of most white Mississippians and the courts they controlled was one of complaisance toward violence among blacks, even toward homicide, as long as it was *intra*racial. There were, Powdermaker reports, convictions for only 30 percent of the homicides recorded in 1933, and of these, 3 percent were sentenced to be hanged, only 1 percent were executed. When whites killed whites the matter was very serious, but when a white man killed a black, it was hardly considered murder. When an African American killed a white man, conviction was assured, provided the case was not settled beforehand by lynching. Powdermaker (1939, 195) notes the gender of lynching, reporting that: "Women fear lynching for their men, but not for themselves. Cases have been known in which women were lynched, but these were so exceptional as to be negligible in terms of chronic fear."

Powdermaker's study does not share the conclusion of the Moynihan Report it would seem to anticipate. In fact, she argues that "there is little if any indication that the fatherless household among these negroes tends to result in the kind of psychological complications which clinical workers have come to associate with middle-class white households where there is no father." Why? Powdermaker speculates that the economic situation is one factor. The black mother usually works away from home during the day or, if she remains at home, she is extremely occupied with her own work (such as sewing for others) or with housework, for instance, washing, some of which she may have also taken in from outside the home. As a consequence, the black mother "lacks time, opportunity, and energy to lavish on her children the overprotection which leads to those emotional difficulties characteristic of certain fatherless white families," repeating a patriarchal homily. Powdermaker also points out that most mothers, even in households without a husband, "do not want for sexual outlet, and therefore are not impelled to seek from their children some substitute for the satisfaction normally derived from a mate" (quoted passages on 197). Finally, she notes that the fatherless home, unlike what it might be in a middle-class white American community, was the norm among African Americans in Cottonville (Powdermaker 1939).

Powdermaker is reluctant to say which family structure is preferable, calling instead for comparative studies. Such research might indicate, she suggests, whether the child's "ultimate adjustment" is made more likely by either type of family structure. She speculates that the "tightly integrated" family may provide a greater foundation of "security," which might better prepare the individual to face an often predatory world. On the other hand, she continues, the "more fluid organization" of the black family may prove superior, as it makes for less discontinuity between the protectiveness of domesticity and the risk in society at large (quoted phrases in Powdermaker 1939, 198).

Illustrative of this "more fluid organization" were black adoption practices in Cottonville. Adoption was almost never made legal; it was referred to as "giving" the child away. Children were frequently given away, probably (Powdermaker speculates) because families frequently broke up. The remaining parent was often unable or unwilling to take care of the children involved. But due to black women's strong commitment to children, Powdermaker found there was always someone ready to take responsibility for these abandoned children. She also found that whatever the circumstances and motivation of the adoption, there was no attempt to conceal these facts from adopted children. As for the children themselves, Powdermaker found that black children in Cottonville contributed strongly to the cohesion of the family group. Given that the black family was organized informally and flexibly, children's role as a cohesive force was more powerful than that of white children: "For they [the children] are the chief effective nucleus of family life" (Powdermaker 1939, 219).

White readers should not conclude, as did many who read the Moynihan Report some forty-five years later, that the fluidity of these parenting arrangements meant that parental expectations for children's success were low. Powdermaker (1939, 211) found that among the middle and lower classes mothers were "most ambitious for their children and most unstinting in their zeal." It was considered "normal and natural" for parents, especially mothers, to work seemingly without pause for the sake of their children, hoping to provide for them opportunities they themselves never had (213). She found that the majority of parents hoped that their children would become teachers. Powdermaker comments: "Despite the low salary, this profession has a strong appeal for people who two generations ago were denied the privilege of reading and writing" (215).

Black parents realized the greatest impediments their children faced were white Mississippians. She found that this fact required blacks to know more about whites than whites typically knew about blacks. Given the racial politics of the period, most blacks performed deferential behaviors when in the presence of whites, so much so that Powdermaker (1939, 329) understood that "the average white person in this community seldom realizes the extent to which this group questions his superiority." Especially among the younger generation, those African Americans in their teens, twenties, and thirties, Powdermaker found that "resentment is keen and outspoken" (331). This generation would provide the nucleus of the 1960s civil rights movement.

Demasculinized Superstuds?

Hannerz (1977, 38) cites Powdermaker's study (as well as Burton and Whiting's [1961]), observing that ghetto mothers do have male lovers and friends with whom they express some of their affection, providing, he writes (reverting once again to the psychoanalytic paradigm he wants to reject) "an oedipal situation in which boys' object of envy is another male. ... Again the necessity of identity only with the mother is not quite as obvious as it might have appeared at the outset." He concludes:

> There is no need to claim that all interpretations of ghetto masculinity in terms of misidentification with mother, followed by compulsive masculinity, are so culturally naive. As we have pointed out above, the facts remain which favor such an interpretation. ... It may well be that neither the thesis criticized here nor the one outlined as an alternative can alone provide an understanding of how ghetto boys become ghetto men; they, and perhaps other interpretations as well, may be needed as complementary perspectives rather than as alternatives. (Hannerz 1977, 59)

I am offering one such interpretation here, namely that any understanding of contemporary black masculinity is partial without an appreciation of the historical significance of lynching and the homoerotic character of white racism.

There are others who, like Hannerz, reject outright psychoanalytic schemas of African-American male sex-role socialization, or at least try to. Robert Staples (1977, 134) judges mainstream narratives of black male sex-role socialization as nothing more than the white production of "stereotypes." Any depiction of the black male, he asserts, "as psychologically impotent and castrated [even when] perpetuated ... by social scientists ... [and] the mass media" represents an "assault on black masculinity." Such attacks on black men are made "***precisely because black males are men***," he counters, not because they are "impotent" (134). He quotes sociologist Jessie Bernard (1966, 69) who declared: "Negro men have been more feared, sexually and occupationally, than Negro women." Bernard argued that the black man had to be destroyed *as a man* to "protect" (73) the white world. But this, Staples (1977, 134) insists, is only a "myth of ... demasculinization."

Staples dismisses "demasculinization" as a myth, then, oddly enough, moves to restore it. He argues that historical evidence suggests that post-Reconstruction segregation was directed more at the black man than at the black woman. Perhaps he was thinking of lynching statistics when he asserts, very broadly and without evidence, that "black women, in a very limited way, were allowed more freedom, suffered less discrimination and were provided more opportunities than black men" (Staples 1977, 136). In more recent times, Staples finds that "the structural barriers to black manhood were great. In a capitalistic society, being able to provide basic life satisfactions is inextricably interwoven with manhood" (136). He continues: "White society has placed the black man in a tenuous position where manhood has been difficult to achieve. Black men have been lynched and brutalized in their attempts to retain their manhood. They have suffered from the cruelest assault on mankind that the world has ever known. For black men in this society it is not so much a matter of acquiring manhood as a struggle to feel it as their own" (137). He quotes black psychiatrists William H. Grier and Price M. Cobbs (1968, 49):

> Whereas the white man regards his manhood as an ordained right, the black man is engaged in a never-ending battle for its possession. For the black man, attaining any portion of manhood is an active process. He must penetrate barriers and overcome opposition in order to assume a masculine posture. For the inner psychological obstacles to manhood are never so formidable as the impediments woven into American society.

So it appears that Staples *does* believe black manhood is a contested terrain, not to be taken for granted. It is because white men have made black men suffer in a gendered way, that is, by making manhood itself a struggle, that other white men (Staples characterizes them as "ideological bearers, the social scientists") continue to make black manhood difficult when they declare black males are not "men." They are, he complains, misreading object relations theory,

> various sociological and psychological studies which purport to show how black males are de-masculinized, in fact may be latent homosexuals. The reason they cite is that black males reared in female-centered households are more likely to acquire feminine characteristics because there is no consistent adult male model or image to shape their personalities. One sociologist stated that since black males are unable to enact the masculine role, they tend to cultivate their personalities. In this respect they resemble women who use their personalities to compensate for their inferior status in relation to race. (quoted passages in Staples 1977, 137)

Such "reasoning seems weak and unsubstantiated," Staples concludes (137). That it does.

The fact of the matter—Staples retreats now to common sense—is that black men are men. No, actually they are supermen, he asserts. Staples now introduces what seems to be the other side of the same coin that insinuates that black men are homosexuals. While the image of the black man as stud may be stereotypic and thereby racist, Staples is not timid in reminding us that "according to the Kinsey Institute ... three times as many black males [as white males] had penises larger than seven inches in length" (Staples 1977, 141). What's he getting at? "In a concrete sense," he writes, "this means that black men do not moderate their enthusiasm for [hetero-] sex relations as white men do" (142). Now he has retreated completely to what amounts to a black reiteration of white stereotypes: "[W]hite men when confronted with their woman's state of sexual readiness may say business first, pleasure later. The black man when shown the black woman's state of sexual excitation manages to take care of both the business and pleasure task. If one task is left unfinished, it is unlikely that the black woman is left wanting" (142). Here he seems to be providing anecdotal evidence for his earlier assertion that "the attempt to emasculate the black male was motivated by the fear of his sexual power" (140). But he doesn't believe that himself, as soon after he adds: "Sexual fears, however, do not totally explain the attempted castration of black men" (142). Sexual fear equals (inverted) desire?

Those black men who attempt to perform others' fantasies of them as superstuds travel an uneasy path. Calvin Hernton (1965/1988) has suggested: "It is not uncommon to discover that many of the [black] men who constantly strive to project such mammoth sexuality around white women are lonely men. In fact, they are sexual failures with black women, if not repressed homosexuals" (78). Staples seems to think demasculinization—at once mythic, at once real—is only a political tool of racist oppression; he fails to understand that "manhood" itself, white or black, is finally illusory, that white men don't have it either, and that in their struggle to be what they are not, that is, "men," white males relocated their disavowed unconscious desire, not only upon "women" but upon black men as well. "Demasculinization" was not the consequence of racism in general; it was a specific response to that white male sexual assault which informed white racism, and which was sometimes explicit in the practice of lynching.

Hortense Spillers seems to suggest that black men embrace matrifocality. Rather than seeing the "female" strictly only as "other" to black manhood, Spillers's (1987) re-visioning of psychoanalytic theory suggests that black men regard the "female" as a valued aspect of the repressed in the black male self. In his effort to fashion "a non-phallocentric black male feminism," Michael Awkward (1995, 51) draws upon Spillers, terming her essay "the most provocative, enlightening, and inviting moment in feminist or in 'womanist' scholarship." For Awkward, "feminism represents a fruitful and potentially not oppressive means of reconceptualizing, of figuratively birthing twice, the black male subject" (57). The alternative is hypermasculinity, with its cycle of misogynistic and homophobic homosociality and violence.

Others agree with Staples in blaming the "crisis" of black masculinity not on intrapsychic gender politics but on the culture of white racism in America. Lynn Curtis (1975) is generally regarded as the originator of the "contraculture" theory of black-on-black violence. Curtis argued that disproportionate rates of criminal violence among African Americans represents a cultural response to political, economic, and social conditions. Especially for lower-class black males, racial and class stratifications have complicated and, for some, blocked entry into mainstream American life. Kept on the economic, social, and political margins, many lower-class black males are unable to perform the masculine role as it is defined by the dominant, that is, white culture (Oliver 1994).

Denied sublimated expressions and affirmations of hegemonic masculinity, lower-class African-American men tend to perform physicalized forms of manhood, what several scholars have termed "compulsive masculinity." Such masculinity represents in part a compensatory response to exclusion. Contraculture theorists such as Curtis regard the persistence of compulsive masculinity and the concomitant violent contraculture as following from a male-to-male subcultural transmission of norms that emphasizes toughness, sexual exploitation, manipulation, and thrill-seeking. Young black males learn these norms and behaviors as they are generationally reproduced through processes of differential association, identification, and imitation (Oliver 1994).

Both contraculture theorists and subculture-of-violence theorists argue that disproportionately high rates of violence among African Americans have very much to do with black males' submersion in a culture of masculinity that affirms violence-prone activities such as verbal challenges, sexual promiscuity, manipulating others, heavy drinking and drug abuse, gambling, and hanging out on street corners and in bars and other settings regarded as "dangerous places" (Curtis 1975, 18). Insults—interpreted, always it seems, as threats to masculinity—as well as romantic jealousy are primary factors in a relatively high frequency of violent confrontations between black men (Oliver 1994). Such a defensive and compensatory masculinity does not surprise bell hooks (1994); she suggests that the pattern represents resistance to emasculation. To illustrate, she quotes Richard Mohr's analysis of white gay male fascination with hegemonic masculinity. In *Gay Ideas*, Mohr (1992) suggests that "under the burden of inherited sexual typographies, liberation is found in a working through of past oppression, a working through in which the constituents of oppression become morally diffused by being incorporated into and transformed in the self-creation of an oppressed minority's development of a positive ideology of and for itself" (quoted in hooks 1994, 132). Is black hyper- or compulsive masculinity such a tactic? Is it, then, a contemporary and male form of "miming"?

VI. Compulsive Masculinity

After slavery ended, black men were constructed as feminine by white supremacist rhetoric that insisted on depicting the black male as symbolically castrated, a female eunuch. In resistance to this construction, black males cultivated and embraced the hypermasculine image.

—bell hooks, "Feminism Inside: Toward a Black Body Politic" (1994)

Hypermasculine and hyperfeminine behaviors designed to forge an identity have as their corollaries prejudice against homosexuals, who represent the feared possibility.

—Elisabeth Young-Bruehl, *The Anatomy of Prejudices* (1996)

I could either be a man or a pussy.

—Kevin Powell, "Ghetto Bastard," in Herb Boyd and Robert L. Allen, eds., *Brotherman: The Odyssey of Black Men in America* (1995/1996)

Can we say that white men have driven black men mad?

—William H. Grier and Price M. Cobbs, *Black Rage* (1968)

Many social scientists have constructed theories of delinquency and violence that employ the concept of "compulsive masculinity" as an important variable. Criminologists have tended to regard it as an intervening rather than as an independent variable in the explanation of violence. How is it defined? Compulsive masculinity refers to patterns of toughness, sexual conquest, manipulation, and thrill-seeking, all culturally coded as "masculine." Parsons (1947) introduced the concept as part of an effort to identify the sources and patterns of aggression in the Western world. He drew upon psychoanalytic notions of masculinity, specifically on the idea of the "latency period," that is, a period during adolescence when boys repudiate their identification with their mothers in order to establish masculine identities. As we have seen, this identificatory process is key in the formation of gender identity (Chodorow 1978, 1994).

Let us review this psychoanalytic narrative introduced earlier in the discussion of the matrifocality of black ghetto families. Recall that this narrative, object relations theory, has the effect of blurring the differences between black ghetto and middle-class families, at least as they function in the psychosexual development of children. The absent father in the black ghetto family is matched by the absent father in the middle-class suburban family, black and white. Parsons (1947) and others tended to see the absent father as a problem, for both white and black boys. Parsons pointed to certain structural features of industrialized societies, in particular the occupational system, which make masculine identification problematical. Why? Boys identify with their mothers, a psychological fact intensified due to the absence of their fathers from the home and from child rearing. As they enter adolescence, boys' identification with their mothers becomes intolerable, as during this developmental phase they must become "men," which is to say, not women. They experience intense peer pressure, and that gendered anxiety is linked with fears that other boys will perceive them as physically or emotionally weak, that is, not "men." As a consequence, many boys adopt attitudes and personality characteristics exactly antithetical to those associated with femininity, and in so doing seek safety from the gender policing, even harassment, of their male peers. Masculinity becomes defined in terms of toughness, emotional detachment, independence, sexual conquest, and competitiveness—whatever qualities are coded as not feminine (Parsons 1947; Oliver 1994). What are men? Men are not women.

Following Parsons, social scientists have tended to accept these adjectives as defining masculinity, although many have preferred different terms, among them compulsive masculinity, overt masculinity, conspicuous masculinity, machismo, macho. Other social scientists have focused less on definitional issues and more upon etiology (Oliver 1994). As noted earlier, psychoanalytic narratives have been controversial, especially among certain black intellectuals such as Robert Staples (1977), who dismisses them as another white-male assault on black men. But, as we have seen, even Staples's resistance to this narrative has taken forms which tend to reiterate it.

The origin and maintenance of compulsive masculinity continues to be a major area of debate among students of the phenomenon. Parsons argued that compulsive masculinity is not a functionally dominant pattern associated with the adult masculine role, but rather a momentary reaction-formation marking a male's transition from boyhood to manhood, including his subsequent participation in the occupational system. For Parsons, compulsive masculinity is for most boys a temporary state, diminishing in significance as they mature and move into the occupational structure (Parsons 1947; Oliver 1994).

Parsons's perspective is usually characterized as a structural one. In the decades since his research, structuralist students of compulsive masculinity have tended to de-emphasize the rejection of mother-identification that was key to Parsons's formulation. Structuralists after Parsons have tended to emphasize the impact of structurally induced marginality in explaining why individuals become compulsively masculine. For example, Toby (1966) argued that compulsive masculinity is more common among lower-class males due to their inability to wield symbolic power, that is, influence and prestige derived from family background, educational achievement, income, social and political connections, and material acquisitions.

Others locate the origins and maintenance of compulsive masculinity in culture rather than in social structure. Culturalists argue that those who become compulsively masculine are enacting their cultural milieu, one that requires males to become tough, emotionally detached, sexually aggressive, manipulative, and thrill-seeking. Compulsive masculinity is understood as a cultural outlook and lifestyle that is grounded, some might say submerged, in the present. As Miller (1958) defined it, compulsive masculinity involves a "positive effort to achieve states, conditions, or qualities valued within the actors' most significant cultural milieu" (quoted in Oliver 1994, 12–13). In sum, culturalists argue that social disorganization and cultural traditions are the primary factors contributing to the origins and maintenance of compulsive masculinity (Oliver 1994).

The concept of compulsive masculinity describes, William Oliver (1994, 13) argues, "a compensatory adaptation that many lower-class black males adopt to cover up their inability to meet the standards of the traditional masculine role." Unable to cope with racial discrimination, economic exclusion, and low self-esteem, young black men become compulsively masculine. Such a genderization is "dysfunctional" and "compensatory" (Oliver 1994, 13), since it creates additional problems and fails to solve the original ones. (This analysis sounds not unlike a racial version of Paul Willis's [1977] analysis of working-class lads in Britain.) To illustrate, Oliver points to high rates of black teenage pregnancy (25 percent), children born out of wedlock (55 percent), divorce (220 per 100,000), and female-headed families (50 percent). Contributing to these phenomena, he suggests, is black males' loyalty to the sexual conquest norm.

Does not this norm represent as well a defensive and compensatory response to the experience of disavowed homosexual desire from white men? Is "compulsive masculinity" in part a recoded form of "homosexual panic"? While not addressing specifically this issue, Young-Bruehl (1996) does underscore the gendered nature of racial oppression, noting that "men who have been victims of racism, with its assaults directed specifically upon their masculinity, its emasculating parricidal and sibling rivalry dynamics, will often respond with various kinds of hysterical hypermasculinizing, including homophobia" (Young-Bruehl 1996, 431).

Several major criminological theories suggest that compulsive masculinity is a major factor contributing to the high rates of violence among black men. Black males' compulsive masculinity, for example, is included in the poverty-social disorganization theory of black-on-black violence. Frazier (1949), Miller (1958), and Moynihan (1965) argued that the cultural values and norms of lower-class black men result in high rates of crime among blacks. Moreover, they argued that the high rates of violence among black men are a function of their inadequate socialization and specifically the failure of ghetto institutions such as the family to encourage lower-class black boys to value conventional definitions of manhood (Oliver 1994). This argument especially as expressed in the Moynihan Report, as we have noted, has provoked a loud and long controversy, including debates between black men and women (Christian 1985; Wallace 1978; Hutchinson 1997; Rainewater and Yancy 1967; Spillers 1987).

The racial-oppression/displaced-aggression theory of black-on-black violence understands compulsive masculinity as a compensatory adaptation or style that black men adopt in order to cope with those structural pressures—that is, white racism—that prevent them from enacting traditional male roles. Moreover, this theory suggests that the dominant white social structure encourages black males' compulsive masculinity through its tolerance of those black men who commit violent acts against other blacks (Oliver 1994). With increasing rates of black-male imprisonment and the increasing costs of prison construction and maintenance, white society may not encourage black-on-black violence, but it does tolerate it more than black-on-white violence. Clearly, whites expect black crime.

The subculture-of-violence theory makes extensive use of the concept of compulsive masculinity in explaining high rates of interpersonal violence among African Americans. In a frequently quoted statement regarding the relation of compulsive masculinity to homicide, M. E. Wolfgang (1958, 188–189) wrote: "Quick resort to physical combat as a measure of daring, courage, or defense of status appears to be a cultural expectation, especially for lower socioeconomic class males of both races. When such a culture norm response is elicited from an individual engaged in social interplay with others who harbor the same response mechanism, physical assaults, altercations, and violent domestic quarrels that result in homicide are likely to be relatively common." In other words, in a culture of machismo, men appear compelled to hurt each other as well as women and children.

Critics of the compulsive masculinity thesis tend to use the same arguments against it that have been employed against the subculture theory of violence. For instance, Erlanger (1974) studied whether members of the lower class in fact subscribe to values different from the middle class, concluding that they do not maintain distinct values that condone violence. In another study, Brownfield (1987) attempted to test the Moynihan version of the compulsive masculinity thesis by analyzing the self-reports of 1,500 white males and 1,000 black males. These men were asked about their family background and personal involvement in criminal behavior. Moynihan (1965) had argued that the disproportionate number of female-headed families among blacks is causally related to crime and delinquency. Brownfield found otherwise. Contrary to Moynihan's version of the compulsive masculinity thesis, Brownfield found that the physical absence of the father is unrelated to the self-reported crime and violence patterns of black and white boys. Rather than mothers being the key variable, Brownfield found that fathers were. Those black and white boys whose fathers had a history of unemployment were more likely to engage in violent behavior than were sons of fully employed fathers. Oliver (1994) points out that while Brownfield's findings refute Moynihan's version of the compulsive masculinity perspective, they do not invalidate versions of the thesis that consider compulsive masculinity to be an adaptation to structural pressures. Oliver believes that compulsive masculinity is more of a symbolic display, enacted via a wide range of behaviors, than it is an unmediated direct compulsion to violence. Many lower-class black men rely on such symbolic displays to communicate their commitment to compulsive masculinity.

Where do these symbolic displays of compulsive masculinity get enacted? Oliver points to bars. What is a "bar setting"? The term refers to a wide range of after-hours places of encounter, including "greasy spoon restaurants, poolrooms, gambling parlors, street corners, alleys, and parking lots that are generally located adjacent to licensed public bars" (Oliver 1994, 5).

Bars are, Oliver argues, important sites of interaction because many black communities lack other institutions which provide opportunities for meeting and engaging in "status-enhancement activities." Many lower-class black men, then, resort to bars and "bar settings" (also know as "clubs") in order to

> exhibit their ability to dress and dance well, to attract the attention of members of the opposite sex, to control and manipulate the behavior of others, and to demonstrate their knowledge of controversial issues and worldly activities such as male-female relationships, childrearing, race relations, politics, sports, gambling, alcohol, and drugs. ... The bar is located at the center of lower-class black social life. (quoted passages in Oliver 1994, 21)

Other students of African-American social life have also concluded that the bar is a key institution in lower-class black communities. Lewis (1955) and Samuels (1976) suggested that the black bar is as important as the black church in the social organization of the African-American lower-class communities. Men in such communities, Oliver (1994, 22) concludes, frequently use black bars "as social stages in which they act out rituals associated with compulsive masculinity." Prior to "going out," Oliver reports, many men spend considerable time "coordinating their clothing, cultivating their physical appearance, and mentally going over the way they will enact their self-presentation." Going to bars is "akin to a manhood rite of passage." There, black men engage in "symbolic displays of compulsive masculinity," which is to say, they perform their masculine self-image and social identity (quoted phrases in Oliver 1994, 23).

Lower-class black men, Oliver emphasizes, define masculinity as toughness: physical prowess, emotional detachment, and the willingness to resort to violence to resolve interpersonal conflict. These men perform "toughness" by appearing and remaining "cool" in social encounters that are potentially threatening to their reputation, self-image or physical safety. Frequented by such men, the lower-class bar *is* a high-risk social setting, providing the likelihood of threats to reputation, self-image and/or physical safety. Symbolic displays designed to communicate toughness are essential features of masculine self-presentation in this setting (Oliver 1994).

Coolness is, as we have seen, a primary medium by which black men symbolically perform their version of the "tough guy." Recall that coolness, as Lyman and Scott (1970, 145) suggested, "is defined as posing under pressure. ... [It] refers to the capacity to execute physical acts, including conversation, in a concerted, smooth, self-controlled fashion in risky situations, or to maintain affective detachment during the course of encounter involving considerable emotions." For Folb (1980, 127), the term *cool* is less precise, as it "connotes a variety of things depending on context." For instance, it could be regarded as a strategy to "make yourself interesting and attractive to others so that you are better able to manipulate their behavior along lines that will provide some immediate gratification" (Rainwater 1970, 206). As you recall, Majors and Billson (1992) understood it as a form of racial resistance, that is, never allowing the white man to see the black man stressed. Inter- or intraracially, to be cool involves the presentation of oneself as "tough." It requires men to assert independence, control, and emotional detachment (Oliver 1994).

African-American culture has often been characterized as an oral culture, due to the unique emphasis placed upon verbal skills and storytelling. Sociolinguistic research has suggested that many African Americans can be very sensitive to the power of words to comfort, to wound, to sexually arouse, as well as to enhance social status. This sensitivity is evident, Oliver suggests, in black bars and bar settings, where lower-class black men often engage in "tough talk." A common theme of "tough talk" narratives is the storyteller's triumph in a tense, conflict-ridden situation. The storyteller underscores the gravity of the event by telling how he successfully managed a threat to his self-image and/or physical safety. "Tough talk" stories tend to depict conflicts over a wide range of interpersonal relationships, including arguments with friends, acquaintances, strangers, girlfriends, wives, social workers, police. Anyone who poses a challenge to a man's manhood or autonomy is an enemy within this culture of hypermasculinity. The "tough guy," the "player of women," the "thrill-seeker," and the "hustler" are typical "manhood scripts" many lower-class black males perform. These roles are typified by violence, the emotional and economic exploitation of women, as well as participation in high-risk activities such as hanging out on a street corners and in bars, heavy consumption of alcohol and drugs, gambling, and petty crime (Oliver 1994).

Violence is not usually the first option exercised by a threatened man. Many lower-class black men, Oliver reports, when first confronted by another man in a way that challenges his manhood, will attempt to deflect the challenge by ridiculing or "sounding" on the transgressor. If ridicule fails to stop the event or fails to repair the damage done to a man's identity or reputation, he may then resort to violence. Students of sociolinguistics report that some black men refer to the nonviolent move in this game of identity defense/promotion as "woofing." Cooke (1972, 44) described woofing as "a style of bragging and boasting about how bad one is." Its purpose, Kochman (1981, 49) suggested, "is to gain, without having to become violent, the respect and fear from others that is often won through physical combat. To accomplish this, it is necessary for a man to create an image of being fearless and tough, someone not to be trifled with." Woofing is, Oliver (1994, 26) summarizes, "primarily a symbolic act in that it is a form of talk designed to advertise one's willingness to engage in violence." Such a willingness to engage in violence is a prerequisite to being a "man."

A man who is interested in "sizing up" another man's manhood, that is, his ability to perform the "tough guy" script, for example, will attend closely to the other man's demeanor, including his posture, style of walking, and "tough talk." How he handles himself when talking to women, gambling, or drinking indexes his masculinity. Those males who are unable or unwilling to engage in symbolic displays of toughness are often dismissed as "weak" or "chumps." Once this characterization is shared by others, the defamed individual is no longer eligible to participate as an equal in the primary peer groups that hang out at various bars. Oliver (1994, 26) comments: "[I]dentity challenges and woofing are frequently employed to check an individual's masculinity credentials."

Because manhood and heterosexuality are synonymous, among the various identity functions of the lower-class bar, none is more important to lower-class black men, Oliver reports, than meeting heterosexual women. Because many lower-class black men define masculinity as sexual dominance and conquest, the "player of women" is the primary script through which they symbolically perform their manhood. To succeed in the eyes of his fellow man, the "player of women" must attract more than one woman, must maintain exclusive sexual access to most if not all of the women with whom he is involved, then exercise emotional and economic control over them. Within bars and bar settings, black men perform sexual conquest more often than any of the other compulsive masculinity scripts (Oliver 1994).

There are subscripts in the sexual conquest story. Lower-class black men may engage in a series of symbolic displays in order to communicate to other males their ability to manipulate or "play" women. These may include attention to their "personal dress and grooming, peer group announcements, raps and semiprivate conversations, socializing with women, and escorting women to and from bars" (Oliver 1994, 27). As in most forms of compulsory heterosexuality, it is clear that for many lower-class black men, women are a symbolic currency in a male-male exchange system, what Rubin (1975, 175) termed the "traffic in women."

In addition to dress, grooming is, Oliver (1994) points out, an important element in lower-class black males' masculinity performance. Many lower-class black women become adept at distinguishing hustlers and pimps from those who are not as committed to these expressions of compulsive masculinity. The ability to assess men based on their personal dress and public presentation is a skill that many black women cultivate in order to protect themselves from those who are likely to the exploit them (Oliver 1994). While many black women reject relationships with men who are more compulsively masculine, Hannerz (1969) observed that there are black women who are attracted to the "flashy" and masculinized self-presentations that successful pimps and hustlers often perform.

No small portion of male-male conversation and repartee in black bars is comprised of announcements of sexual conquest. Men boast often and loudly of their ability to dominate and control women by means of sex appeal, seduction, and emotional manipulation. On occasion, a listener may challenge a man's announcement, precipitating a strained relationship and, not infrequently, rapidly escalating interpersonal conflict. On most occasions, however, peer group announcements of one's exemplary performance as a "player of women" as well as peer challenges to such announcements amount only to "verbal entertainment and cultural sharing." Both claiming and debunking claims to sexual conquest are discursive elements in the ghetto-specific code of male-male interaction. Loud verbal exchanges and contests often typify those social occasions during which men regard themselves as "having a good time" (quoted phrases in Oliver 1994, 29).

The sexual conquest of women has a specific meaning within a male-male social system. Less important than the sexual episode itself is its public confirmation: "A man might escort a woman out for a night on the town for the *sole* purpose of symbolically communicating to other males ... his sexual access to her" (Oliver 1994, 31, emphasis added). On those occasions when a man has not announced a sexual conquest, his primary peers will allow him time to consummate. Men who do not have visible heterosexual relationships about which to brag, and especially those who have failed at initiating a heterosexual relationship, are subject to ridicule (Oliver 1994).

Lower-class black men attach considerable importance, Oliver (1994) reports, to the ability to outwit, manipulate, and control others through cleverness. Language is often employed to perform this aspect of compulsive masculinity. Signifying is one such linguistic complex of discursive moves and strategies. Signifying is "the black term for what in classical European rhetoric are called the figures of signification," or stated differently, "the indirect use of words that changes the meaning of a word or words" (Gates 1988, 81). Signifying takes numerous forms, including capping, loud-talking, the dozens, reading, going off, talking smart, sounding, joaning (jonesing), dropping lugs, snapping, woofing, styling out, and calling out of one's name (Nero 1991).

A Baton Rouge native who came to lead the Student Nonviolent Coordinating Committee (S.N.C.C.) during the 1960s, H. Rap Brown explained: "[B]efore you can signify you got to be able to rap. ... Signifying allowed you a choice—you could either make a cat feel good or bad. If you had just destroyed someone or if they were down already, signifying could help them over. Signifying was also a way of expressing your own feelings. ... Signifying at its best can be heard when the brothers are exchanging tales" (quoted in Gates 1988, 44).

Recall that structuralism purports to explain patriarchy without recourse to biology. According to Lévi-Strauss, relations between the sexes share the deep structure of a language, indeed *are* a sexed language. But men and women do not regularly engage in dialogue: men speak with men and women are the spoken, the sign. This is so taken for granted that Lévi-Strauss feels he must remind his (male) readers that "woman" is not *only* a sign in a world of men. She is, he acknowledges, after all [!] a person (Lévi-Strauss 1963, 1966, 1977, 1979; Boa 1996). Women exist in men's imagination. Are they, as they "exist" in men's minds, substitutions for men's primary attachment to each other? "Why can't a woman be more like a man?" complains Professor Higgins in *My Fair Lady*.

The regime of compulsory heterosexuality cannot accept this possibility. Heterosexual men continue to insist that their primary interest is women, all the while subjecting them to neglect, abuse, not to mention stalking, rape, and murder. Of course heterosexual men *are* interested in women, but as Oliver's research shows, as they contribute to heterosexual male identity (by becoming sexual conquests communicated to male peers). Women are in this homosocial system possessions confirming male power. As such, they are in fact exchangeable with other possessions. Observe this dynamic operating in Oliver's interview with two lower-class black males.

> INTERVIEWER: Why do brothers hang out? Why do brothers spend so much time hanging out on the streets and in bars like Galaxy and Frank's?
> TROY: Women, women, man!
> INTERVIEWER: Women?
> TROY: It is either women or drugs. ... It's drugs. If you got drugs, you get women.
> INTERVIEWER: Why?
> TROY: It's what the women want.
> (Oliver 1994, 58–59)

Several of the men who were over thirty years old told Oliver that the rules of the street were changing, especially among the "young boys"—that is, males between 16 and 25 years of age. These young men de-emphasize the significance of women; many appear to take women and drugs for granted. Drugs, making money, and power: these seem to Oliver to be the major commodities exchanged by the young African-American males he studied. Many of his older respondents regarded the younger men as more violent than they were when they were that age.

> JOHNNY B: These young boys don't care about women. I never see them with a main woman.
> I: So there's less fighting over women?
> JOHNNY B: Right.
> (Oliver 1994, 65)

In fact, it would appear that for some younger men drugs have replaced women as the symbolic currency in the male exchange system:

> I: Do you think there are more fights over drugs today than there are over women?
> MAC: I think there's more fights over drugs than women. There's more violence over drugs. Half of the guys don't care about girls, they just want drugs.
> (Oliver 1994, 66)

Chronic alcohol use, Oliver found, is common among lower-class black males. While the men Oliver interviewed believed that violence among black men is primarily a function of drug disputes, conflict over women, and masculinity challenges (the informants coded these as "disrespect"), alcohol intoxication was cited as a factor. Of course, being in a bar it is unsurprising that alcohol consumption was routine. But Oliver (1994) found that it was not uncommon for the respondents and their peers to use alcohol, marijuana, and cocaine concurrently during the course of a particular period of "hanging out."

These men struck Oliver as "particularly sensitive" to insults that they experienced as raising questions about their masculinity. To be called a "punk"—in prison equivalent to "bitch"—was regarded as the ultimate insult. More than any other action, calling another man a punk was likely to lead to violence:

> HOUSTON: The word *faggot* or something like that is used to take your manhood away.
>
> I: Why do you think that so many fights among black males are centered around manhood?
>
> HOUSTON: I believe with us, the black man, that our manhood is very important to us. That's about the only thing we have to hold on to, besides our families, is our manhood. And when that's threatened, it's time to fight. "I'm going to show you that I'm not a punk," "I'm going to show you that I'm not a faggot"—you know, that sort of thing. I've seen fights where words were exchanged for at least ten, fifteen minutes and they just stood there and exchanged words with one another, and one guy told the other guy, "Look, just leave me alone," and the other guy just kept on you know, "Fuck you, punk," and the other guy was getting tired of the exchange of words, being called punk, faggot, sissy, so forth, that he just went on ahead and punched the guy, and a fight occurred.
>
> I: What would you say is the most important factor contributing to fights between black males?
>
> Houston: Manhood—you know, a challenge to their manhood.
>
> (Oliver 1994, 90)

In one violent incident Oliver investigated, the decision to use violence appeared to be influenced by several factors. One respondent claimed that he hit the other in defense, as he thought that the other man was about to assault him. Later in the interview, the respondent restated his rationale, saying that the insults directed against him by the other man constituted an attack on his manhood. It was too much for him to tolerate:

> DOX 2: He called a man bitches, punks, and faggots. And a man can only take so much. He tried to take my manhood. I mean, he was taking my manhood. How many bitches and faggots can I be?
>
> (Oliver 1994, 91)

The homosexual subtext of heterosexual manhood is evident in yet another passage. Heterosexuality, in this respect, is a simple metaphorization of the literal, not forgetting that metaphors are also meant literally:

> PAUL 1: If you go back to the first time when he told me to fuck you, I don't let anybody tell me to "Kiss my ass and fuck you." I don't disrespect another man. I don't tell anyone to kiss my ass, and I ain't going to let anybody else tell me to kiss their ass.
>
> (Oliver 1994, 106)

And in another the ass symbolizes both a masculinity challenge and a generalized assault:

> I: Why did you hit him?
>
> Paul 5: He had the look. You can tell by that look. A look like, "In two seconds I am going to get busy on your ass." So I decided I better go on and blast him.
>
> (Oliver 1994, 108)

But the main point of sensitivity would appear to be anxiety over heterosexual identity:

> I: What would you say was the main thing he was saying to you?
>
> PATTERSON I: Your brother's going to prison, and he won't be nothing but a faggot when he gets out.
>
> (Oliver 1994, 112)

Several of Oliver's respondents defined manhood in terms of their willingness to resort to violence, especially in order to defend a relative or friend:

> BUTCH 1: *I am one hundred percent man,* and if anybody ever disrespects anybody that I love, I got to go and see about it. I am a champ, and I love my family.
>
> (Oliver 1994, 116, emphasis added)

When the gaze is queered, it is clear that homosexuality, as a subtext related to assault, is a primary preoccupation of these men. Oliver recodes threatened heterosexuality as an issue of autonomy. He argues that one of his most significant findings is that "violent confrontations between lower-class black men are often precipitated by verbal statements or behaviors that are defined as autonomy transgressions" (Oliver 1994, 149). But it seems clear that "autonomy" is a cover for "heterosexuality" which is then conflated with "masculinity." In his ethnographic study of lower-class blacks in Washington, D.C., Hannerz made a similar association. Hannerz (1969, 82) reported: "it seems that most of the violence which occurs has the form of brawls following arguments. Meddling, scorn, and condescending manner come into conflict with the men's feeling for autonomy. 'He's a man and I'm a man, and, I don't take no shit like that,' is how street corner men tend to defend or explain their fighting responses." If you're a man and straight, you're autonomous. By this binary logic women are dependent. But Oliver and Hannerz—they are hardly alone—strip the sexual content from these exchanges, recoding them as (only) autonomy disputes.

Oliver's findings appear consistent with Palmer's earlier observations regarding the association between masculine identity threats and violent confrontations between black men. Palmer (1972) had found that "[i]t is the unreciprocating slights of his masculinity that so often trigger violence. Any disparagement of masculinity is cause for the male to aggress, especially if he is of the lower class and black. ... When it appears to him that one or more [men] threaten through unreciprocity to destroy whatever *fragile identity* he possesses, he takes violent action against them" (59, emphasis added). Is this not in general consistent with psychoanalytic narratives of masculinity production that indicate that heterosexual identity is necessarily "fragile"? Why are we surprised when "men" feel they must engage in violence in order to maintain their reputations as "men" when violence characterizes what they did to those (feminine, mother-identified) aspects of themselves to achieve this identity in the first place? For some black men, in whom traces of sexualized assault must linger from generation to generation (history is past but not gone), would not "manhood" be especially poignant?

These psychosocial and sexualized dynamics are hardly restricted to lower-class black men. For instance, the observation that an autonomy transgression is a major issue in violent confrontations between lower-class black men is also consistent with Horowitz's (1985) findings regarding the association between dishonor and violence among Chicano men. Horowitz found that Chicano men tended to justify the use of violence against others by invoking an honor/dishonor distinction. As for white southern men a century before, these words represented these men's sense of themselves as masculine, as exhibiting integrity. Is that what "honor is"—being straight, the top guy? This is the case in many Latin cultures, where homosexuality as defined by the choice of a sexual partner of one's own sex does not exist. Instead, the system of sexual categorization is "based on a configuration of gender/sex/power that is articulated along the active/passive axis" rather than upon the sex of the object choice. Within this Latin sexual system, for example, as Tomas Almaguer describes it:

> [It] is primarily the anal-passive individual (the *cochon* or *pasivo*) who is stigmatized for playing the subservient, feminine role. His partner (activo or machista) typically is not stigmatized at all and, moreover, no clear category exists in the popular language to classify him. For all intents and purposes, he is just a normal ... male. ... The active party in a homosexual drama often gains status among his peers in precisely the way that one derives status from seducing many women. (quoted passages in Bordo 1994, 289)

This association of penetration with agency and masculinity obtains in American prisons too, as we will see. The former director of Stop Prisoner Rape Stephen Donaldson (1993b) pointed out:

> The sexual penetration of another male prisoner by a man is sanctioned by the subculture [of the prison], is considered a male rather than a homosexual activity, and is considered to validate the penetrator's masculinity. ... The prisoners ... insist that the difference between the experience of entering a female mouth and of entering a male mouth is not significant, that the experiential difference between entering a vagina or a female anus and a male anus is not significant. (quoted in Scarce 1997, 39)

Among the Chicano men Horowitz (1985) studied, "honor" referred to "a person's ability to command deference in interpersonal relations," again a notion not entirely different from nineteenth-century southern white men's conception of "honor" as reputation, especially men's reputation among other men (Stowe 1987). Horowitz found that violent confrontations among these men were often precipitated by acts of dishonor. These acts represented challenges to their honor that could not be ignored; otherwise they would be perceived as exhibiting "a failure of manliness or the physical capacity to maintain claims to precedence among peers" (quoted passages in Horowitz 1985, 23). So vulnerable, so provisional, dominant forms of manhood can only be propped up, like a dictator, by violence.

Interestingly, rather than understanding what he saw and heard as illustrative—albeit an extreme example—of the phenomenon of "masculinity," Oliver (1994, 136) perceived only class and culture. He concludes that

> Findings presented in this study strongly suggest that interactions leading to violent incidents among black males are influenced by role orientations and lifestyles associated with ghetto-based definitions of manhood. Therefore, violence-prevention strategies directed toward violence participation among black males must attempt to change the social context in which young black males enter into manhood.

He suggests that "black male schools and classrooms" be established (Oliver 1994, 160) and that "mentoring manhood development programs" should be developed and/or expanded (161), advice similar to that given by other black male students of black masculinity (see, for instance, Madhubuti 1990).

Oliver does not recommend the questioning of masculinity itself, exposing, for instance, its performative elements, how it mutilates the personality it presumably exists to express. Not to mention how it mutilates other men, women, and children. To confront "masculinity" as a social problem: that is an unacceptable agenda for any mainstream American community, for to be American is to be heterosexual. For many African-American men, to be an American means to be a "man," if not in its civic or capitalistic sense, at least in its gendered one. Brian Phillip Harper remembers Michael Jackson's statement to Oprah Winfrey, made during a live television interview, that "I am proud to be a black American." What, Harper (1996, ix) asks, can this statement mean? The answer points to the complexity of black machismo:

> For while Jackson's profession of racial pride was most obviously meant to counter judgments that his physical appearance is unacceptably "white," it also spoke to a widespread suspicion that his feminized demeanor signals a lack of self-respect, the "feminine" still strongly connoting degradation even at this late historical moment. Jackson's assertion carried this dual significance because the abiding worry over his sexual and gender identities is itself also a manifestation of concern about the status of his blackness.

Harper points out that pride and self-respect are widely viewed as keys to a healthy African-American identity. But such identity is perceived to be fundamentally undermined wherever black masculinity appears to be compromised. Rarely articulated, he suggests, is the conflation between a healthy African-American identity and a virile black masculinity. It is "nonetheless real and pervasive. Its primary effect is that all debates over and claims to 'authentic' African American identity are largely animated by a profound anxiety about the status specifically of African American *masculinity*" (Harper 1996, ix). What on earth could that "profound anxiety" be about?

VII. Black Male Feminism

> *On what basis, according to what ideological perspective, can an Afro-American heterosexual male ground his notions of the female? Beyond its heterosexual dimension, can the "female" truly come to represent for a traditional black male-in-crisis more than a protective womb from which he seeks to be "birthed" again? Can it serve as more than a site on which to find relief from or locate frustrations caused by his inability to achieve putatively normative American male socioeconomic status?*
>
> Michael Awkward, *Negotiating Difference: Race, Gender, and the Politics of Positionality* (1995)

> *[C]ontemporary black male intellectuals claim to challenge the hegemony of a racialized social formation; most fail to challenge the hegemony of their own assumptions about black masculinity.*
>
> Hazel Carby, *Race Men* (1998)

> *It is the heritage of the mother that the African American male must regain as an aspect of his own personhood—the power of "yes" to the "female" within.*
>
> —Hortense J. Spillers, "Mama's Baby, Papa's Maybe: An American Grammar Book" (1987)

Recently there have been articulations of a black heterosexual male feminist position, expressed perhaps most prominently by Michael Awkward (1995, 1996), but I will focus here on the work of Gary Lemons (1998). Drawing on Alice Walker's famous notion of "womanist" as "a black feminist or feminist of color ... committed to survival and wholeness of an entire people, male *and* female" and bell hooks's call for "reconstructing black masculinity," Lemons connects sexism and racism, insisting that black men must come to appreciate that the struggle for civil rights in the United States has for too long been focused on black men. He is not alone; he points to the efforts of black male undergraduates at Morehouse College who founded the organization Black Men for the Eradication of Sexism (B.M.E.S.). He recalls that during the weekend of September 28 and 29, 1996, a year after the Million Man March, "they (we) made history" (quoted passages on 43). At a conference entitled "Black, Male and Feminist/Womanist," devoted to the subject of black men's relation to feminism/womanism, African-American men organized this group to make a public declaration of their commitment to the eradication of sexism. In their mission statement they proclaimed:

> We believe that sexism is a global form of oppression of no less importance than any other form of oppression. All forms of oppression, including sexism, racism, classism, homophobia are interconnected and support each other. *For too long the struggle for the liberation of African people in the united states* [sic] *has been centered on the liberation of black men.* This male-centered analysis inhibits us from fully confronting the oppression we constantly face and perpetuate within and without the black community. The struggle against sexism must become an issue of primary importance if we are to advance as a people. (quoted in Lemons 1998, 44, emphasis in original)

The establishment of Black Men for the Eradication of Sexism suggests to Lemons the possibility of a broader movement of antisexist black men. Acknowledging the necessity of a critique of black sexism, B.M.E.S. declared:

> We believe that sexist oppression against women pervades every aspect of our communities and must be eradicated. ... Although it has often been said that black women are held in high regard by the black community, the reality is that black women are either denigrated as whores and enemies or placed on a confining pedestal as superwoman. The humanity of our sisters is lost in these classifications which only succeed in further dividing our people and preventing us from dealing with other forms of oppression. Sexism is a radical problem that requires a radical solution. ... We support feminism/womanism and all efforts to eradicate sexist oppression. We ultimately demand a complete and revolutionary change that eradicates oppression based on sex, race, class, and sexual orientation, both within and without. (quoted in Lemons 1998, 44–45)

Such a "womanist" declaration, Lemons (1998) acknowledges, "goes against the grain of the racist and sexist mythology of black manhood and masculinity in the United States." Such "mythology" is, he suggests, historically grounded in white supremacist patriarchal ideology; it still communicates the idea "that we pose a racial and sexual threat to American society such that our bodies exist to be feared, brutalized, imprisoned, annihilated—made invisible" (Lemons 1998, 46). Given his heterosexism, Lemons cannot easily see that black male bodies are also and perhaps most fundamentally, desired. Fear and desire are two sides of the same racialized coin.

If we understand homosexual desire (and rape, as in the case of lynching) as threatening to compulsory male heterosexuality, we can appreciate that the fear of emasculation follows from such desire, especially in its deformed, mangled forms such as lynching. Such "emasculation" has typically been interpreted as a recoding of civic disempowerment, which of course took concrete historical forms, that is, slavery and late nineteenth-century disenfranchisement. But it must be recoded in literal terms, as an actual fear of castration, literal or symbolic, due to the omnipresence of white male homosexual desire for the black male body. Lemons (1998, 46) repeats part of this equation, writing that:

> The fear of emasculation originates in the history of black male lynching; the power of white (male) supremacy performed itself in the ritual act of castration (the violent sexual *dismembering* of our bodies) as a tool "to put/keep us in our place," expressed because we were *black* and male—to "feminize" us. Thus, *it is the fear of feminization in the minds of many black men that has led us to overdetermine our sexuality*, believing that our identity as men resides only in the power of our penises. (last emphasis mine)

It is this analysis which informs Lemons's call for black male feminism, which he understands is not a form of "political correctness" and is more than an expression of solidarity with black women. It is, as well, a reconstruction of masculinity, a making over of "ourselves over again in our own image." Such a reconstruction must not amount, however indirectly, to a reproduction of that

> [m]ythology that sexually demonized our bodies as the scourge of white womanhood; rather, it must free us *to be black* in the most radically revolutionary manner, *to be male* in the most nonoppressive, antisexist way, *to be feminist* in the most supportive, nonpatriarchal way to bring about an end to the domination, subordination, and mistreatment of women because they are women. (Lemons 1998, 46; emphasis in original)

For Lemons, Alice Walker's notion of "womanism" suggests such a tripartite remaking of black masculinity, a psychosocial and political labor which requires, he writes, "focusing on the historical impact castration and lynching have had on the black male psyche and on ways we construct our identity as men." Such labor may disclose to black men why "[we] have internalized racist sexual myths of black manhood and masculinity such that images of 'black macho' and the supersexual 'buck/stud' have prevailed in black communities as legitimate representations of black male power" (Lemons 1998, 51). Lemons quotes bell hooks's (1992) observation that "black men who are most worried about castration and emasculation are those who have completely absorbed white supremacist patriarchal definitions of masculinity" (93). Lemons appreciates that "the black buck stereotype" originates "in the white racist imagination during the period of slavery" (51), but fails to add one additional modifier which, I think, would clarify this picture even further: "male." The social construction of black manhood originates in white male racist imagination, an imagination many white women accepted as "true" but which did not belong to them in the primary way that it did to men. It was white men who found the fantasy so compelling that they constructed an imaginary scenario of sexual violation that required their participation.

White men's imaginations have been key to the construction of social reality, and their fantasies regarding black men continue to influence forms of black manhood well into our time. Lemons notes the "phallic representation of black masculinity in the Black Power movement of the 1960s" reappeared in multiple forms of popular culture in the decade following. He is thinking of those performances of hypermasculinity evident in the blaxploitation films in the 1970s, a genre most remembered perhaps by the movie *Shaft,* which exhibited the "superfly" or the hypercool parody of black manhood. He sees the historical throughline between these contemporary expressions of black machismo—the persisting image of the black man as "supersexual savage"—and the need "to control black men during slavery" (quoted passages in Lemons 1998, 51). I would draw another throughline between contemporary images of black men and white masters' employment of enslaved black men as "breeders" *and* as objects of homosexual victimization.

The reproduction and perpetuation of a hypersexualized black manhood and masculinity is culturally affirmed through stereotypical portrayals of black men on television, in film, throughout the white-controlled media. Such "sexually overdetermined" images of black manhood that have "essentialized" black men throughout American history are still played out in contemporary popular culture, where, Lemons points out, "the 'dick-clutching' posture of many black rappers has obtained as a status symbol of male power in hip-hop" (1998; quoted passages on 52).

Lemons (1998) denies that "black manhood and masculinity are about a 'dick thing'." "Progressive black men" reject "sexist, misogynist, and patriarchal practice against women," including "the 'dick thing' mentality," and in so doing "begin to mediate the painful historical memory of our own dehumanization." By rejecting the white fantasy of the "super dick"—a fantasy, Lemons acknowledges, "many black men have internalized as a symbol of black male power"—black men can reject "the racist/sexist sexual mythology created to control us," a mythology that would "have us believe that we are no more than one big collective 'walking, brutalizing phallus'." When black men appreciate that this mythology is not the source of black male power but the expression of "oppressive power over us, we start to perceive the interrelated ways racism and male supremacist privilege work together to dehumanize all black men." "Understanding the link between white privilege and male privilege," Lemons continues, "realizing that empowered images of black manhood do not rest in the reclamation of lost phallic power (the preeminent fallacy of manhood thinking in general), black men come to experience transformative, liberatory power as men" (quoted passages on 52).

In so doing, Lemons suggests, black men may come to understand that feminism is no alienating force in black lives. The mass of African-American men are not there yet: "to many black men feminism represents a threat to their vision of black masculinity and manhood," including male claims to "familial and cultural authority, responsibility, nationhood," even "manliness" itself. Lemons acknowledges that many black men dismiss feminism as an expression of "white supremacy that attempts to reenact the sexual 'unmanning' of black men as the prime spectacle of lynching." "It is any wonder," he asks, that "we remain mistrustful of feminism?" (quoted passages on 53).

Committed to a progressive feminist perspective, Lemons (1998, 59) regards his "teaching as a process of remembering in which African American literary narratives become agents of social healing across the boundaries of race, gender, class, and sexuality." He thinks of his teaching as a form of "mothering"—"a strategy of nurturance"—in contrast to the authoritarianism of the mythological Father. There are autobiographical as well as ideological antecedents here: "I grew up in a patriarchal household where my father's experience as a military officer informed the masculine rigidity of its day-to-day operation. As an often withdrawn, timid little boy, I came to fear, despise, and later resist his notions of manhood, manliness, and masculinity. More than anything, my sympathies were aligned with my mother." His mother, he goes on to tells us, worked for a time as a housekeeper and cook in the homes of privileged white families. "I often think," he muses, "about the powerlessness she must have felt, working tirelessly at the whims of her wealthy employers, always having to enter the back doors of their elegantly appointed homes to perform what they believed themselves unsuited to do" (59–60).

Lemons's mother was by no means defeated by this physical and psychosocial stress, and in fact Lemons (1998, 60) remembers that "it is my mother's sharp tongue, her resolute will to struggle, her critical understanding of the way race shaped her experience as a black, female, working-class mother and wife that have informed how and what I teach." He rejects any notion that his fidelity to feminism implies any loss of masculinity, recalling Sara Ruddick's (1989) notion of the maternal man:

> The fear of becoming "feminine" ... is a motivating force behind the drive to master women and whatever is "womanly." ... [G]rown men should confront the political meaning of "femininity" and their own fear of the feminine. A man does not, by becoming a mother, give up his male body or any part of it. To be sure, by becoming a mother he will, in many social groups, challenge the ideology of masculinity. (45; quoted in Lemons 1998, 60)

In so doing, feminist men, as Lemons understands, run the "risk of having their masculinity called into question; this is the point exactly," he adds. For a man to teach feminism, and in a feminist manner, requires "breaking through barriers of manhood and masculinity inscribed in patriarchy, which devalues the qualities of nurturance and mothering." Once again recalling Ruddick, Lemons asserts that the very notion of the maternal is a "transgendered" one (quoted passages on 60). This transgression is not lost on his students:

> When I tell students I am a feminist, they always react in complex ways, depending on their race, gender, and sexual affiliations. But a feminist

> black man in (or outside) the classroom is always already an oddity. First of all, I am at odds with many white students' fear of black men and racist attitudes about black people in general. Second, I am at odds with many black students whose rage against and contempt for all white people blind them to the possibilities of progressive coalition movements across racial boundaries in resistance to racism, when we begin to de-essentialize blackness. I am also at odds with male students especially (of color and not) who buy into male supremacist ideas of manhood and masculinity. They view me as a traitor to mankind, a misanthrope of the worst kind! (Lemons 1998, 60–61)

Lemons is adamant that black men "can no longer use the myth that feminism is a racist ploy to emasculate black men while we assert our power as men to oppress women." Even if not explicitly and aggressively feminist, progressive black men, he asserts, must divest themselves of male privilege and position themselves in solidarity with black women. Black male opposition to sexism and misogyny, he reminds, resides in a long history of feminist and abolitionist struggle. But he understands that more knowledge of history and appreciation of politics is required, that black men must begin by "confronting the fear of the feminine that feminism represents to many men" (quoted passages on 62). Moreover, black men "must vigorously denounce black male antifeminist rhetoric that reduces the feminism of black women to a diatribe against black men" (Lemons 1998, 63).

What is required, Lemons concludes, is "men of color must be[come] traitors to patriarchy," which means, in part, "refusing to bond with men at the expense of women." "In spite of the structural inequalities of racism we experience as black men," he continues, "patriarchal thinking would lead us to believe that male supremacist power is rightfully ours as a form of racial justice," pointing to that conflation of "the struggle against racism with a struggle for manhood rights" evident in the current "black power movement" led by Louis Farrakhan. Whatever their class location, men of color must repudiate what many white men mean when they affirm manhood, namely the interest in "keep[ing] women in their place." Black men must understand that "the history of black male experience in the United States necessitates an analysis of the interrelation of race and sex oppression" (Lemons 1998, 63). Indeed.

VIII. Black, Male, and Gay

I'd heard my calling by age 6.
We had a word for boys like me.
(Punk)
Punk not because I played sex with other boys—
everybody on the block did that.
(Punk)
But because I didn't mind giving it away.
(Punk)
Other boys traded—"You can have my booty
if you gimme yours"—

but I gave it up,
free,
(Punk).

Marlon Riggs, "Tongues Untied," in Essex Hemphill, ed., *Brother to Brother: Collected Writings by Black Gay Men* (1991)

[T]rue niggers ain't gay.

—Ice Cube 1991; quoted in K. Thomas, "Ain't Nothing Like the Real Thing: Black Masculinity, Gay Sexuality, and the Jargon of Authenticity," in Marcellus Blount and George P. Cunningham, eds., *Representing Black Man* (1996)

Because of my sexuality, I cannot be black. A strong, proud, "Afrocentric" black man is resolutely heterosexual, not even *bisexual. Hence I remain a Negro.*

—Marlon Riggs, "Black Macho Revisited: Reflections of a SNAP! Queen," in Essex Hemphill, ed., *Brother to Brother: Collected Writings by Black Gay Men* (1991)

One of the most serious challenges facing black gay intellectuals is the development of a progressive view of homosexuality in the African American community.

—Ron Simmons, "Some Thoughts on the Challenges Facing Black Gay Intellectuals," in Essex Hemphill, ed., *Brother to Brother: Collected Writings by Black Gay Men* (1991)

Black gay subjectivity is complex and contradictory; it behooves one then to explore it in all of its complexity and contradictions.

—Arthur Flannigan-Saint-Aubin, "'Black Gay Male' Discourse: Reading Race and Sexuality between the Lines" (1993)

If lower-class black masculinity is "compulsive" and compensatory, if middle-class hegemonic masculinity is often heterosexist and homophobic, one would expect considerable anxiety within African-American culture over homosexuality. That anxiety might take the form of political leaders' and intellectuals' attacks on homosexuality. There is evidence of that. Minister Louis Farrakhan and his (at that time) deputy Khalid Abdul Muhammad, for instance, have condemned homosexuality. It would appear that Farrakhan has even condoned violence directed at gay men. On May 20, 1990, in Oakland, California, Farrakhan spoke of the need to "sacrifice the individual for the preservation of a nation." He told his male listeners that they had better "hide" their effeminate behavior, reminding them that the "penalty" for homosexual activity in the Holy Land is "death" (quoted phrases in Boykin 1996, 153).

As Keith Boykin (1996) points out, there are those Islamic scholars who have taken issue with Farrakhan's claim that Islamic civilization and religion have always been antihomosexual. Perhaps Farrakhan, like many others, is simply a victim of homophobia. According to Ron Simmons (1991, 211), a gay black man and former Howard University professor, among African Americans "'homophobia' is not so much a fear of 'homosexuals' but a fear that homosexuality will become pervasive in the community." Why would *that* fear have currency?

In a 1983 speech at Morgan State University, Farrakhan listed imprisonment and the lack of positive male role models as two major causes of homosexuality among black men. Sounding for a moment like the Moynihan Report, he declared: "Those of you—who are homosexual—you weren't born [that] way brother—You never had a strong male image. ... [These] are conditions that are forced on black men. You're filling up the jails and they're turning [you] into freaks in the jails" (quoted in Eure and Jerome 1989, 138; in Simmons 1991, 213). As we will see in the next section, the research on prison rape suggests otherwise.

In *Afrocentricity*, Molefi Asante (1980) too points to "prison breeding" for the "outburst of homosexuality among black men." He is indignant that "black gays are often put in front of white or integrated organizations to show the liberalism of the group." For Asante, homosexuality is a "white decadence" that cannot be condoned. It can, however, be "tolerated until such time as our families and schools are engaged in Afrocentric instruction for males." Such instruction is, for Asante, heteronormative. For the sake of "the people" everyone must be straight: "Afrocentric relationships are based upon ... what is best for the collective imperative of the people. ... All brothers who are homosexuals should know that they too can become committed to the collective will. It means the submergence of their own wills into the collective will of our people" (quoted passages in Asante 1980, 65; quoted in Simmons 1991, 213).

In his *Black Masculinity*, Robert Staples (1982, 88) repeats the fantasy that the "nation's prisons are the main places where homosexual preferences are evident—because of the unavailability of women." After their release, some black men continue the "homosexual lifestyle" for various reasons, "ranging from a desire to escape family responsibilities to acquiring money through prostitution." The increasing visibility of black lesbians, Staples charges, is a result of "the shortage of black men—or the conflict in male/female relationships." He also contends that black homosexuals are "deeply involved in the white homosexual community" (90). Neither Asante nor Staples, Keith Boykin (1996) notes, explains the increasing visibility of homosexuality in the nonprison black population. Simmons (1991, 215) is clear that the issue is broader than simple homophobia among black intellectuals:

> Confronted by racial oppression in the larger society and sexual oppression in our own community, black gay intellectuals face formidable challenges.

> [W]e must not allow ourselves to be paralyzed by the hurt, anger, and rage we may feel toward homophobic and heterosexist scholars. Rejecting us is their loss—and it comes back to haunt us *all*. We have the right to criticize their erroneous ideas and to help build a better world for everyone. We know the reality of our lives. We know that we are not gay because of "prison." The vast majority of black gay men have never been near a prison. For Staples, Farrakhan, and Asante to suggest that most black gay men are gay because of prison shows a serious lack of competent insight and scholarship. (emphasis in original)

Staples (1982) has also suggested that black men's involvement in crime and drug use amounts to a self-destructive "solution" to problems created by white racism in America, a contemporary parallel to the suicide of slaves during the Middle Passage. While not doubting this claim, Isaac Julien and Kobena Mercer (1991, 171) want to say to Staples that "another negative strand in this process [of self-destruction], homophobia and anti-gay attitudes, allows us to examine the ways that such definitions of black manhood have limited the agenda of black politics at a collective level." In other words, black homophobia contributes to an ongoing sense of black cultural crisis by undermining efforts at black cultural mobilization and political collectivization.

Nathan and Julia Hare (1984, 64) cite ancient Greece and the modern Western world as examples of civilizations in a "state of decay" where sex norms and moral values are confused, and "people are alienated and set part from their natural origins. [In such societies] there emerges a breakdown in childrearing and socialization. ... Without a solid core to their personalities, children grow up confused—develop[ing] problems of identity, most notably that of gender confusion. Homosexuality accordingly will proliferate." There have been Africans too who have fantasized homosexuality as a "white" phenomenon, notably Zimbabwe's President Mugabe (Duke 1995). The history of African peoples reveals a different story (Sweet 1996).

Truth sometimes disappears in the politics of racial identity. "You have to understand something," explained Professor Griff of the controversial and highly popular rap group Public Enemy: "In knowing and understanding black history, African history, there's not a word in any African language which describes homosexual, y'understand what I'm saying? You would like to make them part of the community, but that's something brand new to black people." Marlon Riggs (1991b) comments: "And so black macho appropriates African history, or rather, a deeply reductive, mythologized view of African history, to rationalize homophobia" (quoted passages on 256).

Evidently ignorant of African history, Nathan and Julia Hare (1984, 2) succumb to homophobia and heterosexism. They lament: "Where once there were pretty women and working men, there are now pretty men and working women." Capitalism would not seem to be to blame, however. Whites are. For instance, the Hares and other critics such as Jawanza Kunjufu (1989) charge that black boys become homosexuals due not to prison but to the preponderance of white female schoolteachers. The Hares (1984, 66) allege that "white teachers infiltrate black child centers, nurseries and primary schools, compelling black boys to play with blonde dolls in the name of progress." Ron

Simmons (1991, 213) is not persuaded by the Hares's gender analysis: "Nathan and Julian Hare's homophobic raving does not negate the fact that there may be racist genocidal plots against the black community, or that black men are systematically destroyed. Our homosexuality, however, is not part of such plots and our love is not genocidal. It is their divisive homophobic and heterosexist reactions to our natural sexual expression that play into the plot of divide and conquer."

In his *Enemies: The Clash of Races*, Haki Madhubuti (1978) repeats an old white fantasy that there is a preponderance of homosexuals in the higher socioeconomic groups—for his purposes, the black bourgeoisie. Madhubuti (1978) pronounces homosexuality backward, abnormal, and "rampant in significant parts of the black community." Of course, it is not "indigenous" to black folk; it is a consequence of the (white) system:

> It is a profound comment on the power of the system that [it] is able to transform black men into sexual lovers of each other. ... On many black college campuses [and in] the black church, homosexuality and bisexuality [have become] an accepted norm. And far too often these homosexual black men, because of their sensitivity, talent and connections are found in the most sensitive positions of responsibility in the ... working world ... actually directing many community, political and educational programs. (quoted passages in Madhubuti 1978, 148)

In a footnote, Madhubuti (1978, 148) does acknowledge what he calls the "human complexity of homosexuality." Calling for understanding and dialogue, he thinks out loud: "Black homosexuality is on the rise and the question becomes do we enlist them in our struggle, or do we continue to alienate and make enemies of them? [I]f we are truly conscious adults we have to show a sensitivity to their personal differences as well as the political and cultural differences of our people." Such a tactical tolerance is not limited to Madhubuti, as Ron Simmons (1991) observes. Nathan and Julia Hare (1984) also suggest a tactic of tolerance:

> On the other hand—and this is crucial—we will refuse to embark on one more tangent of displaced contempt and misdirected scorn for the homosexualized black brothers or sisters and drive them over to the camp of the white liberal-radical-moderate establishment coalition. What we must do is offer the homosexual brother or sister a proper compassion and acceptance without advocacy. ... Some of them may yet be saved. And yet, we must declare open warfare upon the sources of [their] confusion. (65; quoted in Simmons 1991, 214)

Such "tolerance" is drenched in heterosexism and homophobia. Twelve years after he published *Enemies*, Madhubuti published *Black Men*. After reading this second book, Simmons (1991, 214) judged Madhubuti as "hopeless" in understanding black men who are gay. In fact, in this second volume there is even some backward movement on the gay issue. Whereas that footnote in *Enemies* called for "dialogue" and "sensitivity," in *Black Men*, "Madhubuti offers no insight whatsoever on homosexuality" (Simmons 1991, 215). Apparently he does not even include gays as black men: "Much of the current black studies have focused on either the black family, black women, Afrika, the black homosexual community, or Europe's and America's influence on the black world. Few black scholars or activists have given serious attention to the condition of black men" (Madhubuti 1990, 60). Black men are straight men. "Very" straight, as Madhubuti appears to endorse polygamy.

Madhubuti may want more than one black woman but he remains focused on white men. He quotes Michael Bradley (1981) approvingly: "The problem with the world is white men" (quoted in Madhubuti 1990, 65). He understands homosexuality as a white political strategy. In a list of the "most prevalent tactics [used by the] U.S. white supremacy system to disrupt black families and neutralize black men," he asserts that one tactic is to make black men into "so-called 'women,' in which cases homosexual and bisexual activity becomes the norm rather than the exception. Men of other cultures do not fear the so-called 'woman-like' men of any race" (73–74). As Simmons (1991, 215) observes: "Madhubuti seems incapable of envisioning black gay men as anything other than effeminate men who pretend to be women." He continues:

> We know we are not gay because of "white oppression." Too many of us realized we were "different" during preadolescence before we knew what racism was or who white people were. Our feelings for other males were not taught by white schoolteachers or white dolls. America has done everything in its power to make black men hate themselves. Black men have been taught for hundreds of years that they are worthless. Yet despite this, black gay men love each other. We have protected, comforted, and cared for ourselves, and for thousands of our brothers, in a white society that despises our "blackness" and in a black community that condemns our love. When black men love each other in an environment that negates, it is not a sign of sickness. It is a sign of health. (Simmons 1991, 215–216)

The beauty and power of black men loving, not killing, black men seem lost on many black intellectuals. Many insist that only whites are gay, that "real" black men cannot be. Of those who attribute black homosexuality to whites, Amiri Baraka may be the most memorable. In his 1965 essay "American Sexual Reference: Black Male," Baraka claimed that "most American white men are trained to be fags" (1965/1966, 216). Former Black Panther Eldridge Cleaver (1968) said much the same. Author of the imaginative *The Isis (Yssis) Papers*, iconoclastic black intellectual Frances Cress Welsing (1991) blames black homosexuality (which is caused by whites) for what she perceives to be as the black community's decline. Simmons (1991, 215) comments:

> The lack of insight about African American homosexuality displayed by some of our heterosexual intellectuals is tragic. Their simplistic and shortsighted analyses promote ignorance and confusion in the African American community, and the oppression of black gays and lesbians. This oppression cripples the vital resources of the community inasmuch as it requires a tremendous amount of energy to hate one another, as opposed

> to utilizing our differences constructively toward empowerment of the African American community.

Suggesting forgiveness and unwilling to abandon the possibility of broader coalitions, Simmons (1991, 212) advises: "we must not allow the hurt and anger we may feel toward such scholars to cause us to dismiss them or their ideas on other issues that we may agree on."

Black gay men have been nearly invisible in mainstream—that is, heterosexual white—America. Often the only mention they receive occurs when "crossover" black male comics such as Arsenio Hall and Damon Wayans make fun of them. "Yet behind the laughs," Cornel West (1993, 89) writes, "lurks a black tragedy of major proportions: the refusal of white and black America to entertain seriously new stylistic options for black men caught in the deadly endeavor of rejecting black machismo identities."

Why would black machismo be so pervasive, so insistent, so conflated with blackness itself? Criticized for his homosexuality in the 1960s by men of the moment such as Baraka and Cleaver, James Baldwin (1985, 290) knew what was circulating in that question:

> I think I know something about the American masculinity which most men of my generation do not know because they have not been menaced by it in the way I have been. It is still true, alas, that to be an American Negro is also to be a kind of walking phallic symbol: which means that one pays, in one's own personality, for the sexual insecurity of others. The relationship, therefore, of a black boy to a white boy is a very complex thing.

Indeed.

Being gay and black means two strikes against you, as Keith Boykin points out, and as Baldwin no doubt experienced. Boykin tells a tale of two cities in which African-American gay men and lesbians suffered discrimination within the black community. The first city is Winston-Salem, North Carolina, where in August 1993 a performance ensemble called the Postmodern African American Homosexuals—better known as Pomo Afro Homos—applied to participate in the third biennial National Black Theater Festival. This award-winning group had played to sold-out audiences across the country. In Winston-Salem it wanted to perform its show *Fierce Love: Stories from Black Gay Life*, but its application was rejected (Boykin 1996).

Later that month, not 250 miles away in Washington, D.C., another controversy was under way, this one having to do with the inclusion of black lesbians and gay men in an event representing, presumably, the entire black community. The 1993 March on Washington for Jobs and Justice marked the thirtieth anniversary of the historic 1963 march at which Martin Luther King, Jr., had delivered his legendary "I Have a Dream" speech. Black lesbians and gay men had requested an opportunity to speak. March organizers had agreed. On the afternoon of August 28, 1993, as the lengthy speeches left everything behind schedule, the march organizers, only to save time, they said, decided to eliminate the lesbian and gay speakers. Exhausted by a long afternoon in the unrelenting summer sun, Phil Wilson, living with AIDS, nearly accepted the decision. But he, in consultation with other black queer leaders, declined to be excluded. Keith Boykin (1996, 179) comments:

> The scenario seemed all too familiar; ten years before, noted lesbian writer Audre Lorde had to fight just to be able to speak at the twentieth-anniversary March on Washington. Wilson had come all the way from Los Angeles so that black homosexuals would be represented, and they were determined to see him speak. When the organizers saw that the gay group would not relent, they placed Wilson at the end of the long program. As the day drew to a close and Wilson was finally announced on-stage, only a small sliver of the huge crowd that had gathered that morning remained on the Mall. But Wilson's mere presence broke the thirty-year silence of the black civil rights establishment, which had excluded another black man, Baynard Rustin, from a more open and significant role in the first March on Washington.

Perhaps the situation is changing, slightly, on occasion. During the October 1995 Million Man March organized by Minister Louis Farrakhan, two hundred black gay men and lesbians participated. Himself among the marchers, Keith Boykin (1996, 206) reports: "no one in the crowd reacted adversely." If there is greater tolerance, perhaps more young black men will survive the AIDS crisis. During the decade ending in June 1991, some 179,694 persons in the United States were diagnosed as having Acquired Immune Deficiency Syndrome. Of that number of total reported cases, 41,179—roughly 23 percent—occurred in African-American men. Black males comprise less than 6 percent of the total U.S. population (Harper 1996). "The reality is," Boykin asserts, "that AIDS is the leading cause of death for black males between the ages of twenty-five and forty-four" (1996, xiv).

Black gay men have caught it from both sides: racism from whites and homophobia from black men and women. Racism from gay men may seem ironic. After all, as the documentary film *Before Stonewall* shows, gay liberation in America copied its strategies from the civil rights struggles of the 1960s. As Audre Lorde points out in the film, the 1960s black movement became the model for the others: women, peace, gays, ecology. While taking inspiration from the struggle for black liberation, white male gays have "failed to return the symbolic debt, as it were, by proceeding to ignore racism" (Julien and Mercer 1991, 168).

Isaac Julien and Kobena Mercer (1991) illustrate the exclusion of race from the white male gay agenda by focusing on the issue of "coming out." Calls by white gay and lesbian activists to reject the heterosexist norms of the nuclear family are, they allege, ethnocentric. They neglect the fact that for many black lesbians and gay men, their families are needed to provide support and protection from everyday white racism, racism experienced on the street, at school, from the police, and from the state. Julien and Mercer acknowledge that "our families are contradictory spaces," that while "sometimes we cannot afford to live without the support of our brothers and sisters, mothers and fathers," still

> we also need to challenge the homophobic attitudes we encounter in our communities. But white gays have passed all this by because race is not an issue for them. Instead, the horizon of their political consciousness has been dominated by concerns with individualized sexuality. Here, other aspects of gay white racism have surfaced, most clearly in debates on desire and pleasure focused around photography. (quoted passages in Julien and Mercer 1991, 168)

Julien and Mercer are referring, of course, to the sexualized objectification of the black male body evident in the photography of Robert Mapplethorpe.

Recalling Fanon's (1967) argument in *Black Skin, White Masks*, Julien and Mercer remind us that, historically speaking, European myths about the aggressive, violent, and animalistic "nature" of black sexuality communicated the concealed anxieties and denied fantasies of the all-powerful white "master." In Mapplethorpe's imagery, they argue, "the stench of racist stereotypes rotting in the soil of violent history is sanitized and deodorized by the clinical precision of his authoritative, aestheticizing master vision" (Julien and Mercer 1991, 169). "As black men," they continue,

> we are implicated in the same landscape of stereotypes in the gay subculture, which is dominated by the needs and demands of white males. Black men fit into this territory by being confined to a narrow repertoire of types—the supersexual stud and the sexual savage on the one hand, the delicate and exotic "Oriental" on the other. The repetition of these stereotypes in sexual representations betrays the circulation of "colonial fantasy," and traces the way the contours of this landscape have been shaped by mainstream cultural legacies of slavery, empire, and imperialism. (Julien and Mercer 1991, 169)

Later, Mercer (1994a, 189) would rethink his criticism of Mapplethorpe, not "because those arguments were wrong, but because I have changed my mind, or rather, I should say, I still cannot make up my mind about Mapplethorpe." This is not the place for a detailed examination of Mercer's partial revision of his earlier critique; suffice to say that for Mercer the mutual identification between artist and models and their shared status as oppressed gay men complicates his earlier view that the relation was necessarily exploitative simply because it was interracial. Mercer quotes comments by Ken Moody, one of the models in Mapplethorpe's *Black Book*, which imply a sense of reciprocity: "I don't honestly think of it as exploitation. ... It's almost as if ... and this is the conclusion I've come to now, because I really haven't thought about it up to now—it's almost as if he wants to give a gift to this particular group. He wants to create something very beautiful and give it to them. ... And he is actually very giving" (quoted in Mercer 1994a, 197).

The present repertoire of images of black male sexuality, from docile Uncle Toms to superstud rap stars, comes to us through centuries of slavery, colonialism, and imperialism. Like Robert Staples and others, Isaac Julien and Kobena Mercer (1991) recall that one central strand of the "racial power" exercised by the white male slave master involved the denial of traditional masculine prerogatives such as authority, dignity, and familial responsibility. As a consequence of this historical experience, they argue, black men have adopted certain patriarchal postures which emphasize physical strength and sexual prowess. These postures represent strategies by means of which black men might "cope with the repressive and destructive power of the plantocracy and the state." Black macho becomes "a site of struggle" within contemporary "regimes of truth" (quoted passages in Julien and Mercer 1991. 171). To illustrate, they cite sports, where performances of black machismo often coincide with white expectations. In this respect, macho performances of black male gender identities are, they suggest, a contradictory process, disclosing both race-affirmative and race-betraying elements (Julien and Mercer 1991).

The paradoxical position many black men inhabit is indicated in the "choice" faced by black men who love men. As Charles Nero indicates, that "some African American brothers become 'black gay men' while others become 'gay black men' ... often underscores painful decisions to have primary identities either in the black or in the gay community" (1991, 244). Arthur Flannigan-Saint-Aubin (1993) criticizes the collection of prose and poetry entitled *Brother to Brother* (in which the Nero piece appears, among others I have quoted in this section) for emphasizing the differences between gender and racial oppressions. He quotes Essex Hemphill's introduction to the collection to suggest "it would have been equally informative to interrogate where they interlock" (Flannigan-Saint-Aubin 1993, 475). Hemphill observed: "I tried to separate my sexuality from my negritude only to discover, in particular instance, that they are inextricably woven together" (1991, xvi). Flannigan-Saint-Aubin is also critical of the collection for addressing itself primarily to white gay men and heterosexual black men, in effect erasing black female subjectivity (1993, 473–474).

The fantasized place black men occupy in the white male imagination is explicit in American gay life. Here homoerotic desire is performed not in a distorted and mangled fashion, but straightforwardly (as it were). After Stonewall many white men became interested in black men, but strictly as sexual objects. In the white male gay community, black men were welcomed, if they remained in their "place," still a sexualized place, but one, this time, that required no "lady," imaginary or otherwise. Essex Hemphill (1991, xix) comments:

> At the baths, certain bars, in bookstores and cruising zones, black men were welcome because these constructions of pleasure allowed the races to mutually explore sexual fantasies and, after all, the black man engaging in such a construction only needed to whip out a penis of almost any size to obtain the rapt attention withheld him in other social and political structures of the gay community. These sites of pleasure were more tolerant of black men because they enhanced the sexual ambiance, but that same tolerance did not always continue once the sun began to rise.

Sex was desired, but companionship and interracial love was not. While white gay men spoke of "liberation," they dismissed other white men who preferred black men as "dinge queens." Black men who preferred white men were dismissed as "snow queens." Obviously, Hemphill observes, the gay community "could not be trusted to believe its own rhetoric concerning brotherhood, fellowship, and dignity" (1991, xix). He concludes:

> What is most clear for black gay men is this: We have to do for ourselves *now*, and for each other *now*, what no one has ever done for us. We have to be there for one another and trust less the adhesions of kisses and semen to bind us. Our only sure guarantee of survival is that we create for our own self-determination. White gay men may only be able to understand and respond to oppression as it relates to their ability to obtain orgasm without intrusion from the church or state. White gay men are only "other" in this society when they choose to come out of the closet. But all black men are treated as "other" regardless of whether we sleep with men or women—our black skin automatically marks us as "other." (Hemphill 1991, xx; emphasis in original)

White racism, then, constructs the gay black man as "other" in both gender and racial terms. Even when white gay men lust after black men, black male subjectivity is erased, and black men remain fantasies in the white male imagination. As Fanon knew: "the man who adores the Negro is as 'sick' as the man who abominates him" (1967, 8). Within the black community, his "homosexuality" constructs the gay black man as "other" to many African Americans. As Brian Phillip Harper (1996) and others have argued, black identity in the United States is strictly straight. Homosexuality is that non-African, exclusively European disease no "real" black man suffers. To that myth Ron Simmons replies: "We should also include homophobia as another attitude that black males have adopted largely from white culture" (1991, 221). Essex Hemphill (1991, xxix) explains:

> The black homosexual is hard-pressed to gain audience among his heterosexual brothers; even if he *is* more talented, he is inhibited by his silence or his admissions. This is what the race has depended on in being able to erase homosexuality from our recorded history. The "chosen" history. But these sacred constructions of silence are futile exercises in denial. We will not go away with our issues of sexuality. We are coming home.

"Home" is where white men in America have imagined themselves to be. Until recently.

15 ❖ WHITE MEN

I DON'T EVEN KNOW WHO I AM

I. Strangers to Ourselves?

For out of the counterfeiting of the black American's identity there arises a profound doubt in the white man's mind as to the authenticity of his own image of himself.

—Ralph Ellison, *Shadow and Act* (1964/1995)

[T]he white man's masculinity depends on a denial of the masculinity of the blacks.

—James Baldwin, *The Price of the Ticket* (1985)

Complete masculinity is like complete whiteness; it is a chosen falsehood, a form of denial.

—Lewis Gordon, *Bad Faith and Antiblack Racism* (1995)

As men, we often grow up to be strangers to ourselves.

—Victor Seidler, "Masculinity and Violence" (1996)

It has become clear to a few white male intellectuals, as it has been clear to gay and lesbian peoples black and white, that "masculinity" and "manhood" are social—and racially problematic—constructs that require analysis. Various feminisms have challenged taken-for-granted formations and expressions of "manliness." The majority of men have declined, even rejected, this challenge, but there are a few men, black and white, who have taken seriously feminism, who have become, not always to welcoming arms, "feminist men."

Like Kaja Silverman and others, Sandra Harding (1989) has spoken of the need for theoretical work by men who are committed to feminism. Such men would "speak specifically as men, of themselves, of their bodies and lives, of texts and of politics, using feminist insights to see the world." She warns that the task will be "difficult and painful" but that it is very important for men to come to self-understanding of their experiences as men, just as women have done, especially during the early stages of the feminist movement (quoted in May, Strikwerda, and Hopkins 1996, ix). Such self-understanding is part of a larger project of "rethinking masculinity ... in light of feminism" (May, Strikwerda, and Hopkins 1996, ix).

Landmines are everywhere, especially if such labor is performed only because women have requested or demanded it, or if it is a strategy by means of which heterosexually identified men attempt to placate or seduce heterosexually identified women. "No profeminist man can claim with a straight face that he has rid himself of all sexist beliefs," Lucy Candib and Richard Schmitt (1996, 226) agree. More broadly, probably no man, gay or straight, white or black, including those who have worked (autobiographically, theoretically) on masculinity, can claim to be free of heterosexist, homophobic, misogynistic sexism. And, as I trust it is now clear, for black and white men all of this is mixed up in "race relations," themselves gendered and sexualized.

Larry May, Robert Strikwerda, and Patrick D. Hopkins (1996) discern two endpoints on the continuum of contemporary efforts to rethink masculinity. At one end is John Stoltenberg (1989, 4) who, in his *Refusing to Be a Man*, called "for the end of manhood as we know it." While judging many of Stoltenberg's proposals "laudable," May, Strikwerda and Hopkins complain that Stoltenberg "leaves us with very little to grasp hold of once we have refused to be a man" (xi). (Christine A. James [1998, 189] insists that "Stoltenberg's position is more subtle than May and Strikwerda's description.") Nor are they drawn to what they perceive as the other end of the spectrum, a model of masculinity associated with Robert Bly, to which we will return briefly in the final chapter. This model seems to function, finally, as an affirmation of manhood, archetypally if not stereotypically defined. The project to rethink masculinity remains in its early stages, especially for self-identified heterosexual men.

Gender, Brian Pronger points out, "is deeply personal" (1990, 55). In the next sentence, however, he suggests that one's relation to gender is a matter of one's relation to power, not an especially "personal" concept. "The fundamental meaning of being a man or being a woman in our culture," he continues, "lies in their relative mythic powers." "Mythic" by definition is universal not specific, the abstract not the concrete. He notes that "it is difficult to think about another person without thinking of his or her gender. For example, if you meet a person briefly you may well forget most everything about them; it is very unlikely, however, that you will forget whether they were a man or a woman" (55). True enough, but is not what is individual about each of these—one's relation to power, one's enactment of gender myths, one's presence in a sexed body—the individuated expression and reformulation of each? If one conforms to compulsory heterosexuality or, if gay, to stereotypic conceptions of homosexuality, is one's gender "personal"? Is it not, on the contrary, self-alienating, even self-obliterating?

Could homosexual repression, even the conscious refusal to be gay, be a piece in the puzzle? To put the matter a different way, are misogyny and homosexual repression related? Perhaps it is not intrinsic to heterosexuality, but in our time is it not true, as many feminists have explained, that (heterosexual) men tend to hurt the women they presumably love and desire? Is it any accident, as Guy Hocquenghem (1978, 126) has suggested, that feminist and queer political struggles have been co-extensive: "Experience in Europe and the U.S.A. has shown that the women's movement and the gay movement have coincided. It is as if society could not bear to see in man what it demands to see in women, as if to dominate women and to repress homosexuality were one and the same thing." Without the experience of homosexual desire, men are left with its sublimated residue: homosociality.

The fact of homosociality refers, of course, to the fact that many men tend to prefer the company of other men. Especially self-identified heterosexual men tend to prefer the company of other (self-identified heterosexual) men. Women are for sex. While this binary appears to be breaking down somewhat, it remains the case, especially among lower-class men, and it reverberates throughout the lives of all men, across strata of class or race. The fact of homosociality, interwoven as it is with heterosexism and homophobia, remains an important cornerstone in the edifice that is the contemporary sex/gender system (Sedgwick 1985).

Men appreciate the importance of having a man in one's life. Among self-identified heterosexual men, this sexually stripped and sublimated relationship is called the "best friend." In Alice Walker's (1989) *The Temple of My Familiar*, Mr. Hal makes the point precisely: "Life is so very different when you have a good friend. I've seen people without special friends, close friends. Other men, especially. For some reason men don't often make and keep friends. This is a real tragedy, *I think, because in a way, without a tight male friend, you never really are able to see yourself.* That is because the shaping of ourselves is done by others; and a lot of our shaping comes from that one close friend who is something like us" (114, emphasis added). Unfortunately, the function of male-male friendship may often be to mirror the other, to support a self-structure that in itself may be self-alienated and unself-conscious. If male-male friendships were different, then relationships between women and men would be different (L. Thomas 1996).

If men could be emotionally free and expressive with each other, what would male "bonding" look like? There is no going back to a nineteenth-century version of "romantic" friendship; the "innocence" of that model of unself-conscious male-male involvement has been destroyed forever. No great loss, if you ask me, as it left intact the structure of racial, gender, and economic oppression. Now that "sex" is primary, what if, in the context of the historical present, masculinity in itself were not a self-alienating structure? What if in order to be a "man" boys did not have to repudiate their pre-oedipal identifications with their mothers and fabricate an imaginary identification with relatively absent fathers, a identificatory process which appears to leave the "man" clueless as to he is, and who others are? "Is it really so awful," Mark Simpson (1994, 15) asks, "that men should love one another in a maternal fashion?"

What would friendship among men look like then? Would it be characterized by intimate exchanges, self-reflexive articulations of how one felt about oneself and others? Would such men stop forcing women and black men and other "others" into the places they imagine for them? Would sharp distinctions between notions of "men" and "women" blur; would racialized "othering" fade as well? We know that many "men" today, desperate to be "men" (i.e., not a woman, not a sissy), recapitulate the self-alienated structure of the de-individuated self, and thereby remain dedicated to maintaining "the temple of the familiar," in this case "manhood," obliterating the lived ground of bonded relational experience underneath, to use phenomenological language. Can we be surprised that, for instance, in 1985, after a ten-year study of 5,000 American men and women, Michael McGill concluded: "To say that men have no intimate friends seems on the surface too harsh. ... But the data indicate that it is not far from the truth. ... Their relationships with other men are superficial, even shallow" (quoted in May and Strikwerda 1996, 80).

Friendships among most men today are rarely about self-exploration and interpersonal intimacy, as these threaten the self-alienated edifice of hegemonic masculinity. Still, are not both necessary to feeling, being alive? Perhaps some men "sneak in" intimacy (or a hint of it) while appearing to be engaged in something relatively depersonalized, for instance, a shared activity. May and Strikwerda argue that this is in fact the case. Male friendships, they suggest, often resemble those relationships typical among young children, especially boys, who engage in "parallel play." These boys, they write, "want to be close to each other in the sandbox, for example, but they just move the sand around without sharing or helping and *usually* without hurting each other. They don't really interact *with* each other; they merely play side-by-side—hence the term parallel play" (1996, 81; emphasis in original).

Boys grown tall—men—have friends and comrades, often involved with each other in versions of "parallel play." Comrades, May and Strikwerda point out, are not necessarily intimate friends; they are often bound to one another as generalized others, not in terms of who each one is as a unique individual. But if they are not individuated, that is, individuals themselves, how could they perceive the individuality of the other? Comrades are loyal to each other *not* out of concern for the particularity of the individual other, but out of an undifferentiated respect for "people" in a certain situation: fellow soldiers, teammates, fraternity brothers, coworkers, and so on. "Comradeship," May and Strikwerda (1996, 83) explain, "is a deontological regard for a generalized other and, in this sense, is quite different from intimate friendships, which are based on a regard for a particularized other and where consequences and contexts matter quite a bit."

If men are opaque to themselves, predictably many friendships among men also lack self-understanding and the self-disclosure that permits and supports intimacy. It is a commonplace that many women form friendships characterized by self-revelation and self-exploration. Most men tend to form friendships based on common interests and activities, often work-based or sport-focused, with self-revelation not exactly basic to any of it. How could this change? In order to experience strong emotions for another person, as well as to risk self-disclosure, it is, as May and Strikwerda (1996, 87) point out, necessary for "both to have such feelings and to express them." Self-expression, they continue, requires trust. In the culture of men, however, competition rather than trust tends to characterize relationships between men. Competition bonds soldiers, fraternity brothers, and teammates, but, May and Strikwerda acknowledge, "it also makes men reluctant to reveal things about themselves that would make them vulnerable, and hence cause them to risk being taken advantage of" (87).

Now what could "being taken advantage of" mean? Many things, of course: stealing stock tips or, perhaps, a girlfriend. But, there is a bottom line of distrust and self-alienation that friendships hide: "men in American culture are clearly stymied in pursuing intimacy with other males because of fears involving their sexuality, especially culturally inbred homophobia. As teenagers, we learned not to display feelings toward other boys on pain of being ridiculed as 'queers'" (May and Strikwerda 1996, 87). Henry Louis Gates, Jr. (1996, 83), remembers: "Daddy and Rocky would make heavy-handed jokes about queers and sissies. I wasn't their direct target, but I guess it was another form of masculine camaraderie that marked me as less manly than my brother. ... And while I didn't fantasize about boys," Gates reassures us, "I did love the companionship of boys and men, loved hearing them talk and watching their rituals, loved the warmth that their company could bring." Homosociality/homosexuality: two sides of the same coin.

The interrelated nature of homosexuality and homosociality is evident in the issue of touching. Except for the firm public handshake, American men are, in general, prohibited from touching each other, although this may be changing somewhat. Among family members and best friends one does find, on occasion, constrained forms of touching, such as the "hug." The taboo against male-male touching, May and Strikwerda (1996) point out, expresses the truncated character of men's emotional expressiveness. In sports, they note, there are clearly accepted exceptions to these taboos, such as hugs and other embraces, and, of course, slapping one's teammate's backside. A student reporter assumes her version of the anthropologist's gaze to report the barely sublimated forms of physical expression among athletes, in this case, college baseball teammates. Probably only a female reporter could get away with such candor:

> The most fascinating aspect of the match—oops, game—was the affection so blatantly shown between player and coach on the field. From where I sat, directly behind first base, I could see quite clearly the nice little rear ends of the players waiting for their turn to follow the white line to second. Maybe they were just feeling especially frisky Sunday, but they didn't just give a little congratulatory pat like I thought they would. They grab. Those coaches, and I'm not just talking bout the guys from Kentucky, really take hold of a bun and squeeze. It is so cute.
>
> I'm sure they get so excited about their player taking a base that they just want to grab them and squeeze. That's understandable. Many times I've found myself squeezing babies' cheeks (the ones on their faces) when I just don't know what else to do because their cuteness has made me so

> happy. Only, on the baseball field the babies are grown men and the happiness overflowing out of the coaches isn't brought on by the players' cuteness but their physical strength and control. So, naturally, the thing to grab is the tougher of cheeks—the buns of steel.
>
> This whole butt-grasping aspect of the game was probably so fascinating to me because I rarely get to see boys behave like this in public. Everybody knows real men aren't supposed to get tickled pink, so they don't—not openly anyway. Or at least that is what I thought until Sunday. There must be some accompanying rule to the one above, which limits tickled-pinkness, that says affectionate displays of excitement are acceptable only when intermingled with shows of extreme physical prowess. (Pike 1995, 4)

Gore Vidal understood: "The only time when heteros may openly enjoy what they secretly dream of is when watching handsome young men playing contact games" (quoted in Pronger 1990, 182). Speaking of another sport but of the same dynamic, Gregory Woods once remarked: "Wrestling ... is the heterosexually acceptable form of homosexual foreplay" (quoted in Pronger 1990, 184).

Sports fans, the majority of whom are probably male, will be the last to know, given the power and scope of sublimation and homosexual repression. Millions of American men watch young (mostly) male athletes, often in revealing costumes (I mean uniforms), streak across the screen. Many of those who watch are white men; many of those who perform, muscles rippling, are black. Making a different but (inadvertently) allied point, Haki Madhubuti quotes Richard Gilder's *Naked Nomads: Unmarried Men in America* (1974):

> Millions of reckless men feed on the masculinity of a few heroes—boxers, football players, politicians, rock stars. ... Male aggression and violence animate our movies, T.V. shows, magazines, newspapers, politics, culture. ... Our city schools are terrorized by it. "Liberated" women obsessed by it—laboring through hours of karate, palavering endlessly through rap sessions on rape. It would be better to confront the reality and address the real problem, which is the lack of ways for men to achieve sexual identity and express aggression. (quoted in Madhubuti 1990, 81)

Could this inability to achieve sexual identity, the accumulation of unexpressed aggression, and a (denied) homoerotic identification with young (often black) male athletes all be related? Could the repression of homosexual desire be the thread that binds these together, which alienates the individual male from himself and from his fellow men? "Homophobia," May and Strikwerda want to believe, "is not an insurmountable obstacle to male intimacy, but it certainly does contribute to the difficulties that men have in expressing their deeply held feelings" (1996, 88). They quote Aristotle: "self-knowledge depends upon knowledge of others," a formula that surely can be reversed as well. Aristotle is also quoted as writing: "[F]or the friend is ... a second self" (quoted passages in May and Strikwerda 1996, 89). But s/he should not, at least for men, function to shore up already self-constricting, self-starving, self-estranging structures of "masculinity."

If homophobia limits authentic intimacy among "straight" men, and if homophobia is an integral feature of compulsory heterosexuality and compensatory or hypermasculinity, could it be that intimacy among men—which, if we believe Aristotle, also means (male) self-knowledge—is stymied by contemporary structures of hegemonic masculinity? To become masculine means to become a man, an imaginary ideal, albeit with many (but not unlimited) variations. Judith Butler (1993, 99) puts the matter this way: "Identification is a fantastic trajectory and resolution of desire; an assumption of place; a territorializing of an object which enables identity through the temporary resolution of desire, but which remains desire, if only in its repudiated form." To identify as a "man" requires repudiation of what is "woman" and repression of desire for what is "man." Identification, then, is a defensive revalorization of what has been bleached from desire but becomes the "place" to occupy—that is, what is "manly"—while making the female into his object of "repudiated desire." Compulsory heterosexuality is, in part, a recodification of homosexual desire denied.

To become an abstraction is to become what one is not, to become something abstract and in fact alien: a "man." But it feels so natural ... right, guys? But the pre-oedipal symbiotic relationship with the mother sketched in object relations theory makes clear that the psychological bedrock of men—our identificatory foundation—is the mother. Men are in an foundational sense women, underneath their social surface, that is to say "from behind" (Hocquenghem 1978, 87). Alas, boys "must" become men, and in becoming "men" they repudiate what is female as well as sublimate their longing for the relatively absent father. That's what a man is, of course: not a woman. A man whose desire for other men remains strong but is stripped of sexual content is "a man's man," and this consolation prize—the homosocial—is taken as "natural," the norm. Given the crime statistics, and in particular the rates of crime against women, the abuse and neglect of children, can we continue to take this "norm" for granted?

Of course, there is nothing inevitable here, nothing necessary: we're talking culture and history. Boys could come of age without repudiating that identification with the mother. In David Gilmore's (1990, 11) review of cross-cultural research, *Manhood in the Making*, the "category of achievement" is described as a central component of masculinity in many cultures; he finds a "constantly recurring notion that real manhood ... is not a natural condition that comes about spontaneously through biological maturation [as femininity is imagined] but rather is a precarious or artificial state that boys must win against powerful odds." Perhaps he overgeneralizes, but, as Susan Bordo (1994) suggests, Gilmore has a point, which is evident too in the testimonies of "feminist" men such as Larry May and Robert Strikwerda. These testimonies make clear that heteronormative masculinity is something alien, something alienating both intrapsychically and interpersonally. And racially. Something to be achieved. As Norman Mailer (1959, 222) has observed: "Being a man is the continuing battle of one's life." Apparently it is a battle that is never over, as

Mailer (1985, 168) acknowledges, in another place, that a man can "hardly ever assume he has become a man."

Masculinity in its contemporary, compulsory forms often feels threatening or threatened. As Victor Seidler (1996, 64) acknowledges: "Masculinity is never something you can feel at ease with. It is always something that you have to be ready to defend and prove. You have to prove that you are as much a man as everyone else." Why? Because somewhere in masculinity circulates unresolved issues of power and sexuality, issues which, as Robert Simon (1996) points out, surface in nearly all men's fantasies and in more than a few men's actions. Culturally and economically they circulate through forms of competition. Adorno, Seidler notes, was right to remind us that "in fact, competition itself never was the law according to which middle class society operated. The true bond of bourgeois society had always been the threat of bodily violence. ... In the age of the concentration camp, castration is more characteristic of social reality than competitiveness" (quoted in Seidler 1996, 65). In chapters 16 and 17 we see that the unspoken threat in homosocial society becomes explicit in prison.

II. The Sex/Gender System

> *[B]eing a man is a state of constant negation, there being nothing to avow* that is as significant as the disavowal.
>
> —Mark Simpson, *Male Impersonators: Men Performing Masculinity* (1994)

> *"There you have the world that men have made, and it would make me want to be a woman if it weren't that women fall in love with men."*
>
> —Ulrich to Agathe in Robert Musil, *The Man Without Qualities* (1960/1961/1979)

> *Men produce a universe built upon the erasure of the bodies and contributions of women/mothers and the refusal to acknowledge the debt to the maternal body that they owe. They hollow out their own interiors and project them outward, and then require women as supports for this hollowed space. Women become the guardians of the private and the interpersonal, while men build conceptual and material worlds.*
>
> —Elizabeth Grosz, *Space, Time, and Perversion: Essays on the Politics of Bodies* (1995)

The sex/gender system which sustains such binaries (threaten or be threatened) and convolutions (the association of masculinity with the "doer" not the "done to," the penetrator not the penetrated, the desiring sexual subject rather than the "receiver" of the desires of another) is not exactly a recent invention in Western culture. Susan Bordo (1994) traces it to Aristotle, who characterized the male principle (as well as the male contribution to reproduction) as the "effective and active" element. The woman was relegated to the role of passive, penetrable "matter." Such characterizations are, of course, the very substance of sexism; partly because they construct reality in terms of a gendered duality (active male/passive female) but, more importantly, because they so powerfully privilege the active, as in the following passage from Hegel's *Philosophy of Right* (1821/1952):

> The difference between men and women is like that between animals and plants. Men correspond to animals, while women correspond to plants because their development is more placid and the principle that underlies it is the rather vague unity of feeling. ... Women are educated—who knows how?—as it were by breathing in ideas, by living rather than acquiring knowledge. The status of manhood, on the other hand, is attained only by the stress of thought and much technical exertion. (263–264; quoted in Bordo 1994, 288)

Because "manhood" is imaginary, of course it requires "stress of thought" and "much technical exertion."

In contemporary studies of masculinity, various elements are emphasized (Allen 1993; Franklin 1988; Pleck 1984; Marshall 1993). But there would seem to be a common, unifying theme: the acceptance and expectation of aggression, even violence, as we have seen in the statistics cited at the beginning of chapter 13. Aggression and violence might be "necessary" to achieve typically masculine objectives such as: (1) independence (from relationships); (2) lack of sentimentality; (3) heterosexual success (meaning access to numbers of different women, as well as getting women to do things men do not want to do); (4) physical toughness; and (5) worldly success (as measured in dollars or achievements) (O'Sullivan 1993).

Clearly, not only lower-class black men who "hang out" in bars subscribe to the values described as "hypermasculinity" or "compulsive masculinity." For perhaps a majority of European-American males, these characteristics typify, in some measure, what it means to be a man: (1) toughness, fearlessness, and fighting; (2) preoccupation with developing an athletic physique; (3) sexual athleticism and the concept of women as conquest objects; and (4) defiance of authority (Scully 1990; Candib and Schmitt 1996). The four are interrelated: the repudiation of the "feminine" makes its repossession necessary, usually through sex, and the suppression of homosexual desire returns in sublimated forms such as homosociality. Fighting each other is the other side of fucking each other; defiance of authority converts desire for the father into identification with him. The result is a "man," and his tendency toward violence—performing socially the intrapsychic violence that produced him—leaves all of us at risk (Pinar 1998a).

Here is another list that intersects with the other ones; once again the demands of "manhood" are four in number: (1) No Sissy Stuff (avoid behaving in any manner which can be perceived or labeled as feminine); (2) Be a Big Wheel (strive for dominance, power, wealth and success); (3) Be a Sturdy Oak (be independent, controlled, unemotional; show no vulnerabilities); and (4) Give' em Hell (take risks, be daring) (Brannon and David 1976). In each of these lists is embedded a notion of manhood which "normalizes" violence for men. Echoing nineteenth-century advocates for coeducation (Pinar et al. 1995, chapter 7), George Gilder describes men as "barbarians" who must be "tamed" by women who create "civilization" by "transforming male lust into love." For Gilder, rape and other gendered forms of violence are outcomes of the failure to "civilize" men (Gilder 1986, as cited by Capraro 1994, 24).

Maybe men have to "civilize" themselves, become (small "d") democrats sexually. Richard Mohr (1992) argues that there is something deeply subversive of sexism in homoerotic practice, something akin to a "democracy" of sexual position, in which active/passive roles appear as easily reversible and none is especially or definitively privileged. Susan Bordo argues that such sexual subversion is not intrinsic to gay masculinity, pointing to various sadomasochistic practices which reproduce dualized sexuality. She thinks of homosexuality as it is performed in many Latin countries, where, as we noted earlier, it is not defined by the gender of one's partner, but by the "active" or "passive" position one assumes in the sexual act. The one who penetrates (so-called top men) remains a "man" while the one who is penetrated (the so-called bottom) is derided as "feminine."

The Latin view has its antecedents, as Brian Pronger (1990) suggests. The ancient Greek system was pedophilic; the older man, being superior by virtue of his age and wisdom, was, upon entering the anus of the young man, imparting his learning and manliness. It was unacceptable for a mature man to be penetrated, as this would place himself in a position of inferiority. David Halperin (1990) contests the use of the concept "homosexual" in referring to ancient Greek sexual practices, practices which, he argues, did not coincide with contemporary ones.

Despite the ability and preference of many gay men to exchange positions without attaching value or permanence to any one of them, such "democracy" is not the cultural norm. Pronger (1990, 139) argues that "for a man to be like a woman in our culture is considered contemptible because it is a step down; the greatest insult one can give a man is that he is like a woman. Getting fucked, therefore, is the deepest violation of masculinity in our culture." Clearly, this would seem to be so in American prisons. Bordo (1994) points out that in order to challenge the "penetrable woman/impenetrable man" duality that "maintains the system of gender stereotypes" (as Mohr characterizes it), "it is not enough to simply portray men as penetrable. ... It is necessary to re-think and 're-vision' the qualities of penetrability and impenetrability themselves—and, I would argue, in terms of their broadest meanings: emotional, intellectual, and social as well as sexual" (quoted passages in Bordo 1994, 289–290).

To do so, Bordo (1994, 290) focuses on the surface of the male body, arguing that "we use the surface of our bodies to code superior will power, control over desire, and the ability to manage and shape one's own life and those of others." Bordo suggests that "muscles today are the mark of mind over matter" (291). Incidentally, Bordo points out that the word "muscle" itself is derived from the Middle French word *mus*, which meant mouse. Presumably, women of the *ancien régime* fainted at the sight of both. Or is that another relocated narrative of male-male desire?

Pronger (1990, 145) suggests that muscles highlight masculinity in a heterosexual culture by underscoring the physical power men have over women as well as the power they have to resist other men. Homosexuality, he continues, make muscles ironic, as they function "as enticements to homoerotic desire. … Paradoxical masculinity invites both reverence for the traditional signs of masculinity and the violation of those signs." While recent fascination with "body styling" permits the eroticization of "hardness" in women, softness in men is still unacceptable (Bordo 1994). "Do we need to replace the reign of the hard with the new regime of the soft?" Bordo asks. She answers:

> I think we need to refuse that old opposition as a guide. Here the repressed penis … can stimulate the imagination. Let's not look to the figure of the "soft" penis. This would seem the most obvious route to revision; but we're trying to refuse "hard/soft" now. So let's rather allow the imagination to play with the figure of the *aroused* penis—aroused (as in a state of *feeling*), rather than "erect" (as in a state of accomplishment and readiness to perform). (Bordo 1994, 296; emphasis in original)

Bordo finds Regnault's photography evocative of what she proposes, as it depicts eros in a more general, perhaps classically Freudian, sense, "as the urge for attachment, for connectedness, of building larger human unities out of the atoms of separate selves. Perhaps because the most verboten cultural context for such attachments is between men and men, I find that it is precisely images of men (both homosexual and heterosexual) openly loving each other, in couples and in community, that are the most stimulating to my imagination of a 'revisioned' masculinity" (Bordo 1994, 299). Loving each other would be revolutionary, would it not? In his film *Tongues Untied* (1989), Marlon Riggs declared (after Joseph Beam) that "black men loving black men is the revolutionary act" (see Riggs 1989). But so might white men loving black men, a mode of relation in which white men consciously eroticize and thereby subjectivate their long-standing, if convoluted, cathected relation to black men.

III. "The Drag Ball Production of Realness"

Masculinity assumes, essentializes, naturalizes, and privileges heterosexuality.

—Patrick D. Hopkins, "Gender Treachery: Homophobia, Masculinity, and Threatened Identities" (1996)

Sadomasochism is fueled and motivated by a restless desire to somehow, in some way, procure recognition from the other.

—Lynn Chaucer, *Sadomasochism in Everyday Life: The Dynamics of Power and Powerlessness* (1992)

Waiting numbly for a train in a place where there are no tracks.

—Paul Monette, *Becoming a Man: Half a Life Story* (1992a)

Bordo speaks of "revisioning" masculinity. Accompanying that political act is the analytic act of understanding masculinity. How do men imagine themselves to be men? "[I]dentifications," Judith Butler stresses, "belong to the imaginary; they are phantasmatic efforts of alignment, loyalty, ambiguous and cross-corporeal cohabitation" (1993, 105). Identifying with the man means an imaginary loyalty, perhaps to the father, one which then splits off what is now repressed onto what is desired, now attached to other bodies, both positively and negatively. For the heterosexually identified boy, the trauma that is masculine identification means his pre-oedipal, relatively symbiotic relationship with the mother is sealed over, imprisoned in the unconscious. But what is repressed is not gone. Robert I. Simon (1996, 194) gives a simplified account of the psychodynamics of identification, typified by dissociation and repression:

> Dissociation can be thought of as a "horizontal" separation, in which memory and the intense emotional trauma are split from one another. Thus disconnected and defused like dynamite sticks from their fuses, the traumatic memories and feelings can be stored safely out of awareness, unless an external or internal trigger reconnects and ignites them. Severe psychological trauma may predispose persons to dissociate. By contrast, repression is a "vertical" separation mechanism that banishes unacceptable ideas, fantasies, feelings, impulses, or memories from consciousness, or that keeps in the unconscious dangerous thoughts and feelings that have never been conscious. Psychological conflict is often a precursor of repression. Repressed material is not subject to voluntary recall, though repressed memories may sometimes emerge in disguised form. Suppression, the conscious, temporary setting aside of a painful memory, may be a way station to permanent, unconscious removal of memory through repression.

Simon is discussing childhood sexual abuse, but the trauma of masculine identification, with its violent repression of the pre-oedipal symbiotic relationship with the mother and the consequent dissociation from the "feminine," is not dissimilar. Even when the boy becomes a man, what has been repressed "returns" in various forms. Simon (1996, 194) explains:

> As with a piece of flotsam that is carried down a river, snags on the river bank, and gradually sinks into the mud, childhood memories and associated feelings of abuse become separated—they dissociate—and are carried downstream and become buried in the back channels of the mind. It is not until some abuse survivors are in their thirties and forties, and in therapy for depression, anxiety, or other personality disorders, that they are able to unearth or recall their abuse.

Being a man feels normal, biological, God-given, but these are not only phenomenological feelings following from identification; they are as well defensive, compensatory affirmations of what is inherently fragile and unstable, the residue of trauma.

The "return of the repressed" (Rieff 1966a, 1966b) appears inevitable. For more than a few it occurs in the so-called midlife crisis when a man's masculinity must be reaffirmed through sexual conquests of younger women; perhaps he will become gay; perhaps he will remain married but commence cross-dressing. Dominant forms of masculinity production guarantee that the masculine identification typified by both dissociation and repression cannot remain intact. Its repressed, dissociated elements necessarily "unsettle the 'I'—they are the sedimentation of the 'we' in the constitution of any 'I,' the structuring presence of alterity in the very formulation of the 'I.' Identifications are never fully and finally made; they are incessantly reconstituted and, as such, are subject to the volatile logic of iterability. They are that which is constantly marshaled, consolidated, retrenched, contested, and, on occasion, compelled to give way" (Butler 1993, 105). In lynching, white men simultaneously affirmed the remnants of their own disappearing masculinity while fantasizing that it had regathered itself in the bodies of young black men.

This illusion of stability, requiring constant reconsolidation of an unstable ego's remains (also known as a man's personality), makes for ritualistic performances of manhood. It is not enough to make love to a woman one loves: one must "score" with a "beautiful babe" and, before the news becomes stale, report to friends—well, in the case of lower-class bars, to anyone who'll listen—this latest conquest, yet another confirmation of one's masculinity and manhood. It is, as Butler (1993, 107) points out, in the performance that gender identity is achieved. "Generally speaking," she explains,

> a performative functions to produce that which it declares. As a discursive practice (performative "acts" must be repeated to become efficacious), performatives constitute a locus of discursive production. ... Indeed, a performative act apart from a reiterated and, hence, sanctioned set of conventions can appear only as a vain effort to produce effects that it cannot possibly produce.

This linkage of gender identity with performativity suggests, Butler observes, that "sexed positions" are not stable sites but, rather, "citational practices instituted within a juridical domain—a domain of constitutive constraints" (1993, 108). She recalls Foucault's point in *The History of Sexuality* (1976/1978/1980) that the juridical or regulative law, in its prohibition of certain acts, practices, and subjects, "provides the discursive occasion for a resistance, a resignification, and potential self-subversion of that law" (Butler 1993, 109). Because contemporary masculinity bans from its performance those acts, practices, or subjects suggestive of what is feminine or homosexual, it constitutes itself as a regulatory gender identification. Regulation creates, indeed guarantees, transgression.

When right-wing fundamentalists and politicians such as Pat Robertson or Jesse Helms or Trent Lott denounce homosexuality, they not only reconsolidate the fragile, unstable gender positions of their sympathetic listeners. They not only distance the queer subject-identification and its (fantasized) sexual practices as far removed from the internal self-system of the "righteous." They also create an undertow: "The enumeration of prohibited practices not only brings such practices into a public, discursive domain, but it thereby produces them as potential erotic enterprises and so invests erotically in those practices, even if a negative mode." Hating homosexuals, or black men, or both, contains and expresses the desire it denies and tries to relocate. Under specific circumstances, desire returns, if in mangled and deformed ways: the black man is stripped, cut, castrated. The incarcerated white boy is raped and made into a "woman." As Butler (1993) points out: "prohibitions can themselves become objects of eroticization, such that coming under the censure of the law becomes what Freud called the condition for love" (quoted passages on 110).

The little boy who feels, in his original identification, his mother's affection, even desire, but who in his manhood feels only a reconstituted desire for her substitute, is a casualty of contemporary male sex-role socialization. Like the victims of other childhood trauma, the consequences are lifelong. Butler understands exactly: "In the drag ball productions of realness, we witness and produce the phantasmatic constitution of a subject, a subject who repeats and mimes the legitimating norms by which it itself has been degraded, a subject founded in the project of mastery that compels and disrupts its own repetitions" (1993, 131). Right-wing calls for women's "gracious submission" testify that it is already too late. Once again, southern white boys are talking only to themselves.

Are we clear now that "men" are women in drag? Being a "man" comes at a psychological cost that must be paid. Sometime, somewhere, in some way, men will reenact the violence they experienced as boys being forced to become other than they were. But this calculation of masculinity production is incomplete if we understand its psychodynamics vis-à-vis the mother only. Men, American men at least, are a racialized gender. "What would it mean," Butler (1993, 167) asks:

> to consider the assumption of sexual positions, the disjunctive ordering of the human as "masculine" or "feminine" as taking place not only through a heterosexualizing symbolic with its taboo on homosexuality, but through a complex set of racial injunctions which operate in part through the taboo on miscegenation. Further, how might we understand homosexuality and miscegenation to converge at and as the constitutive outside of a normative heterosexuality that is at once the regulation of a racially pure reproduction?

Miscegenation and homosexuality converge in the American literary imagination (Sollors 1997), as I will elaborate in volume II. "Passing" racially and "passing" as a "man" turn out to be not unrelated performances of racially gendered identification (Johnson 1912/1960; Griffin 1961/1962; Harper 1996). Of course there are, as Butler acknowledges, compelling analytic and political reasons for keeping "race" and "sex" separate. At the same time there are compelling reasons for "asking how and where we might read not only their convergence, but the sites at which the one cannot be constituted save through the others" (Butler 1993, 168). If being a white man in America required the castration—political, literal—of the black man (his "feminization" as an object of white male sexual aggression), should it surprise anyone that black masculinity is complicated in precisely that gendered way, and that, when the opportunity finally presented itself, black political revenge sometimes took the form of homosexual rape? Can whites honestly pretend innocence and shock when they read accounts by 1960s black activists and intellectuals screaming that the emperor has no clothes, that he is, in Baraka's blunt language, a "fag"?

When Butler argues that gender identity is a matter of performativity, what does she mean? Despite the wink toward "drag ball production," it is clear that in her view "the reduction of performativity to performance would be a mistake" (Butler 1993, 234). It includes performance, but more significantly, it emphasizes a specific sense of script, not only learning one's lines but believing in them, enacting what others have stipulated as "normal" and "natural" or even "divinely ordained." She writes:

> Performativity is neither free play nor theatrical self-presentation; nor can it be simply equated with performance. Moreover, constraint is not necessarily that which sets a limit to performativity; constraint is, rather, that which impels and sustains performativity. ... I would suggest that performativity cannot be understood outside of a process of iterability, a regularized and constrained repetition of norms. And this repetition is not performed by a subject; this repetition is what enables a subject and constitutes the temporal condition for the subject. This iterability implies that "performance" is not a singular "act" or event, but a ritualized production, a ritual reiterated under and through constraint, under and through the force of prohibition and taboo, with the threat of ostracism and even death controlling and compelling the shape of the production, but not, I will insist, determining it fully in advance. (Butler 1993, 95)

The script becomes phenomenologically "real"—one actually experiences heterosexual desire, in the body, directed outward, toward the "opposite" sex.

This sense of performativity as socialized accommodation to extant norms is, I think, insufficient to explain gender identity. If it were, homosexuality could never occur, prohibited and policed as it is. Clearly, there are "intrapsychic" dimensions or scripts, which merge, in complicated, contradictory, compromising ways, with scripts of social norms. These intrapsychic substrata of gender formation are implied in the following passage: "The straight man becomes (mimes, cites, appropriates, assumes the status of) the man he 'never' loved and 'never' grieved; the straight woman becomes the woman she 'never' loved and 'never' grieved. It is in this sense, then, that what is most apparent as gender is the sign and symptom of a pervasive disavowal" (Butler 1993, 236). In this topsy-turvy world, then, is one's gender a sign of grief, of loss, a loss of an object relation one denies in the very structure of the gendered self? "Performativity," Butler (1993, 241) concludes, "describes this relation of being implicated in that which one opposes." You are (also) what you are not.

This sense of being implicated in that which one opposes—what one is not—is an important principle of gendered racial analysis. It permits us to see white male desire embedded in the racial hatred that sometimes led to lynching, as well as the desire in the black male for the revenge that is performed in prison rape. It allows us to understand why those who are most homosocial—many athletes, for instance—tend to be the most homophobic and misogynistic. In several paragraphs in a dated study of prisons, paragraphs which were scripted to pathologize homosexuality, we see this paradoxical movement, a conscious devaluation that affirms not pathologizes homosexuality, not unlike, in discursive structure at least, the disavowal of the gendered and racial "other" that the macho man performs. In their 1967 study of *Problems of Homosexuality in Corrections*, Clyde Vedder and Patricia King manage to "normalize" homosexuality while declaring it abnormal, and in so doing perform the homosexual desire embedded in homophobia and heterosexism. Let's watch them work.

Pigeons

Homosexually identified persons have been dismissed as "birds of a different feather." How different, how unusual, are we? Vedder and King (1967, 3) begin their exercise in contradiction by acknowledging that, like many pests, "homosexuality seems to have been known since recorded time," adding that the practice "is found among many living creatures, especially pigeons." Pigeons? That was a new one for me. I knew, for instance, about the red-billed black swans that nest in the lakes of Australia and New Zealand. The most successful parents among these birds tend to be male couples. By combining their strength, a male black swan duo, mated for years or life, stakes out prime territory sometimes 100 times as large as taken by their heterosexual neighbors. A male couple interested in offspring becomes involved with a female, then drives her away after she lays eggs. Or the homosexual couple takes over an egg-filled nest. Despite the absence of "ethics," the male couples perhaps redeem themselves in swan society by their rate of success in raising chicks: while just 5 percent of swan pairs are homosexual, they parent 20 to 25 percent of all surviving chicks (Price 1999).

The conviction that human homosexuality is somehow "unnatural" is accompanied by an equally unfounded belief that animals in the wild never flirt, court, or bond sexually with creatures of the same sex. In his *Biological Exuberance: Animal Homosexuality and Natural Diversity*, Bruce Bagemihl (1999) reports evidence of homosexuality in more than 450 species. "The nuclear heterosexual family, if you look across the whole animal species is really the exception, rather than the rule," Bagemihl said in an interview (quoted in Price 1999, 27). In some species, such as California's northern elephant seal, 90 percent of males never pursue females. Pairs of male walruses cuddle like vertical spoons as they float in the sea while napping. Lesbian rhesus monkeys play "kiss and run" and other courtship games specific to them. A homosexual bottlenose dolphin takes his lifelong mate on a erotic joyride, propelling him through the water while sexually satisfying him. Male giraffes sensually "neck" only with each other. Among grizzlies, at least 9 percent of cubs have two mothers. Inventive pygmy chimps known as bonobos, generally bisexual, have a dozen hand signals to call to their varying sex partners. Homosexuality and bisexuality among the animals has been long known to researchers, a fact some have found distressing, as in the instance when one man lamented a "lowering of moral standards" among butterflies. Others have followed lament with abuse: scientists have tortured homosexual animals in experiments to find out what's "wrong" with them (Price 1999).

Well, then, Mr. Vedder and Ms. King, we may be "birds" but not with such uncommon feathers. Indeed we read in your next line that as with the pigeon, "[h]omosexuality has been found in all civilizations and among all peoples" (Vedder and King 1967, 3). OK, so homosexuality is everywhere; it has existed during all historical periods. Hello. ... Would not that fact in itself lead one to some degree of acceptance of this victim-less "crime"? Not exactly, as Vedder and King (1967) rush to point out that "[i]n early times sex offenders were often castrated or decapitated." Well, not in ancient Greece, were they. But historical accuracy is not the objective here. Rather it would appear that the objective is to show how enlightened we (that is, they) in the corrections business, at mid-twentieth century, have become: "Today, they [homosexuals] are regarded as persons suffering from sexual maladjustment. Homosexuality represents a deep-seated and unresolved neurosis. It is not a congenital anomaly, but rather an emotional aberration, a disorder of psychological, rather than genetic, origin, and therefore should be treated by psychological methods and techniques" (Vedder and King 1967, 3). Like electroshock therapy?

The "cult of the expert" is clearly visible here, a cult in which regulatory and punitive grids are disguised as an expert knowledge designed for "helping." But not one sentence after pronouncing "homosexuals" as patients in need of treatment, there comes a qualification, a qualification that would seem to disqualify the medicalization move just made: "Homosexuals are considered abnormal only in the sense that their sexual behavior represents a regression to childhood, an escape from those biological responsibilities assumed by one who is heterosexual" (Vedder and King 1967, 3). So homosexuality amounts to a state of arrested gender development, characterized by the effort—is it volitional?—to escape the adult responsibility to couple with those designated as the "opposite" sex and then reproduce. What about the romantic idea of childhood as somehow ideal, as "father to the man"?

Concluding the paragraph, it all comes unraveled, as Vedder and King (1967, 4) acknowledge: "Every normal person is, neurologically, potentially capable of gaining sexual gratification from homosexual practices." So in what sense are we "homosexuals" maladjusted? From this paragraph is it is clear that homosexuality is universal, a "naturally" occurring phenomenon, as James Twitchell (1987, 14–15) for one has pointed out: "Homosexuality has not been 'bred-out' of the human species. Homosexuality must therefore in some sense be 'natural'." But because (as Vedder and King imagine) it involves a refusal of adult responsibilities, it must be condemned and punished and corrected or healed. If we were to change our minds about that point, apparently we could all enjoy ourselves homosexually. I knew that.

Having pledged allegiance to the 1960s majority view and professional opinion that homosexuality is pathological (before it was depathologized by various professional organizations, most notably by the American Psychiatric Association in 1973), Vedder and King seem to have "normalized" it. Now, a paragraph later in fact, they refer to it as "this ambivalence" which they trace to the Greeks (the ancient ones, presumably) and "their liberal ideas on sex life."

This ancient and formative homosexual culture in Greece was snuffed, obviously, and so they acknowledge, relying on Gordon Westwood (1953):

> T]he sex code of Western civilization is inherited almost entirely from the Jews through the Christian churches. The outstanding feature of ancient Jewish sex life was the desire for offspring. They encouraged polygamy and were proud of the fact that Solomon had a thousand wives. The many "begats" in the Old Testament and the levirate reflect this cultural bias. The Christians took over this attitude from the Jews and under Christianized Roman Law, homosexuals were either burnt to death or reeds were driven into their bladders until they died of torture. (Vedder and King 1967, 4)

Ancient Jewish men must have been very strongly attracted to one another if homosexuality had to be so aggressively suppressed. But Leviticus follows its condemnation of homosexuality by demanding also death for mediums and adulterers (Comstock 1991).

By now Vedder and King (1967) have, by historicizing sexuality, completely undermined the popular prejudice against homosexuality they had psychologistically scripted in the opening paragraph. Having started with this historical unraveling of a modern popular prejudice, they continue, relying still on Westwood (1953). From ancient Rome they cite his depiction of antihomosexual prejudice in early England, when ecclesiastical courts (always the church, it seems) "decreed that sodomy was a crime for which the penalty was death, and this penalty remained for over 275 years, until abolished by Sir Robert Peel in the 1830s" (quoted in Vedder and King 1967, 4). Curiously, in light of nineteenth-century lynching events, in the thirteenth century in Europe, the main mode of punishment for same-sex acts shifted from castration to burning or other forms of whole body elimination like hanging followed by burial (Young-Bruehl 1996).

That story stays untold as Vedder and King return to the "corrections" theme, noting the problem that Morris Ploscowe (1951) identified. One of the basic canons of criminal procedure, Ploscowe had pointed out, is that a defendant is entitled to know the particulars of the crime charged against him so s/he can prepare a defense. "But," he continues, "when a man is charged with sodomy or a crime against nature, an indictment in the language of the statute is enough. Ever since Lord Coke's time, the attitude of judges has been that sodomy is 'a detestable and abominable sin among Christians not to be named'" (Ploscowe 1951; 197; quoted passages in Vedder and King 1967, 4–5). The sin that dare not speak its name?

The statutes instituted during the reign of Henry VIII—no homosexual he—comprise, Vedder and King (1967, 5) inform us, the basis of contemporary law "in this area," a genital area as it were, as those statutes "prohibited buggery with mankind or beast under penalty of death." Seems simple enough, but there was a complication:

> But buggery includes only genital contact between man and man or between man and woman, and what is now termed bestiality-genital

> contact with animals. For some reason, these earlier statutes failed to include fellatio (oral-genital contact) or cunnilingus (oral-vaginal contact). According to Ploscowe, because of the above omissions in these statutes, a defendant convicted of sodomy by an English court, in 1817, for an act of fellatio with a child was directed to apply for a pardon.

So Clinton didn't have sex with "that woman"?

Vedder and King conclude their comments on homosexuality—which you recall are introducing a study of the problem of homosexuality in prisons—by once again referring to Gordon Westwood (1953). They note that Westwood pointed out "that throughout history, the harsh treatment of homosexuality has had very little effect. It is even possible that the heavy penalties have added an extra spice to the pursuit of these practices" (Vedder and King 1967, 5–6). A Foucauldian spice, as one might characterize it.

During the 1960s those who protested against the war and in favor of civil rights were often accused by right-wingers as unpatriotic. One form that accusation took was unforgettable, as it maligned both one's politics (one was suspected of being a Communist) and one's gender (one was suspected of being a homosexual). "Pinko commie fag" was the colorful if viciously intended epithet. Something of this conflation is captured in the phrase "gender treachery," used by Margaret Atwood (1986) in her dystopian novel, *The Handmaid's Tale.* Set in a post-fundamentalist Christian-dominated United States, the novel tells of criminals who are executed and hanged on a public wall with the name of their crime around their necks for citizens to see. Homosexuals bear the placard "gender traitor."

One need not travel to the future, of course, to witness such nightmarish nonsense. The past will do, as Aquinas, the Christian exemplar, viewed the "vice of sodomy" as the second worst "unnatural vice," worse even than rape (Gilbert 1985), a view echoed in contemporary legal decisions such as *Bowers* v. *Hardwick* (106 S. Ct. 2841, 1986), which upheld the criminal status of homosexuality (Hopkins 1996). "To form a genuine challenge to homophobia," Patrick Hopkins correctly points out, "will not result from or result in merely increased social tolerance, but will be situated in a fundamental challenge to traditional concepts of masculinity itself" (97). And to form a comprehensive challenge to racism, white masculinity itself must be reformulated.

IV. The Objectification of the Male Body and the Desubjectification of the Male Self

> *[M]ale bonding/comradeship* requires *the stunting of individuality.*
>
> —Mary Daly, *Gyn/ecology: The Metaethics of Radical Feminism* (1978)

> *Flesh is only the thermometer of a becoming.*
>
> —Gilles Deleuze and Félix Guattari, *What Is Philosophy?* (1994)

Whether it be beefcake or cheesecake, it's still cake.
—Sam Fussell, "Bodybuilder Americanus" (1994)

My final prayer: O my body, make of me always a man who questions!
—Frantz Fanon, *Black Skin, White Masks* (1967)

Masculinity comprises the structure of the contemporary male self; it is in part the scaffolding that comprises that structure. To refashion masculinity requires restructuring European-American male self-formation, as it is the structure of the self which makes homophobia and racism so likely, if not inevitable. In such work, as Patrick Hopkins knows, one's personal identity is at stake: "Because personal identity (and all its concomitant social, political, religious, psychological, biological, and economic relations) is so heavily gendered, any threat to sex/gender categories is derivatively (though primarily non-consciously) interpreted as a threat to personal identity—a threat to what it means to *be* and especially what it means to *be me*" (1996, 98; emphasis added). The masculinized me, I submit, is in fact not "me," but represents a self-obliterating, gender-standardizing superstructure of performativity. It is herdlike, collective, ganglike ... not nuanced, individuated, relational. Rather than a gendered medium for self-development, masculinity is in its heteronormative, macho form, a tool of self-deformation, as the crime statistics suggest. The macho man is fundamentally a self-alienated creature, as Harry Brod, for one, appreciates.

Brod begins with Marx. "Just as capitalists as well as workers are alienated under capitalism according to Marxist theory, so men," Brod writes, "and in particular male modes of sexuality, are also alienated under patriarchy" (1996, 240). Marx's (1964) concept of alienation, Brod reminds us, describes a process whereby one becomes a stranger to oneself, and one's own powers work against one. He follows Marx to understand alienation not primarily as a psychological state dependent on the individual's sensibilities or consciousness but as a condition caused by living within a system of economic and, he adds, gender alienation. To illustrate, he points to two consequences of men's alienated—what he specifies as pornographic—sexuality. The first Brod calls the objectification of the body; the second involves the loss of subjectivity.

Pornography, "a window on elements of the normative construction of male sexuality in our culture" (Bordo 1994, 273), characterizes men's alienated sexuality under patriarchy. It reduces male sensuality to a genital, performance-oriented sexuality. "Men become," Brod writes, "sexual acrobats endowed with oversized and overused organs" (1996, 240). In this regard he recalls a chapter title in Zilbergeld's (1978) book on male sexuality: "The Fantasy Model of Sex: Two Feet Long, Hard as Steel, and Can Go All Night." Using penile performance as an index of male strength and potency contradicts biology, Brod asserts. "There is no muscle tissue in the penis," he notes. "Its erection when aroused results simply from increased blood flow to the area. All social mythology aside, the male erection is physiologically nothing more than localized high blood pressure" (Brod 1996, 240–241). Focusing our sexual attention on one organ desensitizes other parts of the body that might otherwise be regions of pleasure. For Brod, "the basic male sex organ is not the penis, but the skin" (1996, 241). Is that why lynchers burned their victims after castrating them?

Men's subjective experience is shallow and recast in self-alienation; "being" is replaced with "having." Brod finds the essential points in two sentences in Marx (1964, 159–160; 164–165; emphasis in original): (1) "*all* the physical and intellectual senses have been replaced by the simple alienation of *all* these senses; the sense of *having*" and (2) "the wealthy man is at the same time one who needs a complex of human manifestations of life, and whose own self-realization exists as an inner necessity, a need." Here, Brod points out, Marx understands alienation as a loss of sensuous fulfillment—one thinks of Cleaver's (1968) administrators—replaced by a pride of possession. In the exchange there is a poverty of self-consciousness and an attenuation of one's own "real" desires and abilities.

Brod notes that "the male ego feels uniquely beleaguered today," but that such talk regularly surfaces in American history. He thinks of the 1890s when, as we have seen, there was a keenly experienced "crisis" of white masculinity caused by the rise of the "New Woman" as well as economic, racial, and other developments. We saw how brilliantly Ida B. Wells exploited this "crisis" in her struggle against lynching. Recall this was also a period of intense debate over coeducation (would the presence of girls civilize or effeminate boys?), of obsession over masturbation (cf. Kellogg's cereal), and, of course, the zenith of lynching. Brod (1996, 245) argues that this period marked the transition from patriarchy to fratriarchy:

> [I] believe that much of the culture, law, and philosophy of the nineteenth century in particular can be reinterpreted as marking a decisive turn in this transition [from patriarchy to fratriarchy]. I believe the passing of personal patriarchal power and its transformation into institutional patriarchal power in this period of the interrelated consolidation of corporate capitalism is evidenced in such phenomena as the rise of what one scholar has termed "judicial patriarchy," the new social regulation of masculinity through the courts and social welfare agencies, which through new support laws, poor laws, desertion laws and other changes transformed what were previously personal obligations into legal duties, as well as in the "Death of God" phenomenon and its aftermath. … I believe the loss of the personal exercise of patriarchal power and its diffusion through the institutions of society is strongly implicated in the death of God the Father and the secularization of culture in the nineteenth century, as well as the modern and postmodern problem of grounding authority and values.

"Tentatively" and "preliminarily," Brod (1996) suggests that "fratriarchy" might reflect this shift in the nature of patriarchy characterized by the deindividualization and the collectivization of male power. That is, rather than speak simply of advanced capitalist patriarchy—the rule of the fathers—the rule of the brothers is more precise. Fratriarchy, Brod (1996) argues, depicts more specifically what he takes to be one of the key issues in understanding contemporary masculinities, that is, the disjunction between the facts of public male power and the inner feelings of individual male powerlessness. He recalls Alan Soble's interpretation of men's preoccupation with pornographic fantasy as a compensation for their powerlessness in the public world. So understood, "pornography is therefore not so much an expression of male power as an expression of their lack of power" (1996, 82). Brod argues that by "differentiating levels of power one should more accurately say that pornography is both an expression of men's public power and an expression of their lack of personal power" (1996, 246). For many women I am not sure this is a comforting distinction; violence that compensates for a felt weakness is still violence.

In more reductionist and determinist strains of Marxism, Brod continues, pornography as ideology would be located in the superstructure of capitalism. Brod argues that pornography is not so much a part of patriarchal capitalism's superstructure as of its infrastructure. He points to the commodification of the body and of interpersonal relationships which support an "ever more penetrating ingression of capitalist market relations into the deepest reaches of the individual's psychological makeup" (1996, 247). He reads the feminist slogan "the personal is political" as not only a declaration that what has before been compartmentalized as private or personal should now be viewed as public and political, but also as an acknowledgment of the increasing politicization of personal life in general. In our time, with the public sphere so degraded as to be meaningless, significant political action occurs within the self.

The Marxist concept of imperialism also helps us to comprehend the objectification of the body, Brod suggests. A classical Marxist analysis suggests two factors are at work in imperialism: (1) the exploitation of natural resources, and (2) an extension of the market. Brod understands pornography as a kind of imperialism of the body. As pornography extends its reach from the "soft-core" pornography of much commercial advertising to the greater availability of "hard-core" pornography, the market more completely colonizes the body. The increasing use of the male body as a sex symbol in contemporary culture suggests, Brod believes, the market's appropriation of masculinity to promote images of men as consumers as well as producers. He understands current debates over the meaning of masculinity as a struggle between "new" and "radical" styles of masculinity more suited to advanced, consumerist patriarchal capitalism and those conservative styles which express a yearning to return to idealized versions of "traditional" masculinity, appropriate for a more production-oriented, entrepreneurial patriarchal capitalism. As I suggested in a paper on Boy George in 1983, the contemporary workplace will probably produce a new "culture club" of feminized masculinity more suited to corporate rather than industrial capitalism (Pinar 1994).

Of course, Marxist explanations are not comprehensive or definitive. Susan Bordo (1994) suggests that pornography is a context in which the "repressed penis, haunted by old guilt and embarrassments about secret masturbation, wet dreams, unwanted erections and ejaculations, taught that what spurts out of the body is disgusting, can come out of hiding and exhibit itself without shame or fear of rejection." In Bordo's reading of pornography, "it is the penis which has the stake here, *not* the phallus; for despite 'the pervasive presence of erections' in pornography, these are erections that are exposed precisely in order to be validated. Their validation—the transformation of embarrassed penis into proud phallus—is the point of the pornograph" (quoted passages in Bordo 1994, 275; emphasis in original). This phallic function of heterosexual pornography satisfies a man-sized yearning to be a "big guy," to travel from boys to men.

Is the Penis a Phallus?

The construction of "history" as comprised of "events" such as wars and reigns may be related to the production of contemporary self-alienated "masculinity." Calvin Thomas (1996) appears to be suggesting something like this when he writes that the "hailing" of "men as masculine subjects in history" turns on "a certain repression and disciplining of the male body, of the bodily in the male." The central dynamic in this repression, he suggests, "is the conversion of an arguably indifferent bodily organ, the penis, into the primary or transcendental signifier, the phallus." He quotes Kaja Silverman (1992), who wrote that the "collective make-believe in the commensurability of penis and phallus" so overdetermines "our 'dominant fiction'"—the "ideological belief [through which] a society's 'reality' is constituted and sustained, and [through which] a subject lays claim to a normative identity" that "our society's entire 'reality' depends upon the maintenance of that equation" (15, 8; quoted in Thomas 1996, 34).

Could the dominant fiction and normative identity be reconfigured by disrupting the equivalence or commensurability of penis and phallus? Thomas quotes Jane Gallop, who wrote that the phallus in the Lacanian sense is "neither a real nor a fantasized organ but an attribute: a power to generate meaning" (1988, 126). Guy Hocquenghem refers to the phallus as "the dispenser of meaning between the sexes" (1978, 65), a public organ that separates not only women from men but the men from the boys. Judith Butler argues that "insofar as the male genitals become the site of textual vacillation, they enact the impossibility of collapsing the distinction between penis and phallus" (1993, 61). The incommensurability of penis and phallus might, then, be key in the formation of the historical male subject, a man above the crowd, men who image other individuals as crowds, men for whom others are imaginary. Hocquenghem emphasizes that "only the phallus dispenses identity; any social use of the anus, apart from its sublimated use, creates the risk of a loss of identity" (87). Thomas concludes: "[p]hal*logo*centrism ... is not primarily a denial of power to women (though always that) but a denial of the value of powerlessness, and of meaninglessness, of nonidentity or disidentification, in both women and men" (1996, 35; emphasis in original).

Phallogocentrism, then, is not an essentialism. Commenting on "the endless repetition of failed efforts to clearly distinguish phallus and penis" (127), Gallop (1988, 125) observed that "if the phallus is distinct from the penis, then feminism's battle against phallocentrism is not a battle against men. But if it is nearly impossible to keep the distinction phallus/penis clear, that may account for the constant return of the assumption that men are the enemies of feminism. ... To distinguish penis from phallus would be to locate some masculinity that does not necessarily obliterate the feminine. Yet it remains an open question … whether there is any masculinity that is beyond the phallic phase." Gallop (1988, 131–132) concluded:

> I cannot disintricate the penis from phallic rule but neither is it totally synonymous with the transcendent phallus. At this point in history I don't think they can be separated, but to insist on bodily masculinity is to work to undo the heterosexist ideology which decrees the body female, to be dominated not by a male body (too disorderly to rule) but by an idealized transcendent phallus. I want to render that idealization impossible.

To return bodies to men, then, one have might to abandon the phallus for the penis. In object relations terms, this suggests a (relative) reidentification with the pre-oedipal mother. Less ambitiously (perhaps), would it not mean a subjectification of the body, its transposition from "tool" to embodied subjective self? But many men are imprisoned in masculinized structures of the self, rendering them, in effect, disembodied, imaginary (to themselves), dangerous to others. Calvin Thomas (1996, 36) comments:

> I agree with Gallop that at this point the two cannot be distinguished; the production of (non)meaning can take place only within structure still dominated by the phallic generation of meaning, the meaning of a still predominantly phallic generation (men, that is, are for the most part still a bunch of mean-ies, not to mention outright enemies of feminism, that any male effort to de-mean the phallus, including this one, should remain suspect). At the same time, I also agree that one of the most productive ways of rendering phallic idealization impossible would be to insist on bodily masculinity, to insist on a male body that is too disorderly to rule—that is, both too disorderly to be ruled and, more important, too disorderly to allow the easy assumption of the subject position of the one who is supposed to rule.

Embodiment may prove too much for men now. Perhaps it needs to be subdivided into steps, incremental, nonthreatening. No, forget it: an embodied subjectively existing man is … utopian. That would seem the sentiment of an exasperated Stephen Heath (1987, 26; emphasis in original), who complained that "the truth about men and their bodies *for the moment* is merely repetitive … the regime of the same, the eternal problem of the phallus, etc. … Taking men's bodies away from the existing representation and its oppressive effects will have to follow women's writing anew of themselves: for today, telling the truth about the male body as freeing subject is utopian, about the female body *actuality*." Cary Nelson (1987, 158) agrees with Heath that Alice Jardine's suggestion that men learn to speak and write their bodies is utopian. Nelson allows that such a project promises "to overturn our whole notion of academic writing" and if successful, "the social construction of gender will itself begin to change," but, he despairs; Jardine's suggestion is "a utopian aim [that] we are unlikely to achieve … for some time. It is useful as provocation and a basis for reflection and self-critique, but it is unrealistic as a condition for feminist writing by men."

Surely Heath and Nelson are right if defeated, but Calvin Thomas is not sympathetic: "I am suspicious of these caveats and wonder whether they are not themselves indentured to a certain inherently phallogocentric maneuver." For Heath, Thomas continues, the "male body is elevated to the realm of an ideal, unseen, unrealistic utopia, whereas the question of actuality (corporeality or materiality) gets displaced onto the feminine." Heath (1987, 14) quipped that "female sexuality is a bad question from a rotten history," whereas "'male sexuality' [note the scare quotation marks] is a good question from a rotten history that could not pose it." Thomas (1996) comments: "His simplification is that history is still too rotten for feminist men to pose the question of male sexualities, male bodies. I suggest that it is not simply that history is still too rotten for men to pose the question but rather that men's refusal [is] to think, speak" (quoted passages on 36).

Men may decline to pose "the question" of male sexualities, but they do like to pose, do they not? Strike a pose: in writing, in film, although there only the woman is present, presumably. The woman *must* be there, to argue over, to disguise the object of the gaze, the gaze of men looking at men. In a heterosexist regime, women are too often the pretext of male-male encounter, in film, in text, in that extremely expansive sense of the term which led Derrida to declare "*il n'y a pas de hors-texte*" (1967, 227). It was an imaginary and one-way "traffic in women" that rationalized the sexual mutilation of young black men. And it is the staged pleasure of female sex workers that rationalizes (straight) men watching other (straight) men come.

V. The "Money Shot"

Pornography tells lies about women. But pornography tells the truth about men.

—John Stoltenberg, *Refusing to Be a Man* (1989/1990)

In both gay and straight porn the "come-shot" is the sign of virility that is sought.

—Mark Simpson, *Male Impersonators: Men Performing Masculinity* (1994)

Consider those scenes of ejaculation in heterosexual hard-core pornographic films, the so-called money shots. In such scenes, the male sex worker typically withdraws his erect penis from whichever orifice of the female worker's body he has occupied, then ejaculates visibly onto some other body part, sometimes the face, sometimes the breasts, sometimes the buttocks. Following Foucault, Linda Williams (1989, 101) characterizes pornography less as a representation of repressed pleasures and more as a specific deployment of sexuality, a mode of power/knowledge that attempts to document "the visual evidence of the mechanical 'truth' of bodily pleasure caught in involuntary spasm; the ultimate and uncontrollable—ultimate because uncontrollable—confession of sexual pleasure in the climax of orgasm." In the attempt to display this confession, however, pornography encounters "the very limit of the visual representation of sexual pleasure," for the truth of bodily pleasure that heterosexual pornography wants to show is that of women. In general, in contrast to men's very visible ejaculation, women's orgasms cannot be documented. But they can be faked (C. Thomas 1996).

The irony of the money shot, then, is that the male sex worker's ejaculation substitutes for the woman's unrepresentable spasm. In this respect, the penis and its semen are feminized by virtue of representing—substituting for (presumably, for straight male viewers)—the woman. To avoid that unfortunate (from a phallocratic point of view) conclusion, viewers must accept that, as Williams explains, "the sexual performers within the film want to shift from a tactile to a visual pleasure at the crucial moment of the male's orgasm," or that "the woman prefers the sight of the ejaculating penis or the external touch of the semen to the thrust of the penis inside her" (1989, 101). The fact, as Calvin Thomas (1996, 20) observes, is that both participants are excluded from the "uncontrollable" pleasure that the money shot purports to display:

> [H]is ejaculation becomes the verifiable sign of the orgasm she is not really having (and could not visibly prove even if she were), while her performed convulsions signify the uncontrollable *jouissance* to which he, as a man, has no access (except through watching her). For men, as they are constructed in and out mainstream (straight) pornography, do not have involuntary, uncontrollable spasms; they do not have, or at least are not represented as having, pleasures that fall outside the margins of control. Arguably, men are not represented as having sex at all; rather, they are represented as having power.

Moreover, "most men don't like [hetero] sex. They like being powerful and when you have good sex you lose all power" (Acker 1982, 111).

There is, then, a gendered opposition between a "bad power" that may have little to do with sex and a "good sex" that only exists at some utopian remove from the effects of power. Calvin Thomas suggests that this opposition is a problem not simply because men like power more than sex, although, he grants, that is the form the problem assumes and through which it is culturally reproduced. The problem inherent in this opposition between "bad power" and "good sex" ensures "a tense oscillation between power and powerlessness to which all bodies are subjected but that is culturally split into the gendered subject positions by and as which men and women are ideologically interpellated" (C. Thomas 1996, 20). In such a system, somebody sometimes gets hurt, as Hearn's, Simon's and others' research indicates (see chapter 13).

Phallocratically the proof of male potency, semen, may be feminized when it is displayed (substituting for the woman's undocumentable orgasm), but it nonetheless reassures the heterosexual male viewer that a man is still a man, even when feminized. Male anxiety about the lack of value, lack of power, and lack of masculinity—including so-called performance anxiety—is assuaged. In this respect heterosexual porn functions within a homosocial economy. While the visibility of semen in the money shot locates it outside the frame of normative reproductive heterosexuality (insemination necessarily being invisible; presumably it's gay men who like to watch men come), the money shot depends on the woman's passive and waiting body to reproduce masculine power, ensuring that semen always ends up where it "belongs" ... and in compulsory heterosexuality that's not in the eye of the beholder.

The presence of the female sex worker—she must not appear perfectly passive but in a state of "aggressive acceptance" (McDonald 1990, 41)—functions to guarantee the heterosexuality of the erotic visual exchange between the male sex worker and the male spectator. Additionally, and for Calvin Thomas more importantly, her presence functions to conceal the (heterosexual) male devaluation that occurs in the self-dissolving moment of ejaculation. "In her performance," Thomas writes, "she positions her body as a reassuring surface for the male's ejaculatory inscription—reassuring precisely because powerless, valueless, convulsive, involuntary, out of control—and so reaffirms the male, both worker and spectator, in the position of power and value from which she herself is excluded" (1996, 22–23). Voilá, the penis becomes the phallus.

As in lynching, the woman is imaginary for many "straight" guys watching hard-core porn. Heterosexuality—is this why so many heterosexual women feel so often disappointed?—is often not about women; it is about men. In the money shot, as Williams points out, "it is always quite evident that this spectacle is not really for her eyes. She may even close her eyes if the man comes on her face; and, try as she might, she cannot possibly see the ejaculate when he comes, as frequently he does, on her buttocks or the small of her back. The man, in contrast, almost always sees himself ejaculate; the act seems much more clearly intended for his eyes and those of the viewer" (1989, 101). The camera colludes with the male performer and the male viewer but cuts away just before the masturbating (heterosexual) male spectator appreciates that in fact he's beating off to the sight of another man coming.

The shot fades too, as Thomas observes, at just that inevitable moment, which pornography rarely shows, "when the ejaculate must finally be wiped away" (1996, 22), when it is not the occasion for potency but instead what Bataille called an "object of horror" or anguish, a "fetid, sticky object without boundaries, which teems with life and yet is the sign of death" (1991, 95). The money shot ends, then, as the camera's cut conceals "that moment when the essence of masculinity assumes the status of valueless, powerless, and hence feminized waste" (Thomas 1996, 22). The phallus has become a penis again, limp, spent, an organ of excretion not power.

What the money shot makes explicit, Calvin Thomas argues, is the status of "woman" in those practices of specularization by which men manage to see themselves when the sex worker ejaculates, to be able to identify (with) themselves in the first place. Given the conflation of femininity with waste on which the money shot depends, Thomas (1996, 23; emphasis in original) suggests (after Bataille and Kristeva) that "an archaic *anal* eroticism subtends any (gendered) subject/object binary opposition." Are men subconsciously thinking of each other's anuses when they obsess over women's vaginas? Hocquenghem's (1978) linking of the anus with the (repressed, out of sight, male) self recalls Freud's declaration that "what is 'anal' remains the symbol of everything that is to be repudiated and excluded from life" (1905/1953/1995, 187). The function of the money shot is ultimately to protect the heterosexually identified man from any change in value or identity, to maintain the distinction between phallocentrism and abjection, "to help keep the processes of specularization that produce masculinity from turning it into shit." The price of the heterosexual male self's coherence is the "shattering, disintegration, and humiliation of the other; the terms of accession to the *corps propre* of the phallicized ego are the abjection or fecalization of the other" (quoted passages in C. Thomas 1996, 23). As Judith Butler observed, abjection is "the mode by which Others become shit" (1990, 134). And the "man" himself threatens to become (as straight men so often remind themselves) an asshole.

Disembodiment

So, to be a man means losing not only your body but your self as well. That self-self relation of abjection is projected outward; it is the man who imagines others as abject, and such split-off fragments populate his world of mirrors in which he imagines he sees what is. In turning others into shit he is hiding from himself his own condition. He himself may be dead, in the sense of a subjectified and embodied subject, a zombie but a "man" even so. While the gender binary may kill men subjectively, it murders women objectively. As Rosi Braidotti (1994b) understands, "[t]he issue men need to confront is their disembodiment" (202).

Judith Butler (1993) elucidates the objectification of the male body as a consequence of self-splitting, the production of "reason" and the exclusion of everything else, imagined then as "life." What is not quite rational, not quite human "bounds the figure of human reason, producing that 'man' as one who is without a childhood; is not a primate and so is relieved of the necessity of eating, defecating, living and dying; one who is not a slave, but always a property holder; one whose language remains originary and untranslatable." For Butler, then, "man" is a figure of "disembodiment, but one which is nevertheless a figure of a body." He is, in his self-dissociated relation to his own flesh, "a bodying forth of a masculinized rationality, the figure of a male body which is not a body," hence, she understands, "a figure in crisis, a figure that enacts a crisis it cannot fully control" (quoted passages on 48–49).

The objectification of the body signifies, then, the loss of subjectivity. And while the result is a "man"—tough, aggressive, hard—he is unstable. When he comes he's done. Because what is "man" is a "peculiar institution" resulting from intrapsychic violence (typified by processes of dissociation and self-splitting), he is never "at one" with himself, he is always spilling out of himself, ejaculating into the social world. He is always finding what he has repudiated in himself out there in the world as he "sees" it, which is to say, as he imagines it. He lives in a world populated by the debris of his own self-mutilation. That black man wants my woman. Faggots want my dick. Both are split-off self fragments, reversals of an intolerable white male desire that dare not speak its name.

Heterosexist homophobic male reason is an achievement and consequence of (especially European and European-American) civilization; it is what is left over once the organic has been repressed. Civilization and life are not mutually exclusive, of course. But historically masculine "reason" has become, as Butler (1993) understands, a "disembodied body." The imaginary morphology of masculine reason, she continues, is drawn through the exclusion of other bodies. This "materialization of reason" requires the "dematerialization"—lynchings for example—of other bodies. It requires rape of the feminine,

> for the feminine, strictly speaking, has no morphe, no morphology, no contour, for it is that which contributes to the contouring of things, but is itself undifferentiated, without boundary. The body that is reason dematerializes the bodies that may not properly stand for reason or its replicas, and yet this is a figure in crisis, for this body of reason is itself the phantasmatic dematerialization of masculinity, one which requires that women and slaves, children and animals be the body, perform the bodily function, that it will not perform. (Butler 1993, 48)

Faggots perform the bodily function, homosexual desire, that the dematerialized, imaginary straight boy has repressed in order to become a "man."

Can it be that homosexual desire returns the straight man to his body, against his will? Is that why he detests the gaze of gay men in locker rooms? The gay gaze is not only a reminder we're not all "just guys," as it interrupts the processes of normalization that persuade "guys" that the world is exactly as they imagine it to be. The gay gaze also threatens the structure of a heterosexualized, masculinized self-formation predicated upon desubjectification, upon the exclusion of the body, the abjection of the "other." As Lacan knew: "[T]he body in pieces [*le corps morcelé*] finds its unity in the image of the Other" (quoted in Butler 1993, 75). Conversely, gay men find that dissociated, relocated subjectivity hiding in the hetboy's muscled arms, his pecs, his penis partially erect as he stands in the shower glaring at any man who dares to look at what he dares not see but which his body contains and, in its nakedness, reveals.

What he dares not "see" is his body, the subjectified male body. The social construction of masculinity, Calvin Thomas argues, requires a repression of the male body. He acknowledges the feminist observation that, in Western culture, the "excessive" question of the body tends to be displaced onto the "feminine." Not unlike the male gay body, femininity becomes the repository not only for the body "but the excessive as such, for everything that masculine subjectivity cannot admit or accept about itself" (1996, 2). Thomas argues that this displacement of the bodily onto the feminine is especially evident in matters of representation, for instance, writing.

Like ejaculate in the money shot, writing "is both an act and appearance, both process and visible, material result." Moreover, "writing can be thought of as a scene of gender ambiguity, and thus cause of anxiety, for any author invested in preserving the boundaries, institutional or otherwise, of gendered identity and ego coherence" (C. Thomas 1996, 2). I shall pursue these "male matters" in a later volume; suffice to say for now that compulsory hegemonic heterosexuality banishes the male body, retooling it as an instrument of power, relocating it as a site and subjectification of desire onto the surface of female and black bodies. The male body remains invisible, the repository of a repressed and denied male subjectivity, which is then physicalized, sublimated in behavior: "*men act* and *women appear*" (Berger 1973, 47; emphasis in original). Is that why the gay male gaze is psychologically threatening but the straight male gaze is physically dangerous?

> When a gay man looks at another man in the showers or locker room, it is never from the position of power that straight men have when they look at women at the beach or on the street. In fact, the erotic world that is invoked in homosexual voyeurism is one of equality in the gender myth and the paradoxical *violation* of masculine power rather than the orthodox, heterosexual *confirmation* of power difference that is fundamental to heterosexual desire. ... Those who want to cling to their orthodox masculine power usually prefer to dis-emphasize the homoeroticism of their athletic environments. (Pronger 1990, 205–206; emphasis in original)

So men pretend they have no bodies, looking intensely only into each other's eyes. Nowhere is this studied, accomplished dissociation performed more carefully than in the locker room. Break the rules of not noticing, and you've got trouble, as this story makes clear:

> I had never seen a penis as large as his, mesmerized by its buoyant, almost jovial swing from leg to leg as he walked dripping wet from the showers to his locker. The testicles swung in their long, loose sack. The shaft was rolled with veins, like it had been wrapped with flesh-colored leaves. The greyish-purple head bounced happily between Macowski's strides, as if saying "Hello, foot. Hello, foot." There was a springy power in it, a living heft, a rubbery weight or force that was hypnotic. When he stopped in front of me, I didn't even notice.
>
> "What the fuck you smilin' at?"...
>
> "I said, what the fuck you smilin' at?"
>
> Everyone stopped dressing, all eyes on the naked shapes of Mac and me. ...
>
> "What are you, Keiser, queer?"
>
> "Mac, maybe he likes you."
>
> "Oh yeah!" said Mac, taking the bait. "Is that right dicklick?
>
> Well, why don't you show me how much you like me! He grabbed his penis with one hand, gave it a shake. "Come on, sweetheart, I'm ready!"
>
> I sat there, big-eyed, staring at Macowski. Mountainous, fearsome, articulate, Polish Mac. The adrenalin surged, tingling my fingers and toes. ...
>
> "Back off, shithead," I said, standing up.
>
> Then he hit me. (Sewell 1994, 106)

Many years later these locker-room boys are reunited. Mac is now a stud passé, buried under family, job, responsibility. Brad Sewell has not forgotten the locker-room incident: "Cruel that the body never forgets its past" (1994, 118).

The threat the gay male gaze poses to the heterosexually identified man standing naked in the gym shower room is the potential shattering of his violently constructed identity. The threat the straight male gaze poses is not just psychological but physical. Rape or other forms of physical violence may well follow straight boys' need to physicalize what they cannot bear to feel, unable to acknowledge, will not accept. So they must "act" to escape what they decline to accept. No passive subject, no object of entry, occupation or abjection are they. Drawing on Brian Pronger's and Richard Mohr's argument that acts and images of male anal penetration constitute the key "moments" when orthodox heterosexual masculinity is violated, Susan Bordo suggests the threat has to do with this "specific sexual meaning of the homosexual gaze," namely anal penetration. "What exposure is feared most in the shower?" Bordo (1994, 285; emphasis in original) asks.

> Not the scrutiny of the penis (although this prospect may indeed make heterosexual men uncomfortable), but the moment when one bends down to pick up the soap which has slipped from one's hands. It is in the imagination of this moment that the orthodox male is most undone by the consciousness that there may be homosexuals in the shower, whose gaze will define him as a passive receptacle of *their* sexuality, and thus as "woman." For although it is the imagined effeminacy of homosexual men that makes them objects of heterosexual derision, here it is their imagined *masculinity* (that is, the consciousness of them as active, evaluating sexual subjects, with a defining and "penetrating" sexual gaze) that makes them the object of heterosexual fear.

Prison is the place, white boys fantasize, where this fear will be realized. That fantasy turns out to be true.

In chapter 6 we saw that the nineteenth-century "crisis" of (white) masculinity was accompanied by a masturbation panic, fueled by worries that masturbation would lead to, among other terrible ends, homosexuality and impotence. These were not isolated fears. Dr. William Robinson's *Sexual Impotence* (1912), for instance, went through thirteen editions. Robinson argüed that "older doctors" had exaggerated the threat of masturbation; it was not, he asserted, the cause of impotence. In fact, men were not to be blamed for impotence at all. Who was? Why women of course, since it was women's lack of responsiveness to male sexual interest which exacerbated and sometimes even caused impotence (Kimmel 1996). The problem of impotence in men was, as he coined the term, "frigidity" in women, which "will not call out his virility" (quoted passages in Kimmel 1996, 131).

The fear of masturbation is long gone, but men's concern over impotence remains intense. Statistics indicate that more than half of all men will experience impotence for shorter or longer periods sometime during their lifetime. Between 7 and 9 percent of all men are permanently impotent, a percentage that increases significantly after age 50. There is some controversy over the accuracy of these figures, but there is no controversy over the fact that regardless of the incidence of impotence, "the fear of it is pervasive among men. Men are deathly afraid of being impotent" (Candib and Schmitt 1996, 211). Why? As

Candib and Schmitt suggest: "[T]o be a man requires, as a necessary and perhaps even sufficient condition, that one have an ever-erect, big, hard penis" (1996, 221).

While this must strike some as overstatement, Candib and Schmitt insist it is not. "For many men," they argue, "life is not worth living if they are impotent." Nor is such nonsense recent. They cite a passage in the Old Testament which implies that God punished Abimelech with impotence for thinking about having sex with Sara, the wife of Abraham. A punitive patriarchal God tells Abimelech, "You are as good as dead" (quoted passages in Candib and Schmitt 1996, 213). Among the patriarchs of the Old Testament, Candib and Schmitt remind us, impotence was regarded as a devastating punishment. There must be children, many children, to ensure the survival of an endangered people. Why else would impotence, and homosexuality, be feared and condemned?

In the medicalized, secularized present, there is Viagra. But there is little enlightenment: still, for many men, "the erection—instantaneous, hard, enormous, and indefatigable—is the center of their manhood" (Candib and Schmitt 1996, 213). Is it unsurprising then that what men fear most is the loss of what is a mythical, that is, fantasized, sexual power? Without an erection, Bernie Zilbergeld (1992) reports, most men feel they are "nothing," which is to say, not a man. For these men, certainly it is inconvenient that "male potency is always precarious" (Candib and Schmitt 1996, 213). This physiological reality translates predictably into psychological terms as Judith Butler explains: "[I]f men are said to 'have' the phallus symbolically, their anatomy is also a site marked by having lost it; the anatomical part is never commensurable with the phallus itself. In this sense, men might be understood to be both castrated (already) and driven by penis envy (more properly understood as phallus envy)" (1993, 85). So one "lucky" white male lyncher would keep the castrated penis of the mutilated young black man who, in being denied his civic manhood gained the mythological status of being a real man, at least in the minds of white men who gazed at his dick as they murdered him, then took that body part as their special souvenir.

Is Jake Barnes, the hero of Hemingway's *The Sun Also Rises*, a white version of "everyman"? Barnes was wounded on the Italian front in World War I. His wound left him impotent. As Lucy Candib and Richard Schmidt point out in their discussion of Barnes's situation, "impotence is so frightening that you could not possibly talk about it." The word "impotence" appears only once in the novel when Jake's friend Bill tells him that everyone thinks that he is impotent. Jake's line is that he "just had an accident." Bill agrees: "That's the sort of thing that can never be spoken of." While Jake is recovering in the hospital, the Italian liaison colonel consoles him: "You have given more than your life" (quoted passages in Candib and Schmitt 1996, 214).

Jake is in love with Lady Brett Ashley, and she with him, but his impotence makes any permanent relationship between them impossible: "Hemingway assumes that without a functioning penis, sexual relations are impossible" (Candib and Schmitt 1996, 214). Butler notes: "Castration could not be feared if the phallus were not already detachable, already elsewhere, already dispossessed; it is not simply the specter that it will become lost that constitutes the obsessive preoccupation of castration anxiety" (1993, 101). In this sense is Jack Barnes every man? At least every white man? Certainly he not unusual; one physician reported that: "In my experience, barely half of all civilized men enjoy normal sexual potency" (Stekel 1971, 6; quoted in Hoch 1979, 65).

"[W]hy [does] being a man," Candib and Schmitt ask, "require fearlessness in the face of danger and the threat of dying, but allows and even encourages in men a mindless panic at the very thought of impotence" (1996, 219). They answer, sounding for the moment like Butler, that for many men "sexuality is something like ... performance" (200). As such, being a "man" represents an ever-present "challenge that one can meet ... more or less adequately, or more or less successfully" (220). The point, as it were, of vulnerability, is the penis, and not just any penis, but "an ever-erect, big, hard penis" (221), the need for which cannot be compromised. How surprising is it that the white man obsessed over the black man's penis, which he imagined as so much larger, so much more powerful, so much more desirable than his own? It threatened his "lady," not a real woman with autonomy and agency, but an imaginary split-off resignification of his own feminine sexed position: "[T]he phallus (re)produces the specter of the penis only to enact its vanishing, to reiterate and exploit its perpetual vanishing as the very occasion of the phallus. This opens up anatomy, and sexual difference itself, as a site of proliferative resignifications" (Butler 1993, 89). Others' bodies, female, black, became and remain Rorschach screens for the wildly projective manchild in the promised land.

The pamphlet of Impotents Anonymous, a support organization for impotent men, advises us to "understand chronic impotence for what it is—a treatable condition—like heart disease or a broken leg" (quoted in Candib and Schmitt 1996, 231 n. 7). Why, Candib and Schmitt ask, do men boast about their potency while they rarely volunteer that they do not have a broken leg, or are free of heart disease? Sexuality not focused on the penis is easy to imagine for many women; why do men obsess over erections? Could it be that men are interested in the penises of other men? The power of the prohibition against looking in communal showers, such as gymnasia and locker rooms, would tend to suggest so. Straight men talking while showering after a workout look with steady unbroken determination into the eyes of their buddy: steady as she goes. The truth of the matter, however, is that

> [s]traight guys do just as much comparison and cruising as anybody does. I've noticed that a lot of guys will not shower anymore in the gym, they refuse to. If you ask them why—"too many faggots around here." ... Anybody who's that homophobic, I automatically question their sexuality. What are they worried about, "You've got twenty-inch biceps, fella!" It tells me they are really uptight about their sexuality and have problems dealing with it. Anyone who is sure about themselves isn't going to be concerned when someone is looking at them. (Pronger 1990, 196–197)

Of course they are not sure of themselves.

While erections represent manhood for many men and are thereby (over)valued, there are occasions when an erection is a problem for men and not just for women. Laurence Thomas points to those occasions when men must not reveal sexual interest, as when an erection could function as a kind of public polygraph test. Imagine a homosexual scene in a film: in a female-female scene, a woman could very well experience what Thomas terms "shadow arousal," but unless she articulates her arousal no one else need ever know. With men, there is a problem, as "shadow arousals" might well produce erections. "Hence it is no accident," he concludes, "that there are virtually no male-male erotic scenes in movies for the general public. For an erection would force the issue that either or both male actors found the scene arousing" (L. Thomas 1996, 263). Shirley Steinberg (1998) has noted that both gay men and lesbians are played by "straight" actors; women have sex in these movies, men do not. Straight men are spared the embarrassment of "shadow arousal."

Susan Bordo (1994) also points out that it remains rare for male genitals to be shown in mainstream movies, even for a fleeting moment. True, she acknowledges, male strip-shows—for women only mind you—are rationalized breezily as "what's good for the goose is good for the gander," but the Chippendales and other male strippers, in the United States at least, never exhibit themselves fully naked to women, as female strippers routinely do to men. "What is eroticized in the male stripper routines is not the strip, not the exposure of nakedness," Bordo concludes, "but the teasing display of phallic power, concentrated in the hard, pumped-up armor of muscle and the covered frontal bulge, straining against its confinement. Their penises they keep to themselves" (Bordo 1994, 269). Indeed.

Is that because men know that these self-presentations of "power" are inflated, that, as Bordo puts it, "the phallus is haunted by the penis"? The congealed hardness of power is not matched by the reality of the penis, which, Bordo emphasizes, is not "one" or self-identical. The truth of the matter is that the penis has no unified social identity; it differs according to race, class and culture. Even the illusion of the "ever-ready" hard dick is a (man's) fantasy: "Rather than exhibiting constancy of form, it is perhaps the most visibly mutable of bodily parts; it evokes the temporal not the eternal. And far from maintaining a steady will and purpose, it is mercurial, temperamental, unpredictable" (Bordo 1994, 266).

The realization that the penis has, in a sense, a life of its own can be rather unnerving. In that "shower room with other men, every male knows that the one thing that he absolutely must not do, whatever else he might do, is have an erection" (L. Thomas 1996, 263). Despite this possibility of an erection embarrassing its owner, the possibility is better than no erection at all. Eunuchs, for instance, were presumed to lack both subjectivity and agency; they existed completely as "other," bodies for sport, sex, status, guards, servants, and administration. They were regarded as irredeemable physically, spiritually and socially (Harris 1996).

Coming of age, boys know (even when they do not know the term) that "eunuch" is not an option. There is, then, a definite, pervasive, intense social pressure to become a "man." As boys, Victor Seidler recalls, "we have to be constantly on the alert. We always have to be ready to defend ourselves." Such vigilance, he argues, accumulates tension and anxiety which then gets recorded in the very organization of the body. Accumulated tension makes relaxation difficult, without "medication" such as alcohol. Rather than living through our bodies, men are encouraged to treat the body as an efficient machine, to be used instrumentally. This alienated relation to the body, Seidler believes, "deeply marks our sexuality." Often, he continues, men have mostly utilitarian relationships with their bodies. They do not regard them as lived sources of joy or satisfaction. "We are estranged from our bodies," he concludes, making

> it easier for us to use them in an unfeeling way. Sexuality becomes an issue of conquest. It becomes a question of how many women you can get off with and how many times you can screw them. In this sense, sexuality is closely identified with power. For men, it can become almost second nature. Often it becomes connected to violence. This is partly because this form of sexuality can leave us frustrated and unfulfilled, and it can be easier to take that out on others than to look at ourselves. The roots go very deep. (quoted passages in Seidler 1996, 65)

While gay men are not exempt (they are, after all, men), this seems to me to be a strong statement of the straight man's dilemma.

VI. "Hey Girl!"

> *For hundreds of years white men had written and spoken about how the black man was "hung like an ape," about how he fucked like an animal. The big black prick pervaded the white man's nightmare.*
>
> —Michelle Wallace, *Black Macho and the Myth of the Superwoman* (1978/1979)

> *For after all the Negro Question in America today is the white man's problem.*
>
> —Charles Lemert and Esmé Bhan, *The Voice of Anna Julia Cooper* (1998)

> *The straight mind might be thought of as a sublimation of this privileging of difference.*
>
> —Leo Bersani, *Homos* (1995)

Patrick Hopkins narrates an episode associated with his high-school student days which illustrates pointedly these psychosexual dynamics of compulsory masculinity production. In it we hear "the unconscious speak" and in particular the structure of male self-formation suggested by object relations theory, namely that the psychological foundation, the primary site of identification for both girls and boys, is the mother. Heteronormative masculinity is, as we have seen, an obliteration of this reality, which, in the violence of its repudiation, guarantees a violent internal structure of masculinity, unstable, always searching (for what was lost), projecting (what cannot be tolerated as not "masculine"), fighting (what I have—my manhood—hangs by a thread). In prison these psychosexual dynamics of gendered identification become nightmarishly explicit.

In fact, we can think of Hopkins's story as a school version of the prison tale I will tell in the next chapter, namely that all men know that being a "man" is always a reversible formation. Any "man" can be made into a "woman," to use the binary logic fundamental to the contemporary sex/gender system. Not only inmates know this fact; evidently Hopkins's fellow students and teachers in a so-called Christian high school were quite clear about the reality, rather, the unreality of "manhood." Hopkins recalls his senior year of high school and, in particular, his American government class. In that class the "brains" sat up front and at the edge; the "jocks" sat at the back and in the center. "Every day before and after class," he remembers:

> the male jocks bandied insults back and forth. Typically, this "good-natured" fun included name-calling. Name-calling, like most pop-cultural phenomena, circulates in fads, with various names waxing and waning in popularity. During the time I was taking this class, the most popular insult/name was used over and over again, ad nauseam. What was the insult?
>
> It was simply, "girl."
>
> Suggestively, "girl" was the insult of choice among the male jocks. If a male student was annoying, they called him "girl." If he made a mistake during some athletic event, he was called "girl." Sometimes "girl" was used to challenge boys to do their masculine best ("don't let us down, girl"). Eventually, after its explicitly derogatory use, "girl" came to be used among the male jocks as merely a term of greeting ("hey, girl"). (Hopkins 1996, 95)

Close your eyes and it sounds like you're in a rather festive gay bar. No, that's right, we're in a "Christian" high school.

What is clear here is that while "girl" connotes many things, specifically that you're not a man, at base perhaps it suggests that one is, after all, merely "human." To be a man, in some sense, is to be a machine; it is to be errorless, predictable, mythic, that is, inhuman. Incidentally, this occasion of the unconscious speaking is not limited to the boys themselves. As Hopkins observes in a footnote: "[M]any male teachers and coaches call their students and team members 'girls'" (1996, 112 n. 2). Socratic pedagogues perhaps?

Because Hopkins's high school was conservative and "Christian," no profanity was permitted. "Bad" words were sinful, and using them was strictly against the rules; transgressions were immediately and formally punished. There was, he remembers, "a regulated lack of access to the more commonly used insults available in secular schools." What insults were these? What terms seem to be always on boys' minds? Hopkins writes:

> "Faggot," "queer," "homo," or "cocksucker" were not available for use unless one was willing to risk being overheard by school staff, and thus risk being punished. However, it is important to note that, for the most part, these words were not restricted because of any sense of hurtfulness to a particular group or because they expressed prejudice. They were restricted merely because they were "dirty" words, "filthy" words, gutter-language

> words, like "shit" or "asshole." "Girl" was not a dirty word, and so presented no risk. It was used flagrantly in the presence of staff members, and even used by staff members themselves. (Hopkins 1996, 96)

As Mary Douglas (1966, 1968, 1973) has shown, "dirt" is a universal western symbol of excluded or excreted material, imagined to have no relation to the signifying self.

There is in Hopkins's story a familiar politics of the body. Being a male homosexual and being a girl are, for many straight guys, not completely different. Body armor toughened and ready for combat, the knight in shining armor points his phallus toward his opponent, hoping to pierce his armor, penetrate his body, or, in street talk and prison language, fuck him good. As Guy Hocquenghem (1978) pointed out twenty years ago, the anus signifies entry to the (male) body, to the interior sanctum that is the hidden, repressed, inner self. The penis/phallus signifies his public power. Hopkins is clear that these terms all circulate in the same psychosexual system that is "manhood":

> "Girl," as an allowable, non-profane substitute for "faggot," "homo," and "cocksucker," mirrors and thus reveals a common essence of these insults. It signifies "not-male," and as related to the male speaker, "not-me". ... "Girl," like these other terms, signifies a failure of masculinity, a failure of living up to a gendered standard of behavior, and a gendered standard of identity. (1996, 96)

It is this standard of behavior, this standardization of behavior, this abstracted quality of masculinity which not only erases access to his infancy and childhood, it precludes, finally, individuality itself. To be a man is to become a version of a standardized psychosocial sex role; it precludes that nuanced individuation associated with autobiographical study and development. That is why serious autobiography can be "queer" (Miller 1998); it can challenge the self-alienating, self-obliterating nature of "manhood." It can help a man become his "other," and in so doing, just possibly become himself.

Young Torless, Robert Musil's fictional student at a fin-de-siècle military academy in what is now Germany, was not so blocked. Torless remembers:

> In his skin, all over his body, there awoke a sensation that suddenly turned into an image in his memory. When he was quite small—yes, yes, that was it—when he was still in pinafores and had not yet begun to go to kindergarten, there had been times when he had had a quite unspeakable longing to be a little girl. And his longing too had not been in his head—oh no—nor in his heart either—it had tingled all over his body and gone racing round his skin. Yes, there had been a moment when he so vividly felt himself a little girl that he believed it simply could not be otherwise (Musil 1905/1955, 128).

Think of the film "Europa, Europa" and the blatantly homoerotic character of the German soldiers' affection for the beautiful boy they think is Aryan but we viewers know is the Jewish boy Sorel. In this film we see that the creation of "other" and suppression of the homosexual desire are intertwined. When he is first captured by the Germans, when he realizes that being Jewish means being dead, Sorel throws his identity papers to the ground. Realizing they're not safe there, he retrieves them. He sticks them in his shorts, where his penis (his Jewish identity) is. Standing there among other prisoners, he overhears one of the German soldiers ask how the other can tell who is a Jew; his comrade suggests he examine the penis. For Sorel, as for many men, penis equals identity.

Why, Sorel asks the commander who is taking quite a liking to his young Aryan (Jew), are Jews the enemy? The commander answers: "We must liberate Europe from the Jews." The commander wants to keep this beautiful boy, to possess him. He offers to "adopt" Sorel; we watch him take a photo ..."for the wife" ... of course. Then there is that scene on the train, when Sorel is being accompanied by a formidable-looking woman to the elite Nazi school to which he has been admitted. Now a "war hero," having made a favorable mistake, he is bound for glory at school. On the train the Nazi guardian constructs this young, handsome "war hero" as Fuhrer. The "other" slides easily in the German imagination, from Jew to Aryan, beautiful boy to Fuhrer. [They share the same birthdate.] She fucks him.

What we educators might recall most vividly is the classroom scene. The teacher's description of Nordic man is clearly homoerotic, and the (male) students know it. Sorel is called to the front of the room to illustrate skull science, a German achievement which allows precise and infallible identification of Jews. What relief when, after a moment's silence, he passes. He always passes. Does homosexuality suppressed become fascism? At least fascism is compelled to suppress homosexuality, as in 1934 when Ernst Rohm and other homosexuals in Hitler's entourage were eliminated. When men know they're acting can they then be gay? Sorel's older lover—whose death precedes his train ride—is an actor. Is masculinity only an act? And because it is so do real men require a science of skulls in order to know who is who? Do white men have any idea who they are?

A Man's Man

To be a man requires other men to agree, to testify, that you are no eunuch, no girl, no faggot. One has to be a man among other men, a "man's man" it is sometimes phrased, a status of homosocial admiration sometimes known as "honor." To earn such a reputation one must allow other men to watch one's "accomplishments." In gang rapes men get to prove they are erect, that they can perform. One is a man among men. As a bonus, gang rapes are safely heterosexual settings in which the straight boy gets to not only peek but "look excessively" (without penalty) at the erect penis of his buddy:

> Among some male peer groups the social expectation of sequential or group sex with an anonymous female—a "gang bang"—reveals that being able to have sex on demand in the company of male peers regardless of the wishes or condition of the woman is a criterion of membership in the group. The relationship among the men is what is important here; they are doing it in each other's company and showing support for the group value

> of domination over women and the ability to have sex at the group's behest. (Candib and Schmitt 1996, 222)

Are gang rapes, like lynchings, repressed, mutilated (and mutilating, especially to the female victim) redirected expressions of homosexual desire?

The "traffic in women" travels the route of suppressed homosexual desire. As Victoria Davion (1995) points out, men engaging in forced sex are not interested in the woman (who after all may be unconscious) but "are far more interested in impressing each other," a barely sublimated version of homosexual desire. Depersonalization is necessary, not only to perform the gang rape but to "be a man." Davion reports that she was able to foil a group attack by connecting personally with one attacker who looked apprehensive. When she managed to bring his subjectivity to the surface, the assault was interrupted. The price he paid was that he was, in the eyes of his buddies, no longer a man. So his pals turned on him, dismissing him loudly as a "pussy." Their rage escalated as his subjectivity spilled out into the room; they began to beat him. Aroused, now they threatened to rape *him*. Finally, Davion was able to escape. Such performances of masculinity are supported, as we have seen, by homosocial structures such as fraternities. "In fact," she notes, "the ability to have sex in this setting may be used in some male peer groups to 'prove' masculinity—e.g., the ability to have and use erection is socially mandated to be part of peer group" (quoted passages in Candib and Schmitt 1996, 222).

The erect penis is a weapon of terror in a rape situation. But, as Candib and Schmitt argue, even those who do not use their erections to dominate women still benefit from being the "good guys" or the "protectors." In this sense, "all men have some responsibility for the climate in which rape is prevalent because all men benefit from this climate" (Candib and Schmitt 1996, 223). Apparently most men experience sexual fantasies in which violence plays some part (Simon 1996). In contrast to what occurs with the sexual fantasies of "normal" men, in rapists "fantasies of control, domination, humiliation, pain, injury, and violence are acted out" (Simon 1996, 75). When men's fantasies are performed, women are raped, stalked, murdered. So are men, primarily gay men. Even straight men suffer, if secondarily, as the culture of masculinity creates and maintains the fear of impotence and homosexuality (Candib and Schmitt 1996).

"Rape will continue unabated," Robert I. Simon writes, "as long as society and culture empower men at the expense of women" (1996, 90). That "empowerment" is a function of misogyny, we know; is it also a function, in our time, of repressed homosexual desire? Is patriarchal political privilege the consolation prize for homosexual desire denied then sublimated? "If masculinity itself is a construction premised on, parasitic on, gender *difference*," Susan Bordo observes, "then gender sameness is a violation of masculinity" (1994, 285). But it is no simple violation; homoeroticism is paradoxical because it "both embraces and violates masculinity" (Pronger 1990, 71). I would say homoeroticism violates masculinity *as* it embraces it.

In lynching we have seen how heterosexual fantasies of big black bucks raping helpless white ladies represented, in part, recodings of a homosexual desire relocated onto the muscular young bodies of politically vulnerable black men. We see this complex move in Edvard Munch's "Cleopatra and Her Slave"

(1916/1920). A naked reclining white woman looks at a naked black man, who stands against the wall next to a dog and a stove (with a stack), three phallic symbols in a row, the objects of an apparently feminine gaze. Given the title, the black man is well in hand, no threat to the naked queen. But recall that this is a white man—a Norwegian—imagining, then painting, this scene. He and the woman are in a parallel positions, both looking out onto, in his case the canvas, in hers, a wall. Structurally Cleopatra (here portrayed as a white woman) stands in for Munch, who can now safely gaze uninterrupted, as he is disguised as a white woman (a "queen" no less), at the body of the naked black man. The strange fruit on this planet are white men.

One hundred years ago the white woman was incapable of desiring the black man (apparently only Ida B. Wells knew differently), and so the relocated desire still must be relocated again, this time transformed into a threat. So the white man's desire gets heterosexualized by taking female form, then undergoes a reversal by becoming the rapacious and uncontrollable black male desire for the white woman. In Munch's painting and in nineteenth-century American society, the women were imaginary; they were symbolic currency in homosocial economy. Finally a few white women (such as Jesse Daniel Ames) understood "the affair" was not about them, that in fact chivalry and lynching had nothing to do with them. These were only boys' games. Like war, lethal. Is being at war with each other the other side of the same coin that is desiring one another? Perhaps compulsory heterosexual desire itself is not what it seems, as Susan Bordo has observed: "What *did* men want? My conclusion was that while I wasn't quite sure what it was, it seemed clear that there was something about *me* that it *wasn't*" (1994, 273; emphasis in original).

What do men want? Especially many straight white men seem to have little clue. Could that be because they are emptied of subjectivity, alienated from their bodies, using women to disguise what they cannot bear to feel, to desire? "Who *are* these people?" asks Delease Wear (1999, 175). They are injured, often violent, creatures lost in a world they made but which hides the world that is, stillbirths in the world that might be. They cling to each other—how straight guys love to be together (fraternities, etc.)—to maintain the illusion that the world is as they imagine it to be. It is "really" the woman's pleasure that is important in sex; it is really the "lady" we must protect by teaching these black beasts a lesson they'll not soon forget? Different from but sharing similarities with racism and misogyny (intersecting categories, as this study suggests), the absence of autobiographical consciousness, of subjectivity, is the "mass" man, the conformist, the mob member. In the social production of compulsory masculinity wherein the pre-oedipal identification with the mother is traded for an imaginary identification with a relatively absent father (absent materially, psychologically, and as a subjectively-existing and embodied person), the son, in becoming a "man," is deindividuated. This is clear when he reaches adolescence, and not just for lower-class black boys. Whatever shreds of personal identity that remained are now replaced by an identification with the goals and actions of the group, the male group, sometimes gangs, sometimes fraternities, sometimes just (male) buddies. The social production of (especially hegemonic) manhood requires the individual to become less aware of his or her own values and behavior. Instead he focuses on the group and the situation as defined and constructed by the group (Diener 1980). He has lost himself, but he has gained the world, the world he imagines. Now he is a man's man.

In a group whatever residues of individual responsibility, autonomy, and morality get lost in the power and solidarity of the male mob. As we saw in lynching mobs, in fraternities, in the military, and (as we will soon see) in prison, when among other men, men often feel quite free to perform their rage. Why? One student of this phenomenon makes two points: (1) individuals who identify with a crowd acquire a sense of invincible power which allows them to override internalized control and to succumb to the group mind, and (2) being in a crowd renders the individual anonymous; he acts now in concert with his male brothers (Zimbardo 1970). Of course, such male bonding and solidarity usually requires an "other." Women, for instance.

How are women made into the "other"? In object-relations theory there is, as we have seen, a psychological narrative which answers this question. In terms of social not psychological processes, Chris O'Sullivan (1993) suggests that the story can be told this way. In groups men experience (1) the "outgroup homogeneity effect" (the belief that all members of the outgroup, that is, any not in one's own group, are alike); (2) an inherent sense of "ingroup superiority"; and (3) "groupthink" (a faulty decision-making process of groups, especially elite groups, which includes an inflated belief in the group's righteousness, an exaggerated belief in the inferiority of the opposition, and a squelching of dissent via ostracization of critics and self-censorship of doubt). O'Sullivan concludes: "These cognitive processes give group members a sense of invulnerability and entitlement, as well as a disdain for nonmembers that makes it easier to victimize them" (1993, 26). The gendered and racialized fantasies of Nazi youth, boys' clubs with weapons, white men, straight white men, straight to hell.

The erasure of subjectivity produces a monolithic self-structure, impervious to self-criticism, inner conversation, self-reflexivity. Such a (male) self is easily threatened, easily threatening, especially if merged with (male) others. What drives men into groups? Why do groups so easily turn ugly? Michael Kimmel is curious too: "What is it about groups that seems to bring about the worst in men? I think it is because the animating condition for most American men is a deeply rooted fear of other men—a fear that other men will view us as less than manly" (1993, 127). Such was the essence of "honor" in the patriarchal South. Before visiting contemporary prisons, let us revisit, just for a moment, a nineteenth-century one, the antebellum South.

Honor

There and then honor and masculinity were very much intertwined. To aspire to honor in the South—as white men in all social classes did—was to be ever aware of one's public reputation. Men were socialized to attend to the eyes of other men, not to their own subjective experience: "Honor demanded that a person always see himself through the eyes of others because personal worth was determined not by self-appraisal but by the worth others conferred" (Brundage 1993, 50). Because men disagreed over the worth of other men, the code of honor gave license to, indeed demanded, violence. After all, one's honor, one's self-worth, required defense. From duels to street corner brawls, antebellum men were often at war with each other. Not only did one have to defend one's own honor as an individual, each man was committed to defend his family's honor. If one's family honor was impugned, then one's individual honor was simultaneously at stake (Brundage 1993).

During the latter half of the nineteenth century, a number of developments, among them Emancipation, military defeat, gender shifts, feminism, economic diversification, urbanization, and industrialization, undermined the culture of honor in the South. In the ensuing "crisis" of white masculinity, "honor" became racialized. Dishonor became associated with blacks, and required the maintenance of white supremacy, that is, black inequality and subordination. As honor became racialized, the practice of lynching became more widespread and vicious. As the century ended, whites intensified their subjugation of blacks; they came to see them as not just dishonorable, but as criminal. Blacks were believed to be deteriorating as a race now that they were outside the civilizing influence of their white male masters. Black savagery and black racial extinction were inevitable, widely held views which supported white attitudes toward lynching and legitimized a mob violence that one would have thought would have challenged the very idea of "civilization" in the South (Brundage 1993).

Key in the deterioration and transformation of the southern code of honor was an ongoing "crisis" of masculinity. Indeed, honor and masculinity were intertwined, versions of homosociality that foreshadowed contemporary fraternities, the armed forces, and athletic teams. After their defeat in the Civil War both southern honor and masculinity were imperiled. "In the years immediately following 1865," Earl Thorpe writes, "the castrated South despaired of ever recovering its masculinity. Emasculated and made effeminate by gun and sword, it was through the use of the same weapons that such groups as the Ku Klux Klan hoped to restore the region's manhood" (1967, 154). Is it any wonder that white racism in the United States has been, continues to be, a sexualized phenomenon? "For a long time," Thorpe admits, "it was often through efforts to keep the long emasculated Negro effeminized that the white South sought to keep a semblance of its old masculinity" (154). But the black man was never in fact emasculated, despite the lynchings. In the mind of the southern white boy the black man remained the stud, always a threat, always the object of his sexual fascination. Black men seemed to have understood this sexual dynamic exactly. When the opportunity for political revenge presented itself, many black men knew just what form it must take.

16 ❖ IT'S *a* MAN'S WORLD

I. Technologies of Penal Power

Is it surprising that prisons resemble factories, schools, barracks, hospitals, which all resemble prisons?

—Michel Foucault, *Discipline and Punish: The Birth of the Prison* (1979/1995)

The prison, like the urban school, has undergone a massive demographic transition.

—James B. Jacobs, *New Perspectives on Prisons and Imprisonment* (1983)

[T]he specific apparatuses and instruments of punishment—the technologies of penal power—correspond with larger relations of political power.

—Mark Colvin, *Penitentiaries, Reformatories, and Chain Gangs* (1997)

[E]ach prison segment (inmates, guards, administrators, treatment personnel, and so forth) reflects society's systems of stratifications.

—James B. Jacobs, *New Perspectives on Prisons and Imprisonment* (1983)

Prisons do not exist in a vacuum, of course; they are part of the political, social, economic, and racial order. That order is informed by the history of racial violence and politics in America. I argue that prisons are no alien world severed from our own, but continuous with our world. The physical absence of women in prisons mirrors their status as imaginary in most men's minds, men who still believe that *the* world is *their* world, a man's world. Moreover, mob violence in prisons is key, as was lynching, to disentangling contemporary conflations of race, gender, and class. Since Emancipation, criminalization as been profoundly racialized in the United States, as "legalized lynchings" came to replace the extralegal kind (Wright 1990). In the late nineteenth century, black men were imprisoned for nearly any reason, and once imprisoned, exploited in a vicious convict-lease system that made slavery almost look attractive (Ayers, 1984; see section II). A century later, black men are still imprisoned for almost any reason, victims of a racialized "war on drugs," which, as we will see in section III, is, in effect, a war on young black men (Miller 1996). At this point, this should come as no surprise. Black men have been and remain the obsession of white men, white men who remain determined to keep black men incarcerated, if not in their minds, certainly in their jails. There, however, black men have effected a racial and gendered reversal, often coming out "on top."

In our time the distinction between "society" and "prison" blurs. A policeman named David Lemieux told Haki Madhubuti (1990): "There's dope in the penitentiary. There's everything else in the penitentiary. Sometimes it becomes a blur whether the community is an extension of the penitentiary's life-style or the penitentiary is an extension of the community's life-style" (45). This view is mirrored in the research on prisons. For instance, what has been learned about the organizational life of prisons is not peculiar to the institution but reproduces various aspects of the racialized and gendered social order outside the institution. What has happened and happens still in prisons is definitely not separate from life outside, as students of the institution have acknowledged: "living and working conditions, the legitimacy or illegitimacy of various disciplinary mechanisms, and the structure of punishments and rewards all depend upon how the prison articulates with the political, economic, and legal system of the whole society" (Jacobs 1983, 17–18).

Origins

In early part of the nineteenth century, in Auburn, New York, obscure officials pieced together a prison program that would be copied throughout America and Europe. The Auburn plan required neither total solitary confinement nor the indiscriminate mixing of inmates, the two extremes typifying earlier penological practice. Instead, the Auburn plan confined prisoners to separate cells at night and brought them together, to work in silence, during the days. Character reformation was effected, presumably, by the daytime silence combined with nighttime isolation. Economic efficiency, that is, profits as well as labor control, was made possible by the coordinated labor of inmates under constant supervision. Despite its apparent novelty, "the Auburn plan was as much a culmination as a new beginning" (Ayers, 1984, 40).

There were critics. Inmate life was austere: the convicts worked from dawn to dark six days a week; only on Sunday were they permitted to gather for a sermon and perhaps to walk in the prison yard and chew the tobacco they had earned by their good behavior. Yet reformers in Pennsylvania argued that the New York prison was not austere enough. Only the silence of total isolation, day and night, could truly reform criminals, they argued. One group of educated and influential southerners were also suspicious of the penitentiary, if for different reasons. Ministers of evangelical Christian churches regarded the institution as a threat to the rule of God. After all, the Bible never mentioned a penitentiary (Ayers 1984).

Gustave de Beaumont and Alexis de Tocqueville, James Jacobs (1983) suggests, were the first students of the American penitentiary. In 1833, they linked this penal innovation to the culture, social structure, and political system of the young American nation. They compared them to prisons in France, and observed the following differences: (1) in the United States philanthropic and religious traditions gave rise to the penitentiary movement; (2) the relative egalitarianism of American society appeared to be responsible for the absence of class privileges inside the penitentiary; and (3) American public opinion influenced prison policies and conditions. They speculated that perhaps order was more easily maintained in the American penitentiary due to a more widely shared commitment to law and order in American society, lamenting that "this spirit of submission to the established order does not exist in the same degree with us. On the contrary, there is in France, in the spirit of the masses, an unhappy tendency to violate the law, and this inclination to insubordination seems to us to be of a nature to embarrass the regular operation of the [prison] discipline" (De Beaumont and de Tocqueville 1964, 121). Despite that observation, in 1833 de Tocqueville was able to say: "While society in the United States gives the example of the most extended liberty, the prisons of the same country offer the spectacle of the most complete despotism" (quoted in Cardozo-Freeman 1984, 320).

It was in the 1840s that institutions for delinquents were first established (Bartollas, Miller, and Dinitz 1976). In *The Discovery of the Asylum*, David Rothman (1971) portrays the options considered by communities in the late 1700s and early 1800s when juveniles (as a category) transgressed the boundaries of community propriety. Before the nineteenth century, youth did not know the meaning of incarceration. Nor, for that matter, did anyone else. Local jails were used to hold offenders until it was decided what to do with them. Even punishment was not generally considered useful, as the colonists "placed little faith in the possibility of reform. Prevailing Calvinist doctrines that stressed the natural depravity of man and the powers of the devil hardly allowed such optimism" (Rothman 1971, 53). Sinfulness was why juveniles broke the law (Bartollas, Miller, and Dinitz 1976); what was required was the healing power of God, not the rehabilitating potential of prisons.

Between 1790 and 1830, the rapid growth of towns as well as the settlement of "new" territories rendered older techniques of social control ineffective. Rapid growth had the effect, Rothman (1971) argues, of social disorganization. The perceived causes of delinquency shifted from the natural depravity of humankind to an unsettled and unsettling environment. How might order and predictability be restored, not only to the lives of young people but to all? The nineteenth-century answer was the house of refuge, "the well-ordered asylum," an institution which used the family as its model of organization. Family equals prison?

Not only wayward youth were sent to these institutions, but wayward adults as well. In one facility, as in one family, one might find the aged, the mentally ill, vagrants, orphans, unwed mothers, the lame, and the poor. All were instructed to reorder their lives, then return to society as productive and socially responsible members. The point of the asylum was simple: to provide an opportunity for those incarcerated there to find their way back to "right" ways of living. Right ways of living excluded transgressions of all kinds, but especially sexual ones. Asylum officials were, presumably, models of right living. However, as we see in the following passage describing the Boston Asylum and Farm School (1845), the "return of the repressed" operated then as it does now:

> No sooner did they [young offenders] enter the institution than they were stripped, washed, their hair cut to a standard length, and put into common dress. Managers appropriately claimed that the refuge's main object, that of reformation, is never lost sight of, in any of its regulations, and in all its discipline. From the entrance of the child, he becomes subject to a routine of duties ... order and method. (11; quoted in Rothman 1971, 266)

As we will see in the next chapter, the bodies of the young have always seemed to appeal to prison officials.

The jail as institution dates back at least to medieval England; it was a special structure, erected and administered by the local authorities, specifically the sheriff, for the sole purpose of holding persons to be delivered to the royal courts for judgment. Sheriffs began building jails in the early eleventh century or slightly before. By 1166, Henry II "enjoined all sheriffs to ensure that in all counties where no gaols existed gaols should now be built" (quoted in Irwin 1985, 3). The history of punishment in Europe from the twelfth to the twentieth century has been sketched by Georg Rusche and Otto Kirchheimer (1939). They emphasize the relationship between a country's penal system and its economic system, especially as the latter evolved from feudalism to mercantilism to industrial capitalism. The prison can also be understood as an institutionalized response to complex demographic shifts, which by the nineteenth century had resulted in a situation of chronic surplus labor. By the mid-nineteenth century, the economic function of workhouses—the precursors of the modern prison—was becoming clear: industrialization required plentiful and cheap labor. The modern prison functioned to keep the working poor disciplined, and encouraged them to work for less than adequate wages in less than adequate job settings (Jacobs, 1983).

By the late nineteenth and early twentieth century, there was, Rusche and Kirchheimer argue, a wider acceptance of a "sociological" understanding of criminality. Now "society" was said to be responsible for crime. What "criminals" needed was not so much punishment as "scientific treatment"—that is, "rehabilitation." Jacobs (1983) argues that one cannot understand what is at stake in contemporary debates about penal policy without appreciating the history of rehabilitation as an ideology. Certainly the apparent decline of this "ideology" during the conservative backlash of the past thirty years might help explain the popularity of capital punishment as well as highly punitive policies such as California's "three strikes" law.

Contemporary scholars do not tend to study prisons from as broad and comparative a perspective as did de Beaumont and de Tocqueville or Rusche and Kirchheimer. Certain research on the German concentration camps and on prisoner-of-war camps, however, does illustrate selected efforts to study prisons in terms of politics and society. This research linked concentration camps not only to the racial policies of National Socialism but to the economic requirements of the German war economy, where slave labor and genocide intersected. H. G. Adler (1958, 514) understood that a variety of political, racial, and economic forces were at work in the Holocaust:

> In a world made vulnerable, or at least strongly influenced, by the ideas of the Enlightenment, the purely secular state, the new democracy, and secular socialism, the fate of the man who dissents from the guiding principles and idea of the ruling group has become important: how he is to be rendered innocuous as soon as the ruling group feels threatened by him and how, under whatever pretense, that group discards all protections granted by the constitutional state and the democratic guarantees for personal inviolability. The dissenter is excluded from the community of those who conform, sent to the concentration camp, or killed. This approach to the study of the concentration camp would begin with the position of the ruling group, paying particular attention to political and economic conditions.

The Holocaust, as Marla Morris (in press) brilliantly argues, cannot be so simply comprehended.

American law does not recognize political crimes, although many prisoners—for instance, a number of 1960s political dissidents—have claimed that their imprisonment was in fact political. Other Western democracies, such as France, do have explicit designations for political crimes and special prisons for political prisoners, for instance, La Santé in Paris. In the United States it is assumed that the political institutions of society are flexible enough to resolve all legitimate political conflict. It is a major and often unwarranted assumption. There have always been American prisoners who have defined themselves and who have been defined by their fellow prisoners as political, such as George Jackson (1970). Robert Chrisman discerns a throughline from enslavement to imprisonment: "The first black prisoners in America were the Africans brought to these shores in chains in 1619. Like our brothers in prison today—and like ourselves—those African ancestors were victims of the political, economic and military rapacity of white America" (1995/1996, 414).

The majority of whites insist that the American prison is not a political institution. Prisoners are not regarded as enemies of the state and/or as offenders against the political order; instead they are presumed to be "criminals" unable to live peacefully in the socioeconomic order. Consequently, the American political system has tended to regard prison as punishment for misdeeds or as institutions of rehabilitation (Jacobs 1983). This "psychologization" and "medicalization" of imprisonment sidesteps rather than confronts the political elements of "crime." Worse, the prison appears to encourage what it was designed to suppress. As Foucault (1988, 143) has observed:

> The result was meant to be the reform of prisoners. It soon became clear that prison had exactly the opposite result, that it was on the whole a school for delinquency and that the more refined methods of the police system and the legal apparatus, far from insuring better protection against crime, brought about a strengthening of the criminal milieu, through the medium of prison itself.

The new era of prisoners' rights began in the early 1960s in the wake of the civil rights movement. In prisons, it was the Black Muslims who initiated the struggle for prisoners' rights. The Nation of Islam had been recruiting prisoners as members ever since Elijah Muhammad, the sect's leader, had been convicted and imprisoned briefly for his draft resistance during World War II. By 1960 Black Muslim membership was estimated at 65,000 to 100,000 nationwide, including a relatively high number of prison inmates (Cummins 1994).

The Muslims filed lawsuits throughout the country in the early 1960s, asserting racial and religious inequality. With the assistance of jailhouse lawyers, they sometimes succeeded, and in so doing provided a model for using the law to challenge prison policy. Moreover, their successes regarding constitutional issues of free exercise of religious rights brought the federal courts into the prisons (Jacobs 1983; Genders and Player 1989). "The prisoners' rights movement," Jacobs reports, "made it more difficult to maintain control over prisoners" (1983, 57). Other factors were at work, including an increasing politicization of "race" in prison life. For instance, the Montgomery and MacDougall (1984) study discovered a wide variety of causes for prison riots that occurred between 1971 and 1983, but the most common cause was racial (34.2 percent).

By the late 1950s and early 1960s African Americans constituted a majority of the prisoners in many northern prisons and in some, especially southern, states. The political consciousness of many prisoners had been raised by the civil rights movement; in this regard it is unsurprising that this generation of black prisoners would demand its rights, even behind bars. By the late 1960s, black prisoners, such as Eldridge Cleaver (1968), George Jackson (1970), Claude Brown (1965), and Malcolm X (1965), had achieved extraordinary prominence. Each would point to the political and educational significance of the Black Muslims in American prisons during the late 1950s and early 1960s. With the exception of Claude Brown, each of these writers were themselves politicized through their contacts with the Black Muslims in prison (Jacobs 1983).

An Imprisoned Society

In recent decades the penal system in the United States has expanded at an unprecedented rate. In 1972, there were 196,092 prisoners housed in state and federal institutions; the number grew steadily to 1,127,132 in 1995, a 475 percent increase. Women have been especially affected by this increase; while male imprisonment grew by 458 percent from 1972 to 1995, the number of imprisoned women increased by 993 percent. Arrests for women have risen in recent years (by 37 percent between 1984 and 1993), but not nearly at the pace of their imprisonment (181 percent between 1984 and 1993). Much of this increase in women's incarceration is due to recent antidrug legislation which mandates longer prison sentences (Colvin 1997).

The United States now incarcerates a greater proportion of its population than any other nation, except possibly Russia: one in every 167 U.S. residents was incarcerated in local jails and federal and state prisons at the end of 1995, up from one in every 453 U.S. residents at the end of 1980. Never before has such a high proportion of the American population been imprisoned. If those on probation and parole are included, the total number of people under correctional supervision grew from 1,832,350 in 1980 (1 in every 124 U.S. residents) to 5,100,000 in 1994 (1 in every 57 U.S. residents) (Colvin 1997).

This astonishing growth in rates of incarceration and correctional supervision would lead one to believe that the growth in crime has been astronomical as well. Rising crime, Mark Colvin (1997) argues, explains little, if any, of the explosive growth of the American penal system. What does account for its growth? Since the early 1970s, Colvin answers, the United States has embarked on a "get tough" policy in dealing with offenders. The "war on drugs" of the 1980s and 1990s brought millions of offenders into the penal system, though drug use had already peaked in 1979 and 1980. Some have alleged that the "war on drugs" is "a war on black males," suggesting that whites are just as involved in drugs, if not more so, than blacks but much less likely to serve time if caught. When whites are arrested they are more than likely to be characterized as victims of addiction, "not [as black] thugs who [should] spend the rest of their lives in prison" (Hutchinson 1997, 123; see Miller 1996).

This view is supported by self-reported studies of criminal behavior and drug use which indicate that racial differences in both areas are slight, especially when controlling for income and education. That should predict slight differences in rates of incarceration for blacks and whites. In fact, however, the rate of imprisonment for black males is seven times that of white males. The rate of execution is also disproportionate: from 1930 to 1969, 2,066 black people were executed, compared to 1,751 whites (Chrisman 1995/1996). By the mid-1990s, one in three African-American males, ages 20 to 29, was under some form of correctional supervision at any given time. In America, the criminal justice system has produced, in Colvin's words, "a new type of apartheid." "This is not surprising," he continues, "given that the 'get tough' approach had its origin in the backlash to the civil rights advances of African Americans" (1997, 272).

African-American men are not the only sector of American society disproportionately represented in prisons. There is as well a disproportionate incarceration of the poor. This is evident in comparisons of unemployment and imprisonment statistics. In 1983, for instance, 47 percent of the jail inmates were unemployed prior to arrest; this contrasted with 9.5 percent of the general population. The median pre-arrest income of inmates with income in 1983 was $5,486, as compared to a general population median income of $14,631. And in that same year, the average pre-arrest income of black prisoners was $4,000 (Sbarbaro and Keller 1995).

Crime is crime, right? We must get the murderers off the street. But over half of those incarcerated are not imprisoned for serious crimes such as murder, rape, and assault. Austin and Irwin (1990) found that 52.6 percent of those sent to prison are there for petty offenses, such as minor property theft, drug and disorderly conduct violations. Austin and Irwin determined that 58 percent of the offenders admitted to prison were not following criminal careers. Only 4 percent could be judged as having lost the capacity to live in "civilized" society. The truth is simple if unexpected: "The vast majority of the persons who are arrested, booked, and held in jail are not charged with serious crimes. They are charged with petty ones or with behavior that is no crime at all. And the jail, unlike the prison, has little to do with serious crime. Its primary purpose is to receive and hold persons because they are 'offensive'" (Irwin 1985, 18).

There are, Edward Sbarbaro and Robert L. Keller (1995) point out, two myths about crime and punishment in the United States. The first myth is that the poor and minorities, who are overrepresented in the prison population, are in fact the criminal element. The truth of the matter is that crime is ubiquitous; it is committed by people in all social and economic strata of society. Of course, those who occupy different levels of the social system are likely to commit different types of crime. A wealthy person, for instance, may have no interest in carjacking but may well find securities fraud tempting. Ignoring the ubiquity of crime and focusing only on the lower classes leads to "explanations" of crime in terms of biological, racial, psychological, or cultural pathology. Because they fly in the face of the facts, such explanations are not only mistaken, but classist and racist as well (Sbarbaro and Keller 1995).

The second myth is that prisons are a direct response to crime in society. Recent as well as historical data show, however, that the size of the prison population cannot be adequately explained by crime rates. These two myths are perpetuated, Sbarbaro and Keller (1995) allege, by the criminal justice system and the media. They quote Jeffrey Reiman, who argued that the criminal justice system "[r]efuses to define as 'crimes' or as serious crimes the dangerous and predatory acts of the well-to-do [for example, white-collar crime]—acts that ... result in loss of hundreds of thousands of lives and billions of dollars. Instead, the system focuses its attention on those crimes likely to be committed by the members of the lower classes. Thus, it is no surprise to find that so many of the people behind bars are from the lower classes" (Reiman 1990, 114).

This bias is evident, Sbarbaro and Keller (1995) argue, in the Uniformed Crime Reports (U.C.R.). The U.C.R. is the most widely used source of crime data. The U.C.R., however, is not an independent audit of the criminal justice system. The contrary is the case: those agencies and people who stand to gain from a rise or fall in the crime rate are the same people who collect and compile the crime data. Could this fact have something to do with the white fantasy that violent crime has swung out of control in this country? According to the F.B.I.'s National Crime Survey, homicides and other violent crimes have decreased steadily since the mid-1970s (Rose 1994).

The main focus of the U.C.R. is street crime, specifically assault, murder, rape, robbery, larceny, car theft. These are crimes to which the police respond. "Street crime," Tricia Rose (1994) observes, "lends itself to personal portraits of loss and horror. Unlike corporate or economic crimes against people, it has clearly identifiable victims and villains, even when no villain is caught" (149). Street crime, Sbarbaro and Keller (1995) agree, is not the only type of crime in society, nor the most serious in terms of harm or lost money. In general, street crime comes under the jurisdiction of the police, while regulatory agencies are responsible for crime committed, we might say, in suites, that is to say, government and corporate crimes. These so-called white-collar crimes cost taxpayers more and are more harmful to more people than street crime (Reiman 1990). Thanks to the racist sensationalism of the media and misrepresentation by politicians, the public has come to fear street not corporate crime. While it is not true, the public perceives street crime as the most serious threat to their individual as well as social well-being (Sbarbaro and Keller 1995).

For too long, Sbarbaro and Keller (1995) complain, the U.C.R. has served as the undisputed recorder of the facts concerning crime. Its distortions, they continue, influence both public policy and criminological theory. When the U.C.R. emphasis on street crime is accepted uncritically, the pervasiveness and greater harmfulness of white-collar crime disappears in the public hysteria over street crime. This amounts to class warfare, as it is the crimes of the lower class that become the only type of crime that exists in the public imagination. It is the poor, the public is sure, and only the poor who are the criminal element in American society. Eager to exploit public anxiety and fantasy, politicians succeed in implementing a "get tough" stance on street crime, which means more prisons, not more schools, are built. This is not new; criminalization in the nineteenth century was also racialized, as we see in section II. In section III we will see how racial politics are embedded in contemporary patterns of criminalization.

In that section, focused on the "war against drugs," it will become clear that contemporary criminalization is highly racialized. The demonization of young black males in the popular media, by some black and many white leaders, and among law enforcement officials, helps keep circulating in the white imagination images of young black men that are at least a century old. "For all the public hue and cry about some categories of crime," Tricia Rose points out perceptively, "rarely are Americans exposed to an informed exploration of the relationship between some kinds of crime and the extraordinary institutional violence done to the nation's poorest children of color" (1994, 151). "Institutional violence" includes: massive unemployment (for young black men, their parents, their relatives); constant police harassment and violence against their peers, coupled with limited police success against, and in some cases, participation in, the drug trade; routine arrests for "suspicious" behavior (the police often equate suspicious behavior and young black men ... so-called profiling); substandard housing, sometimes none at all; limited access to legal or political protection; and aggressive state bureaucracies, which demand, for example, that welfare parents continually study the ads for affordable apartments in order to keep their monthly rent coupons, even while those lowest market rentals cost two or three times more than their coupons can cover; and economic shifts that have further depressed economic activity in lower-class black neighborhoods, offering now only tenuous, low-pay, dead-end service jobs (Rose 1994). Is it any surprise that of all black men between sixteen and sixty-two, 46 percent are not in the labor force? (Guerrero 1994)

Contrary to white fantasy, crime is not some pathological aberration of the American way, committed only by a special category of psychopaths called "criminals," nearly all of whom live in black ghettoes or trailer parks. Crime has been and is now widely and somewhat evenly distributed throughout all social and economic classes. Furthermore, breaking the law would appear to be deeply rooted in basic American values and relationships. The most serious crimes—those that result in the greatest financial losses, the most serious personal injury or death, not to mention the corruption of society's morals and political processes—are committed by "reputable" people (Irwin 1985). Certainly this was regularly the case in lynching.

Colvin (1997) acknowledges that Foucault's primary interest in *Discipline and Punish: The Birth of the Prison* (1979) was not the prison per se but the elaboration of the intricate and pervasive processes of control in contemporary society (using the penitentiary as his conceptual point of observation or, we might say, panopticon). Yet Colvin argues that profound insights into the nature of prison discipline and punishment are embedded in Foucault's work. Colvin points specifically to Foucault's appreciation that the nature of punishment reflects the nature of power relations in society. While split off from everyday life, the prison is not some alien institution with no meaningful relation to those of us who imagine ourselves as completely outside questions of crime and punishment. More specifically, Colvin suggests that "the specific apparatuses and instruments of punishment—the technologies of penal power—correspond with larger relations of political power" (1997, 19). In other words, what occurs in prisons cannot be dismissed as only a function of prison life itself. While it is that, too, prison rape is a performance of male-male relations in larger society, a key and imprinting performance of racial politics and violence in America.

II. The Racial Politics of Criminalization in the Nineteenth Century: "New Slaves" and the Convict-Lease System

[F]orms of black behavior that might spark white retribution in one region went unnoticed in another.

—W. Fitzhugh Brundage, *Lynching in the New South: Georgia and Virginia, 1880–1930* (1993)

The lynchings and their aftermath gave South and North alike a further opportunity for reunion—linked again over what was perceived to be the criminality of "lower" races.

—Eric Sundquist, *To Wake the Nations: Race in the Making of American Literature* (1993)

The discourse of race was not on parallel track with the discourse of the nation but part of it; the latter was saturated with a hierarchy of moralities, prescriptions for conduct and bourgeois civilities that kept a racial politics of exclusion at its core.

—Ann Laura Stoler, *Race and the Education of Desire: Foucault's History of Sexuality and the Colonial Order of Things* (1995)

Our Civil War freed the slaves in name only. It left them illiterate, homeless, and penniless, and at the economic mercy of their former masters. Masses of them entered a new slavery in which there was neither legal nor moral obligation on the masters; there was not even so much as a financial interest in the "new slaves."

—James Weldon Johnson, Jr., *Along This Way* (1933)

Curiously, one of the first penitentiaries built in the South anticipated Foucault's emphasis upon the panopticon. Influenced by the writings of Beccaria and Bentham, Thomas Jefferson persuaded Virginia officials to build a prison, perhaps to suppress the practice of lynching which had begun in that state (see chapter 3). Opened in 1800 near the navigable part of the James River at Richmond, this prison resembled Bentham's panopticon design. It stood "near a stagnant pool where the sewage of the city accumulated, the cells had no heat, and prisoners could not work in their dark isolation" (Ayers 1984, 38). The workshops were unprofitable; disorder and escapes were common. State government starved the institution of funds, yet constant complaints from lawmakers about its expense continued uninterrupted for six decades. In 1858, Virginia leased its free black convicts to railroad and canal companies. This experiment anticipated the convict-lease system that was practiced in nearly all southern states after the Civil War, as we will see momentarily. A similar use of convicts was made at Auburn, New York, during the construction of the Erie Canal from 1817 to 1825, but it was the South which found this method of "punishment" irresistible. Nearly all of the former Confederate states would develop a convict-leasing system by the 1880s (Ayers 1984; Mancini 1996; Colvin 1997).

Louisiana built a 100-cell prison in Baton Rouge in 1835 modeled after the prison built in upstate New York. It included a cotton mill and shoe factory (Colvin 1997). Not every antebellum southern state built penitentiaries, but even in those that did, the prison affected relatively few offenders. As we have seen in the case of lynching, informal systems of private justice were preferred to institutionalized procedures. "As long as slavery held the vast majority of the region's poor under rigid control, the South could afford a weak state, could afford to leave most white men alone, could afford to treat even accused criminals with leniency" (Ayers 1984, 137; quoted in Colvin 1997, 212). After the Emancipation, the failure of Reconstruction, and the accomplishment of "redemption" or "home rule," that situation would change.

In the decade following the war most of the large southern cities adopted uniformed police. These cities copied each other; soon one southern police force differed little from another. The situation in Savannah illustrates. There an ex-Confederate officer, General R. H. Anderson, served as chief of police from 1865 until his death in 1888, a sharp contrast from the antebellum practice, when the chief changed with every political administration. The police force General Anderson led, observed a visitor in 1875, resembled "a military organization, clothed in Confederate gray, subject to strict discipline, armed with rifles, revolvers and sabers. ... It is one of the great prides of the city." The visitor also observed: "the negroes no longer have any voice whatever in political matters, and are not represented in the city government" (quoted passages in Ayers 1984, 173). Republican administrations in other southern cities sometimes hired black policemen, but with the collapse of Reconstruction, Savannah's preference for white police supported by white citizens had become the pattern in every southern city. Throughout the South, black citizens were persecuted by the entire machinery of government, and the police stood as the most visible and aggressive element of that government. White supremacy in Savannah was most effective; five years after the war, nine out of ten blacks in Savannah still owned nothing (Ayers 1984).

Absolute poverty, political powerlessness, and a police force supported by white supremacy meant a dramatic increase in black prisoners. Without funds for facilities, state legislators passed the buck. In 1866 the Georgia legislature, for instance, passed a series of laws transferring the punishment of many criminals from the state penitentiary to the counties. Counties were authorized to work the convicts on public roads or hire them out to private contractors. Other southern states followed suit. The birth of the chain gang transformed the punishment of black "crime" from a heavy expense for the state to a revenue-increasing opportunity for the counties. In one set of legislative moves, the entire criminal justice system of the South became redirected. Before the war there had been almost no black convicts, only white. Before the war, a county lost money by prosecuting a minor criminal, but after the adoption of the chain gang, the incentives—racial as well as economic—were rather different. Black chain gangs reduced the imprisoned population (taking the pressure off overcrowded, understaffed jails) and provided labor for primitive, sometimes impassible roads (Ayers 1984).

The chain gang also meant the reenslavement of black people in America. Southern white men were quick to act on their advantage. Now even a misdemeanor could be used to white economic advantage: "a defendant, convicted of a misdemeanor, may be, and frequently is, sentenced to ten days hard labor for his crime, and to three, six or eight months, for costs," observed an Alabama legislator. "In such cases, his poverty seems to be punished more severely than his offense against the law." Or as a black New Orleans newspaper bitterly and accurately complained about sentencing, "three days for stealing, and eighty-seven for being colored" (quoted in Ayers 1984, 178).

As we have seen in chapter 9 (section I), by 1870 the Ku Klux Klan had become a strong force in nearly every southern state. It intimidated the black base of Republican support and suppressed much of the Republican vote (Colvin 1997). By the second Grant administration a broad retreat from Reconstruction was well under way. By the mid-1870s Supreme Court decisions had further undermined federal enforcement of Reconstruction laws. Perhaps the key decision followed federal prosecutions for violations of the civil rights of those African Americans murdered in the 1873 Colfax Massacre in Grant Parish, Louisiana. Black citizens had attempted to protect a duly elected Republican parish government from armed seizure by white Democrats following a contested governor's race. After a three-week siege, the defenders were overwhelmed and a slaughter ensued, including the mass murder of 50 African Americans who had disarmed under a truce flag (Foner 1988).

Federal indictments of the white men who had committed these atrocities were sought under the 1871 Ku Klux Klan Act. Arguing on behalf of the victims, lawyers alleged that a conspiracy existed to deprive their clients of their civil rights. Despite what would appear to be a straightforward case, federal prosecutors were able to obtain only three convictions. In 1876, the Supreme Court in *U.S.* v. *Cruikshank* overturned these convictions, ruling that the law did not prohibit acts by private citizens, only acts by state governments. Federal prosecutions of terrorist acts committed against African Americans were no longer possible. Now black citizens were forced to rely on local officials for protection, and, as Colvin reminds, "only in a very few places were local law enforcement able and willing to provide such protection" (1997, 231).

Now with federal acquiescence, the South slowly avenged its military defeat, not upon the North but upon the formerly enslaved and recently freed. Widespread terrorism plus economic growth in the 1880s combined to support an increase in black migration throughout the South. This movement of African Americans was especially pronounced among young men who searched for the best wages possible, hoping to escape the quasi-slavery of sharecropping. White men, especially planters, determined to maintain a reliable and cheap labor force, were furious. The issues may have been economic but a sexual image often seems to appear when white men speak of black men: "Our young negro men are becoming tramps, and moving about over the country in gangs to get the most remunerative work" (quoted in Ayers 1992, 24; Colvin 1997, 235).

Free black men created such uneasiness among whites that white people became determined to distance themselves as much as possible. One thinks of the pouty rage of a jilted lover: don't come near me! Segregation in the South took time; it did not follow immediately after Reconstruction in the 1870s. In fact, the term "segregation" is a twentieth-century concept (Ayers 1992). But the southern system of racial separation was evident by the 1880s when the railroad became a common means of transportation. Recall that Ida B. Wells was forcibly ejected from a white car on the Chesapeake, Ohio, and Southwestern Railroad. Racial segregation was not only gendered; it was sexualized (Ayers 1992). In those places where only men or only women were likely to interact, racial separation tended to be more relaxed. But in places, such as railroad cars or eating establishments, where both men and women were likely to be present, racial separation became strictly enforced. Segregation followed from "the nearly hysterical fear that black men might have sexual relations with white women" (Colvin 1997, 236).

Young black men were not the only ones on the move in the late nineteenth century. Whites moved too. In fact, they left the South at a much higher rate than black men and women. Poor whites were driven from the countryside by the crop lien and indebtedness. Many migrated within the South, moving from rural to urban areas. As economic opportunities in trade and law expanded in southern cities and towns, the grown children of wealthy planters began leaving plantations to participate in the emerging town-based southern economy (Colvin 1997).

White migration from plantations to southern towns and cities reflected a fundamental shift in the structure of economic and political dominance. The old planter class declined as a new commercial-industrial class expanded and asserted its interests. In many cases, however, planters and the town-based business class overlapped to the extent that they were often one and the same. Still, these white men had changed; a calculating ethic, presumably new to the South, began to spread. Rarely without pretensions of representing the "Old South," the University of Virginia, through its student newspaper, lamented in 1891, "it is very sad to see the old freedom from mean mercenary motives passing away, and instead, growing up in the breasts of our fellow southerners, the sordid, cold blooded, commercial money idea that has always been the marked characteristic of other sections of the country" (quoted in Ayers 1992, 26). A market revolution was well under way in the South as the nineteenth century drew to a close. "But unlike the market revolution that occurred in the North from 1815 to 1845," Colvin notes, "the southern version was not tempered with the spirit of benevolence" (1997, 236).

In the heated electoral contests between Democrats and Populists, blacks often held the swing votes. Populist candidates, most notably Tom Watson of Georgia, appealed directly to black voters by emphasizing their common economic interests with white farmers, tenants, and workers (Ayers 1992). "In their platforms southern Populists denounced lynch law and the convict lease and called for the defense of the Negro's political rights" (Woodward 1951/1971, 257). The Populist strategy "made blacks a potent political force, one that needed to be made quickly impotent if white elites were to survive politically" (Colvin 1997, 240).

The Populists failed to bring about a South that protected the economic interests of both black and white workers, nor were they able to work through even their own internal racial divisions. The Populists won a number of impressive victories at the local level in 1890, but these were short-lived. In Arkansas, where the Populists had been strongest, Democrats defeated Alliance members by characterizing them "race traitors" (Ayers 1992, 244), a term used by a contemporary journal of the "new abolitionism." Fueled by success, Democrats intensified their racist campaign to splinter the Populists. With characteristic southern insensitivity, Populist Tom Watson acknowledged in

1892: "The argument against the independent political movement in the South may be boiled down into the word—'nigger'" (quoted in McMath 1993, 173). Watson himself apparently decided if you can't beat 'em join 'em, but that is a story for another occasion.

The short-lived success of Populism precipitated waves of antiblack hysteria that supported white supremacy. This wave of southern racism succeeded in separating Populist blacks and whites, guaranteeing the demise of the movement. Not unlike racial politics today, this hysteria focused primarily on black crime, both real and imagined. This hysteria expressed itself in many forms, not the least of which was lynching. Other forms included the use of chain gangs and convict leasing (Colvin 1997).

It is true that the late 1880s and early 1890s saw rising crime in the South (Ayers 1992). Statistics were unreliable or unavailable, making it easier for whites to fantasize that it was blacks, especially black men, who were responsible. Many whites were unable to distinguish between law-abiding from lawbreaking African Americans. In 1876, John T. Brown, the principal keeper of the Georgia Penitentiary, spoke for many southern whites when he declared: "The only difference existing between colored convicts and the colored people at large consists in the fact that the former have been caught in the commission of a crime, tried and convicted, while the latter have not. The entire race is destitute of character" (quoted in Tolnay and Beck 1995, 17). Even University of Michigan Professor James Cutler was partially seduced by this white fantasy of black criminality, writing in 1905 that

> [l]ynching has been resorted to by the whites not merely to wreak vengeance, but to terrorize and restrain this lawless element in the negro population. Among southern people the conviction is general that terror is the only restraining influence that can be brought to bear upon vicious negroes. The negroes fear nothing so much as force, and should they once get the notion that there is a reasonable hope of escape from punishment, the whites in many parts of the South would be at their mercy. (quoted in Tolnay and Beck 1995, 19)

This white fantasy of black criminality became "fact" thanks in part to lurid stories of black violence printed in southern newspapers. "Virtually every issue of every southern newspaper contained an account of black wrongdoing; if an episode from nearby could not be found, episodes were imported from as far away as necessary; black crimes perpetrated in the North were especially attractive" (Ayers 1992, 153). But not just the North of course; in early August 1898, Richard Thurmond was lynched in Tippah County, Mississippi. According to the Memphis *Commercial Appeal*, "His cold stiff body [was] an object lesson to the worthless bucks that lounge around there" (quoted in Tolnay and Beck 1995, 43). As Colvin puts the matter, a "demonization of blacks was taking place in the press, fed by both white hysteria and, no doubt, a real increase in criminal activities among some blacks" (Colvin 1997, 241). The truth of the matter was more likely that, in the 1880s and early 1890s, homicide increased dramatically among *both* European- and African Americans (Woodward 1951/1971; Colvin 1997).

What fueled this white fantasy of black criminality? Brundage (1993) suggests a combination of factors were at work: dread of social amalgamation, contempt for and resistance to black education as well as for black efforts toward advancement in general. A new generation of white supremacists were fired by the conviction that blacks, especially those members of the new generation unschooled in "appropriate" behavior by slavery, were retrogressing into savagery. For these postbellum whites it was indisputable (despite the facts) that a new class of criminal blacks was responsible for the epidemic of crime that threatened to overwhelm the region (Brundage 1993).

The fantasy of black criminality was (and remains) impermeable to facts. One hundred years ago, southern whites continued to insist that lynchings were the predictable and absolutely necessary consequence of black crime, particularly sexual assaults. Just as the fantasy obscured the reality of lynching, it was impervious to criticism and allowed no hope for a future significantly different from the present. John Temple Graves, the Atlanta newspaper editor, told an astonished Chautauqua audience in 1903 that "it [lynching] is here to stay." Lynchings, Graves and other southern whites speculated, would disappear not because lynchers were criticized, but because blacks might finally become like whites. Only when blacks became law-abiding citizens and no longer posed a threat to whites (specifically to white women), the argument went, would mob violence cease. Graves was sure that "lynching will never hereafter be discontinued in this republic until the crime which provokes it is destroyed" (quoted passages in Brundage 1993, 53).

In imagining crime—especially sexual crimes—as the "difference" between whites and blacks and utilizing that "difference" to disempower African Americans illustrates, in an American context, how Foucault conceived the discourses of sexuality as intersecting with discourses of race. As Ann Laura Stoler (1995) points out, Foucault's earlier focus on the normalization of power described in *Discipline and Punish* broadened in *The History of Sexuality* to a concern with the power of normalization. Sexuality is not necessarily opposed to and subversive of power. On the contrary, in *The History of Sexuality*, Foucault writes that sexuality is a "dense transfer point" of power, charged with "instrumentality" (1978, 103). While writing about Europe, his point extends to the United States, and especially to the American South: "far from being repressed in [nineteenth century] society, [sexuality] was constantly aroused" (1978, 148; quoted in Stoler 1995, 3). Why was sexuality such an obsession of the nineteenth-century bourgeois order? Could it be both a clue to and a cover-up of a sexual crime? Consider the convict-lease system.

The Convict-Lease System

For half a century following the Civil War, convict camps punctuated the southern landscape. Thousands of mostly young black men spent their short lives in the convict-lease system, underground in mines or nearly underwater in swamps during the day, in wet clothes and filthy shacks or cages during the night. Women comprised 7 percent of the South's postwar imprisoned; they were nearly all black. About half of those in the lease system had been sentenced for theft or burglary, often involving petty amounts. White men with capital, from the North as well as the South, bought the labor of these imprisoned, reenslaved black people. The largest mining and railroad companies in the region as well as small businesses fought each other to win the leases. Deteriorating antebellum penitentiaries were few and relatively unpopulated. Only a few white men convicted of murder, a few black men too sick to work, and a few women (white and black) remained in the dilapidated penitentiaries. Wardens had little to do, for the state had become almost irrelevant in the punishment of criminals (Ayers 1984).

On the surface, the convict-lease system was a source of political patronage for local and state politicians, providing jobs for their unemployed party workers (Ayers 1992). The system was thoroughly corrupt; kickbacks and bribes to public officials usually accompanied the awarding of convict leases to private industry (Ayers 1984). Politics in this "New South" of the late nineteenth century was based on patronage; convict leasing became a major "currency" of exchange. There were those southerners who worked to reform or abolish the convict-leasing system, such as Julia Tutwiler of Alabama, but they were inevitably defeated by those state legislators who had personal investments in the system. For example, Senator Joseph E. Brown of Georgia had a 20-year lease for 300 "able-bodied" convicts to work in his Dade Coal Mines, for which he paid 8 cents a day per inmate. He was not alone: Georgia Governor John B. Gordon was part owner of an outfit that arranged for the leasing of convicts; Colonel Arthur S. Colyar, a boss in the Tennessee Democratic party, leased that state's convicts for the Tennessee Coal and Iron Company; and influential businessman J. S. Hamilton won the exclusive right to lease Mississippi's convicts for a monthly fee of $1.10 each, which he quickly subleased to railroads and other contractors for $9.00 a month per convict (Oshinsky 1996, 43–44; Woodward 1951/1971, 215; Colvin 1997, 244). But corruption is only part (and for us the less interesting part) of the story.

The system had an important economic impact. In fact, convict leasing was perhaps crucial in the early transformation of the postbellum South toward industrial capitalism. In the 1880s and 1890s, convict labor was particularly concentrated in mining, especially in Alabama, Georgia, Florida, and Tennessee, the states that leased the largest number of convicts. In 1890 alone, more than 27,000 convicts were leased in the South. The mining states of Alabama and Tennessee enjoyed the most profitable system; convicts there earned approximately $100,000 for the state treasuries every year, almost one-tenth of the states' total revenue. Georgia, Mississippi, Arkansas, North Carolina, and Kentucky made the lesser but still profitable sums of $25,000 to $50,000 each per year (Ayers 1984; Colvin 1997).

The system had an enormous impact on free workers. Not only were their wage rates driven lower by the competition of cheap convict labor, but free workers' efforts to organize labor unions and to employ strikes as tactics in contract negotiations were also effectively undermined (Mancini 1996). In Whitfield County (Georgia), the local newspaper complained in 1893 that "free labor is absolutely driven out" of North Georgia by Senator Joseph E. Brown's convict labor (quoted in Ayers 1984, 213). Workers understood their dilemma; more than twenty strikes were waged against convict labor by coal miners alone in the 1880s and 1890s (Ayers 1984; Colvin 1997). In Birmingham, Alabama, in 1885, workers founded an Anti-Convict League, charging mine owners of using convicts to keep wages at subsistence level, thereby making Birmingham into "the dumping ground for crime ... the Botany Bay of the Commonwealth" (quoted in Ayers 1984, 214).

Worker resistance to convict labor played a crucial role in the history of southern organized labor. The highly visible, viciously unfair, and outrageously corrupt system united fiercely independent miners across the South. In Alabama, black and white miners fought the convict-lease system side by side, carrying banners that read: "We, the Colored Miners of Alabama, Stand with Our White Brothers." In Tennessee, the funeral for a black miner killed in the protest against convict labor was attended by several thousand white men in an act of solidarity. A considerable number of the militiamen sent to smash the miners' struggle against convict labor were in sympathy with their presumed adversaries. Many members of the militia requested leaves of absence during the struggle; others threatened desertion. Aware of the sympathy and eager to encourage it, miners brought militiamen food and invited them into their homes. At one point the miners voted their ostensible opponents "excellent fellows," and when a soldier asked rhetorically, "What's the matter with the miners?" the militia chanted in unison, "They are all right" (quoted passages in Ayers 1984, 216).

Between 1881 and 1900 coal miners struck twenty-two times in protest of convict labor. An 1891 strike in Tennessee was fought by the governor, John Buchanan, who sent three companies of militia to escort convicts back to the mines. But the miners refused to cave in and Buchanan was forced to call a special session of the general assembly. The Tennessee legislature, with Populists in control, did nothing to help the miners. After months of negotiating, the miners, armed and starving, set free all 500 convicts at the mines of the three companies. Other miners followed suit, burning stockades and railroading convicts out of the area. Although state officials replaced the convicts, the price became too high, and the legislature abolished the convict-lease system in Tennessee in 1895 (Ayers 1984).

In many camps, guards aroused the sleeping prisoners at 4:30 in the morning and had them at work within half an hour. They received forty minutes for dinner, and "then worked until after sundown, and as long as it is light enough for a guard to see how to shoot. They are worked every day, rain or shine, cold or wet" (quoted in Ayers 1984, 193). "Obviously," writes Edward L. Ayers, "the roots of such forced labor reached into slavery" (1984, 191). Like slaves, the conditions under which convicts lived and worked were, at best, brutal (Woodward 1951/1971). These inhuman conditions disclose the intersections between race and sexuality in postbellum southern society, and, in particular, the prison. There is no hint of rehabilitation in these examples of southern living. In rolling iron cages, "prisoners slept side by side, shackled together, on narrow wooden slabs. They relieved themselves in a single bucket and bathed in the same filthy tub of water. With no screens on the cages, insects swarmed everywhere. It was like a small piece of hell, an observer noted—the stench, the chains, the sickness, and the heat" (Oshinsky 1996, 59). The men were supervised by armed guards "notorious for shooting with little provocation" (Ayers 1992, 126).

Many mining companies which exploited convicts used the "task system," in which a group of three inmates had to mine a certain amount of coal each day, or the entire group would receive several floggings. In Alabama, prisoners leased to mining companies were subjected to torture, including being "hung from makeshift crucifixes, stretched on wooden racks, and placed in coffin-sized sweatboxes for hours at a time" (Oshinsky 1996, 79; see Mancini 1996, 76, 115, 123 for other reports of torture in convict-leasing camps). In many mining camps convicts were forced to work throughout the winter without shoes; they stood in cold putrid water much of the time. In turpentine camps, convicts, chained together, were forced to work at a trot for the entire workday (Colvin 1997).

The white men who leased convicts felt no incentive to treat them humanely, let alone well. Probably slaves had been treated with greater care, if only because slaves had economic value. As Ida B. Wells (1892b/1969) appreciated: "During the slave regime, the southern white man owned the Negro body and soul. It was to his interest to dwarf the soul and preserve the body. ... The slave was rarely killed, he was too valuable; it was easier and quite as effective, for discipline or revenge, to see him 'Down South.' But Emancipation came and the vested interests of the white man in the Negro's body were lost" (7). Indeed, black convicts had no value and were easily replaced. Under convict leasing, replacement of injured or dead convicts involved little if any extra expense for the lessee, who could count on a constant supply of able-bodied convicts from the criminal justice system (Mancini 1996). Leased convicts suffered continual illness, brutal punishments, starvation, and for many, death (Colvin 1997).

Prison conditions were documented by officials who made only occasional inspections. Alabama penitentiary inspectors found prisons packed several times beyond their capacities; they were "as filthy, as a rule, as dirt could make them, and both prisons and prisoners were infested with vermin" (quoted in Woodward 1951/1971, 213). Officials reported that convicts were cruelly punished, often without pretext, often excessively. The sick were neglected. A Mississippi grand jury reported that "most of them [convicts] have their backs cut in great wales, scars and blisters, some with the skin peeling off in pieces as the result of severe beatings. ... They were lying there dying ... [with] live vermin crawling over their faces" (quoted in Woodward 1951/1971, 214; Colvin 1997, 247). More often prison officials tried to hide the reality of the system; their reports were exemplary instances of obfuscation and officialese. Reports in Alabama, for instance, praised the "good order" of the convict camps, yet even a glance at the statistical tables accompanying these reports indicated that during some years almost half of the prisoners were dying (Ayers 1984).

During 1868 and 1869, respectively, as the system was instituted, 17 and 18 percent of Alabama's convicts died. This jumped to 41 percent in 1870 (Ayers 1984). By 1880, the death rate dropped to 11 percent (Mancini 1996), but in 1883 a doctor estimated that in Alabama most convicts had died within three years (Adamson 1984; Oshinksy 1996). As a study of Alabama's county penal system reported in 1886, the failure of prison officials to keep records of those leased out meant that many convicts simply "disappeared as completely as if the earth had opened and swallowed them. The very fact of their existence has been forgotten, except for the few at the humble home, who still wait and look in vain for him who does not come" (quoted in Ayers 1984, 226). The disappearance of convicts was well known among African Americans; wives of prisoners worked frantically for the release of their husbands. Black women sought out local white men of influence and wrote letters pleading with the governor (Ayers 1984).

In 1881, the death rate among Arkansas prisoners was 25 percent (Woodward 1951/1971). At some railroad camps and mines, the death rate ranged as high as 36 and 53 percent of convicts (Adamson 1983; Oshinsky 1996). In Texas, the official death rate was not as high; an average of 102 state convicts died each year between 1878 and 1900, a rate of approximately 3.5 percent, but this figure is questionable. Many more prisoners must have died—"unofficially"—in a system where the average life of a convict was seven years (Oshinsky 1996; Walker 1988). The southern states had an average death rate among its prisoners that was nearly three times the rate in northern states; in Mississippi alone in the 1880s, it was 9 to 15 times the northern rate (Ayers 1984; Mancini 1996; Oshinsky 1996; Colvin 1997).

Two-thirds to three-fourths of the convicts working and dying in the convict-lease system were in their twenties or younger. In Mississippi, for example, black children and adolescents comprised one-fourth of all convicts leased to private entrepreneurs. Sexual assaults in convict-lease camps were common. Boys and young men were continually assaulted by older convicts. (In the southern states no distinction was made between adult criminals and juvenile delinquents.) One investigating committee reported that Tennessee's branch prisons were "hell holes of rage, cruelty, despair, and vice;" homosexual rape of young boys occurred daily and "gal boys" were in constant demand (quoted in Ayers 1984, 200). Women were only occasionally separated from men when leased out. Men and sometimes women were chained together, pressed together on the same bunks. Like boys and young men, women prisoners too were regularly raped (Ayers 1984; Mancini 1996; Colvin 1997; Oshinsky 1996; Woodward 1951/1971).

There was little pretense that the convict-lease system would somehow rehabilitate the prisoner. Some white men claimed that the system taught blacks how to work (Ayers 1984). But in general convicts' labor was exploited without disguise or conscience. It was pure punishment of the body; what happened in the soul or the mind was of no interest to southern prison officials in the late nineteenth century. Instead of providing these offenders with programs designed to cultivate their intelligence and heighten their moral sense, the prison was designed "to grind them and their race down" (Colvin 1997, 249). As Colvin (1997) points out, the system was not driven by any penological philosophy at all. Economic and racialized exploitation was not disguised by social science or philosophy. The brutal treatment of black convicts required no philosophical justification for the white southern majority. But this was not exclusively a southern penological point of view; southern defenders of convict leasing found receptive audiences among many northerners in the penological community who had become persuaded by "scientific" racial doctrines that had "established" linkages among heredity, race, and crime (Ayers 1984; Colvin 1997).

There was some criticism of the system by northerners, prompting, as usual, southern defensiveness. In 1881 Whitfield County's *North Georgia Citizen* complained that "[t]he North ... has seen fit to condemn the system [convict lease] in unmeasured terms, characterizing it as a relic of barbarism. Now, we do not care a brass farthing what the opinions of the saintly(!) North may be upon this or any other subject" (quoted in Ayers 1984, 218). Even though the majority of white southerners were beginning to grow skeptical of the system's benefits, they could not bear to read their penal practices denounced by northerners. Even those who worked for reform of the system resented the North's criticism (Ayers 1984). As Ayers observed: "Not unlike their antebellum slaveholding predecessors, apologists for the lease rationalized a 'necessary evil' into a 'positive good'" (1984, 219). Indeed, one white southerner asserted that "to the ignorant negro, brought to manhood during the days of slavery, a term in the penitentiary was without question the best lesson he could obtain in citizenship" (quoted in Ayers 1984, 220).

Accompanying the convict-leasing system was the largest number of lynchings in American history. This period was characterized by an intense rape hysteria which swept the South: "Lynching was a form of 'law enforcement' in areas where the legal system was weak, and was driven by many of the same forces that drove the increase in convict leasing. Where convict leasing was used as punishment in more settled areas, lynching was used in more sparsely populated areas" (Colvin 1997, 250–251). In this regard, lynching and convict leasing were two sides of the same coin: white male mutilation of black (mostly) male bodies.

These three interrelated phenomena—lynching, the convict-leasing system, the hysteria over black crime, especially (fantasized) sexual crime—set the stage for the enactment of Jim Crow laws, which established legalized segregation in almost all areas of southern life, except in the bedroom after sundown. "When complete, the new codes of White Supremacy were vastly more complex than the antebellum slave codes or the Black Codes of 1865–1866, and, if anything, they were stronger and more rigidly enforced" (Woodward 1951/1971, 212). As legalized segregation became routine, the insistence on "punishment" (both official and unofficial) receded as white solidarity was reestablished on the foundation of segregation and a renewal of white supremacy. By splitting up, then absorbing populism, the Democratic Party re-energized itself as white unity was restored in a new "solid South." Southern populism then deteriorated toward racism, nativism, anti-intellectualism, and religious intolerance (Williamson 1984; Colvin 1997). Tom Watson and William Jennings Bryan personified in different ways this last development. Watson would become instrumental in the lynching of Leo Frank. In 1925 Bryan prosecuted a Tennessee teacher named John Thomas Scopes for teaching evolution. Scopes, as you recall, was defended by Clarence Darrow (see Pinar et al. 1995, 778).

The convict-leasing system began to decline in the late 1890s and early 1900s. Changing labor market conditions, including the states' demands for higher fees, narrowed the difference between the costs of convict and free laborers (Mancini 1996; Colvin 1997). Like slavery, the convict-leasing system in the South has been compared to the Nazi prison/work camps (Elkins 1959; Woodward 1951/1971). In terms of conditions for inmates/workers, Colvin concurs. "But," he adds, "the southern lease system lacked a key element of Nazi work camps, which Foucault would be quick to point out. Convict leasing in the South did not have the maniacal commitment to rationalization and bureaucracy seen in the Nazi system. Southern lease camps were brutal but somewhat casual and lackadaisical, as reflected in their high rates of escape" (Colvin 1997, 261).

Not until the first two decades of the twentieth century did the South finally discontinue the practice of leasing convicts. Except for Alabama: in 1920 that state had still failed to pass a law ending the control of state convicts by anyone other than the state. "To the eyes of the world," Ayers notes,

> the replacements for the convict lease system seemed virtually indistinguishable from their beleaguered predecessor. Southern states did not erect new penitentiaries, but instead worked their convicts on chain gangs on public roads or on huge state-owned farms. ... The image of black convicts in striped uniforms laboring under the gaze of armed white guards has endured as one of the most telling symbols of the American South. ... From every perspective, even that of prominent southern whites, the convict camps were incontrovertible evidence of the New South's moral failure. (1984, 222)

On May 3, 1995, more than 40 years after it had abolished the practice, Alabama reintroduced the chain gang, a contemporary version of nineteenth-century convict-leasing, as reported in the *Washington Post* for May 4, 1995. As Edward Ayers has pointed out, "crime and punishment, as much as anything else, measure the continuity of the South with the past." He continues:

> [T]he region still leads the nation in homicide and assault rates, still holds the greatest number of men on death row, and still contains the largest number of handguns. For over a century now, the South has seemed to be disappearing—yet it persists in a thousand subtle and obvious ways. The region always manages to resurrect itself in new guises, for among every new generation walk the ghosts of the old. (Ayers 1984, 276)

Now its ghosts haunt the entire nation. In the final two decades of the twentieth century, the political ascendancy of the South—through its coalition with conservative Republicans nationwide—meant that what before had been distinctively southern patterns of racialized criminalization and "legalized lynching" would now become national patterns. Under the cover of a "war on drugs," white men would continue to pursue the bodies of young black men.

III. The Racial Politics of Criminalization in the Twentieth Century: The War on Drugs

[B]lack masculinity is not merely a social identity in crisis. It is also a key site of ideological representation, a site upon which the nation's crises come to be dramatized, demonized, and dealt with.

—Kobena Mercer, "Endangered Species: Danny Tisdale and Keith Piper" (1992)

Media fascination around black masculinity is almost always concentrated in three areas: sex, crime, and sports.

—Thelma Golden, "My Brother," in *Black Male: Representations of Masculinity in Contemporary American Art* (1994)

The evacuation of young black males from the public sphere has proceeded on every front. As dropouts from the educational system, as victims of suicides, homicides, and the penal system, as casualties of the incredible shrinking welfare state, as fatalities of the crack economy and the AIDS emergency, and as targets of new and more virulent forms of racism, the social obsolescence of black male youth has been quite systematic.

—Andrew Ross, "The Gangster and the Diva," in Thelma Golden, *Black Male: Representations of Masculinity in Contemporary American Art* (1994)

The prize is the souls of black men, but the contest is carried out on the body of the black male.

—Clyde Taylor, "The Game," in Thelma Golden, *Black Male: Representations of Masculinity in Contemporary American Art* (1994)

By 1993 local, state, and federal levels of government were spending $31 billion on a failed drug war, in many respects a racialized war, directed primarily at African-American and Latino males. This figure was six billion higher than that spent on A.F.D.C., the whipping boy of the right wing, that symbol of liberal largesse ($25 billion). Whether as a war on young black men or on poor children, "the politics of crime and welfare came with a decidedly racist cast" (Miller 1996, 1). The American public was informed that the reason for this explosion in funding in antidrug activities was an explosion of crime, especially violent crime. However, as we have seen, rates of violent crime have, in general, decreased over the last three decades (Miller 1996).

While violent crime decreased, federal, state, and local funding of the justice system increased during the 1980s. Average direct federal, state, and local expenditures for police increased 416 percent; for courts, 585 percent; for prosecution and legal services, 1,019 percent; for public legal defense, 1,255 percent; and for corrections, 990 percent. Federal spending for justice grew by

666 percent, county spending increased 711 percent, and state spending surged 848 percent. By 1990, the country was spending at least $75 billion annually in direct costs to arrest and incarcerate offenders. However, as Jerome G. Miller (1996) points out, even these figures are grossly understated. With the passage of federal crime legislation and the anticrime frenzy across the nation, the United States was spending in excess of $200 billion annually on the crime-control industry by the mid-1990s.

In 1991, there were an estimated 14,211,900 arrests in the United States. Only one in five of these arrests was for a serious crime. Approximately six million of these arrests were "new admissions"—that is, the arrestee was a first-time offender in that jurisdiction. In 1991, arrestable offenses included everything from forgery (103,700), to public drunkenness (881,100), to curfew and loitering (93,400), to "runaways" (177,000). The largest single category was "other," a flexible category indeed. More than one in five (3,240,000) of all arrests in that year were marked "other" (Miller 1996, 14). Over 90 percent of rural arrests and 82 percent of city arrests had little or nothing to do with violent crime (Miller 1996).

Similar patterns are evident among those arrested for drug offenses. Whereas there had been a modest 8 percent increase in the number of those charged with drug sales during the 1980s, there was a 500 percent increase in those charged with possession during the same period. The percentage of individuals being sent to prison for violent crimes fell progressively from 1980 to 1990, while by 1990, at least 4 million people were being arrested each year for "consensual" crimes. African Americans, Latinos, and other minorities were overrepresented among those arrested. In 1992, for instance, the National Center on Institutions and Alternatives (N.C.I.A.) conducted a survey of young black males in Washington, D.C.'s justice system. The Center found that approximately 75 percent of all the 18-year-old African-American males in the nation's capital could look forward to being arrested and jailed at least once before reaching age 35. The lifetime risk of incarceration of black males living in the District of Columbia was somewhere between 80 percent and 90 percent. In California, black men comprise only 3 percent of the population; they account for 40 percent of those entering state prisons. A 1991 study of the Los Angeles County Adult Detention Center estimated that nearly one-third of all the young black men (ages 20–29) living in Los Angeles County had already been jailed at least once in that same year (Miller 1996).

The Uniformed Crime Reports (U.C.R.), to which I referred in the first section of this chapter, make police overcharging difficult to detect. Also omitted in these reports are such crucial narrative information as arrest summaries, victim statements, and other observational indicators that might help these data make sense. Whereas most European nations report crime statistics on the basis of convictions, the United States, through the U.S. Justice Department, inflates both the numbers and the seriousness of American crime by including complaints and arrests. Most newscasters, politicians, and policymakers ignore the fact that of every 100 individuals arrested for a felony, 43 are either not prosecuted or their cases are dismissed at the first court appearance. One study found that "despite the widely held belief that there was a significant increase in the level of criminal activity during the 1980s, in general, we find that neither data source depicts increasing levels of crime over this period" (quoted in Miller 1996, 29). Another study found that arrests of black men rose during the 1980s after remaining constant during the 1970s, and the public, especially white, perception that crime has gotten worse only seems to intensify (Miller 1996).

While the national homicide rate has remained at about 9 or 10 per 100,000 for the past two decades, rates have always varied from one region to another. Historically, the northern tier from New England to the Pacific Northwest has seen the lowest rates of homicide, whereas the middle states have had somewhat higher rates, but still well below the national average. Homicide rates have always been much higher in the upper coastal south, with the southern Atlantic states averaging 10.9 murders per 100,000, the west south-central suffering a rate of 14.7, Texas a rate of 16.1, and Louisiana, the leader, with a rate of 18.5 murders per 100,000 residents (Miller 1996).

To help us think about these regional differences, Jerome Miller (1996) quotes cultural historian David Hackett Fischer (1989), who locates the sources of regional differences in American violence to the markedly different "folkways" of the four large waves of English-speaking immigrants who settled in New England, Virginia, Appalachia, and the Delaware Valley between 1629 and 1775. Each of these waves of immigrants exhibited distinct cultural traditions regarding violence. Fischer (1989) concludes that homicide rates can be more dependably correlated with what he characterizes as "cultural regions of origin than with urbanization, poverty, or any material factor" (889; quoted in Miller 1996, 31).

The unusually high levels of violence in the South have been well known for centuries. After visiting the newly independent United States in the 1790s, Isaac Weld recounted stories of fighting and eye-gougings he had witnessed in Virginia, reports that were already familiar features of southern travel accounts. "Our national mythology," Edward L. Ayers reminds us, "assumes violence to be a natural outgrowth of the frontier; the explanation seems almost commonsensical to most Americans" (1984, 12). But, he notes, in other English colonies such as Canada and Australia the fact of "frontier" did not mean outrageously high levels of violence among the settlers. The violence associated with the genocide of Native Americans and the violence that characterized many western cattle towns and the open range in the post–Civil War years may well have been southern violence extended westward, especially by way of Texas (Ayers 1984).

Why was (is) the South so violent? Working from the key role culture plays in violent behavior, historians have pointed to several "fatal flaws" within (white) southern culture: among them a "brooding and pervasive sense of grievance and displaced frustration, an undue affection for guns, and a pessimistic evaluation of human nature that automatically assumed violence to be the inevitable—if unfortunate—recourse in the face of intractable problems" (Ayers 1984, 12). The homosocial economy of "honor" played an important role and, no doubt, the unspeakable violence of the slave system reverberated throughout the broader society.

In approximately 68 percent of crimes designated as violent in our time, no physical injury was suffered by the victim. Of those victims of all crime classified as "violent" in 1991, for instance, just over 1 percent required a hospital stay of one day or more. Of course, murder victims do not require hospitalization. But reported homicides in 1992 (22,540) constituted only 0.003 percent of the violent crime incidents across the nation (as reported in victimization surveys). As we have seen, the group most victimized by the police practice of overcharging and most likely to obtain a "felony arrest" criminal record are black men. "My own experience," Miller comments, "in hundreds of criminal cases over the past two decades leads me to conclude that the major actors in the criminal justice drama are increasingly eager to arrest on the highest charge possible, prosecute to the limits of the law, and demand the longest prison terms potentially available" (1996, 36). Part of what is going on, Miller suggests, is an industry intent on producing sufficient numbers of new "clientele" to justify its existence and its expansion, requiring more police, arrests, prosecutions, and prisons.

While this may be "news" to many white readers, black citizens have long been clear about the racial politics of crime. That clarity shows up in polls that indicate that African Americans and Latinos/Latinas view the police rather differently than do whites. For instance, 43 percent of all respondents to a 1994 *New York Times* poll believed that corruption was widespread in the city police force. When these numbers were analyzed by race, however, 58 percent of blacks polled and 51 percent of Hispanic respondents viewed the police as corrupt, compared to only 32 percent of whites (Miller 1996).

In recent years conservatives have claimed that there is an explosion of stranger-on-stranger violent crime in America. Miller finds that the facts do not support the claim. A 1993 study of homicide in the largest urban counties of the nation reported that approximately 80 percent of murder victims and their killers were acquainted with, or related to, each other. Fifty percent of all murder victims had a social or romantic relationship with the murderer, a fact supported by statistics on the gendered violence in the family reviewed in chapter 13. Among black victims, 87 percent were either acquainted with or related to the murderer. Nationally, 94 percent of black homicide victims are killed by other blacks; 83 percent of white homicide victims are murdered by other whites. While it is true that some streets in some of the nation's large cities are more dangerous than they were fifty years ago (although probably not more than they were 100 years ago), this fact does not point to the existence of a "new breed" of violent offender (Miller 1996).

At every stage of the judicial process there is evidence of racial politics. For instance, of all the violent crimes brought to juvenile court from 1985 through 1989, fully 84 percent (202,300) were either handled informally, nonadjudicated, or simply dismissed. But a study conducted by the Florida Department of Corrections and Florida State University discloses a long-standing bias in the handling of African-American defendants during the pretrial period. An employed black male found guilty of drug crimes was six times more likely to be sentenced to incarceration than whites convicted of the same crimes. Nor is this pattern limited to Florida or the South. A journalistic investigation of over 650,000 criminal cases prosecuted between 1981 and 1990 in California showed that at virtually every stage of pretrial negotiations, whites received better treatment than nonwhites. Whites received more lenient sentences and in fact were less likely to go to prison than were African Americans (Miller 1996).

The War on Drugs

Perhaps the war on drugs ought to be renamed, for accuracy's sake, as the war on young black men. Nothing new in that, of course. Even the racialized association of illegal drug use is not new. For instance, there was no indication of disproportionate opiate use among African Americans one hundred years ago. In fact, studies in Florida and Tennessee made during World War I point to less opiate use proportionately among blacks than whites during that time. Facts aside, law enforcement agencies and the press had no doubt that blacks were using cocaine to a dangerous extent. A *New York Times* article from World War I, entitled "Negro Cocaine Fiends Are a New Southern Menace," suggests the links among race, sex, and drugs in the white mind (see Miller 1996, 81). The article reported that southern sheriffs had switched from .32-caliber guns to .38-caliber pistols in order to protect themselves from drug-empowered black men (Miller 1996).

The current "war on drugs" was declared by President Richard Nixon in 1970. Federal and state budgets in support of antidrug activities grew slowly until the late 1980s. Miller suggests that the death of University of Maryland black basketball star Len Bias from a cocaine overdose provided President and Mrs. Reagan the occasion to cast drug abuse as the major problem facing the nation. The "war" began in earnest. By 1992, the country was spending over $30 billion each year on the drug war. A war lost from the beginning, the continuing war on drugs does make explicit the racial politics of the American judicial system. While African Americans and Latinos comprise the overwhelming majority of those being arrested, convicted, and sentenced to prison for drug offenses, 76 percent of the illicit drug users in the United States are white, 14 percent are black, and 8 percent are Hispanic, as estimated by the U.S. Public Health Service's Substance Abuse and Mental Heath Services Administration in 1992. The fact that drug dealing in the city, in contrast to drug dealing in the suburbs, is often transacted in public areas makes it easier for law-enforcement personnel to focus their efforts on young black and Latino men (Miller 1996).

Their efforts have certainly "paid off." In Columbus, Ohio, where black males comprise less than 11 percent of the population, they comprise over 90 percent of the drug arrests. That means that black men in Columbus are arrested at 18 times the rate of whites. In Minneapolis (where a state court ruled that the sentences mandated by the legislature for possession or sale of crack cocaine were racist in their effect), although black men comprised only about 7 percent of the population, they were being arrested at a ratio of approximately 20:1 white males. Such patterns are hardly restricted to the large cities of the Midwest; they are repeated in cities across the nation (Miller 1996).

Penalties follow the same pattern. In 1991, 90 percent of the "crack" arrests nationally were of African Americans and other minorities; three-fourths of the arrests for powder cocaine were of whites. Sentences for possession of crack were usually three to four times longer than those for possession of the same amount of powder cocaine. While many—among them expert witnesses from the Addictions Researcher Center of the National Institute of Drug Abuse—have insisted that crack cocaine is more addictive more than powder cocaine, not one single study supports the claim (Miller 1996).

While failing to curb drug usage in the United States, the war on drugs has intensified urban violence. Jerome Miller (1996) believes "a strong case" can be made for the view that most of the violent gangs now found throughout Los Angeles are a response to a "heavy-handed" and racialized criminal justice system. He suggests that many of the complex social problems associated with poverty, unemployment, and family breakdown have been "birthed and nurtured" in county and state-run juvenile halls, camps, detention centers, reform schools, and prisons. These are all places where gangs quickly form. It is unsurprising that poor children are "fed a culture of violence" in their neighborhood by older children who have learned the tactics of group survival in correctional facilities. In this respect, poor children can be said to have been converted to crime by the criminal justice system: "The so-called war on drugs provides ample evidence that criminal justice procedures have intensified violence in the inner cities" (Miller 1996, 91). Even for adults, studies suggest an inverse relationship between the use of the death penalty and the rise in homicide. Put simply, official violence encourages an increase in unofficial violence (Miller 1996).

By the early 1990s, even researchers at the conservative Rand Corporation acknowledged the dismal results of criminal justice policies based primarily on deterrence. In a 1993 Rand paper on drugs, Robert J. MacCoun commented that "defenders of existing drug laws and enforcement policies need to recognize that their faith in severity-based deterrence is largely misguided and often counterproductive" (quoted in Miller 1996, 95). Yet, the war goes on, and a disproportionate number of black and poor people are sent to prison. Miller concludes: "[t]he prosecution of the war on drugs had done more to shatter the inner cities of America than decades of neglect and ineffective social programs" (1996, 120).

Rites of Puberty?

Especially for young black men, the experience of arrest and imprisonment sometimes seems to have become "something of a puberty rite, a transition to manhood." The experience "comes with deep, historical, racially anchored roots" and often involves a subjective struggle over whether to meekly assume or to aggressively reject the bifurcated identity the ritual demands. It is, Miller continues,

> an ambiguous puberty rite of disrespect and symbolic castration—from "assuming the position": being handcuffed; placed in a police van; moved from place to place; shackled to a line of peers and older African-American males; posed for a mug shot; tagged with an I.D. bracelet attached to a wrist or ankle; confined in crowded "tanks" or holding cells (a common

> toilet or open hole in the middle)—to appearing before a robed judge; being assigned a lawyer who controls one's destiny but whom one seldom meets; having a price set on one's head as bail; and, finally, joining one's peers or anxious relatives outside. (1996, 99)

This is reminiscent of what George Wright (1990) termed "legal lynching," except the death this time occurs slowly, over the duration of a long prison sentence.

While, as Miller indicates, the arrest ritual echoes historically, its damage is expressed in the psychological and social present, and it is specifically gendered and racialized. Because it is shared by many black men, Miller asserts the experience becomes a site of solidarity as well as a mark of subjugation: "This criminal justice rite of manhood confers the label of a renegade (or perhaps a 'weed'), fit to be treated as trash. The 'secrets' of the experience are shared with peers and adult males, the majority of whom have been subjected to the same rites. The experience in this sense touches archetypal memories in both races" (1996, 100). That is the spell under which we live. To bring this point home, that is, to grasp just how inured many—especially middle-class whites—have become to this particular criminal justice ritual, Miller quotes conservative legal scholar and federal judge Richard Posner. "It is curious to reflect," he writes, "that the arrest of Joseph K. in the first chapter of [Kafka's] *The Trial* is immensely more *civilized* than any arrest would be likely to be in the land of freedom on the threshold of the twenty-first century" (emphasis in original; quoted in Miller 1996, 100).

Not only black male solidarity is intensified by the criminal justice system; so also is black male hatred and suspicion. No one knows who is in the employ of the criminal justice system, and the fact that every deal could go wrong turns friends and brothers into potential traitors and enemies. Miller suggests that no single tactic of law enforcement has contributed more to violence in the inner cities than the widespread practice of populating the streets with informers offering deals to "snitches." This is no isolated phenomenon. Inner-city violence increased in a number of cities exactly at the time a large number of informers appeared on the streets. Miller cites an investigation conducted by the *National Law Journal* to suggest the scale of this operation. That study disclosed that the federal government alone paid approximately a half-billion dollars to informers from 1985 through 1993 (Miller 1996).

Law-enforcement agencies regard informers as key to infiltrating criminal organizations. But arrests have become so common in many poor black neighborhoods that they have undermined, in many cases destroyed, numerous families and peer relationships. Consequently, the government's massive reliance on informers threatens much more than criminal enterprise. It erodes and regularly destroys whatever social bonds remain in families, in the community, or on the streets. These loyalties, Miller points out, had in past years limited violence. Increasing the volatility of the situation is the large percentage of young black men who have served time in prisons and jails. The prison snitch, as we will see, is considered less than a "man." For the authorities to make a snitch of a young black male on the street amounts to nothing less than a gendered assault upon his identity as a man, upon his very masculinity. All this leads

Miller to conclude "that the criminal justice system itself has been a major contributor to breakdown in the inner cities" (1996, 10).

As Commissioner of Children and Youth in Pennsylvania, Jerome Miller directed an effort to remove 400 teenagers from an adult prison. While debriefing the young inmates as they were moved from a maximum-security prison to alternative settings, the term "fronting" was used repeatedly. Miller quotes one 16-year-old: "When I first got there this guy threatened me and told me he was going to make me his 'girl.' I yelled that I would beat his butt if he tried. I didn't know it then, but I'd just 'fronted' on him. I had challenged him in front of the others. The other inmates told me that I had only a few days to 'set up' a confrontation with the guy or I was fair game to be gang raped or taken as someone's 'punk'" (quoted in Miller 1996, 106). The young man waited for the occasion when, in front of others, he (falsely) accused the other inmate of trying to steal his toothpaste. He then struck the other man full in the face, breaking his nose. When the fight was stopped, both inmates had suffered injuries and were removed to solitary confinement for a month. But the new kid had publicly demonstrated his capacity to be violent and had thereby established his reputation as a man before the others. When he emerged from the isolation unit, he would be regarded as a "man" (Miller 1996).

This is no exotic prison ritual, unrelated to homosocial rituals outside the walls of the institution. What this young man did was little different than what many a southern white man has done to establish and/or preserve his "honor." Why is it one must prove one's "manhood" in the eyes of other men and by resorting to violence? Could it be that one's internal self-structure has been violently achieved? To demonstrate manhood one performs in the world the violence one has performed on oneself in the process of becoming a "man." The badge of courage is a sign that one has repudiated the pre-oedipal identification with the mother, and is therefore not a "girl." Perhaps in order to end violence "men" must become "girls."

In the meantime men remain obsessed with men, unacknowledged, of course. More specifically, white men remain preoccupied with black men, as, for instance, in the practice of "profiling," wherein police stop "suspicious" cars driven by black men who fit a "profile." More than a few black men serving time were arrested as a consequence of this practice. In prison, black men return the favor, as it were, and "profile" young white men.

A Society of Prisons

Even allowing for some duplication, the fact of 50 million criminal-history records in state files suggests that the United States has become a society of prisons. Approximately 90 percent of criminal records belong to men. As Jerome Miller suggests, the net of criminal justice has been so widely cast that it ensnares a substantial minority of American citizenry and the absolute majority of its minority citizens. Even racist whites can take no comfort in these figures, as studies in several disciplines, including education, indicate that labeling young people tends to create the realities such designations purport only to describe. In the criminal justice system, this means that these massive arrests could have the unanticipated consequence of producing the very criminal behavior it purported to deter (Miller 1996). As Foucault knew: "Detention causes recidivism" (1979/1995, 265).

It is clear that the rehabilitation model of probation has been abandoned. Increasingly, American probation officers, in concert with the prosecution, understand their job as pursuing any means necessary to move the probationer into prison. The motto for this practice was mounted on the office of one of California's chief probation officers: "Trail 'em, Surveil 'em, Nail 'em, and Jail 'em" (quoted in Miller 1996, 131). There has been "success." In 1993, more than one-third of the 120,000 inmates in California's state prisons had been put there by their probation officers (Miller 1996). After all, "[o]ne could not be the object of suspicion and be completely innocent" (Foucault 1979/1995, 42).

The Reagan and Bush administrations plus an intimidated Democratic Congress can take the "credit" for dispensing with any alternative approaches to controlling crime. The funding figures make that conclusion inescapable: federal, state, and local funds for justice (police, judicial, prosecutors, public defenders, and corrections) rose from about $11.7 billion in 1972 to $62 billion in 1988. In 1981, there were 54,422 employees in the U.S. Justice Department; by 1992, there were almost 100,000. By 1988, $3.1 billion was being spent on the federal "war on drugs" alone. By 1989, it was $4.7 billion, and by 1992 the federal government was spending $11 billion annually (Miller 1996).

The massive prisons that have been and are now being built will not easily be dismantled. Inmates will be found to fill them (Miller 1996). As Miller notes: "A self-fulfilling, self-feeding industry has been created—one aimed primarily at the underclass and minorities" (1996, 159). In Texas alone, 76,000 new prison beds were projected for the Texas system for 1995–1996, with 206,000 beds needed within five years. Commenting that only eight Texas cities had populations that large, the auditors commented frankly: "billions of tax dollars change hands; bulldozers kick up dust; walls and bars are mortared in place. It certainly looks like progress" (Miller 1996, 232). An indifferent, often hostile, white majority is fed a daily diet on the nightly news of "images of dark-skinned predators." Consequently, "crime has become a metaphor for race" (both passages in Miller 1996, 149), a continuation of the white obsession with "black crime" that dates back to the postbellum South.

For twenty years victimization surveys have indicated a stable or falling crime rate. Given this fact, the dramatic increase in imprisonment would seem to have little to do with stemming violence. What the war on drugs has done is drag millions of African-American and Hispanic young men accused of lesser offenses into the justice system, young men who in earlier times would have been dealt with informally, by friends, families, churches, schools, and other traditional groups and agencies of socialization (Miller 1996). Now they go to prison.

With prison populations likely to reach three to five million within the next decade, perhaps we will see a revival of the eugenics movement. After all, it is essential that we identify those with criminal "tendencies," if only, as Miller observes bitterly, "to rationalize the national embarrassment over having become a gulag society with the majority of young American men of color in prisons or camps" (1996, 234). For the foreseeable future, rates of arrest will increase, sentences will get longer, more prisons will be built, more juveniles will be tried as adults, and more inmates will be executed. In 1995, there were calls for the putative use of castration in Texas, recommendations of flogging in Mississippi, an increased use of the death penalty nationally, and more juveniles sent to adult prisons. In February 1995, Congressman Dick Zimmer of New Jersey filed a "no frills prisons" bill that would eliminate television sets, computers, and musical instruments, in pursuit of "the least amount of amenities and personal comforts consistent with Constitutional requirements" (quoted in Miller 1996, 223). "Despite its pretensions," Jerome Miller concludes, "modern criminal justice is no more about crime control than it is about rehabilitation. Nor it is about deterrence. None of that matters" (1996, 217). After all, "prisons do not diminish the crime rate" (Foucault 1979/1995 265).

IV. The Racial Politics of Sex in Prison

Attendance at public school, although a rather encompassing experience, is nowhere near as total and pervasive an experience as prison.

—James B. Jacobs, *New Perspectives on Prisons and Imprisonment* (1983)

It's a society, fucked up as it is. It's a society.

—Gene, an inmate, quoted in Imez Cardozo-Freeman, *The Joint: Language and Culture in a Maximum Security Prison* (1984)

The nation's prisons are reservations and shelters for black men.

—Essex Hemphill, Introduction to *Brother to Brother: Collected Writings by Black Gay Men* (1991)

The issue is manliness.

—Hans Toch, *Living in Prison: The Ecology of Survival* (1992)

Because prison tends to be a male world, most regard it as perversely unrepresentative of the larger world. But in a larger world ruled by official, compulsory heterosexuality, could not the all-male prison show men's "true colors"? One would predict the answer to that question to be negative, for sexual regimes do not operate only by legal and social enforcement; they are reproduced psychologically within each individual. In fact, given the political power of heterosexuality worldwide one would expect relatively little change in sexual conduct when men are deprived of the company of women. If you're "straight," you're straight: case closed. That has not tended to be the case. While the political dominance of heterosexuality has prevented a universal homosexuality among inmates, it has been toppled (as it were).

Contrary to expectation, heterosexually identified men have been sexually involved with other heterosexually identified (and homosexually identified) men, contrary to what, for instance, Susan Brownmiller (1975/1993, 267) implies in her discussion of prison rape, that it is only about "mastery" and power. Certainly it is about both of those, but rape is also about sex. In prison, the gender of racial politics cannot be disguised by the physical presence of women.

In the modern prison there has been a fair amount of sex. Decades ago, when prison officials could first bear to notice what was going on, it was assumed that this had to do with higher-than-average incarceration rates of homosexuals. If men are engaging in sexual behavior with each other, they must be homosexual, n'est pas? By the 1970s it was clear to criminal justice researchers that the majority of sexual liaisons involved self-identified *heterosexual* men. In prison sexual assault, the overwhelming majority are heterosexual men who attack other heterosexual men. Rape is about sex, but, as Brownmiller and others have observed, rape is not only about sex. Because sex is always part of a power grid that is social and political and, in the United States, intensely racial, sex is never about sex alone. What we find in the American prison is Claude Neal's revenge.

It is a particular revenge. After all, racial revenge could be taken many nonsexual ways: athletic competition, for instance. But it is unmistakable from the prison and juvenile detention center research as well as from prison-based popular literature that there has been one main expression of racial revenge. It has involved young heterosexual white men being turned into "bitches" by black men. Bitches? It might seem offensive to employ this term that has been used so viciously and manipulatively by men against women. What is clear from the research on prison rape is that it is also, perhaps primarily, a term used by men against men. In fact, even when men call women "bitch" it is circulating as an epithet in a male-male discursive system. This realization does not reduce the obnoxiousness, the hurt and anger the term can induce in women, especially in heterosexual women who "need" men. My use of it here is hardly to deny how offensive, how completely unacceptable it—and hate speech generally—is in the public sphere, in society. The point I make here is that "bitch" is a term in the male imaginary, and when it is used, regardless of the "object" to which it presumably refers, it is circulating in a male homosocial system of value and desire.

"Bitch" is, prison rape research suggests, what every man knows he is if he's not a man. Like the neutral term it is for female dogs, it too refers to the mother with whom, using once again the narrative of object relations theory, he is psychologically identified. All men are, presumably, pre-oedipally and symbiotically identified with their mothers. While this knowledge is drowned (and often recoded in macho denial) in the cultural mainstream, it is half-remembered in speech, in the male-male surveillance that maintains contemporary forms of compulsory male heterosexuality known as "masculinity" and "manhood." If a man doesn't work at being a man, he becomes what he is all along (what not only lower-class black men suspect unless the "evidence"—that is, violence—is performed otherwise), not a man, but a girl, a bitch, a fag. In one sense the prisoner is "signifying" this fact through what Daniel Bell called a "Coney Island mirror caricaturing the morals and manners of society" (1960, 128). From this point of view, the rape of young straight men in prisons reflects the exploitation of human beings (especially women and racialized "others"), animals, and "natural resources" evident throughout the American economic and political system (Cardozo-Freeman 1984). More specifically, prison rape reflects, captures something essential about, racial politics and violence in America.

What are the racial politics of prison? One word sums them up: rape. Homosexual, interracial rape. In contrast to nonprison heterosexual rape, which is overwhelmingly *intra*racial, prison rape crosses the racial line, *the* problem of the twentieth century Du Bois rightly announced, and it penetrates right where the white man hides: his ass, the seat of male subjectivity (Hocquenghem 1978). On rare occasion is it the black man who is raped, who is made into a "bitch." One such young black prisoner was labeled a "nigger punk" and forced into sexual servitude to white men. He later commented: "That was when I realized that my position wasn't too different from my ancestors and that for the rest of the year I wasn't any different from a plantation slave" (quoted in Scarce 1997, 34). The historical throughline is clear here. It is clear too in what occurs much more frequently. In prison it is heterosexually identified black men who make a political point of raping, then converting heterosexually identified young white men into "passive" anally receptive sex slaves, then selling them later to older white men as their "punks."

This is not what I expected to find. While working through the literature on lynching, I half-remembered the quips I had heard over the years about prison. These were always lines referring to young good-looking white guys, something to the effect that "you're going to be popular in prison." I figured, like the rape myth, this was another white man's fantasy about the black man, an even more explicit instance of homosexual desire denied and relocated to the "other," this time without the mythological "white lady" as mediation. While what I found evidently peaked during the late 1960s and early 1970s (Irwin 1985, 64 n.)—coinciding with the Black Power movement more or less—it was no fantasy. It was real, it happened, it happens still. Prison rape is racially laced, often racially motivated, and illustrates that conflation of gender and race that Henry Louis Gates, Jr. (1996, 84), among others, has observed. In the prisons Daniel Lockwood studied, for instance, while 50 percent of the population were black, 78 percent of the aggressors were black: "the same fact holds true for other prisons" (1980, 105). In the often-cited Alan J. Davis study (1968), about which we will learn more later, 85 percent of the aggressors in 129 incidents were black. This fantasy is real; young good-looking heterosexual white men are indeed "popular" in prison.

As it was for those lower-class black men in bars, it is for men everywhere (it seems); in prison "masculinity [is] the overriding concern" (Scacco 1975, 75). Not only are the inmates obsessed with it; policemen on the street as well as correctional officers in prisons are also always "proving their manhood to the inmates" (76). This preoccupation, as on the outside, is intensified among lower-class males, who tend to express themselves in ways they consider to be masculine beyond dispute. These include "possession of strength and endurance and athletic skills ... and a conceptualization of women as conquest objects" (Cressey and Ward 1969, 336). Lower-class males tend to view upper-class males or "upwardly mobile peers as ... fags or queers" (337). It is clear, Scacco concludes: "that the whole genre of pre-institutional and institutional behavior, both for the keepers and those who are kept, is caught up in one orgy whereby both groups are attempting to prove their masculinity to one another while simultaneously seeking not to be emasculated in the eyes of one another" (1975, 77). A racialized, nonvoluntary orgy.

In this sense, how men—especially lower-class men—feel in prison differs little from how they feel outside the institution. One black inmate reported: "it is my contention that a black convict's condition in prison or out of prison is one and the same thing. I mean the condition of the ghetto. And I mean physically and mentally they do not change when he becomes a convict" (quoted in Scacco 1975, 75). Prison is not an alien planet. What happens there cannot be attributed entirely to the institution itself; what is clear from criminal justice research is that the prison reproduces, in fundamental essential ways, the world outside (Jacobs 1983; Cardozo-Freeman 1984; Colvin 1997).

Within the confines of an all-male institution (as they do in the homosocial society outside the prison), the psychological complexities of incarceration often become defined and reconciled as issues of manhood. Doubts about one's identity are simplified in prison to direct questions of manliness. Questions concerning the status of inmates as men is played out by an age-old ritual of testing: who is the weaker individual? This ancient male practice substantiates the strength of those who dominate (Wright 1994). Gibbs (1981, 115) describes the process whereby the adoption of a masculine persona helps ensure survival and status within inmate society:

> This is a world in which legitimate authorities are seldom appealed to, and disputes are settled by vendetta. It is a world in which "male" no longer simply connotes anatomical characteristics. As in many all-male groups, manliness becomes a status continuum. One's place on the continuum is of great importance, and may be determined by demonstrations of "toughness" during the first weeks of confinement.

Clear and Cole (1986) summarize those characteristics of the incarcerated population that make this group particularly violence-prone: (1) age, (2) certain social attitudes such as "machismo," (3) membership in a gang, and (4) racism.

Several studies of male-male rape have suggested that rape in male prisons is relatively rare (Davis 1968; Lockwood 1980; Nacci and Kane 1983, 1984a, 1984b; Wooden and Parker 1982). Some studies found that as few as 0.3 percent of inmates in male prisons are reported as rape victims, but a 1979–1980 study of one California men's state prison found 14 percent of inmates had been sexually coerced. In the early 1980s, prison overcrowding appeared to affect the rape statistics. Struckman-Johnson reported in a 1997 Nebraska prison study that 22 percent of men responding had been coerced into sexual conduct against their will. Likewise, Stephen Donaldson, former president of Stop Prisoner Rape, estimated that up to 530,000 forcible sexual assaults occur each year among the 1.1 million American male prisoners (Hodges 1998). "Prisoner estimates of rape are often inflated," Han Toch suggests, "but the danger is nevertheless real. The rate is more significant when we consider that potential victims come from a minority of the prison population" (1992, 279).

Complicating these estimates is the fact that many studies fail to clearly distinguish among consensual homosexuality, prostitution, and rape. Furthermore, these studies suggest that correction officers may inhibit accurate reporting by treating victims insensitively or by ignoring altogether coerced sexual behavior. Also making the discovery of sexual exploitation difficult is that only rarely will the victimized come forward and "rat" (Bartollas, Miller, and Dinitz 1976, 39). Moreover, it is difficult to determine what effect underreporting has upon these estimates (Eigenberg 1994). Some students of penal institutions have contended that as many as 95 percent of the inmates are involved in homosexual experiences at some time or other during their sentences (Martin 1954). Although few agree that the rate of homosexuality is that high, many agree that more than half of the inmates in the average prison are involved in homosexual relationships (Hopper 1969).

In 1995 the American Medical Association published *Strategies for the Treatment and Prevention of Sexual Assault*, which included a section on the rape of males under the heading of special populations. The A.M.A. concluded that "sexual assault against ... men in prison populations may be significantly underestimated and under-reported. ... Male victims frequently do not seek treatment or report the assault for fear of being labeled homosexual erroneously" (quoted in Scarce 1997, 177).

The advocacy group called Stop Prisoner Rape (for information, see Withers 1999) estimated that an average of 360,000 males are sexually assaulted in American prisons each year. Of this number, at least two-thirds are repeatedly raped, often gang raped, on a daily basis, making the total number of male-male rape events much higher. Prison male rapes are not included in the Bureau of Justice Statistics crime surveys or estimates of reported rape. Nor do other countries include prison rape in their national crime reports, indicative of the low status the problem has for most prison officials worldwide (Scarce 1997). The former director of Stop Prisoner Rape, Stephen Donaldson, in a guest editorial for the *New York Times*, argued that "the fight against rape in our communities is doomed to failure and will remain an exercise in futility as long as it ignores the network of training grounds for rapists: our prisons, our jails and reform schools" (Donaldson 1993a, A11).

Donaldson knows prison rape firsthand, having been arrested at a nonviolent protest in Washington, D.C. During his brief period of imprisonment, Donaldson was orally and anally gang raped by approximately 60 men over the course of 24 hours. Upon his release, he was hospitalized for rectal surgery. Since that day some twenty years ago, Donaldson, Michael Scarce (1997, 36) tells us, "has worked as a tireless advocate for prisoner rights, particularly on issues of sexual assault. The psychological impact of all of this trauma set into motion a pattern of behavior that landed Donaldson in jail on several more occasions throughout his life. Raped countless times across the span of his life, he became infected with H.I.V. and eventually died of A.I.D.S.-related complications in 1996."

What we find reported in the research, much of it done twenty years ago, has not disappeared today. When Diane Sawyer visited the Western Youth Institution in North Carolina in 1997, what she learned suggests a remarkable continuity with what was the case during the zenith of racialized prison rape. Some of the prison language has changed: new prisoners were termed "new jacks" rather than "fish" at this facility, for instance. The "older" inmates—everyone is under 18 in this youth facility—still stare at the new guys, the "new jacks," in what is called "screw-face." To look away is a sign of weakness, so the new ones try to stare back. Seven major gangs operate in the facility; the guards, Sawyer learned, are often violent. Rape, she asked? "It does take place" one young man replied carefully. A black inmate is more direct: "I'm gonna get meat." New jacks must either "tough it out" or seek protection from a gang, which means giving money, sometimes sex to one's protector, the informant admits. If the new guy has trouble, gang members tell their kids, "tell him I'm your man." Racially speaking, "Blacks run this prison." One black inmate admitted: "White boys got it tough in prison." Drugs, Sawyer asked? "Anything you want" came the answer. Visitors smuggle drugs into the prison (20/20 November 18, 1998).

V. Gee, So Many Queers in Here

[E]very year large numbers of boys, adolescent youths, and young men are made homosexuals, either temporarily or permanently, in the prisons of America.

—Joseph Fishman, *Sex in Prison* (1934)

It is interesting to note the exaggerated masculinity affected by many criminals; ... criminality in men is commonly due to reaction-formation against latent homosexuality and passivity.

—John Dollard et al., *Frustration and Aggression* (1939)

Some seventy years ago observers of American prisons concluded that the relatively high incidence of sexual behavior they were observing meant that "[t]here is a greater percentage of homosexuals within the prison than on the outside" (Fishman 1934, 22). What percentage? In response to allegations that rates of homosexuality ran as high as 80 percent in American prisons, Joseph Fishman reassured his readers: "I believe that not more than thirty or forty per cent of the inmates of any penal institution are homosexuals, or have homosexual propensities" (1934, 81–82). But, Fishman confessed, "the actual presence of so many 'fairies' with their feminine carriage, gestures and mannerisms, in itself tends to keep aglow the fire of sex in even the most heterosexual of prisoners" (22). As it was in men's facilities, so it was in women's: "there are more lesbians in women's institutions than on the outside" (28).

There was as well a certain racialization of sex, at least in women's prisons: "[w]hite women who play the passive part in homosexuality are more likely to have affairs with colored women than are white men with colored men" (Fishman 1934, 29). Fishman was not alone in thinking so; both Katherine B. Davis (1929, 245) and Mabel Elliott (1952, 718) reported that homosexual attraction was "stronger between Negro and white women than between members of the same race" and that this interracial homosexual attraction was used to justify racial segregation in prisons. Racial fantasies die hard, although here the subject is evidently black men not women: "Negro homosexuality differs from the white counterpart, by less emotional involvement, seeking primarily physical relief through ejaculation. The Negro's sex drive ... appears to be more simple and direct. Miscegenated homosexuality, especially when a Negro 'jocker' acquires a white 'brat,' may lead to serious racial disturbance" (Vedder and King 1967, 19). I will discuss these and other prison terms in a moment.

Prisons, from Mr. Fishman's perspective some seventy years ago, were filled with homosexuals and that fact made sex a major problem for everybody else, that is, "normal" men and prison officials. What could be done? There were, Fishman concluded: "[T]hree choices ... to suppress it [the sex impulse] entirely by sheer force of will, to sublimate it in some fashion, or to gratify it by masturbation, homosexuality, bestiality, pederasty or some other form of perversion" (1934, 33). The first strategy, suppression, was tried: for instance, prisoners at the Federal Penitentiary at Leavenworth were once forced to wear a large yellow D (for Degenerate) if they were discovered engaged in a homosexual act (Propper 1981). Later, prison officials would think of a fourth option: conjugal visits with wives and girlfriends.

Observing the fragility of "manhood" and "masculinity," prison officials during the 1930s concluded that prisons were filled with criminals who were, in sexual terms, human monsters. Prison was the worst fate possible for a "regular guy," as evidently fragile (from the point of view of sexual identity) young men run a great risk when they are punished for wayward conduct. That risk is that they may not come out (as it were) as they went in. For, you see, this capacity for monstrosity—even for Fishman writing in the 1930s—is not limited to homosexuals or even to criminals: "[T]here are inherent bisexual tendencies in every one, and that *almost any one could be converted into a homosexual if the proper circumstances were present at the right time.* In other words, that every one in a certain period in his life is on the fence of bisexuality, where a little pressure either way may shape his future sexual life. It can be seen therefore what a menace to youth this class really is" (Fishman 1934, 67, emphasis added). Could Fishman hear what he was saying? Heterosexual manhood, he was suggesting, hangs by a thread.

That sentiment did not disappear with the Great Depression. Perhaps heterosexuality is not "set in stone," perhaps sexual identity is more changeable than one imagined. Fifty years after Fishman's admission, a student of rape in prisons quoted Kinsey: "Males do not represent two discrete populations, heterosexual and homosexual. ... The living world is a continuum in each and every of its aspects" (quoted in Scacco 1975, 40–42). Kinsey had reported that 37 percent of American males had had at least one homosexual experience (Scacco 1975, 44), including, it appears, Kinsey himself (Jones 1997).

Maybe there are no strictly heterosexual men who face corruption by homosexual men. Maybe there are only homosexual men who may revert back to their original state when given the chance: "[E]very year large numbers of boys, adolescent youths, and young men are made homosexuals, either temporarily or permanently, in the prisons of America" (Fishman 1934, 83). One can hear his astonishment when Fishman reports:

> A deputy warden of one of the large prisons in the Middle West once showed me a remarkable collection of notes which he had received in one day from various inmates. Each note stated that the undersigned was a relative of a boyish-looking prisoner who had arrived the day before, and requested that for this reason he be placed in the same cell with him. *There were thirty-nine notes in all.* That number of prisoners had seen the boy and had made up their minds that they would like to have him for their "girl." (1934, 85; emphasis in original)

This heterosexualized homosexual relationship has been called "lugging" and often involves "an older inmate taking a youngster as his own" (85). It is not always sexualized. Sometimes the older man is simply being paternal, and in fact protects the younger man from sexual attacks from others. Often, however, this "paternal" protection comes with a sexual price.

To illustrate, in a study of the inmates at Guelph Reformatory in Ontario, W. E. Mann (1967) found the usual "lugging" pattern. The "father," or "old man," was a repeat offender serving a year or more. Older and more aggressive, he seduced the sixteen- or seventeen-year-old newcomer. Now his "sweet kid," he was "adopted" by the older man, even given a cross-and-chain necklace to wear warning other "musclers" to stay away. The "sweet kid" was sometimes expected to kiss or neck (sometimes termed "muscling" or "bluebirding") or have genital sex. Prison relationships between older and younger men are not *only* sexual; they serve multiple functions. In Mann's study, the "sweet kid" received protection from potential rapists, new clothing, and even an enhanced status due to his partnership with a respected older inmate. Besides sex on demand, the "father" enjoyed status from performing the dominant role, which includes having a visible possession, "hence the expression, 'he is my kid'" (Mann 1967, 61). Both men, Mann concluded, benefited from doing each other favors and from their enjoyment of being together.

This practice is, of course, hardly unique to Canada. In his study of American prisons, Anthony Scacco reported: "Whether it be for protection or for sexual reasons, the older male adopts the younger boy and, as a sign of his possession, gives the boy a cross and chain to wear around his neck. This symbol serves as notice to other 'jocks' that the one wearing it is already taken and anyone attempting to assault the boy will have to deal with the older prisoner whose property is clearly marked by the obvious symbol" (1975, 17). It is not only "women" who are possessed by men. Men, it would seem, tend to possess whomever they designate as "theirs." The anatomy of objects of possession change from outside to inside prison, but not the fact of possession. And not the language.

VI. Underground Language: The Gendered Reality of Prisons

What happens in a society is reflected unconsciously in its language.

—Inez Cardozo-Freeman, *The Joint: Language and Cutlure in a Maximum Security Prison* (1984)

For if the word has the potency to revive and make us free, it has also the power to blind, imprison and destroy.

—Ralph Ellison, *Shadow and Act* (1964/1995)

The language of men ... is almost always divorced from any kind of interiority.

—Mary Helen Washington, Foreword to *The Memphis Diary of Ida B. Wells* (1995)

Rape is most fundamentally a symptom in the entire syndrome of sensed male inadequacy.

—Frances Cress Welsing, *The Isis (Yssis) Papers* (1991)

The language of the prison, Inez Cardozo-Freeman (1984) argues, is an "underground language" which expresses in symbolic terms the reality of prisoners' lives. "Prison is," she writes, "obscene, profane, violent, terrifying, grim, cruel, inhumane, impersonal, ruthless, and dehumanizing." And the language of the prison reflects this reality. Prisoners speak without subtlety so that others will not mistake their condition. In this regard, prison language is intended to shock even "to wound the conventional, straight sensibilities of guards and others" with whom they come into contact. The language of the prison is a kind of testimony to the lived experience of imprisonment. Moreover, Cardozo-Freeman continues, prison language conveys prisoners' desire to affirm their existence, to ensure that their presence is felt. Why? "Prisoners live constantly," she writes, "with the dread that they have been buried and forgotten. Prisoners believe that civil death is very close to physical death" (quoted passages in Cardozo-Freeman 1984, 27). Certainly African-American men have experienced a civic subjugation that was very close, indeed intertwined with, physical sexual subjugation.

The lived reality of prisons cannot be communicated in everyday language. Conventional etiquette does not allow certain harsh truths to be expressed vividly. There is, Cardozo-Freeman observes, a tendency for people on the outside to describe certain uncomfortable aspects of prison in euphemistic terms. In contrast, she writes,

> [p]risoners do not do this. They strip language down to its bare bones, revealing it in all its rawness. In these instances, prisoners are truth tellers, stripping away all hypocrisy and patina from meaning in language. Often their language, shocking as it may be, more truthfully reveals the human condition than does much of conventional, proper language usage.

> Because their daily existence is filled with ugliness, they do not fear ugly language. (Cardozo-Freeman 1984, 28)

To study prison language, Cardozo-Freeman conducted fieldwork at the Washington State Penitentiary in Walla Walla from June 1978 through December 1980. She was assisted by Eugene Delorme, then an inmate. She learned then that "underground language is also used as a weapon by imprisoned men. ... [T]he children's chant, 'sticks and stones will break my bones but names will never hurt me,' is grossly untrue" (Cardozo-Freeman 1984, 26). Prisoners experience bodily what they and others say.

Images of violence are pervasive in the "underground" language of American society. Unlike French or Spanish, the English language exhibits little tenderness, Cardozo-Freeman argues (unfairly I think). There is, she continues, little sense of the aesthetic in those English words which depict sexuality. Those words communicative of sex that are nontechnical tend to convey images of violence; she thinks of "fuck you." "To get fucked," "to fuck over," and the closely related "to screw," "to get screwed" are commonly used in everyday American life. They refer, for instance, to certain business tactics, certain political as well as interpersonal events. David Maurer reports that the word "fuck" has been around in print since about 1200; it is derived from the Latin *pugno*, which means dagger; to strike, to stab with a weapon (Maurer 1979; Cardozo-Freeman 1984, 32 n. 80).

Cardozo-Freeman quotes John Ciardi's distinction between obscenity and profanity (or blasphemy). Ciardi suggested that obscenity tends to offend Protestant sensibilities, whereas profanity or blasphemy (profaning the Lord's name) tends to offend Catholic sensibilities. Cardozo-Freeman reports that Protestant sensibilities would seem to be the most at risk in prisoner underground language usage: "Fuck, motherfucker, pissed off (originally an army expression), cocksucker, sonovabitch, bastard, goddam (the Catholic taboo word most often heard), and shit (the prize winner in this prison, which, believe it or not, even surpasses the much loved motherfucker, and which is a street term used for just about anything) are the most commonly used expressions" (Cardozo-Freeman 1984, 25). Regarding the latter, Hannerz (1977) observes, with Abrahams (1964, 261–262), that the word "motherfucker" and its derivatives are used in multiple and ambivalent ways, sometimes as statements of admiration and at other times as denunciation.

These are terms that can be heard every day. Perhaps they are more frequently employed in all-male settings, such as bar settings, locker rooms, playing fields, and prisons. But in prisons the frequency of this underground language is accompanied by another set of terms, some of which are heard on the outside, some of which are not. These new terms plus the "total" character of the institution provide a profound shock to the new prisoner. It was Goffman (1961) who characterized prisons as "total institutions" whose "encompassing or total character is symbolized by the barrier to social intercourse with the outside and to departure that is often built right into the physical plant, such as locked doors, high walls, barbed wires ... [and is] organized to protect the community against what are felt to be intentional dangers to it, with the welfare of the persons thus sequestered not the immediate issue" (4–5).

The prison becomes, for the inmate, a total reality in which future and past disappear. It is to a great degree "a closed and timeless society where days, weeks, and months pass monotonously" (Jacobs 1983, 135). For many inmates, "the present is reality in all its concreteness" (Massey 1989, 9). One's identity on the "outside" recedes. As John Irwin (1970) observed, "one's identity, one's personality system, one's coherent thinking about himself depend upon a relatively familiar, continuous, and predictable stream of events. In the Kafkaesque world of the booking room, the jail cell, the interrogation room, and the visiting room, the boundaries of the self collapse" (quoted in Cardozo-Freeman 1984, 39). Not only do interpersonal boundaries among men become unstable, but within one's body one feels dislocated: "In describing their feelings, such patients refer to anything that happens within their 'flight distance' as taking place literally inside themselves. That is, the boundaries of the self extend beyond the body" (Hall 1969, 13). As Cardozo-Freeman (1984) points out, the likelihood of conflict and violence is greatly increased by the overcrowded conditions in many prisons, further destabilizing those boundaries and collapsing the distance that men are accustomed to maintain between one man and another. She recalls that Edward T. Hall (1969) found that the proper spacing for animals is maintained by an invisible bubble that surrounds each individual creature; presumably, each human individual also is, at least in a psychological sense, surrounded by such an invisible bubble. Such "space" among individuals functions as a protective psychological device for the personality (Cardozo-Freeman 1984).

Ordinary distances between individuals disappear immediately upon incarceration. A sense of suffocating proximity is evident in the choice of terms for the name of the bus that transports convicted felons from county and city jails to the state's reception center and, afterward, to the prisons where they have been sentenced to serve their time. That bus is termed the "chain." Before boarding the bus each man is chained (Cardozo-Freeman 1984). One prisoner described his experience at this first stage of imprisonment this way:

> All of a sudden you are in the city or county jail—the bars, the steel, the doors are clanging; homosexual acts going down by force or by finesse. The ever-increasing domination and rape of young offenders in city and county jails is outstanding. It's one of the most terrible things you can imagine. It usually happens to the young. ... The wolves are waiting like vultures for somebody to come into the tank. ... The tank has anywhere from forty to a hundred men in it and the way these jails are overcrowded with people sleeping on the floor, it's really out of line. (quoted in Cardozo-Freeman 1984, 37–38)

Especially if they are young and white, new prisoners articulate their concern that they may be sexually exploited. While the frequency of sexual assaults has evidently decreased in recent years, they remain a significant element in jail folklore, and inexperienced prisoners remain very fearful of them (Irwin 1985; Hodges 1998). While young white men are concerned about being sexually exploited, young black men express more concern about being "messed over" nonsexually by strong black peers (Bartollas, Miller, and Dinitz 1976,

54). Rarely will whites attempt to exploit a black prisoner; it is almost always young white men who are victimized. Of the sixteen sexually exploited boys Bartollas, Miller, and Dinitz studied, thirteen were white. As we will see, "some imprisoned blacks turn on young whites as scapegoats in prisons and jails out of revenge for what has happened to them in white society" (Cardozo-Freeman 1984, 66).

Those young men who have been sentenced to "serve time" in a captive community for the first time are often known as "fish." The term has been in use since at least 1915 (Cardozo-Freeman 1984). The genesis of "fish" is "sucker" which can be traced to the nineteenth century; it referred to a person who was easily deceived or duped (Maurer 1979). The "keeper" does not prepare the "fish" for the ordeal that awaits him in the "tank"; consequently, anxiety is extremely high when the young men first arrive (Cardozo-Freeman 1984, 60). A common question put to a young new prisoner is "are you a punk?" Scores of older inmates insist: "I bet you're a punk. How about getting down for me?" (quoted in Bartollas, Miller, and Dinitz 1976, 101).

Men who are raped in prison tend to look or be young, are not especially athletic, and are noticeably better looking than their predators (Brownmiller 1975/1993). When one knows he is attractive to other prisoners, one realizes rape is possible, even likely. Sexual remarks, such as the following taken from interview transcriptions, provoke profound anxiety in new inmates:

> "You are cute."
> "Damn, you're a pretty white."
> "Well, you are a fine-looking dude."
> "I want you to be my kid."
> "I want your ass."
>
> (quoted in Lockwood 1980, 20)

In one study the varieties of threat employed by aggressors were tabulated. Verbal threats of sexual assault were the most commonly used, accounting for 56 percent of the total. They included statements such as:

> "Are you going to give it up or get it taken off?"
> "I want your buttocks and if you don't give it to me, it is going to be taken."
> "We are going to fuck you in the ass."
> "I am going to fuck you up and take your pussy."
> "If you don't give it up, you will get your throat cut easy. I got twenty-five years and I don't give a shit."
> "Give it up, Man, or I am going to take it right here and kill you."
> "Look, Man, I have got a knife and we want to see what you have got."
> "Well, if you want to be a dirty bitch, we got to take this pussy."
> "What would you do if I just took it and if I pulled your pants down and just took it?"
> "I'll play rough with you and then after you break, you'll be mine."
>
> (quoted in Lockwood 1980, 22)

All this may seem like so much talk, posturing among inmates with nothing else to do. Of course, there are occasions when it is, but there are many other occasions when inmates mean exactly what they say. Consider the case of "Jeff." While reported in somewhat sensationalistic terms, his story conveys something of the reality new inmates face:

> Nineteen-year-old Jeff was booked into Los Angeles County jail for possession of dangerous drugs. This was his first arrest, and he was an average, scared kid. After the trauma of being arrested and a three-hour book procedure, he was searched, fingerprinted, researched, photographed, stripped, anus checked, showered, and sprayed for body lice. Then he was given a jail-issue set of clothing and processed through a series of holding tanks and finally assigned to a cell. He was sent to a six-man unit where the other five men had been living in the twelve- by ten-foot cell for two weeks and had formed a social bond. Two of these men were black and in prison for armed robbery, one was Caucasian and in for parole violation, and two were Mexican junkies. Into this setting entered Jeff, bedroll in hand, steel bars slamming shut behind him. He immediately encountered cold stares and, as he related to us, "hard vibes." He was, as the convict saying goes, "a sheep for the wolves."
>
> Lights went out at 9:00 P.M. Jeff was lying on his bunk when one of the black ex-cons moved in and sat on Jeff's bunk and asked, "Hey, kid, you ever been in jail before? What you in for?" This was just friendly small talk—a big-brother "come on." The words implied security and counsel, but actually they were part of the strategy of the "snake stalking its prey." The next night the same black told Jeff that those other four guys "wanted his ass" and that they were talking about "taking it" that night. The con told Jeff, "What are you going to do? Listen, kid, I can handle them. But I have been in this hold for six weeks and I sure am horny. I sure could use some head [i.e., fellatio]. How about tonight after everyone is asleep. You take care of me—no one will know—and I'll look out for you while you're here."
>
> It was the old convict game, the classic play, and each man in the cell played along to make it work. They merely waited for Jeff to take the bait and "cop some rod" and then they "awoke" and demanded their fair share. (Wooden and Parker 1982, 102–103)

Among sexual assaults taking place in state prisons, 77 percent occurred within 16 weeks after the young man first entered the state penal system. The "reception center" (a separate facility where new men are processed and given an orientation to prison life) and the first transfer prison (where men go after reception) are therefore the most risk-laden phases of incarceration (Lockwood 1980). Certainly this was true for conscientious objectors who were imprisoned for their beliefs during the Vietnam War. These were often articulate and literate college-educated young men who were vulnerable to victimization because they were young, middle-class, white, and naive. Take the case of Robert A. Martin.

A 28-year-old Quaker pacifist, a former seamen with a background in journalism, Robert Martin held a press conference in front of the White House in the summer of 1973. Arrested during a peace demonstration in front of the

White House, Martin had chosen to go to prison rather than post a $10 bond. His first week in the District of Columbia jail passed uneventfully in a quiet cell block populated by older prisoners, including Watergate burglar C. Gordon Liddy. In the second week he was transferred to Cellblock 2, a tier of "predominantly young black prisoners, many of them in jail for serious crimes of violence." During his first evening recreation period on the new tier, the boyish-looking pacifist was invited into a cell because, presumably, some of the other prisoners wished to speak with him. Once inside, Martin reported, "my exit was blocked and my pants were forcibly taken off me, and I was raped. Then I was dragged from cell to cell all evening." After being raped, Martin was promised protection by two of the men who had raped him. This promise turned out to be a trick, as the next night his "protectors" initiated a second "orgy of oral and rectal rape." The two men—his "protectors" who had raped him the first evening—stood outside his cell, collecting packs of cigarettes from other prisoners who wanted to take a turn. At one point his attackers gave him a moment to rest (Martin was gagging and vomiting), and he was able in this moment to escape. With a guard's help, he was taken from the tier to D.C. General Hospital. The following morning a Quaker friend posted the $10 bond (Martin et al. 1974; quoted in Lockwood 1980, 6; Bowker 1980, Brownmiller 1975/1993).

Teased and threatened by sexual remarks, the lore of prison rape in his mind, the new inmate is further disoriented as the evidence of home-world identities, such as clothes, watches, money, and other personal items, are stripped away, replaced by drab institutional clothing (Bartollas, Miller, and Dinitz 1976). An Arkansas inmate remembers: "The day I come in, they strip me off naked, they took everything I had, man" (quoted in Jackson 1977, 224). Another reports: "When you first hit this place, they line you up out there in the hall and you go in and there's the big major sitting there. They strip you and they spray you. They spray you like you're a fuckin' goat or something" (quoted in Jackson 1977, 228).

The "initiation rite" for young men who are new prisoners is rape. Tradition involves, as we have seen, a young man ("kid") being "turned out" by an older man (wolf) through verbal seduction (finesse) or force. After being turned out, the young man is said to be a "punk," a very low species in prison who must receive protection from his "daddy" to avoid rape. What is the price of protection? Often it is sex on demand. A more contemporary variant has evolved from this tradition: gang rape. Groups of two or more men lure an unsuspecting "fish" into a secluded area where he is overcome by force. Although gang rape is common among all groups, black men were well-known in the prison Cardozo-Freeman (1984) studied for carrying out this "tradition" against young white men incarcerated for the first time. Two white inmates discussed the phenomenon:

> BILL: "I used to sit and watch the Chain come in and the blacks lying off to the kids who come in and rape 'em. They'd say, 'Come into the house and smoke a joint.' And once you get in that house, you ain't goin' nowhere."

> JIM: "Unhuh. Yeah. … I see that happen several times. Yeah, I sure have. I seen that happen right next door to the house where I was livin'. Over there, man, they were just constantly pickin' up some young kid and draggin' him off into the house and fuckin' him. One of the guys is down here right now [in the Minimum Security Building]. Stayed in that one house. They drug him in there off the Chain and he stayed in that house three years that I know of, just constantly getting' abused every day and he never once tried to do anything about gettin out of the situation cause he was scared shitless. But they gave him a break for a while; they drugged some other kid in there and kept him for about six months." (quoted in Cardozo-Freeman 1984, 66)

There are so many dangerous "sharks" who swim in the tank that new "fish" can easily become paralyzed. These new men can become so frightened by the threat of rape or other forms of violence that they sleep fully clothed, and even refuse to leave their cells. They suffer a specific fear of taking a shower since the "carwash," as it is called, is a place where attacks occur frequently. "Terror shapes the worldview of the new 'fish' coming into the 'tank'" (Cardozo-Freeman 1984, 65). Terror would seem to be appropriate:

> DUANE: "There was one kid who came in here last year. I knew what was goin to happen to him, man. He was just a pale, skinny white kid with curly hair. Sure enough, a few days later he was walkin down the tier askin to suck people's dicks. Guys were makin him do that and chargin' for it. He went in with so-and-so and those guys, and they all fucked him that night, made him suck their dicks, and the next day they came around with him runnin him in the cells. Man, everybody fucked him. They did that to him for a couple of weeks. He finally checked into PC. …" [mental ward]
>
> (quoted in Cardozo-Freeman 1984, 371)

How long is this initiation phase? Cardozo-Freeman (1984) reports two inmates discussing this question:

> JIM: "How long did it take before you felt you were no longer a fish?"
> BILL: "About a year."
>
> (quoted in Cardozo-Freeman 1984, 65)

The sex-role categories of men in prison—these are names given by inmates to each other—appears relatively durable, showing little change from the 1930s to the present time. Fishman (1934) again: "[T]hey are of the passive type, known variously as 'punks,' 'girls,' 'fags,' 'pansies,' or 'fairies,' as distinguished from the inmates who take advantage of their favors, that is the active participants. These are known in prison slang as 'top men' or 'wolves'" (59). More recent students of the prison report terms such as "jockers" and "wolves" (Scacco 1975, 15) to refer to "top men." New inmates, as we have seen, are often known as "fish" (Massey 1989, 5).

Even outside the United States, binary gender distinctions prevail in prison. Under the leadership of Podgorecki several studies were made of Polish institutions during 1969–1971, revealing a similar discursive formation:

> [T]hey could delineate a very sharp division of inmates into two clearly dichotomized basic categories, which in juvenile argot and local terminology are called "ludzie" (people) in plural form (cztowiek, "man," is singular) as the dominant "caste," and "frajerzy" ("cad," slaves, or clumsy) referring to the subordinate "caste." The people were found to have their special language and a highly indigenous set of magic, customs, and taboos. Slaves are not permitted to communicate with people in the normal course of daily events, and they are never supposed to use the code of the people in communication with each other. (quoted in Bondeson 1989, 30)

Top guys—"wolves" and "pimps" ("daddies")—deny that they are homosexual. They boast that they "pitch" but do not "catch," defining homosexuality as it is defined in some Latin countries, only in terms of the "female" or "passive" role (Cardozo-Freeman 1984, 375). These terms reproduce the gender binaries extant in Western culture generally. There is, of course, nothing inherently "female" or "passive" about fellating a man or being anally penetrated by him. Those who want to be fellated are sometimes termed "headhunters," "cannibals," and "kid-fruits." The young man ("kid-fruit") fellates the older man. When a younger man is said to be "geared" or "wired up" that means he is available for homosexual relations (Vedder and King 1967, 18). Victims are sometimes described as "lambs" in contrast to their assailants who are then labeled as "wolves." "Lambs" tend to be white (Wright 1994, 107).

Significantly, the "kid" or "punk" is a heterosexual man who has been "turned out," that is, forced to assume a sexually submissive role (Wooden and Parker 1982, 3). Generally, other prisoners regard punks with contempt because "they lack the courage to save their manhood" (Halliday 1976, 572). Even if a young man fights, only to be overpowered and then raped by a gang, the prison population still regards him with contempt. As Cardozo-Freeman points out, this fate is not unlike that of women who have been raped and are then regarded by some men as "spoiled" or "contaminated." Only "stool pigeons" have less status than punks. A punk is thought of as "weak as a woman" and, hence, he is reviled (Cardozo-Freeman 1984, 371). The term is not restricted to prison life; in street parlance, a "punk" denotes "a weak, passive, somewhat effeminate male" (White and Cones 1999, 71).

A "pressure punk" is a heterosexual man (usually young, usually white) who has been forced into sexual behavior. Many are "turned out" against their will, generally out of fear of being killed or injured. A "turn out" is a debut, a coming-out party, celebrating the arrival of "womanhood" (Cardozo-Freeman 1984, 369). The slightly different social role of the "canteen punk" refers to those young heterosexual men who have been raped and afterward continue to perform sexual favors for "topmen" in return for items such as cigarettes obtained from the prison canteen. Sometimes these young men perform sex for drugs. Some researchers have found a greater incidence of canteen punks among lower-class whites than among other class groupings (Bartollas, Miller, and Dinitz 1976).

Canteen punks often have more than one "client." Bowker (1980) reports: "Men who give in to aggressors and are 'punked' may all of a sudden find themselves owned by predatory groups of 'jockers' who not only use them themselves whenever they wish, but who also force the 'punks' to prostitute themselves for profit or to rob the cells of other prisoners" (14). When these young men "turn a trick for a pack," the customer has a choice of how he will be served, "tops or bottoms." "This inmate is not a true homosexual, but by extending such favors to homosexual inmates, is enabled to acquire more commissary items and other luxuries" (Vedder and King 1967, 19).

One of the most famous murder cases of the mid-twentieth century was that of osteopath Sam Sheppard, convicted of killing his wife in suburban Cleveland, Ohio. F. Lee Bailey would appeal and successfully reverse the first decision that sent Sheppard to the Ohio State Penitentiary, but while incarcerated in the Columbus facility Sheppard observed firsthand the sex system of prison life. Commenting on the use of drugs in the seduction routine, he reported:

> The narcotics were usually sought by the "jockers" so they could talk the young men into going to bed or going somewhere to take part in some homosexual activity. They would give these narcotics to a young man so that he would submit. This was occurring daily in the Ohio Penitentiary and involved, for instance, sleeping capsules such as Nembutal and seconal. ... The point is that sleeping pills are given out to patients all over the hospital every night, and they're ... used to seduce younger inmates. (quoted in Weiss and Friar 1974, 86)

Straight boys have long known about the power of alcohol to weaken a young woman's resolve. In the 1990s, so-called "date rape" drugs would become available for just that purpose, just as seconal served the same function in the Ohio State Penitentiary thirty years ago.

Notice how the binary logic of the heterosexual regime is reproduced in prison. The "jocker" or "stud" is by definition those men who have sex with "punks." Jockers or studs (or wolves) assume only the "masculine" role in the sexual encounter (active in anal intercourse and passive in fellatio). They do not define themselves as homosexual, nor do they define these sex acts as homosexual. As mentioned, only the "bottom" gets defined as homosexual, as a faggot, a girl, a bitch. It is by giving "head" or getting fucked that the punk has violated the masculine image; he is now a "broad" or "sissy" (Wooden and Parker 1982, 3).

Wolves or jockers are sometimes known as "boody bandits." This term tends to refer to young (usually 18 or 19 years of age), heterosexually identified black men who have few qualms about coercing weaker and slightly younger white men into submitting to their sexual advances. In the juvenile facility Bartollas, Miller and Dinitz (1976) studied, little distinction was made among (1) boys tending toward a homosexual identity; (2) those heterosexual/homosexual boys forced to participate against their will; (3) those heterosexual/homosexual boys who had ulterior motives for participating. A new inmate can be compelled to commit oral sodomy on several boys who wait in line. Speaking with the aggressors the day after such an attack, Bartollas, Miller, and Dinitz (1976) found no sense of wrongdoing or any empathy for the victim. In fact, these young black men felt that the rape of young white men was justified because blacks have been victimized on the outside. White boys tend to lack the social cohesion many young black inmates appear to experience; they quickly find themselves isolated and paralyzed. Many lower-class white men have been accustomed to feeling superior to blacks; now they find themselves in a strange world, which they have become "black," that is, the denigrated, the hated, the exploited.

There are times, of course, when sex is consensual in prisons. A "handshake," for instance, refers to mutual masturbation. Solitary masturbation, Vedder and King (1967) report, is so common in male prisons that "it should not be classified as a perversion. But mutual masturbation or 'handshaking' would seem to constitute a perverted act" (Vedder and King 1967, 18). Consensual or forced, many inmates feel they must have a "punk in the bunk."

> DUANE: "Got to have a punk in the bunk to take care of the house. A punk in the bunk is like a crack in the shack. Yeah, they wash your clothes, they clean the house, make your bed, wipe you off, wash your back, or you wash their back."
>
> (quoted in Cardozo-Freeman 1984, 370)

> DUANE: "That saying, 'Shit on my dick or blood on my blade,' used to be a kind of standing joke in here but that's just about the way you run it down."
>
> (quoted in Cardozo-Freeman 1984, 371)

So "men" require "wives" wherever they are, even when anatomical females are unavailable for the position. That fact would certainly seem to support those feminist critiques which locate sex-role socialization generally in masculinist prerogatives and ideologies. It is "men" who require "women," and so they are "produced." That would seem to be the strictly gendered significance of prison sex. What is its racial meaning?

17 ❖ CLAUDE NEAL'S REVENGE

I. How Does It Feel, White Boy?

These scars and wounds [lynching, etc.] are clearly etched on the canvass of black sexuality.

—Cornell West, *Race Matters* (1993)

In prison, most aggressors are black; most targets are white.

—Daniel Lockwood, *Prison Sexual Violence* (1980)

Rap is my name and love is my game.
I'm the bed tucker the cock plucker the motherfucker. ...
The women's pet the men's fret and the punk's pin-up boy.

—H. Rap Brown, quoted in Henry L. Gates, Jr., *The Signifying Monkey: A Theory of Afro-American Literary Criticism* (1988)

[W]e [black men] are outlaws.

—Robert Chrisman, "Black Prisoners, White Law," in Herb Boyd and Robert F. Allen, eds., *Brotherman: The Odyssey of Black Men in America* (1995/1996)

Sexual attacks are still feared in prisons today, but no longer do officials and students of the institution imagine that the fact of rape has to do with a disproportionate presence of homosexuals. The head of one agency told Anthony Scacco: "[h]omosexual rapes in prisons are not homosexual at all, but heterosexuals, usually black men raping white boys for power and revenge" (quoted in Scacco 1975, 4). Is this statement another "assassination" of the black male image, as Hutchinson (1997) might suggest? Studies of sexual assaults in jails and prisons conducted during the past several decades conclude that there *is* a disproportionate number of black aggressors and white victims. Perhaps this is because the majority of prisoners today are black? No, "[w]hether or not there is a black numerical supremacy within the walls of a penal institution, the victim is usually not a black but a white or Puerto Rican" (Scacco 1975, 47–48).

When prisoners at the Tennessee Penitentiary were asked about the racial identities of the aggressors and victims in rape incidents, nearly all agreed that the aggressors were black and the victims were white (Jones 1976). Not one of the black prisoners was able to recall a single instance in which a white prisoner had raped a black prisoner. Is this the case in urban institutions with large black populations? The urban institution studied by Bartollas, Miller and Dinitz (1975a, 1975b) was majority black. Rape victims were white. Rudoff (1964) found the same, and subsequent investigations in North Carolina, California, Pennsylvania, Ohio, Rhode Island, and Illinois have all confirmed that, in correctional institutions ranging from juvenile to adult "hardened" criminal facilities, whites are more likely to be victims and blacks the aggressors in sexual attacks (Bowker 1980).

In the prison Daniel Lockwood (1980) studied, about half of the whites in the random sample were targets at one time, compared to about a fifth of blacks and Latinos. When he looked at white men only in youth prisons, the rate was higher: 71 percent. Targets and victims reported the race of the aggressors as follows: most are black (80 percent), some are Latino (14 percent), and a few are white (6 percent). The percentages are predictably reversed when he examined the ethnicity of targets: most incidents had white targets (83 percent), some had black (16 percent), and a few had Latino targets (2 percent). Other studies such as Scacco's (1975) parallel Lockwood's findings: targets tend to be white and aggressors to be black.

What else did Lockwood (1980) learn from the prison he studied? White men were a minority in the population; was it their minority status that made them vulnerable as rape victims? The answer was no: Puerto Ricans were also a minority but they did not tend to be targets. Multiple aggressors—pairs or groups—carried out 44 percent of reported rapes that Lockwood studied. Most informants reported young slender white men were the preferred objects of attack. Young white men were feminized by "jockers." Lockwood (1980) found that aggressors regularly referred to young white men with female pronouns. These young white men often came from lower-class backgrounds and from rural areas, small towns, and small cities. Overall, they were undereducated. Such young men, Lockwood concluded, are at a distinct disadvantage when confronted by tough urban black men. Due to their backgrounds, targets are likely to strongly value a tough masculine image. When aggressors call them "girls" and treat them as such, and when these young white men doubt their ability to protect themselves from black-male threats and/or attacks, they quickly collapse psychologically.

The racial character of sexual attacks intensifies the racism of many white prisoners. One white inmate confessed: "All the time, all I could think about was killing them niggers because of their attitude toward the white dudes. Every time a nigger sees a white dude, they say, 'I am going to make him my kid.' That kind of stuff really makes me sick. I just want to kill them all" (quoted in Lockwood 1980, 79; in Bowker 1980, 92). Another white inmate put it this way: "Blacks have more control in the jails than whites do. They call it revolution. ... They turn the whites into punks. You don't see any black punks around here. ... All blacks here try to be bad and stuff and show their masculinity. ... The blacks want to bring slavery back to us now" (quoted in Bartollas, Miller, and Dinitz 1976, 60). A white inmate named Gene also saw the link between contemporary prison society and the antebellum South: "Anyway, it's just like white slavery going on here. ... People are still paying money for a punk. I mean, rather than just have 'em sell any pussy, you can own it!" (quoted in Cardozo-Freeman 1984, 388).

How do black prisoners understand the black rape of young heterosexual white men? Is it, as whites allege, "reverse racism"? Unlike the short memories of many white prisoners, black prisoners, time and again, speak about interracial rape in historical as well as political terms. One informant said: "Every can I been in that's the way it is. ... It's gettin' even I guess. ... You guys been cuttin' our balls off ever since we been in this country. Now we're just gettin' even" (quoted in Carroll 1974, 174; Bowker 1980, 92). Why would rape rather than fistfighting or gambling, for instance, represent "gettin' even"? Could it be that the black men's political oppression has also been sexual, *homo*sexual? This is suggested by another prisoner who told his interviewer: "The black man's just waking up to what's been going on. Now that he's awake, he's gonna be mean. He's been raped—politically, economically, morally raped. He sees this now, but his mind's still small so he's getting back this way. But it's just a beginning" (quoted in Bowker 1980, 92–93).

A white rape victim named Alan told how his black attackers repeatedly called him a "white punk," a "white bitch," and asked questions like, "how does it feel to have a black prick in you, white boy?" (quoted in Bowker 1980, 93). Such testimony suggests "a direct link between racism and sexual victimization" (Bowker 1980, 93–94). Alan is not an isolated instance. After extensive interviewing, one prison researcher concluded: "The prison is merely an arena within which blacks may direct aggression developed through 300 years of oppression against individuals perceived to be representatives of the oppressors" (Carroll 1974, 184). Another student of prison rape was more cautious: "Putting all these observations together, it seems reasonable to conclude that racism is a major cause of some of the interracial victimization that occurs in prison, but it is not the only cause" (Bowker 1980, 94).

Several investigators seem unsurprised by the racial character of these violent events. In his study of prison rape, Goldfarb (1976) concluded that "[a]t least in isolated cases, gang rapes of inmates are conducted as a special manifestation of deep racial antagonism that exist in society at large and which are exacerbated in jails" (96). A study of the North Carolina prison system (Fuller, Orsagh, and Raber 1977) quantified racial differences in victimization. The black victimization rate was approximately 45 percent lower than the white victimization rate. Approximately four out of every ten incidents were interracial; 82 percent involved a black aggressor and a white victim (Bowker 1980).

The relationship between rape and race, as noted earlier, does not change in those prisons where the majority are white. In his study of an eastern penitentiary, Leo Carroll (1974) found that 22 percent of the men in that institution were black, yet the racialization of rape was quite similar to what Alan Davis (1968) found in the majority-black Philadelphia prison system. Fifty-six percent of rape incidents in Davis's study involved black aggressors and white victims; 29 percent involved black aggressors and black victims, and 15 percent involved white aggressors and white victims. One of Carroll's informants told him:

> To the general way of thinking it's 'cause we're confined and we've got hard rocks. But that ain't it all. *It's a way for the black man to get back at the white man.* It's one way he can assert his manhood. Anything white, even a defenseless punk, is part of what the black man hates. It's part of what he's had to fight all his life just to survive, just to have a hole to sleep in and some garbage to eat. ... It's a new ego thing. He can show he's a man by making a white guy into a girl. (Carroll 1977, 422; Bowker 1980, 9, emphasis added)

Carroll (1977) learned that nearly all of the black inmates in this prison had participated in sexual assault upon whites at some time during their incarceration.

The political character of racialized sexual attack in prisons was evident in eyewitness reports of the famous Attica (N.Y.) riot in 1971. One inmate testified that: "what has not come out yet, but will soon, is that the rebels brutally and repeatedly raped two young white kids (themselves not homosexuals), at knife point. They held knives at their throats and forced them to submit to oral and anal sodomy at the same time. They also did that to several other white kids, but I know the two I write about" (Wiggins 1972, 329). As we will see in section IV, not all racialized assaults at Attica were black on white. But those were hardened criminals, you say, thinking of Attica. Not human in some way ... human monsters. Perhaps. But in his study of adolescents at the Connecticut School for Boys, Anthony Scacco (1975) found much the same.

II. Boys Just Want to Have Fun

A man is a male human who fucks.

—Robert Jensen, "Patriarchal Sex," in Steven P. Schacht and Doris W. Ewing, eds., *Feminism and Men: Reconstructing Gender Relations* (1998)

All rape is an exercise in power.

—Susan Brownmiller, *Against Our Will: Men, Women, and Rape* (1975/1993)

I'm saying that if we treated our bodies the way we treat our souls, none of us would live past twenty .

—Robert, quoted in James Merrill, *A Different Person: A Memoir* (1993)

Juvenile facilities do not receive "good press" in the prison research literature. There is ample evidence that juvenile institutions, like prisons, are "gladiator schools," providing instruction for novice or ambivalent offenders so they may become "stone" criminals (Cardozo-Freeman 1984, 19). Worse than incarceration in separate juvenile institutions, however, would be sending young offenders to prison with adults, "due to the abnormal sexual practices which the authorities cannot control, and which are common to most institutions where substantial age disparities exist among inmates." The danger to young offenders is even greater, Vedder and King (1967) continue, when, due to overcrowding, prisoners are forced to sleep in dormitories rather than separate cells: "Beds are put very close together and the sight and smell of naked bodies, the parading and exposure which is unavoidable, charge the atmosphere with excessive stimulation" (quoted passages on 22). For instance:

> One evening at the Philadelphia Youth Center fifty-four youths overflow into the gym and try to sleep on mattresses on the basketball floor. Many don't get to sleep much. Nine boys sexually molest one victim during the night; then he's bartered to another twenty. They tell him he's lucky. Other sixteen and seventeen-year olds couldn't find sleeping space on the floor of the gym. They've been shipped to the Adult House of Corrections; the prisoners there are considerably more hardened. (Weiss and Friar 1974, 73)

Another inmate testified to the consequences of overcrowding: "Out there ... they have inmates three and four to a cell. Last time I was out there I saw a inmate get raped out there. By force he had to perform two abnormal sex acts. He was forced to commit what you call oral sex on another man, then he was forced to commit anal sex with another man. This isn't the first time that happened" (Jackson 1977, 211). Rape may accompany overcrowding, but it hardly requires it.

The Connecticut School for Boys was not overcrowded. Youthful offenders lived in age-segregated cottages. The institution was controlled, Anthony Scacco (1975) found, by the black inmate population, even though African Americans were in the numerical minority. This fact of control, political and sexual, was acknowledged by the staff as well as by the inmates. When asked why the situation had not been made public, one staff member told Scacco, "What can we do [about the act of sexual aggression]? If we speak out on behalf of the white boys, the public will say that we are being racists" (Scacco 1975, 48). This was not a solitary sentiment. Scacco found that, by their own admission, officers and other correctional personnel were unwilling to go public with their knowledge of sexual assaults on nonblacks "for fear of official and community disbelief that blacks could possibly force whites to commit such unnatural acts while they were in confinement and supposedly in the process of being rehabilitated. Further, since the staff was composed of nearly all whites, this staff member was of the opinion that they would simply not be believed by the public in general. Yet, this aggression did occur and is occurring at present in most correctional institutions throughout the nation today" (Scacco 1975, 48).

The pattern of sexual assault Scacco found in the Connecticut School for Boys in the 1970s is repeated throughout American prisons. Other researchers too found that "these [black] youth will usually follow any possible avenue to sexually victimize new boys" (Bartollas, Miller, and Dinitz 1976, 55). There is more violence in those prisons holding more violent offenders, but the pattern is the same: "Among the older boys in the training school, the white victim was always forced to submit to a black in the presence of others so that the white's humiliation and the black's domination could be witnessed. ... Gang rapes were known to have occurred in this cottage" (Scacco 1975, 49). Other men "of color" also choose to avenge political suffering through sexual means. While Puerto Ricans were in the numerical minority at the training school, Scacco reported, "should they desire a sexual outlet, they invariably choose a white youth to submit to them" (1975, 50).

The black-on-white rape that occurred in the cottage which housed the eleven to fourteen-year-old juveniles was less public than those rapes which occurred in the cottages housing the older boys. While the orifices of preference changed, the fact of racialized sexual assault did not:

> When a sexual attack did take place among the young blacks, it was usually oral rather than anal sodomy that was the price paid by their victims. In the cottage housing the older inmates the reverse was more desirable; for the victim to "take it in the rear" was the ultimate form of humiliation and a sign of domination, one that gave the victim a reputation as long as he remained confined. Also the younger blacks did not always make it mandatory that the white youth submit in front of witnesses, as did the older blacks who seemed primarily concerned with the domination and exploitation on the basis that "now whitey knows it is his turn." (Scacco 1975, 51–52)

In nearly all of these cases the aggressors and the victims were heterosexual. In one of the cottages which housed the younger inmates, Scacco discovered two homosexual boys, one white, one black. The white boy was 15; the young black man was 15½. Scacco reports that

> [t]he black youth was never forced into any sexual acts by the other blacks or whites. ... The young white homosexual was not as fortunate. ... He was small and very good looking, with long blond hair, frail stature, and known by the inmate population, as well as the staff, as being a homosexual. Thus, he was victimized by whoever desired his body for physical release or as an act of domination. ... He was often forced to provide oral sex for an entire gang of inmates because the act was initiated by one aggressive resident. (Scacco 1975, 52–53)

Puerto Rican inmates, too, tended to be sexual aggressors. "[W]hen the black youths in the cottage were not interested in the white homosexual," Scacco reports, "the Puerto Ricans were. One young Puerto Rican inmate organized a group of boys to be orally satisfied by the [white] homosexual on two separate occasions" (1975, 53).

He probably enjoyed it, you're thinking. After all, he *is* homosexual. This is, of course, the classic "blame the victim" nonsense. Even if a young gay man is sexually active, that hardly implies he enjoys forced sex with multiple partners. As other researchers of juvenile facilities have observed: "It is quite a switch to go from occasional anal intercourse to committing oral sodomy on several peers waiting in line." Heterosexually identified rape victims who turn homosexual often try to dissociate themselves from what has happened to them, sometimes by emphasizing that they were forced into homosexuality or that "they now need homosexual relationships and cannot control themselves" (quoted passages in Bartollas, Miller, and Dinitz 1976, 123).

To their surprise, Bartollas, Miller, and Dinitz (1976) found that social workers tended to be less responsive to juvenile victims' pleas for help than were youth leaders. Social workers, they hypothesized, were not close enough to the "interior" life in the cottage to be aware of what happened there; often they became aware of rapes only after the fact. Thus, they concluded, "boys who desperately need the intervention of social workers are deprived of this important resource" (Bartollas, Miller, and Dinitz 1976, 125). Significantly, female social workers seemed to be much less likely to ignore the scapegoat's pleas than were male social workers (Bartollas, Miller, and Dinitz 1976, 128 n. 18).

Could this be because male social workers imagine the raped boy gets what he deserved, what he secretly wants? This appeared to be the case in the Connecticut juvenile facility. The staff, Scacco discovered, believed that the white homosexual boy was in fact guilty of enticement, but the young man insisted that he consented only because he was forced to. If he had not submitted to his attackers freely, he believed he would have been forced to service them. "This giving in," Scacco reports, "is not at all uncommon, and in larger institutions such as prisons, is viewed by the officers as a voluntary commitment on the part of the victim. In reality, however, the inmate desired by the jock or wolf goes along with him in order not to be gang raped at the whim of the marauders wandering within the institution" (1975, 54). Whether the target is female or male, "men" justify sexual assault by insisting that the victim "wants it."

Why were the white boys always the ones who were attacked? When the nonwhite aggressors were questioned by Scacco why they always seem to choose whites to submit to them sexually, their answers were often that "now it is their turn" (Scacco 1975, 48). Given that black men were not raped outside prison, to what prior event can they be referring? Lynching? Or is the entire spectrum of white supremacy and racism laced with white homosexual desire and assault, so that black men feel not only deprived of their civil rights but of their manhood as well? Scacco concludes: "[t]he black man in prison seeks to make the white captors imprisoned with them suffer for the discrimination he has endured. He does this through sexual assault which he believes buttresses his status as a man, a status he is convinced is constantly thwarted by white society" (1975, 75).

The particular reformatory in Connecticut that Scacco studied had a "large number of black sissies" (1975, 60) who were sexually available. While Scacco found that a few of the black inmates took advantage of this opportunity, the majority wanted white boys. "For a black to have sex with another black," he reports, "carried far less status than a black to have sex with a white, especially a white that was forced to become a punk, thereby attesting to the superiority of the black jock" (Scacco 1975, 60). Scacco concluded: "It appears to become an essential ingredient in their concept of [black] manhood to make it known that whites are the sole object of their sexual attacks in the majority of cases" (1975, 61).

There are those who have argued that homosexuality is the "consolation prize" in prison, that given heterosexual availability homosexuality would virtually disappear. But Alan Davis (1968) reported a case in which young black men on their way to trial in a sheriff's van raped a white youth. In sensationalized terms, Weiss and Friar (1974) tell the story:

> Dennis Cujdik is a runaway from home. His parents decide that he needs to be taught a lesson. They have him arrested. He is thrust into the windowless sheriff's van that is leaving the Philadelphia Detention Court. A crowd of prisoners is crammed inside. When the doors clang shut, the van is pitch darkness. The Cujdik boy is plagued by four black teenagers. "This dude ain't wearing underwear!" His tormentors fling a coat over Cujdik's head and commit sodomy on the wildly tossing boy. Cujdik's insides are scraped and bleeding. His head feels fractured. He vomits. Whenever his rapists let up for a moment he cries for help. The packed, lurching mob makes no response. His assaulters gag his mouth. They burn his legs with cigarettes.
>
> The van finally reaches the court. The attackers rip off Cujdik's shirt and use it to mop his blood. They fling him to the rear of the van. They warn him that they'll trap him in the van going back if he informs on them. As the doors open, the four are the first to jump out. Dizzily, Cujdik descends from the van, swaying as he walks. He makes up a tale to explain his bloody condition to the guards. They seem to know he's lying. And so, in spite of his terror of his rapists' threatened revenge, the boy blurts out what has happened. The doctor sets his fractured nose. His broken jaw is set. He is treated for the bleeding in his anus. (71)

"How long," Scacco (1975) asks, "could they [the rapists] have been deprived of a woman, yet they sought out a white male for their aggressive act. They most likely would have committed the same act of aggression on a white if they caught him walking alone through Central Park" (1975, 63).

Alan Davis found widespread sexual assault on those waiting for trial in his study of the jail and prison system in Philadelphia. In one incident a "slender 21-year-old committed to the Philadelphia Detention Center merely for presentence evaluation, had been sexually assaulted within minutes of his admission" (1968, 8). Davis concluded that the conquest and degradation of the victim were a primary factor in the sexual aggression he studied. Black aggressors told their white male victims "we're going to take your manhood," "you'll have to give up some face," and "we're going to make a girl out of you" (16). Several young black inmates reported that they also rape young white men on the outside "just to show them who is the man" (quoted in Scacco 1975, 64). Since the victim of sexual assault is almost always white, "race is the single most important socio-demographic characteristic associated with victimization" (Dinitz, Miller, and Bartollas 1973, 9).

Perhaps making the same mistake Joseph Fishman made (i.e., conflating sexual behavior with sexual identity), Scacco concludes that: "[h]omosexuality is probably more prevalent among Negroes in the population of a large prison than among the white population. Because of this and because blacks take whites as their victims, there is a constant catalyst for racial tension and extreme violence in penal institutions" (1975, 63). One young prisoner in Philadelphia related his experience:

> I was laying in my bed when seven or eight inmates came to my bed, pulled the blanket off me, put it on the floor and told me to pull my pants down and lay face down on the blanket. I said "no" and was punched in the face by one of the inmates. The inmate that punched me stated if I did not get on the floor the other inmates would gang up on me. I got on the floor and my pants and shorts were pulled off. Two inmates spread and held my legs apart while two more inmates held my hands in front of me. While I was being buggered from behind another inmate would make me suck his penis. This continued until all the inmates had attacked me and I heard one of them say it was 1:30 A.M., so let's go to bed. They put me on the bed, covered me with the blanket and one of them patted me on the behind saying "good boy we will see you again tomorrow night." (quoted in Hopper 1969, 87)

Another victim in the Philadelphia system was twenty-four-year-old (white) William McNichol. An eyewitness told Davis:

> That was June 11th. I was assigned to E Dorm. Right after the light went out I saw this colored male, Geronimo—I think his last name is White. He went over to this kid [William McNichol] and slapped his face with a belt. He was saying, "Come on back with us," and the kid kept saying, "I don't want to."
>
> "After being slapped with the belt he walked back with another colored male named Wolfe. They were walking him back into E Dorm. They were telling him to put his hands down and stop crying so the guard will not know what is going on. About twelve fellows took turns with him. This went on for about two hours.
>
> "After this he came back to his bed and he stated, 'They all took turns on me.' He lay there for about twenty minutes and Geronimo came over to the kid's bed and pulled his pants down and raped him again. When he got done, Wolfe did it again, and then about four or five others got on him.

> "While one of the guys was on him, raping him, Wolfe came over and said, 'Open your mouth and suck on this and don't bite it." He then put his penis in the kid's mouth and made him suck on it. The kid was hollering that he was gagging, and Wolfe stated, 'You better not bite it or I'll kick your teeth out.'
>
> "While they had this kid, they also had another kid named William in another section of E Dorm. He had his pants off and he was bent over and they were taking turns on him. This was Wolfe, Geronimo, and about seven other colored fellows. Two of the seven were brothers.
>
> "Wolfie came back and stated, 'Boy, I got two virgins in one night; maybe I should make it three.'
>
> "At this time he was standing over me. I stated, 'What are you looking at?'
>
> "And he said, 'We'll save him for tomorrow night'." (Weiss and Friar 1974, 71–72)

Alan J. Davis was no prison researcher. At the time of his study, he was serving as an assistant district attorney in Philadelphia; he had been appointed by Judge Alexander F. Barbieri to supervise a three-month investigation, to be conducted jointly by the Philadelphia District Attorney's office and the Police Department, of sexual assaults in the Philadelphia prison system. The 103-page report, which would become a landmark study in research on prison rape, revealed that, "nearly every slightly-built young man committed by the courts [was] sexually approached within a day or two of his admission to prison, and that many of these young men [were] repeatedly raped by groups of inmates." Other young white men, due to the threat of gang rape, found protection through a "homosexual relationship with an individual tormentor." They conservatively estimated that 2,000 assaults had occurred in the Philadelphia prison system within a twenty-six-month period. Of these, only ninety-six inmates reported the assaults to the prison authorities, and of these only sixty-four were documented in prison records, and of these only in forty cases was punishment of the aggressor forthcoming. The investigation made it clear that guards in the Philadelphia prison system declined, even refused, to show concern or take responsibility for the prevention of rapes. "One victim screamed for over an hour while he was being raped in his cell; the block guard ignored the screams and laughed at the victim when the rape was over" (quoted passages in Cardozo-Freeman 1984, 401–402 n. 7; see also Brownmiller 1975/1993, 264–265, for a discussion of the Davis study). Alan Davis reported: "We were struck by the fact that the typical sexual aggressor does not consider himself to be homosexual, or even to have engaged in homosexual acts" (1968, 15). Hard to believe isn't it, straight boys engaged in homosexual acts, even if for political reasons? It turns out that straight boys perform homosexual acts for money as well as politics, and on the "outside" too. One insider estimated that 40 percent of actors in male gay porn consider themselves straight (Rupaul Show 1997). "Gay for pay" is not an uncommon phrase in male homosexual communities, as drug-addicted straight guys especially will turn "tricks" to obtain the cash they need for their next fix.

The situation described by Davis is not limited to Philadelphia or to the 1960s. In spring 1981, New York City Mayor Edward Koch criticized a judge who refused to send a white, middle-class student to Rikers Island because he might be homosexually raped. "We take judicial notice of defendant's slight build, his mannerisms, dress, color, and ethnic background," said Judge Stanley Gartenstein. "Ross would be immediately subject to homosexual rape and sodomy and to brutalities from prisoners such as make the imagination recoil in horror" (*New York Times* 9 April 1981 B-5; quoted in Jacobs 1983, 80 n. 1). A year earlier, two white inmate rape victims filed suit in the Northern District of Illinois alleging that Cook County Jail personnel failed to remove them from tiers predominantly populated by black men who threatened rape. This failure to act, they contended, violated their Eighth Amendment rights (Jacobs 1983, 97 n. 16). Sex is political, racial, generational. In prison, as on the "outside," it is often forced.

III. Prisoners of Desire

[O]ne of the effects of prison rapes is to force people to become consensual homosexuals against their will.

—Lee Bowker, *Prison Victimization* (1980)

What men are most afraid of is the body of another man.

—Margaret Atwood, "Alien Terriory," in Lawrence Goldstein, ed., *The Male Body* (1994)

Goddam near a punk in every bunk in this joint, man.

—Pete, an inmate, quoted in Inez Cardozo-Freeman, *The Joint: Language and Culture in a Maximum Security Prison* (1984)

Lee Bowker (1980) tells the story of Allan, a young white victim of a group rape by an inmate named Willie and his friends. After the initial group rape, during which he was degraded verbally as well as raped repeatedly, he was subjected to numerous individual assaults by a large number of black inmates. After suffering these assaults over a period of several months he then accepted the offer of a well-known and powerful white prisoner to become his "kid." Allan agreed to provide his new "mate" and several of his friends with unlimited sexual services in return for cigarettes, store items, and some degree of protection. Bowker terms Allan's experience a "train job" in which a number of offenders attack a single victim. Willie played the role of the "ripper" as he set up Allan for the initial group rape to be followed by additional sexual assaults, which Willie organized. Only after Allan had become completely submissive did the aggressors lose interest in him. It is at this point that Allan—and prison victims generally—can be converted to "canteen punks."

Bowker does not tell us, but Allan may have been sold to the older white man. Inez Cardozo-Freeman (1984) tells us that most of the pimps are black and nearly all the "girls" in their "stables" are white. The most famous pimp in the Washington state prison she studied was a black man named Tall Tim. He was, she says, a "living legend." Tall Tim supplied "girls" to pimps and did little or no ordinary pimping himself. He was a kind of "white-slaver"; he dealt only in white "girls" (387). An informant told Cardozo-Freeman the story:

> You always see Tall Tim at the movies. See, everybody goes to the movies, gettin all ready, man, and the flicks start and you always gotta check Tall Tim sittin there. He sits pretty tall in the saddle. He's a big black dude, fancy dresser and he's always got these little white broads sittin with him. Everybody will walk by, check em out and he sits there like a king, you know, big rooster in a barnyard. You know what I mean? He's got his suit on and a little Stetson hat, man. Boy, he's be dressin down for a motherfucker—that's what he'd say. And he'd come on down to the ole movie, man, and he'd bring his hoes with him. ... He'd strut his stuff around there for a while, man, and then sit down. In a couple of weeks he'd have a couple of new ones. He'd done sold those. Sell em for a hundred bucks a piece or some damn thing, depending on what they looked like.
>
> He makes the bucks by gettin em prepped and ready and sellin em for hard cash instead of gettin out hustlin. They learn how to dress and they learn how to act, and they learn how to make the dough, and by the time he's ready to sell em, they're worth a few bucks. (quoted in Cardozo-Freeman 1984, 387–388)

Significant sums have been paid by one man to own another in the prison Cardozo-Freeman studied. Several inmates reported that as much as five hundred dollars had been paid to Tall Tim for a particularly attractive "girl." Tall Tim was admired by many in the prison as a kind of entrepreneur; he had made himself into a middleman by supplying "girls" to joint pimps. Pimping is carried on not only by individuals; gangs and clubs will buy a "girl" and put her to work. The new acquisition is forced not only to sexually serve the needs of the members of the gang or club, but they may require him to sell himself to others as they wish. These young men—now "girls"—are also required to keep house for club members (Cardozo-Freeman 1984, 388).

How common are organized gangs? In the 1980s the largest number of gang members were in Illinois (5,300), Pennsylvania (2,400) and California (2,050). In the 1980s, as a proportion of all inmates in state and federal prisons, gang members comprised 3 percent (Camp and Camp 1985, vii). Prison gangs are said to have begun in Washington state in 1950. Almost three-quarters of the gangs "project a macho image" (viii). Membership is based first on race, sometimes connected with racial superiority beliefs—for example, Aryan Brotherhood. Second, prior affiliation or association with members in a close-to-home location often influences membership, for example, Vice Lords. Next in importance in gang composition is the sharing of strong beliefs, political and/or religious, for example, Black Guerrilla Family. Finally, sharing a lifestyle of motorcycle "machismo" influences membership, for example, Avengers. There are overlaps in types of gangs. While any of these types may engage in prison rape, these do not include the countless number of informal groupings of men, such as Willie and his friends, who come together for the express purpose of rape. In nearly two-thirds of the gangs, membership is perceived as a lifetime commitment, "blood in, blood out" (ix).

Prison administrators blame the gangs for the much of the drug trafficking in their institutions. But prison gangs hardly limit their activities to drug trafficking: extortion, homosexual prostitution, gambling, and protection are also mainstays. Gangs seem to have become influential in a number of prison systems during the 1970s and 1980s (Camp and Camp 1985). But more than any other activity, "homosexuality causes more quarrels, fights, knifings, and punishment in prison than any other single problem" (Martin 1954, 177). Indeed, Sylvester, Reed and Nelson (1977) reported that homosexual activity is a leading motive for inmate homicides. In a study of twelve murders occurring during a 26-month period among a population of federal prisoners, Nacci and Kane (1983) found that five had a sexual basis, that is, sex pressuring, unrequited love, or jealousy. Hans Toch (1969), among others, reports similar findings. Some prison officers think of homosexuality only in terms of the potential it holds for overt violence or coercion: "If a male inmate has another male inmate that is his 'woman,' he will fight to protect that 'woman' and he'd want to kill anyone that wanted to touch him. They're very possessive about their 'wife' and or whatever you want to call them and they're more physical about it than the women" (quoted in Pollock 1986, 72). Sex is the first motive cited by most staff and inmates for inmate-on-inmate brutality (Fleisher 1994).

The situation facing young men, especially young white men, is made clear in the following account written by an inmate who characterized himself as a "dirty old man who happens to be a lifer in a California prison." During an extensive interview with Wayne S. Wooden and Jay Parker (1982), the inmate offered to write his "take" on issues that most young white men face as they are processed from county jail into prison. The paper, entitled "Decisions," seems to me sensationalistic, but Wooden and Parker (1982) insist that it accurately speaks to the experiences that many of the "punks" described to him. The paper is reprinted here with Wooden and Parker's editing.

> Decisions, decisions, decisions! That is the name of the game for a young, good-looking (or even half good-looking) white male coming to a California prison. The critical period for this youngster is from the minute he reads on the bulletin board in the Guidance Center that he is being transferred to such-and-such a prison, after his six- to eight-week processing. That notice on the bulletin board immediately tells him if he was lucky enough to transfer to a "soft joint" (relatively easy time with a minimal amount of sexual pressure) or to be unfortunate enough to be sent to a "hard joint" (a prison where he will have to literally fight to keep the jackals from making his rectum twice its normal size within one to two days after he steps off the bus at his destination).
>
> Does all this sound overly dramatic, exaggerated, distorted? It is not meant to be, and it is not. It is called "The Facts of Prison Life for Good-

Looking Young Whites." It becomes a "horror" story if he gets transferred to one of the "hard joints" and can be either easy or hard in the "soft joints." The other prisons fall somewhere in between.

The first lesson "Allan" [the inmate's name for the prototypical young white prisoner] has learned in the Guidance Center is that he is surrounded by a high percentage of horny incarcerated felons with little or no moral values, who are bitter and hostile about a variety of subjects. These felons may be mad about not getting county jail or probation; or they just got a "Dear John" letter or divorce papers from the wife; or they would not be in prison if their crime partner had not testified against them ("ratted on him"), etc.

Allan has many propositions thrown his way during his short stay in the Guidance Center. Some are subtle, some not. Some men pretend they want to be his friend; some offer canteen privileges, cigarettes, or some good grass for his body. Some want to fuck him, some want to suck him, some want Allan to suck or fuck them. Some want to make him into a woman by having him pluck his eyebrows, or wear bikini shorts. But, generally speaking, there is no real threat to him—a threat such as being physically beaten up because he would not cooperate, or being raped or having a shank [knife] put to his throat for sexual favors. To repeat, this is generally speaking, because there are physical assaults, there are rapes (single and gang style), and there are threats with weapons.

But the Guidance Centers are usually closely supervised. There is a train-station atmosphere with people coming and going all the time, and a guy can stay in his cell except for meals and ducats [a pass to go somewhere to take a test or to be interviewed].

The second lesson that Allan learns is that all these sex-starved individuals do not seem to pay any attention to the black queens or black homosexuals, nor do they seem to show any interest in the Mexican queens or Mexican homosexuals in the Guidance Center. He soon finds out, also, that all the sex-starved whites are not interested in the blacks (primarily because of the negative peer pressure that would develop in such a situation) and that the Mexican male inmates quickly establish "territory rights" to virtually all of the Mexican gays and Mexican queens. Fully aware of how possessive and "macho" Mexican males are (or appear to be), the white inmates give a wide berth to the Mexican homosexuals.

Then comes the bus trip to the prison where Allan will do most of his time. And now, during the long bus ride, he must make the following decisions:

1) Is he going to hook up willingly with one guy who will keep everyone else off of him?
2) Is he going to get into fist fight after fist fight and not submit to sexual demands? Is he so weak that he has no choice?
3) Which race or ethnic group should he choose to hook up with sexually, or does it matter to him or to the rest of the inmate population? If he is physically strong (good build, healthy), will that hide his mental weakness? Or, conversely, if he is mentally strong, will that overcome his obvious physical passivity?

4) Will he go directly to "Protective Custody," a single cell in a section of the prison where no one will be able to attack him sexually?
5) Will he hook up with one person or with a gang? A gang would probably give him much more and better protection, and also would provide him with drugs, but he would then be passed around to different gang members like "a box of Ritz crackers."
6) Should he hook up with the first decent con who propositions him, one who will treat him as a human being even though Allan will be his "kid" or "punk"?
7) Should he attach himself to a guy approximately his own age, or to an older con who has been around for a while and knows all the game-playing tricks other cons will use to entice Allan into becoming their "kid"?
8) Should Allan look for a con, regardless of age, who makes a full $100 draw a month at the inmate canteen and can supply him any drugs and other items he wants?
9) Or should he go with the guy who will treat him as a human being between sexual encounters?

Questions similar to these will bounce around Allan's head during the bus ride to his new "home" for the next few years. They will also keep him awake at night for the first week or two after he arrives at the new prison. Because Allan is of average intelligence (a good omen), but because he is also a "fish" (a bad omen), there will be many conflicts in his mind in his day-to-day dealings with the sex-starved, psychotic, paranoid, and hostile general inmate population.

The first thing Allan learns in his new "home" is that this general inmate population does not give a damn whether or not he is gay or straight. That comes as quite a shock to him. He asks himself why everyone would expect him to play the game when he is straight. By the same token, a new gay inmate asks himself why everyone expects him to "put out" just because he is homosexual. But Allan, who can be either gay or straight, reluctantly accepts the fact that in prison no one gives a damn what he is sexually. All the mainline cons know is that he is "a good-looking piece of meat" and they want that "meat." And then it *really* sinks into Allan's mind that there is little if any difference between his position if he is gay or straight, since it is his being young and good-looking that is the prized commodity.

Two other questions also plague Allan.

10) Will he permit sex play from another inmate for "X" number of packs of cigarettes (the same as currency in prison) to "turn a trick"? Allan has to size up his economic situation. Can he expect anyone "on the streets" to send him money to buy the basic necessities like deodorants, toothpaste, soap, and shampoo? Or has Allan any skills that can be used to get a prison job with a high pay number (clerk, typist).

> 11) If he hooks up with someone for protection, will he be sold to another convict when his "old man" transfers, or gets locked up in long-term segregation?
>
> Every white youngster coming to prison for the first time must wade his way through this seemingly endless series of questions and then decide what is best for him.
>
> Unless he looks like Dracula. (quoted in Wooden and Parker 1982, 103–106)

A Medium-Security Institution

Wayne Wooden and Jay Parker (1982) studied "sociosexual patterns among inmates" in a medium-security prison for adult male felons during 1979 and 1980. Located in California with a prison population of over 2,500 men, this medium-security institution, unlike the maximum-security prisons, had little if any violent activity or racial tension. The prison was one to which "known" (i.e., effeminate) homosexuals were sent. Inmates were housed in single-man cells as opposed to two-man cells or dormitory-type facilities. Single-celled housing, they noted, is aimed at reducing the frequency of sexual assault and sexual activity generally.

Ten percent of this prison population were self-identified homosexuals, 10 percent identified themselves as bisexual, and the remaining 80 percent identified as heterosexual. Over half (55 percent) of the heterosexual group reported engaging in sexual activity while in prison. What percentage of these men reported being pressured into having sex against their will? Wooden and Parker (1982) found that 41 percent of the homosexuals, 2 percent of the bisexuals, and 9 percent of the heterosexuals reported they had been sexually victimized. The total number of sexually assaulted men represented 14 percent of the sample.

What defense against sexual assault was possible in this prison? For the majority of sexual "targets," Wooden and Parker concluded, "the best and safest coping strategy is to 'hook up' with a jocker, an inmate dominant enough to protect them" (1982, 18). In this prison, they report, "there is an institutionalized social pressure, both overt and covert, toward feminizing homosexuals and the kids" [heterosexual white boys] (Wooden and Parker 1982, 21). To be a positively self-affirmed "gay" person, as opposed to an institutionally enforced "punk," is extremely difficult, given the pervasiveness of antigay attitudes among inmates. However, Wooden and Parker conclude, "the situation in this particular prison is not as acute as it is in the maximum-security prisons ('hard-core joints'), according to our interviews with convicts who had transferred into this prison from these harder 'joints'" (1982, 22). "For the most part," they conclude: "any young, passive, or feminine [guy] is going to be constantly pressured and 'hit on,' and often either threatened or actually physically raped. ... In prison, any homosexual or vulnerable 'marked' heterosexual who is not hooked up is 'fair game'" (Wooden and Parker 1982, 22).

One informant reported that he was the only homosexual on his tier. He reported being propositioned frequently by the other straight inmates in spite of his known relationship with another inmate. The story goes:

> He was sitting in his room when "Larry," a young, muscled, black convict who lived on the same floor but on the other side of the building came to the door. When he opened the door, Larry asked him for a "shot" (two to three teaspoons of instant coffee; inmates are constantly drinking coffee) and started to make small talk. During the conversation, Larry was standing in the doorway to the informant's cell, indicating an erection prominent in his pants. Larry finally asked for a "play," whereupon the informant stated that he was not into it and that he was busy. Larry was persistent, stating something to the effect "Come on, it'll only take five minutes. There's no one around." At this point he unzipped his fly and exposed an erection, stating, "Come on just touch it, I'm as horny as hell." The informant then acquiesced. Larry stepped in and closed the door, and the inmate orally copulated him. (Wooden and Parker 1982, 39)

Wooden and Parker observe: "This is a fairly typical and not uncommon occurrence" (1982, 39).

It is also common for straight inmates to become aroused when alone in the shower with a homosexual, "and an erection usually leads to a proposition" (Wooden and Parker 1982, 40). In juvenile facilities the shower area is an especially high-risk area. Sexual activity can occur within a very short time. The toilet too is high-risk. Boys in juvenile facilities take advantage of the fact that staff often forget that another youth was just granted permission to go to the bathroom; they then request to go themselves. Even when staff do remember that another youth was granted permission to leave the program area, it is easy to forget to check to see if the first boy is safe (Bartollas, Miller, and Dinitz 1976). At quiet times in the medium-security adult facility Wooden and Parker studied, a quick sexual encounter can occur in the shower room, but due to the lack of privacy this is not common. If the homosexual man is agreeable, the participants ordinarily go to one of their rooms. "Since virtually all homosexuals are hooked up," Wooden and Parker report, "these impromptu encounters only occur while the homosexual's 'old man' is at work or not around. ... Since gossip does tend to get around, these types of sexual encounters must be orchestrated very discreetly, at times when other occupants of the tier are unaware" (1982, 40).

From their observations and given the responses of self-identified homosexual men in their survey, gay men in the medium-security prison Wooden and Parker (1982) studied did not report discrimination by the staff, except on occasion by an individual guard who was obviously homophobic. Three-fifths of the gay men surveyed felt that the staff tended to tolerate homosexual relationships between inmates. It appeared that not all of self-identified homosexuals in prison had had prior homosexual experiences, suggesting that some number of men "came out"—that is, assumed a homosexual identity—while in prison. They conclude: "'Gay liberation' has not yet entered prison walls in the sense that two gay men can hook up and be together in a visible way" (Wooden and Parker 1982, 162).

If the younger man is "turned out," made into a punk and becomes the older man's lover, is there affection expressed? Wooden and Parker (1982) found that some heterosexual convicts will "mug" (kiss) their partners, others will not. Like Scacco, Wooden and Parker (1982) found that while the men's prison permitted and even appeared to sanction sexual aggression, affection or love were not acceptable, except in rare instances: "Prison homosexuality is condoned so long as the homosexual assumes the passive feminine role and hooks up with a straight male. Supportive homosexual relationships between two gay men are not condoned or even tolerated in prison" (Wooden and Parker 1982, 161). Very seldom does this affection occur "between the 'straights who use' and their punks or sissies" (115). Instead, aggression is often used by the "jocker" to keep his punk in line. The challenge, they write,

> of turning out a heterosexual youngster is much more exciting than engaging in sex with a willful homosexual sissy who readily appears to conform to the feminized role. Further, since the effeminate homosexual does not resist, opportunities for displacing the jocker's sexual aggression are lessened and thereby the sexual dynamics and release are less satisfying. In this regard both the passive heterosexual and the masculine-defined homosexual remain "prized objects" since force is required to get them to "fall into line" and assume submissive sexual roles. (Wooden and Parker 1982, 115)

The more reliable predictor of homosexual behavior inside prison is heterosexual behavior before sentencing: "How these jockers treat their prison sexual partners is comparable to ways they interacted with their wives and other women on the outside" (Wooden and Parker 1982, 22–23). These "sociosexual patterns" are not reflected in the studies conducted on women inmates, however (Wooden and Parker 1982). "An imitative rape ideology among females is not unknown in the women's institutions," Susan Brownmiller (1975/1993) reports, "although it nowhere matches the male experience" (267).

Many of the heterosexual inmates become quite skillful at "cruising" or "hitting on" younger men. Wooden and Parker characterized the cruising of older men as "steady and low-key." In fact, much cruising is subtle enough that only those who are "tuned in to the game" are aware of it. At the prison they studied, "there are a certain number of (mostly black) straight men who have developed an 'eye' or 'feel' for homosexual cruising games, and participate actively in the sexual pick-up" (Wooden and Parker 1982, 36). Once two inmates have had sex, it is easy, Wooden and Parker found, for them to establish a pattern.

For the heterosexual sample in Wooden and Parker's medium-security prison, 44 percent of the men reported having received fellatio since coming to prison. For those men who engaged in this sexual activity, slightly more than half have participated minimally (on one to three occasions). There were heterosexual men (30 percent), however, who had received fellatio on more than three occasions since coming to prison. According to the data they collected, Wooden and Parker found that married heterosexuals were just as likely as single heterosexuals, and more likely than separated or divorced heterosexuals, to report involvement in prison sexual behavior. Interesting, in light of deprivation theories of homosexual prison behavior (that is, that men choose each other only because women are absent), Wooden and Parker found that:

> [M]arried heterosexuals who received conjugal privileges were in fact the *most* likely to report sexual involvement with male inmates compared to those married men who did not participate in the family visitation program. On occasion, in the visiting day room the two men hooked up would individually be visiting with their respective families while at the same time keeping an eye on the other's activities, all of which were hidden from the inmates' families. (Wooden and Parker 1982, 55)

Wooden and Parker's findings undermine a time-worn assumption that the incidence of homosexuality in single-sex prisons would be decreased by allowing more furloughs and conjugal visits (Burstein 1977; Reid 1979; Pollock 1986). Many have recommended replacing single-sex institutions with coed facilities (Catalino 1972; James 1969; Robbins 1953; Ross et al. 1978; Ruback 1975). Interestingly, no evidence exists showing that having men and women imprisoned together decreases homosexuality. When Alice Propper (1981) compared rates of prison homosexuality in coed and single-sex institutions, she found identical rates of homosexuality in both, including identical rates of homosexuality in coed and female prisons once the effects of preprison homosexuality were controlled. The heterosexism of many researchers is evident, implied in Inez Cardozo-Freeman's declaration that "it is the lack of this important and natural need [heterosex] that makes prison inmates so vulnerable to homosexual experience in prison" (1984, 385). But like many of her colleagues, she immediately undermines her heterosexism by quoting Hopper, who reluctantly conceded that "homosexuality ... gives testimony to the fact that humans can meet their emotional needs with persons of the same sex" (Hopper 1971, 75).

One of the few studies which indicated a decrease of homosexuality in prisons where inmates were permitted conjugal visits is Hopper's (1969), who studied Mississippi's experiment with conjugal visits. When Hopper asked guards to compare homosexual activity among inmates who had conjugal visits with that among those who did not, eleven of the sergeants said that those inmates who were permitted conjugal visits engaged in much less homosexuality. The remaining three rated those inmates permitted conjugal visits as engaging in a little less. All informants believed, however, that, as a group, those receiving conjugal visits engaged in less homosexuality (Hopper 1969). Other countries seem even more determined to preserve heterosexuality; Mexico is one of those countries that allows conjugal visits, not only for wives, but for "sweethearts" as well (Cardozo-Freeman 1984, 366 n. 7). But, as noted, in the medium-security prison Wooden and Parker studied, this strategy did not appear to work.

As noted, in Latin countries "top" men are often regarded as straight even when their sexual partners are male. What matters is who enters whom. In the United States, black men are the "straight guys" in prison, even when they identify themselves as bisexual. For instance, Wooden and Parker (1982) found that whereas for black bisexuals engaged in the dominant roles of receiving fellatio and performing anal penetration, very few reversed the sexual roles. Only 22 percent of the black bisexuals, for example, reported performing oral copulation compared to 67 percent of the Mexican-American and 90 percent of the white bisexuals. Not one of the black bisexuals reported he had been penetrated. Most of the white bisexuals (70 percent), however, did report having been anally entered by another man.

Self-defined heterosexual inmates from lower-class backgrounds exhibited fewer inhibitions concerning sexual activity than did inmates from middle-class backgrounds, as long as they maintained the dominant, aggressive position. Wooden and Parker (1982) cite this pattern in understanding the higher incidence of sexual activity by black and Chicano heterosexuals than their white counterparts. Twice as many black heterosexuals (81 percent) were sexually active in prison compared to white heterosexuals (38 percent); over half (55 percent) of the Chicano heterosexuals were sexually active. Black heterosexual men (62 percent) and Chicano heterosexual men (52 percent) were more likely to have received fellatio; black men, in fact, were twice as likely as heterosexual white men to have received fellatio.

Black men were also twice as likely as white men to have performed anal penetration, although the frequency for this sexual behavior was not as high as that of receiving fellatio. In both of these dominant and "masculine" sexual roles—anal penetration and receiving fellatio—black heterosexual men were the most sexually active, with Chicanos and whites following in that order. Only in the number of submissive sexual roles—active in fellatio, passive in anal intercourse—did white heterosexual men report a higher rate of incidence than did African-American or Chicano heterosexual men. More than a few of the white heterosexuals who reported "passive" sexual activity had been forced into this "punk" role (Wooden and Parker 1982).

In Wooden and Parker's research, a majority of rapes followed the pattern of blacks as aggressors and whites as victims. However, once sexual pairings occurred, the partners tended not to be interracial. Interracial pairings were in fact uncommon in the medium-security prison they studied; they were virtually nonexistent at maximum-security institutions. The reasons for this taboo? Wooden and Parker speculate that the strong racial solidarity that prison gangs enforce prevents the development of interracial relationships which express affection. But if the relationship is one of aggression? "As we have noted, it is rare for ethnic minorities to 'turn out' one of their own. ... Both blacks and Chicanos, however, will turn out a white boy if they get the chance" (Wooden and Parker 1982, 60).

In the prison Wooden and Parker studied no one racial group or gang appeared to be in control. According to several respondents, at some of the maximum-security prisons (where they had served time before being transferred), often the gangs determined who had access to punks and homosexuals (Wooden and Parker 1982). How are the young men approached? As we have seen, many are approached quite directly: "Hey, kid, we want your ass. You can either give it up or we'll take it. It's up to you. You can do it the easy way or the hard way" (quoted in Wooden and Parker 1982, 103). Occasionally if a youngster is physically strong and/or "shows heart" he can win the respect of other convicts and be left alone. Wooden and Parker conclude: "this is rare" (1982, 107).

At some point in their imprisonment, at least 50 percent of young victimized inmates appeal to the staff (Toch 1992). Why is it that all rape victims do not appeal to prison authorities for protection? Appealing to the authorities for help would be considered "snitching." If an inmate is labeled a "snitch jacket"—meaning he has complained to the authorities—he is unable to "walk the main line" (that is, live among the general prison population) for fear of reprisals. His only alternative is to request protective custody, which means isolation from the total prison population, a total lockdown. Protective custody is not an attractive alternative for someone with a long sentence. For almost everyone the isolation of protective custody is psychologically intolerable. Many inmates prefer to "take their chances" of being victimized again rather than being segregated and alone (Wooden and Parker 1982).

The story of "Ray" illustrates this problem. "Ray" was young, white, and heterosexual. Twenty-one years of age, he had just arrived, that is, he was still on "fish row." One Saturday evening when the majority of inmates were at the movie, two black men forced their way into his room and raped him. They took turns; one man kept watch while the other raped. They dared him to complain to prison officials, but after they departed Ray went to the guard office in tears, told the story to the lieutenant on duty, and identified his assailants (Wooden and Parker 1982).

Ray and the two men were all thrown into the "hole," Ray for protective custody and the two others pending their disciplinary hearing and subsequent prosecution in the courts. While the three were physically separated, they were still within yelling distance. The two men threatened Ray, promising him that if he testified against them, their partners on the street would retaliate against his family. More than the threats against his own person, threats against his family intimidated Ray. When the district attorney came to interview him concerning the filing of charges, Ray suddenly was unable to make a positive identification. At the institutional disciplinary hearing, too, Ray was unable to make positive identification. Subsequently the two accused men were found "not guilty," no charges were filed, they were returned to their quad. Ray was sent to another quad where he suffered the same fate, especially now that he had a reputation for having already been "had" once already (Wooden and Parker 1982).

This sequence of events appears very familiar to prison officials, or so it seemed to Ray when he was interviewed by Wooden and Parker. In his view the prison staff was eager to discourage rape proceedings. Prison officials are well aware of sexual assaults. They knew that Ray was going to be threatened, that he would most likely change his story, and that once returned to the prison floor, he would be raped again. Prison officials do not want the "bad publicity" of rape prosecutions. They work to avoid any official documentation of sexual assaults or sexual activity generally. They were eager, or so it seemed to Ray, to sweep the whole affair "under the rug," pretending that it had not happened (Wooden and Parker 1982).

Most of the young men coerced into sexual relations in prison remain self-identified heterosexuals, despite performing countless numbers of homosexual acts. Forced to "hook up," most young inmates maintain a heterosexual identity while engaging in homosexual behavior. Given they act and talk like heterosexual men (i.e., act "butch"), it is often difficult for the prison staff to identify them as "punks," although their constant interactions with their "old man" at meals and on the quad provide clues to those who can see (Wooden and Parker 1982).

Obtaining information from these young men through interview procedures proved to be extremely difficult for Wooden and Parker, partly due to the embarrassment these young men felt at being publicly identified as a "punk." Although it was common knowledge in prison that these young men were "hooked up," this fact was seldom discussed openly. What Wooden and Parker (1982) learned from both observing and interviewing these young men is that, despite their brave front, many of these "punks" were in fact in distress, many of them perhaps clinically depressed. What were the symptoms? Wooden and Parker felt that their body language indicated defeat and humiliation. They did not project a sense of strength nor did they appear to have any positive self-esteem; a situation, Wooden and Parker point out, "that was *not* generally true for the effeminate homosexual group. If anything, these [heterosexual] youngsters appear to be more often quite distraught because of their sexual victimization even though some of them had been fortunate enough to have developed congenial relationships. ... In this regard the prison scene for these kids is bleaker and more destructive than it is for the homosexuals who are exploited" (1982, 112).

Significantly, for some of these men it is not the sexual act *per se* which is most consequential and damaging, but the fear of being labeled a "queer" or "an easy mark" or "just a punk." Thus the "problem for these self-identified heterosexual men appears to be more in the stigma attached to the sexual act than in the actual physical experience itself" (Wooden and Parker 1982, 117). One inmate explained:

> Rape on a man has the very same or worse affect than on a woman. Even if the man is a homosexual, gays are people, too, no matter how strange they are. They have the same feelings as we do; they hurt and even have pride and self-respect of a sort. If they are assaulted and raped, they have nothing and may very well commit suicide or go insane. It's very sad. I see the "girls" that are with the better pimps as much more secure and happier people, with their little purses and fancy hairdo's. They don't hang their heads or lower their eyes. (quoted in Cardozo-Freeman 1984, 386)

There are inmates who can think their emotional way through the trauma that follows a rape event. One white youth reasoned:

> It was like it wasn't my fault. I can just look back at it and say it was an experience that I had. And I look at it as an experience. Getting raped

> doesn't make a girl a whore, and any guy can get ripped off—I don't care who he is. If two or three guys decide to do it, they are goin' to do it, even to a staff member. So I don't feel bad about it anymore. I kinda accept it for what it was—just what the institution was like and I got myself into it so I had to abide by the rules and fight my problem. (quoted in Bartollas, Miller, and Dinitz 1976, 56).

Another inmate tells his story with obvious resignation, in a somewhat dissociated acceptance of what happened to him:

> I went to the rec and this guy says, "Hey, man, a friend of mine wants to talk to you." So I didn't think nothing of it. I looked around and I didn't see nobody else so I just said, "Okay." You know, I was kind of dumb to even go for it. So then, he said, "Sneak through the door and go around. He is on the other side, waiting for you. He wants to talk to you—he has found something out for you." I was trying to find out a way to get some smoke in. I figured I knew what he was talking about. So I got to the door and two dudes jumped out of back of the door and one of them took and put his arm around my chest and put a knife up to me—a shank—a big long shank. And there was three dudes down the other end and there was a dude standing by the cell door—all black—all six of them. It was all set up. They threw me into the cell and ripped my clothes off of me and everyone of them took me off. (quoted in Lockwood 1980, 115)

The injuries are not only physical, they are of course psychological.

Devaluation and Revaluation of Self

Other researchers corroborate that self-devaluation can be swift after rape. Victims report that afterward they cannot face their fellow prisoners; they fear that news of their degradation will get back to their wives and girlfriends and parents. It is, of course, the brutality and disregard of the victim's wishes in a rape which guarantee that there will be some degree of self-devaluation. In the prison setting this is magnified due to the public labeling of rape victims. Aggressors and other inmates declare that victims have become "women" and can never again be "men." Now their only status in the prison is "womanhood." Such comments are repeated constantly about the new "punk" for the remainder of his prison term. In some cases they may continue on the streets when he is released (Bowker 1980). It is as if men know that manhood is an illusion that can be shattered. When destroyed in other men, it somehow makes their own achievement—their own continuing fabrication of manhood—more precious.

We can glimpse some of these dynamics in the following testimony of a middle-class, 19-year-old-man from a Long Island suburb:

> The sex pressure started the second day. Some guy came in and said, "You owe for cigarettes, man, and do you want to give up your ass tonight?" And, I said, "No, man, and anybody that comes in here talking about that I am going to hit him with a chair or something." So, then I seen them

doing it to kids at night that were scared. I was thinking of taking a mayonnaise jar and breaking it in half in case they tried it against me—and using it as a weapon. But then I was thinking if I do that then I will get more time and that is all I could think of—more time.

Well, I was lying on the bed and I was half awake and half asleep. It was hard to sleep that night because the officers would not keep these guys in their rooms. After 10 o'clock you are supposed to be in your room. Because there aren't any doors, they can walk the halls all night. They came when I was sleeping and one guy shook me and he said, "Come with me to the room." And I said that I was not going no place. And then this one guy who weighed about 240 pounds started twisting my arm—and it really started to hurt. And I figured that this guy would really break my arm, so I am going to do it. And that was that. They took me in a room that was two rooms from where I was. They closed the door and a couple of them stood outside to see if the officer came by.

So I went into the room and I lied on the bed and they gave me all this bullshit. They told me that it won't hurt and that I was not a homo and don't worry they won't tell anybody. So, I had about two or three guys that were hanging on top of me and I was very upset that night. I was in there about 20 minutes because I did not scream or anything. I just let them do it and that was it. These guys—they work very fast. They just get on top of the guy and they do it in like three minutes maybe. So that was that.

I felt depressed. At times, I did think of suicide. I was getting a suicide thought because I say, "Hey, man, I am going to be doing this night after night." Like it was just at the beginning of my time and I had not even gone to my parole board. I was really confused, and I cried at night and I was upset. I was thinking about that—suicide. When you have got four guys that are going to fuck you in the ass every night, it is nothing to look forward to. I never thought about killing anyone or anything in my life, but like I was just thinking about going over with a jar and then hitting him and the whole thing would be over. In that week I changed so much. I had all these hostile thoughts. The violent thoughts were that the next time they came over to me I am going to make an example. I am going to take a jar and hit some guy in the back of the head.

I am thinking: What would a real man do in situations like this? I was thinking that I should have taken a chair and I should have just smashed one of these guys. I am thinking if I know these guys they are going to come again, and they are going to screw me and if I let them I am at fault, if I let it happen and I know it is going to happen then it is my fault. Well, I was upset because first of all, most guys consider themselves a man, and you always say that in jail no one is ever going to do that to you. I was very upset about it for about four or five months afterward because I thought that I had lost my manhood. It was just a very painful thing that happened. You just start to get over it—and you say it was not my fault. You just say to yourself you were in an abnormal atmosphere and it just happened. That is about the most painful part of my time. I had thought of telling the officers but they had told me when it happened that if I told the officers—even if I did get to protective keep-lock that they would run

> a wire on me, and get me in the cell down there. Because this was my first time in jail, and I did not know what was happening. (quoted in Lockwood 1980, 88–90)

Despite the brutality of these initial experiences, some heterosexually identified young men become gay. Despite being forced and coerced into sexual relationships, the result can be, in the long term, homosexual preference and identity. Sagarin (1976) interviewed several gay men in bars who had been forced into homosexuality while in prison by threats, intimidation, and rape. These men knew about the concept of "latent homosexuality" and they had begun to think that the term described them: "Maybe they were right. Maybe I was one of them all along. I don't know. But I came out in prison. I know that" (quoted on 253). Of course, their aggressors encouraged this view, claiming that the "kids" who were a "nice piece of ass" really wanted to have sex all along. Aggressors justified their threats and beatings by claiming their victims did not fight them off because it is the nature of "punks" to want sex with a "man." Eventually they would come around, on their own, begging for more (Propper 1981).

Bartollas, Miller, and Dinitz (1974) studied rape victims who, although finding their initial experiences psychologically disgusting and physically painful, still continued homosexual activity without protest. Many inmates in a boys' training school they studied seemed to accept their sexual victimization, including its low status in the prison stratification system, by finding some positive benefits. An interview with the one of the "punks" illustrates, however, that his adaptation was not without ambivalence:

> If you're a punk and you've been a punk for a long time and you want to stop, it's very hard because you've got so many desires in you. If you enjoy what you was doing before and then after you do it, you get a guilty feeling—you don't know where to turn. Like you say, I want to stop and then you get to the point where it's just like you need a woman, you get horny or something like that. It gets to the point where you want to do it again, and you don't know what to do. You say you want to stop, but there's something in you that wants to keep going. (quoted on 91)

Boys who are transferred to a new institution hope to leave their past behind, but somehow word travels with them. Once their peers learn they have been punks before, they pressure the new guys constantly and intensely until they submit: "Few youths with a history of sexual encounters are able to resist the persistent pressures received from the sexually deprived. Finally submitting to the continued harassment, these youths sometimes become committed to homosexuality as a lifestyle before leaving the institution" (quoted in Propper 1981, 70). The following testifies to the force of "reputation."

> He then said that he heard something about me concerning homosexual acts. I told him what he had heard was not true. He then started to threaten me and if I didn't submit to him. Then I hit him with my fist in his face before he could hit me. Then about three more men came into the

> cell and they started to beat me up too. I fought back the best I could and then I fell on the floor and I got kicked in the ribs. Three guys were holding me while the other one tore my pants off; I continued to fight until one of the guys knocked me out. One of the guys was holding me on the floor and had my arm pinned to the floor. And about seven or eight guys came into the cell and they took turns sticking their penis up my ass. When they finished they left my cell, and I was still laying on the floor. (quoted in Bowker 1980, 6)

In his semi-autobiographical novel entitled *Prisoner of Desire* Britt Hagarty (1979) describes how some straight guys become gay during their prison time. Hagarty's friend Randy tells the story of his first homosexual experience. A self-identified heterosexual, at first Randy confined his activity to the "masculine" role, making kids "blow" him, then later "screwin' them in the ass." In the dreariness of the prison such sex seemed inconsequential, something to relieve the boredom of doing time. Hagarty speculates that living in an all-male world perhaps contributed to Randy's difficulty in communicating with women after his release. He explains: "For one thing, they could never understand how I talk. Every time I wanted to say something, I'd have t'stop and think of how to say it in proper English rather than in joint slang. I felt like a real oddity" (159). Randy is sent back to prison; once again he finds himself having sex with guys and, eventually, taking the "homosexual role" (Propper 1981, 70). As a one-time inmate at San Quentin put it: "today's pitcher was tomorrow's catcher" (Johnson 1971, 72).

Those young men who suffer psychological problems are at even greater risk. Inmates of a Washington state prison told Inez Cardozo-Freeman the story of one psychologically troubled young man named Billy:

> Billy was already getting moody by the time I got here. Some of the guys were hitting on him pretty regular. ... I tried to tell him to act normal and quit pouting. ... But he got worse and he was assaulted somewhere along the line. ... When he was raped he went into a slump and started sort of walking with his head down and talking to himself. He quit taking care of himself. ... Maybe he tried to find some safety in the other world of insanity, I really don't know. But I do know that there are people in here that only act crazy to make others stay away from them and for the most part it will work. But it won't work if you're a cute young man. A crazy young man is only more defenseless.
>
> So Billy was used by different guys for a while until he finally ended up on the nutward for good. By this time the convict attendants in the hospital were all using him daily while the free people turned their heads. (quoted in Cardozo-Freeman 1984, 398)

Billy is not an isolated case in the prison Cardozo-Freeman studied. She learned, in fact, that "horror stories about treatment on Third Floor [mental ward] are profuse" (quoted in Cardozo-Freeman 1984, 88). Inmates reported:

TIM: Some of the stories I heard were about guys that they'd feed 'em with a baby bottle and make 'em wear diapers and then they'd come around and the guy would knock the baby bottle on the floor off his bed or off the nightstand and they'd jerk his diapers off him and they'd fuck him in the hospital. And I'm thinkin', oh my God! This whole place is sick. Everybody wants to fuck everybody in the ass.

DELORME: Well it was all those guys up there who were attendants.

TIM: They had these guys in diapers!

DELORME: That was when they had Dr. G. up there. He said, if you act like a fuckin' baby, I'll treat you like a baby. When you quit actin' like it and deal with problems, he'd put your pampers away and let's go back to reality. It worked for a few guys but some guys liked it and stayed that way. (quoted in Cardozo-Freeman 1984, 89)

Cardozo-Freeman reflects ruefully: "Thousands of young men in jails and prisons throughout the United States experience this horror each year. Although most somehow resist retreating into madness, they never recover from the psychic damage done to them. ... [T]he public is ... outraged when men rape women. The demand is that such offenders be sent to prison, yet the rape of men by men in prisons and jails provokes no outcry" (1984, 399).

Rape is not the only form of sexual assault in prison. The "player approach," comprising 29 percent of sexual incidents reported to Lockwood (1980), is typified by a combination of force and verbal threats. When players pursue targets who are heterosexual, typically they attach female or homosexual labels to these men. A younger man, especially if he is slender, must be "squeeze." Even if he denies it, the aggressors reason aloud, he must have "given it up" before. Unsurprisingly, these tactics upset targets who know themselves to be heterosexual. The aggressor is now encouraged; distress, he knows, means vulnerability. For the "player" to perform his trick, he must "feminize" this object of desire. The object of the game is to place naive new prisoners in submissive status positions and then "turn them out." If the "player" wins the game, the target becomes his "girl," now where he wants him, under his domination, in Lockwood's words, a "receptacle for his penis, and a female companion to accentuate his masculinity" (1980, 117). What these guys know is that any man can be made into a "girl," thus affirming Hocquenghem's quip that "from behind we're all women" (1978, 87).

Approximately a third of the aggressors' approaches, Lockwood (1980) learned, were nonviolent requests for sex, simple "propositions." He found that this tactic was employed by those "gorillas" and "players" who feared authorities or who intended to escalate their demands later by the use of force or threats. Several aggressors participated in rapes only to be "sociable," that is, to share in something other inmates did, "parallel play" as it were. "Let's say," one informant told Lockwood, "that you have a bunch of friends and they get to talking about it was good and the person that they had the sex with. And if they are constantly talking about this, you don't have anything in common if you haven't done it. So what do you do—you do it. So that you can have something to relate with" (1980, 121). There may be a multiplicity of motives, but the game seems always the same.

Prison Marriages

Not all sexual relationships in prison are violent and forced. Sometimes relationships form that look very much like genuine love affairs, some of which are long lasting. These prison couples tend to keep to themselves and can be quite devoted to each other, living somewhat like conventional married people might on the "outside." These relationships, at least one prison researcher argues (Cardozo-Freeman 1984), function in positive emotional, psychological, and social ways, enabling the men involved to survive their prison experience with a minimum of psychological scarring. Often the two men do get "married," a ceremony that can include a reception, a cake, a best man, etc. One inmate recalls:

> The last wedding I went to in here was several years ago. Artie was the bride and John was the groom. Both were weight lifters and that's how they met and so they started living together. They worked in the kitchen and I worked there, too.
>
> We used to make pruno [prison-made alcohol] every weekend and about thirty of us would always get down and get drunk. So one day these two sprung the news on us. They said, "man, we think we'll get married." What they were hinting was, "Why don't you guys give us a party?" So it went from there.
>
> The following weekend after most of the workers in the kitchen were gone, we stayed behind and brought out the ole cake and the booze and the ice and the food and we started having a regular little party. There wasn't any ceremony, no prayers or anything like that, but even the cops were in on it, a couple of Old Timers. They showed their good will by watching over us. (quoted in Cardozo-Freeman 1984, 384)

During his three years' experience as an inmate at San Quentin, Johnson (1971) observed that homosexual marriage was more or less accepted in inmate society. Men tended to assume the traditional roles of husband and wife, imitating the sex-role structure men create outside prison. Aggressive men would court younger men by buying them candy and other items, and the romance that sometimes followed would sometimes evolve into a marriage. Weddings were important events in prison life; being invited was an honor. Wedding invitations were sometimes printed and embossed in gold; gifts were expected. The ceremony included a certificate to document the union; sometimes contracts were signed specifying the masculine and feminine roles assumed by each. Morris Caldwell (1956) also found that many prison marriages were preceded by courtship and dating; he identified fifty married pairs in the medium-sized prison he studied. Thomas (1967) provides an example of two men exchanging vows in a New York prison: "'Do you, Claude, take this man to be your lawful wedded husband, to love, cherish, honor, and obey ... ?' 'I do,' Claude said softly, just like any bride anywhere. ... The groom slipped a ring on the bride's finger and the minister said, 'I now pronounce you man and wife,' and the guests offered them congratulations and best of luck" (282; quoted in Propper 1981, 163). Significantly, prison marriages tend to be intraracial.

Queens

"One of the most interesting roles," write Bartollas, Miller, and Dinitz, "is the queen" (1976, 120). Reproducing a popular stereotype, they defined queens as "overt homosexuals" (120). In the prison they studied for four years, six blacks and one white played this role. The status of queens is considerably higher than punks. Queens fall into two categories that correspond very much to the traditional male nonsense that there are only two kinds of women: good and bad. Describing an example of the former, one inmate asserts: "Sandy has class. … She has a man and she wants to be faithful just like his wife. That's one form of class" (379). He continues: "Sandy is proud of her looks and takes care of herself like any self-respecting woman would. She dresses as well as she can. She isn't too gaudy with the makeup. … When we look at a queen for the first time, we either say she has class or she's a dog. So the idea of class comes from personal appearance as well as personal conduct or character" (379). "Dogs" are "queens" whose disloyalty to their men provoke violence or threats of violence (Cardozo-Freeman 1984). Speaking of these, an inmate says: "A lot of queens [who are dogs] have extremely dirty mouths, and some of the twisted shit that comes out of their mouths is even hard for the average convict to take. They are just plain obscene at times" (quoted in Cardozo-Freeman 1984, 379).

In addition to providing sexual services, "punks" also are "persuaded" to keep their men's cells clean. Others are forced to take in laundry and wash other men's clothes, while others are given sewing machines and commanded to learn tailoring. But, like many women imprisoned in the gender system "outside," sometimes these "girls" weary of performing uncompensated labor for men. In the Washington state prison Cardozo-Freeman studied there occurred a "women's movement," led by punks feeling taken for granted and mistreated by their men. Despite decades of oppressive conditions which could have provoked a protest, in this case (as in many social movements—think of Stonewall) a specific incident triggered mobilization.

During summer of 1977, several near-violent incidents occurred as a result of Tall Tim's (see section III, this chapter) methods of buying and selling "girls." On one occasion, after having received money for the sale of a "girl," he ordered her to move back in with him. This maneuver he repeated several times, positioning the "girls" in greater danger than he was himself. Tim's actions happened to coincide with the arrival of several "queens" from Seattle who belonged to a politically radical group called the George Jackson Brigade. In response to Tim's actions, the group immediately set about organizing all the queens and punks into a club called Men Against Sexism, M.A.S. The main complaint was the fact of being bought and sold; the queens wanted freedom from being others' property. They wanted to be free to choose their own men; if they were required to hustle, they wanted to keep the money they earned. M.A.S succeeded in being recognized by the prison administration; the group was able to make some inroads in the gender system before being disbanded by prison officials in 1980 (Cardozo-Freeman 1984).

Cardozo-Freeman seems to identify with the plight of these "feminized" young men. They are, she points out, "seduced, raped, beaten, forced to please men, often in degrading ways and against their will, assigned the usual drudgeries real women have always been assigned, which most men have disdained doing, reviled and gossiped about, particularly if they are considered unattractive or 'bad' women" (1984, 394–395). Cardozo-Freeman is no radical feminist, however, as is evident in the three positive features she sees in the "women's" situation in prison: (1) most of the men are tolerant toward them provided they are not troublesome; (2) "classy bitches" are protected by the population if they are particularly popular or "foxy"; and (3) "the prettiest and most feminine serve as pathetic reminders for the some of the men of the normal masculine-feminine dimension in the world beyond the prison" (394). In fact, she sounds like a rather traditional woman when she complains: "Take men away from women and they will create women out of men, almost in a parody of Genesis II" (370), evidently forgetting that men—remember that God is the Father—have imagined they created women out of men all along.

IV. Who Will Watch the Guards?

The law is clearly a system of desire.

—Guy Hocquenghem, *Homosexual Desire* (1978)

The prison cannot fail to produce delinquents.

—Michel Foucault, *Discipline and Punish: The Birth of the Prison* (1979/1995)

We are creatures of the cruelties we witness.

—Paul Monette, *Becoming a Man: Half a Life Story* (1992a)

Prisoners tend to regard the guards as nonhuman, as "bulls," "dogs," "pigs," "goons," "robots," and "silons" (Cardozo-Freeman 1984). Because many prisons are located in remote rural areas, guards tend to be drawn from the ranks of the unemployed (or the marginally employed) in small towns and farm areas (Jacobs 1983). They tend to be white and undereducated. A consistent demand of prison reformers, national commissions, and rioting prisoners has been the recruitment of minority personnel to replace veteran rural white prison guards, who have been regularly charged with being at best unsympathetic, at worst brutal, sadistic, and racist. But the recruitment of minority prison guards has not proved simple or always helpful in reducing tensions. The National Advisory Commission on Criminal Justice Standards and Goals (1973) observed:

> There are other problems regarding recruitment of minority staff. In the past, those few who were brought into the system felt pressure to become like their white counterparts. By doing so, they suffered an identity crisis with minority offenders. As black, Chicano and Indian offenders have become politicized, they increasingly have rejected traditional minority staff. Extreme conflict has resulted in some institutions. Black inmates

want black staff with whom they can identify. (quoted in Jacobs 1983, 160)

The relationship between guards and inmates has been characterized as one of structured conflict; even racial and ethnic ties do not appear to alter this basic fact, a conclusion of a well-known Stanford experiment (Haney, Banks, and Zimbardo 1973). That experiment involved the random assignment of white Anglo-Saxon male college student volunteers to the roles of guard and prisoner in a "mock prison" constructed in the basement of a university building. Both groups were dressed appropriately. The guards were given simple rules to enforce and were instructed to maintain order. Conflict between the two groups developed, and in fact intensified to the point that the experiment had to be called off. Many "guards" acted in an authoritarian, sometimes sadistic, manner. This experiment is often cited to support the proposition that the behavior of guards and inmates is a function of their organizational roles, independent of such extra-institutional variables such as education, age, political affiliation, and race. In one study of this issue, researchers found, contrary to their expectation, that the less experienced black guards were not consistently more "inmate-oriented" (Jacobs 1983, 165).

Guards have not been much help during many rape events, as noted earlier. In his study of Philadelphia prisons, Davis (1968) learned that prison guards pressured inmates not to report rapes. Guards intimidated rape victims into silence by reminding them how parents and friends might respond to the news of their sexual subjugation (Brownmiller 1975/1993). In another study (Eigenberg 1994), officers reported that they were more willing to protect heterosexual inmates from rape than they were homosexually identified prisoners. While virtually all officers (97 percent) agreed they should try to prevent rape, only about one-half believed that they should write disciplinary reports about inmates who fight back when they are being pressured for sex. Only one-half believed that officers should warn new inmates regarding the risk of sexual assault. Eigenberg also found that officers tended to express stereotypical attitudes toward male rape victims. Approximately one-half of the officers told her that some young men deserved to be raped; approximately one-third said they believed that rape victims were weak, and about one-sixth of them assumed that male rape victims are in fact homosexuals. In fact, attitudes toward women predicted officers' willingness to respond to rape events. Officers who endorsed a conservative role for women tended to be less willing to respond to rape. Older officers tended to be more willing to respond. "[O]fficers," Eigenberg concludes with understatement, "could be more responsive to rape in prison" (1994, 152).

On occasion male guards have been homosexually raped themselves, especially during riots (Jacobs 1983). Female officers have reported they too have been victims of sexually related events (Light 1994). But usually male guards are the aggressors. In fact, prison guards have not been exactly "professional" during the first decades of this century. But continuing efforts to improve the training and standards of prison employees have resulted in a decrease in brutality by correctional officers (Bowker 1980).

Researchers first noticed this change in Illinois in the 1930s; throughout the northern and western states the situation was slowly improving. However, such improvement did not extend to southern prisons until the 1970s. The mistreatment of prisoners in the Arkansas prison system, for instance, has been well documented, including descriptions of the infamous "Tucker telephone" as well as detailed accounts of numerous beatings. In the Tucker telephone, a naked prisoner was strapped to a table; electrodes were attached to his big toe and to his penis. Electrical charges were then sent through his body which, in "long distance calls," were timed to stop just before the prisoner lost consciousness (Bowker 1980). It doesn't take a queer theorist to discern the mangled homosexual desire expressed in this disciplinary practice.

The superintendent of one Arkansas institution reported the following procedure: he would drive a truck at 40 miles per hour with three prisoners draped over the hood, then jam on the brakes catapulting them to the ground. Perhaps he fancied himself a deer hunter. Despite the obvious sadism and perversity, this prison superintendent regarded "trucking" as a unique and effective method of punishment. Reports from Louisiana, Mississippi, Virginia and Florida confirmed that guard assaults on prisoners were hardly limited to the Arkansas prison system (Bowker 1980). In Texas, for instance, at a juvenile facility named the Gatesville School, a kennel of dogs was trained to chase boys who tried to escape. A guard would follow the dogs on horseback, lasso the boy, then drag him back to the school, "sometimes face down through the unfriendly Texas cactus" (Lloyd 1976, 170).

Brutality was widespread in the Texas system through the postwar years. Physical punishments in Texas prisons included beatings with clubs and fists, as well as the use of blackjacks, riot batons, and aluminum-cased flashlights. Then there was the practice of "tap dancing." Was "tap dancing" a form of relaxation? Not exactly: "On one such occasion, the inmate was thrown to the floor by several officers. One literally stood on the inmate's head (called the tap dance) while another 'spanked' him on the buttocks and thighs with a riot baton" (Crouch and Marquart 1989, 79–80).

In early 1951, a released convict from the Louisiana State Penitentiary told a New Orleans newspaper reporter that a number of inmates had deliberately slashed their heel tendons with razor blades to avoid crushing field work and the brutal punishment by guards at the old maximum security prison in Angola (Carleton 1971). The reporter printed the story, and in response, Louisiana Governor Earl Long empanelled a six-member Citizens Committee to investigate the allegations of prisoner mistreatment at Angola. In April 1951, the Committee released its official report stating that here had been 31 cases of heel slashing at the prison that "appeared conclusively to be the result of physical brutality inflicted upon convicts." The report observed that "the practice of brutality was established beyond question on several levels—physical, mental, emotional, and moral" (quoted passages in Carleton 1971, 155).

Such institutionalized systems of brutality remained in place throughout the South during the 1950s and 1960s. In his biography, Oscar Dees—former "Dog Warden" during this era of the Alabama State Prison at Kilby in Montgomery (where the Scottsboro Nine were held; see chapter 12)—described the common use of a "strap about six-feet-long ... that they use[d] to hit a man. The strap was used when he committed a crime—say he cut another prisoner, they found him with a knife, or he quit work" (quoted in March 1978, 31). The attentive Dees discovered that this form of discipline had a different effect on different inmates: "After a man's been spanked, a white man's buttocks turns blue, a nigger's buttocks turns white" (quoted in March 1978, 44). But the strap was not the only method of physical punishment employed under Dees's administration. "I carried a walking stick made out of hickory" said the former warden. "I'd hit a man anywhere I could ... I didn't pick no certain place to hit him. If I took a notion to hit, I hit him" (March 1978, 50; quoted in Hamm et al. 1994, 174).

Solitary confinement (referred to as the "doghouse") was a common feature of discipline in the Alabama State Prison. According to Dees: "The doghouse ... [didn't have] any windows in it. It's dark in there. [Prisoners were put] in there without any clothes ... and handcuffed to a bar" (March 1978, 50). He concluded that "unjustified punishment might have gone on" (March 1978, 75; quoted in Hamm et al. 1994, 173–4).

Not until August 1974 was the Mississippi Department of Corrections forced to abolish its legendary prisoner trust system. Under this system, some 300 designated white convicts were given state-owned guns and whips (known as the "Black Annie"), and asked to maintain prison law and order (McWhorter 1981). This system of discipline was found "deplorable and subhuman" by the Federal District Court in Gainesville, Mississippi (Hamm et al. 1994, 175). While records were sometimes deliberately falsified, it is not wildly speculative to imagine that some of this prison-driven violence was racial. In one study this was evident; one prisoner reported being scalded with hot water by a guard; a paraplegic prisoner testified to being beaten unconscious by guards; two male prisoners reported homosexual rapes by guards; and one prisoner witnessed another prisoner hang himself to death while guards stood by laughing. Slightly more than one-half of the informants reported that blacks were singled out for severe discipline (Hamm et al. 1994).

Not all guard brutality is restricted to the South, of course. One Washington-state prisoner told Inez Cardozo-Freeman (1984) that a guard sodomized another prisoner with a police baton. Such a use of batons was not unknown in that prison; on another occasion, several inmates watched as guards took another inmate inside the strip cell upside down. The prisoner was handcuffed while another guard repeatedly thrust a baton into his rectum.

Substituting a baton for one's penis is an idea still in circulation. In August 1997, four New York City police officers were formally accused of acting on racist motivations in the case of a Haitian immigrant named Abner Louima, aged 31, and another Haitian immigrant, Patrick Antoine. Hospitalized with a perforated colon, Louima alleged he was beaten and sodomized by police. Both black men had been arrested outside a nightclub on assault charges that were later dropped. Officers Justin Volpe, Charles Schwarz, Thomas Wiese and Thomas Bruder were charged with assaulting Louima in a patrol car. Volpe and Schwarz were accused of attacking Louima in the bathroom at a precinct stationhouse, kicking him, and shoving a broom handle into his rectum and mouth while his hands were cuffed behind his back (Associated Press 1997,

1998). When the accused (and self-identified heterosexual) police officers were led out of the courtroom after being indicted, the crowd yelled at them: "Homosexuals! Fags!'" (quoted in Hodges 1998, 94).

As recently as twenty-five years ago, K.K.K. members were employed as prison guards, a situation one cannot assume is not somewhere true today. In the Pendleton Reformatory in Indiana during the winter of 1972, a group of black prisoners refused to return to their cells. One black inmate raised his hand in the black power salute. One white guard was overheard saying, "That one is mine!" The young man was shot five times; he died immediately. Testimony before the United States Senate later revealed that nearly 50 percent of the correctional officers involved in the incident were members of the Ku Klux Klan (Bowker 1980). As we saw in chapter 9, the Klan has long been popular in Indiana.

The events in 1971 at Attica prison in upstate New York, mentioned earlier, are better known. In the four days beginning with the recapture of Attica, New York state troopers and correctional personnel struck, prodded, and assaulted injured prisoners. Other prisoners were stripped naked then beaten, sometimes in the genital area. These "disciplinary" actions are well documented (Bowker 1980). Relying on Tom Wicker's *A Time to Die*, Paul Hoch (1979) points out that guards had been under the impression that rebellious inmates were castrating those guards held hostage. The impression was due to a rumor which spread rapidly among the guards (and which was "corroborated" by state correctional administrators). This completely false rumor was attributed to a particularly muscular inmate with the nickname "Big Black" who was later captured and tortured by white guards who casually applied burning cigarettes to his genitals. Hoch comments: "In other words, the black must be kept 'in his place'—in the white unconscious—and if he threatens to get out of it, his threatening sexual aspect must be removed, by any means necessary" (1979, 56).

In the preface to its Official Report of the New York State Special Commission on Attica (1972), the McKay Commission reported: "Forty-three citizens of New York State died at Attica Correctional Facility between September 9 and 13, 1971. Thirty-nine of that number were killed and more than 80 others were wounded by gunfire during the 15 minutes it took for the State Police to retake the prison on September 13. With the exception of the Indian massacres in the late 19th century, the State Police assault that ended the four-day prison uprising was the bloodiest encounter between Americans since the Civil War" (quoted in Deutsch, Cunningham, and Fink 1995, 48). In ordering that injunctive relief be granted against further brutality, the Second Circuit Court stated:

> [D]etailed evidence was furnished by plaintiff to the effect that beginning immediately after the State's recapture of Attica on the morning of September 13 and continuing at least until September 16, guards, State Troopers, and correctional personnel had engaged in cruel and inhuman abuse of numerous inmates. Injured prisoners, some on stretchers, were struck prodded or beaten with sticks, belts, bats, or other weapons. Others were forced to strip and run naked through gauntlets of guards armed

> with clubs which they used the strike the bodies of the inmates as they passed. Some were dragged on the ground, some marked with an "X" on their backs, some spat upon or burned with matches, others were poked in the genitals or arms with sticks. According to the testimony of inmates, bloody or wounded inmates were apparently not spared in this orgy of brutality. (quoted in Deutsch, Cunningham, and Fink 1995, 55)

Additional testimony indicated that accompanying the physical violence upon inmates were threats of death or brutality. White correctional officers called inmates "niggers" or "coons" and threatened to "get rid of" them (Deutsch, Cunningham, and Fink 1995, 55).

Correctional officers have been known to permit a sexual attack in their presence. Inmates report that guards seem to enjoy the spectacle. In one documented incident, a prisoner screamed for over an hour while he was gang-raped in his cell within earshot of a correctional officer. Not only did the guard ignore the screams but he laughed as the young man, shaken, stumbled from his cell afterward (Bowker 1980). One Arkansas inmate reported:

> [I]t's not as bad as it was. Then, a boy between the age of thirteen, fourteen, fifteen, sixteen, seventeen, they all became homosexuals. I mean they all was took care of by an older man for sexual acts. I seen two boys, they was brothers, they both got stabbed in the heart. They went up to the warden and said, "This man's trying to fuck me back here." The warden said, "Well, you shouldn't be here. You shouldn't a got your time if you didn't want nothing done to you." That's the way the wardens was back in them days. (quoted in Jackson 1977, 188)

In other instances correctional staff members forced prisoners to have sex with one another. A 15-year-old boy reported that a friend of his was coerced by a guard to have sexual intercourse with a known homosexual prisoner. When the friend refused to do so, he was taken to a private room and beaten. After he was made submissive, the counselors brought in the homosexual prisoner, following which the two prisoners had sex while the counselors watched (Bowker 1980).

In one southern institution a prisoner could buy a boy from a correctional officer, even from the deputy warden himself. Young men were used as "gifts" from prison officials to inmate leaders who helped them keep the institution quiet. One ex-prisoner claims to have been presented to "an entire wing of the prison, as a bonus to the convicts for their good behavior. In this wing, any prisoner who wanted his services, at any time and for any purpose, was given it; the guards opened doors, passed him from one cell to another, provided lubricants, permitted an orgy of simultaneous oral and anal entry, and even arranged privacy" (Bowker 1980, 110).

On occasion staff members become sexually involved with inmates. In one incident, several youth accused several officials of forcing them to participate in homosexual relations. The purely exploitative aspects of these incidents are difficult to verify, for after these boys alleged that they were forced into performing sexual acts, they changed their story. In the new version, they admit they were somewhat willing partners (Bartollas, Miller, and Dinitz 1976). One of the boys described his "affair" with a youth leader: "He had some intercourse with me about every two weeks. I did not want to do it, but he talked about getting me out of [here] faster and I wanted to get out because I have been here a long time" (quoted in Bartollas, Miller, and Dinitz 1976, 214).

According to Lee Bowker (1980), perhaps the only serious student of prisons who defends correctional officers has been Daniel Lockwood (1980). Lockwood has argued that the combination of sexually aggressive prisoners, overcrowded conditions, inadequate management and program needs that put prisoners together, not to mention legal limitations imposed by the courts, all add up to a situation in which the ability of correctional officers to prevent sexual victimization is quite limited. Perhaps so, but as we have seen, there are guards who not only do little to prevent sexual assault but in fact participate in the sexual victimization of young men.

In addition to inmate-on-inmate violence and guard-on-inmate violence, there has been, as we noted in the case of Louisiana's Angola prison in 1951, self-destructive behavior among prisoners. Over recent decades these self-destructive assaults have been declining as a percentage of all prison violence. The highest rate of self-mutilation known in contemporary American prisons occurred at Angola, this time during a ten-month period in 1974. A total of 107 self-mutilation cases were heard by the disciplinary board during this period, an average of nearly ten per month. Why do inmates harm themselves? Despair appears to be the primary motive. Why despair? Aside from the obvious depression that might accompany a life sentence, prison despair has been linked specifically to physical, specifically sexual, victimization by correctional officers and by other inmates (Bowker 1980).

The situation has not changed dramatically in recent years. A small-time car thief from the Chicago suburbs, Michael Blucker was sent to the maximum-security Menard Correctional Center in southern Illinois in May 1993. Bucker was a "neutron," unaffiliated with any of Menard's powerful gangs (the Gangster Disciples, the Vice Lords, the Latin Kings, the Gaylords), all satellites of Chicago organizations that might have given him some protection. Blucker was a classic "fresh fish"—young, lean, with the hairless white body much prized in prison. Not long after arriving Blucker was gang-raped (Hodges 1998).

Waiting in his cell for all Vice Lords on "10 Gallery" to line up ahead of him, Blucker was sitting on his bed when his roommate, "Tyboo," reappeared with "Prince Mike" and another gang member Blucker did not know. Suddenly, Tyboo wrapped an electrical cord around his neck; in a low voice, Tyboo told him to take off his clothes. "Trying to fight and breathe at the same time is a little hard," Blucker testified in August 1997, in his $1.5 million civil suit against seven Menard employees he claims failed to protect him. He tried to resist, but as he began to struggle a man he did not recognize pulled open his shirt to show two homemade knives. Prince stripped off Blucker's pants as Tyboo yanked the electrical cord tighter, arching Blucker's head back. "Shit on my dick," Tyboo hissed, or "blood on my knife" (quoted in Hodges 1998, 94).

All three raped him. After they left, Blucker, a heterosexual man married just seven months at the time, collapsed onto his bed. When he stopped crying, he told the jury in East St. Louis, Illinois, "I brushed my teeth and tried cleaning up what I could" (quoted in Hodges 1998, 94). His sexual exploitation was hardly over. A few weeks later, he testified, the Vice Lords sold him to the Gangster Disciples. He was rented out of cell number 180 as a sex slave by "Johnny C.," his cellmate "master." Concerned about possible H.I.V. exposure Blucker asked to be tested a few months later; the results were negative. By the next year, however, he had seroconverted. With before-and-after tests to prove that his infection occurred at the Menard facility, Blucker sued. But calling prison officials to account for tolerating the penal system's "culture of rape" was very much an uphill battle, as Blucker learned when a jury found in favor of five of the seven prison officials he was suing. They deadlocked on the other two, who will be retried (Hodges 1998, 94).

Blucker was rescued from sexual slavery at Menard by his next-door neighbor in cell number 811, Charles Ervin Johnson. The two came to know each other when Blucker overheard Johnson, a Muslim, practicing his Arabic. The day Johnson was transferred out of Menard in 1993, he sent a "kite" (message) up to the administration detailing the sexual abuse his young neighbor was suffering. Not long after, Blucker was transferred against his will into protective custody. Six months later, after Senator Moseley-Braun's office forwarded a letter from Blucker to the Illinois Department of Corrections, Blucker was relocated to a medium-security prison, then released on parole in January 1997 (Hodges 1998).

In September 1998, allegations of abuse, including sexual abuse, in Louisiana's juvenile facilities were broadcast over local television stations. In November 1999, four guards from the nation's most dangerous prison, Corcoran in California, were acquitted of setting up the rape of a prisoner named Eddie Dillard in March 1993 by leaving him in the cell of a well-known sexual predator, Wayne Robertson. Robertson had testified that he had in fact raped Dillard, repeatedly. He said that the guards knew his reputation and employed him regularly to "punish" disobedient inmates. After several failed efforts at bringing charges in the case, a special grand jury had indicted the four prison guards when a former guard, Roscoe Pondexter, broke ranks and testified in support of Dillard (Russel 1998; Stratton 1999).

Robertson was a muscled six-three and 230 pounds, a convicted murderer and serial inmate rapist who was known in the house as the Booty Bandit. The guards knew Robertson would teach "punks" like Dillard "how to do time" (Stratton 1999, 191). Depending upon his mood, Robertson would either beat Dillard or rape him. Dillard fought back, but Robertson overpowered him. While being beaten and/or raped, Dillard screamed, but for two hours no guard responded. When Officer Joe Sanchez did appear and Dillard told him he was being raped, Sanchez laughed at him. During the next two days, Robertson raped Dillard regularly. As we have seen: "If you surrender, you're a bitch, a punk. Bitches are cut loose, cast out of the group to become prey for other gangs" (Stratton 1999, 208).

In prison parlance, Pondexter, the guard who testified on Dillard's behalf, had a seat in the "car," which means that he had earned a position of respect among the guards who ran the prison. That status did not come easy or automatically. To earn it, Pondexter had to "make his bones." To belong to the inner circle of guards known as the "Sharks," Pondexter reported that "everybody did something that was seen as in the gray area." For instance: "There was a guy who was a chronic masturbator and who would not program with female staff." Pondexter and another guard beat the prisoner, dragged him from his cell, and before the other convicts Pondexter "deep-sixed him" while his partner tortured the prisoners' testicles. Finally Pondexter was accepted and given the name "Bonecrusher" (quoted in Stratton 1999, 189). It would seem that little has changed. Prison remains "a man's world," but it tells us more about men than a heterosexist homophobic society wants to know.

V. "The White Man Must Pay"

Is men's desire for other men the great preservative of the masculinist hierarchies of Western culture, or is it among the most potent of threats against them?

—Eve Kosofsky Sedgwick, *Epistemology of the Closet* (1990)

[T]he point of an erection is to use it.

—Lucy Candib and Richard Schmitt, "About Losing It: The Fear of Impotence," in Larry May, Robert Strikwerda, and Patrick D. Hopkins, eds., *Rethinking Masculinity: Philosophical Explorations in Light of Feminism* (1996)

[P]enetration ... seems to constitute the very essence of sexual practice.

—Michel Foucault, *The Care of the Self* (1988)

In his novel *Our Lady of The Flowers*, Jean Genet communicated the political function of sodomy as the preferred mode of sexual dominance. Genet's character Darling, who is buggering Divine, says, "a male who fucks a male is a double male." This is, Anthony Scacco concludes, the view of many sexual aggressors in prison. In his play *The American Dream*, Norman Mailer wrote that "sodomy has a number of possible meanings in Rojack's mind [and] homosexuality [is] ... a forbidden species of sexuality at which he is an expert and over which he holds copyright; or anal rape, which is his way of expressing contemptuous mastery." Himself a prisoner of war during World War II, Sartre characterized this "sex act as the festival of submission, also the ritual renewal of the feudal contract whereby the vassal became the lord's liegeman." Scacco (1975) observes that "the aggressor in prison is certainly not alone in viewing this act as uniquely his, or his own special invention" (quoted passages on 86–87).

In Mailer's *Why We Are in Vietnam*, D. J. Jethron asserts that "buggery confers an extra honor on the 'male' partner conquering a potential equal, 'cause asshole is harder to enter than cunt and so reserved for the special tool,' to be buggered is to be hopelessly humiliated" (quoted in Scacco 1975, 87). "The black man in prison," Scacco believes, "takes up the same reasoning in his attacks on white victims" (1975, 87). "Every study of male rape survivors," Michael Scarce reports, "found that anal penetration of the victim was the most common form of assault" (1997, 18).

A black inmate serving a sentence in the Cook County Jail in Chicago, Billy Robinson has been described as a "powerful political writer in the tradition of Eldridge Cleaver and George Jackson" (Divons and West 1971, 29). His testimony appears to confirm that interracial prison rape is political revenge, as Robinson writes that "the white man must pay, and pay through sexual assault, for the injustices the black man has had to endure" (quoted in Scacco 1975, 89). Is this because what black men endured was sexually charged, as in the case of lynching? Robinson reports:

> In prison, the black dudes have a little masculinity game they play. It has no name, really, although I call it whump of fuck a white boy—especially the white gangsters or syndicate men, the bad juice boys, the hit men, etc. The black dudes go out of their way to make faggots out of them. And I know that by and far, the white cats are faggots. They will drop their pants and bend over and touch their toes and get had before they will fight. So, knowing this, what kind of men did this make us? (quoted in Scacco 1975, 89)

The constant refrain of prison is sodomy. The research on sex in prison reminds "that to reduce a male to the status of a female by forcible rape was the single most dominating thing for the black man, and the most humiliating part for the white inmate" (Scacco 1975, 90). The temptation is to sequester this behavior as specific to prisons, as we have sequestered this presumably wholly separate category of citizens called "criminals." But prison cannot be kept separate from everyday life in America. In his introduction to Daniel Lockwood's study of sexual violence in prison, Hans Toch (1980) observed that: "In the scenes described in Lockwood's book, we see men feeding on men in ways that are not only truly primeval but reflective of advanced rules of our societal games" (xii). Despite the apparent unreality of the prison world, Toch insists that it cannot be split off from everyday life: "The repulsive, disgusting, offensive depravity we must face and reject in Lockwood's account links us disquietingly to ourselves" (1980, xii).

Is it linked to ourselves because we men know that we can change, that the psychosexual positionality of "straight guy" can be "inverted" through "feminization"? Curiously, this feminization of the male into the "bitch" in prison occurs more at the site of the body than, at least initially, at that of the psyche. Many sexually subjugated men appear to remain irreducibly masculine until the point at which their masculinity is, in Leo Bersani's word, "shattered." Bersani is writing about voluntary self-shattering, and, as Kaja Silverman (1992) observes, it is through a penile image—slackness—that Bersani (1987) asks us to imagine the effects of the "self-annihilation" he recommends, since psychic tumescence is his preferred metaphor for the consolidation of the male ego (218). The limp dick is no longer the phallus; the anus is no longer an asshole, but the "grave" for hegemonic masculinity.

"Is the Rectum a Grave?" might thus be said to reverse the terms of classical homosexual "inversion," in that Bersani calls for the redefinition of the male homosexual as "a man's soul in a woman's body," or—in Silverman's words—"for a male psyche put at risk by its pleasurable relation to the vagina/anus" (1992, 351). While no one would advocate forced homosexualization such as occurs in prison, it is nonetheless the case that through anal receptivity—forced or voluntary—the man can "violate" and even demolish his "perhaps otherwise uncontrollable identification" (Bersani 1987, 222) with that gendered positionality which, outside of prison, oppresses him, other men, and the women he presumably desires (Silverman 1992).

In the United States sex is racialized and race is sexualized, homosexualized. While probably thinking of black women, Winthrop Jordan's (1974) observation about the sexualized character of white supremacy might well apply to black men as well: "Sexually, as well as in every other way, Negroes were utterly subordinated. White men extended their dominion over their Negroes to the bed, where the sex act itself served as a ritualistic re-enactment of the daily pattern of social dominance" (72). The sex act did not merely recapitulate the "larger" pattern of social dominance. Sex structured white supremacy, itself a barely sublimated form of sadomasochism. In prison black men avenge themselves.

Women prisoners, evidence suggests, experience far less sexual aggression than imprisoned men. Just as virtually all sexual aggression in American society is committed by (heterosexual) men, so sexual assault in prison is much more common in men's institutions than in women's (Lockwood 1980). Consensual homosexual relationships are much more likely to occur in women's prisons than in men's (Bowker 1980). Another student of the differences between female and male inmates characterizes men's sexual involvement with each other as covert, private, and "cold blooded." In women's prisons, homosexual activities and relationships tend to be "open, shared, and emotional" (Pollock 1986, 118).

The first separate facilities for women appeared in this country in the early 1800s. From the beginning, these institutions were quite different from those established for men. The first institutions for women were often described as "homes," while prisons for men were more often likened to "factories" (Pollock 1986, 19). Officers have complained that "very few people look upon females in the prison system as criminals. Matter of fact, some administrators in the system don't even want you to refer to them as inmates or prisoners" (quoted in Pollock 1986, 49). Is there something about "prison" and "criminality" which is peculiarly and specifically male?

Sexual aggression in prisons outside the United States converges with patterns identified in American institutions. In his study of sexual exploitation in an Indian prison in Uttar Pradesh, S. Srivastava (1974) found that aggressors, or "laundbaajs," coerced "boyish young newcomers" into performing sexual services for older inmates. They employed a range of strategies, from subtle tricks as well as outright force, to achieve the sexual subjugation of their targets, and after their success openly bragged about their exploits. Victims suffered a defamation process not unlike that suffered by young American men who are raped.

Research reporting sexual aggression in Communist Poland tells a story similar to the American one. For instance, the same prohibition against "snitching" obtained. A "man" may never inform on another "man," not even when he is in grave danger, but corresponding norms do not apply to the "people" or "slaves," or, in American parlance, the punks. "The slaves" (the linking of "the people" with "slaves" is an interesting discursive move) are exploited as sexual objects; it is always a one-sided relationship. Nor can there be any upward mobility from status as "slave" to that of "man." An inmate's status evidently follows him not only from one institution to another, but after his release as well. This problem was even more pronounced for juvenile institutions in Poland, but less so for females than males. Polish prison language is also comparable to that spoken in U.S. institutions: "If we modify the terminology of 'men' to include 'jockers,' 'wolves,' and 'daddies,' and alter the term 'slave' to include 'boy' [the parallel with U.S. racial situation seems precise], 'punk', 'queen' and 'queer,' there are some remarkable similarities in the above description of Polish correctional subcultures with those in the United States" (quoted in Bondeson 1989, 31). While homosexuality is a relatively common phenomenon in Polish and American prisons, evidently it is not in Sweden (Bondeson 1989).

American-like gendered patterns of racialization seem to occur to some extent in Britain. Black inmates tend to have attributed to them a "macho image," and they are assumed to enjoy a greater sexual freedom. The same fascination with the black male body appears to obtain as well; one white working-class inmate reports: "I've been arrested with black lads before and I've seen with my own eyes how they get treated. They definitely get a worse deal. I was arrested this time with one black and one white friend. Me and the white lad were allowed to keep our clothes but my black friend was stripped and just had a blanket" (quoted in Genders and Player 1989, 84).

Britain, as is well known, transported criminals to its American colonies. In 1786, having lost these colonies, and suffering from overcrowding in its own prisons, from which typhus threatened to spread into the surrounding communities, the British government decided to create a penal colony at Botany Bay, on the eastern coast of Australia. As Martha Grace Duncan (1996) points out, the mode of Britain's Botany Bay Project points to the defensive nature of its creation. The British took those who were no longer a desirable part of their body politic and cast them out, telling them that they could not return, except after a lengthy period and perhaps never. The analog of this punishment is, she argues, the notion of defecation. In defecation, as in expulsion of criminals, something that was a part of one's "body" is expelled and becomes refuse. The parallel hints at the policy's anal symbolism and, with it, the likelihood that British citizens felt an attraction to as well as an aversion for those now expelled as "criminals" (Duncan 1996).

Evidently, British citizens continued to identify, if negatively, with those they had expelled from their body politic. In 1822 a rumor circulated in London that women had been sent to Australia to prevent men there from committing "unnatural crimes." In 1832 and 1837 Parliament obtained evidence regarding the incidence of sodomy in the Australian colonies. Convicts were evidently calling each other "sods," and adolescent convicts were taking on names like Kitty and Nancy. One chain gang prisoner reported that his companions were "so far advanced ... in depravity" that they openly engaged in "assignations one toward the other" and "kicked, struck or otherwise abused" anyone who dared to condemn "their horrid propensities" (quoted in Percy 1996, 44). Out of sight would not appear to be out of mind.

In sight, however, is definitely in mind. Duncan (1996) tells the story of one particular convict named Charles Anderson. Irreversibly brain damaged, Anderson did exhibit violent tendencies at the time he was convicted of burglary. He was expelled to Goat Island, a rock in Sydney Harbor. For two years he was fastened, naked, to a chain on the rock, his only home a cavity carved out of the stone. Unhealed welts festered on his back, the scars of hundreds of lashings. Residents of Sydney amused themselves by rowing out to his rock and throwing him crusts of bread to eat, staring at his naked body. Duncan's view is "that Australian criminal exiles played an important intrapsychic role for the British noncriminals, serving as externalized aspects of the noncriminals' selves—their disavowed greed, sadism, and hostility to authority" (Duncan 1996, 165).

About 900 miles from Sydney, in the Pacific Ocean, lies Norfolk Island, where officials transported the worst of Britain's convicts. Many convicts died during the voyage to Australia; many were raped by their fellow exiles, most were treated cruelly by the masters to whom they were assigned. Somehow some survived, and some of these criminals, having served their sentences, did manage to make a new life in their place of exile (Duncan 1996). Like Jean Valjean in *Les Miserables*, they found in the "sewer" a place of salvation (Brombert 1984). Such positive experiences reveal the truth in the facetious words of a 1786 ballad describing the Australian prison colony as "this Garden of Eden, this new promised land" (quoted in Duncan 1996, 169).

From the point of view of the law-abiding British citizenry, America then Australia were sewers where human refuge could be safely flushed. This fantasy that what cannot be ingested into the status quo can be expelled is evident in late twentieth-century America, when Republicans have persuaded the public that more prisons, not more schools, can solve the problem of social suffering. Perhaps the ultimate fantasy of removal is indicated in Ellis MacDougall's suggestion that "[h]uge prisons could be built on the floor of the ocean, away from the general population and with little opportunity for prisoners to escape" (quoted in Montgomery 1994, 250).

Even in this fantasy white men are not safe; the "sea" is their "unconscious" and the "black man" has been there all along. As we will see in the next chapter, Leslie Fiedler will notice this fact in his groundbreaking 1948 essay on interracial desire in the American imagination, expressed in canonical novels such as *Huckleberry Finn* and *Moby Dick*: "The Negro as homoerotic lover blends with the myth of running off to sea, of running the great river down to the sea. The immensity of water defines a loneliness that demands love, its strangeness symbolizes the disavowal of the conventional that makes possible all versions of love" (Fiedler 1948/1995, 532).

❦ SIX

The Gender of Racial Politics and Violence in America

18 ❋ "INTO EACH OTHER'S ARMS"

—Leslie Fiedler, *Love and Death in the American Novel* (1966)

I. Neither Gods nor Demons

I have begun to wonder whether the major, much celebrated themes of American literature—individualism, masculinity, the conflict between social engagement and historical isolation, an acute and ambiguous moral problematics, the juxtaposition of innocence with figures representing death and hell—are not in fact responses to a dark, abiding, signifying Africanistic presence.

—Toni Morrison, *Playing in the Dark: Whiteness and the Literary Imagination* (1992)

The American ideal, *then, of sexuality appears to be rooted in the American ideal of masculinity. This idea has created cowboys and Indians, good guys and bad guys, punks, and studs, tough guys and softies, butch and faggot, black and white. It is an idea so paralytically infantile that it is virtually forbidden—as an unpatriotic act—that the American boy evolve into the complexity of manhood.*

—James Baldwin, *The Price of the Ticket* (1985)

It was Hemingway who pointed out that all modern American writing springs from Huckleberry Finn.

—Ralph Ellison, *Shadow and Act* (1964/1995)

Fiedler is my guide to America's fearsome civilization.
—Mark Simpson, *Male Impersonators: Men Performing Masculinity* (1994)

The archetypal American image, Leslie Fiedler (1966) argued, can be found in "our favorite books." What is this American dream? Is it the heterosexual family nestled safely in the suburbs with the proverbial white picket fence? Not exactly. The archetypal American image, Fiedler tells us, is a "white and colored American male flee[ing] from civilization into each other's arms" (1966, 12). Introducing the 1966 edition of his *Love and Death in the American Novel*, Fiedler acknowledges that "certainly, my earliest formulation of this theory in 'Come Back to the Raft Ag'in, Huck Honey' has met with a shocked and, I suspect, partly willful incomprehension" (1966, 12). I will return in a moment to his depiction of *Huckleberry Finn*, but for now suffice to say that Fiedler posits a homoerotic and interracial image at the center of American civilization. And in so doing, he stimulated a refusal to know (Felman 1982; Britzman 1998a, 1998b, 1998c). Despite the incontrovertible evidence in lynching and prison rape that a mangled repressed homoerotic circulates within white racism, no doubt many readers, many Americans, will continue to "refuse to know."

How can this be? How can "[o]ur great Romantic *unroman*, our typical anti-novel, [be] the womanless *Moby Dick*?" (Fiedler 1966, 25). Fiedler answers psychoanalytically, suggesting, as Baldwin (1985) did, that for much of our history Americans—I prefer to restrict the argument to European-American men—have lived their national life at a prepubescent homosocial stage of psychosexual development. "In recent years the situation," Fiedler wrote just before 1960, "appears to have altered radically." Why? "Perhaps," Fiedler (1966) answers, "because the taste of boys has changed, as the 'latency period,' which Freud thought immutable, tends to be abolished." If Edgar Friedenberg (1962) was right, and adolescence was, during this time, vanishing, it would appear that many young men now move directly from childhood to adulthood, which for Fiedler means there is little movement at all. "At any rate," Fiedler (1966, 29 n.) continues:

> the line between "pornography" and respectable literature has blurred; and certain traditional themes of American literature—the love of white and colored males, for instance, and the vilification of women—are rendered with explicit sexual detail. Indeed, such detail becomes required rather than forbidden as American Puritanism learns to stand on its head. It is long way from James Fenimore Cooper to James Baldwin, or from Herman Melville to Norman Mailer; but even if our dreams have become more frankly erotic, the American eros has not really changed. We continue to dream the female dead, and ourselves in the arms of our dusky male lover.

But this candor is recent. For much of American history, Fiedler suggests, sexual desire was inadmissible. Being inadmissible, we converted it to horror. "[H]orror," Fiedler writes, "however shoddily or ironically treated ... is essential to our literature." Terror fills "the vacuum left by the suppression of sex in our novels, of Thanatos standing in for Eros." Key, however, is that

> through these gothic images are projected certain obsessive concerns of our national life: the ambiguity of our relationship with Indian and Negro, the ambiguity of our encounter with nature, the guilt of the revolutionist who feels himself a parricide—and, not least of all, the uneasiness of the writer who cannot help believing that the very act of composing a book is Satanic revolt. "Hell-fired," Hawthorne called *The Scarlet Letter*, and Melville thought his own *Moby Dick* a "wicked book." (quoted passages in Fiedler 1966, 27)

Was the guilt which followed the parricidal aggression at work in the creation of the American nation somehow reexperienced in the act of literary creation?

If we consider the gendered nature of the colonists' perception of British royal authority and power, the presence of an echo might be plausible. Power, Philip Greven (1977) explains, was associated with masculinity; liberty was feminine. In the minds of European-American men, then, liberty was imagined as both innocent and passive, in need of defense and protection against the active, intrusive, masculine aggressiveness of power. The problem the writers of the Constitution faced was not to abolish power but to contain and limit it, to codify secure and reliable boundaries around the exercise of power so that liberty could be protected.

Greven (1977) points to John Adams to illustrate the gendered anxiety and ambivalence that engulfed many victorious "sons" in the oedipal triumph over the "father," King George III. For Adams, the classic fable of Hercules mythologized the choice that he and his fellow Americans faced. As early as 1759, Adams had recorded in his diary: "The other night, the Choice of Hercules came into my mind, and left Impressions there which I hope will never be effaced nor long unheeded" (quoted in Greven 1977, 245–246). The future president decided to compose a fable appropriate to his "own Case," which began with Virtue addressing him with the question: "Which, dear Youth, will you prefer? a Life of Effeminacy, Indolence, and Obscurity, or a Life of Industry, Temperance, and Honour?" Virtue's advice, which Adams then gave to himself, was to "return to your Study, and bend your whole soul to the Institutes of the Law, and the Reports of Cases. ... Let no trifling Diversion or Amuzement or Company decoy you from your Books, that is, let no Girl, no Cards, no Flutes, no Violins, no Dress, no Tobacco, no Laziness, decoy you from your Books" (quoted in Greven 1977, 246).

After two nights "and one day and an half, spent in a softening, enervating, dissipating, series of hustling, prattling, Poetry, Love, Courtship, Marriage," he lamented that "during all this Time, I was seduced into the Course of unmanly Pleasures, that Vice describes to Hercules, forgetful of the glorious Promises of Fame, Immortality, and a good Conscience, which Virtue, makes to the same Hero, as Rewards of a hardy, toilsome, watchful Life, in the service of Man kind" (quoted in Greven 1977, 246). Greven comments: "All of the themes that were to continue to fascinate and haunt Adams for years to come are present in this fantasy: seduction, temptation, effeminacy, manliness, industry, fame, and watchfulness" (1977, 246). These were, of course, hardly his themes alone; so resonant was this imagery that Adams felt no hesitation in proposing that Hercules should be imprinted on the seal being designed for the newly confederated states in August 1776 (Greven 1977).

These gendered politics of self-restraint and temptation seem remarkably "adolescent," even if that category did not exist then. A perpetual adolescence may be, as Fiedler will explain, the oedipal consequence of having "slain" the "father," King George III, and abandoned the "mother,"—England. On their own, in a world they were determined to make "new," that is, one without fathers, these fatherless sons became imprisoned, Fiedler suggests, in a homosocial adolescence filled not with adults but other children, boys and girls, brothers and sisters. Many "sisters" understood the violence in the heart of "man," as evidenced in Abigail Adams's March 1776 letter to her husband in which she asked him to "Remember the Ladies" in "the new Code of Laws" that he and his fellow legislators were writing, and to "be more generous and favourable to them than your ancestors. Do not put such unlimited power into the hands of the Husbands." "Remember," she told him, "all Men would be tyrants if they could." She added, almost as an afterthought: "That your Sex are Naturally Tyrannical is a Truth so thoroughly established as to admit of no dispute, but such of you as wish to be happy, willingly give up the harsh title of master for the more tender and endearing one of Friend. Why then, not put it out of the power of the vicious and the Lawless to use us with cruelty and indignity with impunity. Men of Sense in all Ages abhor those customs which treat us only as the vassals of your Sex." "Regard us then," she urged, "as Beings placed by providence under your protection and in the imitation of the Supreme Being make use of that power only for our happiness" (quoted passages in Greven 1977, 241). The stage was set for the ideology of "separate spheres," and as well for a peculiar—"queer"?—departure from European traditions of heterosexual courtship and marriage, a departure evident in that artifact of the American imagination, the novel.

To understand the American novel, Fiedler tells us, requires reflection on the fate of certain European genres in an alien, "new" world. In this world European courtship and marriage rituals underwent a profound shift. Certain traditional distinctions of class became blurred for the European invaders, who lacked: "a significant history or a substantial past; a world which had left behind the terror of Europe not for the innocence it dreamed of, but for new and special guilts associated with the rape of nature and the exploitation of dark-skinned people; a world doomed to play out the imaginary childhood of Europe" (Fiedler 1966, 31). The American novel, Fiedler explains, "is only *finally* American." To understand the American novel is to grasp that "its appearance is an event in the history of the European spirit—as, indeed, is the very invention of America itself" (1966, 31).

Fiedler then weaves, in virtuoso fashion, a mosaic of this "European spirit" from which America evolved, that "moment in the mid-eighteenth century which gave birth to Jeffersonian democracy and Richardsonian sentimentality alike: to the myth of revolution and the myth of seduction" (Fiedler 1966, 31). These two myths are, he continues, "the two great inventions of the bourgeois,

Protestant mind," which is to say "white" mind. They were created precisely at the moment when that mind "stood, on the one hand, between Rationalism and Sentimentalism, and on the other, between the drive for economic power and the need for cultural autonomy." The creation was marked by a series of historical events, including the American and French Revolutions, the invention of the novel, the rise of modern psychology, and the triumph of the lyric in poetry. All of this "adds up to a psychic revolution as well as a social one." This revolution has, he notes, traditionally been called "Romantic," but Fiedler finds the term "paralyzingly narrow, defining too little too precisely, and leading to further pointless distinctions between Romanticism proper, pre-Romanticism, *Sturm und Drang*, Sentimentalism, *Symbolisme*, etc. It seems preferable to call the whole continuing, complex event simply 'the Break-through,' thus emphasizing the dramatic entry of a new voice into the dialogue of Western man with his various selves" (quoted passages in Fiedler 1966, 32).

This "break-through" is characterized by the splitting off of psychology from philosophy, the displacement of the traditional leading genre by the personal lyric and analytic prose fiction and the consequent subordination of plot to character, of which Virginia Woolf was, perhaps, the master. It is also marked by the formulation of a theory of revolution as progressive in itself and, "most notably perhaps, by a new concept of inwardness." Fiedler is tempted to say that this inwardness signifies the "invention of a new kind of self, a new level of mind; for what has been happening since the eighteenth century seems more like the development of a new organ than the mere finding of a new way to describe old experience" (quoted passages in Fiedler 1966, 32).

It was Diderot, Fiedler argues, who insisted that humankind (or is it specifically "man"?) is *double* to depths of the soul, "the prey of conflicting psyches both equally himself." While the experience of this conflict was hardly new, it had before been described as occurring between man and devil, or flesh and spirit. It was a revolutionary suggestion that the two were separate aspects of the same creature. In *Rameau's Nephew*, Diderot imagined the two as philosopher and the parasite, the rationalist and the underground man, debating endlessly the cause of the head versus the heart. In his pornographic *Bijoux Indiscrets*, Diderot wrote another version of the same dialogue: the enchanted and indiscreet genitals speak a truth which the mouth cannot (Fiedler 1966). "Pornography and obscenity are," Fiedler writes, "hallmarks of the age of the Break-through." The spectrum of fiction, not only pious novels but titillating ones as well, record the surfacing of underground emotions, euphemistically called "the heart" at the time, into high culture. As influential for Fiedler as Diderot or Richardson or Rousseau in "the *bouleversement* of the eighteenth century" is the Marquis de Sade, who occupies the intersection of depth psychology and revolution (quoted passages in Fiedler 1966, 33).

The contributions of de Sade, Fiedler argues, are several. He exposed the "ambivalence of the inner mind," revealing what Fiedler terms "the true darkness and terror" embedded in what the neoclassical age, in its revolt against Christian notions of sin, had celebrated as simple "pleasure" or polite "gallantry" (1966, 33). De Sade may even have provoked the storming of an almost empty Bastille, with which the French Revolution began. Imprisoned in the *Tour de la liberté* of the Bastille, de Sade, through an improvised loudspeaker made of a tube and funnel, screamed to bystanders to rescue his fellow inmates who were being executed. He scattered handwritten leaflets detailing jail conditions to the crowd he attracted below. On July 3, 1789, he was transferred to insure "the safety of the building," but he had already started writing *Justine, or the Misfortunes of Virtue*, that "perverse offshoot of the Richardsonian novel" (1966, 33–34), what Fiedler terms "the first example of revolutionary pornography" (34). In the Marquis de Sade, Fiedler explains, "the Break-through found its most stringent and spectacular spokesman: the condemned man judging his judges, the pervert mocking the normal, the advocate of destruction and death sneering at the defenders of love and life; but his reductio follows logically enough from assumptions shared by Jefferson and Rousseau, Richardson and Saint-Just. Whatever has been suspect, outcast, and denied is postulated as the source of good" (34).

Before this "break-through" few doubted the inferiority of passion to reason, of impulse to law. Before this moment no one thought it possible, in sophistic fashion, to rationalize these eighteenth-century reversals by quoting the biblical verse which decrees that the last shall be first. "Christianity," Fiedler (1966) asserts, "is dead from the moment such a justification is made." Indeed, the "break-through" is "profoundly anti-Christian" though it does not always confess itself so. There is a brief time of transition "when the Enlightenment and Sentimentalism exist side by side," when it is still possible to believe that "true reason and true feeling," the "urgings of passion" and the "dictates of virtue" are not opposed, that all are divine manifestations. But, Fiedler continues, "Sentimentalism yields quickly to the full Romantic revolt." Soon enough, that enemy of Heaven and the family, Don Juan, has been transformed from villain to hero. Soon enough, audiences begin "to weep for Shylock rather than laugh at him from the stage" (quoted passages in Fiedler 1966, 34).

Even the values of language change. The notion of "gothic" changes from a term of contempt to one of description and then of praise. The concept of the "baroque" makes more slowly the same transition. Terms once describing desirable traits—"condescension," for example—now indicate disapproval. "The child," Fiedler continues, "is glorified over the man, the peasant over the courtier, the dark man over the white, the rude ballad over the polished sonnet, the weeper over the thinker, colony over mother country; the commoner over the king—nature over culture" (1966, 34).

What was cause and what was consequence in the complexity of "breakthrough" is, he admits, "hard to say." Everything seems the cause, and consequence, of everything else. Somewhere within the nexus of causes was the "death of God," says Fiedler echoing Nietzsche, even though the masses had yet to notice. Fiedler locates the event somewhere near the beginning of the eighteenth century, and he describes it not dramatically as a "death" but as a "wearing out." This wearing out was not primarily, in Fiedler's estimation, a matter of destruction of the political and social power of the church. Nor does he measure it by the loss of economic power by priests. While political and theological divisions within Christendom no doubt contributed to its demise, Fiedler regards these as manifestations rather than causes. Perhaps most fundamentally, institutionalized Christianity lost its power "when its mythology no longer proved capable of controlling or revivifying the imagination of Europe" (Fiedler 1966, 35).

It is a revolt of "the darker motive forces of the psyche," who now refused to accept those names and lower ranks by which they had been kept subservient for two thousand years. Once worshipped as "gods," Fiedler notes, they had been decreed demons by the new Christian religion, but now they rose up in discontent. In particular, the "Great Mother" who, Fiedler reminds, had been "cast down by the most patriarchal of all religions (to the Hebrews, she was Lilith, the bride of darkness), ambiguously redeemed as the Blessed Virgin and denied a second time by a Hebraizing Protestantism," demanded her rightful place of honor once more. The very distinction between God and Devil, on which, Fiedler writes, "the psychic balance of Europe had for so long been staked," was challenged (quoted passages in Fiedler 1966, 35). Many people, especially women, continued to go to church; there were revivals. But fewer and fewer men lived in adherence to church dogma (Fiedler 1966).

The American nation is, Fiedler reminds, a fact of the imagination as well as of history. As such, the United States was formed by the Age of Reason. As a product of the European imagination, it was hardly a new idea. Europeans had dreamed for centuries—long before the Enlightenment—about the West: Atlantis, Ultima Thule, the Western Isles. The West was an imaginary place of refuge beyond the seas, a new frontier to which the discouraged European hero might retreat in hopes of rebirth. The West was a "source of new life in the direction of the setting sun which seems to stand for death." On the very brink of an age which was to turn this dream into the actualities of exploration, imperialism and colonization, Dante sent that archetypal explorer, Ulysses, to destruction in the West. Ulysses, Fiedler suggests, represents man's refusal to accept the limits that duty and tradition require: "not the sweetness of having a son, nor the pious claim of an old father, nor the illicit love that should have made Penelope rejoice could quench in me the burning to become familiar with the vice of men and men's valor" (quoted in Fiedler 1966, 36–37). This is, Fiedler notes, an apt epigraph, "to represent that lust for experience which made America. There is, indeed, something blasphemous in the very act by which America was established, a gesture of defiance that began with the symbolic breaching of the pillars of Hercules, long considered the divine signs of limit" (37).

The dream of a Republic is, Fiedler points out, very different from that of Revolution. The revolutionary's demand for blood and fire as ritual purification, his tearing down what had been held high, the degrading of timeless images of authority, the imposition of equality as orthodoxy: these events originated in the *Encyclopédie*, Fiedler suggests. There, however, they were abstract ideas; they were lived, he says, as Romanticism: "The Revolution of 1789 (for which ours was an ideological dress rehearsal) may have set up David as its official interpreter, but it left the world to Delacroix; and though it enthroned Reason as its goddess, it prepared for a more unruly Muse" (Fiedler 1966, 38).

Paraphrasing Fiedler seems so very unsatisfactory; it is, after all, impossible to improve upon his prose. The range of his understanding, the lyricism, indeed the poetry, of his prose, the depth of his insight: all of these must be read in the original. But for brevity's sake, paraphrasing and copious quotation will, I suppose, have to do. Continuing this tale, which will conclude on the Mississippi River on a raft occupied by a black man and a white boy, Fiedler (1966) argues that in sentimentalism the age of reason "dissolves in a debauch of tearfulness." Its sensibility of "seduction, and suicide" typified its art "even before ghosts and graveyards take over." What "strange images of darkness," he muses, "to usher in an era of freedom from fear." "And beneath them," he continues, "lurks the realization that the 'tyranny of superstition,' far from being the fabrication of a Machiavellian priesthood, was a projection of a profound inner insecurity and guilt, a hidden world of nightmare not abolished by manifestos or restrained by barricades. The final horrors, as modern society has come to realize, are neither gods nor demons, but intimate aspects of our own minds" (Fiedler 1966, 38).

When Fiedler refers to the "novel" he does not mean any long prose fiction, but specifically the "modern" or "bourgeois" novel. This genre appeared in the second quarter of the eighteenth century composed by writers such as Richardson; Fiedler excludes the long fictions of the Hellenistic period. When the novel appeared, it pretended—Fiedler thinks specifically of Richardson and his followers—to serve verisimilitude above all. Like autobiography, the novel was to tell the truth of daily existence. In the language of eighteenth-century criticism, it was classified as "fictional history." The novel, Fiedler argues, is irrational, "as it is a form without a theory. The result of mixing allegory with the plot structure of sensational drama, the letter book with prose history and 'scandalmongering'" (quoted phrases in Fiedler 1966, 40), the novel seemed both in the service of and a threat to the Protestantism that in many ways inspired it. The novel, Fiedler writes, "paid allegiance in fact to that secret religion of the bourgeoisie in which tears are considered a truer service of God than prayers, the Pure Young Girl replaces Christ as the savior, marriage becomes the equivalent of bliss eternal, and the Seducer is the only Devil" (1966, 45).

The European code of courtly love seemed to slide into heresy, on the one hand. On the other, "it even more strangely merges with homosexuality" (Fiedler 1966, 49). From the start, Fiedler suggests, it is possible to sense in the verse of courtly love "a desire to mitigate by ritualized and elegant foreplay a final consummation felt as brutal, or else a desire to avoid entirely any degrading conjunction with female flesh." Disagreeing with Denis de Rougemont (1956) (in his *Love in the Western World*) that the troubadours were secret sharers in the Albigensian heresy, Fiedler argues instead that "they were heretics of another order—not secret but *unconscious* self-castrators. For surely their exaggerated worship of the lady unmanned them successfully enough to have pleased any of the world-denying Cathari among the Albigensians" (quoted passages in Fiedler 1966, 49).

In the Catholic south of Europe, Fiedler suggests, what may be construed as the "conflict of maternal and paternal, of lust and order," has never achieved resolution, only a negotiated settlement, a compromise. While nominal victory has been awarded to God the Father, he remains invisible, while everywhere is the Virgin with the Child on her lap. "The orthodox Trinity of Father, Son, and Holy Ghost," he continues, "has yielded in art and the popular imagination to the baroque trinity, derived ultimately from Venus, Vulcan, and Cupid, and still, despite the new names of Mary, Joseph, and Jesus, what it always was: an archetypal representation of cuckold, mother, and son, the last degradation of father" (quoted passages in Fiedler 1966, 54).

It was, Fiedler notes, during the religious wars, when "mother-directed Catholicism and father-centered Protestantism" clashed, in France, Germany, and England, that the novel flourished. Rousseau moves back and forth between Catholicism and Protestantism, though finally, Fiedler insists, "his *sensibility* is as Protestant as that of Richardson or Goethe, the other founding fathers of the form." Their commitment to "the northern rejection of the Virgin" functioned to drive these men "to smuggle the mother principle back into their cultures." "They were," he continues, "thus specially qualified to satisfy the secret hunger of the puritanical bourgeoisie, which demanded bootlegged madonnas; it was the function of the early novel to supply them. Here is another source of guilt, added to the original conflicts which underlie the origins of love in Europe" (Fiedler 1966, 56).

Shakespeare's resolution of the contradictions between courtly love and Christianity was, Fiedler argues, "so extraordinary, so alien" that the bourgeoisie has pretended not to notice it at all. Resistance to the homoerotic content of Shakespeare's sonnets began as indifference, as more than thirty years passed between the first and second editions. But the growing popularity of the sonnets turned indifference into outright expurgation, until in the seventeenth century the original male pronouns were quietly changed to the female forms in an effort to disguise the gender of the object of Shakespeare's desire. A few lines from sonnet 144 make the object of that desire explicit:

> Two loves I have, of comfort and despair,
> Which like two spirits do suggest me still;
> The better angel is a man right fair,
> The worser spirit a woman colour'd ill.
> To wine me soon to hell, my female evil
> Tempeth my better angel from my side. ...
> (quoted passages in Fiedler 1966, 57)

Shakespeare's solution would seem to parallel our argument: homoeroticism denied is transfigured into racism and misogyny, in brief, the fabrication of the "other." Fiedler regards Shakespeare's move, of creating "two loves, one angelic, the other diabolic" as a novel restatement of an old problem, "especially when these drives are directed respectively toward a fair youth (loved as purely as any Italian poet of the sweet new style longed for his lady) and the black woman (lusted after in self-hatred and disgust)." But the denial of homosexual desire means that "sentimental salvation is attributed to the male, passionate damnation to the female." Presumably in the service of ladies, the sonnet sequence disavows homosexual desire. "So successful is his subterfuge," Fiedler notes, "that men in willful ignorance have continued for generations to read to their mistresses Shakespeare's antifeminist praises of the youth, for these are truly love poems of great tenderness." Men reading a man's love poems to boys; is this heterosexuality? Yes, it would seem, anything that is not two men fucking qualifies. But Shakespeare's love for male youth is precisely what "modern critics have tended to disregard in their concern with establishing the fact that Shakespeare did not actually have physical relations with boys. Apparently, such critics are not discomfited by the notion that the poet slept with women and considered it filthy, while chastely embracing an idealized male lover" (Fiedler 1966, 58). (Sounds like nineteenth-century "romantic friendship," does it not?) For Shakespeare the system of two loves was not an unsatisfactory compromise, "since the two loves tend to fall together" (Fiedler 1966, 58). The "other" does tend to be an encompassing construction, obliterating what is individual and distinct in favor of what is exotic or "different."

Fiedler reminds us that during the medieval period "marriage did not make sex a holy thing" (1966, 59). Not until the sixteenth century was the marriage ceremony officially declared a sacrament by the church. "To marry rather than burn," Fiedler explains, "to wed for the sake of progeny and companionship, these were standard and acceptable notions." But linking "the feeling which leads to and persists in marriage with the ennobling passion sung by the troubadours, this was a revolutionary step" (1966, 59–60). This new emotional arrangement would not last long.

Between the late sixteenth and the early nineteenth centuries, a sentimental revolution took place, Fiedler tells us, "a revolution carried out in modest silence by the literary form that had in the meantime dethroned poetry—the modern or bourgeois novel" (1966, 61). Men and women go to war. "Superficially," he explains, "the literary war of the sexes reflects a psychological fact of bourgeois self-consciousness, institutionalized in bourgeois life; symbolically, it stands for a more complex sociological phenomenon: for class war in eighteenth-century England." In fact, the seduction novel worked on this political as well as romantic plane, resolving "the conflict of aristocracy and bourgeoisie within the confines of the boudoir." Typically, the male character was a nobleman, the girl he attempts to seduce from a "humbler stock." "The seducer," Fiedler continues, "is sometimes given to antidemocratic speeches in which he scorns the notion of a marriage that will bring him neither profit nor distinction. Against such cold class-consciousness and self-seeking are balanced the arguments of sentimentality: that it is the quality of the soul which counts, that the truest nobility is piety, etc. etc." (quoted passages in 1966, 71). In these terms—self-seeking and sentimentality, soul and profit—one finds the psychosocial and sexual situation which made possible an American Revolution.

II. To the Back of the Cave

Having killed the tyrannical father, American men feared being swallowed by an infantilizing and insatiable mother—voluptuous, voracious, and terrifyingly alluring.

—Michael Kimmel, *Manhood in America: A Cultural History* (1996)

If boys dream of growing up but escaping from the future, men dream of never having grown up and escaping from the present.

—Mark Simpson, *Male Impersonators: Men Performing Masculinity* (1994)

Mark Twain knew that in his America humanity masked its face with blackness.

—Ralph Ellison, *Shadow and Act* (1964/1995)

Seduction and romance in America were profoundly shaped by the conditions of the country's birth. The American nation began in a political repudiation of England, Fiedler reminds us. But King George III is not the only father denied. In fact, Fiedler tells us, the American—and clearly this prototype for Fiedler is male—has denied enough fathers to cast his fate as a fatherless man: "The fatherland abandoned, the Pope rejected, the bishops denied, the king overthrown—only the mother remained as symbol of an authority that was one with love" (Fiedler 1966, 78–79). This original, archetypal American experience was repeated in the experience of the immigrant generations to follow. The children of Slavic peasants, of German revolutionaries and Jewish scholars become heirs of, in Fiedler's phrase, "a handful of Englishmen who settled New England." He quotes Geoffrey Gorer's *The American People* which took note of "the individual rejection of the European father ... [that] every second-generation American had to perform. ... [T]he making of an American demanded that the father should be rejected both as a model and as a source of authority" (quoted in Fiedler 1966, 79).

These gendered politics of revolution left many American men struggling over "manhood." That is evident in the widespread fear of effeminacy suffered by so many. The fear of effeminacy was, Greven argues, "one of the most powerful inner sources for the encircling paranoia that dominated their political consciousness throughout the 1760's and 1770's" (1977, 351). Greven reminds us of "the close association of paranoia with unconscious fears and anxieties over masculine and feminine impulses and feelings" (351), but as I have noted, Freud is more specific. Paranoia is repressed homosexual desire. This formulation decodes more precisely the fear of effeminacy that consumed so many new Americans; it suggests one source for many American men's "paranoid vision of the political world that dominated the politics of the period. Indeed, the political choices that faced British Americans in 1776 involved nothing less than a choice between being or becoming effeminate and being or becoming manly, for monarchies and monarchical styles of life evoked the imagery of femininity, while republics and republican styles of life evoked the imagery of manliness" (Greven 1977, 351).

As "a revolt of the sons against the father" (Kimmel 1996, 18), the American revolution seems to have marked many white men with a certain longing for the father, the collective denial of which congeals into a homophobic, misogynistic homosociality that becomes thoroughly racialized. Did the revolutionary nation represent the fatherless home Parsons and Moynihan would lament two centuries later? Did the internalized guilt of political patricide stimulate American sons into imagining themselves "self-made," motherless as well as fatherless, a hypermasculine and genocidal brotherhood of boys gone bad? The term "self-made man" was an American neologism, Michael Kimmel points out, first coined by Henry Clay in a speech in the U.S. Senate in 1832. Defending a protective tariff that he believed would widen opportunities for humble men to rise in business, he declared that in Kentucky "almost every manufactory known to me is in the hands of enterprising, self-made men, who have whatever wealth they possess by patient and diligent labor" (quoted in Kimmel 1996, 26).

This was a fantasy white men could share and support. By the 1840s and 1850s many imagined themselves "self-made men." White boys consumed popular biographies and inspirational advice books which would, presumably, guide future self-made men to fashion themselves out of their dreams. As a man "on the go," the "self-made man" was, as one lawyer explained in 1838, "made for action, and the bustling scenes of moving life, and not the poetry or romance of existence" (quoted in Kimmel 1996, 17). While it probably did not occur to those who clung to the abstraction, the central dynamic of being self-made involves, by definition, disavowal of any parental influence, including any pre-oedipal identification with the mother and longing for the father. To accomplish this identificatory trick, American men rejected the home as thoroughly feminine and settled on the public sphere, especially the frontier and the workplace, as the sites for coming of age, in gendered terms the proving ground for manhood.

On the frontier and in the workplace, while other men watched, men would test their manhood. By mid-century, Kimmel (1996) tells us, the "self-made man" was the dominant American conception of manhood. Such a conception required "separate spheres" and the ideology of "true womanhood," notions that enabled, for a time, the European-American man to cover-up the fact that a woman had given birth to him, literally and psychologically, a woman who had at some point made love to a man, his father. Imaging himself an orphan, the nineteenth-century white man denied his relations to others and defiantly claimed conception for himself.

"Father never knows best," Leslie Fiedler (1966, 79) quips. And in the symbolic vacuum left by the murder of the Father is "the figure of woman, as Maiden and Mother" (79). The idealization of woman into "maiden" and "mother"—and her shadow, the "fallen woman"—meant that seduction and romance, as they had been understood and practiced in Europe, would live short lives in the American nation. As late as 1803, Fiedler tells us, it was still possible to devote one of the chief commencement speeches at Harvard to the subject of "seduction." But by the end of the century the topic had become taboo on all public occasions, and Fiedler notes that not even a "realist" such as William Dean Howells treats the subject in his novels.

Instead, in American fiction the female is portrayed, Fiedler argues, "as pure sentiment," often tearful. In contrast, the male's identification with the "naked phallus" is repeated endlessly. And this peculiar perversion of the European spirit affected even the figure of the intellectual. In American fiction, Fiedler writes, "he" is travestied in favor of woman's "finer feelings." Still, the male spouts "ideas," but his ideas are depicted as irrelevant to life and even to good sense, "the babble of a bookish child." Fiedler (1966) imagines he can understand why women should have permitted this mythologizing of the woman. It was, initially and on the surface, very flattering. What baffles him "is why men, too, should have accepted this travesty on their nature and role in life; but they did, in fact, accept it, even repeating in their own books the formulas of feminist sentimentality. Perhaps it seemed to them, on one level of consciousness or another, a symbolic restitution for the injustices they had no intention of reforming—rather like the wealthy Victorian's self-satisfied weeping over the plight of the poor" (Fiedler 1966, 90). I will not be the man you need for me to be, and I will make you into a woman you cannot possibly be and whom finally I do not want.

In the end, Fiedler suggests, the American man and woman arrived at a mutual pact, a compromise based on guilt and resentment. Its terms required the castration of the father, "to make him seem a spoiled child rather than a sexual aggressor." The acceptance by the male of the female's characterization of him "first as seducer and blackguard, then (in America) as 'bad boy,' follows naturally upon the female's acceptance of the male's image of her as sexless savior and (in America) eternal Mama; and perhaps, after all, the former travesty is a revenge for the latter one, rather than for the social indignities visited upon woman." As in *Who's Afraid of Virginia Woolf* (Albee 1962), "instances of male humiliation are endlessly multiplied," as the woman resents a contract she does not recall signing. Perhaps "men" and "women" carry "freight"—a denied, relocated sense of class—in addition to a complicated history of gender: "In this country, Fiedler (1966) exclaims, "the only class war is between the sexes!" (quoted passages on 90).

One consequence of this gendered class war is a substitution of terror for love in the nation's imaginative life. Enter the gothic romance, the primary meaning of which, Fiedler insists, is the substitution of terror for love. Instead of offering the titillation of sex, the American gothic romance "offers its readers a vicarious participation in a flirtation with death—approach and retreat, approach and retreat, the fatal orgasm eternally mounting and eternally checked." The gothic, Fiedler explains, "replaces the classic concept of nothing-in-excess with the revolutionary doctrine that nothing succeeds like excess." The Aristotelian formula for achieving the tragic without "the abominable" is reversed; "the abominable" is now made the touchstone of effective art. "Dedicated to producing nausea," Fiedler writes, "to transcending the limits of taste and endurance, the gothic novelist is driven to see more and more atrocious crimes to satisfy the hunger for 'too-much' on which he trades" (1966, 134). This mode of fiction Fiedler characterizes as the "projective," an aesthetic tradition that moves "through Poe and the Surrealists to a modern climax in Kafka." The other major mode of the novel is the analytic, a line discernible "through Flaubert and James to Virginia Woolf, Proust, and Joyce" (Fiedler 1966, 140).

There is in both modes a racial dynamic. From the time of Richardson, Fiedler tells us, the dramatic destination of the novel had been clear: "to carry the torch to the back of the cave." There would be revealed the "hideous Moor" who lurks in its shadows, just beyond the light of day. Richardson's technique is analytic, psychological, but for Diderot this scene is melodramatic and symbolic—in short, "gothic." In *Clarissa*, the "cave" is the heart concealed beneath the exterior actions of a girl and a man living ordinary lives. The "hideous Moor" is the sum total of the "unconfessed, ambiguous motives" that account for their actions, for which the actors have given rather different, socially respectable explanations. "One can imagine," Fiedler (1966, 141) continues,

> a kind of fiction in which the depths of the mind are represented in the text itself as a cave before whose mouth a bewildered girl stands paralyzed with fright; while the hideous Moor in fact leaps from its darkness, his black skin glistening, his white eyeballs bulging, his sinewy arms reached out to clasp and destroy. In such projective or symbolic fiction, character, setting, and incident alike are "true," not in their own right but as they symbolize in outward terms an inward reality.

An inward reality indeed it was, projected then onto the black man: the rape myth.

Why, Fiedler asks, has the gothic held such a strong attraction for Americans? In part, he answers, the success of terror follows from the failure of love in our fiction, its failure in our imaginative life. Deprived of the theme that animated European novelists such as Stendhal or Constant, Flaubert or Proust, the theme that seemed to them *the* subject of the novel, American novelists turned to tales of loneliness and terror (Fiedler 1966). Instead of love there is adventure, triumph, defeat, always horror; are these the narcissistic dynamics of men adrift, split off from themselves, driven to find something—gold?—but consumed by the uncontrolled, the unregulated, the free: the homoerotic frontier?

The California Gold Rush of 1849 represented the zenith of white men's escape westward. Nearly 200,000 men arrived in California in 1849 and 1850 alone; they comprised 93 percent of the state's population. Almost 71 percent of these were younger men, aged twenty to forty, creating a vast "homosocial preserve" (Kimmel 1996, 61). "There was no female society," complained Reverend John Todd, "no homes to soften and restrain." "The condition of the mining population, especially their carelessness in regard to appearances, mode of life, and habits in general," reported C. W. Haskins, an observer, "showed conclusively that man, when alone, deprived of that influence which the presence of woman only can produce, would in a short time degenerate into a savage and barbarous state." A doctor also subscribed to the view that women kept men "civilized," writing that in California, "all the *restrictive influence* of fair women is lost, and the ungoverned tempers of men run wild" (quoted passages in Kimmel 1996, 62). Kimmel suggests that the forty-niners may have been searching for something besides gold: manhood.

Where does the American dream end, Fiedler asks, and the Faustian nightmare begin? Both aspire to break through all limits and restraints, to reach "a place of total freedom where one could with impunity deny the Fall, live as if innocence rather than guilt were the birthright of all men." In Huck's blithe casual calculation, "All right, I'll *go* to Hell," is an American—at least in its "boyish" form—refusal to suffer. We Americans, Fiedler seems to be suggesting, have secretly suspected that damnation is not all it is cracked up to be, that we just might get away with it, "it" standing for all that European Americans have done. "In a strange way," Fiedler writes, "that naturalized Faust legend becomes in the United States a way of denying hell in the act of seeming to accept it, of suggesting that it is merely a scary word, a bugaboo, a forbidding description of freedom itself!" Even the colonists responded passionately to the myth. In the 1680s, Fiedler reports, one Boston bookseller sold more copies of *The History of the Damnable Life and Deserved Death of Dr. John Faustus* than any title deemed "light literature" (quoted passages in Fiedler 1966, 143).

The reign of terror self-divides. One gothic current becomes what Fiedler calls "black" Romanticism, culminating in the *Fleurs du mal.* A second becomes what he terms the "white," climaxing, he says, with Wordworth's *Prelude.* Like "black" or antibourgeois Romanticism, the "white" or philistine kind testifies to the superiority of feeling to intellect, of the heart to the head. For this latter kind, however, the heart is carefully distinguished from the viscera or genitals, the existence of which is hardly even acknowledged. Like his more melancholy counterpart, the "white" romantic is preoccupied with the picturesque and the exotic, with whatever is not everyday middle-class life. In the ballad, in fairy tales, and in the folk epic, the "white" man seeks a source of strength not obviously available to the sophisticated resident of an increasingly complex urban society. In contrast to the "black" romantic, for the "white" romantic "the primitive remains something clean and heroic, immune to the darkness and the demonic" (Fiedler 1966, 162).

Little Eva (in *Uncle Tom's Cabin*) seemed the answer, Fiedler writes, to a "vexing genteel dilemma." How can the female be saved for those polite readers who wanted women but not sex (or as I would put it, those who wanted "ladies" but not women)? This was no easy matter. "The only safe woman is a dead woman," seems to be the answer. But if the deceased happened to be a young and beautiful woman, she is, he notes wryly, "only half safe, as any American knows, recalling the necrophilia of Edgar Allan Poe," lying with Annabel Lee, in her grave by the sea. "The only *safe*, safe female," he writes, "is a pre-adolescent girl dying or dead. But this, of course, is Little Eva, the prepubescent corpse as heroine, model for all the protagonists of a literature at once juvenile and genteelly gothic" (Fiedler 1966, 267).

Where is Fiedler taking us? What does this provocative portrait of the American imagination tell us? It is that the prototypical American male is "sexually as pure as any milky maiden," but "a roughneck all the same." He is at once "potent and submissive, made to be reformed by the right woman." He is, in Fiedler's phrase, a "good bad boy," and this is, he argues, "America's vision of itself." The American man may be "crude and unruly in his beginnings, but endowed by his creator with an instinctive sense of what is right." Given this self-image, "no wonder our greatest book is about a boy and that boy 'bad'!" (quoted passages in Fiedler 1966, 270)

The book is the "astonishingly complicated" *Huckleberry Finn* (with its extension back into *Tom Sawyer*), a novel portraying not one image of the boy but "a series of interlocking ones." Tom Sawyer exists, Fiedler argues, as the projection of that which Sid Sawyer, as "pious Good Good Boy," yearns for and denies (quoted passages in Fiedler 1966, 270). Huck Finn stands for what Tom is not quite rebel ("man") enough to represent. Huck is Tom's "Noble Savage," what Fiedler terms his "sentimentalized id-figure." Huck represents the "Good Bad Boy's dream of how bully life might be without parents, clothing or school" (279). His black friend Jim (Tom's "double" Fiedler suggests, 279) "embodies a world of instinct and primal terror beyond what even the outcast white boy projects" (271).

Twain is, for Fiedler, more than a novelist; he is a poet, "the possessor of deep and special mythopoetic powers, whose childhood was contemporaneous with a nation's; and who, remembering himself before the fall of puberty, remembered his country before the fall of the Civil War." The myth Twain communicates is a myth of childhood, a childhood that is "rural, sexless, and troubled by the shadow of bloody death" (quoted passages in Fiedler 1966, 273). In 1901, Mark Twain recalled that shadowy death when he damned lynching as "this epidemic of bloody insanities" (quoted in Brundage 1997b, 1). The world in which this American myth is told "is one in which passion is less real than witchcraft, ghosts more common than adulterers; but it is also one in which a pure love between males, colored and white, triumphs over witches and ghosts and death itself" (Fiedler 1966, 273).

By "pure love," of course, Fiedler means unconsummated love, reminiscent of Shakespeare's "solution," except in Huck's case he seems altogether celibate: "With Jim, of course, Huck does not dream of any sexual relation, any more than Tom does with Becky." While his love for Jim is profound, Huck does not think of "their union in terms of a marriage. Yet they pet and sustain each other in mutual love and trust: make on their raft an antifamily of two, with neither past nor future, only a transitory, perilous present of peace and joy." For Huck and Jim, as for the black and white men in the American prison, there seems "no possibility of a continuing love." In the novel, "Jim has a family, which will presumably claim him, and Huck must follow the centrifugal impulse which has made and will keep him the 'only independent person ... in the community.' Moreover, he and Jim are separated not by the schoolyard code which forbids the fraternizing of boys and girls, but the profound social gulf between black and white in ante-bellum Missouri" (Fiedler 1966, 282–283).

There is in America a certain refusal to grow up, Fiedler believes. Perhaps it is due to the parricide that characterized the birth of the nation: if fathers are murdered, why would a son wish to become one? Perhaps it is intertwined with sexual repression: if one's heterosexual choices are either Maiden or Madonna, if the safe object of one's affections is a dead adolescent girl, then, clearly, one must not grow up. One must remain a boy. Fiedler thinks of Jack Kerouac, who, even at age thirty-five, was in some way still a "boy." That Kerouac wrote as "one of the boys" seems to Fiedler not very different from those "middle-aged ladies in their bridge clubs" who sometimes refer to themselves as "girls" (quoted passages in Fiedler 1966, 290). Why would one refuse to grow up?

Could it be that one worries one would not be a "man"? Michael Kimmel observes that patricide has its price, including "the loneliness of the fatherless son and the burden of adult responsibilities placed upon his shoulders" (1996, 21). As we saw in chapter 15, fatherless sons often compensate by cultivating a "hypermasculinity." Fatherless after the American Revolution, American men likewise feared effeminacy, then in the form of a fantasized aristocracy and decadence, terms that often connote sexual "experimentation." Samuel Adams expressed this fear in the *Massachusetts Sentinel* in January 1785. "Did we consult the history of Athens and Rome, we should find that so long as they continued their frugality and simplicity of manners, they shone with superlative glory; but no sooner were effeminate refinements introduced amongst them, than they visibly fell from whatever was elevated and magnanimous, and became feeble and timid, dependent, slavish and false" (quoted in Kimmel 1996, 21). In other words, aristocratic effeminacy threatened the Revolution's masculine edge. The post-Revolutionary American man had to be wary lest he succumb to such temptation; he must labor to distance himself from "feminized indulgence" (Kimmel 1996, 21). Better to stay a boy, safe in the innocence of a homosocial childhood.

The American flight from sexuality has led, Fiedler argues, to a literature about children written for adults. Reading such literature supports those adults in holding onto their innermost images of themselves as children. The "good bad boyhood" idea is not just an inner self-image that influences adult life; it has become, like much else in America, a "career." Think of middle-aged men driving Corvettes, surfers well into their forties, a president who evidently enjoys sex with women not half his age. Fiedler thinks of Kerouac, whose characters, like Twain's, have no definite age, if for different reasons. Fiedler (1966, 290) explains.

> Twain blurred adolescence back into boyhood to avoid confronting the problem of sex; the newer writers, accepting the confusion of childhood and youth, blur both into manhood to avoid yielding up to maturity the fine clean rapture of childish "making out." The protagonists of the hipsters have crossed the borderline of genital maturity, but in all other respects they have not left Jackson's Island. *Plus ça change, plus c'est la même chose*—which in American means, "Boys will be boys."

If it is maturity above all that the American (male) writer fears, then marriage might appear as its essential sign. Traditionally, Fiedler suggests, marriage represents not only "a reconciliation with the divided self, a truce between head and heart, but also a compromise with society, an acceptance of responsibility and drudgery and dullness." But, Fiedler continues, there is more. In psychoanalytic terms "marriage also means an acceptance of the status of a father; an abandonment of the quest to deliver the captive mother and an assumption of the role of the ogre who holds her in captivity." But, he thinks, there is no "authentic American" (male) who would not prefer to be Jack rather than the Giant, no "real man" who would not choose to remain "one of the boys" to the very end. The ideal American man understands himself, Fiedler is sure, as the "fatherless man, the eternal son of mother" (quoted passages in 1966, 338). In fact, he continues:

> There is finally no heterosexual solution which the American psyche finds completely satisfactory, no imagined or real consummation between man and woman found worthy of standing in our fiction for the healing of the

> breach between consciousness and unconsciousness, reason and impulse, society and nature. Yet in no nation is the need to heal such divisions more passionately recognized. (Fiedler 1966, 339)

If there is no satisfactory heterosexual solution available to the American imagination, and homosexuality is forbidden, what move is left? There is, of course, impotence. The impotent man avoids sex with women but manages to retain the heterosexual identity; he may not be "red-blooded" but at least he's a "man." But when the American writer does not make impotence his subject—Fiedler terms this the "Hawthorne-James-Faulkner gambit"—he is left to choose between the two archetypes. The first is an "innocent homosexuality" and the second is "unconsummated incest." Put differently, one is left choosing between "the love of comrades and that of brother and sister." Fiedler (1966, 348) disapproves of both:

> Both themes are juvenile and regressive, that is, narcissistic; for where woman is felt to be a feared and forbidden other, the only legitimate beloved is the self. Pure narcissism cannot, however, provide the dream and tension proper to a novel; the mirror-image of the self is translated in the American novel either into the flesh of one's flesh, the sister as *anima*; or into the comrade of one's own sex, the buddy as *anima*.

Fiedler illustrates these dynamics with William Faulkner's characters Quentin Compson and Joe Christmas. As a child, Quentin observes the American adult dialectic of passion and death in Faulkner's "That Evening Sun Go Down." As an adolescent he relives it, this time as a "witness" and "peripheral actor" in *The Sound and the Fury* and *Absalom, Absalom*! Then, on the "verge of manhood," refusing to become a chronological adult by becoming twenty-one, he commits suicide. In contrast, Joe Christmas, in *Light in August*, has managed to reach the age of Christ at his crucifixion, despite his "induction into nausea" when he was five (quoted passages in Fiedler 1966, 345). At fourteen he cruelly kicks the naked black girl with whom he might have lost his virginity; at thirty-three, he decapitates the aging white woman who has made him her lover. The punishment for this crime is lynching.

> Impotence and sadist aggression, suicide direct or indirect; it is not only to Faulkner that those seem the choices for an American whose imagination is fixed forever on one of the two major crises of pre-adolescent emotional life. Yet it is around these crises that our literature compulsively circles: the stumbling on the primal scene, mother and father caught in the sexual act (or less dramatically, the inference of that scene from creaking springs and ambiguous cries); or the discovery of heterosexual "treachery" on the part of some crush, idolized in innocent homosexual adoration. (Fiedler 1966, 345)

In 1926, as noted in chapter 15, in *The Sun Also Rises*, Hemingway portrayed an emasculated Jake Barnes. Barnes may have wanted Brett, but the feeling between them "only erodes, never sparks to life." Thirty years later,

Fiedler notes, a movie version makes the point of Barnes's impotence without ambiguity, not without "some show of daring" (quoted passages in Fiedler 1966, 345). This is not a matter of psychological impotence, mind you; Hemingway makes sure the reader is clear that it was "the War" which devastated Jake with the "absurd wound" which he examines in the mirror, alone in his room. But, Fiedler (1966, 346) complains,

> "the War" is merely a convenient tag for the failure of values and faith which converted a generation of young American writers to self-hatred, bravado, and expatriation. The same forces, at any rate, which have "emancipated" Brett have unmanned Jake; forced him into the role of pimp as well—setter-up of scenes which, beheld or imagined, can only drive him to queasy despair. From the time of Hemingway, impotence has been a central symbol in our fiction, a felt clue to the quality of American life, erotic and spiritual.

It was a slightly earlier version of this American "crisis" of manhood which Ida B. Wells exploited in her British campaign against lynching.

In American mythology, a mythology which disallows both mature heterosexuality and explicit homosexuality, the tie between male and male, Fiedler notes, is not only considered innocent, "it is taken for the very symbol of innocence itself." This homosocial, often homoerotic, but never homosexual relationship is imagined as the only bond in a "paradisiacal world" in which there are no (heterosexual) marriages. Of course, for hardheaded practical Americans "paradisiacal" means "not quite real." And this fact is evident in American fiction, where there is, in Fiedler's words, "a certain sense of make-believe in almost all portrayals of the holy marriage of males, set as they typically are in the past, the wilderness, or at sea—that is to say, in worlds familiar to most readers in dreams" (1966, 350–351).

And, as Fiedler observes, this "holy marriage of males" is often interracial. The classic, essential rendering of this imagined solution to the America dilemma is *Huckleberry Finn* and the sexless marriage between Huck and Jim. Before beginning his discussion of that relationship, Fiedler (1966) notes that in the twentieth century "things have changed radically in this regard." When the relationship of white and black man is evoked now, he says, it is not always so innocent. To illustrate, Fiedler cites the following passage from James Purdy's *Cabot Wright*: "Taking Winter Hart's left hand in his, Bernie held his friend's dark finger on which he wore a wedding-ring, and pressed the finger and the hand. Far from being annoyed at this liberty, Winters Hart was, to tell the truth, relieved and pleased. Isolation in a racial democracy, as he was to tell Bernie later that night, as they lay in Bernie's bed together, isolation, no thank you" (quoted in Fiedler 1966, 350 n.).

In nineteenth-century prose, white characterizations of black characters tended toward the stereotypic (Starke 1971). Individualization of character came later. But Twain's characterization of Jim in *Huckleberry Finn* was, Fiedler argues, complicated enough to rescue him from becoming only a stereotype in the white imagination. And this relative complexity of his character means one cannot reduce him to the status of substitute father. "Sometimes," Fiedler writes, "he seems more servant than father, sometimes more lover than servant, sometimes more mother than either!" (1966, 352). It would seem to be a multigendered if sexless love affair, the black man and the white boy adrift on a river in the new world, ancient with slavery.

Fiedler sees their relationship as a polis, an "impossible society," given that its citizens are an outcast white boy and a black male slave. Despite his relative complexity, Jim, while he exists as an individual for the reader, does not really exist for Huck. That acknowledged, their relationship constitutes, Fiedler argues, "a society in which, momentarily, the irreparable breach between black and white seems healed by love." It would seem to be Jim's love, not Huck's. Early on Huck plays a stupid joke on the sleeping Jim, in Tom's company. On another occasion he almost kills Jim, the consequence of yet another stunt; still later he teases him to the point of tears about the dangers of the river. Finally, Fiedler reminds, Huck joins with Tom yet again to inflict on Jim "a hundred pointless tortures," even putting his life in danger. "And through it all," Fiedler (1966) observes, "Jim plays the role of Uncle Tom, enduring everything, suffering everything, forgiving everything—finally risking a lynching to save 'Marse Tom's' life. It is the southerner's dream, the American dream of guilt remitted by the abused Negro, who, like the abused mother, opens his arms crying, 'Lawsy, I's mighty glad to git you back agin, honey'" (quoted passages on 353).

Where can such an imaginary relationship exist? As Fiedler has pointed out before, "only on the unstable surface of the river and in the dark of the night." Its "proper home is the raft," floating on the "surge of flood-time into the story," a gift bestowed by a non-Christian yet still divine Nature. "There warn't no home like a raft, after all," Huck reflects. "You feel mighty free and easy and comfortable on a raft." Yet, as Fiedler points out, the nature of life on a raft is "unreality." "The motion of the raft is gentle, and gliding, and smooth, and noiseless." Twain wrote in *A Tramp Abroad*: "under its restless influence ... existence becomes a dream ... a deep and tranquil ecstasy" (quoted passages in Fiedler 1966, 353). This "deep and tranquil ecstasy," this dream, always threatens to turn for Twain into a literal nightmare. In 1906, he recalls a recurring dream in which he is once more piloting a boat down the Mississippi: "It is never a pleasant dream, either. I love to think about those days, but there's always something sickening about the thought ... and usually in my dream I am just about to start into a black shadow without being able to tell whether it is Selma Bluff, or Hat Island, or just a black wall of night" (quoted in Fiedler 1966, 353–354).

The love of Huck and Jim is also a dream, Fiedler suggests, at whose heart lurks a nightmare. While they float together under the stars, all about them on the lawless Mississippi, "crime is plotted and violence done." The river itself is often threatening, ready to destroy their world with fog or storm or snag. Thieves and murderers travel this river on which Huck and Jim float in domestic peace. Finally, in the characters of Duke and Dauphin, evil boards the raft itself. Their "floating island paradise" suddenly is a country occupied by others, a refuge for "absurd and sodden scoundrels" who plan crime and avoid retribution, for a time at least. Fiedler (1966) comments:

> There is no way to escape evil forever, no absolute raft; and once the home of Huck and Jim has been invaded, they cannot manage to establish their little Eden again. For a moment after the fiasco at the Wilks's, it seems as if Huck and Jim are about to recapture their first freedom: "it *did* seem so good to be free again and all by ourselves on the big river, and nobody to bother us." But the King and Duke appear at the last minute, and Huck collapses into despair: "it was all I could do to keep from crying." (quoted passages on 354)

This is, Fiedler points out, no father-and-son relationship. Because their union "signifies a coming to terms with the natural and impulsive," it is impossible to think of it in those terms. "[M]uch more suitable," he writes, "is the metaphor of the spouse." "Only marriage," Fiedler (1966) continues, "is a relationship complicated enough to stand for so complicated and ambiguous cluster of meanings; the search for a parent, a master, a slave, an equal, a companion, a soul—a union with one's deepest self which is simultaneously a rejection of the community to which one was born" (quoted passages on 354).

Where can men marry in a homophobic heterosexist culture? On a raft? In a dream? "In America," Fiedler writes, "the earthly paradise for men only is associated, for obvious historical reasons, with the 'West'" (1966, 355). In this specific sense, he says, it is possible to characterize *Huckleberry Finn* as a "Western." Despite certain superficial differences, the novel is not unrelated to the pulp stories, comic books, movies, and television programs in which the "cowhand and his sidekick ride in silent communion through a wilderness of sagebrush, rocks, and tumbleweed." So understood, Fiedler continues, the "western" does not even require an American setting. He sees it reborn, for instance, in Hemingway's *The Sun Also Rises* in Paris and Burguet: "Like the American East, Paris in Hemingway's book stands for the world of women and work, for 'civilization' with all its moral complexity, and it is presided over quite properly by the bitch-goddess Brett Ashley. The mountains of Spain, on the other hand, represent the West: a world of male companions and sport, an anti-civilization, simple and joyous, whose presiding genius is that scarcely articulate arch-buddy, 'good, old Bill'" (Fiedler 1966, 355).

In a heterosexist world of "others," "no man born of woman," Fiedler suggests, "is innocent enough to combat evil without being converted into its image." Each man must be born again, but the second time he will not be associated with what he perceives to be "the murky flood of blood, amniotic fluid, and milk" which he associates with female gestation. The "disgust of the American male at our original birth" requires a very different birth scene. This time he will emerge "out of the immaculate flux of waters which characterizes a birth into the world of men without women. A new birth implies a new family, a wifeless and motherless one, in which the good companion is the spouse and nurse, the redeemed male the lover and child, each his own progenitor and offspring" (quoted passages in Fiedler 1966, 358). Hypermasculinity, perhaps?

In the last lines of the novel, Huckleberry Finn plans his escape, one of the three great themes of American manhood, Michael Kimmel argues. (The other two are exclusion and self-control [1996, 44].) "I reckon I got to light out for the territory ahead of the rest, because Aunt Sally she's going to adopt me and sivilize me, and I can't stand it. I been there before." Huck expresses, Kimmel points out and as we have seen, the sentiments of many young white men in America. For them, women constrained and undermined manhood, demanding of them temperance, Christian piety, sober responsibility, sexual fidelity. Women set the tone of those institutions of civilization—the schoolroom, parlor, church—that questioned masculine prerogatives (Kimmel 1996). What was necessary was escape into a world of "men without women," a phrase Hemingway used once as a title to a collection of his short stories.

A world of men without women: that is the prison, of course. And there, as we have seen, rape is an interracial act of political revenge as well as sexual desire. Prison rape and love are not accidents of gender-segregated institutionalization. A world of men without women, a world of male-male matrimony (however homosexually denied), is a central element in the European-American male imagination. "In the dreams of white men," Fiedler tells us, "the forbidden erotic object tends to be represented by a colored man, such as the 'black pagod of a fellow,' the 'grand sculptured bull,' 'so intensely black that he must need have been ... of the unadulterable blood of Ham' whom Melville evokes for a moment at the beginning of *Billy Budd*" (1966, 365). Or, still with Melville, Ishmael's love for Queequeg: "Thus, when, in our heart's honeymoon, lay I and Queequeg—a cosy, loving pair" (quoted in Fiedler 1948/1995, 530). The black man the white man lynched was the man he desired.

So, Fiedler concludes, in the "communal American dream of love" the idyllic surface hides a subterranean need to transgress taboos. And that taboo is, as Werner Sollors (1997) has shown, the racial dividing line, itself eroticized. In the white male fantasy of intimacy, of "matrimony," the spouse, the antiwife, "is properly of another race, a race suppressed and denied, even as the promptings of the libido are suppressed and denied." Fiedler moves through fictional examples. In the *Leatherstocking Tales* the antiwife is the dispossessed Indian; in *Gordon Pym*, the mad mulatto; in *Huckleberry Finn*, Jim; in *Moby Dick*, the Polynesian (as was the case in *Two Years Before the Mast*, "which may have given Melville his cue"); in Faulkner's "The Bear," the old man, half Chickasaw and half black man. In Sam Fathers,

> son of a Negro slave and a Chickasaw chief, one meaning of the dark skin is made clear; for his coloredness is taken as an ensign of kinship with the wilderness and the beasts who inhabit it. "Because there was," Faulkner writes, "something running in Sam Fathers' veins which ran in the veins of the buck too. ..." Edenic nature, the totem, and the dark spouse: these are three symbols for the same thing—for the primitive world which lies beyond the margins of cities and beneath the lintel of consciousness. (Fiedler 1966, 366)

Could that "primitive" world be the displaced, repressed, disavowed sphere of homosexual desire?

In such a sphere, fantasies take on political (Fiedler terms it sociological) meaning: "Whatever the symbolic necessities which demand that the male *hierogamos* be interracial as well as homoerotic, that marriage takes on, by virtue of crossing conventional colorlines, a sociological significance as well as a psychological and metaphysical one*" (Fiedler 1966, 366). The footnote reads as follows:

> Recently, we have grown more and more aware of how in the Civil Rights Movement the aspirations of Negroes for full freedom and the struggle of homosexuals to be accepted are oddly intermingled. And it is no use protesting (as Ralph Ellison has done, for instance) that they should be kept separate and pure. For better or worse, they are mythically one in our deepest imagination, as, indeed, James Baldwin has tried to make manifest—however shrilly and ineptly—in *Another Country.*

If the homoerotic circulates near the center of white racism, how could it be absent from the struggle for civil rights?

III. Parenthesis: Adrift in Manhattan

The situation of the Negro and the homosexual in our society pose precisely opposite problems.

—Leslie Fiedler, "Come Back to the Raft Ag'in, Huck Honey!" in *Partisan Review* 15 (1948)

The crossroads of racism and sexism had to be a violent meeting place.

—Susan Brownmiller, *Against Our Will: Men, Women, and Rape* (1975/1993)

The relationship, therefore, of a black boy to a white boy is a very complex thing.

—James Baldwin, *The Price of the Ticket* (1985)

Certainly *Another Country* is unsatisfying in some way. But "inept" and "shrill" seem harsh. I wonder if part of the problem is Rufus's suicide; it is an unhappy fate, not only due to the loss of life. Somewhere in the white male imagination suicide means that the black man has managed to escape from him, not only from the white men in the novel whom he knew and who cared for him, but from the white reader as well. A suicide, while death for the black man, is a triumphant, defiant death, as the black man leaves his tormentor/lover (the white man) behind and alone.

Baldwin knows the white male imagination; here he plays into the fantasy of the black man as stud. At the beginning of the novel Rufus is near his end, so we go back to find out what happened. What happened to the handsome young Rufus? It would appear, or so we are led to believe, that his demise had to do with a bad case of "white girl," and what's worse, southern white girl. Rufus meets Leona, a recently divorced escapee from the South whom he takes to a party. One thing leads to the proverbial other and "he entered her. For a moment he thought she was going to scream, she was so tight and caught her breath so sharply, and stiffened so. But then she moaned, she moved beneath him. Then, from the center of his rising storm, very slowly and deliberately, he began the slow ride home" (Baldwin 1962, 21).

But this "ride home" turns out not to be just an orgasm but death, not a particularly original linking, but in *Another Country* the association has, it turns out, a decidedly homosexual cast. Rufus's wound may have been reopened by Leona (we are never told how she manages to drive Rufus to his edge), but it was made by the hands of another, a white male other. Rufus complains that he would not "betray his friend for a woman, as most white men seemed to do, especially if his friend were black" (Baldwin 1962, 36). The oedipal competition here is interracial, and the male matrimony Fiedler has described has been betrayed, once again not by the black man, but by the white.

It turns out that Rufus, while basically heterosexual, has had an affair with a man, a white man named Eric who figures later in the novel. Rufus's internalized heterosexism functions to devalue not only the relationship but also Eric as a man: "He had despised Eric's manhood by treating him as a woman, by telling him how inferior he was to a woman, by treating him as nothing more than a hideous sexual deformity" (Baldwin 1962, 46). Like Cleaver, like Baraka, Baldwin's character seems to understand the homosexualized character of racism. Rufus says to Vivaldo, his best friend, a struggling writer and a heterosexual white man: "They got the world on a string, man, the miserable white cocksuckers, and they're tying that string around my neck, they *killing* me" (Baldwin 1962, 67).

Baldwin understands the homosocial, homoerotic character of the heterosexual world. Rufus goes to a straight bar, a bar filled with men, there to be with each other. There are also men looking to meet women, but they are "lone," evidently left without male buddies, forced to fend for themselves. And in the phrase "college boys" Baldwin has his fun, as this would certainly be a class and perhaps a racial slur. Businessmen are intent on dulling the pain; college boys, while ostensibly out on the prowl, are flirting with each other. There are women in this bar but we don't see them. They are "drifting," here and there. In some essential sense is this not too a world of men without women?

> The bar was terribly crowded. Advertising men were there, drinking double shots of bourbon or vodka, on the rocks; college boys were there, their wet fingers slippery on the beer bottles; lone men stood near the doors or in the corners, watching the drifting women. The college boys, gleaming with ignorance and mad with chastity, made terrified efforts to attract the feminine attention, but succeeded only in attracting each other. (Baldwin 1962, 72)

In America, as Fiedler has told us, class struggle becomes a war between the sexes.

In a heterosexist regime of reason (Leitch 1992), such a war seems inevitable, somehow the natural outcome of essentially different creatures—from Mars and Venus, as it is popularized—who still, even so, despite the odds, must have each other. In such a regime men are convinced women have the upper hand while insisting on performing the pretense that they do. But the truth, as one of Baldwin's characters named Cass says, might be rather different.

> "I mean"—he [Richard] was watching her [Cass]; she sat down again, playing with the glass of whiskey—"a man meets a woman. And he needs her. But she uses this need against him, she uses it to undermine him. And it's easy. Women don't see men the way men want to be seen. They see all the tender places, all the places where blood could flow." She finished the whiskey. "Do you see what I mean?"
>
> "No," he said, frankly, "I don't. I don't believe all this female intuition shit. It's something women have dreamed up."
>
> "You can *say* that—and in such a tone!" She mimicked him: "Something women have dreamed up. But *I* can't say that—what men have 'dreamed up' is all there is, the world they've dreamed up *is* the world." He laughed. She subsided.
>
> "Well. It's true."
>
> "What a funny girl you are," he said. "You've got a bad case of penis envy."
>
> "So do most men," she said, sharply, and he laughed. (Baldwin 1962, 108)

Perhaps, from a certain sensibility, such conversation is "shrill" and "inept." Certainly it lacks subtlety. But it seems true to the characters Baldwin has created, characters recognizably "New York." Not a subtle town, one might say, but in some profound way truthful. Vivaldo, Rufus's closest friend, cannot quite shake the fear that he is in some way responsible for Rufus's suicide. He dates Rufus's sister afterward. Like many straight men, Vivaldo is no stranger to homosexual desire:

> "One time," he [Vivaldo] said, "we got into a car and drove over to the Village and we picked up this queer, a young guy, and we drove him back to Brooklyn. Poor guy, he was scared green before we got halfway there but he couldn't jump out of the car. We drove into this garage, there were seven of us, and we made him go down on all of us and then we beat the piss out of him and took all his money and took his clothes and left him lying on that cement floor, and, you know, it was winter." He looked over at her [Cass], looked directly at her for the first time that morning. "Sometimes I still wonder if they found him in time, or if he died, or what." (Baldwin 1962, 112)

Baldwin does not seem to have much sympathy for Vivaldo; perhaps he *is* in some way responsible for Rufus's end. After all, as the narrator tells us: "He [Vivaldo] was just a poor white boy in trouble and it was not in the least original of him to come running to the niggers. This sentiment had sometimes seemed to stare out at him from the eyes of Rufus" (Baldwin 1962, 133). And Rufus was not the first black man in whose company Vivaldo had relaxed:

> Once, while he [Vivaldo] was in the service, he and a colored buddy had been drunk, and on leave, in Munich. They were in a cellar someplace, it

> was very late at night, there were candles on the table. There was one girl sitting near them. Who had dared whom? Laughing, they had opened their trousers and shown themselves to the girl. To the girl, but also to each other. The girl had moved away, saying that she did not understand Americans. But perhaps she had understood them well enough. She had understood that their by-play had very little to do with her. (Baldwin 1962, 134)

Eric, the white gay man with whom Rufus has had an affair, and whom he had demeaned, fancied himself in love with Rufus. Baldwin knows to be skeptical of interracial relationships. He has Eric ask himself: "But had he ever loved Rufus?" Perhaps Rufus was the object of his racialized sexual desire: "Or had it simply been rage and nostalgia and guilt and shame?" Then Baldwin has Eric face the fact that his desire for Rufus is merged with racism, with the history and culture of white male fantasy regarding the black male body:

> Was it the body of Rufus to which he had clung, or the bodies of dark men, seen briefly, somewhere, in a garden or a clearing, long ago, sweat running down their chocolate chests and shoulders, their voices ringing out, the white of their jock-straps beautiful against their skin, one with his head tilted back before a dipper—and the water splashing, sparkling, singing down!—one with his arm raised, laying an ax to the base of a tree? Certainly he never succeeded in making Rufus believe he loved him. Perhaps Rufus had looked into his eyes and seen those dark men Eric saw, and hated him for it. (Baldwin 1962, 194)

Rufus's sister Ida, whom Vivaldo dates after Rufus's suicide, will not commit suicide. While perhaps in love with Vivaldo, maybe a bit, and while curious about the white world Rufus had inhabited, some of the time, she does not blur her vision. Cass, a white woman who sees her husband Richard and men in general rather clearly, seems blinded to her own racial position, but Ida is not:

> "What you people don't know," she [Ida] said [to Cass], "is that life is a *bitch*, baby. It's the biggest hype going. You don't have any experience in paying your dues and it's going to be rough on you, baby, when the deal goes down. There're lots of back dues to be collected, and I know damn well you haven't got a penny saved."
>
> Cass looked at the dark, proud head, which was half-turned away from her. "Do you hate white people, Ida?"
>
> Ida sucked her teeth in anger. "What the hell has that got to do with anything?" (Baldwin 1962, 350)

This white woman cannot understand what this black woman is saying to her; she misunderstands it as criticism of her. White people never expect to pay dues; dues are what others pay. Except, perhaps, in prison.

IV. Elopement and Healing? Dream On, White Boy

There is a context in which the legend of the sea as escape and solace, the fixated sexuality of boys, the dark beloved are one.

—Leslie Fiedler, "Come Back to the Raft Ag'in, Huck Honey!" in Gerald Graff and James Phelan, eds., *Mark Twain,* Adventures of Huckleberry Finn: *A Case Study in Critical Controversy* (1948/1995)

[S]omeday on American soil two world-races may give to each other those characteristics both so sadly lack.

—W. E. B. Du Bois, "The Souls of Black Folk," in H. Boyd and R. L. Allen, *Brotherman: The Odyssey of Black Men in America* (1995/1996)

Blacks and whites were bound together in a ceaseless struggle.

—W. Fitzhugh Brundage, "The Roar on the Other Side of the Silence: Black Resistance and White Violence in the American South, 1880–1940" (1997a)

The interracial male-male relationship, as Baldwin depicts it, has great risks for the black man, while the white man fails to understand what is at stake. For the black man the white man's affection confirms the place he knows he holds in his imagination, that is, the one who is desired. For the white man it means the masking of his responsibility and guilt, as he seeks the forgiveness of the man he has wronged, and in doing so, the healing of his own rent character. Fiedler hints that these are indeed something of the dynamics between Huck and Jim, Rufus and Vivaldo: "The elopement of the good companions comes, therefore, to stand for the healing of the social conflicts which most irk us, and before which we feel most powerless and baffled. Such a sociological extension of meaning by no means cancels out but rather enriches other, more profound significances and gives to them their peculiarly American form" (1966, 366). Repressed memory amounts to "powerless and baffled" feelings. Rufus is neither. But he is dead.

There is, Fiedler reminds, in the European novel—and in the drama, epic, and romance which preceded the novel—a tradition of pseudomarriage of males, stretching from, say Don Quixote and Sancho Panza through Robinson Crusoe and Friday, to Pickwick and Sam Weller. Fiedler focuses upon *Robinson Crusoe* in particular, which, he argues, seems to express that same "archetype which haunts our classic fiction." So much so, he says, "that one is tempted to think of it as an American novel before the fact. The protagonists are not only black and white, but they exist on the archetypal island, cut off from the home community by the estranging sea. Cannibal and castaway, man-eater and journal-keeper, they learn to adapt to each other and to domesticity, on what is surely the most meager and puritanical Eden in all literature" (Fiedler 1966, 367). Adam and Steve, not Adam and Eve.

In *Robinson Crusoe*, Fiedler notes, the relationship "is kept rigidly within the European class-patterns of master and man" (1966, 366), a pattern that is broken in, say, Forster's (1971) *Maurice*. And in Michel Tournier's (1969) rewrite of the Defoe novel, entitled *Friday*, the erotic elements of Crusoe's relationship to Friday (and to the island) are made rather explicit. When Robinson realizes that Friday has what he wants, he prays, not to Jesus but to Friday. Is the muscular young black man the European's sexualized fantasy of Jesus? Does he want to be held in the sinewy muscular arms of his Master? Like the ancient Egyptians, he looks to the source of life on earth, begging: "O Sun, cause me to resemble Friday" (Tournier 1969, 202). This white man is crazy about this black man:

> As I think of it, there is nothing very astonishing in the almost crazed intensity with which I watch Friday. What is unbelievable is that I should have lived so long in his presence without, so to speak, seeing him at all. How can I account for that blind indifference, when for me he is the whole of humanity assembled in one person, my son and my father my brother and my neighbor? I must concentrate every emotion that man feels for his fellows upon this sole "other," because what would otherwise become of my ability to feel? (Tournier 1969, 208)

Is Crusoe in some sense every white man, unable to stop gazing at the body of the young black man?

This elopement and attendant healing are of course a fantasy, a white male fantasy. As Fiedler observes, there are "forces in our life," he terms them "profound and aboriginal"—I would add historical and sexual—which "work against such a concept" (1966, 368). Fiedler writes:

> The North European white, blue-eyed stock, which originally settled in the United States, shabby as it was in its origins, soon set itself up as a ruling class eager to protect its hegemony and its purity, a purity especially identified with its pale, genteel women busy in schools and churches. The drama of an equal meeting and mating of Caucasian and colored men was remanded quite early to a *mythical state of nature*, or at least to the nearest equivalent of that state, the frontier, where trapper and Indian guide bedded down together. In the settlements, such equality could scarcely survive beside the facts of social organization: the Negro confined to his ghettos, the Indian harried and driven continually westward, the Polynesian sailor restricted to the waterfront city of cheap saloons and brothels. (368)

And just as this interracial male-male fantasy operates to disguise the ugly facts of history and social organization, it functions to maintain a heterosexist regime which has held in place in the West since, some suggest, the Roman Emperor Constantine. Fiedler notes that "there is an almost hysterical note to our insistence that the love of male and male does not compete with heterosexual passion but complements it." The love of buddy for buddy could not be "homosexuality in any crude meaning of the word." It is friendship, "a passionless passion, simple, utterly satisfying, yet immune to lust—physical only as a handshake is physical, this side of copulation." This explanation, insistent even demanding, does not, cannot remain in place forever. "[W]e can never shake off the nagging awareness," Fiedler (1966, 368–369) writes,

> that there is at the sentimental center of our novels, where we are accustomed to find in their European counterparts "platonic" love or adultery, seduction, rape, or long-drawn-out flirtation, nothing but the love of males! What awaits us are the fugitive slave and the no-account boy side by side on a raft borne by the endless river toward an impossible escape; or the pariah sailor walking in the tattooed arms of the brown harpooner on the verge of some impossible quest. To emphasize the purity of such unions, the fact that they join soul to soul rather than body to body, they are typically contrasted with mere heterosexual passion, the dubious desire which threatens always to end in miscegenation. Yet, though such confrontation seems only to contrast the homoerotic and heterosexual ways of joining white and black, they suggest disconcertingly a general superiority of the love of man for man over the ignoble lust of man for woman.

Disconcerting to heterosexist loyalists, perhaps, but it is clear to many of us: homosociality sublimates a denied yet pervasive and persisting homosexuality. And in the wake churned by its denial and disavowal, misogyny and racism follow.

Is this the reason, Fiedler asks, that "the colored rival of the wife" is often portrayed with the "stigmata of something dangerous and disgusting as well as forbidden"? He points out that Chingachgook wears a "death's-head on his chest and a scalp at his belt," while Queequeg is heavily tattooed and carries with him "a phallic god and shrunken head." And Twain's Jim, who possesses no repugnant qualities, first appears "with his head muffled in a blanket—scaring Huck half to death—and is dyed, before the voyage is over, a sickening blue." But the most "monstrous of all the dark companions" is, Fiedler (1966) maintains,

> Poe's hybrid Dirk Peters, who assumes in the course of Poe's description of him not only a bestial aspect but something of the appearance of a gnome or kobold, which is to say, the surviving image in the mind of *homo sapiens* of the stunted proto-men that they destroyed, the first dispossessed people, whose memory survives to haunt our fairy tales and nightmares. But the Neanderthal gnome is also the model for popular notions of "devils" or "demons," quite properly assimilated to the primordial figure that symbolizes our broken link with the animal world. For better or worse, our love-affair with the "Black Man" carries with it diabolic implications, hints of a union with infernal forces, as well as salvational overtones, promises of psychic redemption. (quoted passages in Fiedler 1966, 369)

Is this not a very strange thing to say, after slavery, segregation, lynching, the prison? Not that we white men are not obsessed with the black male body: that much should by now be obvious. What seems so strange is the notion of "love affair," implying a voluntary association, as if black men might somehow, by their own volition, choose to be involved with white men. History interferes not at all with the persistence of certain white male fantasies, apparently. Fiedler puts the matter this way: "the locus of our deepest response to the conflict of races is legend." He goes on: "we find it easy to believe that our dark-skinned beloved will rescue us from the confusion and limitations of a society which excludes him." Dream on, white boy. So he does, as Fiedler (1966, 388) reminds us: "Certainly, our classic writers assure us that when we have been cut off or have cut ourselves off from the instinctive sources of life, he [the black man] will receive us without rancor or the insult of forgiveness. He will fold us in his arms saying 'honey' ... he will comfort us, as if he knew our offense against him were only symbolic—an offense against that in ourselves which he represents—never truly *real*."

Never truly real? Perhaps not for the white man, hidden behind white sheets, watching burning crosses while cutting the flesh, clutching the castrated penis, of the one he loves. Are we not talking about a race of mad men here? If the white man ever comes to reality, that is, clearness about the homosexual character of his racism, will he then be overwhelmed with guilt, destroyed by his dissociated self-hatred now come home to roost? Or will it all work out, somehow, in some dreamscape, a raft on a river, two men in a bed? Fiedler suggests:

> The immense barrier of guilt between white men and dark men is not more mitigated in our classic fiction than is the gulf of color and culture itself; both, indeed, are emphasized to the point of melodrama, so that the final reconciliation may seem more tender and miraculous. The archetype makes no attempt to deny the facts of outrage or guilt; it is nurtured by them. It merely portrays them as meaningless in the face of a passion immune to what Melville calls "that climax which is so fatal to ordinary love." "It's too good for true, honey," Jim says to Huck. "It's too good for true." (quoted in Fiedler 1966, 390)

In American prisons it is.

"A Passion Utterly Uncontrollable"

During his short, intense career as a journalist, book reviewer, short-story writer, poet, and critic, Edgar Allan Poe wrote two full-length novels, *The Narrative of A. Gordon Pym* (1837–38) and *The Journal of Julius Rodman* (1840). These were, presumably, "chronicles of American exploration on sea and land" (Fiedler 1966, 391) but "seem in large part symptoms rather than achievements" (423). *The Narrative of A. Gordon Pym* is based upon accounts of pioneering expeditions to the South Seas, and especially a South Polar expedition projected by an acquaintance of Poe named J. N. Reynolds. *The Journal of Julius Rodman* borrows extensively from the journals of Lewis and Clark, imagining a trip across the Rockies before theirs.

The Narrative of A. Gordon Pym describes a relationship of Pym and Peters, a white man and a dark man. Indeed, Peters is "a very ogre: such a monster, one of Poe's critics describes him, as ... a nightmare out of our racial beginnings." The "climax" of their relationship, as Fiedler puts it, comes when the two are trapped on the Island of Tsalal. Their companions have lost their lives in an artificial landslide caused by "bloodthirsty black aborigines." The two men are trying to find a way to escape. The dramatic moment comes when Pym is suspended in terror upon a sheer cliff wall. Fiedler quotes from the novel:

> For one moment my fingers clutched compulsively upon their hold, while, with the movement, the faintest possible idea of escape wandered, like a shadow, through my mind—in the next my whole soul was pervaded with a *longing to fall*; a desire, a yearning, a passion utterly uncontrollable. I let go at once my grasp upon the peg, and, turning half round from the precipice remained tottering for an instant against its naked face. But now there came a spinning of the brain; a shrill-sounding and phantom voice screamed within my ears; a dusky, fiendish and filmy figure stood immediately beneath me; and, sighing, I sank down with a bursting heart, and plunged within its arms. (quoted in Fiedler 1966, 396)

"Its" arms? Doesn't Poe mean "his" arms? And who can the "dusky, fiendish ... figure" be? He is, of course, Peters, the half-breed. Fiedler (1966) observes: "The studied ambiguity of the passage, in which the language of horror becomes that of eroticism, make it clear that the *longing to fall* and the desire for the dark spouse are one, a single perverseness. Peters is not made an angelic representative of instinct and nature even at this critical instant; he remains still a fiend, even in the act of becoming a savior" (396).

"Still a fiend"? Gee, what's in this for the black guy? What kind of fantasy is this? The white guy *is* the helpless virginal white girl he once imagined the white lady to be, and his fear of her rape by the black man is (by now) a transparent disguise of his desire for the very same. In the present instance, Fiedler explains, "the tale of *Gordon Pym* projects through its Negroes the fear of black rebellion and of the white man's perverse lust for the Negro." Is not fear of rebellion a cousin of the rape myth? Somewhere in the white man is a desire for reversal, to be the black stud's servant, no, his slave: "Insofar as *Gordon Pym* is finally a social document as well as a fantasy, its subject is slavery; and its scene, however disguised, is the section of America which was to destroy itself defending that institution. It is, indeed, to be expected that our first eminent southern author discovered that the proper subject for American gothic is the black man, from whose shadow we have not yet emerged" (Fiedler 1966, 397). *Whose* shadow?

Poe himself is an interesting character, a former student at the University of Virginia (where his dormitory room is preserved, mausoleum style, on the "west range" of residences, just down the driveway from the Upper and Lower Mews behind the Lawn), in some (perverse) way a prototypical white man. His image in the American mind, Fiedler thinks, is that "image of failure and impotence so necessary to us in a world of success and power: an image of one who is the victim of society and of himself." More specifically and "perhaps essentially," Poe stands for "the *poet as drunkard*, the weak-stomached, will-less addict, forever swearing off and forever succumbing again" (Fiedler 1966, 427). Frances Willard and her W.C.T.U. colleagues knew that.

Certainly Poe did drink. In a letter he once wrote: "For more than ten days I was totally deranged. … All was hallucination" (quoted in Fiedler 1966, 427). He married a thirteen-year-old child, then watched her die painfully. He believed himself the victim of D.T.'s, and yet continued to drink, frantically sometimes, especially, Fiedler tells us, "when faced by sexual problems he could not solve." At the end he was picked up in the streets of Baltimore, senseless. Despite medical attention, Poe died four days later of alcoholic poisoning (Fiedler 1966). Is Poe a white man who comes to ruin simply due to excess drinking? Or is his demise somehow a consequence of interracial longing denied? Does desire denied sometimes seek resolution in booze?

That practitioner of what Fiedler calls "black Romanticism," Baudelaire, regarded Poe as a victim, but not of booze. It was, Baudelaire suspected, America itself that did the white man in. He wrote: "Some of the documents which I have seen persuade me that Poe found in the United States a large prison from which all his life he was making desperate efforts to escape." To the French poet, Poe seemed as a "second Christ whose cross was alcohol" (quoted passages in Fiedler 1966, 424). "I say without shame," Baudelaire confessed, "because I feel it springs from a profound sense of pity and affection, that I prefer Edgar Poe, drunk, poor, persecuted and a pariah, to a calm and virtuous Goethe or Walter Scott. I should willingly say of him and of a special class of men what the catechism says of our Lord: 'He was suffered much for us!'" (quoted in Fiedler 1966, 424–425). In the prison-house that was nineteenth-century America, perhaps Poe too was interracially raped. Not *en personne*, but in the imaginary, where desire denied, as in the formula for the gothic which Fiedler elaborated early on, becomes terror. Terror turns in on the subject, who then becomes undone. Desperate, he seeks healing, or at least a drink. Baudelaire's suffering too would seem to be, to an extent, more narrowly gendered, although the result was not so very different.

What if the white man acts on his fantasy, at least in its cultural sense, and becomes in some way "black"? Fiedler provides another example of what becomes of a white man who strays from his "race." This white man is imaginary, a product of Nathaniel Hawthorne's fantasies. He is "the white doctor and man of science, so oddly at home in the alien world of the primitive." It is the well-known Chillingworth whom Hawthorne describes in the following terms: "By the Indian's side, and evidently sustaining a companionship with him, stood a white man, clad in a strange disarray of civilized and savage costume"; "old Roger Chillingworth, the physician, was seen to enter the market-place, in close and familiar talk with the commander of the questionable vessel." From his native captors and friends, Chillingworth "has learned a darker 'medicine'" which complements his European science. He is, Hawthorne tells us, "the misshapen scholar … eyes … bleared by lamplight," whose "scientific achievements were esteemed hardly less than supernatural." On the one hand, Fiedler notes, Chillingworth is portrayed as having gained access to the lore of the "savage priests"; on the other, he is presented as a student of the black magic of "Doctor Forman, the famous old conjurer." Fiedler (1966) continues:

> To represent the horror of Europe, however, Chillingworth must be white, while to stand for America he must be colored; he is, in fact, a white man who grows black. Even the other protagonists notice his gradual metamorphosis ("his dark complexion seemed to have grown duskier ...") into the very image of the Black Man, which is to say, Satan himself: "a striking evidence of man's faculty of transforming himself into a devil ... if he only will ... undertake a devil's office." (quoted passages on 436)

Part of that undertaking would appear to be a homosexual liaison with dear ole Dimmesdale (Derrick 1997).

Despite the terror of the metamorphosis resulting from race blending, the white man seems willing to risk hell itself for the sake of the black man's love. Fiedler recalls when Huck tries to write a letter to Miss Watson, to let her know where he is, to assuage his conscience. Although doing so allows him to feel "washed clean of sin for the first time," Fiedler tells us,

> his love for Jim returns. He remembers not some abolitionist slogan or moral tag about the equal rights of all mankind, only how Jim "would always call me honey, and pet me, and do everything he could think for me. ..." and he decides not to send the letter. "[I] studied a minute, sort of holding my breath, and then says to myself: 'All right, then I'll go to Hell' —and tore it up." (quoted in Fiedler 1966, 460)

Somehow the white boy knows it's not hell where he'll go, despite what "god-fearin' folk" tell him. Hell is where he is.

V. This Side of Copulation

Memory resides nowhere, and in every cell.

—Saul Schanberg, Duke University medical researcher, quoted in Elizabeth Alexander, "'Can You Be BLACK and Look at This': Reading the Rodney King Video(s)" (1994)

What's so interesting about claiming that, after all, Huck and Jim are just good pals?

—Christopher Looby, "'Innocent Homosexuality': The Fielder Thesis in Retrospect" (1995)

The Negro is a toy in the white man's hands.

—Frantz Fanon, "The Fact of Blackness," in David Theo Goldberg, ed., *Anatomy of Racism* (1990)

Despite the power and suggestiveness of Fiedler's book—situating in civilizational terms my simple argument that white racism is in some profound distorted way "queer"—there are critics who take issue with Fiedler's point of view, especially as expressed in the 1948 *Partisan Review* essay which anticipated by twelve years the first edition of *Love and Death*. Christopher Looby argues that Fiedler's thinking takes place "within a deeply homophobic and gay-baiting structure of assumptions" (1995, 536). Before he specifies this charge, Looby acknowledges that the "archetypal image" that Fiedler identified, that of the white and black man as a "couple," surfaces in countless artifacts of American popular culture, testifying to its "inexhaustible resonance" (36). Looby adds several more contemporary examples: partners Andy and Bobby in television's *Hill Street Blues*, the Mel Gibson/Danny Glover pairing in the *Lethal Weapon* movies, Chris the (white) DJ in *Northern Exposure* and his (black) brother Bernard. Fred Pfeil (1995) reminds us of the somewhat sadomasochistic interracial relationship between the characters played by Richard Gere and Lou Gossett in *An Officer and a Gentleman* (1982) as well as the "partnership" of the urban and professional F.B.I. agent played by Sidney Poitier and the Northwest mountain man played by Tom Berenger in *Shoot to Kill*, recalling specifically that scene in which, "wisecracking steadily, the ... duo lie cheek to cheek on top of one another in a snow cave" (5).

There are, it turns out, countless examples. Mark Simpson (1994) recalls the racialized nature of the relationships between the character (Ron Kovic) played by Tom Cruise and the hospital staff in the *Fourth of July* (1989). As a paraplegic, Kovic's impotence is, Simpson suggests, both literal and symbolic, evident "in the gruesome morning ritual where the shit is washed out of him by black male nurses. He lies naked on a rack surrounded by other men, all with enema bags piping water into their colons. Kovic complains that he is 'done,' but an orderly sarcastically reminds him of his total helplessness by making him wait before attending to him. The white Marine war hero, America's finest, the ultimate 'fucker,' has to endure the shame of his rectum being at the mercy of a black man who is literally shoving Vietnam up his ass" (Simpson 1994, 240).

I think of *The Defiant Ones* (1958), in which two convicts—a white man (named Joker Jackson played by Tony Curtis) and a black man (Noah Cullen played by Sidney Poitier)—escape from prison handcuffed to each other. Not subtle, but the movie does make vivid the bonds that bind white to black men. More recently, there was the astonishing and powerful pairing of Denzel Washington and John Lithgow in *Ricochet* (1991), in which the violent character of the white man's sexualized obsession with the black man is made horrifyingly obvious. Both are narratives of interracial male-male relationships; both illustrate in various ways the general pattern Fiedler discerned. In this genre of film, as Pfeil (1995, 16) points out, "[the] depiction and deployment of women is ... ambivalent at best." In fact, it would appear that women are irrelevant to these homosocial interracial couplings. These films declare the "perfect adequacy of this all-male couple and, accordingly, the relative superfluity of all those around who remain merely biologically female."

Looby suggests that the Tom Hanks/Denzel Washington pairing in the movie *Philadelphia* achieved "some kind of culmination in this tradition: the black attorney as savior of gay white A.I.D.S. sufferer" (536). Fiedler's basic insight—that male homoeroticism and love between nonwhite and white were "fused ... into a single thing" (quoted in Looby 1995, 537)—"remains powerfully suggestive but still largely neglected." It is as well, he insists, "intensely problematic" (537).

But Looby is not quite ready to get down to elaborating that last sentence, and he returns to praise: "Simply for Fiedler to utter, in 1948, in the pages of the *Partisan Review*, the name of the unspeakable love, took some bravado." He notes that "the simple transgressive power of this utterance should not be causally underestimated (the many horrified reactions to his thesis attest to its violation of a taboo)." Moreover, Looby wants us to know that his "analysis of the problematic qualities of the form that utterance took is not meant to detract from the real service Fiedler performed in opening a discussion on some important questions" (Looby 1995, 537–538). Now Looby is ready to begin; the trouble is, he says, that Fiedler's "elliptical" essay doesn't quite know what it's saying. It simultaneously claims—scandalously—that works of classic American fiction are filled with erotically charged interracial male same-sex relationships while it warns us against misunderstanding the nature of those relationships. These relationships, Fiedler insists, are "innocent" homosexual friendships, but Looby quickly asks: "as opposed to what?" The implication is, as Looby understands, that there is some other, "guilty," form of homosexual relationship (537). In a footnote Looby points out that while Fiedler intended "innocent" here to denote sexually chaste and therefore morally blameless, the root sense of "innocent" is "unknowing" or "uncomprehending" and this sense works even better (535 n. 2).

Of course, if "homosexuality" was not invented until the late nineteenth century, then relationships Fiedler details in, say, Twain, cannot be by definition homosexual, as Looby later notes. And from what we know about nineteenth-century "romantic friendship," "homosexual" is not quite accurate, although there were clearly physical dimensions to many of these "innocent" male-male intimacies. The explosiveness of Fiedler's thesis has to do, I think, less with the "sexual" elements of the relationships (such as between Jim and Huck) and more to do with their interracial character. What Fiedler's provocative and insightful analysis forces us to recognize is that hatred is often the opposite side of the same coin as love, and that "race relations" have been characterized, in the United States at least, by a definite "marital" and "conjugal" quality, all mixed up with politics, culture, and economics.

Part of what disturbs Looby is, I think, how the Fiedler thesis plays today, on the contemporary playing field of identity politics. He complains that "readers of the essay have tended to forget the overwhelmingly normalizing force of Fiedler's reassurances." His employment of the rhetoric of scandal (which exploits the explosiveness of discovering a secret truth) is balanced by a countervailing justification of Jim and Huck and the others by showing that "there is nothing scandalous after all." But, Looby asks, "what's so interesting about claiming that, after all, Huck and Jim are just good pals?" (quoted passages in Looby 1995, 538).

What makes their relationship so interesting is that it is, below the surface, conjugal. But in Fiedler's view, all male-male bonds, such as "the camaraderie of the locker-room ..." exhibit an "astonishing naiveté" on the part of their participants (Fiedler quoted in Looby 1995, 540). Looby asks, wickedly: "Don't they know sex is lurking?" (540)

This is, I think, Looby's main gripe with Fiedler, namely that he, Fiedler, wants to preserve this "believed-in" myth of chaste male passion, even though he has already characterized it as a juvenile dream. The alternative is, evidently, in Fiedler's mind, worse: "He [Fiedler] flinches at the prospect of recognizing physical homosexual love as a simple (albeit "stubborn") social fact, a fact that doesn't compromise, destroy, or contradict anything except the homophobic fantasy on which male heterosexual identity in modern American society is precariously built" (Looby 1995, 540–541). Indeed, Fiedler is most assuredly *not* saying that Huck and Jim, Ishmael and Queequeg, and Natty and Chingachgook are "queer as three-dollar bills," as he would later learn those who heard of his essay "at second or third hand" were saying. But Fiedler *is* saying, Looby insists, that "American writers unwittingly and unfortunately privileged a form of love that was dangerously mutable, potentially transformable into outright queerness" (542).

I disagree with Looby here; I think Fiedler is acknowledging that there *is* a sexual element, buried but very much alive and circulating, in the chaste, unknowing homosocial love of "straight" men. Yes, Looby is right to criticize Fiedler for "trad[ing] on the scandalous power of his claims even as he denigrates the unworldiness of those who would be scandalized. He pushes Huck and the others to the brink of the abyss of homosexuality only to pull them back to 'this side of copulation'" (Looby 1995, 542). Yes, Christopher, you're right: Fiedler does want it both ways, simultaneously "an iconoclast and a defender of heterosexual propriety" (542).

So Fiedler enacts the very same paradoxical American heterosexuality he describes as operating in interracial "romantic" friendships in canonical nineteenth-century American literature. I think his infraction, while worth pointing out, warrants no trial, no meting out a sentence of obscurity. And Looby is not suggesting such, I think. Overall Fiedler's accomplishment is great: his panoramic view of American literature and its European antecedents requires us to gasp at its scope and sensitivity. I share Mark Simpson's assessment: "Leslie Fiedler's *Love and Death in the American Novel* ... remains a work of startling insight" (1994, 16). Somewhat inadvertently and not without ambivalence, Fiedler shows that the queer character of American race relations is hardly limited to lynching and prison rape, but resides deep in the civilizational psyche of the nation. It is that which I hope to explore in the next volume, starting with Genesis 9:24 and what happened inside Noah's tent.

As we have seen, the white man's fascination with the black male body was no fiction. Quite aside from lynching, it is clear, despite the fragmentary evidence, that sexual relations between black and white men in nineteenth-century America did not always stop "this side of copulation." Not only female slaves suffered an especially traumatic experience of enslavement because they were subject to the sexual abuse of their masters. It is no accident that one of the most common signs of the twentieth-century civil rights movement was the simple I AM A MAN. A civic category yes, but a gendered one as well, one that underlines that racial subjugation was thoroughly sexualized. I am reminded of Earl E. Thorpe, who characterized white male rape of slaves as "free love," even though, as he acknowledges, the "love" was directed one way: "And although in the Old South a larger number of white men practiced free love than at any other time in the history of Western Christendom, this uninhibited sexual life was limited to black bodies only" (Thorpe 1967, 26).

It is not Thorpe's outrageous misrepresentation of sexual slavery as "free love" that brings this passage to mind; it is his reference to "Western Christendom." Unwittingly I suppose, Thorpe is comparing the antebellum South with ancient Greece and Rome, and no queer student of history cannot help but point out that "free love"—just as phony a category then as it was in the nineteenth-century South—then included erotic relationships between men. On that point, Thorpe is, unwittingly accurate. Another (but responsible) student of slavery, Orlando Patterson, has remarked that "anyone acquainted with the comparative ethnohistory of honorific cultures" such as the Old South would know that "homosexuality is pronounced in such systems, both ancient and modern. Southern domestic life most closely resembles that of the Mediterranean in precisely those areas which are most highly conducive to homosexuality" (1984, 29; quoted in Looby 1995, 543).

There are, Looby points out, a number of "imaginative witnesses," among them William Faulkner and Toni Morrison, who intuited the queer character of the peculiar institution. In *Absalom, Absalom!* (1936) Faulkner narrated Thomas Sutpen's fondness for fighting naked with his black male slaves in the stables. In *Beloved* (1987), Morrison "watched" how male slaves, chained in a coffle in the morning, would be made to kneel before their white male masters whose "whim" it might be to feed the chained black men some "breakfast" in the form of their penises to fellate. "Occasionally a kneeling man chose gunshot in his head as the price, maybe, of taking a bit of foreskin with him to Jesus." One slave escapes sexual assault only because he vomits as he witnesses the sodomization of the man next to him; the white man passes him by for fear of his clothing getting "soiled by nigger puke" (Morrison 1987, 108; quoted in Looby 1995, 543). Sodomy, slavery, and civil rights: the alliterative string is held together by one other: sex.

19 ❖ "I AM *a* MAN"

THE QUEER CHARACTER OF RACIAL POLITICS AND VIOLENCE IN AMERICA

I. Self-Division and the Multiplication of Others

I find the situation we have been explicating genuinely mythic.

—Leslie Fiedler, "Come Back to the Raft Ag'in, Huck Honey!" *Partisan Review* 15 (1948)

The Negro is idealized into a symbol of sensation, of unhampered social and sexual relationships.

—Ralph Ellison, *Shadow and Art* (1964/1995)

[Today] the black body is celebrated as an instrument of pleasure rather than an instrument of labor.

—Paul Gilroy, "One Nation under a Groove: The Cultural Politics of 'Race' and Racism in Britain," in David Theo Goldberg, ed., *Anatomy of Racism* (1990)

[B]eing a man is a game, albeit a deadly one.

—Mark Simpson, *Male Impersonators: Men Performing Masculinity* (1994)

So if only white men could allow themselves to feel what they feel for black men, and if only black men could somehow forgive them for four hundred years of not knowing what they feel, racism would end. Ah, were it so easy. Or precisely that difficult. But as the experience of black gay men testify, white men who do feel their desire for black men are not free of the tendency to objectify the black male body; they simply revalorize it. The black "rapist" of the late nineteenth century has evolved now into "the stud," a promotion, perhaps, but still a figment in the white male mind. Who black men are white men seem to have no clue. Nor do they seem especially interested, as long as they are entertained by their physical prowess, as in professional sports.

Could it be that white men have no clue who black men are because they have no clue who they are? Opaque to themselves, how might they see others? To begin: it would seem, would it not, that white men are neither. "White" is a complicated imaginary constructed in relation to blackness, specifically because there was, whites imagined, something primitive and bestial they identified as "black." White men constructed themselves oppositionally to what they imagined white women and black men and women to be. To be a man meant living in a "separate sphere" from women, a rugged sphere of the frontier (whether that be literal or metaphoric) in which men were "self-made." Around the turn of the century "manliness" evolved into "masculinity," a more sexualized version of the gendered myth of character by which white men had measured themselves earlier. Trapped within their own imagination, men mistook their fantasies—about themselves, about "others"—as real. To maintain the fantasy of white-male supremacy (that "whiteness" and "masculinity" even existed in any essential sense) required suppression of those whose agency, volition, and independence all threatened the fragility of white men's minds.

As we have seen, a certain "crisis" of white masculinity was under way during the final decade of the nineteenth century which left many white men uneasy. Shifts in the economy, the political and social gains of African Americans and of white women (including the campaign for suffrage), the disappearance of "romantic friendship," and in the South an ongoing racialization of a defeated white manhood: all contributed to white men feeling besieged, uncertain, indignant, frightened. Not committed to working through such changes self-consciously and psychologically, the majority of men resorted to defensive and compensatory distractions, among them bodybuilding, sexual restraints (especially of adolescent boys), reactionary racial and gender politics (although both the suffrage and the civil rights movements continued), a "muscular" Christianity, and the construction of compulsory "heterosexuality." Like whiteness, this fantasy of hypermasculinity functioned as a standard to which all men must aspire; it was an ideal few men reached. To be a "man" now required exertion and self-policing and continual demonstrations, even violent; one must *prove* that one was a "man."

The year before the Chicago World's Fair displayed the White City—the presumed "accomplishments" of "manly white civilization"—young black men were lynched at an unprecedented rate. Everywhere throughout the South, it seemed, there was "strange fruit" hanging from southern magnolia trees, while even stranger "fruit" walked away, not infrequently with black male body parts in hand. Who *were* these people? "Men." White men. White men defending white women. Right.

What is a "man"? Not a woman? So it would seem. From the discourses on matrifocality and object relations theory, we may understand that becoming a "man" in any machismo sense requires a defensive and compensatory denial of femininity. That is, to become a "man" requires a repudiation of the son's pre-oedipal symbiotic identification with his mother (or caretaking figure). This is not a rewriting, in different terms, of that nineteenth-century "pedestalization" of mothers as saints. True, in some depictions of the pre-oedipal period there can be what appears to be a fantasy of wholeness, harmony, and completion in the mother-child bond, a nirvanic sense of fullness revealing "a longing to return to unchallenged narcissism, to which psychoanalysts give the name 'primary narcissism,' a deep regressive pull: 'we are all alike here'" (Young-Bruehl 1996, 133). But as Lacan has reminded us, the pre-oedipal phase is also a time of psychological tension and bodily disruption, as the infant experiences her or his separateness from the maternal body once experienced as one's own. It is a time of corporeal fragmentation and incapacity, the genesis of the imaginary order, birthed in frustration and aggressivity (Grosz 1995).

These disruptive, identity-forming moments of separation and vulnerability become complicated and intensified for the son as he must forsake his genesis as female, as the mother in all of her complexity, concreteness, and individuality. This masculinized process of self-immolation and self-creation is performed in order to forge an imaginary identification with the absent (or relatively absent) often abstract father, an identification based on observation and didactic instruction, usually not everyday contact, contact which is often dissociated in any case given twentieth-century prohibitions against male-male touching and intimacy. To be a man, in this binary sex/gender system, is not to be a woman, the woman in fact he is. Such a construction of gender identity, based as it is in negation, often leaves the heterosexually identified male subject unstable, often violent.

This analysis is not to suggest that the pre-oedipal period, while imprinting, is the only time that matters in one's life as a gendered being. Elisabeth Young-Bruehl (1996) rightly worries that feminist appropriations of object relations theory have meant for some that developmentalism has been forgotten. By focusing so exclusively on very early childhood, on the pre-oedipal period and the establishment of gender identity, some feminist theorists, Young-Bruehl argues, have neglected the significance of the oedipal period, not to mention puberty and adolescence and later life. Certainly I am not suggesting that these later periods are unimportant; in chapters 13 and 14 we saw how relatively autonomous cultures of masculinity normalize compulsory heterosexuality, racism, misogyny, and homophobia. Adolescent and especially adult stages are also important as opportunities for education. However wrenching the process, "men" can learn to vacate sites of hegemonic masculine identification.

In fact, men must. Divorced from their psychological and phenomenological grounding and isolated in egos whose boundaries must be patrolled and whose fantasies get projected onto others, heterosexually identified men tend to be misogynistic (in part a hatred of the repressed feminine inside the male psyche), intensely homophobic (as the sexualized love of another male threatens the entire edifice of negated mother-identification and unrealized and unrequited father love), and racialized (as unconscious homosexual desire circulates in the sexualized economy that is race in America). It would appear that in father-absent homes this complex and convoluted process is sometimes exaggerated, and, when combined with certain forms of street culture, class location, and a gendered racial culture, hypermasculinity results. All men tend to suffer psychologically from their lack of self-knowledge, their imprisonment in a sex/gender system which demands continual demonstrations of manhood. But it is women and children and gay men who are abused, raped, and murdered, as the crime statistics reviewed in chapter 13 remind us.

Add to this volatile mix the history of Africans in the "new world." From the Middle Passage to the auction block to the plantation, black bodies existed in subjugation to white bodies, specifically white male bodies, except for the Civil War years when, as Drew Faust (1996) points out, white women were forced to assume the male position. As Saidiya V. Hartman (1997) has explained, white men—even abolitionists—imagined, and in fact psychologically inhabited, black bodies, specifically black male bodies, as extensions of their own economic, political, and sexual desire. Not only black women were raped by white men. As the southern apologist Earl Thorpe (1967) suggests, there was in the antebellum American South a carnal sensuality unknown in the West since ancient Greece. Hardly the achievement Thorpe takes it to be, there was in fact a parallel: in both cases only white men were citizens and while women were wives, young men were very much on old men's minds. The effects of this sexualized subjugation echo throughout contemporary masculinity: "[e]very forty-six seconds of the school day, a black child drops out of school, every ninety-five seconds a black baby is born into poverty, and every four hours of every day in the year a black young adult, age twenty to twenty-four, is murdered, and one realizes that the much discussed crisis of the black male is no idle fiction" (Gates 1994, 12).

Black subjugation in America has been, of course, multidimensional; it remains simultaneously economic, political, psychological, and gendered. When Africans in America became "free"—however illusory, as Hartman notes, that freedom was—white people, especially white men, responded with a bitterness reminiscent of jilted lovers. Many were, of course. Certainly southern white men were defeated men, not only given their loss of black bodies, not only in the eyes of their Yankee victors, but perhaps most painfully in the complicated eyes of their wives, mothers, daughters, and sisters. They were as well, no doubt, defeated men in their own eyes. In an important sense, after 1865 southern white men were "men" no more.

An intolerable thought, so intolerable that southern white men busily began the cover-up. Now, no longer having legal access to the bodies of those black women, men, and children whom they had just a moment ago (it must have seemed) possessed, living in the ruins of the Confederacy, temporarily invaded (during Reconstruction) by triumphant Yankees, southern white men appear to have displaced their sense of vulnerability and emasculation onto women—white women that is. In the decade after Reconstruction, out of the blue it seemed, white women were no longer "safe" in the South. The sense of emergency rapidly intensified, intertwined as it was (in white men's minds) with politics, economics, black progress and resolve. Persuading white women that they too were at risk, white fear became white hysteria.

No longer able to indulge their sexual whim with subjugated black bodies, southern white men became enraged, permanently it seemed, and what Joel Williamson termed "radical racism" ruled the day, resulting in segregation, disenfranchisement, and lynching. White men would punish black people, black men in particular, by castrating them, politically, economically, and literally. In America, "race" is intertwined with "sex," including sex between men. In America, the gender of racial politics and violence is in some essential and nightmarish sense "queer." Later, when African Americans articulated what was at stake in the struggle for civil rights, there was no hesitation: it was "manhood." The protest signs read simply: "I AM A MAN." Now why would black men have to assert *that*? As Daniel Black (1997, 4) acknowledges: "[B]lack men have wrestled with the concept and the attainment of manhood since the days of their enslavement by Europeans."

Black men have had to assert their "manhood" because racial subjugation has been, continues to be, sexualized, *homo*sexualized. (It is, of course, heterosexualized as well, but that is a subject for another day.) Not only white gay men are interested in black male bodies. Straight white men continue to gaze upon them, a gaze sublimated into, for instance, "sport." The imaginary status of white women in the nineteenth century continues, not unchanged of course, but men still resist egalitarian encounters with independent and articulate women. The various feminisms have produced some political progress and suffered much reactionary resistance, witness the crime statistics, continued discrimination in the public sphere, the sometimes hysterical efforts of men, especially politically and religiously conservative men, to block that progress. Enough progress has been made, evidently, so that we are now witnessing a new "crisis" of masculinity. Feeling besieged by assertive women and out gays and lesbians, no doubt missing that forgotten nineteenth-century "romantic friendship," some straight guys are now busy bonding with each other, even across the racial divide (still to a limited extent, that is, in imaginary ways), in reactionary reaction to those who seek equal rights for women and gay men.

A century ago black men had to assault white women only in white men's minds in order to get lynched. Of course, it was never really about "her" in the nineteenth century, as Jesse Daniel Ames and her colleagues in the Association of Southern Women for the Prevention of Lynching understood, a little late perhaps, by the third decade of the twentieth century. Black women—Ida B. Wells at least—knew from the outset that lynching was not about obtaining "justice" for assaulted white women, rather real creatures, as black women knew, who sometimes acted according to their own desires, which sometimes involved black men, white men's feelings and fantasies be damned. The white woman rarely paid the price for indiscretion; it was her black lover who paid for her agency, as the case of Edward [Mc]Coy in 1892 illustrates. When his white female lover, forced by white men to cry rape at what had been a consensual and ongoing relationship, came over to start the lynching fire, "Coy asked her if she would burn him after they had 'been sweethearting' so long" (Wells 1892a/1969, 10). Indeed she would.

White women, even social reformers such as Frances Willard, were often complicit with white men's fantasies, at least some of them, some of the time. For Willard, the category of "men" loomed so large that race receded; she suspected they were all barbaric "under the influence," although black men, she assumed in racist fashion, were worse. Many white women at least pretended to believe what white men said was true, although even conservative white women, as the very different cases of late nineteenth-century Christian feminism and the early twentieth-century W.K.K.K. indicate, found ways to appropriate men's rhetoric for their own purposes. Many conservative Christian women had faith in what conservative Christian men said ... up to a point. They mimed male discourses to their own advantage, gaining the moral and sometimes political upper hand within a "separate sphere" that soon seeped into the public sphere. White women in Indiana evidently joined the W.K.K.K. not only to affirm their husbands' hatreds but also in order to articulate their own experience as wives, mothers, and working women. While their vituperative "poison squads" were models of effective political action, they murdered few others (if any), they stripped no one, castrated no one, they carried no body parts around as souvenirs. The gender of racial violence in the America, as Katherine M. Blee (1991) perceptively observes, is masculine.

The point bears emphasis. There was no white female analog to lynching. Even when white women knew white men were sleeping with black women, they devised no rituals of sexual torture and mutilation to "teach them a lesson." There is no evidence of white women collecting themselves in mobs, roving the countryside in search of black female (or male) "criminals" accused of sleeping with white men. Whatever white female sexual subjugation of black women occurred—apart from prison sex, and there such interracial sexual relationships are often consensual with black women often playing the "butch" roles—there seems to have been no sexual identity-threatening consequences to white female racism. Moreover, there seems no analog to black "hypermasculinity," no hyperfemininity that is driven by a compensatory effort to erase historical experience, a hypersexuality of denial which guarantees a homoerotic undertow. While there is homosociality among women, it seems to lack any parallel to the misogyny—the group violence—of male groups. Women, black or white, do not gang rape men or women.

What is it about "men"—"men" who imagined themselves "white"—which required them to split white women into either madonnas or whores, black men into harmless uncles or rapist/superstuds, and black women into mammies or sluts? What is it about white men that they made black men the intense object of their obsession; why did those Europeans who first discovered Africans feel compelled to enslave them? The place black men have occupied in the imaginative life of European-American writers is profound and constant, as Leslie Fiedler's remarkable commentary makes clear: "[W]hat they [these books] celebrate, all of them, [is] the mutual love of *a white man and a colored*" (Fiedler 1948/1995, 531). That mutuality is in the white male mind only. At the center of American civilization as a patriarchal, homosocial civilization is the desire and longing the white man has felt and feels still for the black.

If only white men could feel what they have repressed, would the four-hundred-year nightmare be over? Would racism disappear? The experience of black gay men with white suggests not. Still the surface of black male flesh shines with the desire white men feel; black male subjectivity remains effaced by the white objectification and commodification of the black male body. Of course, being a sex object is a promotion over being a slave, but as women know, not fundamentally, as objectification enslaves as well. The contemporary "superstuds"—actors, rappers, athletes, models—are at least paid for strutting their stuff, but the historical throughline is clear. Black men still strip, sweat, and move their muscles while white men watch. "The prize, the turf of struggle," Clyde Taylor asserts, "may be focused less today on free black labor, only to shift to black experience as packaged and commodified in popular culture and entertainment" (1994, 168). Elizabeth Alexander sees the throughline as bodies in pain: "Black bodies in pain for public consumption have been an American spectacle for centuries. This history moves from public rapes, beatings, and lynchings to the gladiatorial arenas of basketball and boxing" (1994, 92).

Nor is this situation an especially happy one for white men. Socially isolated, psychologically stunted, driven and alone, many white men, especially heterosexually identified men, must struggle daily to maintain some semblance of stability. Too many have lost any felt or autobiographical sense of themselves to an obsessive careerism, to alcoholism, to drugs, to authoritarianism, to violence, to abuse, especially of spouses, but of girlfriends, children, gay men and lesbians as well. It is not gay-identified men who rape women. It is not gay-identified men who rape men. The prisons are filled with straight men, not gay, although that distinction seems to fade inside the walls of the big house.

Prisons are not alien womanless worlds in which men resort to unimaginable acts. Prisons disclose the profoundly womanless worlds most men in fact inhabit, in which women are fundamentally fictive, units of currency in a homosocial economy. What the fact of homosociality indicates is that the prison is not unique, that many perhaps most men "live" in an all-male world intrapsychically from which women are aggressively banished. It is a sign of manhood. For most men, only fortunes and men's eyes are real. In prison black men act out sexually the civic subjugation, the political emasculation, they have suffered since the Middle Passage. Straight black men could have figured out many kinds of revenge, could they not: physical maiming for one, murder for another. But somehow black men knew exactly what form revenge must be once they were "on top," the same form that "race relations" have taken (and continues to take) in the United States. "Race" has been about getting fucked, castrated, made into somebody's "punk," politically, economically, and, yes, sexually.

None of this is inevitable, nor is it universally true. There are many—perhaps a majority—of heterosexually identified men who are not violently misogynistic and homophobic, not visibly racist, not dangerously unstable. That this is true is remarkable, given the intrapsychic dynamics of hegemonic masculinity production. This "achievement"—I use that word to underscore that such masculine stability hardly comes "naturally"—is possible sometimes through the psychological labor and commitment of caring and loving women. I am thinking not only of mothers and wives, but aunts, grandmothers, sisters, daughters and friends. Such love, carefully and consistently expressed, sometimes allows the unruly male to accept, in a kind of psychological sleight of hand, the maternal foundation of his character, and in a relatively (however vigorously denied) feminized state he can more easily and fully participate in domesticity, child rearing, relationship. But why should women have to work so hard to tame the beast?

Religion too can help produce such men—"brides of Christ" as it were—although the more extreme versions, such as evangelical or fundamentalist Protestantism, have historically been associated with misogyny, racism, and homophobia. And lynching, slavery, and segregation. And imperialism, colonization, and, of course, capitalism. Perhaps churches whose members promote hatred should lose their tax-free status, for starters. Is there something so patriarchal about the cultural forms Christianity has taken that men's egos tend to be inflated by their imagined intimacy with the "almighty"? Is "salvation" his imaginary compensation for the life he has lost, now fantasized as somewhere else, sometime later, when the dead man in the loin cloth on the cross climbs down and takes him into his arms? Is that the second coming?

In Christianity the love of man for man remains a sublimated dream of the hereafter; in this "straight" world the partially clad man remains limp, hanging dead on the cross: our "father" who art in heaven. Mark Simpson puts the matter this way: "The resistance of the religious Right to [homosexuality] is absolutely correct: this is very much a 'cultural war for the soul of America.' What Christianity brought about and what patriarchal power has relied upon in Western civilization since the time of the Holy Roman Emperors is the symbol of male power—the phallus—remaining hidden. For as long as it is hidden it cannot be challenged" (1994, 13–14). The success of patriarchal power—here Simpson quotes Foucault—"is proportional to its ability to hide its own mechanism ... for its secrecy is not in the nature of an abuse; it is indispensable to its operation" (1988/1990, 86; quoted in Simpson 1994, 13). It is time to make visible the loin-clothed man on the cross; he is "man" himself. Awaken him with a kiss.

There are men who help each other to be responsible husbands, fathers, and sons, who work against the cultural current, and strive to foster a responsible masculinity. We see that now especially among a number of African-American men: "in every black community in the United States, there are strong, quiet heroes" (White and Cones 1999, 79). But even these men remain in a man's world, doing the right thing as a "man," for the sake of other men's respect. All too often heterosexually identified men find themselves imprisoned in a culture of manhood which sentences them to positions of competitiveness, accomplishment without contentment, resented responsibility, social isolation, and self-dissociation that amounts to a life of "quiet desperation," a desperation that sometimes results in violence, psychological as well as physical. Heterosexually identified men—as a racialized, gendered category—are, as the crime statistics underscore, a problem for themselves and for the rest of us.

Straight white men pose a special problem, given that they have succeeded in making their dreams come true, that is, made them into the public world the rest of us are forced to inhabit. The problems they pose for black men and women and children are hardly restricted to the forms of racialized and gendered subjugation we have examined here. While gay men are hardly exempt from racism and misogyny, it is straight men who must bear the burden of responsibility for the nightmare that is the lived material reality for millions of battered and abused women, a world in which the care of children is too often incidental, a world characterized by masculinized nationalisms and economic competitions which take incalculable tolls in human life and suffering and threaten to destroy the sustainability of the planet itself. The straight world is a world in which the love of men for men is, unbelievably, a crime. Is it any surprise that this self-hating world many heterosexually identified men occupy is a predatory one? Can it be a surprise that these haunted and driven creatures resist anyone who reminds them the world could be otherwise? In one sense the violence of (especially heterosexually identified) men represents a reenactment, this time involving often innocent others, of their own self-mutilation, those complex and self-eviscerating processes they have suffered on the developmental path to becoming a "man."

How we need today Ida B. Wells, Jane Addams, Jesse Daniel Ames! The courage, clear-sightedness, and determination of these crusaders for justice are needed again, here and now. Thank god lynching is past, but the struggle for racial justice in America remains very much under way. On occasion white men kill black men, as in Jasper, Texas; more often it is black men who kill black men. Now black men are "legally lynched," that is, kept imprisoned, often for petty drug offenses, for much of their lives. White men perpetuate fantasies of black rapists and black criminality well over a century old, persuading white voters to support the construction of more prisons while university budgets are cut and public education remains underpaid and undervalued "woman's work."

Should we be surprised when it is southern (mostly white, straight, and male) politicians who lead the battle against civil rights for all Americans? Regionally if not genealogically, these present-day reactionaries are the descendents of those same white men who enslaved and tortured black people, who, after African Americans were freed, kept (and keep) them in economic and political subjugation, who lynched, disenfranchised, segregated those they exploited. Busy weren't they, but not too busy to thunder against women's suffrage. Now these southern straight white men, still defeated and defensive psychologically, still compensating for those losses of manhood their great-grandfathers incurred and which, at some unconscious level, they evidently still feel, now these men work for the "gracious submission" of women, call for boycotts of Disney or Apple Computer or American Airlines for conferring basic civil rights to gay and lesbian employees. Why on earth should we be surprised that these men—these "white" presumably heterosexual, oh yes, god-fearing southern men—pound the Bible and presume to know what is natural and what is perverted? Theirs is a centuries-old delusion in which their own repressed desires are sublimated, recoded, then mistaken for God's will. These men are the strange fruit now.

There *are* progressives south of the Mason-Dixon—such as Morris Dees and the Southern Poverty Law Center in Montgomery—although they are altogether too few, too timid, too sensitive to the opinions of their not very progressive neighbors and friends. If only white progressives could align themselves with black voters, something resembling social progress might get under way in the Deep South. But, as many black southerners know, white alignment with black in the Deep South happens mostly after sundown, in the bedroom not in voting booths, never in front of disapproving white neighbors. There is hell yet to pay in the South, and the salve that is relative economic progress will not put out the fire next time. Strangely but perhaps predictably, my Yankee friends seem to understand none of this, self-enclosed in northern smugness, mistaking their own regional prejudices for social reality. Little do my progressive colleagues in the North understand that their social, political reality is dependent on southern caste, class, and racial subjugation. Northerners get to feel righteous because southerners are so outrageous. Like one hundred years ago, northerners watch while southern white men claim for themselves life, liberty, and the pursuit of happiness.

As a nation we remain submerged in a thirty-year-old reaction to the progressive and sometimes revolutionary politics that characterized the 1960s. The majority of Americans remain too conservative, on too many occasions, downright reactionary. How one would like to believe that, to borrow a phrase first used thirty years ago by the right, there is a "silent majority" of Americans whose contempt for official reality keeps them at home on election days. If everyone voted, there might be a majority of Americans who find the Southern Baptist idea of "gracious submission" laughable, for whom race is a positive difference, and gay people are interesting if not cool. The power elites will never enact such legislation, but if all Americans were required to vote, the nonsense of the right wing, dominated now by white southerners, might quickly fade into an Orwellian past.

But in Washington we are submerged in their fantasies, still ruled by a fragile but effective coalition of religious crazies, right-wing extremists, and corporate interests, sometimes intersecting categories. With the help of the mass media, this coalition evidently succeeds in persuading many who do vote that (by the lure of prosperity) American business, and business "thinking," is our salvation. Many are so thoroughly seduced by this fantasy they evidently think what works for American business ought to work everywhere, even in fundamentally nonbusiness organizational forms such as the schools. There the dominant thinking remains "corporatist," preparing students to live in a consumer economy which commodifies everything. What is needed, as I trust this study implies, is much more attention to innovative, interdisciplinary humanities curricula understood and taught as forms of social and cultural psychoanalysis (for one example, see Pinar 1991). Students, especially "white" students, need to know the gender of racial politics in this country. They need to understand the racialization of gender as well as the gender of violence. Parents need not fear some homosexual virus will infect their children if they learn that racism has been in some essential way "queer." The homoerotic "virus" is quite already there, everywhere, since the beginning of time. I would say that the point is to experience it, celebrate it, not to suppress it, push it into some subterranean sphere from which it someday resurfaces, mixed and mangled almost beyond recognition, violent, defiant, no longer love but hate: lynching, for instance, or prison rape.

Interdisciplinary humanities curricula conceived as social psychoanalysis must aspire to teach how nefarious gender totalitarianism is, how the contemporary regime of heterosexism not only victimizes queers but self-identified "heterosexuals" as well, especially women and children. The contemporary suppression of homosexual desire, its imprisonment and segregation in "homosexuals," not only creates self-delusion as to one's own gender identity and sexual potential, but relocates desire onto others, skewing perception, deforming experience. Self-division leads to the multiplication of "others." And "others" sometimes get "offed."

I am not suggesting that everyone is "naturally" bisexual; from studies in the history of sexuality we can appreciate that that category is too limited, reified, finally illusory, like "heterosexuality" and "homosexuality." Probably Freud's notion of "polymorphous perversity" is a more serviceable idea. But "sexuality"—itself evidently a twentieth-century phenomenon, at least in terms of its role in identity formation—is now so thoroughly politicized that we cannot make such statements neutrally, "objectively." As Elizabeth Grosz has noted: "There is no pure sexuality, no inherently transgressive sexual practice, no sexuality beyond or outside the limits of patriarchal models" (1995, 181). Given the hegemony of heteronormativity, "bisexuality" is probably politically progressive. The educational task is not to educate children to understand a prehistorical, biologistic or "natural" bisexuality; it is to understand how their phenomenologically real but thoroughly constructed and variable feelings of desire are implicated in a complex gendered history of racial violence and oppression in America.

What is important to teach now is that there is a racial politics of masculinity that historically has relegated women to units of currency in a homosocial economy of desire. It may be so that men have, since some prehistorical matriarchal period, not "recognized" women apart from their need for them, including their repudiation of them. It is also true that men have succeeded, to different degrees, in various cultural settings and historical moments, in persuading and/or forcing women into psychosocial and sexual roles men wished women to assume. Footbinding in China, genital mutilation in Africa, the persecution of "witches" in the West, and widow-burning in India are only four examples (Dworkin 1974). To what extent have women been complicit in this alienated system of male homosocial desire, even while finding spaces for survival and self-affirmation, creating opportunities to cultivate creativity and fashion love, perhaps cannot be known. The worldwide if culturally variable history of misogyny, and women's resistance to and transcendence of it, is another very complicated story. Where it intersects with the tale I have told here is that men's commodification of women, and in particular, white men's fictionalizing of white women, functioned not to protect women from rape; it functioned to rationalize "heterosexual" male sexual assault ... upon other men. Nineteenth-century white men used white "women" as provocations to sexually mutilate black men. Desire denied becomes paranoia, Freud taught, and lynching would seem to be an illustrative if complex instance of that point.

Black women were fictionalized as well by white men, slandered as lascivious. The first woman who publicly declined, and in rather spectacular fashion, this fictional status, this reduction to a figment in the white man's imagination, was Miss Ida B. Wells. This is not the place to speculate why Wells was the first. It may have been fortuitous, the simple consequence of the 1892

Memphis lynching "at the curve." She was not the only black woman who knew that white men were blowing not just steam when they obsessed over black men raping white women. It is true that Wells had a certain orientation, we might even say "commitment," toward black men: she assumed some responsibility for her brother, who was sometimes in difficulty; she took on an all-male Sunday School class later in Chicago and organized settlement houses there for new and homeless (mostly male) migrants from the South, which is to say she felt some moral responsibility toward black men. It is clear from her Memphis diaries (DeCosta-Willis 1995b) that she was hardly uncritical of men; her skepticism of and refusal to participate in the taken-for-granted romantic customs of the time underlines that fact.

Nor was Wells uncritical of what the gender system did to women: she did not decline to record how bourgeois black women (without using that phrase) were sometimes guilty of gossip and pettiness, a phenomenon that undermined racial solidarity as it kept women competitive, isolated, and ornamental. After the British campaign, she did marry and gave birth to four children; she took her duties as mother very seriously. In her autobiography it is clear that her children came first, even before her commitment to crusade for racial justice. Still she found time, however, to continue to fight lynching, as we saw in chapters 10 and 11.

As Hazel Carby (1987) points out, Wells has been called a leader without a movement, "a lonely warrior," a spokesperson for protest in "the age of accommodation," whose life's work can be judged "a limited success" (quoted in Carby 1987, 108). Many historians regard her as a minor figure compared to Du Bois and Washington; suffering under such comparison, her political ideas, strategies, tactics, and analyses have been appreciated primarily in relation to the achievements of these men. As Carby notes, Wells was no imperfect copy of Washington or Du Bois and should not be considered in relation to either. Perhaps there is a historical throughline here, too; she suffered one hundred years ago because men found her "difficult," which is to say "unladylike," unwilling to compromise her strong voice for the sake of men's comfort (Carby 1987). She suffers still, in contemporary remembrances of her.

A public schoolteacher like Anna Julia Cooper, Ida B. Wells found her true calling in protesting with the pen, and she became a militant journalist and antilynching activist. For whites and some black men, Wells was, as Carby (1987) reminds us, an "uppity" black woman with a strong analysis of the relations among political terrorism, economic oppression, and conventional codes of sexuality and morality. For Carby, Wells's analysis "has still to be surpassed in its incisive condemnation of the patriarchal manipulation of race and gender" (1987, 108). Carby finds the influence of Wells's work in the writing of black women from Pauline Hopkins to June Jordan and Alice Walker who, like Wells, have labored to understand how rape and lynching were used as interlocking tools of political, social, and economic oppression.

Wells's commitment to fighting racial injustice appears to have begun when she was thrown off that Chesapeake and Ohio train, but after the loss of her friend at the curve, she concentrated on the outrage, the crisis, that was lynching. What also might have been at play in her commitment, in her courageous assault on white male fantasy, was her refusal to accept the imaginary status of women, in particular white women. Like Frances Harper, Wells did not believe that "white women are dewdrops just exhaled from the skies" (quoted in Roediger 1998, 254). She knew that the white male fantasy of the virginal, morally unreproachable white "lady" was just that—a fantasy; she suspected and discovered that in some cases the "rape" white men were "avenging" by lynching was a voluntary relationship between two consenting adults. And in some cases it seemed that the white woman had been the sexual aggressor. White women were not ornaments on the shelves of the white male mind; they were, she knew, human individuals with minds and passions of their own. Sometimes, however stubbornly, white men refused to accept the fact that white women had decided to go against the prevailing white "wisdom" in order to pursue passion, and, no doubt, love, with men and women who were black.

White men were not only wrong about white women, they were just as wrong about black men and women. Of course, Wells knew that black men were not brutes, sexual fiends, slaves to their "animal" passions—passions which, white men were sure, focused exclusively on white women. Like the "money shot" in heterosexual pornography, lynching used the presence (however imaginary) of women to camouflage homosexual desire. Not only white women were imaginary in this process; black men were fictionalized too, and at every opportunity Ida B. Wells contested that "place" in fantasyland to which they had been consigned by white men. By so doing, she also contested the place black women had been assigned. In England many, especially British, female reformers, "saw" her, but back home even northern newspapers condemned her, predictably, as a harlot.

As perhaps America's greatest pedagogue, Ida B. Wells realized that her "students"—European Americans—could not learn the lesson she had to teach, not from a black woman at least. She tried to reach them, you recall, but even northern newspapers would print nothing she had to teach. In the 1890s few European Americans could see how topsy-turvy their world was, as the racial mythology in which they were submerged was too powerful, too totalizing. And so, undefeated and undaunted, Wells shrewdly appealed to those whom she thought might command a hearing, might shock her resisting refusing students to confront what they were so determined to deny. She took her cause to the British, Americans' political and, for some, cultural parents. As we saw in chapters 7 and 8, Wells, with the help of British women reformers, did succeed in persuading many in Britain that lynching was barbaric, that white men were the uncivilized ones, which in the conflations of the period, meant they were not "men." The British in turn communicated that to their wayward American "children"; it was an allegation that hit home.

It would take another forty years before a white woman would surface who would contest the fictionalized status of women which lynching presumed. Jessie Daniel Ames knew that southern women were not fragile, passive, helpless victims of black male desire. She knew that white men's invocation of chivalry functioned to restrict women's freedom as much as it did to prop up an unstable and fragile male ego. Ames had fought for women's right to vote; after her participation in that important victory, she continued to struggle for women's rights, including the right not to be reduced to an ornament: the southern white "lady." She tackled this considerable problem bravely, challenging women's relegation to white men's trophy case while intervening in the murderous practice that the possession of such "ornaments" presumably justified: lynching.

Men's battle against lynching, what became a primarily black-male struggle led by the N.A.A.C.P., de-emphasized the gendered nature of the practice, predictably so, given the invisibility of men as gendered to the male mind. Walter White saw the problem as primarily economic, although the explicit gender dimensions of racialization portrayed in James Weldon Johnson's 1912 *The Autobiography of an Ex-Colored Man* implies that Johnson sensed that more was at stake in lynching than economic manipulation, political power, and white supremacy. The still shockingly absolute refusal of white men to enact federal legislation to end the practice underscores how powerful a symbol of white/black male relations lynching was. As they had for a century and would continue to the present day, white southern men led the reactionary refusal to protect the basic civil rights of all Americans, this time disingenuously crying "constitutionality" and "states' rights" to prevent federal intervention in southern barbarism. A masculinized symbol system par excellence, law and legislation were in this struggle symbolizations—disguised tools—of male-male desire (Hocquenghem 1978; Grossberg 1990). Southern white men were not about to keep other southern white men away from black men's bodies.

These racialized sexual dynamics, camouflaged in Congress by three-piece suits and abstract argumentation over God, country, and states' rights, become unmistakable in prison. No longer can the social preference of men for men—that sublimation of homosexual desire Eve Kosofsky Sedgwick (1985) termed homosociality—be disguised by the physical presence of women, however imaginary they often remained in many men's minds. In prison the fundamentally sadomasochistic and sexualized character of white/black male relations is unmistakable. Lynching was a kind of rape, a distorted, mangled, nightmarish expression of sexual desire. In prison Claude Neal would be avenged.

Prison rape is political revenge in racial terms, but in psychological terms, it is, I believe, also an expression of the western male's unconscious self-structure, a matrifocal structure requiring the repudiation of that symbiotic union with the mother to become something "other"—a "man." Through rape men act out their internalized self-self relations, performing on women and other men the crimes of gender formation they endured as boys and adolescents in order to become and continue to be "men." Is that why the category is so unstable, so fragile, so imaginary? Compulsory heterosexuality necessarily suppresses an omnipresent homosexual desire, relocating and imprisoning it in "homosexuals," themselves now gender criminals whose fantasized distinctiveness supports the binary between gay and straight, allowing heterosexually identified men to continue to believe the delusion that they themselves are "normal."

Straight is normal, natural, God-ordained. The intensity of the (especially white male) reaction against calls for the protection of the basic civil rights for a fragment of the population the right wing insists is only 1–2 percent suggests otherwise. The protection of the civil rights of gay and lesbian Americans gets recoded as the granting of "special rights," a rhetorical strategy racists used successfully against African Americans one hundred years ago. The lady doth protest too much. The dangers of homosexuality are evidently so powerful, so multiple, so appealing that only constant legal and political suppression can keep them contained. When those who are imaginary "others" must stay "in their place," it is clear that what is at stake is the structure of the white male imagination, recoded as "morality" or "godliness" and most fundamentally as "real." As Alan Sinfield notes: "In many ways, of course, we already don't have traditional heterosexuality. That is why (neo)-conservatives go on about it so much: urgent ideological work usually signals the failure of a system, not its dominance" (1994, xi). When the right wing begins to battle homosexuality, the war is lost. But our victory, perhaps already achieved, is like the light of a distant star: it will take a very long time for the light to reach us on earth. Not in my lifetime.

The European-American male self structure, in its repression and self-splitting, constructs a series of "others," each with its distinctive history of suffering and struggle, each with its own casualty list, but sharing a convoluted place in the white male mind. "Prejudice" may be a discredited concept today, but only because it was too narrowly attitudinal, obscured too much of the complexity of those internal dynamics as well as social relationalities, historical and civilizational legacies, economic pressures, and cultural formations that are all visible in any serious study of racialized, gendered, religious, and classed oppression (Allport 1958; Young-Bruehl 1996). I shall pursue this point in volume II.

Why do "men" create "others"? Could it have something to do with the processes of their own identity formation, specifically that they themselves, as "men," are imaginary? Because they themselves, in order to become "men," are fictionalized, are they then condemned to perceive others in fictional terms as well? The formation of male identity in a regime of compulsory heterosexuality requires repudiation of the pre-oedipal symbiotic identification with the mother (white men projected onto black men their own matrifocality in debates about the black family). In so doing, men structure a male self that is dissociated from the body and emotion (except rage), from that viscous, sensual, phenomenological experience which allows one access to, intimacy with, not only separated and individuated others, but to oneself as well. Could it be that this repudiation of the mother and imaginary identification with a relatively absent father—and here I mean not only the father who works but the prototypical, mythological "father" in a patriarchal society which denies him feeling and "femininity"—congeals a state of self-dissociation in which "othering" is inevitable? Does this self-division require the multiplication of others?

In prison we glimpse how these processes and structures of masculine self-deformation get performed in the construction of social reality. Men feminize younger men, not as substitutes for absent women—the research reported in chapters 16 and 17 make clear that even when prison officials provide conjugal visits with spouses and girlfriends straight men continue their sexual involvement with other men—but because straight men need "bitches," a residue of the repudiated, repressed, then projected feminine within. Of course how men construct "the opposite sex" varies according to class, culture, and historical moment; in prison the "opposite sex" to men is still men. "Why can't a woman be more like a man?" echoes Professor Higgins's famous question. Prison is no weird alien planet; prison provides a glimpse, for those who can bear to see, what (straight) men do everywhere. In prison men assume—some voluntarily, many against their will—the roles that in society women are required to play.

In prison we see racial and class hierarchies reversed. In prison it is good-looking, young, heterosexual white guys who are the losers, inverting (as it were) the gendered racial hierarchy outside. But being "losers" in the man's world that is the prison means having been made over into "punks," that is, "girls," a reproduction of the gender hierarchy on the outside. "Gender and race conflate in a crisis," as Gates (1996, 96) observes, an ongoing crisis at least four hundred years in duration that continues to support heterosexually identified white men's delusion that what they imagine is real. In prison it is black men's fantasies that become real, that become social reality.

Lynching and prison rape disclose the conflation of gender and race in the white male mind. These two events, key imprinting events we cannot set aside as bizarre and exceptional, require us to reconceptualize how we understand "race" in America. What must be concluded from the intolerable facts of these phenomena is that, to a considerable extent, the gender of racial politics and violence in America is queer. Women have been involved, sometimes complicit, often reworking white men's racism toward their own ends, and in several spectacular cases—Ida B. Wells most prominently—taking leadership is fighting white men's violence. But that violence has been sexualized, homosexualized, violence that has left twentieth-century African Americans having to insist: "I AM A MAN."

I am not suggesting that racism can be reduced to latent homosexual desire, or that if we could somehow uncork homosexual desire racism would disappear in an orgy of reconciliation and love. Still, it might help. If white men could allow themselves to experience how their persisting fantasies about black men are intertwined with suppressed desire, racism would at the very least be reconfigured. The racism of white gay men who desire black men is instructive here. The focus remains on the black male body, but now it is revalorized as desirable: the "rapist" is now "stud." Black male subjectivity remains erased as the white male gaze remains fixed onto the same dark skin, the same muscled black body that those sixteenth-century European invaders of Africa found so amazing and overwhelming that they wanted it for themselves, in sexualized subjugation.

To understand the queer character of racism we must appreciate how relations between black males and white males are those of a "romance" gone terribly wrong, as Fiedler's remarkable analysis makes clear. Not that the black man ever reciprocated the desire of his pursuer: his enslavement meant he was never free to negotiate the terms of the relationship, at least from the position of social and political equality. But the subtext of desire experienced and rejected gets expressed in the myriad of ways the two "bounce off" each other, as every effort to find a new rapprochement is undermined by the bitter echoes of the past. If we are to "teach tolerance," to engage in any antiracist education worthy of the name, we teachers—in classrooms, in corporate boardrooms, on the street, in Congress—must appreciate that the educational projects of tolerance and multiculturalism are inextricably intertwined with feminist and queer theory, not just conceptually but historically. The gender of racial politics and violence in America is queer.

II. Beasts, Bestiality, and the Historical Imagination

> *[T]he repeated castrations of lynched black men cries out for serious psychocultural explanation.*
>
> —Cornel West, *Race Matters* (1993)

> *[T]he speaking subject is also the subject about which it speaks.*
>
> —Michel Foucault, "Maurice Blanchot: The Thought from Outside," in *Foucault/Blanchot* (1987)

> *[D]oes the relation to oneself have an elective affinity with sexuality, to the point of renewing the project of a "history of sexuality"?*
>
> —Gilles Deleuze, *Foucault* (1986)

> *That's the South's trouble. Ignorant. Doesn't know anything.*
>
> —Lillian Smith, *Strange Fruit* (1944/1972)

As Joel Williamson (1984) understood, several developments during the late nineteenth century combined to support what he termed racial "radicalism," typified by disenfranchisement, segregation, and the horrifying, widespread racial violence such as lynching. While in the scholarly lynching literature Williamson sometimes seems relegated to a prescientific past that has now been surpassed by the demography and sociology of lynching, in my view his analysis, while heterosexualized, remains the most sophisticated, the most comprehensive, the most perceptive of all historians. In the passage I quote at some length below, notice how the distinguished historian appreciates that a convergence of factors—economic, psychological, and gendered—made possible the madness that was racial hatred in America in the 1890s. He writes:

> Had there been no great world depression in and after 1893, had the material pie not been drastically reduced, people might have felt fulfilled in their images of themselves, and there would have been no Radical revolt. Had there been no industrial revolution, there would certainly have still been exploitation and there would have been racism, but it might never have achieved the vicious fillip that it attained in the turn-of-the-century years. Even more centrally, had there been no Victorian era in the South with exaggerated roles assigned by gender, had white men not seen themselves bound by God to the comfortable material support of their families and the domestication of their women, there probably would have been no Radical rage. (Williamson 1984, 305–306)

Other historians have also focused upon how these developments affected white men, theorizing a "crisis" in white masculinity, however problematic its periodization and variable its expressions (Carnes and Griffen 1990). Such a concept helps convey that white men—in the South their "crisis" of masculinity was intensified by their memory of defeat in the Civil War and the South's subsequent cultural marginalization—could not easily cope with the burdens of being "white" and "men." Recall that "romantic friendship" was ending now that "homosexuality" and "heterosexuality" had been invented, as men became more self-conscious of homoerotic expression. By choosing a more stylized, defensive, and displaced heterosexuality, most men were left without the physical and emotional comforts of other men, and more sublimated forms of male-male intimacy were now required: sport, bodybuilding, "muscular" Christianity, for instance. Women pressed against their enforced "domestication," as Williamson mentions—not only secular feminists who rewrote the Bible and demanded suffrage, but Christian feminists who recast God as feminine and nurturant, positioning themselves as God-like in the process. And, thanks to the efforts of Ida B. Wells, from Britain came cries of "barbarism" and visits from missionaries to "save" the "unmanly" former colonists who lynched helpless black men.

For perhaps a majority of southerners, especially southern white men, it was all too much. As the twentieth century began, they retreated to "An Unreal World" of "Race and Sex in the Modern South," as Williamson (1984, 306) perceptively entitles a section near the end of his classic *The Crucible of Race*. The last decade of the nineteenth century had seen a "horrendous, seemingly unending depression," which mixed with "two vastly powerful currents in the society, the one unreal (exaggerated sex roles) and the other all too real (the loss of material security as the economic depression lengthened), bore this strange, this peculiar and bitter fruit" (Williamson 1984, 306). What "fruit" was this? Yes, the same "fruit" about which Billie Holiday sang, and which I have borrowed to entitle chapter 1 of this study. But there was another kind of "strange fruit" as well, white men who fantasized about the retrogressing black man who was condemned to become more violent, more sexual, more primitive, some said even to disappear as a species, now that "he" was free from the "civilizing" restraint of slavery. That fantasy, as Williamson notes, "finally expired of its own weighty untruth and fell by the wayside" (306).

White southerners continued to retreat from the material and historical world into a fantasy one, one that was admittedly "gone with the wind," but one in which they were determined to believe as fiercely as religious faith can permit. The horrible white racism, with its denied homoerotic, and embittered "romantic" elements (Williamson does not name these), "promoted a loss of southerners of their grasp on reality" (Williamson 1984, 306). Southerners increasingly retreated into evangelical, fundamentalist Protestantism, which provided, presumably, divine legitimation for the unreal racial world they doggedly created, one in which African-American citizens were denied life, liberty, and the pursuit of happiness. Not that black citizens succumbed, but southern whites, especially southern white men, tried very hard to force them to. "But probably nowhere," Williamson understands,

> was the unreality so widely divorced from the reality as in the specific image of the black beast rapist. That mythical being, ***so totally the creature of the white male imagination***, has labored for white people in and after the Radical era probably as no real black person has ever done. If we can understand how he came to be and how he functioned, we will understand much of the history of the Southern white male mind, and, indeed, of Southern culture. It is a case of unreality, ***in extremis***. (Williamson 1984, 306, emphasis added)

Racial "radicals" were obsessed with muscular young black men. These were not closeted "homosexuals" working out their sexual frustrations, although perhaps a few might be so described. The majority of lynchers accepted mainstream sexual norms but as Williamson perceptively understands, "had painted themselves into a sexual corner" (1984, 306).

What "corner" could that be? Despite his brilliance, Williamson does not see what "castration" means in the lynching ritual. To his credit, it is practically the only point he misses. For instance, he appreciates, as feminist historians have demonstrated, the power of the "separate spheres" in nineteenth-century gender relations, how, especially in the antebellum South, white men "had pedestalized white women in their minds. In so doing they had violated the equal humanity of women and removed them, in some degree, from possibilities of real intimacy with themselves" (1984, 306–307). Women were not real to men in the South; men assumed, among other things, that they were more sexual than women. Specifically men imagined "that women (in the South, white women only) did not enjoy sex, that sexual relations were painful to them and allowed only out of a sense of love and duty" (307). With this fantasy mistaken for reality, southern white men who expressed their desire

> upon their wives violated them. They were beasts who, brutish and totally physical, satiated themselves at the expense of the very persons whom they had sworn before God to protect. It seems unlikely that white men, in fact, much denied themselves sexual pleasure with their wives or with white women in general. However, if they did deny themselves, they felt tension; but if they did not, Victorian mores led them to feel tension of another sort, namely, guilt. Whatever they did, they were caught in a trap of their own making. (Williamson 1984, 306)

Williamson has the story right, almost. White men did feel passion toward their wives, did feel tension, did feel guilt, all aggravated by an already diminished sense of "manhood," one in "crisis." But while the white "lady" may have been an abstract unit in a male homosocial economy, "men" had not been such a unit, as we saw in depictions of male-male physical intimacy in nineteenth-century romantic friendship.

Working within a heterosexist logic, Williamson still reconstructs the situation with acumen. He reminds us that in the antebellum period if elite southern white men denied themselves frequent and passionate sex with their wives, they did have other options, and the evidence suggests that there were many who exercised them. Indeed, in the Old South, if a white man were monied and predisposed, he could purchase the sexual services of a woman or women, without any fear of the law and little fear of his neighbors' condemnation, if there were neighbors nearby. Here Williamson's heterosexualized fantasy slips slightly away from him, and he adds, unnecessarily: "If he had enough money he could buy a very desirable woman" (1984, 307). We knew that.

In slavery, slave owners had full access to black bodies, female and male. Williamson thinks only of female bodies, and points out that among whites the "myth arose that Negro women were especially lusty creatures, perhaps precisely because white men needed to think of them in that way" (1984, 307). With emancipation, he notes, white men's legal access to black women ended. But, he might have added, it continued as white men then exploited black female domestics as well as those black women who were economically impoverished and politically vulnerable (Gwaltney 1993; Guillory 1999). Here once again Williamson allows his heterosexual desire to surface slightly, as he tells us that "black men, now free [sic], denied white men access to the heretofore ultimately satisfying alternative, black women, while white men continued to see black women as superbly sexual creatures, uninhibited, unlimited in venereal appetites and potential satisfactions. Black men were now mates to the sexual earth mothers" (Williamson 1984, 307). This was not exactly the case, as black women working as domestics in white homes were still vulnerable to white men's sexual assaults (Guillory 1999).

No doubt white men, especially southern white men, went crazy after being drubbed by the dreaded Yankees, now that southern women could not always hide their disappointment in them. Now southern white men had to struggle without enslaved black bodies to plant crops, feed their families, satisfy their lusts. No doubt sexual frustration built, all mixed with economic hardship, political calamity, and crisis after crisis. Somehow, amidst all this gendered complexity, the buried and mangled homoerotic relation of white man to black resurfaced, albeit disguised as concern for the white woman. Suddenly white men viewed black men not as childlike "Sambos" of antebellum myth, but rather

> as the insatiable satyr, specially built both physically and mentally for the libidinal women they served. The satyr sought all women, and at his most outrageous he sought especially the white woman heretofore denied him. The white man in the black belts found himself alone and often lonely—his women angelic above him, the black male—fully supported by black women below—and he was strapped with the largely unrewarding task of holding the two apart. Of course, it was a task where success went unnoticed and unrewarded, and his inevitable failure from time to time was conspicuously marked and condemned. One careless moment and another black man crashed through the white lines, plunged into the interior and devoured another fair maiden. The black beast was the only man on earth who had sex with southern white women without inhibition, to the exhaustion of desire, and, *mirable dictu*, without guilt. Black men had achieved what white men, in the Victorian infatuation, had lost—"no-

> fault" sex. Simple death, clearly, was too good for them. (Williamson 1984, 307–308)

In this vividly imagistic passage we see the conflations of race and gender which so typify, complicate, and confuse "race relations" in the United States. Note two items, please.

First, note the spatial imagery of black men "below" and white women "above him." These are imaginary subject positions which white men had assigned to each, places in their imagination. By so positioning white women and black men, white men were indicating their sexualized bond with each, a structurally symmetrical bond. Both were positioned in terms of sexuality, one positively valorized, one negatively. But both were positioned sexually. This imagined symmetry indicates that white men were drawn to both, however repressed was this fact, however determined he was not to admit (to himself or others) the object of his desire. The denial (absence?) of sexual attraction to white women situated her toward the angelic in his mind; the same mechanism of repression operated "inversely" with black men. Black men were not stripped of sexual desire; indeed they became saturated with it. In order to protect themselves from facing their desire for black male bodies, white men positioned the black man as rapaciously desiring the white woman, who was, in fact, the white man himself, if in imaginary drag. In this fantasized drama, both the "white woman" and the "black man" were dissociated but bonded and sexualized elements in the white male mind. Neither was real. Both were coerced into remaining in the place assigned to them.

The second especially striking image in the Williamson passage involves the white man's fantasy of the two imaginary elements coming together, the terms of the black man's alleged rape of the white woman. To describe this "violation" Williamson employs, revealingly, imagery associated with homosexual, specifically anal, rape. As Guy Hocquenghem (1978) has suggested, the anus in the male imaginary symbolizes the interior private self, the opening into a subjectivity denied, camouflaged by the more public phallus. When Williamson imagines what the nineteenth-century white man felt, it was this: that the black man might "plunge into the 'interior'." Given that all this is happening inside the white man's head, it is his *own* interior he is naming. And given that there is no evidence that black men did plot to rape white men, just as there is no evidence that black men plotted en masse to rape white women, this "fear" is unfounded. As imagined, this fear represents inverted desire. As Freud suggested, paranoia masks repressed homosexuality.

For Williamson, the notion of "projection" is sufficient to summarize these slippery psychodynamics, all the more so without the congealing knowledge of queer theory. He writes: "Black leaders who explained the alleged epidemic of rape in the South as the work of white men disguising themselves as Negroes with burnt cork in order to achieve sexual satisfaction and yet escape punishment were not, after all, very far wrong. There was a beast abroad in the land, but he lived in white mind rather than black. White men were projecting upon black men extravagant sexual behavior because they were, at varying levels, denying ordinary sexual behavior to themselves" (1984, 308). The incompleteness of Williamson's view is evident in that last sentence, in the phrase "ordinary sexual behavior." The "beast" may well have been passionate heterosexual desire. But given the actions of white men upon black men at many lynching events, it seems obvious that it was also, perhaps even primarily, disavowed homosexuality, which at that time was commonly referred to as bestiality or sodomy. The "beast" was not the historical, concrete, subjectively alive black man, but the repressed "bestiality" that was the white man's desire for him.

For whatever reason—his own sexual preference?—this fact escapes the renowned historian. Instead he heterosexualizes the phenomenon, insisting that the white man is merely projecting onto the black man the desire he himself feels for the angelic white lady. Working within this heterosexual logic, he puts the matters thusly:

> To paint the black as ugly and then to destroy him was to destroy the evil within themselves. To punish the black was to punish themselves, without hurting themselves, a rare and pleasurable power. Excessive punishment of the sin constituted high penance and ensured re-entry into the communion. If black men were, in essence, having sex with angels while white men abstained, then the punishment of black men must be as awful as the white men's guilt in contemplating himself in the same act, compounded by his frustration in abstaining. Never before had white men in the South elevated white women so high on the pedestal as did this first generation of boys born to Victorian mothers, and never before had they punished any men, white or black, as horrendously as they punished some black men in those years. (Williamson 1984, 308)

If this were the whole story, if black men were only substituting for the white man's dammed-up heterosexual desire for white women, when the break in the dam of repression came, would not *this* desire, heterosexual desire, burst through? Would not the crime of the late nineteenth century—"America's national crime" in Wells's words—be women raped on a massive scale? Of course, white and black women were raped by white men in the final decades of the nineteenth century, but the rape of black women has been obscured by the history of silence regarding black women, specifically black women's sexuality (Guillory 1999; Hammonds 1994). What does surface, what dominates the landscape of late nineteenth-century America, is white men's lynching of black men. The desire kept dammed up by the black rapist fantasy was the desire of white men for black men.

Perhaps the most common form repressed desire can take is identification. As Norman O. Brown has observed: "We make the identification with the lost object by introjecting or incorporating it, not really incorporating it, but passively by making ourselves like it" (1959, 49). The son remakes his desire *for* the father (or best friend) into a desire to *be like* his father (or best friend). It is the consolation prize in my view, but it's the prize straight men accept. Of course, for their sacrifice and patience they receive a mother-substitute later, but that is another story. Given the violence of many heterosexually identified men, they don't seem entirely happy with the arrangement either. For women and children, (straight) men's sexual formation is less a matter of happiness than it is of survival, as the rage of heterosexually identified men is most commonly expressed at the women they "love" and the children to whom they are "devoted."

In the nineteenth century, in the aftermath of slavery and with the rationalizations provided by so-called scientific theories of racial superiority, the rage of straight "white guys" (Pfeil 1995) was aimed at black men. First, black guys had to be set up. Not on a pedestal—that seems to happen a century later in Boston, when their penises are compared to "missiles" (see Disch and Kane 1996); in the late nineteenth century black guys were not yet "studs." Then they were "rapists." Williamson explains: "Thus black men were lynched for having seemingly achieved a sexual liberation that white men wanted but could not achieve without great feelings of guilt. In their frustration white men projected their own worst thoughts upon black men, imagined them acted out in some specific incident, and symbolically killed those thoughts by lynching a hapless black man. Almost any vulnerable black man would do" (1984, 308). Now that last line is not entirely true, as mostly young black men were selected. Nor is the first, as black men could not be said to have "achieved" any "sexual liberation." Liberation from what? Puritanical sexual repression? What did white men know of black men's sexuality anyway ... except from watching ... or participating. This is another white man's fantasy, in this case, the historian's own it would seem.

"In effect," Williamson continues, "the black man lynched was the worst part of themselves" (1984, 308). Was it the gay part? Williamson cannot go there, so he goes to another sanctum of sublimation: the church. "A function of lynching," he offers, suddenly waxing theological, "if not indeed the primary function, was to offer up a sacrificial lamb for the sins of white men." He reminds: "Only about a third of the lynchings had anything at all to do with rape" (308). In reality, there were many fewer instances; Williamson is referring here, if we can rely on Tolnay and Beck's statistics, to the frequency with which lynch mobs claimed lynchings had to do with rape, not to the actual incidence of rape or alleged rape. Despite the fictional character of the rape claim, "yet for more than a decade southern white men insisted that lynching was especially for that crime, and they became blindly furious when Sledd [see chapter 7] and others charged otherwise. White men needed to count every lynching against the awful crime because they needed every such performance they could get to quiet the boiling seas of emotion within themselves" (308–309). Gee, what could those "boiling seas" be?

Very much to his credit, Williamson acknowledges lynching as a sexual passion. Once white men had a taste of a young black man stripped, tortured and castrated, evidently they wanted more: "There could hardly be enough of lynching." And like a young man whose sexual conquest circulates as the coin of the realm of manhood, lynchers, Williamson continues, felt compelled to brag about them: "to get the most out of each, lynchings should be reported widely and in the closest detail as to what the black man did to the victim and what the lynchers did to him." Once again, Williamson uses sexualized imagery to depict the assault, although quickly converting the event into theological terms. So converted, lynching becomes a kind of macabre communion ceremony in which flesh and blood, forever sealed in the Christian mind as the enfleshment of forgiveness, become the occasion for cleansing: "The lynchers, active and passive, needed constant assurance that the evil had been destroyed, precisely because it had not. Castration was an ordinary part of the lynching ritual as applied to alleged rapists, and genital dismemberment was not unheard of. That symbol worked to declare that the evil was abolished permanently from the earth" (all passages in Williamson 1984, 308). In Christ's name, amen.

At this point Joel Williamson recalls William Faulkner's *Light in August* (1932/1968). Faulkner, Williamson tells us, demonstrated an "unflagging instinct for truth about the South," enabling him to capture the sense of lynching "perfectly" in the novel (1984, 308). Percy Grimm, a twenty-five-year-old white man, a bachelor, and a captain in the Mississippi national guard who had missed his true calling by having been born too late to have fought in World War I, hunts down the black Joe Christmas and shoots him. Before Joe dies, Grimm takes a butcher knife and cuts away his genitals. Throwing away the bloody knife, he declares, "Now you'll let white women alone, even in hell" (Faulkner 1932/1968, 439–440). As Williamson points out somewhat acidly, "Percy Grimm himself certainly let white women alone in the body all of his life, but God only knows at what cost or what he did with women in his mind" (1984, 308). Amiri Baraka (1965/1966) knew why Grimm let women alone, why he focused on the black man's genitalia: "Most American white men are ... fags" (216). The former LeRoi Jones ought to know; he may well have "experimented" himself (Simmons 1991).

But a lynching was no ordinary rape; it was gang rape. Mobs of white men—and sometimes white women and children, who, in general, watched—exhibited, in Williamson's (1984) words, "a generalized restlessness before the alleged crime that brought on the lynching." Was this the mob's version of "foreplay"? There was, Williamson continues, often a "weirdly silent proceeding of the mob." And, as Baldwin captures so vividly in his short story excerpted in chapter 1, after the thrill of the castration moment, the white mob experienced a "feeling of satisfaction, of peace, that followed the event," like an orgasm, it is almost too obvious to note. "[A]nd, finally, the fact that if a community had done it once they were likely to do it again" (Williamson 1984, 309). Once you've tried interracial gay snuff sex, there's no going back?

In the myth of the black beast rapist, mutilated and castrated at the lynching tree, race and sex were conflated in ways that would continue, albeit in different—in prison more explicit—forms throughout the twentieth century. Southern white men and women ascribed a mythological sexual potency to black men, which, in their state of civic emasculation, they could not easily ignore, given that they lacked the political means to break through the white fantasy of "their place." White men converted their desire into sexual vulnerability, then relocated it to the white woman. The "return of the repressed" took the form of white men's obsession by what they were sure was the constant threat of rape of helpless white women by sexually rapacious, superstud black men (Williamson 1984). The lynching era is gone now, but the myth of the black man as superstud, as criminal, even as rapist, has faded only a little. More than a few black men themselves have come to believe the myth, as those studies of black hypermasculinity reported in chapter 14 indicate. The fact of having been raped, in intersecting and conflated civic and sexual senses, still reverberates through black masculinity today; the "crisis" continues, a "crisis" only exacerbated by white men's insistence on believing what *they* fantasize.

For the South, Williamson notes, racial "radicalism" was a kind of "rehearsal for unreality" (1984, 309), which characterized the twentieth-century South. The black beast rapist did not exist, Williamson notes; neither did the white notion of racial retrogression. But southern whites were imprisoned in their fantasies long before the 1890s; in the antebellum South they had concocted the apparitions known as "Sambo," the black as the stereotypical child, and "Mammy," the black female nurturer. By the 1890s, Williamson writes, southern whites had "almost totally lost control of their material and mental worlds" (310). That is quite clear in southerners' refusal to pass federal antilynching legislation, reported in chapter 11. Having lost their minds, their grasp of reality, many southerners retreated from this world to the next. Protestant fundamentalism, evangelism, and other forms of "radical" religion spread across the region. In psychoanalytic terms, religion derives from the "ego ideal," that "substitute for longing for the father," the psychogenesis of homosexual desire (Freud 1977, vol. 11, 372; quoted in Simpson 1994, 41). In historical terms, Williamson argues, the idea of the South as "the Bible belt" is a twentieth-century phenomenon. It occurred to no one to describe the South as a Bible Belt before the Civil War. Perhaps the War was the turning point:

> The modern retreat of the South into the City of God might have had its beginnings on the bloody battlefields of the Civil War. That war brought southerners from high to low very suddenly, perhaps, that they are as yet unable fully to absorb the fact of their defeat. ... The retreat of the South from reality might have been furthered by the seizure by the Yankee barbarians and the black defectors of the bodies of the southern states during Reconstruction. ... When southern life recrystallized again after 1915, religion was at stage center. (Williamson 1984, 316)

The "recrystallization" has not dissolved today, as the South remains more politically conservative than the rest of the country, with a few urban exceptions such as Atlanta. Fundamentalist and evangelical religious faiths, especially sects of Protestantism such as the Southern Baptists, remain influential. There are many who believe they must deprive gay men and lesbians of their civil rights to honor "God's will," who still, certainly privately, have their ongoing "reservations" regarding "race." There are still "educated" southerners who resist evolutionary biology, an issue upon which Williamson focuses, recalling the famous "Monkey Trial" in Dayton, Tennessee, in 1924 to underscore "the retreat, the withdrawal of southern culture into otherworldliness" (1984, 316). In perhaps the most contentious curriculum confrontation in American history, the court had upheld a state statute banning the teaching of Darwin's theory of the origin of the species in the public schools. For Williamson (1984), the South's reactionary refusal to enter the twentieth century, personified in William Jennings Bryan's prosecution of teacher John Scopes (defended by Clarence Darrow), marked the South's estrangement from the rest of the country.

> The South held firmly to its cloud, and it would not come down to earth. Neither the whole subjects of science, economics, politics, or race would hold even half the charm for them as a whole people that several dozen evangelists would hold. Further, at least in regard to these men, piety and purity had become a male province, while domesticity and submissiveness was certainly left totally to women. Southerners had, in a sense, shuffled off this moral coil, and they lived, really lived (and by their lights thrived) in that other world. Southern strength in national councils in the twentieth century might, in part, be precisely a function of that talent. The Southerner is, in a sense, the other American distinguished from the real, body-built, getting-in-this-world American. The Southerner is the idealistic American as personified, for instance, in Billy Graham, Sam Ervin, and Jimmy Carter, men who perceive Truth as transcendental. When our armies are defeated on the frontiers, when the crops are burning in the fields, when the barbarians sit steaming, bloody, and furious at the gate, it is southerners who sometimes seem to offer the ultimate haven, the world of the spirit where no hard and violent hand can touch. (Williamson 1984, 316–317)

Perceptive for half the paragraph, Williamson himself succumbs from the southern dissociation from reality in the second half.

There is, of course, something attractive about such a remove from the hustle and bustle of the everyday, the marketplace, of sordid politics and business. But I cannot associate it, as Williamson seems to, with southern culture. Without focusing on the three men Williamson cites—one could just as easily point to Jesse Helms, Jerry Falwell, Pat Robertson, David Duke—I cannot help but conclude that religion in the South may provide psychological solace for troubled white people but it also provides support for their reactionary politics. Southerners have used the Bible to justify not only depriving queer Americans of their civil rights; a generation or so ago the "Good Book" was exploited to justify segregation, and before that lynching, and before that slavery. Now southern white men have to content themselves with the "gracious submission" of their wives, the control of women's bodies (the fanatical campaign against abortion), and of the bodies of other men (obscene self-righteousness over "the homosexual lifestyle," a fine southern phrase if there ever was one). Without denying its private therapeutic functions—I say do whatever gets you through the night—I see little to praise in southern religion. Certainly it plays no major role in moral and civic courage, as Williamson appears to imply, at least for many southern whites.

For African Americans living in the South, the story is somewhat different. As Lillian Smith says through one of her characters in *Strange Fruit*: "Nobody but colored folks believe in heaven. White folks believe in hell" (Smith 1944/1972, 49). Be that as it may, African Americans in the South have used religious inspiration to fight political as well as moral battles. From slave days, the black church provided a separate space wherein black culture could be affirmed and performed free of white surveillance, individual and collective spirits could be revitalized, and hope could be kept alive (see, for instance, Wilmore [1983]). In particular, many nineteenth-century black women were inspired by their religious experience to teach and preach and agitate against seemingly overwhelming odds, as the cases of Ida B. Wells, Sojourner Truth, and Anna Julia Cooper, among others, testify. However, at least one historian of the civil rights movement, Adam Fairclough (1995/1999, 71), believes that historians have exaggerated the importance of the black church in racial politics.

As we saw in chapter 5, even middle-class white women were able to employ conservative Christianity to affirm women's experience, miming the words of conservative men to further the cause of women and children. But for southern white men, religion, while perhaps a personal comfort, has been in its public manifestations consistently disastrous, a rationale for a variety of violences. Fooled into thinking they enjoy direct access to God and that they themselves are His (always His it seems) personally appointed representatives on earth, religion for many southern white men has been primarily pathological. As an educator, it occurs to me that what southerners, indeed, what Americans require, is a systematic program of self-reflection and re-education, a curriculum of social psychoanalysis. Perhaps that would help return us to *this* world, a world of fantasy, flesh, and desire.

III. Men in "Crisis" (Again? Still?)

The white ego insists upon control.

—Michael Awkward, *Negotiating Difference: Race, Gender, and the Politics of Positionality* (1995)

Psychoanalytic concepts now float freely in debates on cultural politics, but there is still a stubborn resistance to the recognition of unconscious fantasy as a structuring principle of our social, emotional, and political life. ... It is in the domain of race, whose violent and sexy fantasia haunts America daily, that our need for an understanding of the psychic reality of fantasy, and its effect in the body politic, is greatest.

—Kobena Mercer, *Welcome to the Jungle: New Positions in Black Cultural Studies* (1994a)

The fears of feminization ... have haunted men for a century.

—Michael Kimmel, *Manhood in America: A Cultural History* (1996)

Since the prime of the Victorian era, men had been in retreat.

—Peter G. Filene, *Him/Her/Self* (1998)

Peter Filene's judgment, you will recall, leaves his colleagues Mark Carnes and Clyde Griffen uneasy (1990; see chapter 6, section I). How can we use the concept of "crisis" when it cannot be delimited in time? When we understand that masculinity as it has evolved species-wide is constructed, is compensatory, defensive, and rests upon an identification with the mother that must be denied, then we understand that masculinity has been in crisis from its mysterious origins in human history (Gilmore 1990; Lerner 1986). We saw in chapter 14 that black masculinity continues to be in crisis, a crisis intensified and complicated by the burdens of racial oppression, itself sexualized and gendered. In this section I want to focus on the ongoing crisis of middle-class, primarily (although not exclusively) white masculinity.

If men are in retreat from their audacious and violent insistence that the world coincide with their fantasy life, then we can be encouraged. Certainly there are men—straight, gay, sexual identity unknown—whose modesty, sensitivity, and (racial and gender) politics give one heart. But these are uncommon; most men are still, in some combination, misogynistic, homophobic, heterosexist, racist. Filene (1998, 228–229) sees the continuities between late nineteenth-century men and late twentieth:

> When the ladies jumped off their pedestals and invaded the male provinces of politics, higher education, employment, and sexuality, men grudgingly gave ground while clinging to whatever privileges they could claim. When the occupational world became increasingly bureaucratized, men still held to the notion of work as their primary source of self-esteem. When the wild West became buried under city streets and suburban lawns and when war was waged by computerized missiles, men still sought the strenuous life by turning the pages of James Bond's murderous exploits or watching twenty-two padded, helmeted athletes collide and tackle every Sunday on the television screen. (228–229)

In the 1970s, most middle-class men were still playing at the "manly" roles their Victorian great-grandfathers had played. Whatever shifts in sex roles had occurred between the three generations of men, Filene (1998) argues, were the result of pressures outside the culture of masculinity, such as pressures from women and changing socioeconomic conditions. "Men changed grudgingly," Filene writes, "making no more than adjustments in order to preserve as much as possible of their privilege and supposed superiority. They reacted, in other words, as most elites do in response to insurgence: defensively rather than creatively, regarding innovation as a loss of power rather than a gain of possibilities" (1998, 229).

Even the radical young men associated with the New Left and the civil rights movement were, by and large, unwilling to revise traditional masculine identities. In the early 1960s, college students and others of student age fought nonviolently for civil rights, were beaten by police and national guardsmen during protests, and when drafted to fight in Vietnam or arrested on a civil rights march, demonstrated their courage in jail or in exile to Canada. The "counter-culture" featured men who espoused peace and wore long hair and loose clothes. But in trespassing the boundaries between masculine and feminine, most of these young male protestors were focused on the injustices of race and imperialism, not of gender (Filene 1998).

The student movement, especially in the North, was run by men. Almost all the leaders were men; women were relegated to errands. When women in both the antiwar and civil rights movements began to protest, men reacted defensively and arrogantly. Stokely Carmichael announced that "the only position for women in S.N.C.C. [the Student Nonviolent Coordinating Committee] is prone" (212). One young man declared after the 1968 uprising at Columbia University, "to be busted is to have balls—to come out on top" (quoted in Filene 1998, 229). For these men, the revolution was not a gendered one.

It became gendered, however. Filene remarks that the contemporary feminist movement was born in these frustrations of movement women in the 1960s. Perhaps, although there are obvious antecedents—among them Betty Friedan's *The Feminine Mystique* in 1957, Simone de Beauvoir's *The Second Sex* in 1947, Elizabeth Cady Stanton and Susan B. Anthony in the nineteenth century—to black and white women's insurrections during the 1960s. Feminism engendered gay liberation, and, clearly, by the early 1970s, another major shift in gender and sex roles was taking place. The impact upon domestic roles was, however, negligible. Working women performed fewer hours of housework per week during the 1970s (for the first time in fifty years), and their husbands performed more. But the division was far from equitable. Husbands performed one-third of the domestic responsibilities—up from one-fifth in the 1960s—but far from fifty-fifty. Moreover, these men typically took care of tasks that could be done at their convenience: yard work, house repairs, and so on. Their wives' household duties, such as preparing meals and child care, had to be done every day, when the situation demanded (Filene 1998). Filene observes: "Instead of seeking equal treatment, most women struggled to be superwomen" (231).

Some men got the point, or tried to. Some began speaking of "men's liberation." Between the 1980s and the 1990s, several "men's movements" emerged, all offering different analyses of the "crisis" of masculinity. The first was launched by those few men inside the New Left who had been deeply influenced by feminist ideas. "We, as men, want to take back our full humanity," proclaimed the Berkeley Men's Center in 1973. "We no longer want to strain and compete to live up to an impossible, oppressive masculine image—strong, silent, cool, handsome, unemotional, successful, master of women, leader of men, wealthy, brilliant, athletic, and 'heavy'" (quoted in Filene 1998, 233–234). By the 1980s, thirty additional men's centers had opened, and several hundred men were meeting each year at a national Conference on Men and Masculinity (Filene 1998).

Just as the 1960s women's movement had taken inspiration from the civil rights movement and the New Left, the profeminist and gay men's movements were descendants of those three forebears (for a succinct history, see Sears 1998). The American Psychiatric Association removed homosexuality from its list of mental disorders, more than half the states repealed their sodomy laws, the Civil Service Commission lifted its ban on hiring homosexuals, and in 1980 the Democratic Party endorsed gay rights. But this modest progress would be short-lived, as would many gay men. In 1982, ten new cases of AIDS were reported each week; in 1984 there were 100. By 1988, there were 62,000 reported cases, and one-half of the infected had died. With the 1980 election, a backlash against "the sixties" was gaining full force, in politics, in religion, and in gender. Conservative women—led by Phyllis Schlafly's STOP-E.R.A. campaign—joined with conservative, recalcitrant men to defeat the Equal Rights

Amendment. Among men there would be several reactionary movements, each attacking feminism and civil rights for gay men and lesbians (Filene 1998).

"I am angry," announced a founder of the National Coalition of Free Men, "that in the name of eliminating sex-stereotyping, feminism has reinforced some of the most fundamental and devastating stereotypes of all: the man as predator ... stalking ... powerful ... base and insensitive ... exploitative and untrustworthy" (Haddad 1985, 285–286; quoted in Filene 1998, 237). If women were victimized by sexism, men were now, many (straight) men felt, being victimized by "the new sexism" created by feminists. Men were being blamed for violence, racism, and the environmental crisis, among other social evils; as chapter 13 makes clear, the charges stand. But whining, middle-class, mostly white men couldn't—can't—see it. It's all a series of "myths," these disingenuous men insisted, in books entitled *The Myth of Male Power* (Farrell 1993); *The Myth of the Monstrous Male* (Gordon 1982); *The Hazards of Being Male: The Myth of Masculine Privilege* (Goldberg 1976).

In fact, these writers explained, most men are saddled with the lifelong economic support of others, military service to the nation, not to mention a self-destructive need to achieve. That men displayed a higher incidence of alcoholism, crime, and disease, culminating in death ten years earlier than for women was not, for these gender reactionaries, evidence that heteronormative masculinity itself was problematical. No. Imagination intact, Warren Farrell claimed that "men are hurting more than women. That is, men are, in many ways, actually more powerless than women" (quoted in Filene 1998, 237). Exhibiting once again that paranoia often masks desire, the author of *The Myth of the Monstrous Male* proclaimed: "Men need their own lobby ... because we're really getting screwed, guys" (quoted in Filene 1998, 238).

These men enjoyed considerable political success, in particular the passage of joint-custody bills in forty-three states and an increased willingness of courts and legislatures to punish mothers who refused visits by fathers. But the main problem concerning divorced fathers was not discrimination against them but delinquency by them. True, mothers were awarded custody of children 70 percent of the time, but that was because fathers never bothered to ask for it. When fathers did ask for custody, much of the time they won it. The fact of the matter was that all too many fathers left their families financially and emotionally stranded. Despite increasingly tough measures against "deadbeat dads" (such as confiscating drivers' licenses and income tax refunds), one-fourth of all custodial mothers in 1991 were not receiving the child support their ex-husbands were obligated to pay, and many others were receiving far less than owed. Even more fathers defaulted on emotional obligations. According to a study that followed 1,000 children of disrupted families during 1976 through 1987, more than 42 percent had not seen their father at all during the previous year; 80 percent had not slept in their father's house during the previous month (Filene 1998).

If a large segment of middle-class, mostly white men felt deprived, Peter Filene (1998) points out, theirs was not political, economic or legal deprivation; it was emotional and spiritual. While their complaints often focused upon their rights as fathers, their underlying need evidently had to do with healing their wounds as men, as sons in particular. But "[i]nstead of exploding masculine myths," Filene comments wryly, "they were hungry to learn the mythology of masculine archetypes and rituals" (1998, 239). Instead of working to ruin the masculinity that left them wounded, they, like their predecessors one hundred years ago, were determined to rebuild it.

Amid chants, tears, dancing, and the beating of drums, poet Robert Bly, storyteller Michael Meade, and Jung psychologist James Hillman exhorted gatherings of men to find their "true selves." "We are living at an important and fruitful moment now," Bly wrote, "for it is clear to men that the images of adult manhood given by the popular culture are worn out; a man can no longer depend on them" (1990, ix; quoted in Filene 1998, 239). Men were feeling anguished and impotent because they had failed to trust themselves and experience their "deep instinctual masculine energies" (Filene 1998, 239). Bly is theorizing here, as Fred Pfeil points out, "an ahistorical, transcultural, and openly mythological definition of full-fledged masculinity, the deep and holy truths of the masculine psyche—that, and a set of instructions for how we readers can get access to it, too" (171). The stages of initiation Bly extracted from his fairy tale sound familiar. First separate from mother, let yourself be mentored by a wise father figure, accept your woundedness and experience your sadness, honor the father energy, find your playfulness and creativity, act on your warrior energy, suffer another wound (probably from the fathers), meet your princess, and become yourself: Wild Man, King, and Lord (Bly 1990; Pfeil, 1995).

Key in this sequence, in object relations terms, is the repudiation of the mother identification and an active identification with the father, reproducing heteronormative, oedipal structures of self, family, and society while individuality is effaced. Bly is clear about the role homosociality plays in this gender formation; when the boy separates from the mother and goes into the wilderness, as well as later on when he leaves it, there must be "older men" to "welcome the young man into the ancient, mythologized, instinctive male world" (15). Whether the boys in ancient Greece, or those in New Guinea who are forced to fellate older men in order to become men (Gilmore 1990), or the male initiates in nineteenth-century American fraternal rites (chapter 6, section V), it is clear older men want to be alone with younger men.

This "ancient" and "instinctive male world" is accessible only outside the culture, in the wilderness; and inside the psyche, through one's "wound." In the course *Iron John* the wilderness evokes a fantasy of preindustrial European and non-Western cultures, the two taken, Pfeil notes, "in classic racist fashion as co-equal and conjoined in the same invariant and wise tradition stretching from African tribal custom to Greek mythology and Old Norse Myth" (1995, 173). Within this "wilderness"—more accurately, within these white male fantasies of past cultures recoded as wilderness—man-hungry young men may take as Iron John guides and mentors, either those imagined elders of non-Western or preindustrial cultures who knew and revered men's ways and wisdom, or their contemporary representatives, such as Bly himself (Bly 1990; Pfeil 1995).

Despite this obvious preference for homosociality, Bly insisted he had no interest in "turn[ing] men against women, nor to return men to the domineering mode that has led to repression of women and their values for centuries;" nor did the men's movement "constitute a challenge to the women's movement" (1990, x). But, as Pfeil reminds us, Bly also argues that feminism, in tandem with the emasculating effects of what Bly (1990) termed "the mode of industrial domination" (1990, 98), has produced a feminized masculinity that is "too weak, too listlessly soft and peaceloving—that is, no real masculinity at all" (Pfeil 1995, 171).

The media tended to present the men's movement in a skeptical light; feminists, too, tended to be critical, pointing out that these gatherings failed to address women's suffering specifically and gender inequities generally. Other feminists accused Bly and other men's movement leaders of supporting the worst features of masculinity, including its aggressivity, misogyny, and homophobia. Queer theorist Mark Simpson insisted: "Bly's *Iron John*, for all its careful prevarication and prefaces, its airy-fairy 'mythopoetics' and its earnest scholarliness, is really a paean to male violence: 'show the sword,' 'get in touch with the wild man,' 'accept what's dark down there,' 'bust them in the mouth'" (1994, 259)! Accept what's "dark"?

I share these criticisms. However, I agree with Peter Filene (1998) that "we should also pay attention to what else lay behind the drumming and dancing" (1998, 240), even if he and I will quickly disagree with what lay "behind" it. Filene takes these men at their word, not always a methodological error. He quotes the president of the Men's Center of Raleigh, North Carolina, in 1989 who said, after a crowd of 200 attended a two-day event with Bly: "I think most men who come [to our programs] are yearning. There's a kind of piece missing. A lot of it has to do with father. Ninety-five percent of the men who come are feeling this distance, a disconnectedness, never having had the interaction with Dad" (quoted in Filene 1998, 240). I start with these men's words, but underscore that while this "distance" and "disconnectedness" may have to do with the absent fathers Moynihan associated with black families, they are also, to some extent, the inevitable consequence of trading desire for identification. To that point I will return at the end of this section.

Bly himself, as Filene points out, welcomed such a focus as he recounted his own coming of age with an adoring mother and a forbidding, alcoholic father. He claims that he became a "soft" kind of guy, unafraid of "his feminine side" and, in shame and anger toward his father, repudiated his masculine side. Only in late-middle age did he appreciate, he said, that his father was a victim of social, specifically women's, expectations. After that realization, Bly continued, he could begin to work out a relationship with his father and, more generally, with his own "masculine energy," what he named "the Wild Man." As Filene observes, "Bly's story turned out to be the story of countless other men" (1998, 240).

Bly's *Iron John* (1990) stayed on the hardback best-seller list for more than a year, and Bill Moyers's P.B.S. profile of Bly ("A Gathering of Men") sold 27,000 videocassette copies and 10,000 transcripts. This was no one-man show, however. By the mid-1990s, men could subscribe to twenty-four different mythopoetic journals and walk into more than forty men's centers. In the classified ads of *Wingspan: Journal of the Male Spirit* (circulation, 120,000), they were invited to attend numerous men's gatherings (Filene 1998).

While many of the participants in the men's movement, such as Fred Pfeil (1995), viewed it as a continuation of the cultural and political movement of the 1960s, there were other men who, in the 1990s, were committed to a rejection of that movement. These gender reactionaries echoed turn-of-the-century "muscular Christianity" advocates (see chapter 5, section VIII) by asserting that Jesus was a macho man. "Christ wasn't effeminate," declared televangelist Jerry Falwell. "The man who lived on this earth was a man with muscles ... Christ was a he-man!" (quoted in Kimmel 1996, 312). As men did one hundred years ago, the current crop of "Christian" gender reactionaries complain about the "chronic absence" of men from church. Approximately one-third of American men report attending church; almost one-half of all American women attend. As did their predecessors, these church promoters worry that the statistics indicate the long-term and disastrous effects of the cultural feminization of the church (Kimmel 1996).

Among the most vigorous campaigners for the current version of "muscular Christianity" are so-called Christian athletes. "You think because I've accepted Christ into my life, I'm passive," baseball player Brett Butler told a reporter. "I play hard. If Christ played this game, he'd slide right into the second baseman, and then he'd help him up. Christ was no wimp" (quoted in Kimmel 1996, 313). Other "Christian" athletes have managed to convert "muscular Christianity" into a second career. Bodybuilder John Jacobs founded "the Power Team," a group of muscled converts who appear to think their feats of "manliness"—breaking through a stack of bricks with one's bare hands, for instance—testifies to the existence of God and the power of their faith. "Jesus Christ was no skinny little man," Jacobs assert. "Jesus was a man's man" (quoted in Kimmel 1996, 314). Singer Michael English doesn't seem to sublimate his love for Jesus; his sexy style suggests he takes the centuries-old formulation of believers as "brides of Christ" somewhat sensually.

For others, contemporary religious experience is gender-coded as a heroic quest. The battle for men's souls is, presumably, no girl's game; spirituality is "not equated with prissiness," and "Jesus, the Bible, and the house of God are not just for sissies and girls" (quoted in Kimmel 1996, 313). The astonishing response to the Christian men's organization called the Promise Keepers testifies to the scale of the current "crisis" of masculinity and to the continued homoerotic appeal of a "muscular Christian" response to it (Kimmel 1996).

Organized by former University of Colorado football coach Bill McCartney, the Promise Keepers embrace conservative Christianity. These men assert that "real men," that is, Christian men, must exercise moral leadership in their families, respect their wives and provide for their children, mirroring Jesus's strength and sexual purity. "We're calling men of God to battle" against promiscuity and permissiveness, McCartney declared. He hit a nerve; more than 20,000 men gathered in the University of Colorado's Folson Stadium in 1992, and 50,000 a year later (Filene 1998). By 1995, more than 700,000—like Bly's adherents these almost all white, middle-aged men—were paying fifty-five dollars each at thirteen sites around the country in what one journalist called "a combination Super Bowl game and revival meeting" (quoted in Filene 1998, 242).

Like the earlier anti-E.R.A. movement leaders, the spokesmen for Promise Keepers focused on feminists, declaring that they had undermined God's plan for the family. The first step every Christian man must take, Tony Evans asserted, "is sit down with your wife and say something like this: 'Honey, I've made a terrible mistake. I've given you my role. ... Now I must reclaim that role.' Don't misunderstand what I'm saying here," Evans continued. "I'm not suggesting that you *ask* for your role back, I'm urging you to *take* it back." This nonsense found a receptive, even eager, audience among conservative men. As a United Methodist minister remarked: "You don't come here and feel like you're losing your masculinity because of your faith" (quoted passages in Filene 1998, 242), a statement echoing conservative men's efforts to "re-masculinize" Christianity nearly one hundred years ago (see chapter 5, section VIII).

A Scatological Transsexualism

The year 1993 may well come to be seen as a key year in the current "crisis" of masculinity. As we have just reviewed, throughout the 1980s there had been ongoing discussion regarding a "crisis of masculinity," this one (like the one in the 1890s) stimulated by the advances of women and African Americans and the increased visibility of queers, mixed with those traumatic economic upheavals of post-Fordism (heavy "male" industries were sent south as "female" service industries replaced them). Incontrovertible evidence of the "crisis," Mark Simpson (1994) suggests, was the furor which erupted in 1993 over newly elected President Clinton's pledge to end the Pentagon's ban on lesbians and gays in the military. Suddenly, gender reactionaries howled, the final manly citadel, the last place where men could be sure that men were men, was also under siege. Adding to masculinist anxiety was that women were being assigned to certain combat positions for the first time in both British and the American armed forces. "[I]f women and queers could be soldiers too," as Simpson phrased it, "then what was there left for a man to do that was manly; where and how was virility to show its mettle?" (1994, 2).

Not only did the military force the commander in chief to back down, but the gay issue helped turn white male voters against the Democratic Party (Filene 1998). The reaction is, of course, the point; how fragile heterosexual identification must be if the thought of sharing showers provokes major panic? "I was not alone," Leo Bersani confides, "in being astonished by the prominence of shower rooms in the erotic imagination of heterosexual American males. Fear on the battlefield is apparently mild compared to the terror of being 'looked at'" (1995, 16). Bersani recalls that the *New York Times* reported on April 3, 1993, that a radar instructor who chose not to fly with an openly gay sailor, Keith Meinhold, feared that Meinhold's "presence in the cockpit would distract him from his responsibilities." The instructor "compared his 'shock' at learning that there was a gay sailor in his midst to a woman discovering 'a man in the ladies' restroom'" (quoted passages in Bersani 1995, 16). Bersani (1995, 16–17) comments:

> Note the curious scatological transsexualism in our radar instructor's (let us hope momentary) identification of his cockpit with a ladies restroom. In

> this strange scenario, the potential gay attacker becomes the male intruder on female privacy, and the "original" straight man is metamorphosed, through another man's imagined sexual attention, into the offended, harassed, or even violated woman.

We've seen such a relocation of desire before.

The compromise policy that was finally adopted ("don't ask, don't tell, don't pursue") suggests, Bersani points out, that even more dangerous than the presence of homosexuals in the military (we've been there for as long as anyone can remember) is the prospect of admitting that we're there. Why? Bersani answers by suggesting that the homoeroticism already pervasive in military life risks being made explicit to those many men who at once deny and enjoy homoeroticism. The game is up when self-confessed gay men decline to deny what is essential to the military, the pleasure of physical and psychological intimacy among men. Worse, and here he seems to be relying on a Butlerian notion of "performativity," Bersani suggests the most serious danger in queer Marines being open about their preferences is that they might begin "to play at being Marines. Not that they would make fun of the Marines. On the contrary: they may find ways of being so Marine-like that they will no longer be 'real' Marines" (1995, 17–18). After all, it is a certain unself-conscious machismo that keeps recruits thinking muscles not sex when they pass the sign at Camp Pendleton: "Stay hard!" (Zeeland 1996, photograph opposite 101).

For Susan Bordo (1994), one of the most revealing elements of the debate has to do with the fact that those who have argued against the disclosure of sexual orientation readily admit that there have always been gay men in the military, not to mention straight men being gay, as we saw in chapter 14 (section V). As Bersani points out, these men do not seem to mind gays in the shower as long as they can't recognize them, as long, that is, as they can suppress their knowledge that homosexuals are indeed in there with them, as long as they can continue to deny the fact that homosexuality is present in them. What is obvious to Bordo is that the arguments against "integrated" locker rooms and showers are not about regulating gay behavior; they are about "protecting *heterosexual* men from certain unacceptable thoughts and feelings of their own. … Described bluntly, this is a situation in which it is being proposed that the civil rights of one group are less worthy of protection than the *illusions* of another" (Bordo 1994, 283; emphasis in original).

Key to the current crisis in masculinity is the continued political progress of women (both lesbian and "straight") and of queer men, a progress that while slight still throws hegemonic masculinity into a panic. That panic, I trust is clear by now, carries within it both a racial and sexual fear, the fear that straight white guys will realize they are neither straight nor white. Bersani's (1995, 27–28) analysis hints at this mixed, convoluted, pervasive fear:

> Blacks are a dangerous and inferior race, and they may destroy us. But not even racists could ever fear that blacks will seduce them into becoming black. Homophobia, on the other hand, is precisely that: to let gays be open about their gayness, to give them equal rights, to allow them to say who they are and what they want, is to risk being recruited. … The

> pleasure promised by that recruitment must be very great indeed in order to offset the fear of possible death from A.I.D.S. after the recruitment is successful. ... In his curious conviction that thousands of heterosexuals could easily be converted to the homosexual cause, the homophobic male must be "remembering" a lost jouissance (that is, female sexuality as a male body has in fantasy experienced it).

In the white male mind, women (black and white) and black men have been intertwined for a very long time. But I am not so sure white men don't fear they might become black. Not literally of course, but in terms of those features of black masculinity which they imagine as so appealing, against which they defend themselves so aggressively. For some white men—think of Norman Mailer's (1957) "white negro"—a "transracialized" identity is explicitly appealing.

Or is it black men themselves who are so appealing to white men? Certainly that is Leslie Fiedler's impression, as we saw in the last chapter. Fiedler attributes white fantasies of interracial male bonding to a guilt-ridden search for redemption; no doubt there is plenty of guilt (denied) to stimulate searches galore. Michael Kimmel suggests these white male fantasies are "screens" against which white manhood is projected, against which it is defined. "The nonwhite male," he continues, "stands in for women" (1996, 66). Well, perhaps not as women, although certainly as "other," for as Kimmel notes, this interracial "homoerotic passion is never the passion of equals; the nonwhite is either the guide or exemplar or the Rousseauinan 'noble savage' who, in his childlike innocence, is more susceptible to the wiles of civilization" (66). In this fantasized inequality is revealed the white obsession with subjugation. In the positionality of "master" resides a split-off, repressed identification with "slave." In prison it would be performed.

A New Leaf?

When black intellectuals say black masculinity is in crisis today, they are, as we saw in chapter 14, speaking not only of psychologically wounded sons, as Bly articulated. They are speaking of physically wounded, murdered, and dead sons. They are speaking of incarcerated sons, whose lives have been taken away from them by the same system of racialized criminalization their great-grandfathers suffered in the South's convict-lease system and in other forms of "legalized lynching." The current crisis of black masculinity is not only psychological, not only a matter of existential meaning and well-being, it is a matter of life and death. Without doubt the institutionalized forms of racism—poverty, politics, education, and so on—crush black men and black women in the United States. But black men face something extra. Like black women, they too are exploited in sexual ways, but for black men that exploitation positions them homosexually in a heterosexist, homophobic, patriarchal culture. As "men," heteronormative black masculinity is necessarily in "crisis," predicated as masculinity is upon the denial of lack and specularity and alterity (Silverman 1992). But this "crisis" is aggravated by the racial politics of masculinity in America, the unacknowledged homoerotic lacing the white-male gaze of subjugation. If black men too have been "raped" by white men, is it any surprise some become enmeshed in compensatory and sometimes sexualized patterns of violence?

So American "men"—black and white—remain in "crisis," a crisis that is simultaneously racial, gendered, psychological, and political, all intersecting categories of historical experience and scholarly analysis. "Still" and "again" white men especially worry over their status as "men" and look to black men with a convoluted mix of fear and yearning. Some white men try to become "wild men" as some black men try to become the dignified patriarchs they imagined their precolonial, West African predecessors to be (see chapter 14, section II). Other white men imagine themselves as stand-ins for God, vis-à-vis whom wives are to be positioned in "gracious submission." What do these various events add up to? "Not *a* movement," Peter Filene judges, "but certainly a commotion" (1998, 242). A remarkable number of middle-class men, both black and white, have been raising basic if muddled questions about themselves in the world. Why? Filene (1998, 242–243) makes clear the parallels with the nineteenth-century "crisis" of masculinity, then points to a difference:

> Prodded by the women's movement, gay liberation, and economic pressures, they were asking what it meant to "be a man." They had done the same a century earlier and had emerged with ambivalent answers: acknowledging "the new woman" while stigmatizing homosexuals as "inverts" and clinging to fantasies of the strenuous life. But the late-twentieth-century questions were not simply an episode of *déja vu*. Amid traditional stereotypes and ambivalence one also saw men beginning to perforate the partition between "masculine" and "feminine" identity. (242–243)

If that is true, here is where our pedagogical work might begin. But, if Fred Pfeil is right, it won't be easy. First there is the profound defensiveness of many heterosexually identified men, Pfeil, on occasion, included. That is evident in his cautionary note regarding the likelihood of straight guys changing. "But notice," he writes quite rightly if defensively, that in many critiques "white straight masculinity comes in only one flavor ... and it is bad; and white straight men must stop putting and living it out, and put out something else instead" (Pfeil 1995 ix). Of course, "hegemonic" masculinity is variable; not all heterosexually identified men are violent. It is also true, as Pfeil observes, that one's gender script cannot be rewritten as easily as text can be moved around on a computer screen. Of course "heterosexuality" is suspect to those of us who appreciate its instability and its lie—that there can be pure heterosexual desire that isn't, in America, also repressed racialized homosexual desire. But I must say Pfeil seems a bit whiny when he mourns that "it is by no means clear to me that there is much room within progressive culture for any version of white straight masculinity to take its place in the ensemble of other racial, sexual and gender identities as 'simply one identity among others'" (Pfeil 1995, ix). That day is long off, but not due to lesbians' and gay men's intolerance; that day is postponed because you straight guys can't give it up. You insist on staying on top, playing it straight. You have to, perhaps—it's all you've got.

Yet, curiously, playing it straight—italicize the *playing*—may parody heteronormativity, the "drag ball production of realness," as Butler (1993, 131) so memorably phrased it. The notion of playing at being a "man" or a "woman" recalls the miming of Christian feminists, or Jim Crow–era African Americans, who played roles expected of them with sufficient force as to destabilize them. Contemporary feminist theory has employed this idea, conceived as mimicry, in ways which suggest how playing it straight, or being "black" might help give birth to a new age. The mimic, Luce Irigaray (1985) writes, "must assume the feminine role deliberately. Which means already to convert a form of subordination into an affirmation, and thus to begin to thwart it" (76).

As Carole-Anne Tyler (1994) has pointed out, what Irigaray is suggesting is not "taking it on" but "putting it on" so as to display the feminine role as a put-on, a fake rather than the natural or real thing. The mimic mimes masculinist fantasies of the feminine, Irigaray continues, but "so as to make 'visible,' by an effect of playful repetition, what was supposed to remain invisible: the cover-up of a possible operation of the feminine in language" (1985, 76). This is, as Tyler observes, "a femininity under the sign of ironic negation; the woman is not what she appears to be, not where she appears to be" (1994, 235). For, mimicry points to the "elsewhere" which is the "real" location of women even as she seems to be in her usual place (Irigaray 1985, 76; Tyler 1994, 235). Suddenly it seems "men" are impersonating "men" rather than being, simply, authentically, "themselves." Like simulacra, would "race" and "gender" begin to destabilize in exaggerated performative representations of themselves?

The political and pedagogical possibilities of miming await further elaboration. For now, let us be clear about the problem, the problem of hegemonic masculinity: racialized, misogynistic, homophobic. As feminist psychoanalysis—object relations theory in particular—has suggested, the problem with men is not that they have not separated enough from mother, but that they have separated *too much*. As Michael Kimmel (1996) observes, the structure of a "self-made" masculinity, of a manhood constantly tested, to be proved, requires the repudiation of femininity, a repudiation at times almost hysterical in its shrillness: hypermasculinity. In the nineteenth century this process of male self-division became socially structured in the "separate spheres" ideology, with desexualized, saintly mothers laboring at home, and rugged competitive men at work in a public sphere they controlled and conflated with manhood. Racialized, such manhood denied Victorian femininity to black women, rendering them lascivious and sexually available, and denied manhood to black men, who were castrated symbolically and, on occasion, literally.

What has changed today? Except for those conservative men who apparently yearn for the nineteenth century (and an imaginary one at that), women are no longer on a pedestal. Still, for many men, women are not "real." For many, women remain sexual objects. In object relations terms, because boys, in order to become "men," must abandon those emotional and relational potentials suggested by terms such as nurture, sensitivity, and emotional responsiveness, they become, to variable and changing extents, desubjectified and disembodied, liable to self-division and the multiplication of "others." These projected fragments of their unconscious get mixed with collective fantasies, that is, cultural myths, as well as political exigencies, social structures, economic imperatives, all formed by and expressed in specific historical moments. One hundred years ago this complex admixture erupted in lynching. In our time, in prison—that mirror of outside society undistorted by the presence of the women men use to camouflage their fantasies—the queer character of racial politics and violence is unmistakable.

If mothers embody relationality, that is, the potential for responsibility, care, and nurture, why should men wish to dissociate from them? Why, as Kimmel (1996) asks pointedly, would men's movement leaders counsel men to reject their mothers, run away (on a raft?), and focus on "healing the father wound"? Rather, Kimmel advises, men should heal the *mother* wound, which suggests, in part, reexperiencing the repressed intimacy of the pre-oedipal period. This also suggests reentering the domestic sphere through shared parenting, as Nancy Chodorow (1978) recommended and Kimmel and others endorse. Perhaps through shared parenting, fathers might cultivate modes of relation that would allow their sons to experience nurturance and care as "masculine" as well as feminine. "Such reconnection," Kimmel writes, "is also about responsibility, at work and at home, such responsibilities as nurturance, compassion, and accountability—in short, responsibilities that have become equated with the conditions for emasculation, not demonstration of manhood. Frankly, I'd prefer more Ironing Johns and fewer Iron Johns" (1996, 318).

Quips aside, Kimmel moves to sketch the outlines of "the American manhood for the future," a manhood not based on obsessive self-control, defensive exclusion of others, or frightened escapes to the "frontier," today bifurcated into "inner" and "outer" space. Almost sounding as if he were running for political office, Kimmel (1996, 333) asserts that:

> We need a new definition of masculinity for a new century, a definition that is more about the character of men's hearts and souls than about the size of their biceps or their wallets. A definition that is capable of embracing differences among men and enabling other men to feel secure and confident rather than excluding them. A definition that centers around standing up for justice and equality instead of running away from commitment and engagement. We need a democratic manhood.

How one wishes those lines were uttered from one running for office.

For Kimmel, democratic manhood means a gender politics of inclusion, of opposition to injustice based on difference. He reminds us of profeminist Floyd Dell who wrote that "feminism will make it possible for the first time for men to be free" (1914, 1; quoted in Kimmel 1996, 333). Kimmel is thinking in terms of the politics of the public sphere where profeminist men would join in an alliance—a "rainbow coalition"?—with others working for a restructuring of American society which embraces diversity and ensures equality for women, people of color, and gay men and lesbians. For too long, as Kimmel (1996) reminds, American conceptions of equality have tended to mean the obliteration of difference.

But the "democratization" of American manhood cannot occur solely within political institutions or within educational ones such as the school. It will occur within the human subject. There is a politics of reason within the self, a politics in which modes of identification, of access to experience, of understanding in its multiple forms are privileged, refined, ignored, repressed. While shared parenting is needed and may in fact yield generations of men unafraid of relational bonds, it is insufficient. It is time to think about a conscious education of gender, in which the curriculum might be conceived as *currere*, a running of the course which requires remembrance of things past and brutalities present. Understood as an "autobiographics of alterity," *currere* requires us to focus not only upon the production of whiteness and masculinity and their intersections and conflations, but their dissolution and re-formation. As Fanon knew: "For Europe, for ourselves, and for humanity, comrades, we must turn over a new leaf, we must work out new concepts, and try to set afoot a new man" (1968, 316). To do so requires us to intensify the current "crisis" of masculinity, to cause its collapse, and help midwife, through teaching, a more democratized manhood. That suggests a libidinal politics that few want to face, a politics in which hegemonic oedipal sexual structuring is regressed and earlier maternal identifications reclaimed.

At this historical juncture in the West, a democratization of the white male "self" probably means experiencing the "negative" oedipal complex. If one is heterosexually identified, it means reclaiming projected gendered and racialized fragments as well as repudiated identifications, including that pre-oedipal identification with the mother. Such a process of regressive reclamation—an individuated as well as collective process that is by no means simple or self-evident—would function to negate the most basic premise of male subjectivity: an identification with masculinity. In so doing it lets the genie out of the bottle. Through the privileging of those repudiated "minority" elements of self, a racialized and gendered democratization of self, that is, a progressive self-realization, might begin. Through such self-restructuring a public political program supporting the democratization of society might follow (see Young-Bruehl 1996). That is the progressive dream for our time, a queer progressive dream in which democratization and self-realization imply homosexualization, a gendered historical stage foreshadowing, perhaps, the end of racial violence in America.

IV. Homosexual Panic, Latent Energy, and "[t]he Political Unconscious of White Masculinity"

—Kobena Mercer, *Welcome to the Jungle: New Positions in Black Cultural Studies* (1994a)

We have not yet reached our ideal in American civilization.

—Anna Julia Cooper, "A Voice from the South" (1892/1998)

The principal target of the religious right has been displaced from abortion to homosexuality.

—Leo Bersani, *Homos* (1995)

Every fear is a desire.

—Reginald Shepherd, "On Not Being White," in Joseph Beam, ed., *In the Life: A Black Gay Anthology* (1986)

Why don't we encourage homosexuality in our culture?

—Brian Pronger, *The Arena of Masculinity: Sports, Homosexuality and the Meaning of Sex* (1990)

Homosexuality is a genie that is out of the bottle.

—Mark Simpson, *Male Impersonators: Men Performing Masculinity* (1994)

As Eve Kosofsky Sedgwick has famously observed: "Modern homosexual panic represents, it seems, not a temporally imprisoning obstacle to philosophy and culture, but, rather, the latent energy that can hurtle them far beyond their own present place of knowledge" (1990, 139). Latent energy, indeed. Let us break, continue to break, the silence on homosexuality and release that latent energy. First, it needs to be broken in the elementary and secondary school curriculum. The omnipresence of homosexuality culturally and historically needs to be taught in the humanities, arts, and social studies, across the curriculum whenever possible. As queer theorists of education have insisted, knowledge is, however, not enough (see Pinar 1998a). Simply informing homophobic heterosexist students hardly guarantees "tolerance" for "diversity." Knowledge guarantees nothing except the end of ignorance.

But that *is* something. There will be those who will be moved by the facts, who will not only come to respect homosexuality as significant and crucial in the human experience, but perhaps choose it for themselves, as a political protest, as a deeply satisfying way of life. Ida B. Wells knew the power of knowledge: "The very frequent inquiry made after my lectures by interested friends is, 'What can I do to help the cause?' The answer always is, 'Tell the world the facts.' When the Christian world knows the alarming growth and extent of outlawry in our land, some means will be found to stop it" (1892b/1969, 101). Wells soon came to realize she had overestimated the moral righteousness of the "Christian world," but she never lost faith in telling the truth. Nor must we.

The "outlawry" in our time is the sex/gender system which compels sexuality, gender, and desire, a totalitarian regime in which women are units of currency in a male economy. In the United States, it is a also a racialized economy in which black men remain trapped in the gaze of white men, a gaze effacing black subjectivity and individuality, often leaving black men with two basic options of self-presentation: either "studs" or "criminals." In such a racist regime "white men" imagine themselves to be both "white" and "men," but these are defensive and compensatory, cover-ups. White men are neither, but until the violence, intrapsychic and social, of compulsory heterosexuality ends, men will continue to re-enact the violence they have undergone within; women (black and white) will continue to be stalked, raped, and murdered, children abused, black men imprisoned. All are victims of a sex/gender system that divides the self in binaries and in so doing multiplies "others."

The present sex/gender system can be understood, in part, as the twentieth-century settlement of that late nineteenth-century "crisis" in male gender. Mark Twain lived through that dramatic transformation. In addition (and partly due) to economic, political, cultural (in religion, for instance), racial, and gendered (such as feminism) shifts, there emerged distinct categories of sexual identity (homosexual and heterosexual), that is, sexualities characterized by their same-gender or different-gender preferences, where such sexual identities had not been distinctly recognized before. Twain lived through this massive transformation and experienced some of its effects in himself as well as observing them in others (Looby 1995).

By projecting his castration fantasy onto the black man, the white man disclosed his own subject-position as feminine vis-à-vis the black man. In the nineteenth-century "crisis" of masculinity, the southern white man identified with imaginary white women and "regressed." Intolerable to his (tattered) self-conception as a southern gentleman, he dissociated himself from the process by imagining it as racial rather than sexual. But under the stress of defeat and Reconstruction, it was the southern white man who was the one regressing, from the oedipal toward the pre-oedipal phase, despite the "complicated eyes" of his "mother," that is, the woman who greeted him upon return from war, in the ruins of the life "rebels" had bragged they would defend. Rather than face the facts—political or psychological or racial or gendered—postbellum southern white men fixated on muscular young black men, identifying themselves at the imaginary site of frail white femininity. Shattered, they imagined themselves penetrated, against their will, by supersexual black men who did nothing else but dream of rape. In prison this fantasy came true.

Perhaps the queer character of racial politics is peculiarly American due in part to the circumstances of the nation's birth, in the parricide that constituted the oedipal moment of the former colonies. In murdering the father, as Fiedler observed, Americans became fatherless sons and daughters, brothers and sisters rather than men and women. Focusing on the former, Micheal Kimmel says much the same: "American manhood had been born as the Sons of Liberty threw off the yoke of a tyrannical father. In but one generation the sons had grown to manhood and had turned themselves into fathers without sons" (1996, 58). Is it any surprise that when the nation was perceived to be in racial crisis in the 1960s, white men (in the Moynihan Report) obsessed over matrifocality and absent fathers? Is it any wonder that when (mostly white) men felt themselves to be in "crisis" during the 1990s they yearned for a mythological manhood an absent father had denied them?

Nineteenth-century romantic male-male friendship may or may not have been sexualized in general, but it is clear that during Twain's lifetime *non*chaste homosocial friendship, sometimes interracial, was becoming increasingly visible. That fact may suggest, Christopher Looby (1995) points out, that the relationship between Huck and Jim as Twain portrayed it may represent a more literal reflection on actual social conditions than Fiedler (1966; 1948/1995) may have known. To illustrate, Looby points to an incident reported in 1881 in the *St. Louis Medical and Surgical Journal.* There Dr. William Dickinson discussed a case of sodomy in Mark Twain's hometown of Hannibal, Missouri, a case that involved an eighteen-year-old who was "known to the police as an abandoned character" and a thirteen-year-old "street gamin" (roughly the age and status of Huck Finn) who was partly persuaded and partly pressured into anal intercourse. "This is a crime which however *frequently committed*, is rarely brought to the knowledge of the police," Dickinson observed (quoted in Katz 1983, 179; in Looby 1995, 546, emphasis added).

Foucault and other historians of sexuality refer to the 1860s and subsequent decades as the period when the "homosexual" as a social identity was invented. Looby (1995) notes that the mere temporal coincidence of this emergence of a distinctive homosexual identity within the charged racial atmosphere of these same decades (i.e., the Civil War, Reconstruction, Radical Racism) points to a certain confluence of racial and sexual identity in everyday life, in complicated and often explosive ways. Looby suspects that what Fiedler was sensing was something more than a contingent intersection of sexual and racial categories of the period. He hypothesizes that "the dominant form of subjectivity in this period of America—white heterosexual manhood, whose prescribed object of desire was white heterosexual womanhood—was constituted by perpetually disavowing its homoerotic desire for black men" (Looby 1995, 546).

What is at stake then, in what Fiedler termed the "national myth of masculine love," was not, as Fiedler theorized it, boyish or asexual desire for the black male other, "but a fully sexed desire, a desire on the repression and punishment of which dominant white masculinity was historically founded" (Looby 1995, 546–547). In this respect, then, the "crisis" of nineteenth-century white masculinity was also, Looby is suggesting, primarily a function of the disavowal of desire for the black male body.

Looby reminds us that in the nineteenth century, white men obsessed over black men as erotic threats to white women; popular culture was riddled with images of hypermasculine black men as sexual predators consumed by an irresistible lust for white women. "If," Looby continues, "in the psyches of white men the most charged homosocial rivalry for women was with black men (or, more accurately, with an imaginary black sex fiend), one result would be that the bonds between white man and black (as aversive as they ordinarily were) would then be the bonds at most risk, so to speak, of mutating into homoeroticism" (1995, 547). Recalling Freud's (1911/1963) account of paranoia as a consequence of the repression of homosexual desire, "white men's exaggerated sense of the sexual threat posed to them by black men might well be understood as a defensive response to a wish-fantasy of loving a black man" (Looby 1995, 547).

"My God ... this whole thing a horrible mistake?" asked Judge Horton after learning from one of the examining physicians that Ruby Bates and Victoria Price could not have been gang-raped by nine black men (quoted in Carter 1969/1979, 215; see chapter 12). Is that what white racism is, "a horrible mistake," desire and love disavowed and mixed with politics, economics, and a "crisis" of white masculinity that is structural as well as historical? Is, then, teaching white men to experience (and, preferably but not necessarily, to act on) that desire a key moment in antiracist education?

I am not arguing here in favor of "recruitment," a military idea heterosexists project onto homosexuals which more accurately depicts their own aggressive tactics, demanding that their sons and daughters—everyone's sons and daughters—couple and produce children, children which now threaten to overwhelm the earth's deteriorating ecosystem as the world's population exceeds the capacity of the planet to support it. It bears mentioning that in addition to all the causes of the deepening ecological crisis our children may not easily survive overpopulation is often acknowledged, while its relation to compulsory heterosexuality is not. Of course there is birth control, but that has not been wholly effective. From an ecological point of view, it is imperative that there be a massive shift in sexual orientation.

As ecofeminists know, misogyny and the rape of the earth are not unrelated (Collard 1989; Merchant 1996; Salleh 1997; Spretnak 1997). Paul Hoch also understood: "The rape of nature—and the ecological disaster it presages—is part and parcel of a dominating masculinity gone out of control" (1979, 137). Perhaps a consciously chosen homosexuality can enable men to identify with, not simply exploit and destroy, the earth. As Essex Hemphill tells us, "There was no other way for me to know the beauty of Earth except through the sexual love of men, men who were often more terrified than I, even as they posed before me, behind flimsy constructions of manhood, mocking me with muscles, erections, and wives" (1991, xxviii). The fear of the male body embedded in homophobia functions to dissociate the heterosexually identified male subject not only from his own flesh, but from the skin of the earth as well.

Racism, misogyny, homophobia, ecocrisis: are these not enough to encourage us to stop propping up heterosexuality as "natural," "God-given" and "moral"? Compulsory heterosexuality is none of these. Given divorce rates, crimes against women and children and demonized racial "others," not to mention those unrecorded moments of misery that remained buried with the deceased, can we not say that compulsory heterosexuality, with its misogyny and suppression of homosexual desire, is an ongoing social disaster? Granted, homosexuality is no "magic" cure to the problems of humanity. By itself it will not make human evil disappear, although I do think it would break its spell. Certainly the rape of women would stop. More than a few gay men dislike women, but this form of misogyny is much milder and more easily corrected through education and cultural politics than the profound resentment those men forced to desire them feel, deny, then express, often violently.

Frantz Fanon understood the queer character of white racism. In *Black Skin, White Masks* he asserted simply: "[t]he Negrophobic man is a repressed homosexual" (Fanon 1967, 156). But that's not all "he" is, of course, and so racism will not disappear if, suddenly, all men could reclaim their mothers and become gay. Some white gay men still deride those who pursue black men as "dinge queens," and those white men who fixate on black men still efface black male subjectivity as they lust after black bodies. But these are hardly equivalent to the vicious political and material exploitation and emasculation of black men at which straight white men are experts. On a "queer planet" (Warner 1993), black men may for a time still suffer entrapment within the white male gaze, but being desired sexually is not exactly the problem that lynching was, that being imprisoned is, that being trapped in compulsive hypermasculinity is. A new regime of voluntary heterosexuality and chosen homosexuality cannot be worse than the current heterosexualized crisis of black masculinity. Then too, if the world were queer, "queer" would change.

No, global homosexualization will not eradicate human evil, would not dispel the multitude of problems we face as a species. Of course, each of these must be understood and acted upon multidimensionally, never reduced to any one element, homosexual or economic or religious. Homosexualization is not utopian; in fact, after Morris (1999), we might term it dystopian. But acknowledging intellectually and psychosocially the homosexual dimensions of racism and misogyny in their various cultural and historical specificities can only help us. First we must formulate a curriculum for human survival, one supporting a "queering" of the species.

In schools we need a queer curriculum that challenges the heterosexual matrix, provides a curricular version of affirmative action for homosexual topics and subjects, including interdisciplinary explorations of conceptually intersecting problems, such as race and gender. Why is lynching and the struggle against it so underemphasized, even omitted altogether in more than a few high-school American history courses? Why is prison rape a subject for jokes only? Why are sports extracurricular rather than as a serious subject for feminist and gender analysis all might study? When will the high schools problematize, not celebrate, "sport"?

No time soon, of course. The world appears nowhere ready to acknowledge that gender is socially constructed, and that in its present constructed forms it is intertwined with racism and misogyny. In the United States the so-called religious right appears to have lost the battle to control women's bodies, that is, the abortion issue, at least for the moment. Do they feel cornered, desperate for an issue which they fantasize will bring down God's wrath and make America the heavenly state they imagine it was always meant to be? Homosexuality appears—I write this in July 1998, a week after the newspaper campaign of "compassion" in which "Christians" call for homosexuals to seek God's help to change—to be that issue. Does this issue come to the surface now in these reactionary groups because the other two elements of the "triumvirate," "race" and "women's bodies," are beyond their grasp? No longer able to claim constitutionality and "states' rights" to protect lynching, no longer able, except criminally, through murder, to possess women's bodies, the right wing clings to what's left of their hatred, that is, what's left that they can express publicly: that which is the "queer."

We "queers" remain in a defensive position, criminalized in most states, deprived of basic constitutional protections in all. Still, it is important not to succumb to those embattled and embittered positions to which the right wing presses us. We should take heart from battles and struggles far worse than ours. Remember the mutilated bodies of black men swinging from southern trees. Remember the unbelievable courage of Ida B. Wells, the determination of the N.A.A.C.P. and those who led it: W. E. B. Du Bois, Walter White, James Weldon Johnson. Recall the leadership of Jesse Daniel Ames. We gay men know straight men are liars, we know some—many?—have had gay experiences, that all of them know it's not a far distance to travel from one pole to the other (as it were). After all, gay men are "men."

As such, we, especially we "white" gay men, cannot privilege ourselves, as a relatively oppressed group, in a morally superior position. First of all, we are liars too. The truth is it is not such a far distance for us to travel to the heterosexual side. Many of us have been there, are there now. We are not alone. How many married men, loving husbands and devoted fathers, have, despite themselves, the occasional if unwelcome gay fantasy? How many wives daydream about the woman next door? Certainly we know that many men can't seem to get enough of watching muscular young men on the T.V. screen—yes, "sport" it's called. The "religious" right is right on this point—we could change. For some it would be more difficult than for others. The point is we won't: the right wing—in their vicious self-delusive righteousness, stubbornly literalistic (mis)reading of the Bible—are the ones who will do the changing. Or at least behave themselves. Perhaps we should take out ads offering God's help in their struggle to escape the prisons such "respectable" people misunderstand as "normal" and "righteous." After all, God forgives them their miming of biblical texts to enrich and empower themselves at the material and spiritual expense of the very ones Jesus made a point to embrace. Is not God thankfully promiscuous in her love and forgiveness? Is not promiscuity an appropriate model for a queer sensual ethics?

Second, we queers, white men specifically, suffer racism and misogyny too, although I think for many of us, despite our privileged class positions, the experience of oppression makes for many some degree of humility. But like antiracist and antimisogynist educators, we cannot rely on psychological change alone if we work for social justice. Progressive politics and ethics must be taught and further elaborated, and the relations among the three major great movements of the late twentieth century—civil rights, feminism, queer struggle—made clear, in bars, in the streets, in the classroom, and in bed. While the course ahead may be unclear and the odds overwhelming, we can take heart (and perhaps tactics) from the struggles of one hundred years ago.

Ida B. Wells poked holes in the white man's imagination by inverting the politics of "true manhood" and linking black men's oppression through lynching to black women's oppression through rape. Both were forms of racism, a sexualized subjugation in which men exploited black bodies not only for sexual pleasure, for profit, but for the psychological inflation of beleaguered male egos. As Hartman observes, white abolitionists imagined themselves as suffering slaves, thought they knew who African Americans were, and in so doing mistook their fantasies for reality. By breaking this spell, by reworking late nineteenth-century racial and sexual ideology, Ida B. Wells not only challenged whites' assumption that they were civilized and men's assumption that they were "manly," she started the antilynching campaign while claiming new authority for black women as a consequence of her moral, physical, and intellectual courage.

Wells's assertion that white women sometimes seduced black men anticipates the racial divide in contemporary feminism/womanism, evidenced, for instance, in the difference in point of view between Susan Brownmiller and

Angela Davis regarding the case of the Scottsboro Nine, as we saw at the end of chapter 12. Wells's campaign also anticipates the contemporary complaint by black feminists regarding the "mystique" of white women, a mystique that is more, or should I say less, than it seems. Eldridge Cleaver was explicit that raping white women was a means to "get back" at the "man," a savage substitution of female bodies for male. Assertive, independent, that is, "real" women are unwelcome in patriarchal homosocial worlds, white or black. The "lady" is an imaginary construct, designed to marginalize by idealizing; its contrary concept—slut—functions in parallel fashion. In part it was this knowledge—that the "lady" lynchers were protecting was not real—that so enraged Wells and horrified Ames. In the U.S. Congress white men refused to abandon their constitutional "right" to fantasize about white women and black men, insisting that any federal protection of black male bodies was an invasion of southern states' rights, namely the right of a southern white man to do with a black man whatever he pleased. We are now, I trust, quite clear about the nature of that "right."

Perhaps the major difference between white women's participation in racial politics and white men's was the tendency of the latter to sexualize "race." White women did not look upon black women as sexual "rivals" in the same violently homoerotic ways white men often regarded black men. They did not obsess over black female genitalia as white men did over black men's. White women were—are—often awful to black women, but they didn't track them down, strip them, sexually torture and mutilate their bodies, keeping parts as souvenirs. The castration event says something crucial not only about the difference between white men's and women's participation in American racial politics; it says something as well about the nature of white men's sexual formation in America, namely that repressed homosexual desire has often returned as racialized desire disavowed as "prejudice," itself no monolithic, unchanging, ahistorical phenomenon (Young-Bruehl 1996).

Luce Irigaray (1992) has reminded us that structure of hegemonic or phallocratic masculinity has meant the erasure of men's debt to those from whose bodies they were born, those whose realities they feel compelled to usurp. Irigaray is not talking about specific men (although I am), nor even a general tendency in men (although, in my view, it is there, an inevitable byproduct of men's self-formation as heterosexually identified "men"), but rather, a tendency in phallocentric thought to deny and cover over the debt of life and existence that all subjects owe to the maternal body. In her instructive discussion of Irigaray, Elizabeth Grosz observes that this tendency involves men's "elaborate attempts to foreclose and build over this [maternal] space with their own (sexually specific) fantasmatic and paranoid projections" (1995, 121).

Certainly we have seen that process at work in nineteenth-century southern white men's fantasies of powerless white women and sexually rapacious black men. But Irigaray, and Grosz, want to argue that the entire production of a (male) world has embedded in it "the systematic and violent erasure of the contributions of women, femininity, and the maternal" (Grosz 1995, 121). Such erasure is the foundation or ground upon which a thoroughly masculine universe is constructed, although he doesn't know, fantasizing himself as a "self-made" man: "He can only touch himself from the outside. In order to recapture that whole sensation of the inside of a body, he will invent a world. But the world's circular horizon always conceals the inner movement of the womb. The imposition of distinctions is the mourning which their bodies always wear" (Irigaray 1992, 15).

When women become "real," that is, no longer figments of the white male imagination but separate individuals with agency and their own agendas and the capacity to see through the charade (what Butler called the "drag ball production of realness") that is "masculinity"—for instance, a sports reporter in a male locker room—then they are "out of place." They must be ejected. If not a "lady," then she's a "bitch," as in the case of sports reporter Lisa Olson (Disch and Kane 1996). Then the "lady" can be safely expelled, that is, without disturbing the structure of men's homosocial imagination.

What is homosexual desire? Perhaps I should use instead "homoerotic," as that term is more diffuse in its meaning, less genitally-focused, and does not imply "identity" and "way of life." Genitally focused or not, that men desire other men seems ubiquitous and unchanging, although how that desire is expressed, the cultural forms it assumes as it is sublimated and denied, obviously varies considerably (Gilmore 1990). "Romantic friendship" evidently substituted emotion for sexuality, although I suspect historians understate the extent to which these friends were also lovers. Freud's notion of "polymorphous perversity" is probably right, although such an "essentialized" view of desire is currently out of fashion, replaced by a radical constructivism associated especially with the work of Foucault, which insists "desire" is only a cultural mirage and political medium (Jagose 1996). But when men's need for each other is forcibly denied, as it is in contemporary forms of compulsory heterosexuality, it does not disappear as one might predict in a constructivist model. Rather, when men's desire for each other is frustrated instability, turbulence, even violence follow.

Irigaray argues that what psychoanalysis articulates as the imposition of oedipalization is in fact the (re)production of a circuit of symbolic exchange in which women function only as objects, commodities, or goods; where women serve as the excuse, the intermediary as it were, the linkable point between one man and other. As evidence, she cites the fascination of many men with prostitution, with the idea of sharing a woman that other men have "had" (Grosz 1995, 178).

Moreover, homosexuality is persecuted in part, Irigaray (1992) claims, because gay men make explicit the fundamentally homosocial or, in Irigaray's neologism, *hommosexual* nature of exchange itself, including the exchange as the codification of desire. They make clear that the stakes do not involve women themselves. "If desire is a lack," Elizabeth Grosz points out, "and if it functions by way of the substitution of one impossible/unsatisfying object for another, then what is significant about desire is not the objects to which it attaches itself; but rather the flows and dynamics of its circulation, the paths, detours, and returns it undergoes" (1995, 178). From this formulation it is an inescapable conclusion that homosocial circuits of exchange, like "desire" and "sexual difference," are socially constructed in patriarchal cultures, are structured around the banished male body, that is, the phallus men pretend is "power."

These circuits of exchange are, to use Irigaray's term again, *hommosexual* or, in Sedgwick's (1985), homosocial; they are for and between men (Grosz 1995). The de-eroticized presence of "the 'self-same' body has traditionally functioned as the necessary support for the dream of masculine omnipotence" (Silverman 1992, 269). Its eroticization may help to awaken men to a world in which power is not dreamt but shared, organized horizontally across negotiated terrains of concrete relationalities.

Until power becomes sexualized and the penis is no longer the phallus, women will remain figments in men's imagination, units in their homosocial economies. Racially, white men in America will still obsess over black men. Inevitably the obsession will surface, as it does in James Baldwin's remembrance of an encounter with a white southern politician, who, having drowned his inhibitions in alcohol, tried to pick Baldwin up in a newly integrated Little Rock, Arkansas, washroom.

> When the man grabbed my cock, I didn't think of him as a faggot, which, indeed, if having a wife and children, house, cars, and a respectable and powerful standing in the community mean anything, he wasn't. I watched his eyes, thinking with great sorrow, *the unexamined life is not worth living*. The despair among the loveless is that they must narcotize themselves before they can touch any human being at all. ... That most men will choose a woman to debase is not a matter of rejoicing either for the chosen women or anybody else; brutal truth, further, forces the observation, particularly if one is a black man, that this choice is by no means certain. That men have an enormous need to debase other men—and not only because they are men—is a truth history forbids us to labor. And it is absolutely certain that white men, who invented the nigger's big black prick, are still at the mercy of this nightmare, and are still, for the most part, doomed in one way or another, to attempt to make this prick their own: so much for the progress which the Christian world has made from the jungle in which it is their clear intention to keep black men treed forever. (Baldwin 1972, 63; quoted in Young-Bruehl 1996, 500–501)

Like "heterosexuality," "homosexuality" is everywhere, an essential feature of the human species. In America it is racialized. As Freud knew: "[A]ll human beings are capable of making a homosexual object-choice and have in fact made one in their unconscious. Indeed, libidinal attachments to persons of the same sex play no less a part in normal mental life ... than do similar attachments to the opposite sex" (1977, 56–57; quoted in Simpson 1994, 7). As Mark Simpson appreciates, "the significance of Freud's refusal to assign homosexuality to a 'third sex,' to designate homosexuals a 'race apart,' has yet to be fully realized. By insisting that 'homosexual object-choice' was something that all men [and women] were capable of and had made, albeit unawares in most cases, and something that played 'no less a part in factors of normal mental life' than heterosexual object-choice, Freud overturned the idea that heterosexuality and thus masculinity was noncomplex or unproblematic" (1994, 7–8). And, as we saw in chapter 13, is it ever problematic. Masculinity is the gender of violence.

Perhaps there is, in a certain sense, only one gender—woman—with limitless variations, including anatomical and sexual differences. As men (especially heterosexually identified men) are constituted now, masculinity is often a self-destructive and sometimes even homicidal repudiation of the woman's gender, the mother identification as this inevitably remains, however denied and repressed, within "men." In patriarchy, matrifocality is a social problem, not an identification to be cultivated. It is the absence of fathers patriarchal men imagine as the problem. But that, I suggest, is a problem only for those who insist on sublimating same-sex desire. For men who remain in relative identification and relation with women and thereby eroticize anatomical sameness not difference, the "father" is no longer absent. "He" is here, in my arms. Women would no longer be objectified as sexual commodities, but loved as sons might love their mothers and sisters or, if sexualized, as women might love women. Let us dream a queer progressive dream of a postpatriarchal regime in which they are only "women," albeit some with penises (although not phalluses, those homosocial weapons of power and subjugation), but all of us with openings, for entry, psychological as well as physical: "from behind we're all women" (Hocquenghem 1978, 87).

Due to its omnipresence, homosexual desire in itself is, in a certain sense, not the issue. What people do with their bodies, how consenting adults express love and desire, what can it matter? What *is* the issue is the violent suppression of men's homoerotic desire, the pathological intensity and duration of efforts nearly worldwide to suppress it. In whose interest is this suppression? Not women's, including heterosexually identified women who suffer daily. It is not in lesbians' interest, who also suffer directly and indirectly from the rage of heterosexually identified men. Certainly it is not in gay men's interest. Given how such suppressed desire resurfaces in mangled ways, mixed with other dynamics, as in the case of lynching, such suppression is not in the interest of African Americans and other marginalized peoples whose bodies have become objects of white men's obsession and sadistic desire. Is it in the interest of "straight" men? I suppose, although given their tendencies toward psychological instability, social isolation, and emotional suffering, the price they pay for political and economic and gender domination is high indeed.

In decades past, when African Americans conflated political progress (i.e., the protection of black civil rights) with "manhood" not only a sense of civic emasculation was being expressed. That emasculation was literal in the case of lynching victims, symbolic in later twentieth-century racial politics. In an essay on Harlem, "Fifth Avenue, Uptown," first published in the July 1960 issue of *Esquire*, James Baldwin tried to teach a largely white male readership what was at stake in the emerging civil rights movement: "Negroes want to be treated like men: a perfectly straightforward statement, containing only seven words. People who mastered Kant, Hegel, Shakespeare, Marx, Freud, and the Bible find this statement utterly impenetrable. The idea seems to threaten profound, barely conscious assumptions. A kind of panic paralyzes their features, as though they find themselves trapped at the edge of a steep place" (Baldwin 1985, 211–212; quoted in Kaplan 1996, 27). The same steep place Poe's character Pym found himself? What could that panic be?

White men cannot treat black men as "men" because black men are somewhere, everywhere, in the white imaginary, sexualized. The subjugation of both black men and women was and remains sexualized. It is no accident that the simple and yet somehow incomprehensible phrase "I AM A MAN" expressed the black demand that white subjugation must end. What may not have been so clear then is how psychologically defensive and sexually compensatory white (male) supremacy was, how the late nineteenth-century civic and sexual exploitation of African Americans was an evil born, yes, in economic and political domination, but in also in the defeat, humiliation, and collapse of southern white male patriarchy after the defeat at Appomattox. Southern whites, especially southern white men, missed what they had lost in the Civil War; they missed those on whom they had depended economically, culturally, psychologically, and sexually. In their worst moment, a time of utter and complete defeat, white men looked bitterly and longingly from a distance at the black bodies to which they had before unlimited access. If we were only on a raft, you and me, free on the Mississippi: that has been the white man's dream.

What a psychologically intolerable experience it must have been for southern white men, exhausted by four years of bitter fighting, wounded (over half of the Mississippi state budget in 1866 went to purchase artificial limbs for its shattered Confederate veterans), failures not only in the eyes of Yankee men but their wives and children too. No longer were they propped up by black bodies. In this moment of self-loathing, depletion, and abjection to miss the muscular black bodies by means of which they had farmed the land, fed their children, built their dwellings, experienced social importance, "honor" in the eyes of other southern white men: in this moment to look across the distance of "emancipation" at black bodies no longer at their whim: what a moment of self-dissolution, of psychological dismemberment, of bitter desire that must have been. Can we be surprised that a racialized "patriarchal" reversal (see Disch and Kane 1996) was undertaken, first by the Ku Klux Klan, then by random white male mobs? Certainly the once proud Confederate soldier—and nearly every white male from age 12 to 60 had served by 1865—could not easily admit to himself that he could not go on without those black bodies he had fought so hard to keep as his own. After two years of exhaustion, white southerners remobilized and defeated Reconstruction; by 1877 they had restored black economic and political subjugation. "Redeemed," white boys began to lynch.

Black women as well as men were still raped after "emancipation," but now that "bestiality" could not be hidden in the privacy of one's own barns, on the edge of one's own field, with slaves whose complaints meant only torture even death, now no longer sated, that desire went to their heads. There white men could not allow themselves to experience it, so it was "relocated" and "reversed." It was black men who desired (the relocation), not them of course (now the reversal), but their "ladies." Where there had been relatively little desire expressed before there was now desire of tidal proportions, so alarming to white life and honor that bands of white men formed like rain clouds to "punish" black male efforts at rape. Overwhelmingly their victims were young black men. Strip the bastard, tear out his flesh, and as James Baldwin knew, take what white men wanted most of all. Not orally, not anally ... such forms of sodomy were intolerable (in public at least) in southern "Christian" and "white" "civilization." No, cut it off, take it home, where one could forever remember the feel of it, the look of it, the power of it. Then the crowd could sigh, light the cigarette ... no the pyre, and the body, the atrocity, goes up in smoke. Souvenirs are collected. One young white boy carried Zachariah Walker's finger in his pants pocket for six weeks (Downey and Hyser 1991).

If the white man had to have the black man's phallus, would not fellatio or anal intercourse have been preferable to lynching and castration? If your answer to that question is negative, even for a moment, if (homo)sex seems worse than murder, can you not see how homosexual repression is intertwined with white supremacy and mob violence? If your answer is positive, can you not see that desire for the black man's body is intertwined with racial subjugation and racism, as his subjectivity, his individuality are effaced, lost in your gaze, evaporated in your desire? We white men still fantasize a physical intimacy with black bodies, especially black male bodies, imagined today primarily as a fear of crime, of being robbed, raped, or murdered. Still we imagine a black man in our bedroom. Or if our valorization of the black male body is positive, we imagine lying with him, the macho rapper, the handsome actor, the hot model. For those of us whose positive valorization is more sublimated, perhaps we imagine working with poor black children, as teachers, social workers, perhaps we even adopt a black child. In early twentieth-century settlement houses, at least those in which Charles Stover and John Elliott worked, such pedagogical and social commitments evidently required no sublimation. Sublimated or sexualized, there remains a certain white occupation of the black body, an occupation Saidya Hartman (1997; see introduction, this volume) so brilliantly analyzes, an empathy, a "caring" and "concern" in which black subjectivity and individuality disappear into white "need." Can we white people ever see through centuries of "whiteness"—that film on our corneas—to those concretely and subjectively existing individuals whose bodies so excite, alarm, terrify us? Experiencing the latent energy suppressed by the heterosexual matrix might, as Sedgwick (1990) suggests, help us to do so.

As the racialized heterosexualized social surface cracks, buried genealogical layers of sedimented history become exposed. For Americans—so young, naïve, just ending our adolescence, perhaps—there is a civilizational story to be told, a story which connects us to ancient but continuing atrocities, events which reverberate in our dreams as well as our waking lives. It began, one can say, one night long long ago, a night of wine, of family, a night of sex, culminating in a curse, the genesis of homosexualized racialization in the West, a night narrated in the first book of the Old Testament. To that civilizational story I turn next.

APPENDIX

“[T]HE GREAT LONG NATIONAL SHAME”:

—H. J. Spillers, “Mama’s Baby, Papa’s Maybe: An American Grammar Book” (1987)

SELECTED INCIDENTS OF RACIAL VIOLENCE IN THE UNITED STATES

—adapted from M. Newton and J. A. Newton, *Racial and Religious Vviolence in America: A Chronology* (1991)

1526 November. Georgetown County, South Carolina. Black slaves revolt against their Spanish captors on the Waccamaw River, escaping to live with local Indians, who had helped with the uprising.

1619 August 20. Jamestown, Virginia. The first enslaved Africans arrive in Jamestown, Virginia.

1663 September 13. Virginia. Authorities learn of a revolt planned by slaves and indentured servants. Several leaders are beheaded, their skulls displayed on chimney tops.

1708 Long Island, New York. A small band of slaves revolt at Newton; seven whites are killed. Four slaves, including an Indian and a woman, are sentenced to death; the three men are hanged; the black woman is burned.

1712 April 9. New York City. An estimated thirty slaves, including two Indians, revolt; they set fire to a downtown building, then wait for settlers to respond to the alarm. Nine settlers are killed and six others are wounded before the revolt is crushed. One of the insurgents commits suicide after killing his wife, but twenty-seven are captured and sentenced to die. Authorities pardon six of the condemned, including a pregnant black woman, but kill the other twenty-one.

1718 New Orleans, Louisiana. Plans for a slave rebellion are discovered. As punishment, the leader, Samba, and seven others, are broken on the wheel. The black woman who exposed the plot is hanged.

1732 New Orleans, Louisiana. Authorities crush a plot devised by slaves and Natchez Indians. Four men are broken on the wheel and one woman is hanged then decapitated; their heads are displayed on poles at the city limits.

1781 Williamsburg, Virginia. One white man dies as slaves set fire to several buildings, including the state capitol.

1787 The foreign slave trade is suspended for a period of three years; the ban is continuously renewed until 1803. The smuggling of slaves continues; many slave dealers turn to the domestic breeding of enslaved people.

1803 December 17. Foreign slave trade resumes; more than 40,000 slaves are imported during the next four years.

1814 Legislators pass a law requiring the death penalty for any slave who willfully sheds a white person's blood.

1819 Philadelphia, Pennsylvania. Three white women stone a black woman to death on the street.

1819 Augusta, Georgia. One white man is killed in a crushed slave revolt; the black leader, Coco, is hanged. Another slave, Paul, is sentenced to be branded on one cheek and his ears are cut off; 250 lashes are administered over a period of thirty days, in three-day intervals.

1819 Williamsburg County, South Carolina. Whites attack a fugitive slave community, murdering three slaves and capturing several others. One white man is injured in the assault.

1826 Cincinnati, Ohio. Six hundred ninety African Americans are driven out of town by rioting whites.

1826 May, at sea. Twenty-nine slaves en route from Maryland to Georgia on the ship *Decatur* kill two members of the crew and demand to be taken to Haiti. The ship is captured and taken to New York, where all of the slaves manage to escape. One slave, named William Bowser, is recaptured and executed in New York City on December 15.

1829 July–August. Cincinnati, Ohio. White attacks on black residents climax on August 22 when a mob attacks the black quarter, with many casualties. By year's end, racist violence has prompted at least 1,200 blacks to desert the city; many depart for Canada.

1831 January 7. Wilmington, North Carolina. The press reports that "there has been much shooting of Negroes in this neighborhood recently, in consequence of symptoms of liberty having been discovered among them" (quoted in Newton and Newton 1991, 86). Two companies of militia are stationed in the area to ensure that future slave insurrections can be quickly crushed.

1831 August 20–22. Southampton County, Virginia. Nat Turner's slave revolt claims approximately sixty lives before armed whites mount a counterattack. More than 100 blacks are killed in the fighting, with an equal number of innocent blacks massacred for revenge after the rebellion is crushed. Of fifty-three blacks arrested, twenty are hanged, twelve are sold to out-of-state buyers, and twenty-one are acquitted. Nat Turner and three of his lieutenants are hanged on November 11.

(Other slave revolts occurred elsewhere in Virginia and North Carolina at about the same time, but details have not survived.)

1834 At least fifteen mob attacks on abolitionist groups and speakers occur during the year, all in northern states.

1834 Jefferson Parish, Louisiana. A runaway slave named Squier is shot and wounded by slave hunters in a swamp near New Orleans. As soon as his wound has healed, Squier escapes. This time he organizes a band of fugitive blacks and renegade whites to terrorize New Orleans and environs for the next three years. Taking the name of Bras Coupe, Squier becomes a feared figure, leading bloody raids on outlying homes and plantations.

1834 Summer. Philadelphia, Pennsylvania. Five hundred whites attack a black amusement area, rioting and causing extensive damage before they are driven away. While violence continues over the next two days, with at least one black man, Stephen James, murdered by rampaging whites. Whites destroy thirty-one black homes and two churches during the outbreak.

1834 July 4–11. New York City. Violence by white racist rioters destroys sixty homes and six churches, damages other churches and meeting halls before National Guardsmen restore order. The riots begin on Independence Day, when hecklers disrupt an abolitionist rally. On July 5 two men are arrested for fighting, which follows an argument about slavery. On the night of July 7, whites storm a black meeting at Chatham Street Chapel, forcing those assembled to flee. The next day, arsonists set fire to a building housing a store owned by abolitionist John Rankin, and whites disrupt an integrated meeting at Clinton Hall. Three outbreaks of violence are reported on the evening of July 9; major rioting by whites occurs on July 10 and 11. Black-owned property valued at $20,000 is destroyed in the riots; a store owned by abolitionist Lewis Tappan is also destroyed. The churches damaged or destroyed have all gone on record supporting the abolition of slavery.

1834 August. Philadelphia, Pennsylvania. Christians stage a violent "Passover riot" against Jews.

1834 September. Canterbury, Connecticut. Whites destroy a black school run by local abolitionists.

1835 September. Aiken, South Carolina. A white abolitionist is lynched.

1835 October 21. Boston, Massachusetts. Abolitionist William Lloyd Garrison is dragged through the streets with a rope by pro-slavery advocates. Police rescue him from the white mob and place him in jail for his own protection.

1835 December. East Feliciana, Louisiana. A planned rebellion by forty armed slaves is discovered.

1836 Over sixty-four incidents of mob violence against abolitionists in northern states occur during this year.

1836 Marblehead, Massachusetts. Abolitionist Amos Dresser is attacked by racist whites. A few days later, Dresser is attacked again, this time struck in the head by a rock while addressing an abolitionist church meeting in Circleville, Ohio.

1837 Jefferson Parish, Louisiana. Fugitive slave leader Bras Couple is shot and wounded in an ambush by two white hunters near New Orleans. The corpse of Bras Couple is delivered to local authorities by one of his cohorts, Francisco Garcia. Despite a standing $2,000 reward for the slave, Garcia receives only $250 and is ordered to leave town at once. Coupe's body is placed on public display for two days.

1838 Philadelphia, Pennsylvania. White rioters burn a shelter for black orphans, stone one black church, and attempt to burn another. Violence against blacks spreads to other Pennsylvania cities.

1843 Pendleton, Indiana. Frederick Douglass is attacked and severely beaten by local racist whites.

1847 Harrisburg, Pennsylvania. Whites disrupt a speech by Frederick Douglass, throw stones, firecrackers, cayenne pepper, garbage, and rotten eggs throughout the auditorium.

1849 New York City. Armed with guns and throwing stones, German immigrants prevent Jews from holding a funeral in a local cemetery.

1850 New York City. Racist whites disrupt an abolitionist meeting led by William Lloyd Garrison.

1850 New York City. Racist whites disrupt a speech by Frederick Douglass.

1850 New York City. Inflamed by false rumors that Jews have killed a gentile girl, 500 Christian men raid a Jewish-occupied tenement on Yom Kippur, vandalizing the apartments, beating and robbing their residents.

1862 St. John the Baptist Parish, Louisiana. An armed slave revolt ends after the Union commander of New Orleans threatens to suppress it with military force.

1863 New York City. Antidraft riots, numerous African Americans murdered by rioting (mostly Irish) whites. At least two black men are genitally mutilated.

1867 Nashville, Tennessee. A year-old social club, the Ku Klux Klan, is reorganized along fraternity and military lines by a convention of Confederate veterans. Within a year the K.K.K. will spread to twelve states, attempting to destroy Reconstruction by armed force. No reliable figures are available, but congressional hearings suggest that Klansmen, riding from 1868 to 1871, murdered at least seventy-four persons in Georgia, 109 in Alabama, and 235 in Florida. In a single Mississippi county, Kemper, at least thirty-five were murdered by Klan members between 1869 and 1871. During a six-month period of 1871, the South Carolina Klan is guilty of thirty-five murders, 262 floggings, two rapes, and another 101 victims wounded, mutilated, or driven from their homes.

1867 Louisiana. In May, whites organize the Knights of the White Camellia in St. Mary Parish to undermine Reconstruction and prevent African Americans from exercising their civil rights. In many parts of the South, the Knights will work hand in hand with Klansmen to terrorize and murder black citizens and Yankee sympathizers.

1868 Louisiana. Beginning in May and for the duration of the summer, crimes against blacks are reported from Bienville, Bossier, Caddo, Claiborne, Franklin, Jackson, Morehouse, Richland, and St. Landry parishes. In Bienville Parish, a black Republican is dragged from his home, then decapitated by whites.

1868 September 22. New Orleans, Louisiana. Rioting breaks out after racist Democrats fire on a Republican political parade.

1868 September 28. Opelousas, Louisiana. Emerson Bentley, a white teacher at a school for black children, is beaten in front of his class by three members of the racist Seymour Knights.

1868 November 3. Pulaski, Tennessee. A Confederate veteran who cast a Republican ballot is attacked by a mob and placed on an auction block for mock sale as a "white nigger" (quoted in Newton and Newton 1991, 200).

1869 April. Garrard County, Kentucky. A black man is lynched by members of the K.K.K.

1870 September. Greene County, Alabama. Guilford Coleman, a black Republican, is dragged from his home by Klansmen, shot to death, then mutilated almost beyond recognition.

1870 Fall. Moore County, North Carolina. A black school is burned by the K.K.K.

1870 October. Spartanburg County, South Carolina. Klansmen whip a Republican election official and a black couple, forcing the former to perform degrading acts before the Klansmen mutilate the black man with a knife. Several of the raiders are arrested, then released on bond, and never prosecuted. Those responsible for arresting them are then flogged by the K.K.K.. In a subsequent raid, sixty-nine-year-old John Genobles is beaten until he renounces his Republican affiliation.

1870 November 15. Marianna, Florida. Klansmen attack Richard Pousser, a black Republican constable. They strip and beat him.

1871 January. Frankfort, Kentucky. Abducted by Klansmen, two black men are robbed of a watch and $30, then forced to lie in ice until their clothes freeze. Upon their release, they are warned to leave the county or they will be lynched.

1871 March. Walton County, Georgia. Local Klansmen ban black schools, then publicly burn one teacher's collection of books.

1889 January 15. Pratt Mines, Alabama. George Meadows, a black man accused of rape, is lynched.

1889 January 15. Arkansas. Dean Reynolds, a black man accused of rudeness, is lynched.

1889 January 21. Bolar, Mississippi. Henry Thomas, a black man accused of murder, is lynched.

1889 January 25. New Iberia, Louisiana. Samuel Wakefield, a black man accused of murder, is lynched.

1889 January 26. Wadis Station, South Carolina. William Brewington, a black man accused of murder, is lynched.

1889 February 1. New Iberia, Louisiana. White men lynch a black man named Rosemond, who is accused of theft.

1889 February 7. Amite County, Mississippi. An unknown black man is charged with rape and lynched.

1889 February 10. Houghton, Louisiana. Hayward Handy, a black man who defended himself against white men who attacked him without cause, is lynched.

1889 February 19. Liberty, Texas. Two unnamed black men, accused of murder, are lynched.

1889 February 22. Artesia, Mississippi. D. H. Smith, a black man who founded a black commune, is lynched.

1889 February 23. Port Gibson, Mississippi. Thomas Wesley, a black man accused of attempted rape, is lynched.

1889 February 28. Port Gibson, Mississippi. A black man named Perkins is lynched. No cause given.

1889 March 8. Texarkana, Arkansas. J. E. Robinson, a black man accused of rape, is lynched.

1889 March 14. Tasley, Virginia. Magruder Fletcher, a black man accused of rape, is lynched.

1889 April 3. Abingdon, Virginia. Martin Roland, a black man accused of murder, is lynched.

1889 April 15. Hempstead, Texas. George Driggs, a black man accused of rape, is lynched.

1889 April 18. New Iberia, Louisiana. A black man named Hector, who is suspected of murder, is lynched.

1889 April 19. Bayou Desard, Louisiana. An unidentified black man, accused of rape, is lynched.

1889 April 23. Oklahoma. An unknown black man is lynched.

1889 April 23. Halifax, Virginia. Scott Bailey, a black man accused of rape, is lynched.

1889 May 17. Mt. Carmel, South Carolina. A black man, Tut Danford, is lynched.

1889 May 17. Millican, Texas. An unidentified black man, suspected of rape, is lynched.

1889 May 18. Columbia, Louisiana. An unknown black man accused of burglary is lynched by white men.

1889 May 19. Forrest City, Arkansas. A. M. Neeley, a black man, is lynched as a result of "political troubles" (quoted in Newton and Newton 1991, 242).

1889 May 20. Wickliffe, Kentucky. Joseph Thornton, a black man accused of rape, is lynched.

1889 May 21. Kosciusko, Mississippi. James Mitchell, a black man charged with rape, is lynched.

1889 May 22. Walnut Grove, Alabama. Noah Dickson, a black man accused of rape, is lynched.

1889 May 27. Port Huron, Michigan. Albert Martin, a black man charged with rape, is lynched.

1889 May 31. Thomastown, Mississippi. Accused of rape, an unknown black man is lynched.

1889 June 1. Eureka, Mississippi. Robert Herron, a black man, is lynched. No reason given.

1889 June 5. Tangipahoa, Louisiana. Two black men, Dick Conley and a man called Huey, are lynched. No reason given.

1889 June 11. Petersburg, Virginia. John Forbes, a black man suspected of rape, is lynched.

1889 June 13. Pine Bluff, Arkansas. Armstead Johnson, a black man accused of theft, is lynched.

1889 June 21. Tiptonville, Missouri. Alfred Grizzard, a black man accused of gambling, is lynched.

1889 June 22. Ridgewater, South Carolina. Andy Caldwell, a black man accused of rape, is lynched.

1889 June 28. Union County, South Carolina. A black man, A. McNight, accused of quarreling with white men, is lynched.

1889 July 11. Tunnel Hill, Georgia. Martin Love, a black man accused of rape, is lynched.

1889 July 11. Iuka, Mississippi. Prince Luster, a black man charged with rape, is lynched. Swan Burres, a black man charged with murder, is lynched.

1889 July 11. Lafayette, Louisiana. Felix Keyes, a black man accused of murder, is lynched.

1889 July 11. Waco, Texas. Henry Davis, a black man, is lynched. No reason given.

1889 July 20. Warsaw, Indiana. Willis Peter, a black man charged with rape, is lynched.

1889 July 20. Clinton, Mississippi. Three unidentified black men, suspected of killing a white man, are mobbed and lynched.

1889 July 23. Covington, Kentucky. Daniel Malone, a black man accused of rape, is lynched.

1889 July 23. Paris, Kentucky. James Kelly, a black man charged with rape, is lynched.

1889 July 26. Belen, Texas. George Lewis, a black man accused of poisoning a well, is lynched.

1889 July 28. Greenville, Texas. George Lindley, a black man, is lynched. No reason given.

1889 July 31. Clinton, Mississippi. Thomas Talbot, a black man accused of rape, is lynched.

1889 August 3. La Plata, Missouri. Benjamin Smith, a black man accused of rape, is lynched.

1889 August 14. Aberdeen, Mississippi. Keith Bowen, a black man suspected of rape, is lynched.

1889 August 14. Orange, Texas. A black man accused of rape, James Brooks, is lynched.

1889 August 23. Luccalena, Mississippi. Sherman Lewis, a black man charged with rape, is lynched.

1889 August 30. Fayetteville, West Virginia. John Turner, a black man accused of murder, is lynched.

1889 September 2. Montevallo, Alabama. Two unidentified black men, charged with murder, are taken from jail and lynched.

1889 September 4. East Point, Georgia. Warren Powers, a black man accused of rape, is lynched.

1889 September 9. Hiawatha, Kansas. Richard Fisher, a black man charged with stealing a horse, is lynched.

1889 September 9. Le Flore County, Mississippi. George Allen, a black man suspected of arson, is lynched.

1889 September 9. Stanley Creek, North Carolina. John Sigmond, a black man accused of rape, is lynched.

1889 September 11. Morgantown, North Carolina. David Boone, a black man suspected of murder, is lynched.

1889 September 12. Shell Mound, Mississippi. Lewis Mortimer, a black man charged with murder, is lynched.

1889 September 16. Bluefield, Virginia. Samuel Garner, a black man accused of rape, is lynched.

1889 September 17. Columbia, Missouri. A black man accused of rape, George Burke, is lynched by white men.

1889 September 27. Birmingham, Alabama. John Steele, a black man accused of murder, is lynched.

1889 October 1. Spring Place, Georgia. John Duncan, a black man who lived with a white woman, is lynched.

1889 October 4. Alabama. Suspected of murder, a black man named Stark is lynched.

1889 October 12. Jesup, Georgia. William Moore, a black man accused of throwing stones in public, is lynched.

1889 October 12. Hernando, Mississippi. Robert Biggs, a black man accused of rape, is lynched.

1889 October 21. Lake Cormorant, Mississippi. An unidentified black man, suspected of rape, is lynched.

1889 October 26. Columbus, Mississippi. A black man accused of rape, Joseph Harrold, is lynched.

1889 November 8. Leesburg, Virginia. Owen Anderson, a black man charged with attempted rape, is lynched.

1889 November 10. Midville, Georgia. John Thomas, a black man charged with rape, is lynched by white men.

1889 November 15. Hazelhurst, Mississippi. Two black brothers, accused of murder, are lynched.

1889 November 16. Magnolia, Mississippi. A black man accused of rape, George Washington, is lynched.

1889 November 16. Lincolnton, Georgia. John Anthony, a black man accused of attempted rape, is lynched.

1889 November 16. Hazelhurst, Mississippi. Accused of murder, an unknown black man is lynched.

1889 November 18. Vidalia, Louisiana. An unidentified black man, accused of arson, is lynched.

1889 November 23. Petersburg, Virginia. Robert Bland, a black man, is lynched. No apparent motive.

1889 December 19. Owensboro, Kentucky. Doc Jones, a black man charged with murder, is lynched.

1889 December 26. Jesup, Georgia. Two black men, William Hopps and Peter Jackson, are lynched. No apparent motive.

1889 December 27. Tuscaloosa, Alabama. Bud Wilson, a black man charged with attempted rape, is lynched.

1889 December 28. Barnwell, South Carolina. Eight black men, suspected of murder, are lynched.

1890 August 22. Baton Rouge, Louisiana. William Alexander, a black man charged with attempted rape, is lynched.

1892 February 20. Texarkana, Arkansas. Ed [Mc]Coy, a black man accused of rape, is lynched.

1893 July 18. Memphis, Tennessee. Acting on rumors of an attempted rape, white men kill one black man and jail another. On July 22, suspect Lee

Walker, a black man, is dragged from the jail by a white mob, stabbed repeatedly, hanged from a tree, then mutilated and burned.

1911 August 13. Coatesville, Pennsylvania. Zechariah Walker, a black man charged with killing the town constable in a fight, is dragged from his hospital room and burned alive by a mob. Pieces of his charred bones are afterward distributed as souvenirs.

1921 March 14. Eagle Lake, Florida. William Bowles, a black man accused of upsetting a white woman, is lynched.

1921 May 31. Tulsa, Oklahoma. Dick Rowland, a nineteen-year-old black man, is jailed and charged with attempted rape after he stumbles and falls accidentally against Sarah Page, a white forty-three-year-old divorcee, stepping on her foot. Armed black men appear at the jail after rumors circulate that a lynch mob of white men has gathered there; a shoot-out results. Whites then run amok, burning the mile-square black neighborhood. At one point, white men who have been deputized raid a nearby munitions dump for dynamite, commandeer several airplanes, then drop dynamite from the air on the black neighborhood. Twenty-five whites and at least sixty blacks lose their lives. (The director of a civilian burial detail reports that at least 150 African Americans died.) Black residents who fled the area to avoid the riot are rounded up by local deputies and state militia as they return home and placed in a "camp" where the men, women and children are separated. They are finally allowed to leave the camp to work, but now must carry a "green card" and produce it whenever requested by local law authorities. Thirty whites are charged with looting, and on June 25 a grand jury indicts seven civilians and five policemen—including the chief of police—on criminal charges linked to the riot. On February 4, 2000, a state commission recommends reparations be made to survivors (Yardley 2000).

1931 March 25. Scottsboro, Alabama. National Guardsmen protect nine black youths accused of rape from a white lynch mob as they are convicted by an all-white male jury.

1931 July 17. Camp Hill, Alabama. Violence erupts following black protests over recent verdicts in the Scottsboro "rape" case. One African American is killed and five others are injured; seventeen are arrested. Rioting whites burn the home of a black family.

1932 November 7. Birmingham, Alabama. Klansmen attack black crowds gathered to protest the Scottsboro "rape" verdicts.

1932 November 19. Wisner, Louisiana. William House, a black man arrested for insulting two white women, is abducted from police custody by a gang of white men. His body is found hanging from a tree the next day.

1934 March 17. New York City. Five thousand riot during a rally held in Harlem to protest the Scottsboro "rape" case.

1934 July 9. Bastrop, Louisiana. Andrew McLeod, a black man charged with attempted rape, is taken from jail by a white male mob. He is hanged on the courthouse square, his throat slashed.

1934 July 16. Bolton, Mississippi. James Sanders, a black man, is shot to death by three white men on accusation of "writing an indecent letter to a white girl" (quoted in Newton and Newton 1991, 408). Three relatives of the girl confess to the murder, but their case is dismissed by local prosecutors.

1934 July 24. Pelahatchee, Mississippi. Henry Bedford, a black man, is taken from home and flogged by white men for "speaking disrespectfully to a young white man." He dies on July 25. Four white men are arrested but no indictments are returned.

1934 September 8. Princess Anne, Maryland. White rioters drive the entire black population out of town.

1934 October 26. Brewton, Alabama. Claude Neal, a black man accused of rape and murder in Marianna, Florida, is abducted by a gang of white men from the jail where he has been transported for safekeeping. The mob returns Neal to Marianna, where he is tortured and mutilated and the body hanged in front of the courthouse.

1937 October 3. Milton, Santa Rosa County, Florida. A black man, J. C. Evans, is accused of an "unnatural crime" against a white boy. He is taken from Sheriff Joe Allen and lynched (Brownmiller 1975/1993; Ames 1942).

1948 March 2. Wrightsville, Georgia. Three hundred robed Klansmen parade, declaring that "blood will flow in the streets of the South" if blacks seek equality (quoted in Newton and Newton 1991, 424). On March 3, election day, not one of the town's 400 registered African Americans attempts to vote.

1948 May 9. Jackson, Mississippi. Gov. Fielding Wright, in a radio address, urges those Mississippi blacks seeking equality to "make your home in some state other than Mississippi" (quoted in Newton and Newton 1991, 424).

1949 September 4. Peekskill, New York. White rioters, including policemen and members of the American Legion, stone and beat spectators as they leave a concert performance by black singer Paul Robeson. While claiming to be anticommunists, the rioters shout racist, anti-Semitic epithets at their victims during the assault.

1955 May 7. Belzoni, Mississippi. George W. Lee, a black man and an N.A.A.C.P. officer, is shot and killed by night riders on a rural highway.

1955 August 28. Mississippi. Emmett Till, a fourteen-year-old black boy visiting from Chicago, is kidnapped, beaten, shot, and dumped in a river for allegedly whistling at a white man's wife. His killers are acquitted by a jury, then sell their confessions to the murder to a national magazine.

1967 August 28. Milwaukee, Mississippi. N.A.A.C.P. demonstrators are stoned by white men shouting "We want slaves!" and "Get yourself a nigger!" Marchers are attacked again on August 29 while arsonists destroy a Freedom House in the black district, and snipers harass firefighters summoned to put out the blaze.

1967 October 28. Oakland, California. Patrolman John Frey is killed and a second officer wounded during a shoot-out with Huey Newton, founder of the Black Panther Party. Newton is also wounded in the exchange; he is convicted of manslaughter on September 8, 1968, but the verdict is overturned on appeal, after the disclosure of evidence that Frey apparently provoked the shooting in an attempt to kill Newton.

1968 February 3. Miami, Florida. A white patrolman resigns after charges of stripping a young black man and dangling him from a freeway overpass.

1968 April 4. Memphis, Tennessee. Rev. Martin Luther King, Jr., is assassinated. An ensuing riot in Memphis leaves more than thirty persons injured, with reports of sniping and at least three major fires. Nationwide, rioting erupts in 125 cities over the next week, leaving forty-six persons dead (one of them in Memphis, on April 6), 2,600 injured, and 21,270 arrested. Damage from arson and vandalism is estimated at $45 million; taxpayers spend another $5.38 million to deploy 36,000 federal troops in urban riot zones. Insurance companies report a total loss of $67 million in the riots.

1968 April 5–6. Oakland, California. Police report scattered incidents of looting and vandalism, sparked by racial fights at area high schools. Property damage is $265,000. On the night of April 6, Bobby Hutton, a young Black Panther, is killed during a ninety-minute shoot-out with police that leaves four others wounded and eight persons in custody, including Eldridge Cleaver.

1968 October 23–24. Berkeley, California. Two hundred persons are arrested in rock-throwing incidents sparked by the cancellation of scheduled lectures by Eldridge Cleaver (Newton and Newton 1991, 539).

1969 April 9. New Orleans, Louisiana. Six students at predominantly black Southern University overpower security guards, lowering the U.S. flag and raising a "black power" flag in its place. Crowds stone police after one of the men is arrested; three persons are injured and twenty-seven are arrested (Newton and Newton 1991, 550).

1970 December 4. Chicago, Illinois. Police raid Black Panther headquarters and kill Fred Hampton and Mark Clark, wound four others, and arrest seven persons. Two officers are also injured in the raid, which N.A.A.C.P. investigators describe as a deliberate "search and destroy" mission. Law enforcement officers are charged with conspiracy, but win acquittal in court (Newton and Newton 1991, 568).

1971 August 21. San Quentin, California. Violence erupts at the state prison, with five white guards and three black inmates killed in an apparent escape attempt. One of the dead convicts is "Soledad Brother" George Jackson. Three other guards and two inmates suffer nonfatal wounds during the outbreak. Weeks later, a police informant reports that Jackson had been deliberately "set up" for assassination by law enforcement officers (Newton and Newton 1991, 586).

1972 October 16. New York City. H. Rap Brown and three other black militants are captured during a shoot-out with police following the robbery of a local tavern (Newton and Newton 1991, 588).

1973 November 6. Oakland, California. Marcus Foster, the black superintendent of schools, is shot and killed by radical Symbionese Liberation Army (S.L.A.) gunmen (Newton and Newton 1991, 595).

1980 February 5. Oakland, California. Darline Cromer, a white woman, admits strangling Reginald Williams, a five-year-old black, expressing her belief that "it was the duty of every white women to kill a nigger child" (quoted in Newton and Newton 1991, 613).

1986 November. Concord, California. Timothy Lee, a gay black man, is found hanged two blocks from the site where robed Klansmen assault two other black men. Civil rights leaders reject the official verdict of "suicide" in Lee's death (Newton and Newton 1991, 638).

1988 February 7. Amherst, Massachusetts. Five whites assault two black men walking with a white woman on the local university campus. Two hundred blacks retaliate by occupying the campus New Africa Hall on February 14, demanding better security and the expulsion of the attackers from the school (Newton and Newton 1991, 647).

1997 August 23. New York City, New York. Four officers are formally accused of acting on racist motivations in the case of a Haitian immigrant—Abner Louima—who says he was beaten and sodomized by police. Louima told investigators that officers repeatedly called him nigger and beat him after he was arrested during a scuffle outside a Brooklyn nightclub on August 9 (Associated Press 1997, B16).

1998 Jasper, Texas. James Byrd, Jr., 49, was chained at the ankles to a pickup truck and dragged to pieces by three white men: John William King, 24, Lawrence Russell Brewer, 32, and Shawn Allen Berry, 24.

REFERENCES

A&E television. (1997). Goebbels: A biography. A&E's Biography.

Abbey, A. (1991a). Acquaintance rape and alcohol consumption on college campuses: How are they linked? *Journal of American College Health Association* 17(2): 108–126.

———. (1991b). Misperception as an antecedent of acquaintance rape: A consequence of ambiguity in communication between men and women. In A. Parrot and L. Bechhofer (Eds.), *Acquaintance rape: The hidden crime,* 96–111. New York: John Wiley.

Abrahams, R. D. (1962, July). Playing the dozens. *Journal of American Folklore* 75: 207–220.

———. (1964). *Deep down in the jungle—Negro narrative folklore from the streets of Philadelphia*. Hatboro, PA: Folklore Associates.

Acker, K. (1982). *Great expectations.* New York: Grove Press.

Adamson, C. (1984). Punishment after slavery: Southern state penal systems, 1865–1890. *Social Problems* 30: 555–569.

Addams, J. (1893/1969). The subjective necessity for social settlements. In J. Addams et al., *Philanthropy and social progress,* 1–26. New York: Books for Libraries Press.

———. (1899, May). A function of the social settlement. *Annals of the American Academy of Political and Social Science* 13: 323–345.

———. (1901, January 3). Respect for law. *Independent* 53: 18–20.

———. (1901/1977). Respect for law. In J. Addams and I. B. Wells, *Lynching and rape: An exchange of views,* 22–27. Ed. B. Aptheker. Chicago: University of Illinois, Occasional Paper No. 25.

———. (1902). *Democracy and social ethics.* New York: Macmillan.

———. (1912, November). The progressive party and the negro. *Crisis* 5: 30–31.

Adler, H. G. (1958). Ideas toward a sociology of the concentration camp. *American Journal of Sociology* 63: 513–522.

Adorno, T. W., et al. (1950). *The authoritarian personality.* New York: Harper.

Albee, E. (1962). *Who's afraid of Virginia Woolf?: A play.* New York: Pocket Books.

Alexander, E. (1994). "Can you be BLACK and look at this": Reading the Rodney King Video(s). In T. Golden (Ed.), *Black male: Representations of masculinity in contemporary American art,* 91–110. New York: Whitney Museum of American Art (Harry N. Abrams).

———. (1996). "We're gonna deconstruct your life!" The making and un-making of the black bourgeois patriarch in *Ricochet.* In M. Blount and G. P. Cunningham (Eds.), *Representing black man,* 157–171. New York: Routledge.

Allen, M. (1993). *Angry men, passive men.* New York: Fawcett.

Allen, S. S. (1977). The ironic voice in Baldwin's *Go Tell It on the Mountain.* In T. B. O'Daniel (Ed.), *James Baldwin: A critical evaluation,* 30–37. Washington, D.C.: Howard University Press.

Allport, G. (1958). *The nature of prejudice.* New York: Anchor Books. [Originally published in 1954 by Addison-Wesley.]

Althusser, L. (1971). *Lenin and philosophy.* Trans. Ben Brewster. New York: Monthly Review.

Ames, J. D. (1942). *The changing character of lynching.* Atlanta: Commission on Interracial Cooperation. (Reprinted in 1972 by AMS Press, New York.)

Andrews, W. L. (Ed.). (1993a). *African American autobiography: A collection of critical essays.* Englewood Cliffs, NJ: Prentice Hall.

———. (1993b). The representation of slavery and the rise of Afro-American literary realism. In W. L. Andrews (Ed.), *African American autobiography: A collection of critical essays,* 77–89. Englewood Cliffs, NJ: Prentice Hall.

Angeles, P. A. (1981). *Dictionary of philosophy.* New York: Barnes and Noble.

Appel, S. (Ed.). (1999). *Psychoanalysis and pedagogy.* Westport, CT: Bergin and Garvey.

Apple, M. W. (1996). *Cultural politics and education.* New York: Teachers College Press.

Aptheker, B. (1977). Introduction. J. Addams and I. B. Wells, *Lynching and rape: An exchange of views,* Chicago: University of Illinois, Occasional Paper No. 25.

Aries, P. (1962). *Centuries of childhood.* New York: Alfred Knopf.

Asante, M. K. (1980). *Afrocentricity: The theory of social change.* Buffalo: Amulefi.

Ashmore, R. (1896). *Side talks with girls.* New York: Charles Scribner's Sons.

Asika, N. (1997, June 15). Male rape victims hide in shame. New Orleans, LA: *Times Picayune,* A-27.

Associated Press. (1997, August 23). Officers indicated in torture case. Saskatoon, Saskatchewan: *StarPhoenix,* B16.

———. (1998, November 18). Nearly 18 percent. ... Baton Rouge: *Reveille,* 2.

Atwell-Vasey, W. (1998a). *Nourishing words: Bridging private reading and public teaching.* Albany: State University of New York Press.

———. (1998b). Psychoanalytic feminism and the powerful teacher. In W. F. Pinar (Ed.), *Curriculum: Toward new identities,* 143–156. New York: Garland.

Atwood, M. (1986). *The handmaid's tale.* Boston: Houghton Mifflin.

———. (1994). Alien territory. In L. Goldstein (Ed.), *The male body,* 1–7. Ann Arbor: University of Michigan Press.

Austen, R. (1991). *Genteel pagan: The double life of Charles Warren Stoddard.* Amherst, MA: University of Massachusetts Press.

Austin, J., and J. Irwin. (1990). *Who goes to prison.* San Francisco: National Council of Crime and Delinquency.

Awkward, M. (1995). *Negotiating difference: Race, gender, and the politics of positionality.* Chicago: University of Chicago Press.

———. (1996). A black man's place(s) in black feminist criticism. In M. Blount and G. P. Cunningham (Eds.), *Representing black man*, 3–26. New York: Routledge.

Ayers, E. L. (1984). *Vengeance and justice: Crime and punishment in the nineteenth century American South.* New York: Oxford.

———. (1992). *The promise of the new south: Life after Reconstruction.* New York: Oxford.

Bagemihl, B. (1999). *Biological exuberance: Animal homosexuality and natural diversity.* New York: St. Martin's Press.

Bailey, B. (1988). *From front porch to back seat: Courtship in twentieth-century America.* Baltimore: Johns Hopkins University Press.

Baker, B. E. (1997). North Carolina lynching ballads. In W. F. Brundage (Ed.), *Under sentence of death: Lynching in the South,* 218–245. Chapel Hill: University of North Carolina Press.

Baker, Jr., H. (1987a). *Modernism and the Harlem Renaissance.* Chicago: University of Chicago Press.

——— (1987b). Modernism and the Harlem Renaissance. *American Quarterly* 39(1): 84–97.

———. (1988). *Afro-American poetics: Revisions of Harlem and the black aesthetic.* Madison: University of Wisconsin Press.

Baker, P. (1990). The domestication of politics: Woman and American political society, 1780–1920. In E. C. Du Bois and V. L. Ruiz (Eds.), *Unequal sisters: A multicultural reader in U.S. women's history,* 66–91. New York: Routledge.

Baker, R. S. (1905a, January). What is a lynching? A study of mob violence, South and North. *McClure's Magazine* 24: 299–314.

———. (1905b, February). What is a lynching? A study of mob violence, South and North (cont.). *McClure's Magazine* 25: 422–430.

Baker, W. J., and J. A. Morgan. (1987). *Sport in Africa: Essays in social history.* New York: Africana Publishing Company.

Bakhtin, M. M. (1981). *The dialogic imagination.* Ed. M. Holquist. Austin: University of Texas Press.

Baldwin, J. (1961). *Nobody knows my name.* New York: Dial Press.

———. (1962). *Another country.* New York: Dial.

———. (1963/1985). *Go tell it on the mountain.* New York: Dell-Laurel.

———. (1965). *Another country.* New York: Dell. Trudier Harris quotes from this edition.

———. (1965/1998). *Going to the meet the man.* New York: Dial Press.

———. (1972). *No name in the street.* New York: Dell.

———. (1984). *Notes of a native son.* Boston: Beacon Press.

———. (1985). *The price of the ticket.* New York: St. Martin's Press.

———. (1990). *Jimmy's blues: Selected poems.* New York: St. Martin's Press.

———. (1998). Going to meet the man. In David R. Roediger (Ed.), *Black on white: Black writers on what it means to be white,* 255–273. New York: Schocken Books.

Bandura, A. (1973). *Aggression: A social learning analysis.* Englewood Cliffs, NJ: Prentice-Hall.

Banks, J. A. (1997). *Educating citizens in a multicultural society.* New York: Teachers College Press.

Banner, L. W. (1988). *Elizabeth Cady Stanton: A radical for women's rights.* Boston: Little, Brown.

Bannister, R. C. (1966). *Ray Stannard Baker: The mind and thought of a progressive.* New Haven: Yale University Press.

Baraka, I. A. [L. Jones]. (1965/1966). American sexual reference: Black male. In *Home: Social essays,* 216–233. New York: William Morrow.

Barker, P. (1888). *The secret book containing private information and instruction for women and young girls.* Brighton, UK: P. Baker.

Baron, A. (1990). Acquiring manly competence: The demise of apprenticeship and the remasculinization of printers' work. In M. C. Carnes and C. Griffen (Eds.), *Meanings for manhood: Constructions of masculinity in Victorian America,* 152–163. Chicago: University of Chicago Press.

Barthes, R. (1974). *S/Z.* Trans. R. Miller. New York: Hill and Wang.

———. (1988). The discourse of history. In *The rustle of language,* 127–140. Trans. R. Howard. Berkeley: University of California Press.

Bartollas, C., S. J. Miller, and S. Dinitz. (1974). Becoming a scapegoat: Study of a deviant career. *Sociological Symposium* 11: 84–97.

———. (1975a). Staff exploitation of inmates: The paradox of institutional control. In E. Viano and I. Drapkin (Eds.), *Exploiters and exploited: The dynamics of victimization,* 157–168. Lexington, MA: D. C. Heath.

———. (1975b, January). The inmate code in juvenile institutions: Guidelines for the strong. *Southern Journal of Criminal Justice* 1: 33–52.

———. (1976). *Juvenile victimization: The institutional paradox.* New York: Wiley.

Bataille, G. (1991). *The accursed share, vols. II and III: The history of eroticism and sovereignty.* Trans. R. Hurley. New York: Zone.

Bauer, J. L. (1997). Conclusion. The mixed blessings of women's fundamentalism: Democratic impulses in a patriarchal world. In J. Brink and J. Mencher (Eds.), *Mixed blessings: Gender and religious fundamentalism cross culturally,* 221–256. New York: Routledge.

Bauman, Z. (1978). *Hermeneutics and social science.* New York: Columbia University Press.

———. (1991). *Modernity and the holocaust.* Ithaca, NY: Cornell University Press.

Beard, G. M. (1881). American nervousness: Its causes and interpretations. New York: G. P. Putnam's Sons.

Beck, E. M., and S. E. Tolnay. (1997). When race didn't matter: Black and white mob violence against their own color. In W. F. Brundage (Ed.), *Under sentence of death: Lynching in the South,* 132–154. Chapel Hill: University of North Carolina Press.

Beckett, S. (1980). *Company.* New York: Grove Press.

Bederman, G. (1989, September). The women have had charge of the church work long enough. *American Quarterly* 41: 435–440.

———. (1995a). *Manliness and civilization: A cultural history of gender and race in the United States, 1880–1917.* Chicago: University of Chicago Press.

———. (1995b). "Civilization," the decline of middle-class manliness, and Ida B. Wells' antilynching campaign (1892–94). In D. C. Hine, W. King, and L. Reed (Eds.), *"We specialize in the wholly impossible": A reader in black women's history,* 407–432. Brooklyn, NY: Carlson.

Bell, D. (1960). *The end of ideology.* New York: Free Press.

Bell, Q. (1972). *Virginia Woolf: A biography.* New York: Harcourt Brace Jovanovich.

Benjamin, J. (1983). Master and slave: The fantasy of erotic domination. In A. Snitow, C. Stansell, and S. Thompson (Eds.), *Powers of desire: The politics of sexuality*, 280–299. New York: Monthly Review Press.

———. (1998). *In the shadow of the other*. New York: Routledge.

Benstock, S. (Ed.). (1988a). *The private self: Theory and practice of women's autobiographical writings*. Chapel Hill and London: University of North Carolina Press.

Berger, J. (1973). *Ways of seeing*. New York: Viking.

Bernal, M. (1987). *Black Athena: The afroasiatic roots of classical civilization*, vol. 1, *The fabrication of ancient Greece, 1785–1985*. London: Free Association Books.

Bernard, J. (1966). *Marriage and family among Negroes*. Englewood Cliffs, NJ: Prentice Hall.

Bernheimer, C. (1992, Spring). Penile reference in phallic theory. *Differences: A Journal of Feminist Cultural Studies* 4(1): 116–132.

Bersani, L. (1987). Is the rectum a grave? *October* 43: 197–222.

———. (1995). *Homos*. Cambridge, MA: Harvard University Press.

Bérubé, A. (1983). Marching to a different drummer: Lesbian and gay GIs in World War II. In A. Snitow, C. Stansell, and S. Thompson (Eds.), *Powers of desire: The politics of sexuality*, 88–99. New York: Monthly Review Press.

———. (1990). *Coming out under fire: The history of gay men and women in World War Two*. New York: Free Press.

Beveridge, A. (1905). *The young man and the world*. New York: Appleton.

Black, D. P. (1997). *Dismantling black manhood: An historical and literary analysis of the legacy of slavery*. New York: Garland.

Blackwell, J. E. (1977). Social and legal dimensions of interracial liaisons. In D. Y. Wilkinson and R. L. Taylor (Eds.), *The black male in America*, 219–243. Chicago: Nelson-Hall.

Blake, L. D. (1883). *Woman's place today*. New York: J. W. Lowell.

Blassingame, J. W. (1979). *The slave community*. New York: Oxford University Press.

Blee, K. M. (1991). *Women of the Klan: Racism and gender in the 1920s*. Berkeley: University of California Press.

Blewett, M. H. (1990). Masculinity and mobility: The dilemma of Lancashire weavers and spinners in late-nineteenth-century Fall River, Massachusetts. In M. C. Carnes and C. Griffen (Eds.), *Meanings for manhood: Constructions of masculinity in Victorian America*, 164–177. Chicago: University of Chicago Press.

Blinch, R. (1997, January 6). Canadian hockey in shock over sexual assaults by coach. Reuters Newswire.

Block, A. (1992). *Anonymous toil: A re-evaluation of the American radical novel in the twentieth century*. Lanham, MD: University Press of America.

Block, M. (1967). *Apologie pour l'histoire*. Paris: Armand Colin.

Bloom, J. (1990, April 6). Brockton officials may seek charges in hazing. *Boston Globe*, Metro section, 22.

Blos, P. (1979). *The adolescent passage*. New York: International Universities Press.

Blount, M., and G. P. Cunningham. (1996). Introduction: The "real" black man. In M. Blount and G. P. Cunningham (Eds.), *Representing black man*, ix–xv. New York: Routledge.

Blumin, S. M. (1989). *The emergence of the middle class: Social experience in the American city, 1760–1900*. Cambridge: Cambridge University Press.

Bly, R. (1990). *Iron John: A book about men*. Reading, MA: Addison Wesley.

Boa, E. (1996). *Kafka: Gender, class, and race in the letters and fictions*. Oxford: Clarendon Press.

Bohmer, C., and A. Parrot. (1993). *Sexual assault on campus: The problem and the solution*. New York: Lexington Books.

Bonacich, E. (1972). A theory of ethnic antagonism: The split labor market. *American Sociological Review* 37: 547–559.

———. (1975). Abolition, the extension of slavery, and the position of free blacks: A study of split labor markets in the United States, 1830–1863. *American Journal of Sociology* 83: 601–628.

Bond, H. M., and J. W. Bond (1997). *The Star Creek papers*. Ed. A. Fairclough. Athens: University of Georgia Press.

Bondeson, U. V. (1989). *Prisoners in prison societies*. New Brunswick, NJ: Transaction Publishers.

Bontemps, A. (1947). The Harlem renaissance. *Saturday Review*, 30.

Bordin, R. (1981). *Women and temperance: The quest for power and liberty, 1873–1900*. Philadephia: Temple University Press.

———. (1986). *Frances Willard: A biography*. Chapel Hill: University of North Carolina Press.

Bordo, S. (1993). *Unbearable weight: Feminism, western culture, and the body*. Berkeley and Los Angeles: University of California Press.

———. (1994). Reading the male body. In L. Goldstein (Ed.), *The male body*, 265–306. Ann Arbor: University of Michigan Press.

Boston, M. (1994/1998). Iola's letter. In K. A. Perkins and J. L. Stephens (Eds.), *Strange fruit: Plays on lynching by American women*, 368–408. Bloomington: Indiana University Press.

Bostwick, T., J. DeLucia-Waack, and D. Watson. (1995). Perceptions of dating behaviors and reasons offered to justify date rape. *NASPA Journal* 32(2): 123–129.

Bowker, L. H. (1980). *Prison victimization*. New York: Elsevier.

Boyarin, J. (1994). *Storm from paradise: The politics of Jewish memory*. Minneapolis: University of Minnesota Press.

Boykin, K. (1996). *One more river to cross: Black and gay in America*. New York: Anchor Books.

Brackman, H. D. (1977). The ebb and flow of conflict: A history of Black-Jewish relations through 1900. Los Angeles, CA: UCLA. Unpublished Ph.D. dissertation.

Bradley, M. (1981). *The iceman inheritance*. New York: Warner.

Braidotti, R. [with J. Butler]. (1994a). Interview: Feminism by another name. *Differences* 6(2+3): 27–61.

Braidotti, R. (1994b). Revisiting male thanatica. *Differences* 6(2+3): 199–207.

Brannon, R., and D. S. David. (1976). *The forty-nine percent majority: The male sex role*. Reading, MA: Addison-Wesley.

Brawley, B. (1921). *The Negro in literature and art*. New York: Duffield and Co.

Braxton, J. M. (1989). *Black women writing autobiography: A tradition within a tradition*. Philadelphia, PA: Temple University Press.

Brent, L. (1973). *Incidents in the life of a slave girl*. Ed. L. Maria Child. New York: Harcourt Brace Jovanovich.

Brien, P. M. (1995, August). *HIV in prisons and jails, 1993*. Washington, D.C.: U.S. Department of Justice, Bureau of Justice Statistics Bulletin.

Brink, J. (1997). Lost rituals: Sunni Muslim women in rural Egypt. In J. Brink and J. Mencher (Eds.), *Mixed blessings: Gender and religious fundamentalism cross culturally,* 199–208. New York: Routledge.

Britzman, D. P. (1998a). *Lost subjects, contested objects: Toward a psychoanalytic inquiry of learning.* Albany: State University of New York Press.

———. (1998b). Is there a queer pedagogy? Or, stop reading straight. In W. F. Pinar (Ed.), *Curriculum: Toward new identities,* 211–231. New York: Garland.

———. (1998c). On some psychical consequences of AIDS education. In W. F. Pinar (Ed.), *Queer theory in education,* 321–335. Mahwah, NJ: Lawrence Erlbaum.

Brod, H. (1996). Pornography and the alienation of male sexuality. In L. May, R. Strikwerda, and P. D. Hopkins (Eds.), *Rethinking masculinity: Philosophical explorations in light of feminism,* 237–253. Lanham, MD: Rowman and Littlefield.

Brombert, V. (1978). *The romantic prison: The French tradition.* Princeton, NJ: Princeton University Press.

———. (1984). *Victor Hugo and the visionary novel.* Cambridge: Cambridge University Press.

Brown, C. (1965). *Manchild in the promised land.* New York: Macmillan.

Brown, H. R. (1969). *Die nigger die!* New York: Dial Press.

Brown, N. O. (1959/1967). *Life against death: The psychoanalytical meaning of history.* Middletown, CT: Wesleyan University Press.

Brown, R. M. (1971). Legal and behavioral perspectives on American vigilantism. *Perspectives in American History* 5: 95–146.

———. (1975). *Strain of violence: Historical studies of American violence and vigilantism.* New York: Oxford University Press.

Brown, R. W. (1965). *Social psychology.* New York: Free Press.

Brown, W. W. (1853/1969). *Clotel; or, the president's daughter: A narrative of slave life in America.* Introduction by William Edward Farrison. New York: University Books/Carol.

Brownfield, D. (1987). Father-son relationships and violent behavior. *Deviant Behavior* 8: 65–78.

Brownmiller, S. (1975/1993). *Against our will: Men, women, and rape.* New York: Fawcett Columbine.

Bruce, P. A. (1889). *The plantation Negro as freedman.* New York: Putnam's.

Brundage, W. F. (1993). *Lynching in the new South: Georgia and Virginia, 1880–1930.* Urbana: University of Illinois Press.

———. (1997a). The roar on the other side of the silence: Black resistance and white violence in the American South, 1880–1940. In W. F. Brundage (Ed.), *Under sentence of death: Lynching in the South,* 270–291. Chapel Hill: University of North Carolina Press.

——— (Ed.). (1997b). *Under sentence of death: Lynching in the South.* Chapel Hill: University of North Carolina Press.

Buchanan, J. R. (1851). The sphere of woman. In *Proceedings of the woman's rights convention.* Cincinnati: n.p.

Buckley, J. H. (1984). *The turning key: Autobiography and the subjective impulse since 1800.* Cambridge: Harvard University Press.

Bulhan, H. A. (1985). *Frantz Fanon and the psychology of oppression.* New York and London: Plenum Press.

Bullough, V., and M. Voght. (1973). Homosexuality and its confusions with the "secret sin" in pre-Freudian America. *Journal of the History of Medicine* 28: 143–155.

Burstein, J. Q. (1977). *Conjugal visits in prison: Psychological and social consequences.* Lexington, MA: Lexington Books.

Burt, M. (1991). Rape myths and acquaintance rape. In A. Parrot and L. Bechhofer (Eds.), *Acquaintance rape: The hidden crime*, 26–40. New York: John Wiley.

Burt, M., and R. Albin. (1981). Rape myths, rape definitions, and probability of conviction. *Journal of Applied Social Psychology* 11: 212–230.

Burton, R. V., and J. M. W. Whiting. (1961). The absent father and cross-sex identity. *Merrill-Palmer Quarterly* 7: 87–90.

Bushnell, H. (1870). *Woman suffrage: The reforms against nature.* New York: Scribners.

Butler, J. (1990). *Gender trouble.* New York: Routledge.

———. (1992). The lesbian phallus and the morphological imaginary. *Differences* 4(1): 133–171.

———. (1993). *Bodies that matter: On the discursive limits of "sex."* New York and London: Routledge.

Butterfield, S. (1974). *Black autobiography in America.* Amherst, MA: University of Massachusetts Press.

Bystrom, D. G. (1996). Beyond the hearings: The continuing effects of Hill vs. Thomas on women and men, the workplace, and politics. In S. L. Ragan, D. G. Bystrom, L. Lee Kaid, and C. S. Beck (Eds.), *The lynching of language: Gender, politics, and power in the Hill-Thomas hearings,* 260–282. Urbana and Chicago: University of Illinois Press.

Caldwell, M. G. (1956). Group dynamics in the prison community. *Journal of Criminal Law, Criminology and Police Science* 46: 648–657.

Calhoun, K. S., and R. M. Townsley. (1991). Attributions of responsibility for acquaintance rape. In A. Parrot and L. Bechhofer (Eds.), *Acquaintance rape: The hidden crime,* 51–69. New York: John Wiley.

Calhoun, Sandra L., J. Selby, and L. Warring. (1976). Social perception of the victim's causal role in rape: An explanatory examination of four factors. *Journal of Human Relations* 29: 517–526.

Camp, G. M., and C. G. Camp. (1985). *Prison gangs: Their extent, nature and impact on prisons.* South Salem, NY: Criminal Justice Institute.

Campbell, K. K. (1989). *Man cannot speak for her: A critical study of early feminist rhetoric.* Vol. 2. New York: Praeger.

Candib, L., and R. Schmitt. (1996). About losing it: The fear of impotence. In L. May, R. Strikwerda, and P. D. Hopkins (Eds.), *Rethinking masculinity: Philosophical explorations in light of feminism,* 211–234. Lanham, MD: Rowman and Littlefield.

Cantril, H. (1941). *The psychology of social movements.* New York: John Wiley.

Capeci, Jr., D. J. (1998). *The lynching of Cleo Wright.* Lexington, KY: University Press of Kentucky.

Capraro, R. L. (1994). Disconnected lives: Men, masculinity, and rape prevention. In A. D. Berkowitz (Ed.), *Men and rape: Theory, research, and prevention programs in higher education*, 21–33. San Francisco: Jossey-Bass.

Caraway, N. (1991). *Segregated sisterhood: Racism and the politics of American feminism.* Knoxville: University of Tennessee Press.

Carby, H. V. (1987). *Reconstructing womanhood: The emergence of the Afro-American novelist.* New York: Oxford University Press.

———. (1993). "Hear my voice, ye careless daughters." In W. L. Andrews (Ed.), *African American autobiography: A collection of critical essays,* 59–76. Englewood Cliffs, NJ: Prentice Hall.

———. (1998). *Race men.* Cambridge, MA: Harvard University Press.

Cardozo-Freeman, I. (1984). *The joint: Language and culture in a maximum security prison.* Springfield, IL: Charles C. Thomas Publisher.

Carleton, M. T. (1971). *Politics and punishment: The history of the Louisiana State penal system.* Baton Rouge, LA: Louisiana State University Press.

Carnes, M. C. (1990). Middle-class men and the solace of fraternal ritual. In M. C. Carnes and C. Griffen (Eds.), *Meanings for manhood: Constructions of masculinity in Victorian America,* 37–52. Chicago: University of Chicago Press.

Carnes, M.C., and C. Griffen. (1990a). Introduction. In M. C. Carnes and C. Griffen (Eds.), *Meanings for manhood: Constructions of masculinity in Victorian America,* 1–7. Chicago: University of Chicago Press.

——— (Eds.). (1990b). *Meanings for manhood: Constructions of masculinity in Victorian America.* Chicago: University of Chicago Press.

Carroll, L. (1974). Race and sexual assault in a prison. Paper presented at the annual meeting of the Society for the Study of Social Problems.

———. (1977, January). Humanitarian reform and biracial sexual assault in a maximum security prison. *Urban Life* 5: 417–437.

Carson, C. (1981). *In struggle: SNCC and the black awakening of the 1960s.* Cambridge, MA: Harvard University Press.

Carson, M. (1990). *Settlement folk: Social thought and the American settlement movement, 1885–1930.* Chicago: University of Chicago Press.

Carter, D. T. (1969/1979). *Scottsboro: A tragedy of the American South,* rev. ed. Baton Rouge: Louisiana State University Press.

Cash, W. J. (1960). *The mind of the South.* New York: Vintage.

Cashin, J. E. (1997). A lynching in wartime Carolina. In W. F. Brundage (Ed.), *Under sentence of death: Lynching in the South,* 109–131. Chapel Hill: University of North Carolina Press.

———. (1998). A northwest passage: Gender, race, and the family in the early nineteenth century. In L. McCall and D. Yacovone (Eds.), *A shared experience: Men, women, and the history of gender,* 222–244. New York: New York University Press.

Cassity, M. (1984). *Chains of fears: American race relations since Reconstruction.* Westport, CT: Greenwood Press.

Catalino, A. (1972). Boys and girls in a coeducational training school are different—aren't they? *Canadian Journal of Criminology and Corrections* 14: 120–131.

Cavell, S. (1994). *A pitch of philosophy.* Cambridge, MA: Harvard University Press.

Célestin, R. (1996). *From cannibals to radicals: Figures and limits of exoticism.* Minneapolis and London: University of Minnesota Press.

Cell, J. W. (1982). *The highest stage of white supremacy: The origins of segregation in South African and the American South.* New York: Cambridge University Press.

Center for Disease Control and Prevention. (1986). Web site: http://www.cdc.gov

Chadbourn, J. H. (1933). *Lynching and the law.* Chapel Hill: University of North Carolina Press.

Charter, S. P. R. (Ed.). (1981). Introduction. Spinoza's *The Ethics.* Santa Barbara, CA: Joseph Pangloss Press.

Chaucer, L. (1992). *Sadomasochism in everyday life: The dynamics of power and powerlessness.* New Brunswick, NJ: Rutgers University Press.

Chauncey, G. (1994). *Gay New York: Gender, urban culture, and the making of the gay male world 1890–1940.* New York: Basic Books.

Chideya, F. (1993, August 30). Endangered family. *Newsweek,* 16–27.

Chodorow, N. J. (1978). *The reproduction of mothering.* Berkeley: University of California Press.

———. (1986). Toward a relational individualism. In T. C. Heller, M. Sosna and D. Wellbery (Eds.), *Reconstructing individualism: Autonomy, individuality, the self in Western thought,* 197–207. Stanford, CA: Stanford University Press.

———. (1989). *Feminism and psychoanalytic theory.* New Haven, CT: Yale University Press.

———. (1994). *Femininities, masculinities, sexualities: Freud and beyond.* Lexington, KY: University Press of Kentucky.

———. (1996). Gender as personal and cultural construction. In R.-E. B. Joeres and B. Laslett (Eds.), *The Second* Signs *Reader,* 3–26. Chicago: University of Chicago Press.

Chopp, R. S. (1989). *The power to speak: Feminism, language, God.* New York: Crossroads.

Chrisman, R. (1995/1996). Black prisoners, white law. In H. Boyd and R. L. Allen (Eds.), *Brotherman: The odyssey of black men in America,* 414–417. New York: Ballantine/One World.

Christian, B. (1980). *Black women novelists: The development of a tradition 1892–1976.* Westport, CT: Greenwood Press.

———. (1985). *Black feminist criticism: Perspectives on black women writers.* New York: Pergamon Press.

———. (1987). The race for theory. *Cultural Critique* 6: 51–64.

———. (1990). What Celie knows that you should know. In D. T. Goldberg (Ed.), *Anatomy of racism,* 135–145. Minneapolis: University of Minnesota Press.

Churchill, W., and J. Vander Wall. (1988). *Agents of repression: The FBI's secret wars against the Black Panther Party and the American Indian Movement.* Boston, MA: South End Press.

Clark, L. D. (1992). *A bright tragic thing: A tale of Civil War Texas.* El Paso, TX: Cinco Puntos Press.

Clarke, C. (1995). Race, homosocial desire, and "mammon" in *Autobiography of an ex-coloured man.* In G. E. Haggerty and B. Zimmerman (Eds.), *Professions of desire: Lesbian and gay studies in literature,* 84–97. New York: Modern Language Association of America.

Clarke, E. C. (1873). *Sex in education, or: A fair chance for the girls.* Boston: James Osgood.

Clatterbaugh, K. (1996). Are men oppressed? In L. May, R. Strikwerda, and P. D. Hopkins (Eds.), *Rethinking masculinity: Philosophical explorations in light of feminism,* 289–305. Lanham, MD: Rowman and Littlefield.

Clear, T. R., and G. F. Cole. (1986). *American corrections.* Monterey, CA: Brooks/Cole.

Cleaver, E. (1968). *Soul on ice.* New York: Dell.

CNN. (1998, August 3). *2,000 children died via child abuse in 1997.* CNN News.

Cobbe, F. P. (1881). *Duties of women* 8th Am. ed. Boston: George Ellis.

Cogan, F. B. (1989). *All-American girl: The ideal of real womanhood in mid-nineteenth-century America.* Athens: University of Georgia Press.

Cohen, A. (Ed.). (1956). *The five books of Moses with Haptharoth.* London: Soncino Press.

Cole, D. (1999). *No equal justice.* New York: New Press.

Collard, A. (with J. Contrucci). (1989). *Rape of the wild: Man's violence against animals and earth.* Bloomington: Indiana University Press.

Collier, R. (1995). *Masculinity, law and the family.* London: Routledge.

Collins, J. (1926). *The doctor looks at love and life.* New York: Doran.

Collins, P. H. (1991). *Black feminist thought: Knowledge, consciousness, and the politics of empowerment.* New York: Routledge.

———. (1993). It's in our hands: Breaking the silence on gender in African American studies. In L. Castenell, Jr., and W. F. Pinar (Eds.), *Understanding curriculum as racial text: Representations of identity and difference in education,* 127–142. Albany: State University of New York Press.

Collins, W. H. (1913). *The truth about lynching and the Negro in the South.* New York: Neale Publishing Co.

Colvin, M. (1997). *Penitentiaries, reformatories, and chain gangs.* New York: St. Martin's Press.

Comer, J. P. (1972). Beyond black and white. New York: Quadrangle.

Commager, H. S. (1950). *The American mind.* New Haven: Yale University Press.

Comstock, G. D. (1991). *Violence against lesbians and gay men.* New York: Columbia University Press.

Cook, B. (1977). Female support networks and political activism: Lillian Wald, Crystal Eastman, Emma Goldman. *Chrysalis* 3: 43–61.

Cooke, B. G. (1972). Nonverbal communication among Afro-Americans: An initial classification. In T. Kochman (Ed.), *Rappin' and stylin': Communication in urban black America,* 32–64. Urbana: University of Illinois Press.

Cooper, A. J. (1892/1998). A voice from the South. In C. Lemert and E. Bhan (Eds.), *The voice of Anna Julia Cooper,* 51–196. Lanham, MD: Rowan and Littlefield.

Cornell, D. (1992). What takes place in the dark. *Differences* 4(2): 45–71.

Cott, N. F. (1977). *The bonds of womanhood: "Woman's sphere" in New England, 1780–1835.* New Haven: Yale University Press.

———. (1990). On men's history and women's history. In M. C. Carnes and C. Griffen (Eds.), *Meanings for manhood: Constructions of masculinity in Victorian America,* 205–211. Chicago: University of Chicago Press.

Couto, R. A. (1993). *Lifting the veil: A political history of struggles for emancipation.* Knoxville: University of Tennessee Press.

Cox, O. C. (1948/1970). *Caste, class, and race: A study of social dynamics.* New York: Monthly Review Press. First published by Doubleday.

Cremin, L. A. (1961). *The transformation of the school: Progressivism in American education, 1876–1957.* New York: Alfred A. Knopf.

Cressey, D. R., and D. A. Ward. (1969). *Delinquency, crime and the social process.* New York: Harper and Row.

Crimp, D. (1993). Fassbinder, Franz, Fox, Elvira, Erwin, Armin, and all the others. In M. Gever, P. Parmar, and J. Greyson (Eds.), *Queer looks: Perspectives on lesbian and gay film and video,* 257–274. Toronto: Between the Lines.

Crocco, M. S., P. Munro, and K. Weiler. (1999). *Pedagogies of resistance: Women educator activists, 1880–1960.* Foreword by Nel Noddings. New York: Teachers College Press.

Crosset, T. J. Benedict, and M. McDonald. (1995). Male student athletes reported for sexual assault: A survey of campus police departments and judicial affairs offices. *Journal of Sports and Social Issues* 19(2): 126–140.

Crouch, B. M., and J. W. Marquart. (1989). *An appeal to justice: Litigated reform of Texas prisons.* Austin: University of Texas Press.

Cummins, E. (1994). *The rise and fall of California's radical prison movement.* Stanford, CA: Stanford University Press.

Curtis, L. A. (1975). *Violence, race and culture.* Lexington, MA: Lexington Books.

Curtis, S. (1990). The son of man and god the father: The social gospel and Victorian masculinity. In M. C. Carnes and C. Griffen (Eds.), *Meanings for manhood: Constructions of masculinity in Victorian America,* 67–83. Chicago: University of Chicago Press.

Cutler, J. E. (1905). *Lynch law: An investigation into the history of lynching in the United States.* New York: Longmans, Green.

Dabbs, J. M., R. L. Frady, T. S. Carr, and N. F. Besch. (1987). Saliva testosterone and criminal violence in young adult prison inmates. *Psychosomatic Medicine* 49: 174–182.

Daly, M. (1973). *Beyond God the father: Toward a philosophy of women's liberation.* Boston: Beacon Press.

———. (1978). *Gyn/ecology: The metaethics of radical feminism.* Boston: Beacon Press.

———. (1984). *Pure lust.* Boston: Beacon Press.

Dance, D. (1978). *Shuckin' and jivin': Folklore from contemporary black Americans.* Bloomington: Indiana University Press.

Dateline. (1997, June 17). I gotta be me. New York: NBC News.

Davidson, B. (1994). *The search for Africa: History, culture, politics.* New York: Random House.

Davion, V. (1995). Rape, group responsibility and trust. *Hypatia* 10: 153–156.

Davis, A. (1983). *Women, race and class.* New York: Vintage.

Davis, A. J. (1968, December). Sexual assaults in the Philadelphia prison system and sheriff's vans. *Trans-Action* 6(2): 8–16.

Davis, D. B. (1968). *Homicide in American fiction, 1798–1860: A study in social values.* Ithaca and London: Cornell University Press.

Davis, F. J. (1991). *Who is black? One nation's definition.* University Park: The Pennsylvania State University Press.

Davis, K. B. (1929). *Factors in the sex life of twenty-two hundred women.* New York: Harper and Brothers.

Dawsey, D. (Ed.). (1996). *Living to tell about it: Young black men in America speak their piece.* New York: Doubleday.

Day, B. (1977). The hidden fear. In D. Y. Wilkinson and R. L. Taylor (Eds.), *The black male in America,* 193–206. Chicago: Nelson-Hall.

Dayton, D. (1976). *Discovering an evangelical heritage.* New York: Harper and Row.

De Beaumont, G., and A. de Tocqueville. (1964). *On the penitentiary system in the United States and its application in France.* Carbondale, IL: Southern Illinois University Press.

De Certeau, M. (1980, Fall). On the oppositional practices of everyday life. *Social Text* 3.

de Lauretis, T. (1990). Eccentric subjects: Feminist theory and historical consciousness. *Feminist Studies* 16(1): 115–150.

de Rougemont, D. (1956). *Love in the Western world.* New York: Pantheon

DeBerg, B. A. (1990). *Ungodly women: Gender and the first wave of American fundamentalism.* Minneapolis: Fortress Press.

Debord, G. (1977). *The society of the spectacle.* Detroit: Black and Red.

DeCosta-Willis, M. (1995a). Introduction. *The Memphis diary of Ida B. Wells* (1–16). Boston: Beacon Press.

——— (Ed.). (1995b). *The Memphis diary of Ida B. Wells.* Boston, MA: Beacon Press.

DeCoy, R. H. (1967). *The nigger bible.* Los Angeles: Holloway House Publishing Co.

Delany, M. (1860/1969). Official report of the Niger valley exploring party. In H. H. Bell (Ed.), *Search for a place: Black separatism and Africa.* Ann Arbor: University of Michigan Press.

Deleuze, G. (1986). *Foucault.* Trans. and ed. S. Hand. Minneapolis: University of Minnesota Press.

———. (1993). *The fold: Leibniz and the Baroque.* Trans. T. Conley. Minneapolis and London: University of Minnesota Press.

Deleuze, G., and F. Guattari. (1987). *A thousand plateaus: Capitalism and schizophrenia.* Trans. B. Massumi. Minneapolis: University of Minnesota Press.

———. (1994). *What is philosophy?* Trans. H. Tomlinson and G. Bruchell. New York: Columbia University Press.

Dell, F. (1913). *Women as world builders.* Chicago: Forbes.

———. (1914, July). Feminism for men. *Masses,* 19–20.

———. (1921, October). Feminism and socialism. *New Masses* 345–353.

Delphy, C., and D. Leonard. (1992). *Familiar exploitation: A new analysis of marriage in contemporary Western societies.* Cambridge: Polity.

D'Emilio, J., and E. B. Freedman. (1983). *Intimate matters: A history of sexuality in America.* New York: Harper and Row.

Derrick, S. S. (1997). *Monumental anxieties: Homoerotic desire and feminine influence in nineteenth-century U.S. literature.* New Brunswick, NJ: Rutgers University Press.

Derrida, J. (1967/1976). *Of grammatology.* Trans. G. Spivak. Baltimore, MD: Johns Hopkins University Press. Originally published in French, 1967.

———. (1992). *Given time: 1. Counterfeit money.* Chicago: University of Chicago Press.

Deutsch, M. E., D. Cunningham, and E. Fink. (1995). Twenty years later: Attica civil rights case finally cleared for trial. In E. P. Sbarbaro and R. L. Keller (Eds.), *Prison crisis: Critical readings,* 47–57. New York: Harrow and Heston.

Dewey, J. (1916). *Democracy and education.* New York: Macmillan.

DeWitt, B. P. (1915). *The progressive movement: A non-partisan comprehensive discussion of the current tendencies in American politics.* New York: Macmillan.

Diener, F. (1980). Deindividuation: The absence of self-awareness and self-regulation in group members. In P. B. Paulus (Ed.), *Psychology of group influence,* 209–242. Hillsdale, NJ: Erlbaum.

Dinitz, S., S. J. Miller, and C. Bartollas. (1973, September 2–6). Inmate exploitation: A study on the juvenile victim. A paper presented to the First International Symposium on Victimology. Hebrew University.

Dinnerstein, L. (1968). *The Leo Frank case.* New York: Columbia University Press.

Dionne, Jr., E. J. (1996). *They only look dead: Why progressives will dominate the next political era.* New York: Simon & Schuster.

Disch, L., and M. J. Kane. (1996). When a looker is really a bitch: Lisa Olson, sport, and the heterosexual matrix. In R.-E. B. Joeres and B. Laslett (Eds.), *The second* Signs *reader: Feminist scholarship,* 326–356. Chicago: University of Chicago Press.

Divans, K., and L. M. West. (1971). Larry M.: Prison or slavery. *Black Scholar* 3(2): 6–12.

Dixon, T., Jr. (1905/1970). *The clansman: An historical romance of the Ku Klux Klan.* Lexington, KY: University of Kentucky Press.

Dobash, R. E., and R. P. Dobash. (1992). *Women, violence, and social change.* London: Routledge.

Dobash, R. P., R. E. Dobash, K. Cavanagh, and R. Lewis. (1996). *The evaluation of programmes for violent men.* Edinburgh: Scottish Office.

Dodge, M. [G. Hamilton]. (1868/1972). *Woman's wrongs: A counter-irritant.* New York: Arno Press.

Doll, M. A. (1995). Mother matters. In *To the Lighthouse and Back,* 18–27. New York: Peter Lang.

———. (1998). Queering the gaze. In W. F. Pinar (Ed.), *Queer theory in education,* 287–298. Mawah, NJ: Lawrence Erlbaum.

———. (in press). *Like letters in running water: A mythopoetics of curriculum.* Mawah, NJ: Lawrence Erlbaum.

Doll, Jr., W. E. (1993). *A post-modern perspective on curriculum.* New York: Teachers College Press.

Dollard, J. (1937). *Caste and class in a small southern town.* New Haven, CT: Yale University Press.

Dollard, J., et al. (1939). *Frustration and aggression.* New Haven, CT: Yale University Press.

Dollimore, J. (1991). *Sexual dissidence: Augustine to Wilde, Freud to Foucault.* Oxford: Oxford University Press.

Donaldson, S. (1993a, December 29). The rape crisis behind bars. *New York Times,* A11.

———. (1993b, February 4). Sex among American male prisoners and its implications for concepts of sexual orientation: A million jockers, punks, and queens. Lecture delivered at Columbia University.

Doty, A. (1993). *Making things perfectly queer.* Minneapolis, MN: University of Minnesota Press.

Douglas, A. (1977). *The feminization of American culture.* New York: Knopf.

———. (1988). *The feminization of American culture.* Rev. ed. New York: Anchor Press.

Douglas, K. A., J. L. Collins, C. Warren, L. Kann, R. Gold, S. Clayton, J. G. Ross, and L. J. Kolbe. (1997). Results from the 1995 National College Health Risk Behavior Survey. *Journal of the American College Health Association* 46: 55–66.

Douglas, M. (1966). *Purity and danger: An analysis of concepts of pollution and taboo.* New York: Praeger.

———. (1968). Pollution. *International Encyclopedia of Social Sciences* 12.

———. (1973). *Natural symbols.* London: Penguin.

Douglass, F. (1845/1984). *Narrative of the life of Frederick Douglass, an American slave: Written by himself.* New York: Modern Library.

———. (1855/1968). *My bondage and my freedom.* New York: Arno Press.

———. (1881/1983). *Life and times.* Secaucus, NJ: Citadel Press.

———. (1892, July). Lynch law in the South. *North American Review*, 17–24.

Downey, D. B., and R. M. Hyser. (1991). *No crooked death: Coatesville, Pennsylvania and the lynching of Zachariah Walker.* Urbana: University of Illinois Press.

Dubbert, J. (1979). *A man's place: Masculinity in transition.* Englewood Cliffs, NJ: Prentice Hall.

———. (1980). Progressivism and the masculinity crisis. In E. Pleck and J. Pleck (Eds.), *The American man.* Englewood Cliffs, NJ: Prentice Hall.

Duberman, M. B. (1989). "Writhing bedfellows" in antebellum South Carolina: Historical interpretation and the politics of evidence. In M. Duberman, M. Vicinus, and G. Chauncey, Jr. (Eds.), *Hidden from History: Reclaiming the Gay and Lesbian Past,* 153–168. New York: Meridian.

Du Bois, E. C. (1984). The limitations of sisterhood: Elizabeth Cady Stanton and division in the American suffrage movement, 1875–1902. In *Women and the structure of society: Selected research from the fifth Berkshire conference on the history of women.* Durham, NC: Duke University Press.

———. (1987). The radicalism of the woman suffrage movement: Notes toward the reconstruction of nineteenth-century feminism. In A. Phillips (Ed.), *Feminism and equality,* 127–138. New York: New York University Press.

Du Bois, W. E. B. (1901, June 16). The evolution of Negro leadership. *Dial* 31: 53–55.

———. (1903/1982). *The souls of black folk.* New York: New American Library.

———. (1919, May). Opinion. *Crisis* 18: 13–14.

———. (1927, August). Mob tactics. *Crisis* 34(6): 204.

———. (1940). *Dusk of dawn: An essay toward an autobiography of a race concept.* New York: Harcourt, Brace.

———. (1968). *An autobiography of W. E. B. Du Bois: A soliloquy on viewing my life from the last decade of its first century.* New York: International Publishers.

———. (1995/1996). The souls of black folk. In H. Boyd and R. L. Allen (Eds.), *Brotherman: The odyssey of black men in America,* 36–40. New York: Ballantine/One World.

duCille, A. (1993). *The coupling connection: Sex, text, and tradition in black women's fiction.* New York: Oxford University Press.

Ducrot, O., and T. Todorov. (1979). *Encyclopedic dictionary of the sciences of language.* Trans. C. Porter. Baltimore: Johns Hopkins University Press.

Duke, L. (1995, September 9). Mugabe makes homosexuals public enemies. Washington, D.C.: *Washington Post,* A19, A24.

Dunbar, P. L. (1920). "We Wear the Mask." In *The complete poems of Paul Laurence Dunbar.* New York: Dodd, Mead.

Duncan, J. (1999, September 11). Hazing apparently in the past at LSU, Tulane. New Orleans, LA: *Times-Picayune,* D-6.

Duncan, M. G. (1996). *Romantic outlaws, beloved prisons: The unconscious meanings of crime and punishment.* New York: New York University Press.

Dunlap, D. W. (1995, March 19). Shameless homophobia and the "Jenny Jones" murder. *New York Times,* 16E.

Duster, A. M. (1970). Introduction. Ida B. Wells, *Crusade for Justice,* xiii–xxxii. Chicago: University of Chicago Press.

Dworkin, A. (1974). *Woman hating.* New York: E. P. Dutton.

———. (1981). *Pornography: Men possessing women.* New York: E. P. Dutton.

———. (1983). *Right-wing women.* New York: Coward-McCann.

Dyer, R. (1988, Autumn). "White." *Screen* 29(4): 44–65.

———. (1992). Don't look now: The male pin-up. In *Screen,* M. Merck (Ed.), *The Sexual Subject,* 265–276. New York: Routledge.

Dyer, T. G. (1997). A most unexampled exhibition of madness and brutality. Judge Lynch in Saline County, Missouri, 1859. In W. F. Brundage (Ed.), *Under sentence of death: Lynching in the South,* 81–108. Chapel Hill: University of North Carolina Press.

Dyson, M. E. (1995). *Making Malcolm: The myth and meaning of Malcolm X.* New York: Oxford University Press.

———. (1995/1996). Reflecting black. In H. Boyd and R. L. Allen (Eds.), *Brotherman: The odyssey of black men in America,* 158–168. New York: Ballantine/One World.

Eakin, P. J. (1993). Malcolm X and the limits of autobiography. In W. L. Andrews (Ed.), *African American autobiography: A collection of critical essays,* 151–161. Englewood Cliffs, NJ: Prentice Hall.

Earhart, M. (1944). *Frances Willard: From prayers to politics.* Chicago: University of Chicago Press.

Earle, W. (1972). *The autobiographical consciousness: A philosophical inquiry into existence.* Chicago: Quandrangle Books.

Easthope, A. (1983). *Poetry as discourse.* London and New York: Methuen.

———. (1986). *What a man's gotta do: The masculine myth in popular culture.* London: Paladin.

Eastman, M. (1912). *Is woman suffrage important?* New York: Men's League for Woman Suffrage.

———. (1914, March). What do you know about this? The *Masses.*

———. (1936). *The enjoyment of living.* New York: Harper.

Edwards, H. (1973, November). The black athlete: 20th century gladiators for white America. *Psychology Today* 7: 43–47, 50, 52.

———. (1982). Race in contemporary American sports. *National Forum* 62: 19–22.

———. (1984). The collegiate athletic arms race: Origin and implications of the "Rule 48" controversy. *Journal of Sport Sociology International* 8(4): 4–22.

Edwards, S. (1989). *Policing domestic violence*: London: Sage.

Ehrenkranz, J., E. Bliss, and M. H. Sheard. (1974). Plasma testosterone: Correlation with aggressive behavior and social dominance in men. *Psychosomatic Medicine* 36: 469–475.

Eigenberg, H. M. (1994). Rape in male prisons: Examining the relationship between correctional officers' attitudes toward male rape and their willingness to respond to acts of rape. In M. Braswell, S. Dillingham, and R. Montgomery, Jr. (Eds.), *Prison violence in America,* 145–165. Cincinnati, OH: Anderson.

Elias, M. (1981). Serum cortisol, testosterone, and testosterone binding globulin response to competitive fighting in human males. *Aggressive Behavior* 7: 215–224.

Elkins, S. M. (1959). *Slavery: A problem in American institutional and intellectual life.* Chicago: University of Chicago Press.

Elliot, P. (1996, Spring). Working through racism: Confronting the strangely familiar. *Journal for the Psychoanalysis of Culture and Society* 1(1): 63–72.

Elliott, M. (1952). *Crime in the modern society.* New York: Harper and Brothers.

Ellison, R. (1940, July 2). The birthmark. *New Masses* 36: 16–17.

———. (1952). *Invisible man.* New York: Signet.

———. (1964/1995). *Shadow and act.* New York: Random House. [Reprinted in 1995 by Vintage.]

———. (1964/1995). The world and the jug (1963–1964). In *Shadow and Act,* 107–143. New York: Vantage Books.

———. (1967, March). A very stern discipline. *Harper's,* 81–88.

Eppert, C. (1999). Learning responsivity/responsibility: Reading the literature of historical witness. Toronto: University of Toronto, Ontario Institute for Studies in Education. Unpublished Ph.D. dissertation.

———. (2000). Personal communication.

Epstein, B. L. (1981). *The politics of domesticity: Women, evangelism, and temperance in nineteenth-century America.* Middletown, CT: Wesleyan University Press.

Erenberg, L. A. (1981). *Stepping out: New York nightlife and the transformation of American culture, 1890–1930.* Chicago: University of Chicago Press.

Erikson, E. (1975). *Life history and the historical moment.* New York: Norton.

Erikson, K. (1966). *Wayward Puritans: A study in the sociology of deviance.* New York: Wiley.

Erlanger, H. S. (1974). The empirical status of the subculture of violence thesis. *Social Problems* 22: 280–291.

Eskenazi, G. (1991, February). Male athletes and sexual assault. *Cosmopolitan* 220–223.

Eure, J., and R. Jerome (Eds.). (1989). *Back where we belong: Selected speeches by Minister Louis Farrakhan.* Philadelphia: PC International Press.

Evans, S. (1989). *Born for liberty: A history of women in America.* New York: Free Press.

Fairclough, A. (1995/1999). *Race and democracy: The civil rights struggle in Louisiana, 1915–1972.* [Paperback edition: 1999.] Athens: University of Georgia Press.

———. (1997). Introduction. H. M. Bond and J. W. Bond, *The Star Creek Papers,* xvii–xxx. Athens: University of Georgia Press.

Fanon, F. (1967). *Black skin, white masks.* Trans. C. L. Markmann. New York: Grove Weidenfeld.

———. (1968). *The wretched of the earth.* Trans. C. Farrington. New York: Grove Press.

———. (1990). The fact of blackness. In D. T. Goldberg (Ed.), *Anatomy of racism,* 108–126. Minneapolis: University of Minnesota Press.

Farrell, J. C. (1967). *Beloved lady: A history of Jane Addams' ideas on reform and peace.* Baltimore, MD: Johns Hopkins University Press.

Farrell, W. T. (1993). *The myth of male power: Why men are the disposable sex.* New York: Simon and Schuster.

Faulkner, W. (1936, rpt. 1987). *Absalom, Absalom*! New York: Vintage Books.

———. (1954). *The Faulkner reader: Selections from the work of William Faulkner.* New York: Random House.

———. (1932/1968). *Light in August*. New York: Random House.

———. (1992/1987). *Light in August*. New York: Garland.

Faust, D. G. (1996). *Mothers of invention. Women of the slave-holding South in the American civil war*. Chapel Hill: University of North Carolina Press.

F.B.I. Uniform Crime Reports. (1992). Web Site: http://www.fbi.gov

Feagin, J. R., and V. Hernan. (1995). *White racism: The basics*. New York: Routledge.

Fellows, Jr., J. (1997, August 14). Ill-gotten wealth and the damage of slave trading. Los Angeles*: L.A. Watts Times*.

Felman, S. (1982). Psychoanalysis and education: Teaching terminable and interminable. In B. Johnson (Ed.), *The pedagogical imperative: Teaching as literary genre*, 21–44. New Haven, CT: Yale University Press.

Felman, S., and D. M. Laub. (1992). *Testimony: Crises of witnessing in literature, psychoanalysis, and history*. New York: Routledge.

Ferguson, M. (Ed.). (1987). *The history of Mary Prince, A West Indian slave, related by herself* (1831). London: Pandora.

Ferrell, C. L. (1986). *Nightmare and dream: Antilynching in Congress, 1917–1922*. New York: Garland.

Fichte, H. (1996). *The gay critic*. Trans. K. Gavin. Introduction by J. W. Jones. Ann Arbor: University of Michigan Press.

Fiedler, L. A. (1966). *Love and death in the American novel*, Revised edition. New York: Stein and Day.

———. (1948/1995). Come back to the raft ag'in, Huck honey! In G. Graff and J. Phelan (Eds.), *Mark Twain*, Adventures of Huckleberry Finn: *A Case Study in Critical Controversy*, 528–534. Boston and New York: Bedford Books of St. Martin's Press. Originally appeared in *Partisan Review* (1948), 664–711.

Filene, P. G. (1998) *Him/her/self*, 3rd edition. Baltimore, MD: Johns Hopkins University Press.

Finnegan, T. (1997). Lynching and political power in Mississippi and South Carolina. In W. F. Brundage (Ed.), *Under sentence of death: Lynching in the South*, 189–218. Chapel Hill: University of North Carolina Press.

Fiorenza, E. S. (1993). Transforming the legacy of *The Woman's Bible*. In *Searching the Scriptures*, vol. 1. *A feminist introduction*. New York: Crossroads.

Fischer, D. H. (1989). *Albion's way: Four British folkways in America*. New York: Oxford University Press.

Fishman, J. F. (1934). *Sex in prison*. No city given: National Library Press.

Fitzgerald, M. (1993). The religious is personal is political: Foreword to the 1993 edition of *The Woman's Bible*. *The Woman's Bible* by Elizabeth Cady Stanton. Boston: Northeastern University Press.

Flannigan-Saint-Aubin, A. (1993, January). "Black gay male" discourse: Reading race and sexuality between the lines. *Journal of the History of Sexuality* 3(3): 468–490.

Flax, J. (1987, Winter). Re-membering the selves: Is the repressed gendered? *Michigan Quarterly Review* 26(1): 92–110.

Fleisher, M. (1994). Scenes of violence. In M. Braswell, S. Dillingham, and R. Montgomery, Jr. (Eds.), *Prison violence in America*, 73–95. Cincinnati, OH: Anderson.

Folb, E. A. (1980). *Runnin' down some lines: The language and culture of black teenagers*. Cambridge, MA: Harvard University Press.

Foner, E. (1988). *Reconstruction, 1863–1877*. New York: Harper and Row.

Fones-Wolf, E., and K. Fones-Wolf. (1983). Trade-union evangelism: Religion and the AFL in the Labor Forward Movement, 1912–1916. In M. H. Frish and D. J. Walkowitz (Eds.), *Working class America,* 153–184. Urbana: University of Illinois Press.

Forster, E. M. (1971). *Maurice.* New York: Norton.

Forten, C. L. (1862, December). Interesting letter from Charlotte L. Forten. *Liberator* 19: 7.

———. (1864). Life on the sea islands. *Atlantic Monthly* 13: 587–596.

———. (1893, June). Personal recollections of Whittier. *New England Magazine* 8: 472.

———. (1953). *The journal of Charlotte L. Forten.* Ed. R. A. Billington. New York: Dryden Press.

———. (1968). *The journals of Charlotte Forten Grimké.* Ed. B. Stevenson. New York: Oxford University Press.

Foster, F. (1981, Summer). "In respect to females ...": Differences in the portrayal of women by male and female narrators. *Black American Literature Forum* 15: 66–70.

Foucault, M. (1976, 1978, 1980). *History of sexuality.* Trans. R. Hurley. New York: Vintage.

———. (1978). *The history of sexuality, vol. 1: An introduction.* New York: Random House.

———. (1979/1995). *Discipline and punish: The birth of the prison.* Trans. A. Sheridan. New York: Vintage.

———. (1987). Maurice Blanchot: The thought from outside. In *Foucault/Blanchot,* 7–58. Trans. B. Massumi. New York: Zone Books.

———. (1988). *The care of the self: volume 3, The history of sexuality.* Trans. R. Hurley. New York: Random House.

———. (1988/1990). *Politics, philosophy, culture: Interviews and other writings 1977–1984.* Ed. Lawrence D. Kritzman. New York and London: Routledge.

Fox-Genovese, E. (1988). My statue, my self: Autobiographical writings of Afro-American women. In S. Benstock (Ed.), *The private self: Theory and practice of women's autobiographical writings,* 63–89. Chapel Hill and London: University of North Carolina Press.

Frankenberg, R. (1993). *White women, race matters: The social construction of whiteness.* Minneapolis: University of Minnesota Press.

———. (1997a). Introduction: Local whiteness, localizing whiteness. In R. Frankenberg (Ed.), *Displacing whiteness: Essays in social and cultural criticism,* 1–33. Durham, NC: Duke University Press.

——— (Ed.). (1997b). *Displacing whiteness: Essays in social and cultural criticism.* Durham, NC: Duke University Press.

Franklin, C. W. (1988). *Men and society.* Chicago: Nelson-Hall.

Franklin, J. H. (1970). Foreword. Ida B. Wells, *Crusade for Justice,* ix–xi. Chicago: University of Chicago Press.

Frazier, E. F. (1949). *The Negro family in the United States.* Chicago: University of Chicago Press.

Frederickson, G. M. (1965). *The inner civil war: Northern intellectuals and the crisis of the union.* New York: Harper.

——— (1971). *The black image in the white mind.* New York: Harper and Row.

———. (1988). *The arrogance of race: Historical perspectives on slavery, racism, and social inequality.* Middletown, CT: Wesleyan University Press.

Frei, H. (1974). *The eclipse of biblical narrative: A study in eighteenth- and nineteenth-century hermeneutics.* New Haven: Yale University Press.

Freud, S. (1899/1989). Screen memories. In P. Gay (Ed.), *The Freud reader,* 117–128. New York: Norton.

———. (1905/1953/1995). *A case of hysteria, Three essays on sexuality and other works, of Sigmund Freud. Standard Edition,* vol. 7. London: Hogarth Press and the Institute of Psycho-Analysis. General Edition of J. Strachey in collaboration with A. Freud.

———. (1911–1913). Remembering, repeating and working-through. (Further recommendations on the techniques of psycho-analysis II.) *Standard Edition* 12, 145–156. London: Hogarth Press.

———. (1911/1963). Psychoanalytic notes upon an autobiographical account of a case of paranoia (Dementia Paranoides). In P. Rieff (Ed.), *Three Case Histories,* 103–186. New York: Collier.

———. (1915). The unconscious. In *Standard Edition,* vol. 14, 166–204. London: Hogarth Press.

———. (1955). *Beyond the pleasure principle: Complete psychological works,* vol. 18. London: Hogarth Press

———. (1966). T*he interpretation of dreams.* In *Standard Edition,* vol. 5, 509–621. Trans. J. Strachey. London: Hogarth Press.

———. (1923; 1977). *The ego and the id.* Penguin Freud Library. Vol. 11. New York: Penguin.

———. (1977). *Three essays on sexuality.* Penguin Freud Library, Vol. 7. London: Penguin.

Freyre, G. (1946). *The masters and the slaves.* New York: Knopf.

Friedenberg, E. (1962). *The vanishing adolescent.* New York: Dell.

Friedman, L. J. (1970). *The white savage: Racial fantasies in the postbellum South.* Englewood Cliffs, NJ: Prentice Hall.

Friedman, S. S. (1988). Women's autobiographical selves: Theory and practice. In S. Benstock (Ed.), *The private self: Theory and practice of women's autobiographical writings,* 34–62. Chapel Hill and London: University of North Carolina Press.

Frye, M. (1983). *The politics of reality.* Trumansburg, NY: Crossing.

Fuller, D. A., T. Orsagh, and D. Raber. (1977). Violence and victimization within the North Carolina prison system. Paper presented at the annual meeting of the Academy of Criminal Justice Sciences.

Funk, R. E. (1994). *Stopping rape: A challenge for men.* Philadelphia: New Society Publishers.

Fussell, S. (1994). Bodybuilder Americanus. In L. Goldstein (Ed.), *The male body,* 43–60. Ann Arbor: University of Michigan Press.

Gallop, J. (1988). *Thinking through the body.* New York: Columbia University Press.

Gates, Jr., H. L. (1987). Frederick Douglass and the language of the self, in *Figures in black: Words, signs, and the 'racial' self.* New York: Oxford University Press.

———. (1988). *The signifying monkey: A theory of Afro-American literary criticism.* New York: Oxford University Press.

———. (1992). *Loose canons: Notes on the culture wars.* New York: Oxford University Press.

———. (1994). Preface. Thelma Golden (Ed.), *Black male: Representations of masculinity in contemporary American art,* 11–14. New York: Whitney Museum of American Art (Harry N. Abrams).

———. (1995, May 28). A dangerous literacy: The legacy of Frederick Douglass. *New York Times Book Review* 3, 16.

———. (1996). *Colored people: A memoir.* New York: Alfred A. Knopf.

Gay, P. (1984). *The bourgeois experience: Victoria to Freud,* vol. 1 of *The Education of the Senses.* New York: Oxford University Press.

Gayle, A., Jr. (Ed.). (1971). *The black aesthetic.* Garden City, NY: Doubleday.

Geertz, C. (1973). Deep play: Notes on the Balinese cockfight. In *The interpretation of cultures: Selected essays of Clifford Geertz,* 412–453. New York: Basic Books.

Gelles, R. J. (1974). *The violent home.* Beverly Hills, CA: Sage.

Genders, E., and E. Player. (1989). *Race relations in prisons.* Oxford: Clarendon Press.

Gendzier, I. L. (1973). *Frantz Fanon: A critical study.* New York: Pantheon Books.

Genovese, E. D. (1976). *Roll, Jordan, roll: The world the slaves made.* New York: Vintage.

Gibbon, E. (1776–88/1946). *The decline and fall of the Roman empire.* Ed. J. B. Bury. New York: Heritage Press.

Gibbs, J. J. (1981). Violence in prison: Its extent, nature and consequences. In R. Robert and V. Webb (Eds.), *Critical Issues in Corrections,* 110–149. St. Paul, MN: West Publishing.

Gibson, D. (1996). Chapter 1 of Booker T. Washington's *Up from slavery* and the feminization of the African American male. In M. Blount and G. P. Cunningham (Eds.), *Representing black man,* 95–110. New York: Routledge.

Gifford, C. D. (1993). Politicizing the sacred texts: Elizabeth Cady Stanton and *The Woman's Bible.* In E. S. Fiorenza (Ed.), *A feminist introduction.* New York: Crossroads.

Gilbert, A. N. (1985). Conceptions of homosexuality and sodomy in Western history. In S. J. Licata and R. P. Peterson (Eds.), *The gay past: A collection of historical essays,* 57–68. New York: Harrington Park Press.

Gilder, G. (1974). *Naked nomads: Unmarried men in America.* New York: Quadrangle/New York Times Books.

———. (1986). *Men and marriage.* Gretna, LA: Pelican.

Gilmore, D. (1987). *Agression and community: Paradoxes of Andalusian culture.* New Haven, CT: Yale University Press.

———. (1990). *Manhood in the making.* New Haven: Yale University Press.

Gilmore, L. (1994). *Autobiographics: A feminist theory of women's self-representation.* Ithaca, NY: Cornell University Press.

Gilroy, P. (1990). One nation under a groove: The cultural politics of "race" and racism in Britain. In D. T. Goldberg (Ed.), *Anatomy of racism,* 263–282. Minneapolis: University of Minnesota Press.

———. (1994, Fall). "After the love has gone": Bio-politics and etho-poetics in the black public sphere. *The black public sphere.* Special issue of *Public Culture* 7(1), 49–76.

Ginzberg, L. D. (1990). *Women and the work of benevolence: Morality, politics and class in the nineteenth-century United States.* New Haven: Yale University Press.

Ginzburg, R. (1962/1988). *100 years of lynching.* Baltimore, MD: Black Classic Press.

Giroux, H. A. (1999). *The mouse that roared: Disney and the end of innocence.* Lanham, MD: Rowman and Littlefield.

Gitlin, T. (1992, May 3). "World leaders: Mickey, et al." *New York Times* 2; 30.

Gladney, M. R. (Ed.). (1993). *How am I to be heard? Letters of Lillian Smith.* Chapel Hill: University of North Carolina Press.

Glissant, E. (1989). *Caribbean discourse.* Trans. J. M. Dash. Charlottesville, VA: University of Virginia Press.

Goffman, E. (1961). *Asylums.* New York: Anchor Books.

Goldberg, H. (1976). *The hazards of being male: Surviving the myth of masculine privilege.* New York: Nash.

Goldberg, J. (1993). Sodomy in the new world: Anthropologies old and new. In M. Warner (Ed.), *Fear of a queer planet: Queer politics and social theory,* 3–18. Minneapolis: University of Minnesota Press.

Golden, T. (1994). My brother. In T. Golden (Ed.), *Black male: Representations of masculinity in contemporary American art,* 19–43. New York: Whitney Museum of American Art (Harry N. Abrams, Inc.).

Goldfarb, R. (1976). *Jails: The ultimate ghetto of the criminal justice system.* Garden City, NY: Doubleday.

Goldstein, L. (Ed.). (1994). *The male body: Features, destinies, exposures.* Ann Arbor: University of Michigan Press.

Good, G. E., M. J. Hepper, T. Hillenbrand-Gunn, and L.-F. Wang. (1995). Sexual and psychological violence: An exploratory study of predictors in college men. *Journal of Men's Studies* 4(1): 59–71.

Goodchilds, J., G. Zellman, P. Johnson, and R. Giarusso. (1988). Adolescents and their perceptions of sexual interactions. In A. W. Burgess (Ed.), *Rape and sexual assault,* Vol. II, 245–270. New York: Garland.

Gordon, J. (1982). *The myth of the monstrous male—and other feminist fables.* New York: Playboy Press.

Gordon, L. (1994). *Pitied but not entitled: Single mothers and the history of welfare.* Cambridge, MA: Harvard University Press.

———. (1995). *Bad faith and antiblack racism.* Atlantic Highlands, NJ: Humanities Press.

Gorn, E. J. (1985, February). "Gouge and bite, pull hair and scratch": The social significance of fighting in the southern backcountry. *American Historical Review* 90: 37–58.

———. (1986). *The manly art: Bare knuckle prizefighting in America.* Ithaca, NY: Cornell University Press.

Gossett, T. F. (1963). *Race: The history of an idea in America.* Dallas, TX: Southern Methodist University Press.

Gould, S. (1857). *A golden legacy to daughters, or, advice to young ladies.* Boston: Higgins, Bradley and Dayton.

Goyer, P. F., and H. C. Eddleman. (1984). Same-sex rape of nonincarcerated men. *American Journal of Psychiatry* 141(4): 576–579.

Graczyk, M. (1999, September 24). Dragging participant gets death sentence. Baton Rouge, LA: *Reveille,* 16.

Graham, R. (1989). Autobiography and education. *Journal of Educational Thought* 23(2): 92–105.

———. (1991). *Reading and writing the self: Autobiography in education and the curriculum.* New York: Teachers College Press.

Graham, S. (1834/1974). *A lecture to young men.* New York: Arno Press.

Gramsci, A. (1971). *Selections from the prison notebooks.* Ed. Q. Hoare and G. Nowell Smith. New York: International Publishers.

Graves, A. P. (1879). *Twenty-five letters to a young lady.* Philadelphia: American Baptist Publication Society.

Graves, R., and R. Patai. (1964). *Hebrew myths: The book of Genesis.* Garden City, NY: Doubleday.

Gray, J. G. (1996). The enduring appeals of battle. In L. May, R. Strikwerda, and P. D. Hopkins (Eds.), *Rethinking masculinity: philosophical explorations in light of feminism,* 45–62. Lanham, MD: Rowman and Littlefield.

Green, A. (1986). *On private madness.* London: Hogarth Press.

Greenberg, D. F. (1988). *The construction of homosexuality.* Chicago and London: University of Chicago Press.

Greene, N. (1990). *Pier Paolo Pasolini: Cinema as heresy.* Princeton: Princeton University Press.

Greven, P. (1977). *The Protestant temperament: Patterns of child-rearing, religious experience, and the self in early America.* Chicago: University of Chicago Press.

Grier, W. H., and P. M. Cobbs (1968). *Black rage.* New York: Basic Books.

Griffin, C. (1990). Reconstructing masculinity from the evangelical revival to the waning of Progressivism: A speculative synthesis. In M. C. Carnes and C. Griffen (Eds.), *Meanings for manhood: Constructions of masculinity in Victorian America,* 183–204. Chicago: University of Chicago Press.

Griffin, J. H. (1961/1962). *Black like me.* New York: Signet/NAL.

Griffin, L. J., P. Clark, and J. C. Sandberg. (1997). Narrative and event: Lynching and historical sociology. In W. F. Brundage (Ed.), *Under sentence of death: Lynching in the South,* 24–47. Chapel Hill: University of North Carolina Press.

Griffith, E. (1984). *In her own right: The life of Elizabeth Cady Stanton.* New York: Oxford University Press.

Grimké, F. J. (1899, June). *The lynching of negroes in the South: Its cause and remedy.* Washington, D.C.: Self-published.

Griswold, R. L. (1990). Divorce and the legal redefinition of Victorian manhood. In M. C. Carnes and C. Griffen (Eds.), *Meanings for manhood: Constructions of masculinity in Victorian America,* 96–110. Chicago: University of Chicago Press.

Grossberg, M. (1990). Institutionalizing masculinity: The law as a masculine profession. In M. C. Carnes and C. Griffen (Eds.), *Meanings for manhood: Constructions of masculinity in Victorian America,* 133–151. Chicago: University of Chicago Press.

Grosz, E. (1995). *Space, time, and perversion: Essays on the politics of bodies.* New York: Routledge.

Groth, N. (1979). *Men who rape.* New York: Plenum.

Grumet, M. R. (1988). *Bitter milk: Women and teaching.* Amherst: University of Massachusetts Press.

Guerrero, E. (1994). The black man on our screens and the empty space of representation. In T. Golden (Ed.), *Black male: Representations of masculinity in contemporary American art,* 181–189. New York: Whitney Museum of American Art (Harry N. Abrams).

Guillory, N. (1999). Personal communication.

Gunn, J. (1982). *Autobiography: Towards a poetics of experience.* Philadelphia, PA: University of Pennsylvania Press.

Gunning, S. (1996). *Race, rape, and lynching: The red record of American literature, 1890–1912.* New York: Oxford University Press.

Gusdorf, G. (1980). Conditions and limits of autobiography. In J. Olney (Ed.), *Autobiography: Essays theoretical and critical,* 28–48. Princeton: Princeton University Press.

Gutman, H. G. (1976). *Work, culture and society in industrializing America.* New York: Vintage.

Guzman, J. P. (Ed.). (1952). *Negro year book, 1952.* Tuskegee: Tuskegee Institute.

Gwaltney, J. L. (1993). *Drylongso: A self-portrait of black America.* New York: The New Press.

Haddad, R. (1985). Concept and overview of the men's liberation movement. In F. Baumli (Ed.), *Men freeing men: Exploding the myth of the traditional male,* 281–288. Jersey City, NJ: New Atlantis Press.

Hagarty, B. (1979). *Prisoner of desire.* Vancouver, BC: Talonbooks.

Hall, E. T. (1969). *The hidden dimension.* Garden City, NY: Anchor Books.

———. (1981). *Beyond culture.* Garden City, NY: Anchor/Doubleday.

Hall, J. D. (1979). *Revolt against chivalry: Jessie Daniel Ames and the women's campaign against lynching.* New York: Columbia University Press.

———. (1983). "The mind that burns in each body": Women, rape, and racial violence. In A. Snitow, C. Stansell, and S. Thompson (Eds.), *Powers of desire: The politics of sexuality,* 328–349. New York: Monthly Review Press.

Halliday, M. A. K. (1976). Anti-languages. *American Anthropologist* 78: 570–584.

Halperin, D. M. (1990). *One hundred years of homosexuality.* New York: Routledge.

Hamm, M. S., et al. (1994). The myth of human imprisonment: A critical analysis of severe discipline in U.S. maximum security prisons, 1945–1990. In M. Braswell, S. Dillingham, and R. Montgomery, Jr. (Eds.), *Prison violence in America,* 167–200. Cincinnati, OH: Anderson.

Hammatt, N. F. (2000). Personal communication.

Hammonds, E. (1994). Black (w)holes and the geometry of black female sexuality. *Differences* 6(2+3): 27–61.

Hampden-Turner, C. (1968). *Radical man.* Garden City, NY: Anchor Books.

Handelman, S. (1991). *Fragments of redemption: Jewish thought and literary theory in Benjamin, Scholem, and Levinas.* Bloomington: Indiana University Press.

Haney, C., C. Banks, and P. Zimbardo. (1973). Interpersonal dynamics in a simulated prison. *International Journal of Criminology and Penology* 1: 69–97.

Hannaford, I. (1996). *Race: The history of an idea in the West.* Baltimore, MD: Johns Hopkins University Press.

Hannan, K. E., and B. Burkhart (1993). The topography of violence in college men: Frequency and co-morbidity of sexual and physical aggression. *Journal of College Student Psychotherapy* 8(3): 219–237.

Hannerz, U. (1969). *Soulside: Inquiries into ghetto culture.* New York: Columbia University Press.

———. (1977). Growing up male. In D. Y. Wilkinson and R. L. Taylor (Eds.), *The black male in America,* 33–59. Chicago: Nelson-Hall.

Haraway, D. (1991). *Simians, cyborgs, and women: The reinvention of nature.* New York: Routledge.

Hardesty, N. (1981/1982). "Minister as prophet? Or as mother?" In H. F. Thomas and R. S. Keller (Eds.), *Women in new worlds: Historical perspectives on the Wesleyan tradition.* 2 vols. Nashville: Abingdon Press.

———. (1984). *Women called to witness: Evangelical feminism in the nineteenth century.* Nashville: Abingdon Press.

Harding, S. (1989). After the end of philosophy. Paper delivered at Purdue University's Matchette Conference.

Hare, N. (1971, June). Will the real black man please stand up? *Black Scholar* 2 (10), 32–35.

Hare, N., and J. Hare (1984). *The endangered black family: Coping with the unisexualization and coming extinction of the black race.* San Francisco: Black Think Tank.

——— (Eds.). (1989). *Crisis in black sexual politics.* San Francisco: Black Think Tank.

Harper, P. B. (1996). *Are we not men? Masculine anxiety and the problem of African-American identity.* New York: Oxford University Press.

Harris, B. (1978). *Beyond her sphere: Women and the professions in American history.* Westport, CT: Greenwood.

Harris, L. (1996). Honor, emasculation, and empowerment. In L. May, R. Strikwerda, and P. D. Hopkins (Eds.), *Rethinking masculinity: Philosophical explorations in light of feminism,* 275–288. Lanham, MD: Rowman and Littlefield.

Harris, T. (1984). *Exorcising blackness: Historical and literary lynching and burning rituals.* Bloomington: Indiana University Press.

Harry, J. (1992). *Hate crimes: Confronting violence against lesbians and gay men.* Newbury Park, CA: Sage Publications

Hart, H., Director. (1971). *Fortune and men's eyes.* Metro Goldwyn Mayer of Canada.

Hartman, S. V. (1997). *Scenes of subjection: Terror, slavery, and self-making in nineteenth century America.* New York: Oxford University Press.

Hass, A. (1996). *In the shadow of the Holocaust: The second generation.* New York: Cambridge University Press.

Haupt, H. A., and G. D. Rovere. (1984). Anabolic steroids: A review of the literature. *American Journal of Sports Medicine* 12: 469–484.

Haymes, S. N. (1995). *Race, culture, and the city: A pedagogy for black urban struggle.* Albany: State University of New York.

Haynes, C. A. (1998). *Divine destiny: Gender and race in nineteenth-century Protestantism.* Jackson: University Press of Mississippi.

Hearn, J. (1998). *The violences of men: How men talk about and how agencies respond to men's violence to women.* Thousand Oaks, CA: Sage Publications.

Heath, S. (1987). Male feminism. In A. Jardine and P. Smith (Eds.), *Men in feminism,* 1–32. New York: Methuen.

Hegel, G. (1821/1952). *Philosophy of right.* New York: Oxford Clarendon Press.

Heger, H. (1980). *The men with the pink triangle: The true life and death story of homosexuals in the Nazi death camps.* Trans. D. Fernbach. New York: Alyson Books.

Heilbrun, C. G. (1986). Woman's autobiographical writings: New forms. In P. Dodd (Ed.), *Modern selves: Essays on modern British and American autobiography,* 14–28. London: Frank Cass.

Hemingway, E. (1926/1996). *The sun also rises.* New York: Simon and Schuster.

Hemphill, E. (1991). Introduction. Essex Hemphill (Ed.), *Brother to brother: Collected writings by black gay men,* xv–xxxi. Los Angeles: Alyson Books.

Henriques, F. (1974). *Children of Caliban: Miscegenation.* London: Secker and Warburg.

Herman, D. F. (1989). The rape culture. In J. Freeman (Ed.), *Women: A feminist perspective,* 4th edition, 20–44. Mountain View, CA: Mayfield Publishing Co.

Hernton, C. C. (1965/1988). *Sex and racism in America.* New York: Doubleday Anchor.

———. (1987). *The sexual mountain and black women writers.* New York: Doubleday Anchor.

Herrnstein, R. J., and C. Murray (1994). *The bell curve: Intelligence and class structure in American life.* New York: The Free Press.

Hietala, T. R. (1985). *Manifest design: Anxious aggrandizement in late Jacksonian America.* Ithaca, NY: Cornell University Press.

Higginbotham, E. B. (1993). *Righteous discontent: The women's movement in the black Baptist church, 1880–1920.* Cambridge, MA: Harvard University Press.

———. (1996). African-American women's history and the metalanguage of race. In R.-E. B. Joeres and B. Laslett (Eds.), *The second* Signs *reader,* 3–26. Chicago: University of Chicago Press.

Higgins, L. A., and B. R. Silver. (1991). Introduction: Reading rape. In L. A. Higgins and B. R. Silver (Eds.), *Rape and representation,* 1–11. New York: Columbia University Press.

Higham, J. (1970). The reorientation of American culture in the 1890s. In J. Higham (Ed.), *Writing American history,* 73–102. Bloomington, IN: Indiana University Press.

———. (1971). *Strangers in the land: Patterns of American nativism 1860–1925.* New York: Atheneum.

Hill, Jr., P. (1992). *Coming of age: African American male rites-of-passage.* Chicago: African American Images.

Hille, W. (Ed). (1948). Billie Holiday's "strange fruit." In *The people's songbook,* 124–125. New York: Boni and Gaer.

Hirsch, K. (1990, September/October). Fraternities of fear: Gang rape, male bonding, and the silencing of women. *Ms.*, 52–56.

Hoch, P. (1979). *White hero, black beast: Racism, sexism and the mask of masculinity.* London: Pluto Press

Hocquenghem, G. (1978). *Homosexual desire.* London: Allison and Busby.

Hodes, M. (1992). Wartime dialogues on illicit sex: White women and black men. In C. Clinton and N. Silber (Eds.), *Divided houses: Gender and the Civil War.* New York: Oxford University Press.

———. (1993, January). The sexualization of Reconstruction politics: White women and black men in the South after the Civil War. *Journal of the History of Sexuality* 3(3): 402–417.

Hodges, M. (1998, March). Caged heat. *Out,* 92–95, 110.

Holiday, B. (1973). *Lady sings the blues.* London: Barrie and Jenkins.

Hong, L. (1998). *Redefining bates, booze and brawls: Men against violence—a new masculinity.* Baton Rouge: Louisiana State University, College of Education, unpublished Ph.D. dissertation.

hooks, b. (1981). *Ain't I a woman.* Boston: South End Press.

———. (1990). *Yearning: Race, gender and cultural politics.* Toronto: Between the Lines.

———. (1992). *Black looks: Race and representation.* Boston: South End Press.

———. (1994). Feminism inside: Toward a black body politic. In T. Golden (Ed.), *Black male: Representations of masculinity in contemporary American art,* 127–140. New York: Whitney Museum of American Art (Harry N. Abrams).

Hope, T. (1994a). Melancholic modernity: The hom(m)osexual symptom and the homosocial corpse. *Differences* 6(2+3): 174–198.

———. (1994b). The "returns" of cartography: Mapping identity-in(-) difference. *Differences* 6(2+3): 208–211.

Hopkins, P. D. (1996). Gender treachery: Homophobia, masculinity, and threatened identities. In L. May, R. Strikwerda, and P. D. Hopkins (Eds.), *Rethinking masculinity: Philosophical explorations in light of feminism,* 95–115. Lanham, MD: Rowman and Littlefield.

Hopper, C. B. (1969). *Sex in prison: The Mississippi experiment with conjugal visiting.* Baton Rouge: Louisiana University Press.

———. (1971). Sexual adjustment in prisons. *Police* 15: 75–76.

Horkheimer, M., and T. Adorno. (1944/1972). *Dialectic of enlightenment.* New York: Seabury Press.

Horowitz, R. (1985). *Honor and the American dream: Culture and identity in a Chicago community.* New Brunswick, NJ: Rutgers University Press.

Horsfall, J. (1991). *The presence of the past: Male violence in the family.* North Sydney: Allen and Unwin.

Horsman, R. (1981). *Race and manifest destiny: The origins of American racial Anglo-Saxonism.* Cambridge, MA: Harvard University Press.

Hovland, C. I., and R. H. Sears. (1940, April). Minor studies of aggression: VI. Correlation of lynchings with economic indices. *Journal of Psychology* 9: 301–310.

Howard, C. (1890). *Why man needs woman's ballot.* New York: National American Woman's Suffrage Association.

Howard, W. T. (1995). *Lynchings: Extralegal violence in Florida during the 1930s.* Selinsgrove, PA: Susquehanna University Press.

Howe, F. C. (1905). *What the ballot will do for women and for men.* New York: National American Woman's Suffrage Association.

Howe, J. (1883/1974). *Excessive venery, masturbation and continence.* North Stratford, NH: Ayer.

Huebner, D. E. (1999). *The lure of the transcendent.* Mahweh, NJ: Lawrence Erlbaum.

Hufsmith, G. W. (1993). *The Wyoming lynching of Cattle Kate, 1889.* Glendo, WY: High Plains Press.

Huggins, N. (1971). *Harlem Renaissance.* New York: Oxford University Press.

Hughes, J. S. (1990). The madness of separate spheres: Insanity and masculinity in Victorian Alabama. In M. C. Carnes and C. Griffen (Eds.), *Meanings for manhood: Constructions of masculinity in Victorian America,* 53–66. Chicago: University of Chicago Press.

Hull, G. T. (1987). *Color, sex and poetry: Three women writers of the Harlem Renaissance.* Bloomington: Indiana University Press.

Hunt, A. (1998). The great masturbation panic and the discourses of moral regulation in nineteenth- and early twentieth-century Britain. *Journal of the History of Sexuality* 8(4): 575–615.

Hurston, Z. N. (1935/1990). *Mules and men.* New York: Harper Perennial.

Hutchinson, E. O. (1997). *The assassination of the black male image.* New York: Touchstone (Simon and Schuster).

Hwu, W.-S. (1997). Curriculum, transcendence, and Zen/Taoism: Critical ontology of the self. In W. F. Pinar (Ed.), *Curriculum: Toward new identities,* 21–40. New York: Garland.

Hyde, J. (1998, September 15). Talk show murder sentence thrown out. Baton Rouge: *The Reveille*, 6.

Ide, A. F. (1992). *Noah and the ark.* Las Colinas, TX: Monument Press.

Ingall, R. P. (1988/1993). *Urban vigilantes in the new south: Tampa 1882–1936.* Gainesville, FL: University of Florida Press.

———. (1987, November). Lynching and establishment violence in Tampa, 1858–1935. *Journal of Southern History* 53: 613–644.

Irele, A. (1995). Dimensions of African discourse. In K. Myrsiades and J. McGuire (Eds.), *Order and partialities: Theory, pedagogy, and the "postcolonial,"* 15–34. Albany: State University of New York Press.

Irigaray, L. (1985). *This sex which is not one.* Trans. C. Porter. Ithaca, NY: Cornell University Press.

———. (1992). *An ethics of sexual difference.* Trans. C. Burke and G. C. Gill. Ithaca, NY: Cornell University Press.

Irwin, J. (1970). *The felon.* Englewood Cliffs, NJ: Prentice Hall.

———. (1985). *The jail: Managing the underclass in American society.* Berkeley: University of California Press.

Irwin, J. T. (1975/1980). *Doubling and incest/repetition and revenge: A speculative reading of Faulkner.* Baltimore and London: Johns Hopkins University Press.

Island, D., and P. Letellier. (1991). *Men who beat the men who love them.* Binghamton, NY: Harrington Park Press.

Jackson, B. (1976). Richard Wright in a moment of truth. In *The waiting years: Essays on American Negro literature,* 129–145. Baton Rouge: Louisiana State University Press.

Jackson, B. (1977). *Killing time: Life in the Arkansas penitentiary.* Ithaca, NY: Cornell University Press.

Jackson, G. (1970). *Soledad brother: The prison letters of George Jackson.* New York: Bantam Books. Republished in 1995 by Lawrence Hill Books.

Jackson, O. [Ice Cube]. (1991). Horny lil' devil. *Death certificate.* Priority Records.

Jackson, R. C. (1981). *Gifts of power: The writings of Rebecca Jackson, black visionary, Shaker Eldress.* Ed. J. M. Humez. Amherst: University of Massachusetts Press.

Jackson, S. (1990). *Unmasking masculinity: A critical autobiography.* London: Unwin Hyman.

Jacobs, A. (2000, March 5). Hazing in high school turns more violent, in step with society, educators say. *New York Times*, 30.

Jacobs, H. A. (1861/1987). *Incidents in the life of a slave girl, written by herself.* Ed. J. F. Yellin. Cambridge, MA: Harvard University Press.

Jacobs, J. B. (1983). *New perspectives on prisons and imprisonment.* Ithaca, NY: Cornell University Press.

Jacoby, R. (1987). *The last intellectuals.* New York: Basic Books.

Jagose, A. (1996). *Queer theory: An introduction.* New York: New York University Press.

James, C. A. (1998). Feminism and masculinity: Reconceptualizing the dichotomy of reason and emotion. In S. P. Schacht and D. W. Ewing (Eds.), *Feminism and men: Reconstructing gender relations,* 183–201. New York: New York University Press.

James, H. (1969). *Children in trouble: A national scandal.* Boston: Christian Science Publishing Society.

Jardine, A. (1987). Men in feminism. In A. Jardine and P. Smith (Eds.), *Men in feminism*, 54–61. New York: Methuen.

Jensen, R. (1998) Patriarchal sex. In S. P. Schacht and D. W. Ewing (Eds.), *Feminism and men: Reconstructing gender relations*, 99–118. New York: New York University Press.

Johnson, A. (Ed.). (1929). *Dictionary of American biography*. 15 vols. New York: Scribner.

Johnson, C. (1994). A phenomenology of the black body. In L. Goldstein (Ed.), *The male body*, 121–136. Ann Arbor: University of Michigan Press.

Johnson, C., and J. McCluskey, Jr. (Eds.). (1997). *Black men speaking*. Bloomington: Indiana University Press.

Johnson, E. (1971). The homosexual in prison. *Social Theory and Practice* 1: 83–95.

Johnson, J. W. (1912/1960). *The autobiography of an ex-colored man*. New York: Hill and Wang.

———. (1927, Nov.). The practice of lynching: A picture, the problem and what shall be done about it. *The Century Magazine* 115(1): 65–70.

———. (1933). *Along this way*. New York: Viking.

———. (1973). *Along this way*. New York: Da Capo Press.

Johnson, P. E. (1978). *A shopkeeper's millennium: Society and revivals in Rochester, New York, 1815–1837*. New York: Hill and Wang.

Johnson, P. E., and S. Wilentz. (1994). *The kingdom of Matthias: A story of sex and salvation in nineteenth-century America*. New York: Oxford University Press.

Jones, C., and E. Aronson. (1973). Attribution of fault to a rape victim as a function of responsibility of the victim. *Journal of Personality and Social Psychology* 26: 415–419.

Jones, D. (1976). *The health risks of imprisonment*. Lexington, MA: D.C. Heath.

Jones, J. (1985). *Labor of love, labor of sorrow: Black women, work, and the family, from slavery to the present*. New York: Vintage.

Jones, J. H. (1997, August 25/September 1). Dr. Yes. *New Yorker*, 98–113.

Jones, J. W. (1996). Introduction. H. Fichte's *The Gay Critic*, vii–xx. Ann Arbor: University of Michigan Press.

Jordan, W. D. (1968). *White over black*. Chapel Hill: University of North Carolina Press.

———. (1974). *The white man's burden: Historical origins of racism in the United States*. New York: Oxford University Press.

Juan, Jr., E. San. (1995). *Hegemony and strategies of transgression: Essays in cultural studies and comparative literature*. Albany: State University of New York Press.

Jukes, A. (1993). *When men hate women*. London: Free Association Books.

Julien, I., and K. Mercer. (1991). True confessions: A discourse on images of black male sexuality. In E. Hemphill (Ed.), *Brother to brother: Collected writings by black gay men*, 167–173. Los Angeles: Alyson Books.

Jung, C. G. (1953 ff). *The collected works*, Bollingen Series 20, vols. 1–20. Princeton: Princeton University Press and London: Routledge and Kegan Paul.

Kaplan, C. (1996). "A cavern opened in my mind": The poetics of homosexuality and the politics of masculinity in James Baldwin. In M. Blount and G. P. Cunningham (Eds.), *Representing black man*, 27–54. New York: Routledge.

Kappeler, S. (1986). *The pornography of representation*. Minneapolis: University of Minnesota Press.

Kasson, J. F. (1978). *Amusing the millions: Coney Island at the turn of the century.* New York: Hill and Wang.

Katz, J. (1995). Reconstructing masculinity in the locker room: The mentors in violence prevention project. *Harvard Educational Review* 65(2): 163–174.

Katz, J. N. (1983). *Gay/lesbian almanac.* New York: Harper and Row.

Keil, C. (1977). The expressive black male role: The bluesman. In D. Y. Wilkinson and R. L. Taylor (Eds.), *The black male in America,* 60–84. Chicago: Nelson-Hall.

Kelley, R. D. G. (1993, June). "We are not what we seem": Rethinking black working-class opposition in the Jim Crow South. *Journal of American History* 80: 75–112.

———. (1994). *Race rebels: Culture, politics, and the black working class.* New York: Free Press.

Kellogg, C. F. (1967). *NAACP: A history of the National Association for the Advancement of Colored People,* vol. I: *1909–1920.* Baltimore, MD: Johns Hopkins University Press.

Kemper, T. (1990). *Social structure and testosterone: Explorations of the socio-bio-social chain.* New Brunswick, NJ: Rutgers University Press.

Kent, G. E. (1993). Maya Angelou's I know why the caged bird sings and black autobiographical tradition. In W. L. Andrews (Ed.), *African American autobiography: A collection of critical essays,* 162–171. Englewood Cliffs, NJ: Prentice Hall.

Kimmel, M. S. (1987). The contemporary "crisis" of masculinity in historical perspective. In H. Brod (Ed.), *The making of masculinities: The new men's studies.* Boston: Allen and Unwin.

———. (1990). Baseball and the reconstitution of American masculinity, 1880–1920. In M. A. Messner and D. Sabo (Eds.), *Sport, men, and the gender order,* 55–65. Champaign, IL: Human Kinetics.

———. (1993). Clarence, William, Iron Mike, Tailhook, Senator Packwood, Spur Posse, Magic ... and us. In E. Buchwald, P. R. Fletcher, and M. Roth (Eds.), *Transforming a rape culture,* 119–138. Minneapolis: Milkweed Editions.

———. (1994). Consuming manhood: The feminization of American culture and the recreation of the male body, 1832–1920. In L. Goldstein (Ed.), *The male body,* 12–41. Ann Arbor: University of Michigan Press.

———. (1996). *Manhood in America: A cultural history.* New York: Free Press.

———. (1998). From "conscience and common sense" to "feminism for men": Profeminist men's rhetorics of support for women's equality. In S. P. Schacht and D. W. Ewing (Eds.), *Feminism and men: Reconstructing gender relations,* 21–42. New York: New York University Press.

Kincheloe, J. L., and S. R. Steinberg. (1998). Addressing the crisis of whiteness: Reconfiguring white identity in a pedagogy of whiteness. In J. L. Kincheloe, S. R. Steinberg, N. M. Rodriguez, and R. E. Chennault (Eds.), *White reign: Deploying whiteness in America,* 3–29. New York: St. Martin's Press.

Kincheloe, J. L., S. R. Steinberg, and A. D. Gresson III (Eds.). (1996). *Measured lies.* New York: St. Martin's Press.

Kincheloe, J. L., S. R. Steinberg, N. M. Rodriguez, and R. E. Chennault (Eds.). (1998). *White reign: Deploying whiteness in America.* New York: St. Martin's Press.

King, M. C. (1973). The politics of sexual stereotypes. *Black Scholar* 4(6–7): 12–23.

Kinsey, A. C., W. B. Pomeroy, and C. E. Martin (1948). *Sexual behavior in the human male.* Philadelphia: W. B. Saunders.

Klein, H. (1983). African women in the Atlantic slave trade. In C. C. Robertson and M. A. Klein (Eds.), *Women and slavery in Africa,* 29–38. Madison: University of Wisconsin Press.

Kleppner, P. (1979). *The third electoral system, 1853–1892: Parties, voters, and political cultures.* Chapel Hill: University of North Carolina Press.

Kliebard, H. (1986). *The struggle for the American curriculum 1893–1958.* Boston, MA: Routledge and Kegan Paul.

Kochman, T. (1981). *Black and white styles in conflict.* Chicago: University of Chicago Press.

Koss, M. P., C. A. Gidycz, and N. Wisniewski. (1987). The scope of rape: Incidence and prevalence of sexual aggression and victimization in a national sample of higher education students. *Journal of Consulting and Clinical Psychology* 55: 162–170.

Kostelanetz, R. (1969, Spring). The politics of passing: The fiction of James Weldon Johnson. *Negro American Literature Forum* 3(1): 22–24.

Koven, S. (1992). From rough lads to hooligans: Boy life, national culture and social reform. In A. Parker et al. (Eds.), *Nationalism and sexualities,* 365–391. New York: Routledge.

Kozol, J. (1991). *Savage inequalities: Children in America's schools.* New York: Crown.

Kraditor, A. (Ed.). (1965). *Up from the pedestal: Selected writings in the history of American feminism.* Chicago: Quadrangle.

———. (1968). *The ideas of the woman suffrage movement, 1890–1920.* New York: Columbia University Press.

Kreuz, L., and R. M. Rose. (1972). Assessment of aggressive behavior and plasma testosterone in a young criminal population. *Psychosomatic Medicine* 34: 470–471.

Kunjufu, J. (1989). Not allowed to be friends and/or lovers. In N. and J. Hare (Eds.), *Crisis in black sexual politics,* 109–112. San Francisco: Black Think Tank.

Lacy, D. (1972). *The white use of blacks in America.* New York: Atheneum.

Lamon, L. C. (1977). *Black Tennesseans, 1900–1930.* Knoxville: University of Tennessee Press.

Lane, C. (1996, Spring). Beyond the social principle: Psychoanalysis and radical democracy. *Journal for the Psychoanalysis of Culture and Society* 1(1): 105–121.

Langness, L. L., and F. Gelya. (1981). *Lives: An anthropological approach to biography.* Novata, CA: Chandler and Sharp Publishers.

Laplanche, J. (1999). *Essays on otherness.* New York: Routledge.

Laplanche, J., and J. B. Pontalis. (1973). *The language of psychoanalysis.* Trans. D. Nicholson-Smith. New York: Norton.

Lasch, C. (1984). *The minimal self: Psychic survival in troubled times.* New York: Norton.

——— (Ed.). (1965). *The social thought of Jane Addams.* Indianapolis, IN: Bobbs-Merrill.

Lather, P., and C. Smithies. (1997). *Troubling the angels: Women living with HIV/AIDS.* Boulder, CO: Westview Press.

Laws, G. M. (1964). *Native American balladry.* Philadelphia: American Folklore Society.

Le Clair, T. (1981, March 21). "The language must now sweat": A conversation with Toni Morrison. *New Republic,* 75–78.

Ledbetter, M. (1996). *Victims and the postmodern narrative or doing violence to the body: An ethic of reading and writing.* New York: St. Martin's Press.

Lee, Rev. L. (1853/1984). Woman's right to preach the gospel. A sermon, preached at the ordination of the Reverend Miss Antoinette L. Brown. In D. Dayton (Ed.), *Holiness tracts defending the ministry of women.* New York: Garland.

Leitch, V. B. (1992). *Cultural criticism, literary theory, poststructuralism.* New York: Columbia University Press.

Lemelle, Jr., A. J. (1995). *Black male deviance.* Westport, CT, and London: Praeger.

Lemert, C., and E. Bhan. (Eds.). (1998). *The voice of Anna Julia Cooper.* Lanham, MD: Rowan and Littlefield.

Lemons, G. (1998). To be black, male, feminist: Making womanist space for black men on the eve of a new millennium. In S. P. Schacht and D. W. Ewing (Eds.), *Feminism and men: Reconstructing gender relations,* 43–66. New York: New York University Press.

Lerner, G. (1986). *The creation of patriarchy.* New York: Oxford University Press.

Lessing, D. (1976). *The grass is singing.* New York: NAL Dutton.

Lester, J. (1969). *Search for the new land.* New York: Dial Press.

Lévi-Strauss, C. (1963). *Structural anthropology.* New York: Basic Books.

———. (1966). *The savage mind.* Chicago: University of Chicago Press.

———. (1977). *Tristes tropiques.* New York: Washington Square Press.

———. (1979). *The origin of table manners.* New York: Harper and Row.

Levinas, E. (1966). On the trail of the other. Trans. D. Hoy. *Philosophy Today* 19: 34–36.

———. (1969). *Totality and infinity: An essay on exteriority.* Trans. A. Lingis. Pittsburgh, PA: Duquesne University Press.

———. (1991). *Otherwise than being.* Trans. A. Lingis. London: Kluwer Academic Publishers.

———. (1994). *Beyond the verse: Talmudic readings and lectures.* Trans. G. D. Mole. Bloomington: Indiana University Press.

Lewes, K. (1988). *The psychoanalytic theory of male homosexuality.* New York: New American Library.

Lewis, D. L. (1979/1997). *When Harlem was in vogue.* New York: Penguin.

Lewis, H. (1955). *Blackways of Kent.* Chapel Hill: University of North Carolina Press.

Light, S. C. (1994). Assaults on prison officers: Interactional themes. In M. Braswell, S. Dillingham, and R. Montgomery, Jr. (Eds.), *Prison violence in America,* 207–223. Cincinnati, OH: Anderson.

Lionnet, F. (1989). *Autobiographical voices: Race, gender, self-portraiture.* Ithaca, NY: Cornell University Press.

———. (1993). Autoethnography: The an-archic style of Dust Tracks on a Road. In W. L. Andrews (Ed.), *African American autobiography: A collection of critical essays,* 113–137. Englewood Cliffs, NJ: Prentice Hall.

———. (1995). "Logiques métisses": Cultural appropriation and postcolonial representations. In K. Myrsiades and J. McGuire (Eds.), *Order and partialities: Theory, pedagogy, and the "postcolonial,"* 111–136. Albany: State University of New York Press.

Lipsitz, G. (1988). *A life of struggle: Ivory Perry and the culture of opposition.* Philadelphia: Temple University Press.

Lloyd, R. (1976). *For money or love: Boy prostitution in America.* New York: Vanguard Press.

Lockwood, D. (1980). *Prison sexual violence.* New York: Elsevier.

Loh, E. (1995, June 22). N. O. jury convicts Graves. Baton Rouge: Louisiana State University, *Daily Reveille*, 6.

Lomotey, K., and S. Rivers. (1998). Models of excellence: Independent African-centered schools. In W. F. Pinar (Ed.), *Curriculum: Toward new identities,* 343–354. New York: Garland.

Looby, C. (1995). "Innocent homosexuality": The Fiedler thesis in retrospect. In G. Graff and J. Phelan (Eds.), *Mark Twain*, Adventures of Huckleberry Finn: *A Case Study in Critical Controversy,* 535–551. Boston and New York: Bedford Books of St. Martin's Press.

Lorde, A. (1982). *Zami: A new spelling of my name.* Trumansburg, NY: The Crossing Press.

Loveland, A. (1986). *Lillian Smith: A southerner confronting the South.* Baton Rouge: Louisiana State University Press.

Lowry, M.D., T. P. (1994). *The story the soldiers wouldn't tell: Sex in the Civil War.* Mechanicsburg, PA: Stackpole Books.

Lyman, S. M., and M. B. Scott. (1970). Coolness in everyday life. In S. M. Lyman and M. B. Scott (Eds.), *A sociology of the absurd,* 145–155. New York: Appleton-Century-Crofts.

Lyotard, J.-F. (1984). *The postmodern condition.* Trans. G. Bennington and B. Massumi. Minneapolis: University of Minnesota Press.

MacCannell, D., and J. F. MacCannell. (1993). Violence, power and pleasure: A revisionist reading of Foucault from the victim perspective. In C. Ramazanoglu (Ed.), *Up against Foucault,* 203–238. London: Routledge.

Macfadden, B. (1900). *The virile powers of superb manhood.* New York: Physical Culture Publishing.

MacKinnon, C. A. (1983, Summer). Feminism, Marxism, method, and state: Toward feminist jurisprudence. *Signs* 8(4): 635–658.

Madhubuti, H. R. (D. L. Lee). (1978). *Enemies: The clash of races.* Chicago: Third World Press.

———. (1990). *Black men.* Chicago: Third World Press.

Mailer, N. (1957). *The white negro.* San Francisco: City Lights.

———. (1959). *Advertisements for myself.* New York: Putnam.

———. (1985). *Prisoner of sex.* Boston: Little, Brown and Co.

Majors, R. (1995/1996). Cool pose: The proud signature of black survival. In H. Boyd and R. L. Allen (Eds.), *Brotherman: The odyssey of black men in America,* 783–789. New York: Ballantine/One World.

Majors, R., and J. M. Billson. (1992). *The dilemmas of black manhood in America.* New York: Lexington/Macmillan.

Malcolm X and A. Haley. (1992). *The autobiography of Malcolm X.* New York: Simon and Schuster. [First published in 1965 by Ballatine Books.]

Mancini, M. J. (1996). *One dies, get another: Convict leasing in the American South, 1866–1928.* Columbia: University of South Carolina Press.

Mann, W. E. (1967). *Society behind bars: A sociological scrutiny of Guelph Reformatory.* Toronto: Social Science.

Manning, M. (1983). *How capitalism underdeveloped black America: Problems in political economy and society.* Boston: South End Press.

March, R. A. (1978). *Alabama bound: Forty-five years inside a prison system.* University, AL: University of Alabama Press.

Marcuse, H. (1971). *Eros and civilization.* Boston: Beacon Press.

Marsden, G. (1980). *Fundamentalism and American culture: The shaping of twentieth-century evangelicalism, 1870–1925.* New York: Oxford University Press.

Marsden, J. B. (1991). *Ill-gotten gains.* Spats films.

Marsh, M. (1990). Suburban men and masculine domesticity, 1870–1915. In M. C. Carnes and C. Griffen (Eds.), *Meanings for manhood: Constructions of masculinity in Victorian America,* 111–127. Chicago: University of Chicago Press.

Marshall, D. L. (1993). Violence and the male gender role. *Journal of College Student Psychotherapy* 8(3): 203–218.

Marshall, M. (1999, September 25). Dees sees new racists hiding behind religion. Baton Rouge, LA: *Advocate,* 1E–2E.

Martin, J. B. (1954). *Break down the walls: American prisons: Present, past, and future.* New York: Ballantine Books.

Martin, P. Y., and R. A. Hummer. (1989). Fraternities and rape on campus. *Gender and Society* 3: 457–473.

Martin, R., et al. (1974, October 1). The account of the white house seven. *Friends Journal,* 484–499.

Martin, T. (1993). *The Jewish onslaught.* Dover, MA: Majority Press.

Marx, K. (1964). *Economic and philosophical manuscripts of 1844.* Ed. D. J. Struik. Translated by Martin Milligan. New York: International Publishers.

Massa, M. S. (1990). *Charles Augusta Briggs and the crisis of historical criticism.* Minneapolis: Fortress Press.

Massey, D. (1989). *Doing time in American prisons: A study of modern novels.* New York: Greenwood Press.

Mauer, M. (1990). *Young black men and the criminal justice system: A growing national problem.* Washington, D.C.: The Sentencing Project.

Maurer, D. (1979, June 18). Correspondence with Inez Cardozo-Freeman.

May, E. T. (1988). *Homeward bound: American families in the Cold War era.* New York: Basic Books.

May, L., and R. Strikwerda. (1996). Male friendship and intimacy. In L. May, R. Strikwerda, and P. D. Hopkins (Eds.), *Rethinking masculinity: Philosophical explorations in light of feminism,* 79–94. Lanham, MD: Rowman and Littlefield.

May, L., R. Strikwerda, and P. D. Hopkins (Eds.). (1996). *Rethinking masculinity: Philosophical explorations in light of feminism.* Lanham, MD: Rowman and Littlefield.

Mazur, A., and T. A. Lamb. (1980). Testosterone, status and mood in human males. *Hormones and Behavior* 4: 236–246.

McCall, N. (1995/1996). Makes me wanna holler. In H. Boyd and R. L. Allen (Eds.), *Brotherman: The odyssey of black men in America,* 426–433. New York: Ballantine/One World.

———. (1998). *Post-colonial book.* New York: Routledge.

McDannell, C. (1986, Fall). "True men as we need them," *American Studies,* 19–36.

McDonald, S. (1990). Confessions of a feminist porn watcher. In M. S. Kimmel (Ed.), *Men confront pornography,* 34–42. New York: Meridian.

McDowell, D. (1993). In the first place: Making Frederick Douglass and the Afro-American narrative tradition. In W. L. Andrews (Ed.), *African American autobiography: A collection of critical essays,* 36–58. Englewood Cliffs, NJ: Prentice Hall.

McFeely, W. S. (1997). Afterword. In W. F. Brundage (Ed.), *Under sentence of death: Lynching in the South,* 318–321. Chapel Hill: University of North Carolina Press.

McGovern, J. R. (1982). *Anatomy of a lynching: The killing of Claude Neal.* Baton Rouge: Louisiana State University Press.

McKay, C. (1953). *Selected poems of Claude McKay.* New York: Harcourt, Brace, and World, Inc.

McKeever, W. (1913). *Training the boy.* New York: Macmillan.

McLaren, P. (1997). *Revolutionary multiculturalism.* Boulder, CO: Westview.

McLoughlin, W. (Ed.). (1968). *The American evangelicals, 1800–1900.* New York: Harper and Row.

McMath, Jr., R. C. (1993). *American populism: A social history, 1877–1898.* New York: Hill and Wang.

McMillen, L. (1993, Sept. 8). New theory about Mark Twain's sexuality brings strong reaction from experts. *Chronicle of Higher Education,* A8, A15.

McWhorter, W. L. (1981). *Inmate society: Legs, half-pants and gunmen: A study of inmate guards.* Saratoga, CA: Century Twenty One.

Mehlman, J. (1974). *A structural study of autobiography: Proust, Leiris, Sartre, Levi-Strauss.* Ithaca: Cornell University Press.

Mercer, K. (1992, Summer). Engendered species: Danny Tisdale and Keith Piper. *Artforum* 30.

———. (1994a). *Welcome to the jungle: New positions in black cultural studies.* New York: Routledge.

——— (1994b, April). Fear of a black penis. *Artforum* 32.

Merchant, C. (1996). *Earthcare: Women and the environment.* New York: Routledge.

Merrill, J. (1993). *A different person: A memoir.* New York: Alfred A. Knopf.

Messerschmidt, J. W. (1993). *Masculinities and crime: Critique and reconceptualization of theory.* Lanham, MD: Rowman and Littlefield.

Messner, M. A. (1988). Sports and male domination: The female athlete as contested ideological terrain. *Sociology of Sport Journal* 5(3): 197–211.

———. (1990). Masculinities and athletic careers: Bonding and status differences. In M. A. Messner and D. Sabo (Eds.), *Sport, men, and the gender order,* 97–108. Champaign, IL: Human Kinetics.

———. (1992). *Power at play: Sports and problem of masculinity.* Boston: Beacon Press.

———. (1998). Radical feminist and socialist feminist men's movements in the United States. In S. P. Schacht and D. W. Ewing (Eds.), *Feminism and men: Reconstructing gender relations,* 67–85. New York: New York University Press.

Meyer, S. (1996). *Imperialism at home: Race and Victorian women's fiction.* Ithaca and London: Cornell University Press.

Michaels, W. B. (1995). *Our America: Nativism, modernism, and pluralism.* Durham and London: Duke University Press.

Michasiw, K. (1994). Camp, masculinity, masquerade. *Differences* 6(2+3): 146–173.

Miedzian, M. (1992). *Boys will be boys.* London: Virago.

Miller, J. G. (1996). *Search and destroy: African-American males in the criminal justice system.* New York: Cambridge University Press.

Miller, J. L. (1998). Autobiography as a queer curriculum practice. In W. F. Pinar (Ed.), *Queer theory in education,* 349–364. Mahwah, NJ: Lawrence Erlbaum Associates.

Miller, W. (1958). Lower class culture as a general milieu of gang delinquency. *Journal of Social Issues* 14: 5–19.

Mills, C. W. (1996). Do black men have a moral duty to marry black women? In L. May, R. Strikwerda, and P. D. Hopkins (Eds.), *Rethinking masculinity: Philosophical explorations in light of feminism,* 135–158. Lanham, MD: Rowman and Littlefield.

Mintz, A. (1946). A re-examination of correlations between lynchings and economic indices. *Journal of Abnormal Social Psychology* 41: 154–160.

Mintz, S. W., and R. Price. (1976/1992). *The birth of African-American culture.* Boston: Beacon Press

Misgeld, D., and G. Nicholson. (1992). Editor's introduction. In *Hans-Georg Gadamer on education, poetry, and history: Applied hermeneutics.* Trans. L. Schmidt and M. Reuss. Albany: State University of New York Press.

Mitchell, W. J. T. (1994). *Picture theory: Essays on verbal and visual representation.* Chicago: University of Chicago Press.

Modleski, T. (1988). *The women who knew too much: Hitchcock and feminist theory.* New York: Methuen.

Mohan, R. (1995). Dodging the crossfire: Questions for postcolonial pedagogy. In K. Myrsiades and J. McGuire (Eds.), *Order and partialities: Theory, pedagogy, and the "postcolonial,"* 261–284. Albany: State University of New York Press.

Mohr, C. L. (1986). *On the threshold of the freedom: Masters and slaves in Civil War Georgia.* Athens: University of Georgia Press.

Mohr, R. (1992). *Gay ideas.* Boston: Beacon Press.

Moi, T. (1989). Men against patriarchy. In L. Kauffman (Ed.), *Gender and theory: Dialogues in feminist criticism,* 181–188. New York: Basil Blackwell.

Monette, P. (1992a). *Becoming a man: Half a life story.* San Francisco, CA: Harper.

———. (1992b). *Halfway home.* New York: Avon.

Montgomery, R., and E. MacDougall. (1984). *American prison riots 1971–1983.* Monograph. Columbia, SC: University of South Carolina.

Montgomery, R. H. (1994). American prison riots: 1774–1991. In M. Braswell, S. Dillingham, and R. Montgomery, Jr. (Eds.), *Prison violence in America,* 227–251. Cincinnati, OH: Anderson.

Moon, M. (1987, Summer). "The gentle boy from the dangerous classes": Pederasty, domesticity, and capitalism in Horatio Alger. *Representations,* 87–110.

———. (1989). Disseminating Whitman. In R. R. Butters, J. Clum, and M. Moon (Eds.), *Displacing homophobia: Gay male perspectives in literature and culture,* 235–254. Durham, NC: Duke University Press.

———. (1995). Memorial rags. In G. E. Haggerty and B. Zimmerman (Eds.), *Professions of desire: Lesbian and gay studies in literature,* 233–240. New York: Modern Language Association of America.

———. (1996). Screen memories, or, pop comes from the outside: Warhol and queer childhood. In J. Doyle, J. Flatley, and J. Esteban Munoz (Eds.), *Pop out: Queer Warhol,* 78–100. Durham and London: Duke University Press.

Moreland, R. C. (1990). *Faulkner and modernism: Rereading and rewriting.* Madison: University of Wisconsin Press.

Morris, M. (1999). Curriculum and the Holocaust: Competing sites of memory and representation. Baton Rouge, LA: Louisiana State University, Department of Curriculum and Instruction, Ph.D. dissertation.

———. (in press). *Curriculum and the Holocaust: Competing sites of memory and representation.* Mahwah, NJ: Lawrence Erlbaum.

Morrison, K. (1988). *I am you: The hermeneutics of empathy in Western literature, theology and art.* Princeton: Princeton University Press.

Morrison, T. (1982). *Tar baby.* New York: New American Library.

———. (1987) *Beloved.* New York: Knopf.

———. (1989, winter). Unspeakable things unspoken: The Afro-American presence in American literature. *Michigan Quarterly,* 1–34.

———. (1992). *Playing in the dark: Whiteness and the literary imagination.* Cambridge, MA: Harvard University Press.

Moynihan, D. P. (1965). *The Negro family: The case for national action.* Office of Policy, Planning and Research, Department of Labor. Washington, D.C.: Government Printing Office.

Mudimbe, V. Y. (1988). *The invention of Africa: Gnosis, philosophy, and the order of knowledge.* Bloomington: Indiana University Press.

Muller, K. (1980). Introduction. In H. Heger, *The men with pink triangles: The true life and death story of homosexuals in the Nazi death camps,* 7–16. Trans. D. Fernbach. New York. Alyson Books.

Muncy, R. (1991). *Creating a female dominion in American reform, 1890–1935.* New York: Oxford University Press.

Munoz, J. E. (1996). Famous and dandy like B. 'n' Andy: Race, Pop, and Basquiat. In J. Doyle, J. Flatley, and J. E. Munoz (Eds.), *Pop out: Queer Warhol,* 144–179. Durham and London: Duke University Press.

Munro, P. (1998). *Subject to fiction.* Open University Press.

———. (1999a, Fall). Personal communication.

———. (1999b). Political activism as teaching: Jane Addams and Ida B. Wells. In M. S. Crocco, P. Munro, and K. Weiler, *Pedagogies of resistance: Women educator activists, 1880–1960,* 19–45. New York: Teachers College Press.

———. (in press). *Engendering curriculum history.* New York: Teachers College Press.

Murphy, D. D. (1995). *Lynching—history and analysis: A legal studies monograph.* Washington, D.C.: Council for Social and Economic Studies.

Murphy, K. P. (1998). Socrates in the slums: Homoerotics, gender, and settlement house reform. In L. McCall and D. Yacovone (Eds.), *A shared experience: Men, women, and the history of gender,* 273–296. New York: New York University Press.

Musil, R. (1905/1955). *Young Torless.* Preface by A. Pryce-Jones. New York: Pantheon.

———. (1960/1961/1979). *The man without qualities.* Trans. E. Kaiser. London: Secker and Warburg.

———. (1990). *Precision and soul: Essays and addresses.* Ed. and trans. B. Pike and D. S. Luft. Chicago and London: University of Chicago Press.

Myrdal, G. (1944/1962). *An American dilemma: The Negro problem and modern democracy.* New York: Harper and Row.

N.A.A.C.P. (1919). *Burning at the stake in the United States: A record of the public burning by mobs of five men, during the first five months of 1919, in the states of Arkansas, Florida, Georgia, Mississippi, and Texas.* New York: National Association for the Advancement of Colored People.

Nacci, P., and T. Kane. (1983). The incidence of sex and sexual aggression in federal prisons. *Federal Probation* 7: 31–36.

———. (1984a). Sex and sexual aggression in federal prisons: Inmate involvement and employee impact. *Federal Probation* 8: 46–53.

———. (1984b). Inmate sexual aggression: Some evolving propositions and empirical findings, and mitigating counter-forces. *Journal of Offender Counseling, Services, and Rehabilitation* 9(1–2): 1–20.

Naipaul, V. S. (1987). *The enigma of arrival.* Harmondsworth, Middlesex; New York: Viking.

National Center for Health Statistics (1994/1996). Web Site: http://www.cdc.gov/nchswww/nchshome.htm

National Institute of Justice. (1996, April). *Research in brief: HIV/AIDS and STDs in juvenile facilities.* Washington, D.C.: U.S. Department of Justice, National Institute of Justice.

Neal, L. (1968). Malcolm X—an autobiography. In L. Jones and L. Neal (Eds.), *Black fire: An anthology of Afro-American writing,* 315–317. New York: William Morrow.

Nealon, J. T. (1997, February). The ethics of dialogue: Bakhtin and Levinas. *College English* 59(2) 129–148.

Nelson, C. (1987). Men, feminism: The materiality of discourse. In A. Jardine and P. Smith (Eds.), *Men in feminism,* 153–172. New York: Methuen.

Nero, C. I. (1991). Toward a black gay aesthetic: Signifying in contemporary black gay literature. In E. Hemphill (Ed.), *Brother to brother: Collected writings by black gay men,* 229–252. Los Angeles: Alyson Books.

New York Times. (1894, August 19). China cares not to borrow. ... If they believe all that they read, it is not surprising English busybodies talk of forming societies to civilize us, 1, 4.

———. (1997, November 16). Inquiry begun on Klan tie to college icon, 12.

Newburn, T., and E. A. Stanko (Eds.). (1994). *Just boys doing business? Men, masculinities and crime.* London: Routledge.

Newcomb, H. (1856). *Christian character: A book for young ladies.* London and New York: T. Nelson.

Newton, M., and J. A. Newton. (1991). *Racial and religious violence in America: A chronology.* New York: Garland.

Niebuhr, H. R. (1967). *The meaning of revelation.* New York: Macmillan.

Noll, M. A. (1985). Common sense traditions and American evangelical thought. *American Quarterly* 37 218–235.

———. (1986). *Between faith and criticism: Evangelicals, scholarship and the Bible in America.* San Francisco: Harper and Row.

Nora, P. (1989, Spring). Between memory and history: Les lieux de memoire. *Representations* 26: 7–25.

Nordan, L. (1993). *Wolf whistle.* Chapel Hill, NC: Algonquin Books of Chapel Hill.

O'Leary, C. E. (1996). "Blood brotherhood": The racialization of patriotism, 1865–1918. In J. Bodnar (Ed.), *Bonds of affection: Americans define their patriotism,* 53–81. Princeton: Princeton University Press.

Oliver, W. (1994). *The violent social world of black men.* New York: Lexington Books (Macmillan).

Olney, J. (1972). *Metaphors of self: The meaning of autobiography.* Princeton, NJ: Princeton University Press.

———. (1993). The value of autobiography for comparative studies: African vs. Western autobiography. In W. L. Andrews (Ed.), *African American autobiography: A collection of critical essays,* 212–223. Englewood Cliffs, NJ: Prentice Hall.

——— (Ed.). (1980). *Autobiography: Essays theoretical and critical.* Princeton, NJ: Princeton University Press.

Omi, M., and H. Winant. (1983). By the rivers of Babylon: Race in the United States. *Socialist Review* 13(5): 31–65.

Omolade, B. (1983). Hearts of darkness. In A. Snitow, C. Stansell, and S. Thompson (Eds.), *Powers of desire: The politics of sexuality,* 350–367. New York: Monthly Review Press.

O'Neill, E. (1955/1979). *Long day's journey into night.* New Haven and London: Yale University Press.

O'Reilly, B. (1881). *The mirror of true womanhood: A book of instruction for women in the world.* New York: Peter F. Collier.

Oshinsky, D. M. (1996). *"Worse than slavery": Parchman Farm and the ordeal of Jim Crow justice.* New York: Free Press.

O'Sullivan, C. S. (1991). Acquaintance gang rape on campus. In A. Parrot and L. Bechhofer (Eds.), *Acquaintance rape: The hidden crime,* 140–156. New York: John Wiley & Sons.

———. (1992, August 10). Navy resembles a fraternity in its sexism. *New York Times,* letter to the editor, A 16, col. 2

———. (1993). Fraternities and the rape culture. In E. Buchwald, P. R. Fletcher and M. Roth (Eds.), *Transforming a rape culture,* 23–30. Minneapolis: Milkweed Editions.

Ottenberg, S. (1989). *Boyhood rituals in an African society.* Seattle: University of Washington Press.

Painter, N. I. (1988). "Social equality," miscegenation, labor, and power. In N. V. Bartley (Ed.), *The evolution of southern culture,* 47–67. Athens, GA: University of Georgia Press.

Palmer, L. (1995, May 28). Her own private tailhook. *New York Times Magazine,* 22–25.

Palmer, S. (1972). *The violent society.* New Haven, CT: College and University Press.

Paquet, S. P. (1993). West Indian autobiography. In W. L. Andrews (Ed.), *African American autobiography: A collection of critical essays,* 196–211. Englewood Cliffs, NJ: Prentice Hall.

Parent, A. S., Jr., and S. B. Wallace. (1993, January). Childhood and sexual identity under slavery. *Journal of the History of Sexuality* 3(3): 363–401.

Park, R. (1950). *Race and culture: Essays in the sociology of contemporary man.* Glencoe: Free Press.

Parsons, T. (1937, 1942). *The structure of social action.* New York: McGraw-Hill Book Company.

———. (1947). Certain primary sources of aggression in the social structure of the Western world. *Psychiatry* 10: 167–181.

Parsons, T., and R. F. Bales. (1955). *Family, socialization and interaction process.* Glencoe, IL: Free Press.

Patterson, O. (1967). *The sociology of slavery.* London: MacGibbon and Kee.

———. (1984). The code of honor in the Old South. *Reviews in American History* 12: 24–30.

Patton, C. (1994). *Last served? Gendering the HIV pandemic.* London: Taylor and Francis.

Peck, J. T. D. D. (1857). *The true woman, or, life and happiness at home and abroad.* New York: Carlton and Porter.

Pecora, V. P. (1989). *Self and form in modern narrative.* Baltimore and London: Johns Hopkins University Press.

Peiss, K. (1986). *Cheap amusements: Working women and leisure in turn-of-the-century New York.* Philadelphia: Temple University Press.

Pellauer, M. D. (1991). *Toward a tradition of feminist theology: The religious thought of Elizabeth Cady Stanton, Susan B. Anthony, and Anna Howard Shaw.* Brooklyn: Carlson.

Penley, C., and D. Haraway. (1991). Cyborgs at large: Interview with Donna Harraway. In C. Penley and A. Ross (Eds.), *Technoculture,* 1–20. Minneapolis and Oxford: University of Minnesota Press.

Percy, W. A., III. (1996). *Pederasty and pedagogy in archaic Greece.* Urbana and Chicago: University of Illinois Press.

Perkins, K. A. (1998). The impact of lynching on the art of African American women. In K. A. Perkins and J. L. Stephens (Eds.), *Strange fruit: Plays on lynching by American women,* 15–20. Bloomington: Indiana University Press.

Perkins, K. A., and J. L. Stephens (Eds.). (1998). *Strange fruit: Plays on lynching by American women.* Bloomington: Indiana University Press.

Pfeil, F. (1995). *White guys.* London: Verso.

Pfister, J. (1995). *Staging death: Eugene O'Neill and the politics of psychological discourse.* Chapel Hill and London: University of North Carolina Press.

Phillips, C. D. (1987). Exploring relations among forms of social control: The lynching and execution of blacks in North Carolina, 1889–1918. *Law and Society Review* 21: 361–374.

Pickens, W. (1916/1969). *The new Negro: His political, civil and mental status and related essays.* New York: Negro Universities Press.

Pike, B. (1961). *Robert Musil: An introduction to his work.* Ithaca, NY: Cornell University Press.

Pike, J. (1995, April 13). Players, fans entertain unsuspecting spectators. Baton Rouge, LA: *Daily Reveille,* Louisiana State University, 4.

Pilder, W. (1974). In the stillness is the dancing. In W. F. Pinar (Ed.), *Heightened consciousness, cultural revolution, and curriculum theory: The proceedings of the Rochester conference,* 117–129. Berkeley, CA: McCutchan.

Pinar, W. F. (1983/1994/1998). Curriculum as gender text: Notes on reproduction, resistance, and male-male relations. *JCT* 5(1): 26–52. Reprinted in Pinar (1994).

———. (1991). Curriculum as social psychoanalysis: On the significance of place. In J. L. Kincheloe and W. F. Pinar (Eds.), *Curriculum as social psychoanalysis: Essays on the significance of place,* 167–186. Albany: State University of New York Press.

———. (1993). Notes on understanding curriculum as a racial text. In C. McCarthy and W. Crichlow (Eds.), *Race, identity, and representation in education,* 60–70. New York and London, England: Routledge.

———. (1994). *Autobiography, politics, and sexuality: Essays in curriculum theory 1972–1992.* New York: Peter Lang.

———. (1996). Parenting in the promised land. In J. L. Kincheloe, S. R. Steinberg, and A. D. Gresson III (Eds.), *Measured lies,* 227–236. New York: St. Martin's Press.

———. (1997). Regimes of reason and male narrative voice. In W. G. Gierney and Y. S. Lincoln (Eds.), *Representation and the text: Re-framing the narrative voice,* 81–113. Albany: State University of New York Press.

——— (Ed.). (1998a). *Queer theory in education.* Mahwah, NJ: Lawrence Erlbaum.

———. (1998b). Notes on the intellectual: In praise of Maxine Greene. In W. C. Ayers and J. L. Miller (Eds.), *A light in dark times: Maxine Greene and the unfinished conversation,* 108–121. New York: Teachers College Press.

———. (1998c). Introduction. W. F. Pinar (Ed.), *The passionate mind of Maxine Greene,* 1–7. London: Falmer Press.

———. (1999). After Christianity. *Educational Researcher* 28(3): 39–42.

———. (2000). Strange fruit: Race, sex, and an autobiographics of alterity. In P. Trifonas (Ed.), *Revolutionary pedagogies,* 30–46. New York: Routledge.

Pinar, W. F., W. M. Reynolds, P. Slattery, and P. M. Taubman. (1995). *Understanding curriculum: An introduction to historical and contemporary curriculum discourses.* New York: Peter Lang.

Piper, A. (1992). Passing for white, passing for black. *Transition* 58: 4–32.

Pitt-Rivers, J. (1968). Honor. In D. L. Sills (Ed.), *International encyclopedia of the social sciences,* 8 vols. Vol. 6, 503–510. New York: Macmillan Company/Free Press.

Plant, R. (1986). *The pink triangle: The Nazi war against homosexuals.* New York: Henry Holt and Co.

Pleck, E. (1987). *Domestic tyranny: The making of social policy against family violence from colonial times to the present.* New York: Oxford University Press.

Pleck, J. H. (1984). *The myth of masculinity.* Cambridge, MA: Massachusetts Institute of Technology Press.

Ploscowe, M. (1951). *Sex and the law.* New York: Prentice Hall.

Plummer, W., and J. Johnson (1993, December 13). Fit to be tied: The hazing humiliation of a high school athlete has a Utah town in a snit. *Time,* 52.

Poe, E. A. (1957). *The Viking portable Edgar Allan Poe.* New York: Viking.

Pollock, J. M. (1986). *Sex and supervision: Guarding male and female inmates.* New York: Greenwood Press.

Pope, B. S. (1993). In the wake of Tailhook: A new order for the Navy. In E. Buchwald, P. R. Fletcher, and M. Roth (Eds.), *Transforming a rape culture,* 301–309. Minneapolis: Milkweed Editions.

Poussaint, A. (1972, August). Sex and the black male. *Ebony,* 116–117.

Powdermaker, H. (1939). *After freedom: A cultural study in the deep South.* New York: Viking Press.

Powell, K. (1995/1996). Ghetto bastard. In H. Boyd and R. L. Allen (Eds.), *Brotherman: The odyssey of black men in America,* 151–154. New York: Ballantine/One World.

Price, D. (1999, April 26). Scientist documents sexual diversity in animal kingdom. *Liberal Opinion Week* 10(17): 27.

Pronger, B. (1990). *The arena of masculinity: Sports, homosexuality and the meaning of sex.* New York: St. Martin's Press.
Propper, A. M. (1981). *Prison homosexuality: Myth and reality.* Lexington, MA, and Toronto: Lexington Books.
Pugh, D. (1983). *Sons of liberty: The masculine mind in nineteenth-century America.* Westport, CT: Greenwood Press.
Rabinowitz, P. (1987, Winter). Eccentric memories: A conversation with Maxine Hong Kingston. *Michigan Quarterly Review* 26(1): 177–187.
Ragan, S. L., D. G. Bystrom, L. L. Kaid, and C. S. Beck (Eds.). (1996). *The lynching of language: Gender, politics, and power in the Hill-Thomas hearings.* Foreword by J. T. Wood. Urbana and Chicago: University of Illinois Press.
Rainwater, L. (1967, April). Work and identity in the lower class. In S. H. Warner (Ed.), *Planning for a nation of cities,* 105–123. Cambridge, MA: Massachusetts Institute of Technology Press.
———. (1970). *Behind ghetto walls: Black families in a federal slum.* Chicago: Aldine.
Rainwater, L., and W. Yancy (Eds.). (1967). *The Moynihan report and the politics of controversy.* Cambridge, MA: Massachusetts Institute of Technology Press.
Rajiv, S. (1992). *Forms of black consciousness.* New York: Advent Books, Inc.
Ransby, B. (1992). The gang rape of Anita Hill and the assault upon all women of African descent. In R. Chrisman and R. L. Allen (Eds.), *Court of appeal,* 169–175. New York: Ballantine Books.
Raper, A. F. (1933/1969). *The tragedy of lynching.* Montclair, NJ: Patterson Smith. First printing 1933, University of North Carolina Press.
Reed, J. S. (1968, Fall). An evaluation of an anti-lynching organization. *Social Problems* 16: 172–182.
Reed, J. S., G. E. Doss, and J. S. Hulbert. (1987). Too good to be false: An essay in the folklore of social science. *Sociological Inquiry* 57: 1–11.
Reed, S. (1994, March 15). *London Voice.*
Reich, W. (1970). *The mass psychology of fascism.* Trans. V. R. Carfagno. New York: Straus and Giroux.
Reid, S. T. (1979). *Crime and criminology,* second edition. New York: Holt.
Reiman, J. (1990). *The rich get richer and the poor get prison.* New York: Macmillan.
Resnikoff, P. (1933, October). A psychoanlytic study of lynching. *Psychoanlaytic Review* 20: 421–427.
Rich, A. (1980, Summer). Compulsory heterosexuality and lesbian existence. *Signs* 5(4): 631–660.
Rieff, P. (1966a). *Freud: The mind of the moralist.* New York: Harper and Row.
———. (1966b). *The triumph of the therapeutic.* New York: Harper and Row.
——— (Ed.). (1956). Sigmund Freud's *Delusion and dream and other essays.* Boston: Beacon Press.
Riggs, M. (1989, 1985). *Tongues untied.* Produced and directed by M. Riggs. Videocassette, 55 minutes.
———. (1991a). Tongues untied. In E. Hemphill (Ed.), *Brother to brother: Collected writings by black gay men,* 200–205. Los Angeles: Alyson Books.
———. (1991b). Black macho revisited: Reflections of a SNAP! queen. In E. Hemphill (Ed.), *Brother to brother: Collected writings by black gay men,* 253–257. Los Angeles: Alyson Books.
Robbins, M. (1953, October). The inside story of a girls' reformatory. *Colliers* 30: 74–79.

Robertson, W. J. (1927). *The changing South.* New York: Boni and Liveright.

Roediger, D. R. (1991/1994). *Wages of whiteness: Race and the making of the working class.* London: Verso.

——— (Ed.). (1998). *Black on white: Black writers on what it means to be white.* New York: Schocken Books.

Rogers, J. B., and D. D. McKim. (1979). *The authority and interpretation of the Bible.* New York: Harper and Row.

Roper, C. S., M. Chanslor, and D. G. Bystrom. (1996). Sex, race, and politics: An intercultural communication approach to the Hill-Thomas hearings. In S. L. Ragan, D. G. Bystrom, L. L. Kaid, and C. S. Beck (Eds.), *The lynching of language: Gender, politics, and power in the Hill-Thomas hearings,* 44–60. Urbana and Chicago: University of Illinois Press.

Rorabaugh, W. (1979). *The alcoholic republic.* New York: Oxford University Press.

Rose, J. (1986). *Sexuality in the field of vision.* New York: Verso.

Rose, T. (1994). Rap music and the demonization of young black males. In T. Golden (Ed.), *Black male: Representations of masculinity in contemporary American art,* 149–157. New York: Whitney Museum of American Art (Harry N. Abrams).

Rose, W. L. (1982). *Slavery and freedom.* New York: Oxford University Press.

Ross, A. (1994). The gangsta and the diva. In T. Golden (Ed.), *Black male: Representations of masculinity in contemporary American art,* 111–118. New York: Whitney Museum of American Art (Harry N. Abrams, Inc.).

Ross, J. G., E. Heffernan, J. R. Sevick, and F. T. Johnson. (1978). *National evaluation program: Phase 1 report: Assessment of coeducational corrections.* Washington, D.C.: National Institute of Law Enforcement and Criminal Justice.

Ross, S. J. (1985). *Workers on the edge: Work, leisure, and politics in industrializing Cincinnati.* New York: Columbia University Press.

Rothman, D. J. (1971). *The discovery of the asylum.* Boston: Little, Brown.

Rotundo, E. A. (1983, Summer). Body and soul: Changing ideals of middle-class manhood, 1770–1920. *Journal of Social History* 15: 23–38.

———. (1990). Boy culture: Middle-class boyhood in nineteenth-century America. In M. C. Carnes and C. Griffen (Eds.), *Meanings for manhood: Constructions of masculinity in Victorian America,* 16–36. Chicago: University of Chicago Press.

———. (1993). *American manhood: Transformations in masculinity from the revolution to the modern era.* New York: Basic Books.

Rout, K. (1991). *Eldridge Cleaver.* Boston: Twayne Publishers (G. K. Hall).

Rowe, G. C. (1894, February 1). How to prevent a lynching. *Independent* 46: 131–132.

Ruback, B. (1975). The sexually integrated prison: A legal and policy evaluation. *American Journal of Criminal Law* 3: 301–330.

Rubenstein, W. (1997). Foreword. Michael Scarce, *Male on male rape,* vii–xi. New York: Insight Books/Plenum Publishing Corporation.

Rubin, G. (1975). The traffic in women: Notes on the "political economy" of sex. In R. Reiter (Ed.), *Toward an anthropology of women,* 157–210. New York: Monthly Review Press.

Ruddick, S. (1989). *Maternal thinking: Toward a politics of peace.* New York: Ballantine.

Rudoff, A. (1964). Prison inmates: An involuntary association. Ph.D. dissertation, University of California, Berkeley.

Rudwick, E. M. (1964). *Race riot at East St. Louis, July 2, 1917.* Carbondale: Southern Illinois University Press.

Rupaul Show. (1997, July 8). *Forty percent of actors in male gay porn are straight.* A&E television.

Rusche, G., and O. Kirchheimer. (1939). *Punishment and social structure.* New York: Russel and Russel.

Russel, K. (1998, November 9). Guards acquitted of staging prisoner's rape. Baton Rouge: Louisiana State University, *The Reveille* 1–3.

Russett, C. E. (1989). *Sexual science: The Victorian construction of womanhood.* Cambridge: Harvard University Press.

Ryan, M. P. (1981). *Cradle of the middle class: The family in Oneida County, New York, 1790–1865.* Cambridge: Cambridge University Press.

Rydell, R. W. (1984). *All the world's fair: Visions of empire at American international expositions 1876–1916.* Chicago: University of Chicago Press.

Sagarin, E. (1976). Prison homosexuality and its effect on post-prison sexual behavior. *Psychiatry* 39: 245–257.

Said, E. W. (1993). *Culture and imperialism.* New York: Alfred A. Knopf.

———. (1996). *Representations of the intellectual: The 1993 Reith lectures.* New York: Vintage.

Salleh, A. (1997). *Ecofeminism as politics: Nature, Marx and the postmodern.* London: Zed.

Sampson, A. (1977). *The arms bazaar: From Lebanon to Lockheed.* New York: Viking.

Samuels, F. G. (1976). *The Negro tavern: A microcosm of slum life.* San Francisco: R&E Associates.

Sanchez-Appler, K. (1988, Fall). Bodily bonds: The intersecting rhetorics of feminist and abolition. *Representations* 24: 28–59.

Sanday, P. R. (1990). *Fraternity gang rape: Sex, brotherhood, and privilege on campus.* New York: New York University Press.

Sandeen, E. R. (1970). *The roots of fundamentalism: British and American millenarianism, 1800–1930.* Chicago: University of Chicago Press.

Sandler, B. R., and J. K. Ehrhar. (1985). *Campus gang rape: Party games?* Washington, D.C.: Project on the Status and Education of Women, Association of American Colleges.

Sartre, J.-P. (1981). *The family idiot: Gustave Flaubert 1821–1857.* Trans. Carol Cosman. Chicago: University of Chicago Press.

Sayers, J. (1856). *Women's rights: or, a treatise on the inalienable rights of women, carefully investigated and inscribed to the female community of the U.S. of America.* Cincinnati: Applegate.

Sbarbaro, E. P., and R. L. Keller. (1995). Introduction. E. P. Sbarbaro and R. L. Keller (Eds.), *Prison crisis: Critical readings,* 1–16. New York: Harrow and Heston.

Scacco, A. M., Jr. (1975). *Rape in prison.* Springfield, IL: Charles C. Thomas.

Scarce, M. (1997). *Male on male rape.* New York: Insight Books/Plenum Publishing Corporation.

Schacht, S. P., and D. W. Ewing. (1998). The many paths of feminism: Can men travel any of them? In S. P. Schacht and D. W. Ewing (Eds.), *Feminism and men: Reconstructing gender relations,* 119–145. New York: New York University Press.

Schechter, P. A. (1997). Unsettled business: Ida B. Wells against lynching, or, how antilynching got its gender. In W. F. Brundage (Ed.), *Under sentence of death: Lynching in the South,* 292–317. Chapel Hill: University of North Carolina Press.

Schraufnagel, N. (1973). *From apology to protest: The black American novel.* Deland, FL: Everett/Edwards.

Schulz, D. A. (1977). Coming up as a boy in the ghetto. In D. Y. Wilkinson and R. L. Taylor (Eds.), *The black male in America,* 7–32. Chicago: Nelson-Hall.

Schwartz, M. D., and W. S. DeKeseredy (Eds.). (1997). *Sexual assault on the college campus.* Thousand Oaks, CA: Sage Publications.

Scott, J. (1991). The evidence of experience. *Critical Inquiry* 17: 773–797.

Scott, J. C. (1989). Everyday forms of resistance. In F. D. Colburn (Ed.), *Everyday forms of peasant resistance,* 3–33. Armonk, NY: M. E. Sharpe.

———. (1990). *Domination and the arts of resistance: Hidden transcripts.* New Haven: Yale University Press.

Scully, D. (1990). *Understanding sexual violence: A study of convicted rapists.* Boston: Unwin Hyman.

Seale, B. (1994). *Seize the time: The story of the Black Panther Party and Huey P. Newton.* Baltimore, MD: Black Classic Press.

Sears, J. (1998). A generational and theoretical analysis of culture and male (homo)sexuality. In W. F. Pinar (Ed.), *Queer theory in education,* 73–105. Mahwah, NJ: Lawrence Erlbaum.

Sedgwick, E. K. (1985). *Between men: English literature and male homosocial desire.* New York: Columbia University Press.

———. (1990). *Epistemology of the closet.* Berkeley and Los Angeles: University of California Press.

Sedgwick, E. K., and A. Frank. (1995). Shame in the cybernetic fold: Reading Silvan Tomkins. In E. K. Sedgwick and A. Frank (Eds.), *Shame and its sisters: A Silvan Tomkins reader.* Durham, NC: Duke University Press.

Seel, P. (1997). *Liberation was for others: Memories of a gay survivor of the Nazi Holocaust.* New York: DeCapo Press.

Seidler, V. (1996). Masculinity and violence. In L. May, R. Strikwerda, and P. D. Hopkins (Eds.), *Rethinking masculinity: Philosophical explorations in light of feminism,* 63–75. Lanham, MD: Rowman and Littlefield Publishers, Inc.

Sellers, C. (1992). *The market revolution: Jacksonian America, 1915–1846.* New York: Oxford University Press.

Senechal de la Roche, R. (1997). The sociogenesis of lynching. In W. F. Brundage (Ed.), *Under sentence of death: Lynching in the South,* 48–76. Chapel Hill: University of North Carolina Press.

Sewell, B. (1994). If it was you instead of me. In L. Goldstein (Ed.), *The male body,* 106–118. Ann Arbor: University of Michigan Press.

Sewell, D. (1995, August 27). Teen's slaying galvanized civil rights drive. Knoxville, TN: *Knoxville News-Sentinel,* A-5.

Shapiro, H. (1988). *White violence and black response: From Reconstruction to Montgomery.* Amherst: University of Massachusetts Press.

Sheldon, W. D. (1906, September). Shall lynching be suppressed, and how? [No periodical given], 225–233.

Shepherd, M. (1998). Feminism, men, and the study of masculinity. Which way now? In S. P. Schacht and D. W. Ewing (Eds.), *Feminism and men: Reconstructing gender relations,* 173–228. New York: New York University Press.

Shepherd, R. (1986). On not being white. In J. Beam (Ed.), *In the life: A black gay anthology*, 46–57. Boston: Alyson Publications.

Shillady, J. (1919). *Thirty years of lynching in the United States, 1889–1918.* New York: N.A.A.C.P.

Shohat, E. (1991). Ethnicities-in-relation: Toward a multicultural reading of American cinema. In L. D. Friedman (Ed.), *Unspeakable images: Ethnicity and the American cinema,* 215–250. Urbana and Chicago: University of Illinois Press.

Showalter, E. (1987). Rivers and Sassoon: The inscription of male gender anxieties. In M. R. Higonnet, J. Jenson, and M. Collins (Eds.), *Behind the lines: Gender and the two world wars,* 61–69. New Haven, CT: Yale University Press.

Siegfried, A. (1927). *America comes of age.* New York: Harcourt, Brace.

Silverman, K. (1983). *The subject of semiotics.* New York: Oxford University Press.

———. (1992). *Male subjectivity at the margins.* New York and London: Routledge.

Simmons, R. (1991). Some thoughts on the challenges facing black gay intellectuals. In E. Hemphill (Ed.), *Brother to brother: Collected writings by black gay men,* 211–228. Los Angeles: Alyson Books.

Simon, R. I. (1996). *Bad men do what good men dream: A forensic psychiatrist illuminates the darker side of human behavior.* Washington, D.C., and London: American Psychiatric Press.

Simpson, L. (1983). *The dispossessed garden.* Baton Rouge: Louisiana State University Press.

Simpson, M. (1994). *Male impersonators: Men performing masculinity.* Foreword by A. Sinfield. New York: Routledge.

Simson, R. (1983). The Afro-American female: The historical context of the construction of sexual identity. In A. Snitow, C. Stansell, and S. Thompson (Eds.), *Powers of desire: The politics of sexuality,* 229–235. New York: Monthly Review Press.

Sinfield, A. (1994). Foreword. M. Simpson, *Male Impersonators,* ix–xii. New York: Routledge.

Skaggs, W. H. (1924). *The southern oligarchy: An appeal in behalf of the silent masses of our country against the despotic rule of the few.* New York: The Devin-Adair Company.

Sklar, K. K. (1973). *Catherine Beecher Stowe: A study in American domesticity.* New Haven, CT: Yale University Press.

Smead, H. (1986). *Blood justice: The lynching of Mack Charles Parker.* New York: Oxford University Press.

Smelser, N. (1963). *Theory of collective behavior.* New York: Free Press.

Smith, A. B. (1893/1988). *An autobiography: The story of the Lord's dealings with Mrs. Amanda Smith, the colored evangelist.* Ed. H. L. Gates, Jr. Introduction by J. E. Dodson. New York: Oxford University Press.

Smith, B. (1980). *Toward a black feminist criticism.* Brooklyn, NY: Out and Out Books.

Smith, E. O. (1851/1974). Woman and her needs. In L. Stein and A. K. Baxter (Eds.), *Women in America: From colonial times to the twentieth century.* New York: Arno Press.

Smith, H. W. (1870/1985). *A Christian's secret of a happy life.* Westwood: Barbour.

Smith, L. (1944/1972). *Strange fruit.* San Diego, CA: Harvest.

———. (1949/1963). *Killers of the dream,* revised and enlarged edition. Garden City, NY: Anchor Books.

Smith, V. (1987). *Self-discovery and authority.* Cambridge: Harvard University Press.

Smith-Rosenberg, C. (1978). Sex as symbol in Victorian purity: An ethnohistorical analysis of Jacksonian America. *American Journal of Sociology* 84 (supplement).

Snitow, C. S., and S. Thompson (Eds.). (1983). *Powers of desire: The politics of sexuality.* New York: Monthly Review Press.

Soble, A. (1986). *Pornography: Marxism, feminism, and the future of sexuality.* New Haven: Yale University Press.

Sollors, W. (1997). *Neither black nor white yet both: Thematic explorations of interracial literature.* New York and Oxford: Oxford University Press.

Spillers, H. J. (1987). Mama's baby, papa's maybe: An American grammar book. *Diacritics* 17(2): 65–81.

Spitz, L. (1959, Winter). Politics and realms of being. *Dissent* 6(1), 56–65.

Spivak, G. (1993). *Outside in the teaching machine.* New York: Routledge.

Spock, B. (1946). *Common sense book of baby and child care.* New York: Pocket Books.

Spretnak, C. (1997). *Resurgence of the real: Body, nature, and place in a hypermodern world.* New York: Addison-Wesley.

Srivastava, S. P. (1974). Sex life in an Indian male prison. *Indian Journal of Social Work* 3: 21–33.

Stanko, E. A. (1994). Challenging the problem of men's individual violence. In T. Newburn and E. A. Stanko (Eds.), *Just boys doing business? Men, masculinities, and crime,* 32–45. London: Routledge.

Stannard, D. E. (1980). *Shrinking history: On Freud and the failure of psychohistory.* New York: Oxford University Press.

Stanton, E. C. (1894). *Bible and church degrade women.* Chicago: H. L. Green.

———. (1895). *The woman's bible.* New York: European Publishing Co.

Staples, R. (1977). The myth of the impotent black male. In D. Y. Wilkinson and R. L. Taylor (Eds.), *The black male in America,* 133–144. Chicago: Nelson-Hall.

———. (1982). *Black masculinity: The black man's role in American society.* San Francisco: Black Scholar Press.

Starke, C. J. (1971). *Black portraiture in American fiction. Stock characters, archetypes, and individuals.* New York: Basic Books.

Stein, G. (1937). *Everybody's autobiography.* New York: Random House.

Stein, N. (1995). Sexual harassment in school: The public performance of gendered violence. *Harvard Educational Review* 65(2): 145–162.

Steinberg, S. R. (1998). Appropriating queerness: Hollywood sanitation. In W. F. Pinar (Ed.), *Queer theory in education,* 187–195. Mahwah, NJ: Lawrence Erlbaum.

Stekel, W. (1971). *Impotence in the male.* New York: Liverwright.

Stember, C. H. (1976). *Sexual racism: The emotional barrier to an integrated society.* New York: Harper Colophon Books.

Stepan, N. L. (1990). Race and gender: The role of analogy in science. In D. T. Goldberg (Ed.), *Anatomy of racism,* 38–57. Minneapolis: University of Minnesota Press.

Stephens, J. (1998). Lynching dramas and women: History and critical context. In K. A. Perkins and J. L. Stephens (Eds.), *Strange fruit: Plays on lynching by American women,* 3–14. Bloomington: Indiana University Press.

Sterling, D. (1995). Afterword. *Memphis diary of Ida B. Wells,* 191–199. Ed. M. Decosta-Willis. Boston, MA: Beacon Press.

Stetson, E., and L. David. (1994). *Glorying in tribulation: The lifework of Sojourner Truth.* East Lansing: Michigan State University Press.

Stocking, G. W. (1987). *Victorian anthropology.* New York: The Free Press.

Stolcke, V. (1994). Invaded women: Gender, race, and class in the formation of colonial society. In M. Hendricks and P. Parker (Eds.), *Women, "race," and writing in the early modern period,* 272–286. New York: Routledge.

Stoler, A. L. (1995). *Race and the education of desire: Foucault's history of sexuality and the colonial order of things.* Durham, NC: Duke University Press.

Stoltenberg, J. (1989/1990). *Refusing to be a man.* Portland, OR: Breitenbush Books. Reprinted in 1990 by Meridian.

———. (1998). "I am not a rapist!" Why college guys are confronting sexual violence. In S. P. Schacht and D. W. Ewing (Eds.), *Feminism and men: Reconstructing gender relations,* 89–98. New York: New York University Press.

Stone, A. E. (1993). After *Black Boy* and *Dusk of Dawn*: Patterns in recent black autobiography. In W. L. Andrews (Ed.), *African American autobiography: A collection of critical essays,* 171–195. Englewood Cliffs, NJ: Prentice Hall.

Stowe, S. M. (1987). *Intimacy and power in the Old South: Ritual in the lives of the planters.* Baltimore, MD: Johns Hopkins University Press.

Strategies for the treatment and prevention of sexual assault. (1995). Chicago: American Medical Association.

Stratton, R. (1999, September). The making of a bonecrusher. *Esquire,* 187–191, 208, 212.

Straus, M. A., R. J. Gelles, and S. Steinmetz. (1980). *Behind closed doors: Violence in the American family.* New York: Anchor Press.

Sumner, W. G. (1913). *Folkways: A student of the sociological importance of usages, manners, customs, mores, and morals.* Boston: Ginn and Company.

Sundquist, E. J. (1993). *To wake the nations: Race in the making of American literature.* Cambridge, MA: Harvard University Press.

Suttie, I. D. (1935). *The origins of love and hate.* Harmondsworth: Penguin; (1988) London: Free Association Books.

Sweet, J. H. (1996). Male homosexuality and spiritism in the African diaspora: The legacies of the link. *Journal of the History of Sexuality* 7(2): 184–202.

Sydie, R. A. (1987). *Natural women, cultured man.* Milton Keynes: Open University Press.

Sylvester, S., J. Reed, and D. Nelson. (1977). *Prison homicide.* New York: Spectrum.

Taliaferro, D. (1998). Education for liberation as (an) African American folk theory. Baton Rouge, LA: Louisiana State University, Department of Curriculum and Instruction, unpublished Ph.D. dissertation.

Tannenbaum, F. (1924). *Darker phases of the South.* New York: Putnam.

Taylor, C. (1994). The game. In T. Golden (Ed.), *Black male: Representations of masculinity in contemporary American art,* 167–174. New York: Whitney Museum of American Art (Harry N. Abrams, Inc.).

Taylor, E. D. (1998). Chivalrous men and voting women: The role of men and the language of masculinity in the 1911 California women suffrage campaign. In L. McCall and D. Yacovone (Eds.), *A shared experience: Men, women, and the history of gender,* 297–322. New York: New York University Press.

Taylor, P. (1995). Narrative, pluralism, and decolonization: Recent Caribbean literature. In K. Myrsiades and J. McGuire (Eds.), *Order and partialities: Theory, pedagogy, and the "postcolonial,"* 137–151. Albany: State University of New York Press.

Taylor, R. L. (1977). Socialization to the black male role. In D. Y. Wilkinson and R. L. Taylor (Eds.), *The black male in America,* 1–6. Chicago: Nelson-Hall.

Terborg-Penn, R. (1978). Black male perspectives on the nineteenth-century woman. In S. Harley and R. Terborg-Penn (Eds.), *The Afro-American woman: Struggles and images,* 28–42. Port Washington, NY: Kennikat Press.

———. (1991). African American women's network in the anti-lynching crusade. In N. Frankel and N. S. Dye (Eds.), *Gender, class, race, and reform in the progressive era,* 295–312. Lexington: University Press of Kentucky.

Terrell, M. C. (1904, June). Lynching from a Negro's point of view. *North American Review* 178(6): 853–868.

Thayer, W. M. (1858/1866). *The good girl and true woman; or, elements of success.* Boston: Gould and Lincoln.

Thomas, C. (1996). *Male matters: Masculinity, anxiety, and the male body on the line.* Urbana and Chicago: University of Illinois Press.

Thomas, G. M. (1989). *Revivalism and cultural change: Christianity, nation-building, and the market in the nineteenth-century Untied States.* Chicago: University of Chicago Press.

Thomas, K. (1996). Ain't nothing like the real thing: Black masculinity, gay sexuality, and the jargon of authenticity. In M. Blount and G. P. Cunningham (Eds.), *Representing black man,* 55–69. New York: Routledge.

Thomas, L. (1996). Erogenous zones and ambiguity: Sexuality and the bodies of women and men. In L. May, R. Strikwerda, and P. D. Hopkins (Eds.), *Rethinking masculinity: Philosophical explorations in light of feminism,* 255–271. Lanham, MD: Rowman and Littlefield.

Thomas, P. (1967). *Down these mean streets.* New York: Knopf.

———. (1974). *Seven long times.* New York: Praeger.

Thompson, T. (1998, July 20). Warped by criminal activity, college athletics tries to regain perspective. Baton Rouge, LA: *Reveille,* 1, 6–8.

Thorpe, E. E. (1967). *Eros and freedom in southern life and thought.* Durham, NC: Seeman.

Tilton, T. (1863). *The Negro: A speech by Theodore Tilton.* New York: Anglo-African Office.

Toby, J. (1966). Violence and the masculine ideal: Some qualitative data. *Annals of the American Academy of Political and Social Science* 364: 19–27.

Toch, H. (1969). *Violent men.* Chicago: Aldine.

———. (1980). Foreword. D. Lockwood, *Prison Sexual Violence,* xi–xii. New York: Elsevier.

———. (1992). *Living in prison: The ecology of survival*, revised edition. First published in 1977 by The Free Press. Washington, D.C.: American Psychological Association.

Todd, Rev. J. (1867). *Woman's rights*. Boston: Lee and Shepard.

Todorov, T. (1984). *Mikhail Bakhtin: The dialogical principle*. Minneapolis: University of Minnesota Press.

Tolnay, S. E., and E. M. Beck. (1995). *A festival of violence: An analysis of southern lynchings, 1882–1930*. Urbana: University of Illinois Press.

Tonkovich, N. (1995). Advice books. In C. Davidson and L. Wagner-Martin (Eds.), *Oxford companion to women's writing in the United States*, 12–15. New York: Oxford University Press.

Toomer, J. (1975). *Cane*. New York: Liveright.

Tournier, M. (1969). *Friday*. Trans. N. Denny. Garden City, NY: Doubleday.

Trachtenberg, A. (1982). *The incorporation of America: Culture and society in the Gilded Age*. New York: Hill and Wang.

Trelease, A. W. (1971). *White terror: The Ku Klux Klan conspiracy and the southern reconstruction*. Baton Rouge: Louisiana State University Press.

Trott, N. R. (1995, November 5). Teacher loses job after promoting gay tolerance. New Orleans: *Times-Picayune*, A-13.

Truth, S. (1878/1991). *Narrative of Sojourner Truth; a bondswoman of olden time, with a history of her labors and correspondence drawn from her "book of life."* Ed. H. L. Gates, Jr. New York: Oxford University Press.

Tucker, D. M. (1971, Summer). Miss Ida B. Wells and the Memphis lynching. *Phylon* 32: 112–122.

Turner, J. D. (1995). Personal communication.

Turner, V. (1969). *The ritual process: Structure and anti-structure*. Ithaca, NY: Cornell University Press.

Twardowski, L. (1997, September). Greek mythology. *U: The National College Magazine*, 16–17.

20/20. (1997, November 6). *Sexual harrassment of men by men*. New York: ABC News.

———. (1998, February 27). *Retail racism*. New York: ABC News.

———. (1998, November 4). *Black men and their mothers*. New York: ABC News.

———. (1998, November 18). *Hard time*. New York: ABC News.

———. (1999, April 28). *Sorority hazing*. New York: ABC News.

Twitchell, J. B. (1987). *Forbidden partners: The incest taboo in modern culture*. New York: Columbia University Press.

Tyack, D., and E. Hansot. (1990). *Learning together: A history of coeducation in American schools*. New Haven, CT: Yale University Press.

Tyler, C.-A. (1994). Passing: Narcissism, identity, and difference. *Differences* 6(2+3): 212–248.

Tyler, R. W. (1950). *Principles of curriculum and instruction*. Chicago: University of Chicago Press.

Urban, W. (1989). The graduate education of a black scholar: Horace Mann Bond and the University of Chicago. In C. Kridel (Ed.), *Curriculum history*, 72–88. Lanham, MD: University Press of America.

———. (1992). *Black scholar: Horace Mann Bond, 1904–1972*. Athens, GA: University of Georgia Press.

U. S. Department of Justice. (1983). Web site: http://www.ojp.usdoj.gov

Valois, R. F., M. L. Vincent, R. E. McKeown, C. Z. Garrison, and S. D. Kirby. (1993). Adolescent risk behaviors and the potential for violence: A look at what's coming to campus. *Journal of the American College Health Association* 41: 141–147.

Van Deburg, W. L. (1984). *Slavery and race in American popular culture.* Madison: University of Wisconsin Press

———. (1997). *Black Camelot: African-American culture heroes in their times, 1960–1980.* Chicago: University of Chicago Press.

van der Post, L. (1955). *The dark eye in Africa.* New York: Morrow.

———. (1975). *Jung and the story of our time.* New York: Vintage Books.

Vance, N. (1985). *The sinews of the spirit: The idea of Christian manliness in Victorian literature and thought.* Cambridge: Cambridge University Press.

Varney, J. (1997, August 30). Hazing was brutal, former pledge says. New Orleans: *Times-Picayune,* A1, A17.

Vedder, C. B., and P. G. King. (1967). *Problems of homosexuality in corrections.* Springfield, IL: Charles C. Thomas.

Verene, D. P. (1991). *The new art of autobiography. An essay on the life of Giambattista Vico written by himself.* Oxford: Clarendon Press.

Volosinov, V. N. (1986). *Marxism and the philosophy of language.* Trans. L. Matejka and I. R. Titunik. Cambridge: Harvard University Press.

Von Hentig, H. (1940). Criminality of the Negro. *Journal of Criminal Law and Criminology* (30): 662–680.

Wacker, G. (1982). The demise of biblical civilization. In M. A. Noll and N. O. Hatch (Eds.), *The Bible in America: Essays in cultural history.* New York: Oxford University Press.

Wade, W. C. (1987). *The fiery cross.* New York: Simon and Schuster.

Walinksy, A. (1995, July). The crisis of public order. *Atlantic Monthly,* 39–54.

Walker, A. (1973). *In love and trouble: Stories of black women.* New York: Harcourt Brace Jovanovich.

———. (1983). Gifts of power: The writings of Rebecca Jackson. In *In search of our mother's gardens: Womanist prose by Alice Walker,* 71–82. New York: Harcourt Brace Jovanovich.

———. (1989). *The temple of my familiar.* New York: Harcourt Brace Jovanovich.

———. (1999/1966). *Jubilee.* New York: Houghton Mifflin.

Walker, D. R. (1988). *Penology for profit: A history of the Texas prison system, 1867–1912.* College Station, TX: Texas A & M University Press.

Walker, L. E. (1979). *The battered woman.* New York: Harper and Row.

Walker, P. F. (1978). *Moral choices: Memory, desire, and imagination in nineteenth century American abolition.* Baton Rouge: Louisiana State University Press.

Wallace, M. (1978/1979). *Black macho and the myth of the superwoman.* New York: Dial Press. Published in London in 1979 by John Calder.

———. (1988, April). Who dat say dat when I say dat? Zora Neale Hurston then and now. *Village Voice Literary Supplement.*

———. (1990). *Invisibility blues: From pop to theory.* London: Verso.

Waller, W. (1932). *The sociology of teaching.* New York: John Wiley and Sons.

Walling, W. E. (1908, September 3). The race war in the North. *Independent* 65: 529–534.

———. (1913). *The larger aspects of socialism.* New York: Macmillan.

Walvin, J. (1973). *Black and white: The Negro and English society 1555–1945.* London: Allen Lane.

Ward, E. (1900). *Women should mind their own business.* New York: National American Woman's Suffrage Association.

Ware, V. (1992). *Beyond the pale: White women, racism and history.* London: Verso.

Warner, M. (Ed.). (1993). *Fear of a queer planet: Queer politics and social theory.* Minneapolis: University of Minnesota Press.

Washburne, C. (1942). *Louisiana looks at its schools.* Baton Rouge: Louisiana Educational Survey Commission.

Washington, M. H. (1995). Foreword. *Memphis diary of Ida B. Wells,* ix–xvii. Ed. M. Decosta-Willis. Boston, MA: Beacon Press.

Watson, J. B. (1928). *Psychological care of the infant and child.* New York: Norton.

Wear, D. (1999). Writing with/in leftovers. In M. Morris, M. A. Doll, and W. F. Pinar (Eds.), *How we work,* 171–186. New York: Peter Lang.

Webster, R. (1995). *Why Freud was wrong: Sin, science, and psychoanalysis.* New York: Basic Books.

Weed, E. (1994). The more things change. *Differences* 6(2+3): 249–273.

Weintraub, K. J. (1978). *The value of the individual.* Chicago: University of Chicago Press.

Weiss, C., and D. J. Friar (1974). *Terror in prisons.* Indianapolis, IN: Bobbs-Merrill.

Weiss, J. (1998). Making room for fathers: Men, women, and parenting in the United States, 1945–1980. In L. McCall and D. Yacovone (Eds.), *A shared experience: Men, women, and the history of gender,* 349–367. New York: New York University Press.

Wells, I. B. (1892a/1969). *Southern horrors: Lynch law in all its phases.* In *On lynchings.* New York: Arno Press/New York Times.

———. (1892b/1969). *A red record. Tabulated statistics and alleged causes of lynchings in the United States, 1892–1893–1894.* In *On lynchings.* New York: Arno Press/New York Times.

———. (1892c/1969). *Mob rule in New Orleans. Robert Charles and his fight to the death.* In *On lynchings.* New York: Arno Press/New York Times.

———. (1892/1991). Southern horrors: Lynch law in all its phases. In T. Harris (Ed.), *Selected works of Ida B. Wells-Barnett,* 14–45. New York: Oxford University Press.

———. (1894). *A red record: Tabulated statistics and alleged causes of lynchings in the United States, 1892–1893–1894.* Chicago: Donohue and Henneberry.

———. (1901, May 16). Lynching and the excuse for it. *The Independent* 53: 1133–1136.

———. (1901/1977). Lynching and the excuse for it. In J. Addams and I. B. Wells, *Lynching and rape: An exchange of views,* 28–34. Ed. B. Aptheker. Chicago: University of Illinois, Occasional Paper No. 25.

———. (1970). *Crusade for justice: The autobiography of Ida B. Wells.* Ed. A. Duster. Chicago: University of Chicago Press.

Wells, I. B., and F. Douglass. (1893). *The reason why the colored American is not in the world's Columbian exposition: The Afro-American's contribution to Columbian literature.* Chicago: Ida B. Wells.

Welsing, F. C. (1991). *The Isis (Yssis) papers.* Chicago: Third World Press.

Welter, B. (1976). *Divinity convictions: The American woman in the nineteenth century.* Athens: Ohio University Press.

West, C. (1993). *Race matters.* Boston: Beacon Press.

Westbrook, R. B. (1991) *John Dewey and American philosophy.* Ithaca, NY: Cornell University Press.

Westwood, G. (1953). *Society and the homosexual.* New York: E. P. Dutton.

Wexler, P. (1996). *Holy sparks: Social theory, education and religion.* New York: St. Martin's Press.

White, H. (1987). *The content of the form: Narrative discourse and historical representation.* Baltimore, MD: Johns Hopkins University Press.

White, J. (1999, August 31). Study says 80 percent of college athletes hazed. Baton Rouge, LA: Louisiana State University, *Reveille,* 13.

White, J. L., and J. H. Cones III. (1999). *Black man emerging.* New York: W. H. Freeman.

White, J. W., and J. A. Humphrey. (1991). Young people's attitudes toward acquaintance rape. In A. Parrot and L. Bechhofer (Eds.), *Acquaintance rape: The hidden crime,* 43–56. New York: John Wiley.

White, W. (1929). *Rope and faggot: A biography of Judge Lynch.* New York: Alfred A. Knopf.

Whites, L. (1992, Summer). Rebecca Latimer Felton and the wife's farm: The class and racial politics of gender reform. *Georgia Historical Quarterly* 75: 368–372.

Whitford, M. (1991). *Luce Irigaray: Philosophy in the feminine.* London: Routledge.

Whiting, J. M. W., R. Kluckhohn, and A. Anthony. (1958). The function of male initiation ceremonies at puberty. In E. E. Maccoby, T. M. Newcomb, and E. L. Hartley (Eds.), *Readings in social psychology,* 350–370. New York: Henry Holt.

Wideman, J. (1974). *The lynchers.* New York: Laurel.

Wiegman, R. (1993, January). The anatomy of lynching. *Journal of the History of Sexuality* 3(3): 445–467.

———. (1995). *American anatomies: Theorizing race and gender.* Durham, NC: Duke University Press.

Wiggins, F. (1972, March 31). The truth about Attica by an inmate. *National Review* 24: 327–333, 363.

Wilde, O. (1905/1969). *The rise of historical criticism.* Folcroft: Folcroft Press.

Willard, F. E. (1886/1987). How to win: A book for girls. In C. De Swarte Gifford (Ed.), *Women in American Protestant religion,* vol. 5. New York: Garland.

———. (1889/1978). *Woman in the pulpit.* Washington, D.C.: Zenger.

———. (1889). *Glimpses of fifty years: The autobiography of an American woman.* Introduction by H. Whitall Smith. Boston: G. M. Smith.

Williams, J. A. (1995/1996). The man who cried I am. In H. Boyd and R. L. Allen (Eds.), *Brotherman: The odyssey of black men in America,* 768–776. New York: Ballantine/One World.

Williams, Linda. (1989). *Hard core: Power, pleasure and the "frenzy of the visible."* Berkeley: University of California Press.

Williamson, J. (1984). *The crucible of race: Black-white relations in the American South since emancipation.* New York and Oxford: Oxford University Press.

Willinsky, J. (1998). *Learning to divide the world: Education at empire's end.* Minneapolis: University of Minnesota Press.

Willis, P. (1977/1981). *Learning to labour.* Hampshire, England: Gower. 1977 edition published by Saxon House, Farnborough, England.

Wilmore, G. S. (1983). *Black religion and black radicalism: An interpretation of the religious history of Afro-American people,* second edition. Maryknoll, NY: Orbis Books.

Wilson, H. E., Jr. (1983). *Our Nig: Sketches from the life of a free black.* New York: Random House.

Winslow, H., and Mrs. J. Sanford. (1854). *The benison: The lady's manual of moral and intellectual culture.* New York: Leavitt and Allen.

Wise, D. (1851/1987). "Bridal greetings: A marriage gift in which the mutual duties of husband and wife are familiarly illustrated and enforced." In C. De Swarte Gifford (Ed.), *The American ideal of the "True Woman": Women in American Protestant religions.* New York: Garland.

Withers, R. (1999). Personal communication. Stop Prisoner Rape, Inc. can be reached at P.O. Box 198, Fort Bragg, CA 95437. Tel. 707-961-1953. www.roanne@mcn.org

Wittig, M. (1992). *The straight mind and other essays.* Boston: Beacon Press.

Wolfgang, M. E. (1958). *Patterns of criminal homicide.* Philadelphia, PA: University of Pennsylvania Press.

Wood, C. (1924). *Manhood: The facts of life presented to men.* Girard, KS: Haldeman-Julien.

Wood, J. T. (1996). Foreword: Continuing the conversation about Hill and Thomas. In S. L. Ragan, D. G. Bystrom, L. L. Kaid, and C. S. Beck (Eds.), *The lynching of language: Gender, politics, and power in the Hill-Thomas hearings,* ix–xiii. Urbana and Chicago: University of Illinois Press.

Wooden, W. S., and J. Parker. (1982). *Men behind bars: Sexual exploitation in prison.* New York: Plenum Press.

Woods, G. (1987). *Articulate flesh: Male homoeroticism and modern poetry.* New Haven, CT: Yale University Press.

Woodward, C. V. (1951/1971). *The origins of the new South, 1877–1913.* Baton Rouge: Louisiana State University Press.

———. (1960). *The burden of southern history.* Baton Rouge: Louisiana State University Press.

Woolf, V. (1919/1957). *A room of one's own.* New York: Harcourt Brace.

Worth, R. F. (1998, Spring). A legacy of a lynching. *American Scholar* 67(2): 65–77.

Wright, E. (1996, Spring). Review of Renata Salecl's *The Spoils of Freedom: Psychoanalysis and Feminism after the Fall of Socialism. Journal for the Psychoanalysis of Culture and Society* 1(1): 146–148.

Wright, G. C. (1990). *Racial violence in Kentucky, 1865–1940: Lynchings, mob rule, and "legal lynchings."* Baton Rouge: Louisiana State University Press.

———. (1997). By the book: The legal executions of Kentucky blacks. In W. F. Brundage (Ed.), *Under sentence of death: Lynching in the South,* 250–270. Chapel Hill: University of North Carolina Press.

Wright, K. N. (1994). The violent and victimized in the male prison. In M. Braswell, S. Dillingham, and R. Montgomery, Jr. (Eds.), *Prison violence in America,* 103–120. Cincinnati, OH: Anderson Publishing Co.

Wright, R. (1935, July–August). Between the world and me. *Partisan Review* 2: 18–19.

———. (1938). Big boy leaves home. In *Uncle Tom's children.* New York: Harper.

———. (1940/1968). *Native son.* New York: Grosset and Dunlap. [Also published by Perennial 1966].

———. (1945). *Black boy.* New York: Harper and Brothers. [Republished by Pereniall Classics 1998].

———. (1958). *The long dream.* New York: Doubleday.

———. (1977). Afterword. *American hunger.* New York: Harper and Row.

Wyatt-Brown, B. (1982). *Southern honor: Ethics and behavior in the old South.* New York: Oxford University Press.

Yack, B. (1986). *The longing for total revolution: Philosophic sources of social discontent from Rousseau to Marx and Nietzsche.* Princeton, NJ: Princeton University Press.

Yacovone, D. (1990). Abolitionists and the "language of fraternal love." In M. C. Carnes and C. Griffen (Eds.), *Meanings for manhood: Constructions of masculinity in Victorian America,* 85–95. Chicago: University of Chicago Press.

———. (1998). "Surpassing the love of women." Victorian manhood and the language of fraternal love. In L. McCall and D. Yacovone (Eds.), *A shared experience: Men, women, and the history of gender,* 195–221. New York: New York University Press.

Yang, J. S. (1991, August 18–25). Article on Paul Broussard. *Gay Community News* 19(6): 1.

Yardley, J. (2000, February 5). Panel urges reparations for Tulsa riot survivors. New Orleans: *Times-Picayune*, A-13.

Young, F. W. (1962, January). The function of male initiation ceremonies: A cross-cultural test of an alternative hypothesis. *American Journal of Sociology* 68: 381–386.

Young, L. (1996). *Race, gender and sexuality in the cinema.* London: Routledge.

Young-Bruehl, E. (1996). *The anatomy of prejudices.* Cambridge, MA: Harvard University Press.

Zangrando, R. L. (1980). *The N.A.A.C.P. crusade against lynching, 1909–1950.* Philadelphia: Temple University Press.

Zeeland, S. (1996). *The masculine marine: Homoeroticism in the U.S. Marine Corps.* New York: Harrington Park Press (Hawthorn).

Zikmund, B. B. (1982). Biblical arguments and women's place in the church. In E. R. Sandeen (Ed.), *The Bible and social reform,* 85–104. Philadelphia: Fortress Press.

Zilbergeld, B. (1978). *Male sexuality: A guide to sexual fulfillment.* Boston: Little, Brown.

———. (1992). The man behind the broken penis: Social and psychological determinants of erectile failure. In R. C. Rosen and S. R. Leiblum (Eds.), *Erectile disorders,* 27–51. New York: Guilford.

Zimbardo, P. G. (1969). The human choice: Individuation, reason and order versus deindividuation, impulse and chaos. In N. J. Arnold and D. Levine (Eds.), *Nebraska symposium on motivation, 1969,* 237–307. Lincoln, NB: University of Nebraska Press.

———. (1970). The human choice: Individuation, reason and order versus deindividuation, impulse and chaos. In N. J. Arnold and D. Levine (Eds.), *Nebraska symposium on motivation, 1969,* xxx. Lincoln, NB: University of Nebraska Press.

Zizek, S. (1989). *The sublime of object of ideology.* London: Verso.

———. (1995). Debate with Judith Butler: The Theory Seminar Series. Charlottesville: University of Virginia.

———. (1996, Spring). Re-visioning "Lacanian" social criticism: The law and its obscene double. *Journal for the Psychoanalysis of Culture and Society* 1(1): 15–25.

INDEX

F

G

M

O

T

U

X

Y

Z